May 26ᵗʰ 1890

congratulate you upon
outh. A telegram from
ormed us of difficulty —
ll is on. During the
of Sabine Pass, we pr—
en, and with considerate
the collin lay at
or tide. The Seminole,
nchor on the (say, starboard)
t, by veering a long

Letters and Papers
of
Alfred Thayer Mahan

OTHER TITLES IN THE NAVAL LETTERS SERIES

Aboard the USS Monitor: 1862
Aboard the USS Florida: 1863–65
From the Fresh-Water Navy: 1861–64

Rear Admiral Alfred Thayer Mahan

NAVAL LETTERS SERIES

LETTERS AND PAPERS
OF

ALFRED THAYER MAHAN

VOLUME III

1902-1914

Edited by
Robert Seager II
and
Doris D. Maguire

NAVAL INSTITUTE PRESS
ANNAPOLIS, MARYLAND

Library of Congress Catalogue Card No. 73–91863
Complete Set ISBN 0–87021–339–3
Volume I ISBN 0–87021–341–5
Volume II ISBN 0–87021–343–1
Volume III ISBN 0–87021–344–x

Printed in the United States of America

Contents

Volume I
1847–1889

Publisher's Preface	vii
Acknowledgments	ix
Key to Repositories of Letters and Papers	xv
Letters	1
Diary Kept on Board the USS *Iroquois* and USS *Aroostook*, 1868–1869	145
Letters	333

Volume II
1890–1901

Key to Repositories of Letters and Papers	xi
Letters	1

Volume III
1902–1914

Key to Repositories of Letters and Papers	xi
Letters	1
Papers	553
Memorandum of a Conversation with James E. Jouett on the Battle of Mobile Bay. March 1883.	555
Answers to Questions on Examination for Promotion to Captain. October 15, 1885.	557
Contingency Plan of Operations in Case of War with Great Britain. December 1890.	559
Practical Words: An Address Delivered at the Naval War College. September 1892.	577
The Battle of the Yalu: An Interview with *The Times*. September 25, 1894.	583
Memorandum on the Cost of Coal at Gibraltar. November 20, 1894.	586

Memorandum on the Cost of Alcohol at Málaga.
  November 23, 1894.   587

Memorandum on the Cost of Coal at Algiers.
  February 19, 1895.   588

Memorandum on the Cost of Coal at Gibraltar.
  March 6, 1895.   589

A Statement on Behalf of the Church Missionary Society
  to Seamen in the Port of New York. April 10, 1897.   590

The Sinking of the USS *Maine*: Remarks to the New
  Jersey Chapter of the Society of the Cincinnati.
  February 22, 1898.   592

Expenses Incurred While Traveling Under Orders from Rome,
  Italy, to New York, April 27–May 7, 1898. May 1898.   595

A Distinction Between Colonies and Dependencies:
  Remarks to the New York State Chapter of the
  Colonial Order. November 30, 1898.   596

Presentation to the Annual Meeting of the Church Missionary
  Society to Seamen in the Port of New York.
  December 13, 1898.   597

Address Delivered at Holy Trinity Episcopal Church,
  Brooklyn, New York. March 1899.   598

The Navy and the Philippines: Remarks to the Associate
  Alumni of the College of the City of New York.
  February 24, 1900.   603

The English-Speaking Race: Summary of an Address to
  a McGill University Convocation. May 18, 1900.   604

The Well Being of the Seaman in Port: A Speech Delivered to
  the Church Missionary Society to Seamen in the Port of
  New York. March 21, 1902.   605

Personality and Influence: A Commencement Address at
  Dartmouth College. June 24, 1903.   608

Statement Before the Senate Commission on the
  Merchant Marine. November 25, 1904.   620

Comments on the Seizure of Private Property at Sea.
  February–March 1906.   623

The Work of the Naval War Board of 1898: A Report
  to the General Board of the Navy. October 29, 1906.   627

Some Practical Considerations Concerning the Spiritual
Life: An Address Before the Episcopal Church Club
of Philadelphia. February 25, 1907.   644

Excerpt from a Statement to the American Movement.
May 28, 1907.   657

The Advantages of Subig Bay Over Manila as a Base in
the Philippine Islands. October 25, 1907.   658

Reminiscences of Service at the Naval War College.
March 24, 1908.   663

Jottings from Pocket Notebook. May–August 1908.   668

Statement on Naval History Archives and Repositories.
November 24, 1908.   671

Statement of Expenses on a February 4–6, 1909,
Visit to Washington, D.C. March 1, 1909.   675

Testimony Before the House Committee on the Library.
January 5, 1910.   676

Statement of Expenses on a January 4–6, 1910,
Visit to Washington, D.C. January 7, 1910.   678

Comments on the Armament of Battleships.
November 17 and 18, 1910.   679

Thoughts on the Words of St. Peter. July 7, 1913.   682

Thoughts on the Righteousness of War. July 23, 1913.   683

Why Not Disarm? September 1913.   685

Introduction to K. Asami's Biography of Tasuka Serata.
Summer 1913.   688

The Purpose of a Life Work: An Essay Written for the
Board of Missions of the Episcopal Church. 1913.   693

The Origins of the European War: An Interview with
the *New York Evening Post*. August 3, 1914.   698

The British Navy: Fragment of a Newspaper Interview.
Early August 1914.   701

About What is the War?: Draft of an Unpublished Article.
Mid-August 1914.   702

Sea Power in the Present European War: An Article Published
in *Leslie's Illustrated Weekly Newspaper*. August 1914. 706

Summary of a *New York Times* Editorial. August 30, 1914.   711

Woman's Suffrage: A Speech.   712

The Christian Doctrine of the Trinity: An Essay.   714

Appendices   717
  Recollections of Ellen Kuhn Mahan   719
  Note on Mahan's Bibliography   731
  Index of Omitted Letters   733
  Collections and Libraries Searched for Mahan Materials
      Without Success.   751

Index   755

KEY TO REPOSITORIES
OF LETTERS AND PAPERS

APS   American Philosophical Society, Philadelphia, Pa.

BPL   Boston Public Library

CHS   Church (Episcopal) Historical Society, Austin, Tex.

CIW   Carnegie Institution, Washington, D.C.

CorUL   Cornell University Library
       Andrew D. White Collection

CROCS   County Record Office, Chichester, Sussex, England

CUL   Columbia University Library
       Frederick William Holls Papers
       Seth Low Collection
       Brander Matthews Papers
       Edmund C. Stedman Collection
       General Manuscript Collection
       Special Manuscript Collection

DCL   Dartmouth College Library

DUL   Duke University Library
       Samuel A'Court Ashe Letters

FRCS   Federal Records Center, Suitland, Md.
       (Transcripts of courts-martial in which Mahan
       participated)

HSD   Historical Society of Delaware, Wilmington, Del.

HSP   Historical Society of Pennsylvania, Philadelphia, Pa.
       Dreer Collection
       Gratz Collection

HUL   Harvard University Library
       A.T. Mahan Collection
       W.H. Page Collection

JHU   Johns Hopkins University Library
       Daniel C. Gilman Collection

LC   Library of Congress
       American Historical Association Collection
       Nelson W. Aldrich Collection
       Joseph H. Choate Collection
       Grover Cleveland Collection
       William Conant Church Collection
       John A. Dahlgren Collection
       Josephus Daniels Collection
       George Dewey Collection
       George Dewey Collection (Naval Historical Foun-
       dation—NHF)

LC (continued)	Felix Frankfurter Collection (W.H. Moody Letters)
	John Hay Collection
	J. Franklin Jameson Collection
	Library of Congress Archives
	Stephen B. Luce Collection (NHF)
	Alfred Thayer Mahan Collection (includes letters collected from various persons and places by the late Captain William D. Puleston, USN)
	William McKinley Collection
	William H. Moody Collection
	John Bassett Moore Collection
	Richard Olney Collection
	Charles O'Neil Collection
	Horace Porter Collection
	Mary Edith Powel Collection
	Joseph Pulitzer Collection
	Herbert Putnam Collection
	Whitelaw Reid Collection
	Theodore Roosevelt Collection
	Elihu Root Collection
	William Sims Collection
	Charles Sperry Collection
	Benjamin F. Tracy Collection
	U.S. Naval War College Collection (NHF)
	Henry White Collection
MCGUA	McGill University Library Archives
MHS	Massachusetts Historical Society, Boston, Mass.
	William C. Endicott Collection
	Henry Cabot Lodge Collection
	John D. Long Collection
	James F. Rhodes Collection
NA	National Archives
	Record Groups 19, 23, 24, 26, 37, 38, 45, 57, 59, 74, 78, 79, 80, 84, 153, 156, 217, 313, and 405.
NDL	Navy Department Library
NHS	Newport (R.I.) Historical Society
NMM	National Maritime Museum, Greenwich, England
	C.A.G. Bridge Collection
	William H. Henderson Collection
NWC	Naval War College Library, Newport, R.I.
	Alfred Thayer Mahan Collection (includes Mahan Family Papers)
	Naval War College Archives

NYHS	New-York Historical Society, New York, N.Y.
	Charles S. Fairchild Collection
	Naval History Society Collection
NYPL	New York Public Library, New York, N.Y. (Astor, Lenox, and Tilden Foundations)
	Anthony Collection
	John S. Billings Collection
	Century Collection
	Alfred Bushnell Hart Collection
OANHD	Operational Archives, Division of Naval History, Navy Yard, Washington, D.C.
	General Board File
	Z.B. File, Alfred T. Mahan
PAC	Public Archives of Canada
PUL	Princeton University Library
	Robert Mountsier Collection
	Charles Scribner's Sons Archives
RL	Redwood Library, Newport, R.I.
SCI	Seamen's Church Institute Archives, New York, N.Y.
SHSW	State Historical Society of Wisconsin, Madison, Wis.
UML	University of Michigan Library
UNC	University of North Carolina Library
	Silas McBee Collection
USNAM	U.S. Naval Academy Museum (includes correspondence of the U.S. Naval Institute)
UVL	University of Virginia Library, Charlottesville, Va.
UWL	University of Wisconsin Library
YUL	Yale University Library
	Knollenberg Collection
	Penniman Collection
	Pruden Family Collection
Letters in Private Collections	Identified, cited, and acknowledged at point of entry.
Letters to Editors	Identified and cited at point of entry.
Printed Letters and Excerpts	Identified, cited, and acknowledged at point of entry.

Note: All letters, manuscripts, notes, materials, clippings, photocopies, and other Mahan and Mahan-related data collected during the preparation of these volumes have been presented by the editors to the Naval War College Foundation for deposit in the U.S. Naval War College Naval Historical Collection in Newport, Rhode Island.

Letters and Papers
of
Alfred Thayer Mahan

To Andrew D. White

160 West 86th Street, New York, January 2, 1902 [CorUL]

My dear Mr. White: I have found it necessary to reopen my correspondence with Mr. Holls, on account of certain new matter which appeared to me to require explanation. I consequently enclose to you, as I have to the rest of my former colleagues, two letters addressed to him by me, dated respectively Dec. 10 and 23.[1] I presume he will have sent you his own letters in this connection.

Regretting the necessity of again troubling you, and with much respect I am [etc.].

To Hamilton Holt

University Club, New York, January 3, 1902 [LC]

My dear Sir: A letter from Mr. George, of the *Baltimore American*, received this morning, is my first information of your having published in the current *Independent* my name in connection with a remark made by me in a private letter to you.

It was perfectly optional to you to quote the remark, as from a correspondent, without mentioning my name. The latter you had no right to do, even were I in a civil capacity; but in the case of naval officers, under strict bonds always, and now especially, not to express opinions for publication on naval matters, and our naval matters particularly, this was doubly improper.

My letter on its main subject was in direct reply to one from you on a

---

1. A memorandum, dated January 17, 1902, in the Andrew D. White Papers in the Cornell University Library reads: "My recollections on the whole matter referred to in the correspondence between Messrs. Mahan and Holls is that the first suggestion of difficulty to arise from the Commissions d'Enquête on account of the Monroe Doctrine was made in our delegation by Captain Mahan; but of what occurred in the Committee regarding the matter, I know nothing of my own knowledge, not having attended its sessions."

business proposition.[1] In declining it tentatively, I mentioned one reason which would make declination final. Certainly, if a man cannot enter into correspondence with an editor without security that his name & words will not be published, without first consulting him, there will quickly be an end of all confidence and with it of the editor's business. True, I did not mark the letter confidential. I would as soon have thought of locking up my letters if I happened to leave you in the room.[2]

To avoid further misunderstanding, I will say that I consider that letter private, and never till today had any suspicion it would be otherwise regarded. If its contents[3] reach the public, it will be because you see fit to disregard the implied confidence with which I wrote.

To Charles H. George[1]

University Club, New York, January 3, 1902 [LC]

Dear Sir: I have looked up the *Independent* of this week. The letter from which Mr. Holt quotes[2] was wholly private, on business, in reply to a proposition from him. His publishing the remark alone would have been harmless; attaching my name to it publicly is in my judgment a breach of confidence.

As regards your particular request,[3] the matter alluded to is one on which the Government, most properly, in my opinion—have forbidden officers to express opinion, or comment, in public. It is therefore impossible for me to concede the permission you ask, and I have written Mr. Holt that I shall consider its reaching the public a breach of confidence on his part.

---

1. That Mahan comment on Park Benjamin, "The Schley Court of Inquiry," *The Independent* (September 5, 1901).
2. A paragraph inserted here, but struck through, reads: "Your action in the premises appears to me aptly to illustrate the difference between an error in judgement and an error in conduct, which Mr. [Park] Benjamin has found so hard to appreciate." *See* Mahan to Holt, December 22, 1901.
3. A parenthetical phrase here, struck through, reads: (though I remember them but vaguely).

1. A reporter for the *Baltimore American* attached to that newspaper's New York City Bureau.
2. *See* Mahan to Holt, December 22, 1901, on the Sampson-Schley controversy.
3. George requested Mahan's permission for *The Independent* to answer questions from him (George) relating to Mahan's opinion of the decision of the Court of Inquiry in the Schley case. *See* George to Mahan, January 2, 1902, in the Library of Congress.

To Hamilton Holt

160 West 86th Street, New York, January 6, 1902 [NDL]

My dear Sir: I am glad to know, from your letter of Saturday, that I may depend upon nothing further of my letter[1] being given out. Your expression of regret is sufficient satisfaction to me for your other action, as matters stand, but it is best to point out that I might have been seriously compromised by what was at once construed by a biassed press to be a grave indiscretion on my part. You yourself could scarcely have enjoyed the situation that my indiscretion had consisted in simply trusting you.

I think, if you will refer to my letter,[2] you will find I made upon you no "demand" for a retraction. I had neither right nor power to enforce such demand, so it would have been weak to make it. What I said was, (as I remember) that I considered you had seriously misled your readers, and that unless you corrected your statements, it would affect my action, which *is* under my control, to the extent that I could not associate my name with the *Independent* by writing for it. As this was said in connection with a suggestion from you that I might comment on Benjamin's paper,[3] this was neither threat nor demand, but a statement of my position.

As it seems likely that we will not have any further correspondence, I hope you will not take it amiss if I say that, as far as my knowledge of naval war and of naval practice goes the *Independent* has quite failed to appreciate the naval issues really at stake in this unfortunate controversy. You best know upon whom it depends.

To James Brander Matthews[1]

160 West 86th Street, New York, January 8, 1902 [CUL]

My dear Mr. Matthews: It will give me great pleasure to lunch with you and to meet President Butler,[2] on Saturday January 18th at 1:30.

---

1. Mahan to Holt, December 22, 1901.
2. Mahan to Holt, January 3, 1902.
3. Park Benjamin, "The Schley Court of Inquiry," *The Independent* (September 5, 1901).

1. Professor of literature and drama at Columbia University.
2. Nicholas Murray Butler, President of Columbia University, 1902–1945. In 1901 he served as acting president of the university while President Seth Low was Mayor of New York.

To J. Franklin Jameson

160 West 86th Street, New York, January 8, 1902 [LC]

My dear Sir: I have the honor to acknowledge your letter of the 6th notifying me of my election as President of the American Historical Association for the year 1902, and to say that I have the pleasure of accepting the same.

I note also that the next meeting is to be in Philadelphia & that Prof. McMaster[1] is appointed Chairman of the Committee on programme.

To John D. Long

160 West 86th Street, New York, January 16, 1902 [LC]

My dear Mr. Long: You will believe, I am sure, that I was extremely vexed at the appearance of indiscretion attributed to me in the press a fortnight ago, in connection with a letter to the editor of the *Independent*. I decided not to write you, however, until it was evident that the matter would not take such shape as to force you to ask the explanation I was ready to give.

The circumstances were as follows: About Dec. 20, the editor sent me advance proofs of a criticism on my last book—*Types of Naval Officers*—by Park Benjamin, directed especially against the distinction drawn therein between "errors of judgment" and "errors of conduct." He asked if I would like to reply in the same issue. In answer, I made some running comment on Benjamin's positions, and intimated that I might perhaps give them a few lines, tracing the genesis of the distinction in my own mind, and pointing out that it was not so new as Benjamin supposed, having been drawn by me in my *Lessons of the Spanish War* in 1899. But, I continued, as the *Independent* has misled its readers in the matter of the Schley Court, by speaking of the *majority* report, when it was the report of the whole Board, except where qualified by Dewey, I cannot associate my name again with it unless it corrects a statement essentially so false.

This it was which the editor saw fit to publish with my name. Correspondence with editors about articles is of course frequent with me, and it is needless to say is confidential in the same way as any other business correspondence. My letter was before Christmas, & the part published was given out on January 2, over ten days later, a period which allowed ample

---

1. John Bach McMaster, historian of the United States and professor at the University of Pennsylvania.

time to consult my wishes. In addition, the editor communicated other parts, just what I don't know, to a correspondent of the *Baltimore American*,[1] whose application to me for permission to use it (which the editor's aroused sense of propriety forbade) was the first intimation I had. I wrote at once to the editor, putting the whole matter under the bar of confidence, and I added, "I did not mark my letter confidential. I would as soon have thought of locking up my letters if I had happened to have you in the room."

The editor—Mr. Hamilton Holt—has made such expressions of regret as remedy, as far as may be, the fault of his action. As he did not see fit to correct the misstatement involved in the expression "majority report" after his attention was called to it, my relations with the magazine ceased. There is nothing further to say that occurs to me. Whatever your opinion of the transaction, as thus stated you will now know the facts. If the President[2] was in any doubt as to what I had done, under conditions that demanded unusual care on the part of officers, you will doubtless do me the favor to let him know the truth.

To Leopold J. Maxse

160 West 86th Street, New York, January 24, 1902 [LC]

My dear Mr. Maxse: I had hoped by this to have heard from the editor of the *International Monthly*, to whom I wrote immediately on receipt of your last;[1] but as the mail goes tomorrow I write this line of bare acknowledgment.

My decision rests in some degree upon the outcome of my letter to him. In case of cooperation between you & him on the lines suggested, it would pay me to take time from my principal work in hand to write three or four articles this year; otherwise scarcely. I should be disposed, however, without yet committing myself to a distinct promise, to give you a couple of articles, selected for subject out of those mentioned by you, or my own as to the interests and sentiments that should promote & assure Imperial Union.[2] This & the effect upon the Monroe Doctrine of the acquisition of the Philippines recommend themselves most to me at present.[3] If, however, under these conditions of uncertainty on my part, you would do me the favor to indicate sources of information on the questions of the Persian Gulf & of the

---

1. Charles H. George. *See* Mahan to George, January 3, 1902.
2. Theodore Roosevelt had become President on September 14, 1901, when McKinley died, victim of an assassin's bullet.

1. *See* Mahan to Maxse, December 26, 1901.
2. Later published as "Motives to Imperial Federation," *National Review* (May 1902).
3. Later published as "The Monroe Doctrine," *National Review* (February 1903).

Distribution of the Navy any discussions in Magazines on those subjects, it might modify my views by arousing particular interest.[4]

[Aide-mémoire on letter above]
1. Motives tending to consolidate Union of Br. Empire
   The Foundation of Union in the British Empire
2. The Present Position of the Monroe Doctrine { Policy of Monroe Doctrine
   { Its reasons and extension
3. The strategic Importance of the Persian Gulf
4. The Problem of the Far East (Yangtse Valley etc)
5. The Strategic Distribution of European Navies }
   The Real Objective of the Br. Navy }
6. Commerce-Destroying Question of Immunity from Capture of Goods
   Embarked for Coml. purposes during War

To Theodore Roosevelt

160 West 86th Street, New York, January 25, 1902 [LC]

My dear Mr. Roosevelt: That you should in the past, before you became President, have given consideration to some of my opinions in matters upon which I might be supposed to know something, is a poor excuse for intruding where I cannot be thought to have particular knowledge. I hope, however, that certain general considerations may make this step less inexcusable than it might appear.

I have been, frankly, frightened by the very drastic recommendations of Judge Taft,[1] foreshadowed in his free communications to the Press, concerning the reduction of the force in the Philippines; and my suggestion is this: Would it not be well to ask of the Philippine Commission, and of the Commanding General in the Philippines,[2] separate estimates, itemized as an Appropriation Bill would be, of the force necessary; not in general terms only, but by localities? The total would be determined by the aggregate of the particular forces thus calculated.

This would amount in effect to a kind of plan of campaign, contemplating the possibility of a more or less extensive insurrection, among a people naturally treacherous and so lately in general revolt. The distribution of force for such a contingency, its localization in numbers, the capacity of

---

4. "Conditions Governing the Dispositions of Navies," *National Review* (July 1902); and "The Persian Gulf and International Relations," *ibid.* (September 1902).

1. Federal Circuit Judge William Howard Taft, head of the Second Philippine Commission.
2. General James Franklin Bell.

localities for mutual support, all have to enter into consideration. Upon these, too, there needs to be allowed a margin of safety.

This of course is a calculation essentially military, while Judge Taft's ideas proceed on his conceptions of the civil condition. He has, however, in his reported interviews, committed himself to specification of numbers. Where does he get it?

I need not appeal to your historical knowledge of the disastrous effects of insufficient power at a needed point, as in British India in 1857. All would doubtless agree that it will be more economical for the United States to keep 20,000 men too many, five years longer than they are needed, than to remove the same number six months too soon. As for the islands themselves, and their welfare, even more is at stake in the alternative between internal quiet and intestine strife. Nor can a people that have endured Spanish soldiery three centuries feel ours as an indignity; however petty chiefs, impatient of restraint, may resent them.[3]

To Leopold J. Maxse

160 West 86th Street, New York, January 28, 1902 [LC]

My dear Sir: From some cause as yet unexplained, I have to this moment had no reply in writing to my letters to the Editor of the *International Monthly*, but to day have received a telegram acceding to my proposition made to you, & accepted by you. He said he has written, but as there is a mail tomorrow, and none again till Saturday, Feb. 1, I write to say that I am having the Military Rule of Obedience copied,[1] to send you by the Saturday steamer. It is about 5,000 words; very closely so.

I will take up the other matters as rapidly as possible. I assume you will scarcely want me to preach oftener than alternate months. The first thing however is to produce another article, & in the meantime an arrangement can be developed as to the future appearances, in this tripartite matter.

[P.S.]   I understand that he proposes this present paper for the March number but I will write fully by the Saturday steamer.

The *International* Editor is Frederick A. Richardson. It is published at Burlington, Vermont, a place comparatively small but within 12 hours of New York, and I understand has plenty of money behind it.

---

3. On January 28 George Cortelyou forwarded this letter to Elihu Root, Secretary of War.

1. "The Military Rule of Obedience," published simultaneously in the *National Review* and in *International Monthly* in March 1902. This, however, was the only such dual arrangement between the two journals with respect to Mahan's articles. *See* Mahan to Maxse, May 23, 1902.

[7]

To Leopold J. Maxse

160 West 86th Street, New York, January 30, 1902 [LC]

My dear Sir: I send you herewith Ms. of the Military Rule of Obedience. I have to regret the delay, for there was no reason that I should not mail a week earlier, except that I could not get word from the Editor of the *International*. I have heard at last, and it seems that his silence was due to serious illness, during which his physician would not let him see his correspondence. The excuse is sufficient, though most inconvenient to you and to me. He publishes in his March number, & as this gets off, as it is, a few days earlier than my former to you did, I anticipate it will be in time; as I was able to notify you of its length by last mail.

Mr. Richardson enters very heartily into the general scheme. It will be my study to bring the order of the articles, as well as their individual contents into proper relations & also to facilitate your editorial management by ample time in finishing & sending them. May I remind you of my request for suggestions,[1] as they may occur to you, where to look for material on the Persian Gulf question, & also as to opinions concerning the distribution of your Navy. The latter topic, I own, I rather shrink from, as being for me ultra vires.

To Bouverie F. Clark

160 West 86th Street, New York, February 8, 1902 [LC]

My dear Clark: It has been shabby of me to leave yours of Dec. 18 so long unanswered, but I have been more or less in a state of devilment with work all this winter; and as work with me means largely pen in hand, the tire of it shows in reluctance to write any more for any reason whatever. I had seen your retirement from the Transport Office, and with something of a start of surprise; for, though I knew the limit of your term, I was hardly able to realize that you had put it all in. You see it has all taken place since I really saw anything of you, in Plymouth, and then you had still some time to run there. I did have a couple of flying looks at you in '99, as I went and came from the Hague, but the visit at Plymouth remains clearer. Leisure such as you have, absolute freedom from the necessity to work, does seem to me now one of the most desirable of conditions. I get awfully tired at times of ransacking my brains, and working up what little they yield into readable form. To wake in the morning and feel I need do nothing, not

---

1. *See* Mahan to Maxse, January 24, 1902.

even get up if I dont choose, seems the height of bliss; but I suppose I might soon tire of that, and probably be considerably more bored. The comfort for you is that your repose comes not too late to cultivate successfully the habit of amusing yourself. We Americans live in such strain, that our successful men apparently cant quit working without collapsing. I fancy London is the place for your money. One gets upon the whole more enjoyment and more life in a big city, if you can afford to stay at all; and people dont care how you live, provided you are good to meet. You speak of the Chamberlains. I remember very well lunching with him on board the *Heroine*, with Blackburn,[1] (or was it Blackwood?) in Panama; also his daughter, a very showy girl of striking appearance, as I remember. As regards the canals I have always been a Nicaragua man, though without any personal knowledge of the merits of the case. It has been the American idea all along; intensified later by a spirit of opposition, I fancy, to the French undertaking. I have therefore been somewhat surprised to find our present Commission,[2] which has been studying the matter on the spot for over two years, favor Panama, if the French will sell their work so far done for a reduced price. I am satisfied, however, to accept either solution on competent testimony, & I think our Commission a good one. Certainly their bias, if any, would be toward Nicaragua in the outset. It is very hard to get the matter started at all, and for that reason I regret the change of recommendation, though necessitated by the conditions. I believe your trouble in S. Africa is really nearing its end; it seems as if so much could be read between the lines, and is substantiated by Milner's summary of the reviving conditions of civil life in the Transvaal. Your War Bill is immense; but the real question is whether, as an investment, you will be repaid by a renewed South Africa, and by the increased weight of the Empire in the councils of the world. I think you will; & if so, while I could wish your bargain had been cheaper, it is a good one none the less. All this talk about the *costliness* of war is nonsense, except where one pays too dearly for the result, or when the result is worthless. Such a bargain is bad in any line of life. A railway run through a region that wont pay one per cent on the investment is as bad a bargain as a resultless war. Of course it is a pity results cant be had without killing people and unsettling trade; but one has only to say Kruger, and realize that some bad things cannot be settled except by fighting. The death of our President was sad in its utter uselessness & folly. If the scoundrel[3] had tried, he could not better have demonstrated the absurdity as well

---

1. Captain R. F. Blackburne, R.N., commanding officer of the *Heroine* in 1885.
2. The First Isthmian Canal Commission (1899–1902) was composed of J. G. Walker, Louis M. Haupt, and Colonel Peter C. Hains; Alfred Noble, Emory Johnson, Lieutenant Commander Sidney A. Staunton, and others were added later. The Second Commission replaced it in 1904, and lasted until 1914.
3. Leon Czolgosz, who shot President McKinley on September 6, 1901. McKinley died eight days later.

as wickedness of the crimes of which his is one instance. McKinley was at the very crown of his career. He could not have got higher; success had attended him throughout and he had fairly reached the end of one set of difficulties. Another was opening before him, but as yet nothing had happened to dim in the least the lustre of his success. He was not only honored, but had conquered a singular affection in the whole community. Life could have brought him no more; the murderer simply secured him his safe place in our history. As regards the nation, the feeling of security was no more affected than it would be by the killing of the Emperor of Austria. I think there is a general feeling that Roosevelt is even a better man for the immediate future. Now as to Buller, of whom you speak, I dont know if I ever said my say to you, but he seems to me the most colossal failure of your war.[4] I met him several times in 1894, and was much impressed by him. Never so astounded as by his actions; not only by what seemed to me mistakes in generalship, but also by a certain seeming indecision—notably in his dealing with Warren.[5] As regards popularity with his own command, we had singular evidence of the same sort in our civil war in McClellan; a man of the highest repute before, who proved a most signal failure, but whose men always swore by him, and probably still do. Like Buller, he too was a man of exceptional personal gallantry.

I had not heard of Lady Clark's illness, but rejoice to know that all promises well. Please remember me to her most cordially, and say I always remember my visit to you at Plymouth. And now my dear fellow, if I have been long in replying, I fear you will say I am longer in winding up, so I will stop here—short.

[P.S.]   I must add I like your photo. The appearance of age is simply, I think, that you allowed your beard too long.

To John D. Long

160 West 86th Street, New York, February 9, 1902 [LC]

My dear Mr. Long: This letter will introduce to you the Right Revd. Charles Henry Brent, who I hope will have the opportunity of presenting it in an approaching visit to Washington. Bishop Brent has been recently consecrated to the charge of the Missionary jurisdiction of the Philippine

---

4. During the Boer War, Buller had injudiciously split his forces and expended three months and five thousand men in the relief of Ladysmith.
5. Lieutenant General Sir Charles Warren's indecisiveness at Spion Kop in January 1900 was not dealt with firmly by Buller. *See* Mahan, *The Story of the War in South Africa*, pp. 256–262.

Islands[1] and I need not say how advantageous to him and his work will be the countenance of the Navy Department, so far as it can be properly extended in its various offices in the Philippines. As a Bostonian, you will have the means of knowing from personal observers the high character of the work done by Bishop Brent in his recent charge of St. Stephens Church in Florence St., which to the estimation of his clerical qualities by the Church at large the selection of him for his present office is sufficient testimonial. In view of these, it is scarcely important to add that for both Bishop Brent and his future work I personally have the utmost value.

To Augustus T. Gillender

160 West 86th Street, New York, February 12, 1902 [HUL]

My dear Mr. Gillender: Your letter of the 7th, to which I replied immediately upon receipt on Monday morning, gave me no information as to *where* the Master in Chancery is before whom hearing is to take place on Thursday at 2 p.m. I asked information in my note of Monday, but never has been recd. by me. Unless therefore, I hear to the contrary, I shall be at the Cortlandt St Ferry at 1:30 p.m. Thursday where according to your letter I will expect to meet either you or Mr. Mumford.[1]

To Leopold J. Maxse

160 West 86th Street, New York, February 21, 1902 [LC]

Dear Mr. Maxse: I have notified the Editor of the *International* that I expected to be able to give him the article on the Motive (or Motives) to Imperial Federation by April 1st, and it will be my endeavor so to finish it as to mail it to you, so as to reach you by that date.[1]

Of the other subjects suggested by you he has expressed his choice of the strategic dispositions of the Navies and the future of the Monroe Doctrine. Concerning these I have told him I must *not* be considered *under promise*. I intend to supply them, if possible, but I never work so well under the burden of positive obligation.

---

1. The Episcopal Missionary Diocese of the Philippines.

1. W. W. Mumford, Gillender's law partner.

1. The *International Monthly* did not publish this article; *see* Mahan to Maxse, May 23, 1902. It was, however, published in *National Review* for May, 1902.

These and the Persian Gulf (as well as the Motives) are so far cognate, that I hope the study of one may make all develop in my mind, and that I may consequently be enabled, perhaps without great additional effort, to meet your wishes about the Persian Gulf. I had noted the *Quarterly* article[2] in the Club, and meant to read it, but it will be more convenient to have it at home, where I read evenings and where I write. I think the *Spectator* has in this connection taken much the line you indicate as yours. The demonstration of hostility by the German people to you has been portentous, & introduces a very modifying factor since I wrote my *Problem of Asia*. Nevertheless, Russia's illimitable field for expansion, and her already immense population, make her ultimately the greater danger; & although at first blush inclined to applaud your recent treaty with Japan,[3] second thoughts make me rather wish you had concentred your opposition upon the Gulf. For in China—Manchuria—her efforts would be naturally antagonized by Japan, and by us if trade exclusion were attempted, while, in the Persian Gulf, not only does she, if established there, flank your route to India—a much more dangerous condition to you than having her sea access in Eastern Asia—but you have no natural allies; none whose interests will lead them to contest Russia, unless possibly Germany. Were the latter friendly, I dont know what better condition there could be for you than to encourage her to stretch *by land* right along the western border of Russia, through Constantinople, to the Euphrates. It would entail enduring friction between her and Russia, and cripple Germany's advance to sea power—by the burden of landward defence etc entailed. Even with the present hostility, I cannot bring myself to look upon Russia and France as other than your inevitable enemies, through propinquity in Europe and in Asia, & through tradition, as well as alienage of blood etc. All this however is premature discussion of several elements of the complicated problem I have undertaken to study.

To Leopold J. Maxse

160 West 86th Street, New York, March 7, 1902 [LC]

My dear Mr. Maxse: It will not be possible, I fear, to get my article on Motives to Imperial Federation in less than 8,000 words. I see that this limit, if I keep fairly near it, does not exceed, nor even reach, the space you have occasionally allowed, but I have thought best to notify you at once. The article approaches completion, but is subject to interruption; at times

2. "Persia and the Persian Gulf," *Quarterly Review* (January 1902), p. 245.
3. The Anglo-Japanese Treaty of January 30, 1902.

from external causes, at times because I fancy the head clears for dropping a matter two or three days.

I read last night, consecutively, the article of ABC in the *National* for Nov.,[1] & that in the January *Quarterly* on the Persian Gulf.[2] My convictions as yet remain with the latter. The Gulf flanks your communications with India & the East, as with Australia. It is the *centre* of your line. China, most important as it is, is on the flank, less hazardous to you and more exposed to Russia, for it is distant from the centre of her strength, accessible from the sea, and confronts an accumulation of influences hostile to her *exclusive* policy. To this add on my part a deep-rooted distrust of the Slav—especially under the Czardom—and a great faith in *permanent* conditions, such as Teutonism vs. Slavism, the geographical situation of Germany & Russia, the exceeding numerical preponderance of the latter, etc., and you can understand my bias must be strong. Russia I believe far more dangerous to you than Germany, & the latter has ever Russia on her back .

I am reading diversely and desultorily on the whole question & its cognates, fleet distribution, European politics, colonial statistics etc, my mind being more and more impressed with a certain solidarity of the whole. I trust this will facilitate and better my treatment of the whole. I would be ambitious to give a push to Federalism.[3]

To George F. W. Holls

160 West 86th Street, New York, March 12, 1902 [HUL]

Sir: I have received yours of the 8th inst. Enclosed with it I find copy of a letter addressed by you to my four colleagues in the late Hague Conference.

In the latter, I accept of course, and unqualifiedly, the statements of M. Lammasch,[1] M. Martens, M. Destournelles,[2] as to their present recollection of your words, as given on p. 167 of the proceedings of the Comité d'Examen. As a matter of evidence, it remains that their recollections are now two and a half years old, and that over against them stands the fact—which I do not find contradicted—that although the Secretariat got at the time the first half of your utterance, they did not get the second half. This is the more singular, if M. Destournelles's memory is accurate in saying that he translated your words for the information of the other members. While

---

1. A.B.C. Etc., "British Foreign Policy," *National Review* (November 1901).
2. "Persia and the Persian Gulf."
3. Of the British Empire through imperial federation.

1. Heinrich Lammasch, Austro-Hungarian delegate.
2. Paul Henri Benjamin d'Estournelles de Constant, French peace leader and delegate to the Conference.

this precision of detail undoubtedly gives force to his personal recollection, it adds perplexity to the failure of the Secretariat.

Nevertheless, as the matter stands, and after such deliberation as time permits, I am persuaded that, if considering the evidence in a case wholly without interest to me, I should decide that you did use substantially the words in question at the time mentioned.

As regards the remainder of your letter to my colleagues, so far as it relates to your general attitude towards the Monroe Doctrine, and your reasons for your particular course in the management of Article 27, I have no comment to make. Your general attitude I am not aware that I ever questioned. Your particular action in Article 27 I certainly did, vigorously and vehemently; but the discussion between us on that matter, so far as I am concerned, ended with my letter to you of last April.

To turn now to your letter of the 8th inst. to myself. I, of course, shall not formulate a charge at your dictation, nor admit, as mine, imputations which I have not made. Neither will I, at your "challenge," deny the correctness of the official minutes, of which I have no knowledge. My statement (Dec. 10 and 23) was that I had proof, to me satisfactory, that the passage I there quoted was not in the original minutes of the Secretariat of the Comité d'Examen. This, I added, admits of denial or disproof, for which I give you opportunity. If I rightly understand, you did not contradict this in December, and do not now; but you now bring before me, the evidence, above accepted by me, that you used the words.

Beyond a careful statement of facts, as I had reason to believe, and still believe them to be, I made no imputation, as you call it, "outrageous" or other. I confined myself to facts. Had I gone on, as I understand you now call upon me to do, and turned inferences, however plausible, into a charge or an imputation, I should have been justly censurable. If the facts, stated by me, gave rise in any quarter to impressions unjust to you, it is due, in my opinion, to your failure to realize how delicate a matter it was to add to the minutes words upon which you based so much of your claims, without at the same time providing for the demonstration of your own integrity in so doing.

I cannot afford to pass over your stigma upon my sources of information. As far as known to me, they have been absolutely straight and above board; and I have permission to give the name and communication of my first and principal informant,[3] if I judge necessary.

Finally, touching the expressions of your letter, as distinct from its substance and tone. It is easy to answer words with words. I note yours; but I am satisfied that I may disregard them, resting upon the presentation of the facts in our correspondence, without assuming the appearance of a discomposure which I do not feel.

---

3. Jarousse de Sillac.

To Andrew D. White

160 West 86th Street, New York, March 13, 1902 [CorUL]

My dear Mr. White: I enclose copy of a letter I have had to write to Holls, in reply to documents which you have probably received from him. I faintly hope that I may not again have to trouble my former colleagues with a correspondence that can interest them but very little.[1]

With my compliments to Mrs. White, believe me [etc.].

To George F. W. Holls

160 West 86th Street, New York, March 17, 1902 [LC]

Sir: Your letter of March 14 has been received. Its last paragraph reminds me that, contrary to my custom, I failed to mention that a copy of mine of March 12 had been sent to each of my former colleagues. In correcting this omission, I wish not to be understood as asking that you should furnish them a copy of yours of the 14th, as you express your willingness to do. I conceive that to be a matter that concerns you, not me.

To Leopold J. Maxse

160 West 86th Street, New York, March 22, 1902 [LC]

My dear Mr. Maxse: I forward herewith the Ms. of my promised article—Motives for Imperial Federation. As it slightly outruns the 8,000 words, which I had notified you would be its probable length, I have indicated in blue pencil on p. 10–11 an omission, which you can make or not as seems to you most expedient.

I have kept before me, as you will perhaps recognize, the interesting our own people on this side in these questions, believing that the promotion of sympathetic interest—with entire absence of gush—desirable for both us & you. In my reading and thinking I have been impressed with some leading & significant facts, which may be worth your attention as an editor. In

---

1. On January 17, 1902, White, who sponsored Holls at the Peace Conference, had written Mahan, "I . . . deeply regret the shape the whole matter therein referred to has taken. . . ." and, struck through, "My hope is that some explanation from Mr. Holls may meet the question, harmonize the statements on both sides." Andrew D. White Papers, Cornell University Library.

1892, (about, I have mislaid my reference) Ld. Brassey[1] wrote "It is significant that of the total commerce passing the Suez canal, over 80 p.c. is British." It is otherwise significant that, by the data I now find, in 1898–9 only 67 p.c. is British. This confirms the inference which Ld C. Beresford has lately drawn from your shipbuilding figures. Again, the population of Australia has very far from realized the increase anticipated twenty years ago, and this I gather is due to the policy of the workingmen, who control, discouraging immigration. This, if true, strikes at the very life of the Colony, stunts its growth, and institutes premature decay. Our protection is bad enough in my eyes, but we at least encourage the multiplication of population, the basis of state power, by reserving the home market. This Australian system protects by removing home competition. The Australian workman has an easier time by excluding other workmen, but he purchases this at the expense of the power of the state, and sacrifices the future to the present. Does not the Prince of Wales's advice to wake up apply especially to the British Press? Who are the watch dogs, if not they?

To John Bassett Moore

160 West 86th Street, New York, April 9, 1902 [LC]

My dear Mr. Moore: I have today received the six volumes of your monumental work on International Arbitrations,[1] for which I am indebted to your kind interposition with the Department of State. I had no idea before that it was so gigantic an undertaking, and I thank you most sincerely for having procured me a copy.

Referring to our correspondence about Holls, would you care to see a correspondence I had with him, about the account given in his *Hague Conference* of the origin of the Declaration made by the United States Delegation, in appending their signature. The matter is of no great importance, save as a piece of inside history in a matter which of itself cannot but be interesting to you. It may also have the further utility of enabling you to form a judgment, for yourself, of the candor of a man whose ambitions, I think, point to a public career in the line of diplomacy and international law which are the subjects of your own special interest. I shall not of course wish you to express any opinions to me; but if you would like to see the correspondence and can spare a couple of hours for its perusal I should very gladly put it in your hands.

1. Thomas, 1st Earl Brassey, author of *The British Navy* (1882–1883) and compiler of *Brassey's Naval Annual* (1886– .) He was a persistent advocate of a strong navy, naval reserve force, and merchant marine.

1. John Bassett Moore, *International Arbitrations to which the United States Has Been a Party*. Washington, D.C.: U.S. Government Printing Office, 1898.

To Leopold J. Maxse

160 West 86th Street, New York, April 10, 1902 [LC]

My dear Mr. Maxse: With reference to payment for my articles when running up to 8,000 words or so, I think my understanding with you was £50, or $250, for each article, provided the *International Monthly* also took, and paid me. While the arrangement holds, and for the articles now under my consideration, I shall feel myself adequately paid at this rate, unless indeed some special difficulty arise in my way. "Motives to Imperial Federation" at all events will go at that rate; and I expect the others also, which you both take. The *International* has not signified its willingness to take "The Persian Gulf," if written. In that case I may ask *you* more; but it is a case more of trouble to me than of number of words. You see, all these subjects are new to me, as regard particulars and details. They have therefore been unusually troublesome, as I anticipated they would.

I have been a little encouraged to see in your journals utterances, here and there, so far in line with what I have said in "Motives," that I hope the article may prove opportune. Necessarily, in the partial ignorance to which I allude above, I am feeling my way to conclusions, not yet formed. I am open to conviction, therefore, on the Persian Gulf question, but I own to an obstinate feeling that permanent, inevitable conditions will force Germany to your side, despite the raging of the people. I see even Mommsen,[1] the old Anglo- & American-phobe, is out advocating the cooperation of Germany, England & U.S. I believe the old fellow is honest, & his historic sense compels him to recognize fundamental truths, despite his prejudices. See me supplied with information in your line. In my Club we have all your leading periodicals, I believe, except the service magazines, but call my attention where necessary.

[P.S.] There is no prospect of my going abroad this year.

To John Bassett Moore

160 West 86th Street, New York, April 16, 1902 [LC]

My dear Mr. Moore: I send you my correspondence of last spring with Holls, and enclose a memorandum of the sequence of the letters, to facilitate your reading. As my plan of campaign involved a copy for each of my colleagues of the delegation, besides the one sent Holls, and as my only

---

1. Theodor Mommsen, the German historian to whom Mahan earlier attributed, in part, his discovery of the influence of sea power on history.

typewriter is my wife, you will understand and excuse the roughness of the drafts retained for myself.

In Holls's, the blue and red pencil marks are simply annotations by me, for my reference in replying.

In my last letter of this series, I may explain to you that of the five men who, I say, understood the meaning of Holls's book to be as I contend it to be, three were my colleagues, Low, Newel, and Crozier. Before beginning the correspondence, I wrote to them to know whether the account given in the book tallied with their recollection of the facts—gave a correct impression. All said most distinctly, No; but that of course does not commit them to my argument. I believe, however, I am strictly accurate in saying they all attribute to me the initiation of the Delegation's action, which issued in the Declaration. It happened, in the winter following the Conference, on the evening of the day when the Senate confirmed the Government's adhesion to the Conference, Low and I dined at the Alumni Dinner of the University of N.Y. He said to me "I see the Senate have confirmed our action, thanks to you." This may attach undue weight to the importance of my action, but it shows positively how it was regarded by him.

I have never had the slightest intention of putting in any claim, nor had the matter dwelt much in my mind, until my attention was called to what I consider Holls's adroit and audacious assumption of credit to himself. Nor have I now any purpose of raising an issue. But I am pleased to put the facts before a man of your distinguished reputation, and association with matters of this kind. In saying that I expected no opinion from you, I wished merely to free you from any idea that I wished to do more than put you in possession of the facts, to form your own judgment upon them, without any feeling that I expected you to impart it to me.

I have understood indirectly that President Butler is one of the seven cited by Holls, as not finding his words to imply, to assert, what I say they *do* intimate to the reader.

I ascertained, subsequently to this correspondence, that the passage in the text of the Procès, to which Holls referred me as evidence, p. 167, had been inserted by him in the proof reading. In Dec. last I called his attention to this fact. After a lapse of ten weeks, he replied by a letter to me, abusive in tone, & enclosing a copy of a letter addressed by him to the other delegates. In this he stated that he had received letters from several members of the Comité d'Examen, whom he named, stating that they distinctly recalled his then using the words thus introduced. Replying to the whole, I said that I accepted, unqualifiedly, their statement as to their recollection; that as a matter of evidence, it was recollection now 2½ years old, & that it was singular that the Secretariat should have got the first half of his remarks and not the second. Nevertheless, I accepted it as proving that he had used the words. I have doubted whether you would care to read this second correspondence, but it is entirely at your service, if you wish it. Holls gives in it a long explanation of what he had intended to do, had not I cut in [sentence struck through]. This is a mistake of mine; the explanation occurs in the enclosed.

Personally, I believe that he went to the Conference choke full of the sense that he must safeguard the Monroe Doctrine, and that he was instant, in season and out of season, in enforcing it on the Comité; but I remain entirely unable to believe, from my recollection of the occasion of my raising the particular matter, of his bearing throughout, and the whole *general* impression left on my mind, that he in the least realized the blunder (as I and the others considered it) involved in Art. 27. That he, by his own admission in the accompanying letters, never used this so called reservation, never again alluded to it, convinces me that his use of the words was a matter of routine, probably so often repeated that the Secretariat did not note it. This, however, you will observe is merely an expression of my personal opinion, in no way an assertion of fact.

Retain the papers as long as you wish, but you will understand that, as I have no copies, I trust you will take care of them, especially in returning.[1]

[Enclosure]

1. Mahan to Holls, March 11, 1901
2. Holls to Mahan,   "   15   "
3. Mahan to Holls,   "   23   "
4. Holls to Mahan,   "   30   "
5. Mahan to Holls, April   9   1901
6. Holls to Mahan,   "   10   "

March 11, 1901, Mahan called Holls's attention to the account given by a letter in his book on the Peace Conference, pages 268–270, touching the origin of the reservation made by the American delegation in signing the convention for the pacific settlement of disputes Mahan claimed the credit of originating the reservation and repelled Holls's apparent claim of credit for it.

Holls replied March 15, 1901, in a long letter. He defends the statement made in his book and says he does not see how he could have avoided "saying just what I did." He says that when he made the reservation in the *comité de examen* he "had in mind" a declaration to be made later on "in the committee, or possibly in the *acte finale*," and that by Captain

---

1. On this letter Moore wrote: "I note in Mr. Holls's letter of the 15th of March the statement that he did not at the meeting on the morning of the 22nd of July mention the reservation which he had made 'personally' in the *Comité d'Examen*. I also observe his statement that when you inquired whether he did not consider Art. 27 a very serious, fundamental and important provision, he replied that 'in itself' he could not so consider it."

Mahan's "vigorous intervention," and "entirely independent of anything which was said or done in the *comité de examen*, the declaration was appended to the treaty itself. Nevertheless, it covered, he says, "the point which I had in mind on July 3, and hence, from the point of view of a history of the conference, it was the declaration for which I had made a reservation."

Mahan replied March 23, 1901, and returns to the charge that in Holls's text there is "the clear implication that there was a connection between your reservation and the action of the delegation in deciding to make a qualifying declaration." Mahan returns to the charge and declares that Holls's statement that he had "made a reservation for the declaration afterwards formulated," is not consistent with the facts.

Holls responds, March 30, 1901, and says that he evidently has not succeeded in making himself understood "with entire clearness." In this letter he says: "So far as my narrative produces the impression that I had foreseen, and, in the *comité de examen*, provided against the abandonment of the Monroe Doctrine, and so far as it indicates that I was, during the whole conference and from the beginning, greatly impressed with the necessity of safeguarding the Monroe Doctrine at the proper time and in the proper manner, it is entirely correct, and I am fairly entitled to whatever credit, as a negotiator or otherwise, is due for this foresight and my individual action. Of course, I distinctly deny that my narrative does produce this impression, or give such indication." Again, in the same letter, Holls, after affirming his great interest and activity in protecting the Monroe Doctrine, says: "To my mind article 27 afforded the best immediate occasion to make a reservation, but it did not, according to my view, make so material a difference as you, and, I am bound to add, the other members of our commission seemed to think." Further on he says: "There is nothing whatever in the narrative on pages 268–270 indicating that my reservation of July 3, as well as the declaration afterwards formulated, were not both simply emanations from the American commission or Government." Holls declares that if he had said "a declaration covering the point raised in the reservation made by Mr. Holls on July 3 was afterwards carefully formulated," Mahan must admit that from his own point of view he could not object to one word of that language, although it would by implication have given Holls the credit of originality to which Mahan objected.

Mahan rejoins April 9, 1901, and says that the question now "stands perfectly clear, and shorn of all confusing details." The question is simply this: "Does the narrative of your book convey a truthful impression of the occurrences connected with the American declaration? Or does it, as I have alleged, by suppression, combined with arrangement and implication, convey the idea that your course—personal or public—in the *comité de examen*, led to, or materially contributed to, the declaration? In short, the declaration has a history; has your narrative limited itself to the suppression of that history, or has it suggested an alternative history, devoid of foundation? " In his concluding paragraph Mahan says that he shall await with interest to the end of the current week to learn "whether you are disposed to rectify this impression, which I maintain results from the tenor of your narrative which you have given to the public. Failing to receive such intimation from you, I shall then assume that you identify yourself with this account, maintaining that it conveys a true impression of the history of the declaration."

Holls, April 10, says that Mahan's letter, "by its closing paragraph" seems to call for a reply, however brief. He says that Mahan is correct in stating that the question has become one which "simply involves the meaning of language," and that, "in view of our substantial agreement as to the facts, this means, in other words, that the question is whether I have been successful in expressing the meaning which I certainly wish to convey." He says that seven different persons, including leading publicists and writers, as well as one of the ablest international lawyers in the country and "one of the foremost educators and masters of style in this city," all agree that his language cannot be properly taken to imply that his reservation was "the originating source of the American declaration," or that there was "a connection between my reservation and the action of the American delegation in deciding to make a qualifying declaration," beyond the undoubted and important fact that the declaration covered the ground of the reservation.

In the first letter of March 11, 1901, Mahan states that according to his recollection, two days, or so, subsequent to the adoption of article 27 by the Full Third Committee, his eye was caught by an editorial in the *Manchester Guardian*, rejoicing over the extreme results insured by the adoption of that article. "I then went to the printed minutes, supplied to the delegates, and read the Article; which I had not before done, not being on the Committee immediately concerned. After brief reflection, I became satisfied that it was compromising, as then worded, to our settled national policy, and I decided to bring the subject at once before our Delegation at the meeting which was to be held that forenoon, by appointment. This I did, and an animated discussion followed; all the members being present, and all accepting my views almost immediately. Mr. White, I especially remember was particularly impressed with the urgent necessity of rectifying the matter. You, however, argued against my contention, and stood out for some time against the admission that the article, for the acceptance of which you among us were primarily responsible, would in operation have the practical effect that I alleged. The matter indeed had gone inconveniently far; it was extremely awkward for us, the Conference then nearing its close, to ask to revise, or to dissent from, an article to which our consent had been given, not only in subcommittee but in full committee as well. If, however, you had mentioned to us this reservation, of which your book speaks, our path would have been clear and simple; our retreat would have been kept open. No such mention was made to me then, or at any subsequent time; nor did I ever hear any allusion, by any member of the delegation, to such reservation by you, at that time or afterwards.

"The discussion in our delegation resulted in a decision to gather several of our principal foreign associates at a breakfast, to discuss the way out of our dilemma. It is not necessary to pursue farther the history of the reservation, as finally framed, for it is with its origin only that I am here concerned.

"If the facts be as I state above,—and my memory of them is very clear,—it is hard to reconcile them with either the general coloring of your account, or with the specific assertion that you qualified your approval in sub-committee by 'reserving the right to make a declaration * * * after consultation with your colleagues.' At our meeting when I brought up the matter, no one present mentioned any previous consultation by you on the matter, and I certainly had not been consulted; though, if the importance of the matter had been realized, as your account implies, I was certainly entitled, as a délégué plénipotentiaire, to be consulted. And at no subsequent stage of the proceedings, at the breakfast, or elsewhere, did I ever hear any mention of this antecedent reservation, or of any antecedent consultation."

To Robert W. Neeser[1]

160 West 86th Street, New York, May 5, 1902 [YUL]

My dear Sir: I was extremely concerned that a mistake of the maid allowed you to be turned away yesterday. If you will call tomorrow, Tuesday, between 6 and 6:30, it will give me pleasure to see you.

To Leopold J. Maxse

160 West 86th Street, New York, May 12, 1902 [LC]

Dear Mr. Maxse: I am extremely glad to know that the article[1] this month has drawn as much interest as appears from the *Times* you sent me,

---

1. American naval historian, author of *Statistical and Chronological History of the United States Navy* (1908), *Our Navy and the Next War* (1915), *Ship Names of the U.S. Navy* (1921), and other books. At the time of his call on Mahan, Neeser was eighteen years of age.

1. "Motives to Imperial Federation."

and from a copy of the *Morning Post* I have recd. through our attaché in London.[2] I shall be glad also to hope that it may have any effect that it ought upon the approaching Colonial gathering. There is of course always a possibility of such a measure proceeding too fast; but the more probable danger is that it will go too slow. One caution, however, I think there is. It is better that the various members feel the evils arising from want of federation, than those which may spring from a federation too rapidly matured. Let a more perfect union wait upon the experience of the communities that what they already have is not enough. The clock strikes twelve some time, but it is perhaps better that it first have struck the smaller hours.

I have been at work on the question of the Disposition of the Fleet, and incidentally of the European Navies,[3] & have already written more than enough for an article, without finishing my work. Condensation will be needed. Meanwhile, though I confidently expect to send you this, do not consider me *promised*, either for it or the Persian Gulf.[4] My intentions are yours, but I cant bind myself.

May I ask of you permission to republish in book form the articles I have, and yet shall, send to the *National*; subject, in your interest to acknowledgment to the *Review*, and not to appear until two months after the number in which you publish them. Please answer this soon.[5]

I shall carefuly consider all you say about Germany.

[Enclosure]

Received from L. J. Maxse, Two Hundred and Fifty Dollars, in payment of the Article "Motives to Imperial Federation," in *National Review*.

To John M. Brown

160 West 86th Street, New York, May 12, 1902 [LC]

My dear Mr. Brown: I hope my past years have established for me a decent reputation as a correspondent, for I am covered with confusion at my delay in answering yours of last week which was followed in two days by the promised photograph. The latter I find excellent; there are few men to whom it is given to make so good a showing at sixty, & I congratulate

---

2. Captain Richardson Clover.
3. "Conditions Governing the Dispositions of Navies."
4. "The Persian Gulf and International Relations."
5. The answer was affirmative. The articles were published by Little, Brown and Company later in 1902 under title *Retrospect and Prospect, Studies in International Relations, Naval and Political*.

you on the way time has dealt with you. I myself have anticipated you by eighteen months in reaching that period, concerning which one is in doubt whether most to congratulate a friend that he has safely covered so much of life's journey, or to exchange condolements that so much is over and gone. However, it is best that optimism prevails. It is so with me; for, after all, the end we may hope will be but the beginning of a better.

As regards a book this year, I cannot speak certainly. My production through the year has been fragmentary and laborious, dealing with magazine subjects that, while timely and important in themselves, have demanded from me an unusual degree of thought and labor. If I can complete one now in hand and another which somewhat hangs to it, the entirety may make a small book, and if so I will notify you at once. To make full confession of my status, I have been distracted this twelvemonth between two or three purposes, when I ought to have definitely made up my mind to one. As a result I am somewhat empty handed. The Amn naval biographies could not be handled in time, for I should have to collect the data.

[P.S.] The second photo arrived this a.m.

To J. Franklin Jameson

160 West 86th Street, New York, May 17, N.D.   Probably, 1902 [LC]

My dear Prof. Jameson: I quite agree with you that the publication of the Virginia Co. records would be rather ultra vires for the Commission, and that, as regards the Council, a sound decision is more likely to be reached by open discussion in assembly, than by expression of individual opinion, without full consultation & debate.

As yet, however, I do not recall having had the proposition submitted to me.[1] If it is done, I shall take your ground.

To Robert U. Johnson

160 West 86th Street, New York, May 19, 1902 [NYPL]

My dear Mr. Johnson: In taking account of my literary purposes—if I may so call them—I have been struck with a sense of mortification at re-

---

1. In his capacity as President of the American Historical Association.

membering that several years ago, in conversation with yourself and Mr. Gilder,[1] I had promised to prepare for the *Century* a series of some half-dozen naval battles of historical celebrity. I have been mortified, for the interview was a formal one, and I have never kept my promise. I recognize a certain excuse, for the intervention of the Spanish War, and a year later of the Hague Conference called me off; and incidental to the former was the request with which the *Century* honored me to prepare some papers on the war, in which McClure by an accident anticipated you.

Qui s'excuse, s'accuse. I have no hesitation in accusing myself of breach of engagement, without excusing. I can only say that the matter assumed unconsciously to my mind the impression of lapsed by mutual consent, un-expressed. It has not been on my conscience, though it should have been.

My object in writing now is to ask how the matter stands in your mind; whether the *Century* would still like to have the articles and if so at what time—approximately?[2] If you would, I recognize, now, what I ought to have recognized before, the precedence of your claim in this upon me, and I wish now to observe my obligation in adjusting my work in contemplation, to this claim.

It will be more convenient to me to have a good deal of latitude as to time, and from my experience with the *Century* I imagine your issues are filled up some time ahead.

To Leopold J. Maxse

160 West 86th Street, New York, May 23, 1902 [LC]

My dear Mr. Maxse: I have to thank you for a large number of cuttings, from which I am glad to see that "Motives" has attracted favorable comment in England. I hope it may also have affected favorably the *National Review* in some measure.

I hope to mail you by steamer of the 27 or 28 the next article, which I have styled "Considerations Governing the Disposition of Navies." Partly by natural bias, partly from a semi-conscious indisposition to appear to instruct your officials, I have given the subject a more general treatment than you perhaps have expected. I have thought it more useful and more suggestive to the 'man in the street,' thus put; and also, if in any way novel—which I doubt—that it will be more influential, because less offensive to your powers that be, than the more direct expressions of a foreign officer

---

1. *See* Mahan to Johnson, February 14, 1898.
2. The *Century Magazine* declined Mahan's offer and never again published his work.

[25]

are likely to be. Above all, I have in view the possible discussions on the subject of military and naval aids by the colonial representatives at the Coronation. If the article appear in your July number it will in this respect be timely, so far as any value it may possess.

This explanation of my motives is probably best kept between you and myself. I fear you may find the paper a little long. It is about 10,000 words; but to keep within this compass I have cut down and left out a good deal that is to my mind superfluous only because there is no reasonable room for it. You have been indulgent in promising toleration as to space.

I fear that I shall have to stop here for the present, for the subjects I have handled for you have made unusual demand upon my cerebral processes, and I am tired. I propose to quit writing at all for at least several weeks. I am sorry to say that the Editor of the *International*[1] has broken his engagement with me, on account of other arrangements he has made. This he did, at a moment's warning, without any previous intimation, although our agreement was of three months' standing. This is not the determining factor in my decision to stop writing for the moment, although it has of course some influence. Fatigue, and again a little shrinking from intruding my opinion on a question like the Persian Gulf have both affected me. As far as I remember I have with you only a conditional promise, not absolute. If you will, let it stand so for the present; I may see my way better after rest.

I hope I may soon hear from you that you are willing I should republish the articles in book form[2] next autumn.

[P.S.] The coming article[3] is all typewritten, only awaiting final revision, so that mailing on date named is fairly certain.

To Leopold J. Maxse

160 West 86th Street, New York, May 27, 1902 [LC]

Dear Mr. Maxse: As I wrote you Friday, I am distressed over the length of the enclosed, though somewhat encouraged by the assurance in one of your letters that you would bear with me in the matter of length. I may say that omission and condensation have been used, to much expenditure of my time.

---

1. Frederick A. Richardson.
2. *Retrospect and Prospect.* See Mahan to Maxse, May 12, 1902.
3. "Conditions Governing the Dispositions of Navies," *National Review*, July 1902. *See* following letter.

After writing you to catch Saturday's steamer, I became troubled with the apprehension that I might have given you more positive assurance than my memory recalled, as regards other papers from me. If there is such in my letters to you, let me know, for I keep no copies of my own—as a rule. I want not to break any word I have given.

The Persian Gulf question has to me two aspects, both primarily military. First, that it is more dangerous to Great Britain's position to have a possibly hostile power on the line of her communication with India, than in equal or greater force in the Far East. Second that Russia *must* reach unfrozen water somewhere. It follows that it is far better for G.B. that she—Russia—should establish herself at Port Arthur etc. She cannot for two generations be in force at both places; and in fact, as far as I can foresee, by developing her ambitions in Manchurian waters, she institutes a condition, substantially *permanent*, most favorable to you; off your flank, and committed to the maintenance of her power in a region where she meets *permanent* opposition —besides yours; to wit, Japan, the U.S., and probably Germany. Neither Japan, nor we, have direct interest in the Persian Gulf. Now it is possible that after a month's rest I might develop a paper on these lines, if you should wish it, in time for your September number. You can let me know if you think it worth while.

[P.S.] The above argument was in my *Problem of Asia*, in skeleton.

To William H. Henderson

160 West 86th Street, New York, June 1, 1902 [NMM]

My dear Henderson: Thank you for your letter.[1] It was kind of you to write, and I may say timely, so far as I am personally concerned, for I feel at times a sense of discouragement, & have been so lately. It is I suppose a common enough experience, but I have written with a sense of fatigue which is apt to translate itself into dissatisfaction with what is written. Consequently, your assurance has been particularly welcome. In forwarding the federation of the Empire,—so far as I may,—I quite conceive myself to be working for my own country, and, incidentally, for the rest of the world. "The rest" I daresay, dont see it; but for the U.S., it is to me perfectly plain that whatever makes for your naval strength works for us. Every interest of

---

1. Henderson had written to congratulate Mahan on his "Motives to Imperial Federation" in the May 1902 *National Review,* and to assure him that history would some day recognize him "as one of the greatest Empire-makers" that had existed because his work was "one of the foundation stones, not of one but of two" empires.

yours prompts you to be friends to us. We on the other hand profit by your navy, for you must keep it at a standard of force which we never will, in this generation, attempt; and its international weight unavoidably tells in our favor because in the great international questions of the day, your interests and ours are common. On the other hand, while I am not prepared for international federation between us—by alliance—I hope and believe that the outside world will see in the community of interests between us a warning that by attacking one they may arouse both.

As regards your politicians, I think they are wise in allowing public opinion to keep ahead of them. The difficulties are so great—in point of form and effective machinery—that Federation must wait upon felt necessity for that vital spark of full conviction and consent without which its formal realization would be insecure. On the other hand it is most important to keep the subject alive by frequent presentation of its advantages and existing disadvantages.

I have had the pleasure of meeting Dr. Parkin some time ago at a small lunch, and I know his enthusiasm in this cause.

I congratulate you greatly on your appointment & to that lovely country. Of course I know little about the Yard proper, but I stayed once a few days with Bouverie Clark when at the Barracks, and had the luck to lunch at Mt. Edgecumbe and go over the grounds, as well as to visit some other localities.[2]

To Seth Low

160 West 86th Street, New York, June 9, 1902 [CUL]

My dear Mr. Low: Will it be too much trouble to ask of you to propose, for membership of the University Club, my son, Lyle Evans Mahan? He graduates at Columbia on Wednesday, the 11th, and then becomes eligible for nomination. I shall ask Mr. Bishop[1] of the *Commercial Advertiser* to second him. As you know, he is not eligible for election for three years but I wish to get him started as soon as may be.

---

2. *See* Mahan to Henderson, August 12, 1902. Henderson forwarded this letter to his friend Fawkes (Admiral Sir William Hawksworth), and suggested that he show it to Lord Selborne, First Lord of the Admiralty. Henderson to Fawkes, June 22, 1902.

1. Possibly, Joseph Bucklin Bishop, who was on the staff of the *New York Evening Post* 1883–1900, of the New York *Globe* 1900–1905, and was Secretary of the Isthmian Canal Commission, 1905–1914.

To Leopold J. Maxse

Slumberside, Quogue, Long Island, June 12, 1902 [LC]

My dear Mr. Maxse: I am at my summer home till Oct. 1, and my address as above. The "Slumberside" is an unnecessary frill, for an address.

I received your letter of May 29 some days ago, & was rather surprised that I had conveyed to you the impression that you might not get the article on the Disposition of Navies. By reference to my register receipt, however, I find that it was mailed to you May 27, so I hope it arrived in time enough for July. May I ask you, if practicable, to send me a copy of first proofs, or advance sheets, instead of waiting for the copy of the magazine itself—though I shall hope to receive that also. If I carry out my present purpose of republishing, by your kind assent given, I wish to incorporate the matter I had to leave out, and even further to develop it, as opportunity serves. In order to do this, I should like to have it before me, in print, as early as possible.

I thank you sincerely for the permission to republish. I have not abandoned the hope of preparing the article on the Persian question; the more so that I cannot but think that your just exasperation, at the tone of the German people, is unduly biassing your judgment as to the real political conditions. We Americans consider Germans, European Germans—and especially Prussians, to be endowed with peculiar faculties for irritating, which they have developed shockingly towards England. The Russians on the contrary are what the Spaniards call "simpatico"; all the same I think your danger lies there.

The subject has for me increasing attraction & I have therefore brought my notes down. I shall hope, however, that, if I can mail you by July 25, for publication in Sept. No., that you will so far relax as to allow me to publish in the book Oct. 15. Two months space after all the other articles is easy enough; but my publishers grumble at late issues before Christmas. Moreover, this article, if worth space at all in your pages will be worth wider circulation, especially here. The subject is coming to the front in our press.

Our friend of the *International*[1] I learn is changing his monthly to a quarterly. This does not however excuse his ordering the article from me, and refusing it (unseen) three months later, when practically ready for delivery.

---

1. F. A. Richardson.

To Edward K. Rawson

My dear Mr. Rawson: Could you do me the favor of sending me to the above address the books named on the other page?

[Enclosure]
1. Goldsborough, *U.S. Naval Chronicle*[1]
2. Commodore Morris, *Autobiography*[2]
3. Sir J. Barrow, Autobiog. *Memoirs*[3]
4. Sir R. Vesey Hamilton, *Naval Administration*[4]
5. Remarks on British Naval Administration since 1815[5]
6. Inquiry into necessity of reorganizing U.S. Navy[6]
7. Reply to hints on reorganization of U.S. Navy[7]

To Leopold J. Maxse

Slumberside, Quogue, Long Island, June 20, 1902 [LC]

My dear Mr. Maxse: I will undertake the Persian Gulf article on the terms of your letter of June 3d—$500. I was already inclining strongly towards it, my interest being increasingly aroused against my previous reluctance; but the double incentive of the honorarium & your assurance that the other articles were pretty generally acceptable in England, has overcome the indisposition that I entertained, partly through shrinking from additional labor, and partly from the feeling that I was intruding unwelcome opinion.

I hope you may be able to publish in September & accord me permission to republish in my proposed book Oct. 15, instead of Nov. 1.

---

1. Charles Washington Goldsborough, *The United States Naval Chronicle*. Washington, D.C.: J. Wilson, 1824.
2. *Autobiography of Commodore Charles Morris*. Boston: A. Williams, 1880; and in the U.S. Naval Institute *Proceedings*, VI, No. 12, 1880. J. R. Soley wrote the preface for the *Proceedings* edition.
3. Sir John Barrow, *Autobiography*. London, 1847; G. F. Staunton, *Memoir* [of John Barrow]. London, 1852.
4. Sir Richard Vesey Hamilton, *Naval Administration: The Constitution, Character, and Functions of the Board of Admiralty, and of the Civil Departments it Directs.* London: G. Bell and Sons, 1896.
5. Not found.
6. Not found.
7. *A Reply to Hints on the Reorganization of the Navy*, N.P., 1845. An answer to *Hints on the Reorganization of the Navy, Including an Examination of the Claims of its Civil Officers to an Equality of Rights*. New York: Wiley and Putnam, 1845.

To Bouverie F. Clark

Slumberside, Quogue, Long Island, July 7, 1902 [LC]

My dear Clark: I was much startled as well as greatly grieved to see the notice of Lady Clark's death in the *Guardian*. It met my eye by the merest chance, just as I was about to send the paper on to a friend, so that I have been longer than I otherwise would have been in writing you. There is very little one can say, after all. I have not been called upon to bear the same, but I can by imagination put myself a little in touch with your bereavement, coming as it has done when your active career had in great measure closed, and your wife's affection and society, and your common interests, remained as the chief factors in your life. It must be a satisfaction to you that she lived to know and share the appreciation and reward of your services by the Government. I happen to know how deeply she was concerned in your burden of work during the war, in its success and its acknowledgment. Believe me, my dear fellow, that though no man can pretend to enter fully into the feelings of one who has suffered such a loss, that I do think of you with very sincere friendship and sorrow for your sorrow.

To Stephen B. Luce

Slumberside, Quogue, Long Island, July 9, 1902 [LC]

My dear Admiral: The criticism alluded to was in a series of articles published in *McClure's* from Dec. 1898 to April, 1899. I cannot give you the exact number; but for reference you will probably find it simpler to turn to the publication in book form, *Lessons of the War with Spain*, which I daresay is in the College Library. The particular comment there occurs pp 164–170,[1] but of course the narrative which furnishes the material for criticism is more extended. I would suggest your collating with it a quotation from Sampson's older report, p. 116.[2]

With kind remembrances to the ladies [etc.].

---

1. Pages 164–170 deal with the alternatives of fleet action before Havana in May 1898. Mahan argued that the eastward voyage of the Havana division to San Juan was unfortunate, since it violated the principle of war that condemns "eccentric" movements, i.e., those away from the center. By it both Havana and Cienfuegos were left uncovered. Cervera's fleet slipped undetected into Santiago on May 19.
2. *Lessons of the War With Spain*, p. 116, in which Sampson gave his reasons for leaving San Juan on May 12 and shaping course toward Havana. *See also Sampson-Schley Official Communications to the U.S. Senate*. Washington, D.C.: U.S. Government Printing Office, 1899.

To John S. Billings

Slumberside, Quogue, Long Island, July 14, 1902 [NYPL]

Dear Sir: Will you be good enough to inform me on enclosed addressed postal card, between what dates the Astor branch of the Library will be closed, if at all this year, for cleaning etc?

To Leopold J. Maxse

Slumberside, Quogue, Long Island, July 14, 1902 [LC]

Dear Mr. Maxse: I have finished the article on the Persian Gulf, for which I propose the title "The Persian Gulf and International Relations." For, though I keep pretty closely to the Gulf itself and its immediate surroundings, the above title would more accurately express the scope and intention of my treatment. It is now being fair copied and I may get it off by the mail of Saturday, 19th; more likely however by that of July 23. By rough count it will be about 8,000 words.

I do not look upon your opinion as a fad, and I know that it is shared by a great many of your people. I have not the least doubt, either, of the hostile feeling of the German people toward you, & in a slightly less degree toward ourselves. My view merely is that the permanent facts are too strong, and must eventually bend Germany, people and rulers, to their force and tendency. I think the Emperor already sees this. I do not acquit him of having done much to foster the beginning, that he was "trying it on" in his dispatch to Kruger,[1] and since then in the beginning of the war, to see how far Europe might be prepared to go, with the purpose of getting what he could out of the scramble, if any came. Prussia has a miserable back history, to which I was sorely tempted to allude. Silesia in 1740, the course of 1795, 1805 and 1806, Bismarck's shameless cynicism, all justly lead us to look upon her politics as worse than selfish—shameless. Despite all this, some condonement may be allowed for her extremely difficult position, Russia & France on the Continent, Great Britain, U.S. & Japan on the sea. The great fault is not that she is self interested—that her *govt.* ought to be—but that, having decided what her interests demand, she trusts to chicanery & twisting instead of to a straightforward course. But for us, we must regard the permanent factors, the problem as a war game, & having decided

---

1. On January 3, 1896, the Emperor telegraphed his congratulations to Kruger on the defeat of the Jameson Raid.

our course hold to it—sleeplessly vigilant, but not hating. After all the single eye is easier to us than to her.

[P.S.]   I ran across the enclosed slip,[2] after my article was finished. You will see my views coincide.

[Enclosure]

July 14

Received from L. J. Maxse, Two Hundred and Fifty Dollars, in payment of article Disposition of Navies in the *National Review*.

To Edward K. Rawson

Slumberside, Quogue, Long Island, July 21, 1902 [NA]

My dear Mr. Rawson: I have today returned by register mail Barrow's *Autobiography*, that of Com. Morris, and the volume of British Naval Tracts kindly loaned me, and beg to thank you again for them. If Vesey Hamilton's *Naval Adminstration* should turn up, or be acquired, I should feel it a great favor if lent to me for a fortnight.

To Leopold J. Maxse

Slumberside, Quogue, Long Island, July 22, 1902 [LC]

Dear Mr. Maxse: I am indebted to you for a number of cuttings from English newspapers which have been very welcome. The general consensus has been very gratifying to me, & the more so that the one seeming dissentient, the *Manchester Guardian*, does not fairly state my argument from which it dissents. I confess to some surprise at the favorable result, in view of the diffidence I certainly felt as to making the attempt.[1]

The article "Persian Gulf etc" went by registered mail from here the 17th, & so by steamer of 19th. I mention this because I have kept a corrected copy; so that, in case it fail to reach you in due course, a cable to me here would enable me to mail copy in time for your Sept. No. I have decided to modify slightly one of the paragraphs near the close, and enclose copy,[2] as altered, and as I wish it to appear. Though satisfied that the Germans

---

2. Slip not found.

1. Reference is to his "Motives to Imperial Federation" which appeared in the *National Review* for May 1902.

2. Enclosure not found.

hate us only next to you, I cannot on reviewing my grounds for that belief find within my knowledge the positive evidence, without which I dislike to make even qualified assertions. I have therefore struck out that sentence, which in no way strengthens my argument. I was reluctant to do this, for my hope was so to intimate the feeling of at least a large & thoughtful class of Americans, as should make Germany realize betimes that she is entering on a doubly dangerous path. Possibly, however, the rest of the paragraph shows sufficiently my personal attitude. I have also some sympathy for the perplexities of Germany in the ever present incubus in Russia.

Do you recall this passage in Seeley's *Expansion of England*,[3] The possession of India gives us . . . "a leading interest in the affairs of all those countries which lie upon the route to India. This and this only involves us in that *permanent* rivalry with Russia, which is to England in the nineteenth century what the competition with France for the New World was to her in the 18th." Writing in 1883, Seeley had not in view the phenomenal recent growth of Germany but though he lived to 1895, he never corrected in subsequent issues; but I conceive the permanent conditions are not altered, nor do I anticipate for Germany a sustained rate of progress. The remark (*Edin. R.* April, p. 416) "Her progress will naturally appear to be rapid until she finds her level,"[4] appears to me sound.

To Leopold J. Maxse

Slumberside, Quogue, Long Island, July 25, 1902 [LC]

Dear Mr. Maxse: It is a great satisfaction to know that so competent an authority as Mr. Spenser Wilkinson[1] has thought well of my last article, and I thank you very much for letting me know. It is a matter of encouragement which no man is worse for. I had attributed the *Times* article[2] to Thursfield, whom I know quite well, and who in times past has honored me with his approval.

---

3. Sir John Robert Seeley, *The Expansion of England*. Boston: Little, Brown and Company, 1900. (This was a reprint of the original 1883 edition.)
4. "British Policy in Persia and Asiatic Turkey," *Edinburgh Review* (April 1902), pp. 398–428. This was an unsigned review of seven books. The quotation in context read, "It must be remembered that Germany is a new competitor in this field and that her progress will naturally appear to be rapid until she finds her level."

1. Chichele Professor of Military History at Oxford, and later author of *Britain at Bay*. (London: Constable, 1909.)
2. The article, in *The Times*, London, July 2, 1902, p. 9, agreed with Mahan on the importance of open lines of communication between Britain and the Far East, and with his analysis of the function of self-governing colonies in Imperial defence.

I will repeat in this letter the request, made in one of Tuesday last, that in publishing the Persian Gulf article you will omit the words (p. 28 or 29) "I believe further that the popular attitude (German) toward the people of the U.S.... has been prejudiced, inimical & unjust." Also for "purposeless," three lines lower down, put "can serve no good end." As this is only a precautionary duplicate request, I will not repeat my reasons for it.

I have not considered the need of a map & have therefore no recommendations ready. I had imagined the general geographical knowledge of people, supplemented by atlases readily accessible, would be sufficient. I should suppose, speaking hastily, that if a map at all, what would be desirable would be one showing the southern shore line of Asia, and east to China, the Red Sea & the Levant to include the Suez Canal. The map in my book *Problem of Asia*, between the equator & 40° N., and 30° & 130° E. gives my idea; for details I would enter no topographical features, except the great rivers, but I would incline to put in steamer routes, the existing & proposed railway lines, (especially to the Gulf); and I would clearly show the dividing line between Persian & Turkish territory at the Gulf, and perhaps distinguish the semi-independent communities at Koweit, Muscat and elsewhere. You will observe I do not discuss strategic details touching the Gulf itself, though I hold strongly that Great Britain should hold her own at Koweit, & in the system of communications *everywhere* in the vicinity of the Gulf. All roads from the North should end in a system controlled by British capital.

As regards our future arrangements to which you kindly allude. It will give me pleasure to contribute further to the *National*, as occasion arises, without however committing myself to a promise to do so. Our relations have been in every way satisfactory to me. After getting off the Disposition of Navies, I laid by from all but reading for three or four weeks, and this with my transfer here set me up so that I wrote the Gulf article with an ease that surprised myself. I recd. about this time a letter from Mr. Marston of Sampson Low, asking if I would contribute to the *Nineteenth Century* an article. Though shrinking from extra work, I consented conditionally upon terms I stated, from which I have not heard.[3] Without affecting an absence of personal interestedness, I have long standing personal and literary arrangements with Mr. Marston, which predisposes me always to accept propositions that come through him, if I think he himself wishes them, as in this case & the review of the London *Times* S.A. War history.[4] He has been to me always such that the wish to oblige him is a strong motive. This communication you will of course consider confidential. I have made it only

---

3. No article by Mahan appeared in the *Nineteenth Century and After* during 1902 or later.

4. *The New York Times*, May 30, 1902, p. 5, published Mahan's review of the first of seven volumes of L. S. Amery, ed., *Times History of the War in South Africa*. London, 1900–1909.

[35]

because, in case of writing, you might very naturally think my profession of fatigue contradicted.

As regards future contribution to the *National*, I continue to feel that the position of a foreigner writing articles of this nature is delicate, & may easily appear intrusive. I have besides undertaken a considerable historical labor for next year. The two reasons combine to make me think that if I write for you, it should be at longer intervals than this year. I would therefore suggest that you decide at your leisure two or three subjects—if you have so many—to be published at intervals of about four months, for which you would be willing to pay me $500 each, with permission to republish two months after the appearance of the last of the three. When I know your views so far I shall probably be able to reply more definitely.

To William H. Henderson

Slumberside, Quogue, Long Island, August 12, 1902 [NMM]

My dear Henderson: Thank you very much for your letter anent the article on the Disposition of Navies. It is always a help to know from competent readers and observers that an article has struck true, for I at least find it hard to fancy a man independent of that kind of support, through entire conviction of his own adequacy.

I am glad to know that you find your new duties to your liking.[1] It is the happiness of life to have congenial work. The surroundings of Plymouth, as I have seen them, have always been to me extremely pleasing, due largely no doubt to Mt. Edgecumbe, and to my outlook being from the anchorage and not the never agreeable outskirts of a dockyard. Still, I stayed a few days with Bouverie Clark in 1894, and the glimpses I got from time to time of the country round left a very pleasant impression, as did Devonshire generally as far as have seen it.

Wishing you all good luck and realized happiness in your new billet, believe me [etc.].

[P.S.] Mrs. Mahan thanks you for your remembrances which she bids me also return with her own.

---

1. *See* Mahan to Henderson, June 1, 1902.

To Leopold J. Maxse

Slumberside, Quogue, Long Island, September 15, 1902 [LC]

My dear Mr. Maxse: I write a line to acknowledge the receipt of draft for $500.00 which came to day, and for which I beg to thank you.

Your brief note written immediately upon your return from France has also been received and I shall look forward with pleasure to hearing again from you. By the time you receive this, you may as well note my address as again 160 West 86th St., N.Y.

I am extremely glad to hear the article[1] has been so successful and shall have much interest in seeing the cuttings, when you send them.

To John S. Billings

Slumberside, Quogue, Long Island, October 2, 1902 [NYPL]

Sir: May I ask to be kindly informed, on enclosed postal, whether the Library has in one of its branches a full file of *Niles Register?*[1]

To Leopold J. Maxse

Slumberside, Quogue, Long Island, October 3, 1902 [LC]

My dear Mr. Maxse: I am in receipt of yours, suggesting an article on the Monroe Doctrine with reference to particular contemporary considerations and opinions.[1] The subject would require delicate handling on my part, in an English periodical especially, for I cannot speak as an authority, either from my official position, or from my technical knowledge from the point of view of an international legist. In one of our own I could speak more freely. It is, however, very possible that I may be able to give you something from my own point of view; which is, that the principle of any policy which is essentially correct survives—is the permanent factor— but no one can foresee the particular applications that may arise with changing circumstances. Without therefore committing myself to a definite undertaking, I will take the matter into consideration. This is a very busy year with me, and I must bespeak your forbearance if I seem to fall behind; but

---

1. "The Persian Gulf and International Relations."

1. *Niles' Weekly Register* . . . . Baltimore, 1811–1849.

1. Published as "The Monroe Doctrine," *National Review* (February 1903).

I think I can undertake that for the year 1903. I shall not write for any other English magazine on subjects cognate to those I have given you, provided you give me three on the terms proposed.

I have to thank you for cuttings concerning Persian Gulf. There seems to be a variety of opinions, which is a healthful condition; but there should be less uncertainty as to what are the permanent, essential, features of the situation. These, not transient gusts of emergency or feeling, are the guiding lights of policy.

To Theodore Roosevelt

Navy Department, Washington, D.C.,[1] October 16, 1902 [NDL]

There is much to be said on the side of individual power for battle ships, as well as on the side of numbers. Therefore, it is not an unqualified certainty, but only a preponderance of argument that can be adduced for limiting size in favor of numbers.

The primary consideration is that the battle ship is meant always to act with others, not alone. Strategically, and yet more tactically, this demands homogeneousness. In the battle ship, one is designing a class, not a unit. This imposes upon the designer conditions other than those of the single ship, especially in tactical qualities, such as dimensions, speed and turning power. These should be harmonized by an antecedent determination of a size, to which battle ships must conform during a measurable future. This object may be attained by designing a class, forming a tactical unit, to be completed simultaneously. This is the least demand; but I believe calculation could be pressed to the further extent of controlling shipbuilding hereafter; nearly as the recognized 74 once did, admitting variations in gun power, but not in nautical qualities.

In my *Lessons of the War with Spain*, pp. 36–42, I have stated, with detail and illustration, the arguments for numbers against size—given the same aggregate tonnage—as clearly as I think I now can do. These are summarized in the words: "War depends largely upon combination, and facility of combination increases with numbers. Numbers therefore, mean increase of offensive power, other things remaining equal." By a comparison made by me when then writing, I found that from the 10,000 to the 15,000 ton

---

1. During this trip to Washington Mahan was the guest of the William Croziers.

ship (in the British Navy), there was, as my memory now serves me, little more broadside gain than one six-inch rapid fire gun. In conversation with the present Chief of the Bureau of Equipment[2]—an extremely able officer—I understood him to admit this, but to advocate increase of size on account of coal endurance. This is a very important consideration; but to my mind, it can in no wise justify an increase of nearly fifty per cent in tonnage with less than ten per cent of offensive power. All questions of communications—which coal supply essentially is—are subordinate to the offensive power to which they minister. The inconvenience of coal renewal can be alleviated, but not obviated; and the extent of alleviation should not overpass absolute necessity, if offensive power thereby suffers.

The same remark applies to speed. Beyond a certain point, not difficult of approximation, it should not be purchased by increase of size. Speed is under distinct limitations as a strategic quality, and as a tactical unit it can be sufficiently insured—for chase, for example—by the armored cruiser; that is, by a class of battle ship—relatively few—in which speed is purchased by some sacrifice of fighting strength;—an exception, for exceptional purposes.

The conflict of interests in the organs of administration, I believe to be the main cause of increasing size. The chief object appears to be to satisfy all demands. Here enters an underlying administrative defect. Professional opinion is not represented; and no conception of a *standard* battle ship is framed or even imagined. It cannot be, for a majority consensus does not exist; much less has received formulation. To illustrate: The old 74 represented a professional consensus, reached by long experience and accepted, if not formulated. It therefore controlled the ship building, intrusted to a civil administrative board. We have now neither the experience, nor the time, our predecessors had. We must therefore, be at pains to supply by reflection what they gained by experience. Size and other qualities are now determined by administrative officers. The sea-officer is not represented, except as he finds place in the administration proper. As soon as he does so, he represents a particular interest—speed, or armor, or coal endurance; what not. He becomes an advocate, on the board which decides qualities. What is needed supremely is an organ, wholly detached from administration, to evolve conclusions which shall stand for the professional opinion of the instructed sea-officer; of the man who cares nothing about the administrative processes, but simply for the fighting efficiency of the ship. Such an organ, be it one man or many, might conceivably realize,—what a group of administrative officers never will,—that a ship is not an aggregation of functions, each of which gets all it can—(in order to which, each ship must be bigger than the last)—but that it has, according to its class, one dominating object to which all others must be subordinated. Like war in general, a

---

2. Royal B. Bradford

[39]

war ship is a work of art, a unit in conception; not an aggregation of incompatibilities.

A distinguished British naval architect—Scott Russell,[3] I think—once defined the relative function of the sea-officer and the naval architect, thus: Let the naval officer tell us what he wants—nautical qualities, guns, armor, coal endurance, etc., and then leave us to produce the article. The production of the article is the administrative function; for the function of conception, for ascertaining what the sea-officer needs, no provision exists, either in accepted professional opinion, or in such an organ as I suggest. Yet this is what the Navy requires. Needless to say, it is not to be attained by polling the service, or by promiscuous discussion. These may offer useful side lights; but decision can only be had by consultation among a very few really enlightened officers, the essence of whose position in this respect should be that they are entirely unconcerned in administration, and look only to the purpose which the particular ship is to serve in the fleet in campaign. Let them define her qualities.

To Leopold J. Maxse

Library, Navy Department, Washington, D.C., October 17, 1902 [LC]

Dear Mr. Maxse: I have asked my American publishers to send you 'from the author' a copy of *Retrospect & Prospect*, which I beg you to accept with my regards. You will find some amplification of my articles for the *National*, chiefly in Dispost. of Navies; and in the Boer War article I eliminated what I said about exclusion of Boer leaders and language. I have not changed my opinion; but the terms of your government having been formulated & granted, I saw no reason to contribute my mite to prolonging bitterness.

I enclose a letter recd. yesterday.[1] It is impossible to weigh the value of an anonymous letter, but along with a certain Gallic bumptiousness, there seems here an indication of national feeling that may be useful to you in estimating currents of feeling. There is nothing otherwise in it, and of course I dont send it for quotation, especially in connection with my name.

---

3. John Scott Russell, shipbuilder and engineer, Vice President of the Institution of Civil Engineers, and a guiding spirit in the Institution of Naval Architects, was an early proponent of iron ships. For the influence of his ideas, *see* K. C. Barnsby, *The Royal Institution of Naval Architects, 1860–1960.* London: Royal Institution of Naval Architects, 1960.

1. Enclosure not found.

To Walter Hines Page

160 West 86th Street, New York, October 28, 1902 [HUL]

Dear Mr. Page: On returning home, I find your book[1] and note of the 21st awaiting me. Please accept my thanks for both. Of course, we who are busily occupied in writing know that the pleasure of reading books has to wait its chance, yielding the pastime to the business of writing them.

To William H. Moody[1]

160 West 86th Street, New York, November 1, 1902 [LC]

Dear Mr. Moody: Believing that you were to be absent from Washington during the current week, I have delayed till now answering the question of your letter of Oct. 23.

I should expect that the expenditure of officers and men in time of war, owing to incidents of service, would be nearly parallel, except in the higher grades, those of command, where the feeling of responsibility, coming also upon years advanced probably much beyond the prime of life, would be likely to induce a much larger percentage of break downs. With this exception, I think—it is my personal forecast—that the material of the navy will be liable to more frequent and more extensive inquiry than the personnel. Accidents will be more frequent, and will more often entail the laying of a ship aside for periods of varying length.

No difficulty is to be apprehended as to the supply of admirals and captains of *average* competency. All competent lieutenants of over thirty will be fit to command a ship; and would need only the experience of commanding a single ship to fit them for flags.

The trouble will be, and historically almost always has been, to have a sufficiency of watch & division officers. This is the trouble the Department is now feeling acutely, and of course would in still higher degree in war. If fully met, by adequate numbers of lieutenants & midshipmen, there ensues infallibly the congestion, of which the "hump" with its evils was an example, unless some relief can be found.

---

1. Walter Hines Page, *The Rebuilding of Old Commonwealths, being Essays towards the Training of the Forgotten Man in the Southern States.* New York: Doubleday, Page, and Company, 1902.

1. Secretary of the Navy, 1902–1904; Attorney General, 1904–1906; and Associate Justice of the Supreme Court, 1906–1910. H. C. Taylor to Moody, November 5, mentions an earlier letter from Mahan to Moody on the cessation of ship construction, but it has not been found.

Probably no effective remedy, no complete remedy, I should rather say, can be found. My own has been rather scouted by officers. *I* would train at the Academy a large additional number of men, with the provision that they should fulfill two complete years of service, on a battle-ship in commission, after graduation. I would then relegate them to civil life, with the provision that during a term of years, say five, they should be liable to a call for service in war, and that during the same time the Government would pay them a yearly stipend—say $500. They could be carried on the Register as a reserve.

A man well trained as above would not lose his requirements in five years; after that his usefulness would deteriorate rapidly. This is not so much a remedy as an amelioration. In the nature of things a dilemma exists, because enough lieutenants, say five to each commanding officer, means that the captains and the admirals can't get out of the way fast enough to insure reasonable promotion; and reasonable promotion is as necessary to efficiency of the navy as adequate numbers are. The question of promotion is not a personal one.

Of course, my scheme is to be regarded more as the statement of a general principle, than as a precise detailed method.

Selection of course, if thoroughly capable, is the true solution. It is better to have a captain of forty with lieutenants of fifty years, than a captain of fifty and lieutenants of forty. The same I believe to be true, perhaps truer, as regards admirals & captains.

To Alonzo H. Clark[1]

160 West 86th Street, New York, November 1, 1902 [LC]

My dear Sir: About a month ago I received from Mr. Alcée Fortier, president of the Louisiana Histl. Society, a letter in which he said he would like to become a member of the Am. Histl. Assocn., and asked me to present his name for membership "for the year 1903."

I told him I would do so in time sufficient. As I am not familiar with the custom of making elections, will you do me the favor of putting this matter in train, or notifying me what has to be done?

---

1. Editor for the Smithsonian Institution, 1881–1918, and Secretary of the American Historical Association, 1889–1908.

To James Brander Matthews

160 West 86th Street, New York, November 5, 1902 [CUL]

My dear Professor: Thank you very much for your witty and instructive treatment of the difficulties and necessities of speakers, which I have read—your part of it—with amusement & benefit. The appendix I reserve.

I feel myself constrained to the written word, never yet having been able to think on my legs for over five or ten minutes; about as far, in fact, as one long mental breath will carry me. As I fear that so much brevity would scarcely be felt to fit the solemnity of any dolorous occasion, there is nothing for it but paper.

To James Ford Rhodes

160 West 86th Street, New York, November 10, 1902 [MHS]

My dear Mr. Rhodes: Since my return home a fortnight ago, I have been purposing to thank you for the clippings from the *Times* you sent me during the summer, a thoughtfulness which I very much appreciated.

Meanwhile I have had the pleasure of accepting through the Secretary the invitation of yourself and Mr. Adams[1] to dinner on Nov. 28, in which I think I scarcely err in recognizing another instance of consideration towards myself.

I trust your European trip has brought you back rested and refreshed for the continuance of your very important and successful work. For myself, though I have stuck to the oar it has been in reasonable moderation, and I am better for the summer.

With kind remembrance to Mrs. Rhodes, believe me [etc.].

To Seth Low

160 West 86th Street, New York, November 17, 1902 [CUL]

My dear Mr. Low: Mr. Strachey,[1] the editor of the London *Spectator*, is in town for this week only, and is to lunch with me on Thursday at the University Club, at 1:30. Will you not spare a couple of your very busy hours to join us? I expect only a company of six.[2]

---

1. Either Charles Kendall Adams, first President of the American Historical Association in 1889, or Henry Adams, President in 1894. No account of Rhodes's dinner has been found.

1. John St. Loe Strachey.
2. In the margin of this letter Low wrote: "Rapid transit meeting that afternoon. Sorry."

To James Brander Matthews

160 West 86th Street, New York, November 17, 1902 [CUL]

My dear Mr. Matthews: Will you give me the pleasure of lunching with me at the University Club on Thursday next at 1:30, to meet Mr. Strachey, of the London *Spectator*.

As he is only just arrived in the city and for one week, my notice has to be short, but I trust you will *make* it convenient to come.

To John Bassett Moore

160 West 86th Street, New York, November 19, 1902 [LC]

My dear Mr. Moore: Will you not give me the pleasure of your company at lunch tomorrow, Thursday at 1.30, at the University Club, to meet Mr. Strachey, the editor of the London *Spectator*.

To R. M. Holden[1]

160 West 86th Street, New York, November 24, 1902[2]

Sir: I have had the honor to receive your letter of the 10th instant, notifying me that I have been unanimously elected an Honorary Member for Life of the Royal United Service Institution.

It gives me very great pleasure to accept this election, and I beg that you will convey to the Council my thanks for the honor done me, and my very high sense of the terms of appreciation in which it has been pleased to speak of my contributions to the naval literature of the British Navy.

To John Bassett Moore

160 West 86th Street, New York, November 25, 1902 [LC]

My dear Mr. Moore: I observe that Wharton[1] quotes a letter from Everett to Mr. Rives, Dec. 17. 1852, alluding to "steps taken by Great

---

1. Secretary of the Royal United Service Institution.
2. From the Royal United Service Institution *Journal*, XLVI (1902), p. 1637.

1. Francis Wharton, ed., *The Revolutionary Diplomatic Correspondence of the United States*. 6 vols. Washington, D.C.: Government Printing Office, 1889. Mahan was preparing his "The Monroe Doctrine," *National Review* (February 1903).

Britain, France, and United States to preserve the tranquillity and integrity of the eastern part of Santo Domingo."

Can you give my any fuller reference to these steps? for I find nothing in the President's Message or published documents. Or do you know whether this was a convention of any kind for joint action? The natural inference would be that it was an agreement, formal or informal, concerning action, several or joint, or else a pledge to abstention. All this too would seem in line with the general tendency of the Taylor-Fillmore term, to observe indeed the general policy of the country against entanglements, but all the same to yield for special purposes, of which the Clayton-Bulwer treaty was the conspicuous example.

To John Bassett Moore

160 West 86th Street, New York, November 27, 1902 [LC]

Dear Mr. Moore: Thank you exceedingly for the paper you have sent me. There seems to have been a great aberration in our general policy in 1850; the Clayton-Bulwer and this S. Domingo business. In the former there was something apparently to gain though we paid high for it, but there seems almost nothing in the latter. At that stage of our national fortunes it might have led to anything.

To Charles H. Haskins[1]

160 West 86th Street, New York, December 2, 1902 [LC]

My dear Mr. Haskins: In looking forward to the Philadelphia meeting, it has occurred to me, as probably extremely expedient, that there should be arrangement beforehand for some one in particular to preside over each of the sectional meetings.

If this be so, my great lack of acquaintance with the personnel of the Association makes me very unfit to choose. The duty is very nominal for any one, whose interest in the particular subject will lead him to be present at all. Still, some persons like even that little prominence, and there is a fitness in selection.

If you can help me by any suggestion I should be greatly indebted. I

---

1. Professor of History at the University of Wisconsin and chairman of the program committee of the American Historical Association.

do not mean that any notifications should be sent out beforehand, but only to be myself in measure prepared to ask suitable persons.

I presume there is some one, or more, occasions, on which the President should take the chair, and I shall be ready to act on such, where I can. One only exception I shall wish to make, and that is Saturday evening. I wish to secure that evening and Sunday with friends in the country, leaving town by 6, after attending the reception programmed.

To Andrew C. McLaughlin[1]

N.P., N.D.   Probably, New York, December 12, 1902 [LC]

My dear Sir: Yours of the 9th is to hand. I see no reason why I should not hand you my MS. during the Philadelphia meeting if you are there, or send it to you immediately afterwards, for publication at your convenience.[2]

To Andrew C. McLaughlin

160 West 86th Street, New York, December 17, 1902 [LC]

My dear Sir: I have received a letter from the editor of the *Atlantic Monthly*, asking to publish my address to be delivered at Philadelphia. He tells me this has been done by Mr. Rhodes and other recent presidents of the Association.

I am prepared to consent to this, provided it does not conflict with the prior claims of the *Review*.[1] Probably the circulation of the two magazines does not cross to any extent that would make the double issue injurious to either. I do not remember what has been the practice in previous cases, except that of Mr. Adams,[2] which I know the H.R. published.

May I ask you for a speedy reply.

---

1. Managing editor of the *American Historical Review*, 1901–1905.
2. Mahan's presidential address to the American Historical Association, "Subordination in Historical Treatment," was published in the Annual Report of the Association for 1902, pp. 47–63. Retitled "Writing of History," it appeared again in the *Atlantic Monthly* (March 1903) and was reprinted in *Naval Administration and Warfare* in 1908.

1. The *American Historical Review*.
2. Henry Adams.

To Bliss Perry[1]

160 West 86th Street, New York, December 17, 1902 [HUL]

My dear Sir: With the instances of Mr. Rhodes and others before me, I assume there can be no objection on the part of the *American Historical Review* to the *Atlantic* publishing my address, which the *H.R.* expects to publish in its April issue.[2]

Assuming the assent of the editors, I shall be very glad to put it in your hands. It is in length 6,000 words, and I should consider its value under the circumstances to be $150.00.

I have written a line to the managing editor of the *A.H.R.*,[3] asking his acquiescence. Assuming it I should be glad to know when you would wish the manuscript.

To Bliss Perry

160 West 86th Street, New York, December 19, 1902 [HUL]

Dear Sir: I wrote at once to Dr. McLaughlin, the Managing Editor of the *A.H.R.*, and may hope to hear soon from him. Equally with yourself, I see no reason for his objecting. There will be no difficulty about my placing copy in your hands by Jan. 10. We may therefore consider the matter settled, subject only to the remote chance of an objection.

To Bouverie F. Clark

160 West 86th Street, New York, December 19, 1902 [LC]

My dear Clark: I have no particular occasion for writing to day beyond that of sending my cordial best wishes for the Christmas and New Year season, during which I may expect this letter to reach you. My life has been, if anything, rather more quiet and preoccupied with routine work than usual; but the recurrence of these periods consecrated to general and particular good will has the advantage of calling to mind old friends of whom one wishes to know.

I have not seen or heard any mention of you since your last. It gave me

---

1. Editor of the *Atlantic Monthly*, 1899–1909.
2. Because Mahan promised his paper to another journal, "Subordination in Historical Treatment" was not published in the *American Historical Review*.
3. A. C. McLaughlin.

pleasure to read, I cannot now recall just where, that some further formal notice of the excellence of the transport service had been taken; if I remember right, by recognition extended to the transport captains. In the column or so of comment which I read I was somewhat surprised not to see you named; but anything said on the subject cannot but reflect back to you, very much as admirals have a share in all prize money. Making every allowance for the general merit of the system when you took it, it must always remain that efficient superintendence was the essential condition of success. It was a tremendous job, an expansion beyond all precedent, especially in the pace that had to be kept up. It was also the basis upon which the success of the campaign rested, and it is a great thing for you to look back on, that it was the service which beyond all others demonstrated its efficiency by the amount of work done, & the fewness of mishaps.

My past year has been very successful, though I find literary work like all others becomes something of the dray horse business, when the first freshness is worn off. I think, however, that in return I write more quickly and evenly; travel the daily round with less friction, if with less ardor. I am on the point of beginning a history of our war with you in 1812, which will complete my series of Sea Power books as originally designed. I had expected to do this nearly ten years ago; but other issues turned up, and the immediate advantage of magazine writing has shunted me more than it ought.

The year has been marked to you by one of those great sorrows[1] which cannot be forgotten, even if one desired to; which few would wish, I think. I trust, nevertheless, that by this time has done somewhat of its merciful healing work; not impairing the memory of the loss, nor disguising its greatness, but relieving in measure the soreness of a wound which if not so alleviated would be insupportable.

To John S. Billings

160 West 86th Street, New York, December 20, 1902 [NYPL]

My dear Dr. Billings: Three or four years ago I became involved in a polemic with a Mr. Badham concerning Nelson's action at Naples, 1799. In the course of it I had to procure a number of books, or pamphlets, which I have hitherto retained, in case of the controversy reopening; but as I have heard nothing from Badham since January, 1900, and Dr. Rawson Gardiner, then in health and Editor of the English *Historical Review*, assured me I

---

1. *See* Mahan to Clark, July 7, 1902.

need take no further account of him, as a disputant, I am disposed to give the collection to the Public Library, if you care to accept them.[1]

I enclose a list. They are all paper bound, but I believe complete. I make of course no stipulations; but I should be glad, if feasible, if Nos. 12, 13, and 14 could be bound together. They contain either the substance of the controversy, or else all necessary reference to previous papers by Badham or myself. My refutation of Maresca's paper is much more important than that of Badham, as the former is an authority, the latter not.

If you care to have them, and will so notify me, I will fix a time when they will be ready for a messenger, who I suppose could be sent for them.

[P.S.] Foote's *Vindication* is only the 1st ed.; the second is of consequence to this matter.

[Enclosure]

1) *Storia della Republica Partenopea*, G. G. Pahl 1889; 2) *Maria Carolina, Carteggio con Lady Hamilton*, R. Palumbo 1877 (Documenti inediti); 3) *Histoire de la Revolution Dans les deux Siciles*, Saint Denys 1856; 4) *Vigliena* (Rivoluzione Napal. del 1799) F. Pometti 1894; 5) Fabrizio Ruffo, *Rivoluzione e Contro. Riv. 1798–1799*, Helfert 1885 (Italian translation from German); 6) *Il Cattivo Genio di Nelson*, C. Segre 1898; 7) Nelson, *Caracciolo e la Rep. Nap.* (1799) P. Villari 1899; 8) *Il Cavaliere Antonio Micheroux*, B. Maresca 1895; 9) *Nelson e Caracciolo e La Rep. Nap. 1799*, F. Lemoni 1898; 10) *Memorie Storiche sulla vita del Cardinale Ruffo*, D. Sacchinelli 1895; 11) *I Borboni di Napoli*, 10 volumes, A. Dumas 1863; 12) *Nelson at Naples*, 1799 (pp. 48), F. P. Badham 1900; 13) *Gli Avvenimenti di Napoli, June 13–July 12, 1799*, narrati del Cav. A. Micheroux, B. Maresca 1900; 14) *Nelson at Naples*, A. T. Mahan 1900; 15) *Captain Foote's Vindication* (first editn.) 1807.

To Leopold J. Maxse

160 West 86th Street, New York, December 22, 1902 [LC]

My dear Mr. Maxse: I enclose herewith an article upon the Monroe Doctrine for which you expressed a wish.[1] The subject seems to lead naturally on to the consideration of the fact that recent and present conditions—present history, if I may so say—conspires with the Monroe Doctrine to withdraw European activity from this hemisphere. That is to say, the questions of the Levant, Egypt, and China, in which the Mediterranean

1. *See* Mahan to Billings, September 8, 1905.
1. *See* Mahan to Maxse, October 3, 1902.

is also necessarily involved, give European countries with their mutual jealousies quite enough to occupy all their attention.

I had written some lines in that direction with especial application to Great Britain in this sense. That her position in Egypt, India, and Australia, with the related interests (Persia, China etc), and her preeminent commerce, made it distinctly her interest to support—morally and tacitly—the general policy of the U.S. formulated in the Doctrine. I am never in favor of formal agreements in such matters between states, unless imperative, which I do not see to be the case here; but I am a convinced believer in the expediency of drawing out the motives, which should lead states to support one another, and especially in this case in a kind of division of labor, we taking this end of the pole, Great Britain the other. To do this would have run the article too long; but I suggest it for your consideration as a matter of present lay policy with a probable, and to my mind very certain, bearing on the immediate future.

I am sorry Great Britain has associated herself with any other power in the Venezuela business.[2] The action of the two powers does not contravene the Monroe Doctrine; but I fear the *joint* action will excite a popular sentiment here injurious to both. In this I care nothing about Germany; but I do care about Great Britain, both because I have a regard for you and because *our* policy requires cordial relations. It is illogical to object to two Powers doing jointly what there is no objection to either doing singly; but feeling takes little heed of logic, and I am not myself sure that the one is a less good guide than the other. However, I should not complain, for I see the facts are influencing Congress to authorize two more battle-ships.

To John S. Billings

160 West 86th Street, New York, December 23, 1902 [NYPL]

My dear Dr. Billings: The pamphlets etc[1] are now packed ready for the messenger. The bundle, of extemporized materials & made up by myself, is somewhat archaic, but can go its short journey safely.

I have put the three I would like bound together, in the same elastic; but you will use your own judgment as to a matter that concerns rather the convenience of readers than my personal preference.

Renewing good wishes for Christmas & New Year [etc.].

---

2. A joint Anglo-German show of naval force against Venezuelan dictator Cipriano Castro in December 1902 to collect overdue financial obligations.

1. *See* Mahan to Billings, December 20, 1902.

To John S. Billings

160 West 86th Street, New York, January 5, 1903 [NYPL]

My dear Dr. Billings: Noting what you said of a group of publications on a given subject, I have a consecutive series of British Parliamentary Blue books (7), containing correspondence on the troubles which led to the South African War, extending from August 1897, to after the outbreak of the war, and nearly to January 1900. It contains Milner's full report of the Bloemfontein Conference, and all that the British Government published up to the latter date; including the Boer Government's letters as well. With these I have also the official text of the Praetoria (1881) and London (1884) Conventions, on which the argument mainly turned. And there is also a supplementary No. on the Defenses of Natal in the beginning of the War.

I dont know whether the Library possesses these. If not, they are gladly at your service.

To Andrew C. McLaughlin

160 West 86th Street, New York, January 11, 1903 [LC]

My dear Mr. McLaughlin: I enclose the proof of my address[1] for such summary as you may care to make; after which I will ask you to send it to the Chairman of the Committee charged with the publication of the Proceedings of the Association; as I understood they wished it.[2]

The title I chose for my Address was "Subordination in Historical Treatment." The *Atlantic* has made it the "Writing of History," and excised the first opening words which I have attached in copy sent you.

To Bliss Perry

160 West 86th Street, New York, January 13, 1903 [HUL]

My dear Sir: I return herewith the corrected proof of my article.[1] I am entirely satisfied with the the title you have chosen, and merely mention

---

1. Presidential address to the American Historical Association.
2. On January 3, 1903, McLaughlin asked Mahan to prepare a short précis of "Subordination in Historical Treatment" for the *American Historical Review*, since he himself had not been present.

1. *See* Mahan to Perry, December 17 and 19, 1903.

the one set by myself, "Subordination in Historical Treatment," in case you should think it better. In my own judgment the latter is more precise, though limited; yours more general. Please suit yourself.

To Stephen B. Luce

160 West 86th Street, New York, January 13, 1903 [LC]

My dear Admiral: Thank you for your letter. The main thesis of my *War of 1812* must necessarily be the sufferings of the country through the inadequacy of the Navy as compared with the actual power of the country to have made better preparation.

I will endeavor however so to word my comment as not to give offense such as you mention. I own to thinking that the paragraph as a whole is good for our public; and that the navy can only complain of the expression you quote by severing it from the context, which enlarges—perhaps not sufficiently—upon the merits of the navy and the demerits of the nation towards the service.[1]

To John S. Billings

160 West 86th Street, New York, January 17, 1903 [NYPL]

My dear Dr. Billings: As the Public Library is already provided with the substance of the Blue Books, of which I wrote you,[1] I have decided to place them in the University Club Library.

To Leopold J. Maxse

160 West 86th Street, New York, January 27, 1903 [LC]

My dear Mr. Maxse: I have been much concerned latterly at not hearing at all from the Ms. "Monroe Doctrine," mailed to you Dec. 22 by register mail. Taking the steamer of Dec. 24, I calculated there would be

---

1. On this letter Luce wrote: "In answer to letter of mine calling attention to *Interest of America in Sea Power* pages, 149–50, stating that never was blood spilled more uselessly than in the frigate fights of War of 1812."

1. *See* Mahan to Billings, January 5, 1903.

time for it to appear in Feb. number;[1] when, from outlook then, & still more now, whatever value it might otherwise possess would be enhanced by opportuneness.[2] I still trust you have recd. it, for I find on inquiry that return registry receipt is not sent back over the Atlantic, unless specially asked by sender. I need only add that I have a rough draft of that sent; though somewhat imperfect it can serve to reproduce adequately.

To Samuel A. Ashe

160 West 86th Street, New York, February 1; April 12, 1903 [DUL]

My dear Ashe: I have for some time been intending to ask you whether you have ever known anything of the history of your quondam roommate—Hackett.[1] He is, I think, the only one of the twenty of our class who graduated, of whom I have never heard since the beginning of the war. Probably you may know that he resigned from the Service on the outbreak of the Civil War, on account of his sympathy with the South; but I do not even know whether he went so far as to take arms on your side. You were good friends as roommates, but I fancy there was no very particular sympathy between you. At graduation, he and Averett,[2] under whose influence he was greatly, would not speak to me on account of a quarrel, of which you may remember to have heard at the time.

Last year I had a letter from Jeff Slamm,[3] who was of the 55 date. Am I mistaken in the impression that, the year before I came, you and he roomed together? He was turned back in 56, bilged that year again, and had to leave. His father was purser of the *Congress*, in which Claiborne, Cenas, Spencer, Wiltse[4] and myself made our first cruise; & he had influence to have Jeff appointed a master's mate, so that he was in our mess two years, June 1859 to August 61. During the war he served in our volunteer navy, and then secured a place in the revenue cutter service, in which he has passed his life. I have not met him in all these years, but he wrote me to certify to his *Congress* service, in order to secure retiring rights, or pay, involved. He remembered that he & I alone were left of the mess; & as it seemed he might have some information of the others, which I had not, I wrote to ask. He

---

1. It did appear in the *National Review* in February 1903.
2. As the result of the Anglo-German intervention in Venezuela in December 1902.

1. S. H. Hackett, from Pennsylvania, did not participate in the Civil War.
2. S. W. Averett, CSN, from Virginia, went south in 1861, and died in 1898.
3. Jefferson A. Slamm.
4. H. B. Claiborne, from Louisiana, who went south in 1861, and died in 1873; H. Cenas, from Louisiana, who became a lieutenant in the Confederate States Navy, and died in 1877; T. S. Spencer, who was a lieutenant commander when he resigned in 1867; and G. C. Wiltse, who died as a captain in 1893.

told me that Claiborne, who was abroad most of the war, died soon after returning to New Orleans; that he had visited his grave. Cenas he had met at Richmond, at the time it was taken possession of. Wiltse was also there at the time, so the three met. Some years later, Slamm was in New Orleans, and there again met him [Cenas]. He was quite seedy, doing nothing, and looking dissipated. Slamm had need to go to a telegraph office, and in paying for his message laid down a $20 bill. When the change was given, Cenas, who always had bullied J. [Jeff], drew it towards him and kept $5, saying "you dont know how much I need this." Later in the day J. saw him drunk in the street—I suppose the proceeds of the $5. He never saw him afterwards, but knew of his death, and had met one of his sisters at a later day. They supported him and themselves by keeping a school. Cenas had begun to drink before leaving the *Congress*—a habit unusual in a Creole—& when luck ran against him, I suppose could not resist. Poor "Fan" Spencer, Slamm wrote, also died of drink. On the *Congress* he was always perfectly steady, but increasingly indolent, rather disposed to plume himself on it; but the trait grew on him till he became perfectly worthless as an officer. About 1867 it led to a row between him & his captain, in consequence of which he resigned; whether there was then any rum in the matter I dont know. Of course, laziness may go in government service up to a certain point; but in the competition of civil life it spells ruin. I asked about him once or twice from his brother in law, "Tom" Walker—do you remember him?—who married his sister; but Tom would never give definite reply. He spoke vaguely of his putting his head down, and butting straight at his troubles; but I fancy he made little of it. He ended by marrying a woman with some money, but I imagine socially very inferior, got to drinking & so died. After you—a very long distance after you—I cared more for him than any man in the class. Two years in the same room, and two in the same mess, and from that day to this I could count on one hand the times I have seen him.

I have fancied that in this "evening of our life" it might interest you to hear somewhat of those who to you can be but dim figures of a distant past. Wiltse died ten years ago. He took part in the abortive flag-raising at Hawaii, which Cleveland disavowed; & it has been said that concern and disappointment hastened his end. He had, however, become very obese, & I doubt if he were destined to old age. He had some little property, and married a good bit more; always more or less of an ass, yet withal a man of pluck and resolution.

Butt,[5] the fiddler, I heard of more than once. He was at one time in the Peruvian Navy, stationed at a yard they maintained on the east of the Andes, at the head waters of the Amazon. In 1872 I was on my way to Rio, and the ship stopping at Pará, at the mouth of the Amazon, a Peruvian captain came on board who had been with him there. The next time I heard of him

---

5. W. R. Butt became a lieutenant in the Confederate States Navy, and died in 1885.

was from Loyall Farragut, who knew of his death in California, at the house (I think) of a connection of Farragut's, also related to you. His habits I understand had become very bad. Certainly he died before his time.

Of Averett's death I heard very casually about four years ago. A cousin of his—a woman—wrote me that he had died—age about 60—and that she wanted data for a memoir. She said he had given himself to educational work in Virginia, and I gathered had had hard work to make the ends meet.[6]

Of those who "went South"—seven, including Hackett—there remain Hall and Borchert.[7] Of the former you probably know more than I. I have heard nothing of him since I left him consul at Nice, where I doubt he was much of a success. Concerning Borchert, the detailed report reached the country of his being murdered, I think before 1870, by a revolutionary mob in one of those South American countries where he had sought service. He had been in N.Y. a short time before, at the same time with myself, and there had been an arrangement to meet; but something prevented.

Of those who remained in the Navy in 1861, there are now alive only four. Nine have departed. The four are Remey, Farquhar, Kane[8] and myself. Remey alone is on the active list, and now the senior rear-admiral—only *the* Admiral, Dewey, above him. He retires, I think, during the current year. I know very little of him, no one of the class has crossed my way so little. He married, I believe a woman of means, and has children; but I have never seen his family, and himself only at long intervals. He has recently returned from a full tour of duty on the China Station. He was one of the cabal that coventried me in the last year, but that was a recollection tacitly dropped by both.

Farquhar retired for age last year. I met him two months ago on a street corner in Washington, on his way to church with his wife. He was looking well, but with that pathetic combination of likeness and unlikeness to one's former self, which so strikes us in those we have not seen for some time. He and I, however, have always kept friendly touch. The only interesting circumstance in his career, probably unknown to you, is that he married— quite early—during the war, after only two weeks acquaintance with his wife to be. The marriage has been perfectly happy, and they have several children.

Kane was retired, rather against his will, some five years ago, for nervous

---

6. Averett College, in Danville, Virginia, has in its archives a pamphlet titled *In Memoriam, Samuel Wooton Averett, President Judson Institute*. (Montgomery, Alabama, 1896). Mahan does not seem to have been among the anonymous contributors to that work.

7. W. B. Hall; and G. A. Borchert, from Georgia, who became a lieutenant in the Confederate States Navy.

8. G. C. Remey, who survived until 1928; N. H. Farquhar, who retired as a rear admiral, and died in 1907; and T. F. Kane, who retired as a captain in 1896, and died in 1908.

breakdown. Some of those associated with him thought him hardly treated; that he would have recovered, if given time; but in the Spanish War he was called on for some administrative shore duty, urgent & distracting in its demands, and I understood he went to pieces in very short order. He also married young, a woman I knew pretty well, and liked very little. I believe, however, it has turned out very well. He has three sons, and makes N.Y. his home. I see him semi-occasionally, but scarcely to know him. I hear he is morbid at times.

Mackenzie, Swasey, and Prentiss[9] were killed in action; Swasey on the Mississippi in 1862, Prentiss at Farragut's entrance to Mobile Bay in 1864. They were too young to have a history, though Prentiss was already married. I went passenger in the same transport with him from N.Y. to New Orleans, in 1863; and it is a curious fact that, on arrival there, I asked to be ordered to the ship on which he met his death a few months later. It dont follow I should have got in the way of the same ball, but the incident struck me. His captain told me he was quite useless in the action, and I infer from what I heard that he went into it oppressed with a presentiment of death. I was a pall-bearer at Swasey's funeral.

Mackenzie was killed on the island of Formosa, in 1867. A punitive expedition had been sent to visit retribution on the savages for some injury to an American vessel or crew. The only man hurt was poor Mac. I was at the time on my way to the station, looking forward to seeing him. He also was one of those who broke with me, but he wrote me a very candid & straightforward letter of regret a couple of years before he died.

Dana Greene committed suicide about 1884. There was, I think, some specific physical cause that induced the brain trouble, which was aggravated by a controversy he got into over the *Monitor* & *Merrimac* fight. He was first lieutenant of the *Monitor* on that occasion, & was highly complimented by his captain for his conduct. His father died here four years ago at the age of 98; on the other hand his son lost his life under most distressing circumstances a year later. He and his wife were skating together after nightfall; the ice broke with them and both were drowned, not only unhelped but unheard.

Beatty Smith[10]—do you remember Beatty Peshine barely five feet high?— also became worthless as an officer, and upon coming up for promotion to commander was rejected, and dropped from the list. I think he made no effort to have the action reversed. His father had been to Japan as a legal advisor to the Govt., I believe, and Beatty was one of the few who really got a good bit of prize money. I fancy he was quite comfortable. I met him

---

9. A. S. MacKenzie, who was killed during the expedition to revenge the *Rover* affair; C. H. Swasey, who was killed while serving in the *Scioto*; and R. Prentiss, who was killed while serving in the *Monongahela*.
10. B. P. Smith, who left the service in 1874 and died in 1886.

once, probably now twenty years ago, in the lobby of a N.Y. hotel. He was perfectly straight, and I fancy still lounges through life. I have never since heard of him.

April 12

The interval between dates will inform you as to my habits of correspondence. In fact, however, though I write many letters, I have no correspondent, since mine with you dropped off. An off Sunday, as today, is the only occasion on which I am fresh enough from my daily drudgery of writing to indulge in conversation by letter. The delay in this case was specifically due to the fact that I knew there were 20 to graduate, & my tally ran only to 19. I could not recover the missing man, & finally wrote to Washington to a friend to consult an 1859 *Register*. The missing man proved to be C. Marius Schoonmaker; the C. standing for Cornelius and not for Caius, as might naturally be inferred. He continued through life what you would expect if you recall his personality; heavy and phlegmatic in external characteristic, but attentive kindly and faithful. A good officer, not brilliant, but thorough to the extent of his abilities. He lost his life in command of a ship, the *Vandalia*, in the great hurricane at Samoa in 1889. She dragged ashore, but my impression is few lost their lives by drowning, and he was killed by being thrown off his feet and striking violently on his head.

This completes the story of the "date" so far as it graduated. But no—there is one whom I had not forgotten, but also not mentioned—McCook.[11] He remained always coarse—was so essentially; goodhearted enough, a tolerable officer as far as I know, but coarse to the marrow. This is a condition which gets much worse when it dont get better; and I fancy that drink made things worse than they would otherwise have been. He managed to keep in the service, however, and died in it, a commander; but he was not fifty when he departed.

That *does* "finish the account." If you can add anything to it of your own knowledge, I should be very interested to hear. Hackett is the only one of whom I had never known anything; but of those of whom I have heard a little, you may know more, especially of those who "went South." They had very hard times, for as Billy Parker[12] said in his book, other men lost property, but the Southern naval officers lost a profession, by the results of the war. It was a profession, too, that did not lead up to anything else, so that concurring with the poverty of their section for so many years their case was peculiarly hard. I ran across one curious exception, however. When I was writing my volume on the Navy in the Civil War,[13] I learned that John

11. R. S. McCook retired in 1885, and died in 1886.
12. William Harwar Parker, *Recollections of a Naval Officer, 1841–1865*. New York: Charles Scribner's Sons, 1883.
13. *Gulf and Inland Waters.*

Grimball, graduate of 58, was practising law in N.Y.[14] As he had served in the *Arkansas*, I hunted him up to ask some questions. When I entered his office I could not believe my eyes. If you remember him, he was short, almost diminutive. He had grown a man of at least five feet ten; it rarely happens that such a change takes place after 18. He looked well to do, but although I saw him once in church a few weeks later, we have not met since, and I dont find his name in the telephone directory; a pretty sure sign he is not practising here.

About myself you know pretty much all the externals, though you have not the run of my way of life, nor I of yours. It is so far a quiet enough evening tide, with abundance of occupation, still sufficiently congenial, although not with quite the abundance of interest it once had for me. I am at present at work on the War of 1812. It is a very old story, often told, and not a brilliant episode, nor one of which, as a whole, the United States can feel proud. It remains to see whether I can give any such novelty of presentation as to justify another telling.

With undiminished regard believe me, my dear Ashe [etc.]

To Leopold J. Maxse

160 West 86th Street, New York, February 7, 1903 [LC]

My dear Mr. Maxse: I have to thank you for the draft for $500, in payment of the article on the Monroe Doctrine, which is duly to hand.

Several of the closing paragraphs of the article were cabled to the *N.Y. Sun,* and have to some extent been commented on by the press. Several persons have also expressed to me their interest in the matter, so that this article may seem to share the characteristic of opportuneness which you kindly noted in some of its predecessors.[1]

It has seemed to me probable, particularly in view of the dissent expressed —as we hear—to some of my conclusions by the English press, that it might be advantageous to devote a paper to a consideration of the relations of the Doctrine to world politics, under some such title as "The U.S. and International Relations." I have as yet no intimation of your views as to further subjects, beyond what I understood to be a general willingness to accept initiative from me, subject of course to your approval as to suitability for the magazine. I am myself increasingly impressed with the idea that the Monroe Doctrine, in its inception and in present scope exclusive, is arriving at a stage where, without change in essential *internal* character, it is becoming

---

14. Grimball, from South Carolina, died in 1922.

1. Maxse himself wrote a critical review of the article in the same issue of *National Review* (February 1903).

a shaped and chiselled piece, fitted for a place in the general scheme of world wide relations; and that this particular place, for which the years have fashioned it, is becoming increasingly apparent.

I have also some views as to another matter which I will lay before you in due time—that is when I shall have time to overhaul what I already have in hand, written upon it.

Finally, I may say that I dont want to have another article ready before time for the June number unless you particularly desire it.

To Leopold J. Maxse

160 West 86th Street, New York, April 28, 1903 [CROCS]

My dear Mr. Maxse: Your letter of March 31 was received in due course, and has been allowed to lie in my mind for occasional reference & gradual maturing—if attained—which is my usual method of reaching conclusions. I cant say, however, that the international status of Holland, however interesting in itself, commands itself yet to me as a matter I am likely to deal with successfully and it would be impossible for me and I think intrinsically premature to advocate the U.S. taking part in any plan of mediatization as such an arrangement would involve alliance of a very permanent nature, and also U.S. intervention in European probity, both of which are contrary to our national conviction as well as to my own, personally; and I fear I am too old to change. Would there not be a curious analogy between the guarantee of Holland's independence as the seat of International Arbitration; and the Pope's claim of temporal power as necessary to the Divinely appointed arbiter among churches and nations? International Arbitration & the Papacy always seem to me cognate ideas, and I am not in love with either.

I have been so much engrossed in the preparation of my work on the War of 1812 that I have not been able adequately to think of my promised articles for the *National*. This would be unfair to you were it the result of other than miscalculation on my part. I engaged that *1812* should be ready for serial publication by Sept. 1 of this year, and I thought I could be so forehanded as to get in also two of the three articles for the *National* by that time. The Monroe Doctrine I wrote before seriously buckling to *1812*, and when I had mailed it I thought I had a clear path cut; but my forecast has proved wrong. I have, since the past four weeks have been forcing this conviction upon me, comforted myself in part by reflecting that you were probably in no pressing want from me, and that clearly nothing was occurring in my special lines.

I intend of course that, with your acquiescence, this means only delay;

not non-fulfillment. If you really want anything from me briefly, I can propose a possible makeshift for your consideration. A year ago our *Scribner*'s asked of me an article on Naval Administration. I wrote it last summer but on sending it in the editor found that my treatment, showing "the philosophy of the thing," to use his own expression when he asked it, was too "academic." That is, I had treated it by analyzing its principles, and illustrating by an historical comparison of the development, and existing character, of the contrasted systems of Great Britain and the United States. He wanted me to change it, and give him something more concrete and American, by showing actual working in our past experience. Rather than change I wrote an entirely new article,[1] which appears in the current (May) number of the magazine. If you should like, I can give you the first article[2] together with the *Scribner*, and by examining the two you could decide if the former is fresh and interesting enough for your readers. I personally think it good.

Otherwise, I still think the effect of the Monroe Doctrine as making for universal peace the subject just now most likely to excite in me the interest essential to good writing. Possibly, events are preparing something else for us.

To Herbert Putnam[1]

160 West 86 Street, New York, May 9, 1903 [LC]

My dear Mr. Putnam: I have the pleasure of enclosing to you the Ms. of my address,[2] as desired. I leave it in the entirely rough state, as I believe such value as these things possess is as much in the indication of the author's methods as of his handwriting.

To Leopold J. Maxse

160 West 86th Street, New York, May 12, 1903 [CROCS]

Dear Mr. Maxse: Your cable was received today, and I hope before this reaches you, you will have heard from me by cable that the articles are on

---

1. "The United States Navy Department."
2. Maxse accepted this article and it was published as "Principles of Naval Administration," *National Review* (June 1903).

1. Librarian of Congress, 1899–1939. The Putnam correspondence is in the Library of Congress Archives.
2. "Subordination in Historical Treatment."

their way. The one offered to your consideration will need some changes for an English magazine, having been written with an American clientele in view. I have been too occupied today to look it over, but expect to tackle it tomorrow and put it into shape for you.

To Stephen B. Luce

160 West 86th Street, New York, May 12, 1903 [LC]

My dear Admiral: Your early days must have been contemporary with some who had the traditional reports of 1812. Have you ever heard any comment on the fact that the *United States* and the *President* both arrived in the United States in December 1812, and did not go to sea again till the spring, thus throwing away the winter months for getting out? The *United States*, particularly, returning from the capture of the *Macedonian*, was by Decatur[1]—after the action—pronounced fit to continue her cruise. Yet she acted as above, & so never again got to sea during the War.

I have now worked through the three first frigate actions. I am somewhat surprised to find each having its own distinct individuality, though I cannot yet but grudge the time I have to spend on them. More interesting and important is the individuality of the captains, betrayed more by continual impression than by particular expression. John Rodgers had, in my judgment, the soundest military conceptions. I have been led to comment somewhat at large upon them. Yet, although he made four cruises in the *President*, averaging over three months each, & was therefore at sea longer than any captain during the war—except Porter[2]—he accomplished almost nothing. Why? *I* dont know. Bad luck will account for many things, but so much bad luck seems to justify the French proverb that it is a bêtise. Decatur seems very much what I thought him to be—more heart than brains. I remember Adml. Goldsborough[3] telling me the trouble with him was he was not a seaman. Pendergast[4] said the same; but then the Barron[5] tradition entered there. Bainbridge[6] impresses me unpleasantly; indefinably so, yet distinctly. Selfseeking I should think, and not over adventurous. Any side lights from your reminiscences of the old times would be welcome.

---

1. Stephen Decatur was in command of the frigate *United States* at the time of the capture.
2. David Porter, who commanded the frigate *Essex* during the War of 1812.
3. Louis M. Goldsborough.
4. Austin Pendergast, class of 1853.
5. James Barron was court-martialed in 1808 for surrendering the frigate *Chesapeake* to HMS *Leopard* in 1807.
6. William Bainbridge, who commanded the frigate *Constitution* during the War of 1812.

To Leopold J. Maxse

160 West 86th Street, New York, May 15, 1903 [LC]

Dear Mr. Maxse: I enclose the article, to which I have given the title "Naval Administration, historically considered." I am not wholly satisfied with that title; but to catch tomorrow's steamer, I let it go at that, and if anything better occurs I will write again. On page 40, I have indicated an "End," in deference chiefly to your space, and partly also to my own preference. To the latter consideration, you may justly ask, Why then send it at all? My only reply is a doubt as to whether it is essential to completeness. If your editorial opinion demand it, I shall be satisfied; but if you prefer to exclude it, I shall be more satisfied.

The May number of *Scribner's*, containing the other article[1] goes by the same mail.

To Leopold J. Maxse

160 West 86th Street, New York, May 29, 1903 [LC]

My dear Mr. Maxse: I write a line to say that my address till October 1st will be Quogue, N.Y.

If you continue your kindness of sending me the *National* please have it sent there. Letters are forwarded me but other class matter is more than doubtful.

Wishing you a pleasant summer, [etc.].

To William J. Tucker[1]

Slumberside, Quogue, Long Island, June 8, 1903 [DCL]

My dear Sir: I am much indebted for the information in your letter of the 2d., which I found awaiting me on my return Saturday. I will communicate with you in ample time concerning the time of my arrival, being here at an inconvenient distance from New York—for starting. It is needless to say that it will give me great pleasure to accept the kind invitation of Mrs. Tucker and yourself to be your guest.

I also accept with many expressions of obligation the proffer of the

---

1. "The United States Navy Department." *See* Mahan to Maxse, April 28, 1903.
1. President of Dartmouth College.

Trustees of the Degree of Doctor of Laws. This I presume takes place on the forenoon of the 24th. It will be necessary for me to return towards New York as immediately as possible after the conference of the degree, and it has occurred to me to ask you to ascertain with reference to getting the night boat from either Albany or Boston or Providence, as being an easier mode of travel. For New York you will doubtless know.

On referring to Dr. Smith's letter of February 9th, I see he asks to be informed as to my subject. "Personality and Influence"[2] is the tentative title I have affixed to my leading thought; but as the words remain to be written I cannot be more explicit now.

To Leopold J. Maxse

Slumberside, Quogue, Long Island, June 11, 1903 [LC]

My dear Mr. Maxse: I have received this week a request from Sir Percy Bunting,[1] for an article upon the general subject of the late excitement in Great Britain over the revelations concerning German forwardness etc. It is quite impossible for me to undertake this, consistently with other obligations now upon me; but had I been at leisure I should have felt a little embarrassed, in view of an impression I have that you, in view of the large payment the *National* has been in the habit of giving for my former articles, had signified—and I thought reasonably—that I should not at the same time be contributing to its possible competitors.

Under ordinary circumstances I should have looked upon my relations with the *National* as resting upon this somewhat tacit basis; but, in view of such a very live naval topic arising, your not showing any wish for an article from me suggested to me the idea that possibly you had receded, either from the wish for my articles, or from the willingness to pay the price.

The information concerning Germany's action—as given in the Parliamentary debates—impressed me so strongly as interesting the U.S., that I sat down to a letter to one of our leading dailies, to set forth the facts & what I thought the U.S. public should realize. This, developing farther than I intended, I ultimately sent to one of the weeklies—*Collier's*—which has a large circulation; wide-spread as well as large.[2]

I am, as I think, bound down for the time to certain work which I have

---

2. *See* Paper, "Personality and Influence," June 24, 1903.

1. Editor of *Contemporary Review*. No article by Mahan was ever published in the *Review*.

2. *Collier's Weekly* did not publish this paper.

in hand, & excluded from other for the moment. But this I hope will cease with the summer, & it seemed to me advisable, with reference to my future course, to ascertain whether my status with the *National* was the same as before. Of course, I feel free in the U.S. to write for whom I please, but I have not felt quite the same as to Great Britain.

To Stephen B. Luce

Slumberside, Quogue, Long Island, June 17, 1903 [LC]

My dear Admiral: I have intended all along to answer your last letter, not because it absolutely required reply, but because I think you misapprehended the drift of my query.[1] It was not the failure of our frigates to get away after the spring—say April—1813; but that, with a difficulty so plainly to be foreseen, why they—notably the *President* and *United States*—should have remained, apparently supinely, during the preceding three months. After April the difficulty, except for light draught vessels, was almost insuperable.

After his action with the *Macedonian* Decatur wrote that his damages would not prevent his continuing his cruise; that he came back only to see the prize into port. He arrived Dec. 4. 1812, and the *United States* losing the next four months, never again got to sea. The *President* arrived Boston Dec. 31. She did not sail again till late in April. Since writing you I have come across a misplaced letter of Decatur's, March 10, 1813, "the new mainmast of my ship will be finished today, and the principal cause of my detention in port so long be thus removed." If, as is probable, but I cannot just now verify, the condemnation of the old mainmast was due to a scrape from the enemy's shot, the *Macedonian* could claim that she had, though beaten, closed the *U.S.*'s career. Rodgers mentions excessive cold in part cause; but so far, though quite willing to believe that there were reasons, wholly satisfactory, for the loss of time not to be regained, I have not met them.

As regards the surrender of the *President*, I know Roosevelt's general ground,[2] but have purposely refrained from studying his reasons till I shall have formed my independent conclusions. Decatur has always been a hero to me; all my prepossession is in his favor. The question of when to give in is always difficult. Hull's surrender at Detroit and Porter's defense of the *Essex* mark extremes; granting for argument's sake, what is very disputable,

---

1. *See* Mahan to Luce, May 12, 1903.
2. Theodore Roosevelt, *The Naval War of 1812*. New York: G. P. Putnam's Sons, 1882.

that Hull needed to surrender at all. His excuse was "to save life." Porter unquestionably would have been justified in surrendering sooner than he did for the same reason. Whatever specific justification exists in a particular case, I suppose we would all agree in the general rule that it is better to hold out too long than too short.

To Charles W. Stewart[1]

Slumberside, Quogue, Long Island, June 26, 1903 [NA]

My dear Mr. Stewart: On my return home last night from a four days absence, I found awaiting me the registered package of books sent from the Library. I enclose a receipted list, to guard against the possibility of any mistake in either sending or receiving.

I am greatly indebted to you for your kindness in thus favoring me. In these days, of just demand for a somewhat exhaustive examination of sources on the part of an historian, it is an immense help to have at hand such valuable material as the Library presents. I have also received copies of some important papers from the British Archives, & fear I shall be put to the further expense of not only getting copies but of personally visiting Ottawa; not however, if I can avoid so doing. You will be interested to know that among the Canadian Records is the letter of instructions of our Navy Dept. to Lawrence for the projected cruise of the *Chesapeake*, frustrated by her capture, and doubtless taken in her.

Again thanking you, believe me [etc.].

[P.S.]   Would you mind having word sent me what volumes are charged against me, *prior* to enclosed.

[Enclosure]
Niles Register Vols. 4, 5, 6
Cooper's *History U.S. Navy*[2]
Maclay, *History American Privateers*[3]
Biographical Notice of J.D. Elliott Phila., 1835[4]

---

1. Chief Clerk, Library and Naval War Records, Department of the Navy, 1898–1902, and Superintendent, 1902–1920. He edited *The Official Records of the Union and Confederate Navies*, 1898–1920.
2. James Fenimore Cooper, *History of the Navy of the United States of America*. London: R. Bentley, 1839; also various American editions.
3. Edgar Stanton Maclay, *A History of American Privateers*. New York: D. Appleton and Company, 1899.
4. This Jesse Duncan Elliott item has not been found. There is, however, *Correspondence* relating to the controversy between Commodore Elliott and General Towson, and a *Defence* by George M. Dallas at his court-martial.

Cooper, *Battle of Lake Erie*[5]
Burgess,　　　＂　　　　[6]
Mackenzie, *Life of Perry*[7]
Documents Relating to Difference between Perry & Elliott[8]
Elliott, J.D., Speech delivered in Hagerstown[9]
Soley, *Naval Campaign of 1812*[10]
Emmons, *Navy of U.S.*[11]
Anon, *Impartial*, etc, *History of War of 1812*[12]
Ingersoll, *History of War of 1812*[13]
James, *History British Navy*—Volume containing 1812 only[14]

To Charles O'Neil[1]

Slumberside, Quogue, Long Island, June 30, 1903 [LC]

My dear O'Neil:　On these days of progress, does the Bureau possess any tabulated data as to the range of such very old time guns as 24 pdr & 32 pdr.

---

5. James Fenimore Cooper, *The Battle of Lake Erie: or, Answer to Messrs. Burgess, Duer and Mackenzie*. Cooperstown: H. & E. Phinney, 1843.
6. Tristram Burgess, *The Battle of Lake Erie, with Notice of Commodore Elliott's Conduct in that Engagement*. Philadelphia: William Marshall and Company, 1839.
7. Alexander Slidell Mackenzie, *The Life of Commodore Oliver Hazard Perry*. New York: Harper, 1840.
8. *See Port Folio*, December 1814, pp. 529–539, and C. O. Paullin, *The Battle of Lake Erie ... Documents* (1918), pp. 27; 206–210.
9. *Speech of Commodore Jessee Duncan Elliott, U.S.N., Delivered in Hagerstown, Md., on 14th November, 1843*. Published by the Committee of Arrangement of Washington County, Maryland. Philadelphia: G. B. Zieber & Co., 1844.
10. James Russell Soley, *The Boys of 1812 and Other Naval Heroes*. Boston: Estes and Lauriat, 1887.
11. George Foster Emmons, *The Navy of the United States, from the Commencement, 1775 to 1853, with a Brief History of Each Vessel's History and Fate ...* Washington, D. C.: Gideon & Co., 1853.
12. Possibly, *Sketches of the War, between the United States and the British Isles, Intended as a Faithful History of All the Material Events from the Time of the Declaration in 1812, to and including the Treaty of Peace in 1815, Interspersed with Geographical Descriptions of Places, and Biographical Notices of Distinguished Military and Naval Commanders*. Rutland, Vermont: Fay and Davison, 1815. The Library of Congress entry attributes this work to G. M. Davison and to the Reverend Samuel Williams.
13. Charles Jared Ingersoll, *Historic Sketch of the Second War between the United States of America, and Great Britain ...* Philadelphia: Lea and Blanchard, 1845–1849. (Two volumes of three published.) Continued by "Second Series," embracing the events of 1814 and 1815. Philadelphia: Lippincott, Grambo & Co., 1852.
14. William James, *The Naval History of Great Britain, from the Declaration of War by France in 1793, to the Accession of George IV*. New ed. London: R. Bentley, 1847.

1. Chief of the Bureau of Ordnance.

carronades, and also of long 12s and 24s; from level up to, say 5° elevation.

Of penetrative power I think no account was, or very well could, have been taken, except in the most general way.

If there be among your archives data on these points, they would be very useful to me in answering some matters relating to 1812, on which I am now busy.

To Charles O'Neil

Slumberside, Quogue, Long Island, July 10, 1903 [LC]

My dear O'Neil: I am much indebted for the tabulated information which I fear caused you more trouble than I anticipated when asking .

To Mr. Gauss[1]

Slumberside, Quogue, Long Island, July 23, 1903 [NA]

Dear Mr. Gauss: If you are still in Washington, or when you are, will you consult for me Perry's report, *at length*, of the battle of Lake Erie, and verify whether the words, (very near the opening), are as follows: "At 10 A.M. wind hauled to S.E.; formed the line and *brought up*." Brought up is not good nautical English for anything that happened; it means stopped by some external obstacle, e.g. the ground. In this place it should be either "brought *to*," or "*bore* up." The latter is much more congruous to the general current of incidents, and is given in some publications; the other is more frequently found.

I am not sure the letter is on the files, but in *Captain's Letters*, 1813, Vol VI, there is from Perry *No 33* Sept 10, and *No 41* Sept. 13; also *No 72*, Sep 20. September 13 is the date of the report, but 41 seems by my notes to deal with other matters.

---

1. Gauss, not further identified, may have been an employee of the Navy Department Library and Naval War Records.

To Stephen B. Luce

Slumberside, Quogue, Long Island, July 29, 1903 [LC]

My dear Admiral: I read your pamphlet on Naval Administration,[1] which you kindly sent me, with much interest; and I need scarcely add with entire concurrence. Should the views you advocate find legislative adoption, which now seems possible, no one will have done as much as yourself in putting the administration of the Navy on an efficient basis. The present scheme, to my mind, derives directly from the War College, through Taylor's experience there; and the institution of the College, due entirely to yourself, was, when taken in connection with the state of the services at that time, a singular instance of prescience. If the History of the Navy as a whole, from beginning to end, ever find a philosophic historian, one capable of freeing himself from trivialities and seeing things in their true proportion, he will give a very large place to that incident, even if it be necessary to sacrifice a few skirmishes to give it the room due.

I want to ask you if you can make time to read critically my discussion of the *Chesapeake-Shannon* action. I have taken a somewhat different point of view—a different ground—from the other narratives known to me; basing myself upon my analysis of times and incidents. Before myself accepting it as a finality—to myself—I should be glad to have the judgment of a person upon whose professional ability I can rely as upon yours. When I tell you that I wrote it three times, and was a week over it, you will see I found the task not light; but the truth is explaining defects is a nuisance—at least to me.

To Stephen B. Luce

Slumberside, Quogue, Long Island, August 3, 1903 [LC]

My dear Admiral: I am much obliged for your consent to look over the *Chesapeake* business, which I enclose. I have not meant to trouble you with ascertainment of facts, though I shall be happy to have any correction or suggestion you can make; but to ask you how far the narrative and comment stand criticism, assuming the facts as stated. For facts I have thought best to depend primarily upon James, as a distinctly hostile historian; comparing with some data in *Niles Register*. Roosevelt I think took his data from

---

1. Luce wrote three papers on Naval Administration. They were all published in the U.S. Naval Institute *Proceedings*: XIV (1888), pp. 561–588; 727–737; XXVII (1902), pp. 839–849; and XXIX (1903), pp. 809–821.

James. Comdr. Eaton[1] of our navy read a paper before the Mass. Military Histy. Society, in 1901, in which he practically endorsed Roosevelt with an introduction of some new data, unpublished, of a Comd. Raymond,[2] R.N., a master's mate of the *Shannon*. This I have not yet seen, but have looked somewhat askance at some of Eaton's particulars e.g. "of the *150* men stationed on the *spar deck* of the *Chesapeake more than 100* were laid low by the first discharge." Who counted them? The C. lost *148* all told, and we know particularly that many of them were on the gun deck, that she had 14 guns in broadside there, and only 10 on the spar deck, and fired low. There is very little doubt under the weather conditions that as many of the gun deck guns took effect on the C's gundeck, as of the carronades on the spar deck. Two guns were dismounted on each deck. Eaton makes a funny inadvertence. At 5.30 the *Chesapeake* was three miles distant; on the following page at 5.40 she was at fifty yards, having gone three miles in ten minutes—18 knots per hour, under topsails. (If you find any such in mine, please warn me ere I get into print.)

There is a point which I fancy will occur to you, that had Lawrence, Ludlow,[3] or the master survived, the cutting of the topsail tie and jib sheet would have caused in the Court a query as to whether there was a preventer or stopper of any kind in either case. The loss of so many officers leaves us badly off for evidence.

I rather wonder Chadwick fell into his mistake;[4] but I have to correct so many statements of my own—*before* I publish—that I can understand somewhat.

To Charles W. Stewart

Quogue, Long Island, August 4, 1903 [NA]

My dear Mr. Stewart: Among my memoranda made in Washington last October, but overlooked since, is a letter from Com. Bainbridge Feb. 13. 1814 (*Captains' Letters*, 1814, I, 110) "Court of Inquiry on loss of *Chesapeake* has finished." Is there no trace of this Court's proceedings? James

---

1. Joseph Giles Eaton, class of 1867. His paper, *The Chesapeake and the Shannon*, was published for the Military Historical Society of Massachusetts. Boston and New York: Houghton Mifflin & Co., 1901. It was also published in the Society's *Papers*, Vol. XI, pp. 141–164.
2. George Raymond.
3. James Lawrence was commander of the *Chesapeake*; Augustus C. Ludlow was Acting First Lieutenant.
4. Chadwick might have erred on some point in his address to the Naval War College, June 4, 1902, which appeared in the U.S. Naval Institute *Proceedings*, XXVIII, pp. 251–268, or in his letter relating to the training of seamen, *ibid.*, pp. 85–87.

alludes to it as published, & quotes part of its finding. It is *not* the same as that on Cml. [court-martial] of which *Decatur* was president.

I hope very shortly to return all the Erie & Perry books.

To Stephen B. Luce

Slumberside, Quogue, Long Island, August 10, 1903 [LC]

My dear Admiral: I am much indebted for your letter and comments, and have made some changes in consequence of them. As regards the squaring the main yard, your judgment would be decisive, did not my own agree as to its impropriety; but I fear the evidence too strong that Lawrence came up with such way on that only so could he prevent shooting by. I did not know that James's first edition did not mention it. The one I have is explicit, and also mentions that Broke[1] waited with way on, but maintopsail shaking. Budd,[2] second lieut. of the C., had the forward maindeck division, and was doubtless watching the approach from the bridle port. He testified before the Cox court that the S. was lying with her yards aback, (evidently, the condition noted by James), and that the C. came up "with considerable way." The backing of the C's main topsail he would not know, of his own knowledge; but he swears that his guns fired three rounds, after which they no longer bore, the ship having ranged too far ahead. A man on the main deck at such a time could only know relative positions, and I fancy that this being ahead was compounded of a forward and a luffing movement. However that be, it seems to me probable, independent of James's statement, that Lawrence *had* to back something or else go so far ahead as that his guns could not bear, and also give the chance of raking.

Your criticism seems to me so just that I have recast my treatment, bringing out the evidence more fully: that it may appear that Lawrence probably did as alleged, because of his first error of coming up with too great way. I shall not make this comment, I only arrange the evidence. James lived till 1827, and I have no doubt, from his painstaking ways, he got his account from Broke who died about 1840, subsequent to the first edition of the history. My account is not yet final, for I have learned that the record of the Court of Inquiry, Bainbridge senior member, is at the Department, and I shall see it or a copy. I dont expect much from it, because no spar deck officer of rank survived. I may also send for the S's log, though my experience of logs of that time is that they differ little from the Captain's report.

---

1. Captain Philip B. V. Broke, commanding officer of the *Shannon*.
2. George Budd.

To Whitelaw Reid[1]

Slumberside, Quogue, Long Island, August 20, 1903 [LC]

My dear Mr. Reid: I have not here a copy of *Retrospect and Prospect*, but presume my ideas on the matter you mention are there stated, and rest, upon the general ground that maritime commerce bears to national power the same general relation that the communications of an army do to its vigor of action. I have never written in extenso on the subject, but make it a rule never to let slip an opportunity, which offers naturally, for supplying a corrective to what I consider an error, due to prepossession and irreflection. I am extremely glad to learn that doubts have arisen in the mind of one of those fitted to guide and influence public opinion.

I find, in looking over the books I have here, the following references in my writing

Interest of America in Sea Power—pp. 126–134

Problem of Asia, 51–55, 124–126

May I add for your consideration that in the Civil War the blockade of the Southern Coast was simply a special form of commerce destruction; and that in 1812, the only reply we could make to the British blockade was by preying on their trade. The one and the other were commerce destruction, and both extremely influential, *and little destructive of life.*

Capt. C. H. Stockton, a very capable officer, contributed to the *North American* a paper on this subject.[2] I have not read it, but it was about five years ago.

To Leopold J. Maxse

Slumberside, Quogue, Long Island, August 21, 1903 [LC]

Dear Mr. Maxse: With reference to the two subjects suggested by your letter of August 3, it seems to me that the political side of Mr. Chamberlain's proposition[1] is so closely intertwined with economical considerations and details as to be a good deal beyond my scope. If commercial interchange between Great Britain & the colonies can be placed on such a basis of mutual preference as shall tend to strengthen and solidify the bonds of Empire, I

---

1. Owner and editor of the *New York Tribune*. An earlier letter from Mahan to Reid (1899), quoted in Royal Cortissoz's biography of the latter, is not in the Reid collection in the Library of Congress.
2. Charles Herbert Stockton, "Capture of Enemy Merchant Vessels at Sea." *North American Review* (February 1899).

1. In a speech in Birmingham on May 15, Joseph Chamberlain had proposed an inter-imperial tariff plan.

should say that the Empire was not called upon to consider what other people think—least of all Mr. Carnegie. The question whether such preference can be established is, however, chiefly economical. I mean that it will, in my opinion, be of little or no use to establish it unless it really conforms to mutual commercial & economical interest—to the interest of both. Whether it will do so or not, depends upon many commercial details, intricate in their mutual effects, mastery of which I do not possess. I do not think people in this age can be induced to undergo immediate commercial inconvenience for the sake of a political advantage—Imperial Federation—which may seem remote.

For other people to object to British measures, promotive of British interests, will certainly be wholly unreasonable; I am not sure, however, that resentment may not be felt, merely because unreasonable. If I were a British statesman I should endeavor to minimize offence and injury to foreigners, but I certainly should not for that reason abstain from anything I thought beneficial to the Empire.

As regards the "Limits of International Arbitration," I feel much more at home, having convictions, in which I believe, contrary to the prevailing furor. I gave them voice, however, pretty fully in 1899, after the Hague Conference, in the *North American Review*.[2] For several reasons I think it would be better to postpone, at least, an immediate utterance. In the first place I doubt if the opportune moment has arrived; for I think your people will be too full of Chamberlain's proposition to entertain seriously any international matters *not forced upon them*, until the next general election. I should suppose too that M. D'Estournelles de Constant's ingenuous proposal, to call a conference for limiting *naval* armaments between France, Russia and England, will have opened the eyes of your politicians to the true inwardness that underlies most of these proposals for notions to fetter their future action by present engagment.[3] You may rely upon it the hand of Russia underlies the whole business. Constant is honest, I daresay, he is a very decent little fellow, but he is Frenchy to the marrow, and has a maggot on the brain in the matter of binding nations hand and foot by precedent engagements concerning a future of which they now can know nothing. It

2. "The Peace Conference and the Moral Aspect of War," *North American Review* (October 1899).
3. Paul Henri Benjamin d'Estournelles de Constant was also active politically at the time of the Second Hague Conference. Among his published speeches and writings were: *A French Plea for Limitation of Naval Expenses.* Speech in the French Senate on the 11th of April, when the Navy budget was under consideration. Boston: The American Peace Society, 1905. *International Conciliation: The Organization of Peace.* Address delivered on the 11th of April, 1907 . . . at Pittsburgh at the inauguration of the Carnegie Institute. Pittsburgh (?), 1907. *Program of the Association for International Conciliation*, by Baron d'Estournelles de Constant, président fondateur. New York: American Branch of the Association for International Conciliation, 1907. *The Results of the Second Hague Conference.* With David J. Hill. *Ibid.*

was he, chiefly, who fathered the French idea, formulated in Article 27 (or 26) of the Hague Conference, which our man Holls, who I see passes as a great international legist in the *Times*—was weak enough or blind enough to allow in Committee; the detection of which in its consequences by our Delegation, led to the declaration qualifying our signatures, & safeguarding the Monroe Doctrine.

I should rather rejoice in returning to this field of warfare, but I think I am candid in believing that, unless further circumstances arise the matter had better wait & with this concurs the fact that I am much behindhand in my other engagements. *The War of 1812* has proved much more embarrassing and complicated than I expected; and my calculation, expressed to the editor of *Scribner's*,[4] that I should be ready by Sept. 1 of this year finds me now several months out. I shall indeed be ready to start on time, but not with my work finished, as I hoped, and it is my wish now to conclude this before I undertake anything else.

If it please you, I will keep the matter in mind, and also watch the papers for new developments, so as to be prepared as far as possible to write, if occasion arise. My mind once possessed with a matter, and matured, I write rapidly. I am extremely jealous of all attempts to fetter a nation's—as a man's—actions by precedent promises, and there is no subject on which I would more gladly write, did circumstances demand.

To Theodore Roosevelt

Slumberside, Quogue, Long Island, September 7, 1903 [LC]

My dear Mr. Roosevelt: It gave me much pleasure to know that you had found my books worth rereading, and still more to know that you had found time for holiday. A man may damage his private work by overwork if he like; but public affairs demand that officials keep their brains & faculties unjaded.

I do not now recall particularly the De Ruyter letters you mention. The only life I had was Gerard Brandt's huge folio[1] of the seventeenth century when men had time to build monuments. I wonder whether the one you mention has the curious incident that, at the beginning of one of his many collisions with the English, he felt so perturbed with fear that he was unable to command his faculties. Finally, he retired to the cabin & said his prayers; after which his customary composure returned.

I doubt whether full justice has ever been done, or will be done him. He

---

4. William Crary Brownell.
1. Gerard Brandt, *Life of De Ruyter*. Amsterdam, 1687.

was, I imagine, better appreciated in his own day than ever since. As regards our own two instances you mention, there cannot be the slightest doubt, what the verdict of naval history will be. The Schley Court settles that, even if the unsworn testimony before had been insufficient. What has amazed me most is that after the Court—Dewey included—had found his coal reports "inaccurate and misleading," men of intelligence and position have been found to give him open welcome; ignoring what those words mean, if put into plain English. One of Dewey's officers said to me, "Upon the whole, I think I would rather have been found guilty of cowardice; for that may be the result of uncontrollable constitutional infirmity."

As regards Miles I know the matter only superficially. An incident which occurred immediately after my recall to Washington, in 1898, shook my faith in him; and what little I saw afterwards confirmed the impression. After this began his singular semi-political actions. Concerning these, I need only say that to my mind the end stamps the career. If Finis Coronat Opus, doubtless it may be that Finis discoronat opus. I daresay this Latin is impeachable, but you will know what I mean. I entirely went with you in your omission of words of commendation.

Your administration bids fair to have accomplished two fundamental successes on the military side—Root's reorganization and the Naval General Staff Bill. As regards the latter, which I hope will pass in principle, it appears to me of the utmost importance that the designing of ships—their classes, numbers, and qualities—should be brought into direct relation with the naval policy and strategy of the country. This can never—in my judgment—be the case while these decisions are left to Bureau Chiefs. The General Staff having digested what will need to be done in time of war, can best and can alone pronounce the relative importance of the several qualities; subject to the revision of the President and Secretary. This or that man's views may be more or less valuable; but an organized body can alone impart accuracy, clearness and fixity, lasting from adminstration to administration.[2]

[P.S.]   The kindest remembrances from Mrs. Mahan and myself to Mrs. Roosevelt.

---

2. This is the only Mahan-Roosevelt letter between 1902 and December 1904. The "Chronology" in E. E. Morison's *Letters of Theodore Roosevelt* shows that Roosevelt lunched with Holls twice in 1900, had dinner and lunch with him in 1901, and was his host at Oyster Bay in 1902. He apparently regarded Holls as his expert on Russia. Mahan is never mentioned in the "Chronology," even for the dates of his two known visits to Oyster Bay. Mahan never mentions the Holls dispute to Roosevelt.

To Augustus T. Gillender

Slumberside, Quogue, Long Island, October 15, 1903 [HUL]

My dear Mr. Gillender: As I wrote you before, I am glad to think that if you are elected there will be a man on the Board of Aldermen, upon whose integrity and knowledge of City conditions I can feel assured.[1]

At the same time you will doubtless realize that personal esteem is not by itself sufficient to decide a vote, & especially where difference exists on a matter of fundamental civic principle. In incidental conversation you have told me with considerable emphasis that you do not believe in the administration of a municipality by men not identified with, and responsible to, a great party organization, political in character. I have no quarrel with any man for holding that opinion, but it is diametrically opposed to my own, and I think it dangerous to good municipal government. Were it an opinion merely personal to you, moreover, and you ran on a ticket holding my view, that national politics should have no relation to city government, I could most gladly support you, for I should feel you would subordinate your personal judgment to that of the platform. It is needless to say that the Tammany candidates distinctly state that the object is to have government of the city by a national party, with a view to affecting the next presidential election. This amounts to saying that considerations of what is good for the city are of less importance, *in a strictly municipal election*, than considerations of national politics.

I am sensible of my own lack of familiarity with city men and city happenings; but I am not ignorant of the general character of many city men, because in many cases it is matter of notoriety. I feel reasonably satisfied that men of the stamp I believe in, Democrats in national politics, are more and more holding this view, and that nothing has forced it upon them more certainly than the long record of Tammany. That the Republican organization, as such, would gladly turn municipal politics to its own advantage, I am quite ready to believe; but I think it has realized that the other is the winning view, that it is best for its own interests to adopt it, and honestly to forward it. The Tracy experience taught it a lesson, and the Republican party learns; which is the reason why it holds power, despite the solid South. Whatever the Republican leaders would like, I am satisfied that they are, and will, cooperate *honestly* for non-partisan government, because they see it is *good policy* from the national standpoint.

Pray pardon a rather unwarrantable set-forth; but I feel deeply and should take many pages more were I to speak all my mind.

---

1. The list of candidates given by *The New York Times*, October 7, 1903, p. 2, does not include Gillender.

We returned to town only day before yesterday. Mrs. Mahan & I spent a week at West Point, from which we got little good because of the rains. Kind regards to Mrs. Gillender & yourself from us both.

To Charles W. Stewart

160 West 86th Street, New York, November 5, 1903 [NA]

Dear Mr. Stewart: I have today returned by Registered mail vols 5 & 6 of *Niles Register*, and thank you much for bearing with my long detention of them. I hope by the end of this week to send Cooper also; but I hope you can bear with my keeping the other books yet a little while.

To Joseph H. Chapin[1]

160 West 86th Street, New York, November 5, 1903 [PUL]

Dear Sir: I have delayed returning the accompanying map from the thought it might bear some insertions useful for following articles.[2] I have concluded the scale will not admit this, and accordingly transmit with a few additions and suggestions.

1. As to your question with reference to the peculiar position of the drawing as related to the border lines, I appreciated the inconvenience of not having the cardinal points of the compass follow the top and side lines; and suggested this arrangement simply with a view to getting everything within a magazine page. I think those who care to consult the map will find no difficulty, *provided* you insert a compass with the four principal points. I have inserted such *approximately*; please see made exact.

2. If practicable, extend border to left, (blue mark), to admit so far Florida boundary line, and mark 'Florida Line.'

3. Insert names Albany, Buffalo, L.(ake) Oneida, Wilmington (N.C.), Delaware Bay.

4. It would I think add to clearness if the initial (or last) letter of a town name were brought close to the town mark, and the name thrown as much as possible away from the geographical lines. Montreal, e.g., nearly meets my idea; I have indicated (in ink lines) how I would have Toronto, Kings-

---

1. Art editor of *Scribner's Magazine* and in charge of book design for Charles Scribner's Sons.
2. *Scribner's Magazine* published Mahan's *War of 1812* in eleven parts, the monthly installments beginning in January 1904 and concluding in January 1905.

ton, Quebec, Erie, Charleston, Savannah, Philadelphia lie; and I incline to think Chesapeake Bay and Delaware Bay had better be thrown to sea, as Narragansett Bay now is.

I have inclosed in red lines a map which I think should accompany Art. *3*, and will be useful in Art. *4* equally. The width, east to west, to be that which a magazine page will admit; side lines to be due north and south.

I also suggest a map of the Atlantic Ocean to be bounded by Lat. 55° N, 35° S; Longitudes 5° West and 82° West.

The latter, if approved, would include the positions of all the ocean duels fought by our ships of war in 1812; for it takes in Valparaiso, where the *Essex* fought in the Pacific, and the mouth of the English Channel. I should propose to enter upon such the position of each battle, and in certain selected cases, the tracks of characteristic cruises, which led up to engagement—or not.

From a look at the World, Mercator projection, in the *Century Atlas*, I think a magazine page would sufficiently accommodate this; which also should appear in Art *3* with *Constitution* & *Guerrière*. In subsequent articles, reference could be made, "Position shown in map accompanying March number."

I apprehend the map in red lines will in like manner suffice for the military operations, not only in Art *3* but in all others involving the Lake frontier.

Will you consult Mr. Burlingame, and ascertain whether the magazine will wish these maps for the third—March—pages. I will not make up data till I hear.

[P.S.] It looks to me as if west part of Nova Scotia were a little out of drawing. Will you see?

To Joseph H. Chapin

160 West 86th Street, New York, November 9, 1903 [PUL]

Dear Sir: The maps being decided on, I enclose memoranda for the one marked by me in red border.

My practice is to reduce both features and names to the smallest number consistent with the requirements of the text. There will probably be needed a few other names to make this map serve the purpose of the following articles (after IV); but until I get the galleys of these I cannot complete the list. At the same time it will be expedient to develop enclosed as soon as convenient; for it will guide me as to what is possible for such further insertion.

For completeness, the text would require that I should place in the map the "Black Swamp," which "stretched from the Sandusky River on the East to the Indiana line on the west, some forty miles in width." This seems to have disappeared under drainage and cultivation, and I have not yet found a map old enough to give this topographical feature of that day. If your experience can help thereto, I shall be greatly indebted; and if found it may also bear on its face "Hull's Road," laid by that unlucky general in the summer of 1812, which I want to get in.

The Atlantic Map need be only an outline of the shores, within the limits of latitude and longitude given. I fancy both maps will have to go back and forward between us twice or thrice.

I have found the glazed surface of the map sent me a little inconvenient for work either with ink or pencil. Beyond that I have no suggestion to make.

To Joseph H. Chapin

160 West 86th Street, New York, November 22, 1903 [PUL]

Dear Sir: I return the print of map for second article. In it I note two points only for correction.

1. The line of the Detroit River appears to me lacking in distinctness; chiefly from the shading along it. The Niagara River shows properly; & Detroit should resemble it.

2. The West and South boundaries of Pennsylvania should make a right angle. A glance at an atlas will show that the one follows a meridian & the other a parallel of latitude. I may add that the jog in the N.W. corner of the state lacks distinctness of outline. It might be well in this connection to look to all north and south boundary lines.

These are the only corrections I note. I would further suggest a title: The Atlantic and Lake Frontiers of the U.S. in War of 1812.

To Charles W. Stewart

160 West 86th Street, New York, December 2, 1903 [NA]

Dear Mr. Stewart: In examining the list of letters you have been good enough to send me, I find none to Com. Chauncey[1] in *1814 between May 27 and July 20.* This particular period was very critical, and caused much

---

1. Isaac Chauncey, who commanded the U.S. naval forces on Lakes Ontario and Erie during the War of 1812. He failed to establish U.S. naval supremacy there.

dissatisfaction with Chauncey. From the sequence of the list sent me, I infer it has been followed seriatim, and without omission, from the correspondence preserved; yet I must ask if there have by chance been any omission at the period named.

On June 7 of that year the Cabinet adopted a plan of campaign, based upon expectations of naval support, which were not realized. The plan ought to have been communicated to C. [Chauncey] and some precise instruction given as to what he was expected to do. *His* letters, of which there are several, give no indication of such, but on the contrary imply entire discretion on his part as to the manner in which the squadron should be employed for the general interest. At the same time it will be a favor to me if you will have the correspondence examined, and let me know if there be a letter, or letters, between May 27 and July 20, from the Dept. to him. You will note that on Aug 5 orders [were] issued relieving Chauncey, probably on account of health, & ordering Decatur in his place.

I wish I were in Washington to read over the papers myself, but their contents are pretty clearly inferrible from the briefs you sent, and my knowledge of what the officers did; e.g. to Sinclair[2] May 19, 1814. There are, however, a few I may ask Mr. Gauss to copy.

I want again to thank you for this most useful memorandum.

To Henry C. Taylor[1]

Lenox Library, New York, December 7, 1903 [LC]

My dear Taylor: Your letter reached me two hours ago, and as you want an immediate reply I write from my desk at the Lenox Library.

The question of widely divergent interests is incidental to most military conditions. It has always confronted Great Britain; is no new thing, and therefore should not be allowed to disquiet judgment.

No general ever met such conditions with greater skill than Bonaparte. No ruler was ever more careful to minimize their danger beforehand, by preparation of adequate force, than was Napoleon. *Moral*, we should provide diligently force adequate to make head in both fields.

This, however, is not the question you propose to me. Being ignorant of the immediate cause of its being raised now, I cannot consider it as one of proximate military urgency, but of general policy; of statesmanship, to which the disposition of the fleet is accessory.

---

2. Arthur Sinclair who, in 1814, was commander of the U.S. naval force stationed on Lake Huron.

1. At this time, Chief of the Bureau of Navigation.

In considering possible wars with the great nations of the world, it seems to me inconceivable that any one of them should expect seriously to modify, or weaken, our position in this hemisphere. Naval success of a moment there might be; but our position, numbers, and wealth, etc., etc., must forbid to any European state the hope of permanent assertion against us on this side the Atlantic. Great Britain has abandoned the idea; who better than she could maintain it?

In the East—and that means all the Pacific—the case is very different. All of them have there interests and aspirations common to them and us; and are, some more, some less, in a position to maintain them. Concerning that field, embracing not the Philippines only, but Hawaii, and all the commercial interests of the Pacific, much remains to be determined. Further, and as a military consideration more important, all of them have in the Pacific exposed remote interests, *against which we can take the offensive*, always the desirable attitude. The danger of those positions will constrain the action of each country—I forbear names.

To remove our fleet—battle fleet—from the Pacific would be a declaration of policy and a confession of weakness. It would mean a reversion to a policy narrowly American, and essentially defensive, which is militarily vicious. Had we assured control of an Isthmian Canal, the Caribbean might be regarded as a central position, for movement in any direction; but even so the outbreak of war would at once raise the question—How direct the fleet? Should not the answer be—At some enemy's interest? We cannot so do towards Europe; and, save Great Britain or France, no European state can towards the Caribbean, for want of coal stations; but both they and we can attack in the Far East.

In brief, the American question, the Monroe principle, though not formally accepted, is as nearly established as is given to international questions to be. The Pacific and Eastern is not in that case, and is the great coming question, as far as one can easily foresee.

Has it been considered what would be the effect upon the Pacific slope of such an abandonment of an interest primary with them?

I shall send this as it stands. You will need to have it copied, I fancy, if you desire to use it. In that case will you return me the original—or a copy?

To John M. Brown

160 West 86th Street, New York, December 13, 1903 [LC]

My dear Mr. Brown: It is difficult for me to reply very definitely to your inquiry about the size of *1812*, or the date of publication; for the work is not yet finished, although very far progressed. I made a rough estimate last night that it would be about 190,000 words, the first *Sea Power* having been 220,000. That would make the new book rather more than 4/5 of the first. This seems a curious lack of proportion, as the first covered 120 years, and this nominally only 3. In truth, however, this will consist of two parts. The first 40 to 50,000 words concern the antecedent history of the war, in about four chapters. The remainder only will be the war proper. The whole forms a perfectly consecutive narrative, in my purpose; but it differs from the first two of the series in having necessarily much more detail. I may add that the book will embody much more than the magazine articles,[1] though I do not know whether *Scribner's* would care to have this known.

I hope to conclude all except the battle of New Orleans—which strictly is a mere episode—by Jany 1. But, independent of revision, I fear I shall not be satisfied as to permanent publication until I have looked up certain points—probably in England. I hope to get my magazine articles completed, and proofs read by April 1, and that I may be able to go abroad with my family before April 30. It will be my purpose to spend two months—probably August & September—in England and there to examine certain records. I have had a number of copies made already, but personal inspection may better my files, and I have found so many minutiae to embody that I want to make the *book* as near perfect in that respect as I can. I have already spent some time in Washington & Ottawa.

You probably know that I am to deliver some Lowell Lectures, beginning Jan 4 and ending Feb 4. I shall have the opportunity thus of seeing you in Boston.

I should regret very much any thought of taking the English publication from Sampson, Low. Mr. Marston has been very kind to me at all times, as well personally as in business relations, and I believe it is his wish to continue publishing my books. Nothing has ever occurred that would make me wish a change.

To Joseph H. Chapin

160 West 86th Street, New York, December 27, 1903 [PUL]

Dear Sir: The plan—for the *War of 1812*—of the Niagara peninsula will not be required before the June number; probably not before July. But as I shall be out of town a great deal during January, it has occurred to me to ask whether it would commend itself to you to send one of your draughtsmen to see me at the Lenox library, on *Tuesday, Dec. 29*, between 10 and 12, noon. I in that event could show him certain drawings of the

---

1. *See* Mahan to Chapin, November 5, 1903, Footnote 2.

district in question, from which the contemporary conditions could be built up.

If not convenient, you can communicate by telephone here tomorrow.

I have ascertained also that there are in the Archive Office, Ottawa, Canada, certain plans of the lakes, by a British naval surveyor, in 1816; among them apparently the Niagara peninsula. I propose tomorrow to copy the names of these plans and send them to you. You can let me know whether you can arrange for copies of them, if expedient. There will be no difficulty by the Canadian authorities, I feel sure.

My wish is to embrace in one map, of fairly large scale, the contemporary conditions—roads etc—of the Peninsula, without copying from any historical work, but depending upon contemporary surveys, official if possible. I think the data can be had.

P.S. Can you send me shortly a copy—no matter if rough—of the map for Art. *3*, embracing only the Lake Region—Ontario and Erie? I need it to have a drawing for stereopticon, of lectures I am to give in Boston, on the basis of the magazine articles, with Mr. Burlingame's consent.

To Joseph H. Chapin

160 West 86th Street, New York, December 28, 1903 [PUL]

Dear Sir: In accordance with my letter of yesterday, I enclose a list of plans & maps stated to be now on file in Archive Offices, Canada.

The object I proposed to you was the construction of a map of the Niagara Peninsula, from a few miles *east* of Niagara River, westward, to include the west end of Ontario and lower course of Grand River. I should say the *East and West limits* would be the meridians 78 ½° and 80° west. *North and South* the width would not exceed 45 miles.

I doubt if we can find a wholly satisfactory map, (contemporary), and think our result would have to be reached by a comparison of those I hope to show your draughtsman tomorrow; reinforced perhaps by some of these herewith included.

Before leaving town I hope to send you a diagram of the action between *United States* and *Macedonian*, for Article *5*.

To Scribner's Magazine

160 West 86th Street, New York, December 29, 1903 [PUL]

Gentlemen: I enclose the proofs of maps sent me yesterday, with following comment:

1. In that of the Lakes, Chrysler's I think is spelt Chrys*t*ler's, and I think it would be expedient to insert Plattsburg.

In the table of dates, and in the placing of figures to which they correspond, it seems to me it would be neater to observe the chronological order on Ontario. This would place 2 where 4 now is in the table, and 3 where 2. The figures, however, are perfectly correct in their reference, as they stand.

The title of this map might be: Map of Lake Frontier. If desirable, would add "to illustrate campaigns of 1813 & 1814," but I dont [think] this essential.

2. In Ocean Map, the positions and names are correct; but *Peacock* and *Epervier* seems spelt wrong (is indistinct also) and *Pelican* likewise, as near as I can detect. I would insert also the names St. Helena and Tristan d'Acunha.

Title: Map to illustrate Ocean cruises and battles.

Rough copies like the enclosed would sufficiently serve my purpose, as furnishing copies for draughtsman in Boston, and saving on the labor of re-editing the data. With your permission, therefore, I will retain the proofs *first corrected* by me, and returned by you with the enclosed. If you need them, however, they shall be sent you at once.

I should be glad also to receive clear copies when ready. As my lecture 3 in Boston is January 11, my time is rather short.

[P.S.] The *Constitution* & *Guerrière* plan is correct by my drawing; but a modification is needed which causes me to retain it. I hope I may get it to you by this evening's mail.

[Enclosure]
References (additional) for Map Niagara Peninsula
I Lenox Library
   1. *Map of Canada* (Cabotia) Publ. J. Whittle, London, Oct. *1814*
   In 4 sheets; of which S.W. sheet has general map of Upper Canada, including of course the peninsula; and N.W. has an inset map of Peninsula
   2. *Map of Canada* by Ed. Staveley, *1844*. Has map of surroundings of Niagara Falls in which are some names not found in *1*.
   3. James's "*Military Occurrences*"[1] (1812) Vol. I. Frontispiece is map of Niagara River from L. Erie to Ontario, contemporary with 1812; and opposite p. 131 is Sackett's Harbor, also contemporary.
II Canadian Archives[2]

---

1. William James, *A Full and Correct Account of the Military Occurrences of the Late War between Great Britain and the United States of America*. London, 1818.
2. Mahan corresponded with the Archivist of the Canadian Archives on October 7 and 14, 1902, and later visited Ottawa for research. Only the briefs of these letters survive.

1. Archive Reference Q.128-1, p. 39a Sketch of Niagara frontier
2.   "   "   153A Sketch of action, July 25, 1814
3.   "   Q.128–2, p. 289a Sketch of route Ft. Erie to Ft.
                                    George.

To Scribner's Magazine

160 West 86th Street, New York, December 30, 1903 [PUL]

Gentlemen: I return plan of *Constitution* & *Guerrière*.

The principal correction to be made is my own error, I think. In the position *last but one*, the yards of *C.* should be as they are in the *last*. I have marked in pencil the inclination they should have to the ship's length. This change is necessary to conform to the text.

In the last two positions of *G.* you have put the middle yard, the main too near the forward. The mainmast of a ship of those days was usually a little abaft the middle of her length; nearer the mizzen than the fore.

I was sorry that the man from Poates did not show up at the Lenox yesterday. I waited for him till 11.55. I enclose a memorandum of maps I intended to show him, also one or two additional Canadian references. These complete all that I at present can furnish relative to Niagara Peninsula.

I shall in time, for which there is now abundance, draw up more particular instructions as to names, features, etc. to be inserted.

P.S.   Please send me as soon as you can a corrected *Constitution* & *Guerrière*; *or*, my own original draft.

To John M. Brown

St. Botolph Club, Boston,[1] January 18, 1904 [LC]

My dear Mr. Brown: Would you kindly read the enclosed[2] and give me your opinion of it, *as a simple business proposition*—would there be money in it? I have no desire to do the work, which does not commend itself to my taste, & should comply, if at all only from motives of kindness. Naturally, I dont care to waste my time over unremunerative work, with the only object of doing a favor, which might after all amount to nothing pecuniarily.

---

1. Mahan was in Boston during most of the period January 4–February 4, 1904, to deliver the Lowell Lectures. He lectured on aspects of the War of 1812.
2. Enclosure not found.

To Seth Low

160 West 86th Street, New York, January 26, 1904 [CUL]

Dear Mr. Low: Thank you very much for the list you have been kind enough to send me. It is indeed a matter of great gratification to me that so many men, & among them, besides yourself, so many men of distinction should have done me so much honor.[1]

To John M. Brown

St. Botolph Club, Boston, January 29, 1904 [LC]

My dear Mr. Brown: I was very sorry not to see you yesterday, for, as I go to the Welds[1] at Dedham today, it is at best doubtful whether I shall be in Boston again this year, except for my two remaining lectures. If I dont see you, goodbye and good luck.

In looking over the copy of *Nelson* sent from you to the Club, I find that, although the new matter is now in the *text* of the 2 vol. edition, the preface to the 2d—Revised—edition is not incorporated. Would it not be well to state to that effect in future make-ups? Though of secondary importance to the text revision, it is not without appositeness.

To J. Franklin Jameson

160 West 86th Street, New York, February 10, 1904 [LC]

Dear Mr. Jameson: I am much indebted for the reference. The extract from the *Lawrence*'s log (the original of which is lost) bears internal evidence of accuracy; and luckily for me only confirms, does not shake, my previous conclusions.

To Scribner's Magazine

160 West 86th Street, New York, February 11, 1904 [NYPL]

Gentlemen: I do not know upon what authorities you base the map of Black Bay and Sackett's, herewith re-enclosed. It differs considerably

---

1. Mahan had been elected to the Academy of Arts and Letters.
1. Stephen Minot Weld, head of Stephen M. Weld and Company, cotton merchants, director of various corporations, and Overseer of Harvard.

from *Century Atlas*, and from the map of Sackett's in James's *Military Occurrences*, to which I referred you. From the latter, specifically, in showing Horse Island as detached from the mainland, instead of connected by a fordable neck; an important detail. The contour of island also differs.

As regards surroundings, the projecting point off Henderson's Harbor (Stoney Point) reaches so near Stoney Island as to be, in my judgment, incompatible with the following words of Com. Chauncey, in May, 1814: "Five British sail are now anchored between Pt. Peninsula and Stoney Island, about ten miles from the Harbor, *and two brigs between Stoney Island and Stoney Pt.*, completely blocking both passes." This tallies completely with outlines such as in *Century Atlas*, but not with the submitted sketch.

In returning, I have marked in blue pencil what I conceive to be better boundaries for the completed plan. North of Chalmont Bay and West of Black Bay are immaterial to my narrative; but Stoney Pt., Stoney Crk., and Sandy Crk. may be, probably will be, useful, in view of an incident I am likely to incorporate in a later article.

If in doubt as to actual outlines, I would suggest that application to U.S. Coast and Geodetic Survey, Washington, would procure you an authoritative plan.

[P.S.] With reference to positions, 1, 2, 3, which you ask me to locate I am unable to do so. They are in no wise essential to my story. I would advise omitting them and changing the other numbers. Possibly James may help you.

To the Editor of The New York Times

New York, February 11, 1904[1]

Having unadvisedly permitted a reporter from *The World* to speak with me a few moments I find myself announced in headlines as saying that torpedoes are irresistible.

I suppose I could now stand the imputation of a certain amount of idiocy, without serious harm, but still I shall be obliged by allowing room enough in your columns for the statement that I never said anything of the kind.

---

1. From *The New York Times*, February 12, 1904, p. 8.

To John Bassett Moore

160 West 86th Street, New York, March 1, 1904 [LC]

My dear Mr. Moore: I doubt how far any moral right exists for troubling with questions so busy a man as yourself; yet if you can spare time, I will only ask very categorical replies.

1. Upon receiving the U.S. declaration of War in 1812, the British Govt., desiring to arrest hostilities, "forebore to issue letters of marque and reprisal," but did direct "the commanders of ships of war *& privateers* to bring into port all vessels belonging to citizens of the U.S." Later, convinced that the war must go on, the Govt. ordered "that general reprisals be granted etc etc etc." What is the distinction? My first impression was that they abstained from authorizing privateers; but the underlined words dispose of that.

2. Is the difference between "privateer" and "letter of marque" that the latter is primarily a cargo ship, but with the authority to attack and make prize, if the opportunity offer?

3. I have been puzzled by the evident fact British cruisers captured vessels sailing from U.S. blockaded ports, although provided with licenses. Lately I have met the statement that this was because, by maritime law, the permitting of a licensed trade from a blockaded port abrogated the blockade. This seems reasonable, as towards neutrals at any rate, but is it correct? Has not a power maintaining an effective blockade the right to waive the belligerent rights thus acquired? This, as I understand, was Fox's[1] method in 1806. In those lawless days it seems to me improbable that British practice would have been affected by any nice technicalities.

To John Bassett Moore

160 West 86th Street, New York, March 6, 1904 [LC]

Dear Mr. Moore: I am much indebted to you for sparing so much of your busy time to reply.

The explanation of the two reprisal measures of the British Government to my mind meets the tenor of their words.

As regards the singular fact that, after proclaiming a blockade, they captured American vessels which had sailed with British licenses, which puzzled me a good deal, the technical propriety of their action doubtless

---

1. Charles James Fox, British Foreign Secretary for a few months before his death in 1806.

rested on the principle in the quotation you give me: that a belligerent may *not* "with a view to the interests of his own commerce, permit enemies' ships to bring him cargoes from their own ports, though he at the same time insists upon a blockade of such ports against neutrals."

Nevertheless, they must have whipped the devil round the stump in some way, in their desire for American flour; for certainly American vessels continued to sail from the Chesapeake and "throw themselves," to use Captn. Morris's expression, into the hands of the enemy. The subject is rather incidental than vital to my treatment of the war; yet, as I design never wholly to separate the political from the military, it has not only attracted my attention, but compelled some notice. Croke,[1] at Halifax, decided in case of an American vessel sailing from N.Y. under license, before the blockade was known there, was not good prize; but that, which is doubtless known to you, appears to rest upon the innocence of knowledge in the offender.

The whole manipulation of the licensed commerce would be an interesting study; but I doubt if it would pay me to go beyond the *obvious* motives and methods.

To Stephen B. Luce

160 West 86th Street, New York, March 29, 1904 [LC]

My dear Admiral: On returning from Washington I find a letter from Mr. Brown, agreeing with me that it would be very desirable to have the plate you suggest for the book. If you will kindly send me the photograph I will forward to him.

I write unavoidably away from my own desk, and beg you to excuse deficiencies in paper and pen.

Thanking you for the thoughtfulness of your suggestion.

[P.S.]   I receive occasional expressions of satisfaction with the treatment of *1812*, so far.[1]

---

1. Sir Alexander Croke, judge of the vice-admiralty court at Halifax, 1801–1815.

1. *The Influence of Sea Power in its Relation to the War of 1812.* Boston: Little, Brown and Company, 1905. *Scribner's Magazine* began serialization of the book in January 1904.

To Stephen B. Luce

160 West 86th Street, New York, April 8, 1904 [LC]

My dear Admiral: By one of those vagaries to which members of families seem liable, the packet containing "The Chase of the *Constitution*"[1] was placed in a corner where it escaped my knowledge till last evening. I opened it this morning. It is a splendid picture—using the adjective not loosely, but advisedly; instinct with life and movement. I never saw the original—that I know, but I imagine it loses little in photograph. If I could venture a criticism, it would be that the conspicuous figure of the *Constitution*, the just center of interest, would not have been diminished in effect, while the urgency of her situation would have been more impressive, had the artist permitted the leading British ship to emerge a little more clearly from the haze. This is a detail, however, the work as it stands is noble.

I shall forward very shortly to Messrs. Little & Brown, with strong terms of appreciation.

[P.S.]   I dont know whether I have before mentioned that we expect to go to Europe May 10, returning at the end of September.

To Edward P. Mitchell[1]

160 West 86th Street, New York, April 29, 1904 [NYHS]

My dear Sir: I return corrected proofs of the Review of Morris's Diary, together with a receipt for the honorarium, for the amount of which, and for its prompt remittal, I beg to express my thanks.

If practicable, it will give me pleasure to contribute the signed article you ask; but my agreement with *Collier's* calls for a third article,[2] on which I am now engaged, and treating precisely the question you suggest. If it can be managed, with *Collier's* consent, to send you such a treatment as shall not conflict with his prior rights, I will gladly do so, upon the same general terms as I usually write—$50 per thousand. I shall probably know today,

---

1. Stephen Salisbury Tuckerman's "*The Chase of the Constitution*" is the frontispiece to Mahan's *War of 1812*.

1. Editor-in-chief of the New York *Sun*.
2. "Torpedo Craft vs. Battleships," *Collier's Weekly* (May 21, 1904). The two earlier articles were "Appreciation of Conditions in the Russo-Japanese Conflict," Parts I and II, published February 20 and April 30, 1904, respectively. *See* Mahan to New York *Sun*, May 9, 1904.

or tomorrow, whether I can so separate *particular* discussion from *general*, as to make a treatment practically distinct for the two journals.

May I ask the further favor that a copy of the issue containing the Review be sent to Sir F. Maurice, whose address I add on next page.

[P.S.] Major General Sir J. F. Maurice, 9 Gwenwr Road, West Kensington, London, England.

To Edward P. Mitchell

160 West 86th Street, New York, May 9, 1904 [NYHS]

Dear Mr. Mitchell: The enclosed has been read carefully though under pressure. I must trust the proof-reader, especially for spelling of *Petropavlovsk* (?).

May I ask you to send me two copies to the North German Lloyd Steamer *Princess Alice*. As we do not sail until 1, there will be ample time for delivery on board. I should also esteem it a favor, if you could send a copy, with my name, to Mr. Albert Lee of *Collier's*. I want him to see, as from me, that I had not traversed the ground of my article for them.[1]

To the Editor of the New York Sun

New York, May 9, 1904[1]

The destruction of the Russian battleship *Petropavlovsk* by contact with a submarine mine has given a renewed impetus to the contention, never wholly quiescent, that the large, heavily armored ship of war is obsolescent and an anachronism, because liable to vital injury or total loss by means so inexpensive relatively to her own cost. It has apparently occurred to no one similarly to contrast the relative intrinsic value of the rifle bullet with that of the trained soldier, or accomplished general, whom it slays. The results to be expected from the torpedo are set forth as seductively as the prospectus of a new corporation, promising the largest conceivable profits with expenditure inconceivably small. The trouble with these calculations is that they fail to take accurate account of what the desired result is in naval operations; the necessary, indisputable aim of which, in the unanimous opin-

---

1. "Torpedo Craft vs. Battleships."

1. From the New York *Sun*, May 11, 1904, under the caption "The Probability of the Survival of the Battleship: Captain Mahan's Conclusions."

ion of all competent judges, is the control of the sea. The disabling or destruction of battleships, one or many, is a means to this end doubtless; but it is itself only a means, not an end, and the two cannot be confounded without vitiating any course of reasoning based upon such initial confusion. Because an expensive battleship may be removed from the field of action by an inexpensive torpedo, it by no means follows that control of the sea can be maintained by vessels differing radically from the historical class, of which in our day the battleship is the type.

The question, in short, is not, as commonly understood, battleship *versus* torpedo. It is big ships *versus* small ships, as means for *controlling the sea*, in the full sense of that expression. It is bigness of the battleship, the extent of the loss, military and pecuniary, that produces the impression under the influence of which so much editorial writing and platform speaking are done. Now, I wish to begin by saying that I myself have long held, and in writing maintained, that from sound military considerations there is a limit to the size which should be given to battleships. The mechanical skill of the day, the materials for shipbuilding at our disposal, remove all limit upon the size of a nautical construction due to difficulties of building. These no longer exist; but, in my opinion, there are already good military reasons, irrespective of torpedoes, for not overpassing certain limits of size. With these reasons I am not here concerned, and allude to them only to show that, in supporting the general position that control of the sea can be secured only by fleets of big ships, I am sensible that the proposition carries with it certain qualifications.

Upon what does military efficiency, both sea and land, depend in matters of material, as distinct from personnel? Upon two principal factors: concentration of force, and mobility. Most have heard the homely rendering of these great principles, true in all ages: "Get there first, and with the most men." The ocean, the scene of naval warfare, from the vastness of its extent, and the consequent great distances to be covered, makes a special demand upon mobility, the getting there first; but also it is upon the sustained power of the individual ship to do this that arriving with the "most" men—the most ships—also depends. Exactly in the case of the forced march of troops to seize a military position, the arrival in adequate numbers would depend upon the marching of the men—not merely at what rate each one can go a mile, but how long most of them can sustain the arduous exertion. Under favorable conditions the torpedo vessel for a limited time has speed from 50 to 75 per cent. greater than that of the battleship; but a few days ago a Russian officer, estimating the length of time for the Baltic fleet to reach the East, was quoted as saying: "Two months, if without torpedo vessels; with them, three months."

In the matter of speed for battleships, again, I am not an extremist. Much of the exaggerated speed demanded for vessels of that class I look upon as a frill; for the same reason that the rapid march of a detachment of troops depends, not upon the powers of a few athletic walkers, but upon the average rate the whole body can maintain without serious straggling. Battleships are meant to act strictly in concert with others; an isolated battleship is an anomaly; and a speed much below the highest is all that is likely to be got from several together, because causes particular to one or two will retard the others. For all this, however, it remains true that a speed high for an average of several ships—for a fleet—should be sought, and can be obtained. Now the speed of ships, whether of war or peace, is of two kinds: for the moment, a spurt of three or four hours, or "over a measured mile"; and the sustained sea speed under various conditions of weather. In the former a small vessel, with weight of hull thinned down to the utmost, and crammed with machinery, can in smooth water far outrun the armored ship. Under such conditions she can get there first; but her "most men" will depend upon the ability to plant her torpedo. In rough seas speed depends upon momentum, and momentum means weight; consequently the torpedo vessel, under conditions at which the battleship laughs, loses speed rapidly and becomes hopelessly slower.

Nor is it due to rough seas only that the torpedo vessel is less fast for long distances. She has to renew her supply of coal much more frequently. This means either friendly ports at short intervals—a condition to be realized only in a very restricted field of warfare; or else coaling at sea, an operation always difficult, but many-fold so for small light vessels, which the swell tumbles about mercilessly because of their lightness, and which for the same cause are very easily stove.

For the reasons adduced, the small ship is, always has been, and always will be greatly inferior in speed to the large one—in the long run. Particular circumstances may at a moment favor her; but in a few thousand miles of distance, or a year of time, she must prove inferior in that element of force which we call mobility. It remains then to consider how she will compare in point of concentration of power.

It may be contended that, if her torpedo is capable of sinking a battleship, you have in that alone as striking a concentration of power as can be desired. I think, however, that it will be readily seen that this is not so; I mean that the ability to reach striking distance, and to obtain any certainty of aim, is by no means probably within her control. It makes no difference how great a power is, unless it can be applied. The Russians have had a dozen torpedo vessels, of large size for their class, in Port Arthur, and Admiral Makaroff was committed to the general statement that command of the sea was never wholly lost, so long as such means remained in hand; but no Japanese battleship has suffered, although known to be present, to the number of six, within a restricted radius of the port; while weather conditions, in the course of nearly three months, could scarcely have failed to be at times propitious. As I have gone largely into details concerning these matters about Port Arthur in an article which is shortly to appear in *Collier's Weekly*, I will not here dwell further upon this point, but confine myself to stating a serious doubt as to the power of the small vessel, singly or in numbers, to insure her weapon striking a proposed victim. Of course, instances will happen, just as instances of overcoming almost any difficulty do occur; but that is not insuring or assuring. It is a happy chance.

To assure delivering a decisive blow at a man, or a ship, which you mean seriously to injure, you must be able to "stand up" to him, or it. Of course, there is lurking in dark corners, and striking from behind; and that is the role of the torpedo vessel as at present constituted. She is an assassin; using the word not as a term of reproach, for which there is no occasion, but as a metaphor. It is, in fact, the role ascribed to her by her warmest advocates, and a perfectly proper one; for the element of treachery is not in it. But all the same it is the policy of the weak, and there has never yet appeared any reason to suppose for it a success, on large or decisive scale, greater than that which has ever attended such a policy. Now and again a great man, or a great ship, may be so struck; but neither nations nor fleets are thus destroyed. It is the concentrated power which can come out into the open that wins in the end, and this the Japanese battle fleet has proved. Of course such original superiority may be frittered away, by inferior military ability or precautions, allowing a force to be cut up in detail, until it becomes inferior. History is full of such instances, before torpedoes were ever dreamed of.

It cannot be too clearly or too firmly kept in mind that the rivalry here is not between a weapon and a big ship; but between small ships and big ships. The automobile torpedo is a weapon which any class of vessel may carry, and which can be used by all, with the chances of accurate use favoring the larger and steadier. It is a weapon having certain very formidable attributes, and also certain inherent defects. Its strength is that its effect depends upon an explosion produced with slight momentum, needing little force of impact; but above all its greater danger to the opponent lies in the fact that to the end of its flight it ranges the water at a constant depth, which I understand can be as small as ten feet. Any floating body crossing its path and immersed more than ten feet, will therefore receive the full shock of the charge; with what fatal results the *Petropavlovsk* has shown, although in her case the mine was stationary, not automobile.

Accepting ten feet as the depth of submersion, it follows that to be immune from the torpedo a vessel must draw less than ten feet of water; with a further deduction in that the movement of the waves, which may not affect the weapon, may lower her to its depth. Under such limitation as to draught, I presume naval architects would consider it impossible to produce seagoing ships possessing the initial speed, the weight with consequent momentum, and the coal carrying capacity which are the three principal factors of that sustained speed which constitutes the mobility of the battle fleet. But even could this be effected within the draught named, there must be a tonnage which would involve some superstructure, something above the waterline; and, in fact, sustained high speed through heavy seas of itself demands this. The instant you have such superstructure you have a target for guns; and the presenting of such target induces guns upon the enemy, and armor on oneself for protection against them. With these you are at once again on the high road to the battleship. It is interesting to note, in connection with this, that when the torpedo vessels of the contending fleets at Port Arthur have met, they have fought with guns. "As soon as the Japanese destroyers discovered her (a Russian torpedo-boat destroyer) they went in pursuit, cut her off, and then destroyed her in ten minutes *with their 6-pounder guns.*" But their own weakness, such as has been here insisted on, was apparent immediately after. Another destroyer was seen, but escaped: "for it was now light, the cruiser *Bayan* was in sight, and it was impossible for the second division of Japanese destroyers to tackle the *Bayan*'s quick firers." Power concentrated in one vessel prevailed over power dispersed among several.

Power so concentrated, if equally well handled, will always prevail; not only against an equal amount, but even against a decidedly superior amount dispersed among several. This is elementary military experience; appearing in another form in the commonly understood virtues of central position, interior lines, massed forces and single command. This is, in brief, the argument for the battleship; single command and concentrated force. There is further the utterly unappreciated, in fact wholly ignored, factor of economy. It is much more expensive to put the same aggregate tonnage into two ships than into one. Speaking within limits, you get less military efficiency at higher cost. You need two captains for one; nearly twice as many officers; and crews which, while they might not be the double of the one ship, will exceed it by a very large percentage. And the more you divide your tonnage—say ten or twenty torpedo vessels for one battleship—the greater the economical loss. This was the fatal economical error of Jefferson's seductive cheap gunboat policy, a measure which insured a minimum of military usefulness at a maximum of pecuniary outlay.

Is there then any limit to the size of the battleship? Logically, perhaps not, on this line of reasoning; but practically there is, and until we can do without war altogether the nations may be grateful to the torpedo for suggesting, and even imposing, a stop upon a progressive development of size, which has begun to seem endless. For purely military reasons, while big ships have the advantages named, the battle fleet requires, in its several members, numbers as well as individual power. Therefore, if the tonnage for a navy is limited, there must be a compromise between the two. Numbers are necessary in order to distribute a total force in accordance with the exigencies of successive situations. They are needed also to facilitate combination, for combination is the essence of military art—strategy or tactics; and, mathematically, the power to combine increases with numbers. Despite these evident considerations, various motives, subordinating, as I think, military policy to administrative views, have been inducing in most nations a constant gradual increase of size in battleships. To this tendency the fate of the *Petropavlovsk* comes with the old warning not to put too many eggs in one basket, reinforcing the military suggestion to increase numbers by putting some limit on size.

In my opinion nothing has occurred so far in this present war to confirm the opinion that torpedo attacks by small vessels against battleships will be frequently successful. However, even as a matter of mere good luck, success at times must be expected; hence it is desirable so to regulate the size of the battleship that the loss of one may not be excessively felt. It will be impossible to contest contol of the sea with vessels exempt by their draught from torpedo injury; and control of the sea is the one thing needful. For the most part, attack by torpedo vessels will be confined to coasts and the neighborhood of ports, where they will generally be encountered, and in measure checked, by vessels of their own class.

I have not here entered into the question of the use of the torpedo by battleships themselves. Important as this subject is, it is other than that before us, which is the effect of the torpedo upon the continuance of battleships as a factor in naval war. Its use by them of course presupposes such continuance, the probability of which I have sought to establish by a different line of argument. Unquestionably, there is room and occasion for a fundamental reconsideration of the torpedo as a weapon, and its effect both upon the armament of battleships and upon their tactics. The *Petropavlovsk* incident, though exceptional, is ominous. It cannot be considered in the least indicative of the probable successful use of the automobile torpedo, for it is not a case of such; but the entireness of the destruction, which it does suggest, demands consideration. In default of experience only a careful re-study of the probabilities of the gun and torpedo, not by technical but by military experts, can reach a safe conclusion as to their relative values, considered as factors in the armament of battleships; and this again must be determined by a similar study of the tactics imposed upon fleets by the two weapons in their present state. Armament should embody a clear tactical preconception. Under whatever modification of tactics or armament, however, I consider the continuance of the battleship certain.

To Leopold J. Maxse

SS *Prinzess Alice*, At sea, May 14, 1904 [LC]

My dear Mr. Maxse: If, as I hope, the *National* purposes to continue me on the list of those receiving complimentary copies, may I ask you the favor of forwarding it for the present through B. F. Stevens & Brown, 4 Trafalgar Square. They already send me regularly certain periodicals, and I shall keep them informed of my address while in Europe.

I left N.Y. with my family May 10, and we are due to land at Cherbourg May 19. I expect to be in England in July, but our movements will depend much upon the health of Mrs. Mahan, who had a very severe illness in the spring, & is still far from restored to health.

Somewhat—in fact wholly—to my surprise, a day or two before sailing, I saw reproduced in the *Times* an article written by me for a N.Y. weekly[1] anent the current war. There was in this no breach of faith, for I had written unconditionally, and the paper belonged to the buyer; but I was somewhat chagrined that I should appear to be writing for an *English* daily—or other English—upon a subject closely cognate to those for which I was under a prior obligation to you. The facts are—that at the outbreak of war I was asked by *Collier's Weekly* for 3 articles, totalling 7,500 words, for which they offered a handsome payment. I accepted, *conditionally* upon my intended sailing for Europe, as affecting the completion of my prior contract with *Scribner's* concerning *1812*, which had stood in the way of my fulfilling my promise of a 3d article to you last year. Had our original date of sailing, April 23, stood, I could have written only one paper for Collier; but the postponement enabled me to complete the two others, of which the second appeared in the *Times*. By April 21, I had barely scraped through my completion for *Scribner's*.

In point of mental effort the past twelvemonth has been for me very arduous, & I am much enjoying the leisure of shipboard. I do not much care for the daily news from the war, but do for the details of operations as affecting naval problems & still more world problems. I saw a very startling suggestion somewhere, that England should facilitate a peace by offering Russia compensation in the Persian Gulf for concessions to Japan in the Far East. I can scarcely conceive the origin of such a purpose; for in the Far East the cause of Great Britain is that of a dozen other States, all more or less necessarily allies. In the Persian Gulf, with all it means, you would be practically alone against Russia. Why try to direct her thither?

I met casually at the Club, three nights before sailing, the Russian Con-

---

1. *Collier's*. The London *Times* had reproduced Part II of "Appreciation of Conditions in the Russo-Japanese Conflict," which *Collier's Weekly* published in its April 30, 1904, issue.

sul General; a benevolent looking old gentleman of Tartar physiognomy. He was mildly cheerful over all their reverses, expecting ultimate triumph—the glacier movement, etc.; but you and he could have struck hands, for he assured me the War & all that led to it was the work of *Germany*. How? asked I. By taking Kiao-Chow he replied. His English, though good, was not facile, and I failed to grasp the connection of ideas; though doubtless the united action of France, Germany & Russia *is* responsible for the present issue.

To Bouverie F. Clark

SS *Prinzess Alice*, At sea, May 16, 1904 [LC]

My dear Clark: I have been a fig to leave your last letter so long unanswered, but it is the old excuse; not merely pressure of time, but weariness of the particular occupation of which letter-writing is an extension—penwork. I have besides this year been under the necessity of finishing a series of articles for one of our big illustrated magazines, before leaving the country at a date which was originally fixed at April 23. Unfortunately, my wife's health, which was a chief determining cause for going abroad, received a severe shock by an attack of influenza in February, which affected the heart—never a very strong member with her. We had some days of great anxiety, a trained nurse for over a month; and in her weakened condition inherited gout got an inning, from the grip of which we cannot yet release her. Although without immediate anxiety, I am not without fear as to ultimate results; gout involves serious possibilities, especially when the heart is not strong. We could not sail before Tuesday last, and our movements will be governed by her condition; her response to change of air & scene, etc. We land at Cherbourg on the 19th, and are going first to a small sea side resort, Dives, on the French Channel coast. If she does not improve decisively, we shall very likely go to London for a day or two to consult a specialist, whose name I dont now recall, as to whether she can take any cure at any of the baths; the question involving her strength to endure a treatment as well as its character. Otherwise, we shall probably remain on the Continent till July. Whenever likely to be in London, I will notify you beforehand, or look you up upon arrival. Other than this record of illness, I have little personal news. The past winter & year has been a steady grind with the pen; not unpleasant, except as one tires of everything. The season itself has been the severest that I can distinctly recall. During the worst of it, in Jan., I was in Boston, utilizing my magazine articles for a course of lectures; thus turning an honest penny twice over, to nobody's harm. The extreme cold seemed actually to kill the material for colds—that is, for the healthy; but the death-rate in our cities generally has, I believe, greatly increased, certainly in N.Y. I have been following the war with interest, both general and special; the latter because it brought me engagements to write on good terms. I am thankful for the latter, not only for pecuniary reasons, but also because the obligation to write enforces close attention to details which otherwise I am sure would escape me. One of my American articles was reproduced in the London *Times*, I presume by arrangement with the Amn. publishers; certainly without my foreknowledge, though I had no cause to object.[1] You may possibly have seen it. The *Petropavlovsk* affair of course threw the great majority of our non-naval world off its head, and my last work[2] before leaving, rushed off at a sitting, was an extensive statement of reasons why battleships—or what may correspond to them in general size and purpose—are not destined shortly to disappear. The leading Committee-man in our Upper House on naval matters,[3] announced the profound opinion that the character of ships should not be determined by experts, but by Congress. He himself, by his personal party influence, at the opening of the Spanish War, forced the building of four new low freeboard monitors; contrary, I believe, to the judgment of 99 out of every 100 officers of the navy; also it was said, though this I dont *know*, gave the Navy Dept. no rest as to providing local protection for the coast of Maine; the which, if you know anything of the coast of Maine was absolutely protected by its own military insignificance. Another case of St. Vincent's "old women, in Parliament and out," whose fears must be calmed. No one of course questions the right and duty of Congress, or Parliament, to decide; but of their capacity to decide, without expert opinion, the above are instances. We are having a good passage, as pleasant as a North Atlantic passage is ever likely to be; cold always, and passing the ice belt, with a clear keen northerly wind, though we saw no ice, I was nearer frozen than all last winter. Good bye, my dear fellow.

To Leopold J. Maxse

Bad Nauheim, Germany, June 17, 1904 [LC]

Dear Mr. Maxse: The agitation for a Channel Tunnel, if it assume any real proportions, will doubtless be a matter of transcendent importance, and

1. *See* Mahan to Maxse, May 14, 1904.
2. *See* Mahan to New York *Sun*, May 9, 1904.
3. Eugene Hale.

one on which I would very willingly express an opinion, because the security of Great Britain is now a question too important to America to be lightly regarded by us. My fear would be that there is scarcely matter for a Magazine article in length; the question, though vital, can be so briefly stated. Over ten years ago, at the request of Mr. R. B. Marston, of Sampson, Low, I gave him a résumé of the argument, as it presented itself to me, which he subsequently published; and he has since reproduced it in the *Sphere*, of June 11 last.[1] One cannot tell how long one's pen may run, when started; particularly my pen, for my brain seems to work best when my pen is in hand. You will readily understand that travel & pen are not mutual supports, especially when one has proposed to one's self a holiday; but, if I find myself settled for two or three weeks, I feel now inclined to resume work.

My own attention is preferentially centred as yet upon the Far East war, and the unknown future to which it points. I have noted two papers which combine to give food for thought to my mind: One is the "Genesis of the War," for use in Russian schools, which I find in the *Weekly Times* of June 3; the other a really remarkable pamphlet by H. J. Mackinder on the effect of geography on history,[2] concluding with a speculative forcast of the relative future of Russia & the Sea Powers. The question is, "Can Russia be content as a Power shut out *militarily* from the sea?" You know my feeling has been that it is to the interest of Great Britain that she should retain Port Arthur, because the effort there will exhaust all her surplus energy, & will so withdraw her from the Persian Gulf, where *you* would have no ally, whereas in the Far East every commercial nation confronts Russia. But, on the other hand, you cannot at this point of the game consider anything but your ally's interests. I confess I as yet see no solution, but the matter greatly engages my concern.

Like you, I have a certain strong feeling for the Russians as a people, individually & collectively; but it seems to me that in Finland & in Korea & Manchuria, the course of their government has been little short of shameless, and this, combined with their, or its, ludicrous inefficiency, places it in a position as unrespectable physically as it has been morally. Altogether both my judgment & my sympathies are in a somewhat chaotic state; but chaos, after all, is a boiling of materials, which may at last run out into a mould, in proper proportions.

How the war hangs at present!

---

1. R. B. Marston, "Captain Mahan and Our Navy," *The Sphere*, XVII (June 11, 1904), p. 250.
2. Halford J. Mackinder's "The Geographical Pivot of History" was read before the Royal Geographical Society, London, in 1904 and was published in the *Geographical Journal*, XXIII (1904), pp. 421–444.

To William H. Henderson

Bad Nauheim, June 18, 1904 [NMM]

My dear Henderson: I was very glad to hear of and from you again. I expect to be in London the first part of July, but alone and on business[1] which will not let me run down to Devon. It was part of our plan to have given a fortnight or more to that of England, but Mrs. Mahan's unfortunate illness modified all our plans by making them subservient to her treatment here & after-care. If we can, I think we may probably revert to this part, as salvage from the general wreck of our intentions, for it is a part of the world all of us wish to know better. If we come at all, that way, I shall certainly let you know betimes. I am glad to say Mrs. Mahan is benefiting rapidly. She ought to, for she is a most subordinate and disciplined patient.

To Leopold J. Maxse

Grand Hotel Axenfels, Lake Lucerne, Switzerland, August 11, 1904 [LC]

Dear Mr. Maxse: I have made sufficient progress on an article to write you about it.[1] It aims to treat discursively, in military fashion, the general trend of events in the present war, with running comment on some leading features, as far as developed. If you will care to have it, I will be obliged to send it to you, when ready, in somewhat rough manuscript, having here no facilities for a smooth copy. It will be legible, however, and final correction can be done as well, or even better, on the rough proof sheets.

I write now, so that, in case you wish it, you can indicate time when it should be received in MS, and when the final proofs should be in your hands. I should hope to finish about Aug. 20—*my* draft, that is. Meanwhile, as you may be out of London in this holiday season, I write a little early that the letter may find you sooner.

[P.S.]   Be as liberal in allowance of time as the circumstances admit, for I am under considerable disadvantage here in that arrangement of working hours which at home I control. I have written about 3,000 words, & expect to run to about 8,000.

---

1. On July 6, Mahan was the guest of honor at a banquet given in London by the Imperial Federation League. He spoke on American interest in Federation, stating, as reported in *The Times* of London, that "the union of the United States and the federation idea were forces that were working together toward the period when all the nations would live in mutual peace."

1. "Some Considerations of the Principles Involved in the Present War," *National Review* (September 1904). Retitled "Principles Involved in the War Between Japan and Russia" and reprinted in *Naval Administration and Warfare* (1908).

To an Unidentified Addressee[1]

Grand Hotel Axenfels, Lake Lucerne, August 12, 1904 [NYPL]

My dear Sir: Your letter reached me too late to write to your hotel.

I am disposed to write for you, can I find a subject. I do not recall any such incident as you indicate, and picturesque description is not in my usual line. I am here away from all my notes, & have no means to refresh my memory as to possible matters of interest.

How would it impress you, as suitable, for me to prepare a raisonné account of the lake campaigns of 1812–14, for young readers; giving an account of the transactions and their setting in the general history of the war. Having (as I believe) a natural turn for teaching, I think I could make such an article interesting; and it would carry with it a certain amount of incidental information as to conditions in that day which would be educational as well as—I think—interesting. The two principal events, Lake Erie & Lake Champlain, have an interest of their own, and the protagonists, Perry and McDonough were young, though certainly not boys.

The two could not well go into one article however; but you can take the one & leave the other. Erie is probably the better, Champlain having less antecedent and concomitant.

To Leopold J. Maxse

Grand Hotel Axenfels, Lake Lucerne, August 16, 1904 [LC]

Dear Mr. Maxse: I dont know whether it will be necessary for me to telegraph immediately. I have received yours and will mail on Saturday aftn. the MS. in the condition in which it then finds itself. I suppose from the tenor of yours you must be intending for the September number, while I had anticipated the October, and so having time to read proofs. Of course the Russian sortie from P. Arthur hangs up matters until we can have clearer details, but I expect no difficulty in mailing Saturday.

I will telegraph you Saturday and sooner should any hitch occur.

---

1. Probably, William Henry Rideing.

To Leopold J. Maxse

Grand Hotel Axenfels, Lake Lucerne, August 19, 1904 [LC]

Dear Mr. Maxse: Here is the rest of the article.[1] Do have care given to the proof reading; for being fussy by nature, I feel nervous at having to let it go without my usual amount of re-reading, and not type-written.

You have formerly been good enough to send me some half dozen copies of numbers containing my own articles. May I ask you in this case to send simply, and direct, to the addresses opposite; my own still to 4 Trafalgar Square.

General Crozier
War Department
Washington   U.S.A.

David B. Ogden
Bar Harbor
Maine   U.S.A.

Captain C. S. Sperry
Naval War College
Newport
R.I.   U.S.A.

To Leopold J. Maxse

Lake Lucerne, August 20, 1904 [LC]

Dear Mr. Maxse: Unluckily I mailed my Ms. yesterday instead of waiting for today; not that I wish to change anything, but the tenor of the London papers I have seen would have led me to insert something, *somewhere*, to this effect: "The defence of Port Arthur must not be looked upon as an isolated consideration, dependent upon its particular merits, but as part of a general plan of operations. Every day it holds out is a gain, not perhaps for itself, but for Russia. No principle of warfare is more fundamental than that no one position stands, or falls, for itself alone, but for the general good."

If any of your staff can find a place for this, I should be pleased. If not, it is not absolutely material, being but a categorical, positive enunciation of the general drift of my argument. Yet it would be advantageous to public understanding; for it is really preposterous to see how people talk of sparing

---

1. "Principles Involved in the War Between Japan and Russia."

bloodshed, and having done enough for honor, as if Stoessel[1] had only to think of himself and his troops, not of Kuropatkin or Russia.

I omitted to say that I am leaving here to resume wandering, & that my address will revert to 4 Trafalgar Square.

May I ask that a copy of the September number be sent my brother, Major Mahan
51 Avenue Montaigne
Paris.

To Charles W. Stewart

160 West 86th Street, New York.   Probably, October 14, 1904[1] [LC]

My dear Mr. Stewart: I received a few days ago the roll of page proofs of Gleaves's book,[2] which I had begun to fear you had forgotten. I am much obliged to you for it.

As I am today reading my last proofs of the *Chesapeake* affair for *Scribners*, I have read in connection Gleaves' account of the same. Of the principal features of the action itself there is little dispute. I have preferred to follow James in the main, because, dying as he did in 1827, his authorities are necessarily partly contemporaneous, and he is known to have been painstaking. My principal difference from Gleaves will be in more serious criticism of Lawrence's action in *seeking* battle when he did. In this I think that Gleaves, with the usual bias of a biographer, overlooks the bearing of some of his own statements. He lays stress on the readiness of the *Chesapeake* for battle, based upon casual statements of Lawrence & Ludlow (pp. 167, 168); but overlooks the force of Lawrence's remark in a letter to the Secretary[3] (p.175) that he had been detained for men (elsewhere spoken of as "a few" from Portland); and that on the evening of the fight, when these few had presumably joined, he asked Bainbridge to fill his vacancies (p. 173). In my judgment, the bearing of this is not so much upon the

---

1. General Anatoli M. Stoessel, commander of the Russian garrison at Port Arthur. When General Aleksei N. Kuropatkin ordered him to abandon the city, he suppressed the order and remained, withstanding siege from November until January.

1. This letter from the Gleaves Collection is a typed copy dated April 14. The original has not been found. Since Mahan's description of the *Chesapeake* engagement appeared in the October issue of *Scribner's*, the editors have tentatively re-dated the letter October. *See* Mahan to Gleaves, November 4, 1904.

2. Albert Gleaves, class of 1877, was the author of *James Lawrence, Captain, United States Navy, Commanding the Chesapeake. . . .* With an Introduction by George Dewey. . . . New York: G. P. Putnam's Sons, 1904. The biography has a subtitle, *American Men of Energy.* Luce had been of great assistance to Gleaves in the collection of material and the preparation of the manuscript.

3. William Jones, Secretary of the Navy.

question of more or fewer, as upon the question of organization; and on this Gleaves makes a decisive remark, for which I presume he has authority that Lawrence dropped down to President Roads, May 30, intending to lie there a few days *to shake down*. This is precisely my comment. He should have taken some days to shake down; and that he intended to do so contradicts Gleaves's statement, in the same paragraph, that "his orders were peremptory." If they were peremptory in the sense that he had to sail because the *Shannon* appeared, they were equally peremptory against his remaining as he intended, but for her appearance. It is only necessary to read the Secretary's order to see that he did not fetter the captain's judgment. Jones was in fact too practical, common-sense, a man for such arbitrary indiscretion.

The fact is to me clear that the *Chesapeake* had an excellent crew, used to guns etc, and wanting only that element of organization perfected, *by association together*, to be a very formidable fighting body. But it is in evidence that the 3rd and 4th lieutenants had just joined in that capacity, the 3rd mustered at his quarters for the first time the morning of the fight, and he did not know his men. The Captain & 1st Lieut. were equally new—almost—to their positions.

While I differ from Gleaves here, from my glance over his pages he has produced a very readable book, and a valuable addition to our naval history.

[P.S.] My final book will develop my treatment, with reasons, to an extent the magazine cannot accommodate.

To Charles S. Sperry

160 West 86th Street, New York, October 18, 1904 [NWC]

My dear Sperry: A copy of the circular[1] was sent my daughter by the daughter of Mrs. Schott of Newport, to whom it had been sent. This I put in the waste paper after reading, without much thought about the matter. Two or three days ago I received a letter from Pennington,[2] disclaiming any part in the matter. This I was quite prepared for, as I knew it had passed out of his possession; in consequence, I believe, of a kind of bankruptcy on his part. Afterwards, about two years ago—I received two visits from parties who were interested in it as a piece of property. One thought I

---

1. Soliciting funds for the purchase of a painting of Mahan to be presented to the Naval War College. *See* Sperry to Mahan, October 7, 1904, in the Naval War College Library.
2. Harper Pennington, American portraitist.

would like to buy it myself, the other wanted me to recommend it as a portrait satisfactory to myself. *I refused both,* not caring to meddle myself with the hawking about of a portrait of myself.

I sat for the portrait at Pennington's request—if I remember rightly, Mr. Sheldon happened in at one or two sittings; not in the least as interested in it, but as people do into artists' studios. I received the impression from Pennington at the time—perhaps erroneously—that some persons had indicated a wish for a portrait of me for the College, & inferred that he hoped, if successful, it might be so bought; but he of course could have had no interest in its sale now, not being his, & he is not at all the sort of person to be mixed in what now looks like an audacious swindle.

The portrait was not thought at all satisfactory by my family. I thought better of it myself, but one is not a judge of one's own likeness, and so far as any expression of opinion should adopt theirs as mine.

To Herbert Putnam

160 West 86th Street, New York, October 30, 1904 [LC]

My dear Mr. Putnam: In considering the antecedents of the War of 1812, I come across the mention of the Report of a Committee of the Privy Council concerning the condition and trade of the British West Indies, about the year 1785–7. Does this exist in any form in the Library of Congress, and if so could it be loaned to me for a time?

To Albert Gleaves

160 West 86th Street, New York, November 4, 1904 [LC]

My dear Sir: You were, I think, absent from the country when I returned from Europe a month ago, and found awaiting me the copy of the *Life of Lawrence,* which you had left with Mr. Stewart for me. I beg to express to you my thanks and my appreciation of the service done to the Country and the Navy, by thus recalling the services of a distinguished officer, together with much information likely otherwise to be lost, and which certainly should be preserved.

To George Dewey

160 West 86th Street, New York, November 9, 1904 [LC]

My dear Dewey: I doubt if there be between the Commission[1] on which you are about to sit, and that of which I was a member, any such resemblance as would make our experience useful as a precedent in procedure. Yours will be of the nature of a Court, deciding questions of fact, and pronouncing judgment. Ours was a Convention, or Congress, similar to those assembled for making a treaty; our business simply that of reaching agreements, after discussion, as to the best mode of meeting certain difficulties, or certain wishes, entertained by our principals. The formulated articles, the result of our discussion, needed the ratification of our principals; whereas your *judgment*, I apprehend, will be binding on the governments who submit the case to your decision.

I think, therefore, that in the State Department you will find better advisers than either Crozier or myself are likely to be. If you still wish my opinion on the points you name, I think you will find that both governments will be represented by counsel, who will argue the case before you. I doubt your needing legal aid as a Court—such for instance as the Judge Advocate of a Court used to be. As to your needing it for your personal guidance, in any matter of doubt, *I* scarcely think it will be necessary; but there again the State Dept. can better judge than I. So as to a secretary; our Commission, being a national body of delegates, had a secretary, provided by our Government; but I think yours, being an international tribunal, the Secretary, if any, will probably be appointed by the Court itself, on assembling, and his expense fall on the governments—of Russia and Great Britain.

As to personal & official expenses, as our Commission was purely the agent of our government, all our expenses were borne by our State Department. As our Govt. is wholly without concern in this matter, I presume all expenses will be borne by the nations immediately interested. It may be, however, that as a point of dignity our Govt. may prefer to pay the expenses of the officer loaned by them, at least to & from the place of meeting. Here again the State Dept. must be your informant.

The report of your Court will I fancy, be transmitted to and through the permanent organization maintained, I believe, at the Hague. As to your Secretary, I doubt his being necessary to you in your Hague capacity; but I also think an officer of your rank and distinction ought to be accompanied

---

1. The Santo Domingo Commission. An international body called together by President Roosevelt in February 1904 to study the debt structure of the Dominican government and to ascertain the ability of that government to meet its foreign financial obligations.

by such an aide, & that he might be needed to keep you in touch with the important duties here, which you for the moment leave. I should think from that point of view the Navy Dept. would order him.

To Herbert Putnam

160 West 86th Street, New York, November 11, 1904 [LC]

Dear Mr. Putnam: The Report for which I asked must have been made in 1787, if, as I understand, it was the basis of an Act passed in 1788. This may however be substantially the same, or a second edition; for it seems to me improbable that a second report would follow so soon upon the first, which was clearly intended to be exhaustive for the moment.

In any event I would like to see it, and at my house, according to your kind offer; for the convenience of having it here would greatly exceed that of either public library.

To the Editor of The New York Times

New York, November 14, 1904[1]

In one of the minor editorial paragraphs in your Sunday issue I see certain comments upon the siege of Port Arthur which appear to me less than just to Genl. Stoessel, both personally and in relation to the bearing of the heroic defense of the port upon the general war. It is scarcely fair, in advance of knowledge, to assume that his personal hardships have been less than those of the soldiers he commands. As a matter of fact, the leaders who have received such following as he has, have usually obtained their backing through the sense of their subordinates that they shared on equal terms the sufferings and privations which they exacted from those beneath.

There is the familiar story of Elliott, who was Governor of Gibraltar during the three years' siege. The enemy's commander sent him a present of game and fruit; he accepted the courtesy, with the reply that there must be no more of it, as he could not receive what his soldiers lacked. I do not remember, but imagine the contents of the basket went to the hospital. You altogether omit, also, to mention the tremendous burden of responsibility which Stoessel alone, of all the garrison, has had to bear. How often and pitifully must he not have asked himself: "How much more must I ask of them?"

---

1. From *The New York Times*, November 16, 1904.

There appears to me a very general failure on the part of the public to recognize that, appealing as is the misery of these brave soldiers to our every sentiment of humanity, they are not dying—have not died—in vain. Whatever the upshot, they have given their lives, or are still giving their endurance, not merely to save a barren fortress, but to hold in check, by the imperious necessity laid upon the enemy to reduce the place, a body of foes, in army and in fleet, whose hands would otherwise be at the throats of Kuropatkin or Vladivostok. It is no idle sentiment of military punctilio, as you seem to imply, but the strong demands of a military situation that justify, nay compel, the resistance, which whatever may hereafter befall, will cover Stoessel and his troops with undying honor.

And in view of such suffering, shall those who have in it no part save sympathy, risking little above idle sentiment, advocate interference, as we hear from time to time? Have not the men who have done what Kuropatkin and Stoessel and their valiant soldiers have done, a right to demand "hands off" till their Government seeks interposition? I am no partisan in this matter; so far as I could understand the situation, Japan had no recourse but to declare war, and at the moment she did. But unless the paramount interests or the national honor of other nations are at stake, they have no right to interfere; least of all, we might say, one which, within the memory of numbers of us still living, has twice seen the shadow of intervention looming over our righteous quarrel. Let there be fair play.

To Herbert Putnam

160 West 86th Street, New York, November 15, 1904 [LC]

Dear Sir: I beg to acknowledge your letter of Nov. 12, just received, & also the copy of the Report.

I find in it mention of a previous Report on the same subject, May 31. 1784. Has the Library that also?[1]

Expressing my great thanks for the loan of the book, I am etc.

---

1. A note in the margin reads: "The Library of Congress does not possess a copy of the Report of May 31, 1784." *See* Mahan to Putnam, October 30, 1904; November 11, 1904.

To Leopold J. Maxse

My dear Mr. Maxse: I find I have not kept the copy of the *National* containing my paper on Naval Administration; about *June 1903* I think. Can you let me have one now?

I have not forgotten the *National* and the War, but it is the old cry of preoccupation. I must get the *War of 1812* in shape for book publication, before committing myself to any other serious work. As a matter of possible preparation, however, I have now begun to read up history in the columns of the *Weekly Times*, which I have neglected. I fancy, from my recollection of à Court,[1] that I detect in his writing the effects of his unhappy mistake in life; a bumptiousness & dogmatism, not without flippancy, I should not have expected. But some of the *Times* correspondents are excellent.

My own feeling, rather instinctive than reasoned, is that the Japs are pretty near fought to a standstill; and even if not, that they have not the *man* needed to carry them successfully on. Naturally, as a prophet, I see fulfilled my diagnosis of the effect of Port Arthur; and I see the *Times* Special *With Kuroki*[2] written after Liao Yang, "The fall of Port Arthur now appears necessary to insure the success of the Japanese, who perhaps have tried to do too much." Depend upon it, he has heard that in the camp.

Personally, I still think, as I always have thought, that though Japan is your ally, the interest of Great Britain is that Russia should remain engaged in Manchuria & a Pacific seaport. She cannot tackle both that and the Persian Gulf.

To John Bassett Moore

160 West 86th Street, New York, November 22, 1904 [LC]

My dear Mr. Moore: In treating the subject of Impressment, I have made the statement that the visitation of American vessels in British ports, within municipal jurisdiction, and the impressment of seamen really British, was not an illegal action. It might be complained of as vexatious, and a re-

---

1. Probably, Charles à Court, who was British military attaché at The Hague in 1899.
2. General Tamemoto Kuroki was in command of the Japanese First Army, which defeated General Zasulich at the Yalu, and General Kuropatkin at Liao-Yang.

quest made concerning it, but could not be treated as a wrong. Is this correct? I infer from the published diplomatic correspondence that our ministers did not venture to question the legality of the action, though careful also to make no troublesome admissions.

I had no doubt of my correctness till lately, nor can I say I have now; but, having had one or two narrow escapes from a serious blunder, when this occurred to me I thought I would appeal to an authority.

To John Bassett Moore

160 West 86th Street, New York, December 3, 1904 [LC]

Dear Mr. Moore: I am afraid I have been guilty of the incivility of not thanking you for your kind and comprehensive reply to my question. I was suddenly called to Washington by the Department,[1] and although my absence was short, my correspondence was somewhat thrown out.

It is a relief to have my statement rest on the solid basis of your detailed knowledge, & I am very thankful to you for it.

To Charles W. Stewart

160 West 86th Street, New York, December 5, 1904 [NA]

Dear Mr. Stewart: Not until now have I been able seriously to consider the list of Masters-Commdrs' letters you were good enough to send me. I have gone over them carefully. Some of the most interesting I have come across in Mackenzie's *Perry*, & others in *Niles*; but, until I received your list I had to lament very serious gaps in the continuity of Macdonough's command. For this reason the appended list of letters I would like to receive contains many more of his than of Perry's.

There is no great haste in the matter. If they can be sent me by January 1, it will be abundance of time.

I am glad to learn by a letter from the Secy, & from the service papers that the collection of records is authorized at once.

---

1. Mahan was ordered to Washington on November 23 to testify before the Senate Commission on the Merchant Marine on November 25. *See* Paper, Statement Before the Senate Commission on the Merchant Marine, November 25, 1904.

[Enclosure]

Letters desired

[P.]   *Perry*

90   July 27, 1813
93   Aug.   4   ″
115   Sep.   2   ″
116   ″   ″

Macdonough

106   Aug. 14, 1813
122   Sep   9,   ″
144   Oct   18,   ″
169   Nov. 23,   ″
187   Dec.   9,   ″
       ″   18,   ″
       ″   28,   ″

Vol. X

48   Feb.   7, 1814
115   April 30,   ″
126   May   13,   ″
128   ″   14,   ″
129   ″   18,   ″
143   June   8,   ″
145   ″   11,   ″
146   ″   19,   ″

Vol. XI

25   Aug. 27
41   Sep.   7

Your briefs of contents have been of great value to me, & I am much obliged for them. For British information I have a good many of their own papers—in full or in brief—seen by me in Ottawa.

To John S. Billings

160 West 86th Street, New York, December 5, 1904 [NYPL]

My dear Dr. Billings: I am extremely indebted to you for the list of naval works, just received. It will be very useful; but—what is to happen to authors of the next generation, save those of fiction who spin from their own insides?

To James Ford Rhodes

160 West 86th Street, New York, December 12, 1904 [MHS]

Dear Mr. Rhodes: It has given me much pleasure to carry out your wish, as far as in me lies. To day I entered your name as candidate for admission, wrote the letter required by the Club[1] rules to the Committee on Admissions, & sent word to Prof. Sloane[2] that I had done so.

It was a matter of much regret to me that I was unable to attend the meeting and dinner, and the more so that I learned afterwards that Mr. Adams did not receive betimes the letter I was careful to send him, notifying my inability. I consequently remained for some days under the appearance of a grave discourtesy to him & his company. On the Wednesday I received a telegram from the Navy Dept., ordering me to appear on Friday before the Merchant Marine Commission in Washington.[3] I had of course no option, & equally it was impossible to return in time.

To John S. Billings

160 West 86th Street, New York, December 22, 1904 [NYPL]

My dear Dr. Billings: The book marked on the enclosed slip[1] struck me as possibly valuable, unless you have something that covers the ground—possibly even more fully. I have no use for it myself; but I potter with interest about such subjects when they come in my way, and am always attracted by them, even when out of it.

To Theodore Roosevelt

160 West 86th Street, New York, December 27, 1904 [LC]

My dear Mr. President: I have seen with concern that in issuing the invitation to a second Hague Conference, the United States puts in the foreground of subjects for consideration, the exemption from capture at sea of "private property." This proposition was, it is true, advanced by us

---

1. The University Club in New York City.
2. William Milligan Sloane, Seth Low Professor of History at Columbia.
3. *See* Mahan to Moore, December 3, 1904, Footnote 1.

1. Enclosure not found.

at the first conference; but we then were not the initiating power, nor was this the subject of the call. It was a side-issue entirely, introduced by President McKinley as part of the traditional policy of the United States. This it is; and for the very reason that it is traditional demands consideration, as to whether it may not have lost the fitness it possibly once had to national conditions.

That measures which tend to exempt commerce, finance, and, so far, the general community, from the sufferings of war, will *not* make for peace seems to me a proposition scarcely worth arguing. The furor of war needs all the chastening it can receive in the human heart, to still the mad impulses towards conflict.

I must not attempt, however, to occupy the time of so busy a man with general considerations. I take the liberty of enclosing a few pages from the introductory chapters to my forthcoming *War of 1812*, in which I have —not developed—but outlined the argument, which I conceive makes inexpedient and illogical such a change in the laws of war.

Should you find time to read these, I would like to add that the general situation of the United States, in the world policy of today, appears to me to make most impolitic this change. Circumstances almost irresistible are forcing us & Great Britain, not into alliance, but into a silent cooperation, dependent upon conditions probably irreversible in the next two generations. Our united naval strength can *probably* control the seas; but there is always a remaining chance of a combination in the East—the *Western Pacific*—which might approach an equilibrium. The future & policy of China remains uncertain. It may very well be that under such conditions the power to control commerce,—the *lawful* right international precedent now confers,—may be of immense, of decisive, importance. Also, this may *not* be; but what is there in the present state of the world to compel us to a proposal, which in itself does not involve a *moral* issue. There is no more moral wrong in taking "private" property than in taking private lives; and I think my point incontestable, that property employed in commerce is no more private, in uses, than lives employed on the firing line are private. One is at the communications in the rear, the other at the front.

The question is one of expediency; and what was expedient to our weakness of a century ago is not expedient to our strength today. Rather should we seek to withdraw from our old position of the flag covering the goods. We need to fasten our grip on the sea. I need not, I suppose, assure you that all this in no wise changes my known position about "commerce destroying." From the first, as now, I have held it "a most important *secondary* operation, not likely to be abandoned till war itself shall cease"; but as a *primary* measure a delusion (*Sea Power*, p. 539.).

It has occurred to me, as an agreement tending to lessen the expense of armaments, that nations might agree on a limitation of the tonnage of single ships. Doubtless this would be only an amelioration, but I think it would have a tendency to introduce a slight brake, a little modification, which might eventually be felt as a relief all round. The question of limiting armaments is very thorny; it will not be helped, I think, by allaying fears that commerce, men's pockets, will suffer in war.

To John Bassett Moore

160 West 86th Street, New York, January 2, 1905 [LC]

My dear Mr. Moore: You will remember my questioning you about letters of marque.[1] I have lately come across the following in Jefferson's *Works*[2] vol. 5, p. 23, to Gallatin: "I have today consulted the other gentlemen on the question whether letters of marque were to be considered written within our interdict. We are unanimously of opinion that they are not. We consider them as essentially merchant vessels; that commerce is their main object, and arms merely incidental and defensive." The latter adjective I should cavil at, but Jefferson's ideas about arms seldom strayed beyond defense. Elsewhere, p. 273, he says that they have thus been considered since 1703, but of this I made no memorandum.

I have still a question to ask. Can you refer me to any source of information for the number of vessels arrested and *condemned* under the Orders in Council of Nov. 1807? J. Quincy Adams speaks in his reply to Pinkney[3] of millions of property; but I fancy condemnations were really few, that our people put their pride in their pockets, obeyed orders, and paid duties in English ports. I have found a few typical cases in newspapers of the day, for illustration, but as yet no summary. Equally I should be glad to hunt up the numbers of Napoleon's sequestrations, if you can guide my search.

To Andrew C. McLaughlin

160 West 86th Street, New York, January 3, 1905 [LC]

My dear Prof. McLaughlin: In connection with the *History of the War of 1812*, upon the issue of which in book form I am now engaged, I am much interested in what you have written in the *Diplomatic Archives of the*

---

1. *See* Mahan to Moore, March 1, 1904.
2. Thomas Jefferson, *Writings*. Paul L. Ford, ed. 10 vols. New York, 1892–1899.
3. William Pinkney, U.S. Minister to England, 1807–1811.

Dept. of State (p. 16) just received.[1] My work is of course primarily & chiefly military in character, but I have always tried to associate with such treatment a sufficient account of political matters so as to give some inkling at least of the connection of the war proper with other current events.

For this reason I have prepared some four chapters on the antecedents of the war, as I see them. The fourth and last deals with the period to which Russell's[2] letters—both from France & England—relate. Can you give me an approximate estimate of the number of words I would need copied, in order to cover such letters as are really decisive; I mean, illustrative rather, of the general character of Russell's correspondence. You will not need to be told how much iteration, not perhaps of precisely the same facts, but of a general trend of action, occurs in such a series; & you mention yourself (p. 17) four dispatches as especially illuminating.

There is one point of detail at which I would like to get. Have you found any numerical statement—or any probable indication—of the *number* of Amn. vessels condemned under the Orders in Council, or the Berlin & Milan Decrees? And incidentally I would like to ask if you have certain authority that the British ministry were really preparing to withdraw their Orders, prior to the false Decree of Napoleon withdrawing his decrees.

While in London last summer, I obtained permission from Lord Londonderry to look over the Castlereagh papers, with reference more particularly to the influence of European complications upon the British ministry's attitude toward the U.S., & upon the peace negotiations of Ghent. I had a number of private letters copied not of primary importance, but yet interesting as showing how distinctly we were indebted to extrinsic influences for getting out of our scrape in 1814 with a whole skin & bones unbroken. Do you think Adams's Ghent dispatches would change materially the views of a person consulting his personal diary at that time?

To John Bassett Moore

160 West 86th Street, New York, January 12, 1905 [LC]

Dear Mr. Moore: Thank you very much for your letter of yesterday. It is I who should apologize for troubling you with a question, the answer to which in most part could be found in the State Papers. I now remember having seen this report, but it had slipped my mind. Naturally, also, I wanted somewhat more of specific information; for of the 389 after the Orders in

1. Publication #22, *Report of the Diplomatic Archives of the Department of State, 1789–1840.*
2. Jonathan Russell, U.S. chargé d'affaires in Paris and London, 1810–1812, and member of the U.S. delegation at the peace negotiations in Ghent, 1814.

Council many doubtless were condemned on other grounds. Rummaging through the *Evening Post* for 1808, I have struck a few items of interest, & also in Parliamentary Debates. It is astonishing however how hard it is to find specific statements, & how plentiful are glittering generalities. In this respect your reference to your *History of Arbitrations* is most acceptable, the more so as, thanks to your past thoughtfulness, the volumes are on my shelf.

Again thanking you, I am [etc.].

To Andrew C. McLaughlin

160 West 86th Street, New York, January 17, 1905 [LC]

My dear Prof. McLaughlin: Your very full letter should sooner have received the thanks to which it is entitled from me. I will not plead preoccupation with a man probably even busier than myself, but a certain degree of hesitancy has delayed me. The Antecedents of the War are subordinate & introductory only to the War in itself, as I plan, and I have doubted whether it was incumbent upon me for a treatment which does not pretend to be exhaustive in the particular field, to give the time and money necessary. While money is always a consideration with me, I doubt whether I should accept from the Institute[1] a defrayal of which others equally deserving have probably greater need.

I could not in any event go to Washington before February 6—Monday —and meantime, as my treatment of the particular years develops, I can better judge whether it is necessary to my treatment to examine the files. My present impression is that it is; not so much for the correction of details, which to my scheme is very secondary, as for the general impression—the atmosphere, if I may so say, of the day. For instance, your remark about Russell, wanting to believe Napoleon, and suspicious toward England, is doubtless a correct appreciation; but its greatest value is that it reproduces in miniature the whole power of mind of the Republican party—to which I presume he belonged. It runs straight down from Jefferson's attitude toward the X.Y.Z. business, Madison's toward the letter withdrawing the Decrees of Napoleon etc. The British course was overbearing & lawless, but their statesmen were above a direct lie, and upon the whole even above very bad equivocation.

Public Documents are necessary and invaluable; but at an early stage in my life as an attempting writer of history, I made up my mind that truth

---

1. The Carnegie Institution of Washington, D.C., where McLaughlin was a Research Associate.

was most surely to be attained by access to private letters, subjecting them to the cross-examination of comparison with one another and with all other evidence. In private correspondence, men speak carelessly, which is against truth, but they also speak freely which is for truth; and the gain is greater than the loss, granted reasonable insight & faculty for cross-examination. Particularly, they reveal motives which are perhaps even more important to history than are acts. I would never rely upon the public dispatch of an unsuccessful general, and I fancy statesmen are much the same. Neither will lie, both will suppress and color; perhaps unconsciously.

Should I decide to go on, I will trouble you betimes with a letter and ask of you to do what in you lies to facilitate my work, to the saving of my time. Meantime I beg again to express my very sincere obligation.

[P.S.] As regards the proposed article for the *A.H.R.* I will bear it in mind, and if I find anything that is worthy and suitable—not already published—I will gladly give it you.[2]

To Herbert Putnam

160 West 86th Street, New York, January 28, 1905 [LC]

Dear Mr. Putnam: Three or four days ago I returned the Report of the Committee of the Privy Council which the Library was good enough to loan me, & I am glad to know by return register receipt that it arrived safely.[1]

It has been of much use to me, as well as of particular interest & I am greatly indebted to you for it.

To John Bassett Moore

160 West 86th Street, New York, February 3, 1905 [LC]

My dear Mr. Moore: I should like to have you meet Baron Kaneko[1] if I can get him for lunch at the University Club next week. Could you come on either Thursday or Friday—the 9th or 10th. I ask you before I ask him,

---

2. From Mahan's research on the War of 1812 came "Negotiations at Ghent in 1814" which the *American Historical Review* carried in its October 1905 issue.

1. *See* Mahan to Putnam, October 30, 1904.

1. Japanese Baron Kentaro Kaneko, through whom Theodore Roosevelt helped negotiate the calling of the Portsmouth Conference. Kaneko and Roosevelt had been students at Harvard together.

because first I want you to meet him in this way, and second I want him to meet you. I think it probable you have met already, but it is so apt to be in a crowd, and both you and he are men to meet more quietly, with time for talk, such as a lunch gives.

Will you let me know as soon as you can whether you will accept for one, or either of these days, and I will then ask him. I shall not ask more than one office hour—1:30.

[P.S.] You may catch me on telephone, 3994 Riverside.

To John S. Billings

160 West 86th Street, New York, February 13, 1905 [NYPL]

My dear Dr. Billings: I have purposed to go systematically through the list of naval works you were good enough to send me; but having failed to do so thoroughly I will not wait longer to offer two or three suggestions—others perhaps later.

1. I find only the first edition of my *Nelson*. There was a second, published in 1899—embodying a certain amount of new matter, & what to my mind is more important, a much ampler treatment of Nelson's action at Naples, elicited by Badham's attacks. The 2d Ed. is in two forms: a one-volume, popular price of $3.00 and the 2 vol revised at $6 or $8. I forget which. If you choose the latter, be sure it is a revised copy—the chief changes are at the end of Vol I.

2. Elkins *Naval Battles* (p. 9) should be Ekins. Here also, *I think*, there is a later edition, taking in the Battle of Algiers, 1816, at which Ekins commanded a ship.

3. To a great American library I should think advisable, for completeness, copies of the Courts Martial of the British commanders on Lakes Erie and Champlain. These have been published. There is no evidence so generally satisfactory as Courts Martial Records. I have copies, which I intend to present to the Navy Dept. Library, and I can answer for their utility to a naval student. If you would like to make copies from mine, I should be very glad to lend them to you for that purpose, if you can send a messenger for them. It may be more satisfactory to you to have copies from the originals in London—the only objection I know being that, I believe, neither typewriter nor ink is permitted in the rooms.

There are other Courts Martial that have never been published. I have those in the captains of the *Guerrière* and *Macedonian*, and somewhere also that in the captain of the *Serapis*, Paul Jones's opponent. These of course have not the real historical importance that squadron actions possess. Besides the published Courts, in the incident of Matthews and Lestock (1744), of which I see you have several, there is that upon Matthews himself, the Commander-in-chief, who was cashiered. This has not been published, and is a valuable historical document. In connection with this, I may mention that the Navy Records Society will publish, in a future number, the journal of a French officer, who was on board the Spanish flagship in that action. In your future lists it might be helpful to collate this with the Matthews-Lestock papers. The original document (or book) is in the Boston Athenaeum, with whom I made arrangements to have it copied for the N.R.S.[1]

I must not close without congratulating you on the eminent success of Saturday's dinner.

To John S. Billings

160 West 86th Street, New York, February 13, 1905 [NYPL]

My dear Dr. Billings: This evening I have found time to run over the English list and I miss the following:

1. Life of Nelson; more exactly: *Nelson, His Public and Private Life* by *G. Latham Browne*, Fisher Unwin, 1891. I dont think well of it; but the present Earl Nelson gave me a copy, saying he thought it the best then out.

2. Commander *Jeaffreson Miles* of the British Navy published in 1843 a vindication of Nelson against the imputations on his conduct at Naples.[1] I cannot recall the title.

3. *Naval Researches*, by Capt Thomas White R.N.[2] Published in 1830. A *very* useful work, by an officer who took part in many of the fleet actions in our War of Independence.

4. The Nelson-Hamilton correspondence. Printed about 1893 by Alfred Morrison,[3] but now, I believe, put on the market. It is in two volumes, and comprises a large number of letters never published elsewhere. Morrison was a collector, and in some way obtained these, upon which Pettigrew

---

1. Navy Records Society.

1. Jeaffreson Miles, *Vindication of Lord Nelson's Proceedings in the Bay of Naples.* London, 1843.

2. Capt. Thomas White, *Naval Researches, or a Candid Inquiry into the Conduct of Admirals Byron, Graves, Hood and Rodney, in the Actions off Grenada, Chesapeak, St. Christopher's, and of the Ninth and Twelfth of April, 1782, Being a Refutation of the Plans and Statements of Mr. Clerk, Rear Adm. Ekins, and Others. . . .* London: Whittaker, Treacher, and Arnott, 1830.

3. Alfred Morrison, *Catalogue of the Collection of Autograph Letters and Historical Documents formed between 1865 and 1882 by A. Morrison.* Compiled and annotated under the direction of A. W. Thibaudeau. 6 vols. 1883–1892: Second Series. *The Hamilton and Nelson Papers.* 2 vols. 1893–1894.

based most of what was new in his *Life of Nelson*.[4] They relate chiefly to the Hamilton episode, but not without side lights on many matters. Morrison sent me a copy, when in England ten years ago. I believe he is now dead, but probably a copy may be picked up. The work is essential to a complete Nelsoniana.

To John Bassett Moore

160 West 86th Street, New York, February 20, 1905 [LC]

My dear Mr. Moore: Having occasion lately to look up the case of the privateer *General Armstrong*, I ran through your account in the volumes on Arbitration. You noted, without comment, what I had elsewhere seen, the assertion that the affair, by delaying the British ships involved, delayed the New Orleans expedition, and so decisively affected the issue at the city. This struck me as militarily so improbable, that I devoted an afternoon to chasing it up; and as a man interested in his work appreciates all details, I think you may this, though so wholly foreign to your subject.

The fact is 1, that the expedition proper, from the Chesapeake and elsewhere, rendezvoused at Negril Bay, Jamaica, on the 22d or 24th of November; and 2, the ships engaged in the attack on the *Armstrong* had reached Kingston, on the other side of the island, Nov. 14—eight or ten days before.

Statement 1 rests on Gleig's *New Orleans' Campaign*,[1] which I have not before me, and so only remember generally was about ten days. The 2 is from a contemporary Kingston dispatch, quoted in *Niles' Register* vol. 7, p. 255.

And two U. S. Senators—Voorhees and Evarts[2]—endorsed the claim for delay.

---

4. Thomas Joseph Pettigrew, *Memoirs of the Life of Vice-Admiral Lord Viscount Nelson.* 2 vols. London, 1849.

1. George Robert Gleig, *A Narrative of the Campaigns of the British Army at Washington, Baltimore, and New Orleans, under Generals Ross, Pakenham, and Lambert, in the Years 1814 and 1815....* By an Officer who Served in the Expedition. London: J. Murray, 1821.

2. Daniel Wolsey Voorhees, of Indiana, a senator from 1877 to 1897; and William Maxwell Evarts, of New York, a senator from 1885 to 1891. The reference is obscure. *See* Mahan to Stewart, September 25, 1905.

To Andrew C. McLaughlin

160 West 86th Street, New York, February 21, 1905 [LC]

Dear Mr. McLaughlin: I have to thank you for your letter of the 15th, and enclosed list of papers. I have been gradually reaching the conclusion that I must go to Washington, to look over the papers about which I first wrote you,[1] and these others can then be looked over. Just when to come is uncertain, owing to a number of personal and family complications, together with the inaugural week, when Washington is an impossible place for a mere worker. Should the suggestion of publishing my views on the Jackson controversy materialize,[2] I presume the *Historical* has an issue about July; the latest before my book is intended to come out—in early fall. After reading several of the prominent speakers in Congress, in connection with the affair, I own to surprise at Adams's treatment;[3] particularly coming from a family from whom one rather expects novel views. In connection with the general controversy, I have stumbled across a point of view concerning the Administration's action upon the Cadore[4] letter of Aug. 5, 1810, which had not before arrested my attention. Adams may have it, & I overlooked. This I have not yet verified. Should the article[5] be otherwise short, this may eke it out. Both points are rather for historical students than ordinary readers; and if I finally judge them sound, I shall not be sorry to put them out in the magazine.

I presume the time of my going to Washington would be immaterial to you. Should I come I will write betimes to ask you to make any arrangements practicable to expedite my work.

To John S. Billings

160 West 86th Street, New York, February 26, 1905 [LC]

My dear Dr. Billings: I cannot lay my hand on the Courts Martial of the *Guerrière, Macedonian* or *Serapis*. I have looked through all my papers, & fear these are at my country home in Quogue, where I have not been

---

1. *See* Mahan to McLaughlin, January 3, 1905.
2. The overbearing actions of British Minister to the U.S., Francis James Jackson, in 1809–1810 which led to a virtual break in diplomatic relations between the two governments in September 1810.
3. Henry Adams, *History of the United States during the Administrations of Jefferson and Madison.*
4. Jean Baptiste Nompère de Champagny, 1st Duc de Cadore, French minister of foreign affairs, 1807–1811.
5. The article, instead, dealt with "Negotiations at Ghent in 1814," *American Historical Review* (October 1905).

since a year ago last summer. I could not have destroyed them, & they will doubtless turn up. Luckily, the more important—Lake Erie and Lake Champlain—are here, and I send them. As some of the annexed papers might puzzle a copyist, I have bound together those which belong together. I will ask you to instruct the persons concerned to be very careful, so that they may be returned to me all right; as I shall have to use them again in foot-noting the text as it passes through my hands in proof.

I shall not require them before April 1, which will, I think, allow you ample time for copying.

To John Bassett Moore

160 West 86th Street, New York, March 2, 1905 [LC]

My dear Mr. Moore: I am really ashamed to trouble you again, and can only hope that your general interest in such questions may in some measure excuse my importunities.

I find in Monroe's correspondence with the British minister Foster,[1] in 1811, a frequent assertion that Great Britain had *pledged* herself to repeal the Orders in Council, *pari passu* with the repeal of Bonaparte's Decrees. Now I cannot find this pari passu, nor any equivalent for it, in the *published* correspondence of G.B. (State Papers) from first to last; and I have, I think, detected decided instances of Madison putting words into his opponents' mouths. Hence I am more suspicious of pari passu than I otherwise might be.

I hope to give a week to Washington ere long to run over the unpublished letters, but meanwhile this difficulty bothers me.

Dont undertake any search, but if, out of the fullness of your knowledge you can direct me, I will be greatly obliged.

To Andrew C. McLaughlin

160 West 86th Street, New York, March 5, 1905 [LC]

My dear Professor McLaughlin: I now hope to go to Washington on Wednesday next, and write merely to say that I hope you will do whatever may be done to enable me to see the papers in the State Department with as little delay as may be possible, as for several reasons I wish to get back with the least detention.

1. Sir Augustus John Foster, minister plenipotentiary to the United States, 1811–1812.

As soon as I know where I am to stay, and that I am certainly going, I will telegraph you my address; and ask you to favor me with a line to it, to know where and what hour I can see you, on the day I name—if convenient to you.

To John Bassett Moore

160 West 86th Street, New York, March 5, 1905 [LC]

My dear Mr. Moore: I had not overlooked the letter, copy of which you kindly send me; but with attention you can scarcely fail to admit that it does not bear out the "pari passu" put upon it by Monroe. By it the British Government undertook to repeal, when the "commerce of the *world*" is restored etc; the "commerce of neutral nations" (no exception); and when the enemy "shall retract the principles" which, in British estimation, rendered the Orders in Council necessary.

Monroe—which I apprehend means also Madison—desired to construe this into a promise, binding in the case of remission by France towards the United States; and so affirms that Great Britain has "pledged herself to proceed *pari passu* with France in the revocation of their respective acts" (State Papers 111.445 which is not the only use of that phrase, which I have also found in a Congressional speech—I think Calhoun).

It seems to me clear that the British letter you send me says, beyond possibility of mistake, that H.M. will abandon his system, (not pari passu, but) when the commerce of the world, the commerce of neutral nations, is restored; and the principles of the Berlin & Milan Decree are retracted. If so, the assertion of pari passu is unwarranted and, it seems to be, is a somewhat gross instance of putting into an opponent's mouth, not in hasty speech, but with the deliberation of writing, words which the opponent never used—nor any equivalent to them.

Am I wrong?

To Andrew C. McLaughlin

160 West 86th Street, New York, March 20, 1905 [LC]

Dear Prof. McLaughlin: The regret that we did not meet is mutual, but I trust you will feel that I received through your office[1] every attention that I could desire. Your assistants found me both place and books. I did not call upon them for further assistance, because, now knowing where to

---

1. Department of Historical Research of the Carnegie Institution in Washington, D.C.

go, I obtained such further volumes readily as I needed; nor did I ask for writing, because the great majority of the letters had only here and there passages valuable to my treatment. It was shorter therefore to copy them in my rough short hand, than to tell another where to find them.

There are, however, five letters which I wish to have complete. Of these I enclose a memorandum; and if you feel justified in copying them for me I shall be greatly indebted. You will of course subject them to the Department's inspection in order that I may be authorized to use them. I have already sent back in fair hand, for inspection, copies of my extracts in short hand.

I have found nothing that appears to me in the least improper to publish; but it does appear to me that all our agents were placed in a weak position, which they had to support more or less discreditably, by Madison's precipitancy in accepting Cadore's letter. Further, the internal evidence appears to me to show that this weakness was recognized by them, all the time that they were asseverating to England their absolute confidence in that dirty trick. The State Papers themselves seem to me to have been edited under influence, cognizant of the discreditable diplomatic position, in which Madison had placed the country. Passages are suppressed, and letters omitted, which strongly suggested this idea to me.

There is one point which I had not time to look up, and to which I found no clue in the papers I turned over. I very much wish you could look it up. In the State Papers, vol iii. p. 440, Monroe to Foster makes this remarkable assertion: "It was stated also that the British Government would proceed *pari passu* with the Government of France in the revocation of her edicts." Now, in the *first* formal communication of the Orders in Council to our Government, by Erskine,[2] Feb. 23, 1808 (S.P. iii, p. 210) the announcement is that "His Majesty is ready to abandon the system which has been forced upon him, whenever the Enemy shall *retract the principles* which have rendered it necesary." Doubtless, in so important a matter, Erskine copied Canning's[3] own words; and they were reiterated by Canning's successor, Wellesley[4] (S.P. iii, 366), as the standard of British determination. Whence then comes Monroe's *pari passu?* It is a convenient and even forcible argument, in favor of Great Britain's revoking the Orders in Council as to the United States, and on the sea, when Napoleon had withdrawn so much of his Decrees; but when and where did the British Government say it? In all that has been published, or that I read in Washington, there is no previous use of the expression; & it is certainly entirely

---

2. David Montagu, 2nd Baron Erskine, Minister Plenipotentiary to the United States, 1806–1809.
3. George Canning, British Foreign Secretary, 1807–1809.
4. Richard Colley, 1st Marquis Wellesley, British Foreign Minister, 1809–1812.

alien to the consistent haughty tone, and great caution concerning yielding an inch, that is conspicuous alike in Canning & Wellesley.

It has occurred to me as possible that the words may have been used, or their equivalent understood, by Monroe, when Minister in England; and *might* be found in his letters to the Secretary of State, between Dec. 1806, and his return to the U.S., about November, 1807. They may have been spoken, or even written, by the more liberal ministry which issued the Order of January 7, 1807. If not found there it may be in their letters to Erskine, for which I will have to inquire in England.

So far, as it stands, it is another instance of putting into an opponent's mouth words he did not use, as, in my judgment, was done to Jackson. Could one of your office staff undertake to run over Monroe's correspondence with the State Department (Dec. 1806–Nov. 1807) with particular attention to the month of January, and the communication of the order of that month?

At what time would you want the paper on Jackson.[5] I feel I had better send for Canning's instructions to him, & at the same time I may have the British Government's letters to Erskine run over, in search of pari passu.

Will you kindly express my thanks to your assistants for their politeness to me.

To John Bassett Moore

160 West 86th Street, New York, March 20, 1905 [LC]

My dear Mr. Moore: Your letter of the 12th was forwarded to me in Washington. During my stay I ran over Pinkney's and Russell's correspondence 1808–1812; they being the object of my visit. The pari passu, while not the originating purpose of my search, was always in the background of my thought, and, while I found no trace of it, it caused me to observe the extreme guardedness of Canning and Wellesley against yielding an inch, or saying anything that implied yielding. Wellesley's reference back to Erskine defining the British position, consistently held from Feb. 23, 1808; & doubtless Erskine's own exposition of so thorny a subject.

It has occurred to me that if the phrase, as applied, had any origin outside of Monroe's imagination, it is to be found in the interviews between him, Pinkney, & the British Commissioners, at the time of the latter making the Declaration appended to the Treaty of Dec. 31, 1806. Lord Holland[1]

---

5. *See* Mahan to McLaughlin, February 21, 1905.

1. Henry Richard Fox, 3rd Baron Holland, who concluded an unratified treaty with Monroe and Pinkney in 1806 which accepted limited U.S. trade with France but failed to resolve the impressment issue.

afterwards charged the Portland[2] Government with allowing the United States to remain under a deception as to the Order of January, 1807; as to the restrictions intended upon voyage from port to port of hostile Europe, and the general tone of the Grenville[3] government was more likely to utter some such conciliatory phrase as pari passu. Of the words themselves Monroe seems to have a monopoly.

If the expression cannot be found, it would appear that we have another instance of putting words into an opponent's mouth. I think, indeed I am sure, I have found two others.

Did it ever strike you that the State Papers, when published, were edited by someone interested in Madison.

To John T. Lee

160 West 86th Street, New York, March 25, 1905 [SHSW][1]

Dear Sir: I hope the enclosed[2] may sufficiently meet the wish expressed in your letter of March 22.

Thanking you for your kind expressions concerning my writings, believe me [etc.].

To Andrew C. McLaughlin

160 West 86th Street, New York, March 29, 1905 [LC]

Dear Mr. McLaughlin: I find among my notes taken in Washington, the following imperfectly identified:

Extract from Napoleon's address to the Chamber of Commerce, April, 1811 (March 24, 1811).[1]

"The Decrees of Berlin and Milan are the fundamental laws of my Empire. . . . The fate of American Commerce will soon be decided. I will favor it if the United States conform to those Decrees. In the contrary case their ships shall be repelled from my ports."

---

2. William Henry Cavendish Bentinck, 3rd Duke of Portland, Prime Minister, 1807–1809.
3. William Wyndham, Baron Grenville, Prime Minister, 1806–1807.

1. From the John Thomas Lee Autograph Collection, published with permission of the State Historical Society of Wisconsin.
2. Enclosure not found.

1. In the manuscript "March 24, 1811" is written over the April date.

Can you conveniently have this reference verified for me, sending me letter and date in which it is (I think) quoted. From the order in my notes, it should occur between Russell's letters to the Secretary of State of April 4, and May 8, 1811.

To John M. Brown

160 West 86th Street, New York, March 30, 1905 [LC]

Dear Mr. Brown: I have been wondering lately whether Little, Brown & Co—if they have had time to think of me—have been concerned about my delay in forwarding copy.[1] I have today finished Chap IV (and last) of Antecedents; after which the MS. runs on easily to near the end of the whole book where I propose to introduce a few new concluding pages on the peace negotiations.

I shall now revise Chapter IV, rather hastily, and hope to send it to you within a week for the printer. In the following matter I have some data to be introduced, but think I shall be able to keep well ahead of the printer from then on.

As you perhaps know, the pagination was changed, for some reason, after the page proof was set up and numbered; the opening page being changed from *3* to *1*. In consequence some foot notes "Ante" need correction. I wrote word about this generally, as to *88* pages so altered, and sent me. I observe also, however, on p. *121*, "Ante p. *8*" should be *6*; and p. *125*, "Ante page *9*" should be *7*.

Mrs. Mahan and one of my daughters[2] sailed for Europe on Tuesday, so I am now quite alone. Mrs. Mahan is going to take another course of baths at Nauheim.

To Andrew C. McLaughlin

160 West 86th Street, New York, April 2, 1905 [LC]

Dear Mr. McLaughlin: I think the result of your search after pari passu very satisfactory. The origin appears, as I apprehended, in an informal conversation; but *not*, as I anticipated, by Monroe over that of January 1807. It is evident that pari passu by no means corresponds to the measured phrase used by Erskine in his written communication of the Orders of

1. For *The War of 1812.*
2. Ellen Kuhn Mahan.

Nov. 11; a phrase which I expect to find was by him transcribed from Canning's instructions to him. I have written to Stevens to send me copies of the latter, & of his subsequent instructions to Jackson. They could possibly be had from the British Legation, but I apprehend not without authority from their Foreign Office, so I have written direct.

I would back Madison & Erskine heavily for muddling any matter they engaged in. Both were so eager to achieve their end, that they read into other peoples words, and even letters, what could not be found there. I apprehend that when Wellesley assumed Erskine's words, in his letter of Feb. 23, 1808, as defining the position of the British ministry, he did so because they were Canning's, but, as already known to the Am. Government, they were through Erskine. When Monroe cited pari passu to Foster, the latter did not trouble to deny it, because by his argument (correct, as I think) France had not yet made a single passus.

However, Canning's letters when I get them will probably settle pari passu. Meantime, I am deeply indebted to you, & to your staff, for the assistance rendered me.

To John M. Brown

160 West 86th Street, New York, April 9, 1905 [LC]

My dear Mr. Brown: I wish I could accept your kind invitation for a visit, but I cannot leave my daughter[1] who is suffering from an approach to nervous prostration, & forbidden by the doctor to see more than one visitor a day. Under those circumstances I feel too large a factor in her day to quit her. There is no serious trouble, but entire rest is ordered.

Day before yesterday I sent by express Chapter IV, the last of Antecedents. It will probably require some modification, when I shall receive some copies of documents for which I have sent to London, but as they are far on in the chapter there is time for them to arrive. I am now re-reading Henry Adams on the same period. My point of view is so different, though dealing with the same conditions, that I hope there will be no repetition of treatment— and think there will not. The question will arise— whether a leaf should interpose at end of Chapter IV— and then "The War" begin with Chapter I, or Chapter V. The title of that chapter will be "The Theatre of Operations."

If by chance the receipt of the package has not been acknowledged to me, will you kindly have it done?

---

1. Helen Evans Mahan.

To John Bassett Moore

160 West 86th Street, New York, April 20, 1905 [LC]

My dear Mr. Moore: I think that, regarded *locally* only, the West Side from 72nd St. is one of the best residence quarters of the city. The inconvenience we have found has been the distance, from the shopping and amusement centers, increased in our case by the fact that most of our friends and acquaintances are down town or Eastsiders. The subway has greatly mollified conditions, due largely to the fact that we are near a station; & should you decide to settle in this quarter, I would suggest nearness to a station as a factor of great interest to the ladies of a family. I think we have here great advantage in the air, and the width of the avenues. Personally, I should be content to remain where I am the rest of my life. The ladies had manifested great restlessness till the subway came. This has much reduced their complaint, but I am afraid they may yet move me in order to be nearer where friends can run in & out—rather an illusion in N.Y.

I must tell you that McLaughlin of the Carnegie Instn. got track of pari passu in a letter, not official, from Madison to Pinkney, saying that Erskine had expressed verbally such a view of the British Govt.'s intention. Viewed in the light of Erskine's subsequent action, I incline to think this is a rehearsal antecedent of what he did in 1809. I hope in a few days to receive Canning's instructions to him.

To Andrew C. McLaughlin

160 West 86th Street, New York, April 28, 1905 [LC]

Dear Mr. McLaughlin: I am greatly obliged for the verification of the letter of June 24, 1812, by your letter of April 24. I assume that the "one word in question," would not vitally affect the meaning of the bracketed portion, the effect of which is to throw on Hull[1] almost the entire onus of the crossing to Canada; without, however, excusing the shameful lack of preparation by the Administration & Congress.

You will see by the enclosed—*which please return*—that Mr. Burton[2] declines me the use of the letters. I cannot of course delay my book till he pub-

---

1. General William Hull.
2. Clarence M. Burton, city historiographer of Detroit. McLaughlin had informed Mahan that Burton owned two Hull letters of interest to Mahan's treatment of Hull's surrender of Detroit to the British on August 16, 1812. McLaughlin to Mahan, April 17, 1905, in the Library of Congress.

lishes,[3] & will therefore only be able to refer in a note to the existence of these letters. I do not attach much importance to them, in view of the sworn testimony before the Court. The *finding* of a Court, though under sanction of an oath, is still an opinion, liable to bias; the testimony of unimpeached witnesses is statement of fact, liable doubtless to error, but as near truth as we can usually get here below. Letters of the accused *may* be important, it cannot be denied before they are seen; but at least they are unsworn statements of a deeply interested party, who made at least one untrue statement, viz: as to the ammunition on hand.

I have just recd. Canning's letter to Erskine of Dec. 1, 1807 instructing him concerning the Orders in Council. Mutatis mutandis, Erskine's of Feb. 23, 1808, A.S.P. to Madison is a literal transcript, the concluding words of which were adopted by Wellesley to Pinkney in 1810, as defining the British position. To make assurance doubly sure, I have written Stevens to have examined the entire record from Dec. 1. 1807 to Feb. 1. 1808, for any trace of pari passu, or its equivalent. I have also written Sir Mortimer Durand[4] whether he would feel at liberty to inform me concerning the archives of his office, but as yet have no reply.

Now, my idea of a paper for the Historical[5] was an exhibition of three other such instances of the diplomatic negotiation under Madison; pari passu being a fourth. With the necessary explanatory treatment I suppose this would make a paper of reasonable length and interest. Of the latter it is for you to judge. My book does not appear till fall. Will you wish the article, and if so by what date?

To Andrew C. McLaughlin

160 West 86th Street, New York, May 9, 1905 [LC]

Dear Mr. McLaughlin: With reference to the one unimportant variation in the War Department's letter of June 24, 1812 to Hull, if unimportant, it is unimportant; but is it? I took the extract I sent from the *Defense of Dearborn*, by his son;[1] & as I shall have to use it contentiously, I would be glad to have an exact copy.

---

3. The nearest book in date by Clarence Burton was *Early Detroit: A Sketch of Some of the Interesting Affairs of the Olden Time*. Detroit, 1909.
4. Sir Henry Mortimer Durand, British Ambassador to the U.S., 1903–1905.
5. *See* Mahan to McLaughlin, January 17, 1905; February 21, 1905.

1. Henry Alexander Scammell Dearborn, *Defence of Gen. Henry Dearborn, Against the Attack of Gen. William Hull*. Boston: E. W. Davis, 1824. William Hull attacked Dearborn in *Memoirs of the Campaign of the North Western Army of the United States A.D. 1812. In a Series of Letters Addressed to the Citizens of the U. S. . . . .* Boston: True and Greene, 1824.

With regard to the paper for the *Review*, I can see no difficulty now about preparing it by August; but I am not yet sure when the book may appear.[2] Probably not before October—but by August we will probably know.

I enclose a letter[3] which speaks for itself, which I would have sent to the Secy., had I his name *exactly*. This leads me to suggest publishing the names of the officers of the Histl. Assn. in each number of the *Review*. It would be convenient as reference, and probably otherwise beneficial. Will you send it to him? I replied to the letter saying I was no longer President.

To Leopold J. Maxse

160 West 86th Street, New York, May 30, 1905 [LC]

My dear Mr. Maxse: I have received your letter and am glad to know that the *National* has not forgotten me, as I certainly have not it, although my winter has been one of the most laborious I have known. The article which appeared in the *Times*[1] was written offhand in about three days, to meet, as I thought, a question of current interest, likely soon to be past.

To John S. Billings

Slumberside, Quogue, Long Island, June 15, 1905 [NYPL]

My dear Dr. Billings: Since my arrival here, I have found the Courts Martial of the *Guerrière* and *Macedonian*, but have not laid my hand yet upon that of the *Serapis*. Should you desire the two former, I can send them to you now by express, & they can remain in your hands till after my return to town in October.

I have just received a complimentary copy of the Historical MSS. Commission's "Report on the MSS of Lady Du Cane."[1] It consists substantially

---

2. McLaughlin had suggested that the article on the Ghent negotiations be in his hands in early August if it was to be included in the October 1905 issue of the *American Historical Review*. McLaughlin to Mahan, May 1, 1905, in the Library of Congress.
3. Enclosure not found.

1. *The Times*, London, May 13, 1905, carried Mahan's "The Problems That Rozhdesvensky and Togo Must Solve." *Collier's Weekly* carried the article under the same title in its issue of the same date. *The Times* also ran an editorial on May 13 entitled "The Coming Struggle," which discussed Mahan's point of view.

1. *Report on the Manuscripts of Lady Du Cane.* . . . London: Printed for H. M. Stationery Office by B. Johnson and Company, York, 1905. Lady Du Cane was Georgiana Susan (Copley) Du Cane.

of the correspondence of a Vice Admiral Medley, 1721–1747. There is also
a find of quite a long correspondence of a Chevalier de Caylus[2] of the
French navy of the same period. The whole prefaced by Prof. Laughton.
Although I have made no close examination, I am satisfied that the work
contains a great deal of material incidentally valuable to naval history, in
its broader aspects. It can be purchased from Wyman & Sons, Fetter Lane,
E.C.

To Andrew C. McLaughlin

Slumberside, Quogue, Long Island, June 19, 1905 [LC]

Dear Mr. McLaughlin: Another curious instance of verbal inaccuracy
has come under my notice. Goulburn,[1] British Commr. at Ghent, 1814,
wrote to Castlereagh about Aug. 20. (I have lost my memorandum) "We
have been much embarrassed by finding in the copy of your letter of Nov.
4, 1813, furnished to *us*, that there do not occur the words 'of perfect reciprocity' as quoted by the American Commissioners." You will find the
Am. quotation in their letter of August 24, 1814 (State Papers, iii, 711).

It would be interesting to ascertain, if Castlereagh's note of November
4 to the U.S. Govt. be still on record, and whether it bears the words 'of
perfect reciprocity,' which, as far as the copy of the British Commrs.
went, were an interpolation.

If you can make the inquiry, I anticipate you will find the words, for
I have in Monroe's straightforwardness much more confidence than I have
learned to feel in Jefferson or Madison.

You will notice how large an argument the American envoys base on
the words. Goulburn to Castlereagh could only surmise that if the quotation were honest, it had been inserted in the copy sent to America and forgotten to be made in that retained in the Foreign Office.

Castlereagh's reply to him is not in the published Castlereagh correspondence.

To Herbert Putnam

Slumberside, Quogue, Long Island, June 29, 1905 [LC]

My dear Mr. Putnam: Has the Congressional Library any topographical
data showing the places and roads between the Patuxent River and Wash-

---

2. The letters of the Chevalier de Caylus cover the period 1714–1746.

1. Henry Goulburn, who succeeded Sir Robert Peel as Undersecretary for War and
the Colonies in 1812, and was second commissioner at Ghent in 1814.

ington, in 1812–14? I wish to obtain an outline contemporary sketch, or rather to frame an outline sketch from contemporary data for my *War of 1812*, in which I purpose giving a mere outline of the movements, so brief as to be intelligible.

Adams has such a plan in his *History of the United States*, but I dont think he says where he got it, and I of course dont care to borrow from him, if I can get nearer head waters.

To Herbert Putnam

Slumberside, Quogue, Long Island, July 5, 1905 [LC]

Dear Sir: I am greatly indebted and beg to thank you for your prompt and satisfactory reply to my inquiry.

To John M. Brown

Slumberside, Quogue, Long Island, July 22, 1905 [LC]

Dear Mr. Brown: I have today finished the last chapter of *1812*—The Peace Negotiations—and by a happy coincidence received last night a letter from Stevens in London, announcing that they have dispatched the copies of the last papers I required from them. These have not yet reached me, but coming as Commercial Papers they follow letters, and as my English newspaper[1] by same mail has not come, I surely expect them. Stevens is very careful in mailing, but should delay occur I will write Monday, providing for duplication by cable.

These papers will serve only to modify, by expansion or change the text already written, or printed, in chapters in my hands still.

As regards the Index, laborious though it is, I prefer to give both the labor and the time myself—for it is scarcely less a factor of a book than the text itself. I propose to give my first leisure time to the Table of Contents at the beginning. This will renew my familiarity with the text and be a good foundation for the Index.

Under the circumstances, I will send the copy in detachments, beginning as soon as I see that I can keep it up. You are already informed as to the approximate amount.

I am myself most desirous to finish my part, and also to see the book out.

[P.S.]   As regards a fresh set of proof for Index, I dont know what

---

1. *The Guardian*, an Anglican church paper published in London.

[133]

trouble it may cause. I find in looking over my file that I have not in all cases (apparently) received Cast Proof, and much of what I have is dirty from handling. If not too much trouble a fresh set is desirable.

To J. Franklin Jameson

Slumberside, Quogue, Long Island, July 27, 1905 [LC]

My dear Prof. Jameson: I seem to myself to live in a state of dire uncertainty as to what I can or cannot effect, and this may partially excuse my delay in answering you. It cannot wholly, jaded though I daily am by the close attention to infinite detail which my *War of 1812* imposes, and the pressure of the publishers.

My proposition to Mr. McLaughlin went no further than this: In reply to a suggestion that my study of 1812 might have afforded some available by-products, I said it had not; that I intended to publish substantially all of such character as the *Review* could wish; but as he thought there would be no objection to the *Review* publishing what I intended to reproduce, I suggested that I considered I had pointed out such grave misunderstanding of our Government in the correspondence connected with their refusal to have any further intercourse with the British Minister—Jackson—in 1809, as to be a serious reproach to our diplomacy. I am not willing to leave it out of the book; but I am conscious it will there probably be buried; whereas in the *Historical* it may interest students. If I am right, Adams has not noticed it.

The treatment would require some little preliminary explanation leading up to the facts, and possibly some current development of the matter as treated for the book. Otherwise it will be the text itself.

I do not know how long you can wait for copy. McLaughlin said Aug. 1. This I cannot do. I think that by the end of next week—say Saturday, Aug. 5—I can let you [know] definitely whether I can let you have the article by Aug. 15 or 20. For more than this I fear to undertake.

I dont like to plead baby, but had I foreseen how driven I would be just now I would have been more careful in my offers; but I greatly wanted if possible to send the *Review* the paper.

[P.S.]   I congratulate you heartily upon your new duties.[1] I think you will find them most interesting as well as congenial.

The book is to be published Oct. 10–20 next.

---

1. Jameson was Director of Historical Research of the Carnegie Institution in Washington, D.C., as well as Editor of the *American Historical Review*.

To John M. Brown

Slumberside, Quogue, Long Island, July 28, 1905 [LC]

My dear Mr. Brown: I am very glad to see that the books have done so well; particularly that the *Problem of Asia* has had some notice. I look upon it as good as any of my literary children, but the world has not smiled on it.

I am sorry that Mr. Crowninshield had not the letter, the original of which has disappeared; but as the information was said by *my* informant to come from Adml. Schley, I am not greatly surprised that it proved incorrect. The matter is of less consequence than when I wrote you, for I have since found an official publication which gives it, which I have no cause to doubt is complete & exact.

I am sending today the next chapter of the book for the printer, XVII. Nineteen is complete. Eighteen needs recasting in some particulars on the lines of the last documents I recd. from England, but the end seems almost within arm's length.

To Charles W. Stewart

Slumberside, Quogue, Long Island, July 28, 1905 [NA]

My dear Mr. Stewart: It has been my intention, when *1812* was off my hands, to present to the Department Library the Courts Martial Records which I have had copied: *Guerrière*, *Macedonian*, Lake Erie and Lake Champlain. This would be no excessive acknowledgment of the courtesy and benefit I and my work have received from it in the three years of labor. I intended to ask only one stipulation, that they should be substantially bound.

I have besides quite a number of copies of British correspondence—Warren & Yeo[1] which also I purposed to send you. This is not complete, but could be completed by the means used to get what I have. Stevens & Brown have had copies made for me in the British Records Office, and the men they employ I believe to be entirely capable of any work you require.

In my opinion our Department Library ought to possess a complete series of the Instructions issued by the Admiralty—*Out* Letters—to the commanders of fleets and squadrons in North America, 1812 to 1815; and of the Admirals' replies or communications, known as *In*-Letters. The Admirals

---

1. Admiral Sir John Borlase Warren, Commander-in-Chief of the North American Station, 1813–1814; and Commodore Sir James Lucas Yeo, Commander-in-Chief of the ships of war on the Great Lakes in 1813.

were Sir John Warren and Sir Alex. Cochrane[2] on the coast; on the Lakes Sir James Yeo. *Possibly*, also, the letters between Prevost[3] Governor General of Canada and Bathurst,[4] Secretary of War in England, should be examined prior to May, 1813, when Yeo arrived. Till then Yeo and Bathurst "bossed" the lake navy.

When I get time I will look over my memoranda of Canadian Archives. Much of Yeo's correspondence is there; but it may be that there are copies in London, or those in Ottawa may be copies.

The British correspondence is as essential as the American to any complete data for the war. Of course, there may be many papers of no use—routine returns; but routine papers showing armaments of vessels, crews of vessels, losses, etc are all useful.

I hope your kind anticipations concerning *1812* may prove well founded.

To J. Franklin Jameson

Slumberside, Quogue, Long Island, August 6, 1905 [LC]

My dear Prof. Jameson: I have looked over my material for the article under consideration,[1] and I find that there would be more new work to be done than I had thought. I am really afraid to undertake the preparation in addition to the rest of the brain racket through which I am passing, and have still to pass.

To J. Franklin Jameson

Slumberside, Quogue, Long Island, August 11, 1905 [LC]

My dear Dr. Jameson: The passage marked in the enclosed cutting from yesterday's *Sun*[1] caught my eye. If the mystery really exists, popularly or generally, it may be that the concluding chapter of my *1812* may fill the

---

2. Admiral Sir Alexander Forrester Inglis Cochrane, Commander-in-Chief of the North American Station, 1814–1815.
3. Sir George Prevost, Governor General of Canada from 1811 to 1815. He was recalled after the British defeat at Plattsburg on suspicion of collusion with the French Canadians.
4. Henry Bathurst, 3rd Earl, Secretary for War and the Colonies in Lord Liverpool's ministry.
1. *See* Mahan to Jameson, July 27, 1905.
1. The article, "Ghent and Portsmouth; Some Observations on the Russian Czar's Part in Our Peace of 1814," signed "Strawberry Bane," Portsmouth [New Hampshire], August 7. Enclosure not found.

bill in the *Review*—should time still permit. Last summer I obtained from Lord Londonderry permission to read the Castlereagh Papers in his possession. Castlereagh was in Vienna, during the Ghent negotiations, & as Secretary for Foreign Affairs, though absent, and because absent, there went on a steady correspondence between him and Liverpool (Prime Minr.) and to some extent with Bathurst, acting in For. Affairs. I wish not to exaggerate the importance of this. Because new to me, it is not necessarily so to others. I think merely that it does show clearly why we got off as easily & cheaply as we did, and I think my own presentation fairly clear.

I glanced over Adams yesterday in N.Y. & think he had some of my data, from Wellington's supplementary dispatches; but by no means all.

Should conditions favor your taking this for the October number, I would propose sending the "copy" to my publishers with the request for galley proofs at once. I am only waiting as it is to complete two single ship actions, which end the chapter preceding this last.[2]

I should, moreover, be entirely willing for you to decide, when you see the proofs, whether the article fills your bill, as I am not *anxious* to pre-publish.

[P.S.]   The chapter is 8,500 words perhaps 9,000.

To Ellen Kuhn Mahan

Slumberside, Quogue, Long Island, August 20, 1905 [LC]

My darling Nellikin: When you get this you will know of our poor little Rovie's death. Mamma will have told you how it happened, and I will write only a few little last happenings which you may like to hear. He was lying on the porch, in his usual attitude, when I started for my afternoon ride on Monday; and he followed me round to where I had left my wheel, leaning against the piazza, just abreast the dining room. There was on the green an old bone, which I suppose had been there six weeks, and at which he gnawed from time to time, with half an eye on me; expecting, as happened, that, as I walked by it, I would give a shy at him. I did, & he pranced as usual. It was always a game, reminding me of you at the old College,[1] when I used to rush at you from my office to kick you down stairs. He thought it great fun, as you used to. So I rode, little thinking I had seen him for the last time in life. As I turned the corner by the Morris's, coming home, I saw Mamma, Helen & Mrs. Taylor standing by the bicycle rack, looking intently at something. I little suspected anything serious, but at the

---

2. "Negotiations at Ghent in 1814," *American Historical Review* (October 1905).

1. The old building in which the Naval War College was housed in 1886–1890.

gate mamma met me, saying Rovie had been killed by an automobile. I went at once to him. His little body was not at all mangled, or disfigured, except by a little blood at the lips. The injuries must have been all internal; and they were mercifully so complete that death followed almost immediately. Helen thinks not over five minutes, & Mrs. Al Geer, who was by, says much the same. The poor little man must have had an instant of terror and agony, but in the sum much less than Jomini's week of suffering; and probably the one shock destroyed sensation. Grieved as I was, and much as I miss him, I am glad that my sorrow was for him, for the loss of his days of happy life, & not for my own loss. But if, as we know, not a sparrow falls to the ground without our Father, we may be sure that our Father and his Father had taken this little dog from some sorrow. Sure I am that Christ did not die for man alone. "Dear little man," I said to him, "I wish I could tell you how sorry I am." I then turned to Mary—the upstairs one, & asked her to cover him. She brought the blanket he had at night, and said, "I suppose he will be buried in this"; & so it was. Dr. Carr, who had come in, said he was entirely dead; and Cornelius, coming along about six, dug a grave for him, alongside the fence between us & the Morris's. I told him to send me word when all was ready, & then went out. They wrapped him in his blanket, and Spencer and I stood by while he was covered in. You may think me a sentimental old pagan, but I laid by him the old bone, and a stick on the lawn which he had latterly laid great store by, larking with me, and crunching it. I understand now why people of old laid with their dead what their dead loved in life; and my only regret over the burial is that we did not replace his collar on him; not that he loved his collar, but it belonged to him. The grave was dug deep, no spade or plow will ever go so low; only the foundations of a house could disturb his bones. It is surprising what a blank is left by his absence, he was always turning up somewhere, for something. I am glad that your absence will make this less apparent, perhaps, to you. He had a happy life, though so short; and the approaching separation from us might have been harder for him than we are able to understand. God knows, and He does know.

To John S. Billings

Slumberside, Quogue, Long Island, September 8, 1905 [NYPL]

My dear Dr. Billings: I tried very hard yesterday, in town, to get your office on the telephone, but could not succeed, it not being in the book. We have rented our house in N.Y. for three years, and among my papers I find copies of a large number of letters connected with affairs about Naples in 1799, obtained when I was busy with that subject, on which I sent you a number of pamphlets.[1] The package of papers is now in my house, 160 W. 86, in which the packers are now in possession. I tied to it a tag, "to be given to a messenger from the Public Library should one come." It is in the *bath room, on 3d floor*; but you will have to send at once, as we are scuttling out. Please accredit messenger with a certain note.

The papers are for the most part very disappointing, routine and unilluminating; but if you have a stow hole it will be better than devoting them to destruction.[2]

I came across also the *Serapis* Court Martial, which I will send you. After copies have been made of it, and of the two others now in your hand, I will ask that the three be sent to the Librarian of the Navy Department, Washington. I will ask him to send you penalty addresses, which will frank the packages through the mails.

To Theodore Roosevelt

Slumberside, Quogue, Long Island, September 9, 1905 [LC]

My dear Mr. President: A few days ago I turned up, among my papers, the enclosed clipping from the *Manchester Guardian*, towards the end of the Hague Conference.[1] It is so interesting an indication of the extreme views that have been, and will be, advocated at the Peace Conference, believed to lie again in the near future, that I think it worth your attention.

Article 27 was distasteful to all the powers represented, except France, where I think it voiced the views only of a côterie. Yet it passed, though not without strong protest from small states—notably the Balkan.

It may interest you further to know that the enclosed clipping, coming under the eye of the American delegation, was the immediate cause of the Declaration attached to their signatures, saving the Monroe doctrine.

To John M. Brown

Slumberside, Quogue, Long Island, September 14, 1905 [LC]

My dear Mr. Brown: What is the outlook now for *1812*? I am conscious that much of the delay hitherto has been on my side, though due

---

1. *See* Mahan to Billings, December 20, 1902.
2. Billings wrote on this letter: "Recd. 17 logs & 24 packages of letters, 9.S.05."

1. The article hailed the adoption of Article 27, which related to recommended arbitration, and speculated that had it been in existence in 1898 there might have been no Spanish-American War.

only to the necessity of the treatment, and I must be patient now that it is my turn to wait; having sent the Index "Copy" nearly, if not quite, a week ago I have been wondering about the galleys.

I would suggest that in the prospectus, etc, it might be well to emphasize the fact that this concludes the Sea Power series, as originally projected. I have made that the opening sentence of the Preface, with a view to draw attention to it.

I am to deliver an address on Nelson on Trafalgar Day, Oct 21, in Boston to a British society;[1] and on Oct. 28 expect to sail for Europe for the winter. I am pretty well jaded by the year's work, which has been unremitting since my return last October; but I do not feel as though I ever tired beyond the probability of a speedy recovery, as soon as the steam is quite off. Not only has *1812* called for unusual research & care, but we have rented our N.Y. house for three years, purposing to spend the winters in a milder climate, and the moving has added to my preoccupations.

When the date of publication approaches you will of course let me know, and I shall want to arrange for sending presentation copies direct from the store, to spare myself packing for the mail. I have thought that my visit for Oct 21 might possibly meet this contingency, as I prefer to give autograph copies. Can there be inserted in those I shall send fly leaves on which the ink will not run?

Among the recipients of these copies I hope you will allow me to remember yourself, in memory of the completion of our joint Sea Power undertaking, begun fifteen years ago.

To Charles W. Stewart

Slumberside, Quogue, Long Island, September 14, 1905 [NA]

My dear Mr. Stewart: I am sending you today a package containing *copies* of the *Serapis* Court Martial, and also of some papers relating to naval transactions in Canada and Lake Champlain in 1776, for the Library.

I wish, however, *first* to ask you to send them *at once* to "Doctor John S. Billings, Director N.Y. Public Library, Astor Library Building, N.Y.," to be copied by him for that Library. And with the papers to send return penalty envelopes, that he may send them back to you; *with* the Courts Martial records also in the case of the *Guerrière* and *Macedonian*, now in his hands.

I should like myself also some return penalties.

I have finished *1812*, and hope soon to return you the books.

---

1. The Victoria Club.

To Leopold J. Maxse

Slumberside, Quogue, Long Island, September 14, 1905 [LC]

My dear Mr. Maxse: Your letter of Aug. 29 was received a few days ago. The *National* has been much in my mind all this year, with a feeling of dereliction on my part; but both my own and the publisher's pecuniary interest in the production of the *War of 1812* required my unremitting attention to it, to give it its best chance, & I have had time for nothing else so serious as is my work for your *Review*.

For the present the same must apply to the naval lessons of the War; but as regards Nelson there is a possible chance. Early in the year, when over confident on other matters, I engaged to deliver an address to an English society in Boston, on Trafalgar Day. I apprehend there can be no collision of interest between that delivery, and the November *National*.[1] At all events, should it seem likely to me to suit your columns, I will send a copy as soon as completed, which I should hope you might receive the first week in October, and you can decide whether or not it will satisfy you and your public.

I am expecting to sail Oct. 28 for southern Europe, we having rented our town house for three years, intending to spend the winters in a warmer climate on account of some of my family. I dont know how long the Russo-Jap war can be considered a live topic; but after a rest, which I greatly need, I hope I may turn off something for you.[2]

We hope to spend a month in Pau from about Dec. 5.

To Charles W. Stewart

Slumberside, Quogue, Long Island, September 18, 1905 [NA]

Dear Mr. Stewart: I am sending you today two packages, one containing the British Courts-Martial on the battles of Erie & L. Champlain, the other the correspondence between the British Admiralty & Warren & Yeo, so far as I have thought necessary for *my* history to have them. In

---

1. The address to the Victoria Club in Boston on October 21 was published as "The Strength of Nelson," *National Review* (November 1905); a companion piece, "The Personality of Nelson," was published in the *United Service Magazine* (October 1905).

2. "Some Reflections Upon the Far Eastern War," *National Review* (May 1906). It was also published in *Living Age* for July 14, 1906. Retitled "Retrospect Upon the War Between Japan and Russia," it was reprinted in *Naval Administration and Warfare. Some General Principles.* Boston: Little, Brown and Company, 1908.

package 2 there are some miscellaneous papers—notably some appertaining to L. Champlain, which ought to have gone in *1*.

The Warren and Yeo correspondence ought to have your own attention, with a view to the probability and advisability of supplying the gaps. For my purposes I have had what I thought necessary; but a collection such as the Navy Department Library ought to have a complete set of all the British papers (except mere routine) bearing on the War of 1812, just as it ought to have everything in private collections, like Cooper's.[1]

I don't think I shall ever need these papers again myself—unless some controversy arise, but with a view to such necessity, I should be glad if some brief memorandum should be made that they came from me. It would serve to give me a lien upon their use, should necessity arise, and the Library be then under a management less liberal than yours.

If you will send me the full name of the present Secretary, I think I will write him, recommending the acquisition of papers.

I trust you will see adequate supervision, not only to the binding of these papers, but to their being systematically arranged. In the main, I have sent them in order, but the overlooking of the Champlain papers in *1* shows that my arrangement is not impeccable.

To Charles W. Stewart

Slumberside, Quogue, Long Island, September 23, 1905 [NA]

Dear Mr. Stewart: I send you today some more, and nearly the last of my available copies. There are some miscellaneous papers connected with 1812, most of which speak for themselves. Rufus King's[1] letter is closely connected, and though solitary, deserves to be bound with them. The data concerning British troops in Canada might perhaps be properly communicated to the War Department Library, should it wish to take a copy. The papers connected with the New Orleans expedition give a fairly connected account of its genesis.

I have added a number of papers connected with Nelson's battle at Copenhagen, 1801; including logs of most of the ships; less important than they sound, but still useful. Also, some letters of Rodney, either not given in Mundy's *Life*,[2] or incomplete. I think it would be useful to enter in

---

1. Philip H. Cooper's deposit of the papers of James Fenimore Cooper.

1. Rufus King, U.S. Minister to Great Britain, 1796–1803, and U.S. Senator from New York, 1813–1825.

2. Godfrey Basil Mundy, *Life and Correspondence of the Late Admiral Lord Rodney.* London: J. Murray, 1830.

the *Life* itself a reference where these letters are on the Library shelves, as they have importance, not only to Rodney's life, but in the history of naval tactics.

To Charles W. Stewart

Slumberside, Quogue, Long Island, September 25, 1905 [NA]

Dear Mr. Stewart: In returning you *Naval Miscellany*,[1] Vol. 19, there is a preposterous misstatement in the account of the *Genl. Armstrong*, (p. 31.), claiming that New Orleans was saved by the delay of the squadron, the boats of which were so roughly handled by the privateer. It seems, pp. 32, 33, 58, that this was imposed upon three U.S. Senators, Voorhees, Evarts, & Pendleton.[2]

The facts are, that the British expedition, army and navy, were ordered to rendezvous at Negril Bay, Jamaica, *Nov. 20*; and that the squadron which attacked the *Armstrong* arrived at Kingston, Jamaica, *Nov. 14*, six days before the time appointed for rendezvous!!

It seemed to me so improbable, that an important land expedition would be delayed by the loss of a couple of hundred sailors, that I looked through *Niles* for information; & found in vol VII. p. 255, the contemporary announcement of the arrival of that squadron at Jamaica. I have noted this on p. 31 of the pamphlet, in pencil so light that it can easily be erased; but I suggest, in the interest of truth, that you make in the margin a permanent record of the truth. This you can further re-enforce by reference to Gleig, *History of the Campaign of Washington, Baltimore and New Orleans*, which I also consulted. I have not here a copy, but you will find in it that the main expedition did not reach Negril Bay till a week after the Fayal squadron reached Kingston. I may add that this Fayal squadron belonged to the West Indies. Its meeting with the *Armstrong* was an incident in a cruise. As a seaman you can value the probability of the loss of 200 men affecting the movement of a division which had no naval enemy to fear.

[P.S.]   Minor errors of statement are: Sir Thomas, for Sir Alex. Cochrane; two very different men; and that Pakenham[3] was at Negril Bay. He did not join the army till Christmas day—before New Orleans.

---

1. The Navy Records Society of London started to reprint the *Naval Miscellany* in 1902.
2. George Hunt Pendleton, of Ohio, a senator from 1879 to 1905. *See* Mahan to Moore, February 20, 1905.
3. General Sir Edward Michael Pakenham, who commanded the British forces at New Orleans and was killed in the battle.

To Charles W. Stewart

Slumberside, Quogue, Long Island, September 26, 1905 [NA]

Dear Mr. Stewart: I sent yesterday, by express, to the Library the eight volumes of *Niles' Register*. They are, as to binding, in much worse condition than when they reached me; but it is due to the aged condition of some of the covers at the first, and, if elsewhere, to simple wear and tear in continued handling. Possibly the damp seashore climate, & transition to New York counts for something also.

I enclose herewith also a letter I wrote you yesterday, with reference to a statement occurring in *Naval Miscellany* 19. This volume, together with the *Perry Statue at Cleveland*,[1] and Mackenzie's *Life of Perry*, I hope to return today or tomorrow. I believe these to be all the Library books I have, but would be glad to know from you, if their return makes my account clear.

[P.S.] In reading over I see I have omitted to thank you for the volumes, & to say of how great service they, *Niles'* especially, have been to me.

To Leopold J. Maxse

160 West 86th Street, New York, September 29, 1905 [LC]

Dear Mr. Maxse: In my letter yesterday I had meant to say,—what it is right you should know, though it can in no way affect the article sent,[1]— that I have written short articles, one for the *Graphic*[2] (weekly) of about 2,000 words, and one for the *Army and Navy Gazette*,[3] of about 800. The former concerning Nelson only as a tactician; it in no way touches the point of view taken in the article sent you. That to the *Gazette*, not to speak of its shortness, does not, as far as I can remember, have anything in common with the article. As soon as I knew that the *Gazette* had received it, I destroyed my rough draft; but I can recall its general tenor.

---

1. Cleveland. City Council. *Inauguration of the Perry Statue, at Cleveland, on the Tenth of September, 1860, Including the Addresses and Other Proceedings, with a Sketch of William Walcutt, the Sculptor.* Published by direction of the City Council. Cleveland, Ohio: Fairbanks, Benedict & Co., 1861.
1. "The Strength of Nelson," *National Review* (November 1905).
2. "The Consistency of Nelson as a Tactician," *The Graphic*, LXXII (October 21, 1905), p. 514. The article appears under the general heading, *The Centenary of Trafalgar*.
3. During the Nelson Centenary, *The Army and Navy Gazette* ran many articles on Lord Nelson, all short, all unsigned. On the basis of length and style, "Tactics of Trafalgar," July 29, 1905, p. 708, might be Mahan's contribution.

I am going also to ask you if you will kindly have the copy of the *National* which you have been so good as to send me, addressed to "4, Rue d'Orléans, Pau, France." I do not know just when I shall get there, but in the month of my stay I may get a chance to read, which I certainly shall not find en voyage.

To Charles W. Stewart

Slumberside, Quogue, Long Island, October 2, 1905 [NA]

Dear Mr. Stewart: In a final overhauling among my papers, preparatory to departure, I find the enclosed from Stevens.[1] By comparison with the "copies" on Champlain sent you (and in part "Erie" also) you will see that there are several documents which I did not think necessary to obtain; and especially certain plans. I had to consider expense in relation to utility, & thought that the testimony was as conclusive as plans would probably be. The letter, however, will serve to show you that in London,—and in Ottawa,—there is still much material requisite to a *complete* file of the British documents.

To Little, Brown and Company

160 West 86th Street, New York, October 8, 1905 [LC]

Gentlemen: I have received with much satisfaction the advance copy of *1812* which you have been kind enough to send me. It appears to me in every way satisfactory in workmanship and general turn out. The choice of the *Constitution* under full sail for the cover decoration was a happy thought.

I have to be in Boston Oct 20 and 21,[1] and hope to call on the forenoon of the latter day for the purpose of writing in the copies I purpose for presentation. I find that I will want for this twelve, and probably fourteen (14) copies.

I am to sail with my family for Europe Oct 28, and my address while there will be 4 Rue d'Orléans, Pau, France.

We leave here Tuesday Oct 10, and until sailing letters addressed to 10 East 10th St. N.Y. will reach me.

---

1. B. F. Stevens & Brown to Mahan, London, July 11, 1903, listing War of 1812 letters and documents that might be copied and sent to Mahan.

1. To speak to the Victoria Club on the occasion of the Trafalgar Centennial.

To Leopold J. Maxse

Slumberside, Quogue, Long Island, October 9, 1905 [LC]

My dear Mr. Maxse: I have your letter of Sept. 29, accepting the Nelson paper,[1] & am glad to know that it must, or should, at this writing be in your hands.

With regard to the compensation, under the circumstances, I had given some thought to that. It has appeared to me, in the matter of simple pecuniary value, to the circulation of the *National*, the reason of its production did not lessen it; nor would it be affected by delivery as an address on this side of the Atlantic, antecedent to its publication.

This is, however, more in the province of the Editor to determine than in my own. My experience supplies me with three closely analogous cases. In two the article, or articles, were written for the magazine, and used as addresses by its permission, care being stipulated against press publication. In one case it was required that I should furnish a summary, to prevent the papers reproducing in extenso. The same precaution I have taken for the Nelson article, although it is scarcely conceivable that an address delivered Saturday night Oct. 21 could, or would, reach England to interfere.

In neither of these cases was the magazine payment affected by the question of other compensation. In the third, the article had been prepared for another publication. The magazine, with which I have had considerable dealing, and always found liberal, rather objected to full payment under such circumstances, but the Editor almost immediately named four hundred dollars, instead of five hundred.

So many things go to the value of an article—the occasion, the writer's name, etc, as well as the mere value of the article considered alone,—that precision is impossible. I shall be quite satisfied to receive four hundred dollars, if that seems to you just. I should like it sent in francs, to my address in Pau. I believe I gave you this in my last, but will repeat "*Care F. Leonard Brown, Esq., M.D.,*[2] *4 Rue d'Orleans, Pau, France.*"

We sail October 28, landing at Gibraltar, and proceeding slowly through Spain to Pau, where we hope to arrive about Dec. 15. I think the general Eastern question will engage and interest my attention as soon as my brain

---

2. William Wyndham, Consul at Boston, 1904–1908.
1. "The Strength of Nelson."
2. Husband of Mahan's sister-in-law, Rosalie.

recovers its normal working power. Just at present it is somewhat rattled by the extremely close and sustained attention required by my book; now happily finished and soon to be published.

To J. Franklin Jameson

Slumberside, Quogue, Long Island, October 9, 1905 [LC]

My dear Prof. Jameson: I was glad to see, by the arrival of the *Historical* for October, that the article[1] was out well in advance of the book[2] publication. This is fixed, I understand, for October 21, simultaneous here and in Great Britain; and there is a period between publication & distribution, so that the article gets a fair start.

There is a matter to which I have not hitherto alluded, because I wished the *Review* to have an article from me in any event, entirely unembarrassed with stipulations. That being accomplished, I will mention to you that Prof. McLaughlin, in writing me about an article, said the magazine could, he thought, pay me $100. I decided I would make no claim, and would postpone all mention till after publication, in order that you might feel that there was no promise, or agreement; nothing beyond my understanding of McLaughlin's letter, which I did not press to a stipulation.

Equally you will understand that if, for any reason, attributable either to the article itself or my own self, it would be right to pay me a hundred dollars, I am not in a position to forego it. I hope therefore you will consider the matter purely editorially, as between me and the magazine, to be determined as may be right toward both parties.

I sail for Europe Oct. 28, expecting to be absent six months. Till sailing my address will be 10 East 10th St. N.Y.

To John M. Brown

University Club, New York, October 19, 1905 [LC]

My dear Mr. Brown: I am much obliged to you for putting me down at the Somerset, and so far as I can see I shall be able, as well as most happy, to lunch with you on Saturday. I had at one time in contemplation accepting an invitation from the Victorian Club (before which I am to give an address Saturday night) to lunch on Saturday at the Country Club but in the end

1. "Negotiations at Ghent in 1814."
2. *The Influence of Sea Power in Its Relation to the War of 1812.*

considering how much I wished to attend to unhurried, on that day, and what a complication such affairs, I regretted—the more easily because I have to dine with them.

I enclose the addresses of the persons to whom I propose to send the copies.[1] It will not be needed till after I have written in them, but it will be one thing off my mind, if the proper person have it in hand.

To J. Franklin Jameson

University Club, New York, October 23, 1905 [LC]

My dear Dr. Jameson: In your last letter received, (which I have not here by me), you told me that the payment of the $100 had been already settled. Under ordinary circumstances I should not again trouble you in the matter; but I do not know whether I told you that I am sailing for Europe Oct. 28, (next Saturday), for six months at least. Should it be any way inconvenient to the *Review*, I can wait; but if perfectly convenient I should be glad to have the check sent to *10 East 10th St., New York City*.

In case of necessary delay, my address while abroad will be *4, Rue d'Orleans, Pau, France.*

I am glad to know that the *American Historical* can pay. The English could not, when I last dealt with it;[1] but this you know better than I.

To Leopold J. Maxse

Hotel Reina Cristina, Algeciras, Spain, November 9, 1905 [CROCS]

My dear Mr. Maxse: I have received your letter here, where we arrived day before yesterday. I am extremely glad to know that you liked the article on Nelson,[1] & it is very kind of you to tell me so. When one has written so much on a particular subject, as I on this, doubts naturally arise as to whether the ground has not been worked out. In Boston the address toward the end elicited some signs of weariness from the audience, which were exaggeratedly represented as insulting to me. It *was* too long in delivery; & I was handicapped by a bad light, which impeded my reading and prevented the proper raising of my head, so that I was not myself surprised to find

---

1. Enclosure not found.

1. Mahan's last publication in *English Historical Review* was "Nelson at Naples," in October 1900.

1. "The Strength of Nelson," *National Review* (October 1905).

myself tedious. It is reassuring to know that you have thought well of it. If I succeeded, it is due to my very hearty and affectionate veneration for Nelson himself.

As regards the sending of the honorarium, I fancy it will be best delayed till we get to Pau. I have indeed a plan of procedure, in pursuance of which we start north today, but it is elastic as to times. I should be at a loss to fix a place for receipt, especially in view of the proverbial slackness of Spanish administration, which may affect the P.O. as well. I will give you due notice of my arrival in Pau. Meantime, letters of less consequence may be addressed as your last.

It is my purpose on arriving in Pau to take up the subject of the late war, and to see if I can venture an article of opinions touching it. Somewhere in my luggage I have a number of clippings, and the file of *Weekly Times* is accumulating in Pau.

I write by this mail to ask Messrs. Sampson, Low to send you a copy of my *War of 1812*. The first two chapters, of the Antecedents of the War, seemed to me, while writing them, to have a bearing (mutatis mutandis) upon Mr. Chamberlain's programme. I have understood all along that his aim was primarily political, and only secondarily economical; the welding of the Empire first, regarded as a whole, the economical programme being a means thereto. In this there is a distinct resemblance to the views of your antecessors on the subject of Navigation, as distinguished from Commerce. I have not pointed the moral as regarded Chamberlain, & am now almost sorry I did not. It might be worth while for you, or some of your staff, to see if there be material there for your approaching electoral contest.

To John Bassett Moore

Grand Hotel de la Paix, Madrid, Spain, December 3, 1905 [LC]

My dear Mr. Moore: I learned from my son, who attends to forwarding my mail, that you had been so good as to send me the volumes of your "Diplomatic History,"[1]—so he describes it. I regret that so long a time should elapse before my acknowledging your kindness, but it is one of the inconveniences of going abroad, that friends cannot be notified except by particular letter. In these days of constant wandering, we shall need a column for such advertisements, on the general principles of marriages and deaths.

---

1. John Bassett Moore, *American Diplomacy, Its Spirit and Achievements*. New York: Harper and Brothers, 1905.

Your own letter acknowledging my *War of 1812* came to me here in Spain; but of course I, knowing my movements, could not expect to hear earlier from recipients than I actually hear. In my treatment of diplomatic matters, I was from time to time much indebted to you for advice and information; and when your pressure of work permits reading, I hope you will find I have fallen into no great errors in my estimate of the situation.

I congratulate you on the completion of your *International Law Digest*,[2] a task I should esteem infinitely more onerous—even to you—than my *War of 1812*; and I was very tired of the latter by the time of publication. As a war, it had few redeeming features of interest. Already, however, I find myself wearying [for] want of occupation, and wish myself back at my desk and books. We rented our 86th Street house for three years from October 1. last, and I feel like a vagrant; the more so that I have no settled plan for future action.

I see you have settled yourself near the 72d St. subway. It is a good position and I hope may be found convenient by your family.

To John M. Brown

Grand Hotel de la Paix, Madrid, December 12, 1905 [LC]

My dear Mr. Brown: I have learned from my son that two photos of Captn. Barclay[1] have been received in N.Y.; and I have written him asking to send at once to your firm. I hope they may be incorporated in the future imprints of the book as soon as time will permit, as Mr. P. Barlcay, who gives them, seems to have been at much pains to supply me also details of Capt. Barclay's career. With these I did not think necessary to trouble you.

In connection with these photos there came a letter from Marston, dated about Nov. 9, saying that he had spent a guinea in some way about them, and asking me to mention this to you with a view to his repayment. I was puzzled at his mentioning this to me, but presume that from the smallness of the item he did not wish to write a special letter to you. I tell you of it.

With reference to the February royalties—I shall not need any of it, certainly little, if any, over here, and would prefer to deposit it in New York. Would it be possible for you, on the receipt of a formal request from me asking you to pay the same to Messrs E. & C. Randolph of N.Y., to do so, taking their receipt for the same? If you will write me that this course will be satisfactory to you, I will send such formal request to you, notifying

---

2. John Bassett Moore, *A Digest of International Law*. 8 vols. Washington, D.C.: U.S. Government Printing Office, 1906.

1. Robert Heriot Barclay, who was tried in England in 1814 for the loss of the Lake Erie Flotilla to Perry, and was "most fully and honorably acquitted."

them at the same time, so that they will be prepared to give the receipt in such form as you may wish.

We have had rather bad luck in Spain. Our first two weeks, in Southern Spain were not so bad, although the weather was unusually cold and rainy; but we saw Ronda, Granada, Cordova, and Seville quite thoroughly. After reaching Madrid, two weeks ago, I got an excessively bad cold, and my younger daughter[2] came down with scarlattina [*sic*]. This will so delay us, awaiting her cleansing from infection, that we shall have spent here five or six weeks instead of two. Singularly, here, where we expected bad weather, it has been beautiful, bright sun every day, though we had ice last night. My own cold is due to a severe chilling in a train coming from Segovia, over mountains drenched in snow.

This should reach you somewhere between Christmas & New Year. I wish all the happiness of the season to yourself and family.

My address abroad, I think you know, is Care of F. Leonard Brown Esq, M.D., 4 Rue d'Orleans, Pau, Basses Pyrénées, France.

To Little, Brown and Company

Grand Hôtel Continental, San Sebastián, Spain, January 9, 1906 [LC]

Gentlemen: Your letter of Dec. 19 was duly received. To day, at my first leisure, I have written Mr. R. B. Marston, that my recollection is that he was cognizant, some year or two ago, of the application of M. Izoulet to translate into French *The Interest of America in Sea Power*; that, at his suggestion, the negotiation was carried on through my brother, Major Mahan, because resident in Paris and in touch with Izoulet. In any event, Izoulet paid me 500 francs, and I granted the right of translation. The change of title was made without my knowledge.[1] I have suggested to Marston the insertion of a statement of these facts in the "notes" to the "Publishers' Circular," and if he agrees will prepare such a note. I presume Izoulet thought the title more likely to catch French attention, & and there may have been some Russian sympathy in it; but my consent should have been asked. The book has already been translated into Japanese.

I have also written concerning the German application to translate *1812*; and have asked Mr. Marston to comply with your wish to be put into communication with the German parties.

---

2. Ellen Kuhn Mahan. She also suffered an attack of rheumatic fever at San Sebastián a few weeks later. *See* Mahan to Maxse, January 15, 1906.

1. *Le Salut de la race blanche et l'empire des mers*. Traduction, sommaires, préface et introductions, par Jean Izoulet. . . . Introductions: la Croix et l'épée en Occident; l'Expropriation des "races incompétentes." Paris: E. Flammarion, 1906.

Since leaving the United States, now over two months ago, I have not seen an American newspaper, and should be very glad if you could send me some clippings of the principal notices of the *1812*. There are always a multiplicity of brief "syndicated" notices, which are immaterial; but such as the *N.Y. Sun, Times, Tribune*, the *Boston Herald*, & others of that type I should much wish to read. Mr. Marston was good enough to send me a number of English notices. They struck me as rather colorless, for the most part; though the *Times* and *Spectator* were discriminating. None, however, were unfavorable, and the interest of the book to Englishmen is secondary. Our best sales should be in America this time.

To Leopold J. Maxse

4 Rue d'Orléans, Pau, France, January 15, 1906 [LC]

My dear Mr. Maxse: We have at last arrived here, and, when convenient to you, I shall be glad to receive the honorarium for "The Strength of Nelson," which I had asked you to postpone till our arrival .

I remember writing you once, but I do not recall whether it was before the beginning of the succession of mishaps which have attended us. A few days after reaching Madrid, on Dec. 1, my younger daughter was taken down with scarlatina, involving a delay of a month there, and at the same time I was attacked by severe catarrhal trouble, which descended to and involved the bowels. After getting away from Madrid, my daughter developed inflammatory rheumatism, a not infrequent sequel to the other trouble, I now learn, and she is now laid up again with the prospect at best of a fortnight's suffering, & probably a long convalescence.

It has been my intention ever since starting on my journey, to devote myself at once upon arrival here to the article for which you expressed a wish, based upon the Russo-Japanese War.[1] I am the more disposed to do so, as I have one or two suggestions on questions of naval policy I shall be glad to work in. I cannot make any definite promise beyond the intention to try, but I should be glad if you could send me any information which may probably have escaped my notice. In over two months, I have not seen an American paper, but I have kept fairly track of the London *Times*, daily and weekly, without seeing anything striking. The war is now so much in the past, and your elections & allied matters of such immediate interest, that I fancy it makes little difference whether my article be ready one month or the next.

---

1. "Some Reflections Upon the Far Eastern War," *National Review* (May 1906); published also in *Living Age* for July 14, 1906.

I read with great interest Genl. Barrow's article[2] in one of the *Nationals*. Most able and instructive, but at its end I quite understood Kitchener's objection to him. A colossal *I* should have been stamped on every page.

[P.S.] The *National* you kindly send me has not reached here for January.

To James R. Thursfield

4 Rue d'Orléans, Pau, January 22, 1906 [LC]

My dear Mr. Thursfield: Can you indicate to me any sources of *published* information, relating to the naval operations & occurrences of the Russo-Japanese War, further than that which appeared soon after the Battle of the Japan Sea, in May last. Up to leaving the U.S., Oct 28, I kept pretty good track of them, as I thought, in the *Weekly Times*, which I take; and since my arrival on this side I have looked through the subsequent issues, but I find substantially nothing as regards Togo's disposition of his fleet during the siege of Port Arthur, its rendezvous, depots, scouting etc; nor have I come across any more illuminative details of the great battle, & the preceding engagements (of 1904) than appeared almost contemporaneously. Last June the *Weekly* published an excerpt from Togo's report; but besides being only in part, there were one or two evident errors, doubtless incurred in cable transmission. I presume the next *Brassey Annual* will contain all there is to be known now, but I fear it will not appear before March, and I want my material sooner for an article promised conditionally.

I am on this side for the winter only, in search of a mild climate & quiet for my family. We landed at Gibraltar, to reach this place through Spain. Most unhappily, after a fortnight in Southern Spain, on reaching Madrid one of my daughters developed scarlatina. This involved a delay of a month, and after resuming our journey, acute rheumatism came on, and from that she is now suffering. So we have not thus far the feeling of brilliant success.

In common with the world at large, and I believe with more sympathy than most, I have been watching your elections. Besides my general goodwill toward you, I believe the strengthening of the ties between the different parts of the British Empire to be distinctly to the benefit of the U.S. I regret, therefore, the change of hands in your Government; but I draw satisfaction from the fact that the younger among the Liberal leaders are more "Imperialistic" than the older men, and that Democracy, the grow-

---

2. Sir Edmund Barrow, "The New Balance of Power in the Far East," *National Review* (October 1905).

ing force of which, with you as with us, is apparent, is of the same temper. The end and aim of the two parties, in external matters, will not be greatly different twenty years hence. As to the means & method, I do not believe that such tightening of the bonds of Empire can be achieved by merely drifting and trusting to the development of public sentiment. There must be a ready watchfulness to do something, at an opportune moment; which means to employ some artificial method to draw the parts together. Whether Chamberlain's method fits the case, I dont undertake to say; but his aim I believe holds the promise of the future. The whole effect of my study of the period of two centuries, before the War of 1812, convinced me that the Navigation Acts were just such a purely artificial method, economically unsound, and as bitterly assailed as Preferential Treatment now is, but which yet built up the Empire of the Seas, without which there could have been no British Empire. Having served their turn, they should have been modified earlier than they were; but they were a triumphant proof that at times Protection may protect. Yet I am a free trader by conviction, *provided* others will free-trade.

To James R. Thursfield

4 Rue d'Orléans, Pau, January 31, 1906 [LC]

My dear Mr. Thursfield: I am much indebted for your letter of the 26th, and especially for sending me the *Edinburgh Review*.[1] A moment of self-reproach passed across me when I read the latter intention, for I had addressed inquiries to Laughton as well as yourself, & when the copy appeared, I feared, from the moment of its receipt, that both of you had done the same act of kindness, for which I had not looked. Fortunately, as only one copy has come, I am relieved on that score; and I assure you I very heartily appreciate the facility you extended me by your prompt action, as well as by the other suggestions of your letter. I think I may send for the *War in the Far East*,[2] although I read the various letters of the *Times*'s Military Correspondent as they appeared, while Laughton secured for me Togo's Report through Sir C. Bridge, who had it, together with other data, in a file of the *Japan Times* which he sent me.

With so much professional discussion already, I dont know that I will find any room for useful comment on the particular battle.[3] I feel a greater

---

1. A discussion of the Russo-Japanese War had appeared in *Edinburgh Review*, CXCIX, p. 511.
2. *War in the Far East, 1904–1905*, by the Military Correspondent of the London *Times*. (London: Dutton, 1905).
3. The Battle of Tsushima.

interest, (possibly because of the mystery as yet surrounding), in Togo's dispositions during the siege of Port Arthur, together with what may be gleaned concerning the effects upon Japanese finance, shipping & commerce, from the action of the Vladivostok Squadron, while that had a comparatively free foot. The control of sea-borne commerce is a factor in the policy of naval states which is receiving little attention, and what is given is marred by prepossession and imperfect consideration.

I am much gratified by your appreciation of my *War of 1812*. It will readily be understood that from a merely professional, as distinguished from a national, point of view I found the work rather dry. Indeed, I put more heart into the "Antecedents" than I did into the war itself. The review in the *Times* came early into my hands, and was the cause of much satisfaction to me. I supposed you were the writer, and am glad now to know it. I could have asked nothing better for the work, unless that it wake up my countrymen a bit.

Your articles on "The Nelson Touch"[4] were sent me, though I did not know by whose motion. Nor did I know, until after my arrival on this side, that you were the author. I confess they have not convinced me; partly, perhaps, because I have never considered the attack in column as misjudged. Bridge had sent me a copy of his address,[5] which I read twice before leaving the U.S., and yours I also read as the numbers reached us. Before I saw either, however, I had contributed to the *Graphic* a paper on the subject which appeared in its issue of Oct. 21[6] (the accompanying diagram was not mine and is inconsistent with my text. I dont know whence it came.) I *think* I read the proof, however, in the light of your and Bridge's paper. The fact that Nelson contemplated from the first an attack from leeward, on the same general lines as that actually delivered (by my understanding) from windward, with the additional disadvantage of a slanting approach, longer, equally exposed, and equally unable to reply to the fire of ships towards which the course was directed—a condition, too, in which the loss of spars was of greater moment than with a quartering wind—all convinces me that he would not hesitate to attack in column, which is the onus of the supposed charge against his military judgment. I did not bring your papers with me, but according to my memory the diagram accompanying the last, or next to last, is inconsistent with Collingwood's[7] remark that, when "leading down," both flank ships of the allies was abaft the *R*.

---

4. James R. Thursfield, "The Nelson Touch," *Spectator*, XCV, p. 601.
5. Sir Cyprian A. G. Bridge had recently produced two papers on Nelson: "The Centenary of Trafalgar," *Cornhill's Magazine*, XCII, p. 312; and "Recent Calumniators of Nelson," *United Service Magazine*, XXXII, p. 9.
6. "The Consistency of Nelson as a Tactician."
7. Admiral Lord Collingwood, who succeeded to the command upon the death of Nelson at Trafalgar.

Sovn's[8] beam. Your diagram places the van ally well forward of the beam; and if the reply is that when Collingwood kept away both flanks were abaft the beam, the answer is that, by your thesis he then ceased to "lead," in any natural sense of the word, for the rest of his column then kept away together. But my *Graphic* article, though in no wise intended controversially, gives my own impression of what the Nelson Touch was, in its essential features.

Our movements are still involved in uncertainty, but you may be sure that if I pass through London, or come to England, I shall let my presence be known to you. Meanwhile, renewing my thanks, believe me [etc.].

To John M. Brown

4 Rue d'Orléans, Pau, February 26, 1906 [LC]

My dear Mr. Brown: I received two days ago your letter accompanying the semi-annual statement. It was gratifying to me to see so fair a six months return on the old books, but I own I share your disappointment at the apparent indifference of our people to so notable a period of our history as the War of 1812. I had no very extensive expectations, but I certainly looked for a larger sale than 1,000 copies in America. The experience is however much the same as I had with the *Life of Farragut*, which I wrote for Appletons, although that period was so much nearer to contemporary recollection and interest.

I believe myself that *1812* is in thoroughness and execution a better book than any of its predecessors, but the intrinsic interest of the subject is undoubtedly less. Since the return I have wondered whether a title putting 1812 more forward, and Sea Power more in the rear would have caught attention better. It is significant that Hazeltine[1] has not reviewed it, as he did all the other principal books. Just what this signifies I dont know, but I am confident that had it been assigned him, he would have recognized that in solid achievement it was ahead of the others. Have you any idea why it was not given him?

We are still here—my daughter is convalescent,[2] but not yet in condition to travel. What the upshot will be I cant yet tell, but I am satisfied that either we will go home as intended in April, or else to some baths for Mrs. Mahan and the girl.

[P.S.] I received the clipping that you sent and am much obliged.

---

8. HMS *Royal Sovereign*.

1. Mayo Williamson Hazeltine, literary editor of the New York *Sun*.
2. Ellen Kuhn Mahan.

To Charles W. Stewart

4 Rue d'Orléans, Pau, March 13, 1906 [NA]

My dear Mr. Stewart: Mr. Robert W. Neeser, of New York, but at present a student of Yale University, wishes to consult some documents in the Navy Department, in connection with certain work on which he has been engaged for some years back.

It will give me much pleasure if you will assist him, either in your own department or by introducing him to others in the Navy Department, should that be necessary.

To Elihu Root

Villa Diana, Bad Nauheim, Germany, April 20, 1906 [NA]

Dear Mr. Root: I dislike to trespass on so busy a man; but the matter to which I would ask your attention is primarily one of our external policy, in which I think a long-standing tradition, derived from the expediencies of our early weakness, has been too easily continued by successive Administrations to the present day, and to very different conditions.

I allude to the advocated exemption from capture of so-called "Private Property" at sea. The property thus styled is essentially, *not* private, but the general commercial movement of a belligerent nation in external trade. As such, it is an important factor in belligerent efficiency.

Is it too late to undertake a comprehensive examination of this subject in its civil, legal, and military aspects? Its importance is greater than is commonly realized. During the interim between Mr. Hay's departure in search of health and his untimely death, I enclosed to the President what were then advanced sheets of my since published *War of 1812*. In these, arguing against exemption, I showed that our statesmen of a century ago, under the pressure of contemporary expediency, were prepared to yield the principle of commercial blockades. If this had been done, International Law in 1811 would have forbidden the blockade of the Confederate coast, than which no one measure contributed more powerfully to the success of the Union arms. May we not now, under the influence of prepossession, be contemplating a similar mistake in the measures to be discussed at The Hague?

I ought perhaps to accept as final the adverse reply of the President, and I am constitutionally reluctant to move in matters not of my immediate charge; but, as seen by me, the matter is so important, and the contrary view has so long held the field unchallenged, in our country, that it appears to me a final decision should be delayed until the matter has been threshed out, in a mature reconsideration, by bodies of men expert in its several aspects. Should I succeed in arresting your own attention, I may hope to see the powerful influence of your reputation and office enlisted with the President, in behalf of such consideration; surely not an extreme precaution to take, before committing the nation to an irreversible step. As you know, military regulation forbids me recourse to the Press; a rule correct in principle, though with the drawback of silencing men whose profession may have led them to give special attention to a subject.

The subject has two principal aspects: moral, (or legal), and military. As to the first, the phrase "private property" conveys the idea that seizure is of the nature of robbery, like taking a man's coat and purse. This is not so. The existing law forbids the belligerent to trade; should the prohibition be disregarded, the penalty is confiscation. I need not say, to a man of affairs, that the confiscation of offending property is not robbery.

On the military side, the *general* question is; Does the interruption of his trade sap the resources of a belligerent, diminishing his power to fight? As to this, there can be little doubt. For the *particular* nation, the military question is one of policy. Which is more to my advantage?

The latter could be submitted to a commission of naval experts to consider, and to advise the Government, which retains always the power to accept or reject the conclusions submitted. Such a commission, specially qualified by its present duties, already exists in the General Board, of which Admiral Dewey is president, for the consideration of naval policy in war.

Should the subject recommend itself to your further attention, I enclose some type-written pages, which formed part of an article contributed by me to the English *National Review*, for May.[1] Upon reflection, seeing that they traversed a declared policy of the Administration, I cut them out. In my *War of 1812*, I have in several places stated the general arguments. I have not a copy near me, but, should there be any wish to refer to my statements, I believe the Index will show them under the heads of "Commerce," and of "John Marshall."[2]

---

1. *See* Paper, "Comments on the Seizure of Private Property at Sea," February–March, 1906. The May 1906 article in *National Review* was "Some Reflections Upon the Far Eastern War." The *National Review* published in its June 1907 issue Mahan's "The Hague Conference: The Question of Immunity of Belligerent Merchant Shipping."

2. On May 23, Secretary of State Root forwarded Mahan's letter to Secretary of the Navy Charles J. Bonaparte. His letter of transmittal suggested a careful reexamination of the traditional position concerning immunity before the opening of the Second Hague Conference, and requested the views of the General Board. Bonaparte responded, in effect, that in recent years the stand in favor of immunity had been advocated from moral considerations; and the Board feared that the military or practical considerations had not received the attention they deserved in framing U.S. policy.

[P.S.] I enclose two clippings from the London *Times*, which besides showing the importance attaching to the subject in general, suggest (to me) the further reflection that the positional control of Great Britain over German Commerce is much like our own over the Panama Canal routes, in the future.

To James Ford Rhodes

Bad Nauheim, May 20, 1906 [MHS]

My dear Mr. Rhodes: It was very kind of you to write me the letter which I received yesterday. It is always gratifying to an author to have his work valued; and doubly so by one who has experience of the same kind of labors, and has achieved the success and recognition which your own work has among all competent critics.

I suppose you ought to be congratulated upon the completion of your history,[1] and I do congratulate you most heartily. There is real tragedy when a man is cut off before the completion of a life's work, as was the case with poor Rawson Gardiner,[2] and with Hunter,[3] the best qualified, I suppose, of all historians of India. But on the other hand, there enters the element of sadness, which Gibbon[4] depicted so graphically, when you and your work are parted, and it leaves your hand finally to go into the world. You and I share the same experience at nearly the same time, for, as you know, *1812* completed the Sea Power series, which must remain the chief of any work done by me.

Will you attempt nothing else? The period from 1815 to 1850 is to me the terra incognita of U.S. history. Has any one ever filled it—in extenso? Of course general histories, like Hildreth's[5] and Schouler's,[6] take it with the rest; but has it ever received the elaboration which you have given to the succeeding period, and Henry Adams to the preceding?

---

1. James Ford Rhodes, *History of the United States from the Compromise of 1850.* New York: 9 vols. Harper and Brothers, 1893– ; also London: Macmillan, 1900–1928.
2. Samuel Rawson Gardiner, *The History of England from the Accession of James I to the Outbreak of the Great Civil War, 1603-1642.* 10 vols. (1863–1882). Various editions, including New York: AMS Press, 1965.
3. Sir William Wilson Hunter, *A History of British India.* London: Longmans, Green & Co., 1899–1900.
4. Edward Gibbon, *The Decline and Fall of the Roman Empire.* Various editions.
5. Richard Hildreth, *The History of the United States of America.* 6 vols. New York: Harper and Brothers, 1856–1860.
6. James Schouler, *History of the United States of America, under the Constitution.* 5 vols. Washington, D.C.: W. H. Morrison, 1886–1891.

Our steamers will cross, for we sail from Bremen the 26th.[7] We will spend the summer in Quogue, after which our plans are most uncertain, for we have rented our N.Y. house for three years.

I trust that Mrs. Rhodes and yourself will have a happy year abroad, and you find some new subject for work; for how can we live without it?

To the Editor of the Philadelphia Public Ledger

Probably, Philadelphia, early June 1906[1]

Returning home recently in the North German liner *Barbarossa*,[2] on May 31, about 8 a.m. we passed the Cunarder *Campania*, bound east. When her approach was mentioned to me by a fellow passenger I was just able to see her by craning my head as far as I could over the port rail. She must, therefore, have been nearly right ahead, and she passed so near that her name was read without glasses. The weather at the time being clear, the circumstances presented no difficulty; but four or five hours before, at early daybreak, we had an hour of fog, which recurred also a little later. Under such conditions, which were evidently possible at any time, it is mild to say the situation would have been extremely tense. Being in about longitude 30 degrees, there was no land within 200 miles. The question, therefore, naturally arises why were two steamships, laden with passengers—the *Barbarossa* had 1,500 steerage—following courses which might entail even a remote risk of head-on collision? I have been under the impression that the great companies prescribed to their vessels certain limits to avoid such risk, and that the *Barbarossa* was so governed is inferable from the fact that, after leaving the approaches to the English Channel until reaching those to New York, no steamship was seen, so far as I heard, pursuing a direction other than our own except the *Campania*. That the chances against collision preponderate greatly is nothing to the purpose. Not the slightest needless risk should ever be run, and it is to the public interest that any such meeting should be reported by one or more of the passengers, specifying place and time.

---

7. Mahan stopped over in London on his way home. Ambassador Henry White informed Mahan that King Edward VII wished to see him at four o'clock on the afternoon of May 30. It is not known if the appointment was kept.

1. From the *Army and Navy Journal* (June 16, 1906), p. 1163. Original not found.
2. The Mahans returned to New York from Europe on June 7, 1906. They visited Mrs. Mahan's relatives in Philadelphia prior to going to Quogue for the summer.

To John M. Brown

Slumberside, Quogue, Long Island, June 18, 1906 [LC]

My dear Mr. Brown: We arrived home about ten days ago, and my address will be here till further notice. I dont know whether I told you that we rented our N.Y. house last year for three years, and I have shifted my citizenship to Quogue. What our winter arrangements are cannot yet be foreseen.

I am settled down to work again. A year ago *Harper's Magazine* asked me if I could not furnish them some chapters of Reminiscences, after the so frequent course of our day. The idea seemed to me at first preposterous for so quiet a life as my own; but I have begun an attempt at it, hoping thereby I may turn the few additional honest pennies that I want for current expenses. Along with that I have provided the necessary material for carrying on my study of U.S. History, especially in the periods most unfamiliar to me; having still in view that history of the U.S. of which we have before spoken. Of course, I cannot contemplate exhaustive research, or full treatment, of our now three century record. My hope is to strike a ruling thought, like Sea Power, and to string my account so upon that as to present a more vivid and coherent whole than more elaborate and comprehensive works do—or can do.[1] I hope I have such an idea now. Time will show.

Have you any further notices of *1812*?

[P.S.] Let the U.S. history remain a business secret for the present.

To Charles J. Bonaparte[1]

Quogue, Long Island, June 26, 1906 [NA]

Sir: 1. In reply to the Department's letter G.B.No.401–2, of June 20, 1906, which I have only to-day received, there is no reason to prevent my taking up the work in question now, as well as later. I would therefore suggest that the orders place me on this duty July first.[2]

---

1. Mahan's contemplated survey history of the United States, turning on the "ruling thought" of American expansion, was scarcely begun at the time of his death in 1914.

1. Secretary of the Navy.

2. On June 20, 1906, Admiral Dewey, President of the General Board, recommended to the Secretary of the Navy that Mahan prepare a history of the Naval War Board. On the same day he wrote to Mahan outlining the scope of the project. *See* Paper, "The Work of the Naval War Board of 1898," October 29, 1906.

2. Referring to Section 3 of the Department's letter, the reasons for the organization of the Board, or the scope and nature of its duties, are not known to me, except by inference. I mean that they, being essentially advisory, were never formally stated to me by letter, nor, as far as I now remember, expressly defined and limited by word. Might it not be well to address inquiry to this effect to the Hon. John D. Long, who was then Secretary? If there were formal orders, specifying the scope of the Board's duties, I do not remember them. I retain, it is true, a clear impression of the nature of the duties, from the actual discharge of them, and of such I can give an account.

3. I did not report until about May 10, 1898, some time after the Board began its duties. Rear Admiral Barker had been a member until my arrival; and Rear Admiral Crowninshield had then also been a member, and continued to be to the dissolution of the Board. They have therefore a personal knowledge of that earlier period which I have not.

To Little, Brown and Company

Slumberside, Quogue, Long Island, June 30, 1906 [LC]

Gentlemen: Will you kindly send me here a copy of the *one* volume (popular edition) of the *Life of Nelson?* Also, one copy, each, of *Retrospect & Prospect*, and *Types of Naval Officers*.

I should like also to see a proof of the likeness of Captn. Barclay which was received too late, for publication in the first impression of *1812*. Have you yet been able to incorporate it in any bound volumes?

I have received and looked over the notices of *1812*, kindly sent me by you, and shall mail them back to-day. I do not find among them one by the *Athenaeum*[1] which I saw while abroad. It is one of the most discriminating—I dont mean eulogistic—that I have seen.

To J. Franklin Jameson

Slumberside, Quogue, Long Island, June 30, 1906 [LC]

Dear Mr. Jameson: Owing to my migratory life the past twelvemonth, I have not received the April number of the *Historical Review*. Will you kindly have a copy sent me here, & have this, *Quogue, N.Y.*, noted as my address.

---

1. An unsigned review in *Athenaeum* (March 10, 1906), pp. 290–292.

I have only recently returned from Europe, but look forward to being a fixture for some little time.

[P.S.]   I of course expect to pay for the April number, if it has gone to another address than this. If sent here, first notify me that I may inquire.

To Stephen B. Luce

Slumberside, Quogue, Long Island, July 11, 1906 [LC]

My dear Admiral: I am more gratified than I can tell you to hear that after such a lapse of time you still have so high an opinion of my Strategy Lectures.

The thought of publishing has at times passed through my mind, but never to the extent of forming a purpose.[1] When I retired, it was with the expectation that I could more than recover for my family the loss of prospective increases of pay; I had also the secondary motive of believing that I could do better for my own ambition, and for the navy, than by remaining. The first reason has been always dominant with me, and would at any time hitherto have deterred me; and, as it is, I will not undertake it until I am in receipt of the increased pay which I gather the late bill will give me.[2]

Should this occur, I at present [have] a distinct inclination to take up the work, should the conditions you speak of also concur. I speak only to disposition at present, without yet committing myself to a final determination. In the matter of ambition, I am as likely to lose as to gain by new efforts; as to gain, the pecuniary side, I should not be advantaged beyond, if up to, what I make at my worst; but I think the work would be congenial, (which is the very best thing work can do for you), and as far as I can now see it will by next winter fit in with my projected occupations for the next year or two.

I am deeply thankful to you for the interest which has prompted your action, as well as for your kind expressions towards me; and may I congratulate yourself on the power of sustained interest in outside matters, which is, to my mind, the chiefest of life's blessings.

[P.S.]   The Dept. has just ordered me (Dewey requesting) to draw up an account of the reason and proceedings of the War Board of 1898.

---

1. The lectures were revised and published by Little, Brown and Company in 1911 as *Naval Strategy, Compared and Contrasted With the Principles of Military Operations on Land.*
2. This legislation promoted to the next higher rank on the Retired List those retired naval officers who had served in the Civil War. *See* Mahan to Clark, January 15, 1907.

To George Dewey

Quogue, Long Island, July 13, 1906 [OANHD]

Sir: I have received from the Secretary of the Navy orders directing me to report to you by letter for "the duty of preparing for the Navy Department a record of the studies and conclusions of the Naval War Board in the War with Spain, etc."

This duty will be undertaken by me in accordance with your letter to the Department, June 20, 1906, copy of which has been forwarded to me.

To George Dewey

Quogue, Long Island, July 19, 1906 [OANHD]

Sir: In a letter received today from Hon. J. D. Long, former Secretary of the Navy, in reply to mine asking for information as to the reasons for the organization of the War Board of 1898, and its relation to the Department, he briefly refers me to his history of the *New American Navy*,[1] pages so and so.

May I ask to be furnished with a copy of that book, for pursuance of the work assigned me under your orders.

To Theodore Roosevelt

Quogue, Long Island, circa July 20, 1906 [LC]

Dear Mr. President: When at Oyster Bay,[1] I mentioned to you my wish to be free to write for publication concerning matters that might come before the approaching Hague Conference; notably the question of exemption of private property, so called, from maritime capture.

A very proper and necessary regulation of the Navy forbids officers discussing publicly matters of policy on which the Government is embarked. The question arises, however, is the Hague Conference a body where measures are to be advocated as national policies; or whether they are to be advanced for discussion, with a view to reaching improved conditions of the code, common to all, which we call International Law.

It is by no means necessary that any Government should formally an-

---

1. John D. Long, *The New American Navy*. New York: The Outlook Company, 1903.

1. On June 30, 1906, the Navy Department telegraphed Mahan to report to the President at Oyster Bay, Long Island.

nounce either of the above as its own attitude; but should the second construction be adopted by our own, there could be no impropriety in a public officer contributing a properly worded argument on either side. Taking the particular measure I mention, our Government, I understand, has advanced it; but, in so doing, is it as a matter of national advantage so pronounced that opposition is improper, or is the matter one so far open to consideration that light may be welcomed, whencever coming.

It must be obvious to you that the present prepossession of the public mind in most countries is such that the question of War itself, and of questions incidental to War, are in danger of being prejudged and "rushed." One side only is clamorous. A special element of danger in this direction is the present British Government, with its huge heterogeneous majority to keep placated. With a Conservative Government there, we might afford to be persistent in our old national policy, safe that it would not be accepted, but would go over to a further conference; with the present, you will on military questions be playing with fire. But especially to be considered is the *popular* attitude in Germany towards the English speaking communities, and the effect of the exemption of private property upon her ambitions at their expense. Maritime transportation, and commercial movement, which is what so-called "private property" really amounts to, is now one of her great interests, and is steadily growing. Great Britain, and the British Navy, lie right across Germany's carrying trade with the whole world. Exempt it, and you remove the strongest hook in the jaws of Germany that the English speaking peoples have; a principal gage for peace.

British interests are not American interests, no. But taking the constitution of the British Empire, and the trade interests of the British Islands, the United States has certainty of a very high order that the British Empire will stand substantially on the same lines of world policy as ourselves; that its strength will be our strength, and the weakening it injury to us. Germany is inevitably ambitious of transmarine development. I dont grudge it her. As proof, after the Spanish War I refused a suggestion to use my supposed influence against her acquisition of the Carolines, etc.; but her ambitions threaten us as well as Great Britain, and I cannot but think that final action on the question of so called private property at sea would be better deferred, and the question be thrown into the arena of discussion, that action when taken may be in full light. As yet the public has heard but one side. The instance I quoted before to you is in clear point. No doubt our Government a century ago would have signed away the right of commercial blockade, which so helped us in the Civil War.

When to Germany are added the unsolved questions of the Pacific, it may be said truly that the political future is without form and void. Darkness is upon the face of the deep. We will have to walk very warily in matters affecting the future ability to employ national force.

To George Dewey

Quogue, Long Island, July 21, 1906 [OANHD]

Admiral: I have to apologize that in reporting to you by letter on the 12th [13th] inst., in obedience to the Department's order of July 1, I neglected to enclose those orders for your information and endorsement. I herewith enclose them, and respectfully request that they may be returned to me endorsed to enable the paymaster to enter me on his books accordingly.

To J. Franklin Jameson

Quogue, Long Island, July 25, 1906 [LC]

My dear Dr. Jameson: Your letter of the 18th arrived rather late, just as I was concluding the enclosed,[1] for which I presume you can find room. If you note anything objectionable in the tone of my comment, I shall of course be glad to modify; but I dont think you will. I see Mr. Hunt is put down as "Editor," which I suppose means journalist, and his review is very journalistic.[2]

With regard to your proposition anent Jamestown,[3] the subject lies so far outside my particular study in the past that I cannot at once appreciate the situation or my own possibilities. If I knew the authorities, still more had them at hand, I daresay I could estimate the situation. My Gardiner, which would doubtless give some hints, is packed, out of reach, and no historical literature touching the period is here accessible, unless in Fiske's *Old Virginia*.[4] In short, I am disposed to write the paper, but must for the moment fall back on you to tell me where the data are to be found. Moreover, after this statement of ignorance, you may think better to ask some one else, who has made the period his own. If so, dont fail to do so. My acceptance must be delayed in any event till I can see what I have to chew on.

As regards my former letter my impression is I asked a copy of the *April, 1906* number to be sent. If I did, it has not been received; but that my address was duly noted for the July number came.

1. *See* following letter.
2. Gaillard Hunt, who edited *The Writings of James Madison*, 9 vols. New York: G. P. Putnam's Sons, 1900–1910; and the letters of Mrs. Samuel Harrison Smith, *The First Forty Years of Washington Society* New York: Charles Scribner's Sons, 1906. He was active in the American Historical Association. Hunt's review of *1812* appeared in the *American Historical Review* (July 1906).
3. Jameson had suggested an article for the *American Historical Review* commemorating the tricentennial of the Jamestown settlement.
4. John Fiske, *Old Virginia and Her Neighbors*. Boston and New York: Houghton Mifflin, Co., 1897.

To the Editor of the American Historical Review

Quogue, Long Island, July 25 1906[1]

In the issue of the *Review* for July, in the review of my *War of 1812*, your reviewer, Mr. Gaillard Hunt, has fallen into an inadvertence of statement which I cannot afford to leave uncorrected. He writes:

"The naval victories on Lake Champlain and the military victories at New Orleans are treated as events irrelevant to the objects and outcome of the war."

As to New Orleans, this is exact as regards the outcome: scarcely so, I think, as regards the objects. As to Lake Champlain, it is entirely contrary to what I explicitly stated. Thus, in concluding my account of Mac-Donough's victory, Vol. II, p. 381, I say:

"The battle of Lake Champlain, more nearly than any other incident of the War of 1812, merits the epithet decisive."

This is certainly not saying that the battle was irrelevant to the outcome of the war; and that this was not an accidental comment on my part, but in keeping with my steady point of view, appears both from the preface, which I refrain from quoting, and from the following other extracts:

"As, on a wider field and in more tremendous issues, the fleets of Great Britain saved their country, and determined the fortunes of Europe, so Perry and MacDonough averted from the United States, without further fighting, a rectification of frontier," etc. (Vol. II., p. 101.)

"In 1814 there stood between the Government and disastrous reverse, and loss of territory, in the north, only the resolution and professional skill of a yet unrecognized seaman on the neglected waters of Lake Champlain." (Vol. II., p. 267.)

Whatever may be thought of these two estimates, in themselves, they show that I considered this battle far from irrelevant to "the objects, or the outcome of the War."

The statement of your reviewer affects too seriously my sanity, as an historical writer, to be passed over in the silence with which an author of many years' experience learns to accept differences of opinion. But for it, I should not have written at all; but, as it has drawn me out, I will say further that, in my judgment, your reviewer has failed in another respect to reach the high standard which should be expected in the *Review*. The

---

1. From the *American Historical Review* (October 1906), pp. 183–184. For Hunt's rebuttal, *see ibid.*, pp. 184–185.

obiter dicta of the periodical press are one thing; the *Review* is specialist in aim and character. Mr. Hunt writes:

> "Nor is Captain Mahan without injustice in his treatment of the controversy which terminated in the dismissal of Jackson, the British minister. No minister had ever gone so far in insolence, and no self-respecting government could have done other than dismiss him."

Insolence, doubtless, may be cause for dismissal; the degree that demands it is a matter of opinion. Mr. Hunt says Jackson's insolence reached it; an opinion about which I am not solicitous to differ. But in an historical magazine, should it be thought necessary to express an opinion, the opinion should speak to the facts. The fact is that our Government dismissed Jackson, not on a general charge of insolence, but on the specific ground that in his letters to it he had made, and afterwards repeated, a specific implication, which was false and insolent. The American letter ran thus:

> "I *abstain*, Sir, from making any particular animadversions on several irrelevant and improper allusions in your letter.... But it would be improper to conclude the few observations to which I *purposely limit* myself, without adverting to your repetition of a language implying a knowledge on the part of this Government that the instructions of your predecessor did not authorize the arrangement formed by him."

The abstention, and the limitation, here italicized by me, exclude other grounds for action than the language construed by Madison to imply the meaning which he repelled; and the letter of dismissal rests directly, and solely, upon the same ground: "language reiterating, and even aggravating, the same gross insinuation." After a very diligent examination of the correspondence, I elaborated in the book under review a demonstration that Jackson's language, carefully and fairly scrutinized, did not imply the statement put into his mouth. My conclusion was expressed in these words:

> "Prepossession in reading, and proneness to angry misconception, must be inferred in the conduct of the American side of this discussion; for another even graver instance," etc. (p. 226).

This is simply a statement of opinion, with which any one is at liberty to differ; but, as an opinion, it relates not to a general charge of insolence, but to the specific reason alleged by the American Government for its action, which I endeavored to show was unfounded. The opinions advanced by me currently in my account of the transaction, and summarized in the above abstract, constitute my injustice in this matter to the administration of Madison; that injustice, if it exists, should have been indicated, not by a general sweeping mention, but by the statement that the facts contained in my demonstration failed to sustain the judgment that "prepossession in reading and proneness to angry misconception must be inferred from the American conduct of the discussion." From first to last the action of the American Government was based on a specific implication, alleged to be in Jackson's letter. If that implication was in the letter, fairly and dispassionately read, I have been unjust; if it was not in the letter, but, as I have asserted, and I think demonstrated, was read into it, wilfully or carelessly, I have not been unjust. Either view is open to a reviewer's conscientious conviction; but the conviction, when stated, should be in reference to what I have said, and not to what I have not said.

The matter is of consequence because, if I am right, the whole correspondence throws light on Madison's characteristics, confirming impressions which his other diplomatic letters produce; because the examination of the phraseology which I gave I have found nowhere else, and by it the diplomatic incident is essentially transformed; and, finally, because the character of the *American Historical Review* demands on the part of its reviewers more exactness in stating the position of an author, when they charge him with injustice.

To George Dewey

Quogue, Long Island, July 29, 1906 [OANHD]

Sir: Having written to His Excellency, President Roosevelt, to ask his recollections of the reasons for establishing the War Board of 1898, and its relations to the administration of the Department, in order to meet as fully as possible the requirements of the Department's orders to me of June 20 and July 1, he has replied by asking me to see him personally at Oyster Bay, July 31.

Will you kindly ask the Department to issue the requisite orders for travel to Oyster Bay, and return?

To J. Franklin Jameson

Slumberside, Quogue, Long Island, July 31, 1906 [LC]

My dear Dr. Jameson: You have done very right I think in giving Mr. Hunt the opportunity for rejoinder in the same issue with my letter. As the object should be clear understanding, I would suggest that, if you find he has misunderstood me in any case, you might indicate to me the fact and particulars. I am led to this remark, because I see that in one place, speaking of the Champlain incidents of 1814, I call them an episode, like that of New Orleans. It is of course obvious (at least to me) that an attempt may be of the most serious purpose, and yet from faulty execution, and consequent speedy frustration, may in performance amount merely to an episode. The expression might have misled Mr. Hunt, though it is a long way from there to his "events irrelevant to the objects and outcome of the war," and quite incompatible with careful reading of my whole. I indicate this merely as showing how a misconception may arise, in some quite other connection.

I think of course also that you are quite right in seeking another for Jamestown, as I suggested.[1]

To William S. Sims[1]

Quogue, Long Island, August 6, 1906 [LC]

My dear Mr. Sims: I have received your letter of July 28, enclosing the report of general methods and results of the recent improved target practice, and am greatly indebted to you for both. I have heard in a general way of the course of these improvements, which have been attributed mainly to your own concentration of purpose upon this one thing; but I have not before been in possession of any specific data as to the results obtained, and I am therefore doubly glad to have this.

You do not mention specifically any deduction from these results due to ordinary movements of ships in moderate seas. If they have been attained in the face of such conditions they are certainly most remarkable. But in any event they are extremely encouraging, both absolutely and relatively to the British service, and those who fire best under one set of conditions will doubtless show a like superiority under another, if there be otherwise equality between the contestants.

I saw President Roosevelt last week, and in the course of conversation he expressed his great satisfaction at the progress in this matter.[2]

Renewing my thanks, believe me [etc.].

1. *See* Mahan to Jameson, July 25, 1906.

1. Sims, class of 1880, was a lieutenant commander. From 1907 to 1909 he was naval aide to President Roosevelt, and from 1917 to 1919 he commanded American naval operations in European waters.

2. At this time Sims, long associated with the problems of accurate naval gunfire, led a small group of younger officers, most of them ordnance experts, in an attack on

To J. Franklin Jameson

Quogue, Long Island, August 13–14, 1906 [LC]

My dear Dr. Jameson: Although my letter of July 3 is the cause of yours of August 8, with enclosures, I admit that I do not see what I can do to shorten it, (except as hereafter specified). A definition of the word "episode," which misled Mr. Hunt, and a comparison of that with his rendering, "events irrelevant to the objects and outcome of the war," would use space rather than economize it. Readers can do that for themselves. Instead of a frank acknowledgment of a mistake, he grudgingly says his words are "obviously *too sweeping.*" He had not carefully read what he undertook to review.

As regards the Madison matter, I have made two light red-pencil marks in Mr. Hunt's letter, enclosing words which, had they been used in the review, would have been addressed to the statements in my book and obviated all reasonable objection on my part. I might have regretted Mr. Hunt's unfavorable opinion of my conclusion, but the matter would have been fairly before readers. You surely can have no difficulty in seeing this. The words thus red-pencilled are 36, against 43 in the review; and with that falls Mr. Hunt's want of space.

As regards the specific omission you suggest, I can accept part of it, and have bracketed with blue pencil what I think could be omitted. This, however, is only as it is necessary to my personal justification. As bearing upon a matter of historical interest, in a case where prejudice still stands in the place of accurate measurement of words, I think them of consequence to the objects of the *Review*.

This letter of course is not for publication.

Aug. 14

You will note, in the words of Mr. Hunt which I have red pencilled, that the fact that "no one (not even Madison) ever discovered before the meaning, or absence of meaning in Jackson's most insolent letter," is precisely what gives importance to my text. If I were merely adding a reiterated argument, pro or con, already known, it might matter little. Whether Madison discovered the meaning or not, is not the point; personally, I in-

---

Mahan's arguments for mixed-calibre-gun battleships. In spite of Mahan's reputation, Roosevelt supported the Sims insistence on single-calibre main batteries for battleships, particularly after the British launched HMS *Dreadnought* in 1907. As Sims wrote: "When we advocated the single calibre main battery, T. R. said he could not make any headway against the great Mahan; that it was up to us to convince the public that the great Mahan was wrong. This paper was the first attempt to do so. It convinced T. R. . . ." *See* Mahan to Sims, October 3, 1906, and notes; and Mahan to Henderson, January 19, 1907.

cline to the belief that he acted open-eyed; but the real point is, is the true construction of Jackson's letter as I analyze? If so, it is a serious contribution to history. Mr. Hunt does not reason closely.

To Leopold J. Maxse

Slumberside, Quogue, Long Island, August 21, 1906 [CROCS]

My dear Mr. Maxse: The difficulty of which I once wrote you, in reference to my writing for publication on topics likely to come before the Hague Conference, has been overcome.[1] As the matter now presents itself to me, I should like to prepare two articles; one on the general subject of War, and its armaments, etc., as a factor in political progress (and equilibrium); the other on the particular question of the Immunity from Maritime Capture of Private property, so called.[2]

Should this proposition commend itself to you, I will gradually consider the two subjects; but it seems evident, both from the magazine point of view, of immediate interest, and the writer's, of wishing to affect public opinion opportunely, that publication should be deferred till toward the approach of the Conference. If this take place next year, it will scarcely be earlier than May. If so, the Feby to May numbers would be most suitable, in my judgment; but you of course will express your own.

Incidental hereto, I should reach a wider audience if there could be simultaneous publication in an American Magazine; for our country for the most part hears but one side of the argument. Will you in due time give me your views on this matter, and state also if you would prefer any especial magazine. Our illustrated magazines have here an immense circulation; the more weighty, like the *North American* and *Forum*, I believe to be much less. Should such an arrangement be feasible, I should like so to arrange price as to lessen that to the *National*, while somewhat increasing my total honorarium; but while my increasing years make this motive real, it is secondary, and in any consideration of the matter, be assured I am entirely satisfied with the payments of the *National*.

---

1. *See* Mahan to Roosevelt, circa July 20, 1906.
2. These articles were eventually published as "The Hague Conference; the Question of Immunity of Belligerent Shipping," *National Review* (June 1907); and "The Hague Conference and the Practical Aspect of War," *National Review* (July 1907). They were also published in *Living Age* (July 6 and July 27, 1907) and were reprinted in *Some Neglected Aspects of War*. Boston: Little, Brown and Company, 1907.

To Harper & Brothers

Quogue, Long Island, August 29, 1906[1]

I will agree to concede all serial rights in the *Recollections of My Life* (or whatever title chosen)[2] to Harper & Brothers for $3,000 (three thousand dollars), with subsequent book publication, subject to a royalty to me of fifteen per cent. of retail price; with the reservation that after lapse of five years from date of such publication, it will be permissible to include the work in a collected edition of my works by such publisher as I may select.

To John M. Brown

Slumberside, Quogue, Long Island, August 31, 1906 [LC]

My dear Mr. Brown: I have agreed with Harper and Brothers for full serial rights to some Recollections of my life that I have been putting together, and have along with these conceded also to them the book publication. I stood out at first for giving you the book; but in discussion I had to recognize that the entire suggestion of the work came from them, and that it was substantially just to yield the point.

The arrangement was only concluded by their formal letter, accepting my terms, just received. Their representative called me by appointment day before yesterday; but he did not feel authorized to accept definitely the terms that I thought due to myself. So I have lost no time in communicating to you the particulars, as is due to our long association.

I should add that the agreement contains a stipulation that after five years from date of publication the book may be included, in a collected edition of my works, by such publisher as I may select. I dont know that this will ever be needed, but it at least does no harm.

---

1. From Charles C. Taylor, *The Life of Admiral Mahan*, pp. 123–124. Reprinted by permission.
2. The title chosen was *From Sail to Steam.* Harper Brothers published it in book form in 1907 after serializing it in *Harpers Monthly* (February; May; August; October, 1907) and *Harpers Weekly* (September 21, 1907, through December 7, 1907).

To J. Franklin Jameson

Slumberside, Quogue, Long Island, September 1, 1906 [LC]

Dear Dr. Jameson: I am a little shy of Lucas's book;[1] but will look over it, if you like, writing a brief notice if I find I can. I saw the London *Times* review, and fancy that has struck the key note, viz: the effect of the war upon the nationality, so to say, of Canada.

I apprehend that for the rest it will be an elaborate setting forth of the merits of Canadian conduct in various petty scrimmages. Should that prove the case, I could not possibly give the time for investigating the merits. They are not worth it. But if the book have some *general* recognizable trend, and I can detect it, I will be willing to word a review for you.

With this understanding, if you send me the book I will examine it.

To George Dewey

Quogue, Long Island, September 5, 1906 [OANHD]

Sir:

1. Referring to the Navy Department's letter, G.B. No. 401–2, June 20, 1906, and its subsequent order to me, of July 1, to report for special duty to the President of the General Board, I have to report that in pursuance of these instructions I had compiled a statement of between 5,000 and 10,000 words;[1] relying upon my memory, upon such personal information as I could collect, and upon an account published by me in *McClure's Magazine*, within six months of the ending of the War with Spain.

2. At this point, the various uncertainties remaining in my mind suggested writing to Lieut. A.H. Cobb, retired, who had acted as Recorder during my connection with the Naval War Board, to ask whether there might not remain some history of its work, unknown to the Department, as shown by its letter. In reply, Mr. Cobb said that certain letter press and other books, forming a record subsequent to his reporting, May 11, 1898, had been deposited in the Bureau of Navigation.

3. I then applied informally to Mr. E.W. Callahan, now Chief Clerk of that Bureau, who in 1898 was associated with, and under Mr. Cobb. He, after diligent search, has found, and reports to me, certain letter press copy books containing a seriatim record of the Board's proceedings. These were

---

1. Sir Charles Prestwood Lucas, *The Canadian War of 1812*. Oxford: Clarendon Press, 1906. *See* Mahan to Jameson, September 10, 1906.

1. *See* Paper, "The Work of the Naval War Board of 1898," October 29, 1906.

accompanied by a letter from Rear Admiral Sicard, of which a copy has been furnished me, dated August 24, 1898, when the Board's meetings ended. This letter specified the above books, by title and number, and contained also some pertinent but not very important, details concerning the personnel of the Board.

4. I would respectfully suggest that these letter press books, and Admiral Sicard's letter, be examined under the direction of the present General Board, to ascertain how far their contents would modify the Department's impression "that no history of the work of the Naval War Board of 1898 exists," and might affect its consequent instructions to me of June 20.

5. My statement, as so far prepared, speaks partly to facts which however are of imperfect memory, and thus less authoritative as to "the work" of the Board than such records. On the other hand, it gives my own recollections of the Board's general view of situations as they arose, and its reasons for advice given, as distinct from the advice itself. It may therefore assume to meet, so far, the Department's requirement concerning "general conclusions on strategical situations." I have embodied also such information as I could gather from President Roosevelt, (formerly Assistant Secretary), Ex-Secretary Long, Rear Admirals Barker and Crowninshield, and my own recollections, concerning "the reasons for the organization of the Board, its duties, and their relation to the administration of the Department."

6. It may become necessary for me myself to consult these records in order to correct any imperfections of my own memory; in which case I shall have to ask orders to Washington. But as both heat and traveling knock me up a good deal, at my present age, I will have to ask the Board's indulgence not to go on for that object until toward the end of the present month.

7. It has occurred to me, as an alternative to my going on, that typewritten copies of the books, specified in Admiral Sicard's letter as Letter Books A and B, and Strategy Board No. 1, might be made at no greater expense than my mileage to and from, and would preserve duplicates of papers important both officially and historically. Should such duplicates be made, they could be sent me by mail for use, and returned to the Department for preservation apart from the originals.

To J. Franklin Jameson

Slumberside, Quogue, Long Island, September 10, 1906 [LC]

My dear Dr. Jameson: I have received Lucas, also yours of the 7th. I have looked over the book, not indeed thoroughly, but as it were a reconnaissance. As far as I see, it is simply a narrative of the war, in the main quite accurate as far as my own knowledge goes, and accompanied by a running comment which also seems judicious, as far as it goes. But I find in it no indication of any salient features other than those judiciously selected by the *Times* reviewer; nothing to show that it is more than a last version, painstaking and impartial, of a thrice told tale.

Reviewed from this point by a man who has just published a work on the same subject, comment based on this estimate might easily seem the damning with faint praise by a jealous rival. I think better for myself and the *Review* that the task should go to another.

Lucas in his preface says this is an installment of Canadian history. As such it is sufficient; regarded as a history of the war it seems to me commonplace. The test of a history of Canada will come, I imagine, in the formative period preceding & culminating in Lord Durham's[1] administration—a process which I presume, from my most elementary knowledge, was parallel to and contemporaneous with our own subsequent to 1812. If Lucas so sees it, he may produce a great work.

I will send on the book as you ask.

To John M. Brown

Slumberside, Quogue, Long Island, September 29, 1906 [LC]

My dear Mr. Brown: Have you ever considered the possibility, from a pecuniary point of view, of producing by itself the chapter I contributed to Sampson, Low's *History of the Royal Navy*; taking some such title as "The Movements of the (Navies) (Fleets) during the War of American Independence."[1]

Prof. Laughton, one of the foremost naval historians in England, once expressed a wish to me that this might be done; adding that it would be a classic. In its present position, it is lost in a very unhandy, heavy volume; it could be produced in one light to the hand. Further, with a view to any collection of my works, this in my own opinion would be among the most valuable.

I wrote more than once to Marston to this effect, but casually. He never even replied to the question. This may have been due to their embarrassments, still more to cut under their weighty book early in its career. But I see now that this volume (it came out by volumes) was published in 1898. A re-

---

1. John George Lambton, 1st Earl of Durham, High Commissioner and Governor General of Canada (1838–1840), whose reforms, following the Canadian rebellion of 1838, looked forward to dominion status for Canada within the Empire.

1. It was published separately by Little, Brown and Company in 1913 under the title, *The Major Operations of the Navies in the War of American Independence*.

production therefore cannot be in less than nine years. Moreover, the Editor, Sir W. Clowes having died, may remove a possible objector.

There would probably be omissions, possibly some additions; but nothing of consequence. Will you consider the matter with a view, say, to Christmas, 1907. Marston's permission of course would be necessary.

[P.S.] Please note my address: Woodmere, N.Y. after Oct. 3d.[2]

To Charles W. Stewart

Slumberside, Quogue, Long Island, September 29, 1906 [NA]

My dear Mr. Stewart: Will you look up for me the following bits of information:

1. Date of the burning of the Steam paddle wheel frigate *Missouri*, in Gibraltar. This in Emmons, *Ships of U.S.N.*[1]

2. Number of midshipmen entered in 1841, as shown by the *Navy Register* of 1842. This is the famous "Forty-One Date."[2]

3. The number in my class, Third Class, at Naval Academy as shown by the *Register* of 1857. This is the class, and the first occasion, on which my name appears in the *Register*.

I have some minor questions of a similar character which I may put to you, unless I can find the books in N.Y., when we leave here.

I hope the hot summer has not treated you very badly.

To William S. Sims

Quogue, Long Island, October 3, 1906 [LC]

My dear Mr. Sims: I return herewith the confidential papers with which you kindly favored me two months ago. I have to regret that despite the

---

2. Having leased their home at 160 West 86th Street for the three-year period 1906–1909, the Mahans spent the winter of 1906–1907 at Woodmere, Long Island, in a house leased by Mrs. Mahan's brother, Hartman Kuhn Evans.

1. George Foster Emmons, *The Navy of the United States, from the Commencement, 1775 to 1853; With a Brief History of Each Vessel's Service and Fate. . . .* Comp. by Lieut. George F. Emmons . . . under the Authority of the Navy Department. To Which is Added a List of Private Armed Vessels, Fitted Out under the American Flag. . . . Also a List of the Revenue and Coast Survey Vessels, and Principle Ocean Steamers, Belonging to Citizens of the United States in 1850. Washington, D.C.: Gideon and Company, 1853.

2. The date of 1841 produced 135 graduates, thus creating a "hump" which was still felt during the later years of the century. The date of 1842 produced only 7; and 1845, only 3.

time elapsed I have been able to pay little attention to it, my time is so much occupied with my other work. I had, however, read some parts, and had noted some questions which suggested themselves to me; but those I have found answered in the main in the paper prepared by you for the President,[1] at his request, in reply to my article in the Naval Institute,[2] which he sent to me; so that I am deprived of that evidence of interest shown by questioning.

I assure you, none the less, that I have greatly appreciated your attention in sending me the papers, and that they have not been neglected, though less studied than they deserve.[3]

To Theodore Roosevelt

Quogue, Long Island, circa October 8, 1906 [LC]

Dear Mr. President: Your letter enclosing Sims's paper[1] arrived on Saturday, at a moment most unhappy for me. Not only was I crowded with work promised for the next three months, which made even the reading of his 26 close-spaced pages a task, but I am moving my household hence to-morrow.

In these three working days left me this week, I tried to frame a short

1. "The Inherent Tactical Qualities of All-Big-Gun, One-Calibre Battleships." Among those to whom Sims sent his paper, originally marked "Not to be published—For private circulation among U.S. Naval Officers only," were a number of Army officers and politicians. The paper then appeared in the U.S. Naval Institute *Proceedings* for December 1906, in *Brassey's Annual* for 1907, and in *Size of Battleships ... Naval Papers* by Capt. A. T. Mahan, U.S. Navy, and Lieut. Commander William S. Sims, U.S. Navy ... Washington, D.C.: U.S. Government Printing Office, 1907. Mahan's contribution to this last was his article in the U.S. Naval Institute *Proceedings* for June 1906. *See* Footnote 2 below.
2. "Reflections, Historic and Other, Suggested by the Battle of the Japan Sea," U.S. Naval Institute *Proceedings* (June 1906).
3. Sims later wrote, triumphantly, that Mahan "was too busy to reply to my arguments. . . . It is now known that he was wholly mistaken. The *Dreadnought* type became the universal standard." He must have been kept in ignorance of Mahan's letters to Roosevelt of October 8 and 22 below. Among those who congratulated Sims and rejoiced at Mahan's defeat were Fullam, Chandler, Goodrich, Fiske, Sperry, McLean, Hood, and Fisher. Luce, without mentioning Mahan, praised the Sims paper and corrected Sims's grammar. Chadwick and Higginson also were courteous but impersonal. For these letters and other documents on the "All-Big-Gun" controversy in the Navy, *see* the Sims Collection in the Library of Congress.

1. *See* Mahan to Sims, August 6 and October 3, 1906, and notes.

paper of comment. This I have done, but not in such shape as to submit. I must leave this till I am settled again.

Meantime I return his paper, with thanks for the opportunity to read it, and submit a brief of the general argument.

Three facts are obvious:

1. A 12 inch gun is vastly more powerful than, say, an 8-inch.

2. A fleet, A, composed of ships the force of which is 1, is weaker than a fleet, B, of the same numbers, whose force is 1-¼.

3. A fleet, A, the fleet speed of which is three knots less than the fleet B, is at some disadvantage.

These things, as the French say, sautent aux yeux. They are the first broadside of an argument, and produce the proverbial effect of the first broadside. To them are to be added, less obvious at first, that the concentration of force under one hand in one ship is superior to the same force in two or three ships; while economically, the same tonnage in big ships is more economically built and maintained than in smaller.

This constitutes the main weight of the argument against those who, with me, advocate gun-power rather than speed; numbers against size; and an "intermediate" battery in part, instead of "primary" alone. I leave aside the "secondary" now so styled.

The argument above stated is very heavy, to first sight overpowering; and, for this reason, those with whom decision rests should the more gravely consider the less obvious points, urged on the other side. These are:

1. That there must be numbers to a considerable extent; and that, while ten 1½ ships are cheaper than the same tonnage in—say 15—smaller vessels, each 1½ ship costs much more than a 1 ship. Consequently, some time numbers will compel a halt in size, or will themselves become utterly inadequate.

2. That, with numbers, the power of combination increases, and combined action is the particular force of fleets. The problem will not have been adequately handled until a competent, unbiassed, tribunal shall have considered exhaustively the combinations open to fleets, engaging with numbers equal and unequal.

3. That speed confers the power of the offensive: yes; but, if used for long range action, it allows the defensive, inevitably, a wide field of action, with interior lines upon which to manoeuvre, in such mutual support as may be wished; and with abundant power to act at will, so long as a range of, say, 3 miles is maintained. An approach within that range will narrow the field, but bring the intermediaries into surer play.

4. It seems probable that the greatest development of fire, to a fleet acting on an outer circle, is represented by the column, the full broadside

effect. Greater numbers, acting within, can mass effectively against such a disposition.

The above, though longer than I hoped, is but a brief. I do not pretend to be fully equipped in tactical resource, and hold myself retired, as a rule from such discussion, though I present my views when asked. The Institute asked me for a paper.[2] I have now neither time nor inclination for exhaustive study of tactics; and have besides full preoccupation in other more congenial matters. Still, as far as they go, I think my views sound; and if sound, they are pertinent.

In the relation of primary and intermediary guns to fire control, I cannot place my undigested knowledge against that of Mr. Sims. I think, however, that, like most specialists, he overvalues the extent of fire control in battle. I believe the present system, with its admirable results, will in the day of battle justify itself amply; yet not so much by its own particular action as by the habits it will have bred in officers and men. The regularity of the drill ground is felt in the field, not in a similar regularity, but by the induced habit of looking to one another; each part duly remembering the others and the whole; not elbow touch but fire support.

When I am settled again, I will endeavor to send you the paper of comment.

P.S.   I enclose a clipping,[3] and will mention that *Blackwood's* for this month will have an article on speed by Vice Admiral Sir R. Custance.[4] Bridge, lately commanding their China squadron, is of the like opinions.

To Little, Brown and Company

Woodmere, Long Island, October 10, 1906 [LC]

Gentlemen: Replying to your letter of Oct 5, I should much prefer your communicating with Messrs. Sampson Low & Co, and that the transaction be purely business, whatever form it take ultimately.

---

2. "Reflections, Historic and Other, Suggested by the Battle of the Japan Sea," U.S. Naval Institute *Proceedings* (June 1906). Published also in the Royal United Service Institution *Journal* (November 1906).
3. Enclosure not found.
4. "The Speed of the Capital Ship," *Blackwood's Magazine* (October 1906). Unsigned. Custance probably also wrote "The Growth of the Capital Ship," *ibid.* (May 1906) and "Lessons from the Battle of Tsu Sima," *ibid.* (February 1906).

With reference to an ultimate collection of my works, it occurred to me to suggest to you, whether the Sea Power Series might even now be advantageously so collected under the General Title of the "Influence of Sea Power upon History." I enclose a sheet showing the idea.

[Enclosure]

I $\begin{cases} \text{The Influence of Sea Power upon History} \\ \text{1660–1783} \end{cases}$

II $\begin{cases} \text{The Influence of Sea Power upon History} \\ \text{1783–1812} \\ \text{The French Revolution and Empire} \end{cases}$

III $\begin{cases} \text{The Influence of Sea Power upon History} \\ \text{1812–1815} \\ \text{The War of 1812} \end{cases}$

Probably some suitable sub-title for I might be evolved, if desirable.

To Leopold J. Maxse

Woodmere, Long Island, October 17, 1906 [LC]

My dear Mr. Maxse: Will you kindly note the above as my address for this winter?

Replying to your letter of Sept. 27, I will communicate with the Editor of the *North American*, and let you know his reply, when received. My first obligation is to the *National*, and I will not make any other, except with your approval; but if the case of Private Property (so called) be as important as I think, I want, for general as well as personal reasons, to publish on both sides.[1]

I quite agree as to the date of publication being near that of the Hague assembling; and indeed if that be, as in 1899, in May, I should think March and May better months. As it is, work has doubled up on me as usual, and I shall find it hard to be ready for your February, if indeed practicable.

A week ago I received a letter from the Editor of a new periodical, to be edited under the auspices of the Am. Society of International Law, saying that he had seen my "arraignment" of the (Am) doctrine of immunity, and asking me for an article for their first issue—in January.[2] As Mr. Elihu Root

---

1. *See* Mahan to Maxse, August 21, 1906.
2. The *American Journal of International Law*. Mahan published nothing in this Journal.

is president, and it was to him I communicated the views which I cut out of the last article for the *National*;[3] it may be that he suggested this. Of course I know nothing.

To Theodore Roosevelt

Woodmere, Long Island, October 22, 1906 [LC]

My dear Mr. President: I send herewith such comment as I have had time to make upon the general subject which elicited Sims's paper. I regret delay; but, even as it is, it is by sore sacrifice of other work that I have prepared this.

As regards the particular matter of the Battle of Tsushima, he accepts as decisive the testimony of the single witness cited by Lieut. White.[1] Our old professor of astronomy, Chauvenet, a man of standing, used to say, "Never trust one sight, because you think it very good. Average several." I fancy most lawyers would say the same of a comparison of witnesses; as an historian, I certainly should. When I wrote my account,[2] I had Togo's official report, some others already published, and in addition the advance sheets of a work by Captain Klado of the Russian Navy, in which he had collated several, from Russian sources.[3] It was from Togo's report that I assumed a Russian speed of 12 knots, against which Mr. White's witness says 9.

I presented, however, no account of the battle. I simply constructed, from the data, a plan of its probable opening scenes, in order from them to discuss the tactical question of speed. Mr. Sims's discussion begins by misunderstanding my statement, which he gives thus: "Shortly after the fleets sighted each other, the Japanese changed course *from S.W. to East*, while the Russians were steering N.E.; and the Japanese speed was slower than that of the Russians; 2 or 3 to the Russians 4." This assumption of mine, as to relative speeds, applied only (see my text, p. 449) to the time the Japanese, by Togo's report, were steering S.W.; not to their steering East,—an entirely different condition. White's Russian witness says that, after

3. "Some Reflections Upon the Far Eastern War." *See* Paper "Comments on the Seizure of Private Property at Sea," February–March, 1906; and Mahan to Root, April 20, 1906, and notes.

1. Richard Dace White, class of 1899. The source mentioned here is "With the Baltic Fleet at Tsushima," *Scientific American* (August 11, 1906).
2. "Reflections, Historic and Other, Suggested by the Battle of the Sea of Japan."
3. Nikolai Lavrentievich Klado, *The Battle of the Sea of Japan.* . . . London: Hodder and Stoughton, 1906.

[182]

the Japanese countermarched to East, both fleets were steering about N.N.E. My memory is that Togo makes no such statement; he gave no course, between East and the subsequent countermarch, *after* the battle began. Indeed, as regards Japanese speed, after the first shot, I made no positive statements; only assumptions, for my argument on a general problem.

My impressions of "the nature of the action," (beyond the opening scene), had therefore nothing to do with the "reasoning by which Captain Mahan assumes Togo was influenced—in taking a position (across the head of the enemy's column) which he did not take." (Sims p. 4.) I do not believe the closest scanning of my article will detect an expression implying that Togo took a position across the head of the enemy's column; unless it be that I said that, when first seen, the Japanese were ahead of the Russians; or, as White's witness says, "on the starboard bow." In this sense I did say "he had headed him," (p. 456); and had he not? But that is very different from taking a tactical order, for battle.

Deductions from the actual fighting of the battle, unless of a very technical character, e.g. the falling of funnels, are much vitiated by the Russian inefficiency. They did not enjoy, what Farragut called the best defense, "a rapid (and accurate) fire from our own guns." The Japanese in large measure had *target* practice of them. We therefore can scarcely be said to have a fair test of the *battle* efficiency of fire control. For this reason, while Mr. Sims is in some measure correct in saying that the three conclusions he attributes to me (p. 1.) are, in my judgment, supported by the battle, he is mistaken in saying that they were derived from it. A careful reading of my article will show that the reasoning is largely *a priori*, supported only by inferences from the occurrences of the battle. (See my page 451). My reasoning far antedated the battle.

The view Mr. Sims attributes to me, (p. 1), that "in designing battleships of certain displacement we are never justified in increasing the speed, within reasonable limits, at the expense of gun power," is an exaggeration. See my pages 455, 456, 461, 469. Even at the expense of often seeming to hedge, I try to qualify my statements against exaggeration. Caricatures no man can avoid.

The opposite sides of the contention, on which Mr. Sims and I stand, are that one believes in size of ship, the others in numbers. The one believes in a few very heavy guns, the other prefers more numerous lighter ones. Let neither attribute extremes to the other. Mr. Sims does not believe in a navy of one huge ship, nor I in a thousand vessels of five hundred tons. Neither do I believe in ships of five knots speed; nor in a battery of smooth bore twenty-fours; nor yet in one primary battery of today. There must be adjustment.

[183]

Further, while I believe in volume of fire, I also believe in fewness of calibres. I would have one "primary" calibre, and one "intermediate"; being led thereto long ago by considerations, not of fire control, but of battery supply. Here, incidentally, let me remark that the several indexes of powder mentioned by Mr. Sims, (p. 10), if avoidable, would seem to call for simplification.

Also, while I deplore the present tendency, in size, as in speed, I admit that no one nation can wholly resist it. It compels by a power like gravitation; just as the stronger is in some measure compelled by a weaker enemy,— unless hopelessly weak. It does not therefore follow, however, that no modification of a tendency, no brake, is possible; and it was to this I looked in the words that the "willful premature antiquating of good vessels is a growing and wanton evil." To an extent which might be lessened, nations are compelled to throw out of the line of battle ships otherwise good, which must be quickly replaced. The length of time, and the expense, required to build a battle-ship, are now the sole hindrance to the process of total discardment. In a measure Germany has just been compelled to such a discardment. (See article by "Excubitor" in one of the September British monthlies.[4] Yet Brassey, in the passage I have marked in red, seems to show Great Britain suffers from the recoil of her own measures.) This harmful progress is possible only by bigness. Each step is by an increase of size, now that men have overcome the mechanical limits formerly imposed by their materials. There being now no limit to their wills, they exercise these, as most powerful persons do, indifferent to circumstances of reasonable consideration. I have seen as yet little evidence of any reasonable consideration of the fact, that somewhere numbers and size must have a head-on collision.

For this reason I suggested, in an article in the *National Review*, May, 1906,[5] that in the approaching Hague Conference an artificial limit be attempted on the bigness of ships of war. Eliminate bigness beyond a certain tonnage, and men, having a limit in that direction, will turn their attention to the proper dispositions of the permitted tonnage, and to its tactical management. Bigness will no longer be a refuge from every difficulty, or a recourse from every embarrassment.

In matters of fire control, and reasonable deductions from practice in it, I must cede to the far greater familiarity of Mr. Sims. Of course, I do not mean by this that I unconditionally accept his inferences. For instance, Mr. White's calculation, which Mr. Sims makes much of, after giving the *Orel*'s injuries, goes on "the *Suavaroff must have been* struck, etc." "*Allowing* a little over thirty-five each for the *Alexander III*, etc." "It is *hardly possible* that these guns, etc." Such assumptions are perfectly permissible

---

4. "Command of the German Ocean," *Fortnightly Review* (September 1906).
5. "Some Reflections Upon the Far-Eastern War."

for making approximate inferences; but they remain assumptions, which qualify the conclusions. From such consideration as I have been able to give his paper, I cannot yet feel convinced as to the effect of volume of fire under battle conditions, as distinguished from target practice. That far better results will be achieved in battle, owing to the eminent work done by Mr. Sims and associates, I cannot doubt. I believe in it unconditionally. But I believe also in the probability that a fleet such as I would favor could, by dint of numbers, effect tactical combinations quite balancing mere weight of metal in the individual ship; could in the end enforce closing, when volume of fire would tell—probably tell also before.

In arguing, I have the right, within the limits of the possible, to choose the proportion of inferiority I accept for my battleship. I am on record as favoring in 1898 a maximum of 12,000 tons. It need not follow, if other nations now insist on 20,000, that I will deny that in measure we must follow,—force of gravitation. I need not, however, accept a fleet double in number and half in individual size; nor yet dispositions putting half my fleet out of action.

To illustrate my views, as regards tactical combinations open to numbers, I present a diagram showing 12 ships, A, opposed to 8 B; the aggregate tonnage to be approximately the same. This would make each A ship two-thirds, or sixty-seven per cent, the size of each B. I give the A fleet three knots less speed,—fleet speed,—than the B; and I assume that, by this sacrifice of speed, and if necessary of some proportion of other qualities, the offensive gun power of A is three-fourths, 75 per cent, that of B. Whether this proportion can be reached, I do not know; but as I am informed by competent authority that the *Lord Nelson*, on one-eighth—twelve per cent— less tonnage, and three knots less speed, than the *Dreadnought*, carries an equal weight of battery, I presume my supposition may not overpass possibility. If it does, I would sacrifice something else to gun power. This would make the total gun power of A, to that of B, as 9 to 8.

The four rear ships of A are given two positions—blue and red. The interval between two adjacent blues, in the direction of the fleet's progress, is 250 yards; while in the line of bearing on which the blue are ranged the interval is 850 yards. For the red the distance 250 is doubled,—500. Any interval intermediate between 250 and 500 is of course permissible. The nearest blue is 1.6 miles from the rear enemy; the nearest red 1.9 miles. The distance between the main bodies (1–8 inclusive) is 6,000 yards,—three miles. The nearest red ship has to give most forward train to her guns; but the angle, 37°, is well within feasibility for a broadside.

The dotted lines show one method of concentration. By it the four rear B ships receive each the attack of two vessels, of .75 per cent their force, or a total against them of 1.5. The four leading A are pitted against a force which is to their own as 1.33 to 1.

[185]

It is to be observed that, if the B fleet mean to fight at the range of 6,000 yards,—now apparently favored,—it cannot prevent the A from assuming this formation; nor can it escape from the dilemma by its superior speed, except by making its four rear ships retire. It may retire altogether; but then that is not fighting. A moves on interior lines, with such an advantage of distance in its favor that B (granting the range) cannot control him. B, to maintain position and range, must accommodate himself to the speed A chooses to observe. He can abandon position and range, and by virtue of speed bring A to action; but that presents another problem. If A has a speed of 15 knots, and chooses to steam at 12, or 10, B, to keep position, must do the same. A therefore can give his blue ships ample reserve of speed for manoeuvring. If B try to circle round A, A is master of that situation; for upon concentric arcs of small radii, three miles apart, a speed of at least 2 to 1 is necessary for the fleet on the outer circle. The radius of the inner circle is at the choice of A; and he can, if he choose, impose such a condition that B, to keep abeam, (or any fixed bearing), and the range, will need a speed of 3, or even 4, to 1. The blue ships of A, not to speak of their reserve of speed, also occupy inner position; and the advantage of their main body (1–8) remains with them in greater part, though diminished. The two fleets can circle indefinitely, keeping this formation. Any change must proceed from B, or from the accidents of battle.

I do not for a moment imply that B is tactically helpless; every thrust has its parry; but I conceive he is confronted "with a condition, not a theory." He cannot prevent A making that disposition; and if B wishes to engage at 3 miles he must accept it. Will B by steaming ahead, superior speed, withdraw his rear ships? Then he, in measure, takes his leaders out of position. Will he meet this by circling round A? But A can circle also, and on an inner circle. I subjoin a table, showing in three sets, five miles apart, the comparative diameters and circumferences of two concentric circles, the radii of which differ by 3 miles—the engaging range.

Radius	Diameter $\pi=3.1$	Circumference	Speed needed
Inner: 1 mile	2 miles	6 miles	4:1
Outer: 4　"	8　"	25　"	
Inner: 6 miles	12 miles	37 miles	
Outer: 9　"	18　"	56　"	2:1
Inner: 11 miles	22 miles	68 miles	5:4
Outer: 14　"	28　"	87　"	20:16

If A chooses to circle with a radius of one mile, diameter two, he has a circumference of six against B's twenty-four; to keep abreast B must have four times the speed. Passing by the intermediate case it is plain that should A, being free to choose, choose even so large a circle as twenty-two miles diameter, B to keep abreast must steam as 5 to 4, or as twenty knots to sixteen. Now, without committing myself to any particular speed, I think I have never hinted at accepting this disparity. My argument has been: Where speed counts really for so little, why this mad race for speed? It has, for battleships, no reference to the great world of action, normally outside military matters, but which military control affects; it is little decisive in military matters; why maintain it?

The tactical advantage constituted by superior speed is this: it confers the offensive. A great advantage, admittedly; but the defensive is not made hopeless. Defensive campaigns are the highest test of merit. But, tactically, as shown by the table, if the offensive wishes long range, nothing can deprive the defensive of interior lines. He cannot prevent the assailant closing, nor taking short cuts; but, on the supposition of long range, he has tactical freedom and short lines for any combination or change he desires. If part of his battery is intermediate, he will wish closing; and it is thereby excluded to the offensive. Accepting the range, and the 3 knots difference of speed, the defensive has a circular area of not less than fifteen miles diameter within which he moves at will and compels the assailant—force of gravitation.

The second disposition of two A ships off the head of the column, I leave to speak for itself. It is a mere alternative suggestion.

The above has reference only to speed and a *total* weight of battery. The distribution of the latter, primary only, or primary and intermediate, is another, and to me more difficult, matter. I have presented certain arguments on this; Mr. Sims others. Decision belongs elsewhere. If Mr. Sims is correct in his inferences as to the accuracy of intermediates, and the effect of funnel injuries, and of the gases from explosion, he has certainly damaged much of my argument in favor of more numerous lighter pieces. The enclosed clipping from the N.Y. *Sun* of Oct. 19 seems, however, to leave still some hope for 6-inch intermediates at two miles.[6]

As regards the comparative loss to a fleet by accident, coaling, etc., I suppose, in a matter of pure chance, the theory of probabilities would say that in twenty smaller vessels the chance of an accident would be double that in ten larger. Yet I imagine that a careful investor, dealing with a hundred thousand dollars, would feel safer if he had placed it in ten companies than in two, or in five. The clipping I enclose seems to show this opinion in the present Lord Brassey; who is, I believe, conspicuous alike as a business man and as a lay expert in naval matters.[7] In administrative processes, such as coaling, docking, etc., I cannot but think a real advantage

---

6. Headed " 'Superior Speed' in Battleships," the article generally sustained Mahan's pessimism about the tactical advantages of speed per se in the new battleships under construction. "Captain Mahan likens the attempt to secure higher speed than your neighbors have to the chase of the will-o'-the-wisp, which constantly entices and constantly eludes the chaser."
7. Enclosure not found.

obtains to numbers. Administration is not chance, and is largely combinative; combination proceeds with numbers; and I believe a good administrator would keep more force at the front with twenty ships than with ten. The question of numbers must also be considered with reference to the whole navy, not to a particular fleet only. If, for distribution of force in a fleet, twelve ships be only as good as eight, does it follow that for the general war forty-eight are not more advantageous than thirty-two? You have several stations, or you wish quickly to transfer a decisive detachment from one place to another. An instance in point was when we expected to detach Watson from before Santiago against Camara. From Sampson's seven armored ships we might send two; but suppose, with the same tonnage, he had had only five. Taking into consideration coaling, accidents, etc., would three be sufficient to watch Cervera?

I have replied more at length than I could have wished, Mr. President; but I felt that when you had done me the honor of placing a paper before me, there was imposed upon me some recognition beyond mere acknowledgment. You will readily perceive that, in dealing with such questions, while engaged as I have been for years in work foreign to them, I am necessarily in the matter of details at a disadvantage, as towards men whose chief occupation is with present problems. The question may arise,—it presents itself to me,—whether under such circumstances it would be better for me to withdraw from discussions, in which I must limit myself chiefly to general principles. The only reply is that it is to be presumed that the men with whom executive decision lies will weigh all arguments, in the full light of all the evidence. This they are always able to command, from experts on all sides. The tactical diagram and explanation I present, is cognate with my paper for the Institute, in that it represents one example of a use of numbers, familiar to my life-long line of thought; which, though unexpressed, underlay much of my argument. It is merely a specific instance of division, combination, and consequent "Grand Tactics," as the expression used to be. There cannot but be many dispositions similar in principle, and to be carried out more certainly than ever before, because of greater certainty of motive power, and, in measure at least, of clearer vision due to smokeless powder. The field is one which should be exhaustively explored by men younger and less occupied than I; by the coming men, in short, rather than by one of the past.

I will be permitted to guard myself against being understood to imply more than I say. The illustration given is assuredly one of many tactical expedients. Equally assuredly, there are tactical repartees to it and them; every thrust has its parry, and may be followed by a return; yet duels end in one winning. But will an exhaustive study of tactical situations place superiority of speed in so decisive a situation as to warrant sacrifice of gun power to it?

Enclosures:

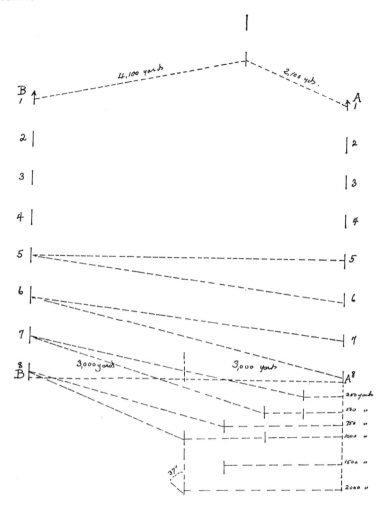

1. Diagram of Fleets.
2. Clipping from N.Y. *Sun*, October 19, 1906.
3. Clipping from *Weekly London Times*, September 28, 1906.

To Theodore Roosevelt

Woodmere, Long Island, October 24, 1906 [LC]

My dear Mr. President: Owing to my change of address to this place for the winter, your letter was somewhat delayed in reaching me.

I shall be only too glad that you should use any of my writings in any manner that may be serviceable to you, or that you may think serviceable to the country.[1] The question of credit in such connection is to me quite immaterial.

Judging by the sales, the book[2] has not been very widely read in this country. Great Britain rather better.

To Samuel A. Ashe

Woodmere, Long Island, October 25, 1906 [DUL]

My dear Ashe: The Church Board of Missions, of which I have been a member for several years, has lately placed me in an off shoot from it called the American Church Institute for Negroes; the object being thereby to coordinate the several Church undertakings for negroes. In pursuance of this Mr. Geo. Foster Peabody[1] has invited us to a tour of inspection in his private car, and I for one have consented to go. We leave here Sunday night, and by the schedule sent me are due to arrive in Raleigh, Tuesday, the 30th, at 3:05 A.M., leaving again Wednesday, 31st, at 1:20 A.M. This means that we spend the day of Tuesday in Raleigh, to visit St. Augustine School.

I do not know how our "official" time will be disposed of; but circumstances may admit our shaking hands once more. We are pretty old fellows now, and must be prepared for something of a shock in changed appearance, should we now meet after 35 years. From 31 to 66 is a tremendous chasm; not one, however, quite empty in our two lives.

Please remember me very cordially to that pretty daughter of yours,[2] the only one of your family, save yourself, that I have met. She was very like what you were in face, when you wore a midshipman's jacket a half-century ago.[3]

---

1. *See* Mahan to Little, Brown and Company, December 6, 1906.
2. *Sea Power in its Relations to the War of 1812.*

1. Trustee of the American Church Institute for Negroes.
2. Probably, Mary Porter Ashe. *See* Mahan to Ashe, March 28, 1876, Footnote 1.
3. A message, the text of a telegram from Ashe to Mahan, at the top of the letter reads: "Delighted. We expect you to be my guest while in Raleigh. Will call for you at half past Eight . . . expect you to breakfast."

To Summer E. Kittelle[1]

Dear Mr. Kittelle: Your letter[2] was received yesterday, as I was going down to Quogue to vote. I fear my memory can supply nothing, beyond the wholly negative testimony that I cannot recall the influence of Admiral Dewey's telegram, on the decision of the Board to advise Watson's squadron. My memory has been continuous, that it was the Board's own action; and such fragmentary incidents as my efforts can now recall go to affirm that it was taken instantly upon the news that Camara had actually sailed, and been sighted so far east as to indicate his ends.

The Department was in constant communication with agents in Spain—by cable. So that Camara's preparations were known, and his purposes considered; and I presume, though as to that I do not remember, that our alternative courses were considered, whether he went east or west.

But surely there must be some more certain evidence available than the notoriously deceptive memory of a man of my *years then*, and now. The memories of my youth I find singularly correct, but you yourself were witness that I did not clearly remember concerning the *Monadnock*, though it is evident from my *Lessons of the War With Spain* (p. 196) that I then understood the facts. I find in the same book (p. 198) that Watson's flagship was the *Newark*. Cannot the log be consulted as to the date of her leaving her then station, or arriving off Santiago? Will not the file of telegrams to Sampson, or Remey at Key West, or Watson, show when the orders were issued? There is nothing like contemporary documents.

That the same idea should have occurred coincidently to a man of Admiral Dewey's military instincts, pondering the same military conditions, is what might be expected. Personally, the situation presented itself to me precisely as one I used to use in lecturing at the College—Napoleon's instructions to Marmont at Salamanca, opposed to Wellington at Almeida. I quote from memory, you can find the letter in the *Correspondance de N.*, beginning of 1812: "Dispose your army in divisions within a day's march of Salamanca. Should W. attempt to move South, concentrate at S., and advance upon Almeida, and he will return. Indeed, so long as you maintain these dispositions about S., he is too able a man to attempt a serious movement of the kind". It was with reference to this that, in my report to Dewey, I said it would be pedantic to cite precedents.

The right thing to do, in order to obtain for the Admiral the recognition

---

1. Secretary of the General Board of the Navy.
2. The letter referred to was not from Kittelle to Mahan, but from Captain Nathan Sargent, class of 1870, to Mahan. It raised certain historical questions about the proposal to dispatch Watson's squadron to attack the coast of Spain in 1898.

due him, if the Board's action resulted from his suggestion, would be to search the telegrams and logs *exhaustively*. I find it hard now to think that, Cámara having sailed the 16th, and Dewey's telegram despatched from Hong Kong the 26th, we remained uncertain during the ten days.

To Leopold J. Maxse

Woodmere, Long Island, November 9, 1906 [CROCS]

Dear Mr. Maxse: Your letter expressing disinclination to the *N. American* arrived, unluckily, two days after I had made my proposition. I waited long for a reply, the delay being attributed to absence of the Editor in Chief. The proposition was then declined, on the ground that the *N.A.* published also in England, and the *National* here.

The matter therefore rests where it did, and I now incline to publish with you only;[1] for a similar difficulty is likely to obtain with all magazines. As between England and U.S., yours is the strategic position; for our people have hugged their delusion so long, a single paper cannot hope to stop action at the Hague; the more, if, as our press states, the immunity of so-called "private property" has already been stated as one of our propositions. To England, the position she occupies across the approaches of all trade to N. German harbors, the interdiction of all German shipping in war, makes the maintenance of the present law imperative. This view needs strong enforcement at the proper moment. As a people, *we* are interested in you, as in great measure bound to the same interests as ourselves; and we have besides our own reasons for maintaining the law. But the central reason is the grip you, our almost certain cooperator, have on German shipping.

A new periodical devoted to International Law is about being started here, and I have already recd a letter from the editor asking an article on this subject. I declined; but it is barely possible a coincident publication, say next April, might be effected.[2] I dont think it will be able to pay; but in the general interest it might be well to develop my argument before experts. I believe it novel. In *strict confidence*, I may say to you that the President's consent to my writing rests as a special exception, (as to naval officers), grounded on the value attached to my previous writing on public, as distinct from military, subjects. This of course does not mean *great* value, but some. Meanwhile, there is no hurry.

---

1. *See* Mahan to Maxse, August 21, 1906.
2. Mahan did not publish in the *American Journal of International Law.*

To R. Stein[1]

Woodmere, Long Island, November 10, 1906 [NWC]

Dear Sir: I have received your letter, and subsequently the proposed petition and argument.

While I do not affect to have detailed knowledge, as to the means by which Mr. Rockefeller[2] accumulated his millions, the public discussion of the same has given me such a profound distrust of the moral integrity of his methods, that it would be impossible to put my name to any request to him for money.

The proposed scheme does not recommend itself to my judgment. I greatly doubt its having any tendency towards the end you desire; nor will that, if reached, eliminate other burning questions, but rather facilitate their development. Further, I do not believe that the time has yet arrived when the decrease of the warlike spirit, and of preparation for war, among the nations of Europe, will conduce to the peaceful settlement of the questions, the approach of which you think discernible in the future. Yet could such a settlement as you forecast be reached, with the consequent relief from immediate apprehension of danger from neighbors, the cry for disarmament would be irresistible, and would leave the white world weaponless before peoples of very different ideals, should the contingencies which you expect arise.

Fortunately—from my point of view—the ambitions of the white nations are too varied and active, to be stilled by any such measure as you propose.

To William S. Sims

Woodmere, Long Island, November 16, 1906 [NYDC]

Dear Mr. Sims: I beg to thank you for the copy of your revised article.[1]

I have lost so much time by various outside causes this autumn, that I fear it will be long before I can revert to this matter, but I am much obliged all the same.

---

1. Robert Stein, Arctic explorer, pacifist, and internationalist.
2. John Davison Rockefeller, Sr.

1. *See* Mahan to Sims, August 6 and October 3, 1906. This note was apparently Mahan's last direct correspondence with Sims.

To Stephen B. Luce

My dear Admiral: Yours of Nov. 26 was received just as I was leaving home for a couple of days. My address for this winter is as above.

I should hesitate to commit myself finally and definitely between the two ports; perhaps because my first prepossessions have favored N.Y. In my judgment, strategic value depends not upon *position* only, but upon *resources*. Under the latter head come (N.Y.) two exits; and also (Newport) facility for issuing.

In noting your details, I think perfectly sound that, granting suitable defences at Plum Id. &c, an enemy could not remain within L.I. Sound; his supply vessels & colliers being threatened both by the forts and by a fleet in Narragansett, flanking his communications. This effect however would equally be produced by a body of vessels much smaller than our main fleet.

The congested state of New York Harbor could, I think, be satisfactorily met by moving the fleet ten miles up the Hudson—less than an hours steaming. In case of blockade there would be much less congestion.

Save for the illimitable growth in battleships, my prepossessions would continue to favor N.Y. because of the immense naval resources of a great commercial port, and the back communications of which the Hudson is the type; and especially the *two exits*. But wireless telegraphy has made much more possible for an outside enemy to occupy a central position, sufficiently at hand for either exit; a fact which much lessens the advantage of the two, without however wholly removing it.

The increasing size of vessels will probably throw New York out. The one exit is now not available at all stages of tide; the other is so tortuous as to be dangerous. Upon the whole, I incline at first sight now to Narragansett Bay; trusting to torpedoes and submarines to enforce upon an enemy a distance so respectable as to enable our fleet within to get out and form order of battle unmolested which is the utmost support a port can give to an offensive naval movement. The same distance would also favor evasion, if desired; though not so well as two exits do.

I should say that the question had now advanced so far that dry dock provision in Narragansett Bay, to the extent at least of simultaneous docking of two battleships, was imperatively necessary; for it seems probable we may be forced to abandon New York through the steady increase of draft.

This is rather an appreciation of conditions than a definite opinion. The latter I am reluctant to form, much more to express, without a more prolonged examination than I now have either time or data for. It might be well for you to consider whether the defences of Narragansett Bay, and Fisher's Island Sound, could not be so extended as to insure our fleet passing from

Narragansett to Long Island unseen. That would be two exits [and] entrances; indeed three, for it could come out by Sandy Hook.

As regards War Boards (or Strategy) the Secy. must usually be incompetent to original strategic decision. The remedy, in my judgment, is that the head of the General (or Strategy) Board should be singly responsible for all advice given. Let him consult as much as he wishes—like a commander-in-chief; but let the conclusion he submits be his alone. The admirals afloat must grow to consider themselves his subordinates, and may so be delivered from the jealousies which no Board can escape. To this day Dewey is credited with having secured telegraphic communication with Washington, as one of his greatest achievements.

[P.S.] I think I wrote before that I would not willingly accept orders before my supposed promotion and increase of pay; and even then without a clear understanding that I must be at liberty to give time at my disposition to other objects. If I seek, or accept an offer, of orders, unconditional, I bind myself to the exclusive dedication of my time, which might be a pecuniary loss as well as an abandonment of topics preferable to me.

To Little, Brown and Company

Woodmere, Long Island, December 6, 1906 [LC]

Gentlemen: I enclose herewith a large number of clippings which were secured by me from my son, some six weeks ago. I presume they must have come from you to him during my absence in Europe,[1] but owing to his prolonged illness during the summer they lay neglected. I trust you will pardon the delay, and that it has not occasioned inconvenience.

Did the N.Y. *Sun* ever publish its intended second notice? I presume you have seen that the President alluded to the book in his message,[2] and also made some quotations from it. He had written me before that it would be impossible specifically and individually to acknowledge these and to ask if I would object to such use.[3] Of course I was only too pleased.

---

1. Mahan, his wife, and two daughters were in Europe from November 1905 to June 1906.
2. Roosevelt's December 3, 1906, Annual Message to Congress cited Mahan's *War of 1812* to the point that naval preparedness was a means of preserving peace. *See* Mahan to Roosevelt, October 24, 1906.
3. *See* Mahan to Roosevelt, October 24, 1906.

To Henry E. Rood[1]

Woodmere, Long Island, December 6, 1906 [DUL]

Dear Mr. Rood: The enclosed galleys[2] were received this morning, and are herewith returned. In 2, the editor's omissions made a hiatus of my meaning, which I think I have sufficiently remedied by an insertion of six words.

During a recent trip South, I found the southerners are making a point of calling the Civil War, "The War between the States." This somewhat disturbed me; for, if generally accepted, it struck at the constitutional theory on which the North maintained the Union. Mr. Charles Francis Adams suggested to me the War of Secession, which I here adopt,[3] and introduce as the best title I have heard. It can offend neither party; for while slavery caused the war, the right of Secession was the political bone of contention.

I cannot from the galleys judge what omissions the Editor has made from my Ms.; but I recognize at least one. I trust therefore the Ms. is carefully kept. With whom should I communicate as to book form, and the expectation as to whether it is to be set up from my Ms., or from the galleys?

To Charles W. Stewart

University Club, New York, December 10, 1906 [NA]

Dear Mr. Stewart: Can you ascertain for me about the date at which the *Essex, Enterprise,* & *Huron* class appear first on the *Navy Register?* from which they long since disappeared. It was, I think about 1870–5.

Also have you in the Library a Bowditch of 1855 to 1860?[1] and if so can you refer to it for me, and verify my recollection, that in getting out from the tables the combined parallax & refraction of the moon, we had, at some stage of the proceeding—the end, I think—to add or subtract 59′42″. This is an odd question, but I have a reason. This is all the questions I think of at present; so, as the old letters said, no more at present from [etc.].

[P.S.]   My address is Woodmere N.Y.

---

1. Assistant editor of *Harper's Magazine.*
2. For *Harper's* serial publication of *From Sail to Steam.*
3. "Our Navy Before the War of Secession," *Harper's Monthly* (May 1907).

1. Nathaniel Bowditch, *The New American Practical Navigator.* 26th new stereotype edition. New York: E. and G. W. Blunt, 1856. The 27th edition appeared in 1857, and the 29th in 1860.

To Bouverie F. Clark

My dear Clark: Your last letter struck me on my birthday, Sept. 27—
when I was sixty-six, and I shall try to get this in on you on Christmas or
thereabouts. I congratulate you upon your new lease of the house in Francis
St., which I remember you were fearing to lose when I last saw you. It
struck me as about what a man alone would need, and a convenient walking
distance from your two clubs, which to me is always a recommendation.
Besides, for the Senior at least, the omnibuses must be plenty. I suppose the
automobile as an omnibus must be as objectionable as it is apt to be to out-
siders in the other relations of life. We have now only one omnibus line
in N.Y., by Fifth Avenue, which as a swell residence street objects to
trams. Otherwise our transportation systems are all on rails. We have
however a most curious development of the 'bus; I wonder has it reached
your backward people. It is called the "Seeing New York Coach"; a huge
auto, with perhaps 14 to 16 seats, thwartships, each rising a little above the
one in front like a theatre. It takes no way passengers, only the full course
to view the points of interest. At the head stands the sight-shower with a
megaphone. "This building on the right is the Roman Catholic cathedral,
on the left next above is the house of Mr. —— Vanderbilt etc." Never having made the round, I cant vouch for particulars of description.

Your letter spoke of the President's spelling reform, there I suppose a
new thing. Todays paper announces that the Lower House has passed a
resolution contrary to it, & the President has "come down."[1] With his
usual luck, I suppose this will increase his popularity; it will probably take
immensely "bowing to the will of the people, as expressed by their representatives." He deserves it, however, he is a thoroughly good fellow all
round; honest and immensely shrewd. Better judges than I say he is one of
the most sagacious "politicians" in the country; but from beginning to end
his strength with the people has been his downright courage, to which they
are little used in public men.

Our house in N.Y. being still under lease, we are passing this winter at
Woodmere, essentially a summer resort, an hour from town, but with a
considerable society in itself, or in two or three other similar settlements,
contiguous, which run into one another. The house is under three years
lease to Mrs. Mahan's brother, who only spends the summer months and
offered it us. As the thermometer has been down to 6° already with high

---

1. The Chairman of the House Printing Committee introduced a resolution forbidding
the use of simplified spelling by the Public Printer, and also by President Roosevelt
in public documents. Roosevelt did not wait for Senate action, but ordered the
printer to abolish the abbreviated forms.

N.W. wind, we can feel pretty safe as to the heating; and while we have neighbors, we are yet substantially "in the country."

You will be amused to hear that at the request of one of our big publishing houses I am writing my Recollections. At first I laughed, "Nothing ever happened to me"; but what with old naval yarns etc etc, and incidents of one sort or another I am surprised how many words I have written. It will come out, joints at least, in *Harper's Monthly*, beginning February; ultimately, the carcass whole will be served in book form; the whole ox— or hog.

I say nothing to my family but have an internal intention—they consenting—to spend the summer of 1908 in England. Otherwise we are a fixture here till May, and then Quogue for the summer.

Goodbye and Good Luck; Merry Xmas and the rest.

To Stephen B. Luce

Woodmere, Long Island, December 15, 1906 [LC]

My dear Admiral: Thank you very much for your kind congratulations.[1] There is no one from whom they could come more acceptably to me, for I have never forgotten that to you I owe my start upon whatever success I have had.

I have no doubt that the Department would show me all possible consideration, but I hesitate to ask for orders just now, when the other work I have in hand would make impossible for me to give a quid pro quo. I think I see daylight ahead some time next spring, & my present inclination is, when I shall have finished that to which I have alluded, to make to the Department the suggestion which you have made to me. I suppose, indeed, if the lectures[2] have the value you kindly attribute to them, the Government might esteem their revision & publication worth the years difference of pay to me, irrespective of the particular amount of labor I put upon them.

I have, besides the College lectures, some other material, more particularly some Lowell lectures delivered in 1897. They are not now fresh in my mind, but I think there is in them a good deal that might bear republication. I

---

1. Mahan had been promoted to rear admiral on the retired list.
2. The lectures on naval strategy that Mahan had delivered at the War College over the years. Luce's suggestion that Mahan seek active duty for a year for the purpose of revising and publishing them under Navy Department or War College auspices was not acted upon. Little, Brown published the revised lectures in 1911 under the title *Naval Strategy, Compared and Contrasted with the Principles of Military Operations on Land*.

will see what kind of a blend the two promise. Revision will mean to me addition as well as correction.

With kind remembrances to Mrs. Luce and your daughters believe me [etc.].

To Stephen B. Luce

Woodmere, Long Island, December 21, 1906 [LC]

My dear Admiral: The question of revision takes on a somewhat different light in what you have last written me. I will keep the matter in mind so as to be ready when brought before me, should it be. I understand that your letter does not in any way commit the authorities of the College or Department.

To John M. Brown

Woodmere, Long Island, January 1, 1907 [LC]

Dear Mr. Brown: I heartily echo your good wishes for the coming year and thank you for them.

I may as well reply to you, as more formally to the firm, concerning the material contributed by me to the *Royal Navy*. The sole question is whether you and I are willing to pay a sum which they will consider compensation for damage to the sale of their book. If they are still out several thousand pounds it is manifest we can do nothing to help nearly recoup that. Marston paid me between $2,000 and $2,500—at the rate of 25 to 30 dollars per thousand words. I have presumed it was the best paid and am glad to know they consider it the most important in the book. I remember Mr. Roosevelt telling me the rate of payment was excessively small, but he did not mention the amount. I presume from two offers made to me that £2 per thousand is the usual tender.

I believe they are mistaken in thinking the separate publication would injure the main work; but that of course is for them to judge. As our chief object is to obtain the right to print in connection with a future edition of my "Works," I should be satisfied with that understanding to surrender to them the English royalties. I think the offer to share my American royalties should be held in reserve; for should I do that I doubt if I could attempt any serious revision, such for instance as bringing the naval events into relation with the transactions on land which might be attempted for our home market.

I am sorry about *1812*, but not surprised. In my own estimation, it is the best bit of historical writing I have ever done; superior by far in research, in treatment and in style. But nothing could redeem the essential flatness of the theme. I hope the result will at best not be disastrous to you, that the prestige of the other books may have floated this enough. For myself, it was the serial publication and Lowell lectures that repaid me for three years of my most faithful work.

Upon reflection I will write a formal letter to the firm.

To Little, Brown and Company

Woodmere, Long Island, January 1, 1907 [LC]

Gentlemen: I have received yours of December 27, enclosing letter from Mr. Tyrrell, managing Director of Sampson Low & Co.

I feel it would be quite impossible for me, and I presume also for you, to make any offer based upon the proposed separate publication, or otherwise, that could go far towards recouping a loss of several thousand pounds. My contribution to the *History of the Royal Navy* was made upon terms fixed by myself, at a price less than that usually paid me when writing to order. The *War of 1812* of course does not come in any way into the present consideration.

The most I see my way to doing is to offer to surrender to them, *for five years*, my royalties upon the English sales; it being made clearly understood that in return we have full copyright privileges and right to republish after five years in any collected edition of my Works. I doubt if I could be ready for Christmas, 1907.

P.S.   I will be glad to receive the *1812* clippings, but should there be any among them you should wish to keep, please do.

To John S. Billings

Woodmere, Long Island, January 10, 1907 [NYPL]

My dear Dr. Billings: I duly received your letter notifying me that the Library had kindly presented me and dispatched a copy of the *Naval Let-*

ters of Percival Drayton.[1] I have waited to reply, hoping I might by the same letter acknowledge receipt; but it has never come. Your letter did not specify way sent. I have followed up one delusive P.O. clue, which brought me Park and Tilford's catalogue in reply for four cents deposited; and one U.S. Express notification which has resulted so far in nothing.

Drayton was an old captain of mine, and a kindly friend. I shall be glad to see his letters. Meantime my thanks to you remain all the same. The miscarriage is due ultimately to my new address, as above but for this winter only—till May 1.

I was sorry to hear somewhere that you have been ill, but trust you are now quite recovered.

To Philip R. Alger[1]

Woodmere, Long Island, January 10, 1907 [LC]

Sir: Have you seen a translation from the Russian of the *Battle of Tsushima*,[2] with preface by Sir George Clarke,[3] Secretary of the British Defence Committee, in which he is said to sustain the position as to the 8 in. and 6 in. guns at Tsushima, which I advanced?

I saw it noted in the *Athenaeum* of Dec. 22 (p. 799). I have about determined that I cannot keep sufficiently close to technical details to justify my entering into discussions; but this interested me because Clarke (whom I know well) is from his official position well behind the scenes so far as Japan opens her heart to her ally.

I had a strong letter from R. A. Sir Hedworth Lambton,[4] the Ladysmith man, sustaining my article specifically in this particular.

---

1. Percival Drayton, *Naval Letters from Captain Percival Drayton, 1861–1865.* Printed from the Original Manuscripts Presented to the New York Public Library by Miss Gertrude L. Hoyt, 1906. Originally printed in the *Bulletin* of the New York Public Library, November–December 1906.

1. Secretary of the U.S. Naval Institute.
2. Vladimir Ivanovitch Semenov, *The Battle of Tsu-shima between the Japanese and Russian Fleets, Fought on 27th May, 1905* ... translated by Capt. A. B. Lindsay, with a preface by Sir George Sydenham Clarke. London: John Murray, 1906.
3. Clarke, a major force in planning the defense of the Empire, was First Secretary of the Committee of Imperial Defence.
4. Commander of the naval brigade throughout the siege of Ladysmith, 1899–1900.

To Theodore Roosevelt

Woodmere, Long Island, January 10, 1907 [LC]

Dear Mr. President: I fear I may trespass on your indulgence, but the statement in a morning paper that four of our best battleships are to be sent to the Pacific has filled me with dismay.

In case of war with Japan what can four battleships do against their navy? In case of war with a European power, what would not the four battleships add to our fleet here?

I apprehend, should war with Japan come before the Panama Canal is finished, the Philippines and Hawaii might fall before we could get there; but, had we our whole fleet in hand, all could be retrieved. Between us and Japan any hostilities must depend on sea power. Invasion in force is possible to neither.

I had inferred from the recent sustained withdrawals of our battleships from Eastern waters, that this was the policy of our Government; and it may be I should at once apologize for writing upon a mere newspaper statement.

Have you chanced to see in the *Athenaeum*, December 22, (p. 799) some comments attributed to Sir George Clarke, Secretary of the British Defence Committee, sustaining the opinion advanced by me concerning the 8 in. and 6 in. guns at Tsushima?

To John S. Billings

Woodmere, Long Island, January 13, 1907 [NYPL]

My dear Dr. Billings: The long missing Drayton letters[1] turned up last evening, and I again express my thanks to you for thinking of me in connection with them.

I am delighted to learn from your letter that you are well again.

To Bouverie F. Clark

Woodmere, Long Island, January 15, 1907 [LC]

My dear Clark: Would you kindly glance your eye over the enclosed,[1] and let me know if it accord with truth? You can understand that in my

---

1. *See* Mahan to Billings, January 10, 1907.

1. Enclosure not found.

Recollections, and particularly, of my stay in England in 1894, I am divided between the wish not to seem to make too much of the attentions showed me, and the equal desire to recognize all that they were in themselves. Of these, among the most valued by me was the Royal Navy Club, because of the closeness with which it has guarded guestship. The compliment of being the first foreigner to be entertained by it was very great. Some things of course I cant say. Sir N. Salmon[2] when walking round with me to the general dinner given to the officers of the *Chicago* said to me "You know we would have liked to make the occasion more special to you and your books, but it was impossible to overlook your admiral." This of course could not be said, nor have I ever before mentioned it even privately outside my family—nor will you please. Some one, I think you, once sent me a little blue book about the Club, but that is packed up with my other belongings now our house is let.

You will congratulate me, I am sure, on promotion to *rear adml retired*, a more substantial incident being that it increases my pay by something over £200.[3] For the other, "Captn Mahan" has become almost a nom de plume for me, and I am a little perplexed about changing it. Eight years ago, to aid promotion, Congress passed a law allowing retirements with an advance in grade and pay, but expressly excluded from benefit those already retired. The consequence was that men who had served the four years Civil War were outranked and outpaid by men without war service. I having retired voluntarily felt no grievance so long as the terms were observed; but it was unfair to those retired compulsorily for age or health. In the rectification, however, I share as above.

I received your letter of Dec. 26. I am quite with you as regards Chamberlain and your present government. In the latter I have little confidence. As regards naval matters I am too old and too busy to keep up, and have about made up my mind to leave it all to younger men.

To William H. Henderson

Woodmere, Long Island, January 19, 1907 [NMM]

My dear Henderson: I am glad to hear from you again, though regretful about the employment. As we crawl to the top of the tree, however, the vacancies become fewer. I do not know how far the change from Plymouth to London may suit your personal tastes, but I feel very sure that your temperament is too active to enjoy unlimited repose. By the way, your

2. Admiral Sir Nowell Salmon, commander-in-chief at Portsmouth, 1894–1897.
3. *See* Mahan to Luce, November 18, 1907.

former command at Jamaica is feeling the want of repose with a vengeance. The recent painful disaster must have for you a very particular and personal interest.[1]

I am glad you liked my paper.[2] You can appreciate under what sense of difficulty a man writes on that subject, unless he is one of the lucky ones who can only see one side. I am apt to be painfully conscious of the possible retorts of an opponent, and as I am not fond of argument I dislike papers that may involve it, as this did; but now that our President has come out definitely in favor of the *Dreadnought* type,[3] and I believe the preponderant opinion of our service goes along, I intend to withdraw from the discussion, and leave facts and experience to work out the conclusions. Somewhere, the need for numbers and the increasing cost will enforce a halt on size, if no other way by bankrupting some of the competitors.

With other leading features of your naval policy I am in general accord. The redistribution of your fleets and the recasting of your educational programme I think in the main correct. I have not attempted to master details.

My present address is for this winter only. We rented our N. Y. house a year ago for three years, and this winter my brother-in-law offering the use of this we are trying a country winter—about an hour from town. I like it very well, though somewhat disconcerted by a heavy snowfall.

Mrs. Mahan thanks you very much for your remembrances, and sends her own, and with best wishes for the future believe me [*etc.*].

To Leopold J. Maxse

Woodmere, Long Island, January 22, 1907 [LC]

Dear Mr. Maxse: Have conditions so developed that you know when you will wish my proposed article? Will there be a Hague Conference this year? If so when would it be best to publish?

---

1. Fire and an earthquake had devastated Kingston on January 4, 1907.
2. "Reflections, Historic and Other, Suggested by the Battle of the Sea of Japan," U.S. Naval Institute *Proceedings* (June 1906) and the Royal United Service Institution *Journal* (November 1906).
3. Roosevelt had warned the House Naval Committee concerning the possible loss of world political power and position if ships of the *Dreadnought* type were not built. On this occasion, he sent the Committee Sims's "Tactical Qualities of the *Dreadnought* Type of Battleship." At the President's request, Sims prepared a summary of his article, which was directed not only to George Edmund Foss, Chairman of the House Committee, but also to Senator Hale, Chairman of the Senate Committee.

I have completed an article with the title "The Practical Aspect of War,"[1] but I should prefer to keep it in hand for modification or correction till you need it. By my proposition it was to be followed by one on the question of the Immunity from Capture of so-called Private Property at Sea.[2] My idea has been that if the Conference was held this year it would meet in May; in which event the first article might appear aptly in your April number, and the second in May.

You might well keep your editorial eye on the matter of the private property upon the strong control the position of Great Britain can exert over all German maritime routes. It is a great safeguard of peace should trouble arise.

I fear your present government. It has some strong men but as a whole I think it lacks balance.

To the Editor of the New York Sun

Woodmere, Long Island, January 28, 1907[1]

The editorial in your issue of this morning, "A Short Sighted Philippine Policy," caused me to read the article upon which it is based, "The Philippines, the Key to the Open Door," by Mr. Benjamin Baker, in the new naval periodical, the *Navy*,[2] for January.

In my judgment Mr. Baker has made a serious and valuable contribution to American thought upon the subject of the Philippines, and I am the more sorry that there seems to be in his paper a ground, implicit rather than explicit, favoring one of the measures recommended in your editorial, which says, "At least three battleships could be spared from the Atlantic fleet and ordered to Pacific waters."

From a correct military standpoint the reasonable reply to this is: Of what avail would three battleships be against the strongest navy in eastern

1. "The Hague Conference and the Practical Aspect of War," *National Review* (July 1907). Published also in *Living Age* (July 27, 1907). Reprinted in *Some Neglected Aspects of War*. Boston: Little Brown and Company, 1907.
2. "The Hague Conference: The Question of Immunity of Belligerent Merchant Shipping," *National Review* (June 1907). Published also in *Living Age* (July 6, 1907), and reprinted in *Some Neglected Aspects of War*.

1. From the New York *Sun*, January 31, 1907.
2. Published by the Navy League. There is no indication that Mahan ever was a member of the League, or submitted material for publication in *The Navy*. It seems to have been an organ for the officers who espoused Sims's cause.

Asian waters, and how valuable a reenforcement are they to the Atlantic fleet, with which they are at this moment united?

The *Sun*, again following Mr. Baker, who, however, is far more guarded in his words, says: "Our present fleet arrangement is based upon the idea that we have more to fear from an attack upon the Atlantic coast than from a raid on the Philippines." I do not know how far the *Sun* speaks from inside information of the Government's policy; but it seems to me most reasonable to assume that the Government, under a president who has knowledge of military principles, and advisers such as the General Board, over which Admiral Dewey presides, would reason that to send three battleships to the Philippines would be to put ourselves exactly in the position in which Japan caught Russia; with a navy in the aggregate superior, divided into two parts individually inferior to the Japanese navy. Should such a misfortune as war arise with any Power able to reach Eastern waters sooner than we, our proposed Philippine fleet would represent that of Port Arthur, and to the Atlantic fleet, if sent subsequently, would be assigned the role of Rojestvensky. I do not, of course, say that exactly similar results would follow, but only that the situation we should needlessly have created would be the same. Absit omen!

That we should have a stronghold impregnable as Port Arthur, as Mr. Baker says, is correct; only, unless adequately manned, it would, by falling into an enemy's hands, enable him to protract resistance should our fleet now concentrated in our own waters succeed ultimately in establishing naval control in the East. The question is one chiefly of naval superiority. For that object, in the present proportions of our navy, the three battleships here are thrice as efficient as they would be in Manila. Mr. Baker's conclusion, "The plain remedy is for us to have enough battleships to allow a proper force in both the Atlantic and the Pacific," is unimpeachable; but I fear a counsel of perfection until we have a new generation which shall be less shy of the word imperialism and its military consequences as well as a broader outlook to the future which Mr. Baker well forecasts.

To Little, Brown and Company

Woodmere, Long Island, January 30, 1907 [LC]

Gentlemen: I beg to acknowledge receipt of your semi-annual statement of account to January 1, 1907, showing due me $2307.82, together with check to that amount for which I have to express my thanks.

To Leopold J. Maxse

Woodmere, Long Island, March 5, 1907 [LC]

Dear Mr. Maxse: Your letter of Feb. 16 evidently crossed mine.[1]

With regard to the dates of publication: Assuming that it appear that the Conference will meet about June 15, I should personally incline to putting the article on the Capture of Private Property in the May number. *If* it carry weight at all, I think it would be well that it should be before your Government anterior to their final instructions to their representatives at the Congress. (In confidence) I have reason to know that they wished to know my opinion on that matter; which makes me doubly wishful that they should have them clearly, from both the moral and military point of view. I want also my own Government to have them betimes; and I should feel indebted if you would send a copy from the very first struck off to President Roosevelt and to Mr. Root (Hon. Elihu Root), Secretary of State.

My first thought was that the other article should precede; but from the point of view of effect—if any is produced—it would perhaps be more effective if it appeared immediately before, or during the early part of the Conference. "The Practical Aspect of War" is intended to suggest, and to make men ponder, certain questions which I believe arbitration cannot settle. If I am successful, it should impart a sobering alterative to the "Hurrah for Peace," represented by Stead,[2] D'Estournelles de Constant, and that ilk.

With this expression of my views I leave the matter to you to settle. I believe the "Practical Aspect of War" may and probably will, tell best when they have met, but the "Private Property" will be decided mainly by the Governments, not the Conference.

You have I think a wretched Government, which may mean only that they differ from me on almost every subject. I sat next Campbell Bannerman[3] at lunch at Mr. Choate's in 1899, just before the last Hague. I had then no propossessions, & he impressed me as a most ordinary person. His only claim to prominence I have been able to detect, is a willingness to take up extreme positions.

[P.S.]   The article on capture of "Private" Property is finished, & being typewritten I shall then revise, and shall send by steamer of not later than Saturday, March 16.

---

1. *See* Mahan to Maxse, January 22, 1907.
2. William Thomas Stead, publicist for the peace movement in England and America, slavophile, and champion of arbitration.
3. Sir Henry Campbell-Bannerman, Liberal leader in the House of Commons when Mahan lunched with him; Prime Minister from 1905 to 1908. In 1907, he spoke with pride of a reduction in the naval estimates of £2,000,000, and made a preliminary offer of unilateral disarmament for the second Hague Conference.

To John M. Brown

Woodmere, Long Island, March 16, 1907 [LC]

Dear Mr. Brown: I have read the letter of the Director of Sampson Low. It puts an end of course to a proposition in which I was interested, but interested to no extraordinary degree.[1]

In my recollection there was no formal agreement between the old firm and me. There was simply an exchange of letters, stating and accepting terms. I do not think there will be found in mine any stipulation beyond furnishing a certain number of words *for* a *History of the Royal Navy*. You might ask Mr. Tyrrell to quote any words from my letters conceding any other use of my contribution than for that book; anything conceding "*all* rights, English, American, Foreign, *serial* and book rights." That this is "obvious" is a mere inference, of a man in a temper over a bad bargain; an inference from the price paid: £500; $25 the thousand at a time when I could command $50 per thousand for magazine writing.

So long as they continue to publish only in the *History*, I should feel it a breach of faith to publish separately here, although we have copyright; but should they attempt a separate publication, I should feel at liberty to publish so here, if it seemed expedient to us. It would perhaps be only advisable with some development to meet American interest.

I see no occasion for saying anything of this to Mr. Tyrrell, unless you do; but I think you might write that I find the terms he proposes inadmissable; that they would not in any way pay us nor me for trouble of revision; and that, *unless he can quote* words committing me to every use they wished of the material, I do not recognize that they have any rights to publish except in the *History of the Royal Navy*.

The allusion to the *War of 1812* is of course absurd; it merely emphasides the man's vexation, apparent throughout.

To J. Franklin Jameson

Woodmere, Long Island, March 22, 1907 [LC]

My dear Dr. Jameson: Thank you very much for thinking of me for the complimentary offer you make me.[1]

---

1. *See* Mahan to Brown and Mahan to Little, Brown and Company, January 1, 1907.

1. As President of the American Historical Association, Jameson had been authorized by the Executive Committee of the National Arbitration and Peace Congress to appoint two delegates to represent the Association at its New York meeting, April 14–17, 1907. Jameson to Mahan, March 21, 1907, in the Library of Congress.

I am prevented from accepting by the fact that I am booked to sail for Europe April 6.

Again thanking you, believe me [etc.].

To Henry E. Rood

Woodmere, Long Island, April 4, 1907 [NYPL]

Dear Mr. Rood: I return Art V. as sent me and I should imagine, despite the somewhat inconclusive appearance of Galley 9, as sent me, that you have here enough for an article of ordinary length.

I presume that as II appears only in May, and you have three more now, the Magazine[1] is adequately provided, till my return about June 30. Should you need to communicate with me, however, my address will be, U.S. Dispatch Agent, 4 Trafalgar Square, London.

To Leopold J. Maxse

Off Cape St. Vincent, SS *Konig Albert*, April 15, 1907 [CROCS]

Dear Mr. Maxse: I wrote you before leaving N.Y. a letter acknowledging yours and your cable, and expressing my satisfaction that "Maritime Capture"[1] should appear in May, the other[2] in June. I write now to renew my wish that copies of May number be sent "with Rear Adml. Mahan's respects" on cover, to President Roosevelt; Hon. Elihu Root, Secretary of State; and Admiral Dewey. Washington will be sufficient address for each. I would like also one similarly sent to Hon. Joseph H. Choate, our late ambassador to Great Britain. I have not his street address, but "New York" will reach him.

My own address is Villa Albion, Bad-Nauheim. You have usually favored me with some half-dozen copies of my own articles. I shall require but one, but I am desirous that those to the gentlemen named get to them as early as possible, and I hope you may dispatch the earliest numbers available to their address.

---

1. Reference is to serialized chapters of *From Sail to Steam* which appeared in *Harpers Monthly* in February, May, August, and October 1907; and in *Harpers Weekly* for September 21 and 28, October 5, 19, and 26, November 16 and 23, and December 7, 1907.
1. "The Hague Conference: The Question of Immunity of Belligerent Merchant Shipping" appeared in the June 1907 *National Review*.
2. "The Hague Conference and the Practical Aspect of War" appeared in the *National Review* for July 1907.

To Leopold J. Maxse

Villa Albion, Bad Nauheim, Germany, April 30, 1907 [LC]

Dear Mr. Maxse: I have been rather disappointed at your change in date of publication; but, independently of the fact that the editor must be the ultimate appeal in matters concerning the interests of the Magazine, it is very likely your judgment is better as to date of issue on general principles.

I will only ask that whenever you do send out copies to any English statesmen concerned among whom I think the Secretary for Foreign Affairs should be one, copies should also be sent at least simultaneously to President Roosevelt and to Messrs Root and Choate, as before asked by me.

I see by reports in our home papers that at the recent Peace meetings there, there has been the usual misleading mixture of truth and nonsense talked—the dangerous half-truths. I could wish I had been there to puncture some of the windbags. Very possibly the hard cold sense which I flatter myself I have put in my arguments will have a better chance when the effects of the fizz-stuff have evaporated. Luckily, Roosevelt, Root, and Choate have heads as clear and hard as ice. Their hearts too are all right, especially the President's; but they dont prevent their brains from seeing both sides.

I see nowhere the argument concerning maritime capture presented on the lines I have taken. Whatever its worth, it is novel. I of course believe it is good. The trade policy is traditional, has never been thoroughly searched. I am not without hopes that I may carry conviction in influential quarters which have hitherto accepted tradition without query. For your country, to surrender the control over Germany's action, by your commanding position over her new merchant routes and shipping would be madness.

To Hugh R. Monro[1]

Bad Nauheim, May 7, 1907[2] [USNAM]

Dear Sir: Your letter of April 21 has been so long unanswered, through unavoidable conditions.

I am so heartily in sympathy with the general tenor and objects of your

---

1. Banker and philanthropist; at one time president of the American Tract Society. A devout Presbyterian, he was interested in the furtherance of religious education and ecumenism.
2. Although his letterhead read *Quogue*, Mahan was in Bad Nauheim at this time.

movement, that I can willingly give my name in the support you ask, subject to one understanding.

In the enthusiasm towards Christian comprehensiveness latterly aroused, I see many hopes and but one danger—specific danger, I mean. That danger is—how far are our movers prepared to accept as fellow workers those who deny the eternal Godhead of our Lord Jesus Christ?

In short, are Unitarians, who so deny, to be welcomed as fellow workers? If so, I for one can neither enter on such a movement, nor remain in one which I should unwittingly have joined.

In a most proper and most Christian eagerness to subordinate other points on which we differ, I fear lest the impulse may lead us to ignore this one foundation, apart from which our whole building will rest upon sand. In my apprehension, it is worse than useless to preach Christ, if we preach less than that He is the Only Begotten Son of God, Himself God.

If you can assure me that the proposed movement is confined to the Christian bodies who hold to this truth, you have my hearty acquiescence in the use of my name.

To Leopold J. Maxse

Villa Albion, Bad Nauheim, May 10, 1907 [LC]

Dear Mr. Maxse: I have just returned from mailing you corrected proofs.[1] Owing to my ignorance of German, I failed to accomplish registering; the occasional interpreter not being in the office, but I doubt not the papers will reach you. Should they not, it matters little, for the corrections, though in my judgment improvements, are not vital.

I have never fully shared the degree of your distrust of Germany. Nevertheless, it is important that Englishmen in office should appreciate how much of German carriage is done in German shipping; that this is an increasing factor; and that Great Britain by position has her hand on this. I felt some delicacy in saying this too brutally in the article, but the consideration is there clearly enough for any careful reader.

I shall write Mr. Roosevelt telling him he may expect an early copy of the article.

---

1. "The Hague Conference: The Question of Immunity of Belligerent Merchant Shipping."

To Bouverie F. Clark

Villa Albion, Bad Nauheim, May 20, 1907 [LC]

My dear Clark: When I received your letter and accompanying pamphlet of the R.N. Club, I was expecting to remain at home, and put both aside for acknowledgment and thanks in due course, as I worked through my writing. Upon this supervened suddenly a strong recommendation from my doctor to accompany the family movement to this place, which I fear is destined to be a regular annual function during the life of my wife and myself. I had not at all looked for this, however; he suddenly discovered, or at least for the first time told me, that my arteries & heart were showing signs of age & this place might help. So, although feeling quite as well as usual I packed & left April 6. The immediate effect was the necessity to concentrate on my book work etc, to leave everything ready for the printers during my absence; & letters, among which yours, had to be postponed. The physician here confirms in general terms the diagnosis, which I conceive to be that, as I am nearing sixty seven, wear and tear is evident. I must moderate my pace—literally as metaphorically; come down from the four miles per hour, I have tried to maintain, to three etc. etc. There are of course other restrictions, but none I much mind as compared with exercise.

I dont know whether you know this place. It is dull for most and crowded with cripples—like myself—bathing. The baths—at least the final ones—are like Apollinaris, in outward seeming; lively as champagne. I am loafing unutterably. Baths at 6 A.M.—so as to avoid the crowd, and the indefinite wait for one's turn. Back to bed till 10, and spend the day novel reading, of which I have a debauch, finished and current; exercise—as per prescription above—for two hours off & on, etc. Listen to the band, & view the scenery which is tranquil rolling & pretty, but not striking; just the sort to suit people compelled to keep their hearts quiet. I should have liked to remain on this side, once here; but the family plans and my own work forbid. We are to sail from Bremen June 8. It is a nuisance to have to cross the sea for these brief spells; but, while for that reason I envy the position of Europeans, I am satisfied that one great feature of benefit to us is that the ocean lies between us & our accustomed cares & vexations. Out of sight, out of mind. Your Consul General in N.Y., Sir Percy Sanderson,[1] who is just retiring, told me that head work was incompatible with Nauheim & I have found it so—the only place that so affects me. For my wife it has done wonders; not only did it restore her after a dangerous illness, but now at 55 she is more like what she was at 30 than at 40; and she has had some sharp tests in family illnesses & other worries. At one period I should never have hoped to see her again as well as she now is.

---

1. British army officer and diplomat; Consul General in New York since 1894.

As I said I am sorry that I cant get England in; the more so that three years have now passed since I was there. Traveling, as such, is for me over, at least in intention. My girls say I am getting fussy & irritable in it, which is a good sign to quit. But quiet going to a place & staying, as here, is not travel. So I still hope for the old country again.

I shall have an article in the May & June *National*,[2] should you care to read them.

Good bye my dear fellow for the present & here's to our next meeting.

To Leopold J. Maxse

Villa Albion, Bad Nauheim, May 30, 1907 [LC]

Dear Mr. Maxse: Your telegram and subsequent letter were duly received & have been the means of making for me two very pleasant and pleasing acquaintances, in Lord & Lady Northcliffe.[1] We have seen enough to size one another up, but the semi-invalid restrictions that prevail here have in part hindered us.

I am glad to learn the probable attitude of your government in the matter of maritime capture. It is particularly important at this moment, for, if I rightly understand from the papers, our own is so far committed, by putting the question among its agenda, or proponenda, in the letter of Mr. Hay, suggesting a renewal of the Conference, that I fear it can scarcely entirely withdraw it. Yet I incline to think it would not be greatly disappointed to meet an insuperable objection. The policy is with us traditional, resting partly on interest in bye gone days and conditions; partly on the misnomer "private." I believe, though I do not know, that my exposition has to some extent put the matter in a different light; and I also think there is some appreciation with us of a certain solidarity of interest between you and us, which under expedient you should not surrender the hold your position gives you over German trade-routes. No doubt can exist that, as between you and Germany, we have much more to guard against aggressive action by the latter, hence our interest in your positional opportunity to control German trade—a guarantee of peace. All this is with me matter of inference, not of knowledge. I have no inside knowledge, and I prefer not to have, in order that I may be free to speak when I write, without the fetters of confidential information. What most matters for me is not what a particular government is doing, but the accurate weighing of conditions

2. *See* Mahan to Maxse, April 15, 1907, Footnotes 1 and 2.

1. Alfred Charles William Harmsworth, 1st Viscount Northcliffe, newspaper magnate; from 1908 proprietor of *The Times* (London).

and free setting forth of the same. I believe that if this matter can be staved off this Conference, it is very doubtful if it would be renewed by us at a future one. That it should not prevail is to my mind of the utmost importance to Great Britain.

We have taken passage by steamer from Bremen June 8, and I will ask you therefore when you come to sending your honorarium, in due routine course, to remit mine to Quogue, N.Y.

In view of my failure to obtain publication in an American magazine, I have written to a publication (weekly), known as *Littell's Living Age*,[2] which for more than a half-century has reproduced (in Boston) articles from English periodicals; always giving full credit to the magazine from which copied. As I had your consent for republication of articles in the *National*, after the bloom was off, I felt sure that, in view of the importance of this question, you would approve of its being further brought before the American public. I of course do not know whether my hint will be acted on.

I wish I felt up to writing more, upon the to me menacing appearance of the Japanese questions. I think I have before told you that I thought you had made a mistake in helping drive Russia out of Manchuria. I did not then see the probability of trouble between us & J. arising where it has; but I feel strongly that with the black race question on our hands we must withstand a further yellow one. This of course implies no condonement of the blackguard conditions of San Francisco; but it does point to a time when Great Britain may have to consider her relations to Japan in the light of those to the U.S., and Australia, where the "white" feeling also prevails. But Nauheim weakens the head and I cannot write fully.

[P.S.]   I enclose a *German* pronouncement.[3]

To the Editor of The New York Times

SS *Prinzess Alice*, Southampton, June, 8, 1907[1]

It may be useful to some of your readers, especially Americans returning home, to know that the North German Lloyd Company, after assigning

---

2. Eliakim Littell founded *Littell's Living Age* in 1844. After 1896 the publication was known as *Living Age*. "The Hague Conference and the Practical Aspect of War" was reprinted in *Living Age* (July 27, 1907); and "Maritime Capture in War" in *ibid.*, (July 6, 1907). This last was titled "The Hague Conference: The Question of Immunity of Belligerent Merchant Shipping" in the June 1907 *National Review*.
3. Enclosure not found.

1. From *The New York Times*, June 15, 1907.

rooms to certain first-class passengers on the present trip of the *Prinzess Alice*, has refused to permit them to be occupied as engaged, on the ground that the particular deck, habitually first-class, was for this passage to be used for second-class accommodation.

In my own case, this decision was not made known to me until my arrival in Bremen, the day before sailing. Only by an entire reversal of plan could I escape the annoyance of accepting rooms which I knew by experience to be ill-fitted for my personal convenience and comfort.

How far the company is within its technical rights in this action is quite immaterial. The question is between it and the travelling public. These small arbitrary measures are too often passed over in silent submission. It would be interesting to know to what they may amount in the aggregate, were each one given publicity by those inconvenienced.

To Little, Brown and Company

University Club, New York, June 20, 1907 [LC]

Gentlemen: Will you kindly send me *at once*, a copy, carefully selected for a present, of the *Types of Naval Officers*.

Address: *Quogue, N.Y.*, which please also note as my address till otherwise notified.

I think mail more expeditious, probably, than express to Long Island.

I shall be greatly obliged if you will give this matter the quickest possible dispatch.

To Leopold J. Maxse

Slumberside, Quogue, Long Island, June 28, 1907 [LC]

Dear Mr. Maxse: Your letter, asking where to send the honorarium for the June article,[1] crossed one from me at Nauheim asking that it be sent to me at Quogue N.Y. Three weeks having elapsed since I left Nauheim, and not having heard, I have feared lest my mention, occurring amid several other topics of the letter may not have caught your eye; or possibly there may be something astray otherwise. In any case, remembering your invariable promptness, it seems better to mention the fact.

---

1. "The Hague Conference: The Question of Immunity of Belligerent Merchant Shipping."

I hope you will send copies of the July number[2] to the same persons as the June; but especially to our President. I regret that our Govt. has persisted in presenting the project of immunity; but I know it has felt almost bound to do so. If it should be accepted generally, especially by Great Britain, I fear it will so relieve Germany as to have a tendency to throw the U.S. toward her rather than Great Britain—which would contradict the whole of *my* life policy. Thus: Great Britain is the ally of Japan. Japan and the U.S. have a bone of contention the end of which none can see, in our resolve (like Australia & I believe New Zealand) that we will have no yellow immigration on a large scale. Weaken Great Britain by the concession of immunity, and place her also as the ally of Japan, and it is almost a sure sequitur that we incline to Germany as a counterpoise. I am glad to see Strachey has ranged the *Spectator* right, & he ought from his position on free trade to have considerable influence with your present ill-cemented Govt.

Quogue remains my address till the autumn at least. All our plans after October are of the vaguest. Our N.Y. house is rented, and we literally have no projects for the winter.

To Stephen B. Luce

Quogue, Long Island, July (8?), 1907 [LC]

My dear Admiral: I am preparing for publication some of my experiences in the Service. The work was undertaken as a pot-boiler, upon request; but in process it has engaged my interest, and in any case I always want to put my best foot foremost in writing.

I enclose two extracts, pp. 120–122, and 300–304,[1] which I ask of you the favor to read. In the first, I would like to know whether your memory contradicts mine as to the incident I have margined with blue pencil. I am quite clear, but memory sometimes plays tricks after forty years. The second extract I send mainly because I should like you to know, even beforehand, that I have never been insensible to my debt to you for my start in life; but I should gladly receive any suggestion, if you think my account of the genesis of the college inaccurate or defective.

I have not forgotten, nor discarded, your suggestion as to the revision of my strategy lectures;[2] but it has been postponed necessarily. When I shall have completed the preparation of the recollections, probably by July 15, I have another project which I wish to carry through certainly while I

---

2. "The Hague Conference and the Practical Aspect of War."

1. The latter pages contain a statement of tribute and gratitude to Luce.
2. *See* Mahan to Luce, December 15, 1906.

live,—if I can. Beyond that, while I will not commit myself, I hope to undertake the other. But there is no reason why any other younger man should not undertake the subject off his own bat. Any man's position is outlived, if not in his life time, at least after death; and I am now nearly sixty seven.

Has your attention been drawn to an article of mine in the (English) *National Review* for June on the subject of "private property" at sea in war. I have another in the July number on "The Practical Aspect of War." They have attracted almost no notice on this side of the water, but I hope they may not be without effect on the other. The subjects I know will interest you, though I cannot predict your approval of the treatment. To me this is a day of shams; I think to have exposed one in "private property." I hope also to help demolish another by showing that the avoidance of war depends not upon pious "resolutions," or conferences, but upon a change of heart in mankind. Until that occurs War is inevitable, except by the "practical" expedient of being ready for it. Our Western Coast, Australia, & New Zealand say "No yellow immigration." Japanese coolies, and others, are bent upon immigration. Has War here no practical aspect?

To Charles W. Stewart

Slumberside, Quogue, Long Island, July 8, 1907 [NA]

My dear Mr. Stewart: I have to trouble you again, and am somewhat ashamed to do so, because the necessity arises from certain memoranda which you once sent having been lost in my flittings this year. The questions are all *Navy Register*, however.

1. The numbers of the '41 date of midshipmen shown by the *Register* of 1842.

2. The numbers of the 3d Class, (my class) of acting midshipmen, shown by the *Register* of 1857.

3. (This I think is new) The roster of the officers of the frigate *United States*, Pacific Squadron, shown by the *Register* of 1843, or 1844.

I returned from Europe about a fortnight ago, and have hunted in vain for the data of 1 and 2, which I know you sent me. Others I have.

I trust you have been well in the meantime, and the Library flourishing.

To Stephen B. Luce

Slumberside, Quogue, Long Island, July 15, 1907 [LC]

My dear Admiral: Thank you for your letter. I regret that I should have given you the trouble of writing, but am relieved to have been warned off the mistaken account,[1] which I suppose is to be attributed to my mixing up interviews with you on different occasions. As for the German General Staff, I did not mean, nor I think say, that it immediately influenced either your thought or action, but that the conspicuous success attributed to it in the Wars of 1866 and 1870 had had a profound influence on all military action ever since; had imparted a momentum even where least realized. That of course is an expression of opinion, not as assertion of fact.

In all such results as the War College there is a recognizable, formal, official action, and there is also an antecedent history of exertion by individuals which does not always appear on the files. In recasting the pages I sent you I have said that to your "persistent initiative must be attributed much of the movement" that so resulted—that is, in establishing the College. If you think this is inaccurate, please notify me and I will expunge it; but if not do not trouble to write farther.

To Charles W. Stewart

Slumberside, Quogue, Long Island, July 15, 1907 [LC]

My dear Mr. Stewart: Will you kindly send me word if my recollection is right that the contract speed of the *Chicago*, in 1884, was but 15 knots.

To the Editor of The Contemporary Review

Quogue, Long Island, July 19, 1907[1]

In your issue of July, Sir John Macdonell, in his "Note on the Hague Conference," quotes me thus:—

"The object aimed at by the method of seizing vessels and cargoes at sea is to stop maritime transportation, the increase of the enemy's wealth *in* circulation. This is the essence of the matter."

As I read this I underwent some perturbation of mind. Is it possible, I asked, that in proof-reading I passed "*in* circulation?" Upon referring to the *National Review*, in which my article appeared, I found written what I meant, "*by* circulation."

---

1. Of a point connected with the founding of the Naval War College which he wished to recount in his autobiographical *From Sail to Steam*.
1. From *The Contemporary Review*, September 1907.

The increase of an enemy's wealth *in* circulation does not necessarily imply an increase in his aggregate wealth, but only a difference of proportion between that stationary and that in movement. Increase *by* circulation can mean only an increase of the total, through the process of circulation called Commerce. The whole drift of my article was that maritime Commerce increased wealth, increased the financial power of a belligerent, notoriously the sinews of war; and that to curb this by the process caricatured as "the seizure of private property" was an effective and proper belligerent method for reasons elaborated in my argument.

Having thus travestied my proposition, Sir John proceeds to this comment:—

> An obscure deliverance, not expressed in terms of ordinary political economy and not easily reconcilable with good sense. Why merely stop "wealth *in* circulation"?[2]

To this repeated misquotation I propose no reply. To the proposition "Why stop the increase of wealth *by* circulation?," I refer those interested to my article in the June *National*.

I trust you may be able to find place for this letter in your August issue.

To Stephen B. Luce

Quogue, Long Island, July 20, 1907 [LC]

My dear Admiral: Please forgive delay in replying to your very kind and flattering letter. I have had to write two controversial retorts, which I thought did not admit delay, to misrepresentations of my article contesting the prohibition of capture of (so called) private property at sea.

Before going farther, let me thank you for the copies of your two papers,[1] which have both been carefully read.

I remember very distinctly the report of the Board composed of yourself, Sampson, and Goodrich[2] though more than fifteen years have now passed since I have had occasion to refer to it. At the time of my presidency, I naturally looked more to its recommendations, as bearing upon my conduct

---

2. Macdonell agreed, in reply, that the word was *by* rather than *in* but argued that Mahan's conception of value added to wealth by circulation (commerce) was economically naive. *The Contemporary Review* (September 1907), p. 456.

1. Probably, "War Schools," U.S. Naval Institute *Proceedings*, IX (1883) and "The United States Naval War College," *The United Service Magazine* (January 1885).

2. This Board, which was called into existence by Secretary Chandler on May 30, 1884, was ordered to study the feasibility of postgraduate education for naval officers. On June 13, 1884, it recommended the establishment of the Naval War College and outlined a proposed course of study.

of affairs, than to the antecedent reasons which led to the establishment of the College. Also, this immediate precedent movement, including your report, took place while I was out of the country. Consequently, my knowledge of it was second hand; and in the course of time has evidently got mixed up with things said to me by you, after my return. E.G. The remark as to the double meaning of tactics, which to me at the time was novel.

Nevertheless, I cannot but think that my impressions, though confused as to chronology, are substantially correct in attributing to you the initiative, both in the movement leading to the College, and in my own dawning comprehension of military matters. You helped start me. Except Napier, no one else did this. The passage marked by you in your article, touching the illumination you received from Sherman, is directly in line with the remark about tactics. They show the working of your mind which underlay the movement toward the College, of which movement you were the soul.

I think I appreciate fairly well what I myself have done. That after all these years no one else has undertaken for the College the expansion of my Strategy lectures,[3] of course speaks strongly for my work. I am not acting under any private self-denying ordinance as to my own merits; upon which, however, it is not for me to dilate. I merely affirm that whatever my capacity, or my subsequent work, it was you who laid the train, in my orders, and afterwards touched it off. I don't fear but that I shall have justice enough. Indeed, I have had; and in incidents which only I know and cannot tell. But to be just all around, it is essential that your part be known. I attempted it in the pages I sent you; blunderingly, as it appears, although, as "impressionist," I fancy not far out. I have rewritten in the sense of your letter correcting my mistaken apprehensions.

[P.S.] My two articles, in *National Review*, *Littell's Living Age* republishes. Nos. July 6 and July 27 (future).

To Leopold J. Maxse

Slumberside, Quogue, Long Island, July 30, 1907 [LC]

Dear Mr. Maxse: Yesterday I received your letter of the 18th, and today from Messrs. Baring of N.Y. the second $500.00. I am sorry that the uncertainty of my whereabouts should have caused you any unusual trouble —but such things happen.

---

3. Luce had urged Mahan to update, expand, and publish his War College lectures. This, argued Luce, would more likely assure Mahan's professional reputation than the publication of many "pot-boilers." Luce to Mahan, July 15, 1907, in the Library of Congress. *See also* Mahan to Luce, December 15, 1906.

I am very glad to hear, on account both of the *National* and myself, that the articles have made a good impression. During the Conference I am taking the daily *Times*, and I see that Sir E. Satow[1] quoted them in his argument concerning immunity. I have no knowledge of Mr. Roosevelt's present views, but I greatly doubt that our Government will seriously regret the rejection. I know that some men in high political life have doubts as to the real expedience of carrying on, as a present policy, what is to us chiefly a political tradition dependent upon other times and conditions. But, in any case, I think it must be realized by our intelligent statesmen that, in the present conditions of German ambitions and German commerce, it would be suicidal madness for England or France to surrender the control their position gives over German commerce in war. I have said this here, where I thought advisable; but it will belong to your journalists to see that your people do not forget it. Our newspapers make much of the number of votes for immunity, Switzerland, Cuba, Belgium, etc. against G. B., France, Russia, Japan, etc. It is much as the votes of Rhode Island, Delaware, Nevada, etc., etc., in the U.S. Senate outweighing New York, Pennsylvania & Ohio.

As regards the Japanese question, I hope you will look beyond such blackguard performances as San Francisco,[2] and realize that Australia, and I understand Canada, are as set against Japanese *coolie* immigration as is our Pacific slope. With this view I entirely agree. Open the doors to immigration, & all west of the Rocky Mountains would become Japanese or Asiatic. It is not a question of superior or inferior race; but of races wholly different in physical get-up, and in traditions wholly separate during all time, up to a half-century ago. The problem is yours—through Canada—as much as ours; and with Australia backing Canada, Imperial Federation will be up against the question of Japanese alliance, *if* the Japanese insist upon freedom of immigration. As you know, I have never approved of your alliance, from the point of view of British interests, as I see them. Your play, as I always thought, was to favor Russia engaging herself deeply in Manchuria. Australia is probably for the moment safe, as Japanese labor will prefer not to cross the tropics, if it find America open, either with us or Canada. If Canada objects, will you, can you, insist? As for us, the Western slope is to us much as Canada and Australia to you—outlying parts of the Empire, although, unlike your colonies, federated with it. What it wishes in this matter, our Government must accept; nor do I for a moment imagine that the majority of our Eastern and Middle people would favor immigra-

---

1. Ernest Mason Satow, second British delegate to the Second Hague Conference in 1907.
2. The San Francisco Board of Education in October 1906 ordered the segregation of all Oriental pupils, an act which, combined with related anti-Japanese demonstrations, contributed to the American-Japanese war scare of 1907. The question of U.S. restrictions on Japanese immigration was a major contributor to the crisis.

tion, were the question posed on its merits. It has been little discussed; but it is chiefly our "little Englanders" in the press who favor placing Japanese immigration on the level of European.

There need not be war, unless Japan insist upon the right of immigration. If she does, there will be, sooner or later; and Great Britain will then find Canada favoring the American view.

To John S. Barnes

Slumberside, Quogue, Long Island, August 3, 1907 [NYHS]

My dear Captain Barnes: I have been much delighted by the receipt of your very pleasant letter; and the more so because my impression of the incidents I mentioned, but which I did not know at first hand, is in the main confirmed by you. I shall insert the two verses you give me, when the articles are published in book form.[1] In the magazine the editor has cut and hacked them a good deal, with the Procrustean object of fitting them to the space he can allow. Consequently, the author sees a certain mutilation of coherence, which possibly may escape the notice of a reader.

Poor dear Crosman![2] I saw a good deal of him the last fall and winter of the war, 1864–5. It was impossible not to admire a certain chivalrous daring and directness of character, despite the foible you mention and which never wholly left him. I liked and esteemed him greatly, and was sincerely grieved when I heard of his death, though we then had not met for several years.

I intend to recast the round house incident so as to bring in the more exact knowledge you have been good enough to give me. Do you see any objection to my mentioning Crosman's name, and you as authority?[3] It is not a matter of importance to ordinary readers, to whom a name will convey nothing; but possibly other naval people, ignorant like myself hitherto, may be interested in fitting the cap.

Thanking you again very heartily for the trouble you have taken in writing, believe me [etc.].

[P.S.]   The two additional verses had wholly escaped my memory.

---

1. *From Sail to Steam: Recollections of a Naval Life.* (New York: Harper Brothers, 1907), pp. 59–60.
2. Alexander Foster Crosman, class of 1855, Barnes's roommate at the Academy. He died at Greytown, Nicaragua, in April 1872, while commanding the *Kansas.*
3. *From Sail to Steam,* pp. 58–60.

To Julian S. Corbett[1]

Quogue, Long Island, August 12, 1907[2]

Acting upon my suggestion, the American publishers of my works have written, requesting permission to incorporate your article in the *Nineteenth Century*, upon the Capture of Private Property at Sea,[3] in a small book, containing certain articles of my own under the title *Neglected Aspects of War*.[4]

I preferred that this request should come to you through them, as a business proposition; but equally I am unwilling not to accompany it with an expression of keen appreciation and admiration with which I read your article at the time of its appearance. I have ventured to hope that yours and mine, coming out simultaneously, reaching the same conclusion by different paths, have reinforced and complemented one another.

It was not till some time later that the thought of book publication occurred to me. My aim is, while the memory of the Hague Conference is still fresh, to bring together, easily accessible, the arguments based upon existing international conditions, which shall awaken public attention to the inevitable part War necessarily must play in the present state of the world. Our public, busy with their private affairs, hurrahs for Peace without any reflection as to the difficulties. I think it is time for some opposition to a movement so largely represented by men like Stead and Carnegie—that is to public eye in America.

P.S.   My own articles will be: "The Practical Do [Aspect of War]." (*National*, July); "War from the Christian Standpoint";[5] and that on private property, etc.

---

1. Corbett was the author of *Drake and the Tudor Navy* (1898), *Successors of Drake* (1900), *The Campaign of Trafalgar* (1910), and *Some Principles of Maritime Strategy* (1911). He was editor of many volumes for the Navy Records Society, and a lecturer at the Royal Naval War College and at Oxford.
2. Mr. Brian Tunstall, Corbett's son-in-law, kindly hand-copied this letter for the editors from his collection of Sir Julian's papers and added editorial material.
3. "The Capture of Private Property at Sea," *Nineteenth Century* (June 1907).
4. Published as *Some Neglected Aspects of War* by Little, Brown and Company in 1907.
5. Written in November 1900 and not previously published.

To John M. Brown

Slumberside, Quogue, Long Island, August 30, 1907 [LC]

Dear Mr. Brown: I am glad to hear of the consents of Pritchett[1] and Corbett. It will be desirable for me to see their letters, *in case* they make any stipulations as to the manner in which I shall in the preface limit their responsibility to their own articles.

The time is convenient for me, as I hope to conclude the galley proof reading[2] for *Harper* by Sept 5.

To Little, Brown and Company

Quogue, Long Island, September 3, 1907 [LC]

Gentlemen: There are certain questions connected with *Neglected Aspects of War*, especially the papers of Messrs. Corbett and Pritchett, which I wish to bring up now.

1. I presume Mr. Pritchett will be willing to read proofs of his paper. If not, and also in the case of Mr. Corbett, especial care should be taken to insure accuracy of reproduction.

2. About the Title-Page. I shall make a full acknowledgement to them in the Preface; but should there not appear in the title some explicit mention?

3. If so, how? I enclose a first approximation in which I put Corbett before Pritchett, because (1) he is a foreigner, and (2) Pritchett's paper comes first in the order proposed for the articles.

4. Corbett may have some preference as to which of his works shall be attributed to him. If time admits, the question might be asked him. The list of his works (chiefly naval) will be found in an English "Who's Who."

5. Pritchett also should be designated, and his wishes followed. I should think Ex-Prest. of the Tech would please him, and convey more to purchasers; but he may have other preference.

These suggestions are purely tentative, as yet. Mr. Corbett has written a very cordial reply to my letter, but beyond his assent has expressed no wishes.

[P.S.] In Table of Contents acknowledgement of course will be made to all the Magazines concerned.

---

1. Henry S. Pritchett was President of the Massachusetts Institute of Technology, 1900–1906, and of the Carnegie Foundation for Advancement of Teaching, 1906–1930. His paper in *Some Neglected Aspects of War* was "The Power that Makes for Peace"; Corbett's was "The Capture of Private Property at Sea."
2. Of *From Sail to Steam.*

To Little, Brown and Company

Quogue, Long Island, September 5, 1907 [LC]

Gentlemen: I enclose herewith Preface to *Neglected Aspects of War*. It lacks only a final paragraph, of recognition and thanks to Messrs. Corbett and Pritchett, which I retain for the moment.

It will be well to have galley proofs sent me as soon as possible.

To Bouverie F. Clark

Slumberside, Quogue, Long Island, September 6, 1907 [LC]

My dear Clark: I have been meaning to write to you ever since my return now over two months ago; but I have been doubly busy, in that I have no longer quite the power of work I had. The Nauheim baths left me quite languid, as I found when I attempted to begin, after arrival, and it is only quite lately that this has in some measure disappeared. My physician says that the treatment there has benefited me markedly. So far, so good.

I do not understand why *Harpers* has made so little serial use of my recollections;[1] for they paid a very good price for such use. They are to appear, however, in book form some time this autumn; and as I intend you a copy dont buy one prematurely. I have written purposely for the public, not for the profession; to amuse, and if possible make the book sell. I did not and do not fancy greatly writing about myself and hope I have minimized the ego. You will probably find in it simply a phase, in another service, of the experience and anecdotes you have known in your own. The last one or two chapters are more directly personal.

Besides this, I am going to publish some of my articles under the title *Some Neglected Aspects of War*; and have obtained permission from Corbett, and from an American named Pritchett to join with them one, each, of theirs. My leading object is to provide in cheap and accessible form some of the reasons why Arbitration cannot be the panacea some of its advocates seem to think, and that there are present questions, easily recognizable, which can be settled only by War, or, what is the same thing by being so ready that the other fellow wont fight. Are there people capable of believing that the question of Japs settling in California, Australia, or British Columbia, can be settled by arbitration? Yes, there are; but such people can believe anything they like. Your government, I fear, is in a mess in

---

1. As of September 6, 1907, *Harper's Monthly* had published one chapter (August 1907) and *Harper's Weekly* none. But by December 1907, a total of ten chapters had been published in serial form, two in the *Monthly*, and eight in the *Weekly*.

British Columbia, in overriding the local desire to exclude. You will lose it, and perhaps Canada, unless you can find a way around your alliance, and authorize exclusion. British Columbia, I am sure, is thoroughly loyal now; so were the U.S. before the Stamp Act; but, if forced to accept Japanese, local sympathy on this issue will put them in line with our Pacific States, and behind the latter will stand our nation as a whole. I think, too, that Eastern Canada, when the issue becomes acute, will realize that it must back Western, or lose it. If so, there can be no doubt of the choice. Before long, I understand we have to make a new treaty with Japan,[2] and it may try to insist on the right of immigration for its coolies. This would fetch us mighty close to War. I for one, would accept war to-morrow, rather than concede a claim which would soon fill our country west of the Rockies with another race, involving interminable trouble. But I greatly mistake our countrymen if they will permit this.

I have no knowledge why our battle fleet is going to the Pacific, but believe that [it] is not in apprehension of war, but merely as a matter of practice, to encounter now the difficulties, run our heads against them, so as to know how to manage all questions of supply, should War some day come. After my concern as to permitting yellow immigration, my great anxiety is as to the effect upon our relations with you. It does seem an awful pity that your treaty[3] may force you into a position of apparent antagonism. I never believed in the treaty; not for these reasons, which I did not anticipate, but because I thought from the first that it was to the interest of G.B. to allow Russia to engage herself so deeply in Manchuria that she would have neither time nor money to spend on Constantinople or the Persian Gulf.

Well, I did not mean a political letter, but if it wake some of you up to the way things are going, it wont be amiss.

[P.S.] Of course, I am not defending mob work in San Francisco—though the J's did some of that two years ago in their own land.

To John M. Brown

Slumberside, Quogue, Long Island, September 7, 1907 [LC]

Dear Mr. Brown: I sent off this morning the concluding paragraphs to Preface;[1] since which I have received yours of yesterday:

---

2. Projected renewal of the 1894 American-Japanese Commercial Treaty in which Japan had accepted the U.S. right arbitrarily to regulate Japanese immigration in conformity with national law.
3. The Anglo-Japanese Treaty of 1902.
1. To *Some Neglected Aspects of War.*

I quite agree that "Lectures in History &c" would be the best thing to append, subject to Mr. Corbett's approval; and I would suggest enclosing in the letter a copy of the paragraph from the preface, relieving him of responsibility.

I have assumed that you have the consents of the *Atlantic* and *Nineteenth Century*, as well as of the two writers.

To John M. Brown

Quogue, Long Island, September 7, 1907 [LC]

My dear Mr. Brown: I enclose herewith, additional to the Preface, of which copy has already been sent, the final paragraphs of acknowledgement. Upon this particularly I wish your comment or amendment.

As regards time of publication, I have no wishes; unless, from the ethics of the publishing business, Harper's book, being first contemplated and engaged, should be conceded priority. The subject matter of the two is so entirely different that there can be no collision between them. Harper has intended to publish in October, by my last information. I have read about half the page-proof.

I would be glad if one or two of your firm, or discreet employees, would read, in Preface, the anonymous letter and my comments, there introduced. I have feared a little that these may be bad taste; the intrusion of too much personal element. Yet the fact and the comment are both pertinent.

Farragut (by Appleton) and *Sea Power in French Revn.* both appeared in the same season.

To Samuel A. Ashe

Slumberside, Quogue, Long Island, September 9, 1907 [DUL]

My dear Ashe: To communicate a death is perhaps a doubtful reason for a letter; but if I am right in thinking that Jeff Slamm was your room-mate during the fourth class year of the '55 Date, you may be interested still to know that I have seen his death, on August 3, in the Puget Sound country. To you, of course, he must now be among the most distant of memories; to me only somewhat less so, but for two years we were messmates on board the *Congress*, 1859–1861, since which time I also have never seen him. His father was purser of her, and had influence enough to get him the position of master's mate; as which he did midn's duty. He was a man of no mark, either in character or intellect, but a good fellow. He remained in the navy as a volunteer till after the War of Secession, and then was appointed in the Revenue Marine, in which he passed his life. You will recall my sending you some information obtained through him of our old classmates.

One other of these has died recently, Farquhar. I had gone abroad for some baths in the spring, and it was during my absence, I think, that his death occurred. There now remain in the Navy only Kane, Remey, and myself, & I believe I have heard the deaths of all who graduated, except Hall, of whom I have known nothing since I left him Consul at Nice, in 1894.

Since I saw you last fall, the doctors have discovered that my heart and arteries are deteriorated. This apparently means as yet merely that I must live more quietly as to exertion; but the very fact of abandoning the somewhat violent exercise to which I had accustomed myself has let me down, as regards the general plane of vigorous action upon which I have lived till last March. All this, however, is but the common lot of man, and at your and my age we must slack up on the racket.

My kind regards to the young ladies, your daughters, of whom I retain very pleasant recollections.

To Little, Brown and Company

University Club, New York, September 11, 1907 [LC]

Gentlemen: I shall be at the above address for the rest of this week; so it will be best, should any proof remain to be sent to send it here. I will notify you duly in case of change.

I received first installment last night. As regards the papers of Pritchett and Corbett, I must throw myself absolutely on the proof readers for accuracy.

To John M. Brown

University Club, New York, September 20, 1907 [LC]

My dear Mr. Brown: I have mailed to day under separate cover, the galleys containing "War from the Christian Standpoint"; and I will mail tomorrow the Preface to our proposed book.[1]

---

1. *Some Neglected Aspects of War.*

These two papers stand first, in my estimation of the need for revision and correction; and I have wanted therefore to get them first back, so that, if possible, I might read them under their altered form.

This applies particularly to "War from Christian Standpoint," because that defends a central part of my thesis.

Upon it, as it goes back revised, I wish two points impressed on the proof reader and printer:

1. That I have made War to spell with a capital, where, and only where, I have used it in a *general* sense.

2. The marginal notes in *red ink* are all *foot-notes*, references to the Bible in support of the statements.

Should it be possible, without further expense, to set up these pages, or corrected galleys, and get them to me by Wednesday next, I could give a final (page proof) reading; and should the above be impossible, I will ask only that the proof-readers give special care to these two papers, that my meaning be rendered.

If possible, I will correct galleys of my three other articles; but, if I dont, they can go just as they stand in the Magazines. I shall not attempt to touch those of Pritchett or Corbett.

To Little, Brown and Company

University Club, New York, September 21, 1907 [LC]

Gentlemen: I mailed you yesterday corrected galleys of "War from Christian Standpoint," with letter of advice & requests; and I have today mailed corrected galleys of "Preface."

As I said yesterday, these two alone I proposed carefully to scrutinize. *I should be glad to hear from you the receipt of the corrected proofs.* The other articles of my own I will read as I can, & forward; but they can be published as they stand, subject only to careful reading by your proof readers.

To John M. Brown

University Club, New York, September 23, 1907 [LC]

My dear Mr. Brown: I have succeeded today in reading and correcting two of the remaining articles: "The Moral Aspect," and "The Practical Aspect"—of War. I have not revised, as may be seen; only corrected. To-

[229]

morrow I hope I may send "The Question of Immunity for Belligerent Merchant Shipping," but if I fail it remains, as of the two sent today, that with care by proof reader, my reading is unnecessary. But what shall I say when the proof reader passes "normal" for "moral"?

I would suggest that, not only in the Table of Contents, but also at the heading of each article in the *body of the book* should appear the name of the Magazine, & the *date*. I am led to urge this because I find, in "Moral Aspect," a censorious allusion to Russian Finland, in 1899, which might carelessly be taken to be pointed at Japan in Korea, 1907. I have guarded against this by a foot note, but I think my suggestion also good.

In the use of capitals I find consistency difficult, but I have had reasons throughout.

Should an operation be decided on,[1] I go to the hospital Wednesday—after which no work till discharged.

[P.S.]   Articles will be mailed with this.

To Little, Brown and Company

University Club, New York, September 23, 1907 [LC]

Gentlemen: I cannot recall whether I called your attention to the enclosed "Contents" not giving the *name* of the Magazine, and the *date* of *issue*, for the several articles.

As I shall not be able to attend to any business for the next three weeks, I ask your special care to the due acknowledgments.

I have also written Mr. J. M. Brown to say, that for reasons assigned, I think the same acknowledgment better inserted at the head of each article in the body of the book.

[P.S.]   I take for granted that a copy of the book will be sent to Messrs. Pritchett & Corbett, at the same time as those to me.

To Samuel A. Ashe

University Club, New York, September 23, 1907 [DUL]

My dear Ashe: I have no time to do more than tell you that I will not be in Richmond this year. I am just about to put myself in the doctors' hands

---

1. A prostatectomy.

for a pretty severe course of treatment, involving an operation which will keep me quiet & off all duty for the better part of a month. In any event I was not a delegate to this Convention,[1] though nearly elected despite myself, which happened once before.

Kindest regards to the young ladies, whom I remember always with pleasure [etc.].

To Little, Brown and Company

University Club, New York, September 24, 1907 [LC]

Gentlemen: I am sending you today the corrected galleys of the last of my articles: Question of Immunity for Belligt. Shipping. This completes my revisions. Under the same wrapper I send the galleys of Messrs. Pritchett and Corbett, as read by your proof readers, and the text of the latter's article from the *Nineteenth Century*, as requested by you.

I regret I cannot find the *Atlantic* "copy" of Mr. Pritchett's article, and fear I have destroyed it.

I have not attempted myself to read either of the other gentlemen's proofs; but am glad that I have been able to read all my own.

The further management of the matter I must now leave in your hands, having made I believe, all the suggestions that occur to me.

To Little, Brown and Company

Lawrence, Long Island,[1] October 28, 1907 [LC]

Gentlemen: I received yesterday yours of Oct. 25, with enclosures. I entirely agree with you that we should not print the article without Knowles's[2] consent.

Should that not meanwhile be received, I should strongly urge that in communicating the necessary decision to Mr. Corbett, you send him a copy

---

1. The Annual Convention of the Protestant Episcopal Church, which Mahan had previously attended as an elected layman in the House of Delegates.

1. The Mahans rented a house in Lawrence in which they lived during the winters of 1907–1911. The West 86th Street house was leased again, to 1911.

2. Sir James Thomas Knowles, founder and editor of *Nineteenth Century*. Little, Brown and Company had approached Corbett directly for permission to reprint his "The Capture of Private Property at Sea" which had originally appeared in *Nineteenth Century* in June 1907. Knowles, annoyed, withheld consent for a short time.

[231]

of yours to Knowles. Yours is entirely the letter of a gentleman, full and explicit as to an action evidently clear of any willing discourtesy or disregard of rights of another; the more noticeable that you had before you his extremely provocative language. That of Sir James is such as a gentleman might write in anger, but could not but recall after your clear explanation. That he has not done so is excusable only on the score of illness or insanity. He could reject, without yielding his property rights.

The omission of Corbett's article need in no way affect Pritchett's; retain it by all means.

The only changes I see necessary are 1, in the pagination, shifting my last article to where his [is]; 2, the change on the title page; 3, in the Preface, from which I must either eliminate allusion to Corbett, or say that "owing to unexpected obstacles we have been unable to include &c &c," but that I recommend it to those interested in the question treated. I incline to the latter, but would like your opinion. My desire is to educate public opinion in a matter wherein it is uninstructed.

It will be well to send me *page* proof of Preface, for I can thus make changes which will leave pagination unaffected.

I have some indistinct recollection of seeing in English newspapers the question of property right between author and magazine judicially determined. My impression is that it remains with author; the publisher has it only for the publication, he has no property right except for the magazine issue. This of course is too vague for any certainty.

My own opinion would favor waiting till Thursday to hear from Knowles. Not hearing, I should write Corbett, by Saturday's steamer, and proceed with book without him.

But send me Preface at once. I am still too weak for steady work, but can do odd jobs.

To Bouverie F. Clark

Lawrence, Long Island, October 31, 1907 [LC]

My dear Clark: A few days ago I mailed you a copy of my reminiscences, which the publishers have called *From Sail to Steam*; a title I accepted, but did not originate. You will find in it little new. My aim was to be readable for the general public, & to a certain extent to contravene erroneous ideas about naval matters, which are more dangerous in our country than in yours, except when we have a man like Roosevelt, who really has sound military ideas.

Since writing you last, I have had to undergo a severe surgical operation, which kept me four weeks in hospital, whence I only emerged a week ago. I am still weak and somewhat sore;[1] but the general gain is obvious, and I am led to hope for complete restoration by the new year. Of course, at sixty-seven, recuperation is slower than once; but my progress, now that I am at home and in country air, is indisputable.

Still, I have to limit my writing, the more that my arrears of correspondence is large. I am slowly working it off. My address till May is as at the head of the letter. I doubt if we shall ever again live in New York. Our house is satisfactorily rented for three years more, and I am here only a little over an hour from my club.

With regards & best wishes [etc.].

To John P. Merrell[1]

Lawrence, Long Island, November 16, 1907 [NWC]

My dear Merrell: About eighteen months ago—I being then abroad—I received a letter from Sperry, asking that I should put in writing some account of the early fortunes of the College while I was president. This I said I would do, when I could find leisure. I then was beginning some Reminiscences for Harpers;[2] and meaning in them to say something about my assocation with the College, I thought the same data would in great measure fill the account which Sperry wished, as I understood for the College records.

I can now undertake the paper,[3] and write to ask if there be any particulars upon which you would wish me to touch especially, as my memory serves.

To Stephen B. Luce

Lawrence, Long Island, November 18, 1907 [LC]

My dear Admiral: Your experience of duty pay on the retired list is governed by the fact that you retired as a R.A.; and consequently you have not run up against the fact—as I have—that an officer retired & promoted, if assigned to duty, gets the duty pay only of the grade held before retirement,

---

1. Mahan's prostatectomy was complicated by adhesions which required further surgery early in December 1907.

1. Admiral Merrell, class of 1867, was President of the Naval War College.
2. *From Sail to Steam.*
3. *See* Paper, "Reminiscences of Service at the Naval War College," March 24, 1908.

in my case Captn. My duty pay as Captn. is just the same as my retired pay as R.A. Being ignorant of this canny provision, when I was promoted last Dec, taking rank from June, I supposed I would get the difference between R.A. & Captn's duty pay for those months, during which I had been on unsolicited duty.[1] The Paym. at the N.Y. yard referred my claim & it was decided as I tell you; so I got nothing except the allowance for quarters &c during the period. Nor should I, if ordered to the College.

While it is possible that the duty pay of R.A. would decide me, if wavering, I am certain I would not be deterred from the work you suggest, had I completed that of which I spoke before. You have misunderstood me, or I have unwittingly misled you, if you have thought *From Sail to Steam* the work that stood in the way. I do not wish you to mention it, but I had in view the collating and systematizing a number of thoughts on religious subjects which had occurred to me, and which I have imagined fit for modern "difficulties."[2] I was very full of this when you first wrote me; at present I am greatly discouraged, my own practical piety having broken down miserably under some recent troubles, so that I doubt my fitness. Yet I am loath not to try. Just now I am recovering from a very severe operation, which kept me in hospital four weeks; and while my general health is nearly restored, the local troubles persist obstinately, taking out of me life and energy through persistent disappointment.[3] While in hospital, I was greatly excited & enraged by the Sims comments on the movement of the fleet to the Pacific; and receiving soon after a request from the *Scientific American* to write an article on the subject, I was able to do so.[4] Beyond this I have done nothing, and am doing little but lie on the sofa and read novels.

In short, as soon as my mind regains its tone I want to undertake the work of which I spoke. If I finish it, or when I abandon it, I see now no reason why I should not next undertake the Revision of the Strategy Lectures.[5] I shall do it chiefly from a feeling of duty, dependent upon your opinion of the value of the work; and I recognize that some one ought to do it. But you will recognize that to bring the treatment down to date will require a great deal of reading and thought, and books which I suppose the College may supply, at least in part.

---

1. Mahan was placed in active duty status from July 1, 1906, to December 11, 1906, for the purpose of writing a brief account of the activities of the Naval War Board in 1898.
2. This project became *The Harvest Within: Thoughts on the Life of a Christian*, which Little, Brown and Company published in 1909.
3. *See* Mahan to Clark, October 31, 1907, Footnote 1.
4. "The Value of the Pacific Cruise of the U. S. Fleet," *Scientific American* (December 11, 1907). Reprinted in *Naval Administration and Warfare* (Boston: Little, Brown and Company, 1908).
5. *See* Mahan to Luce, July 20, 1907.

To Stephen B. Luce

Lawrence, Long Island, December 3, 1907[1] [LC]

My dear Adm'l. Luce: Mr. Mahan rec'd your letter on Sunday and was able to smile a little as I read it to him between the paroxysms of pain. He has suffered so intensely for the past two weeks that the surgeon said there was nothing for it but to submit to a second operation. The first wound had healed in such a peculiar way (very unusual they say) that it formed an almost impassable barrier and the last state was worse than the first. They operated yesterday afternoon—he stood it wonderfully well, quite remarkable when one considers the intense agony of the past fortnight, passed quite a comfortable night and is much refreshed this morning, and is so happy to be free from the dreadful pains; he says, tho' it might not be comfortable to another man, to him it is bliss to lie on his back & doze and feel he is not to be roused by pain. It is a trial to him of course to have the dressings changed, but it does not last long & is not very frequent.

Forgive the length of this epistle but I thought you would like to know about Mr. M—— and would wonder that you did not hear from him.

With love for Mrs. Luce, Mrs. Noyes and Mrs. Walter I am [etc.].

To Stephen B. Luce

Lawrence, Long Island, December 12, 1907 [LC]

My dear Adm'l Luce: Thank you very much for your letter—I read it to my husband, but I dont think he at all grasped the contents—his brain is very weak, at times clouded and wandering. Today, however, he really seems more like himself than since the operation, and is much quieter than he has been—he does not suffer except from debility and general misery, but he is very unhappy most of the time.

I feel sure he *will* like to see what the author of *La Guerre Sur Mer*[1] has to say about him when he is able to read—but that will not be for some time yet. Thank you very much for offering to send him the book.

With very kind regards for you all, in which Mr. Mahan would join did he know I am writing, believe me to be [etc.].

---

1. Both this and the following letter are signed "Ellen L. Mahan."

1. Gabriel Darrieus, *La guerre sur mer, stratégie et tactique. La doctrine.* Paris: Challamel, 1907. Translated as *War on the Sea*, by Philip R. Alger. Annapolis: U.S. Naval Institute, 1908.

To Stephen B. Luce

Lawrence, Long Island, January 27, 1908 [LC]

My dear Admiral: Your kind letter of inquiry to Mrs. Mahan was recd. yesterday, and I answer in person, that you may see I have so far progressed towards recovery. I am still confined to two rooms, which together afford me a promenade of about fifty feet. There was talk of my getting out for a walk last week, but the snow has stopped that for some time. It is four months to day since my first operation, which, had it run in normal course, would have left me well by this; but, as it has panned out, I have had a dead beat, head wind and lee tide. I think a few more tacks will fetch, but dont expect full restoration before spring gives good weather.

With you I have watched interestedly the course of naval affairs since the beginning of the Brownson imbroglio.[1] In my judgment the President, confident in his knowledge of naval matters and of his profound interest in the service, has made the grave mistake, since Moody, of filling the Secretary's chair with figureheads, expecting to run the machine himself.[2] Necessary result, hasty and mistaken decisions, for the Navy is now so big a thing as to demand the sole attention of a first class man for a full official term. No man can run it and the Presidency together. The letters to Brownson, or about him, should never have been written by any one but the Secy., though the President might have seen them. With reference to the merchant skipper for the hospital ship, has any one recalled the behavior of the transport captains off Santiago, as stated by Chadwick (*Encyc. Am.*)?[3]

---

1. W. H. Brownson resigned as Chief of the Bureau of Navigation because President Roosevelt upheld a recommendation of Surgeon General Presley M. Rixey (also his personal physician) that surgeons be assigned to the command of hospital ships. During the same week, on December 27, 1907, Roosevelt removed Brownson from a joint Army and Navy Board which was then debating the fortification of Subig Bay rather than Cavite, and replaced him with Captain R. Wainwright. Since the latter was at sea, the Navy's position in the Philippine fortification debate was weakened. Early in January, Roosevelt publicly characterized Brownson's letter of resignation as "unseemly and improper," and "injurious to the service," and appointed Captain John E. Pillsbury, class of 1867, as his replacement at the Bureau. Sims was accused by the *New York Tribune* of endorsing and supporting Rixey's proposal, an allegation which he publicly denied. "A Review of the Naval Situation," *The Navy* (January 1908) gives an excellent account of the Brownson resignation and removal, with a chronology and all pertinent correspondence.
2. W. H. Moody was Secretary of the Navy from 1902 to 1904. He was followed by Paul Morton in 1904; Charles J. Bonaparte in 1905; Victor H. Metcalf in 1906; and Truman H. Newberry in 1908.
3. "Great difficulty was experienced through the wretched conduct of many of the transport captains who were under no proper control and wandered over the sea at will. Hours were spent in finding some of them and when found they would insist upon lying miles from a shore which they could have approached with safety within a ship's length." From French E. Chadwick, "*United States—War with Spain,*" *Encyclopedia Americana*, 1927 edition.

[236]

I trust you and Little may long scan the papers in vain for your detachments.

Kind remembrances to Mrs. Luce [etc.].

To William H. Rideing

Lawrence, Long Island, March 2, 1908 [NDL]

Dear Mr. Rideing: I kept no copy of my letter to the Ed *Windsor Mag*,[1] but my recollection is that, he having written that I probably knew that the article was to be republished there, I replied that I had no such knowledge.

I think I scarcely could have said "there is no reason" etc., for I had had experience of McClure selling an article of mine in like manner. I was wholly indifferent in *this*. What I did object to was the having proof sent me to read; for I considered my work done, & did not choose to accept the implication that I was in any way bound to correct again. I said this with great distinctness, but not in my opinion rudely.

At your request, I have written the Editor, disclaiming any such contestation of your rights. As to the "apology" suggested by the Author's Syndicate, that is of course out of the question unless I see my letter again & recognize in it just cause for apology.

To George B. Balch

Lawrence, Long Island, March 4, 1908 [UNC]

It was very pleasant to me to see again, after so long a time, your well remembered signature, and to see in the firmness of your hand how well you are carrying the years to which you have attained.[1] I wish you many more of happiness.

Immense indeed has been the progress, as well outside as within the Navy, of the period since we were shipmates in the old *Pocahontas*. The publishers wanted to call my book "The Old Navy and the New"; but I refused, for I said I have had nothing to do with the *new* Navy, the Navy of

---

1. *Windsor Magazine*: An Illustrated Monthly for Men and Women. London, 1–90, 1895–1936. The details of the issue discussed in this letter are obscure.

1. Admiral Balch, then eighty-eight years old, wrote Mahan a letter on February 27, praising *From Sail to Steam*, and thanking him for his "commendatory notices" in it. In 1861 Balch had relieved Drayton as commanding officer of the *Pocahontas*.

to day. I did witness the transition from sail to steam; but my last command, though so late as 1895 (the *Chicago*) is already *old* navy.

Though much younger than yourself, the fleeting years have brought me almost within touching distance of the Psalmists term of life. I was sixty seven my last birthday.

With much regard, and renewal of my prayers for many happy years, believe me, my dear Admiral [etc.].

To John P. Merrell

Lawrence, Long Island, March 13, 1908 [NWC]

My dear Merrell: Immediately after writing you in October, I began writing the Recollections of my experience.

Unfortunately, I had no sooner started when I was taken ill, and throughout the winter have been unable for serious headwork.

Though not yet fully restored, I have now completed the account, which I enclose in rough draft, trusting that you can have it copied in typewriting and sent back to me for revision and signature.[1]

Concerning this draft one explanation is needed. When the word "over" appears as an insertion, the reference is to the back of the page, where, according to a habit of long standing with me I have made an insertion too long to be put on the front.

To Little, Brown and Company

Lawrence, Long Island, March 13, 1908 [LC]

Gentlemen: You will probably have seen the enclosed,[1] which is as "unexpected" to me as to the publishers in England.

The occasion prompts me to ask if you have received any notices of the book which you could permit me to see.

---

1. The final version did not differ substantially from the draft enclosed with this letter. *See* Paper, "Reminiscences of Service at the Naval War College," March 24, 1908.

1. A notice from the British publication *The Publisher's Circular*, February 29, 1908, which announced that owing to the "unexpected demand" for Mahan's *Some Neglected Aspects of War* further copies could not be supplied by the publishers until March 7.

To John M. Brown

Lawrence, Long Island, April 6, 1908 [LC]

Dear Mr. Brown: I am glad to know you have succeeded in your arrangement with the new Sampson Low people, come-down though it is pecuniarily. I have rather a distaste for them, owing to their persistent grumbling over *1812*. The deal had been made before they took over the business, and was part of their bargain in so doing. Why then whimper? Natural, but absurd. They are, too, narrow in refusing the separate publication, after now ten years, of my paper in the *Nav. Histy. of G.B.* I have not, of course, the business experience to judge certainly; but I believe the advertisement the separate publication would give would outweight any possible injury to a book, so huge in size and cost that all individuals & libraries likely to require it must now have it. It can only be a book of reference, & I doubt its being first rate as that. Their tone seemed to me more colored by sulkiness over *1812*, than by candid estimate of the separate publication.

My health is nearly restored, but there is an element of uncertainty still as to permanency.

To Stephen B. Luce

Lawrence, Long Island, April 6, 1908 [LC]

My dear Admiral: Thank you very much for your kind letter of congratulation. I am very much better, and able to do most things as before, but have not yet full health or weight, and what is worse am not *sure* that I am quite out of the woods.

I have seen the first installment of Alger's translation of Darrieus's book,[1] in the N.I. *Proceedings*, but not yet the book itself. As regards Custance's book,[2] I was in correspondence with him while its contents were appearing serially in *Blackwood's*, and he modified my already adverse views on armored cruisers to worse, in the article I contributed to the Nav. Institute.[3] When the book was published he sent through me a copy to Mr. Roosevelt.

With kind remembrances to Mrs. Luce, and to your daughters, if either are with you, from Mrs. Mahan & myself [etc.].

1. *See* Ellen L. Mahan to Luce, December 12, 1907, Footnote 1.
2. Sir Reginald Neville Custance, *The Ship of the Line in Battle*. Edinburgh: W. Blackwood & Sons, 1904–1905.
3. "Reflections, Historic and Other, Suggested by the Battle of the Sea of Japan."

To James Ford Rhodes

Lawrence, Long Island, April 8, 1908 [MHS]

My dear Mr. Rhodes: The enclosed explains itself. I have written on the back the names of the Committee on Admissions,[1] as far as known to me; one third having gone off in March, and their replacers I dont know.

I have not been able to find on the lists of members of the Club any that I knew to be acquaintances of yours; while in the matter of knowing members of the Committee, I myself know but one, Hobart Porter.

I am obliged therefore to await some word from you. Should you be in Boston, please reply speedily, for I am at present ignorant whether you have returned from abroad. Should this reach you abroad, I will have done meanwhile what I can in your interest.

To Charles W. Stewart

Lawrence, Long Island, April 9, 1908 [NA]

My dear Mr. Stewart: I have been appointed a member of a Committee on Documentary Historical Publications of U.S. Govt., working under the Com. on Department Methods. Our business is to consider the question of unpublished documents, and to make recommendations as to which should be published.

To me has fallen the naval portion of this job, one part of which is to state what has already been published.[1] In this connection, I have received Van Tyne and Leland's "Guide to the Archives,"[2] in which I find mention of Neeser's forthcoming book *Statistical and Chronological History of U.S. Navy*. If you have a copy of this, can you send it to me for the purposes named?

This work, though initiated by the Am. Histl. Assn., has been adopted by the Govt., by which Mr. Ford[3] of the Congl. Library has been named Chairman.

---

1. Of the University Club. The names listed are: O. H. Payne, H. L. Terrell, E. F. Baldwin, all of New York, T. J. Coslidge, and James H. Crafts.

1. Frederick Jackson Turner agreed to do the same for U.S. economic and social history. *See* Mahan to Turner, May 9, 1908.

2. C. H. Van Tyne and W. G. Leland, *Guide to the Archives of the Government of the United States in Washington*. Washington, D.C.: Carnegie Institute, 1904.

3. Worthington Chauncey Ford, Chief of the Division of Manuscripts, Library of Congress. Ford was assigned the task of making recommendations on the publication of documents in the areas of U.S. finance, banking, currency, and foreign commerce.

To James Ford Rhodes

Lawrence, Long Island, April 11, 1908 [MHS]

My dear Mr. Rhodes: I had forgotten that Sloane was your seconder, but in the event of your being abroad I had decided to write him on the matter. He has a much larger acquaintance than I, and I am glad to hear of what he has undertaken.

I may possibly see you in New York, though I cant speak certainly. I am living an hour out of town, and this winter has been to me one of serious illness consequent upon a succession of operations—thrice under anaesthetics. I am now in pretty good shape but very quiet; go to town once a week, for the day, and returning early. Of course, at my age, past sixty seven, I can hope for only a fair share of vigor, and that I hope to regain.

To James C. Young[1]

Lawrence, Long Island, April 13, 1908 [YUL]

Dear Sir: I have received a notification from Adams Express, 2753 ½ Broadway, N.Y., that they have a package for me, weight 16 oz.

I do not know whether this can be *From Sail to Steam*, the dispatch of which you notified me; the more so that you lately recd a letter from me from *here*, and I have therefore no reason to suppose that you would send to my former address in N.Y. But as the book has not reached me I think best to write you, as perhaps you may have sent by express and to N.Y.

To John M. Brown

Lawrence, Long Island, April 17, 1908[1] [LC]

My dear Mr. Brown: In your last letter you said you would like to hear if I had any plans. At the moment I had nothing immediate; but it has since occurred to me that the following six magazine articles have never been published:

---

1. A Minneapolitan bibliophile who collected autographed books by celebrated living authors. *See* Mahan to Young, April 28, 1908.

1. This was Mahan's last letter to Brown, who died April 28, 1908, at age 66.

Monroe Doctrine	*National Review*	End of 1902 or beginning of 1903
Russo-Japanese War	" "	Sep. 1904
"	" "	April or May/06
Naval Administration (British)	" "	May (?) 1903
" (U.S.)	*Scribner's*	"
The Strength of Nelson.	*Natl. Review*	November, 1905

I think they would bear republication, because the treatment is so general, deals so with *principles*, that they are as useful now as when written.

I am not sure whether I have, at Quogue, copies of all these. I am quite sure I have of some, but fear others are packed with my New York books. I would suggest therefore, if you could conveniently send to the Public Library, and ascertain if—on a pinch—they could be obtained from there. If you will let me know about this, I will, when I go to Quogue, about May 10, write to Maxse to see if he can supply me missing numbers. Please send me *dates* of each, as my own (above) are from memory only.

To John S. Billings

Lawrence, Long Island, April 20, 1908 [NYPL]

Dear Sir: I enclose herewith a clipping (blue pencil) from the N.Y. *Sun*, in which I have neglected to note the *year* of the issue.[1]

The date otherwise is (from the reverse side of the clipping) about January 20; and I am reasonably certain it is within the last 3 years.

If not too much trouble, may I ask that the year be ascertained from your bound volumes of the *Sun*, and marked in colored pencil on the clipping itself. I enclose stamped envelope for return.

To H. M. Lydenberg

Lawrence, Long Island, April 23, 1908 [NYPL]

Dear Sir: I beg to thank you for your prompt and kind reply to my recent inquiry.

---

1. The enclosure was not found, but its correct date was January 20, 1907. H. M. Lydenberg to Mahan, April 23, 1908, in the New York Public Library. Lydenberg was Assistant to Billings.

To James C. Young

My dear Sir: Shortly after dispatching to you *From Sail to Steam*, I picked up the card of "requirements," which had accompanied your letter of advice.

This card being undated, I cannot affirm that I never before saw it; but certainly I never before read it so carefully as to appreciate the contents.

If you will carefully weigh its wording, I think you can scarcely fail to perceive that such expressions as "to *entitle* a book to a place in my literary collection," "it is *required*," the frequent repetition of "*should*," convey an entirely erroneous conception of the relation between yourself and the authors, of whom you ask the favor which you so often have of me.

The clear implication, the natural meaning of the words, is that entrance into "your literary collection" is a privilege, which you dispense to authors upon requirements laid down by you.

Such language is inconsistent with the respect due to those of whom you have asked a favor. In my own case compliance with your requests has been due always to a good natured wish to comply with what I looked upon as a fad; a compliance in which, so far from seeing a privilege, I recognized only a momentary trouble which I would gladly have been spared.

I think you would do well to recast your card. Had I appreciated the spirit its words indicate, I certainly never would have conceded your requests.

To Leopold J. Maxse

Slumberside, Quogue, Long Island, May 7, 1908 [LC]

My dear Mr. Maxse: I am purposing to publish this fall a collection of some half-dozen articles,[1] most of which have appeared in the *National*; but on overhauling my files, I find two are missing, viz: The Monroe Doctrine, which appeared in February, 1902, and one on the Russo-Japanese War in September, 1904. I do not know whether your method of preserving back numbers is such as to make *convenient* to you to furnish me duplicates of these. Should it be entirely convenient, I should be greatly helped; but I beg that you will not allow yourself to be inconvenienced, as copies can be made from bound volumes in our libraries, if not otherwise procurable.

---

1. *Naval Administration and Warfare. Some General Principles.* Boston: Little, Brown and Company, 1908.

Since you last heard from me I have undergone prolonged illness, consequent upon a series of operations. This has entailed full five months of entire inactivity, mentally; a period which enabled me to read the *National* more exhaustively than I usually am able to do. I must congratulate you upon the recent successes of your party, which I can do the more heartily because I think in preferential tariff and incidental protection you have the right of the matter. You are not Balfourist; but he has a happy knack at phrasing, and he defined for himself a point of view which is absolutely mine. Like him, I am a free trader by conviction; but in these times Englishmen who want free trade must come down into the arena, & fight for it with the weapon of protection and retaliation. The world is protectionist.

I am now substantially recovered, and am taking up my work again, embarrassed by heavy arrears; rather, I should say, by the necessity of doing as rapidly as may be work which ought to have been done during my enforced idleness.

To Frederick Jackson Turner[1]

Quogue, Long Island, May 9, 1908[2] [LC]

It appears to me that first in utility *at present* would be the collection and publn. of data bearing upon the manner in which national resources have been used, are being used; with estimates of their present value; water power &c.

A prominent impression made upon me by this Report is the impossibility of a Govt. doing more than supplement the labors of the *private* investigator. No Govt. scheme can supply the *interest* of the hobbyist.

To Little, Brown and Company

Slumberside, Quogue, Long Island, May 9, 1908 [LC]

Gentlemen: I have yours of May 7, with enclosures, & beg to thank you for the information contained.

---

1. American historian, professor at the University of Wisconsin, 1885–1910, and at Harvard, 1910–1924, best known for his work on the significance of the frontier in U.S. history.
2. These comments are marginalia on page 1, Part I, Preliminary Report of Professor Turner, Committee on the Documentary Historical Publications of the United States Government, May 9, 1908. *See* Mahan to Stewart, April 9, 1908.

I have no difficulty in acceding to the wishes of Messrs. Chatto and Windus,[1] on the understanding of acknowledgement, as expressed by them.

The two articles you mention—South African War and Persian Gulf—have already been republished in *Retrospect and Prospect*.

As I wrote before, I have thought of republishing a short article of perhaps 3,000 words on the recent voyage of our fleet to the Pacific,[2] and it has since occurred to me that my address as President of the Amn. Histl. Assn., on "Subordination in Historical Treatment," in 1902, might bear re-issue. It will number about 5,600 words. With your estimate of six articles, sent me, this would total about 62,000 words. I think likely, by the 1st June, when I may hear from *Natl. Review*, I may think of something else.

To Charles W. Stewart

Slumberside, Quogue, Long Island, May 16, 1908 [NA]

My dear Mr. Stewart: I am intending to republish certain of my articles this fall; and among others one of which I have no copy, but believe to be in the Nav. Institute *Proceedings* of 1892, or 1893.[1] It was delivered at the War College in the late summer of /92.

If you find it to be in the Institute *Proceedings*, could you loan me the volume to have a copy made, for the purpose I mention.*

As I am writing, I may add a request I should otherwise postpone: to be informed as to the published information concerning the Russo-Jap War, especially the *official naval* accounts. Adml. Luce has been urging me to revise and publish the Lectures on Naval Strategy delivered at the War College twenty years ago, bringing the illustrations down to date, including our war with Spain & the other.

Many books and narratives had been published, but so far as known to me official Japanese data are much to seek. I dont yet know where Togo headquartered his fleet while watching the Russians in Port Arthur.

*If you should prefer to have a copy made instead of sending the volume.

---

1. A British publishing house.
2. "The Value of the Pacific Cruise of the U.S. Fleet, 1908. Prospect," *Scientific American* (December 7, 1907), and "The Value of the Pacific Cruise of the U.S. Fleet, 1908. Retrospect," *Collier's Weekly* (August 28, 1908) were both reprinted in *Naval Administration and Warfare. Some General Principles.* The book also contained "Subordination in Historical Treatment" under its alternate title "Writing of History."
1. "The Practical Character of the United States Naval War College," U.S. Naval Institute *Proceedings* (June 1893).

To Edward L. Burlingame

Slumberside, Quogue, Long Island, May 18, 1908 [PUL]

My dear Mr. Burlingame: I am proposing to republish certain of my articles, and wish to include among them that on Naval Administration—"The Navy Department"—which appeared in *Scribner's* in May, 1903.[1] As you once gave permission for its reproduction in pamphlet form, I might presume the same in the present case, but prefer to assure myself.

The due acknowledgment to *Scribner's* would of course be made.

To J. Franklin Jameson

Slumberside, Quogue, Long Island, May 18, 1908 [LC]

Dear Dr. Jameson: I am proposing to publish a collection of my articles, and wish to include among them my address as President of the Histl. Association. I presume the Association will have no objection, the fact of its origin being duly stated.

Will you kindly let me know?

To Little, Brown and Company

Quogue, Long Island, May 21, 1908 [LC]

Gentlemen: I have had before me for a week your letter of May 12. The question of title bothers me a little; but for the purposes of announcement, subject to modification, I think "Public Opinion and General Principles" might answer.

The leading principle of the book is summed up in words of Sir John Seeley, which occur in one of the articles, and which I purpose using in the Preface: "Public understanding (opinion) is necessarily guided by a few large, plain, simple ideas. When great interests are plain, and great maxims (principles) of government unmistakable, public opinion may be able to judge securely even in questions of vast magnitude."

This quotation might be used in the announcement; and by naming therewith "Some Consideration of *Principles* in Russo-Jap War," "*Principles* of Naval Administration," with the suggested title, the general scope of the Collection would be shown.[1]

---

1. "The United States Navy Department."
1. The title settled upon was *Naval Administration and Warfare. Some General Principles.*

To Charles W. Stewart

Slumberside, Quogue, Long Island, May 23, 1908 [NA]

Dear Mr. Stewart: Thank you very much for the pamphlet, the possession of which is very useful to me at the present moment; also for the big bibliography of the Japanese War.[1] The trouble of future historians is going to be not the lack of material, but the super-abundance of chaff to wheat, and the labor of sifting the little valuable out of the mass of rubbish.

Please express to Miss Barney also my indebtedness for the trouble she has taken.

To John P. Merrell

Slumberside, Quogue, Long Island, May 25, 1908 [NWC]

My dear Merrell: In the summer of 1888 I delivered a presidential address at the annual opening of the War College. This was printed in pamphlet, by myself, and distributed somewhat widely among those we wished to make friends, of which the College then stood in serious need. Within a year or so I retained a copy, but it has unaccountably disappeared.

May it possibly be that the College still has a copy? for I presume I certainly would have placed one or two in the library. If so, and especially if there be a duplicate, could it be lent me? I have in view including it, with another address of 1892,[1] in a volume of magazine articles I intend to republish.

To the Navy Pay Office

Quogue, Long Island, June 3, 1908 [LC]

In obedience to the above order, I left my home at Quogue, N. Y., May 30, 1908, proceeded to Washington, D. C., and, having performed the special temporary duty required of me, returned to Quogue, June 3, 1908.[1]

---

1. *See* Mahan to Stewart, May 16, 1908.

1. The two addresses were "The Necessity and Objects of a Naval War College" and "The Practical Character of the United States Naval War College." They were published in the U.S. Naval Institute *Proceedings* in December 1888 and June 1893, respectively, and both were reprinted in *Naval Administration and Warfare*.

1. This notation appears below Roosevelt's personal order to Mahan for special duty.

To John P. Merrell

Slumberside, Quogue, Long Island, June 5, 1908 [NWC]

My dear Merrell: I am greatly indebted for the copy of my 1888 address. My carelessness in preserving such matters does not deserve the indulgence I have experienced from others.

With reference to revising the Strategy lectures,[1] I recognize an obligation; but it is one balanced by other necessities. If the law gave me the pay of a retired rear admiral, I would begin immediately [when] the work, now in hand (which has great priority in my mind) is finished; which I hope to be by autumn—easily. But as things stand I have to consider also the pecuniary side. Up to my illness my pen has added to my income an amount of substantial importance to my family and I hesitate to contract the *obligation* to write which orders would entail. I might perhaps reconcile myself to such desultory application as, by the length of time, would raise my compensation. To do so would be pecuniarily just, for I should get no more than I have done from other sources abandoned for the nonce; but somehow I dont like it.

You will recognize that it would be impossible to ignore the Russo-Jap War; but to master it, collecting the material, on both sides, much probably unpublished, means an effort for which $720 a year is poor pay. The addl. thousand would be another matter.[2]

In short, mere revision, based on present knowledge, would be comparatively simple. I will turn the matter over, making some inquiries, and should I feel able, will write you. I may add the project of such publication has been long in my mind.

To Charles W. Stewart

Quogue, Long Island, June 5, 1908 [NA]

Dear Mr. Stewart: I have undertaken to deliver the address at the unveiling of a window to Adl. Sampson at the Academy next fall.[1] As part of my data I need a chronological statement of his service, and orders, after

---

1. Merrell, along with Luce, Sperry, and others, had urged Mahan to revise and publish his lectures on naval strategy, hoping that Mahan would undertake this task "for the good of the College and the service." Merrell to Mahan, May 29, 1908, at the Naval War College.

2. *See* Mahan to Luce, November 18, 1907, on pay for retired captains and rear admirals recalled to active duty.

1. Sampson died in May 1902. In July of that year *McClure's Magazine* published Mahan's "Sampson's Naval Career." Published also as "Rear Admiral Wm. T. Sampson," *Fortnightly Review* (August 1902).

graduation. I fancy Hamersley[2] will give all I need in this respect; and if so, can you send me a type written copy from his book, which I have not.

I shall greatly appreciate the suggestion of any other material for his life known to you.

To Little, Brown and Company

Quogue, Long Island, June 6, 1908 [LC]

Gentlemen: I have received through the kindness of the *National Review* a copy of the issue of Sept. 1904 containing Principles Involved in Russo-Japanese War. I have thus in hand copies of all the proposed articles for republication—as per list enclosed—except that on the Monroe Doctrine. As this has not been sent, I fear the *National* found no copy; and it may be well to seek it through your agents, or to have a type written copy made.

Besides the enclosed, I am preparing an address to be delivered in the occasion of unveiling a memorial window to the late Admiral Sampson, to take place probably between Oct 15 and Oct 30 this year. I expect to have it ready by July 1, and that it might find place at the end of this volume; provided, of course, that no publicity would ensue from the printing, and that actual publication did not take place till after the delivery. If proper secrecy can be maintained in this respect, the book could be made up and printed ready for immediate issue after the ceremony—say October 31.

With reference to title, I fail to see why it should necessarily suggest my previous work. "Retrospect and Prospect" labors under the same disadvantage, if such it be. Still, by placing in the fore-front the articles on the Japanese War, and those on Naval Administration, the title might read "Certain (or Some) General Principles touching Naval Warfare and Administration."

The general motive of the Work is expressed by a sentence of Sir John Seeley, author of *The Expansion of England*, which I propose to quote in the Preface. "Public Understanding is necessarily guided by a few large, plain, simple ideas. When great interests are plain, and great maxims unmistakable, public opinion may be able to judge securely even in questions of vast magnitude." Hence my suggested title—"Public Opinion and General Principles."

Should you wish, I will send you the articles now, but they would have to come back to me for editing. I think to add somewhat to the fleet's "Voy-

---

2. Lewis R. Hamersly, *The Records of Living Officers of the U.S. Navy and Marine Corps*. Philadelphia: L. R. Hamersly & Co., 1870, 1878, 1890, 1894, 1898, 1902.

age to the Pacific," and that I shall be able to begin revision by June 30, ending by July 31. Manuscript could be forwarded as fast as each article is revised.

[Enclosure]

		Words
	1. Some Consideration of Principles Involved in the Russo-Japanese War	9,335
	2. Some Reflections upon the R.–J. War	9,703
	3. Principles of Naval Administration American & British systems contrasted historically	9,367
	4. The United States Navy Department	9,537
Addresses {	5. Specific Purpose of the Naval War College, (1888)	7,000
delivered {	6. Practical Character of Naval War College (1892)	5,000
	7. True or Military Significance of the Cruise of the U.S. Fleet to the Pacific ? 3,500 words }	3,000
	8. The Monroe Doctrine	8,647
	9. Subordination in Historical Treatment	5,842
	10. The Strength of Nelson	6,826
		74,257
?	11. Admiral Sampson	? 6,000

To Stephen B. Luce

Slumberside, Quogue, Long Island, June 17, 1908 [LC]

My dear Admiral: Your letter of June 9 was duly received. If I am able to take up the Revision,[1] I should not attempt any history, properly so called; but I should wish to furnish my mind with adequate knowledge of recent hostilities, so as to be able to give illustrations, as well new as old, and those the most adequate I can find.

Possibly your idea of simple revision may be best. I had contemplated, vaguely, the preparation of a fairly elaborate treatise on the subject of Naval Warfare; but perhaps the old lectures, as a trial balloon, might be advisable first, in publication.

---

1. Of his War College lectures on Naval Strategy for possible publication.

To Leopold J. Maxse

My dear Mr. Maxse: The number of the *National* for September, 1904, was received a few days before your very kind letter of June 2. That for Feb. 1902 has not arrived.[1] If gone astray in the mail, or troublesome to get at, I hope you will not further trouble, as I can procure here a typewritten copy; if the Manager by inadvertence omitted sending, I should be glad to have it in print. Only dont take trouble.

My health is very much restored, though I feel it still needs the summer's rest to be confirmed. I am working much as usual in time, pace a little slower; and I shall make no attempt to cover arrears. The lost time is lost.

Your expression concerning Japan—that she has bitten off as much as she can chew,—was an odd reminder to me of these precise words used to me over ten years ago by the late Durham W. Stevens, the American counsellor in Japanese Service, in Korea, who you may remember was murdered by a Korean in San Francisco a few months ago. Stevens was then speaking of the attitude which Japan had for a moment taken as to our occupation of Hawaii, an incident which I know remains in the mind of one at least of our most accomplished international lawyers, as *significant* of the possible inclination still held; not by the lower classes only, but by statesmen. Dont allow yourself to forget it, for it cannot but remain in the background of thought over here. Since Stevens' remark Japan has bitten off a good deal more; and I myself recognize, not her future will—though I prefer to believe it, and at least act accordingly—but her lack of power for some time to come. I think, too, that China, formless and inert though she still is, and though with cause of complaint against our western hoodlums, recognizes the really excellent good will of our govt. and people generally toward her territorial interests, and that near Japan is to her more troublesome than distant America. From the nature of things Japan is to us a kind of Germany; cannot but be.

As regards Prest. Roosevelt, I have no present knowledge of his thoughts about Germany, though he is so open a talker that I have little doubt he would tell you just what he thinks. I do know that a decade ago, before thought of for the Presidency, he was fully awake to her possible ambitions; and I dont believe him in the least a man to be long hoodwinked. It will not matter much, however, provided his notorious policy of maintaining the Navy in full force and efficiency is persisted in. As for Great Britain and us, of course anything *may* happen; but if conditions count for anything it is scarcely possible to see where a clash can arise. Your col-

---

1. *See* Mahan to Maxse, May 7, 1908.

onies even would raise an outcry; for they are mostly Pacific states and the day is easy to foresee when our Navy will seem to them that of an ally. Even Canada has British Columbia to deal with. Japan is a very big factor in your imperial policy, because of the way your colonists regard Orientals.

[P.S.] I see I forgot to say "Thank you" for the magazine; but I meant it.

To Charles W. Stewart

Slumberside, Quogue, Long Island, July 3, 1908 [NA]

My dear Mr. Stewart: I am deeply indebted to you for the record of Sampson's orders. I believe that I now have all the data I need for the occasion of the unveiling.

I am going to ask if you will verify a quotation for me, from the autobiography of Commodore Morris (Soley's?)[1] apropos, I think, of his being ordered to the command of the *Brandywine*, in 1825. As I have it, it reads: "I believed that the exercise of military duties of a captain, whilst holding a *district* commission of a civil character, would be disagreeable to the feelings of the officers, even if legal."[2] The word "district" seems to me odd; could it be a mistake for "distinct"?

To James Ford Rhodes

Slumberside, Quogue, Long Island, July 4, 1908 [MHS]

My dear Mr. Rhodes: I share your satisfaction at your election to the University,[1] which I had already learned by a casual meeting with Prof. Sloane. It is to me a much more useful club than the Century, which I hold to only on account of the monthly Saturdays, where I meet a few persons I value but never see at other times; but for weekdays, Sundays and holidays, board & lodging I depend on the University. I doubt too whether the Century, outside its Saturdays, has maintained the cachet it once had. The University membership is quite as good.

[P.S.] Thanks for your kind wishes—I continue very well so far.

---

1. James Russell Soley, ed., "The Autobiography of Commodore Charles Morris, U.S.N.," U.S. Naval Institute *Proceedings*, VI, No. 12, pp. 115–218.
2. *Ibid.*, p. 200.

1. *See* Mahan to Rhodes, April 8 and 11, 1908.

To Charles W. Stewart

Slumberside, Quogue, Long Island, July 11, 1908 [NA]

Dear Mr. Stewart: I am enlightened, as well as much obliged by your informing letter on the subject of "district." The word in that connection is novel to me.

As Morris used it, I shall let it stand, and probably subjoin a note with the information you give me. I still find it hard to reconcile the word with the idea of "civil" which I infer was substantially what Morris had in mind. I wonder are Light House Inspectors officers in Civil Employment.

To Robert Mountsier

Slumberside, Quogue, Long Island, July 14, 1908 [PUL]

Dear Sir: I regret that I see no possibility of accepting the invitation with which you have honored me, to deliver an address before the university body of the University of Michigan. Independent of the fact that a six months illness has left me heavily in arrears with contemplated work, I see little likelihood that my strength will permit me hereafter to do anything in the way of platform work.

Renewing the expressions of my sense of the honor done me by the invitation of the Students Lecture Association, believe me [etc.].

To Little, Brown and Company

Quogue, Long Island, July 16, 1908 [LC]

Gentlemen: I enclose herewith the list of articles for the proposed book, in the order which under the circumstances seems advisable.[1] As given, the titles are meant primarily for the fly-leaves which, in previous books, precede each article in its place in the succession. The Sub-titles in each case are explanatory, and it has seemed to me might well be in small italics; but of that you will judge. The same titles may probably serve for the Table

---

1. Enclosure not found. The book was *Naval Administration and Warfare*.

of Contents; while for the successive article headings, the sub-titles can be omitted.

I should now be entirely ready to send you all the Copy, revised; but unfortunately promised data has not yet arrived two instances: The Monroe Doctrine and the Pacific Cruise.

Concerning the former, the editor of the *National Review* wrote he had ordered it sent me with that on the Principles, Russo-Jap War. As it did not arrive with the other, I so notified him, hoping it was an oversight. Should it not reach me this week, I will write or telegraph you, by Monday next, to have type-written copy made; but if possible I much prefer to have it before me in print.

Concerning the Pacific Cruise, some interesting data of its experiences have been furnished me, which I have written up and intend to append under the sub-heading Retrospect.[2] Unluckily, [the] other[3] is to be sent, which keeps me hung up.

This of course cannot continue. I propose therefore to send you next week the "copy" of the first eight articles, ready for the printer. If the expected data do not reach me by the time I have similarly prepared the Monroe Doctrine I will wait no longer, but send those two together. In view of the lateness of the Admiral Sampson ceremonial, I have decided not to include that address.

In your prospectus to the trade you may safely use the following:

The governing idea of the articles is expressed in the words of Sir John Seeley: (Regius Professor of Modern History at Cambridge, England. Died, 1895. Author of *Ecce Homo* and of the *Expansion of England*, etc.)

"Public understanding is necessarily guided by a few large plain, simple, ideas. When great interests are plain, and great maxims of government unmistakable, public opinion may be able to judge securely even in questions of vast magnitude."

Captain Mahan has endeavored thus to govern his treatment with reference to principles which it is most important that the people of the United States should duly weigh. Specifically, the last war between Russia and Japan, and the still more recent cruise of the United States battle-fleet to our Pacific shores, illustrate momentous considerations. To the last the author has been able to supply, not only general principles, but concrete facts drawn from the experiences of the cruise as far as Magdalena Bay.

---

2. "The Value of the Pacific Cruise of the U.S. Fleet, 1908. Retrospect," *Collier's Weekly* (August 28, 1908).
3. "The Value of the Pacific Cruise of the U.S. Fleet, 1908. Prospect," in *Scientific American* (December 7, 1907).

To Little, Brown and Company

Quogue, Long Island, July 19, 1908 [LC]

Gentlemen: There is now no probability that I shall receive the article on the Monroe Doctrine from the *National Review*. I must therefore seek a copy by your kind offices.

Under the superintendency of Mr. Herbert Putnam, the Boston Public Library loaned me for several weeks bound volumes of *Foreign Reviews*. If the volume of the *National* containing this could be so loaned me for a fortnight, I could have a copy made me here, with the additional advantage—as I think it—of seeing how it strikes me in print. Failing this, I will ask you to have a type written copy made and sent me.

I may add that I have received the additional data for the Pacific Cruise paper. It contains nothing I desire to insert. Consequently the Monroe Doctrine is the sole remaining article, and it is desirable for me to get to work at it at once. The Preface also is ready.

To Little, Brown and Company

Quogue, Long Island, July 21, 1908 [LC]

Gentlemen: I send you to-day, by register mail, copy for the first eight, of the ten intended, articles for the new book. Of the eight, numbers *one* and *four* have included between the leaves, but not stuck to them, some type written insertions and additions, with specific instructions as to insertion &c.

I beg you to understand that I have no duplicates of the printed matter, of which the copy chiefly consists. I hope therefore you will give specific instructions against loss.

I enclose also Preface—type written—with other Copy.

To Robert Mountsier

Slumberside, Quogue, Long Island, July 21, 1908 [PUL]

My dear Sir: I have had much pleasure in receiving the kind expression and offer of your letter of July 16, but for the present must confine myself to a simple acknowledgment.

Should opportunity to embrace your offer arise, I will communicate with you duly and promptly, but at present I see no immediate or speedy prospect.

To Little, Brown and Company

Quogue, Long Island, July 24, 1908 [LC]

Gentlemen: I have received the bound volume of the *National Review*, and will return it at the time mentioned in your letter.

I have arranged with *Collier's Weekly* for a publication of the "Retrospect" part of the Pacific Cruise article, with the understanding that the book may appear with it on October 1st.

To Little, Brown and Company

Quogue, Long Island, July 29, 1908 [LC]

Gentlemen: Referring to your letter of July 27, the article on the Pacific Cruise has received about 4,500 words in the *Collier's* article, and about 1,000 in addition, making a total under this head of about 9,000. The Monroe Doctrine article will also have an addition of 2,000. I hasten to give this information, in case it should in any way modify the proposed setting of the type.

All this material is now ready, and the type writing in process. I hope to forward all by the end of the week.

To Little, Brown and Company

Quogue, Long Island, August 2, 1908 [LC]

Gentlemen: I sent you yesterday by registered mail the last two articles: The Pacific Cruise and the Monroe Doctrine. Of these the former is in three parts, but I believe each so numbered and explained as to be easy to set up. The Monroe Doctrine is type-written and runs straight.

I think that the Contents and Fly Leaf titles for the latter should read: The Monroe Doctrine, *a Consistent Development*; instead of *an Historical Summary*.

Have you settled a title for the Book?

I should like Preface sent with first group, and to retain it till third or fourth article has been read, as I think there is a repetition in it from one of them. The Preface has frequently gone in late, and is paged independently.

The bound volume of *National Review* is put up, and will be sent by express to-morrow.

To Little, Brown and Company

Quogue, Long Island, August 6, 1908 [LC]

Gentlemen: I have received your letter of Aug 4, and also two packages galley proofs. The latter will have my speedy attention.

I enclose a title page—suggested. In the difficulty of finding a title at once brief and comprehensive, for a miscellaneous collection, I decided to put the Administration articles first, and make them title articles. The treatment of Warfare is not specifically naval; and by putting Administration first the adjective does not apply so directly to the Warfare, thus corresponding more immediately to facts.

It has occurred to me that as my works are now so numerous as to be a cumbrous category for a title page, it might be expedient to enumerate there only the three Sea Powers, viz: *1660–1783, French Revolution & Empire,* and *1812.* The other works might be given a fly leaf.

I do not remember whether I asked to see the fly leaves before each article, in proof. I should wish to do so.

[Enclosure]

Naval Administration
and
Warfare
Some General Principles
· with other Essays
By A.T. Mahan
Captain &c.

To Little, Brown and Company

Quogue, Long Island, August 15, 1908 [LC]

Gentlemen: I am returning today corrected galleys 49–57, inclusive, comprising nearly the whole of the Pacific Cruise of Atlantic Fleet.

I think that, in the final order of articles sent you, this was to be 9th instead of, as by this, 5th. The change in the particular instance is not very material; but I think it would be a mistake not to keep at least two stronger articles: the Strength of Nelson and Monroe Doctrine—for the last. The three addresses—two War College and one Histl. Association—at the end might look, in dimensions at least, two [*sic*] much like a tail.[1]

To Little, Brown and Company

Quogue, Long Island, August 17, 1908 [LC]

Gentlemen: The enclosed speaks for itself.[1] I am disposed to accede to the request, with the stipulation that Mr. Reinsch[2] should append a note, where "*the part*" selected appears in his collection, to the effect that the entire article is being published (or has since been published) in connection with other articles on kindred subjects, in book form, under the title *Naval Administration & Warfare*.

I leave the decision, however, to your judgment as to the effect upon the book. If favorable, will you please address Mr. Reinsch to that effect. I dont think there will be any clash.

To Little, Brown and Company

Quogue, Long Island, August 22, 1908 [LC]

Gentlemen: In returning today corrected galleys, 58–75, I have marked in blue pencil *certain* quotations which I think had better be printed in somewhat smaller type, and in separate paragraphs. In the "Copy" they were narrow spaced; from which I thought the Printers would recognize the call for a difference, such as is often found in quotations of length.

---

1. The final order of the articles in *Naval Administration and Warfare* was: The Principles of Naval Administration; The United States Navy Department; Principles Involved in the War between Japan and Russia; Retrospect upon the War between Japan and Russia; Objects of the United States Naval War College; The Practical Character of the United States Naval War College; Subordination in Historical Treatment; The Strength of Nelson; The Value of the Pacific Cruise of the United States Fleet, 1908: Prospect; The Value of the Pacific Cruise of the United States Fleet, 1908: Retrospect; The Monroe Doctrine.

1. Enclosure not found.
2. Paul Samuel Reinsch was probably preparing his *Readings on American Federal Government*, to be published by Ginn the following year. He was also preparing *The Young Citizen's Reader* for publication by B. H. Sanborn of Boston.

These galleys have been read apparently by a different proof-reader. I have found overlooked several misarrangements of letters,—more than I think should have been the case. The use of capitals has also been inconsistent with preceding, except where I have detected and changed.

To Little, Brown and Company

Quogue, Long Island, August 22, 1908 [LC]

Gentlemen: It would, I think be advantageous to place an outline *map* of the seat of war in the Far East, *after the fourth article*, "Retrospect on the R–J War." I enclose two maps, by combining which all the needed data would appear. I would like the one marked B to be returned me, as I have no other copy, and my memoranda on it may be useful hereafter.

The simplicity and absence of detail speak for themselves.

To Little, Brown and Company

Quogue, Long Island, August 22, 1908 [LC]

Gentlemen: With regard to Mr. Reinsch's request, it has been my purpose always to leave business arrangements, outside the book itself, in your hands.

In the present case there are two considerations: 1, The fortune of the book, which is common to you and me. 2, Should the permission be granted, whether any payment should be made me.

If you think the proposed use would injure sales, that settles the question, adversely. Should you on further consideration see any possible advantage, as advertisement, I should be very glad that Messrs. Ginn should make fair payment, and should be obliged if you would so present the case.

To Little, Brown and Company

Quogue, Long Island, August 26, 1908 [LC]

Gentlemen: Yours of yesterday is just recd. I hasten to write that the two maps, sent by mine of Aug 22, were meant to be combined, *forming one only*; and not two, as you seem to have inferred. I think if you will refer to my letter you will find this clearly said. The two simply afforded me a convenient means of giving you the data.

I have just taken up the first page-proof, received yesterday. I find, on referring to *rough draft* of a letter to you, date not noted, that I expressed wish that on fly (or blank) leaf *preceding the several articles*, might be noted in full the description of each as in Contents. In the first article, which alone I yet have, this has not been done. I enclose my memorandum (copy) to you and also the fly leaf as sent with page proof.

If you think this inadvisable (as it has not been done in my other Collections) I am not disposed to press the matter; but the articles in this case do stand in need of more explicatory titles than usual, to indicate their drift.

I have written Prof Reinsch, declining his request.

Galley proofs have now all been sent back, corrected.

To Little, Brown and Company

Quogue, Long Island, August 29, 1908 [LC]

Gentlemen: I return proof of Title Page. I suggest no change in its content; but I think that as "Some General Principles" applies to "Naval Adm. & Warfare," they should be closed together; and that "With Other Essays" be moved down. I should think that my name and its accompaniments might also be moved to further this purpose; the point in my mind being to separate the "With Other Essays" from "Some General Principles," the latter relating chiefly to the main title.

Yours of yesterday just received. If you mean to omit the separate preliminary titles, I have no objection; but would suggest for consideration whether to put all that matter at the head of each article will not be heavy in appearance.

If the table of Contents, proof of which I have not seen yet, be full as to magazine's & *full* title, there is no urgent call for repetition. Beyond this suggestion, I leave the matter in your hands.

To Little, Brown and Company

Quogue, Long Island, September 2, 1908 [LC]

Gentlemen: I return enclosed, received today with your letter of Sept. 1. It seems to me unfortunate that you decided to omit the leaves preceding the various articles, and bearing the titles, as was done in *Interest of America in Sea Power, Lessons of War with Spain, Retrospect and Prospect* as well as *Neglected Aspects of War*.

In accordance with this decision, I omitted in proofs the reference in "Preface" to those leaves. I did not, however, omit the statement that the *date* at Chapter heads was *date of writing of article*, not *date of publication*.

In the page you send me the date is relegated to a foot-note, and is the date of publication not that of composition.

Some of the titles in the present book are unavoidably complicated and long. In my first scheme I proposed to utilize the pages preceding the articles, to reduce this inconvenience.

In the case of the article, first page of which you send me, I had proposed that the full title, (within red pencil lines) and magazine publication (also red) should be on the page preceding article; and that for chapter heading should appear only the words "The Principles of Naval Administration" (omitting those which follow within my blue pencil marks). Under these words would be date of my writing the article—February, 1903.

I think this decidedly best, because conforming in plan to my previous books of like character. But, as I wrote you, I am willing to leave details in your hands. Please, however, see that whatever you adopt does not contradict what I have said in the Preface, corrected proofs of which have gone to you.

I wish to add that I have read all galley proofs and returned them; *but* no page proof has been received *for over a week*, and only 29 pages (page) have come at all.

The word "Historically" is essential; and cannot be omitted, unless all the other words within blue lines are also left out.

To Little, Brown and Company

Quogue, Long Island, September 5, 1908 [LC]

Gentlemen: The title page last sent me is to me wholly satisfactory. I enclose it with note to that effect.

The map sent is satisfactory also. I return today by Registered mail; having made only two suggestions for alteration in placing names.

Your decision as to half-titles, and to page preceding the text of each article with full titles etc. mentioned in yours of Sept. 3, is also satisfactory to me.

To Little, Brown and Company

Slumberside, Quogue, Long Island, September 10, 1908 [LC]

Gentlemen: I return herewith signed copy of agreement relative to *Naval Administration* &c.

At the same time permit me to remind you that I have had no page proof after page 29, and that a full fortnight ago.

To Bouverie F. Clark

Slumberside, Quogue, Long Island, September 11, 1908 [LC]

My dear Clark: In the matter of correspondence few of us can throw stones, I fear. I was thinking it was about time for me to write you, when your letter arrived. If, as I infer, my last letter to you was in October, I have a more than usually good excuse. Very shortly after it was written distressing symptoms made their appearance, indicating that the first operation must be supplemented by another, less critical but still severe—the object of both being to clear the urinary canal which was being clogged, first by the prostate, and then by the changes of tissue incidental to old age. There was about nine weeks between the two, but the last fortnight or more of these was characterized by frequent intense pain, so with the double shock and all together I came out of the second pretty well shattered. For two weeks I was practically out of my head, and my strength did not fully return, up to the reasonable mark of my years, before May. I am now however fairly all right; such trouble as remains seems at worst quite manageable, & I can go about my daily stint with entire comfort. But it is useless to pretend to myself that I have not lost a good deal of ground that I am not likely to recover. Two years ago I was substantially fifty; now I am close to my actual age, 68 if I live to Sep. 27. I still ride my wheel but my long rides are those which were daily two years since; and I bathe in the sea, but can stay in less long. But all said I am in as good state as most men of my years and better, I think, than most.

I thank you cordially for your appreciation of our fleet's work. I mailed you two days ago one of our illustrated weeklies, in which is an article on it by me.[1] I had before me a long letter from one of the junior admirals,[2] and considerable information from Evans's aide.[3] The success has exceeded my anticipation, & you will be interested, if not converted, by the experience as bearing on the question of amalgamating the executive and engineer branches. I was one of our pioneers in this branch—though few will re-

1. "The Value of the Pacific Cruise of the United States Fleet, 1908: Retrospect."
2. Either Seaton Schroeder, class of 1868, or Richard Wainwright.
3. Lieutenant Commander Lloyd H. Chandler, class of 1888.

member it; having written a Prize Essay article for our Naval Institute in 1878 advocating the measure.[4] As regards Japan, I had no fears as to the particular movement. The two governments understood conditions perfectly; and it was not conceivable that that of Japan should resent our sending our own fleet where we wished in our own waters. I feared and still fear popular commotion on our Pacific coast & in Japan; and I believe the Jap people in the ferment of their radical changes are more out of hand than even our Pacific hoodlums; but San Francisco is too far from Japan for the mere movement of the fleet to cause excitement. It is forgotten that in their anger over the Treaty of Portsmouth Japanese mobs wrecked some American property, & I shall be more at ease when the fleet gets safely away from Japan without shore rows and the typhoon season, which it is scheduled to meet at the worst time.

I have not been able fully to appreciate the Fisher–Beresford imbroglio; but Sir Percy Scott's signal was so consummately impertinent, that I have sympathized against his crowd, which seems to be Admiralty.[5]

Although myself theoretically a free trader, I am satisfied that the system is impossible today. The world wont have it; and if the world wont it is of no use one nation standing out. I believe you are on the road to what Dizzy[6] conceived as Imperial Democracy. We are much the same; and I believe in it as well as accept it as inevitable.

We have not been abroad and have no present expectations of doing so.

To Caspar F. Goodrich

Slumberside, Quogue, Long Island, September 14, 1908 [LC]

My dear Goodrich: I received your letter Saturday night.[1]

Every statement of fact in the *Collier's* article I had on what I think good and adequate authority.

---

4. "Naval Education," U.S. Naval Institute *Proceedings* (December 1879).
5. Lord Charles Beresford, Commander-in-Chief of the Channel Fleet, suffered the constant depletion of his force in favor of the development of the new Home Fleet, a part of the reorganization plan of Sir John Fisher, then First Sea Lord. Finally, in March 1909, he was ordered to haul down his flag and come on shore. The Channel Fleet, having ceased to exist as a separate command, became the Second Division of the Home Fleet. As Fisher named them, the "Syndicate of Discontent" on this and the Dreadnought issue consisted of Fitzgerald, Lambton, Noel, Custance, Beresford, and Bridge. He was supported by Percy, Scott, Jellicoe, Bacon, and others.
6. Benjamin Disraeli.
1. Goodrich, Commandant of the New York Navy Yard, had written: "Had you known the real history of the trip from Trinidad to Magdalena Bay of the Atlantic Fleet, you would have framed your *Collier's* article very differently. We all look up to you as the model of accuracy. Greatness has its own responsibilities you see." Goodrich to Mahan, September 12, 1908, in the Library of Congress.

The article is on the point of appearing in a book collection, with several others; save for an unforeseen hitch, the final proofs would by this have been read and the leaves in the hands of the binder. I expect to begin reading immediately.

If you have specific misstatements to correct, I shall be prepared to consider the corrections; but in so serious a matter as substantial change, within so short a time, evidence adduced should be not vague, but clear, precise, and such as I shall be at liberty to use and to quote at my discretion, naming my authorities, if I think necessary.

The delivery of the matter should also be prompt, as the publication of the book should not suffer delay for any but the most imperative reasons.[2]

To Little, Brown and Company

Quogue, Long Island, September 23, 1908 [LC]

Gentlemen: The title of map is of no great consequence. If execution has not gone too far, it might be well to place on it "Outline Map of Seat of War in Manchuria"; but if completed, and this cause delay or expense, it may be omitted. To "Contents" might be added: Map—with title as above, and page.

I enclose the title on page 307, from page proof. This corresponds to my suggestion, originally; but when I found that in the first articles there was placed on the corresponding pages nothing more than appeared at the head of the article, I acquiesced without comment, and struck out from Preface the mention that these particulars would be given elsewhere than in "Contents."

I apprehend that uniformity is desirable; and that consequently what has been omitted before should be omitted here. To this there is one exception. In third article, "Principles of R. J. War," it is essential to me that it appear that this was written during, and still refers to the war *as existing.* This is the gist of the paper. I therefore, in returning page proof, inserted *"Written during the War."*

---

2. To this letter Goodrich responded: "It isn't for me to make any 'charges'—but it is for you to be sure of your facts. That's what I mean." Goodrich to Mahan, September 15, 1908, in the Library of Congress. At the bottom of this letter from Goodrich, Mahan countered: "To this I replied that the word 'charges' had not been used by me, as the quotation marks seemed to imply." The letter to Goodrich in which this demur was made has not been found. Apparently Goodrich had misread Mahan's *change* as *charge.* But Goodrich wrote Sims in 1906 that he had abandoned Mahan's way of thinking, and his imputation of inaccuracy is nearly a direct quotation from Sims. *See* Mahan to Loeb, September 30, 1908.

To Charles W. Stewart

Slumberside, Quogue, Long Island, September 23, 1908 [NA]

My dear Mr. Stewart: I wish to ascertain how long Evans was in command of the Atlantic Fleet. The January *Register* gives him "Commanding Atlantic Fleet" since March 31, 1905; but it may be that part of the interval he was in subordinate position.

I have no back *Registers* and my memory does not serve me.

Will you let me know as soon as possible?

To William Loeb[1]

Draft   Quogue, Long Island, September 30, 1908 [LC]

After much consideration, I have decided to ask you if you can find an opportunity to lay before the President the enclosed brief correspondence; asking his judgment as to whether he thinks it in the public interest that, before republication, the article challenged by Admiral Goodrich should be submitted by the President to some person sufficiently cognizant of the facts to correct me, if in error.

I have relied upon the letter of Admiral Sperry,[2] and upon the published letter of Lieut Commander Chandler,[3] in the light of which I have carefully re-read the article. I am now holding up the book, which is otherwise proof-read for publication.

As a copy of *Collier's* may not be immediately available I mail you under another cover duplicate of the article, in book proof.

I presume there wd. be no objection to saying that the press reports simply confirm those antecedently reported by letters from Sperry and other officers.

[Marginalia]   Goodrich first Sep. 12: "Had you known the real history of the trip from Trinidad to Magdalena B. of the Atl. Fleet, you would have framed your *Collier* art. very differently."

Copy from my letter to G. of Sep. 14: "Every statement of fact in the *Collier* article I had on what I think good and adequate authority.

---

1. Private secretary to President Roosevelt.
2. Sperry succeeded to command of the Great White Fleet in May 1908, when Admiral R. D. Evans became ill.
3. The letter constantly referred to in "The Value of the Pacific Cruise of the U.S. Fleet, 1908. Retrospect" was one from Magdalena Bay written by Lieutenant Commander L. H. Chandler to the *New York Herald* and published on March 29, 1908. *See* Mahan to Goodrich, September 14, 1908.

"If you have specific misstatements to correct, I shall be prepared to consider the corrections; but in so serious a matter as substantial change within so short a time, evidence adduced should be not vague, but clear, precise, and such as I shall be at liberty to use and to quote at my discretion, naming my authorities, if I think necessary.

"The delivery of the matter should also be prompt as publicn. of book should not suffer delay for any but the most imperative reasons."

To Little, Brown and Company

Quogue, Long Island, September 30, 1908 [LC]

Gentlemen: I am holding back last page proof—after reading—because I have received from an officer of rank in the Navy, a letter impeaching the accuracy of the *Collier's* article.

As his statement was general, and he has since refused to make it particular, or to give authorities, I have inclined to dismiss it as unworthy of consideration; but upon reflection have decided to submit the whole affair in a quarter from which I may expact an adequate, and I believe speedy, decision. You will believe that I regret a delay such as this, but believe it upon the whole in our common interest.

May I remind you that the "Contents" proof has not yet been sent me.

To James Ford Rhodes

Slumberside, Quogue, Long Island, October 5, 1908 [MHS]

My dear Mr. Rhodes: I have never been particularly interested in our Academy, and in fact resigned membership in the Institute[1] at one time, though I withdrew it upon representation. I made however the mental reservation that my part would be limited to annual dues.

I am constitutionally averse to the unnumbered organizations and societizations which are continually brought before me, and increasing years increases indisposition. I have this month two,[2] and next month two, journeys to take and meetings to attend. I am not willing to add to my liabilities.

I fancy enterprises of this kind must be maintained by those naturally interested; those who go from a sense of must or should—which I do not feel—will probably remain perfunctory.

---

1. The U.S. Naval Institute.
2. One of these was on temporary duty in Washington as a member of the Committee on Documentary Historical Publications, October 22–25.

To Little, Brown and Company

Quogue, Long Island, October 5, 1908 [LC]

Gentlemen: The position for the Map is after the fourth Article—"Retrospect upon the War etc." It should open to the *right*, for convenience of readers of the two articles preceding.

I enclose "Contents" which is all right.

I submitted the article "Retrospect on Pacific Cruise" to competent knowledge of conditions, and shall to day mail you remaining page proof. The only correction necessary—on p. 345—arises from reconsideration of my authorities at the first writing. I find them not perfectly clear that Admiral Evans's physical condition permitted his immediate supervision "throughout," the word used by me. I have therefore changed the wording so as to insure him the credit justly his due, without sacrificing my own literal accuracy. His credit is exactly that of the President of a great company, whose business has run despite an illness. It is perhaps rather more than less, that he can raise his hand for a moment and have the machine run equally well.

On pp. 352, 376, and 407, where a line long, I have made omissions which will reduce to proper 28 lines.

The change on p. 345 should not affect pagination.

The consideration of expense connected with changes in pagination has alone deterred me from adding to this account of the Pacific cruise, a notice of the reports of continued efficiency at Manila. From San Francisco to Manila is, roughly, 11,200 miles, against 13,400 from Hampton Roads to Magdalena Bay. The fact is noteworthy that Admiral Sperry is reported by the press as stating that "the efficiency of the ships has been greatly increased, particularly in the engineering department."

The last page of the article (352) is already full. Addition would therefore involve the change of the numbers of the 55 pages following. It might be expedient to inform me whether this could be done without exceeding the allowance made to me by our agreement; and, if it does, by how much. I am just now at heavy expense, added to that of my prolonged illness, and cannot afford frills. It is matter for consideration that a page with print, 353, would relieve the rather heavy appearance of 352 up against the title "Monroe Doctrine" on 353.

I should like to see again p. 345, as here corrected. Otherwise, the proof today mailed concludes my work as far as known to me.

To Little, Brown and Company

Gentlemen: In response to your to-day's telegram, I send enclosed to be added to Pacific Cruise article.[1]

Had page *352* been but half full, I would have wished a double space before the enclosed, to indicate breach of continuity. As it is, perhaps such allowance may be feasible at top of page 353. I calculate the enclosure will need only 26 lines.

[P.S.] I have not been able to have enclosure type written, as usual.

To Little, Brown and Company

Quogue, Long Island, October 14, 1908 [LC]

Gentlemen: In Cast Proof just received, p. 343, line 9, I see the word "moving" is moying.

As I sent the pages, of which this is one, in duplicate proof to be read with reference to accuracy of statements—for reasons known to you—I cannot say that it was right in page proof. If not, in addition to my own error, it involves the proof reader; and leads me to say, as I think I before remarked to you, that the typographical mistakes uncorrected by the reader, and detected by myself, were more numerous than I can recall in any previous experience.

To Little, Brown and Company

Quogue, Long Island, October 26, 1908 [LC]

Gentlemen: We shall be leaving here shortly for Lawrence, L.I., and, in view of probably unsettled conditions for a few weeks, I write to ask that the copies of *Naval Administration* to be sent to me, *be retained* until I write you to send them.

My address remains Quogue until I notify you of change.

---

1. The addition of 26 lines was made to "The Value of the Pacific Cruise of the U.S. Fleet, 1908. Retrospect" when it was reprinted in *Naval Administration and Warfare*, after the cable reports of the arrival of the Fleet at Manila Bay. Mahan quotes Sperry on the increased efficiency of the warships when deprived of the customary convenience of bases. *See* Mahan to Loeb, September 30, 1908, Footnote 3.

To John P. Merrell

Quogue, Long Island, October 31, 1908 [NWC]

Sir: In obedience to the enclosed orders from the Secretary of the Navy,[1] I have the honor to report to you by letter for duty in connection with the Naval War College.

To Little, Brown and Company

Lawrence, Long Island, November 11, 1908 [LC]

Gentlemen: I enclose application for English copyright, filled, signed and witnessed as directed. The witness is assistant to the librarian at the University Club, N.Y., where I am now writing.

Have you seen the enclosed clipping,[1] from *Publisher's Circular*, Oct 31? Do you know what it means?

My residence now, and I believe permanently, is Quogue, where I vote; but this winter we shall spend in Lawrence, L.I. which I beg you to note as my address until May 1, 1909. When the new book is ready, I will ask you to send the copies there, as we move in tomorrow.

To John P. Merrell

Lawrence, Long Island, November 17, 1908 [NWC]

My dear Merrell: I find in my own copy of the lecture, the original made over twenty years ago, a large number of notes, additions &c, made from time to time during the seasons in which I delivered them; the last occasion being, I think, in 1897. These are of the nature of revision, so far as they go, though I shall doubtless find plenty else.

It has occurred to me, consequently, that it would be well that, if the copy at the College be not required for current use, it be sent me to compare with my own. The latter is in such a confused condition, owing to annotations, &c., that I doubt whether I could make it the body for revision, intelligibly to myself—let alone a copyist.

---

1. Secretary Victor H. Metcalf ordered Mahan to temporary duty at the War College to revise his naval strategy lectures for publication as "required in the public interests."

1. Enclosure not found.

Can you then send me the College copy, either itself or a copy of it? I go to Annapolis on Thursday, being, as you perhaps know, to deliver an address on the occasion of unveiling the Sampson memorial window; but I expect to return here Sunday afternoon.

I do not expect to start work on the lectures until I have reviewed and extended my knowledge of the subject by a certain amount of reading. In connection with this I shall probably have to ask you for books from time to time. Have you for instance Callwell's *Effect of Maritime Command on Land Operations Since Waterloo?*[1] And is there a printed catalogue of the College Library, of which a copy might be sent me?

I will ask you also to send me a package of penalty envelopes for correspondence with you—about 8 or 9 inches long.

To Little, Brown and Company

Lawrence, Long Island, November 17, 1908 [LC]

Gentlemen: I have to thank you for the ten copies of *Naval Administration* &c which have been received.

I am going to ask of you the favor to obtain from Sampson Low & Co., if now procurable, a copy of the English Edition of my account of the *South African War, 1899–1900.*

This was written for Collier's, in New York, and by them published with numerous illustrations. It was republished in England, without illustration, other than maps; I think by Sampson Low.

My reason for asking is that your ordering will save me the trouble of a separate transmittal of the small cost involved; they charging to you, and you to my account. It might be addressed to me direct. I suppose, too, you are in frequent communication with them.

[P.S.] If no copies remain, a second hand copy would be acceptable.

To Samuel A. Ashe

Lawrence, Long Island, November 30, 1908 [DUL]

My dear Ashe: I was in Newport[1] a little over a week ago, to deliver an address on the occasion of unveiling a window to Admiral Sampson's

---

1. Charles Edward Callwell, *The Effect of Maritime Command on Land Campaigns Since Waterloo.* Edinburgh and London: W. Blackwood and Sons, 1897.

1. Mahan meant to write "Annapolis."

[270]

memory,[2] and while there asked to see your son[3] after the ceremony. He may have mentioned it in his home letters, but I wish also to write you what a pleasant impression was made upon me by his appearance—face, manner, and bearing. The natural advantages are improved also by the set up given the midn., to an extent unknown in our day. He has a look of you, recognizable to me, the more so that my best memories of you are at the same age; but the resemblance is not striking, as is that of his sister Josephine.

Since I saw you two years ago I have had a very severe illness, consequent upon operations necessitated by enlargement of the prostate; not an uncommon trouble for men of our years. Practically, I was housebound from the end of Sept. to April 1, though not always so. I believe I may say I am now all right; but I am less strong, not able to walk as fast or as far as once I did. I will give you the warning the surgeon gave me: If you have to rise, habitually, to urinate, more than once in an ordinary seven or eight hours bed period, see a doctor.

I have little else in the way of news concerning myself. I hope you in the South are preparing to throw over Bryan now. He wont get off of his own motion, yet you may be sure that he alone will damage fatally the best Democratic platform in the States centering round N.Y.; barring, of course, some folly on the part of the Republicans which experience gives us reason to expect. He may be absolutely honest, it makes no difference. No one believes him safe, and distrust, I believe amounts to terror.

To John P. Merrell

Lawrence, Long Island, November 30, 1908 [NWC]

My dear Merrell: Have you in the Library, and can you spare me for a time, Julian Corbett's *England in the Mediterranean*?[1] I think that is the title.

While I hope not to keep unreasonably, if sent, I should like an intimation

---

2. On November 21, 1908, a memorial window for Sampson was unveiled at the Naval Academy Chapel. Rear Admiral Chadwick made the presentation address. The *Army and Navy Journal* (November 28, 1908) noted that "R. Adm. A. T. Mahan, who was a classmate of Admiral Sampson, read a paper which was heard only imperfectly." Mahan's "Address" was published in the U.S. Naval Institute *Proceedings*, XXXV (1909).

3. George Bamford Ashe, class of 1911.

1. Julian S. Corbett, *England in the Mediterranean; a Study of the Rise and Influence of British Power Within the Straits, 1603–1713.* London, New York, and Bombay: Longmans, Green, and Co., 1904.

of probable length of time I could retain, without inconvenience to you.

Also, have you Daveluy's *Study of Naval Strategy*,[2] to which Darrieus alludes favorably in his *War on the Sea*.[3]

To John P. Merrell

Lawrence, Long Island, December 3, 1908 [NWC]

My dear Merrell: Thank you for the books which have been received. My address for the winter, till May 1, 1909, will be as above.

[P.S.]   Dec. 4. The two copies of the Lectures are received today.

To Samuel A. Ashe

Lawrence, Long Island, December 9, 1908 [DUL]

My dear Ashe: Your volume of the *History of North Carolina*[1] reached me day before yesterday; but I had to go almost immediately to New York on business which kept me over night and all day yesterday.

I have of course had no time to read more than the Preface; but I gather from it that the work not only has been to you a labor of love and interest, but has been carried on [in] the most approved modern methods of original research. It is thus only that true history can be built up, and any man who deals thus with a specific period in the life of any community does valuable service to general history. I am sorry you do not intend to pursue the work, because of what occupation, when congenial, adds to one's own life and happiness; yet I can well undersand how material accumulates beyond one's power of handling as the period approaches our own. I dont know of course whether that is your reason; I only lament for you the lapse of an absorbing task.

I see your publisher is named Van Noppen.[2] In 1899, when I was at the

---

2. René Daveluy, *Étude sur la stratégie navale.* Paris, Nancy: Berger-Levrault & Cie., 1905.
3. Gabriel Darrieus, *La guerre sur mer, stratégie et tactique.* Paris: A. Challamel, 1907.

1. Samuel A'Court Ashe, *History of North Carolina.* Vol. 1. Greensboro, N.C.: Van Noppen, 1908. Vol. 2. Raleigh, North Carolina, 1925. Both volumes were reprinted by Gregg in 1971.
2. The man whom Mahan met at The Hague was Leonard Charles Van Noppen, a lecturer on Dutch literature in the U.S. and the Netherlands and translator of Joost van den Vondel, "the Dutch Shakespeare." He probably sent Mahan Vondel's *Lucifer*, illustrated by John Aarts and published in New York by the Continental Publishing Company, 1898. Ashe's publisher was Charles Leonard Van Noppen.

Hague, there was a young North Carolinian there greatly interested in Dutch literature. He sent me a volume on a Dutch epic poet, Vondel, from whom Milton is surmised to have drawn some of his material for "Paradise Lost." I wrote at once in thanks; but, not having his address, sent (I think) in care of his publishers. Several months later my letter came back to me— "Not found." I have felt this sense of incivility, though faultless; and should opportunity offer should be glad to have you mention this matter to your publisher.

I hope your son may give you the satisfaction of seeing him graduate into the service.[3] Like all professions, the Navy has its drawbacks; but it is a certainty—beyond most, and there are compensations.

Thanking you sincerely for your thought of me in your gift believe me always, my dear Ashe [etc.].

To John P. Merrell

Lawrence, Long Island, December 20, 1908 [NWC]

My dear Merrell: I have read Corbett's *Mediterranean* with much interest, and am now far advanced in a second reading. I think it will be well also to read his *Seven Years War*,[1] if you can spare it me.

My idea is at present to extend my reading with a view to collect illustration; at the same time comparing my own valuations of situations and events with writers like Corbett, Darrieus, and Daveluy. Later, I will consult Rodgers[2] as to material at the Intelligence Office, with special reference to the Russo-Jap War.

It will be desirable for me to keep books, for reference when I undertake revision formally, until satisfied I have no further use for them; subject always, of course, to your judgment as to the concurrence of the College. The study of War and its illustration, is—as Darrieus and Daveluy [were] not the first to say—primarily and chiefly a study of history.

Like most men, Corbett's theory to some extent runs away with him, but the book is substantial and much of its comment extremely useful. He has, I think, missed one military generalization; much, as he says, England long overlooked the value of the Mediterranean.

---

3. George Bamford Ashe eventually attained the rank of rear admiral.

1. Julian Stafford Corbett, *England in the Seven Years' War; a Study in Combined Strategy.* London, New York, Bombay, and Calcutta: Longmans, Green, & Co., 1907.

2. R. P. Rodgers.

To James W. McIntyre

Lawrence, Long Island, January 7, 1909 [LC]

My dear Mr. McIntyre: During Mr. Brown's life, I often consulted with him in reference to my projects of writing, before finally deciding upon a particular step, and before submitting a business arrangement to the firm. Since his death no occasion has arisen until now; and now, the proposition I am to advance being very different from anything I have hitherto attempted, I wish at the first to confine myself to a single member of the firm. From one or two casual remarks, I gathered that Mr. Brown himself would have indicated you. Also, unless my memory is at fault, it was you who in 1889 first brought my *Sea Power* to Mr. Brown's attention, after your conversation with Mr. Soley.

I have written a book of broadly religious character,[1] in which I think I have been governed by a leading idea, similar, in its influence upon the work, to that which guided me in the Sea Power series. It is now complete, barring a final revision, and will be about 75,000 words.

Two questions arise:

1. In your judgment, would the firm care to undertake publication?

2. Are the business connections of the firm such as to give a work of this character probably as good a chance in your hands as if placed elsewhere? This includes, of course, consideration by you of your knowledge of the conditions as to methods and times which give such a book its best chance of getting public attention, or your facility for obtaining such knowledge.

I much doubt, for example, whether in England the present Sampson Low people are as fit for the English end of the business as some other firms there; e.g. Rivington's, Longman's and Parker's. Religious publication, at least for the Church of England, with which my own line of thought is affiliated, is more specialized there than it seems to be here; and firms identified with the American Episcopal Church seem to me somewhat weak professionally. Still many English houses, I believe, do publish works of this character incidentally to their main business.

The title I propose is: "Fragments that Remain"; being the results of my life's experience.* The sub-title: "Thoughts on the Life of the Christian," though subordinate, expresses more exactly the motive which underruns the treatment.

* I must guard myself from seeming here to imply that I mean to talk about myself, or my personal experience. Reflection, or observations, would perhaps be a better word than Experience.

---

1. *The Harvest Within: Thoughts on the Life of a Christian.*

To Theodore Roosevelt

Lawrence, Long Island, January 13, 1909 [LC]

My dear Mr. President: Your letter of January 8, with enclosure, reached me only yesterday.

I have not yet learned Mr. Newberry's plan,[1] and therefore cannot antecedently busy my mind as I could wish in considering the criticism.

Your letter does not require of me any opinion before the Conference;[2] yet it may save time in ultimate expression to say at once that, as far as I have yet gone, I have never found fault with the Bureau organization, in itself, regarded as a *civil administrative* system. The failure is in the fact that the Secretary, the coordinating factor, as a rule comes to a big business not only without military conceptions, but without that antecedent practical experience of the civil side, which almost in every case the head of a great civil business has gained in subordinate functions. He is therefore, as usually appointed, quite unacquainted with the details, or the general ideas, that underlie his duties.

The only corrective has been the bureaus. They are essentially and almost purely civil offices; with the one possible exception of Navigation. At present, five of the eight are held by persons essentially civil in profession. That is the influence, and the sole influence, officially bearing upon the Secretary from below.

Ideally, the President does, and the Secretary as his lieutenant should, hold in his hands a complete mastery of the diplomatic, military and naval considerations, home and foreign, which for the time being at any moment affect the policy of the Country. Actually, neither the President nor the Secretary ordinarily can thus do, because usually they come new to the military considerations, afloat and ashore. The only means by which such consecutive knowledge can be maintained is by a corporate body, continuous in existence and gradual in change. That we call a General Staff. In my conception, the Chief of Staff can scarcely, with our institutions, hold certainly for as long as, say, ten years. The knowledge, therefore, must be in the general staff at large; but, and here perhaps is my particular point, he should be solely responsible for information, *and for advice*, given the Secretary. He should be compelled to act as President of a Board, composed

---

1. Truman H. Newberry, Secretary of the Navy, sought to reorganize the Navy Department on the basis of modern business methods, especially in navy yard management and procurement. He advocated a General Staff, similar to the Army's, to advise the Secretary.
2. The Naval Conference in Washington was merely a rubber stamp for Newberry's plan. Mahan was present at its session on January 15, and returned to Lawrence the following day.

of his chief subordinates; but the advice he gives must be his, not theirs. The advice must be single, not corporate.

I raised this point the instant I joined the War Board in 1898; and my experience then convinced me that some men will easily roll off personal responsibility; the result being that one man practically decides, but without individual responsibility for the advice. If I rightly read the English press, this is the case now in the Board of Admiralty. We only advised; but with many secretaries advice will practically be decision. Therefore, responsibility for advice should be individual.

For best results, the Chief of Staff should so possess the confidence of the Administration, as to be aware of the relations exisitng between our own Government and the various states interested in a possible theatre of war; and also of the attitude these states bear to one another, and hence their possible action in case of hostilities. All these are military factors. Thus equipped, the two Chiefs of Staff, Army and Navy, would be invaluable understudies to their respective Chiefs and to the President.

Have your read Corbett's *Seven Years War*? It is a good book. He brings out clearly that Pitt, besides eminent ability, had control of all three threads, —diplomatic, military, and naval,—and that in this, concentrated in one efficient man, consisted his great advantage. Jomini taught me from the first to scorn the sharp distinction so often asserted between diplomatic and military considerations. Corbett simply gives the help of putting the same idea into other words. Diplomatic conditions affect military action, and military considerations diplomatic measures. They are inseparable parts of a whole; and as such those responsible for military measures should understand the diplomatic factors, and vice versa. No man is fit for Chief of Staff who cannot be intrusted with knowledge of a diplomatic situation. The naval man also should understand the military conditions, and the military the naval.

Corbett makes another excellent point: that for a military establishment the distinction between a state of war and a state of peace is one of words, not of fact. Nothing so readily as a general staff will insure this. They, or a body like them, should in my opinion decide what the leading features of a ship of war and her armament should be. I would not have a bureau officer have a vote on such a question. I would compel the Staff—or Board—to hear the Bureaus in extenso, as expert witnesses, and their testimony should be recorded, to emphasize the responsibility of the Board; but the decision should be that of a body, or an individual, purely military. No one civil by profession, or by office, should control here, severally or collectively; except, of course, the Secretary or the President.

Do you remember how delightfully Nelson phrased all this in his last order. "The order of sailing is the order of battle." Every day ready for action. I should like to see that framed and hung up before the desk of every secretary who had wit enough to comprehend.

I am sure you understand my general position sufficiently to know that I would neither advocate nor countenance any measure tending to weaken the ultimate power of the Secretary. He should be able to overrule and upset, if necessary, every one beneath him, from Chief of Staff down.

To James Ford Rhodes

Lawrence, Long Island, January 26, 1909 [MHS]

My dear Mr. Rhodes: It will give me much pleasure to dine with you on Saturday, Feb. 13, at 8, at the University Club.

We are living in the country now; and indeed this is the fourth winter we have passed away from N.Y., having rented our house there. But we keep the district P.O. always informed of our address.

Looking forward with pleasure to our meeting, I am [etc.].

To Bouverie F. Clark

University Club, New York, January 28, 1909 [LC]

My dear Clark: It was awfully good of you to remember me at Xmas, and it has been very shabby of me to be so long in acknowledging. I am not sure that "better late than never" is true of such dereliction. The two troubles are, that I had intended to send you a like remembrance, but was disgusted with the cards they had to show us here; and further that increasing years is making me more idle than ever with my pen.

Times are squally, as you say, but our dear peace at any price people will always persist in ignoring facts. Some thirty of them have just petitioned our Congress against an increase of the Navy; among other things, they argue that Japan dont want to fight us, nor we her. Perfectly true, and I hope we never shall; nor you Germany. But, the Japs—the common people—do want to immigrate to us, and to Br. Columbia, and small blame to them; and the Columbians and our slopers object. There is raw human nature, irrepressible—like German trade and colonial jealousy toward you. So long as you and we have big navies, and Japan is in a financial hole, the Jap will do his best to keep his people in order; but weaken our navy, and fill the Jap treasury, and it will no longer [be] worth while for them to be unpopular with their own people. When the people of two nations are antagonistic, because of clashing interests, the peace can only be kept by force; like a policeman arresting two brawlers. As regards absence of armament making for peace, I always say: Look at our North and South, in 61. Never were two communities less ready, but they fought all the same, because interests clashed.

I continue very well, though the surgeon still has to tinker at me. I walk four or five miles every day, eat with relish, and sleep well. I am, if anything, a little more busy than I care to be, but it is better than the ennui of idleness. My family also are well. We have had an open winter, but I hope our last in these latitudes. Mrs. Mahan, though well and vigorous, ought to be where she can live in the open air.

With all best wishes, & hoping we may drift together again before too long [etc.].

To William H. Moody

Lawrence, Long Island, January 28, 1909 [LC]

My dear Justice Moody: I have seen in the morning papers the reconstitution of the Commission, and what purports to be a copy of the President's letter to the individual members.

Assuming these to be as stated, the Commission will doubtless desire you to be at its head; and I therefore venture a few lines in the interest of our proceedings.

The duties towards the community of men in your position, and that of Judge Dayton,[1] will of course have priority of consideration. You are tied down to times, and your functions are of the first importance.

Might it not, however, convenience yourselves, as well as us in minor positions, if a circular letter could be sent to each member, requiring of him a written tentative scheme, embodying his views under the several heads specified by the President. These, being reproduced, and sent to all the members, would enable us when meeting to be much better prepared for discussion, than we possibly can be if we meet without some such prior provision.

From my experience of Commissions, I have found a great loss of time in desultory talk, often vague and purposeless; like a man feeling his way in the dark. The plan I suggest compels each man to formulate to himself his own views, and to correct them—or modify them—beforehand, by ac-

---

1. Alston G. Dayton, former member of the House Committee on Naval Affairs, and an advocate of a strong navy.

quaintance with those of others. The procedure has been that of a Commission on Publication of Historical Documents, of which I have recently been a member.

The clerical force of the Department could doubtless see to the multiplication of the reports.

I own to personal as well as public reasons for desiring economy of time. A long absence in Washington seriously interrupts my other work; whereas in the way suggested I lose only the time immediately needed for the specific purpose. This reason of course is absolutely secondary; but, if needless expenditure of time can be reduced for the Commission itself, it will surely be worth while.

To John S. Billings

Lawrence, Long Island, January 30, 1909 [NYPL]

My dear Dr. Billings: I have been ordered on a Commission upon reorganization of the Navy Dept.,[1] mention of which you may have seen in the Press. Pertinent to the matter in hand, will be an Order in Council of the British Government, in August 1904, giving to the First *Sea* Lord of the Admiralty responsibility for the whole business of the Board; a responsibility previously inhering in the head of the Admiralty, officially styled the First (not Sea) Lord.

If, without too great trouble, you could have me sent a copy of this, which will almost certainly be in a file of the London *Times*, which the Library preserves, I should be greatly indebted. I do not ask for any search beyond the *Times*, nor would I know where else to look.[2]

To Theodore Roosevelt

Lawrence, Long Island, February 1, 1909 [LC]

My dear Mr. President: You will recall Dicey's article.[1] The English friend who sent it to me has sent me also the enclosed, London *Times*, Jan.

---

1. On this date Mahan was advised by Newberry that, by direction of the President, he had been appointed member of a commission on the reorganization of the Navy Department, and should report at the Department on February 5.
2. Billings sent Mahan a transcript of the British Order in Council of August 10, 1904. Billings to Mahan, February 1, 1909, in the New York Public Library.

1. Since two Diceys, Albert Van and Edward, were writing in the periodicals at this time, the reference cannot be identified with certainty.

21, which I think will interest you; both in itself, and as showing that, despite proverbs to the contrary, Truth sometimes catches up with falsehood.[2]

To William H. Moody

Lawrence, Long Island, February 1, 1909 [LC]

My dear Justice Moody: I have been ordered to be present at a meeting of the Commission at the Navy Department on Friday next, at 2.30 p.m.; and incidental thereto am directed to confer with you by letter.

Conference, I presume, can mean little more at this stage than a presentation of my views, in order, as far as possible beforehand, to expedite the business of the meeting. I am scarcely prepared so to present immediately, though I have been giving my attention to that object and hope at least to bring a written tentative formulation to the meeting.

My consideration of Naval Administration hitherto has been historical and critical only; ascertaining facts and thence deducing principles. But as I have never expected to be called upon for constructive work, which is the task of the Commission, I never undertook such for my own amusement or instruction.

Starting from the principle which as yet is to my mind unqualified, that there must not be within the Department organization any check upon the final decision of the Secretary, there has come to mind an analogy which possibly may be worthy of consideration. If I rightly understand, the cabinet of the President is not recognized by the Constitution, perhaps not even by statute, as an organic body. No individual member can in the last resort override a decision of the President. They act in his name, and in virtue of his authority alone—not of their own. In diplomatic correspondence formerly—perhaps also now—the Secy. of State spoke always in the President's name: "The President thinks," "the President directs me to say," etc. Nevertheless, no one doubts the usefulness of Cabinet meetings, that the President is through them a vastly more efficient official—executive—than if he saw the members only separately; and public opinion would be disturbed to hear that a Prest. had resolved to hold them no more.

Could not—might not—some such provision be introduced into our two

---

2. Enclosure not found; but probably an article under the heading "The United States, the President, and the Congress," which described the popular protest against talk of impeaching the President, Representative William F. Willett's "ribald speech," the action of the House with regard to Roosevelt's Secret Service Message, and Senator Benjamin R. Tillman's threat to expose White House graft. It lauded Congress's motion that Willett's speech be expunged from the record, and predicted that president-baiting as a congressional pastime would soon cease.

military Departments? They are especially needed there, just because the average public man understands something of almost every public interest, except the military. Specifically, in the Navy Department, should there be a General Board corresponding to the General Staff idea, would anything be more educative to a Secretary than to meet it periodically, at short intervals, and with it to discuss, and so to master, the military questions, from the military point of view, involved in our political relations with foreign states? Similarly, such questions as the all-big-gun ship, and the position of the armor belt relatively to the mean or external line of flotation. These are of recent memory, and being purely military are for military determination, not for the Bureaus. Ordnance, *in virtue of its office*, has no more to do with the one, or Construction with the other, than a tailor has to do with the thickness I require in my coat, or the number of pockets I desire. His business is merely to furnish what I order.

It is the General Board that I should like to see in Cabinet relations with the Secy. Add to this that, after Dewey retires, that the head of the General Board should be, ex officio—the designated commander afloat of the fleet in case of war, and you have the two leading constructive ideas which have so far reached me. The Head of the General Board, or Staff, should understand all along that he is preparing for war; which, if it come, he will have to conduct. He will be perpetually sowing for a future personal reaping.

Subordinate in idea to this, I would have him the sole *responsible* adviser of the Secy. What I mean is, that, after hearing and discussing with the other members, he should, on vital military questions, say to the Secy "This is *my* advice, not the Board's advice." This does not in the least bind the Secy. to take it, any more than a client is bound to take the advice of his lawyer; but it does fix the sobering sense of responsibility upon both advisor and advisee, without impairing the individuality of either. In case of culpable mishap there can be no doubt where the responsibility lies.

In my apprehension, the work of the General Board underlies the activities of the Bureaus. Knowledge of the theatres of possible war, and the conditions to be met are the data to determine the sizes, qualities and armaments of ships. It is in free and frequent—Cabinet—meetings with that Board that a Secretary will most surely gain, and maintain, mastery of all the rest of the Department work.

You will of course recognize the hasty and crude form into which alone time permits me now to throw some ideas which I cannot pretend yet to have mastered—much less digested.

To John S. Billings

Lawrence, Long Island, February 2, 1909 [NYPL]

My dear Dr. Billings: Thank you very much for the prompt reply to my letter.[1] I believe I told you that the request was on account of a Commission on which I have been ordered by the President, and which, worse luck, will keep me from the Round Table on Friday.

To Stephen B. Luce

Lawrence, Long Island, February 2, 1909 [LC]

My dear Admiral: As soon as I saw the President's letter in print,[1] last Thursday, I wrote to Justice Moody on the assumption he would be again Chairman, suggesting that the naval members be urged to formulate their views, so that we might, by facing the music individually, learn what our exact preliminary position is.

In accordance I have been framing my own, finding it difficult to be at once clear and compact. If you see any others I hope you will urge them to come similarly prepared. The trouble with most Boards is that the mem-

---

1. *See* Mahan to Billings, January 30, 1909.

1. Roosevelt, in a letter of January 27, 1909, to the Senate and the House of Representatives, announced that he had appointed a commission consisting of W. H. Moody, A. G. Dayton, P. Morton, and Admirals Luce, Mahan, Evans, Folger, and Cowles "to consider certain needs of the navy." The members were asked to consider especially: lack of coordination in the work of the Bureaus, the excessive authority of the chiefs of Bureaus, the division of responsibility in the preparation and conduct of war, overlapping functions in Bureau operation, lack of financial accountability, and the encroachment of civilian control. The commission was to submit three reports: on the principles of an organization that would insure effective preparation for war in time of peace; recommendations on changes in the existing organization; and recommendations on the necessary number, location, and facilities of navy yards for maintaining the fleet in a state of readiness. The recommendations of the Moody Board were submitted February 18 through 25, 1909. They condemned the inefficiency of the Bureau system of administration, and proposed an advisory commission of officers to the Secretary of the Navy, to be headed by an officer who would also command the fleet in wartime. The recommendation was an approach to the later Chief of Naval Operations concept advocated by many reformers, including Mahan and Luce. The Board also suggested that the question of yards and bases be studied jointly by senior officers of the Army and the Navy. Roosevelt subsequently appointed a joint commission for this purpose, with Mahan as its chairman and the following members: Rear Admiral C. S. Sperry, Rear Admiral R. Wainwright, Captain C. McR. Winslow, Major General J. Franklin Boll, Brigadier General W. W. Witherspoon, and Brigadier General W. L. Marshall.

bers do nothing before meeting, and not much for some time after. The two things hang together.

I am tired of being away from home before I start.

To William H. Moody

Lawrence, Long Island, February 3, 1909 [LC]

My dear Justice Moody: I recognize my incompetence to advise a man of so much wider familiarity with public conditions than myself; and I am equally not in a position to criticize the President's decision.

Yet I may be justified in submitting to your consideration the importance of getting out, in a form that will carry weight with the public, at the least a brief statement of the principles underlying naval organization; & also a circumstance which you can weigh far better than myself, how far the President is in face of an opposition which may be conservative to perverseness, if not actually reactionary.

No such statement can carry authority, if put forth by a body of line officers, however weighty their individual reputation. In effect, it is absolutely necessary that a decisive element of the Commission be of men in civil life, and of such none can be better than those who in addition to personal reputation otherwise, have had recent experience of the Department workings, in their special capacity—executive or legislative.

Granting the general desirability of the President's scheme, there is no time to lose; for the next administration, besides being new, will have its hands full at once. Yet time is being lost, when the issue at stake is merely the authorizing a Commission; the report of which need not be even read—still less adopted. Why then should the legislature delay acceding to so simple a request? When delay means indefinite postponement, inferences are natural.

My own disinclination to this duty, and the inconveniences it causes me, to some extent extenuates to my own judgment an appeal which I trust you will not find importunate.

To Stephen B. Luce

Lawrence, Long Island, February 11, 1909 [LC]

My dear Admiral: Yours just received. On Tuesday I had a telephone from Mr. Morton,[1] fixing to-morrow, 10 a.m., for a meeting at his house.

---

1. Chairman of a subcommittee of the Moody Commission on Naval Reorganization.

Until that is held, I cannot reply definitely to your query. If we agree to-morrow it will of course expedite matters; but the question, even of principles, is difficult. I will let you know as soon as I see clear.[2]

To William H. Henderson

Lawrence, Long Island, February 16, 1909 [NMM]

My dear Henderson: It was good to hear from you again, to learn your plans and definitive settlement for the years to come. I have been delayed in replying because, while already busy enough, our President, by one of his sudden characteristic resolutions, appointed me on a Commission to consider and recommend changes in the organization of our Navy Dept. I fancied myself to have some appreciation of underlying principles; but when it comes to formulating them, and at the same time adapting them as far as possible to conservative opposition—to sugar coat the pill and get it down—the matter becomes complicated and requires much thought. The work is distasteful to me, which also makes it more wasteful of time.

I think you absolutely right in your choice of residence.[1] Nothing like a big city to keep one alive and young. We have for three years—this the fourth—abandoned our N. Y. home, for reasons of health of the women of my family. We are here an hour from the shopping district of N.Y., and little more from my club; but while advantages preponderate, I am satisfied I am too much out of the world. But, having had a severe illness last year, entailing a series of operations, a quiet life has advantage for me too. I am wonderfully recovered, almost as good mentally and physically as before; which at 68 is a good showing after so hard and prolonged an experience. But I *know* I am older.

We will have to agree to differ about immunity of private property. I dont think our Government as keen about it as it was; while your throttling geographical position towards German trade seems to me a factor of decisive importance in any conclusions reached. My delay in writing permits some enlightenment as to the outward quiescence of your service as con-

---

2. On February 15, W. F. Fullam, Secretary, notified Mahan that the Commission would meet on Friday, February 19, 1909. The cleavage between the young and the old in the Navy, so apparent in the bitter all-big-gun ship dispute, and in the Newport Conference, was at least temporarily healed by a general resentment against the power of the Bureau chiefs, and the belief that the Navy was virtually leaderless.

1. Probably, 22 Richmond Mansions, London, S.W.5.

trasted with the inward. Beresford's detachment,[2] cabled to our press yesterday is, I fancy, an outward and visible sign of interior conditions otherwise than amiable. I was interested to infer, from the dispatch, that it is proposed that the main fleet shall be commanded by one of the Sea Lords; who, it *seems*, is with it to retain his seat in the Board. Interested, I say, because a pet idea of mine has been that the man (U.S.) charged with Fisher's specific duties should be, ipso facto, commander in chief of the concentrated battleship force; hoisting his flag for four summer months.

The worst thing in the naval outlook—to my mind—is the increasing size of ships;[3] not so much on its own account, but because of the coincident rapid scrapping of smaller ships. This is throwing money away, and must end in stopping naval preparations. Personally, I stand aghast. If absence of preparation would stop war, all right; but it wont. Never were two states more devoid of preparation than our North & South in 1861; but there was cause to fight and they fought. Those who think that stopping of preparation will ward off the struggle between the white and yellow races in the Pacific, disagree with me. But how long can we go on, not merely spending money on ships, but spending it to make them worthless in a half dozen years, because outgrown.

To James W. McIntyre

Lawrence, Long Island, February 16, 1909 [LC]

Dear Mr. McIntyre: The dispatch of the Ms. of my proposed new book[1] has been delayed by unexpected orders from the President, placing me upon a Commission; attendance upon which has procrastinated the final revision I thought desirable. It is now made up, and I hope to dispatch to you today, by mail or by express.

I am desirous to place it upon the market as soon as easily practicable, and hope therefore that it may begin to be set up as soon as convenient to you. Last year, this year, and next year, have been and promise to be a period of sustained interest in these matters, among most bodies of Christians; and I have thought to recognize a certain prominence given generally to

2. From command of the no-longer-existent Channel Fleet. *See* Mahan to Clark, September 11, 1908, Footnote 5.
3. Lord Fisher's reorganization plans, stemming from the Order in Council of 1904, firmly established the all-big-gun battleship and cruiser for the British navy.
1. *The Harvest Within.*

the line of thought which I have here put forward independently. I do not flatter myself that I can say much that is new; but I hope that, as in *Sea Power*, I may have put old things in a new form such as may make them more cordially received, because clearer.

This Commission, and other Government employment will make large demands upon my time, for which reason I am the more anxious to begin this work speedily. My revision has been so frequent and minute, that I hope I may spare myself in proof reading, and yet keep up with the printers.

You will observe there is no preface. Should it seem expedient I may submit one later, having indeed one rough-sketched. Also, I may wish to add as a separate article, an address of between three and four thousand words, delivered by me ten years ago,[2] and which summarizes, with the conciseness needed, what I have in the book developed at length. These questions can be decided, as expediency may dictate, while the other work is going forward.

To James Ford Rhodes

Lawrence, Long Island, February 17, 1909 [MHS]

Dear Mr. Rhodes: I want to congratulate on what seemed to me the success of your dinner on Saturday. I certainly derived from it much pleasure, due largely I think to the fact that there were not too many. It was just what I should like to do often, had I the means; and I recall two such before, which I owed to you: one when I met Mr. Olney[1] at the Algonquin Club, and one at your own home in company with Mr. Adams.

To William H. Moody

Telegram Lawrence, Long Island, February 22, 1909 [LC]

I am willing for the modifications.[1]

---

2. "The Practical in Christianity," delivered in the Episcopal Church of the Holy Trinity, Middletown, Connecticut, on March 22, 1899.

1. Richard Olney, Secretary of State from 1895 to 1897.

1. A collect telegram. On February 25 Mahan submitted his preliminary report on the general principles of naval reorganization.

To Spencer Gordon[1]

Claim of A. T. Mahan, Rear Admiral, Retired, for traveling expenses, from February 4 to February 27, 1909, performed under orders of the Navy Department, dated January 30, 1909, with modification dated February 16, 1909; copies of which accompany this claim.

A

Orders January 30, 1909. Travel performed February 4–6.
Left Lawrence, Feb. 4, 2 p.m. Returned Feb. 6, 5 p.m.

R.R. Ticket, Lawrence to New York, and return	.80
″ New York to Washington, ″	10.00
Pullman Sleeper ″ ″	2.00
″ Additional for Compartment (explanation below)	5.00
Single Meal, en route, going	1.25
Tips ″	.35
Transportation of Baggage ″	1.00
Hotel Room one night	2.50
Tips	.50
Single Meals, Hotel, four 7 a.m. Feb. 5, to	2.40
″ Outside, one 3 p.m. Feb. 6.	.40
″ Tips	.50
Cab to Station, returning	.80
Transportation of Baggage, returning	.75
Tips returning	.40
Meal ″	.20
Carfares	.10
	28.95

B

Summoned to New York, by telephone, by Hon. Paul Morton,
Chairman of a Sub-committee appointed by the Chairman.
Left Lawrence 10 A.M. Feb. 12. Returned 6 p.m.

R.R. ticket to N.Y. and return		0.80
Carfares		.10
	Total	.90

1. An attorney retained by Mahan to press his disagreement with the departments of Navy and Treasury on travel cost reimbursement. The case eventually went to the Court of Claims in Washington, D.C.

C

Orders, Feb. 15, 1909. Travel performed Feb. 18–20.
Summoned to Washington for a meeting of the full Commission by
Hon. W. H. Moody, Chairman.
Left Lawrence February 18, 9 A.M. Returned Feb 20, 11 P.M.

R.R. Ticket, Lawrence to New York and return	.80
" New York to Washington "	10.00
Pullman " " " "	2.50
Single Meals, en route, going and returning	.40
Tips " going	.30
Transportation of baggage, going	.60
Hotel Bill room 2 days	5.00
" four single meals	3.25
One single meal (outside Hotel)	.35
Tips, five single meals	.50
Hotel tips—two days	.70
Cab to Station	1.00
Transportation baggage, Washington to Lawrence	.75
Tips, returning	.30
Carfares	.15
	26.60

D

February 23, 1909
Left Lawrence Feb. 23 10 A.M. Returned 6 P.M.
Summoned to New York by Hon. Paul Morton,
Chairman of Sub-Committee. By telephone.

R.R. Ticket Lawrence to New York and return	.80
Carfares	.10
Total	.90

E

Orders, telegraphic, Feb. 24, 1909. Travel performed, Feb. 25–27.
To Washington, by summons, to attend Commission meeting.
Left Lawrence, Feb. 25, 9 A.M. Returned Feb. 27, 11 A.M.

R.R. Ticket Lawrence to New York and return	.80
" New York to Washington "	10.00
Pullman Seat " " "	2.50
Tips, en route, going	.20
Hotel Bill, Washington one day, Room	2.50

Single Meals, two in Hotel	1.60
" one outside	.30
" tips	.30
Hotel Tips	.50
Transportation of Baggage—going	.60
" " returning	1.00
Single Meal returning	1.25
Tips, returning	.30
Room in New York	3.00
Single Meal "	.50
	25.35

Summary

1.	February 4–6	28.95
2.	February 12	.90
3.	February 18–20	26.50
4.	February 23	.90
5.	February 25–27	25.35
		82.60

Lawrence, N.Y., March 1909

I hereby certify that the amounts claimed above have been actually expended by me in pursuance of the accompanying orders, and that they were necessary.

I enclose herewith Hotel receipts; also check receipts of Pullman seats for the trips of Feb. 18–20 and 25–27. Those for February 4–6 I did not retain, because I believed myself to be then traveling under mileage; and I was informed at the Bureau of Navigation that such had been the intention of the orders, which subsequently were modified. No other receipted bills were practicable.

Note. In explanation of the expense for compartment on the night of February 4–5, since a severe illness of a year ago, my physical condition, not to speak of my age, 68, requires absolutely that I have the privacy of a room at night. In taking it I at the time believed myself to be traveling under mileage as before stated.

The justification of my night in N.Y., Feb 26–27, as 'necessary' rests on the fact that Geo. Meyer,[2] as next Secy., wished to talk with me (message by Moody) I could not properly, even if I wished, refuse. The choice was between sleeping in Washn. or in N.Y.—the latter so far on return, no midday meal, 27th.

---

2. George von Lengerke Meyer became Secretary of the Navy on March 6, 1909. He was deeply interested in the application of the methods of scientific management to problems of naval reorganization and administration.

To Theodore Roosevelt

Lawrence, Long Island, March 2, 1909 [LC]

Dear Mr. President: Will it be in any sense improper that you should give a last earnest recommendation to Mr. Taft on no account to divide the battleship force between the two coasts?

As a matter of popular outcry, this is a nightmare to me. With all his peculiarly eminent qualifications for the Presidency, I do not know whether Mr. Taft has a strong military sense; and, as I see it, this is one of the most evident external dangers threatening the country.

Pardon the intrusion.

To William H. Moody

Lawrence, Long Island, March 2, 1909 [LC]

Dear Justice Moody: Your letter, enclosing copy of President's,[1] came back by the same delivery as took out mine to you—of today.

I am much indebted for the copy, having received no other.

To Little, Brown and Company

Lawrence, Long Island, March 4, 1909 [LC]

Gentlemen: I send the enclosed[1] in response to your letter of March 1, asking for a descriptive paragraph, giving the scope of my new book.[2]

When the proof begins to be sent, I would like to be informed of the number of lines on an ordinary page, and also the number on the pages beginning a chapter. Such knowledge sometimes guides in making corrections, preventing paragraphs of awkward length.

To Charles W. Stewart

Lawrence, Long Island, March 19, 1909 [NA]

My dear Mr. Stewart: The Naval Appn. Bill reached me duly, and I am much indebted for it. My chief purpose in asking was, that if both

1. Enclosure not found.
1. Enclosure not found.
2. *The Harvest Within.*

Houses had passed the Senate clause, recommending the division of the battleship fleet between the Pacific and Atlantic coasts, I felt it would be time for naval officers to speak out for the enlightenment of the people on the folly of Congress in dealing with such matters. As you know, the remonstrance of the "one man," the President, with the House Committee helped largely to prevent this suicidal recommendation.

As regards the arguments for naval expenditure, the best newspaper reference I can give you is the London *Times*, for March 1 and 2; especially the later date. To this is to be added, when it arrives, the issue of March 16 or 17, giving the proceedings in parliament, as to the increase of the German navy, not only in numbers, but in a facility for rapid building which bids fair to rival that of Great Britain.

The issue of March 2 gives the projected (statutory) building of Great Britain, Germany, and the U.S., as each now stands; from which it appears, owing to the refusal of Congress to give the four new ships recommended by the "one man," the German Navy will in 1912—in three years—have a stronger battle fleet in A.B.G.[1] ships than we. What then shall we say, upon what shall we rely, if she, on occasion arising, defy us in the Monroe Doctrine? How do we propose to keep that national idol on its feet without a superior navy?

It may be said that in any event the British Navy is far superior to ours; indeed, to a degree that no one proposes to overtake. Granted, for it is true. The reply is that Great Britain is already overloaded with colonial possessions; her present problem being how to bring into a more solid framework of mutual support those she now has; not to acquire more American territory, which is the gist of that to which the Monroe Doctrine opposes itself. The exposure of Canada, in case of war with the United States, would at once bring to an acute stage the question of the future political relations of that Dominion. Besides, we have now a long history of discussion with Great Britain, in which the Monroe Doctrine has been the avowed, or the latent, motive; and it is assured that that country has no reason now, and no disposition, to traverse our position in the matter.

It is very different with Germany. Her commercial and colonial development is a matter of yesterday; and the rapidity in both directions testifies at once to strong national purpose and to masterly organization of effort. But, the colonies she now has are far from the first order of commercial value, and all other land throughout the world is now preempted, and occupied—politically, if not actually. Germany cannot but desire acquisition; and acquisition by war is a legitimate international transaction. In natural resources, as distinguished from the value as a market which an adequate population constitutes, as a body of consumers, South America probably leads the world; and the smallness of present population is an

---

1. All-Big-Gun.

additional advantage from the point of view of colonial acquisition.

In addition, should the hopes of Holland, from the Queen's approaching confinement, be again disappointed, we shall be definitely menaced with the possibility of Germany, with the second strongest navy in Europe, becoming heir to the Dutch colonial system. Is it to be imagined that with a claim so entirely lawful she would respect our position as to the transfer of American territory from one European power to another? She has done so so far; but her navy has not been superior.

In the matter of expenditure, it may be apt to remark that, whatever our various views on the tariff, American legislators are, and necessarily must be, exceedingly sensitive to the consideration of the wages and scale of living of American workmen. That means that we, as a nation, will always have to pay more, much more, for our military preparations, than a nation like Germany with a long history of comparatively meagre remuneration to labor, and with a much larger proportion of working men relatively to the total resources of the country.

The question of expenditure is not that of what we are willing to pay, but whether we are willing to hold our most cherished international dogma —the Monroe Doctrine—at the mercy of a superior navy, the possessors of which may have good reason to disregard our views.

I have developed this so much beyond what I meant when I sat down, that I will ask you to return it to me, together with the enclosure.[2] I may have use for them. You can, of course, keep a copy if you wish.

To Little, Brown and Company

Lawrence, Long Island, March 23, 1909 [LC]

Gentlemen: I have received fourteen galleys, and have corrected the text; delayed a little in returning by the felt expediency of verifying the foot-notes.

Concerning these notes: May I depend upon the proof reader verifying that they correspond with those in the "Copy"? I verified the "Copy" very minutely before sending; and if I can rely that the proof reader will insure correspondence with it, I can postpone further verification on my part to the page-proof.

This I shall desire the more because the printer, in these galleys, instead as heretofore of putting in the notes as he finishes each page of copy, has placed all at the foot of the completed galley. This renders verification much more troublesome.

---

2. Enclosure not found.

In proceeding to page proof, I wish that the page headings, on the even numbered pages, be throughout the book: The Life of the Christian; not Fragments that Remain, as in the specimen page sent me. The odd numbered pages to have simply the Chapter Heading: Power, Likeness, &c.

I note in the leaflet circular accompanying the galleys, that you ask the return of the Ms. with the proofs. If you really wish this in my case, of course I will comply; but as in our long association it has never before been done, I will await your further instructions.

To Little, Brown and Company

Lawrence, Long Island, March 25, 1909 [LC]

Gentlemen: I am returning to day the first fourteen galleys. The trouble in verifying and correcting the references (footnotes) leads me to submit to you again the convenience of returning to the previous custom, of inserting the footnotes as each page of copy is set up.

Your experience may suggest to you reasons to the contrary, not apparent to myself; and I shall accept your decision willingly. The confusion due to my insertions is real, but would be minimized by the practice I suggest.

[Written on attached envelope]:
Contents of this Envelope refer *solely* to lowering price of my books in England. Mr. Brown's final letter, stating pecuniary result *to me*, to be paid May, 1909, is in Elly's keeping.

To Little, Brown and Company

Lawrence, Long Island, March 29, 1909 [LC]

Gentlemen: I had overlooked that it was customary to place the title of the work at the head. You may restore it to its usual position.

The sub-title, "The Life of the Christian," is more consonant to the general purport of the work; but it is a phrase very likely to have been used before. I know, indeed of a book recently published called "The Life of *a* Christian."[1]

The meaning of "Fragments that Remain" will appear in the Preface; copy of which I hope to send tomorrow or Wednesday.

---

1. Charles Mercer Hall, *The Life of a Christian; Some Suggestions for Short Studies in the Spiritual Life* . . . With an Introduction by the Bishop of Milwaukee. New York: Longmans, Green & Co., 1907.

[293]

To Little, Brown and Company

Lawrence, Long Island, March 30, 1909 [LC]

Gentlemen: I enclose herewith the Preface of the new book, and also the Address[1] which, as a separate paper, is to follow the text.

This completes the "Copy."

I have no other copy of these two papers, so that their preservation till set up will need care.

To Little, Brown and Company

University Club, New York, April 1, 1909 [LC]

Gentlemen: I do not know what your plans may be as to binding of my forthcoming book;[1] and it has occurred to me to suggest for your consideration, on the cover, as congruous to the general purport of the book, a monogram—one of those generally recognized as standing for Our Lord.

I have in mind two; of Greek letters. The first is somewhat as follows: the first two (in English three) letters of His Name. The other is the well known Alpha & Omega.

All this is mere suggestion to which I would only add that I prefer the first; and if either be adopted, the simpler the better.

To Little, Brown and Company

Lawrence, Long Island, April 5, 1909 [LC]

Gentlemen: Unless my memory deceives, the articles referred to in the enclosed[1] have never been republished. If so, the writers' request should be addressed to Messrs. Chas Scribner only. Should you write to that effect, will you kindly add that they have my consent, conditional upon that of the Scribner's.

Of the two monograms, I think the Alpha & Omega would be more usually recognized as familiar. I have often seen it, but now can only recall one; in the East window of the Church of the Holy Communion, N.Y. 6th Av. & 20th St. Probably clergymen of the Church of the Advent, Boston, or

---

1. "The Practical in Christianity."
1. *The Harvest Within.*
1. Enclosure not found.

Messrs Copples & Upham, could advise you. It is best, I presume, not to depart too far from the conventional and simple in symbolism. Two forms occur to me: ⚭⚭ . It should be remembered that the two letters should be in all respects of *equal* force in scale and weight. There should not be a predominance in effect of either.

I am glad to know that you purpose to make the book markedly distinct in exterior effect from others.

To W. W. Mumford

Lawrence, Long Island, April 5, 1909 [HUL]

Dear Sir: As one of the residuary legatees under the will of Mrs. J. L. Swift, I hereby request you to turn over to Mr. Lyle Evans Mahan a satisfaction of a mortgage executed by Mrs. Swift to Mr. White in 1873, which mortgage was for the sum of $579.00 dollars.

I also request you to turn over to Mr. Mahan, all papers relating to the estate of Mrs. Swift and also of my mother, Mrs. Mary H. Mahan, and he is authorized to receipt to you for the same.

To Little, Brown and Company

Lawrence, Long Island, April 10, 1909 [LC]

Gentlemen: I am rather disconcerted by the discovery that "Fragments that Remain"[1] has been anticipated as a title: for, while "Thoughts on the Life of the Christian" represents more exactly the spirit and matter of the book itself, the other stands for my own personal relation to the thinking factor in it.

There is, of course, nothing to do but to accept the impossibility of utilizing the phrase, and to accept provisionally "Thoughts &c;" as the main title, instead of, as before, secondary. I would like the question left open, however, till proof reading approaches completion. Something may occur to me; and the only places affected are the title page, and first page of text. There is, it is true, an allusion to Fragments in the preface, but that can be readily handled.

---

1. Maltbie Davenport Babcock, *Fragments That Remain from the Ministry of Maltbie Davenport Babcock, Pastor Brick Church, New York City, 1899–1901, Reported and Arranged by Jessie B. Goetschius*. . . . New York: Fleming H. Revell Company, 1907.

As regards the change falling on p. 77, I have so modified it in the page proof returned, as not to add a line. It is my purpose never to interfere with pagination once set up, unless for very grave cause.

To James W. McIntyre

Lawrence, Long Island, April 12, 1909 [LC]

My dear Mr. McIntyre: The new book is near completion. Have you made any decision as to the English publishers?

As in business judgment generally, I am willing to acquiesce in your opinion; but, unless this is decisively pronounced, I feel strongly that others than the present Sampson Low will be better than they. Such contact as I have had with them impresses me with their being of rather picayune calibre; and their speciality, I apprehend, is not devotional literature, as this aims to be.

Their objection to publishing in separate form my contribution to their *History of the Royal Navy*, has appeared to me to rest, not on any broad views of present expediency, but upon a half-resentful view that I was overpaid for it at the time—ten years ago. As a matter of fact, I was paid about half the rate I was getting for magazine writing.

When the troubles of the late firm came on, before I knew of them, I received letters from three or four English firms asking the agency—or English publication—of my books. Among these was John Murray. The others I forget; but in all cases my reply was that I left such matters with your firm, and moreover (being ignorant of conditions) had no wish to separate from the Marstons.

I do not believe in allowing feeling to enter into business decisions. My wish is to reach the greatest number of readers with this book; and that for many reasons not necessary here to enumerate. So I repeat, that with this object, which necessarily is yours also, I am willing to acquiesce in your judgment; but, unless you are very sure, I would prefer to S. L. & Co some recognized dealers in devotional literature in England.

Underlying all, I have also a feeling that the future agency of my works might be used diplomatically to obtain of them acquiescence in separate publication of the above naval contribution. I have good authority for saying that it is worthy of such publication, and believe it would pay—them as well as us.

To Little, Brown and Company

Lawrence, Long Island, April 12, 1909 [LC]

Gentlemen: It has occurred to me that the title, "The Harvest Within," would be consonant with the leading idea of the book as expressed in the sub-title "Thoughts on the Life etc"; and at the same time would leave rather more individuality than the latter, if used as the only title.

Should this meet your approval, and there be no prëmption, as in "Fragments that Remain," it would only be necessary to substitute for the latter on title page, and first page of text.

To Little, Brown and Company

Lawrence, Long Island, April 15, 1909 [LC]

Gentlemen: I return herewith one copy of Agreement for *The Harvest Within*, duly signed as requested.

Kindly let me know if you will require the original "Copy" of the work returned to you; for, if not, as I leave this house for Quogue, May 1, I should like to destroy it.

To James W. McIntyre

Lawrence, Long Island, April 16, 1909 [LC]

Dear Mr. McIntyre: I am glad that the new title suits. To my own judgment it appears better than Fragments. Had it occurred to me in time, I might probably have been willing to carry it for the page headings; but upon the whole I believe the present arrangement better.

All the page proof of the *text* has now been read and returned. The Middletown address[1] galleys have been corrected, but I have not seen page proof of either it or Preface.

I quite agree that it is inexpedient for *us* to attempt to re-open the question of the Royal Navy article. I do not believe they are acting in their direct interest; but apparently with some vague desire of getting back part of what was paid me. I shall confront very changed conditions before I meet them there.

---

1. "The Practical in Christianity," Holy Trinity Episcopal Church, Middletown, Connecticut, March 22, 1899.

I do not intend to mix feeling with business; but I am much inclined to believe it best to transfer *all* my books to some other English firm; all, that is, of the future. I will ask you to keep this in your mind.

To Little, Brown and Company

Lawrence, Long Island, April 19, 1909 [LC]

Gentlemen: As the book *The Harvest Within* is so near completion, and my time much pre-occupied during the next ten days, I write now to notify you that after April 30, my address will be Quogue, N.Y.

And I request that, if the copies to be sent me should by chance be ready before that time, that *they be not sent* until you hear further from me.

To John P. Merrell

Lawrence, Long Island, April 24, 1909 [NWC]

My dear Merrell: I send today under two envelopes, because one will not hold, written Ms. of a preliminary lecture to the course as it now stands. I have not been able to give to the form as much attention as I could wish; but time presses, and I think matters will be expedited if these pages could be type written and returned to me for revision as to style.

Will you please note that my address after May 1 will be Quogue, N.Y.? and will you send me there another package of official envelopes?

I leave here Tuesday next, and shall remain the week at the University Club, N.Y. going myself to Quogue, Monday, May 3.

To John P. Merrell

Lawrence, Long Island, April 24, 1909 [NWC]

My dear Merrell: After closing the first envelope, I remembered that I had not explained my habit of writing insertions on the back of a page, placing the word "over" at the point of insertion, as notice to the copyist to look at the back.

Also, on pages 27, 28, will you ask Adml Luce to verify my recollection of what he told me, and correct as necessary.

To Little, Brown and Company

University Club, New York, April 25, 1909 [LC]

Gentlemen: As we are moving away from Lawrence for the summer, I thought best to send you yesterday, by mail, the "Copy" of the book. The first page of the Preface is missing.

On p. 233, cast-proof, about line 15 from top, the sentence: "Father into Thy hands I commend &c" has no comma after "Father." It were better it had, but I am too ignorant of processes to know whether it can now be inserted without an expense and delay quite disproportionate to the requirement of the change.

To Stephen B. Luce

Marshmere,[1] Quogue, Long Island, May 6, 1909 [LC]

My dear Admiral: I received your two notes and the accompanying pamphlets at the Club, but have only today found time to read the latter. Merrell will, I suppose, send on the type written copy of the material sent him by me, and I will try then to bring the particular portion into due correspondence with the facts as you state them. My object was merely illustration to which the incident was peculiarly apt; I was not intending a full account such as the very instructive narrative given by you of the proceedings before Charleston.[2]

I have often been told that my detachment from the College, and orders to *Chicago*, in 1893 were due to the Hawaii article.[3] I daresay, though I never inquired. My first informant, as I recall, was an ex-U.S minister under Harrison's administration, who told me in London, coupling with the act the name of Josiah Quincy, Asst. Secy. of State under Cleveland. I have never felt quite sure, for Ramsay had been on my tracks for quite a while, & after Tracy left office I found no sympathizer in Herbert. Still, the article may have been a last straw; the occasion, if not entirely the cause, of my orders. These were one of the luckiest things that have happened in my career, a boomerang for any who wished me ill in them.

---

1. The summer house at Quogue, called "Slumberside," was sold in 1908 and "Marshmere," a substantial year-round residence on the water, was built in 1908–1909. The West 86th Street house remained leased. It was never again occupied by the family and was sold in 1915. *See* Mahan to Clark, July 23, 1909; and Mahan to Henderson, December 26, 1910. The family spent the winters of 1909–1910 and 1910–1911 in Lawrence, Long Island.
2. Stephen B. Luce, "Proceedings before Charleston." Lecture and discussion at the Naval War College, Summer Session, 1899.
3. "Hawaii and Our Future Sea Power."

To John P. Merrell

Quogue, Long Island, May 10, 1909 [NWC]

My dear Merrell: I have received the two type-written copies, and the original, of my proposed preliminary lecture, and hope to return one ready for use by the end of this week.

As regards my lecturing in person, I have for some years past been declining to appear in public speaking.[1] Will you let this stand over for a few days, and let me know meantime when the lectures would begin; fixing the latest date consistent with the College requirements? I have made a certain number of notes for addition to the lectures. In rereading, and inserting these notes, I may find myself sufficiently conversant with the matter as a whole to justify my attempting what you kindly ask.

To William Dean Howells[1]

Marshmere, Quogue, Long Island, May 13, 1909 [HUL]

My dear Sir: After reflection, I think it unadvisable for me to undertake the paper for the meeting of the Academy in December next. This decision is based not merely upon the demands upon my time, which probably are not insuperable, but upon the increasing inexpediency of my undertaking to speak or to read in public at a fixed date.

I am very sensible of the honor done me by your request, and by associating me in it to the other distinguished names which you mention; but I believe it better for the meeting as for myself that I decline.

To John P. Merrell

Quogue, Long Island, May 22, 1909 [NWC]

My dear Merrell: I am glad to find that you have appreciated the impossibility of my completing revision in time for the opening of the Con-

---

1. Merrell had suggested that Mahan "give in person, as you did prior to the Spanish War, your lectures on Naval Strategy." Merrell to Mahan, May 5, 1909, at the Naval War College.

1. President of the American Academy of Arts and Letters, novelist, critic, and editor.

ference[1] this year. Revision, I find, is not unlike repairing a ship; once begun, you dont know where you will end. It is not that I find much to cut out, or even to correct; but the years intervening since 1898, the amount of reading and writing since done, provide material for addition which cannot be introduced without a process much resembling repair; and which, moreover, needs checking and pruning, lest by excess it obscure rather than elucidate.

As regards the immediate proposition: Among the interests and occupations that have accumulated around me in my retirement is one which calls for my presence in New York June 8, to attend a meeting. The preliminary lecture you have had type written, I expect to mail to you on Monday next, May 24, corrected for delivery. Though preliminary to the revision, it has a certain independence of all other lectures, revised or unrevised; and should you care so to order matters, I will come on the 9th June, and deliver it on the 10th.

Meantime, I may be able, probably shall be able, to furnish a few additions to the lectures as they stand; whether read by another or by myself. My reading at all will be somewhat tentative; for I feel my years now, and do not know how far I can stand the continuous strain. I have definitely and finally abandoned all *extempore* speaking; but that carries an additional element of nervous strain, which does not obtain in using manuscript. The latter is only a question of physical endurance.

I shall remember the necessity of your having in hand the clean copy of the lectures as they now stand, and will bear in mind that they reach you before the end of the week, June 5; unless, indeed, you require them sooner. The intervening time I will give to considering whether any, and what, additions may advisably be introduced, having regard to the time at my disposal.

Before leaving the Intelligence Office, Rodgers sent me a lot, I believe all, their material bearing on the Russo-Jap War.

[P.S.] I incline myself to think that my making June 10 (should that meet your views) had better stand by itself; an experiment, determining whether I can read in October, as you suggest.

---

1. The name given at this time to the regular annual session of the College. In July–August 1909, however, there met conjointly with this Conference the so-called "Battleship Conference" or "Newport Conference" especially ordered by President Roosevelt to consider the design of new battleships, with particular attention to the adequacy of armor-plating on the proposed *North Dakota* class. Sixty-seven officers and high-ranking Navy Department civilians, including nine rear admirals, participated in these deliberations. President Roosevelt also attended. The regular session or Conference of the College was resumed on September 1.

To Little, Brown and Company

Quogue, Long Island, May 22, 1909 [LC]

Gentlemen: I enclose a list of names and addresses, to which I would like you to send, direct from your establishment, copies of *The Harvest Within*, when the day of publication arrives. I shall be obliged if you will insert in them a slip, "from the Author," as I see is frequently done; and I will further ask you *to notify me* when this is likely to be done, as I wish to write personally to the several persons my object in so sending.

In addition to the seven copies thus designated, kindly send seven others to my own address; that is fourteen in all, of which ten will be those to be furnished me by the terms of our agreement.

[P.S.] The charge for sending to the several . . . [sentence not completed].

1. Rt. Rev. W. C. Doane, D.D.
   Albany, N.Y.

2. Rt. Rev. David H. Greer D.D.
   7 Gramercy Park, New York

3. Rev. Wm. R. Huntington, D.D.
   Grace Church Rectory, New York.

4. George Wharton Pepper, Esq
   Philadelphia, Pa.

5. Robert E. Speer, Esq
   Presbyterian Board of Missions
   156 Fifth-Avenue, N.Y.

6. Mrs. George Zabriskie
   23 Gramercy Park, N.Y.

7. George Foster Peabody, Esq
   2 Rector St
   New York

To Little, Brown and Company

Quogue, Long Island, May 22, 1909 [LC]

Gentlemen: During the life time of the late Mr. Brown, he spoke to me of a possible eventual publication of all my works—uniform edition. A special stipulation exists with regard to *From Sail to Steam*; and I presume ultimately consent might be had from Appleton's for *The Life of Farragut*, and from Scribner's for *The Gulf and Inland Waters*.

In view of such a contingency, I write to ask whether it would be expedient, and convenient to you, to deposit in your care, copies of casual work—articles &c—not collected in book form; and also copies of printed books, corrected, so far as emendation or addition may seem desirable.

Mr. Brown seemed to think well of such an undertaking in some future time; but I of course do not pretend to estimate its probabilities from a business point of view.

To John P. Merrell

Quoque, Long Island, May 24, 1909 [NWC]

My dear Merrell: I send herewith the typewritten copy (not carbon) of the proposed preliminary lecture. The only changes it will be necessary to have made at the College relate to the quotations from Adl. Luce. It will probably be better for a reader that pp. 12 and 13 be re-typewritten, the overplus being numbered 13a.

At p. 12 I have inserted a substitute slip. For 13 I have noted on opposite blank page the desired change, in a manner which I think will be found sufficiently explicit.

I retain the carbon duplicate; but would be glad also to receive carbons of above.

To Little, Brown and Company

Quogue, Long Island, May 29, 1909 [LC]

Gentlemen: In glancing over the Cast Proof today, I notice that on page 1 the old title, "Fragments that Remain," still stands. Can it possibly have remained overlooked? I cannot remember writing about it, but trust some one has changed it to "Harvest Within."

To John P. Merrell

Quogue, Long Island, May 31, 1909 [NWC]

My dear Merrell: As you will need the old lectures for the opening of the course, I send them back to you, by today's mail.

I find that the first note that I have undertaken, in expansion of the lectures, has led me so far that I shall not be able to complete it in time for use now. In connection with it, and possibly with further illustration—probably—I shall need Corbett's books which I have here. Can you not leave them with me? Even, in case of necessity, get Stewart to let you have them from the Navy Dept. Library?

Indeed, in connection with this I would make a special suggestion for your consideration, viz: that the College might advantageously possess three or four copies of these, & of some other standard books on military & naval science, so that several of those attending the Conference[1] might, if they chose, study them without material interference.

Doubtless, those who will study with good will and ability will rarely be many; but, if interest be excited in capable men, nothing will more conduce to fruitful reading and tangible results for the Service, than historical works; after the leading principles of Strategy and Tactics have been mastered.

No lecturing will equal the results of such independent study.

Can you supply me with three or four pads, preferably without lines, of the general size of this paper on which I am now writing?

I do not know whether the understanding is *settled* that I am to come on the 9th, to lecture on the 10th; or whether you can have orders sent me to go from here hence.[2] I wish you to feel perfectly free to decide either way, as I am by no means bent on going, and it may possibly be best that I remain here, working without interruptions.

To Little, Brown and Company

Quogue, Long Island, June 3, 1909 [LC]

Gentlemen: I received last night advance copy of *The Harvest Within*, for which I beg to thank you. I am entirely satisfied and pleased with the get-up of the book, and have only one criticism to make—not unfavorable, but an instance of curious coincidence—upon the monogram on cover. Artistically and otherwise, it is all I could desire; but one of my daughters, at a hasty glance, read it A.T.M.—my own initials. I would be rather sensitive to such mistake, if it became general; & suggest for your consideration whether in future bindings it might not be well to omit or modify the crossing surmounting the Alpha—the $\overline{/}$.

---

1. *See* Mahan to Merrell, May 22, 1909, Footnote 1.
2. Mahan was ordered to report to the War College on June 9, 1909, to lecture. Merrell to Mahan, June 2 and 3, 1909; Pillsbury to Merrell, Telegram, June 3, 1909, at the Naval War College.

You are quite right, in assigning the English publication, to estimate my wish as being to promote the circulation of the book, rather than immediate returns; nor am I surprised that Longmans should hesitate in their venture. But, if the book should take, I presume that of course you would require, and they be willing, to pay accordingly; that the present price to them is tentative only.

[P.S.] Does my memory deceive me in the impression that you formerly thought Longmans less attentive to pushing books than some other Church publishers?

To Little, Brown and Company

Marshmere, Quogue, Long Island, June 5, 1909 [LC]

Gentlemen: I return herewith application for registration of English copyright.[1] The witness signing is my daughter.
Quogue is my legal residence.

To Little, Brown and Company

Quogue, Long Island, June 28, 1909 [LC]

Gentlemen: In yours of June 24 you do not say whether you had addressed a copy of *The Harvest Within* to the Archbishop of Canterbury,[1] as I asked. Please let me know that this has been done, as I wrote him a copy would be sent him by the *American publishers*.

I return Messrs. Longmans' letter. It is, as you say, conservative—and indifferent. Do you purpose making any comment, or would you prefer me to do so? The London *Weekly Times*, to which I subscribe, has no mention of the book in its issues of June 4, 11, 18; in all which appear, as usual, "Publications of the Week." Messrs. Longmans do not control the *Times*; but how is a book to be known that not only is not advertised, but is not so much as mentioned? As a matter of fact, no book of mine, I believe, has escaped notice, and usually review, in the *Times*.[2] This book, of course,

---

1. For *The Harvest Within*.

1. Randall Thomas Davidson.

2. *The Times Literary Supplement* of December 17, 1908, merely mentioned the receipt of *Naval Administration and Warfare* (1908); it was not actually reviewed until April 1, 1909 (p. 128), when an anonymous critic, although admitting the presence of "precious metal," complained that "he occasionally beats it out rather thin," and criticized the lack of organic cohesion between the essays. *The Harvest Within* passed apparently unnoticed.

is of very different character, but the *Times* deals with every kind. The *Spectator* continually has articles on the same topics as *The Harvest Within*. Failure to advertise in the *Guardian*, however, is the most remarkable. It is by far the leading Church of England paper, and I know it well for over thirty years.

Either you or I must make sure that the book reaches the *Guardian* and the *Spectator*.

To Little, Brown and Company

Quogue, Long Island, July 2, 1909 [LC]

Gentlemen: I have received your letter of June 30, and am glad to know that I had misjudged the delay of Messrs. Longmans in the matter. The explanation is satisfactory to me, and I am glad also to note that you have requested them to send copies to the *Times, Guardian, & Spectator*.

I note also the circular sent out by you. I judge that this is sufficient to insure that the book become known. Beyond that, it must stand or fall as it deserves; and in either event, if duly advertised, I shall have no cause nor wish to complain.

To John P. Merrell

Quogue, Long Island, July 23, 1909 [LC]

My dear Merrell: So far I find that Revision takes the shape rather of Expansion. Since I was in Newport I have read substantially all the material sent me by the Intelligence Office on the Russo-Japan War and have now ready for the type writer my comments, etc, thereon. This, in my apprehension so far, will precede the most part of the lectures, as they now stand; being, in idea, an enlargement of that illustration with which they begin, the explanation of the Archduke Charles, concerning his theater of war.

I do not send, merely because I do not know whether you are yet ready for the typewriting. As soon as I hear from you to that effect I will forward. There must be full 12,000 words.

[306]

To Bouverie F. Clark

My dear Clark: I had been thinking two or three days before your very welcome letter came that it was time some one was getting a move on in the matter of our correspondence; so I was partly glad and partly ashamed when yours was received.

We have had it hot while you were cold; hot as blazes. Luckily, we were here. Two summers ago Mrs. Mahan and the girls decided that our old house was too small. I think the trouble mainly was that in my illness I needed a bigger room than before, and so had to take one needed for other purposes. Anyhow, dissatisfaction having started found many reasons; so they prospected for a new site, out of the way of dust & motors, and with a pleasant outlook and there we proceeded to build a new house. Having abandoned New York this is arranged for early spring & late autumn; indeed for winter, but we do not propose to spend here more than six months—May 1 to November 1. The deuce of the arrangement, however, is a perpetual disarrangement every autumn, looking out for a new house every October, one that shall be suitable in position & convenience—not to add, price. It is with reference to this that we are thinking of a warmer climate. My wife ought to sleep in fresh air, & have it all the time. I need it more and more, *feel* the need of it. My house-keeping daughter ought to escape the nuisance of servants for a time each year. So in short we have a summer home, and for winters are all adrift. Whether we will settle upon Southern Europe, or Bermuda, or such like, I dont yet know nor even surmise. Perhaps we shall not have initiative to go anywhere. Your own feeling about leaving home is shared by us; my wife is as hard to start as a ground tier. I keep a little more limber by going to New York not infrequently for a night at the club; but that is so free and easy, and the accommodation so good, that it rather spoils me than hardens.

I keep a fleeting eye on your naval turmoil, but of course have no inside knowledge beyond your occasional mention. Some one certainly behaved badly when temporizing was permitted on the matter of ship-building. The truth is your present Government has tied itself in the hardest kind of a knot by increasing expenses and antagonizing tariff reform. I am averse to protection myself, but no one Govt. can stick out against some measure of it, in the face of the whole world. As regards Germany I wrote an article for one of our weeklies[1] just after your "panic" of last March, in which I took the ground that it made no difference to us what object she had in view; that her navy was a big fact, that called on us to sit up and take notice, if we were in earnest about the Monroe Doctrine, Panama Canal,

---

1. "Germany's Naval Ambition," *Collier's Weekly*, April 24, 1909.

and some other little jobs. I intend this autumn & winter to follow this up by a somewhat long discussion of international conditions. The Peace and Arbitration people—above all Andrew *Carnegie*—get on my *nerves*. I cant stand talk that blinks all the facts, and exhorts people to ignore facts that stare you in the face. At present my pen is tied down to some work for our Naval College—lectures on Strategy—which command all my time, & grow as fast as I write so that I dont catch up much; but there is an end to everything, and I hope soon for a free hand. My own hope is that our people may be brought to realize that *in our own interest* we may have to back you. One will have to walk warily, and turn your back as you do when leading a horse; but it may be done. I fear, & have from the first believed, that your Govt. backed the wrong horse in the alliance with Japan. It, more than anything else, may handicap us. Your own white folks in Australia etc dont like it any better than we. Well, this is a pretty long story. I have only to add that I am doing well; very well for one who will be 69 in September.

To John P. Merrell

Quogue, Long Island, July 31, 1909 [NWC]

My dear Merrell: I send you today under another cover and by registered mail what I have proposed on the Russo-Jap War. There is I think nothing to say for the copyist, except to remind that the interlineation *"over"* refers to back of page.

Day before yesterday the Intelligence Office asked back two of the papers sent me. Neither was of particular moment to my work; but as I have had the very considerable box-full sent me for very nearly three months, it seems due to return them as soon as may be. I purpose keeping them only till the typewritten copy comes back, and I have read it, with the advantage of correcting with the papers still at hand, if desirable.

My object is to use this and some other historical material as being in line with and immediately following the slight account of the Archduke Charles's work with which the course now opens. When I tell you that that which is so far written is nearly half what I send today, and when completed will nearly equal it, you will see that with the necessary reading and the writing I have not been idle. Whether my time has been fruitfully spent is another matter.

With regard to September I will come if physically and mentally able; I mean if not tired out. I cant work quite as I did; or, if I do, I get worn out.

To Little, Brown and Company

Quogue, Long Island, August 6, 1909 [LC]

Gentlemen: Will you kindly let me know if you have, or see, any objection to my acceding to the request in the within letter?[1] Please return it.

To Little, Brown and Company

Quogue, Long Island, August 11, 1909 [LC]

Gentlemen: I have received your letter, enclosing one to Messrs. Sampson Low, in the matter of the request of Captn. Charles Reade, and have forwarded the one to them.

Thanking you for your trouble in the matter, I am [etc.].

To John P. Merrell

Quogue, Long Island, August 26, 1909 [NWC]

My dear Merrell: I shall send you today by registered mail some Ms. for the type-writer. About as much more will follow in about ten days, and this will complete all I can accomplish for the present session.

Whether more should be done may very well be considered when I come to Newport; and that occasion will be doubly suitable, if Rodgers[1] by that time shall have arrived there.

With regard to my coming, it is imperative that I should be in New York early on Sept. 28, and probably for the 29th as well. It would therefore be most convenient to me if the lectures could be given in the week Sept. 20–25. Until I see them in typewrite I cannot say just how many there will be, but I apprehend not less than four nor more than five.

Those on the Russo-Jap War, already typewritten, come last; those now being sent, first. I took up the Japanese business first, because I could not be sure how long the Intelligence Office could leave in my hands the papers on which largely I depend.

You will remember that over six weeks of the past nine months were cut out by the excursion into naval administration, initiated by Roosevelt.

---

1. Enclosure not found. Possibly, a reprint request from Captain Charles Reade. *See* Mahan to Little, Brown and Company, August 11, 1909.

1. Rear Admiral Raymond P. Rodgers replaced Merrell as President of the Naval War College on October 1, 1909.

Although revision has carried me in somewhat different direction than I expected, and in an ordinary sense has not been effected, my diligence is justified by the *amount* of output. I can only hope the *quality* may not prove defective.

To Little, Brown and Company

Quogue, Long Island, August 26, 1909 [LC]

Gentlemen: I have recd. your two letters of yesterday with Messrs. Longmans *Monthly List*, for which I beg to thank you.

As regards the material found in your vaults, the manuscript copy of *The Harvest Within* may be destroyed. As regards the negatives, photos, &c I am unable to speak before seeing them, and it will be better to send them, though I can scarcely imagine I should wish to preserve them.

To Little, Brown and Company

Quogue, Long Island, August 31, 1909 [LC]

Gentlemen: I have to thank you for the package of plates &c kindly sent me by express, and received. There were in it two or three I am glad to keep.

As I am writing, and in case you have not seen it, I mention that in the (London) *Guardian*, the leading English Church weekly, of Aug 18, *The Harvest Within* is made the subject of a leading article.[1]

This, with the notice in the N.Y. *Churchman* of Aug 21,[2] is as much advertisement—at least in that Church—as I could reasonably expect.

To John P. Merrell

Marshmere, Quogue, Long Island, September 7, 1909 [NWC]

My dear Merrell: I am sending today a registered package, containing the *carbon copy* of part of the manuscript, corrected by me in such places

1. An unsigned editorial review, "Faith in Action," *The Guardian* (August 18, 1909), p. 1286.
2. "Captain Mahan's Interpretations of the Faith," *The Churchman*, C (August 21, 1909), p. 272. The review is probably by McBee, and stresses the importance of the layman's interpretation.

as necessary. There are several typographical mistakes I have not touched, because a stranger could detect them as well as I.

Accompanying this is the greater part of my own Ms., following upon the last page (27) so far typewritten. It will be desirable for me to have this back next Monday or Tuesday, if possible; and, in the pressure of time, Mrs. Mahan has undertaken to typewrite for me all that I do not now send you. Our paper here is not uniform; but should you think desirable, it can be copied by your writers at leisure, after the course.

I thank you very much for your invitation to stay with you, which I gladly accept; regretting that I am not to have the pleasure also of seeing Mrs. Merrell.

To begin on Monday, I must arrive Saturday by the train which leaves N.Y. about 1 P.M.; and on Sunday P.M. I may most probably need to get some map work ready. Of this I will send you all necessary indications later, and in good time.

I am disappointed to find that the material written outruns much what can be given in five lectures. I much want, if possible, to return to N.Y. by the Friday night boat, and think that I can, as often before, condense the material. It will be an advantage, however, from my point of view, to have put down all that I have done. Between this and my coming I shall have read and systematized, which I have not had time yet to do, and by a judicious extrempore exposition may convey in shorter time and space than is possible when writing.

To John P. Merrell

Quogue, Long Island, September 10, 1909 [NWC]

My dear Merrell: I send you by registered mail (1) the carbon copy of the Russo-Jap War, retaining here the first copy; and (2) the remaining Ms., in my own hand, belonging to that sent you some days ago.

As regards the former, I need it chiefly on the principle that duplicates generally should be in separate places. For the second, Mrs. Mahan has made me a typewritten copy. There is therefore no necessity for immediately typewriting at the College. You may think expedient to have it copied, for uniformity, as my typewriting paper is of different size; but my wants are met by the copy made by my wife.

To John P. Merrell

Quogue, Long Island, September 14, 1909 [NWC]

My dear Merrell: I believe I have written you that it is best that I should begin my lectures on Monday, the 20th; and for that reason ought to come to Newport on Saturday, by the train leaving N.Y. about 1 P.M. and due Newport 6:40. I presume my orders can be issued on these data, in general terms; the date of arrival being immaterial to them.

On Sunday p.m., I should like to do some tape and card-board work on the map (general) of Europe which I think you have. I should need, for this, narrow tape of vivid colors: red, yellow, blue about ⅛ in.; and black of ¼ inch. Exact widths and colors are not material. Also, some sheets of thin paper, same colors.

The map of Europe will be principal, and should be best placed for the seeing by the audience; but that of the Gulf and Caribbean, and of the recent seat of war in China (Russo-Jap) will be needed as accessory. Unluckily, some of my most arduous graphic presentation fades on the first lecture.

I shall probably need also a few names printed which I cannot send today, but will before Saturday.

I find, on reading over the lectures to that end, that they will be six; unless I can do condensation, which time now scarcely allows.

Of these, the last will require only simply reading; and, if it can be arranged, I should wish that it be read by some one else, allowing me to leave by night boat, Friday. I can, if necessary, remain over Saturday, leaving by the 1 p.m. train for N.Y.; but, in addition to Saturday being usually an off day at the College, I myself would prefer to use it in town. I leave this in your hands, or to be settled when I arrive.

I had nearly forgotten: An Historical Atlas will be very necessary to me. Have you not Freeman's[1] in the Library, and if so, have it for me at the house? If not, cannot one be obtained from the City or Redwood?[2] I have one here, but very small and elementary.

As I customarily go to Church on Sunday, will you ascertain for me the hour of forenoon service at St. John's, which is nearest the College? I beg you will not allow this to interfere with the breakfast hour of yourself and Miss Merrell, which I heard her say was irregular on Sundays. Also, I shall prefer to walk both ways.

---

1. Edward Augustus Freeman, *The Historical Geography of Europe*. London: Longmans, Green, & Co., 1882, and subsequent editions.
2. Newport City Library and Redwood Library, Newport.

To Charles W. Stewart

Quogue, Long Island, September 14, 1909 [NA]

My dear Mr. Stewart: We have settled here in a new house, which we hope to be our home for the rest of my life. I have here transferred all my books, previously divided between Quogue and N.Y. I find my set of *Records, Union & Confed. Navies*, Series I, complete through volume 22; except vol. *20*. Whether this gap is due to carelessness or accident here, I cant say; but can you send me that volume?

I enclose two photos of Capt. Barclay, who commanded the British squadron on Lake Erie, in 1813. If you have none, I know no place they can be better bestowed than the library. The one nearest contemporary with the action I believe to be that which has the pencil memorandum on the back; to which I have added a statement, desirable for placing its authenticity beyond doubt. Had I received it in time, it would have been bracketed with Perry's likeness in the book, as Yeo and Chauncey are. The photos has been soiled by handling other than mine. It has occurred to me that you might insert it in the Library copy, opposite Perry's, after having cleaned and mounted for that purpose; but that will be at your judgment.

[P.S.] We could get no trace of a portrait of Downie,[1] who commanded at Lake Champlain.

To John P. Merrell

Marshmere, Quogue, Long Island, September 16, 1909 [NWC]

My dear Merrell: From this morning's paper I realize that there will likely be a great jam of travel for N.Y. on Friday the 24th.[1]

Will you act therefore to engage for me betimes a stateroom, *outside* if possible, on Fall River Boat leaving Newport that night, September 24th.[2]

Only so, if I fail in securing my room in N.Y. (already asked) will I be able to come on to Quogue that Saturday.

---

1. British Captain George Downie.

1. As a result of the centennial celebration of Robert Fulton's successful experiment with a marine steam engine on the Hudson River. *See* Mahan to Clark, October 1, 1909.

2. In the margin of this letter is written: "Outside ($2) room engaged—will be held until 12 M. September. 24/09. Total=$4.75."

To John P. Merrell

University Club, New York, September 25, 1909 [NWC]

My dear Merrell: I dont know whether my sixth lecture is to be read by Little today or Monday; but if the latter will you let him see this before it.

In the London *Times Literary Supplement*, Sept. 16, p. 331, which I just picked up, is a notice of *Port Arthur*. Column 1, last paragraph, beginning "During the six years following" there are comments which bear usefully and interestingly, upon the danger of contemplating coast fortresses too exclusively as for coast *defence*, instead of, as my lecture argues, for *offence*, in sheltering a fleet which is ready, and purposes, to act offensively.[1] There is in the review an amount of technical detail foreign to our purpose; but in the point named the article is useful, and possibly Little may see his way to using it.

In any event, I would be glad if he would enter on the Ms. a reference to the work reviewed, which I apprehend you will have in the library, later.

To Bouverie F. Clark

Marshmere, Quogue, Long Island, October 1, 1909 [LC]

My dear Clark: I wonder how you found my birth day; but however it was, it was very nice of you to write me. No man can have had a much happier life than I, so that congratulations are very much in order when sixty nine years of such are settled, and for the good, even though the mere fact of age has in other ways some drawbacks.

Your letter nearly hit the bull's eye in point of date; for, having to be forwarded to me in New York, it reached me the day before the anniversary. I had been a week in Newport, at our College there, the present administration of which had asked me to revise a course of lectures on Naval Strategy which I had written when at its head twenty years [ago]. Having done this, in part, I was asked also to read them again; and it was returning from this that your letter caught me in N.Y. which was then in

---

1. An unsigned review of *Official History of the Russo-Japanese War. Part III. The Siege of Port Arthur.* Prepared by the Historical Section of the Committee of Imperial Defence. London: Wyman, 1909. The specific paragraph concerns Russia's neglect of the land-side fortifications of Port Arthur.

the very beginning of the Hudson Fulton spree. It is calculated that there were, and doubtless still are, a million additional to the ordinary population, visitors drawn by the festivities. I had not intended to go; but it so happened that I had an imperative engagement of long standing for Sep. 28, and I held on to my room, which I luckily got at the Club on the 25, lest at the later date I should find myself homeless at night. The clubhouse is right in the midst of the goings on, streets crowded and noisy, and dirty, but all very jolly and animated. A good deal of bunting over some two miles of length, and some very brilliant illumination in the immediate neighborhood. I did not need a light at night to get about my room. I have met Seymour.[1] He was in Boson in /05 when I delivered an address before the "Victoria" club on Trafalgar Day; he and I being guests in the house of the then British Consul. I have accepted an invite to meet him and other officers at a dinner to be given by several British and a Canadian societies on Oct 5, so I shall see him thus again.

Our new house is all that we can desire, apparently thoroughly well built. We rejected the contract method, and had the work done by a builder we had reason to trust, and by days work. An honest man thereby was relieved of all temptation to scamp his job, and I believe we have done well.

I quite sympathize with your wrath over the government naval policy; and the vacillating course of the admiralty has seemed to me to ignore that a cabinet loaded down with socialistic promises had especial need of firm expression of opinion by professional experts. I received the *National*, for which thanks. I am familiar with Maxse's caustic pen,[2] having, as you know, written often for it in past days. The amusing, yet exasperating, circumstance to me is the abuse of armaments and of war, by those who fail to see that both are the effects, not the cause, of conditions. That the real object to attack are the selfish methods and interests of the people, many of whom are entirely insensible of this selfishness, and regard war etc as a cause in itself, rather than the outcome of commercial wickedness. As for armaments *causing* war, never were two communities less armed beforehand than our North & South; yet we fought like tigers for four years.

Well, good luck again. Years are telling on us, but I trust that you like myself can report well on the whole upon the past, and may find the future as good.

---

1. Sir Edward Hobart Seymour, who commanded a British squadron sent to attend the Hudson-Fulton centennial celebration.
2. In the *National Review* for September 1909, Maxse violently attacked Sir John Fisher and defended Lord Beresford, then "retiring" or "ejected" as Commander-in-Chief of the Channel Fleet.

To the Fourth Auditor of the Treasury

Draft   Quogue, Long Island, October 11, 1909 [LC]

Sir: Under orders from the Navy Department, copy of which is enclosed, I have from November 1908 to present date occupied quarters other than public: at Lawrence, N.Y. from Nov. 1 to April 30, inclusive, and at Quogue N.Y., from May 1 to now. A certificate from the President of the War College, that there were no quarters for me, has been continuously in the hands of the Paymaster, Navy Yard, New York.

Until recently, I have been ignorant of the allowance for fuel and light established by the law of May 13, 1908; and I am informed that to obtain that for fuel, up to and including June 30, 1909, I must make application to your office.

I have receipted bills from the parties who have supplied me with fuel during the period named, and respectfully ask your instructions as to the particular manner of presenting my claim to you.[1]

To J. Franklin Jameson

Quogue, Long Island, October 13, 1909 [LC]

My dear Dr. Jameson: I hate to say No; but unless you can wait longer than I think probable I cannot do it.[1] Circumstances into which it is needless to enter have conspired to harass my work the last three or four weeks, and until I have regained the lost ground I cannot with composure see any increase of my responsibilities for engagements.

Could you not try Rear Admiral C. H. Stockton, or Goodrich of the same rank; both retired. Stockton is the better for the work, a sound and intelligent man, and practised writer. Goodrich also is this, but with an originality which to my mind is rather eccentric than original. Stockton lives in Washington & I think has leisure.

---

1. Jotted on the back of this draft letter are these undated comments: By letter of Genl. Storekeeper Jan. 19/10 it appears that I received *fuel* from govt. from July 1, 1909. Remains therefore Oct. 31, 1908 to June 30, 1909—That is my claim as to fuel. *Light*: Genl. Storekeeper enclosed (Oct. 21, 1909) me a letter for Bu.S. & Accts (106.835 Oct. 15, 1909) that Bureau had referred to 4th Aud, recommendation that I be credited with amount due me for light for *present* (?) qr. Oct.–Dec.

1. Jameson had asked Mahan to review for the *American Historical Review*, William Wood, ed., *The Logs of the Conquest of Canada*, published in 1909 by The Champlain Society. Jameson to Mahan, October 8, 1909, in the Library of Congress.

To Herbert Putnam

Marshmere, Quogue, Long Island, October 21, 1909 [LC]

My dear Mr. Putnam: I enclose a letter from Mr. Thursfield, one of the naval men of the London *Times*, in explanation of a question which you can probably reply to me through one of your assistants.

Mr. Thursfield recently published a paper on Paul Jones in which he accepted & quoted the letters in Buell's Life,[1] which have been impugned by Mrs. De Koven.[2] I myself have felt little interest in the matter because my views about Jones were formed and published years before Buell wrote, and while corresponding with her [about] the letters named, [I] did not in the least depend upon them.

The question I wish to put to you is briefly this: Are Mrs. De Koven's allegations as to the non-existence of the letters correct, and if there be any decisive opinion on the part of the experts of the Library can you have it sent to me for Thursfield's information. The latter has written to the *Times*, asking suspension of opinion till further intelligence.

Ford would be quite the man for this; but I believe he has left you.[3]

To Raymond P. Rodgers[1]

Marshmere, Quogue, Long Island, October 22, 1909 [NWC]

My dear Rodgers: Thank you for your letter communicating to me the Secretary's decision.[2] The understanding you had with Merrell coincides with my own, and I shall expect to give the lecture before the Conference[3] next summer.

What I did in the past year, while fairly under the head of revision, might

---

1. James Richard Thursfield, *Nelson and Other Naval Studies*. London: J. Murray, 1909. And Augustus C. Buell, *Paul Jones, Founder of the American Navy; a History*. 2 vols. New York: C. Scribner's Sons, 1900. Buell's biography of Jones was replete with spurious letters ingeniously concocted by the author.
2. Anna Farwell De Koven (Mrs. Reginald), "A New Page in the History of John Paul Jones," *Harper's Weekly* (April 7, 1906).
3. W. C. Ford had left the Library of Congress to be editor for the Massachusetts Historical Society, and to pursue his lectures at Harvard.

1. Rodgers had relieved Merrell as President of the Naval War College on October 1, 1909.
2. Rodgers had persuaded Secretary Meyer to retain Mahan on temporary duty with the War College during the winter of 1909–1910 so that he could continue revising his naval strategy lectures and prepare another series of lectures for delivery during the summer of 1910. Rodgers to Mahan, October 19, 1909, at the Naval War College.
3. *See* Mahan to Merrell, May 22, 1909, Footnote 1.

more properly be called expansion, & at the beginning I cut out my work both of reading and writing on an over large scale. With this experience I hope to have this year a better sense of proportion & see no reason why I should not be able to accomplish the revision in due time.

My compliments to Mrs. Rodgers. We have not met for a long time.

To the Fourth Auditor of the Treasury

Quogue, Long Island, October 28, 1909 [LC]

Sir: Replying to your letter, 4056–RSJ, of October 27, my permanent residence—where I live half the year and where I vote—is Quogue, N.Y.; but from November 1, 1908, to May 1, 1909, for reasons of convenience, I occupied a house in Lawrence, N.Y.

During the whole period, November 1, 1908, to date, my official connection has been with the War College, Newport, R.I.; but there were there no quarters for me, and my duty,—preparing lectures—did not require residence in Newport.

To Herbert Putnam

Marshmere, Quogue, Long Island, October 30, 1909 [LC]

My dear Mr. Putnam: I beg to thank you, and through you Mr. Hunt,[1] very cordially, for your kind attention to my request. I have forwarded Mr. Hunt's memorandum to Mr. Thursfield.

To the Fourth Auditor of the Treasury

Draft   Quogue, Long Island, November 3, 1909 [LC]

Sir: Replying to your letter of November 2,—4056, R.S.J.—my orders from the Navy Department were to "report by letter" to the President of the War College, which I did on October 31, 1908.

I enclose a certified copy of my orders, endorsed by the President of the College.

---

1. Gaillard Hunt. *See* Mahan to Putnam, October 21, 1909.

To the Fourth Auditor of the Treasury

Draft   Quogue, Long Island, November 3, 1909 [LC]

Sir: Replying to your letter—4056–R.S.J.—of November 2, as I enclosed you in my letter of October 11 a copy of my orders to "report by letter" to the President of the War College, yours raises the general point, whether an officer placed on duty—by orders to report by letter is entitled to commutation for quarters while on such duty.

I have therefore referred the case to the Secretary of the Navy.

To George von L. Meyer

Draft   Quogue, Long Island, November 3, 1909 [LC]

Sir: I enclose a copy of a letter received today from the Fourth Auditor of the Treasury, by which it appears that the amount paid me for commutation of quarters by the pay officer at the New York Yard for the past year—since October 31, 1908—amounting to about one thousand dollars, is suspended "for information as to the date upon which I reported *in person* at the War College."

My orders from the Department, copy of which I enclose for convenience of reference, were to "report by letter" to the President of the War College. This his endorsement shows I did. I had no warrant to go to Newport, or to report otherwise than as I did.

The Auditor having a copy of my orders, his letter apparently raises the point whether under the Department orders I have been entitled to the usual commutation of quarters. This is a general question affecting all orders to report by letter for duty.

"Suspension" means, I believe, that I can receive no pay at all till this question is settled or the thousand dollars worked off. As this will put me to great inconvenience, I trust the Department will have the matter decided soon.

To Stephen B. Luce

Marshmere, Quogue, Long Island, November 12, 1909 [LC]

My dear Admiral: I find in my possession two prints, one of the Chase of the *Constitution*, the other of the Capture of the *President*, both with your name on the back. I am not sure, but think, that they were sent me by Little & Brown, in the shake up attending their recent change of business place. They then sent me a quantity of relics from my book work, accumulated through years; but not till a few days ago did I notice your name on the back. Will you care to have me send them to you? If so, please let me know soon, as we break up here within a fortnight.

You will be instructed to learn that the Fourth Auditor has suspended payment of pay to me, until it shall appear when I reported "in person" to the President of the College, the Department having ordered me to report "by letter." There is a mingling of wrath and amusement that an underling of a Department should possess such a power of ipse dixit in the affairs of an officer of another Department, without the intervention of either Secretary.

To the Fourth Auditor of the Treasury

Quogue, Long Island, November 19, 1909 [LC]

Sir: Referring to the letter of the Fourth Auditor to me, No. 4056–RSJ, I wrote to the Navy Department, enclosing a copy of it, and of my orders. In reply that Department has informed me, by endorsement upon my own letter, that I misunderstood in part the scope of the Auditor's letter.

The endorsement then adds the following paragraphs, which I hope may meet the Auditor's need "for information as to the date upon which I reported in person at the War College."

3. From the copy of his orders enclosed, it appears that Admiral Mahan was in no sense required to report in person at the War College, his place of duty being Quogue, N.Y., where he was clearly entitled to commutation of quarters while on such duty.

4. It is believed that the Auditor's action arises from misunderstanding of the conditions under which Admiral Mahan was performing duty, and that the suspension will be promptly removed upon a statement of the facts being furnished that Office.

I will add that the change of actual residence—as distinguished from customary residence—from Quogue to Lawrence, during the winter months, was with the knowledge and acquiescence of the Navy Department, as shown by official letters addressed by it to me there; notably to a Commission,[1] constituted in January, 1909, by President Roosevelt, in which I am directed after the completion of that duty "to return to Lawrence and resume present duties."

---

1. The Moody Commission. See Mahan to Luce, February 2, 1909, Footnote 1.

To Stephen B. Luce

Marshmere, Quogue, Long Island, November 22, 1909 [LC]

My dear Admiral: I sent by mail last week the two plates about which we exchanged letters, & trust they have reached you in good order. The drawings themselves were all right, though the cardboard on which they were set was a little defaced.

I am now sending you also, with shame and confusion of face, a French pamphlet of yours which I have had for more years than I care to recall. The retention is the result of an accumulation of procrastinations & forgettings, which may be assigned as a cause but not justified as a reason. Sometimes, unhappily, I do such things.

To the Fourth Auditor of the Treasury

Draft Lawrence, Long Island, November 30, 1909 [LC]

Sir: I enclose herewith, filled out, the blank sent me in the Auditor's letter, 4056–RSJ, November 22d, to be filled out by the party, (Mrs.) E. L. Mahan, who, I am instructed by the same letter, is the one who actually furnished me with heat and light.

To Thomas Nelson Page[1]

Lawrence, Long Island, December 6, 1909 [DUL]

Captain Mahan regrets that his engagements for December 14 prevent him from leaving New York, and that he is consequently unable to accept the kind invitation of Mr. Thomas Nelson Page to dinner for that day.

To the Fourth Auditor of the Treasury

Draft Lawrence, Long Island, December 10, 1909 [LC]

Sir: In compliance with your letter of December 8, 1909—4056-RSJ— I enclose copies of orders received by me from the Navy Department since the orders assigning me to duty at the Naval War College.

---

1. Author of essays and novels which romanticized the life and character of the southern Negro and the Old South.

[321]

The orders of January 7, 1909, were followed by other orders in direct sequence of them, addressed to me at Lawrence. These are at my house in Quogue, N.Y.; I having moved to this place for the winter, by permission of the Navy Department.

If the Auditor desire them, copies of these can be obtained; but, as I explained above, they are simply in development and sequence of those of January 15, directing further visits to Washington.

To Robert U. Johnson

Lawrence, Long Island, January 15, 1910 [NYPL]

My dear Mr. Johnson: Replying to yours of Dec. 12, I have already tackled the article, the scope of which (dont fear additional length) grows on me as I think of it. It concerns the beginning of an historical process, in which Japan made a first entry when she wiped Russia off the board—at sea.

I have been undergoing grippe; which, while not severe for grippe, is leaving me much below par. The only thing I feel safe to say is that you shall have the article by Feb. 1; or else a renunciation of it, as impracticable for me, in view of other work from which I cannot properly spare more time.[1]

To Raymond P. Rodgers

Lawrence, Long Island, January 20, 1910 [NWC]

My dear Rodgers: The stray lecture was duly received here yesterday. Many thanks.

As regards the lectures you now have at the College of mine, none are yet ready for manifolding. Merrell had two copies made. Perhaps I had better premise that the old originals, used by me for several years, were taken in hand by him during his incumbency. They were on pages about the size of this on which I write; and on them had accumulated year by year, notes made by me for my own guidance in delivery, intelligible to me at the time, but as time passed less and less even to myself—still less to others. Merrell reduced the mass to such order as he could, had the result type written, and sent me *both first* and *carbon* copies when I began to revise. The first I sent back to him last summer, and it is to that I presume you now refer. I had given so much time to revision in the form of ad-

---

1. The article was abandoned.

ditional matter, that I had had no time for revision more exactly so called.

The carbon copy I still retain, and upon that I am working.

The new, or additional, matter, amounting to seven (7) lectures, (of which you have just sent me the seventh) was also duplicated. One copy is at the College, the other with me. You have therefore one full copy of all my work and I have one copy.

Nothing is yet in your hands ready for the type writer; but, from the state of the work now, I hope to send you early next week the material for the first lecture, and think I shall be able to keep you along so that steadily, yet without undue pressure at any time, your type writers can have the whole done by June.

The preparation for the copyist is itself no slight job, when the author is not at hand for reference, for, besides corrections and omissions, there are many interpolations in the body of the earlier lectures. The new lectures, written last year, I now purpose to introduce bodily, here and there, among the old;[1] and this you can understand will involve a further question of where the divisions among the lectures must fall.

Is your programme for the summer so far fixed, that you can tell me my date nearly?

Where I am just now I find a reference to *Commentaires de Napoléon*, vol ii, p. 191. As I have not the book at hand can you have a copy of the page, or the part referred to, sent me? I think it is to the effect that Brueys[2] suggested to Napoleon sending off a detachment of vessels for some object, and that Napoleon's reply was "If you do and we meet the English tomorrow will we not need the detachment?"

[P.S.] I find I have not been sufficiently explicit as to the readiness of the last summer's (new) lectures. I do not anticipate much change to be made in them, but it would not be expedient to make a clean copy of them till after my next delivery of them. They are in good enough shape for that; and with the experience of another reading, I can leave them with you for such reproduction as you may then desire.

To Raymond P. Rodgers

Lawrence, Long Island, January 27, 1910 [NWC]

My dear Rodgers: The preparation of the manuscript for the copyist has proved more intricate than I anticipated; but I am able to mail it to you

---

1. Published together as *Naval Strategy* (1911). This juxtapositioning of the new and the revised lectures produced an awkwardly arranged book.
2. François Paul Brueys, French admiral.

today in such shape as will require, I hope, only close attention to the particulars.

I will have to ask you to send me half a dozen envelopes, of the proper size to take such an enclosure without folding it. By great good luck I have found the one now used; taken by me from the College last September. I should also wish a dozen penalty officials, the use for which exceeds my anticipations.

The scheme of lectures in my intention stands now as follows: Will begin with the introductory lecture used last June by me. Follows this the present enclosure, down to line 3, page 4; where, as noted, I propose to introduce two lectures, of the new ones, given in September. Upon these two will follow the remainder of the present enclosure, which I estimate will make only one lecture; though possibly, on revision, part of its ending may be thrown upon the succeeding lecture.

This totals four. There are two more of the old now substantially re-vised, but which I prefer to hold on to for a few weeks, as we still have four months to June. Into these I expect to fit another of the new lectures; but into this and the rest of the job it is bootless to enter, until I have settled conditions better in my own mind.

I enclose a separate memorandum for the copyist. May I ask that black ribbon, not blue, and quite white paper, may be used.

I quite agree with you as to the general period of the lectures, and indeed had understood from Merrell that early June was desirable. I only asked as to particular date, if fixed. The postponement to September last year was only because I could not be ready sooner.

When completed, the new copy should be sent to me; for after a certain amount of correction one's appreciation of the mixture becomes confused. But there is no haste about this.[1]

[Enclosure]

I believe that the manuscript is corrected by ordinary usages which will require no explanation beyond the following:

The interlineations "over", when met, refer to the back of the page on which they occur.

In pages 4–12 occurs a large substitution, the leaves of which go loose, at page 4, and are numbered A to R inclusive. The former pages 4–12 are omitted as marked.

Page 17 receives also some loose leaves, which are pinned to one another, and contain corrections, or insertions, for that page.

---

1. On this letter Rodgers wrote: "Captain Little will please cause this copying to proceed regularly & continuously—and will supervise the copying to meet Ad. Mahan's directions."

To Stephen B. Luce

Lawrence, Long Island, January 28, 1910 [LC]

My dear Admiral: I am much obliged to you for the clippings.

I have never myself studied the question of the New York Yard from the point of view of the particular site, nor have I Narragansett Bay. I feel, however, very satisfied, that as a naval *station* New York is unique in having two entrances, the main and the Sound, with the whole splendid sheet of the Sound for covering its movements; granted of course proper fortification at the eastern end. When I have had occasion to touch the question, however, I have always spoken of Narragansett Bay as possible to be comprehended in the same scheme of defense, and of operations; although there is probably a weak point in the stretch round Point Judith for a single vessel or small detachment making a passage, with an enemy outside.

To Raymond P. Rodgers

Lawrence, Long Island, January 31, 1910 [NWC]

My dear Rodgers: I shall be glad if, in the copying of the lectures now, the usual mode of spelling can be followed and I spared in reading the distasteful forms, tho, thru, catalog, & others, which have been used in the material upon which I am now working.

Of course, if the College have a rule, I will acquiesce; but if not, I shall be glad to have my conservatism respected.[1]

To Raymond P. Rodgers

Lawrence, Long Island, February 3, 1910 [NWC]

My dear Rodgers: I find a reference in the lectures "Napoleon to Marmont," which I think would be useful; and, although I have not the volume number, or page, I believe I can sufficiently indicate to be easily found by one of your staff, in the *Correspondance de Napoléon*.[1] The index of letters is very complete, briefing contents.

---

1. In the margin of this letter Rodgers wrote: "This is to be observed."

1. J. B. P. Vaillant, *et al.*, eds., *Correspondance de Napoléon I*. 32 vols. Paris: H. Plon. J. Dumaine, 1858–70. The reference is found in Vol. XXIII, p. 232. Rodgers to Mahan, February 7, 1910, at the Naval War College.

This to Marmont is either early in 1812, or late in 1811; in any event prior to the battle of Salamanca, in which Marmont was defeated by Wellington, and wounded. In it Napoleon directs Marmont to keep Wellington in check by cantonning his army within a couple of marches of Salamanca (or Ciudad Rodrigo). If Wellington makes a move toward the South (against Soult), Marmont is to concentrate and advance against Almeida; upon which instruction Napoleon elaborates an essay on diversions, and control.

I could hunt this for myself in the Astor Library, but, independent of the time needed, that building has become so crowded and air so foul, that I hate in my declining years to expose myself lightly to its germ laden atmosphere.

The length of the quotation will be at the easy discretion of any officer.

To Raymond P. Rodgers

Lawrence, Long Island, February 10, 1910 [NWC]

My dear Rodgers: The arrangement proposed by your letter of the 7th is entirely satisfactory to me.[1] I have received the first part of the new copy; but as the remainder is to follow shortly, I will postpone reading till it is received, and go on with the other work in hand.

I have received also the copy of Napoleon's letter to Marmont, for which I am obliged to you and to Little. It is the one I wanted.

To Raymond P. Rodgers

Lawrence, Long Island, February 16, 1910 [NWC]

My dear Rodgers: I have sent you today by registered mail the second lecture. There are no new comments for the copyist, unless perhaps the advisability of studying out each page (of the original) so as to be sure beforehand where the additions or changes come in. I have done my best to make them clear, but care will be needed as they are unavoidably somewhat complicated in disposition.

I shall probably get off the clean copy of the first lecture by the end of the week.

---

1. For copying Mahan's lectures. Rodgers to Mahan, February 7, 1910; at the Naval War College.

To R. J. Tracewell[1]

Lawrence, Long Island, February 16, 1910 [LC]

Sir: I have received from the Auditor for the Navy Department a letter, 4056-R.S.J., February 15, 1910, disallowing a payment made to me for commutation of quarters, on the ground that I was ordered by the Navy Department to "report by letter" to the President of the War College, and not directed to report in person. The sum disallowed is $414.40.

I beg to submit that the duty assigned me was by request of the President of the College; that it was not by me solicited, but accepted at his request; and that the allowance for quarters was an element in my acceptance of work which I had not desired, and which took me from other congenial occupation.

This doubtless is not to the merits of the case. The nature of the duty, however, is. The duty was the revision of a series of lectures delivered by me in former years at the College. This could be done effectually elsewhere than at the College; it was so understood and accepted by the Navy Department; and the only result of directing me to report in person would have been to cause the Government the needless additional expense of my travel to Newport and return to my residence.

I respectfully request your reconsideration of the matter in the light of the character of the duty, and the fact of its performance under a reasonable expectation of usual allowances.

To Raymond P. Rodgers

Lawrence, Long Island, February 17, 1910 [NWC]

My dear Rodgers: Yesterday I received a letter from the Fourth Auditor of the Treasury, disallowing payments for commutation of quarters made me under my present orders, of October 23, 1908, because they read to report by letter. The matter being purely personal to me, and thinking it important with reference to my future conduct to know as soon as possible whether the decision would stand, I sent direct to the Department a request for revision by the Comptroller.

On the general record of the Treasury Department, I have little doubt of an adverse decision. In order, therefore, to save what I can out of the wreck, in the future, I have made the enclosed statement[1] and application

---

1. Comptroller of the Treasury.

1. Enclosure not found.

which I will ask you to forward with such endorsement as you may think proper.

Should you approve it, there will be sufficient probability of the order issuing to justify asking you to have reserved a state room for me on the Fall River boat for New York on March 1. My plan would be to reach Newport by a train sufficiently early to admit of reporting, and of leaving at that hour.

If this procedure should regularize my status for commutations, in the eyes of the Treasury, I shall then expect to go on with my work and lecture as by the present understanding; but I shall request you, subject of course to your judgment, in one of your visits to Washington, to represent the 'facts, and in view of the grave practical injustice done me, to ask that I be continued on duty with a view to lecturing the following year. I see no other way by which the Government can pay me what it justly owes me; for the work in point of time and labor is worth all that I have been receiving, and it has cut me off from the opportunities which I have heretofore used successfully.

At your leisure will you kindly let me know your views on the matter here set before you.

To Raymond P. Rodgers

Lawrence, Long Island, February 17, 1910 [NWC]

My dear Rodgers: I have sent by mail today the new copy of Lecture I. There are several corrections but none of any great consequence; mostly copyist's errors for which doubtless my handwriting is partly responsible, though I never can understand the true copyist temper which writes down sense & nonsense with equal equanimity. They are all alike in this.[1]

To J. Franklin Jameson

Lawrence, Long Island, February 18, 1910 [LC]

My dear Dr. Jameson: As regards reviewing Paullin's *Life of Rodgers*,[1] it is quite impracticable for me to undertake it. During this winter I have

---

1. In the margin of this letter Rodgers wrote: "When the corrections are made, the copies to be held arranged for binding."

1. Charles Oscar Paullin, *Commodore John Rodgers, Captain, Commodore, and Senior Officer of the American Navy*. Cleveland, Ohio: The Arthur H. Clark Company, 1910.

been worked beyond my mental and nervous strenth, and the burden still resting on me forbids my attempting anything more.

The same preoccupation has prevented my giving consideration to the matter of your letter of January 15. Nothing has occurred to me beyond the general drift of my paper for the Commission on Documentary Publication.[2] I let the matter lie for advisement, but cannot give it at present the necessary thought.

To Raymond P. Rodgers

Lawrence, Long Island, March 4, 1910 [NWC]

My dear Rodgers: I sent revision of Lecture III by registered mail yesterday. By the middle of next week I hope to send also No. IV, unless the final reading disclose some change to be made. It is complete, save for final reading I always give before dispatching.

I feel greatly indebted for the attention and care you gave in smoothing the way of my rapid excursion to Newport, on Tuesday. I trust that by this time Mrs. Rodgers is well restored. Please remember me kindly and express my regret at having missed seeing her.

To Raymond P. Rodgers

Lawrence, Long Island, March 9, 1910 [NWC]

My dear Rodgers: I received your letter from Washington and thank you very much for the trouble you have taken.

The enclosed speak for themselves.[1] I am sorry you should have the trouble even of forwarding them; but it seems best to follow the routine channels.

Lecture IV would probably have been ready for forwarding today, but for the necessity of getting up the elaborate statement to the Comptroller.

---

2. *See* Mahan to Stewart, April 9, 1908. On January 11, 1909, The report of the Committee on the Documentary Historical Publications of the U.S. Government was transmitted by the parent Committee on Departmental Methods. The complete report is in the Mahan Collection in the Library of Congress.

1. Tracewell to Mahan, March 5, 1910, at the Naval War College; and Mahan to Comptroller Tracewell, March 9, 1910. The latter was enclosed in Mahan to Meyer, March 9, 1910, with a request that it be forwarded to the Comptroller.

To R. J. Tracewell

Draft   Lawrence, Long Island, March 9, 1910 [NWC]

Sir: Referring to the Comptroller's letter to me of March 5, 1910—Appeal No. 18472—I have to reply that the President of the Naval War College did not give me any formal written orders upon my reporting to him by letter, beyond the endorsement "Reported by letter, October 31, 1908," upon the orders of October 23, which have been always in the hands of the Fourth Auditor. Such orders could not have been thought by him necessary, in view of the facts in the following statement, which I now lay before the Comptroller; regretting the necessity of troubling him at such length.

In 1886–7, when myself President of the Naval War College, I wrote for the courses then current a series of lectures on Naval Strategy. This was used by myself, both then, and in later years by request, after my immediate connection with the College had ceased, up to 1897; when I had retired from active service. They received from me during this period frequent revision in details, and after 1897 continued to serve as part of the annual Conference, being read by an officer of the College. They had thus been accepted as a standard there, by the successive Presidents; remaining in text as I had left them.

In May, 1908, the President of the College, Rear Admiral John P. Merrell, wrote me asking if I would undertake to revise the lectures in view of the changed conditions of naval warfare, and the accumulated experience and illustration of the principles of Naval Strategy, in the three naval wars which have occurred since they were written. I replied that the private work then in hand forbade my voluntarily undertaking to do this, but that when it was completed I would. In October, 1908, I wrote him that I would be ready at the end of the month, and in result the orders of October 23, to report by letter, were issued by the Department. I may add that Rear Admiral Pillsbury, then the Chief of the Bureau of Navigation, under which the College is, expressed to me his satisfaction that I had undertaken the work.

It will appear from the above that the lectures originally prepared by me were found so far satisfactory to the authorities concerned that no attempt to replace them had been made; and that, when the question of revision arose, it was to me they turned. It follows that my competence in the matter was so far recognized, that no necessity for *orders* as to scope and treatment was apparent. It was of course entirely open to the President of the College to give them, as orders or suggestions; and I myself wrote to ask if he had any to offer. He replied that he preferred in the main to leave the matter in my hands; but where suggestion occurred to him he would give it. He gave none.

All the correspondence, and on one or two occasions conversation, here narrated, was of the character commonly called semi-official; such as the Comptroller will doubtless recognize to be frequent when the question arises of offering, or requesting, work of a person who is left at liberty to accept or decline, as I am satisfied it was meant that I should be. My share of such correspondence has not been preserved by me; but if it be thought necessary to refer to Admiral Merrell, he certainly will confirm my statements.

Had the present difficulty of allowing me commutation and allowances, upon reporting by letter, been foreseen, I would doubtless have been ordered to report in person; and any other question of form, such as orders from the President of the College, could have been arranged easily at the time. But the Comptroller will remember that in the autumn of 1908, when my present duty began, commutation and allowances were new in the Navy, and the particular contention that has arisen in my case was not known to the Navy Department in general. Thus, shortly after reporting, the President of the College sent me the blanks necessary to sign to obtain the commutation; two successive pay officers at the New York Navy Yard, and the General Storekeeper, have paid me it, and allowances, without demur; and when the Auditor in November last notified me of the "suspension" against me, upon my referring it to the Navy Department, the Paymaster General endorsed upon my letter the opinion that I was clearly entitled to quarters. I understand that the Navy Department has certified the Comptroller that, in issuing the orders, it was the understanding of the Department that I would receive the commutation. It is therefore clear that the Department also at the time was ignorant of the particular ruling. I myself shared the ignorance; if I had known, the matter would have gone no farther than myself and the President of the War College, and would have been ended by my declination.

In sum: The duty assigned me by the Navy Department's orders of October 23, 1908, was of a character which it is unusual, as well as generally considered inexpedient, to place upon an officer contrary to this will; it was asked of me because of my recognized particular fitness for the work; the entire arrangement, because of its voluntary character, was carried on by the semi-official methods usual where choice is left to the officer; and the President of the College issued to me no orders concerning the methods of the work, doubtless because it was considered that I was not in need of specific instructions, the original lectures being mine, and myself accepted as an authority on the general subject, not in the United States only, but throughout the world, my other works having been translated into the principal European languages, as well as into Japanese. I have stated already, in my request for revision, February 16, 1910, that the work could be done effectually at my own home, and that this was so understood by the Department. The subject and the necessary treatment were closely cognate to the kind of work which I had been doing for a dozen years past, since my retirement.

As regards the second paragraph of the Comptroller's letter of March 5, the President of the College, as already stated, made me no formal specific assignment. No other order has been given me than that of the Navy Department, of October 23, 1908. This was continuous until revoked; and in October, 1909, shortly after the revision, as far as then carried, had been delivered by me as a course of lectures at the College, the Department decided to continue it; acting in this upon the opinion of the incoming and retiring Presidents of the College. From what has been said above, it will be seen that the duty indicated by that order embraced a well understood general subject, the method, details, and treatment to which were left actually, and for the most part necessarily, to my judgment; much as the faculty of a College leaves the superintendence and development of the several courses to the particular member concerned, or to any expert who may be asked to assist in the line of his special knowledge.[1]

To George von L. Meyer

Lawrence, Long Island, March 9, 1910 [NWC]

Sir: I enclose herewith a copy of the letter from the Comptroller of the Treasury,[1] together with my reply to him, which I request the Department to forward to him.

As my request for revision necessarily went through the Navy Department, it has seemed to me proper that any consequent correspondence should follow the same course. If the Department desire that the correspondence on my part should be direct with the Comptroller, I beg to be so informed.

To Raymond P. Rodgers

Lawrence, Long Island, March 10, 1910 [NWC]

My dear Rodgers: I send you by this same mail Lecture IV, ready for the copyist.

---

1. This letter was enclosed in Mahan to Meyer, March 9, 1910.

1. Tracewell to Mahan, March 5, 1910, at the Naval War College; and Mahan to Tracewell, March 9, 1910.

In writing yesterday, forwarding reply to Comptroller, I meant to explain what may appear a somewhat vainglorious insistence upon my fitness for the work, as evidenced by my reputation. The Comptroller's action, as far as deducible from his letter, rests upon the insufficiency of the Department's orders to place an officer on duty, unless followed by his specific orders and explanations to the Treasury. The point is, it seems to me, untenable, and one the Navy Department for its own self respect should bring to an issue; but as regards the special instance of myself, such specific orders were needless owing to circumstances with which the Treasury is not to be supposed familiar. This needs to be stated, since question is raised, on behalf of the Presidents of the College, that no imputation for not issuing such orders rests on them; though my reason of course is simply to fight my own battle, by putting my claim in the most forcible way open to me.

To Bouverie F. Clark

Lawrence, Long Island, March 10, 1910 [LC]

My dear Clark: Your Christmas card and letter were duly received and gratefully remembered; that I did not reply before now has been due to overwork, yes; but still more that for the first time I am beginning to feel such work in a kind of a fagged mental condition which I have hitherto been a stranger to, at least to such an extent. Contemporaries, and still more younger men, tell me that in appearance I am one of the youngest of the "survivors," and I dont feel that I can complain, but the old enemy comes on all the same.

I have been following your conditions and elections with the keenest interest and sympathy with your difficulties. I did not know what to expect, and have been inclined to look upon the result as an intermediate step to a return of the Conservatives to power. My reason is this, that I think it demonstrated that only so can England be delivered from subjection to the Irish vote, and that realized by the English people will be resented and rejected. We shall soon see, however; for among all uncertainties another General Election seems the one thing certain. Our todays papers say that the Liberal First Lord[1] estimates for seven new battleships. In that case either they are convinced that Germany is drawing ahead, or else Sir Arthur Wilson[2] is already making himself felt. You of course read Sir W. White's

---

1. Reginald McKenna, First Lord of the Admiralty, 1908–1911.
2. First Sea Lord, 1909–1912.

article[3] in the *Nineteenth Century* in which he skinned Fisher rather neatly. We in this country—officers, I mean—would not be let write such an article. I read it with great interest, but was not inclined to attach much importance to those parts of the German declaration of 1900, which he declared necessary to a proper appreciation of it. On the other hand there is no fault to be found with Germany for setting up such a standard for herself; only you fellows will have to take notice.

On this side we are quiet, and no one outside the service taking any account of the fact that Germany has passed us, and is daily drawing farther ahead. We have an admirable new "First Lord,"[4] but he is sorely hampered by antediluvian legislators; one in particular. I incline to think Germany's ambitions are not turned toward our continents, but all the same it is inexpedient for us to allow her to put us so far behind.

I have been busy for the last year working over some old lectures on Naval Strategy, and adding several new ones for use at our College. I have found it pretty hard work; against the grain, and with too little of the free foot which my long retirement had accustomed me to. I think if I could have realized beforehand what it would mean to me I would not have acceded to the request made me to undertake it. But I am in and must see it through despite the nervous strain and irritability which I have been feeling lately.

I saw Stockton[5] in the club the other day, looking a little older. There is a queer tired appearance about face and figure, which are hard to define, but which I fancy you will have noticed come on among your own people; somewhat suddenly too. You meet a man today and he seems much the same as ever; two or three months later you see him again and he has become old. An observant friend of mine once said, People do not grow old *gradually*.

Having been delinquent so long I am timing this letter to hit your birthday as nearly as possible. Unluckily, the steamers which sail Saturday are not fast, but I do my best to be in London a week from that day. There is of my personal news absolutely nothing, nor is there anything in the state of our public affairs which can possibly interest others than ourselves. I notice some symptoms of uneasiness as regards our relations with Japan, and with the feeling of our Pacific coast people, and the sensitiveness of the Japs, there seems to me always the elements of trouble. Certainly we can never accede to opening our territory to Oriental immigration. With so much vacant land we should be swamped in a decade.

---

3. Sir William Henry White, "The Naval Situation," *Nineteenth Century and After* (April 1909).
4. George von L. Meyer.
5. C. H. Stockton, then 65 years old.

To Raymond P. Rodgers

Lawrence, Long Island, March 18, 1910 [NWC]

My dear Rodgers: Can the Library lend me for a short time Semenoff's account of the Battle of Tsushima? *Not* the *Rasplata*,[1] which I have seen and read.

Little told me last year that he thought I had misjudged the tactical order in which Rodzhestvensky[2] approached and I understood based his opinion upon this book, which I have not read.

To Hugh R. Monro

Lawrence, Long Island, March 20, 1910 [USNAM]

Dear Mr. Monro: I have read twice, carefully, the article you sent me. In all main features I am entirely in accord with your position, and your observation tallies with my own.

Mr. John R. Mott,[1] whose name is doubtless familiar to you, wrote me a question much to the same effect as your article. That is, he posed as a question, bearing upon the direction and success of missionary effort, whether the home churches are themselves suffering from a blight, partial or more, which cannot but affect the strength of the missionary impulse.

My reply was that I had for many years back been impressed, increasingly, with what I called the impersonality of the standard held up in the pulpit, and generally before the world, as the motive to Christian action. By that I meant that the Person and sacrifice of our Lord were not put in the forefront, supreme over all other motive; that work was commended for the work's sake and not for the Lord's sake; that good works, activities, were set forth as the be-all and do-all of the Christian man, with little reference to Him who alone is the one sufficient motive and cause. As a further exemplification of this impersonality, on the human side, I mentioned that personal holiness, "perfecting holiness in the fear of God," was no longer considered the first aim of the Christian man; that before it were now placed Christian, or simply benevolent, activities.

In short, that the furrows did not lead up to Christ, to use Spurgeon's

---

1. Vladimir Ivanovich Semenov, ed., *Rasplata (The Reckoning); by Commander Wladimir Semenoff.... His Diary During the Blockade of Port Arthur and the Voyage of Admiral Rojestvensky's Fleet.* Translated by L.A.B. [Louis Alexander Mountbatten]. London: J. Murray, 1909. The book that Mahan sought was Semenov's *The Battle of Tsushima.* London: John Murray, 1906.
2. Zinovi Petrovitch Rodjestvensky, Russian admiral commanding at Tsushima.

1. A member of the International Committee of the YMCA and chairman of the Continuation Committee of the World Missionary Conference, Edinburgh, 1910–1920.

expression.[2] You and I are looking at the same object, Him, from slightly different positions, which in no wise contradict but complement one another. You, if I may so say, are looking from the standpoint of "justification," the sacrifice of Christ for my sins and yours; I by temperament look more to Him as the power that works in us to "sanctification." But undoubtedly, in order both of time and of importance, the pardon precedes the growth in grace; as one of our Episcopal collects runs, Christ "is made to us both a sacrifice for sin and also an example of Godly life."

I think that for completeness your article needs to take account of the absence of "conviction of sin" in our generation generally. To feel the need of a Saviour, to appreciate the greatness of the work of redemption, and to value duly the immensity of the love of which the Cross is the token, one's sins must come home to one; one must feel lost. Certain classes of acts still are held so far wicked, that there is some hope that those guilty of them may realize their fault and welcome a Saviour; but the great mass of us, leading respectable lives, fail to realize our lost condition. The pulpit does little to bring it home to us. My own self I have lately been feeling a sense of utter failure all round, which it has seemed to me gives Him a nearness that I did not feel before. Yet if there be two lines anywhere that have summed up my self appreciation always they are those well known ones

> Nothing in my hands I bring
> Simply to Thy Cross I cling.[3]

The mental unrest of the world begotten by the advances of the last century have driven men to seek assurance in tangible action, rather than in faith. The result is that, there being a vast amount of benevolent action, done for kindly motives in which Christ has no part, we are smugly satisfied that all is right. Sinners! not we; look at our works. Nevertheless, the loss of personal relation to Christ is sin, and the end as sure as a cancer. If your article can stir up the preachers to make the fact of sin come home as a personal concern to the men of our time, you will have done a great good; they will then welcome the Saviour as an ill man does a physician.

To Raymond P. Rodgers

Lawrence, Long Island, April 7, 1910 [NWC]

My dear Rodgers: I have sent today by registered mail Lecture 5 and No. 6, and last of the old ones, will follow next week. As they are sub-

---

2. Charles Haddon Spurgeon, author of many series of sermons, anecdotes, letters, and proverbs, and of an autobiography. This reference is from his *John Ploughman's Talk: or Plain Advice for Plain People*. New York: R. Carter and Brothers, 1884.
3. From the hymn "Rock of Ages," by Augustus Montague Toplady.

stantially one, though too long for a single delivery, I have kept both until I could read them consecutively in their revised form.

I understood that the preceding four were to be sent me for a final reading; but so far that has been done only with the first, which was so read and returned almost at once.

When No. 6 shall have been sent, there will remain to do only a rereading of the new lectures—read last session—and the dovetailing the new with the old in such wise as to make the best consecutive arrangement of the whole. For this purpose it would be desirable for me to have copies of the six old sent me after May 1, when I expect to return to my usual home in Quogue. I have all the new here with me, and as I expect to have little correction to make in them, they ought all to be in final shape by the end of this month. The dovetailing, and the figuring and the method of presentation— what some call the "scenery"—can be done without undue haste during May.

I may say with regard to Nos 5 and 6, of the old,—the one sent today and to go next week,—that there is less need of my seeing them than the others. They form a subject by themselves, and could come anywhere or at any time, *after* the first four of the old, and any of the new.

To Little, Brown and Company

Lawrence, Long Island, April 11, 1910 [LC]

Gentlemen: Replying to yours of March 25, enclosing error detected *re* Nelson's hands by Messrs Sampson Low, I confess to an astonishment at the character of mind which finds a common expression in need of correction because the subject of it happened to have lost a hand.

Since, however, there are such, I have no objection to the "s" being dropped. My impression is that I took it direct from the surgeon's report of the process of decease, and that he used it as he would in case of any dying man, one or two handed, of whose last moments he wrote. I have no time, however, to verify just what he did say. It could be found doubtless in Nicolas.[1]

To Raymond P. Rodgers

Lawrence, Long Island, April 14, 1910 [NWC]

My dear Rodgers: I will send you today by registered mail No. 6, and last, of the old lectures, revised for the copyist.

---

1. N. H. Nicolas, *Dispatches and Letters of Vice-Admiral Lord Viscount Nelson.*

Replying to your letter of the 12th [11th], the arrangement therein proposed suits me entirely.[1] As regards the distribution between myself and Little, I would suggest that he take the *old* lectures revised. He has been long and consecutively familiar with them in their old form; and has not the same familiarity with the new, which he has heard only once.

Between excision and addition I think the old will be found considerably longer than in their first form, and I would suggest for your consideration —in conjunction with Little, if you think well—whether the four days assigned him will be enough. I am too unfamiliar with present arrangements to express an opinion. It may be that he, as reader, may see his way to condense with a few words what in writing requires a larger development.

I said in my last that after arriving in Quogue, in the beginning of May, I would like to have the whole six old, as revised, before me, with a view to dovetail them with the new in order to make the whole as near topical in sequence, and continuous in form as possible. I shall, however, be perfectly able to take up those that have been copied clean, *now* for such revision as I already have given No. 1. If 2, 3, and 4, for instance, are copied I can read and correct, and in this form they may be easier for Little to estimate on. From my experience of No. 1, and recollection of the whole work of revision, I do not think any one of the three would take over one day. The rough revision of course would accompany the clean copy.

To Raymond P. Rodgers

Lawrence, Long Island, April 16, 1910 [NWC]

My dear Rodgers: I returned yesterday, by mail, *England in the Mediterranean*, and *England in the Seven Years' War.*[1]

I have had these books for a very long time in connection with the new lectures. If you happen not to have read them, I venture to recommend them to you to recommend to those of the Conference who are reading men, and interested in the subject of warfare. They deal with matter in itself interesting and the treatment is good and suggestive.

---

1. Rodgers proposed that Mahan deliver in person four of his lectures on naval strategy at the College on June 6, 7, 8, and 9, 1910, and that Little read four others on July 7, 12, 13, and 14, 1910. The final three lectures were to be delivered personally by Mahan on September 6, 7, and 8, 1910. Rodgers to Mahan, April 11, 1910, at the Naval War College.

1. By Sir Julian S. Corbett.

To Raymond P. Rodgers

Lawrence, Long Island, April 17, 1910 [NWC]

My dear Rodgers: I returned Lecture No. 2 by registered mail yesterday. Seeing what a snarl of corrections and insertions was presented by the manuscript from which the copy was made, my compliments are due to the copyist and editor for the success with which it was disentangled and typewritten. The few corrections made are almost wholly on my own matter, and will in no way interfere with the easy use of the material by any lecturer.

I send the enclosed,[1] for forwarding by the same channels as I have maintained all my side of the correspondence with the Comptroller.

[P.S.] I must renew my thanks to you for the trouble taken by you in the Treasury matter.

To J. Franklin Jameson

Lawrence, Long Island, April 20, 1910 [LC]

My dear Prof. Jameson: I have received both your letters, and the Bill; but am ashamed to confess I forgot to write to my M.C. In truth, I dont know who he is.[1] If I had, I would have written instanter; but waiting to ascertain, the matter went out of my head. I trust no failure will result.

I regret the pecuniary provision could not be made. In my judgment, should the bill pass, you will need to find the men sufficiently *interested* to take up the matter. Pay supplies interest; otherwise, I for one would not abandon work to my taste for other less to my taste. Money might incline the balance. I am sure you did what you could.

To Raymond P. Rodgers

Lawrence, Long Island, April 27, 1910 [NWC]

My dear Rodgers: I send by today's mail old lectures 3 & 4, which I have read and made final corrections.

---

1. Enclosure not found. But *see* Mahan to Tracewell, March 9, 1910.

1. Mahan's congressman was W. W. Cox. The legislation was designed to provide an honorarium for the members of the Committee on Documentary Historical Publications. The bill did not pass.

I have so far kept the *rough draft* revised from which these copies were made. Is there any object in keeping them longer; for if not, I shall prefer not to take them away when I leave here.[1]

To Raymond P. Rodgers

Lawrence, Long Island, April 30, 1910 [NWC]

My dear Rodgers: I received last night, addressed to me direct, here, permission to change residence to Quogue on May 6th. The family will move down on that day. I myself intend going on the 5th, for a few days rest, and to see a lifelong friend whose course I fear is pretty nearly run, to *Haverford, Pa.*, where my address will be care Allen Evans,[1] in the unlikely contingency of my being needed. I shall return to New York the 9th and go down to Quogue the 11th.

Lecture 5 has been received and is ready to return, corrected. I hold it back in case of No. 6 coming here in time to be similarly read and returned under same cover. If not, 5 will be mailed before leaving here.

The preparation for Little's part of the programme is now complete, or will be with 6. My own for June are also in shape for my own using, and the time before me in Quogue will suffice fully for such further preparation for delivery as may be necessary. Whether afterwards it will become expedient to make fair copies so as to be as ready for use by another person as they now are for my own, is a question that can wait till after delivery, or till after the Conference; indeed, indefinitely.

To Charles W. Stewart

Quogue, Long Island, May 13, 1910 [NA]

My dear Mr. Stewart: I have just returned here for the summer, and in the course of necessary desk clearing have decided to send you, under another envelope, a number of copies of dispatches (British) which I had made at various times while preparing my *1812.*

They are of two principal classes: (1) from the British Foreign Office files, correspondence concerning *the* Orders in Council of 1807; and (2)

---

1. On this letter Captain Little wrote: "The War College does not need them anymore as it has copies of the unrevised lectures."

1. Son of Mrs. A. T. Mahan's uncle, Edmund C. Evans.

from the Canadian Archives at Ottawa, in relation to military and naval operations on the Lakes and Canadian frontier.

They are of course of very varying degrees of interest, but should you have time to overhaul them you will find some, I think, sufficiently interesting to keep.

I have also enclosed two logs of British vessels covering the period of the action of Sept 5, 1781, off the Capes, which determined the fate of Cornwallis.

To William H. Henderson

Lawrence, Long Island, May 17, 1910 [NMM]

My dear Henderson: I hope you will not be too disgusted at my long neglect to reply to your January letter to favor me with other occasional news of yourself and contemporary feeling in England. On picking up your letter and rereading I have reproached myself doubly for the failure to express at once my sympathy, for yourself as well as for Mrs. Henderson, in the anxious and painful illness through which she was passing. I trust that the recovery which then promised has since been fully realized to her and to you. I can give a personal element of personal experience in such a trouble; for two years ago I passed through a severe operation (prostate) and was believing myself nearly well, when further complications involving further operations reduced me to a wreck, and confined me to the house for the whole winter.

I am not wholly without excuse for my delay in answering. It is not merely that I have been very busy, but that I am forced now to recognize a distinct decrease in the amount of work that I can do consecutively. As I shall be seventy in September, this is not out of the way; but either it has come upon me somewhat suddenly, or else I suddenly waked up to the fact. So long as I have a steady unbroken course of thinking and writing, my mind runs along pretty smoothly and easily; but a succession of minor disconnected calls upon my time, such as administrative work, which you like, so often entails, breaks me up pretty quickly. Passing from one detail to another, the same aggregate of head work tires me very much more. So with vexatious incidents, of which I have had a share lately. I dont worry more than I did, perhaps much less; but the same amount of worry takes more out of me. My physical condition remains good; distinctly above the average of my age, I think. Of the twenty who graduated with me in 1859 at our Naval Academy only one besides myself still hangs out.[1]

---

1. G. C. Remey.

I was particularly interested in your statement that the one calibre gun ship was exploded. I never was a convert; but, as I had held myself aloof from professional discussion I accepted under silent protest what seemed the general verdict. I wish you could have told me that there was any ultimate goal in point of size visible. I fail to see how budgets can stand the pressure. If disarmament meant peace it might be a good thing; but I always cite our War of Secession in disproof of that somewhat plausible proposition. Never were two communities more wholly disarmed in proportion to their population and resources. They fought all the same; the only result of military unreadiness being that the matter took much longer to settle, and at an expenditure of money and blood which present armaments will not entail, either in the matter of preparation in peace, or use in war. The disarmament advocates fail to note that within ten years you have had at least three wars in Europe, which have cost no blood; and no money, beyond the cost of preparations, just because the nations were— or were not—armed. In the Delcassé incident[2] Germany by force made France do her will; in the succeeding Algeciras affair,[3] France having got ready, Germany was reasonable. In the Balkan business[4] two years ago Germany evidently forced Russia to be quiet; and force is war, whether blows be exchanged or not. The ousting of Japan from the Liao Tung by the three nations in the nineties was war, just as really as the subsequent war of 1904–5 by which Japan regained her loss.[5]

In short it is public opinion and public virtue which alone, in case of disarmament, can maintain peace; and nobody I presume sees anywhere such power of enlightened opinion and such virtue as will restrain nations when they have power. Plausible reasons for wrong action have always been forthcoming when policy required. In fact, I have never been quite clear that governments are not bound to forward national interests even when doubtful in legality. Take our Monroe Doctrine. It is policy pure and simply. No one can say it is a *right*, legal or natural, that we exclude European acquirement—if we can—in these continents; but it is greatly to our advantage, because it averts occasions for clashing interests. The mere

---

2. Resignation of Théophile Delcassé, French foreign minister, in June 1906, as the result of British unwillingness to support firmly France's opposition to German economic penetration in Morocco. The crisis resulted in considerable French loss of face.
3. The Algeciras Conference of January-April 1907 which recognized the independence of Morocco but at which French special interests in the area were also generally accepted.
4. German support of Austria's annexation of Bosnia and Herzegovina in October 1908, an act which an outraged Russia nonetheless accepted.
5. By the terms of the Treaty of Shimonoseki of 1895, concluding the Sino-Japanese War, China was to cede to Japan the Liaotung Peninsula. Immediately after the treaty was signed, Russia, France, and Germany decided that the peninsula should be returned to China. Japan, receiving no assurance from London or Washington, submitted to the will of the European powers.

expediency may constitute a moral right for the Government of a nation, as a trustee, to follow a course of action which another Govt. equally as a trustee must oppose. By all means let them agree if they can upon some adjustment; but if not, if both are heavily armed they are more likely to reach such adjustment than if unarmed one sees a chance of getting the advantage. Besides, where in the awakening East can Europeans find the public opinion, or the public law, which to some extent does help in European troubles?

I congratulate [you] on your steady occupation. Administration is not to my taste, but it is to yours; and the only two desiderata in work are that it be enough and congenial. Though very busy, I myself am somewhat puzzled what I shall take up after my present job is finished: but when that bridge is reached, I suppose I shall manage to cross it.

To Raymond P. Rodgers

Marshmere, Quogue, Long Island, May 25, 1910 [NWC]

My dear Rodgers: In going over the four lectures to be delivered by me in June, it has seemed to me that it will be advantageous to open the second one—Tuesday, June 7,—with a brief exposition of a land campaign—that of 1796; which, with the matter already embodied in the three lectures, June 7, 8, 9, will give a kind of trilogy of illustration of their particular subject.

To prepare the graphic illustration on the map, I should need to consult Jomini *Guerres de la Révolution*;[1] but it has occurred to me that possibly Little might be able and willing to get out the few data which are needed, a memorandum of which I enclose. If he can, this will obviate the necessity of sending the volume which contains this particular campaign in Germany.

I lectured on this, in extenso, in former days at the College; but I cannot now find the manuscript, nor yet lectures which I gave on Bonaparte's Italian campaign of the same year. Possibly I turned them over to the College. If they exist, and Little will undertake what I want, they may help him; but French is to him like English, and Jomini is tremendously interesting. Hamley[2] gives much of these data, perhaps all, and is more succinct; but dry as sawdust.

---

1. Henri Jomini, *Historie critique et militaire des guerres de la révolution*. 6 vols. Paris: Anselin et Pochard, 1820, and subsequent editions.
2. Edward Bruce Hamley, *The Operations of War Explained and Illustrated*. Edinburgh: William Blackwood and Sons, 1889, and subsequent editions.

My first lecture will require no illustration; but my Monday afternoon will have to be given wholly to preparing the graphical side of the next day's work. Shortly before leaving here I will write you what maps will be needed.

That of which I now write will not take ten minutes speaking, being merely an explanation of the prepared diagram.

[Enclosure]

Memorandum

In the campaign of 1796 in Germany, data needed:

1. To trace in sufficient outline, i.e. through two or three principal points, the lines of advance of the two French armies, (Jourdan and Moreau), from the point at which each lay immediately before crossing the Rhine to the *farthest* point reached by each one.

2. To mark the simultaneous positions of these two armies, *at the time Jourdan began to retreat*. Jourdan's line of advance will end there; but Moreau, as I remember, advanced several marches beyond the position occupied by him at that moment.

3. To show line of retreat by each army from the point to which it had advanced.

4. To show line of Austrian retreat, (Archduke Charles), from beginning of French movement to his attack in force upon Jourdan, at the point where the latter's retreat began.

5. To have in figures, to the nearest thousand, as given by Jomini:
   a. Austrian force at opening campaign
   b. Jourdan's "   "   "   "
   c. Moreau's "   "   "   "
   d. Austrian force brought against Jourdan
   e. Jourdan's force at that instant
   f. Austrian force detached to oppose Moreau
   g. Moreau's force at that instant

These last four refer to the instant when Charles divided his force and attacked Jourdan, which coincides with the end of Jourdan's advance.

I propose at that instant (corresponding to 2, above) to show the relative forces, in all four divisions, by the means I have commonly used.

My mode of illustration would be:

French advances: Whole green lines, (*light* green preferable).
   "   retreats: Broken   "   "

Austrian retreat: Whole red line. The Austrian pursuit of Jourdan will not be required.

French forces: Green cardboard.
Austrian " : Red   "

To the Editor of The Daily Mail

N.P., N.D. Probably, Quogue, Long Island, circa June 1910[1] [NA]

The huge development of the German Navy within the past decade, and the assurance that the present rate of expenditure, over twenty million pounds annually, will be maintained for several years to come, is a matter of general international importance. Elsewhere and in another connection, I have had occasion to point out, in our American press, that the question immediately raised is not what Germany means to do with this force, which already is second only to that of Great Britain, and for which is contemplated a further large expansion. The real subject for the reflection of every person, statesman or private, patriotically interested in his country's future, is the simple existence, present, and still more prospective, of a new international factor, to be reckoned with in all calculations where oppositions of national interests may arise.

From this point of view it is not particularly interesting to inquire whether Germany has any far-reaching purposes of invading Great Britain, or of dismembering her empire; nor yet whether, on the other side of the ocean, she purposes no longer in future contingencies to show that respect for the Monroe Doctrine which she hitherto has observed, much to American satisfaction. Americans, while giving full credit to Germany for the most friendly intentions towards them, have to note that in the future she can do as she pleases about the Monroe Doctrine, so far as our intended organization of naval force goes, because she will be decidedly stronger at sea than we expect to be, and we have over her no military check such as the interests of Canada impose upon Great Britain.

To Charles W. Stewart

Marshmere, Quogue, Long Island, July 15, 1910 [NA]

My dear Mr. Stewart: *The Daily Mail* has sent me some copies of its issue of July 4, containing the article about which you asked.[1] I send you the page. One paragraph was omitted, by accident they write me, but on

---

1. From *The Daily Mail*, London, July 4 and 6, 1910. This letter was enclosed in Mahan to Stewart, July 15, 1910.

1. Mahan's papers in *The Daily Mail* for 1910 were "The International Significance of German Naval Development," July 4 and 6, and "Britain and World Peace," October 31.

comparison with my rough draft it seems of no moment from your probable point of view. They intended to republish July 6.

The title has been changed from that I assigned;[2] but that is one of the things editors do, unexpectedly.

To James W. McIntyre

Marshmere, Quogue, Long Island, July 30, 1910 [LC]

My dear Mr. McIntyre: I have for over a year past been keeping careful watch upon general international relations, and have now in hand, substantially ready for the press, a sketch of them as now existing, with their bearing upon American interests. For this I would propose, tentatively, the title "The Interest of America in International Relations." The number of words is something over 25,000, divisible probably into three chapters.[1]

The sketch opens with a brief historical summary, eliciting necessarily an allusion to the contrasted European ideas of "Balance of Power" and "Concert of Europe," and proceeds to examine the existing relations between Great Britain and Germany, with the apparent progress of the latter towards the leadership of Europe. A valuation of the balance of forces now existing in Europe leads on to an appreciation of their probable effect upon the United States as concerns our two leading external policies, the Monroe Doctrine and the Open Door.

I believe I have put together a summary of facts with an appreciation of their significance not readily at hand for the average American reader, and calculated, I hope, to arouse an interest too little diffused in our country. Needing only a brief revision, with a few alterations or additions already determined, I can deliver probably by August 15.

I have been so busy with Government work for the past year that I have had little time for my own.

To James W. McIntyre

Marshmere, Quogue, Long Island, August 13, 1910 [LC]

My dear Mr. McIntyre: Your letter of August 5 has been constantly in mind since receipt. At the moment I happened to see that S.S. McClure

---

2. The original title was "Britain and the German Navy."

1. In 1910 Little, Brown and Company published four essays under the title *The Interest of America in International Conditions.*

had embarked for this side, and I send him today a letter asking if he would care to accept the papers for his magazine.[1] Should he do so, the book publication can be postponed; but, as you surmise, I am desirous to get the matters before the public soon, in one form or another. Any occurrence might necessitate modification or enlargement; and in fact, all that now remains not ready for the printer is an addition—at the very end—necessitated by the Russo-Japanese convention of July 4.[2] This is written, but not yet fully revised and concluded.

I have stated my arrangement with you to McClure, requesting in consequence his speedy reply. I scarcely expect it to be favorable to me, but last fall he entered into a correspondence with [me] on this very subject, and it may be he will still think it interesting to the American public, which he has told me is his one standard of value.

Should he decline, the "Copy" will be mailed you at once, with the exception named; which being at the end will be completed before the printers can reach it.

I send you a cutting from the *Daily Mail* (London) containing an article by me,[3] which has made some little stir, favorable or the reverse, on the other side, and which may help this. The *Daily Mail* in fact has asked of me another paper, based upon the words red-pencilled; but I have not yet decided whether I can write it.[4]

To Raymond P. Rodgers

Marshmere, Quogue, Long Island, August 23, 1910 [NWC]

My dear Rodgers: When lecturing last September on Rodzhestvensky's action Captain Little urged upon me that I had not done justice to his order of approach. After my return here last June, I took up at once the lectures for September coming, and in connection with them asked him to give me his views, etc., but at his leisure; knowing that in addition to his usual occupation he had before him the not light task of reading several of another man's lectures. About ten days ago I received from him a very full reply.

---

1. The papers were titled: "The Present Predominance of Germany in Europe. Its Foundations and Tendencies"; "Relations Between East and West"; "The Origin and Character of Present International Groupings in Europe"; and "The Open Door." Mahan and McClure did not reach an agreement. *See* Mahan to McIntyre, August 26, 1910.
2. In which the signatories spelled out further their respective spheres of influence in Manchuria.
3. *See* Mahan to Stewart, July 15, 1910.
4. Published as "Britain and World Peace," *The Daily Mail*, London, October 31, 1910.

I make this explanation in order to account for the late date at which I send the enclosed to be copied if it be convenient so to do. Should the pressure on the clerical force be too heavy, return the papers to me as they stand; for to lecture from a typewritten manuscript, though more convenient, is not indispensable. I should have written first to ask if it were convenient, but seeing how little time is left it seems scarcely expedient thus to consume two more days.

Somewhat more than Little's suggestions have gone into the revision, but I am greatly indebted to him for inserting it by his comment, for it moved me to a closer examination of the whole matter.

To James W. McIntyre

Marshmere, Quogue, Long Island, August 26, 1910 [LC]

My dear Mr. McIntyre: McClure returned my manuscript on Tuesday saying it is a little too close reading and too long for their magazine purposes. I have retained it till today for chapter division and headings, and some revision and now send by registered mail.

I think it quite as valuable, more opportune and easier reading than *The Problem of Asia*, and I hope to excite at least a beginning of public interest. It is better for it to appear as a whole, though less beneficial to me pecuniarily. I hope in September to write an article on the same general subject for the English *Daily Mail*,[1] which has already asked and published an article—which however, I sent you. I trust this may help the book with the British public.

There remains to revise and type write about a thousand words which come at the end of the last chapter. I hope to send them on Monday. At present I contemplate no preface; but probably a Table of Contents to be made out as the page proof comes in.

To Little, Brown and Company

Marshmere, Quogue, Long Island, August 29, 1910 [LC]

Gentlemen: I enclose herewith the concluding pages for *The Interest of America in International Conditions*. They have been rendered necessary by the occurrence mentioned having taken place since the preceding part

---

1. *See* Mahan to Stewart, July 15, 1910, Footnote 1; and Mahan to McIntyre, August 13, 1910, Footnote 4.

was written; and, as indicated upon their face, this should be emphasized by a space between the two.

Barring some other incident requiring a like qualification this concludes the "Copy" for the book.

To Raymond P. Rodgers

Marshmere, Quogue, Long Island, August 31, 1910 [NWC]

My dear Rodgers: There will be no difficulty, I think, in my leaving my lectures with you after delivery, ready for the final typewriting. I have read them two or three times during the summer; and although I am prone to make additions or corrections at every reading, I think, from a glance again this morning, finality may be assumed for the purpose you indicate when I shall have read them on this occasion.

As regards the lecture at which the Secretary proposes to honor me by his presence,[1] I think likely the last is as good as any; perhaps better, inasmuch as the other two are parts of a whole.

To Little, Brown and Company

Marshmere, Quogue, Long Island, September 3, 1910 [LC]

Gentlemen: I am obliged to go to Newport today,[1] to remain there till next Thursday. As I may probably have time for proof reading while there, you may send any proof, addressed to the "Naval War College, Newport, R.I.," up to and including Wednesday, September 7; but, unless Wednesday's is mailed early, a duplicate had better be sent to the University Club, New York, where I shall spend Friday. Mark such "Keep till arrival."

I have mailed this morning galleys 1–6; and have directed any received after my departure to be sent to the War College.

[P.S.] I shall be back here Friday night, Sept. 9.

---

1. A last-minute change in his plans caused Secretary Meyer to miss hearing Mahan's lecture.

1. On August 22, Mahan had received orders to proceed to Newport and report to the President of the Naval War College, there to deliver a course of lectures.

To Raymond P. Rodgers

Marshmere, Quogue, Long Island, September 10, 1910 [NWC]

My dear Rodgers: I write a line to say that I have found the three lectures delivered last June. I think I can send them to you by the end of the coming week, and having regard to your wishes about the copying will send each to you as soon as satisfied with it myself.

To Little, Brown and Company

Marshmere, Quogue, Long Island, September 12, 1910 [LC]

Gentlemen: Acknowledging yours of September 9, I am entirely content with the proposed book title, "America's Interest in International Conditions." I should, however, prefer for the title *page* the longer form "The Interest of America etc," unless you see sufficient reasons to the contrary.

I hope to mail to you to-day through galley 48, and to follow with the remainder tomorrow.

To Little, Brown and Company

Marshmere, Quogue, Long Island, September 13, 1910 [LC]

Gentlemen: I mail you to day galleys 49–55; reserving the last, 56, for a day or two in case it should seem to me expedient to add a few lines relative to the purchase by Turkey of two (or four) battleships from Germany; a fact which has several bearings. Will mail in either event on Thursday.

To Little, Brown and Company

Postcard   Quogue, Long Island, September 13, 1910 [LC]

When next sending proofs, will you also kindly send a half dozen addressed wraps for returning.

To Little, Brown and Company

Marshmere, Quogue, Long Island, September 15, 1910 [LC]

Gentlemen: I enclose corrected proof of last galley, No. 56, and of title page. I will reserve the privilege of adding to the end of the book the paragraph before indicated as the reason for the detaining of the galley; but I have been so pressed with work that I have not been able to attend to it and the indications now are that I will not. It is not essential, though perhaps expedient; but not sufficiently so for any delay.

To Raymond P. Rodgers

Marshmere, Quogue, Long Island, September 15, 1910 [NWC]

My dear Rodgers: I send herewith the second in order of the four lectures I delivered last June. It may be considered in final shape for any one's use, though I never yet saw the occasion in which I have not modified in some way when myself using.

The principal change is the pasting on instructions as to the method of illustration used by me in several cases. In case of my disability, or absence otherwise, these may aid a substitute by suggestion. Little is thoroughly familiar with all my methods.

To Raymond P. Rodgers

Marshmere, Quogue, Long Island, September 17, 1910 [NWC]

My dear Rodgers: I have sent you today the fourth and last of the lectures delivered by me last June. With this I think the College will have a complete set of all that I have done under the project of revision; corrected, and annotated with such directions for graphic illustration as have suggested themselves to me.

To Little, Brown and Company

Marshmere, Quogue, Long Island, September 21, 1910 [LC]

Gentlemen: I observe in the page proof, after the first chapter, the right hand pages are no longer given the page heading "In International Conditions," corresponding to the left hand heading "The Interest of America." The curious right hand headings assigned seem to have been drawn from the Chapter headings, but they really are nonsense in themselves, or reduce the "The Interest of America" to irrelevance.

The proof readers not having made the chapters, other than one, correspond in this to Chap I., I have indicated that the page headings should be *throughout*: Left "The Interest of America" *Right* "In International Conditions"; but I think best to call your particular attention to the matter.

To Philip Andrews[1]

Marshmere, Quogue, Long Island, September 24, 1910 [OANHD]

My dear Andrews: Replying to your letter of August 20, I should first say that during my time on the active list I never was closely associated with the administration of navy yards, except when fitting for sea; and except during the War of Secession never served on our own coast, always abroad. I therefore have no intimate knowledge of the local details of our navy yard positions and less of their present development. This probably may not matter much, as you ask only a general opinion upon the whole field; you can yourself supply corrections necessitated by my ignorance of details.

The question addressed me concerning Naval Yards and Stations has to be viewed from the broad ground of general national policy. One view is that a navy exists primarily for defence only. This, the popular impression, while excessively narrow and inadequate, is so far correct that the safety of the national coast is the primary consideration, if only because the entire coast line is the base of both national defence and offence by naval means; such basic function being localized in particular positions, the superior fitness of which makes them to represent the whole.

The other view, that the navy is essentially for offensive action, that coast defence itself, to be adequate, depends upon the power of the navy to assume the offensive, and which recognizes the existence also of external policies, to the maintenance of which the navy is the necessary arm, is more correct, and the one I shall follow. This view includes the popular saying, "a navy

---

1. Commander Andrews, class of 1886, at this time attached to the General Board, noted on this letter: "Secy Gen Board. This was in response to a query written Adml. Mahan by direction of Secy. Meyer." Mahan's response was designated G. B. [General Board] Document No. 404.

for defence only," as the whole includes its parts; for the provision of bases for home coast defence is conducive, even essential, to the external action of the navy.

The United States has now two principal and permanent external policies: The Monroe Doctrine and the Open Door. The latter of these signifies that trade with Chinese territory by the world outside of China is to be regulated by China herself, and not by external Powers forcibly installing themselves in possession of Chinese territory.

Having reference to naval stations, the Monroe Doctrine centres around the Isthmus of Panama; the Open Door requires positions as far advanced in the Pacific Ocean as is permitted by the local advantages of points now in our possession, and by the general national willingness to maintain a navy and naval bases adequate to our avowed national policies.

As before remarked, the entire coast frontier, like any land frontier, is the national base of operations. Our coast frontier divides into three sections: The Atlantic, the Gulf, and the Pacific. Naval Stations for these must be chosen in accordance with the two principal objects stated: (1) To ensure the safety of the coast; (2) To facilitate external operations in support of national policies.

This is the point to introduce a remark which governs the military determination of navy yards and naval stations; a consideration too rarely distinctly formulated. This is, that navy yards are for war, not for peace; that therefore they are primarily yards for repair and refit, not for construction, because under modern conditions naval vessels must be constructed in peace, the duration of a war not allowing time. The function of naval stations, therefore, is to maintain in efficiency ships already built, and their location should be determined by this consideration, irrespective of facilities for building, whether natural or acquired.

This amounts to saying that the choice and maintenance of naval stations should be determined by strategic considerations, rather than by such as are industrial or economical. Of course, where the three coincide—as in New York—it is a fortunate conjunction; but where there is a collision of considerations the place which is superior by situation,—nearness,—defensive strength, and the possibility of storing resources, is to be preferred to one industrially or commercially greater. Let me add that the chief of all elements of refit is the dock, and suitable ground for docking, or harboring floating docks, is a prime consideration.

The Atlantic seaboard is obviously the most important of the three principal divisions of our sea frontier. Its function in a general scheme of naval provision is largely defensive, because it is not nearest to either of our great external objects of policy. In case of war with a naval power so far superior as to be able to maintain on that coast a navy stronger than our fleet, our fleet would need at least two principal bases; because the existence of two not only provides alternate refuges in case of need, but by that very fact facilitates also the offensive operations of any character, the execution of which is the office of a defendant navy. The question of the Atlantic seaboard, viewed distinctly as a military problem, is therefore simple; nor is there any doubt that Chesapeake Bay and New York represent the two best positions. That the two are principal does not imply that they are equal, or should receive equal development. New York is distinctly the better, because it has two entrances; for New York must be understood to embrace Long Island Sound, and may advantageously be extended to include Narragansett Bay. So extensive an interior sheet of water, covering unlimited resources, with two entrances over a hundred miles apart, each capable of powerful fortification, constitutes a base of naval operations probably unique in the world.

In considering the Gulf Coast we find ourselves at once in face of a complex problem; for there is involved not only local defence and utilization, but the further question of the Panama Canal. This last compels us to assume as a factor a navy at least substantially equal, on the ground in dispute, to any that would venture to encounter us there. With a distinctly inferior navy we cannot protect the Isthmus; the question therefore is: how with equal forces best to insure the safety of the Gulf ports, and their usefulness to the plan of operations?

The reply to my mind seems quite clear that the Gulf Coast is best defended, and because so defended made most useful as a source of supplies to the Isthmus, by the effective occupation of Guantanamo. By effective I mean the establishment of docking resources and defences which will assure the use of the place by the fleet. A fleet pivoted on Guantanamo covers effectually the whole Gulf coast, granting ordinary local defensive fortification against sea attack at the important sea ports,—New Orleans, Mobile, Galveston; because a hostile fleet is debarred from a hasty attack by such local fortifications, and from prolonged operations by the fact that all its lines of communication with the ocean would be flanked by Guantanamo. Precisely the same remark applies to the line of communications from Gulf ports to the Isthmus, essential to the maintenance of the latter; Guantanamo by position covers them all.

For these reasons Guantanamo appears to rank next in importance as a naval station to the Chesapeake and New York; and second to these only because home security bears to external policy the relation of a foundation to its superstructure.

I am inclined to attach value to Key West as a naval station, secondary to Guantanamo; because, being hereafter in communication by land with the rest of the country, it can more rapidly and more safely serve as an intermediate means of supply to Guantanamo. This is, supposing the enemy strong enough to remain in American or Caribbean waters, the sending of supplies directly from Atlantic or Gulf ports would be longer and more exposed than through Key West. If Key West can be sufficiently fortified, and docks built there, Guantanamo and Key West would give the Gulf the two frontier positions which it is generally held are expedient on any frontier, regarded as a base of operations. By the north and south sides of Cuba there are two distinct lines of communication between the two places.

I conceive that such occupation of Guantanamo and Key West, having behind them the Chesapeake and New York, defends the Gulf coast better than it is possible to defend the Atlantic coast; and the more so because the latter, being much the more important commercially, would thereby first invite harassment by an enemy.

The Pacific coast intrinsically is more exposed, in greater danger from an enemy, than either of the others; because, being much the more recent, it has received less development, and is far more removed by land from support by the Atlantic and Gulf coasts than either of these is from the other. There is also much more imminent danger of hostilities in that sea than in the Atlantic, because of the doubtful issue of the Open Door, and the inflammable prejudice of our Pacific population towards the Japanese resident.

I need scarcely enlarge upon the probable disinclination to war of the Japanese government, with its critical engagements in Manchuria and Korea, amid two hostile populations, and with Russia close at hand to improve any opportunity for retrieving recent humiliation and loss. If we can keep our Pacific people in hand, even the Open Door may be maintained for some time to come, despite the apparent purpose of Japan to disregard it as far as she can; a purpose easy to forgive in view of her poverty and financial needs. But, should war come, Japan has an excellent navy, a very numerous army, highly organized, and with a recent experience which will constitute its members available veterans for foreign service for full ten years hence.

Invasion of the Pacific coast is therefore a possibility, which, if transmuted into actuality, we have no organized land force to meet. This means that, should our navy not be able to prevent a landing, our naval bases may be taken out of our hands. The same, doubtless, is true of positions on other coasts; but there is more imminence in the Pacific. Further, we have in the Pacific Ocean two external territorial interests, Hawaii and the Philippines, besides Panama, which is common to both coasts.

Not only, therefore, is a navy doubly essential to prevent attack, but it is more than usually exposed to the loss of positions which are indispensable to its efficiency. Actually, we have not an army capable of operating in Japan, while Japan has an army capable of operating in the United States; granting in each case the capacity to effect a landing. It is difficult to state more forcibly the dependence of an issue upon a navy, and this is the fundamental consideration in determining the question of naval stations, upon which the navy in its turn is dependent.

These considerations govern my reply as to the Pacific. Because of their commercial importance, and as accessory to the defence of the Pacific coast line, also as outlets for supply to the Pacific fleet in general, Puget Sound and San Francisco should remain naval stations. Of these I believe Puget Sound to be distinctly superior to Mare Island; and unless there exist within San Francisco Bay an available site markedly better than at Bremerton, the latter should receive the higher development as a docking yard. But to cover the Pacific coast against a landing, and at the same time protect our other interests in the Pacific,—the Open Door, the Philippines, Hawaii,—Pearl Harbor should receive the development now contemplated, and Guam should be constituted a kind of Gibraltar, if the engineers find that it can be held for six months by works and a garrison which the country would be willing to provide. No situation in our possession equals Guam to protect every interest in the Pacific; nor need it be feared that Japan would attempt an invasion of the Pacific coast, or of Hawaii, nor probably of the Philippines, with a superior or equal American navy securely based upon a point only a thousand miles from its coasts and flanking all its eastward communications.

It has been necessary to give this outline of reasons to account for my reply, that in my judgment, having regard to the military, commercial, and industrial interests of the country, and to its security, there are five principal naval positions to be maintained as naval stations: New York, the Chesapeake, Guantanamo, Puget Sound, Guam. Accessory to these Pearl Harbor in Hawaii, and Key West.

These are the great offensive positions strategically underlying the avowed external policies of our country. All others are defensive only; expected only to stand on the defense against attack by ships. Within them works of construction or repair may be established, and it may be necessary in a representative political system to obtain support for that which is necessary, by conceding maintenance to that which is not similarly essential. No objection, however, can be made to distributing constructional provision, irrespective of war emergencies, provided the war stations are kept up to the necessary adequacy for refit,—especially docking. On the contrary, the distribution of manufacturing employment is in the interests of the country. It realizes Napoleon's motto, "Disseminate in order to live; concentrate in order to fight."

By naval station of the first order I mean one having not only seaward defence, but landward dispositions as well, calculated to insure holding out until the general force of the nation and the navy could come to its assistance. All others, for instance Boston, would require only seaward guns; because, if taken, the efficiency of the positions vital to the national cause would not be seriously impaired. I am inclined to think that Guam so secured would render unnecessary any other first class station, as defined, on the Pacific; except that the large Japanese population of Hawaii would require particular precautions for Pearl Harbor.

To undertake works to defend on the land side the naval stations at New York, Norfolk, and Puget Sound is probably neither immediately necessary, nor under existing political conditions possible. There should, however, be in hand, ready for immediate execution, schemes of such defence, matured by the selection of lines and the elaboration of plans for fortifying them; having in view the character of troops, regulars or citizen, that could be had to man such works. In an emergency, and with the time gained by our great distance from any dangerous enemy, a large force for rapid construction could be at once secured. But for Guantanamo, Pearl Harbor, and Guam, no such day of grace can be expected. If it be determined to fortify them at all, what is to be done should not be begun until everything is ready to press forward to the point of security. The worst of all mistakes would be to prepare them so far as to fall into an enemy's hands well fitted for resistance to recapture. This would resemble what Russia did, by the way she assembled her Port Arthur fleet.

As regards abandonment or modification of existing naval stations, viewed as a purely military question, I should consider that for the decisive operations of war no harbor east of Cape Cod or south of the Chesapeake is of great importance. Guantanamo and Key West, developed as suggested, would eliminate the former Gulf ports, Pensacola and the Mississippi, which twenty years ago, when I first studied the Strategic Features of the Gulf and Caribbean, were of the first class. The increasing size of battle ships as well as our new acquisitions throw them out. The events of 1898 advanced our Gulf frontier to the line of Key West, Guantanamo, Porto Rico. In the Pacific, Puget Sound, Pearl Harbor, and Guam are the only military indispensable positions.

The case of all other existing naval stations, Portsmouth, Boston, League Island, Charleston, Port Royal, the Gulf ports, Porto Rico, San Francisco, the Philippines, is to be determined on administrative and political grounds only. A concentration of energies on those ports alone which are called first class might provoke opposition too strong to be overcome. Construction of all sorts therefore, and the repair and maintenance of torpedo vessels, and cruisers other than armored, submarines, and general manufacturing, might be distributed elsewhere as thought expedient and useful. It may very well be that such distribution would relieve the great stations and so rather increase than diminish efficiency. But as naval stations for war, only the five named, with Key West and Pearl Harbor, need to be maintained. Such provision is not very excessive for a frontier of, I suppose, five thousand miles, and an external policy like the Monroe.

My advocacy of Guam is based upon its position, the assumed sufficiency of its harbor after certain easy improvements, and the further assumption

[357]

that it might be made as secure as Malta, the works of which I was assured on the spot by a distinguished British Engineer, are of very exaggerated development. The question of such defence is of course for the army to decide. Into other reasons for Guam I will not enter further, the more so that at the request of the President of the War College I contributed to the present Conference a fairly full discussion of the matter.[2]

Have you seen the account of the development of Wilhelmshaven and its relations to the general scheme of German naval development in this year's *Naval Annual?*

To Little, Brown and Company

Marshmere, Quogue, Long Island, September 26, 1910 [LC]

Gentlemen: I am returning today the last page proofs, corrected, 189–212. I have been desirous to introduce in the foot note, p. 201, reference to an article which I had not seen and could not have seen, when the Ms. was sent.[1] In order to do so, without changing lining or paging, I have marked for omission two lines of the footnote, which will allow the necessary space; but I have thought to ask you whether by some device, moving the footnote higher, using another form or admitting the irregularity of the note running too low on the page, the words marked for omission could be retained. Further to assist this object it would be admissable to omit from the sentence the words indicated, thus: *The Times* has been (throughout) a (consistent and) strong advocate of the Anglo-Japanese alliance.

To Joseph L. Jayne[1]

Marshmere, Quogue, Long Island, September 28, 1910 [OANHD]

My dear Sir: In looking over some back numbers of the *Naval Annual* I found the following (1905):

"The General Board of the U.S. Navy, October 28, 1904, recommend the *Connecticut* to be the standard as to displacement and dimen-

---

2. Members of the General Board were present at the War College during the summer of 1910 when Mahan lectured there on the strategic importance of Guam.

1. The recent article was "The Mystery of the Status Quo," which *Nineteenth Century and After* carried in its September 1910 issue.

1. Commander Jayne, class of 1882, was Secretary of the General Board of the Navy.

sions . . . and is of opinion that, if found practicable, battleships be given a battery of heavy turret guns, none less than ten-inch, and at least four twelve-inch, without intermediate battery."

Can you inform me whether the above is correct?[2] From the place of its appearance, I assume that the recommendation was made public at the time and that there is no impropriety in my asking about it or your telling me; but if there be any doubt, you will, I hope refer the matter to the President of the Board for his sanction.

To Raymond P. Rodgers

Marshmere, Quogue, Long Island, September 28, 1910 [NWC]

My dear Rodgers: If you still are of the opinion that my lectures should be printed, in whole or in part, I think it would be well to send me a complete set for consideration, when the copies now being made are finished. I understood you contemplated several sets of the whole, one of which doubtless could be spared me for the purpose named.

As lectures simply, they are now complete, and revision final for a measurable period; probably for my life time. But as a matter of publication, several considerations present themselves. Shall all be printed, or only some? for example, only the development and revision of the old lectures,—the part read by Little,—or also the additions which I myself read this summer and last.[1] Also, shall the unconventional lecture style remain, or a more formal book form be adopted? Other questions also may occur.

I myself incline to let the lecture style stand, perhaps because I feel weary of the general subject and shrink from the additional labor of reviewing the whole; for it might amount to that.[2] In the lecture form it would be necessary only to purge redundancies, and to qualify undue unconventionalities of language. Final conclusion on these points can be postponed till the whole has been re-read consecutively.

As regards the medium of publication, I think upon the whole it would

2. Mahan sought this information in connection with the preparation of his article, "The Battleship of All Big Guns," *World's Work* (January 1911). The battleship *Connecticut*, commissioned in 1908 displaced 16,000 tons. She mounted four 12-inch, eight 8-inch, twelve 7-inch, twenty 3-inch guns; and four 21-inch torpedo tubes. Her length was 456 feet, breadth 77 feet, and her twin screws drove her at 19 knots.

1. Beside this sentence Rodgers wrote: "I would say the matter in all should be included." Little, Brown and Company published the whole in 1911 under the title *Naval Strategy, Compared and Contrasted with the Principles of Military Operations on Land.*

2. Beside this sentence Rodgers wrote: "As he prefers."

be better for the work and for myself, that it be through my usual publishers. I should hope that the Department would leave me on duty in connection with the College for the specific object, and allow me also to receive my usual royalties from the publishers.[3] In themselves, the royalties would scarcely repay me for the labor involved, and indeed as a private venture I would not undertake the work; not that I think it would not more than clear expenses, but that the margin would not compensate me for my time.

To Little, Brown and Company

Marshmere, Quogue, Long Island, September 29, 1910 [LC]

Gentlemen: Replying to yours of Sept. 27, the matter of correction to footnote of p. 201, proposed by you is of course satisfactory to me.

The arrangement of the front matter[1] is also satisfactory, except that the "Contents" are *four* chapters, and *not three* as in your letter. I have abandoned the thought of adding at the end, once mentioned to you. The sale of two German ships of war to Turkey, the matter involved, while significant from several aspects seems scarcely to justify special mention; if it had gone on to four, as once reported, it would have been a larger subject in every way.

To Little, Brown and Company

Marshmere, Quogue, Long Island, September 30, 1910 [LC]

Gentlemen: I am just re-reading, with reference to certain future projects, my *Problem of Asia*; and I find in its opening pages so much that seems relevant to the topic of the book going through the press,[1] that I would suggest adding *The Problem of Asia* to the two other works cited on the title page, if not too late to do so.

I presume that it is your intention, as in other instances, to assign a page to a list of my other books.

---

3. Beside this sentence Rodgers wrote: "Write to Secy. about." On October 1, 1910, Rodgers wrote Meyer urging his approval of this royalties arrangement and of the retention of Mahan on temporary duty. Meyer responded on October 11, 1910, agreeing to both recommendations. The Rodgers-Meyer correspondence is at the Naval War College. See Mahan to Rodgers, October 19, 1910.

1. Of *The Interest of America in International Conditions*. See Mahan to Little, Brown and Company, September 13, 1910.

1. *The Interest of America in International Conditions*. On this letter an employee of the company wrote: "Too late. List of books at end of book & also on wrapper."

To Little, Brown and Company

Marshmere, Quogue, Long Island, October 1, 1910 [LC]

Gentlemen: I return herewith one copy, executed, of the contract for *The Interest of America in International Conditions.*

I have no difficulty in accepting the royalty terms as drawn up by you, for the reasons given, but I think it would have been more correct to have notified me, of the necessity felt by you for the reduction, before undertaking the work.

To Little, Brown and Company

Marshmere, Quogue, Long Island, October 8, 1910 [LC]

Gentlemen: Replying to your letter of Oct. 5, let me say that I have no idea of in any way questioning the substantial fairness of your action.

Cases might arise in which I should not think worth while to proceed with work, on account of the probable poor remuneration. In this instance, I should have gone on irrespective of the terms, with which, as I wrote you, I found no difficulty in agreeing, and I continue so to think, with no expectation other than that I have signed. As a matter of procedure, we both agree that a precedent notification of change is proper.

To Little, Brown and Company

Marshmere, Quogue, Long Island, October 14, 1910 [LC]

Gentlemen: When the time approaches for publication of *Interest of America in International Conditions,* will you kindly notify me before sending the ten "author's copies"? in order that I may send certain names and addresses to which I would like copies sent directly from you.

To Little, Brown and Company

Marshmere, Quogue, Long Island, October 14, 1910 [LC]

Gentlemen: In accordance with my rule in such cases I enclose letter and explanatory papers received from Messrs. Blackie & Son, Glasgow, requesting permission to use certain copyright diagrams.

I see myself no objection, but possible advertisement, in the permission. Should you coincide, will you kindly notify Messrs. Blackie directly, giving our joint consent.

To Raymond P. Rodgers

Marshmere, Quogue, Long Island, October 19, 1910 [NWC]

My dear Rodgers: I am ready now to undertake the reviewing and editing of the lectures in order to publish; and will ask you to send me one of the clean copies which I understood were being made.

The questions suggested in my letter of September 28, and touched in your reply of October 17,[1] will receive their best solution in the course of the revision.

I propose not to broach the question of publication to my publishers until revision shall have proceeded so far as to enable me to state the proposition to them with the necessary fullness and precision. They have notified me that the interest in naval works has much fallen off. This must affect their calculations, one element of which will be the number of copies the Government will take.[2] It may also compel me to accept a reduction from my previous royalties; for which, however, the employment by the Government is a compensation.

The preliminary work can be done down here; but I propose with approval of yourself and the Department to remove again to Lawrence, about December 1. It will be an advantage to me to have the New York libraries under my lee in case of verifications, which my habitual caution is apt to multiply when committing myself to print. I return the enclosures of your letter.[3]

To Little, Brown and Company

Marshmere, Quogue, Long Island, October 22, 1910. [LC]

Gentlemen: My daughter has unluckily signed the enclosed as witness in the wrong place. Should it be material please send me another copy, but I should think it ought not to matter.

---

1. The letter conveying Meyer's agreement to Mahan's suggestions on the publication of *Naval Strategy*. See Mahan to Rodgers, September 28, 1910, Footnote 3.
2. Following much correspondence with the Department, Rodgers ascertained that the Navy would guarantee the purchase of 125 copies of Mahan's proposed *Naval Strategy*, and that the book would sell for about $3.50.
3. Copies of Rodgers to Meyer, October 1, 1910; Meyer to Rodgers, October 11, 1910; and Mahan to Rodgers, September 28, 1910, all at the Naval War College.

To the Editor of The New York Times

Quogue, Long Island, October 25, 1910[1]

In its issue of Sunday, Oct. 23, *The Times* renews the charge, frequently before made by you, that Mr. Roosevelt's political action at the present time is on his part "a campaign for the Presidency."

This assumes a knowledge of Mr. Roosevelt's motives that neither *The Times* nor any person possesses, unless some confidant of Mr. Roosevelt. Until something authoritative transpires, motive is unknown. True, as is universally conceded, motive may be inferred from acts. But such inference must be both rational and candid; it has an intellectual and a moral side. A bad motive, such as in this instance one purely personal would be, is not to be imputed when a motive consistent with rectitude is more probable; or even equally probable.

What are the facts as regards Mr. Roosevelt's present line of action? They are these: A man in the prime of life, barely past 50, who in the past has shown consummate ability as a political leader, and who has demonstrated the faculty of gaining great popular support, returns to the country after a considerable absence.[2] He finds his party, which he believes—as all honest party men must—to be, upon the whole, best fitted for the government of the Nation, in a demoralized condition; disturbed by internal faction, and apparently having lost heavily in popular support. Is it the duty of such a man, convinced that the country needs his party, to abstain from action? On the contrary, granting the conviction, and the capacities conceded to Mr. Roosevelt, is it not his duty to strain every personal effort to accomplish at the polls the victory for his party which he is convinced will most conduce to the interests of the country?

There seems to me no question that such a motive is commendable; that it is entirely consistent with the known facts; and that, because so consistent, to impute a lower motive, when the higher is able entirely to account for the facts, is neither rational nor moral. Criticism, whether sound or mistaken, of specific acts or utterances, or of a general line of conduct, is proper. Imputation of motive is not criticism. It is merely assertion of fact; which needs proof as much as any other statement, and without such proof is not consistent with good morals.

All will remember distinctly that when Mr. Roosevelt, as President, decided to sent the American fleet to the Pacific Coast, a large portion of the press attributed to him the motive of desiring hostilities with Japan. I recall the fact here, because it illustrates imputation of motive which was neither

---

1. From *The New York Times*, October 26, 1910, p. 10.
2. Roosevelt had returned to the United States on June 18, 1910, after a fourteen-month trip to Africa and Europe.

rational nor moral. Not rational, because it was not needed to account for the act, which had other abundant justification; immoral, because it was a wanton attribution of wrong purpose.

I am bound by my own argument to infer that the charge freely made by *The Times* is honest. I have no right to charge a wrong purpose in that which I nevertheless consider a very wrong act. We may, however, examine the immediate purpose which *The Times* avows, viz.: to promote the defeat of Mr. Stimson[3] this year, in order to defeat Mr. Roosevelt's purpose charged by *The Times*.

It is by no one claimed that Mr. Dix[4] is an abler man than Mr. Stimson. The public services of Mr. Stimson are known and can be appealed to; the ordinarily well-informed man knows nothing of Mr. Dix, and no evidence of public service in lower sphere is offered as proof of fitness for the Chief Magistracy. Yet this big Commonwealth of New York, of which I am a citizen, is asked to reject as its Chief Executive a man known and tried, in favor of one unknown and untried, in order to affect the Presidential election two years hence. *This, too, when the views of the State on the subject of National politics have at present full means of expression in the vote for Congressmen, which takes place on the same ballot.*[5] The present interests of the State are to be hazarded on a purely conjectural imputation of motive; or, at the best, upon an uncertain calculation of conditions two years hence. This is "New Nationalism" indeed, of a kind; subjecting the probable welfare of the State to the very uncertain assumed benefit of the Nation.

To the purpose—not to the motive—of *The Times* must be applied also the statements, which I have not seen contradicted, that Mr. Dix is the nominee of Tammany Hall, through its leader, Mr. Murphy.[6] If so, and if elected, we will hope he will not be, as Governor, Mr. Murphy's creature; but he will be his creation. The citizens of the State at large must take account of this; Tammany behind the chair at Albany. Was the nomination made because New York can produce no better and abler Democrat? I well remember the eloquent exposition of the late James C. Carter,[7] when opposing Mr. Shepard's[8] candidacy as Tammany Mayor, as to how his election would bear upon the office-filling of the City of New York. Is Mr. Dix a bigger man than Mr. Shepard? If so, how is he known to be so?

---

3. Henry Lewis Stimson, Republican candidate for governor of New York. Following his defeat in 1910, Taft appointed him Secretary of War.
4. John Alden Dix, chairman of the New York Democratic state committee in 1910, and victor in the gubernatorial race of that year.
5. Mahan's emphasis.
6. Charles F. Murphy, a sachem of Tammany Hall from 1902 until his death in 1924.
7. A lawyer and expert on municipal government and common law.
8. Edward M. Shepard, law partner of Mrs. Mahan's cousin David B. Ogden, and Democratic candidate for mayor in 1901.

To advance the supposed interests of the Democratic Party in the election of 1912, the citizens of New York are asked to accept as their Chief Executive a man whose nomination is charged to be due to one of the worst, if not the very worst, element in the Democratic Party; while at the same time it is stated, and will more and more be stated, as the campaign progresses, that when the Republican Party tried to reject one of its members, proved corrupt, from his place in the State Senate, five out of six Tammany Senators voted against the expulsion; that these five are renominated by the same influence that nominated Mr. Dix, and that the sixth that voted for expulsion is not renominated. To this statement of fact, not denied, *The Times* opposes a pure conjecture that Mr. Roosevelt's motive in entering the campaign is to force himself into the Presidency two years hence.

This appeal to prejudgment may possibly defeat Mr. Stimson. If so, but scarcely in the reverse case, the exigencies of the beaten Republican Party may force its most forceful leader to accept two years hence a candidacy which otherwise would be premature, and therefore inexpedient. The future is conjectural, here as always; but it seems likely that two years of repentant experience of its mistake would also bring the State back into the Republican columns.[9]

To Little, Brown and Company

Marshmere, Quogue, Long Island, October 29, 1910 [LC]

Gentlemen: I enclose a letter from Captain G. R. Clark of the Navy, which explains the permissions which he wishes to obtain.[1]

It is very much my wish that he should receive them, for I believe after this lapse of time since the publication of the books, such use cannot injure and possibly may benefit. If you coincide will you kindly write to Capt. Clark to that effect. His address is on his letter.

---

9. Mahan's letter was answered by an editorial on the same page of *The New York Times*.

1. George Ramsey Clark, *A Short History of the United States Navy*, by Captain George R. Clark, Professor William O. Stevens, Carroll S. Alden, and Herman F. Krafft. Philadelphia: J. B. Lippincott Company, 1911. Clark had served under Mahan in the *Wachusett*.

To the Editor of The New York Times

N.P. N.D. Probably, Quogue, Long Island, circa November 2, 1910[1]

I have recently read again the six "contentions" of an argument in favor of immunity for "private property" (so called) at sea, read before the Inter-Parliamentary Union assembled in Brussels at the end of August. In these the separation between "contentions" 1 and 6, by the four intervening, obscures a mutual refutation which contiguity in printing will at once reveal. I therefore so present them, continuously:—

1. That the *pressure* which can be brought to bear on a Continental enemy *is of comparatively small importance*, owing to the network of railways which connects countries and to the fact that the Declaration of Paris permits an enemy to embark his goods, not being contraband, in neutral vessels. This argument will be further strengthened if the Declaration of London is ratified and if the doctrine of "continuous voyage" as affecting conditional contraband is abolished.

6. That the present system is inhuman, from the fact that, while it does not involve loss of life, it brings great suffering upon innumerable traders, *by completely disorganizing the conditions of business.* (My italics)

It appears that "completely disorganizing the conditions of business" constitutes "a pressure of comparatively small importance" upon a nation at war. I will venture the assertion that historically, this is not so; that "complete disorganization of business," which it is urged will result from the exercise of the right of maritime capture, has always constituted a "very important," and often—if not always—a decisive "pressure." To say that the greatness and intricacy of modern industrial and commercial development will cause the pressure hereafter to be greater is reasonably probable, and may safely be prophesied.

To bring the pressure of war to bear upon the whole population, and not merely upon the armies in the field, is the very spirit of modern warfare. It may safely be asserted to be least inhuman of all the inevitable inhumanities of war, because the danger of it deters from war; and because, while hostilities are proceeding, it tends most to make the war unpopular and so to hasten peace.

As a matter of European politics, the right of maritime capture is the principal, if not the only, strong weapon of offence possessed by Great Britain against the nations in arms of the Continent.

---

1. From *The New York Times*, November 4, 1910, under the heading "The Immunity from Capture of Private Property at Sea."

To James Ford Rhodes

Marshmere, Lawrence Long Island, November 15, 1910 [MHS]

Dear Mr. Rhodes: It gives me much pleasure to accept your kind invitation for Wednesday, December 7, at 7.30, and to meet your very judiciously selected company, as well as yourself.

To Raymond P. Rodgers

Lawrence, Long Island, December 15, 1910 [NWC]

My dear Rodgers: Since the Secretary's letter to you from the Pacific Coast,[1] I have looked upon the publication of the lectures as determined and indeed as being the chief reason for my continuance on duty. The matter, therefore, in my mind is settled. I took up at once the question of arrangement, with the other preliminaries of form and necessary revision. Unhappily, early in November, I got a cold which, while at no time severe, was very obstinate and has seriously interfered with my power of attention up to the present. This has not stopped progress, except during some days, but has retarded it quite a good deal. I fear my age counts in this far more than I like; but in my re-reading, which has covered all the lectures except two on the Russo-Japanese War, I have found little occasion to modify my personal opinions. There are, however, a number of statements of fact and deduction which in publishing require a greater precision than is absolutely needed in lecturing; the verification and confirmation of these impose care and deliberateness.

I hope that I may be able by the end of January to communicate with my usual publishers on the project, giving the size of the work and particulars as to maps. An important element in their decisions will be the information as to the number of copies to be taken by the Government, which you give in your letter.[2]

Mrs. Mahan joins me in the good wishes of the season to yourself and family.

[P.S.] I enclose a letter for Little, which I presume had best go through you.

---

1. Meyer to Rodgers, October 11, 1910, at the Naval War College.
2. *See* Mahan to Rodgers, October 19, 1910, Footnote 2.

To William McC. Little

Draft[1]   N.P. N.D. Probably, Lawrence, Long Island, December 15, 1910 [LC]

My dear Little: In reviewing my lectures for publication I find some uncertainties as regards naval movements 1688–1692, which I cannot settle with the references at my disposal here; and will be glad if you can look up the following questions in the library.

I find the French Navy was supreme in Mediterranean in 1688, the year William of Orange landed in England. In 1690, at the Battle of Beachy Head (Beréziers), the French in Channel were superior to Allied English and Dutch. In 1691 French were inferior to the others. In 1692 they were greatly inferior owing to *the non-arrival of the Toulon ships*; so that Tourville with 44 was little, if any more than half as strong as the allies at La Hougue.

The questions are: When, and how many of the Mediterranean ships were sent thence to the Channel after 1688: and the various movements of big detachments, ships of the line, between Mediterranean and Channel 1689–92. Tourville being superior in 1690, his inferiority in 1691 may have been partly due to a natural increase in the hostile navies; but in 1692 the inferiority was abnormal and the absence of the Toulon ships is alleged as accounting for it.

Troude, *Batailles Navales*[2] is the most likely source of information; for he "chronicles," in strict sense of that word. Campbell's *Lives of the Admirals* may help. As you know, the Lives are only part of that book. He gives current narrative of events covering the years in question.

To Charles W. Stewart

Lawrence, Long Island, December 23, 1910 [NA]

My dear Mr. Stewart: Has the Library a copy of the Letters & Dispatches of the Duke of *Marlborough*, published I think by a Col. Murray in 1845?[1]

If you have I know you would lend me such volumes of it as I would

1. Finished version, not found, was sent as an enclosure in Mahan to Rodgers, December 15, 1910.

2. O. Troude, *Batailles navales de la France* ... publié par P. Levot ... 4 vols. Paris: Challamel ainé, 1867–1868.

1. Sir George Murray, *The Letters and Despatches of John Churchill, First Duke of Marlborough*. 5 vols. London: John Murray, 1845.

need; but if you have not, will you ascertain of the War Dept. Library if it has, and will lend under any conditions?

I need it in connection with the lectures I have delivered at our War College, which by request of the College I am preparing for publication.

Merry Christmas and Happy 1911 to you and yours.

To Robert U. Johnson

Lawrence, Long Island, December 26, 1910 [NYPL]

My dear Mr. Johnson: Your letter of Dec. 17, being addressed to 160 West 86th. St. had to follow me round two or three days. I shall be as above till May 1.

I will undertake the article you wish, availing myself of the somewhat wider scope indicated by your words "upon sea power in general."[1] By this I mean that the question of the Pacific is intimately connected with that of the Caribbean and our Gulf Coast, and the whole modified by the changes ensuant upon the war of 1898. Such an article has more than one importance. Our whole naval expenditure is vitiated by the disposition to look upon it as so much plunder; to be distributed, not as a simple military disposition, but with reference to the supposed claims of different localities to have money spent in them. In other words, that the distribution of naval stations is to be not national, but sectional. You doubtless have seen the resentment in certain localities at the present Secretary's effort to change this; and I have little doubt it counts for much in the opposition he encounters.

I do not propose to treat the matter in the least controversially; but simply to summarize the situation as seen from the military—or sea power—point of view.

Will you let me know the latest date at which you will want the manuscript. I should ask for it three hundred dollars.

To William H. Henderson

Lawrence, Long Island, December 26, 1910 [NMM]

My dear Henderson: The reproach of having delayed so long answering your kind letter of last year has remained on my conscience ever since

---

1. "The Panama Canal and Sea Power in the Pacific," *Century Magazine* (June 1911).

I did at last reply; so having a holiday today by the general sense of the community, though I have myself only partially so used it, I determine not to run the chance of a similar lapse this year.

How much has happened to both countries, even since my belated reply got off. Just where you are I confess I cant quite understand. And do ordinary rules apply to so extraordinary a situation? The Veto Bill[1] reduces you to a one Chamber government, surely a tremendous Constitutional change, and the majority which controls—barring the small labor vote which would not give a working majority by itself—is not British but Irish. The very condition that three years are required before the Lower House can pass over the Veto of the Upper is a spur to precipitate legislation; for the expiry of Parliament would leave the fight to be fought again. It seems to me doubtful whether ordinary rules can apply to so momentous a situation.

We have had an overturn too, but there is nothing radical in the situation.[2] It would not have occurred, in my opinion, but for the fact that the legislation of the now expiring Congress was controlled by very old men, men living in a past, unable to keep up with public opinion, or to free themselves from the "privileged" influences which had always dominated their acts. The President unfortunately lacked the courage of what appeared to be his convictions, & did not use a Veto which would have placed him where Roosevelt was.[3] What part the latter played in the general result is doubtful. Popular idols stand on unsteady pedestals, and he has certainly come down to some extent; but it is pointed out that in the localities where he put in his heaviest fighting, the loss of his party was much less than in states where he did not speak. The interests and the privileges were against him. I believe he still has a big future, for he possesses one quality which voters adore,—absolute recklessness of personal consequences. The cautious man is so much in evidence, that an uncautious one appeals to the people.

Personally, my year has been spent in connection with our War College, revising and expanding lectures on Naval Strategy which I first wrote there over twenty years ago. I am now preparing them, by request, for publication; for my lecturing days are coming to an end. I am well in bodily health, very well for my years—I reached 70 last September. I still can do all I used to do, but not quite so fast or so far. My walks and bicycle rides are not so long as five years ago and I rarely feel the inclination to

---

1. The Bill, sponsored by Asquith, ended the power of absolute veto by the House of Lords.
2. The Republican Insurgent reform movement which in March 1910 deprived House Speaker Joseph G. Cannon of his power to appoint the Committee on Rules, and which in November combined with reform Democrats to return a Democratic majority to the House. The Insurgent movement split the Republican Party into separate Taft and Roosevelt factions.
3. Taft signed the Pension Bill, of which he disapproved, for fear that a veto would lose him the soldier vote.

exceed a certain modicum. Mentally I realize what Grote[4] said of himself at the same period of life. I think I can do as well, but not as much, as twenty, or even five years ago. I must have told you that we have abandoned N. Y. as a residence. We have just re-leased the house for three years, and I have no idea we will ever go back to it. Now that both the rivers which bound N. Y. are tunneled, we run straight into the heart of the city; no ferries. One comes straight from Washington to the same place; & from here we dont have to go into the street to reach Washington, or for the matter of that, New Orleans.

I dont clearly see how the naval situation of the world is going to turn out. The increasing power of the working classes seems bent on such social expenditures as make the burden of armaments nearly insupportable. By one means or another, your old age pensions, and our war pensions, etc etc in other countries, the resources of the countries are very mortgaged. My own opinion is that Great Britain and the U.S. have a tremendous start, but that the German social framework [has] the better endurance. The party in this country that has won the late election is traditionally and theoretically against military expenditures; but conditions, especially Isthmian & Pacific conditions, will force their hands. It is tremendously interesting. I hope it may not become painfully so.

It is the season for the exchange of good wishes, & you and yours have mine most heartily. I trust that Mrs. Henderson is quite restored from the indisposition under which she was suffering. Recuperation in such cases is sometimes to better than before. It was so with me; I trust with her also.

To George C. Perkins[1]

Draft N.P., N.D. Probably, Lawrence, Long Island,
January 11, 1911 [LC]

Dear Senator Perkins: Replying to the inquiry which you and Senator Flint have done me honor to address to me,[2] the distribution of the fleet is the immediate function of the Secretary acting under the President. I apprehend therefore that the existing arrangements are to be considered as representing his views, and consequently not open to public comment or suggestion by one of his subordinates.

---

4. George Grote, English historian of Greece.

1. Republican senator from California.

2. Perkins and Frank P. Flint, also a Republican from California, had written to Mahan on January 7, 1911.

For your own information as to my opinion, I may add that the division of the battle fleet into halves, separated by the whole distance between our Atlantic and Pacific coasts, would be to render each fraction inferior to a foreign fleet in either ocean; in the Atlantic inferior to more than one European navy. Such a division, out of mutual support, liable to be attacked by superior numbers before it could possibly be reinforced, is contrary to all sound military opinion and practice. It was what the Russians did in their recent war with Japan, with the consequence that first the Port division and afterwards Rozhestvensky's fleet were wiped out. The two united would have decisively outnumbered the Japanese, and might have prevented the war; certainly should have compassed a more favorable issue.

As a strategic question, this dividing of the fleet, as opposed to concentration, was very thoroughly threshed out at the Naval War College some years ago in a series of war games between parties; the result being a conviction that such a division at the moment war broke out could not be remedied afterwards, and was utterly disastrous. I was not present at this investigation; but the result concurs with all my military reading, and is absolutely coincident with my personal opinion based upon my study of history. The people of the Pacific slope might *feel* themselves safer with half the battle fleet in their harbors, but *actually* they would be in greater peril, because they would have conditions favoring the destruction of our entire navy, in detail.

The position of a concentrated fleet—whether for instance the whole Russian navy prior to the war should have been in the Baltic, or in the Far East—is a separate question. It depends upon a variety of conditions—international policy, administrative readiness, navy yard facilities, etc. all which must be supposed present to a national government, and concerning which, aside from all questions of propriety, its information must be more exact than that of an individual officer. But the military necessity of sustained concentration is as absolutely certain as anything human can be.

To Robert U. Johnson

Lawrence, Long Island, January 28, 1911 [NYPL]

My dear Mr. Johnson: The article can be ready well before the middle of February.[1] It is I think substantially complete now, but I have found it more difficult than I thought, probably because of an attack of grip which not only lost time directly, but has incapacitated me from full working power for many days.

---

1. "The Panama Canal and Sea Power in the Pacific" was published in the *Century Magazine* in June 1911.

I notice you mention the agitation of the question of fortification. This is a distinct question from that proposed by you, "the effect of the completion of the Panama Canal upon Sea Power in the Pacific, or, if you prefer, upon Sea Power in general." I mention this because I have been asked, and have undertaken to write upon the Fortification question for the *North American*, to appear in the March number.[2] I have kept the two carefully separate, which was not difficult, as the treatment—or subjects—are different; the one general, the other specific and technical. It seems proper, however, in view of your later expression to mention this. As regards the *North American* the mention is confidential. I have said nothing to it about my article for the *Century*.

To Little, Brown and Company

Lawrence, Long Island, January 30, 1911 [LC]

Gentlemen: Within the past three years I have been delivering at the War College in Newport, R.I., certain lectures on Naval Strategy. The authorities of the College, with, I understand, the approval of the Secretary of the Navy, wish that these should be published in book form, as more permanent and more generally accessible to the officers who each year attend the annual "Conference,"—from June to October.

The size of the work will be about 145,000 words, or say 150,000; this by an average of some pages. The *first* of the Sea Power series was 220,000 words; so that the proposed now would be about two-thirds the size of the other named.

There would be no *battle* plans such as in the Sea Power books; but there should be a certain number of maps of a purely outline character, no shading nor topographical features. I am not yet prepared to say exactly how many; but as to size I should say not more than three or four full pages.

The text I have been over several times, and think that I shall be able to put the whole of it in your hands by May 1.

The President of the Naval War College has written me that he has been informed by the Navy Department that it will take 125 copies for the use of ships' libraries, and that he himself estimates that the College would want 25 to 30 copies.

Will you kindly inform me whether you will undertake the publication of the work.

---

2. "Why Fortify the Panama Canal?" *North American Review* (March 1911).

To George von L. Meyer

Lawrence, Long Island, February 1, 1911[1]

Your letter of January 27 reached me only the morning of day before yesterday.[2] It will not be expected that in 48 hours I can have given a ripened consideration to the measure (H. R. 29371) in itself, but my mind is somewhat prepared by previous habits of thought and by cognizance of the British committee of defense (or some such title).

The general purpose of the bill seems to me excellent. It would compel the deliberation in common of a number of men whose specialties are closely allied actually, but are not brought into formal cooperation, as the bill provides they shall hereafter be. For the information of each member of the council, and of the whole as a body, and for the subsequent formulation of measures, this method is superior to the appearance of experts before a committee, though it doubtless will not supersede that. Experts before a committee are like witnesses in a box, and confine themselves very closely to the matter in hand, whereas in discussion between equals many collateral facts and considerations transpire because of the freedom of range. Time is not thereby lost, at least to any greater extent than the half-informed questionings of those who are eliciting statements from a witness. I believe that Congress, the ultimate arbiter in matters of military provision, would be enabled to judge much better through the institution of this proposed council.

As to questions of detail, I have very little to suggest. The proposed composition of the council, by ex officio members, seems to me very judicious. In a copy of the bill which reached me from some other quarter, by the same mail as your letter, there is a suggested substitute of "a senior admiral of the Navy," instead of the aide for operations. I think this is a mistake. If I rightly apprehend the functions of this aide, he should ex officio be on the council, because the distribution of the fleet in peace should correspond fundamentally with that deemed probable for war, which the council will determine.

My own prepossessions would have led me to place on the council the chairmen of the two Committees on Foreign Affairs, because the details of military provision depend very largely upon questions of international relations. It has been justly remarked (Corbett's *Seven Years War*) that the strength of Great Britain's action in that war was that the three allied

---

1. In *Hearings Before the House Naval Affairs Committee*, 61st Congress 3d Session, p. 670.
2. Meyer had forwarded Mahan a copy of the bill providing for a Council of National Defense at the request of George E. Foss, Chairman of the House Committee on Naval Affairs.

functions—diplomacy, army, and navy—were in one hand. In my judgment, they should all be represented in the proposed council. The chairman of the Appropriations Committee can contribute little, ex officio, however competent personally, to the military knowledge of the council; but they doubtless can assimilate information which would qualify duly the necessary tendency toward close economy proper to their committees. Also, being specified in the bill, as framed, to omit them now would probably foster antagonism.

It strikes me as somewhat singular that the commander in chief of Army and Navy, the President, should not be on the council. In Great Britain the prime minister is ex officio president of their commission. I do not know whether it would be competent for Congress to legislate the President on to a council, but it seems to me he ought to be there for several reasons; above all, because he sums up in his office the three functions—diplomacy, Army, and Navy.

It appears to me that the provision of only one meeting annually rather belittles the importance of the measure, and that it would be better to provide for a fixed greater number during each session of Congress. Of the feasibility of this, however, I obviously am less capable of judging than the members of the Naval Committee.

To Little, Brown and Company

Lawrence, Long Island, February 1, 1911 [LC]

Gentlemen: Your letter of January 31 is at hand. The terms you propose as to royalties will be entirely satisfactory to me. The net price of the book I shall leave to you to determine as I invariably have done in the past.

If the book meets general professional approval I should think it probable that the sales would be good in Great Britain, where there is a considerable body of interest outside of the Navy as well as in it. There will be a discussion of the Russo-Japanese War, and also of Caribbean conditions; and there is beside a large amount of historical illustration which may make for general interest. I do not know the policy of the British Admiralty as to ships' libraries. If as liberal as our own, they would need more copies.

There is no haste as to the time of putting the book on the market, as it could in no case be ready for the current year's Conference at the Naval War College, where it will form this year a series of lectures as in past years.

To Robert U. Johnson

Lawrence, Long Island, February 2, 1911 [LC]

Dear Mr. Johnson: I have no map ready to be reproduced, and in view of your wishes about space had not contemplated one. I have, however, been using one in an Atlas at the University Club, the reproduction of which, in outline only and with certain features only, which I could indicate, would make the conditions more intelligible to a reader.

In such cases, with my usual book publishers, my practice has been to indicate the N.S.E. & W. limits of a map, and what features in it need to be named, which I always reduce to a minimum. I am going to town tomorrow or next day, and will send you needed particulars next week early, about which time also I hope to send you the MS.[1]

To Robert U. Johnson

Lawrence, Long Island, February 8, 1911 [NYPL]

Dear Mr. Johnson: I send you the proposed article. When the galleys are ready, will you kindly send me *duplicate* proofs for reading, as I have frequently found the convenience of two sets.

I enclose also a memorandum for map, should you think expedient to present one. Such will certainly convenience readers; and I think that my practice of eliminating all names, except those occurring in the text, is a great help to clearness. I have made one exception in the case of the Galapagos Islands. These are not mentioned; but the recent popular demonstration in Ecuador against the lease of them to the United States makes advisable to name them. Has it struck you how this incident illustrates the small ultimate control of governments over people where national feeling is aroused and set, and how powerless in the face of such is the hope for arbitration?

[Enclosure]

Memoranda for Map

Limits
1. North: 60° North latitude; to take in full coast of British Columbia.
2. South: 55° South latitude; to include south shore of Australia.
3. East: 74° West Longitude; to include Guantanamo and Windward Passage.
4. West: 90° East longitude, to include Sumatra.

---

1. Of "The Panama Canal and Sea Power in the Pacific."

British Columbia; Saskatchewan; *United States*; (States of) Washington, Oregon, California; *Mexico*; *Central America*; Colon and Panama, with black line indicating Canal; Cuba; Guantanamo; Galapagos Islands; Hawaiian Islands; Samoa Islands; Fiji Islands; Marshall Islands; Caroline Islands; Guam; Ladrone Islands; *New Zealand*; *Australia*; Sumatra; Java; Borneo; New Guinea; Philippines; Formosa; *China*; *Japan*; Korea; Manchuria.

Although not directly connected with the article, it would be expedient to indicate [thus (Dutch)] that Sumatra, Java, Celebes, Molucca, are Dutch; Borneo largely Dutch, though partly British; New Guinea, Dutch, British, and German. For, there can be little doubt that this vast Dutch colonial possession has much to do with the German desire to incorporate Holland with the Empire, of which tendency the disturbing proposition to fortify Flushing may be another outcrop. Such incorporation might carry Curaçao, with Dutch Guiana; and thus establish the German Navy in the Caribbean. The Ladrone Islands, except Guam, should also be marked (German).

I have marked with blue pencil names which I think should be in heavier type than others.

To Little, Brown and Company

Lawrence, Long Island, February 9, 1911 [LC]

Gentlemen: Replying to yours of February 6, I doubt whether the division into chapters can be determined by Feb. 22; but I can most probably give you sufficient data as to the general scope, and succession of treatment, in the book.[1] Possibly also a tentative title; but this is less certain.

As regards Messrs. Low's attitude towards undertaking the English publication,—at the time the old firm was breaking down, I received letters from more than one publisher, offering to take over the agency for my works. One of these was Mr. John Murray, and about a year ago Mr. Fisher Unwin made advances of a similar character. I have always declined; partly because I have preferred to leave business arrangements in your hands, and largely at the first from feelings of regard for the old firm, from whom, especially from Mr. R. B. Marston, I received various services and courtesies.

I shall be quite prepared for any arrangement you wish to make in the present instance, reserving only a right to give consent, the exercise of which would probably be purely formal.

I should be glad if your representative can ascertain the precise motive of

---

1. *Naval Strategy.*

the present firm in refusing to concede the separate publication of my "Major Operations, 1763–83," in their *History of the Royal Navy*. It has appeared to me not so much a feeling that it would injure the sale of the *History*, as a resentment that I should have been paid what they consider an excessive price for that contribution, and a wish to recover part of it in any new arrangement. As to this, as I have said to you before, the price was fixed by myself, and was at about half the rate I usually got then and now, when paid by the thousand.

My wish in the matter is simply this: What I wrote is now buried in a mass of material, of very varying value, in a number of exceedingly cumbrous volumes. I should be glad to see it published alone, as a matter of personal satisfaction. It would not probably increase my reputation; but it would have a better chance of being seen and known. In the United States, published under some such title as "The Great Naval Operations of the American Revolution," or "of the American War of Independence," it might more than pay its way.[2]

While I desire this, I do not wish it to the extent of conceding any arrangement that implies, however remotely, that I was overpaid for it. It would not have been written at all for any less remuneration. I believe that it is technically a rather unique representation of one of the most interesting naval wars of modern history.

[P.S.] You probably know that they took the opportunity of Mr. Roosevelt's visit to England last year, to publish separately his contribution—the War of 1812.[3]

To Little, Brown and Company

Lawrence, Long Island, February 20, 1911 [LC]

Gentlemen: I should have had ready for you the memoranda concerning the general lines of the proposed book, in great part, if not all; but I was unexpectedly called off by the Government to some urgent work[1] which

---

2. It was republished by Little, Brown and Company in 1913 as *The Major Operations of the Navies in the War of American Independence*.
3. Roosevelt republished Chapter XLI, his contribution to Clowes's *Royal Navy*, as *The Naval Operations of the War Between Great Britain and the United States, 1812–1815*. London: Sampson Low, 1910.
1. Solicited comment on the Naval War College's Strategic War Plan of 1911 treating a hypothetical war with Japan in the Pacific. *See* Mahan to Rodgers, February 22, 1911.

prevented my completing this, involving as it would a careful look through the whole text.

I enclose, however, a sufficiently complete analysis of the Introductory Chapter, done before the Government's call upon me; together with a summary of the remainder of the work. The latter is dependent upon my memory only, and is necessarily brief; but sufficiently exact as to the general tenor of the book.

As regards its value from the professional point of view, you will have to depend upon the general opinion of the numerous officers who within twenty-odd years have listened to the substance of the book in the form of lectures.

I have never disputed the control of Messrs. Sampson Low over the article in their history of the Royal Navy, so far as acquiescing in my desired separate publication. If you have so understood me, I wish to correct the error. My argument is merely that separate publication after this interval could not hurt the *History*, and would probably find a sale among those who value my name in such connection, and may not care to possess all the very voluminous and *very heavy* volumes of the *History*. The present firm, however, did say that I had been very largely paid for the article. This I dispute, on grounds not necessary to repeat; and I am unwilling, on separate publication, to concede anything which implies that I was so paid. I conceive also that the firm has no right to publish separately without my consent; as the article was written expressly and solely for the *History*.

[Enclosure]

Synopsis

Naval Strategy

I. Introductory Chapter. Origin of the lectures (the present treatise). Subsequent development. Changes of conditions in intervening twenty years. Permanence of principles; variations in application. Illustrations of this from history. Value of experience to principles; history is simply experience recorded. Interaction of principle and illustrations. Consequent value of military—or naval—study. Development of such study among naval officers in recent years. Indications in professional literature.

II. Discussion of certain historical episodes as illustrative of strategic principles, as well land as naval: concentration, central position, interior lines, communications.

III. Strategic Positions; Situation, Strength, Resources. Strategic lines. Ocean Frontiers. Historical Illustrations.

IV. Discussion of strategic features of the Caribbean Sea.

V. Relation of Coast Fortresses to naval warfare.

VI. Examination of the naval—and in part of the military—features of the Russo-Japanese War.

To Raymond P. Rodgers

My dear Rodgers: I have read twice very carefully the Strategic Plan submitted to me by you.[1]

It will be recognized that in the ten days the papers have been in my hands I cannot have acquired all the detailed knowledge, much less the familiarity with all conditions, which are essential to judicious final decisions. The comment which I present therefore is rather of the nature of suggestion for the consideration of those upon whom the responsibility of such decisions rests. Several of the suggestions, such as to length of time required to fortify, size of garrisons, proportion of attacking troops to defenders, are army questions, and should be referred to a military opinion.

Estimate p. 2. I think the assumption that Orange could readily project an over-sea movement of 100,000 men is exaggerated. It should be carefully tested by known army standards, as to tonnage needed, which increases largely with the distance. I have seen that, for the short distance from Germany to England, it is held that, for 70,000 men, 200,000 tons of shipping would be required. From Japan to Luzon the same estimate might hold; but from Japan to Honolulu, eleven days at twelve knots, the troops would suffer if similarly crowded. Moreover, greater stowage of provisions and ammunition is required for distant operations. From Yokohama to San Francisco it would be fifteen days.

p. 5. Thirty-five thousand troops *could* be transported, assuming above rate of tonnage; and I presume the reckoning of 25,000 to occupy Hawaii rests upon data which I do not possess. But I cannot think that the detachments named, 5,000 for Guam, 3,000 for Samoa, and 2,000 for Kiska, could securely hold those points, unless already fortified, landward as well as seaward. Even with Blue Fleet in Atlantic, there would not be time so to fortify, by placing in position guns which a modern fleet need regard. Except Hawaii, the others could be picked up in detail by a Blue division of 15,000. For this reason, important as I consider Guam, I would not fortify it, because in the present temper of the Blue nation it would not be adequately garrisoned; while to have it fall to an enemy fortified would be an additional calamity.

p. 9, last paragraph and p. 10, first paragraph. Shows the necessity, which underlies every part of the plan, that Pearl Harbor should be so fortified, garrisoned, and provided with stores, as to be able to hold out at least six months,—or double the time needed for the Blue Fleet to move from the

---

1. The Naval War College's Strategic War Plan of 1911 [Hypothetical Naval War in the Pacific Between Japan (Orange) and the United States (Blue)].

Atlantic to its relief. With Hawaii thus secured, I doubt if Orange would risk even the force necessary to hold Guam, if not fortified. They would not have time to fortify.

p. 14. Would the dispositions recommended suffice to preserve Guam (harbor), if unfortified, from a crushing fire by the whole Orange fleet? What is to prevent Orange from sending 25,000 to Guam, as proposed for Hawaii? and what could the proposed force, 3,000, do against such? In short, is the shipping proposed adequate to resist naval attack, or the troops proposed land attack? If not, like the assumed Orange forces in Kiska and Samoa, they are only a bait to swallow.

Is not Corregidor to be fortified? If so, can it not at least support the shipping which, like the monitors and gunboats, cannot be removed? Will not Guam empty be least of a prize to Orange, and more easily regained by Blue? Will not Corregidor, plus monitors and 3,000 troops, be a more effectual concentration than Guam plus the same?

If time allow, I agree the cruisers had better retreat at once upon Pearl Harbor, and further westward; but betimes. Orange will not make formal proclamation before striking; though Blue by its Constitution must do so.

pp. 15, 16. The Blue Pacific detachment should advance on calculated time to meet Asiatic detachment. The destroyers and submarines should be distributed at San Francisco and Puget Sound.

p. 16. "During period of strained relations." An unexpected blow from Orange may occur at any moment during this period.

p. 19. I concur most emphatically in the underlined paragraph on this page; but these preparations should be made now, not left to strained relations with a Power that has no scruples as to time of striking.

p. 19, line 20. Minorca and Malta do not support the conclusion. Both succumbed to the Power controlling the sea, when it chose to take them. In 1760 the British preferred to regain Minorca by capuring Belle Isle; in 1782 they did not control the sea. Malta in 1800 fell, after two years tenure, because its communications were cut off by the control of the sea.

p. 20, line 2. Ten thousand men are not sufficient, in my judgment; but that is an army question. Navally it is certain that the Blue fleet cannot reach there from the Atlantic in less than three months; whereas Orange can land 30,000 men in three weeks.

p. 20, last paragraph. I entirely agree with this paragraph and that next following it on page 21.

p. 21, last paragraph. If Hawaii be gained by Orange, it becomes thenceforth a possession which it must both defend and supply; as the French did Malta in 1798–1800. That is, it is an exposed point. The Blue fleet once arrived in the Pacific, Kiska and Guam, if unfortified when taken, can be regained; if indeed Kiska be occupied, which I doubt. To hold Hawaii securely, Orange must also hold Guam; and I incline to think that with Blue's superior navy it must be possible from Kiska to act decisively against Guam. In fact, unless Guam falls into Orange hands already fortified, it seems impossible to prevent the occupation of the harbor by Blue; after which the troops on the island are hopelessly cut off. The harbor then becomes a base, both for the battle fleet to operate against Orange possessions, and for the cruisers, armored and others, to attack and to defend the lines of supply. Hawaii cannot harbor the Orange fleet, if its communications are cut off; for in such case, being continually in doubt as to coal, it can threaten but little the Blue communications, which also, in the case of single vessels, may take any one of the many lines possible from the Pacific coast to Guam. I infer, therefore, that a move of Blue fleet to Kiska will compel Orange fleet to fall back from Hawaii, and that it will not stop at Guam, but must retreat to home base.

p. 22, second paragraph. The conclusion that "a southern approach to the Philippines would be the only practicable one," on the supposition that Orange has so occupied Hawaii as to require a long continued direct attack to reduce it, appears to me the crux of the whole plan, and to be very disputable. Much depends upon the harborage available at Kiska, or at Unalaska, as to which my information is inadequate. I know that General Wood[2] has been inclined to look favorably on Unalaska.

The assumption is that Orange has settled himself firmly at Hawaii. As there are, (p. 5), three anchorages in the islands, this assumption implies that he has at *each* at least 30,000 troops; for no less force could hope to resist that which Blue could land within six months after Blue fleet, by arrival, has established command of the sea. If the Blue fleet go to Hawaii, this command of the sea will be localized there. The attempt to regain the islands then would be direct, instead of indirect, by counter attack elsewhere, and by stopping communications. In case of direct attack, say by 50,000 Blue troops, with the superior Blue fleet commanding the water, unless the three anchorages mentioned (p. 5) are all on one island, no one of the three 30,000 Orange divisions can help the other; and it is stated (p. 20 last line, and p. 21 first two lines) that other islands than Oahu may fall and become a supporting point for Orange. Why not for Blue in turn? It will be the case of Kiska, Hawaii, and Samoa reproduced on a larger scale.

If, however, Orange recognizes this dilemma and concentrates his force at one position, say Pearl Harbor, the other anchorages remain open to

---

2. General Leonard Wood, Chief of Staff, U.S. Army, 1910–1914.

Blue from which to institute the strictest blockade, and to throw Orange wholly on local resources for prolonged occupation. Like the French in Egypt, and in Malta, 1798–1800, neither reinforcement nor ammunition could reach them; perhaps scarcely even information, except by wireless. The Orange battle fleet must retire; or else fight, which is what Blue should wish.

If Blue finds direct attack inexpedient, or prefers an indirect attack, that is upon the Orange communications with Hawaii, and upon other Orange interests, the question arises of a new base, other than Hawaii. The Plan (p. 24) dismisses the northern route, on account of "climatic or weather disadvantages during six months of the year." As hydrographic difficulties, of safe anchorage, are not advanced, I presume there are harbors.

I find it difficult to admit that for white men climatic inconveniences of an over-cold climate can equal in ultimate effect those of one constantly over-warm. Also, the southern route seems to depend upon coal renewal at Nukuhiva, Solomon Islands, Admiralty Islands; although these are neutral, and permission so to use them is doubtful. The northern route throughout will be either Blue or Orange in tenure; that is, open to use by a belligerent, conditional only on his power so to do.

Let us examine the strategic position of Kiska, and of Unalaska, with reference to the situation that will exist if Blue finds the Hawaiian group so strongly held as to render a direct attack there unadvisable. Unalaska, with Dutch Harbor, is six hundred miles nearer Bremerton than Kiska is, and the same distance further from Yokohama.

Although my personal opinion is that the Blue battle fleet should be stationed on its Pacific coast at least eighteen months before the expected completion of the Canal, I find it impossible to believe that, if it be ready for instant movement from the Atlantic, Orange can both seize and adequately fortify all anchorages in the Hawaiian islands and Guam before Blue fleet can reach Pacific.

Dutch Harbor is 2039 miles from Honolulu; San Francisco about the same, 2098. Kiska is about 200 miles farther away from Honolulu, but it is only 1800 from Yokohama, 1500 from Hakodate, and 2700 from Guam; whereas from the Hawaiian Islands to Guam is 3312, making the total distance, San Francisco to Guam, 5410, or double that of Kiska, and quite beyond the steaming radius of the fleet.

For position merely, Kiska is better than San Francisco, or than Bremerton. It lacks strength and resources; and, if used, strength must be supplied to protect the resources.

From Bremerton to Kiska is 2400 miles, from Kiska to Guam 2700. Total 5,100, as against the 5,400 of the present route: San Francisco, Honolulu, Guam. I learn from the Plan that 4,000 is the estimated coal endurance of the battle fleet; so that a Bremerton-Kiska-Guam passage would bring it to Guam ready for immediate action so far as coal is concerned,—bunkers one-third full.

It will be understood that I am not advocating the northern route against the central; but against the southern, on the supposition that central is closed, because no anchorage in the Hawaiian group can be secured, and Orange ships there threaten communications by central route. For the entire trip, Bremerton-Kiska-Guam, colliers would have to supply only 1,100 (5100–4000) miles more steaming than the fleet starts with from Bremerton. The colliers also being full on starting, the fleet may be assumed easily filled at Guam itself, should it be attacked. That is, if it can take Guam at all, it can do so before necessary to coal. If thought impossible to capture Guam, it will be neglected and another destination sought.

For such alternate destination it is to be remembered that Yokohama is but 1800 miles from Kiska; Hakodate 1,500. Therefore, the arrival of the Blue Fleet at Kiska, or even at Unalaska, menaces all the home waters of Orange. Amami O Sima itself is but 800 miles from Yokohama; that is, at most, 2,600 from Kiska. In other words Amami O Sima is a little nearer than Guam to Kiska, which menaces both. Kiska is also about 2,300 miles from Honolulu. It presents therefore, as to position, an equal menace to three Orange positions,—supposing Guam occupied as well as Hawaii.

Unalaska is somewhat inferior to Kiska as regards position; but there being the two, Orange must occupy both, as well as all Hawaii and Guam, or else the above strategic reasoning stands. Holding means, of course, guns that a fleet dare not meet, and a garrison which 30,000 men cannot dispossess.

With the Blue Fleet at San Francisco, the inferior Orange may hold on at Hawaii, if still there; but with the Blue at Kiska, its home interests and its communications are too much endangered. Reverse the conditions, giving Orange the naval superiority Blue now has: Would the Blue Fleet remain in Hawaii if Orange advanced to and seized Kiska or Unalaska, threatening Blue's communications with the main land?

In summary, I apprehend that, if the Blue Fleet be in the Atlantic when war begins, Orange could land a large force on the Pacific coast; but I think she will not do so, realizing that the effect would be to solidify popular feeling in Blue, and so entail upon herself a prolonged effort on a scale so huge as to be exhausting. During 1909, the trade of Japan, with a population of 58,000,000 was $400,000,000; that of Australia, with less than 5,000,000, amounted to $580,000,000. The contrast indicates the staying power resting on finance; and it is well understood that the advances of Japan towards peace with Russia in 1905 were attributable to a financial exigency which is not yet dispelled.

At a much less expenditure of force Orange could seize the Philippines and Guam. This would undoubtedly arouse much public feeling in Blue; but it would be neither unanimous, nor so enduring as the presence of a hostile force on Blue's home territory. The War of 1812 illustrated this difference, when Great Britain in 1814 could spare troops for invasion. Hawaii also could probably be occupied without universal popular dissatisfaction; except on Blue's Pacific coast, which as yet has not the numerous voters which cast the scale in representative governments. These facts affect the important consideration of the *energy* of Blue warfare.

I apprehend, therefore, that in case of war, the Blue Fleet being in the Atlantic, Orange might calculate reasonably upon successes which would insure the permanent acquisition of the Philippines and Guam; but could have no equivalent expectations of results from Hawaii, and still less from invasion of Blue's Pacific coast; that she would not attempt the latter; but very probably might Hawaii for several reasons, among which the large Orange population already there.

It is of course incumbent to consider the possibility of invasion; and while I have no criticism to make of the Plan, in its provision for such contingency, I think the military word to the Blue Government is that its fleet should be in the Pacific not later than eighteen months before the Canal is completed. Meantime the docking development of the Pacific should proceed apace.

Like the United States after the War of Secession, there remains to Orange from her late war, and will remain till several years after the Canal opens, a large force of veteran troops available for the various enterprises named: Philippines, Guam, Hawaii, Pacific coast, Kiska, Unalaska, and Samoa, besides that which singly is the most important of all—the Canal. But, even granting the means and the numbers to seize all, it is to me incredible that all can also be fortified, armed, and garrisoned, before the Blue Fleet establishes control of the sea in the Pacific. That is, a base must remain open for occupancy to Blue.

I prefer that that base be one of the three anchorages in the Hawaiian group; because nowhere else can such sure control over the communications of the supposed Orange garrison be established. To this occupancy there can be but one issue in Hawaii, unless Blue loses control of the sea.

This base should be fortified at once against a possible attack by any Orange division. If the Orange battle fleet be in Hawaii, the Blue battle fleet remains there, the armored cruisers proceeding against Guam; this, of course, without awaiting the fortification of the base.

If, as is more probable, the Orange fleet be in home waters, the battle fleet should proceed against Guam at once. Cruisers, armored and otherwise, would remain at the Hawaiian Base to cut off the supplies and reinforcements of the garrison. These cruisers should be kept in prime steaming condition, going to San Francisco or Bremerton by detachments, for cleaning. Until the Hawaiian base gives them security by its works, surprise by an enemy's superior division, though improbable, is possible; and both by

[385]

speed and coal endurance they must be always ready for such contingency.

Should the anchorage at Guam have been so fortified as to make attack dangerous to Blue's naval superiority, a condition I think extremely doubtful, the Blue battle fleet should make its base at Kiska. This alternative illustrates the importance of Guam; for while Kiska is not much farther—500 miles—from southern Japan than Guam is, Guam is greatly nearer Manila and Formosa, to all Japanese communications to those islands, and to Japanese commercial lines, which must be mainly from southern Japan southward, or westward.

This is so evident that it appears to me, if I were at this instant making plans for Orange, I should say the first move would be the seizure of Guam, and the provision now, in time of peace, of guns and mountings, etc. with plans for instant fortification and garrisoning. Hawaii would be to me secondary to Guam, from an Orange viewpoint.

In this connection, it is to be remembered that Kiska is so much nearer Guam than Hawaii is,—2700 miles against 3312—that with a steaming radius of 4,000 miles a fleet from Hawaii will reach Guam dangerously near the limit of its endurance, if compelled to delay entrance to the harbor, or to fight an action, whereas from Kiska the margin of safety would be considerably larger.

I believe that these remarks present sufficiently, though too discursively, my views as to the northern route and its bases. They lead of course towards a blow at the Orange communications, from the island Kiushiu southward. Kiska is merely a Blue advanced home base, a stepping stone to a base in or near the Orange territory, from which the superior Blue fleet can operate offensively as may be judged most expedient. This position attained, Kiska remains a stepping stone, held by the Blue army for the service of the fleet and protected against Orange enterprises on a large scale by the fleet's own position.

As regards further operations from a fixed base,—whether Guam or Kiska,—it is to be remarked that, with so extensive a coast as that of Japan and its dependencies, it seems scarcely probable that no undefended anchorage could be found where the fleet could coal; securely as regards hydrographic conditions, though greatly exposed to attack.

If accompanied by sufficiently many destroyers, however, coaling by daylight only, with nets down by night, and scouts out both day and night, —in short with due watchfulness against an enemy known to be enterprising, —it seems probable the operation could be safely carried out. To act at all, the fleet must anchor somewhere; and, in fact, must advance to and occupy for the war a permanent position suitably chosen. The coaling just spoken of on Orange coast is a minor case of the same.

For this permanent advanced base: it is clear that the Orange fleet cannot be both south and north at the same time, except by an absurd division of force. It has a station at the Pescadores; an Orange army may be in the Philippines; the great naval stations are in southern Japan, Sasebo, Kure, and others not accurately remembered by me now. Kure on the Inland Sea presents such military advantages as to be the most probable choice.

The Lu-Chu islands intervene between Japan and the Pescadores, and are within easy steaming range of all southern Japan, as well as of Orange communications with Guam; not to say of those with Hawaii, if occupied by Orange. An anchorage in the LuChus is the most effective position for the Blue Fleet. Such occupation would demand of the fleet a provision of defences immediately; by mines, booms, and other precautions, as to which the Japanese occupation of the Elliot Islands may offer suggestions. In advancing for such purpose, the fleet should go prepared; not only with material, but with detailed plans, and officers especially familiar with these to place them in the shortest time. This done, and with proper scouting, which will inure from the mere watching of southern Orange ports to oppress their commerce, the fleet while at anchor should be reasonably secure, as security is reckoned in war.

The fleet by its general position, indicated above, would seriously incommode, if not wholly cripple, Orange communications southward. It would probably cause the recall of cruisers based on Guam, and thus secure in great measure its own communications, unless Orange has had time to stock Guam heavily with coal. It would be usually at sea; because cruising is the basis of efficiency, and it must support a blockade of the Orange coast. The blockade will be planned with a view to dislocating traffic as well by land as by sea; for which purpose railway centres and their relations to ports of entry must be studied beforehand. This of course is cruiser work. The aim will be to force an outcry for peace; but it will not be possible to blockade effectively the whole coast-line. Dislocation is the aim.

As detachments must return to coal and to rest crews, the numbers of the Blue Fleet need to be increased to the utmost, disregardful of a certain relative inefficiency in older ships; disregardful also of stripping the Blue coasts as towards other possible enemies. Blue cannot fight Orange and another great naval Power at the same time; so this contingency must be dismissed in favor of concentration against Orange. Blue will in fact have the sympathy of every naval nation except the ally of Orange, all of whose colonies would cry out against any attack on Blue.

The General Scheme here advanced seems to me decidedly stronger than the southern route with base at Malampaya Sound and a Suez line of communications. It must be remembered that nations now tire easily of war; that it is enormously expensive; and that therefore blows must be straight, rapid, and decisive one way or the other. The risk of the scheme here suggested is great; but it is a flank attack instead of a direct one, as from Malampaya; and, while it offers greater chance of a military reverse than the other, it offers also a greater chance of national success, which the other may forfeit even while escaping a particular disaster. Compare the flank march to Blenheim, in its effects, with Marlborough's other victories, Ramillies, Oudenarde, Malplaquet, weighty as they were. Consider Napoleon in Italy in 1796, rushing past the Austrian flank to Piacenza to seize the position in their rear. Consider his movement in 1800 to Marengo, again in the rear; and in 1805 cutting off Ulm. Perhaps more illustrative, read in Grant's *Memoirs*[3] the discussion between him and Sherman concerning the great flank march past Vicksburg, and crossing the Mississippi below to come up in rear, instead of Sherman's suggestion to fall back to Memphis, and thence to advance in direct attack with communications constantly covered by the army's line of advance. It would be an interesting inquiry in military psychology, what effect the Vicksburg campaign had in determining Sherman's March to the Sea, eighteen months later.

To insure success, however, to "get the greatest number of chances in your favor," all details must be carefully thought out beforehand, all alternative schemes searched out, weighed, and as far as may be developed also, so that in case of failure at one step the next best thing may equally be known and at once attempted; if not it, the second best, and so on. Several schemes resemble several lines of communication; if one fails, you have the others.

But all this elaborate and necessary scheming demonstrates only more forcibly that at a not distant date the Blue fleet should be moved to the Pacific, and there remain until the opening of the Canal; that the Pacific ports be duly fortified, and Hawaii secured. There will then be no war; barring some intolerable action, which Blue as a nation will not commit.

To Robert U. Johnson

Lawrence, Long Island, February 23, 1911 [NYPL]

My dear Mr. Johnson: I am very sorry to hear you have read that very troublesome complaint. As you say, it is an excuse for anything: though I have not been aware in this instance of anything needing excuse.

I will of course gladly do anything I can to bring an article into accordance with the views of an editor. The disgustingly indiscreet—not to say worse—utterance of Champ Clark,[1] concerning annexation, has disposed me to consider very carefully what I said about Canada.[2] My interest was

---

3. Ulysses S. Grant, *Personal Memoirs of U.S. Grant*. 2 vols. New York: C. L. Webster and Company, 1885–1886.

1. House Speaker James Beauchamp Clark of Missouri, leading Democratic presidential hopeful in 1912 and sometime advocate of American annexation of Canada.
2. In "The Panama Canal and Sea Power in the Pacific."

very different, but my words must answer to the intent. I always suspect him of being more or less under the influence of liquor, from one four days' observation.

I should like to receive your comments and galley proofs sufficiently in advance of a date you will name, for return of corrected proofs, to give me unhurried time for reconsideration as well as for revision.

To Charles W. Stewart

Lawrence, Long Island, March 3, 1911 [NA]

My dear Mr. Stewart: I cannot help Mr. Cruikshank[1] further than by referring him to the Captains' and other letters in the Department, to *Niles' Register*, and to Mackenzie's *Life of Perry*. As far as I remember these were my sole sources of information; though doubtless others may have escaped my memory.

I do not now recall what final disposition was made of those copies of Letters made for me. They *may* still exist at my house in Quogue; or I may have turned them over, as I sometimes do, to the Astor (or N.Y. Public) Library. If I find them on my return to Quogue the Library will be welcome to them. You have the originals, of course; but the study I made of the whole, for my selection, might well be spared another person.

I want to ask of you the address, and the Editor's name, of the *United Service Magazine* (not *Gazette*).[2] I have to ask him permission to republish a certain article,[3] which I need for the Naval Strategy book I am now preparing for the War College.

To Raymond P. Rodgers

Lawrence, Long Island, March 4, 1911 [NWC]

My dear Rodgers: After reading the paper you handed me on Thursday,[1] I think it better, rather than to reply to it point by point, which might

---

1. Ernest Alexander Cruikshank, who collected and edited the documents concerned with the Canadian side of the War of 1812. His *Documents Relating to the Invasion of Canada and the Surrender of Detroit, 1812* was published by the Government Printing Bureau in Ottawa in 1912.
2. Stewart answered that the editor was Lieutenant Colonel Alsager Pollock and the publisher was William Clowes and Sons, 23 Cockspur Street, S. W. London.
3. "Two Maritime Expeditions," *United Service Magazine* (October 1893).
1. War College Response to Mahan's Critique of Strategic War Plan of 1911, at Naval War College. *See also* Mahan to Rodgers, February 22, 1911.

seem a contentiousness which I am far from feeling, to state the impression left upon my mind as to the general situation.

Many of the facts stated in the last paper are new to me, for my attention for several years has not kept abreast of the detailed advances of naval equipment. That an advanced base can be equipped within a week for holding against a serious attempt at recapture,—serious, of course, means against a considerably superior force, for the attack must always be superior, in a proportion depending upon the position of the defender,—is new to me. The efficacy of mortar batteries, also, I have esteemed less highly by far than the College does; but officers on the active list, specially devoted to such studies, should be better judges than myself.

The broad situation raised by the problem may be stated thus: Blue has a decisively preponderant naval force in line-of-battle ships, in cruisers, and in destroyers,—not in smaller torpedo vessels. Blue, however, has a less protected coast, and several island stations outlying from that coast; none of which are properly defended. Orange, though inferior in naval force, has much the superior army, composed largely of veterans who have known war; a better defended home coast; and means for transporting that army rapidly either to the attack of Blue positions, or to the defence of its own outlying islands, of which there are many.

Under these conditions, the Blue Navy, the presence of which would control operations and transport within the radius of its steaming powers, is actually not less distant than three months steaming from the scene of operations on its own coasts, and nearer outlying islands; while, to reach Orange possessions, two months more at least, for renewal, for preparation, and for transfer of force, would be needed.

In short, despite the superior Blue Navy, Orange controls the Pacific Ocean for four months; during which the Blue fleet is non-existent for counteractive purposes.

When the Blue fleet at last, at the expiration of this period, arrives on the scene, it controls the water within the limit of its sustained steaming power.

One (of several) assumptions of the College is that it will by that time—circumstances being as they now are—find all its islands occupied, and possibly a strong Orange force on its mainland; either in Alaska or in the Pacific states, or in both. Also, that in the islands Orange will have fortified all positions to such an extent as to be inexpugnable to the utmost efforts of the Blue Navy, and of such Army as Blue may in the four months assemble. The result is, that north of Panama Blue will have no base of operations from which to begin. Of course, the islands off Santa Barbara are as open to seizure and occupation as other positions.

Before proceeding, I wish here to note my entire assent to the College position that such lodgments are possible, although I am less convinced of their inexpugnableness; and that it follows with absolute directness that Oahu, and Guam if possible, should be at once so provided as to make rapid seizure impossible. The whole process of the war will depend upon this. If the Blue people will endure the strain, they doubtless have the power to retrieve all the loss; but at an immense additional expenditure over that which would be necessary if Guam and Oahu be preserved.

I differ from the College in that I do not believe it practicable for Orange to occupy *all* possible bases in such manner as to be inexpugnable. It may be that Orange, although knowing that Blue will eventually appear in decisively superior naval force, will scatter her land force, large though it may be, in numerous detachments; which will be isolated from the moment the Blue Navy appears. The existing military land force of Blue is in numbers contemptible; but Blue is extremely rich, as compared with Orange, and history has shown that within a year it can produce forces which would capture one by one every Orange detachment thus exposed. True, the process will take time; but time means money, and Blue, if it has endurance, can bear the strain better than Orange. It is to be remembered that Orange, having once occupied these positions, is tied to supporting them. It might even be urged as a sound policy on the part of Blue, to induce Orange to such distant effort, which would place it in the same position that Blue finds so difficult in trans-Pacific operations.

I cannot believe that Orange can put in position, in six months, in all the positions taken from Blue, as well as in all its own many harbors, guns of a calibre that a fleet could not encounter; and while I know that rifled mortars have a very great increase of accuracy over the old time ones, I conceive that no number likely to be placed in *all* the captured Blue positions, and in Orange positions as yet unfortified, would prevent even a half-dozen armored cruisers from clearing a beach and enabling a landing to be made. Ships under rapid movement, which can be made designedly irregular, are difficult objects even for a flat trajectory; much more for a vertical fall. In short, I believe Blue can recover a base, and gradually recover all captured positions in such order as may seem expedient. Some may be even neglected, as immaterial, in favor of offensive action against the enemy's positions.

For the same reason that Blue, even if more provident militarily than it is, would not attempt to make all its outlying stations impregnable, so I conceive Orange must, if for mere economy, leave some anchorages open, which may, or may not, serve the purposes of Blue. One thing is certain; somewhere Blue must secure a base for any offensive operations for recovery of its own, or for aggression against the enemy's interests. I believe such base can be secured somewhere, no matter what the scene of war.

To what extent modern defences can be rapidly installed, to what extent ships can encounter such rapid installations—a very different matter from twelve and fourteen inch guns deliberately placed,—all the circumstances of covering a landing, of effecting a landing, of the subsequent land operations, are questions for men in the prime of life; and with full knowledge abreast of modern conditions. It must be remembered always, however, that an operation is not impracticable because two or three ships may be sunk, or ten thousand men injured. To five-inch guns, and to mortars, cruisers may be exposed and may prove adequate; reserving battleships for battleship work.

Granting that Orange has possessed himself of all the Blue outlying positions, that the central route is thus eliminated, there may be adopted the northern route as I suggested; but if that prove impracticable, or unadvisable, there remains the southern, or that of Suez. The latter not being mentioned in the Plan submitted to me, I did not consider it, nor even realize for the moment that it was shorter than Magellan, as I now understand.

The southern routes, either Samoa or Suez, reject the plan I advocated, of seizing a central position of the Orange group, in favor of a base at the extreme end (south) of the line of Orange possessions (supposed to include the Philippines by occupation). In case of a southern approach, by either route, this is inevitable. The subsequent process of gradually working northward is more secure than my suggestion, and also slower. It protracts the issue; and leaves Orange unmolested in Oahu, and for a time in Guam. Though safer, it is less decisive. My own opinion is that unless Orange is put in tremor concerning his communications,—threatened at home,—he can hold out till the Blue people weary of the war. If the Blue nation do not weary, Orange will be reduced by exhaustion.

I do not attach major importance to the Blue fleet by position covering the Pacific Coast. Offence against the enemy, war carried to his own possessions, is the best defence. The British people have always been placid under risks to Gibraltar, or even to the West Indies, but terrorized by the allied fleets in the Channel, and by Napoleon's project of invasion. Witness also the present apprehensions of the Pacific coast. Blue cannot attempt a landing in Orange home territory; but even the poor Vladivostok division shut up the native shipping in Yokohama by appearing near-by.

As regards operations against the trade of Orange, this is cruiser work; supported by battleships, whose only share is that of support. They therefore are not divided, but the cruisers are; and the disposition is against commercial centres and coasting trade, to produce, as I said, dislocation, and engorgement of railroads. I do not believe blockade of the whole coast possible. I do believe it probable that dislocation with all its evils can be produced.

If the Blue fleet maintain superiority such as it now has, it can be maintained near the Orange coast. The question of coal supply is a huge administrative question, costly and intricate; but it is not insoluble to money and brains. There is to be but one dominating principle, viz: "To have coal enough, you must have too much." On any plan, northern route or southern, a depot can be secured and fortified against probable molestations by raid. Anything more, as, for instance, such landing as I have considered possible for the reduction of Orange positions scattered in former Blue possessions, demands a force which will not be risked afloat by Orange while Blue is in near-by command of the water.

Everything, however, goes to show, and all argument returns to the point, that Oahu and Guam should be made secure now. Why not now keep in Guam the 3,000, if they be deemed adequate, on the plea of comparative health which should obtain in a small wind-swept island? Granting such garrison, why not now place mortars? And certainly, even now, every feature of the island should be studied and mastered with a view, not only to fortification but, to defence against landings. My objection to the proposed transfer of force from Corregidor was, partly, that I thought it inadequate; partly that I thought, if relations were strained, Orange would prevent it. Both considerations are worthy of weighing. How far does the topography of the harbor of San Luis favor gun positions, and conceal vessels within?

As a last suggestion, with Oahu and Guam in Blue's possession, I presume a fleet leaving the former might, besides colliers, carry a deck load for several days, without tactical risk through meeting an enemy.

In conclusion, the two papers of the College appear to me to present a very admirable digest of the situation of both sides, with a full presentation of the difficulties which Blue must encounter as soon as his campaign is initiated by entering the Pacific. Such full appreciation of all difficulties is absolutely essential to any safe plan. What I miss in the papers is a clear recognition of the difficulties of Orange, of moral effects, of the fact that difficulty does not spell impossibility, and of the truth that the very existence of difficulty has repeatedly proved opportunity, for the reason that the defence is deceived by its apparent security.

Farragut's summary of the difference between Drayton's point of view and his own, and his adoption as his motto of Danton's "de l'audace, de l'audace, et encore de l'audace," will be found in every great military achievement. A very striking illustration of this very quality will be seen in the council he held before passing the New Orleans forts, contrasted with Porter's advice. This will be found in my *Life of Farragut*. (I should mention that Soley in his life of Porter[2] contests the justice of this report, but only as affecting Porter personally, not the question of the two lines of action). Grant and Sherman before Vicksburg presented the same contrast.

---

2. James R. Soley, *Admiral Porter*. New York: D. Appleton & Co., 1903.

In this connection, I question the soundness of Corbett's dictum of not attacking the enemy where he is strongest; and the apparent inference, in the second paper, that "Blue's security lies in an approach on Orange's weakest flank." Corbett relies mainly on Clausewitz, whose authority is of the very first; but I conceive it is not the enemy's local strength, but the chance of success, and the effect produced by success, which should influence. In our Revolutionary War the allied fleets preferred the blockade of Gibraltar, and operations in the West Indies, to the occupancy of the British Channel, or to the support of the American armies on the continent, where the British strength was such that Washington said, "We are at the end of our tether." Actually sixty-odd allies hesitated to attack thirty-five British in an anchorage on the British coast, though there were no torpedoes then; and Yorktown was a fluke, as regarded allied cooperation. Brueys thought that the difficulties of navigation would delay Nelson's approach and give him a night to repair neglects. Yet there seems to me no doubt, that naval support on the American coast, or such an action as offered in the Channel, were the true course, though the heart of the enemy's strength lay there. In short, aphorisms are open to the condition that circumstances alter cases.

To Charles W. Stewart

Lawrence, Long Island, March 6, 1911 [NA]

My dear Mr. Stewart: Will you lend me for a few days the volume of Troude's *Batailles Navales de France* which covers the years 1688–1697.

I want to extract from it certain data, and will need it not more than two or three days.

[P.S.]   I am much indebted for Pollock's name and address.

To Charles W. Stewart

Lawrence, Long Island, March 11, 1911 [NA]

My dear Mr. Stewart: I have been much obliged by the loan of Troude, which I returned yesterday by registered mail, having extracted the information I needed.

I will try to bear in mind your wish to be notified of books or papers interesting from the naval point of view that may come under my notice.

One, by the way, a *Mercantile Marine Atlas*, by George Philip of London,[1]
I lately found very useful at the University Club in N.Y.

[P.S.]   Do you know Beers's books (American) on Colonial America of
the 17th and 18th centuries?[2]

To Raymond P. Rodgers

Lawrence, Long Island, March 17, 1911 [OANHD]

My dear Rodgers: Your letter of March 14 reached me last evening.
Replying to your query, with regard to the comments I sent you upon
the College "Plan," as submitted to me, I am entirely willing that any disposition of the papers be made that may seem expedient.[1]

It will be remembered, of course, that I wrote under limitations of time
which did not permit a full examination of details which might modify the
general line of thought. But the concurrence of opinion, on certain important necessities, between the officers of the College and myself may have
value.

To Robert U. Johnson

Lawrence, Long Island, March 24, 1911 [NYPL]

My dear Mr. Johnson: I write to acknowledge the receipt of two envelopes, containing your letter and the duplicate galleys.[1] Being for the
moment engaged on a subject requiring continuous thought[2] I have post-

---

1. George Philip, *Philips' Mercantile Marine Atlas*. 2d ed. London: G. Philip and
Son, Ltd., 1905. 3d ed., 1909.
2. George L. Beer, *The Commercial Policy of England Toward the American Colonies*.
New York: Columbia University, 1893. *British Colonial Policy, 1754–1765; The
Origins of the British Colonial System, 1578–1660*; and *The Old Colonial System*.
New York: Macmillan, 1907, 1908, and 1912, respectively.

1. Rodgers had requested Mahan's permission to forward his two critiques (February
22 and March 4, 1911) on the Strategic War Plan of 1911 to the General Board.
Rodgers made it clear that he considered Mahan's critique of March 4 to be, in
effect, an optional counterplan to the original NWC plan. Rodgers to Mahan, March
14, 1911, at the Naval War College.

1. Of "The Panama Canal and Sea Power in the Pacific."
2. Mahan was preparing for the *North American Review* four articles dealing with
armaments, international law, arbitration, and diplomacy, viz: "Armaments and
Arbitration" (May 1911); "Diplomacy and Arbitration" (July 1911); "Navies as
International Factors" (September 1911); and "The Deficiencies of Law as an Instrument of International Adjustments" (November 1911).

poned proof reading till that is finished; but from present indications I expect to take it up on Monday, and all that you say in your letter will be carefully considered at the same time, and the article shaped to meet your views to the utmost I can.

The *particular* questions you put do not, at first glance, appear to me affected by the Canal, as distinguished from their status before the Canal. The effect of the Canal is to expedite the arrival of the Navy on the scene— a most important gain; but all the same, once arrived, its action differs little.

To Raymond P. Rodgers

Lawrence, Long Island, March 25, 1911 [NWC]

My dear Rodgers: I have received the chart of Guam, which I shall study with great interest. A year ago I obtained those of Guantanamo and Culebra from the H.O.; but Guam I had, and have, never seen.

I find that in preparing my lectures for the printer some pages will have to be re-typed; and I should be much obliged if you would have sent me two quires of T.W. paper of the same size—not [illegible word follows].

I have read Martin's article once and am just about to re-read. It is an excellent paper, expecially as a brief from one point of view; but it seems to me unduly dominated by the soldier's outlook, as ours doubtless by the seaman's.

To Robert U. Johnson

Lawrence, Long Island, March 31, 1911 [NYPL]

My dear Mr. Johnson: I return the corrected galleys,[1] with a type writ-ten addition marked for substitution on galley 3. This has been written to meet the wishes expressed in your letter of March 21. I have not dealt with the question of the Navy helping to resist an attack on Pearl Harbor. If the Navy be there in force, the attack will not be made; at least not until the Navy has been beaten. If the Navy is not there, the case does not arise.

You may be interested to know that an English colonist from S. Africa,[2]

---

1. "The Panama Canal and Sea Power in the Pacific," *Century Magazine* (June 1911).
2. Probably, Lionel Curtis, one of the authors of *The Government of South Africa*, a two-volume study prepared for the National Convention, which wrote the Constitution of South Africa. *See* Mahan to Johnson, July 6, 1911.

who apparently has been travelling through Australia and Canada with reference to Imperial Defence, and was on his way to London, sought an interview with me in New York. In our talk I mentioned this article as slated for June; at which he expressed regret that it had not been for May, in view of the Imperial Conference meeting May 22. I have had also two letters from Australia asking me for an article on the necessity of rapid immigration to Australia. This I have declined.

You have not sent any map, although by your suggestion I sent you the memoranda for one. This is only in case of oversight; as I leave the expediency to the judgment of the editor.

If time allows, it might be expedient to let me see the enclosed[3] insertion in print.

To Charles W. Stewart

Lawrence, Long Island, April 4, 1911 [NA]

My dear Mr. Stewart: Agreeably to your wish expressed some time ago, I note in the (English) *Publishers Circular*, a book *The Ocean Empire* by Gerard Fiennes;[1] published by A. Treherne & Co. London.

There are two Fiennes, I believe; and I have understood one of them is the "Excubitor" who writes under that nom de plume on naval matters in English monthlies.[2]

To Charles W. Stewart

Lawrence, Long Island, April 6, 1911 [NA]

My dear Mr. Stewart: Could you send me, if possible by return mail, the *aggregate appropriations* for the current fiscal year, ending June 30, 1911; and also the same for the next fiscal year, as appropriated.

[P.S.]   I presume the first are in the Secretary's Report; but I dont [know] just where to turn for the second.

---

3. Enclosure not found.
1. Gerard Yorke Twisleton-Wykham Fiennes, *The Ocean Empire, its Dangers and Defences* (1911).
2. If "Excubitor" was the second Fiennes, he was probably Geoffrey Cecil T. W. Fiennes, author of *Reminiscences*. London: Nisbet and Co., 1925.

To Raymond P. Rodgers

Lawrence, Long Island, April 14, 1911 [NWC]

My dear Rodgers: I have looked over the chart of Guam which you so kindly sent me. I do not know whether you expected any expression of opinion, as you did not ask any; but I submit the following impressions.

The harbor of Apra is at an angle, from which the island extends, in one direction, N.E. about fifteen miles; in the other south about ten miles.

From its latitude, I presume Guam is in pretty steady trade wind weather. This the road development seems to confirm, showing little transportation, and therefore few inhabitants, on east side.

The west and north-west shores, presumably lee as to the prevailing wind, are for the most part steep-to; and in many places, if not indeed for the most part, lined with ledges. There seems only one low sand beach, properly so called; and that of small extent, viz: Dadi Beach at the neck of the Orote peninsula, which forms the south side of Apra anchorage. I see also two beaches, in deep indentations south of Facpi Point, in which the land seems low, but the character of the beach is not shown.

Apra anchorage is open to gun fire from West to Northeast at any distance above one and a half miles, at the choice of an attacking fleet.

Orote Peninsula is two and a half miles long from neck to tip. At the neck it is but one thousand yards wide; from which I infer that, if properly fortified, it could be easily held by a comparatively small garrison against land attack. Its works ought to command Dadi Beach, and landing elsewhere would be difficult.

If supplied with guns that armored ships would fear, Orote peninsula could probably protect vessels at the anchorage; for I cannot conceive battle ships exposing themselves to 12-inch shore guns, so long as an enemy's equal, or nearly equal, battle-fleet is in existence.

I do not read topography well enough to be able to estimate how far a garrison could hold out on the peninsula, if strong enough to resist a land attack, but *without heavy guns* to keep off the fire of armored ships. This question, in fact, is rather military than naval. The land of the peninsula seems of no great height; and from south, by west, to north, it could be covered with projectiles, from which the troops must have protection. Otherwise, the fire of the defence being kept down, there seems no reason why a landing force should not enter by the very harbor's mouth, in vessels of considerable size. Calalan Bank has for the most part four and a half fathoms.

There is further the question of supplies as affecting that of ultimate endurance.

I should sum up by saying that to a nation seriously intending to hold Guam as a basis of operations, Orote peninsula seems well adapted to control the harbor of Apra, at comparatively small expense in numbers of garrison and development of works. The rest of the island could be abandoned to an enemy with indifference, provided Orote can stand off battleships, and resist attack by land. No matter where an enemy may land he has to come to the neck of that peninsula, unless and until he can confront it with siege guns adequate to reduce the defence. Such guns in position on the high ground east of the harbor might effect reduction; but much time will be needed to place them; and with time the Guam fleet should arrive.

I return the chart by this mail with many thanks for the sight of it.

To George von L. Meyer

N.P. Probably, Lawrence, Long Island, April 21, 1911 [OANHD]

Fuel stands first in importance of the resources necessary to a fleet. Without ammunition, a ship may run away, hoping to fight another day, but without fuel she can neither run, nor reach her station, nor remain on it, if remote, nor fight.

The distribution and storage of fuel is, therefore, eminently a strategic question. As regards economical methods of storing, I have no opinion to express; but (1) the positions for storing, and (2) the quantity to be stored at each position, are amenable to strategic considerations, to which I confine myself.

As regards position, there seem to be three principal heads of requirement.

1. Accessibility to the fleet operating in the particular field of maritime operations under consideration. This accessibility may be either for the fleet itself, coaling together or in detachments, or for colliers transporting to a front of operations.

2. Military security; security against an enemy's attack or seizure, while stored.

3. The facility of getting coal to the place of storage, i.e., transportation; the means of storage; and the facility for handling coal when filling the fleet or its colliers.

You may recognize here the three elements of strategic value in any point: Position, Strength, and Resources.

It seems to follow directly that a place suited for a strategic centre of operations for a fleet should equally be the position for a coaling station; because, (1) there it will be near the fleet; (2) it will be under shelter of the fortifications established for the position as a naval base; and (3) at the base should be accumulated all resources of every kind, fuel included.

As an illustration: New York, including certainly Long Island Sound, with also, probably, Narragansett Bay, is a comprehensive water area, which by situation and local conditions is peculiarly suited to a fleet base. It will doubtless be as strongly fortified as any point on the coast; and it possesses peculiar advantages for the accumulation of coal, because the haul thither, from the coal fields, is comparatively short, by a highly organized four-track railway. All this means that New York, regarded as a coaling station, possesses in the nature of things in a high degree the three requisites: Position, Strength and Resources. It is a good example of the desirable.

The comparative facility of transportation to New York affects the military question of the amount of coal to be stored. Under any system of storage, some deterioration progresses; and, moreover, coal stored is money locked up from current expenses, on which perhaps it might be better used at the moment. Where coal can be so certainly and quickly conveyed, the amount to be stored in peace can surely be less, even though it be deemed expedient to provide the storage basins on a war scale.

Conversely to New York (which I now use as an illustration in the reverse sense), a position far removed from the sources of coal supply should be more fully stored; and if it be inaccessible by land transport, so that possibly transportation might be interrupted at a critical moment, the necessity for large storage becomes more urgent. Attention may here be called to the coasting coal trade, upon which I think Narragansett Bay and the eastward depends. Should that be interrupted, the situation of New York, near the coal fields, would be emphasized.

If this be so, positions like Guantanamo, the Panama Canal, Pearl Harbor, and Corregidor stand first in order of importance, in the matter of receiving necessary provision, both by strength of fortification and by fuel storage. The Pacific Coast positions follow them, because they can be supplied by land. Nevertheless, as an economical measure, it would probably be better to store them fully, according to a standard to be fixed; e.g., a month's consumption by twenty battleships at full steam, or at some fixed speed—say 15 knots. The Atlantic strategic ports can more safely rely on the ordinary railway transportation, or on inland water communication, such as Chesapeake Bay, to meet an unexpected emergency.

Again, where transportation is by water only, as to island positions, or Panama, the total distance from our own shores, and the nearness to those of an enemy, will markedly affect certainty and security.

It is perhaps expedient to regard war in the Atlantic or in the Pacific as equally probable—or improbable—from the international point of view; although I personally think the Pacific much more likely, unless our west coast people can be kept steadily in hand. Assuming equal probabilities, the Pacific positions, both continental and island, are much the most exposed, and in provision of fortification and of coal should have precedence.

Until the Panama Canal is completed, accumulation of coal on Pacific points can be safe only in so far as the military preparation insures the holding of a particular point, until the fleet can reach it. Otherwise accumulation is only for the enemy. In case of war in the Pacific,—where there is only one Power with whom war could actively be waged,—it appears to me that the proper disposition is to accumulate no coal, unless where the army can guarantee its security for a determined time, necessary for the fleet to arrive from the Atlantic.

On war occurring in the Pacific, all military effort should be concentrated at the Isthmus, up to the utmost locally needed, to hold it securely. While the fleet, necessarily taking all colliers with it, is passing from one coast to the other, provision can be made to hasten coal to Colon and to transport it rapidly to the fleet when arrived in Panama. Coal also might be advanced during the same period in sufficient quantities to intermediate stations of the trans-continental railroads, to within, say, five hundred or a thousand miles of the Pacific, ready for forwarding. As, however, an enemy could seriously interfere by destroying the railroad near the coast, it would seem better that the colliers should be filled at Panama: the fleet being enabled thus to refill from them. In short, failing full military preparation, dependence for coal supply in case of a Pacific war should be primarily on Panama, until the fleet, arrived and recouped, establishes maritime preponderance. If Pearl Harbor can hold out till then, it should be stored beforehand with at least a month's full steaming for the fleet.

If the Panama Canal reach completion before any war occur, coal in American Pacific ports, owing to the nearness of the fleet, may be considered secure against anything but raids; and such security will be as absolute as military security ever can be. Moreover, if under water storage be used, a raid can effect little destruction, unless by means unknown to me. Panama to Honolulu being more than the steaming distance of the battle fleet, it must go first to San Francisco, or its vicinity, and probably thence to Pearl Harbor. This would imply at Pearl Harbor and San Francisco the standard amount before suggested of coal. I think that Bremerton should have the same.

As regards storing Corregidor, I am in great doubt until the Canal is finished. It is for the army to say whether it can probably hold out for the time needed for the fleet to pass to the Pacific and thence across to the Philippines. If not, coal there is enemy's coal. After the Canal, the chances will be far better. It will then be for the Navy to calculate the time for the fleet to arrive, and for the army how long the place can resist. If the calculation is close, put the coal there; the advantage of having it, if we succeed, is much greater than the disadvantage of losing it, if we fail. The enemy being there near his coal supplies, an amount captured, more or less, signifies little.

I understand that the Japanese in the late war found that coal afloat in colliers was a better administrative provision than coal landed. This applied, I imagine, more especially to an advanced base like that at the Elliott Islands, and would mean that coaling from colliers was best for a fleet thus advanced. It saves additional handling, and facilitates a distant operation, or shifting the base. In actual war, the United States ports of coal storage would serve probably as reservoirs, whence the colliers would draw their supplies to be conveyed to the fleet, obviating the necessity of itself leaving its station merely for coaling. But, whether for filling colliers, or coaling the fleet direct, the provision of basins, of barges, and of amount to be stored, at such several ports will be the same.

My general conclusion is that provision for storing, up to the standard fixed, should be made, first, at San Francisco, Bremerton, and Pearl Harbor; next at the Atlantic terminus of the Panama Canal and at Guantanamo; subsidiary to Guantanamo, at Key West. The Atlantic ports come last, both in provision of basins, etc., and in accumulation of coal for emergencies; because the ordinary activities of the country, and the nearness of the coal fields, make the supply of a fleet surer and easier than at the other stations.

As regards Corregidor, I would neither make preparation of basins, nor accumulate coal beyond peace convenience, before the opening of the Canal, unless the army can assure the probable maintenance of the post, and security of the coal, for eight months after hostilities beginning. Guam is practically about the same distance from the south coast of Japan that Corregidor is, and the communication from Guam, by colliers to a fleet advanced towards Japan, would be less threatened by the Pescadores than communications with Corregidor. Guam could be more easily and safely supplied from U.S. Pacific ports; and from the Atlantic after the Canal is finished. From southern sources of supply, e.g., Australia, Manila is less remote than Guam by some six hundred miles; but Corregidor, unless extremely fortified, garrisoned, and stored, is a most exposed position.

I draw a distinction between the actual accumulation of coal, and provision; that is, the preparation of basins, barges, etc. The preparations will require far more time than the accumulation, for the latter is, after all, only a specific application of the ordinary transportation activities of the country. Moreover, if a port be captured, a coal-less basin is a barren prize. I would lose no time in making preparation, but I would not accumulate the coal on a war footing until either the army, or the fleet by its strategic predominance over the enemy, make it secure in the military sense of security. Whatever else we do, we must not help solve the coal problem of an enemy seeking to operate on our own coasts, by exposing coal to his capture.

The difficulty of discussing in the same paper measures appropriate to no Canal and preparations contemplating a future with the Canal, makes advisable that I should summarize this discursive discussion in definite conclusions.

While awaiting the opening of the Canal, I would carry on to completion a full development of coaling facilities at San Francisco, Bremerton, and Pearl Harbor. I would not at Corregidor, unless with adequate assurances from the army. Similar development should take place at Guantanamo, Key West, and at the Atlantic terminus of the Canal, under the fortifications. War provision at the Atlantic ports should be subsequent in importance to those in the Pacific, and the others named.

As regards oil fuel preparations, I should think the same general principles would apply to the determination of stations. In the current *Naval Register*, I find among active vessels only six T.B.D.'s that use this fuel; and I presume some time will pass before it will be required for vessels bigger than protected cruisers. In general, considering the large number of ports on the Atlantic and Pacific where it is kept stored by private parties, I should think that, except at positions separated by water from the United States, dependence might be placed on these parties. In case of war, contracts made on a liberal scale with them would probably cost less, and be equally efficacious with elaborate Government provision beforehand.

One general remark applies: that the operations of torpedo vessels, submarines, and in general coast defense vessels, and of cruisers, are more widely disseminated than those of battleships. The arrangements for their supplies require corresponding distribution, instead of the concentration of the battle ships; but I incline to think the ordinary amounts in private hands, seconded by Government arrangements with them in case of war, would correspond to the necessities.

As regards wireless stations, my technical knowledge is deficient. I assume that wireless communication, in war, is mainly for cases where telephonic, by wire, is impracticable. The latter I assume to be preferable, because it is confined by the directive force of the wire to the sender and hearer; whereas the wireless spreads in concentric sound waves in all directions, open to whosoever can hear and decipher. That is, wireless is appropriate to water distances where no cable exists; notably, for instance, to scouts, or to single vessels, or to fleets, desiring to keep touch with shore stations, or to come in speediest communication with them; in case, for instance, of returning for supplies or aid, allowing preparations to be made in advance. The same would apply to the approach of an enemy's expedition.

Take the Atlantic coast, and assume the speed of an approaching vessel, scout, or fleet,—or of an enemy—to be 300 miles per diem. I would wish three days' notice before possible arrival; that means 900 miles wireless range. Lay down on the coast a line parallel to the coast, and 900 miles from it. Now, if the wireless can carry 1000 miles, any position upon the coast within 1000 miles of the line laid down, will serve as a wireless station; and I should imagine three stations of such power, with one at Key West, four in all, would cover the whole area intermediate between coast and line. If the country is in a condition of general preparation, such warning of an advancing enemy seems to be all that should be required.

The same method would apply in the Pacific. Guantanamo, the Canal, and Pearl Harbor are so advanced that they should have a wireless for that reason alone; while Corregidor is entitled to it because so widely separated. In a detailed scheme, the distance between Pearl Harbor and San Francisco should be bridged by two vessels, equipped with wireless; like the chain of repeating vessels which by flags alone transmitted to Nelson within three hours that the combined fleets were leaving Cadiz.

My reply has been governed throughout by reference to the general fundamental idea of concentrating preparations, and dispensing with a numerous distribution of them; believing the principle of concentration, construed in spirit and not merely literally, to be upon the whole most efficacious, most secure, and most economical. Preparations must be under a shield of security, and there is a limit to the aggregate amount of security that can be provided. Therefore there is a limit to distribution; or else to adequacy. It would be delightful to have every port impregnable and fully stored but it is impossible. Hence a few points only must be chosen and effort concentrated on them.

To Raymond P. Rodgers

Lawrence, Long Island, April 22, 1911 [NWC]

My dear Rodgers: I hope soon to be able to send to the publishers the greater part of the manuscript of the proposed book,[1] about four fifths, which will more than keep them occupied till June 1, when I hope to send in the remainder.

It will be necessary for this purpose, not only to use but to take apart and rearrange the copy of the lectures upon which I have worked; and in any case it would be diverted from further use in the lecture room. Before doing this, I think it prudent to ascertain from you whether I can proceed as stated, and can also have sent me in Quogue—not before—another copy for use in preparing for the summer lectures.

[P.S.] I enclose receipt for Study of Pacific anchorages.

1. *Naval Strategy.*

To Raymond P. Rodgers

Lawrence, Long Island, May 3, 1911 [NWC]

My dear Rodgers: Not having heard from the Bureau relative to my change of address, and having regard to its letter of April 19, and my own explanation of permanent residence at Quogue, I assume that the permission to reside here, which was only asked for the winter, is construed by it in that sense; and that I do not need a special authorization to resume my "usual" residence.

In any event, my lease here is up, and summer tenants expected shortly. My family will therefore move to Quogue May 8, and I shall follow them on Wednesday, May 10. On Friday coming, I intend to go to the University Club, where you can communicate with me directly, if necessary, until May 10. During the breaking up here and settling there, I can work to better advantage at the Club; and besides there are books which I wish to consult in the Library.

I have not heard from you in reply to my letter, asking whether I was at liberty now to break up the copy of the lectures in my hands, for use by the publishers; counting upon another copy to be sent me in Quogue, for preparation for lecturing this year. The text of more than four fifths is now ready for the printer. I hope in New York to complete the map specifications for the same, which are well advanced; but, alike for keeping watch over the map work, and for preparation for the lecture season, I ought to have a copy in my hands by May 15, at Quogue.

I enclose vouchers for residence here to May 8. Those you returned were drawn up by the Paymaster; but I had no hesitation in signing them as they stood, because in either place I was entitled to the same allowance, and from the previous action of the Bureau had reason to expect authority for residence.

I enclose also acknowledgment of receipt of commission.

To Robert U. Johnson

University Club, New York, May 10, 1911 [NYPL]

Dear Mr. Johnson: Since my line of this morning[1] I have happened to look in the May *Century*, and in the advertisement for June see my article styled "The Panama Canal & Sea Power in the *Atlantic*." Surely this must be a misprint for *Pacific* which must be guarded against.

[P.S.] My address henceforward is Quogue, Long Island.

---

1. This letter has not been found.

To Raymond P. Rodgers

Marshmere, Quogue, Long Island, May 11, 1911 [NWC]

My dear Rodgers: As you see by the enclosed for the Bureau I am now here.

I find that the title of Klado's book which I have is *The Battle of the Sea of Japan*, 1906; and from the Preface I gather that the previous work, which I want to consult is, *The Russian Navy in the Russo-Japanese War*.[1] If the College has this and can spare it me I should be obliged. The Russo-Jap War is what remains to be corrected for the publishers.

The other copy of my lectures has not been received, but I presume it will have been sent by registered mail. I understand fully that it is to remain intact and to be returned to the College after use this summer.

To Raymond P. Rodgers

Marshmere, Quogue, Long Island, May 13, 1911 [NWC]

My dear Rodgers: To my dismay, I find that Klado's Russian Navy in the War with Japan is not the book I wanted, though it will be useful to me to read it. There seems in it no allusion to the phrase "Fortress Fleet." Happily I find in my own *Naval Administration and Warfare*, p. 156, sufficient account of the phrase, and of the advanced sheets I saw in 1906, for me to go on; but I have found also a letter from the translator, J. H. Dickinson, dated *July* 6, 1906, in which he says that the book is to be titled "Naval War," and that it, or its proofs, would be sent me.

Have you such a book as Klado's *Naval War?*[1] I dont remember hearing of it, nor do I recall that any proofs were sent me other than the advanced sheets of which I wrote. Those were in *March*, 1906.

With reference to the Plan,[2] about which we wrote and talked last winter, have you and the College men read Asakawa's *Russo-Japanese Conflict?*[3]

---

1. Nikolai Lavrentievich Klado, *The Russian Navy in the Russo-Japanese War*. . . . Translated from the French text of M. René Marchand by J. H. [Hargreaves] Dickinson. London: Hurst and Blackett Ltd., 1905. His *The Battle of the Sea of Japan*, translated by Dickinson and F. P. Marchant, was published in London by Hodder and Stoughton in 1906.

1. This title has not been found.
2. The Naval War College's Strategic War Plan of 1911. *See* Mahan to Rodgers, March 4, 1911.
3. Kanichi Asakawa, *The Russo-Japanese Conflict, Its Causes and Issues*. Boston: Houghton Mifflin & Co., 1904. Rodgers responded that he had commenced reading the book. Rodgers to Mahan, May 16, 1911, at the Naval War College.

The first chapter more particularly abounds with particulars of military significance as showing the utter dependence of Japan upon the sea and the need of Expansion room.

To Little, Brown and Company

Marshmere, Quogue, Long Island, May 15, 1911 [LC]

Gentlemen: I have sent you to-day by Express prepaid, the manuscript of my Lectures on Naval Strategy, through page 366. The last MSS. page being 434, there remain in my hands 68 pages, in the speedy revision and dispatch of which I foresee no difficulty.

I enclose also memoranda for a number of maps, and there will probably be three or four more. The voluminous memoranda may make them seem more extensive and complicated than they by any means are. The work is almost wholly outline, as you will see; and the voluminousness is due merely to the desire on my part to make everything of a somewhat novel subject, especially Map 2, perfectly clear.

I have received a letter from the President of the Naval War College, asking if I can let him know when you propose to put the book on the market, and what its probable cost. The object of this inquiry is that the Bureau of Navigation, Navy Department, which intends to take 125 copies, wishes to reserve the necessary sum at once, lest it should be infringed upon by other expenditures between now and date of publication.

To Raymond P. Rodgers

Marshmere, Quogue, Long Island, May 15, 1911 [NWC]

My dear Rodgers: I have sent off today to the publishers 366 pages of the 434 which constitute the manuscript of the book, and am also sending them the details for all the most difficult maps, leaving three or four of the simplest (for them) though not necessarily easiest for me.

I am asking their date of publication, and probable cost, which the above data will I think enable them to estimate. As regards title, I have usually left that to the last possible moment, in hopes of the best conclusion, but I suppose "Lectures on Naval Strategy" will answer tentatively, and not prejudice a change if something more suitable turn up.

The publishers are Little, Brown & Co. of Boston.

To Little, Brown and Company

Marshmere, Quogue, Long Island, May 29, 1911[1] [LC]

Gentlemen: I enclose herewith the remaining pages of the manuscript of Naval Strategy.

You will remember to let me know the price of the book, when decided, for the information of the President of the War College and of the Navy Department.

To the Editor of The New York Times

Quogue, Long Island, June 2, 1911[1]

In the issue of *The Times* for June 1, the leading editorial article, entitled "A Roosevelt Incident," quotes the following words from Mr. Roosevelt's address to the veterans on Decoration Day:

> "There are certain questions which we Americans would never think of arbitrating. One is the Monroe Doctrine, and another is the allowing of vast quantities of Asiatics to come here. We have got to stand out against agreeing to do these dangerous things, no matter what the short-sighted, false-peace advocates say."

Upon this the editorial comments:

> "The famous speech of President Taft, which was the starting-point of the extensive and important international movement toward general arbitration now proceeding hopefully among the great Powers, made no mention of these exceptions and reservations. He is, obviously, the very chief of the 'short-sighted false-peace advocates' whom Mr. Roosevelt takes occasion to hold up to public contempt."

The Times thus takes Mr. Roosevelt's speech and by a construction of its own makes of it a cap which it proceeds to fit to Mr. Taft's head.

Having a copy of Mr. Taft's speech of December 17, 1910, before me, I submit that this construction is quite unwarranted by the facts—of that speech. Mr. Taft did not, it is true, specify the Monroe Doctrine and Asiatic immigration as exceptions to the broad general proposition. It is not by

---

1. The lapse of time was caused by Mahan's being ordered to appear before the House Naval Committee on May 19 for hearings on the Council for National Defense. He returned to Quogue on May 26. *See* Mahan to Roosevelt, July 1, 1911.

1. From *The New York Times*, June 5, 1911, p. 10. This letter was reprinted in *The Outlook*, June 17, 1911, under the heading "Misrepresenting Mr. Roosevelt."

elaborating exceptions in an after-dinner speech that such a proposition is initiated; and the overt initiation, as a matter of fact, was by the British Foreign Minister's speech in Parliament of March 13 indorsing that of President Taft. It is in the working out of the proposition that possible exceptions must be met and obviated, if success is to be attained.

Mr. Taft's specific words were: "If we can negotiate and put through a positive agreement with some great nation to abide the adjudication of an international arbitral court in every issue which cannot be settled by negotiation, no matter what it involves, whether honor, territory, or money, we shall have made a long step forward"; but the greater part of his address, two-thirds at least, was devoted to the justification of military preparations, notably the Panama fortification. "The discussion of needed military preparations," he said, "does not sound very well at a peace meeting, but the trouble about a peace meeting is that it seems to me to be just one-half the picture, and I want to introduce the whole picture in order that," &c. And again: "The trouble is that nations are quite as likely as men to violate their obligations under great stress like that of war."

It is difficult to see how such utterances, accessible to any seeker, and doubtless known to Mr. Roosevelt, can permit the speaker to be classed under the head of "short-sighted, false-peace advocates." That such a class exists will scarcely be denied; but the application to Mr. Taft is not in his own words, or in those of Mr. Roosevelt, but in an ill-founded assumption of *The Times.*

Besides the above, it is a matter of common knowledge that Mr. Taft's Administration favors a strong navy, maintained in force by the provision of two new battleships annually. This is not the mark of short-sighted, false-peace advocacy.

Mr. Roosevelt's name seems to make *The Times* see red. Six months ago, in a letter which *The Times* did me the favor to publish,[2] I pointed out that it was stating as a fact its own inference that Mr. Roosevelt, in overruling the machine of his own party, procuring the nomination of Mr. Stimson, and taking an active part in the campaign, was simply and selfishly seeking his own renomination in 1912. This perversion of inference into assertion undoubtedly helped to deprive the State of New York of the services of a Governor whom Mr. Taft has now invited into his Cabinet; a step which, in view of Mr. Stimson's past public career, seems to indicate a certain coincidence of judgment between Mr. Taft and Mr. Roosevelt. While the construction now placed upon Mr. Roosevelt's recent speech does not err in precisely the same way, it does err, and by most injurious intention, in not giving all the facts concerning Mr. Taft's speech. It is only by ignoring those facts that the offensive application of Mr. Roosevelt's words to Mr. Taft can be sustained.

---

2. *See* Mahan to *The New York Times,* October 25, 1910.

To Carter FitzHugh

Quogue, Long Island, June 7, 1911 [LC]

Dear Mr. FitzHugh: For several reasons I am very chary of expressing any views upon the chances of an enemy landing on our shores. The question is very complicated, and I cannot say that I have given it such mature consideration in all its phases as would warrant the formal expression of a public opinion. There are many exposed points doubtless, and we have few trained forces. If we had a large regular army, it could not be omnipresent, though it would greatly modify the situation in case a landing were successfully accomplished. I have heard that Moltke said with reference to a German invasion of England that there were many ways of getting an army in, but he knew of none for getting it out. Whether he ever said so or not, it is probably true that a force once landed would find its chief difficulties, those of military supply, still before it, provided our people had the nerve to hold out. Would they? A hundred thousand trained men could impose submission on large sections of the country, as Napoleon did on Europe; but it seems to me improbable that an attempt to get in would be made so long as we have a navy capable of cutting off retreat. It is deeply to be hoped that our navy will be brought at least equal to that of Germany.

Of course this letter is not for publication, directly or indirectly.

[P.S.] Some years will probably elapse before 10,000 men can cross the British channel, aviating; and more before 100,000 the Atlantic or Pacific.

To Little, Brown and Company

Naval War College, Newport, June 14, 1911 [LC]

Gentlemen: My letters from home inform me that proofs of *Naval Strategy* have begun to arrive; so I write to say that I am absent, and shall not return till Saturday, which will explain failure to read and return.[1]

I hope to begin reading on Monday, or as soon thereafter as I shall be able to clear my desk of accumulation during absence.

I am here on duty, delivering a course of lectures, which itself forms part of the book.[2]

---

1. Mahan reported to the Commandant of the Narragansett Bay Naval Station on the 12th, and returned to Quogue on June 19.
2. There are in the Library of Congress 45 letters addressed by Mahan to Little, Brown and Company during the period June 26 to November 6, 1911, dealing with the mechanics of reading and correcting proofs and the preparation of maps for *Naval Strategy*. The editors consider that the samples reproduced here suffice to demon-

To Theodore Roosevelt

Marshmere, Quogue, Long Island, June 19, 1911 [LC]

Dear Colonel Roosevelt: Your letter of June 8 came just as I was leaving home for Newport for lectures at the War College, and I was there too heavily engrossed to allow a reply. On my return Saturday I found the *Outlook* of June 17, for which I imagine I am indebted to you, and in any case am much obliged by receiving.[1]

Curiously enough, the night before your letter I had been reading John Hay's letters touching the Alaskan boundary question; in which he comments that Lord H—— [Herschel] conducted the British case in the spirit of a lawyer trying to win a case, not in that of a statesman endeavoring to reach an equitable solution. "If a less able lawyer had been sent, a man of diplomatic habit of mind, he might have been able to come to an arrangement." (Vol. III, p. 142).[2]

This is to me the case in a nutshell. I had used equivalent words in the May *North American*, p. 650.[3] Government everywhere is largely in the hands of lawyers; and, like the proverbial leather of the shoemaker, in their eyes there is "nothing like law." This is singular in this country; for admirable as the ideal of law is, here the delays and subterfuges of law have brought it into much disrepute, regarded as an instrument for working purposes. And when a decision of the Supreme Court is by five to four, what moral or intellectual demand is satisfied? We rightly submit, but we are not convinced; and an unconvinced nation is in a dangerous moral frame of mind in an international contention.

As regards Asiatic immigration, has your attention been called to a new British Quarterly, the *Round Table?* The third number has just reached me. It contains an article on the Emigration question in Japan.[4] I have not had time to read thoroughly; but the gist is that neither in Manchuria nor Korea can the Japanese immigrants (there are already 15 to the square mile in Korea) contend economically with the native. What remains? Australia and America; where their economical advantage over the present occupants is greater even than their disadvantage in Asia. I presume you have noted

---

strate Mahan's careful attention to detail when a book of his was going through press. For a listing of the letters not reproduced, *see* the Index of Omitted Letters that follows this collection of letters and papers.

1. Roosevelt sent Mahan this issue because it contained a reprint of Mahan's June 2 letter to *The New York Times*. Roosevelt served as an editor of *Outlook* from 1911 to 1912.
2. John Hay, *Letters . . . and Extracts from Diary*. Washington, D.C., printed but not published, 1908.
3. In his article, "Armaments and Arbitration."
4. An unsigned article, "The Emigration Question in Japan," *The Round Table*, I, No. 3, p. 263.

the undercurrent of Japanese discontent with the latest treaty,[5] indications of which have reached the surface amid all the jubilation over our concessions. This, and the huge strides of the German Navy, should be considered seriously, by all as they are considered by you.

In one particular Sir E. Grey has helped us by enabling our government to insist upon a recognition of the Monroe Doctrine as antecedent to a Treaty of General Arbitration with any Power.

To Raymond P. Rodgers

Marshmere, Quogue, Long Island, June 19, 1911 [NWC]

My dear Rodgers: During my stay in Newport, the first proofs of the contemplated book began to arrive, and quite a number are now here.

In connection with the proof reading, it will be convenient to me to have here, at hand, the drawings or *better still*, if Little can give the time, smaller-scale sketches of the drawings now on hand and used at the lectures, of (1) the march round of a detachment of two separated army divisions, (2) the Mincio (Lonato) dispositions, (3) the illustration of different dispositions for guarding a mountain chain, or river, having several passes.

This description will enable Little to recognize just what I want. In addition it would be convenient for me to have my own lectures on Bonaparte's Italian campaign of 1796, now in the College records.

The sketches are needed only for reproduction by the draughtsmen of the publishers, and therefore need be only rough indications; yet beyond my powers of pencil expression.

To Theodore Roosevelt

Marshmere, Quogue, Long Island, June 24, 1911 [LC]

My dear Colonel Roosevelt: At the wish of the President of the War College, I am revising for publication my lectures there on Naval Strategy. I find in them the statement that in the early stages of the War with Spain "the Flying Squadron was kept in Hampton Roads mainly to assure our

---

5. The American-Japanese Treaty of Commerce and Navigation, signed February 21, 1911.

northern coast that nothing disagreeable should occur." As that squadron left for Key West within a week of my joining the Board, I had not personal knowledge of the previous deliberations of the Department; and I have thought best, before committing myself to print, to ask you whether the statement is substantially correct.

To Raymond P. Rodgers

Marshmere, Quogue, Long Island, June 26, 1911 [NWC]

My dear Rodgers: I have received the copy of my lectures on the Italian Campaign of 1796, together with the two sketches which Little kindly had made for me.

The lectures will be returned as soon as they are no longer needed for my guidance in the book now in hand.

[P.S.]   I enclose memorandum for the reproduction of the missing three passes draught, the (one) which will be needed for my next lectures.

[Enclosure]

Memorandum for Illustration of Mountain Passes

To illustrate the true and the incorrect system of protecting mountain passes, (or river fords), the most impressionist and therefore most suitable that occurs to me is:

Three passes with general mountain topographic features, well separated, and each with considerable length as compared with its width. Thus:

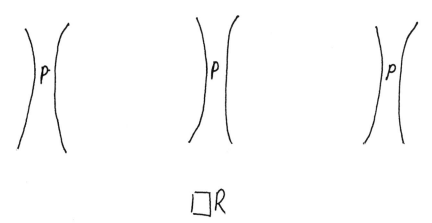

Two of this plan; differing from each other in the respect that of a total force 25 p.c. be pushed well forward (p) in each pass; 25 p.c. kept in reserve.

In the second the same pass system; with 10 p.c. of same total in each pass having in central position (reserve) remainder of force; that is 70 p.c.

The mountain features need to be emphasized in order that difficulty of any one pass coming in support to others may be obvious—impressionist.

To Theodore Roosevelt

Marshmere, Quogue, Long Island, July 1, 1911 [LC]

My dear Colonel Roosevelt: I am greatly indebted for your reply to my letter; with which I was loath to trouble you, but the information which it gives was as essential to me as it is satisfactory.[1]

I should greatly like to talk the matter over with you, but I am tied down by the necessity of reading some 150,000 words of galleys, besides the same amount in subsequent page proof; the whole complicated by some promised magazine writing. It is due the publishers that they be able to get the book out in October. I myself am adequately remunerated by being kept on duty for the particular work.

I wonder whether you ever experience the feeling I from time to time do; a tremor of responsibility for what I have done in supporting naval development and fortification of the Canal. This comes when I reflect that all will be only half done, and therefore perhaps worse than not done at all. The Democratic party in foreign relations still dwells in Jefferson's tomb; and the chairman of the House Naval Committee is a one battleship man from Tennessee, sixty years old; without antecedents and too old to change.[2] I had the satisfaction of telling the Committee[3] that the size of the battle fleet was not a naval question, but an international.

To Robert U. Johnson

Marshmere, Quogue, Long Island, July 6, 1911 [NYPL]

My dear Mr. Johnson: A South African acquaintance, Mr. L. Curtis having written me asking for my article in the June *Century*,[1] I have sent

---

1. *See* Mahan to Roosevelt, June 24, 1911. In a letter dated June 27, Roosevelt confirmed Mahan's statement about the Flying Squadron.
2. Lemuel Padgett, a Democrat.
3. Mahan testified on May 19, 1911.

1. "The Panama Canal and Sea Power in the Pacific."

him the copy kindly sent me by the *Century* at publication, and have therefore to ask you for another for myself.

I enclose Curtis's letter,[2] as well as one from a Mr. Fullerton,[3] which may interest you as Editor and may add that I have also heard from Mr. Roosevelt in equally hearty terms.[4] Mr. Curtis, I think, indeed I am sure, has been in attendance on the Imperial Conference though not probably officially; and I fear from his inquiry that the article had not got before the members.[5]

Dont trouble to return the letters, but please destroy them.

To Little, Brown and Company

Marshmere, Quogue, Long Island, July 8, 1911 [LC]

Gentlemen: I received yesterday your letter of July 6, advising me that certain maps have been forwarded. Your suggestions as to the manner of dealing with them in correcting will be carefully observed.

As regards the larger maps, there is little cause for haste. They stand by themselves, and the places to be assigned them will be determined as page proof goes on. The inserts are different. It is they alone that have prevented me from returning galleys, which I have been reading steadily.

I have now corrected, awaiting dispatch, seventy-two galleys; which by rough calculation I estimate to be about two-fifths of the complete text.

In the last galleys received, the red string, instead of being simply wound round the disk was caught by a loop. This causes trouble to the opener and is unnecessary to safety.

I am obliged to go to Newport on Monday, July 10, for further lectures. From this I hope to return here July 14; after which, as far as the present outlook goes, I shall have no further absence from home before October, and shall be able to give my continuous attention to the book with little distraction to other matters.

The roll with maps this moment received.

[P.S.] A second roll by express, also just recd.

---

2. Curtis to Mahan, June 21, 1911, in the New York Public Library.
3. W. Morton Fullerton to Mahan, Paris, June 23, 1911, in the New York Public Library, praising Mahan for his "The Panama Canal and Sea Power in the Pacific" article in *Century Magazine* (June 1911) and for his "Misrepresenting Mr. Roosevelt" in *The Outlook* (June 17, 1911).
4. Roosevelt to Mahan, June 8, 1911, in Charles C. Taylor, *Life of Admiral Mahan*, pp. 203–204.
5. *See* Mahan to Johnson, March 31, 1911.

To Clarence C. Buel

Marshmere, Quogue, Long Island, July 8, 1911 [NYPL]

Dear Mr. Buel: As I am leaving home for a week tomorrow I must confine myself at present to acknowledging receipt of the MS. sent by you.[1] I will endeavor to read it as soon as possible after my return.

To Little, Brown and Company

Marshmere, Quogue, Long Island, July 17, 1911 [LC]

Gentlemen: I have received your letter of July 14, enclosing correspondence with Sampson Low & Co., concerning republication of my contribution to their history of the Royal Navy.

There is not any money for any one, at least to any amount, in the proposed republication; but I do regret that a work I believe, on good authority, to be worthy of better results should be buried in their ponderous tomes. At the same time I wish to acknowledge, and to thank you for, the trouble you have taken in the matter.

To Charles W. Stewart

Marshmere, Quogue, Long Island, July 22, 1911 [NA]

My dear Mr. Stewart: I am sending you today by mail, in two packages, all the type written copies of Captains' & Master Commdrs' letters in my possession; and in a third envelope certain memoranda of contents of the Commdr. letters, supplied me by your kindness when I was writing *1812*.

I am going to ask the favor of Volume *I* of Corbett's *England in the Mediterranean* for a few days. It is in connection with my forthcoming book,[1] and I ask it of you rather than of the College because in summer it may probably not be in demand with you, whereas it is in the summer Conference of the College.

[P.S.] Please send book at once if possible.

---

1. Manuscript not identified.

1. *Naval Strategy*.

To Little, Brown and Company

Postcard   N.P. Probably, Quogue, Long Island, July 24 [1911] [LC]

Will you kindly instruct the person sending proofs *not* to loop the twine around the disks or elsewhere. I have asked this before; the practice is wholly unnecessary & very disconcerting to the recipient.

To Raymond P. Rodgers

Quogue, Long Island, July 26, 1911 [NWC]

My dear Rodgers: With regard to date of publication, it will depend upon myself as well as upon the publishers; for in revising I find frequently small questions of accuracy of statement arising. These at times give me much trouble, owing to the lapse of time since first written, for which reason the place to which to refer has slipped my memory. These concern almost wholly statements of facts, not material in lectures because not important to the accuracy of impression; but which in publication must be put right for the general credit of the work.

About half the rough proofs are read. The map work also is well along, and I anticipate no delay from it. I do not think there is any possibility of the book being published before October, but that very possibly it may be before November 1.

As regards the number of copies to be taken by the Department,—when proposing publication to the publishers, I communicated to them, according to your letter of December 14, 1910, that the Department had informed you that the Bureau of Navigation would like 125 copies; and that the College would take 25 *or* 30 copies. I trust the Department's order will not fall short of the number then given you.

Please ask Little, when sufficiently disengaged, to send me a copy of the "Three Passes" illustration.[1] The matter does not press immediately, because it comes very near the end of the book.

The title *Naval Strategy* is sufficiently correct. It describes the subject, but some apter idea may modify it.

---

1. Beside this sentence Rodgers wrote: "Will be ready Aug. 1."

To Little, Brown and Company

Marshmere, Quogue, Long Island, August 1, 1911 [LC]

Gentlemen: In your "statement" of July 1, received yesterday, I notice the item, 7 *Lives of Nelson* (Can) charged at 12 ½ cents,[1] while immediately above the same, (Pop), is at 60 cents. May I ask why the difference? If not an oversight, there is some reason which I would like to understand. Below, the same (Can) is at same price as the 13 *French Revolution and Empire* immediately above it.

I noticed also, in memorandum of books sent to Boone,[2] the *War of 1812* is charged at $4.80; where in the statement all copies save one are at forty cents. I am aware of the reduction in retail selling price to which I consented, and if there be any rule by which the book sent to Boone should be at the higher price, allowing me only my usual discount, I have no wish to have an exception in my case; but I have thought best to ask your attention.

To Little, Brown and Company

Marshmere, Quogue, Long Island, August 3, 1911 [LC]

Gentlemen: I will ask you to send again to Mr. J. W. Lott, 281 Fourth Av., N. Y., all my publications by you, *except* those before sent, viz: *Nelson, Sea Power on History, Sea Power in French Revolution,* and *1812.* These four, having already gone, are not to be duplicated. Mark on outside "for Boone University."

Please charge to my account and send me memorandum of prices.[1]

To Little, Brown and Company

Marshmere, Quogue, Long Island, August 3, 1911 [LC]

Gentlemen: I have recently entertained the thought of changing the title of the forthcoming book from "Naval Strategy" to "Comparative

---

1. The recipient of this letter wrote in the margin: "Large quantity on hand" and "Reg. sales in Can[ada]."
2. Boone University, Wuchang, which had the first library school in China.

1. The recipient of this letter wrote on it:

1 Types of Naval Officers	1.80	1 Some Neg. Aspects	1.12
1 Retrospect and Prospect	1.20	1 Naval Admin & Warfare	1.13
1 Interest of America	1.20	1 Harvest Within	1.12
1 War With Spain	1.20	1 Ints Amer Int Con	1.13
1 Prob. of Asia	1.20		

Strategy," with a title page to run: Comparative Strategy, (Being) a Consideration of (the) Principles Common to Warfare by Land and by Sea.

The matter of course must be settled at once, before page proof and headings go further. I will ask you therefore to give me till day after tomorrow (your Monday) for final decision.

I should be glad if you will indicate any serious disapproval, or approval, if such occur to you.

To Raymond P. Rodgers

Marshmere, Quogue, Long Island, August 5, 1911 [NWC]

My dear Rodgers: I have received Little's copy of the "Three Passes" illustration[1] for which I am much obliged. It is entirely satisfactory.

To Raymond P. Rodgers

Marshmere, Quogue, Long Island, August 5, 1911 [NWC]

My dear Rodgers: It has recently occurred to me that, instead of "Naval Strategy," "Comparative Strategy" would be a better title, more really descriptive because so much space is given to and illustration drawn from land warfare. If there be this change in title, I would have the title page read: Comparative Strategy—A Consideration of Principles Common to Warfare by Land and by Sea.

The change seems to me advisable both as conveying the contents more accurately, or comprehensively and also as carrying the suggestion to naval officers that land strategy has its claim upon their attention. The terms Comparative is of course in line with such other scientific expressions as Comparative Anatomy, Comparative Philology.

The question of title I presume is much at my own discretion, but before decision I should be glad to hear if you see any objecton.[1]

---

1. *See* Mahan to Rodgers, June 26, 1911.

1. The full title finally settled upon was *Naval Strategy, Compared and Contrasted With the Principles of Military Operations on Land.*

To Theodore Roosevelt

Marshmere, Quogue, Long Island, August 11, 1911 [LC]

My dear Colonel Roosevelt: I have read very carefully, though without the advantage of legal training, the articles of the Treaty of General Arbitration with Great Britain.

1. If the Senate confirm the Treaty,[1] it retains control in any future case only over the special agreement; and, as to that, not as to its being made at all, but as to its terms. The Editorial of the *New York Times* of August 8, favorable to the Treaty, shows the cloudiness of its terms.

As I read them, the Senate parts forever with its power of advice and consent as to the determination whether a particular question is "justiciable." This power is by the terms of the Treaty transferred to the Joint High Commission of Inquiry. I doubt whether the Senate has the constitutional right thus to limit constitutional powers over international agreements, even its own; but in any event ought its decision to be rushed by popular demand for immediate action, which, if in the present session, cannot but be precipitate?

2. Great Britain reserves the right to obtain the concurrence of any self-governing dominion whose interests are involved. The cases of a self-governing dominion and of a group of our states are not on all fours. Nevertheless, as the protection to a minority, ought there not to be some security that a strong sectional interest, such as that of the Pacific Coast as to Asiatic immigration, should be safeguarded. Article II provides that the Joint High Commission shall be six, Americans three. The Pacific coast could hardly have more than one; while, if all but one of the six decide that the question is justiciable, the decision stands. The Senate is impotent over this decision.

3. These considerations do not affect greatly, if at all, the pending treaty, because with Great Britain we have so much in common. But the question arises whether we can refuse a treaty in similar terms with another country, without making an invidious distinction. In view of Germany's recent action in Africa, could we risk the Monroe Doctrine to a treaty of General Arbitration with her? Sir Edward Grey has already endorsed the Doctrine in words that should be noted, but which are not in the treaty. "It is a postulate of any successful arbitration treaty of an extended kind that there should be no possibility of conflict between the national policies of the nations which are party to it." Asiatic immigration seems to me much less probably justiciable than the Doctrine. The latter to my mind is right, in policy and in morals, but without a shred of legal right.

---

1. The Treaty, signed August 3, was ratified by the Senate on March 7, 1912; but in an amended form that excluded the Monroe Doctrine and Oriental immigration control from its coverage.

4. What I particularly deplore is the attempt to press the Senate to hasty action; for that not only fetters its due regard to its own responsibility, emasculating its functions, but precludes national discussion. All responsibility and power is thus placed in the hands of the negotiators of the Treaty, and taken away from Senate *and people.*

Obstruction on the part of the Senate is one thing, reasonable deliberation another. Few now regret the Senate's rejection of the first Hay-Pauncefote Treaty.

To Raymond P. Rodgers

Marshmere, Quogue, Long Island, August 12, 1911 [NWC]

My dear Rodgers: Yours of the 8th was duly received with enclosure; copy of Department Letter that 125 copies would be ordered.

I have decided to adhere to the title *Naval Strategy,* and expect this decision to be final. The publishers are Little, Brown & Co. of Boston.

I am finding the drawing representing the Archduke Charles' campaign of 1796 somewhat perplexing, and should be helped if the Library can spare me for a week the volume of Jomini's *Guerres de la Révolution,* which contains this operation; and also the Archduke Charles' own narrative. I have the drawing substantially finished, but am a little doubtful as to some questions of numbers, on which Hamley is unsatisfactory.

To Charles W. Stewart

Marshmere, Quogue, Long Island, August 16, 1911 [LC]

My dear Mr. Stewart: I return today by mail the volume of Corbett on the Mediterranean which you kindly lent me.

I am sorry to infer from your last that I may have neglected to acknowledge also the Congressional documents you sent me, notably Hobson's Bill.[1] If so, I can now only express my regrets and apologize.

---

1. Richmond Pearson Hobson, *Fortification Bill.* Speech of Hon. Richmond P. Hobson in the House of Representatives, Thursday, February 18, 1909. Washington, D.C.: U.S. Government Printing Office, 1909.

To Theodore Roosevelt

Marshmere, Quogue, Long Island, August 25, 1911 [LC]

My dear Colonel Roosevelt: I cannot very well write on the subject of the Treaties[1] to the *Outlook*, because I am under an engagement to furnish a half-dozen articles to the *North American*, the third of which, Navies as a Diplomatic Factor, appears in September.[2] It is true, I have much liberty in the choice of my subjects, but these was an express wish that I should consider Arbitration, and therefore, while I may not touch upon the treaties at all, if I do the *N.A.* has a mortgage upon me.

Moreover, I am getting out a book upon Naval Strategy which will probably be my last magnum opus, and which therefore requires so much of my time that I have with difficulty met the promise to the *N.A.*

Curiously, I find more satisfactory accounts of the attitude towards the treaties in the London *Times* than in my own paper—the *N.Y. Times*.

May I make one suggestion? The Senate is spoken of as clinging to its "privileges," "prerogatives," "rights." Is not duty the same word? The Senators may be wrongheaded, but surely they have a duty.

To Little, Brown and Company

Marshmere, Quogue, Long Island, September 29, 1911 [LC]

Gentlemen: As proof reading draws to an end I am prompted to ask you about an Index.

I am preparing constantly a table of "Contents" such as is prefixed to all my Sea Power works; but as regards Index I feel convinced that, if I prepare it, I can not begin till after proof reading is over, in which case I am sure I cannot finish in less than three weeks—probably four.

I have understood that Indexing is something of a profession; and while an author should know his book better than others, I feel so much less power for work of that kind than I did ten, or even five, years ago, that I should undertake the task with considerable doubts as to my rate of progress.[1]

The "Contents" are to me a much more satisfactory presentation of what a book has than an Index; but public opinion seems to demand the latter.

---

1. The arbitration treaties with Great Britain and France negotiated by the Taft Administration in 1911.
2. "Navies as International Factors," *North American Review* (September 1911).

1. The company decided to employ a professional indexer. *See* Mahan to Little, Brown and Company, October 21, 1911.

To Stanley C. Hughes[1]

N.P., N.D. Probably, Quogue, Long Island, September 1911[2]

I have read with interest and profound sympathy the pronouncement of yourself and your brother clergy of Newport on the subject of the non-observance of Sunday, so rapidly increasing among us as a people.

You will expect criticism, the type of which is familiar to us. I beg to express to you my own strong personal admiration of the stand openly taken and my deep conviction of the imminent necessity for it.

To Stephen B. Luce

Marshmere, Quogue, Long Island, October 17, 1911 [LC]

My dear Admiral: A petition such as your letter suggests, could be made only through, or by consent of, the Navy Department. I doubt whether the Department would be willing to take a step which would open again a fatiguing controversy, into which it must inevitably be drawn.

The present Government, without entering upon the old vexed question, has done things recently which would rather incline it—commit it—to the Schley side, if controversy arose. The President sent a strong telegram of sympathy, which conveyed a meaning beyond bare sympathy. Whether by his direction, or of its own motion, the Department brought the Academy battalion to attend the funeral,[1]—a colossal endorsement, though perhaps not so intended. Dewey's influence, which is great, would be on the same side.

I doubt if anything would be made out of the proposed step. The crucial point against Schley, perfectly compromising when fully realized, is his famous telegram about coal compelling him to return to Key West, [which] conflicts with the finding of the Court that his coal reports were "inaccurate and misleading." As one of Dewey's best officers said to me, cowardice is a lighter charge than that. I think upon reference it will be found that Dewey signed this finding, although his prepossessions and conduct in the case were astounding.

The petition might result in vindicating Sampson's fair claim, but I greatly doubt it. I know if I were the Government, I would refuse to re-open

---

1. Rector of Trinity Episcopal Church, Newport.
2. Excerpt from a letter from Mahan to Hughes, as published in the *Monthly Notes* of Trinity Church, and quoted in *The New York Times*, October 3, 1911, p. 6.

1. The funeral of Admiral Schley, who died of apoplexy on a New York City street on October 2, 1911.

the case, and a petition to the Senate will be to reopen it. It is another matter if public recognition of Schley's supposed merits be attempted. That would probably also re-open the question, but the onus would then be on the other side.

To Stephen B. Luce

Marshmere, Quogue, Long Island, October 20, 1911 [LC]

My dear Admiral: I do not take in the *North American*, and therefore do not see every number, although I have written for it this year. In consequence I did not see your October article[1] until yesterday, at my club in New York. I had not understood that by "the victor of Santiago" you meant Sampson, for I had never heard that *his* courage had been questioned, and I understood your last letter to apply the phrase "sarcastic like" to Schley, upon whose courage I had heard aspersions more than once.

I still think that a petition to the Senate would have to be made by consent of, probably also through the Department; but it would not entail the re-opening of the Sampson-Schley dispute, which was the principal reason I had for anticipating a demurrer on the part of the Administration. Applied to Schley, that effect would have followed, in my opinion.[2]

To Little, Brown and Company

Quogue, Long Island, October 21, 1911 [LC]

Gentlemen: On arriving home night before last, I found that the Card Index had arrived that day. Yesterday and to-day I have been able to go through exactly one half of it, pretty thoroughly; but I find as I go on a tendency to note oversights.

Upon the whole it is quite satisfactory; and I think I shall be able to send you the whole on Tuesday the 24th, revised and corrected. I had purposed sending the half to day, if I had finished it; as I actually have. But one or two instances of omissions, detected as I turned over the pages for purpose of verification, led me to conclude it would be better to keep the whole till finished.

Considering the very technical character of the book, and the unusual

---

1. Stephen B. Luce, "The Spanish American War," *North American* (October 1911).
2. On the bottom of this letter Luce wrote: "Next move?"

difficulty which the author himself has experienced in keeping it in mind for Index purposes, I consider the indexer has done well; and the employment of one has certainly much accelerated completion.

The "Contents" proof will be returned Monday together with "Preface." There is little correction in either.

With reference to change on Title Page, suggested in yours of Oct 19, I am quite willing, as far as *form* goes; but as I have held steadily to the title "Captain" as a *titre de plume*, under which I gained my reputation, I prefer to retain it, instead of Admiral.

In sending the Index, I purpose to put it in such shape that the proof reading may be done in Boston, as you desire. It will need great care, however.

[Enclosure]

Naval Strategy
Compared and Contrasted
with
The Principles and Practice
of
Military Operations on Land

Lectures delivered at U.S. Naval War College, Newport, R.I.,
between the years 1887 and 1911
by
&c   &c   &c

N.B. I leave of course the particular arrangement in your hands. I think my name need be followed by only the Sea Power Books (including *1812*) and perhaps *Nelson*.

To Little, Brown and Company

Quogue, Long Island, October 23, 1911 [LC]

Gentlemen: With reference to the sentence on enclosed page,[1] which you have queried, the nominative of the verb "has been pursued" is the relative pronoun "which" that immediately precedes. "Which" itself is either singular or plural; but this particular "which" refers to the word that precedes it —"that"—and it is the singular "that" that governs the following verb as to number.

Apparently, the impression has been that "which" here refers to "studies." Evidently it does not; and the singular "that" was adhered to by me because

---

1. Enclosure not found.

it refers to the one single particular "study" of the Gulf and Caribbean. That study is cited simply as an illustration of the class of studies, of which it is one, and which as a class are recommended to military students.

To Raymond P. Rodgers

Marshmere, Quogue, Long Island, October 25, 1911 [NWC]

My dear Rodgers: The permission to move to New York was sent to me direct. I transmit it for your information, and for dating the vouchers for quarters.

The last proof of the book—Contents and Index—are now out of my hands, on the way to the publishers. The latter expect to publish in November, the exact date as yet not known to me. It has to be fixed with reference to English copyright, to which simultaneous publication is necessary.

I shall return to-day or to-morrow the copies of the Lectures now in my hands, together with my other lectures on Bonaparte in Italy, 1796, all of which belong to the College archives.

To Bouverie F. Clark

Marshmere, Quogue, Long Island, October 27, 1911 [LC]

My dear Clark: It was very pleasant to receive your congratulations upon my birthday; although the rapid passage of time which you speak of makes these frequent recurrences of annual milestones rather ominous, when one has gone by as many as I have. I dont know whether you know Boswell's *Johnson* as well as you ought. If you do you will remember that that old gentleman, who bitterly disliked the very mention of death, consistently resented any reminder of it by notice being taken to him of his birthday. I dont feel that way, however; and am glad to have them remembered.

I think I am substantially as well as when I last wrote you, but I have been under a good deal of pressure to complete a book on Naval Strategy by a fixed time, and this has reacted upon me unfavorably for the moment. Six weeks ago I got to sleeping very badly, & seemed approaching that condition which it is the fashion to speak of as nervous exhaustion. The doctor knocked me off tea & coffee, and I have gradually pulled together again. The last proofs have been read, thank goodness; the rest of the job belongs to the bookmakers, &, while I have work enough on hand, it is of manageable proportions, and I shall be cautious how I get in a like scrape again.

I have followed your national difficulties with interest not unmixed with apprehension. To us Americans, with our written Constitution, fixed two chambers, and a Supreme Court to decide what is constitutional and what not, the emasculating of the Upper Chamber and absence of any standard as final authority to settle constitutional questions seems a very hazardous condition. I trust the political instinct and fitness of your countrymen in general will prove equal to the emergency.

As regards Reciprocity, I understand the economical question too little to be glad or sorry. Otherwise, if it really means a strong tie between Canada & you in the future, I am well pleased. My view for a dozen years or more has been that it was our interest that Canada should remain British, because the Canadian Pacific slope will tend to keep you right (in my view) on the Japanese question. My sympathies with our own side were somewhat alienated at the beginning by the "slopping over" of the President and the Speaker of our lower House.[1] The first was inadvertent, when he spoke of Canada being at the parting of the ways, but statesmen are not permitted inadvertencies. The Speaker was blatant, talking about annexation. I suspect him of having drinks aboard when he said it, not from specific knowledge of the particular incident, but from a few days association with him some years ago. Both remarks were capital campaign material for Borden[2] and his party. Like yourself, I have little confidence in the imperial feeling of Canadians. They are suffering from swelled head just now, and I think more inclined to independence than to cooperation. Annexation in any shape is out of the question, and I think few here want it. I dont, because I dont admire them. Australia and New Zealand will remain true as long as they feel the need of the connection & that will be for a long while.

I expect to spend this winter in New York, but this place is my permanent address, and I trust our home while I live. We are all well and happy here. Neither the heat nor the drought troubled us much here, though the country at large suffered as you did. I bathed every day in the sea, which greatly refreshed me, and despite my 71 years did eight or ten miles on the bicycle four or five days in the week. I suppose you never took up that form of exercise, living in London, and I remember you were a little uncertain about a knee in the old days. Here our bicycles are at the door like so many horses every day, and we go on them everywhere—church, postoffice, beach, friends and all. It is also for me a standard of strength. The long rides of five years ago I never take now, & my long rides are those which then were daily.

1. J. Beauchamp ("Champ") Clark, who saw the 1911 American-Canadian Reciprocity Treaty as a step toward American annexation of Canada.
2. Sir Robert Laird Borden, leader of the Conservative Party and Prime Minister of Canada, 1911–1920.

For bathing I am nearly where I used to be, & go in colder water, remaining as long or longer. Your indisposition to move I share, but conditions compel me as they dont you. We even talked of going to Europe this year but I dont think it will come off. With much regard [etc.].

To Little, Brown and Company

Quogue, Long Island, October 28, 1911 [LC]

Gentlemen: According to my habit, I enclose a communication received from the Funk and Wagnall's Company.[1]

The article in question[2] appears under copyright in *Naval Administration and Warfare*. Personally, I am not disposed to concede republication of a part, only; and especially without remuneration, but would like your opinion as a matter of policy. It will be remembered that not long ago we refused such permission to Mr. Reinsch, in another book.

An ex-justice (retired) of the U.S. Supreme Court wrote me two years ago that the article contained in compact form *all* that the ordinary man needed to know about the Monroe Doctrine.

To Little, Brown and Company

University Club, New York, October 31, 1911 [LC]

Gentlemen: On and after November 7, my address will be Hotel Collingwood, 45 West 35th St, New York City.[1]

With partial reference to this change of address, and the fewer facilities I shall have there than in a house of my own, I write to ask if it will be practicable to send me fly leaves for half a dozen copies of *Naval Strategy*, on which I could write the names &c of persons to whom I propose to give them. These could then be bound in corresponding volumes of the ten to be furnished me, and by you dispatched by mail to the addresses, which I will give you.

I think you obliged me by doing this in the case of *1812*; and I shall

---

1. Enclosure not found.
2. "The Monroe Doctrine."

1. The Collingwood was a new apartment hotel. The Mahans occupied quarters on the ninth floor during the winter of 1911–1912.

esteem it a favor, if it can be so arranged now. I will add that, if so, I will on notification send you the addresses from Quogue, and I should be glad if I could receive the said fly leaves there.

[Enclosure]

Addresses for special copies of
Naval Strategy, sent by the Author

1. Rear Admiral S. B. Luce
   15 Francis St
   Newport, R.I.

2. Rear Admiral R.P. Rodgers
   Naval War College
   Newport R.I.

3. Captain W. McCarty Little
   Naval War College
   Newport, R.I.

4. General William Crozier
   War Department
   Washington, D.C.

5. General Leonard Wood
   War Department
   Washington, D.C.

6. Sir J. K. Laughton
   9 Pepys Road
   Wimbledon, England

7. F. Leonard Brown Esq, M.D.
   4 Rue d'Orléans
   Pau, France

3 copies to A.T. Mahan, Hotel Collingwood, New York.

To Little, Brown and Company

Quogue, Long Island, November 2, 1911 [LC]

Gentlemen: On returning from New York last night I found the Index proof. I return it herewith, under usual wrap. I have found corrections necessary or desirable on the following galleys: Nos. 1, 6, 8, 9, 10, 11, 13, 15, 16, 17, 19, 20. Though on so many sheets they do not aggregate very numerous, and are mostly proof reading oversights. These should be corrected, in any case. Others, if too much trouble may be omitted. Macauley, J. B. is rather a bad break for T.B.

I have marked each of my corrections thus X to catch the eye more readily.

As regards the Funk and Wagnall's business, I will leave that in your hands with the following provisos: (1) Not less than $25; (2) to be acknowledged to the book *Naval Administration and Warfare*; without prejudice, should they so desire, to naming *National Review*; (3) in no sense to interfere with my full possession of copyright to use hereafter in any way it may seem expedient.

To Little, Brown and Company

Quogue, Long Island, November 6, 1911 [LC]

Gentlemen: I have received what appears to be the final page proof of the Index. In looking over it, I find embodied corrections submitted by me in the galley reading. I note, however, three slight errors of spelling

1. P. 464, column 2, line next to bottom "practi*c*e" in text is changed to practi*s*e; whereas on p. 470, col. 2, line 10, "practi*s*e" in text is changed to practi*c*e. The two should be uniform. These are two of the three.

2. P. 469, Col. 1, lines 27 & 28, I cannot tell whether the mis-spelling "Strage*t*ic" is properly notified to printer. Probably it is, but being in doubt I mention it.

To the Editor of the New York Evening Post

New York, November 8, 1911[1]

I am indebted to Mr. Crammond Kennedy for drawing attention, in your issue of November 7,[2] to the inexactness of my words concerning the fortification of the Panama Canal and the action of the United States Senate in relation thereto. The authority which I consulted seemed so to affirm my then impression that I accepted the conclusion too hastily.

Nevertheless, after more careful consideration, I still think that, to repeat my words, "the Senate prevented the nation from committing itself to a

---

1. From the *New York Evening Post*, November 11, 1911.
2. Crammond Kennedy, "Admiral Mahan and the Canal," letter to the Editor of the *New York Evening Post*, Washington, D.C., November 6, 1911, published November 7, 1911.

treaty which might have proved extremely awkward at the present moment, and that the Senate of 1900 saved the situation for 1911."

What are the facts? The Executive of 1900 sent to the Senate for ratification a treaty containing, among other stipulations, the clause that "no fortifications should be erected commanding the canal or the waters adjacent." This clause was seventh, and last, of a number of "rules," which the treaty provided for the observance of the neutrality of the Canal; with the expressed intention of following the provisions in an already existing convention for the neutralization of the Suez Canal. In this treaty there was no reservation of a right for the United States to defend in any way a property of large value, and of a specific national importance exceeding by far the interest of any other one nation.

In this treaty the Senate made three changes: One introduced a sentence providing that the Clayton-Bulwer treaty should be superseded by the new treaty. The second struck out a provision that any other Powers might be invited to adhere to the treaty. This emphasized that the matter was not one of general interest, but specifically American, requiring arrangement with Great Britain only because of the Clayton-Bulwer treaty, under which the nation had chafed for some time. The third change was an insertion introduced after and under rule five of the seven:

> It is agreed, however, that none of the immediately foregoing conditions and stipulations in sections (rules) numbered one, two, three, four, and five of this article, shall apply to measures which the United States may find it necessary to take for securing by its own forces the defence of the United States and the maintenance of public order.

With the changes mentioned the Senate ratified the treaty, *retaining* the clause forbidding the erection of fortifications. Here was my error, properly noted by Mr. Kennedy. Great Britain refused to accept the changes; and, consequently, the treaty fell, owing to the Senate's action.

Undiscouraged by this rejection, the Executive of the United States resumed negotiations, in which its course was evidently influenced by the attitude of the Senate already shown, and probably also by a clearer understanding, through conversations, of what was necessary in order to command the support of the Senate indispensable to success. The changes introduced consequently reflected those made by the Senate in the first treaty. The Clayton-Bulwer treaty was specifically superseded by a distinct article; not merely by an incidental phrase, as in the previous Senate amendment. The invitation to other nations to adhere not only was omitted, but particular care was taken to mould the phraseology so as not in any way even to imply an invitation. Thus the British words "all nations which shall agree ... to observe these rules," was altered by Mr. Hay to "all nations observing these rules." The influence of the Senate's action is clear.

[431]

As regards the question of fortification, the mere omission in the second treaty of the forbiddal in the first is significant; but the intention of the contracting parties, which is decisive in cases of doubt, and the recognition of that intention by the British government, appear conclusively from a passage in a memorandum, dated August 3, 1901, drawn up by Lord Lansdowne, then British minister of foreign affairs. The italics are mine:

> I [have] pointed out the dangerous ambiguity of an instrument (the treaty as approved by the Senate) of which one clause permitted the adoption of defensive measures, while another prohibited the erection of fortifications. It is most important that no doubt should exist as to the *intention* of the contracting parties. As to this, I *understood* that by the omission of all reference to the matter of defence the United States government *desire to reserve* the power of taking measures to protect the canal, at any time when the United States may be at war, from destruction or damage at the hands of an enemy or enemies. On the other hand, I *conclude that*, with the above exception, *there is no intention to derogate from the principles of neutrality laid down by the rules*. As to the first of these propositions, I am not prepared to deny that contingencies may arise when not only from a national point of view, but on behalf of the commercial interests of the whole world, it might be of supreme importance to the United States that they should be free to adopt measures for the defence of the canal at a moment when they themselves were engaged in hostilities.

From these words the reason of the omission of all mention of defence or fortifications in the second treaty appears, and that the British government acquiesced in it. It appears also that the British government recognized that measures of defence do not necessarily mean disregard of obligations of neutrality. The omission therefore concedes implicitly—it might be said explicitly—the right to take measures of defence. The difficulty of avoiding ambiguity appears again in that it is not perfectly clear from Lord Lansdowne's words whether such measures are to be taken only when danger arises, or whether is implied previous preparation, which will meet such a movement better than impromptu measures, and may even avert danger altogether. In reason, however, there can be no doubt. Measures of defence cannot be postponed to the hour of emergency. A nation which sees it needs a fleet cannot wait until war to build; neither can it so wait for passive defence, of which fortification is an incident.

It appears from the above that my original statement, though faulty in an important particular, is essentially correct. The power to protect the Panama Canal was signed away by the Executive, without reservation. The Senate introduced a reservation, which was partial in that it disallowed a very essential element—that of preparation. The discussion which preceded the second treaty evidently developed appreciation, and cleared the minds of all parties; affecting their action, even though it may not have changed all personal opinions. The new treaty was framed under a clear understanding by the British government that, by "omission of all reference to the matter of defence, the United States desired to reserve the power to take such measures," and this result was obtained by the interposition of the Senate, even though for the moment that body failed to see that preparation beforehand—in this case by fortification—is as essential as any steps taken, perhaps hurriedly, in a moment of emergency.

To the Editor of The New York Times

New York, November 21, 1911[1]

In the *Evening Post* of Nov. 18 I observe that the American Peace and Arbitration League has asked clergymen of all denominations throughout the country to observe Nov. 26 as "Unity Sunday," preaching in each church a sermon dealing with the arbitration treaties between the United States and Great Britain and France, now pending in the Senate. It is believed by the League that these treaties "stand in grave danger of failure of ratification, and that these special services should be held to urge the necessity of favorable action." Responses already show a marked willingness on the part of the clergy to support these arbitration treaties. There follows a long list of clergy of this city, who will have such services.

The movement thus avowedly is for the Church to bring pressure to bear upon the State, in the matter of an action which is committed to the State, and is not committed to the Church. In other words, the Church is to be used as an instrument of political agitation. To habitual churchgoers like myself the question arises, what are we to hear in this matter from those set to teach us in spiritual things? If it be in favor of arbitration in the general, the Senate accepts the principle; but if it be to favor the ratification of the clause to which the Senate is believed to object, the pronouncement of the clergy will be upon a subject on which very distinguished constitutional lawyers differ, and upon which the clergy, as such, are not competent instructors, and have no authority to teach.

As generally known, there is between the Executive and the Senate a distinct issue of opinion concerning these treaties, as framed. The Executive negotiated and sustains them. Of the fifteen members of the Senate Committee, the large majority recommended the omission of a clause

---

1. From *The New York Times*, November 24, 1911, p. 12. Published also in the *New York Evening Post*, November 23, 1911.

which in their judgment involved a delegation to others of duties imposed upon the Senate by the Constitution. One only of the committee approved unconditionally. Two assented with a very serious proviso.

As to the correctness of these several opinions, I offer no view of my own. I am not an expert; I recognize the fact, and likewise that there is not laid upon me any duty to take action, as there is upon each Senator. But neither is any such duty laid upon the Church, and she exceeds her legitimate functions, and so do the individual clergy, when, as Church or as clergy, they endeavor to bring pressure to bear upon the State in its own divinely appointed sphere. To use its Master's expression, the Church is intruding into the things of Caesar, the temporal power of His day.

The rashness as well as the impropriety of this step is evident from the fact that neither Church nor clergy, as such, have any expert knowledge, and that experts outside of the Executive and the Senate differ widely. John Bassett Moore, than whom is no higher authority on public law, thinks the disputed clause constitutional. (The *Independent*, August 17.) Mr. Root, Secretary of State under Mr. Roosevelt, also considers it constitutional, yet thinks advisable to introduce a proviso which very seriously modifies the scope of arbitration. Richard Olney, Secretary of State under Mr. Cleveland, discussing the general subject, and analyzing specifically Mr. Root's proposition, concludes that with such "a rider" it is doubtful whether the treaty would be worth ratifying; yet he holds that the Senate cannot constitutionally assent to the clause against which the majority of the Senate reported. (*Independent*, Sept. 21.)

We are used to experts differing. Nevertheless, attention should fasten on the fact that the question before the country is not the advisability of extending arbitration as far as wisely can be done. On this all agree. The question is the wisdom of a particular extension, and whether the method adopted is consistent with the Constitution of the United States. On such a question the Church has no commission to speak, and no competent knowledge. The attempt of the clergy to do so is simply an intrusion into the sphere of the State, recalling the Calvinistic theocracy of Geneva and early New England, and the monstrous claims of the mediaeval Church to decide whether citizens owed allegiance to this ruler or to that.

As a life-long communicant of the Protestant Episcopal Church, I have grieved greatly to see that the Diocesan Convention of New York has ventured thus to pronounce in its representative capacity. It has passed a resolution approving the treaties and asking that the Senate ratify them. This was no general approval of arbitration on Christian grounds—itself of doubtful propriety—but a specific indorsement of the specific method. The introducer, replying to an objection, said that Mr. Root's proviso removed all danger. (*The Churchman*, Nov. 18.)

All the members of that convention, clergy and lay, are citizens as well as churchmen. As citizens it is not only their privilege, but their right, and may be their duty, to do their utmost to forward any measure of public policy that commends itself to their judgment. But when they assume—as they have—to take such action as representative of the Church, they usurp power. They do that for which they have no commission from God or man. They have constituted the Church—whom at the moment they represented —a ruler and a judge in a purely secular matter; and they have done so without excuse of necessity, for as citizens they could have got together during or after convention, and taken the same action while distinctly disavowing representative capacity. As representative, the action was really null; for not only had they no commission for it from their constituency, but that constituency, the Church at large in the diocese, was incompetent to authorize their course. The source of the Church's authority is not the people, but Jesus Christ, and He never gave the Church, nor himself assumed such powers. "Who made me a ruler and a judge?"

To Theodore Roosevelt

University Club, New York, December 2, 1911 [LC]

My dear Colonel Roosevelt: I send you the clipping from the *Globe* of which I spoke to you last night. It came to me through Romeike[1] enclosing it, with a request for my custom (I had not seen it myself); and it would have gone to Mr. Lodge three days ago, but that I had mislaid it for the moment. I hope therefore its history is providentially ordered to draw your attention to what in my mind is one of the worst and most dangerous features of the approaching organized agitation,[2] viz: the attempt to coerce the Senate into acting in accordance with popular demonstration, irrespective of their convictions.

The Globe, as you know, favors the treaties as they stand, and with somewhat brutal candor states the object of agitation. But while a representative body exists to carry out the matured will of its constituency in matters, legally proper, it ceases to be truly representative when it neglects to give to matters of public right the close attention which individual citizens cannot give; and which they therefore perforce turn over to representative agents. If the Senate without conviction, or against conviction, yields in such a matter to popular pressure, it is false to its representative duty.

The more I think, the more certain I am that the Monroe Doctrine is "justiciable," that is that there are settled principles and precedents in in-

---

1. A British clipping service. Enclosure not found.
2. *See* Mahan to Roosevelt, December 13, 1911, Footnote 2.

ternational law which apply; and they apply against the Doctrine. If this be so, the Commission of Inquiry must so decide, if honest; and equally arbitrators when it comes before them must decide against the U.S. This alone, if correct, condemns the treaty as it stands.

I purpose asking your acceptance of a copy of my last book *Naval Strategy*. I dont bank on the strategic part particularly, but there are obiter dicta which I do value. Chiefly that Asiatic immigration is against the spirit of the Monroe D.; because, as they dont assimilate, they colonize, and virtually annex. Permitted, the Pacific slope would be an Asiatic territory in twenty years.

To Little, Brown and Company

University Club, New York, December 4, 1911 [LC]

Gentlemen: I have received and beg to thank you for the three copies of *Naval Strategy* sent to 45 West 35th. I appreciate also your thoughtfulness in inserting in two of them a leaf suited for writing upon.

With regard to the extra charges for changing in text after setting up I have been surprised at the total amount,[1] because I believe the changes to have been chiefly in the galleys, in which in general practice I have had in all quarters a free hand to change; while in the page proof of *Naval Strategy* I took particular care not to involve the pagination, but to preserve it as it stood. The whole matter, however, is somewhat foreign to my experience, having no knowledge of the printer's trade, and I can only accept the result with this expression of my surprise.

Will you kindly inform me whether you wish me to remit the sum due now, or allow it to go to the next semi annual accounting.

In closing, I desire to thank you for your kindness in forwarding to their destination the other complimentary copies.

To the Editor of The New York Times

New York, December 7, 1911[1]

In its editorial columns of Sunday, Dec. 3, *The Times* gives a partial synopsis and a eulogy of a recent address by Secretary of State Knox before the American Society for Judicial Settlement of International Disputes.

Upon that address and its arguments, if before me in full, I should be

---

1. $258.30.

1. From *The New York Times*, December 8, 1911, p. 12.

incompetent to express an opinion, which is not quite the same thing as incompetent to form one. But while recognizing the merits of Mr. Knox, is it impossible in an editorial article to be courteous to the Senate because it has differed from him, and perhaps may continue to differ? Such expressions as "utter futility," "Jingo Senator," "strange objectors," applied to men of the position and calibre of those who have criticized the treaties do not contribute to elucidation, while to the thoughtless part of the public they convey an impression of mere stupid obstructiveness on the part of the Senate, which it may be said that the facts do not warrant.

Most objectionable, however, are the closing words of the article: "This is the argument which the Senate will have to consider before the session closes. We do not believe that it will venture to disregard it." To tell a body of men that they will not venture to do this or that will, with the average man, arouse a strong disposition to do it. But the worst of the expression is that the natural implication to the thoughtless is that the Senate wishes to do wrong and must be coerced into doing right.

It is not too much to say that, though we have not yet the referendum, an equivalent attempt is being made to override by popular outcry the representative character of the Senate: to compel it to yield to clamor, a question not of simple popular will, but one of construction upon which the people generally have not the training nor the time to form competent opinion. We need representative government just because the people cannot in such points decide expertly for themselves; consequently a representative body which allows its judgment to be forced on a matter of strict construction is false to its duty. The fact is disregarded that the questions raised by the majority report of the Senate are so nice that one former Secretary of State, Mr. Root, has thought it advisable to introduce a provision, making for a clearer exposition of the understanding with which the United States enters into the treaties, while another former Secretary, Mr. Olney, considers the proposed delegation of the Senate's powers unconstitutional.

In general expression, the utterances of those who speak or write on this subject imply a conviction that the Senate as a body is motived by a mere desire to assert itself and its privileges. There is another and very different side, little emphasized or even noted. The Senate has a duty imposed by the Constitution, and it has a right to be thought honest until it is shown to be otherwise. In the past the Senate has interposed most usefully. In 1900, in consequence of its action, there was preserved the right to fortify the Panama Canal, desired and exerted by the present Administration, which was abandoned by the treaty then submitted to the Senate for approval. It is possible that the Senate may be right now; but in any event the points raised are such as require calm discussion and clear conclusions, such as Mr. Knox has contributed; but this end is not furthered by denunciation, nor by mass meetings, nor by public dinners.

To an Unidentified Addressee

45 West 35th Street, New York, December 11, 1911 [NWC]

I do not know who the officer is, copy of whose miniature you have sent me. There is something familiar about the face, but I think a kind of generic likeness runs through portraits of the period.

You cannot do better as far as I know, than to refer to the British Admiralty, Whitehall, London; unless possibly to Mr. J. K. Laughton of the United Service Institution who knows more about such matters than probably any man in England. Upon the whole, of the two, I would try the Admiralty.

To Theodore Roosevelt

University Club, New York, December 13, 1911 [LC]

My dear Col. Roosevelt: I am much obliged for the copy of Low's letter which you have been kind enough to send me. It happened that he had himself sent me a copy, but I am none the less obliged for your thoughtfulness in the matter. It is to be regretted that it did not find more place in the *daily* Press, for the people, at least the loudest talkers, seem bent upon going it blind in this matter.[1] I was glad to see in the list of intending speakers last night fewer "eminent citizens" than I had feared might show up on the platform.[2]

To Bouverie F. Clark

University Club, New York, December 15, 1911 [LC]

My dear Clark: I send you a line of Christmas and New Years good wishes, trusting that all is well with you and will so continue during the year before us. We ourselves are all in good case and spending this winter

---

1. Debate on the Arbitration Treaties with Britian and France, 1911–1912.
2. On December 12, a mass meeting at Carnegie Hall under the auspices of the Citizens' National Committee, of which Joseph H. Choate was chairman, to support ratification of the arbitration treaties with Great Britain and France, was broken up by German sympathizers led by Alphonse G. Koelble. Choate, Colonel Henry Watterson and Nicholas Murray Butler had already spoken, but Carnegie could not be heard through the pro-German interference. Choate was obliged to close the meeting. Among the organizers were Butler, Frederic R. Coudert, J. P. Morgan, Chauncey M. Depew, William McAdoo, J. B. Moore, Oscar Straus, and others. (*The New York Times*, December 13, 1911, p. 1.)

in the city for the first time in six years; having taken a small apartment in one of the big apartment dwellings that are springing up all over the town. The position is very central; indeed rather below than above the present center of the shopping district which determines so much in a woman's preference as to localities. Our former house in 86th Street was not only much above, but a good deal to one side; so that although we had excellent public conveyance the ladies found going back and forth troublesome both as to visits and shops. Being in the ninth story the air is much better than the street, though not as good as our old house; and though the quarters are relatively contracted they are good enough and excellent taste. I personally am enjoying a comparative rest from the grind under which I worked until Oct. 15, when the last proofs of my latest book *Naval Strategy* were completed. I have enough to do still, but no pressure. I did not send you a copy for I did not see why you should be bored reading—or thinking you ought to read—a book which is not interesting, and which I myself had come to loathe.

I dont know whether you agree, but I thought Sir. E. Grey's speech[1] (Nov. 2) one of the very best I ever read. I hope things may now go smoother, but I think there is more trouble ahead everywhere than our ignorant optimists believe.

Again wishing good luck [etc.].

To Theodore Roosevelt

University Club, New York, December 23, 1911 [LC]

My dear Colonel Roosevelt: The Senate passed the resolution during the last month or six weeks of your second term.[1] My impression is that it was a joint resolution, and that you procured its suppression in the House by omission. I was much concerned and wrote to Sperry, who was just back, suggesting that his reputation as commander of the fleet would weigh heavily in such a matter, & that he be prepared to express his opinion— which I knew—very clearly, if opportunity required.

I also wrote you, suggesting a recommendation to Mr. Taft on the subject.[2] You wrote a letter to him in consequence; and sent a copy of it to me.

---

1. Probably, the speech delivered by Viscount Grey of Fallodon, British Foreign Secretary, to the Dominion delegates at the Committee of Imperial Defence, 1911: "What really determines the foreign policy of this country is the question of sea power.... If we mean to keep the command of the sea, we should have to estimate a probable combination against us in Europe not of two Powers but of five Powers."

1. To divide the Fleet between the Atlantic and Pacific coasts.
2. *See* Mahan to Roosevelt, March 2, 1909.

The treaties I imagine would die a natural death but for the organized agitation, which cannot last, I think, because it has no strong popular feeling behind it. Root's amendment will take the worst out of them; but then, as Olney says, with that attachment there is not much treaty left.

I am glad you find the book interesting, the more so that I have never been so sick of anything I have written as I was of this before ending it. I hear from the College that they like it there.

Permit me to congratulate you on Sheldon's[3] letter. It was needed for some persons, though not for me as I never doubted. *The Times* seems engaging in the profitable task of proving evident truth to be falsehood; a very dangerous occupation for the soul.

[P.S.] I have just ascertained that at the bottom of p. 395, two or more lines have been left out, so that the first lines of 396 are, so to say, in the air. No serious difficulty is occasioned but it looks very queer.

To Little, Brown and Company

45 West 35th Street, New York, December 25, 1911 [LC]

Gentlemen: I have been informed by the War College at Newport, and correctly, that at the bottom of p. 395 of *Naval Strategy*, as published, two or three lines of text have been omitted.

You can verify the fact by glancing at a copy. My informant has sent me the missing words taken probably from one of the several copies of the original lectures filed at the College.

These words are.

"This quotation illustrates, and should bring conviction of, the value to naval officers of acquaintance with contemporary"

Upon which follow p. 396

"political, or rather international, literature."

How, or when, or through whom, this omission occurred, I have no means at hand to determine. I left at Quogue a full set of page, or cast, proof; but have none here.

Copies sent out are beyond recall, but it is of course desirable that the cast-proof should receive the amendment.

---

3. George Rumsey Sheldon was a banker and a member of the Republican National Committee. His letter to Roosevelt, December 15, 1911, denied an allegation that Roosevelt had improperly requested railroad monopolist E. H. Harriman to contribute to his 1904 campaign fund. Roosevelt supported Sheldon's statement in a letter of December 19. Both letters were published in *The New York Times*, December 22, p. 1.

To Charles W. Stewart

45 West 35th Street, New York, December 29, 1911 [LC]

My dear Mr. Stewart: In printing my book *Naval Strategy* a singular blunder was made by the printers, first discovered by the War College and by it notified to me. Though not very important, it is a blemish. I enclose a letter from the publishers, which I will ask you *to return* to me at the above address.

At the bottom of page 395 two or three lines were omitted; although, as the enclosed shows, they were present even in the *cast*-proof. The words, as furnished me by Captn. Little from the copies of the original lectures on file at the College, are as follows:

(p. 395) "This quotation illustrates, and should bring conviction of, the value to naval officers of acquaintance with contemporary"

upon which follows (p. 396) "political, or rather international, literature" P. 396 is all right.

As I do not know, in the present division of Bureau duties, under whose care ships' libraries come, I will ask you to see the proper chief and explain.

My idea was that the words omitted might be set up and printed, and distributed for insertion in copies already bought by Government. In any case, I hope as little expense as possible may be caused the publishers; for while responsible, they are scarcely personally to blame, and by long dealing I know them to be a careful and trustworthy firm.

To Henry Cabot Lodge

45 West 35th Street, New York, January 6, 1912[1] [MHS]

My dear Mr. Lodge: I am sensible that there is some incongruity in a man of my slight equipment and practice of affairs making a suggestion to one of your long antecedents concerning a provision of the pending treaties;[2] but the following argument has had such weight in my mind that I venture to submit it.

1. By the universal custom of nations it has been, and still is, lawful and proper for nations to acquire or transfer territory, by war, by purchase, by exchange. So invariable has this rule been, that I presume it might claim the

---

1. The handwritten draft of this letter was dated January 5. The typed version was dated January 6. The draft was actually first written in early December 1911. *See* Mahan to Lodge, January 8, 1912.
2. Senator Lodge was instrumental in amending the 1911 arbitration treaties in such manner as to render them virtually innocuous.

standing of a "principle of law," as cited in Article I of the treaties. We acquired the Philippines by purchase, Porto Rico as the result of war. Germany has just acquired a huge African territory by transfer from France.

2. Up to 1823 this principle of law applied in America, as well as in other quarters of the world. Actually, in 1809 and 1810, for instance, Great Britain acquired Martinique and Guadeloupe from France, by conquest, and restored them in 1814. Since 1823, and at present, the United States by the Monroe Doctrine opposes and forbids such transfers, under threat of opposition by us; but how can this policy of a single nation affect a principle of the law of nations, when a case involving such a principle is brought before any tribunal? whether the tribunal be one of ultimate arbitration, or intermediary, such as the proposed Joint High Commission. How can such a tribunal hold that the question of transfer of territory, everywhere recognized and practised, is not "justiciable . . . by the application of principles of law," when such law exists in the shape of established practice and custom everywhere, except in the American hemisphere; and there only because of the pronouncement of a single state, unsupported either by general assent or by treaty?

3. I am told that a matter of government policy is *ipso facto* "not justiciable." If that means that a state will not submit to arbitration a matter it considers one of vital policy, I agree; but it appears to me that such an assertion merely begs the question. Such a state refuses, not because there is no law to govern a tribunal in the case, but because in its mind its vital interests are above law. That is a tenable position, and one on which all states act; an attribute of sovereignty recognized by all. But this does not deprive the existing law of its validity, nor make the matter one that is not "justiciable by means of being susceptible of decision by the application of the principles of law." On the contrary, the matter remains one that is so justiciable, because there is an applicable law, until by some change of law, either by general consent or by specific treaty, it is removed from that category of questions.

4. It appears to me that there is prevalent a mental confusion between a question being non-justiciable, because a state as a matter of policy will not submit it to arbitration, and its being non-justiciable because there is no law that applies to the case. The only reconciling factor that I can see is the general acceptance, as of a fundamental principle, that when a state defines a national determination as a national policy, that policy thereby ceases to be justiciable by law, however long the applicable law may have existed.

5. This is substantially what Italy has lately done,—very rightly in my judgment,—and other states have silently accepted. Such tacit acceptance is a step towards the full acceptance of the principle just stated; but it overturns in so far most of the labored procedure of the Hague Conferences, by leaving each state the final judge in its own case, unbound even by

specific agreements, still less by "principles of law." That a state is such final judge has been an axiom ever since I first studied international law; qualified possibly by treaty obligations, when such exist, but not by the mere consensus which we call International Law.

6. I cannot but think the pending treaties fatally vitiated by a confusion of thought which defines "justiciable" as "capable of settlement by principles of law," yet apparently assumes that any principle of law disappears before a national pronouncement. What then is law?

To Little, Brown and Company

University Club, New York, January 8, 1912 [LC]

Gentlemen: The Librarian of the Navy Department has asked me to obtain from you a cancel sheet of the defective page in *Naval Strategy*.

I enclose his letter, in order that you may see exactly what he wishes, and why; and also because it mentions the steps taken with reference to copies otherwise received by the Navy Department.

You will probably have received the information in some other way, but writing at his request I enclose the letter.[1]

To Henry Cabot Lodge

University Club, New York, January 8, 1912 [MHS]

My dear Mr. Lodge: After much hesitation I have decided to send for your consideration the enclosed two papers. One is a letter to yourself, written nearly a month ago (though dated Jan. 6.) The other is an article I drew up immediately after the Carnegie Hall Mass Meeting, with a view to the press;[1] but I concluded that as an executive officer I had best not appear in direct contradiction to the position of my chief.[2]

Since writing, two considerations have occurred to me. One is that Germany's ambitions are so directed eastward and southward, that, in view of the opposition of our Monroe Doctrine, she feels little temptation to acquisition here, in America; but once give an opening, such as my papers suggest, to acquire by law, she will attempt it, and our resistance, not

---

1. Enclosure not found.

1. Article not found. The Meeting took place on December 12, 1911. *See* Mahan to Roosevelt, December 13, 1911.
2. President William H. Taft.

[443]

known and expected, will in such case excite a bitterness of resentment which will affect relations, if not cause serious trouble.

The other consideration is a remark made to me by a Southerner, in this connection viz: that if the framers of the Constitution had dared to attach to it a specific assertion or denial of the Right of Secession, the trouble of 1861 might have been averted. Why, then not define the Monroe Doctrine, and what else may be necessary, as non-justiciable in the present instruments?

To John Bassett Moore

University Club, New York, January 11, 1912 [LC]

My dear Mr. Moore: Will you do me the favor of dining with me *here* on Monday, January 29. There will be only a small number, five or six, and I should so much appreciate meeting you again.

To Little, Brown and Company

45 West 35th Street, New York, February 6, 1912 [LC]

Gentlemen: I have just received yours enclosing that of Sampson Low & Co relative to the German proposition.[1] I entirely approve your reply and according to your wish have mailed it.

They dont seem to me very pleasant correspondents.

To John Bassett Moore

University Club, New York, February 26, 1912 [LC]

My dear Mr. Moore: I was exceedingly interested and pleased to see in yesterday's paper your categorical explanation of the course open to our Government, in case a European Power should undertake acquisition of territory on the American "continent."[1] As I presume our objections are

---

1. A proposal for a German translation and edition of *Naval Strategy* advanced by Mittler & Son. *See* Mahan to Little, Brown and Company, March 27, 1912.

1. Moore's address took place at a luncheon at the Republican Club on February 24. He said, "You cannot make a treaty under which every question can be arbitrated." But he also argued that the proposed treaties would not interfere in any way with the Monroe Doctrine, and that the United States should not accept the responsibility for checking the peace movement by a refusal to sign the arbitration treaties.

equally to acquisition of American islands would not "hemisphere" be a better word?

I attach importance to your utterance, because I think every statement from eminent international law experts, though unofficial, does help make our position clear beforehand; and this "beforehand" is to my mind of the utmost consequence. Admitting, as you do, that acquisition or transfer of territory is *in general* legal—internationally—I cannot rid myself of the uneasy feeling that a powerful state—Germany, in short—may insist that it is legal not only generally, but always and everywhere. I greatly desire therefore that she should appreciate beforehand that—law or no law—we will not have it. When these pending treaties are signed, one with Germany will follow. If these contain no provision safeguarding the Monroe D. explicitly, neither will that with her. If under the treaty, she raises the point that buying the Danish [Virgin] Islands is determinable by law, therefore justiciable, & we refuse, we shall be much nearer war than if the understanding is clear from the first. Germany will soon have a decisive navy.

If the Monroe D. were simply an instance of national touchiness resembling the English "Narrow Seas" doctrine, I should have nothing to object; but I believe it of the highest importance as tending to exclude European wars from propagation to this side of the Atlantic. I am really deeply concerned about the situation developing from the treaties and the attitude of the Democratic party towards the Navy. If we fail to provide battleships now, our children will have to provide double the number or more.

I looked up Germany's assurances at the time of the Venezuela business. They were eminently satisfactory as regards the matter in hand, and doubtless will furnish material for argument in case of future diplomatic correspondence; but I cannot see that they bind her, as mere words even, to abstain from acquiring the Danish Islands, or Martinique should she wish to do so, as she very naturally would in view of the Panama Canal, having the second merchant shipping.

To Stephen B. Luce

45 West 35th Street, New York, March 9, 1912 [LC]

My dear Admiral: Your letter reached me in due course, but the pamphlets also having been sent to Quogue I had to write for them specially; second class matter not being forwarded. They came to hand only this evening. I am sorry Rodgers[1] did not tell you my address—here till May 1.

---

1. Captain William L. Rodgers, class of 1878, who had relieved Raymond P. Rodgers as President of the War College in November 1911.

I am much obliged to you for them and will read them carefully in connection with the pretty large mass of material Rodgers sent. I hope I shall succeed in boiling it all down, a pretty difficult matter in a space allowed of little, if any, over 5,000 words.[2] Much of the subject is new to me, but I hope for the best.

To Carter FitzHugh

University Club, New York, March 9, 1912 [LC]

Dear Mr. FitzHugh: I am pleased to know that you liked my article.[1] The position of Germany as regards expansion is one that commands much sympathy—so to say. Her ambitions are natural and laudable. As regards the American hemisphere, several years ago I defined my own position: that the Valley of the Amazon indicated a boundary south of which it seemed to me unnecessary to carry our Monroe Doctrine.[2] The region north of it, the Caribbean especially, I should be unwilling to see open. Unfortunately for German ambitions, if such exist, most of America south of that line is too strong for occupation, and would not accept it.[3]

Of course, all political balances are unstable. Time brings constant changes with consequent need of revision. I sometimes think I see possibilities of such change in my own views, but at present they are as above. If a little volume of mine, *Interest of America in International Conditions*, should come your way you may find interest in it.

To Little, Brown and Company

45 West 35th Street, New York, March 10, 1912 [LC]

Gentlemen: I have omitted through oversight to acknowledge yours of March 4, enclosing communication from Messrs. Sampson Low of Feb. 20. There seems no occasion for any suggestion on my part, beyond this acknowledgment of receipt, and to await developments.

---

2. The allowance for the article published as "The Naval War College," *North American Review* (July 1912).

1. "The Place of Force in International Relations," *North American Review* (January 1912).
2. "The Monroe Doctrine," *National Review* (February 1902).
3. In reply to this comment, FitzHugh wrote on the letter: "In an article in June *Century* 1911 ["The Panama Canal and Sea Power in the Pacific"] he forecasts that it will be invited someday."

To Bouverie F. Clark

University Club, New York, March 12, 1912 [LC]

My dear Clark: I am not sure that the recurrence of birthdays, which *seem* to follow one another at intervals increasingly shorter as one grows older, is entirely a matter of congratulation when our time of life is reached. However, the three score and ten which you turn on the 19th is really such a marked event in one's life that an old friend can scarcely pass it unnoticed. At least, I hope and believe that whatever the sorrows of the journey, you, like myself, can say that upon the whole there has been much happiness; and I rejoice to think that your present contains much upon which I can heartily wish you a continuance & many happy returns.

I meant to have brought with me your last letter, in case it offered anything to reply to, but I left it at home. I think, however, there was nothing beyond the passing comment on the events of the day. Since it was written, the coal people in your country have been indulging you with the most alarming excitement that I remember in a long time. We are threatened with something of the same sort in our anthracite fuel, upon which our household economy so largely depends in this country; April 1 being set as the date, if agreement be not reached. Possibly it may spread to the bituminous output also, upon which railways and manufacturers rely. I am selfishly glad to know that our country home is stocked full, every bin filled when we left last November, and there has been no draft save for the small needs of the man left in charge; but I am already contemplating sending down food supplies etc betimes, if things get blacker. I cannot sufficiently appreciate the rights and wrongs on either side to place my sympathies. Judged by our labor pay, the demands of your miners seem moderate, but these things are comparative. What is most gloomy in the outlook is the absolute power apparently in the hands of the coal people over the welfare of the whole community.

I remember that in your letter you spoke hesitatingly about reading my *Naval Strategy*. I sincerely trust you have not felt that friendship required it. I will confess to you that the composing [of] it was the most perfunctory job I have ever done in book writing. There were very compelling reasons for undertaking it, but it alone of all my much writing was felt to be a burden. It was conscientiously done and I hope is not a bad piece of work, but it was against the grain, and I feel probably the last professional large work that I shall attempt. Enough commendation has reached me to make me hope that, with whatever faults, my reputation will not suffer seriously from it.

We have had a very pleasant four months in town. Our central position has been convenient, and circumstances have caused me to see more of the Grand Opera than in twenty years before. From both that and the theatre

I have had much enjoyment. I am also full of occupation, which I take it is one of the chief happinesses of life. I have also been very well, have not had to see a doctor once, and the winter is so nearly over that I am hopeful I shall not. We had some bitter weather in January, & I had one ear frosted in walking only the mile between house and club; but except that one day I have worn only a spring overcoat and gauze under flannels. Fortunately, early in my married life my wife, who is constitutionally warm blooded, persuaded me out of superfluous clothing, and with the thermometer at 20 I get on very well with no overcoat; having great delight in the freer movement, and wonder at seeing men forty years my junior in garments that are about as limber as plate armor, with heavy furs often to boot. I can still walk nearly four miles an hour, though I could not keep it up over an hour.

We are in the most complex political situation here that I can remember. Probably your papers tell you all that you are interested to know about it. The most alarming feature to me is the attitude of our present lower House toward the Navy. The Democratic Party, which there has the control, is strongest in the least rich and least educated—narrowest minded—part of the country. Broad views of external policy cannot be had from it; and with Japan confronting our weakest seacoast, the coast also which from its insufficient development is not the one on which to keep the fleet, I have great fears. Japan cannot but resent our attitude toward immigration, which Australia and Canada both share; and while I do not think she wants war I think she aims to have the superior fleet, which if she gets there is plenty of combustible material to start a conflagration. Unless wisdom come in time to Canada and the U.S.—not to mention Australia—there is a large possibility that the American Continent west of the Rockies may be Asiatic. I should not be surprised, however, if the elections go Republican, because, with some brilliant exceptions, the real brains is on that side.

With great regard [etc.].

To Joseph H. Choate

45 West 35th Street, New York, March 15, 1912 [LC]

My dear Mr. Choate: You will recall speaking to me at the Round Table two months ago about *The Great Illusion.*[1] I have just found in the

---

1. Norman Angell, *The Great Illusion*. London: G. Putnam's sons, 1910. Angell argued that modern man must speedily outgrow war as a means of settling his disputes, and that the idea of arming for peace was really the fact of arming for war.

last *The Round Table*, of this March, two passages,[2] which, if you have not seen them, are in very close coincidence with my own view of the fundamental fallacy of that work, which seems to have escaped the notice of its numerous admirers. The fallacy is serious, if my own view and that of *The Round Table* are correct; viz: that the author presents, as a general current illusion, an attitude of mind, or impression, which in fact does not exist; or, if it exists, has not the motive force attributed to it. In brief, the argument is addressed against a fact which does not exist. Pardon the bull.

The Round Table is of so recent origin,—the March number is only the sixth quarterly issue,—that it may not have come under your notice. It deals specifically with the politics of the British Empire which is practically the politics of the world. I am pleased as well as interested to find this coincidence of view with myself in the March *North American*.[3]

The passages are page 228, and 282 in a different article from the former.

To Joseph H. Choate

University Club, New York, March 19, 1912 [LC]

My dear Mr. Choate: I fear I can be of little help in the direction of your question.[1] I find in *Poole's Index to Periodical Literature*,[2] between 1897

---

2. An unsigned article, "The Balkan Danger and Universal Peace," has a paragraph on the error of the pacifists in failing to explain the true causes of war, which lie not in greed and ambition, but in the very nature of the human race. A second unsigned article, "Lombard Street and War," contains the passage: "Self-interest should lead [the Dominions] to spend every penny they can afford on placing beyond question the supremacy of the British flag at sea. . . . Would the Australians confine themselves to protest while the Chinese landed in their millions in the Northern Territories, or Canada be content merely to reason while the Asiatic flood poured into British Columbia?"

3. "The Great Illusion," *North American* (March 1912), a review of and attack on Angell's book. Notes taken on the book and a detailed draft of the review are among Mahan's papers in the Library of Congress. He regarded Angell as a great threat to realistic thinking on the questions of war and peace.

1. Choate had written to Mahan on March 18 asking for a good account of the work of the first Hague Conference in connection with lectures he was preparing to deliver at Princeton. He was relying on: Frederick William Holls, *The Peace Conference at the Hague, and Its Bearings on International Law and Policy*. Holls also wrote many articles on the subject, 1899–1910. James Brown Scott, *The Hague Peace Conferences of 1899 and 1907*. 2 vols. Baltimore: Johns Hopkins Press, 1909. Scott also edited the texts of the Peace Conferences which were published by Ginn & Co. William Hull, *The Two Hague Conferences and Their Contributions to International Law*. Boston: Ginn & Co., 1908.

2. William Frederick Poole and William I. Fletcher, *Poole's Index to Periodical Literature*. New York: Putnam, 1848. Various revisions and supplements. The material on the Hague Conferences is in the 4th and later supplements.

and 1902, Vol V, under the head "Peace Conference of the Hague," a long list of articles, many of them in monthlies; among which there may be some containing information rather than comment and criticism. In the *North American Review*, No. 169, there were three articles, by M. de Martens, Mr. Low, and myself.[3] My own is of the nature of comment, or discussion of principles, not likely to be of service to your present object; but Mr. Low's, if I rightly remember, is more narrative. I do not send you a copy of the list, merely because it is frankly too long for my copyist powers.

As you are depending upon Holls, it may be not improper to caution you that his language, in speaking of the Declaration which the American Commission attached to its signatures, as a reservation, tends to give the impression that he had a principal share in originating that declaration. The fact is that he was our representative on the particular committee which adopted the article (27, I think) and assented to its appearing without qualification. It was thus in shape to appear before the Conference, and on the point of being presented, when a member of the Commission noticed that it so trenched on our traditional policies as to make very doubtful the consent of the Senate; an opinion justified by the recent Senate action.[4] We brought the matter instantly before the Commission and it was decided to make the declaration, which in its terms was drawn up by Mr. Low, with possible changes in discussion. Holls had nothing to do with it beyond acquiescing in a step which necessarily reflected somewhat on his own vigilance.

This a piece of inside history quite immaterial to your treatment, except so far as you might be led to attribute to his initiative a step which at the moment was very acceptable to our Government. There is no occasion to attribute to any one that which in result was the action of the whole Commission; but to attribute it to Holls would be a disinct error. If the point seem necessary of confirmation, the surviving members of our Commission, Messrs White and Low and General Crozier can doubtless give their recollection even now.

After reading my last note, I remembered that I had left Hamlet out in failing to say that the articles to which I referred you clearly had *The Great Illusion* in the foreground of their thought, though the name was not mentioned.

---

3. F. Martens, "International Arbitration and the Peace Conference at the Hague"; Seth Low, "The International Conference of Peace"; and Alfred Thayer Mahan, "The Peace Conference and the Moral Aspect of War," all in *North American Review* (November 1899).
4. In weakening the general arbitration treaty of 1911 with Britain prior to passage.

To Joseph H. Choate

University Club, New York, March 20, 1912 [LC]

My dear Mr. Choate: I remembered last night that my son a year or two ago prepared an article on Arbitration for a projected encyclopaedia which I believe has fallen still born, or never came to birth. I have asked him if he can suggest any sources of information such as you desired, to write you.

It has occurred to me also that Mr. Andrew D. White's *Autobiography*[1] devotes quite a number of pages to the first Conference, in which he was President of the American Commission.

To Little, Brown and Company

45 West 35th Street, New York, March 27, 1912 [LC]

Gentlemen: I return herewith the letter of Messrs. Mittler & son, enclosed in yours of March 25. There seems no cause for comment at this stage of the proceedings, except to state my satisfaction with your course.

If you have any information as to whether Corbett's recent work on the same subject[1] is being translated into German, I should be interested to receive it.

To William H. Henderson

45 West 35th Street, New York, March 28, 1912 [NMM]

My dear Henderson: Yours of the 9th has been duly received. You have indeed had a most interesting trip. In a very general way I keep track of the doings and conditions of your great dominions; mainly I confess through the tri-weekly *Times*, so that most comes through one channel. I think however one that is fairly full and reliable. Personal observation, such as yours, is more satisfactory. I see you say nothing about the slow growth

---

1. Andrew Dickson White, *Autobiography*. New York: The Century Company, 1905. The second volume of the 1907 edition has excerpts from White's diary kept at The Hague.

1. Sir Julian Stafford Corbett, *Some Principles of Maritime Strategy*. London: Longmans, Green & Co., 1911.

of population in Australia. Viewing the immense area in proportion to the inhabitants, this strikes me as a most unsatisfactory state, though less unsatisfactory than the apparent unwillingness to provide against a condition which to my mind menaces, and if unremedied will ultimately thwart, their wish to make theirs a white man's country. The same danger threatens our Pacific slope, and I am today appalled to see that the party in power in the Lower House has decided to refuse appropriations for battleships.[1] With Japan on one side and Germany on the other, with the Canal near completion, & the inevitable and natural desire of both those to possess near by stations, the Monroe Doctrine will be torn up & thrown in our faces within ten years. If the M. D. were a mere frill I shouldnt care; but it unquestionably tends for peace, so long as *force* stands behind it. If, for instance, Germany & France had come to blows, Germany could have seized Martinique, except for us. This exception will soon cease to exist, at the current rate.

I note what you say about Canada. A very intelligent young South African[2]–English by birth, who passed this way two years ago, told me that Canada was suffering from a good deal of corruption owing to the immense boom, and money-plenty of recent years. He had come by way of Australia & was bound to England for the then approaching colonial conference. I daresay you may be right as to Australia's solving the social questions of the day; though I myself feel less sure. I incline to think that in these matters opinions as well as sympathies are largely matters of individual temperament. We, like yourselves, are passing through a period of adjustment which may take an ultimate solution like that of Australia, which you expect. Whether, under the circumstances, national and race vitality will keep pace with the amelioration of conditions in the community, is to me more than doubtful. The tendency seems to me to destroy the capacity to endure hardness, which has made your country and ours what they have been. Our worthless leisure classes show the tendency. I fear that the Asiatics will, through this and their numbers, attain an ultimate superiority of fighting & resisting force. Things can be too smooth for national security.

I was very sorry to hear of Mrs. Henderson's mishap. She seems to have had rather a run of bad luck of late years, but such things run in spells, and it is open to hope that she will now have a time of repose from evil. We are all well, and have been spending the winter in a small apartment; our first stay in the city for five years or more. The experiment has worked well, because we are here very central. Mrs. Mahan desires to be kindly remembered, & believe me my dear Henderson [etc.].

---

1. 62 Cong., 2 Sess. House Report No. 710, p. 14, recommended a naval appropriation without provision for any battleships. In August, the House compromised with the Senate demand for two such ships by appropriating funds for one.
2. Lionel Curtis.

To the Editor of The New York Times

New York, April 2, 1912[1]

In its editorial column of Sunday, March 31, *The Times* very justly calls attention to the grave mistake made by the Democratic Party, as represented by its Congressional caucus, in deciding to stop the graduated increase of the navy by two annual battleships; a progress which has been in operation for some time past.

The action taken is based on the plea of economy. It neglects the obvious change of international relations, and of our own National exposure, caused by building and owning the Panama Canal, itself an incident of National advance. It is true that the Canal is far from being our only point of serious National exposure, against which a navy is in a sense the sole ultimate provision; but the Canal has this peculiarity, that it constitutes an entirely new strategic centre of the utmost world-wide importance in commercial, and therefore in international, conditions.

Our National remoteness has induced in us a sense of security which has some slight justification, but which in itself alone is a wholly inadequate reliance. We ignore that this remoteness formerly was one not only of distance but of interest, and that with the Canal the remoteness of interest will cease to exist. We look with assurance to a past century of peace, under conditions entirely different from the present, and mock at the thought of conquering the United States. Conquest in the sense of occupation is indeed a wild apprehension. Germany after its colossal victory did not attempt to occupy France. But conquest in the sense of defeat, and of the exaction of terms, as an alternative to unbearable injury, is no impossible dream.

What terms? Well, to name three principal, omitting others: the surrender of the Panama Canal, the admission of Asiatic labor immigration, and the abandonment of the Monroe Doctrine. These may be stated as (1) the surrender of a vital link in our coastwise communications, the principal end for which the Canal has been undertaken; (2) the constitution of a population predominantly Asiatic on the Pacific slope west of the Rocky Mountains—a new race problem; and (3) the suppression of a National policy, the salutary aim of which has been to exclude foreign wars from propagation to the American Hemisphere. For example, had the strained relations between France and Germany last Summer resulted in war, Germany, naturally—and properly—desirous of a naval station near the Canal routes, because of the interest in them of her great merchant shipping, might—I believe could—have taken Martinique. The Monroe Doctrine asserts that such transfer shall not be made. With a competent American navy it therefore would not

---

1. From *The New York Times*, April 4, 1912, p. 12, under the heading "For More Battleships."

be attempted. If the Monroe Doctrine were simply a frill, an arrogant self-assertion, such as England's once claim over the Narrow Seas, I should have no word for it. Its beneficent aspect, however, does claim American homage. The Democratic prophet, Jefferson, once said, long before Monroe: "We begin to claim all within the Gulf Stream as neutral waters." But he rejected a navy and his claim elicited nothing but foreign derision.

With our immense coast line it is vain to think we can have an army adequate to prevent landings, or assaults, with results I have indicated. Several European States—and Asiatic Japan—for sufficient object can land a hundred thousand or more trained troops on our coast, except for our navy; and if anyone imagines that there is in the United States the force to control such a body within a reasonable time, I imagine he will find himself mistaken if the day comes. But with a competent navy this will not be attempted until that navy is beaten; because otherwise a hostile army, even if momentarily successful, cannot be sustained. It will be the navy's business not to be beaten; but it is the country's business to give the ships. Should the present determination be persisted in by the House of Representatives, it assumes the whole responsibility, if trouble comes; for the Executive has stated its needs clearly. To quote words recently used in a different connection, "Ultimate economy is to be desired, not immediate cheapness."

To the Editor of the New York Evening Post

University Club, New York, April 26, 1912[1]

In the *Evening Post* of April 24, Admiral Chadwick passes a distinct approval upon the conduct of Mr. Ismay in the wreck of the *Titanic*,[2] by characterizing the criticisms passed upon it as "the acme of emotionalism."

Both censure and approval had best wait upon the result of the Investigation being made here, and to be made in Great Britain. Tongues will wag; but if men like Admiral Chadwick see fit to publish anticipatory opinions, those opinions must receive anticipatory comment.

Certain facts are so notorious that they need no inquiry to ascertain. These are (1) that before the collision the captain of the *Titanic*[3] was solely responsible for the management of the ship; (2) after the collision there

---

1. From the *Evening Post*, April 27, 1912.
2. J. Bruce Ismay, Chairman of the White Star Line, survived the April 14, 1912 disaster. Mrs. Mahan's niece, Angelina ("Lina") Evans, was among the 1,513 people lost.
3. Edward J. Smith.

were not boats enough to embark more than one-third of those on board; and (3) for that circumstance the White Star Company is solely responsible, not legally, for the legal requirements were met, but morally. Of this company Mr. Ismay is a prominent, if not the most prominent member.

For all the loss of life the company is responsible, individually and collectively; Mr. Ismay personally, not only as one of the members. He believed the *Titanic* unsinkable; the belief relieves of moral guilt, but not of responsibility. Men bear the consequences of their mistakes as well as of their faults. He—and Admiral Chadwick—justify his leaving over fifteen hundred persons, the death of each of whom lay on the company, on the ground that it was the last boat half-filled; and, Mr. Ismay has said, no one else to be seen.

No one to be seen; but was there none to be reached? Mr. Ismay knew there must be many, because he knew the boats could take only a third. The *Titanic* was 882 feet long, 92 broad; the length say, from Thirty-fourth Street to a little north of Thirty-seventh. Within this space were congregated over 1,500 souls, on several decks. True, to find any one person at such a moment in the intricacies of a vessel were a vain hope; but to encounter some stragglers would not seem to be. Read in the *Sun* and *Times* of April 25 Col. Gracie's[4] account of the "masses of humanity, men and women," that suddenly appeared before him, after the boats were launched.

In an interview reported in the *New York Times* April 25, Admiral Sir Cyprian Bridge, a very distinguished officer, holds that Mr. Ismay was but a passenger, as other passengers. True, up to a certain point. He is in no sense responsible for the collision; but, when the collision had occurred, he confronted a wholly new condition, for which he was responsible, and not the captain; viz: a sinking vessel without adequate provision for saving life. Did no obligation to particularity of conduct rest upon him under such a condition?

I hold that, under the condition, so long as there was a soul that could be saved, the obligation lay upon Mr. Ismay that that one person, and not he, should have been in the boat. More than 1,500 perished. Circumstances yet to be developed may justify Mr. Ismay's action completely; but such justification is imperatively required. If this be "the acme of emotionalism," I must be content to bear the imputation.

Admiral Chadwick urges the "preserving a life so valuable to the great organization to which Mr. Ismay belongs." This bestows on Mr. Ismay's escape a kind of halo of self-sacrifice. No man is indispensable. There is surely brains enough and business capacity enough in the White Star Company to run without him. The reports say that of the rescued women thirty-seven were widowed by the accident and the lack of boats. Their husbands were quite as indispensable to them as Mr. Ismay to the company. His duty

---

4. Archibald Gracie, an amateur military historian.

to the ship's company was clear and primary; that to the company so secondary as to be at the moment inoperative.

We should be careful not to pervert standards. Witness the talk that the result is due to the system. What is a system, except that which individuals have made it and keep it? Whatever thus weakens the sense of individual responsibility is harmful; and so likewise is all condonation of failure of the individual to meet his responsibility.[5]

To Little, Brown and Company

N.P. Probably, 45 West 35th Street, New York, May 3, 1912 [LC]

Gentlemen: I beg to acknowledge yours enclosing that of Messrs. Mittler with translation. I have no surmise as to the comments upon which they rest their change of mind.

To John Bassett Moore

45 West 35th Street, New York, May 4, 1912 [LC]

My dear Mr. Moore: Your pamphlet *Contraband of War* and the book *Four Phases of American Development* have arrived almost simultaneously.[1] I am delighted to have them, especially the book, for it deals with a subject the interest of which is to me perennial. I write at once my acknowledgment and thanks, because we are just breaking out here to go to Quogue next week for the summer and autumn. I shall get at the book at the first moment of comparative leisure, which will be soon after this transfer.

With renewed thanks, believe me [etc.].

---

5. Chadwick wrote a long rebuttal of Mahan's attack which appeared in the *Evening Post* on April 29.

1. John Bassett Moore, *Contraband of War*. Philadelphia, 1912. Reprinted from the *Proceedings* of the American Philosophical Society, LI, No. 203 (January–March 1912); *Four Phases of American Development—Federalism—Democracy—Imperialism—Expansion*. Baltimore: Johns Hopkins Press, 1912.

To the Editor of The New York Times

Quogue, Long Island, May 22, 1912[1]

At the present moment the Presidental campaign is in a chaotic condition, the issue of which the shrewdest can scarcely foretell. It may be that this period of chaos, during which the champions only are in the field, not the armies, may permit a momentary yet decisive glance of the people at large to certain things which belong to their peace. After the National conventions have made the nominations, the large internal questions pending will probably absorb public attention. Yet it will be unfortunate if consideration shall not have been obtained for measures which affect our standing in the community of nations, the lack of which may influence disastrously our power to support the policy which assures peace to the American continents, as well as to secure our own extensive interests external to our borders.

The appeal here is to the whole nation; but it lies specifically to the Democratic Party, and especially to its leading men, for by that party it is proposed to discontinue a naval policy with which the Republican Party has been identified for some years. To make on party grounds an appeal such as I wish here to make would be almost a crime; for it would be seeking to prostitute a National common interest to partisan ends. But it is not similarly wrong to point out a tendency to this result, which is glaring, though overlooked. External circumstances are such that the National interest demands a steady naval increase, which the National Executive has calculated and stated, while the action proposed for the Democratic Party, if persisted in even for the current year, will imperil that interest. It is certain that the nation would go to war to sustain the policy summed up in the phrase "The Monroe Doctrine." The resulting questions, "Shall it be necessary to fight?" and "If it comes to fighting, shall the force be adequate?" are really not two, but one; for if the force be sufficient there will be no fighting. That is, the question ultimately is between assured peace and possible war, which indeed summarizes the Doctrine itself.

In Great Britain, long tradition and present evident necessity have established a national policy concerning the Navy which is almost co-extensive with the population. The Navy therefore is there not a party question. The late W. T. Stead, a foremost journalist, who went down in the *Titanic*, was a peace enthusiast; he published a periodical called *War Against War*; but coincidentally, as a peace measure, he advocated laying down two British battleships for each German one, and was largely instrumental in the sustained increase of the British Navy. In the United States the Monroe

---

1. From *The New York Times*, May 24, 1912, p. 10.

Doctrine, if of shorter tradition, is nevertheless a national policy similarly conducive to peace, and equally established in the will of the people, but although there exists a present evident necessity for a Navy, the relation between it and the Monroe Doctrine is not as clear to the apprehension of our people as the relations of the Navy to their insular well-being has been to British citizens since the time of Shakespeare.

Yet the Monroe Doctrine has not a leg to stand on, except the United States Navy. Eminently moral as the Doctrine is, because it makes for the peace and independence of all American states, it has not behind it a shred of sanction from international law. Its assertions are contrary to established international practice. It contravenes particular European interests. It forbids in the American hemisphere the political transfer of territory to or between non-American States, a proceeding which has prevailed everywhere else from time immemorial, and prevails now. And this exemption of American territory from transfer not only has no precedent in law to show, but is without treaty support from any other nation. Eminently wise and equitable as I believe it to be, it rests only upon the will of the American people. How shall that will be sustained?

It is curious that in the concluding debate on the Arbitration Treaties, after the omission of the decisive clause had been voted, a Democratic Senator introduced, needlessly then, as it seemed to me, a further resolution reaffirming the Monroe Doctrine; while almost coincidentally the Democratic caucus has decided to stop the increase of the Navy at a moment when all other navies are growing. This is an inconsistency which gives hope that the party may yet see its mistake.

The Monroe Doctrine, moreover, is only a part of our self-assumed external responsibilities, and not the larger part. The doctrine applies distinctively only to American territory not in our own possession. In territories belonging to us, even though not embraced within our continental borders—as defined by the two oceans, the Gulf, and the Great Lakes—we have the full support of international law for using every right of a sovereign State. However extreme our action, as for instance forbidding labor immigration from Eastern Asia while permitting that from Europe and even from Western Asia, we exercise rights which cannot be questioned on the ground of law. Positions like Hawaii and the Panama Canal are not for this reason less exposed militarily; but they are less a source of friction, because legal ground for contention concerning our action therein does not exist, and has to be found. But in the Monroe Doctrine, so far as law is concerned, the legal ground for resistance is always present the instant that any State decides to resent our attitude, or to reject our claim.

This danger is not imaginary, although as yet it may not be immediately at hand. I follow with some care the straws blown by international impulses; and while admitting them to be straws only, I think they are to be noted. Twice recently, once from Canada, once from an English source in China, has come a suggestion that the present feeling of Germany against Great Britain might by placated by Great Britain repudiating the Monroe Doctrine. This does not mean that Great Britain desires, or should desire, new American territory; but that she should enter into an agreement with Germany that she would not oppose any German project to obtain American Territory, continental or insular. This would be on the same lines by which Great Britain arranged her long-standing territorial difficulties with France, by conceding a free hand for France in Morocco. Of course, we Americans do not wish to depend upon any other nation for support to our national policies; yet we may need it, and probably would not receive it, if we relax our battleship building. Even the intermission of a single year will embarrass the future seriously. Here is the place to mention that very recently an article has appeared in a German magazine, directly assailing the doctrine. If attacked as being without support from international law, and also contrary to German interests, there is no reply except an adequate battle fleet.

I do not for one moment suggest that the motive for the present German naval expansion is interference in America in support of a defined German policy. But I do say that the simple existence of such a fleet as Germany is now providing places the Monroe Doctrine at her mercy; while the completion of the Panama Canal will cause her a strong temptation to violate it by acquiring through purchase or otherwise a position or positions in the Caribbean Sea such as the two other chief naval States, France and Great Britain, possess and have possessed since our colonial period.

In the early years of the present British Administration, an attempt at economy was made similar to our projected discontinuance of battleship building. A marked relaxation was affected, the consequence of which ultimately was a sudden revived apprehension coincident in extent with the whole British people. The result was that which always follows overconfidence; a spasm succeeds lethargy, feverish action the steady processes of a well-organized plan. It will be so with us; but we have not the means, the shipbuilding plant, which Great Britain has. Moreover, she never wholly lost her place, as we are doing.

The thing to be distinctly noted is that what is at stake this year in the Naval Appropriation bills is not primarily the navy, but a great National policy to which the Nation is wedded. A navy is not an end, but a means. He who wills the end—the policy—wills the means. The present situation is deplorable, for it is tending to make a party question of policies cherished by the Nation, not by any one party, yet which can only be maintained by a sufficient navy.

To William L. Rodgers

Marshmere, Quogue, Long Island, May 30, 1912 [NWC]

My dear Rodgers: About Saturday last I received orders detaching me from all duty on June 6.[1] As they came direct I returned the required form in like manner. This closes my prolonged association with the College, and in notifying you of it I wish to express my appreciation of my pleasant relations with yourself, as with all the presidents, and my wishes for your successful term of office.

To Little, Brown and Company

Marshmere, Quogue, Long Island, May 30, 1912 [LC]

Gentlemen: Yours of May 27 received. I find the term "Naval History Article" a little obscure, because I have been under the impression that the present Messrs. Sampson Low had declined entirely to permit publication of that to which I suppose you refer; namely, in the *History of the Royal Navy*, Vol III.[1]

Assuming this to be the article to which you refer, the terms suggested will be acceptable to me; for my desire has been chiefly to rescue the paper from the seven volumes, and I know not how many pages, in which it is now submerged.

As regards the revision I shall of course carefully reread the whole, but I have no intention of doing more; nothing in the way of outside reading or research. The work was very thoroughly done in the first instance, and to attempt more than I indicate would be needless.[2]

Will you kindly inform me whether you have or can without undue expense procure, printed pages of the work? At time of publication you kindly sent me some half dozen copies of the article. Of these I have given away all but one, which I have, bound as well as the copy in the *History* itself; but loose page would be convenient.

When the work is finally determined on I may have some suggestions as to plates other than battle plans &c; as to illustration, in short.

---

1. Meyer to Mahan, May 24, 1912, at the Naval War College.

1. "Major Operations of the Royal Navy, 1762–1783," III, pp. 353–565.
2. The extensive article was published in book form by Little, Brown and Company in 1913 under the title *The Major Operations of the Navies in the War of American Independence.*

My recollection is that the type setting was done in America, as a copyright precaution.

Will you please note that my address now is Quogue N.Y.

[P.S.] I scarcely think that, with my other pre-occupations, the text could be ready for this fall trade.

To Charles L. Slattery[1]

Marshmere, Quogue, Long Island, June 1, 1912 [HUL]

My dear Dr. Slattery: I regret that I cannot comply with your request. Not only have I found myself, through repeated trial, an ineffective speaker, but I was advised some years ago by physicians not to attempt it again.

To John Bassett Moore

Marshmere, Quogue, Long Island, June 1, 1912 [LC]

My dear Mr. Moore: Since moving here three weeks ago I have read twice your *Four Phases*, a copy of which you kindly presented me. Twice partly because of the interest of the book itself and the authority of the author, partly because the line of thought is one that has occupied me already, and now to much more advantage through this work. I have cherished for some years the idea of a history of the United States, connected by the leading thought of expansion; and while at 71 it seems doubtful whether I shall have time to complete such, the task would have the recommendation of certain occupation for the remainder of my working days.

There are perhaps a half-dozen points I would like to put before you, for a reply which I trust you will postpone until wholly convenient.

On pp. 13–14 you speak of the commercial restriction, practiced on the colonies, as felt to be insupportable. There is no doubt that it chafed; but I have gained the impression that the colonists as a whole more than acquiesced in it; as a part of a system of commercial regulation designed, and actually contributive, to the welfare of the whole Empire, and of each part. As a system of commercial regulation adroitly calculated to obtain the greatest good of the greatest number, it indirectly was taxation, and without representation; but the *principle* at stake was not taxation, but adjustment of the parts of a whole. At least so the colonists conceived it;

---

1. The Rector of St. John's Episcopal Church, Providence, Rhode Island.

and being tempered by large and easy smuggling—like despotism by assassination—they accepted it. The system in fact then commanded the suffrages of the world outside of Britain, as the completest realization of the mercantile system, which Adam Smith had not yet undermined.

On pp. 32–33, you speak of the equal representation of the States in the Senate as a compromise. This of course it was; between the two principles of nationalism and statehood. Have you ever formulated to yourself the thought that, while historically certainly a compromise as you say, it established a method of minority representation unusually effective. As far as I know none equally effective exists. There is of course the drawback of a hitch between the two houses at times. But is this a drawback, in the long run?

Is Imperialism the right title for your third chapter? Should it not rather be Nationalism, implying both an opposition to Sectionalism and Individualism? In the first place, with us "Imperialism" as a word has achieved a popular acceptance which must be reckoned with. As an old Spanish grammar of mine said, "The populace is always stronger than Academies," referring to the Spanish Academy. But also this popular use is correct, according to my sense of the word Empire, which I find confirmed in my Webster's *International Dictionary*. *Empire*: "a dominion always comprising a *variety* in the nationality of, or the forms of administration in, constituent and subordinate portions." Several years ago, in speaking, I said that, from the Christian standpoint, the common phrase "Kingdom of Jesus Christ" should more properly be "Empire," because of the variety of "all kingdoms and nations" so claimed by it. Essentially of military derivation, Empire implies unity of a somewhat artificial character, imposed by an external authority, or government. No such variety exists; nor was contemplated by our annexations within the limits of our *continental* dominion, unless as a transition period to full nationality, under a form of government essentially the same throughout.

These, I think, are my only points of difference, and they are very mild ones. On another I should like to feel assured that we are in the accord which I infer from your phraseology. On p. 146, do the words "exceptional but *justifiable* recognition" of the Republic of Panama imply your own judgment as to the justifiableness of the course of our government? Or, is there meant only to indicate Roosevelt and Hay's judgment on the point? Personally, I have held, after reading for this decision the correspondence in your *International Law Digest*, that our course was just from a legal point of view, as laws amongst nations go. My only doubt has been as to whether we violated our treaty agreement of 1846.

I reject, as not applicable, the frequent assertion that right between nations is as clear and simple as between the individuals; and I find in governments no power to waive a national right at all comparable to that of an individual to waive personal rights. But I am tenacious of the view that a national promise is as binding as a personal. In 1885 we stopped fighting at the Isthmus insuring thereby transit; but then the fighting was between parties only, not sectional. Did either succeed there was no transfer of territory. But in 1902 it was a sectional fight; on the one side independence, on the other subjection. We again interfere, and the result is independence of Panama, and loss of sovereignty by Colombia; but our interference in both cases assured the neutrality of the ground and the security of transit. The methods employed were different. In 1885 we used land forces as well as naval, and occupied the ground. In 1903 we used naval force only, preventing the transit of Colombian troops. Our engagement in this respect went only to the insuring of the railroad isthmian transit. We had a further engagement to assure the sovereignty of Colombia; but as far back as 1865, Seward had said that this engagement was only against *foreign* conquest, or invasion. If all this be so, we fulfilled our obligations. We secured transit, and were under no obligations as to method, or as to securing the integrity of Colombian territory against domestic revolt.

The endeavor to state the case to you has gone far to clarify my own mind, and to convince me of the integrity of our action. That men as keen sighted as Roosevelt and Hay should have perceived at once an opportunity, and should have purposed to embrace it, is nothing to the point of law or equity. We have to do only with the act, and that is the discharging of our guaranteed assurance of quiet. It may be that the Colombian force was so overwhelming as to insure submission without disturbance; but as to that our Government was at liberty to form its own conclusions. It was not called upon to permit a landing that might be followed by fighting, nor to sustain Colombia against domestic outbreak.

In apologizing for so long a letter, let me add also my keen appreciation not only of the interest but of the value of your book.

To Horatio G. Dohrman[1]

Marshmere, Quogue, Long Island, June 6, 1912 [LC]

Dear Mr. Dohrman: Reply to your letter of June 1st has been delayed by several causes. I am much obliged to you for copies of telegrams and of your letter to Mr. Underwood.[2] I am myself persuaded that the present attitude of the Democratic leaders imperils seriously the future of the

1. Dohrman, otherwise unidentified, was from Steubenville, Ohio.
2. Oscar Wilder Underwood, Congressman from Alabama, and Democratic floor leader, 1911–1915.

country as regards both the Monroe Doctrine and the security of the Panama Canal in our hands. The only hope at present seems to be that the Senate will insist upon the restoration of the two battleships, expressing their willingness to enter the campaign with that issue among others. I am informed that several Democrats share the views which you and I have.

To Samuel A. Ashe

Marshmere, Quogue, Long Island, June 7, 1912 [DUL]

My dear Ashe: It has been my purpose, ever since I received the announcement of your daughter Josephine's marriage, to write you in congratulation and interest; although it must be somewhat of a trial that her married home should be so far away. I met Loyall Farragut in the street a short time before we left New York for here, and he told me she was to live in Hastings-on-the-Hudson. I do not know the particular locality, except as a railroad station through which I have often passed; but I do know the Hudson Valley very well, having been born as you know some thirty miles above Hastings; in the Highlands. In summer it is hot, but not unbearably so; and I think, as I hope, that she will like it in the experience. For yourself, although it is not exactly round the corner from Raleigh, distances count for little in these days.

Farragut tells me you and he had not met before. He evidently had carried away very pleasant impressions. There is, I think, a roundabout connection between you, through the Loyalls. He himself is a thoroughly good fellow, who I fear has not made much out of life. His wife died when he was just so old as to make re-marriage difficult, and she left no children; so that he has had very little of a home, although he has a house in N.Y. big enough for a family of eight or more.[1] There he inhabits with an old bachelor chum, who is to him more of an anchor and a burden than a pleasure, I fancy.

I have little to communicate about myself & family. Being about the same age, we each know that the other is nearly 72. Yesterday was in every probability the last day of duty in the Navy that I shall ever see. Since 1908 I have been connected with the War College at Newport, as a summer lecturer and winter worker on matters connected with it. A law passed in 1898, in the exigencies of the Spanish War, authorized the employment of retired officers in peace, as well as in war, for 14 years from date. As I had a somewhat unique relation to the theory of naval war, I was asked in 1898

1. He lived at 113 East 36th Street.

to resume my work for the College. This lasted till yesterday, when the expiring of the law ended my job. I am still uncertain what I shall do now; whether apply myself casually to passing topics of interest, letter-writing for the Press, etc, or whether I shall devote myself to some long work of more permanent character. At my age there is the doubt whether time or strength will last for completion of such a task; but the engagement of my faculties is of greater consequence than the mere fulfillment of a project. Being uncertain, I have committed myself to the Divine guidance; the more readily that no man can have been more happily guided than I up till now. On June 11 I shall have been married forty years.

Just now, my interest is absorbed and oppressed by the decision of the House to build no more battleships. To me this is an incredible infatuation, that within a decade will recoil on the heads of those responsible. I had thought so well of Underwood, but his name I fear will be associated with the cause of great disaster within the decade. Few of our public men have the time or the training to keep abreast of world movements, and to realize the dangers we are running. Extravagant though his words sometimes are, Hobson of Alabama seems one of the few Democrats level with the situation. He owes it largely to his former profession,[2] though there must also be natural aptitude. With Germany one one side and Japan on the other, both nations necessarily aggressive because of their need of expansion, a large navy is now our only security. Great Britain and France have on our side positions, which Germany has not and wants; between Japan and us are the questions of immigration and of Hawaii. Both G. & J. are building fast; and while to some extent their surroundings in Europe and in Asia reinforce us, they do not so to an extent which permits us to remain inadequately armed.

What a curious Presidential situation! If Taft is nominated it will be by the southern delegations; that is, the contract will be made by those who cannot deliver the goods—i.e. the state vote. Roosevelt is unquestionably the Republican choice; he can carry the decisive states; yet it is doubtful if he can get the nomination. If he does, he will be elected. In my judgment, Taft cant be elected. As for the prominent Democratic candidates, I should once have liked Underwood. Clark I abhor; both his utterances and what I saw of him in three or four days association on the Board of Visitors at the Naval Academy several years ago. As for Wilson, a governor of a State who gives his time to stump speaking all over the country carries to me no assurance that as President personal interest will not predominate over duty to office.

Well, we shall see! Meanwhile, there is hope above; I see little sign of encouragement in men. All the same I am not pessimist in feeling, though somewhat in intellect. I was not in favor of Roosevelt running again now,

---

2. Richmond P. Hobson, class of 1889, had been an active duty naval officer until 1903.

though I do not share the feeling about a third term, unless consecutive. But I have cause to believe that only he, of all the candidates on either side, has the comprehension & the character to deal with our international relations.

To Samuel L. Parrish

Quogue, Long Island, June 13, 1912[1]

The question of the size of the navy is not a naval question but a diplomatic one, and should be so recognized by being put under the Committee on Foreign Relations; details only appertaining to the Naval Committee. . . .

There is really only one of the present candidates who has any large grasp of foreign policy, and that is Roosevelt. I have not been able to accept his recent propositions concerning recall, &c.,[2] but believing, as I do, that our foreign policies are the most important, I am coming around to him. In this conclusion the naval action of the Democratic caucus has a large share. . . .

To Little, Brown and Company

Marshmere, Quogue, Long Island, June 20, 1912 [LC]

Gentlemen: The sheets of *Major Operations of Royal Navy* were duly received. I have delayed communicating with you more definitely until I could settle my plans with some certainty as to conditions before me.

I am to prepare for publication as soon as possible for Messrs. Harper and Brothers a series of papers published in their *North American Review* during the last eighteen months.[1] I mentioned to them my habit of publishing through your house, but as every article—save perhaps one—had appeared in their magazine, I felt I should defer to their choice in this matter. I shall get to work at once, and hope that I may finish by, or soon after, August first. I shall then take up the *Major Operations* at once.

---

1. Excerpts quoted in Parrish to the Editor of the New York *Sun*, Southampton, Long Island, May 29, 1916. Published in the *Sun*, May 31, 1916. Parrish has not been identified.
2. In his pursuit of the Republican nomination, and as the candidate of the Progressive (Bull Moose) Party in 1912, Roosevelt supported such democratic reform measures as the initiative, referendum, and recall.

1. *Armament and Arbitration, or The Place of Force in International Relations of States.* New York: Harper Brothers, 1912.

If it prove, as I expect, that very little modification will be needed, two months should complete revision. I have written already to Sir John Laughton, who is most up on English Naval History, as it transpires, of any man I know, to ascertain if he can make any suggestion.

As an historical work, touching the long past, this book can wait more easily than that of the articles, the value of which, whatever it may be, is immediate and current. This, combined with your expectations, that next year would be the time, fixed the order of preparation in my mind.

As regards illustration my wishes were very restricted, looking rather to omission than to addition. The title will have to appeal, in this country, to the American Revolution; and my principal idea was to bracket on one page the following opposing admirals—like Chauncey and Yeo in War of 1812—viz: Howe and D'Estaing; Rodney and DeGrasse; Suffren and Hughes. The battle plans of course will all be needed.

To Henry White

Marshmere, Quogue, Long Island, June 28, 1912 [LC]

My dear White: You recognize of course that the questions you raise bristle with conundrums.

My position is this. I believe that Roosevelt was the real choice of the Republican Party. Barring the delegates from Southern States, who cant deliver a single electoral vote, Taft could not have been nominated.[1] Personally, my views are nearer those of Taft than those of Roosevelt, but I have lost faith in the former as able to guide the ship, because he has not commanded the confidence of the people, as I think Roosevelt has. The avowed sympathies of the latter would give him greater power to influence, and to control extravagances.

But he has lost the nomination, and the question urgent in my mind is, Can the proposed third party effect in this election any other result than defeating the Republicans, and bringing the Democrats into power? The time element is conspicuous. Four years hence the new party may be formed; I greatly doubt whether it can do anything more determinate this year than put in the Democrats.

I am satisfied these are not fit to be intrusted with the international relations of the country. Sick as I am of Knox,[2] and of the diplomatic record of the administration, it is clear to me that a *party* which at this juncture can stop building up the navy is *ipso facto* shown to have no grasp of national—or international—issues. And look what a gang of candidates!

---

1. Taft was renominated on June 22.
2. Philander Chase Knox, Secretary of State, 1909–1913.

For all these reasons I hold my decision in suspense, and shall watch events closely. If I see reason to believe that Roosevelt can be carried in by a third party, I shall vote for him and use any influence I can in the same direction. But if I conclude that the only effect of the third party will be to defeat the Republicans and put in the Democrats, I shall vote for Taft.

When I say my opinions are nearer Taft than Roosevelt, I refer to domestic questions chiefly. I have not been able to reconcile myself to the recall, and only partly to the initiative and referendum. His sledge hammer manner of speaking also chills me. But he is a great man; and with my principal interest in external affairs I would prefer him in the Presidential chair to any man prominently named in either party. But I doubt the possibility, this election. For two years back I have in my mind deprecated his running until 1916.

My compliments to Mrs. White.

To Stephen B. Luce

Marshmere, Quogue, Long Island, June 28, 1912 [LC]

My dear Admiral: I enclose a copy of the letter you wish;[1] but as it is the only one I have left, and I need it for reference and possibly for reproduction in another form, I will ask you to return it as soon as possible.

The flaming head lines you will appreciate are not mine but the newspaper's.

To Horatio G. Dohrman

Marshmere, Quogue, Long Island, July 15, 1912 [LC]

My dear Mr. Dohrman: I have received your letter of July 11, with enclosures, for which I thank you.

How far your diagnosis of British motives is correct I cannot estimate. Of one thing I am sure; that while they work first, and properly, to British interests, one of their leading dispositions is to maintain kindly relations with us. This proceeds not only from a general friendliness and the stress of the German competitors, but also from the evident bearing of American power not only upon the security of Canada but of Australia and New Zealand as well.

From every point of view the increase of our navy is imperative, and

1. Enclosure not found.

I am very glad to see that you revert to that in both your letters. All diagnosis is subject to error; but there can be no error in securing our own interests by an adequate "exhibition" of organized power. Armament, not arbitration, is as yet the one sure safeguard of peace.

I note that you have satisfied yourself to vote for Mr. Wilson. I myself am waiting to see the final stand taken on the two-battleship programme by the House. If it persist in refusal, I shall conclude, as I have long held, that the Democracy as a party has not yet risen to that grasp of national issues that make it fit to be trusted with the country's future. I cannot find in Wilson's personality any assurance that he will compensate for his party's shortcomings. His conversion to advanced "progressive" views has synchronized too nearly with his seeking a nomination to convince me of the purity of his motives; and his prolonged absence from his duties as governor of a state to push his personal fortunes has confirmed the unfavorable impression. I may add I am a convert away from him, having once esteemed him highly.

To Little, Brown and Company

Marshmere, Quogue, Long Island, July 18, 1912 [LC]

Gentlemen: I return the enclosed. Considering the length of time which has now elapsed since the *Life of Nelson* was published, as well as the other circumstances of the particular case, I see no objection to the request, and unless you have some—not stated in your letter—I give my cordial consent to Captain Landquist's proposition.[1]

To Little, Brown and Company

Marshmere, Quogue, Long Island, August 1, 1912 [LC]

Gentlemen: It may be well to take up at once the subject of illustration in the proposed separate publication of the *Major Operations*; a title which I shall probably wish to change. No final decision need be reached in the matter of illustration until the revision is completed, or nearly completed; but I think it probably advantageous to submit my views as I go along.

---

1. Not identified.

In first chapter (Chap. XXXV, p. 355) a particular instance requiring management occurs. The length, from southern end of Lake George to Sorel on the St. Lawrence, is so great in proportion to width that, given any proposed page, it will be difficult to make clear. Something can be done by shading the land, both main and islands, throughout. The outlines also seem to me a little heavy.

Again, the plan stands with south at the top of the page. I cannot remember how far I was consulted about this at the time, but I now think it a mistake.

The inset of Valcour Island is so awkwardly placed as to appear at first sight almost a part of the main map. The inset will be required, and had best be separate. I now think it would be desirable to obtain a map from the Hydrographic Office or Coast Survey. Between the island and the west shore is a small shoal of which mention is made in the text. The crossed flags are scarcely discernible on present scale, while the details of channel are so confused as to be unintelligible.

The junction between Lakes George and Champlain is so enlarged that I have been for some moments puzzled as to the nameless stream running east of L. George and nearly parallel to it. It is really the upper part of L. Champlain. The inlet from George to Champlain should be a bare line, perhaps somewhat exaggerated in length in order to convey the impression of separateness of the two lake valleys.

I propose to make the section of Chap. XXXV, dealing with "The Naval Campaign on L. Champlain, 1775–1776" a distinct chapter, first of the book. It is the only purely American naval operation of the work, and therefore should receive most careful elaboration, in addition to the fortuitous advantage of being the first in the war, and therefore in the book.

For this reason, I would suggest the advisability of presenting an illustration of one of Arnold's schooners, the *Revenge*, raised with reference to the recent "Champlain Tercentenary." It will be found on page 352 in book of that title, published by the State of New York,[1] a copy which doubtless is in the Boston Public Library. I recognize that conditions of expense must be narrowly weighed in a book of this character; but it is a question whether a very best foot foremost would not be advisable in this chapter,—such as likenesses of Ethan Allen, Arnold, Schuyler, Waterbury, Carleton, Douglas, Pellew.

On the other hand many of the English portraits, reproductions of medals, &c., further on, might well be omitted from an American point of view. What policy would dictate us towards the English publishers and market, you can better judge.

---

1. New York (State) Lake Champlain Tercentenary Commission, *The Champlain Tercentenary*. . . . Prepared by Henry Wayland Hill. . . . Albany, N.Y.: J. B. Lyon Company, State Printers, 1913.

Finally, as regards Lake Champlain, how far would it be legitimate and practicable to present the plan fifty per cent or less wide in proportion to length? in other words to gain clearness and impression at the expense of literal accuracy.

To Little, Brown and Company

Marshmere, Quogue, Long Island, August 2, 1912 [LC]

Gentlemen: A question applicable to many instances that will arise in revision is illustrated in the last seven lines of p. 373. Is it best to retain the names of these unknown captains? In an exhaustive work like the *Naval History*, much uninteresting detail must be recorded; but should this apply to a more popular rendering, from which mere dryness should be excluded when possible?

The English publishers and American market have both to be considered.

My own opinion is in favor of omission, at my discretion. In the preface the fact might be mentioned, with a reference to the main work. The same would apply to detailed lists of fleets, such as on page 406.

To Little, Brown and Company

Marshmere, Quogue, Long Island, August 7, 1912 [LC]

Gentlemen: Acknowledging yours of August 5, it might perhaps be well if I reserved opinions till fuller consideration; but on the other hand early suggestion to you may be better, as time saving.

With regard to lists such as on pp. 406 and 415, my proposition would be to omit them altogether, depending upon the mention of numbers of vessels in the text. To compensate omission, I would make a general reference in Preface to the *History of the Royal Navy*; and perhaps also a specific foot note in each case, *in loco*, giving the page reference. E.G. "For names of vessels and commanders see *The Royal Navy, a History*. Vol. III, p —. Editor, Sir William Clowes. Sampson Low, Marston & Co." After one or two such foot notes, others could be shortened to: *The Royal Navy*, Vol. III, p—.

I see no reason why any of the medals or tail pieces should be inserted.

As regards portraits, I submit to your judgment. Arbuthnot and Hardy[1] were thoroughly commonplace men, and unknown to all but naval students. Barrington, Cornwallis and Parker were better, but equally unknown to the general public. Howe was a great man, and you already have his portrait in *Types of Naval Officers*; D'Estaing's name being known to our people, I have thought that the two bracketed would be interesting to them. Rodney I would bracket with DeGuichen[2] if the latter be obtainable; Rodney you have in *Types*. Hood with DeGrasse. Suffren with Hughes. I have an alleged Suffren which I could send you, but I think there is one more authoritative in Guérin's *Histoire de la Marine Française*,[3] vol 5.

My general look is towards American interest in this matter. Howe, Rodney, DeGrasse, D'Estaing are names known here.

The maps on pp. 377 and 381 are not to me satisfactory from the point of view of map drawing or of clearness. I think they could be curtailed, and consequently enlarged to advantage; but I will defer suggestion till further consideration. I incline also to think there should be a special map of New York Harbor and approaches; a mere outline, to meet the description of movements, pp. 382–6.

My tentative title would be: Major Operations of the Navies, American, British, French and Spanish in the War of American Independence.[4]

To Charles W. Stewart

Marshmere, Quogue, Long Island, August 10, 1912 [NA]

My dear Mr. Stewart: I am at present engaged upon a revision of the chapter contributed by me fifteen years ago to Samson Low's *The Royal Navy—a History*. The Chapter is "Major Operations 1762–1783."

In connection with this I should like to have at hand for the next two months, Chevalier's *Histoire Maritime, Guerre de L'Independence Americaine*[1] and also Troude's *Batailles Navales*, the volume covering 1775–1782, if you can spare them; which I hope may be easily possible in this off season.

---

1. Marriot Arbuthnot, who commanded the British North Atlantic Station, 1779–1781; and Sir Thomas Hardy.
2. Luc Urbain du Bouëxic, Comte de Guichen, who fought Rodney three times in the Antilles, 1780–1783, without winning a decisive victory.
3. Léon Guérin, *Histoire maritime de la France . . . depuis le règne de Louis XIV jusqu'à l'année 1850*. Paris: Dufour et Mulat, 1851.
4. It was published in 1913 as *The Major Operations of the Navies in the War of American Independence*.
1. Louis Edouard Chevalier, *Histoire de la marine française pendant la guerre de l'indépendence américaine. . . .* Paris: Hachette et cie., 1877.

To Charles W. Stewart

My dear Mr. Stewart: I am much obliged for the books, which have been received. As regards the *Royal Navy*, there has been a misunderstanding as to my wishing it, for I have a copy of my own. I therefore return the volume at once.

[P.S.] I find that instead of Chevalier's *Marine Française pendant La Guerre de l'Indépendence Americaine* there has been sent *Sous la Première République.*[1] I will return this tomorrow. Please send the former.

To the Editor of The New York Times

Quogue, Long Island, August 15, 1912[1]

You recently mentioned editorially the difficulties confronting the "French in Morocco," and their successes in Algeria and Tunis. Certain particulars concerning those successes may interest your readers, to many of whom they are probably as unknown as they were to myself until recently led to the knowledge by particular circumstances. In 1830, the year of the conquest, the entire commerce of Algiers, export and import, was under $1,000,000. Today it amounts to $200,000,000. Tunis, at the date of occupation, 1881, had a commerce of $8,000,000. It has now risen to $40,000,000. As an indication of the methods underlying such development, in the same thirty years 2,000 miles of good roads have been constructed in Tunisia.

The "successes," therefore, are not merely of the sword or of possession. They mean the material redemption of unimproved properties to the benefit of mankind at large.

To the Editor of The New York Times

N.P., N.D. Probably, Quogue, Long Island, August 20, 1912[1]

Those who appreciate the general conditions of international relations at the present time, of which the universal increase of armaments is no mere

---

1. By the same author, published in Paris by Hachette in 1886.

1. From *The New York Times*, August 17, 1912, p. 8.

1. From *The New York Times*, August 21, 1912, p. 8, under heading "Time Ill Chosen for a Weak Navy."

feature but the distinguishing and ominous exponent, cannot esteem too highly the action of those members of the Democratic Party in Congress who have endeavored to obtain from their associates a competent addition to our battle fleet. The people of the United States, whether they realize it or not, owe them gratitude. Unhappily, the fact remains that they have not been able to carry the party with them.

Dr. Eliot, till very recently the honored President of Harvard, has just returned from a round-the-world journey which is commonly understood to have been undertaken under the auspices of Mr. Carnegie's crusade for peace. As reported in the newspapers, Dr. Eliot has found that the Governments of the great States while heartily desirous of peace, are not in favor of a reduction of armaments in their own countries; or even of a near stay in the present movement of augmentation. In short, and to repeat what was said above, the increase of armament is simply a direct consequence of existing international conditions, as apprehended by the men responsible for the welfare of the several nations.

It is the dictate of the simplest common sense that in the practical conduct of life we must accept facts—such as those of the last paragraph—as we find them, not as we wish they were; and must meet them with appropriate measures. To meet the increasing armament of others by decreasing our own is unpractical. Though thus devoid of vision, it is none the less visionary; for it fails to realize that the armaments of other States have a definite object, which object is not war, but the enforcement of National purpose in moments of international crisis by being ready for war if the worst come. Statesmen are arming, not because they want fighting, but because they consider that conditions of which they have familiar knowledge render armament necessary, unless their Nation is willing that National policies—such as the Monroe Doctrine, or the safe tenure of the Panama Canal—be violated by superior power. If the power be sufficiently superior there will be no fighting. Careful observers of international events know how correct this estimate is. The last decade has seen a half-dozen bloodless wars, and decisive victories, effected by adequate armament.

In the approaching elections the voters of the United States also will have to accept facts as they are, not as they may wish them to be: and, like statesmen, they will have to adapt their measures to what is. There are several important internal questions before them, of which it may be said generally that they are common to most civilized nations to-day, and that, also, in regarding them there are in all countries two great divisions, eternal in the history of mankind—the conservative and the advancing. Between these two schools of thought internal questions take care of themselves; not that they do not need attention and action, but because they naturally get these, for the reason that they come home to every man's daily experience. Therefore they will not be neglected, and our daily papers bear hot assurance that they are not. But in every country, except in moments of excitement, external affairs do not enter the daily round of life, and therefore receive little attention. That is sadly the case with us now.

In this the Democratic representatives probably reflect the condition of their constituents. The fact remains, and the voters must deal with it, that the Democratic Party has deliberately refused to provide duly for the organized naval force of the country, and that the grudging concession of a half-measure has been reached only under a considerable pressure exerted on the eve of an important election. It is a fair, though sorrowful, inference that if the party be returned to power for two and four years, it will, in security of office and freedom from pressure, pursue the definite policy indicated by this year's course. In that event, the navy of the country will drop rapidly backward during four years.

The Democratic nominee for the Presidency in his speech of acceptance has refrained from expression of opinion, and is reported to have said, while the matter was in urgent discussion, that he could not with propriety interfere. Yet if elected, as he hopes, the strength of the United States Navy will be a very consequential factor in the international relations of the country, and these are the very especial charge of the Chief Executive. Apparently Dr. Wilson has no present concern as to the conditions under which he will bear this responsibility.

The result is the more imminent because in line with the traditions of the Democratic Party. In our Federal system we have two great historical divisions of thought: That which sees first the Nation, and that which sees first the State lines. All of us recognize the necessity of due co-ordination between the two; but the one which sees first the Nation will seek, and historically has sought, to strengthen the power for external action, which in the original compact the people—or the State—committed to the central Government, thus constituting a Nation where before there was none. There seems no reason why the State-rights school also should not wish adequately to strengthen the central Government, which represents the whole country, for its specific action, which is the international efficiency of the State; but, as matter of fact, to whatever cause due, that school does not so act, and in the instance before us is not now so acting.

It is not that Democratic Presidents have not had to deal with acute international relations, or have not shown great ability in so doing. Where they have failed has been in preparation, with consequential failure of power in negotiation, where issues of great importance were at stake. The first two, and most eminent, Jefferson and Madison, backed by Gallatin, spent years of fruitless argument with Great Britain over gross outrages to our rights; just because they would not prepare a navy, and the British Government realized that the United States neither would nor could fight. To the same lack of preparation were due the disasters of 1812. I hope I need not here contravene again the impression that that war was on our part other than a miserable failure. It is a sustainable, almost a demonstrable, proposition that the United States between 1801 and 1812 could have maintained a navy of such size that the menace would have forced Great Britain to seek an accommodation of differences.

Some days ago Everett Wheeler cited in your columns the concession of Great Britain to Mr. Cleveland's demands as an evidence of needlessness of a strong navy. The evident reply is that the Venezuela dispute was intrinsically of small account to England and that her reluctance to arbitrate was due rather to the truculence of Venezuela than to disinclination to please us. The questions now before the world are of a very different import and the powers interested much more in earnest than ever Great Britain about the Venezuela boundary. They will not desire war with us, but if they see us unprepared they will insist on their demands. In that case, we will either yield or be beaten. The result in either case is the same.

For the past half century, and now, nation after nation is emerging into international life with intensified powers manifested in greater armament. The moment is ill-chosen to weaken the effectiveness of the American Nation, which alone from its intrinsic powers, if properly organized, can maintain the separateness of the American continent from exterior molestation, from the transference hither, of conflicts existing elsewhere.

To Horatio G. Dohrman

Marshmere, Quogue, Long Island, September 2, 1912 [LC]

My dear Mr. Dohrman: Your letter of August 12 has remained too long unanswered, but unluckily I have bitten off more than I can chew in the way of promised writing; and, but for a rainy day stopping my usual necessary exercise, I don't know how even now I could find an opportunity for letter writing.

On the final adoption of the Conference Report, giving one battleship, I wrote a final letter—for this once—to the *N.Y. Times*, pointing out that the Democratic Party as a whole, despite many illustrious exceptions, were fairly committed to inadequate provision for the Navy, and that the same must be expected if they came into power for four years to come. I believe that much pressure like your own was brought to bear. The *N.Y. Times*, *Herald*, and *Sun* all backed the two ships. If under the evidence of public interest and facing an election the party has refused, nothing can be expected from it, if securely seated. On the top of this they have passed the Panama Tolls

Bill[1] which, whether first or not, has demonstrated the need of a navy, by bringing all Europe down on the Monroe Doctrine.

The matter is now up to the voters. As one, I am decided that the first thing is to defeat a party which has thus proved again its incapacity to rise to any conception of our foreign interests. It is no mere temporary aberration, but fundamental; or, as we say of an individual, constitutional. The taint is in the blood; the mess they will make of navy, Panama, Hawaii, and the Philippines is portentous to think of.

I shall watch indications and shall vote for either Taft or Roosevelt, as seems most likely to carry this state against the Democrats. With congressmen the same consideration will dictate. I am the more confirmed in my decision to base my vote on our foreign relations, in that I believe all parties recognize the general necessity of the regulation of domestic industrial relations, which is playing so large a part in the campaign. Methods and points of view differ, but something will be done whoever comes in; and in so large a question I doubt whether anyone can *yet* say which of the several methods is best,—that is, antecedent to experience. Personally I prefer Roosevelt as a man to Taft; but Taft's ideas appeal more to my conservative temperament. It is better to go a little too slow than a great deal too fast in such a matter. On the other hand, Taft has made a most disastrous muddle of our foreign policy. He has less tact than I could have supposed possible,—but at least he, like Roosevelt, stands for two battleships.

As regards your suggestion of an appeal to the money sense of our communities, the ground is lawful and sensible, if not very elevated. If nothing else will arouse us, let that be started; but to tell you the truth I have not much faith in the capacity of a mercantile interest to take broad views, even of its own affairs. I am interested in your idea of an American history written upon the lines of the relation of the citizen to the state. It would be an excellent thing. I have for some years contemplated such a history based upon the idea of Expansion; tracing our gradual advances both in territory and in external influence. But as I am nearly seventy-two, I don't know whether I shall ever really get at it. Contemporary events take up so much of my time.

I believe I have said to you before that I have no confidence in Dr. Wilson. I don't question his personal honesty, but I believe—as you have found— that he is simply after the Presidency—in other words, his own personal advancement. I take a good deal of stock in the valuation of our public men made by the correspondents of English papers, especially the *Times*, whose foreign notes are marked by fullness and judgment. As I remember, two

---

1. The Panama Canal Act of August 24, 1912, which exempted U.S. coastal shipping from payment of tolls. In British eyes, this contradicted a provision of the second Hay-Pauncefote Treaty of 1901 that the Canal should be open to the vessels of "all nations" on a basis of full equality.

weeks ago, its Washington correspondent commented on the vagueness of Dr. Wilson's speech of acceptance. I had myself characterized it as mere generalities.

I cannot presume to advise, much less to urge you; but I hope you will be governed in your decisions by the recollection that Ohio is a very great state, and not improbably very close. Your influence may count for much, and while, as I said, industrial and economical conditions will certainly receive attention, whoever is elected, foreign affairs will almost certainly be mismanaged by the Democrats.

To Edwin A. Alderman[1]

Marshmere, Quogue, Long Island, September 28, 1912 [UVL][2]

My dear Dr. Alderman: I shall write to Professor Dobie[3] that we are considering going abroad this winter, for several reasons; but that if not, which will be decided by Oct 20, it will give me pleasure to accept the invitation proffered. Of course should this necessary delay be inexpedient, I must decline. I should feel it a privilege, perhaps even a duty, to embrace such an occasion, although until recently I had determined that I should do no more public lecturing.

In case of my coming I shall very gladly accept your kind and hospitable offer of being your guest.

To the New York State Public Service Commission

Draft   Marshmere, Quogue, Long Island, September 30, 1912 [LC]

Gentlemen: I do not know how far the following presentation falls within your scope, but submit it.

On Thursday last, Sept. 26, I took a Long Island train, at 7:40 A.M., at Quogue, for New York. The train went by way of Manorville. I found every seat occupied; many who got on board at the same place had to stand thence to Mineola, a distance of fifty-eight miles. The numbers were much increased at Westhampton, the next stop. At Speonk, the second stop after Quogue, there were several passenger cars on a siding. None of these were

---

1. President of the University of Virginia, author of many books, and editor of the *Library of Southern Literature*.
2. From the Alderman Collection, courtesy of the University of Virginia Library.
3. Armistead Mason Dobie, professor of law at the University of Virginia.

attached to the train to relieve the pressure. In consequence, a large number of passengers filling every aisle of the "coaches" had to stand all the way, about an hour and a half.

I went into a parlor car where several seats were vacant, and so continued till I left the car. I took one of these. The conductor demanded a parlor car fare. I objected, on the ground that I had only entered because there was no seat anywhere else. He informed me that your Commission had decided that under such circumstances the law did not permit a seatless passenger to take an unoccupied seat in a parlor car. The matter ended by his getting a passenger in the coaches to give up his seat to me. This of course took away the ground of my contention, and I left the car.

Considering the fact that it is almost impossible for an individual passenger to get any redress from a corporation—a circumstance which makes a voting enemy of each sufferer—does it not seem congruous with your duty to order, or to obtain a law, that in such cases every seat in the train is open to passengers, parlor car fare or not?

To Little, Brown and Company

Marshmere, Quogue, Long Island, October 1, 1912 [LC]

Gentlemen: Owing to a number of circumstances which have commanded my attention unexpectedly, I have not quite completed the revision of the *Major Operations* in the *Naval History*, as I had expected to do by this date. I have, however, read all but the last twenty pages, correcting as I went; so that I can speak with some confidence in saying that the matter requiring some careful reconstruction does not exceed a half-dozen pages.

There will remain, therefore, simply to read the twenty yet unread; to recast, in no extensive measure, the half-dozen; and to make some suggestions as to maps; the present seeming to me in some cases open to improvement. I cannot recall whether originally I passed upon these maps. They seem to me to have been chosen more for antiquarian flavor than for fitness in several instances, and in others to be sketchy and indistinct to a degree never practised in your publications of my works.

Speaking generally, the battle plans taken from my first Sea Power book seem less well rendered in this history than in Sea Power.

During the summer pressure, which has been considerable, I have postponed this work to others because I assumed that in no case would it be published before next spring, and that you might prefer to postpone even to next autumn. I should particularly like to know your wishes, because I am thinking about going to Europe with my family about November 20, to remain absent till May 1. In that case I should expect to place with you before sailing the "copy" complete and corrected, so that any accident to myself need not interfere with publication; but if you prefer autumn, or do not prefer next spring, proof reading might be postponed till my return. In this particular I shall hold myself entirely at your disposal.

To the New York Public Service Commission

Draft   Quogue, Long Island, October 7, 1912 [LC]

Gentlemen: I am obliged to you for your letter of Oct. 4 enclosing copy of that of the President of the Long Island Railroad.[1]

This letter amounts to this: that having in expectation a large passenger traffic they met it so badly that some fifty or sixty persons had to stand up from Quogue to Mineola, nearly sixty miles. No explanation is offered why one or more of the cars on the siding at Speonk were not attached. The crowding by that was not only evident, but extreme.

I do not know whether this satisfies the Public Service Commission. It probably will not any of those who had to stand.

I note that the Commission expresses no opinion upon Mr. Peters' letter; nor as to the use of unoccupied seats in parlor cars without payment for persons treated as were the passengers on that day; nor any purpose to advocate meeting such conditions by this. Abroad, I have frequently been witness to third class passengers being ushered into first class cars under similar conditions.

In short, there is no indication of its being of the slightest use to a citizen to apply to the Commission.

To Little, Brown and Company

Marshmere, Quogue, Long Island, October 12, 1912 [LC]

Gentlemen: In pursuance of the purpose intimated to you in a recent letter, I expect now to sail for Europe on November 9, to be absent until

---

1. Ralph Peters.

the end of April. Before that date I expect to place in your hands corrected "copy" and battle plans, with all suggestions as regards maps; in short, all the material of the book except index. Preface is outlined, and the text chaptered.

I expect to reach Pau, France, by December 15, and to be there a month. If the galley proofs can be sent there (or any part reach me here) proof reading can go on, as opportunity offers. A month should be amply sufficient, and corrected proof will be mailed as finished.

I expect to make a second long stay of nearly a month, probably February, on the Riviera, where perhaps page proof may be read.

I of course do not know how far it may be practicable for you so to expedite printing as to utilize these suggestions, but as I confidently expect to place the materials in your hands by October 22, I notify you in advance. In fact four fifths of the text could be mailed to-day.

My address till otherwise notified will be Care F. L. Brown, Esq. M.D., 4 rue d'Orléans, Pau, France.

To Little, Brown and Company

Marshmere, Quogue, Long Island, October 14, 1912 [LC]

Gentlemen: Referring to the plan on p. 526 of the *Major Operations*, which is substantially the same as that in the first Sea Power book, p. 486, as I come to it anew after so many years, I conceive it will be better to give it the size of a full page of text. The actual distances involved, and the words of the text, make this almost indispensable in order that text and plan correspond more plausibly.

I enclose a sketch of the plan so determined. The border corresponds to the page space of *Major Operations*. I do not yet know the page size of the proposed work; but that will be immaterial, as the draughtsman can proportion.

I will add that the figures B and C (*M.O.* 527, 528) are well enough at the present size and could go on the same page; *north* point to top of page. This will be an advantage, as they represent together a transition moment. Figure D, (p. 529) will be decidedly better at full page size. The space east and west enlarged, and positions altered in proportion, would be better than present size. In this, east and west would take the page *length*; as it is east and west enlargement that is needed.

I find that I shall also need a copy of Plan XIV, *Sea Power*, p. 431, as the rendering in *Major Operations* p. 551 is defective.

[481]

To Little, Brown and Company

Marshmere, Quogue, Long Island, October 19, 1912 [LC]

Gentlemen: I send today by registered mail, the "copy" for the book *The Major Operations of the Navy in the War of American Independence.* I also enclose herewith memorandum as to *maps* for the work.[1] I should have sent also memorandum concerning battle-plans, but may not be able to have it copied in time for the same mail. Moreover, the plans &c, mentioned in yours of Oct. 16 have not yet reached me. I have copies of the above named memoranda which I shall take with me, but I have no duplicate of the revised text; that sent being the only one in existence.

As soon as the battle-plans named in yours of Oct 16 are received, I will enter changes, of which I have full notes, and return them. This will complete the material. The "copy" also contains all changes in battle-plans, and some alluded to in memorandum for maps. These had best be consulted before giving to printer.

[P.S.] The "copy" mentioned in above is the revised and corrected text of *Major Operations* on sheets sent me for that purpose. It would be best to consult this "copy" which goes by registered mail today (19th) before turning it over to printer; although I propose to make the changes on the drawing notified in yours of Oct. 16, which has not yet reached me. I take also a duplicate with me.

To Little, Brown and Company

Marshmere, Quogue, Long Island, October 21, 1912 [LC]

Gentlemen: I enclose complete list of Battle and Other Plans for the Operations of the Navies.[1] The plans themselves will go in this mail, registered.

I have retained the sheets of *Major Operations* sent by you to me, except those carrying plans which have been used in making the above plans. If you wish those other sheets please notify me.

There is being type written now a Preface and an Introduction. The latter was begun for Preface, but in writing I concluded better to separate the two, making the Preface very short. The Introduction I propose now, to precede of course the text, but to form *part of it*; a chapter by itself

---

1. The enclosed three-page "Memorandum as to Maps for Operations of the Navies" has been omitted.

1. The enclosed two-page "Plans, Battle or Other, for The Operations of the Navies" has been omitted.

with arabic numbers, not Roman; my reason being that I want the Introduction *read* and I think the usual disposition is to skip such matter.

The question then will arise whether to call it Introduction, and leave Chapter numbers to stand as now, or to call it Introduction, Chapter I, and modify the subsequent chapter numbers accordingly. I prefer the first course, but will acquiesce in your judgment.

Preface and Introduction will go forward to-morrow, together with proposed Title Page.

To Little, Brown and Company

Marshmere, Quogue, Long Island, October 22, 1912 [LC]

Gentlemen: I enclose herewith Preface and Introduction alluded to in my letter of yesterday. Also, Title Page, the principal point of which is what ones of my now numerous volumes should be mentioned as cognate to the subject of the particular work.

These complete the material for the book, except the Contents and Index, which cannot be undertaken before the paging. I expect to do both these myself.

To Carter FitzHugh

Quogue, Long Island, October 24, 1912 [LC]

Dear Mr. FitzHugh: In a book just published, *Armaments and Arbitration*, pp. 180 and 195, I have expressed the opinion that the U. S. Navy should be second only to that of Great Britain. On the question of annual increase I have confined myself to supporting the recommendations of the Administration, two battleships annually. Granting my first position as a premise, the rate of increase depends upon that of other nations.

I have expressed no opinion on the Panama Canal Tolls, considering the interpretation of the phraseology of treaties as beyond the scope of a naval officer.

In the *N. Y. Times* of April 3, May 23, and August 21, I have developed at length the argument for increase. The first two of these dates depend on memory, but are almost exact. I would send you clippings, but have only one of each. Doubtless, you can in some way, or from some quarter, obtain copies.

[P.S.]   It should be always remembered that the question of increase is not primarily naval, but one of national external policy.

To Bouverie F. Clark

Philadelphia, October 28, 1912 [LC]

My dear Clark: I have been a fig not to have acknowledged sooner your cable and letter on my birthday; both which were duly received. I am not without excuse, however, for I was making a desperate attempt to close up a mountain of work in order to be able to leave manuscript complete in the hands of publishers before sailing for Europe, which we now hope to do Nov. 9, going hence direct to London by an unfashionable line, the Atlantic Transport Co., which is well spoken of by friends who have often used it. We are due Nov. 18 or 19, expect to spend about a week in London, thence to Paris, where I have a brother living, for the same length of time, and to arrive about Dec 15 at Pau where Mrs. Mahan has a sister married to a Scotch resident physician. We intend thence to go on to the Riviera, winding up with Sicily, to leave thence for home in April. I shrink from such an active programme, but it is partly for that very reason I undertake it; also because I have got into such a habit of hard monotonous work that I feel a total change necessary. I am now with friends near Philadelphia, and have already felt the benefit in three days, not only of the idleness but of the absence of the desk and the paraphernalia which keeps work always in mind. I hope the total absence will break up all such associations and perhaps free me from the active interposition in current national naval policies which has added so much to my work this year. We are threatened, and I fear the accession to power of a doctrinaire party—the Democratic—which is dominated by a number of theories which can by no means be made to fit present facts; like the wrong key to a lock. Among others that of keeping the navy below strength, and ignoring all the dangerous contingencies of the present by the simple process of shutting their eyes, and taking a sleeping potion of the doctrines of a man who died near a century ago. Perhaps you know the name Jefferson. He made a hideous mess in his own day, and yet has a progeny of backwoodsmen and planters who think what he taught a great success. I have been slinging brickbats at them for months past, and hope getting away will put them and their rottenness out of my mind. I'm sorry for the country; but if it will take what is bad for it now, it must take its medicine later like a good boy.

I see you accept your quiet rest and home. I do the same yet believe it better not to yield wholly to what is certainly pleasanter and more to the mind of my old age. After this trip I may understand better how to order the future. I trust at least I may so far regain my balance as not to fret if the country persists in going to the devil its own way. I intend to vote for Roosevelt as the best—by far—of the three candidates for the Presidency, and then for the Republican members of the houses, who will serve as a brake upon his too great impulsiveness and who, as a party, sustain the navy, and recognize that we have to reckon with some other nations beside the U.S.

Till then. I will let you know our London address, when I know it.

To Leopold J. Maxse

Hotel de la Trémoille, Paris, France, November 30, 1912 [LC]

Dear Mr. Maxse: Your letter of the 27th reached me too late to be acknowledged in London, which we left at 10 A.M. of the 28th. It revealed also what had been a puzzle as to the source whence Bernhardi's book[1] had reached me. I am much indebted to you for it. I have seen notices and from them inferred its general drift, but the book itself is new to me.

I have not yet communicated with M. Clemenceau,[2] and shall prefer to do so in writing, but am greatly indebted to you for the pains you have taken in the matter. As I have only a week in Paris, I shall not avail myself of Mr. Saunders,[3] for I have so much to do I cannot afford to embarrass my time with engagements, which may clash inconveniently. With many thanks [etc.].

To Little, Brown and Company

4 Rue d'Orléans, Pau, France, December 18, 1912 [LC]

Gentlemen: I arrived here Dec. 15, and have found your various covers transmitting in full the text of *Major Operations*. I confidently hope to complete proof reading, and to return before the end of my stay here—a month hence.

I have recd. also the battle plans, which I have no doubt are complete in number, though I have not verified this. The maps have not yet come to

---

1. Friedrich Adam Julius von Bernhardi, *Germany and the Next War*. Translated by Allen H. Powles. London: E. Arnold, 1912.
2. Former Premier (1906–1909) of France. In 1912 Senator Georges Clemenceau was active in the related anti-German and pro-preparedness movements in France.
3. This might be Albert Saunders, author of *Maritime Law* (London: E. Wilson, 1901), and *The Neutral Ship in War Time: Rights, Duties and Liabilities* (London: E. Wilson, 1898). There was also George Saunders, who succeeded Sir Valentine Chirol as *The Times* correspondent in Berlin.

hand, and from the date of your letter—Dec. 3—I presume they were scarcely to be expected by this writing.

[P.S.] Before arriving here I had received your suggestion as to title. I will reply in due time, merely observing now that between title page and cover title there is a difference which will allow much condensation for the latter.

To Leopold J. Maxse

4 Rue d'Orléans, Pau, December 24, 1912 [LC]

Dear Mr. Maxse: I have written Messrs. Harper and Brothers, of London and New York, asking them to send you a copy of my last published work *Armaments and Arbitration*. The title speaks for itself; but in your influential position I am especially desirous to have in your hands—or within your reach—the two articles on *The Great Illusion* and on Mr. Roosevelt's action at Panama in 1903, in case you should have occasion to comment on either.[1] I will not be so tiresome as to wish—much less to ask—that you should read either as a matter of general interest; but if specific need arise I believe the last named especially should receive consideration.

I am the more moved to this because your experienced Washington correspondent, in your December number, p. 625,[2] seems ignorant that in the correspondence intervening between the first & second Hay-Pauncefote treaties of 1901, Lord Lansdowne[3] explicitly recognized the desirableness to the U.S., & he added, possibly to the general use of the Canal, of our fortifying it. I cannot here give you an exact reference, but I found Lord L's letter in a voluminous govt. work, *Digest of International Law*, by John Bassett Moore; a man of encyclopedic information on the subject. Possibly the same may appear in a Blue Book covering the negotiation of those treaties. The *Quarterly Review* of Oct. last fell into a like error,[4] and I addressed a letter from N.Y. to the editor, pointing out that and another

---

1. "The Great Illusion," *North American Review* (March 1912); "Was Panama a Chapter of National Dishonor?", *ibid.* (October 1912).
2. A. Maurice Low, "American Affairs," *The National Review* (December 1912), pp. 618–628. On pages 625–627 Low discussed questions raised by Stimson's article in the then current *Scientific American* on the "necessity for and reason why the Panama Canal is being fortified."
3. Henry Charles Keith Petty-Fitzmaurice, 5th Marquis of Lansdowne; Unionist leader in the House of Lords.
4. "The Panama Canal," *Quarterly Review* (July and October 1912), pp. 299–323. Mahan's letter to the editor has not been found but the January 1913 issue carried an opinion to the effect that the United States had not intervened in the Panamanian revolution against Colombia in 1903.

error into which I conceived the Q. had fallen in the same article. Prothero[5] has written me here that a reply had been sent to America, but it has not yet come to me here. I think it may accurately be said that, although Great Britain preferred not to sanction explicitly the fortifying of the Canal, the second treaty (H–P) was signed with the clear understanding that we had the right to do so.

I have not yet read Bernhardi's book which you kindly sent me, but I have read attentively your illuminative analysis of it.[6] I was glad to realize that he did not rest his case merely, or mainly, on the material interests of a nation, but on what you rightly call the spiritual motives. My main contention against *The Great Illusion*[7] is that its chief proposition, that nations go to war for material gain chiefly, for the sake of their pockets, is itself an illusion; one which ignores the motive which has underlain every war from, and including, the American War of Secession.

I have not tackled Bernhardi's book because I came abroad for a rest, among other things from too much serious reading and from the strain attendant upon it. My interest in current politics is not academic, but so excessively sympathetic as to constitute a true mental excitement & physical effect which at 72 I cannot disregard. But I am not yet past work, and I shall give myself to Bernhardi as soon as I can do so profitably. Meantime I am glad to know, through you, the character of the book. From casual reviews I had gathered that Bernhardi was simply an unconditional advocate of pure brute force, with no better justification than supposed national advantage.

With much regard, and with best wishes of the season believe me [etc.].

[P.S.] A somewhat disjointed sentence, above, is due to the hair-cutter interrupting me.

To Joseph H. Chapin

4 Rue d'Orléans, Pau, January 7, 1913 [PUL]

Dear Sir: Your letter of Dec. 17 reached me here today. I have no objection to your [Scribner's] supplying The Houghton Mifflin Co. with the plan of the *Bonhomme Richard* & *Serapis* action, as they wish.

---

5. Rowland Edmund Ernle, 1st Baron Prothero, editor of *Quarterly Review* (1894–1899).
6. The review, in the form of an editorial by L. J. Maxse, "Germany's Next War," *National Review* (December 1912), p. 517, stated that Bernhardi's book had become the Bible of the German patriot and had exerted great influence on the Emperor and the Crown Prince.
7. Angell, *The Great Illusion* (1911).

To Little, Brown and Company

4 Rue d'Orléans, Pau, January 10, 1913 [LC]

Gentlemen: I have completed reading the galleys of *Major Operations*, and in connection therewith have examined and corrected battle plans. The maps for the book have not come.

I propose returning the galleys in six separate packets of thirty each, which I shall mail at intervals, to guard as far as possible against a loss of any great extent. The first was mailed yesterday. The battle-plans will be sent in one packet by themselves. In Rodney's actions of April 9 and 12, 1782, I have made such re-arrangements as makes advisable to enclose a separate memorandum.[1] All the others have only usual proof indications; but in some cases I have written comment or explanation on the back of the plan.

The question of page headings has occurred to me; but as no easy solution presents itself, I incline to throughout (left page) Major Naval Operations; (right pages) War of American Independence. Should you prefer otherwise, I will accept any necessary change.

I wish not to read page proof before my return home, which I expect to be about April 20. The effort here has tended to defeat in part the complete refreshment of mind which was my object in coming abroad; and after my return will permit ample time to complete page reading, Contents, and Index by June 15, if not indeed sooner.

My address while abroad remains here, whence letters will be forwarded. I shall notify you betimes of precise date of return, and of U.S. address.

[P.S.] With reference to portraits, I have seen in a window here of a bookseller collector of prints, etc. a likeness of Count D'Estaing. The name is E. Dupuy, Rue des Cordeliers, Pau.

To Little, Brown and Company

4 Rue d'Orléans, Pau, January 16, 1913 [LC]

Gentlemen: I received on the 14th package from you containing five maps, viz: Lake Champlain, New York and New Jersey, Narragansett Bay, Santa Lucia, and Leeward Islands Station.

Having carefully examined these, I enclose a memorandum, of changes,

---

1. This enclosure, "Memorandum Concerning Battle Plans, Rodney and De Grasse, April 9 and 12, 1782," and another, "Memorandum Concerning Five Maps (Proof-read) for Major Operations," have been omitted.

explanatory where needed beyond usual proof corrections.[1] I have been embarrassed as to New York, and Narragansett Bay, by lack here of a suitable atlas, as to U.S. Therefore, while I think the maps as corrected will stand, I suggest they be not considered final until my return in April permits me to verify details by more copious atlas than here attainable.

It was I believe understood that besides these five there were to be the four following: Atlantic Ocean, and Indian Peninsula with Ceylon. These two taken from first Sea Power Book. Also, Fort Moultrie, and Island Martinique, as shown in *Major Operations*.

I have now noted in *duplicate* galleys all changes made in reading proof. Five *originals* have been mailed to you, and the last will be mailed January 18; at which time I expect to send also a packet containing battle plans and above maps.

My address remains here, 4 Rue d'Orléans, but as I shall be travelling, I can do no more work on this side.

To Carter FitzHugh

4 Rue d'Orléans, Pau, January 18, 1913 [LC]

Dear Mr. FitzHugh: I had the pleasure to receive here yesterday your letter of Dec. 29. I had seen the notice in the *Spectator* but am none the less obliged to you for mentioning it.

I am very glad to know that while a member of a Peace Society, the aims of which are admirable, you are still sensible of the difficulties in the way of an immediate entire realization of its laudable purpose. I am persuaded that at the present moment and for many years to come the great preparations for war now sustained are the surest guarantee for the continuance of *actual* peace even among the nations of our European civilization. I am at a loss also to understand the ground of those who would prefer a *nominal* peace, with the atrocities committed under it by the Turks, to a war which at least releases the victims. It is to be remembered too that the major part of mankind still is alien to the ideas of Christian civilization, and in no sense recognizes its standards. To be sure, Christian nations and peoples fall far short of those standards, but all the same they are influenced progressively by them.

As regards the Panama Canal tolls, if my memory serve me, the obnoxious act was passed after most of my proof reading was done.[1] I agree with your

---

1. Enclosure not found.

1. For his "Was Panama A Chapter of National Dishonor?", *North American Review* (October 1912). The Panama Canal Act was passed on August 24, 1912. *See* Mahan to Dohrman, September 2, 1912, Footnote 1.

reading of the words of the treaty, but was impressed also by the fact that so eminent a legist as President Taft thought differently. I felt myself scarcely lawyer enough to venture on a public construction contrary to his, even had I time to write one. I may say that last May I received a pamphlet and letter from a man in Phila., advocating the remission of tolls *or* an equivalent subsidy. My reply, which antedated the act of Congress, was that I did not approve of the remission; that if any allowance were made it should be by subsidy, but that in my judgment the coasting trade was already sufficiently privileged by our interdiction of foreign competition.

To Little, Brown and Company

San Remo, Italy, January 28, 1913 [LC]

Gentlemen: In forwarding corrected galleys from Pau, I omitted to mention that by a good many of the corrections I had placed an asterisk*. It did not occur to me at the moment that this might give rise to perplexity or misunderstanding; but I write now to say that these pencil marks, wherever occurring, were to indicate that the mistakes were by the printer and not in the "copy" he was using.

I believe I have not used the asterisk in any other connection, or for any other purpose, at any time.

[P.S.] My address, if needed, remains 4 Rue d'Orléans, Pau.

To Little, Brown and Company

San Remo, February 10, 1913 [LC]

Gentlemen: My first impulse as to the enclosed[1] was to give consent, but my second is to comply with the usual routine and transmit the letter for your action, signifying my own acquiescence. As the whole book has already been translated into German and into French, I scarcely see the object of his proposed rendering into Dutch, but if he wishes I am willing. I enclose also his order for the necessary stamp, which was decent of him.

I send also my receipt for February settlement, for which please accept my thanks.

---

1. Enclosure not found.

To Little, Brown and Company

San Domenico Palace, Taormina, Sicily, March 8, 1913 [LC]

Gentlemen: I enclose a letter from a young French officer, asking permission to publish a translation of *Naval Strategy* with certain abbreviations.[1] I have written my consent, conditional upon a *general* statement in preface that there has been abbreviation, and also upon your consent. If you consent, will you write him direct, confirming mine, and imposing such pecuniary condition, or other, as you may think expedient. I have thought fifty dollars enough, to assert the principle of payment without bearing unduly hard upon him; the pay of French officers being very small.

The book is too technical to be very remunerative, and the appreciation conveyed by his letter is really worth more than the money. It may interest you to know that when in England Mr. Winston Churchill, the head of the Admiralty, told me he was about to read the book upon the recommendation to him of one of the "Sea Lords."

I expect to sail from Palermo April 6, to be at the University Club from April 20 to May 4, and then to be at Quogue, N.Y.

To Bouverie F. Clark

Hotel Panormus, Palermo, Sicily, March 24, 1913 [LC]

My dear Clark: I have no book of reference for the exact date of your birthday, but unless my memory is greatly at fault it is about this time. At any rate here goes, as well as a poor hotel pen will permit. Intending to do a minimum of writing I brought with me no materials of my own.

We have been leisurely travellers since I saw you. Spent ten days in Paris, where my brother is settled, then five weeks with Mrs. Mahan's sister, married in Pau. Thence to San Remo for three weeks, where an intimate girl friend of one of my daughters makes her winter home, a fortnight in Florence and now a month in Sicily, winding up here where we await the homeward steamer, *Saxonia*, due to sail hence on April 6.

---

1. *Naval Strategy* appeared in French as *Stratégie navale*. Admiral R.V.P. Castex, *Théories stratégiques* (Paris: Société d'Editions Geographiques Maritimes, 1929), pp. 40–41, describes the translation as "particulièrement abstraite et soporifique, non aérée et vivifiée par le recit des faits eux-mêmes comme beaucoup de ses autres ouvrages." And he adds a footnote; "On recueille cette impression dans des traductions françaises faites par quatre traducteurs différents. La question du traducteur paraît donc n'y être pour rien . . . Mahan est aussi lourd dans le texte anglais que dans le texte français."

The conclusion of the whole matter is that I am a hopeless old fogey. I dont like the warm climate as well as our northwest and northeast winds at home; feel more myself at 20° (in winter) than at 60°; and feel bored by seeing things, or rather by feeling that I ought to see them and therefore must see them. Further than Dr. Johnson, I think now that the show things not only are not worth going to see, but scarcely worth seeing when you get there.[1] All which is an awful proof of old age, for seven years ago I loved seeing things. I do enjoy however poking around by myself in the slums of these continental cities, losing myself and finding my way, and noting the old heavy built and heavily decorated palaces, now serving mainly as tenements for the unwashed. I like mingling with the crowds in the street and seeing the scenery, which is very fine here, from car window or from carriage. But "sights" have lost attraction for me.

Things have been moving pretty rapidly since I left London. It has been on my mind, though I have not worried, that any slight slip among the diplomats might land all the fat in the fire, and the Mediterranean be a scene of war before I could get my women folk out,—not to say my gray hairs, what I have of them. Even now I should not be surprised by a *mauvais tour* in the proceedings, but they have been talking so long I fancy now they will be able to settle things without fighting. Nevertheless, as long as Turkey exists she will be perpetually giving rise to "questions." I believe the individual Turk is not a bad sort, but any people more hopelessly unfit for governing it is hard to imagine. I believe the Persians are worse.

I look back with much pleasure to having seen you again for a few meetings, as well as some other friends. From the look of things, I fancy some years will elapse before I again come abroad, and at our time of life a few years means a good deal. I have had my holiday, broken out of my rut, and am now beginning to feel restive for work again, due largely, I think to the fact that the usual diversions of travel have ceased to interest me, and that I have become so attached to the plough that I feel better satisfied with the yoke on my shoulders than off. Yet what to do remains a problem. My vogue is largely over[2]—I am less in demand, and therefore must make work for myself, without security that it will be wanted. Still I have plans and an outlook.

With much regard and kind remembrances from Mrs. Mahan [etc.].

---

1. "Worth seeing? Yes; but not worth going to see." Boswell's *Life of Johnson*. Everyman edition, Vol. 2, p. 291.
2. A year earlier, Fisher wrote jubilantly, "Mahan is an extinct volcano." Albert J. Marder, ed., *Fear God and Dread Nought: The Correspondence of Admiral of the Fleet, Lord Fisher of Kilverstone*. 3 vols. (London: Cape, 1952–1959), II, p. 430.

To Little, Brown and Company

Hotel Panormus, Palermo, April 1, 1913 [LC]

Gentlemen: Yours of March 11 reached me only yesterday. As you have my letters, I suppose I did not answer the question you now repeat. In reply, I should not object to the cover-title of "Major Naval Operations," since the space in such case is limited; but for *title page* I think "Major Operations of the Navies in the War of American Independence" distinctly preferable, and there doubtless would be room there. "Major Naval Operations" conveys the idea of greater coherence and plan than actually occurred, more system and interconnection. Further, the second title, "Operations of the Navies," brings out better the fact that several navies, largely independent of each other, were concerned; viz: American, British, Dutch, French, Spanish.

I sail from here on next Sunday April 6, and am due to arrive in New York, per Cunard Steamer *Saxonia*, April 20. I expect to remain in New York till May 5 or 6 when I shall go to Quogue for the summer. I shall be able to take up page proof shortly after arrival in N.Y. where my address will be University Club, Fifth Ave. & 54th St.

Your two last letters, addressed to France, bore only two-cent stamps. In consequence, double the deficient postage had to be paid here. I thought the first only an oversight, but it would be well to caution the responsible person that Great Britain is the only foreign country with which we have two cent postage.

To Little, Brown and Company

University Club, New York, April 23, 1913[1] [LC]

Gentlemen: I reached New York on my return from Europe day before yesterday, and will be ready shortly to take up the final proof readings of the new book. I remain here until Monday or Tuesday, May 5 or 6, and can begin reading next week. I should prefer, however, waiting until I reach Quogue. In any case, please notify me with the proofs what is your latest date for requiring the completion of them.

The question is the purely business one of the most advantageous moment for publication. As usual, I defer to your judgment on such points, but I want free time for a fortnight to overtake a bundle of accumulated correspondence I find awaiting me.

[P.S.] Address till May 2, as above. From May 2 onward Quogue, N.Y.

---

1. Mahan incorrectly dated this letter April 24.

To Charles Scribner[1]

University Club, New York, May 8, 1913 [PUL]

Dear Mr. Scribner: Returning to my room this evening I found Fullerton's *Problems of Power*,[2] for which your card tells me I am indebted to your kindness.

I am very much obliged for it. International questions have now come to be my chief interest, to the subordination at least of those that are purely naval, with the details of which I have for some years past found it onerous to keep up. I shall therefore have much pleasure and little sense of effort when I take up Fullerton upon my return home next week.

Renewing my thanks, believe me [etc.].

To Little, Brown and Company

Quogue, Long Island, May 17, 1913 [LC]

Gentlemen: All the items specified in your letter of May 9 were found by me in the package, when opened.

Referring to the last paragraph of the letter: I find it on trial rather awkward and hindering to take up the several maps and battle-plans except as they come along in the text. As your desire to have them *all* back with the first installment of proofs seems to depend entirely upon the requirements of your travelers, why should they not take them exactly as they now are, for samples? The changes probably will not be extensive, only in details; and I do not see why buyers for sale should need more than to have the general effect. There will be I think no radical changes of any kind.

I may add that I have read and corrected nearly half the text in three days work together with the maps and plans incident to that half. Unless something very unexpected occur I ought to send all back by June 1.

---

1. Son of the founder of Charles Scribner's Sons publishing house. He became the head of the firm in 1879 and founded *Scribner's Magazine* in 1887.
2. William Morton Fullerton, *Problems of Power, a Study of International Politics from Sadowa to Kirk-Kilissé*. New York: C. Scribner's Sons, 1913.

To The New York Telephone Company

Quogue, Long Island, June 3, 1913 [LC]

Gentlemen: Referring to a letter addressed by me to you, May 21, 1912, I hereby extend the permission for the telephone wires to run across my property, from the pole in Post Lane to that in the Gardiner's grounds, from June 1, 1913 to June 1, 1914.

To Little, Brown and Company

Quogue, Long Island, June 7, 1913 [LC]

Gentlemen: Enclosed I send the Table of "Contents" complete.

With regard to the position of the date, whether at the end of the Preface, or of the Introduction, your suggestion seems to me somewhat technical; but if the innovation,—in the Introduction, which you rightly judge was on account of the allusion to the late Balkan War,—seems too startling, I am willing that the change be made as you suggest. I should regret, however, that readers should imagine that my homily, on the illustration offered by the Turkish Empire in general, depended on my being waked up to the fact merely by the recent hostilities. The Introduction was written weeks before the sudden outbreak. And indeed, the illustration itself suffers, if a reader fails to realize that the conditions of the thirty previous years constituted a danger of universal war, and that the particular incident, or the manner of its breaking out, was relatively immaterial. The failure to provide beforehand against the evident conditions kept all Europe on tenter hooks and in real imminent danger through the last six months; a danger before which arbitration was helpless, because all law was on behalf of Turkey. Armament and war solved in six months a difficulty before which all other means had failed for thirty-odd years but the danger of war becoming universal was avoided only because every state was armed.

I want the United States to wake up betimes.

To the Editor of The Times

Quogue, Long Island, circa June 13, 1913[1]

The three weeks or more of time involved makes it a far cry to criticize from this side of the Atlantic an argument in an English daily, but the com-

---

1. From *The Times*, London, June 23, 1913, under the heading "Japan Among the Nations: Admiral Mahan's Views." *See* Mahan to Roosevelt, July 8, 1913, and Mahan to Root, July 9, 1913.

munication of Sir Valentine Chirol[2] in your issue of May 19, "Japan Among the Nations: The Bar of Race," is of such importance to the American world—in Canada no less than in the United States—and also of such enduring interest to the whole community of European civilization, because affecting the political conditions of territories to which their emigrant population may wish to resort, that it seems expedient to attempt some comment, even though inevitably retarded.

The question discussed by Sir Valentine is based by him upon the Alien Land Bill recently passed by the California Legislature. Upon that particular measure I have no comment to make; it is in fitter hands than mine. It is to "the ultimate issue involved," as construed by Sir Valentine, that I direct my remarks. "The ultimate issue involved," he writes, "is whether Japan, who has made good her title to be treated on a footing of complete equality as one of the Great Powers of the world, is not also entitled to rank among the civilizations whose citizens the American Republic is ready to welcome, subject to a few well-defined exceptions, within its fold whenever they are prepared to transfer their allegiance to it." In brief, this means, I apprehend, whether the attainment by Japan of the position of a Great Power entitles her to claim for her citizens free immigration into the territories of any other Great Power, with accompanying nauralization.

While Sir Valentine does not give a decisive reply to this question, the whole tone of his paper implies an affirmative. In my own appreciation there is no necessary connexion between a nation's status as a Great Power and her right to receive for her people the privileges of immigration and naturalization in the territory of another State; and the reasonings adduced in support of the proposition seem to me defective, both in some of their assertions, and still more in ignoring certain conspicuous facts.

Primary among these facts is that of the popular will, upon which, in the fundamental conceptions of both British and American government, the policy of a nation must rest. Be the causes what they may—economical, industrial, social, racial, or all four; and if there be any other motives— the will of the people is the law of the Government. So far as that will has been expressed in America and in Canada, it is distinctly contrary to the concession of such immigration. With the question of immigration that of naturalization is inextricably involved. There cannot be naturalization without immigration; while immigration without concession of naturalization, though conceivable and possible, is contrary to the genus of American

---

2. Chirol was in charge of the foreign department of *The Times* from 1899 until his retirement in 1912. He had used his influence since 1905 in favor of a strong Anglo-Japanese alliance, the entente with France, understanding with Russia, and firm relations with the United States.

institutions, which, as a general proposition, do not favor inhabitancy without right to citizenship.

Another tacit assumption is that changes of governmental methods change also natural characteristics, which make for beneficial citizenship in a foreign country. Stated concretely, this means that the adoption of Western methods by Japan has in two generations so changed the Japanese racial characteristics as to make them readily assimilable with Europeans, so as to be easily absorbed. This the Japanese in their just pride of race would be the first to deny. It ignores also the whole background of European history, and the fact that European civilization (which includes America) grew up for untold centuries under influences of which Eastern Asia—including therein Japan—experienced nothing. The "Foundations of the Twentieth Century" are not only a succession of facts, or combination of factors. They are to be found chiefly in the moulding of character, national and individual, through sixty-odd generations.

It is, I conceive, this deep impress of prolonged common experience which constitutes the possibility of assimilation, even among the unhappy, poverty-stricken mass often coming to us, which Sir Valentine stigmatizes as "ignorant and squalid." Undoubtedly they constitute a problem, but one with which the immense assimilative force of English institution, especially when Americanized, has been able so far to deal successfully, and I believe will continue able. But there are those who greatly doubt whether, in view of the very different foundations of the Japanese 20th century, and of the recognized strength and tenacity of character of the Japanese people emphasized by strong racial marks, they could be so assimilated. We who so think—I am one—cordially recognize the great progresses of Japan and admire her achievements of the past half-century, both civil and military; but we do not perceive in them the promise of ready adaptability to the spirit of our own institutions which would render naturalization expedient; and immigration, as I have said, with us implies naturalization. Whatever our doubts as to the effect upon national welfare in the presence of an unassimilable multitude of naturalized aliens, the presence of a like number of unnaturalized foreigners of the same type would be even worse.

The question is fundamentally that of assimilation, though it is idle to ignore that clear superficial evidences of difference, which inevitably *sautent aux yeux*, due to marked racial types, do exacerbate the difficulty. Personally, I entirely reject any assumption or belief that my race is superior to the Chinese, or to the Japanese. My own suits me better, probably because I am used to it; but I wholly disclaim, as unworthy of myself and of them, any thought of superiority. But with equal clearness I see and avow the difficulties of assimilation due to the formative influences of divergent pasts and to race. What the racial difficulty entails, even where the past has been one of close contact and common experiences, let the present Austrian Empire testify; and Britons, too, may look to the French in Canada and to the Boers in South Africa, though these latter are of the same general Teuton stock.

Let me say here that Sir Valentine is mistaken in the statement that the United States "within living memory waged the greatest civil war of modern times in order to establish the claim of American negroes to equal rights of citizenship with the white population." With the statement falls necessarily his inference from it, that "a colour bar cannot be logically pleaded as prohibitive." The United States did not wage the War of Secession even for the abolition of slavery, still less for equal rights of citizenship. Goldwin Smith, as a contemporary, held against us that the war, not being for abolition, was one of conquest. Lincoln said distinctly:—"I will restore the Union with slavery or without slavery, as best can be." Myself a contemporary and partaker, I can affirm this as a general tone, though there was a strong minority of abolition sentiment. The abolition proclamation came 18 months after the war began, and purely as a measure of policy. The full rights of citizenship came after the war ended, as a party political measure, though doubtless with this mingled much purely humanitarian feeling. Concerning this legislation a very acute American thinker, himself in the war, said to me within the past two years, "The great mistake of the men of that day was the unconscious assumption that the negro was a white man, with the accident of a black skin." That is, the question was not one of colour, but of assimilation as involved in race character. Now, while recognizing what I clearly see to be the great superiority of the Japanese, as of the white over the negro, it appears to me reasonable that a great number of my fellow citizens, knowing the problem we have in the coloured race among us, should dread the introduction of what they believe will constitute another race problem; and one much more difficult; because the virile qualities of the Japanese will still more successfully withstand assimilation, constituting a homogeneous foreign mass, naturally acting together irrespective of the national welfare, and so will be a perennial cause of friction with Japan, even more dangerous than at present.

Sir Valentine poses the question, "Must the bar of race be permanent? Is her Asiatic descent permanently to disqualify Japan from the enjoyment of the full rights freely accorded to one another by the great nations, into whose country she has already gained entrance on a footing of complete political equality?" The reply to this is that "permanent" is a word so foreign to diplomatic experience that it means nothing. No statesman can look so very far ahead as "permanent" stretches. Each generation must settle its own problem, day by day, step by step.

As a conclusion to so much dissent, may I express my full accordance with the admiration which the long experience of Sir Valentine Chirol has brought him to feel for Japan? I myself in early life was in Japan for more than a year at the time of the revolution which immediately preceded the era of the Meiji. I saw much, though superficially, of the old Japan then on the point of passing away. I had experience of the charming geniality and courtesy of her people, which has endeared them to my recollection, and has been confirmed over and over again by the social occasions in which I have repeatedly met their military officers, diplomats, or private gentlemen.[3] In the 40 years that have elapsed I have followed their progress with sympathy and gladness, and with all the admiration, which has been shared, I believe, by men of science and of politics in all nations, but which in men of the military professions must be peculiarly keen. Should these words fall under the eyes of any Japanese, I trust he will accept these sincere assurances, and will himself sympathize, as far as may be, with the difficulties of the United States in the particular instance. It is not a colour question, though that may emphasize the difficulty. It is the recurrent problem which confronts Germany in Poland, Austria in her Slav provinces, Canada in her French population, South Africa in the Boers. Despite gigantic success up to the present in assimilative processes—due to English institutions inherited and Americanized, and to the prevalence among the children of our community of the common English tongue over all other idioms —America doubts her power to digest and assimilate the strong national and racial characteristics which distinguish the Japanese, which are the secret of much of their success, and which, if I am not mistaken, would constitute them a solid homogeneous body, essentially and unchangingly foreign.

To Little, Brown and Company

Marshmere, Quogue, Long Island, June 25, 1913 [LC]

Gentlemen: I have received Cast-Proof through p. 84 and also duplicate proof of Contents. To-day I have finished the Index; half of which, how-

---

3. On May 17, 1913, Mahan consented to write an introduction to a biography of Japanese Vice Admiral Tasuka Serata by Lieutenant Commander K. Asami, IJN. Serata had attended the U.S. Naval Academy when Mahan taught there in 1877–1880. See C. C. Taylor, *Life of Admiral Mahan*, pp. 267–268; and Mahan's Paper, "Introduction to K. Asami's Biography of Tasuka Serata." The Asami biography, published in 1914, has not been translated into English.

ever, has yet to be type-written. I hope to enclose it to you, with Contents read, by the end of the week.

I have also compiled a glossary of nautical terms used in the book, which I think will add to its completeness. I began with the intention of introducing it in Index, under heading Nautical Terms. I now think it will be better to precede Index as a separate thing, with a reference to it in the Index. I will, however, write fully when I send the whole, as above.

To Theodore Roosevelt

Quogue, Long Island, July 8, 1913 [LC]

My dear Colonel Roosevelt: I send you under another cover a sheet of *The Times* (London) of June 23, containing a letter from myself, and an editorial thereon, which I have thought you may like to see, if you have not already done so.[1]

Mine is a reply, though necessarily at a considerable time interval, to a letter by Sir Valentine Chirol, who is (I think) head of the foreign affairs department in *The Times* office, and also has spent much time in the East as a correspondent of the paper. Under all the circumstances, it appeared to me to present a good and fair opportunity to put before the British "man in the street" a temperate summary of the American position, as I understand it, which I dont think he does. A good understanding with England, and in England, is always useful to us, and I still have a certain personal estimation among them derived from days now past.

I need not, however, pursue explanation with you, whose interest in such matters is always keen, and whose views I believe coincide broadly with my own. We have before us a long controversy with Japan, the outcome of which is in my judgment very uncertain. The formation of a correct and decisive public opinion, not at home only but in the civilized world generally, is important to us. I think I have seen somewhere, latterly, that Japan has been making agreements with Austria and Italy on the subject of land ownership; upon which, I presume, she will try to establish an analogy, and precedent, for a like concession by us, with our less than twenty to the square mile population on the Pacific coast.

I was delighted to read your speech for the Navy at Newport. I feel as if, for the next four years, the country is in the hands of the Philistines— or worse.

---

1. *See* Mahan to *The Times*, London, circa June 13, 1913.

To Newton W. Rowell[1]

Quogue, Long Island, July 9, 1913 [NWC][2]

My dear Mr. Rowell: I have received your letter of June 27, with enclosed Statement of Principles, asking suggestions in modification or enlargement of the same; and also, if I rightly understand, suggestions of a general character, which, if approved, might render more smooth the relations between Missions and Governments, both those of the country in which a particular Mission is established and those of the country whence that Mission originates.

I have nothing to offer in modification or in extension of the Principles as stated; but as cognate to the objects for the advancement of which the Principles have been enunciated—namely, the perfecting and developing of proper relations between Governments and Missions—it appears to me that the ground might now be taken that Missions, by natural development, have become in the present day an actual existent international subject, of which Governments should take more direct and more systematic cognizance than they have in times past,—if for no other reason, because from time to time they give rise to international questions.

Such cognizance, of course, could not apply to the spiritual or religious characteristics of any mission. The separateness between the spheres of religion and of civil government lies at the basis of the Statement of Principles, and pervades each one of them; but the fruits of the spiritual propaganda, as manifested in the effect upon the lives of converts, upon their characteristics as citizens, upon the betterment or injury of their temporal conditions, upon their morals as distinguished from religious faith, of the physical benefit from medical missions,—in a word, the broad, secular results of missions,—are a specific part of the international question, and as such should engage the regulated attention of Christian Governments so as to supply them with a digested mass of information ready for use when specific questions arise for discussion. Not only that, there would arise a general acceptance of proper principles, a familiarity with them, and a development such as follow naturally upon consecutive attention to any class of problems.

As regards the methods of effecting this, I would suggest that our Committee recommend to the Continuation Committee to take under advisement the desirability of asking the Governments of the various States of

---

1. Author of *The British Empire and Independence*. Toronto: Victoria College Press, 1922. Rowell was also involved in the Social Christianity and Christian Missions movements.
2. From *Papers for Continuation Committee, November 1913: Report of Committee Appointed to Draw Up a Statement of the Recognized Principles Underlying the Relations of Missions and Governments*. New York: Protestant Episcopal Church, 1913, pp. 3–4. Pamphlet in Mahan Family Papers, now deposited in Naval War College Library.

the Christian civilization,—broadly, all European and American Governments, citizens of which may be engaged in Missions,—to direct their diplomatic representatives to make periodical investigation into the results of Missions, as evidenced under the various secular heads above enumerated, and under others which doubtless have escaped me; such others, for instance, as educational work done, and, very important, the effect upon the general conditions of the unconverted classes, and upon their attitude towards Missions, as experience of them grows; whether there is salt and leaven in the work, not only affecting converts but influencing the outside community in contact with the missionaries.

The benefits which I think would result from such a measure are, in the first place, that it would compel resident diplomatic representatives to inform themselves, and that under a weighty sense of responsibility. Their conclusions, if favourable, would supply a valuable basis of disproof against the too frequent irresponsible detraction of the occasional traveller, or of the disgruntled resident and hostile foreigner. It would tend to draw the attention of the world of Christian civilization—practically the whole civilized world—to the question of Missions and their work, and to create a body of public opinion which, though probably indifferent to religious aspects, would cordially appreciate beneficent humanitarian outcome. Such incidents as the treatment by Japanese officials of the recent alleged Korean conspiracy,[3] and the conduct of M. Augagneur,[4] when Governor of Madagascar, would be less likely to occur if it was felt that the limelight of an instructed public opinion would be turned upon the transaction. As it was, the things were done; and instead of prevention there had to be an attempt at cure, against all the onus of accomplished facts, and against the strong unwillingness of the doer and of his government to admit wrong done, if it could be buttressed by argument.

In non-Christian lands under control of Christian States, such as India, Madagascar and most of Africa, the same measure could be applied by the several governments instructing the proper officials to obtain and report information on the same lines as those suggested for diplomatic representatives in foreign non-Christian countries.

I cannot but think that it would conduce much to the cordial relations between Missions and Governments, if the better understanding of the benevolent work of Missions, of its great extent, and of its indirect influences, were thus brought to the various Foreign Offices of Christian States. The knowledge would insensibly distil thence into the communities whose agents they are. As it is, such knowledge is too commonly confined to those

---

3. A number of Korean Christians had been arrested on suspicion of conspiring against the life of the Japanese governor-general of Korea.
4. Victor Augagneur, who took measures to curb the Christian churches and missions in Madagascar and to revive the old native cults.

already interested in Missions, with consequent bias. On Missions themselves would be produced that sense of responsibility, of aroused public attention, the beneficial effect of which upon every man and upon his work is a commonplace of our daily experience. I think it probable also that the justly deprecated tendency of some missionaries to have quick recourse to the diplomatic representative of their countries would be checked by the knowledge that such representative had his eyes always steadily turned to all such cases, as matters upon which he was expected to have an instructed opinion. There might even eventually result some check upon the tendency of the Roman Church everywhere to complicate Christian action by ecclesiastical intrusion into the civil sphere.

As things now stand, that separateness between the sphere of Missions and of the secular State, upon which our principles rightly insist, is permitted to entail a sense of mutual irresponsibility, if not alienation, which is scarcely Christian, and which will not aid to solve and determine their proper inter-relations. It seems to me that the recommendation of such a course as that which I have sketched is directly in the spirit to which the appointment of our Committee is due, in that it would further its ultimate necessary end. It may be added that, coming from the missionary body, it would be not only a direct invitation to subject its actions to searching examination, but a conciliatory expression of desire to conform its methods, as far as Christian principle allows, which is very far, to the necessities and embarrassments of international relations.

In conclusion, I may remark that there has been frequent testimony by diplomatic officials to the great and admirable work of Christian Missions. These testimonials, however, have been occasional and for the most part unrelated to one another. Some such method as that here suggested would tend to mass and co-ordinate such witness, as well as to elicit much which otherwise would never appear. I believe that the words of Christ are identically true of Missions to-day—"He that doeth right cometh to the Light, that his works may be made manifest that they are wrought in God."

To Elihu Root

Marshmere, Quogue, Long Island, July 9, 1913 [LC]

My dear Mr. Root: I dont know whether you may have seen at the time a cabled summary of a letter by Sir Valentine Chirol, in the London *Times* of May 19, on the general question of Japan's international position, and consequent claims. I determined at the moment to wait for the full text, and, if it corresponded with the cable, to write a reply. This in due course has been published by the *Times*, and copies reached me. I send you the necessary sheet, on which you will find both the letter itself and an editorial by the *Times*.[1]

I have taken the liberty of thus sending you because of the high regard I have for your mastery of international questions, and for your distinguished occupancy of the position of Secretary of State. I fear we have before us a prolonged controversy and possible tension with Japan; and it consequently seemed to me a fit opportunity for a person with no official position to compromise, and with some acceptance in English opinion, to put before the English public a view which I think is preponderantly held here, as well as one important to themselves. The editorial seems to show that the attempt has been not wholly vain.

You will appreciate the hesitation with which one intrudes one's own composition upon a man of your eminence in the particular field of international relations, but you will feel, I hope, that there is no obligation on your part to comment, nor any expectation on mine that you will do so.

To Garrett Z. Demarest[1]

Quogue, Long Island, July 15, 1913 [NWC]

Dear Sir: Upon receipt of your letter I wrote at once to New York to obtain, if I could, the information you wished. Not having heard in reply, I give the following:

Mary H. Mahan, my mother, died in March 1893. She left a will. For twenty years before death she resided in Elizabeth, N.J. During this time her affairs were mainly in the hands of Augustus T. Gillender, a lawyer of New York City. For half a dozen years past, he has been suffering from paresis, and probably could not be of use to you. I do not know where the will is filed, nor do I remember about the Executors, though I think he was one, if not the sole. The will was settled long ago, without any unusual delay that I know of.

To J. Franklin Jameson

Marshmere, Quogue, Long Island, July 22, 1913 [NA]

My dear Dr. Jameson: Your suggestion in your letter of the 16th encountered in me at once a strong disinclination; for I am averse, for more

---

1. *See* Mahan to *The Times*, circa June 13, 1913.

1. A New York lawyer and Treasurer of Balch Price and Company.

[504]

than one reason, to passing a winter in Washington.[1] I have not settled down as yet to any specific work for my declining years, though for some years past I have had a tentative project of writing a history of the United States from the point of view of expansion; that is, in which expansion should hold some such position as Sea Power has taken in my principal writings.

However, as you say, there is no need for a hurried decision, and I understand your suggestion would apply to the coming winter, or to the following. Unless for unforeseen controlling reasons, I should prefer to spend the coming winter in New York; but particulars as well as funds can await the conclusion of the weeks intervening between now and your passage south. I will keep the matter in mind, and I trust greatly to the effects of unconscious cerebration.

To the Editor of The New York Times

Quogue, Long Island, July 23, 1913[1]

In editorial article of July 22 *The Times* remarks, with reference to the present civil war, it is essential in the Balkans that "the hands of the clock cannot be set back so far now as to permit the Turk to regain his lost possessions."

The immense disappointment felt by many who have, in the recent war, sympathized deeply with the former victims of Turkish misrule, may tend to a violent reaction of opinion. It seems, therefore, useful to quote a very recent statement by an eminent English lawyer, now and for forty years past resident in Constantinople, where he is President of the European bar. Sir Edwin Pears, in the *Contemporary Review* for June, 1913,[2] writes:

> Twelve years ago I concluded a historical study[3] with a sentence, with which I venture to close also this article: "Wherever the dead weight of Turkish misrule has been removed, the young Christian States have been fairly started on the path of civilization, and justify the reasonable expectation of the statesmen, the historians, and the scholars who sympathized with, and aided them in, their aspirations for freedom." I still hold the same opinion.

---

1. Jameson had asked Mahan to become a Research Associate of the Carnegie Institution of Washington "for one winter of five or six months." Jameson to Mahan, July 16, 1913, in the Library of Congress.

1. From *The New York Times*, July 25, 1913, p. 6. *See also* Paper, "Thoughts on the Righteousness of War," July 23, 1913.
2. "Turkey, Present and Future."
3. Sir Edwin Pears, *The Destruction of the Greek Empire and the Story of the Capture of Constantinople by the Turks.* London: Longmans, Green and Co., 1903.

Shameful and distressing as is the present internecine strife between those who lately fought side by side, it is fully permissible to believe that it is but an interruption, to which will succeed the law of progress noted by Sir Edwin Pears. The issues in dispute are not wholly those of mere greed. They are very intricate and involve national interests and racial sympathies, resembling quarrels, very difficult for an outsider to appreciate. Nor should we forget the centuries of bondage, retarding development of healthy national character.

To J. Franklin Jameson

Marshmere, Quogue, Long Island, September 11, 1913
[NA (Copy at LC)]

My dear Dr. Jameson: I shall be delighted to see you as proposed on Sunday 21st.[1] Let the stage bring you direct to this house, and lunch with us.

I may as well say now that as far as present indications go I shall not be willing to spend this coming winter away from New York. Your proposition was for this winter or next. Being 73 this month, I calculate our family movements more from the point of view of my daughters than myself or wife. We were abroad all last winter, and I am not willing another should separate them from their outside friends and relations, upon which much of their lives must depend in the future. But the succeeding winter is another matter; and, which non-committal as yet, I shall much appreciate the opportunity of talking over the matter, and still more the pleasure of seeing you personally.

To William Griffith[1]

Draft   Quogue, Long Island, September 15, 1913 [LC]

Dear Mr. Griffith: When publishing the "Editorial" which I sent you,[2] I will ask you to omit certain words, at the end of the first paragraph; be-

---

1. Jameson had asked permission to visit Mahan. He regretted that Mahan's reaction to his request had not been more favorable and offered the inducement of proximity to the Library of Congress. Jameson to Mahan, September 9, 1913, in the National Archives. *See also* Mahan to Jameson, July 22, 1913.

1. Editor of the *National Sunday Magazine*, 1912–1916. No issues of this weekly have been found.

2. The title of the draft of this article was "Why Not Disarm?" The article was published in the *National Sunday Magazine* for September 28, 1913, under the title "The Folly of the Hague." *See* Mahan to Short, June 24, 1914. The draft version is published as a Paper in this collection.

cause, although I am sure of their substantial accuracy, I relied upon my memory only, and a doubt arising in my mind I have been unable to verify the statement. The words are:

"It is an irony of the present situation that one of the most noisy and self advertising of the advocates of disarmament and arbitration has admitted that the chief effective champion of peace is the "War Lord" of the greatest army and of the second greatest navy now existing."

These words are not necessary to the argument and their omission will not affect it.

To Little, Brown and Company

Marshmere, Quogue, Long Island, September 25, 1913 [LC]

Gentlemen: I have received the advance copy of *Major Operations* which you have been good enough to send me, and have found it both in general appearance and in details very satisfactory.

I gladly avail myself of your kind offer of forwarding by mail such copies as I wish to distribute, and will forward you before long a list of names and addresses, some of the last of which I need to obtain. Meanwhile, I will feel obliged if you will retain all copies due me by our agreement, beyond the one I have just received.

To Newton W. Rowell

Quogue, Long Island, September 27, 1913 [NWC][1]

My dear Mr. Rowell: I have received yours enclosing the letters of Dr. Barbour and Mr. Low[2] relative to mine of July 9. That of Mr. Low is brief, and rests almost wholly upon the general principle of the separateness of Church and State. I scarcely think this sufficient in itself to reject a proposition which looks merely to the State observing through its officials, and without interfering, secular results which influence for better or for worse the circumstances and the conduct of the people affected. The State takes cognizance, when necessary, of Church temporalities in the matter of property or the misuse of property. If such use, or misuse, were directly con-

---

1. From *Papers for Continuation Committee, November 1913* . . . pp. 9–10. *See* Mahan to Rowell, July 9, 1913, Footnote 2.
2. Thomas S. Barbour, former foreign secretary of the American Baptist Foreign Mission Society, and Seth Low, both of whose letters are in *Papers for Continuation Committee, November 1913.* . . .

trary to the well-being of a community, the State would interfere, as it would with any corporation. In fact, the Church has civil standing as a corporation, and if I rightly understand, while the State will not interfere with the right of the Church to prescribe conditions of membership, it will, if called upon, determine whether the treatment of a member conforms to the conditions laid down by the standards of the Church. Indeed, it seems to me not too much to say that while the Church, as Church, not being of this world has no commission to interfere with the procedures of the States, which are secular only, the State, being alone in charge of secular affairs, has the commission to control the activities of the Church when these involve the various civil relations of mankind.

Briefly, then, the principle of separateness of Church and State is not absolute, but is conditioned by questions of expediency. In this Dr. Barbour's letter raises points which appear to me well worthy of careful consideration, and to which I am not prepared at once to reply. The possible sensitiveness of Governments of highly organized peoples, like the Chinese and Japanese, to official opinions expressed concerning the effect produced upon their own people by foreign missions, or by Chrisianity, might be serious. Yet, avoiding comparisons, positive statements as to work done by hospitals and educational institutions, the attitude of the unconverted toward missions in general (of which some very striking instances have been given in China), the standing of missionaries before the public opinion of communities where they have been long established,—such things, I think, might be stated without offence. In other words, the actual work of Missions could be stated and the immediate good effected; even though it be wiser to omit references to direct results upon the neighbourhood.

In less highly organized people, or people less in touch with the world, as Africa and parts of Asia, and even of the Turkish Empire, I should think a greater freedom of expression could do no harm.

My object was and is to initiate steps looking to envolving an instructed public opinion, both in the public at large and in Governments, an opinion firmly based on facts, adequately elicited and competently stated in accessible form. I desire to remove indifference, and to win for missions the general approval which I believe due to them. This, if obtained, will not increase spiritual support, possibly will not; but it would tend to give missions a standing of esteem, and a recognition which at present they do not receive, even from many well-meaning Christian people. I think this result would be beneficial, and the benefits would hereafter be felt in such instances as those I cited before; the alleged conspiracy in Korea, and Augagneur in Madagascar.

The members of our Committee are very busy men, wide apart and not easy to be assembled. The central body in Edinburgh, though busy enough, is, I presume, busy upon subjects cognate to this, and could find time to discuss this proposition maturely, if in their view it possessed any merit, even subsidiary. Considering also the imminent necessity of submitting a report, I would suggest that my letters and those of Dr. Barbour and Mr. Low be forwarded as they stand, with such expression of opinion from yourself as you may think expedient, but without recommendation of the Committee as a whole, which, indeed, cannot well be had now.

After writing so far it occurred to me to refer to the letter of July 23rd of the Rev. Dr. A. J. Brown,[3] Chairman of the Committee on Reference and Counsel, of which you also are a member. You doubtless have a copy. While it contains no specific recommendation such as mine, it asserts copiously, both in general and in specific instances, the entangled interrelations of Missions and International affairs as a positive existing fact, which has to be recognized. My proposition, summarized, is to provide a method by which the most responsible officers of foreign Governments, resident on a scene of Missions, should keep themselves familiarized with the conditions and acquaint their home Governments by reports. The method suggested in one brief letter by one person, without discussion with others, could not fail to err by excess or defect. The real question for the moment is whether some plan should be adopted, to meet by prevision evident exigencies, of which Dr. Brown's letter cites many instances, which may increase in numbers and in complication. Certainly the opinions of resident observers, official in position, trained by the habit of observing Missions and missionaries, but not associated with them, would be a most valuable help in forming correct judgment, when critical difficulties arise between Missions and the local Government or population.

To Little, Brown and Company

Marshmere, Quogue, Long Island, October 4, 1913 [LC]

Gentlemen: Replying to yours of Oct 2, the original "copy" of *Major Operations* has been destroyed, as have also the galleys with which I worked over the page proof; but quite accidentally I have left still untouched the duplicate galleys, which I took with me from Pau and brought home.

These I send you in another packet. The corrections are noted throughout; and, unless by some accidental omission, correspond with the galleys destroyed. In both sets, as a precaution, I noted with an *asterisk* wherever the proof corrections were of printer's errors, not of errors in the "copy." As one such asterisk occurs on galley 162, I doubtless observed this practice throughout the proof-reading.

---

3. Arthur J. Brown, administrative and general secretary of the Board of Foreign Missions of the Presbyterian Church.

To Bouverie F. Clark

Marshmere, Quogue, Long Island, October 6, 1913 [LC]

My dear Clark: Your birthday letter to me made a bulls-eye this time, arriving here on the forenoon of the very day. Had we been in New York it probably would have been a day ahead. Many thanks for your good wishes and remembrance. I am very well, and, for 73, in very good shape; but I certainly lose in a twelvemonth. I have bathed in the sea all summer, and for both surf and swimming still do well enough, but once with a heavy sea and outward drag, I had to signal the bathers to fetch me in. I was keeping afloat all right but my breath was failing me, and when that happens in a seaway you feel scared. So I thought best to signal before I became flustered.

I also still can ride my bicycle, though neither so fast nor so far. It takes indeed over twenty minutes and three or four miles to get heart working right. I dont know whether so inveterate a Londoner as you have taken up the wheel. London streets dont look very suited to such progress, and I have ridden little in our city, outside of the parks. In this flat country we rarely walk anywhere; our wheels are always at the door for use.

My last letter to you must have been from Sicily, and probably from Palermo. We left there April 5 in a very slow Cunarder, the *Saxonia*; but had a delightful voyage, if it did take two weeks. After another fortnight in town we came here and have remained steadily. In fact, it is our home, and as we not only have here all our household goods, but have developed in the five years very attractive surroundings, here, and here only, we are all satisfied for the summer. We have always a blaze of color from flowers, and more sunshine to the square foot and to the week than any place we know. The sea breeze blows five days out of the week, almost perpendicular to the shore, so that excessive heat is almost unknown. We shall go to the city after the next elections, Nov. 5. I remain here to vote.

You must not look for sympathy with your pro-Turk view from me, nor, I believe, from one American in a hundred. The individual Turk I daresay is a very decent fellow when his blood is not up, but I should suppose it as settled as any historical question can be that the Turkish race has no capacity for government, except by the sword. Now the sword is a good thing in the background, but to be the only resource in peace as in war, and upon non-combatants, is not political management. The Balkan peoples have probably behaved very badly also; but they have demonstrated that they can organize, and that they can lick the Turks. It is not the fighting quality of the Turk that has fallen, but the administrative incapacity of the government, with, probably a momentary absence of any single able man, that left the army, so called, a disorganized mob. Turkey is hopeless. Her very return from Adrianople, though the natural thing to do, only mortgages her future more deeply.

Sir Edwin Pears, for forty years resident in Constantinople, and now President of the European Bar there, in an article in the June *Contemporary*, reaffirmed what he had said twelve years before. "Whenever the dead weight of Turkish misrule has been removed, the young Christian states have been fairly started on the path of civilization, and justify the reasonable expectations of the statesmen etc, who sympathized with, and aided them in, their aspirations for freedom." Pears was born in 1835, and so is of an age to have imbibed that old British feeling of the Crimean War, when, as Lord Salisbury said, You backed the wrong horse. Do you at this moment know of a single Mahometan government of which you can say what Pears said above?

Well, we will see what we shall see, though it is doubtful whether men of our age are to see the end, which a year ago I hoped for.

I follow your politics with interest, but I find I cant read as much or as carefully as I did, so that I am less up than I could wish. You always have my best wishes, for your country no less than for yourself.

To the Editor of The New York Times

Quogue, Long Island, October 13, 1913[1]

I have had this recent instructive experience: On Oct. 1 I took a taxi on the street at Sixth Avenue and Thirty-fourth Street for Fifth Avenue and Fifty-fourth Street and paid for the service 60 cents. On Oct. 11 I took a yellow taxi at the Pennsylvania Station, Thirty-fourth Street, between Seventh and Eighth Avenues, and for the same destination paid $1, 66 per cent more.

Upon complaint later in the day to the official in charge at the station, I was told the charge was correct. I did not give, and will not give, a tip in one case, as I did in the other. Might not the public adopt this rule?

To Bouverie F. Clark

Marshmere, Quogue, Long Island, October 23, 1913 [LC]

My dear Clark: I am sending you today, by book post, a copy of my latest, and probably my final book on Naval History. You are not likely

---

1. From *The New York Times*, October 15, 1913, p. 10.

to find anything new in it, because it originally appeared fifteen years ago in Clowes' *History of the Royal Navy*, and is now simply republished in separate form with of course some modification and addition. I dont expect you to read it, but send it simply as a keepsake as it probably is the last work on Naval History I shall ever undertake, such at least is my present purpose.

I have nothing to communicate since my last of a fortnight ago. We go to New York, for the winter, on Nov. 6;[1] but my address remains always Quogue, whence all letters, and, in the case of foreign mail, even printed matter etc is forwarded to my temporary residence, of which Quogue is kept always informed.

Our political situation is now very interesting to a neutral & not wholly benevolent onlooker at the present Administration. The President called Congress together in April, and by constant pressure, at least so the papers say, carried the Tariff measure[2] he desired, according to party platform. Not satisfied with this triumph, he has insisted on non-adjournment till a bill remodelling currency conditions was passed.[3] Consequently Congress has not adjourned, but so many are away the lower House cant command a quorum; even the leader has gone away from the capital. Remains to be seen whether the annoyance of the last personal pressure will not wipe out the personal popularity of the first success. Much will depend on the outcome of the Mexico affair,[4] whether that will justify what to me has been rather amateurish diplomacy so far followed in that matter. Sir E. Grey's stand is not helping our Admn. I dont say this critically; it is a difference of opinion only, but your new minister to M.[5] presenting his credentials at the particular juncture, though only a coincidence, is rather a black eye to the Administration policy, for it practically re-affirms that recognition of Huerta which we have refused. Being of the opposite party to the Admn. I am less concerned than as a patriot I ought to be; but in truth from the beginning of our nationality, in 1789, the Democratic Party has refused the maintenance of a Navy such as necessity, and therefore patriotism, demands. I shall not feel secure while they are in office.

---

1. The family returned to the Hotel Collingwood, 45 West 35th Street, for the winter of 1913–1914.
2. The Underwood Tariff Act, substantially lowering duties, was passed on October 3, 1913.
3. The Owen-Glass Act which established the Federal Reserve System was passed on December 23, 1913.
4. Mexico was torn by revolution under the dictatorship of Victoriano Huerta which threatened American lives and property.
5. Sir Lionel Carden.

To C. B. de Camp[1]

Draft   Quogue, Long Island, October 25, 1913 [LC]

Dear Sir: Referring to your letter of Oct. 23, I think I understand your wishes sufficiently to make unnecessary the trouble of your coming to Quogue. As far as I can estimate my present knowledge of the subject, and the maturity of my own view, I believe I can write a useful article, but I cannot quite take your line, or point of view. I shall have to give merely my own opinion with the reasons for it.

The time, Nov. 10 to 12, would ordinarily present no difficulty, but matters are somewhat complicated by our prospective move from here to New York. However, I can accomplish it, provided full opportunity to read galleys be given me.

If, from the above, you continue to wish for the article, I would name three to four thousand words, and two hundred and fifty dollars, as the terms.[2]

Please let me know if this is satisfactory.

To Little, Brown and Company

New York, November 6, 1913 [LC]

Gentlemen: In breaking up at Quogue for the winter, on Tuesday last, I found to my surprise, under a body of other papers, the first set of corrected galleys, the duplicates of which I sent you some weeks ago. If these will still be of any service to you, for the purposes which you had in view in asking for them then, I have left them ready for sending upon so hearing from you. If you wish them, please address me at *45 West 35th St, New York*, and take note that I expect that to be my address till May 1, 1914.

To William H. Henderson

University Club, New York, November 7, 1913 [NMM]

My dear Henderson: Just before breaking up and out from my country home, last Tuesday, I sent you by book post a copy of a book just published separately *Major Operations of the Navies in the War of American Inde-*

---

1. Associate Editor of *Metropolitan Magazine*, New York.
2. These negotiations failed to produce an agreement.

pendence. As it originally appeared fifteen years ago, as a chapter in the *History of the Royal Navy,* edited by the late Laird Clowes, you may have seen it already; but I send it as a reminder of old friendship and as probably the last historical naval work I shall publish, as I am a little weary of that special form of authorship. If you have not before seen it, there really is little that would be new to you, unless the operations on Lake Champlain should seem to possess the decisive importance I attribute to them. When Clowes named them as part of the subject he wished me to treat, I was astonished and perplexed; but investigation gave them to me the character of an episode at once interesting and decisive. The portraits of some of the red fellows of that day may also add interest to the book.

I am in town for the winter and already a little sick of it, though our early coming here was principally my work. Our *home* is in the country—town, though for half the year, is the interlude, likely to be shortened, I fancy, in the future. The din of the city wearies me, and its restless atmosphere; not to mention the dust which your moister climate keeps down in mud.

I have at present no immediate work in hand, though plenty of odd jobs voluntarily undertaken. The attitude of an interested spectator of current politics, at least of my own country with its new administration, occupies my time fairly, not least by rousing my impatience with what the event may show to be sagacious diplomacy, but to me appears amateurish. With two green hands at the head of external affairs, both, I think, more or less faddists,[1] there is cause for anxiety as to where we will fetch up, and how. They have at their hand one of the most capable and instructed international legists that we possess;[2] but as they are both opinionated, and I fancy dont esteem law as highly as they do their own ideas, I am a little afraid of consequences at once serious and preposterous. A sense of satisfaction that it is none of my responsibility is perhaps a little ignoble, but at my age comforting. The party in power now is likely to be greatly captivated by Churchill's suggested naval holiday;[3] there are already indications of their embracing it as an excuse—which they are always after—to postpone shipbuilding; a postponement which is rarely followed by any effort to regain ground lost. You may gather I am in opposition, and I am. Possibly, our current difficulties with Mexico and Japan may cause a jar or two which will cause the peace party to sit up & take notice.[4]

---

1. Woodrow Wilson and Secretary of State William Jennings Bryan.
2. John Bassett Moore had become a member of the Permanent Court of Arbitration at the Hague in 1912.
3. Churchill's suggestion in Parliament in March 1912 that during 1913 Germany refrain from building her scheduled three capital ships, thus freeing Britain of the obligation of constructing five super-Dreadnoughts. The suggestion was declined by the Emperor in April.
4. *See* Mahan to Clark, October 23, 1913.

I trust this will find you and Mrs. Henderson—to whom I beg you to give my compliments—in good health and happiness. On the latter score I have every reason to felicitate myself, though I have to notice that my strength and staying power are less than they were. I cant do all I wish to, but at 73 one has to accept such as gracefully as he may.

To J. Franklin Jameson

University Club, New York, November 14, 1913 [LC]

My dear Dr. Jameson: I have delayed answering your request that I would review the Spencer Papers,[1] hoping that I should find myself up to the job; but I do not. Since my coming to town ten days ago, I have undergone quite suddenly a degree of nervous agitation and feeling of pressure which forbids at present my adding any avoidable work to my tasks. I have glanced over the book here. To review would mean—to me—to read the whole and I really do not feel up to it.

To Bouverie F. Clark

University Club, New York, January 15, 1914 [LC]

My dear Clark: It was awfully nice of you to remember us on Christmas. Your letter and card found me confined to the house, and much of the time to bed, by an attack of grip. This disease, always bad enough, has been this year very exhausting to its victims, so our doctor tells us; and though I escaped better than most, despite my 73 years, I still after three weeks am not up to the notch in either body or mind. Of course the enforced idleness left me with arrears of all kinds, and still more with an indisposition to work of any kind. All this will explain and I hope excuse my delay in writing.

From the reports your weather in Europe seems to have been of your own getting up; not from this side. Till two days ago, we could scarcely be said to have had any winter at all. Then the thermometer got down to six below zero Fahrenheit, which with a gale of over sixty miles an hour satisfied the most wintry. I was out both days, but not at the worst hours, and I

---

1. George John Spencer, *Private Papers of George, Second Earl Spencer, First Lord of the Admiralty, 1794–1801.* Edited by Julian S. Corbett. London: Navy Records Society, 1913. This was Volume 1 of the Spencer Papers, Volume 46 of the Society's publications; succeeding volumes appeared as Volumes 48, 58 and 59.

am very canny in seeking shelter. Still, I wore ear coverings, and my cheek bones ached. As I write, the first real snowfall of the winter is coming down. Happily scarcely two months for winter remains.

For the most part my family have been well, though one daughter also had grip. There is nothing in our public news to interest you, or for the matter of that ourselves. I have seen that the *Daily Mail* published two weeks ago a letter for which it had asked me.[1] This had a somewhat curious history. They *cabled* for it last July, and I mailed the manuscript July 27. Their not publishing excited my curiosity and I half imagined they were going to suppress it, and had gone over to Lloyd George. They seem, however, to have held it back for a psychological—or political—moment. I was amused at one of our "peace at any price papers" commenting that this moment of distress to English people (Lloyd G.) was *chosen* by Adml. Mahan, etc.

With best wishes for the New Year [etc.].

To J. Franklin Jameson

University Club, New York, January 22, 1914 [NA]

My dear Dr. Jameson: I have received your two letters, and thank you for the kindness of your offer expressed in them. You wrote under the impression that Dr. Woodward[1] had communicated with me. If he did, the letter has not reached me. I have waited for the full proposition to be before me, in order to make a decisive reply.[2]

I do not find myself personally more inclined to the change than I first was, and at present I am suffering the weakness consequent upon an attack of grip which the more disinclines me. I feel as if the past weeks,—now more than six—would have been unbearable if I had any obligations of work, not self imposed, hanging over me. As it is I have had the blessed sense of irresponsibility.

I have not your letter by me but believe it was addressed to 45 West 35th St. In that case, or even otherwise, Dr. Woodward would know from you where to send.

---

1. "Declares British Navy Weak," *Daily Mail*, London, January 4, 1914.

1. Robert Simpson Woodward was President of the Carnegie Institution of Washington.

2. *See* Mahan to Jameson, July 22 and September 11, 1913.

To Little, Brown and Company

Chestnut Hill, Philadelphia, January 29, 1914 [LC]

Gentlemen: Will you kindly send one copy of the *Problem of Asia*, and one of *Retrospect and Prospect* to Prof. *Gino Dallari, Via Alberto da Giussano*, 11, Milan, Italy.

Prof. Dallari has written a comment upon my general trend of thought, in an Italian periodical *La Cultura Moderna*,[1] copies of which he has sent me with the request that I would send him one or other of the two books named.

I take this occasion to acknowledge with thanks receipt of your cheque of $271.79 received today. I am here temporarily only.

[P.S.] Please return enclosed.[2]

To Robert S. Woodward

Chestnut Hill, Philadelphia, January 29, 1914 [CIW]

My dear Sir: Your letter,[1] conveying to me the Resolution of the Executive Committee, appointing me a Research Associate of the Department of Historical Research for six months, dating from November 1, 1914, with an honorarium of $2400, has been forwarded to me here from my New York address.

In reply, I accept the appointment, and at the same time beg to express through you my sense of the honor done me by the Executive Committee.

To Herbert Putnam

Chestnut Hill, Philadelphia, February 2, 1914 [LC]

Dear Mr. Putnam: I hope you may pardon my delay in answering your very kind and only too complimentary letter. You may perhaps have learned by this time that I have accepted the offer extended me by Dr. Woodward.

---

1. *La Cultura moderna; antologia* seems to have been a monographic series. Prof. Dallari's article has not been identified.
2. Enclosure not found.

1. Woodward to Mahan, January 27, 1914, in Carnegie Institution Archives.

The work in itself is far from distasteful; indeed quite acceptable. But you may readily realize that after seventy one hesitates and is reluctant to make a radical change of surroundings, and Washington has to me always been distasteful, my association with it being that of a transient visitor, modified by official contact with the bureaus, which I detest. I had expected never to go there again.

I thank you very cordially for your kind assurances of coöperation, of which I should have felt assured from my former experience. I can only wish that the scene of our association was my own familiar city. But having accepted I cast regrets behind, as far as will goes. I fear, however, I must admit the somewhat sordid motive of pecuniary considerations, to which un-luckily—or luckily—I often have to yield, has weighed with me in the satis-factory tender made by the Carnegie.

Looking forward with much pleasure to our meeting next winter, believe me etc.

To J. Franklin Jameson

45 West 35th Street, New York, February 6, 1914 [NA]

My dear Dr. Jameson: I have two letters from you not yet answered. I thank you for your expression of satisfaction at my accepting the offer of the Institute. You will understand, I hope, that the duty in itself is acceptable to me, that my hesitation lay in my great unwillingness at my age to sever myself from my accustomed surroundings. This I do not think I could have overcome except for the feeling that I ought not to refuse the pecuniary offer. As regards society, my wife and myself live such retired lives that it weighs little with us. It is of course impossible to replace the few intimacies which we have in New York. In the sixties and seventies the circle of friendships does not expand.

I do not yet clearly understand my future duties. As they had pre-sented themselves to me, I had thought to begin with the documents on some subject, arranged between you and me, the process of examining which would probably open out other lines of investigation, as such searches commonly do. On this frequent conferences between you and me would naturally follow, and possibly my huntings would furnish material for talking to the Department Staff. Other than this, or kindred matter, I am at a loss to see how I could "talk informally to them about historical mat-ters." Such talks could not be impromptu, and if weekly would require a degree of preparation which would militate against the time due to research.

Might it not be that at the end of the time a general report, or synopsis of results, would better meet the Department needs.[1]

There is plenty of time to settle all this. I had not anticipated the prosecution of my own work dating the six months given to the Institute—unless by occasional papers elicited by current events. I expected to put all my working hours to documents. Turn these things over in your mind.

To William H. Rideing

45 West 35th Street, New York, February 7, 1914 [NDL]

My dear Mr. Rideing: I have not forgotten the proposed article but until yesterday was at a loss for a subject. I then received a letter from the Secretary of the Society of the Sons of the Revolution, speaking of their purpose to raise a fund for a statue of DeGrasse, as the representative of the French Navy, in connection with the surrender of Yorktown. It then occurred to me as possible that it might not be beyond your readers to comprehend, and be interested by, a sketch of the movements of the armies and navies which combined, and concurred to bring about the crowning success of that war.

Incidentally, sound instruction could be conveyed of the part played by the navies in that war. I think the whole subject could be lucidly presented, with probably enough of anecdote etc. to be easy reading.

Will you let me know how this strikes you.[1]

To Mary E. Phillips

University Club, New York, March 11, 1914 [BPL]

Dear Miss Phillips: The book which you so kindly sent me,[1] with the very gracious inscription with which you have accompanied the gift, did not reach me until some days after your letter. I have read a good part of it, and will not delay acknowledgment and thanks until I have finished it.

---

1. Jameson had outlined the arrangements, including his hope that he might have the "privilege of a little talk" with Mahan every day and that, perhaps once a week, Mahan would talk informally to the staff of the Department. Jameson to Mahan, January 31, 1914, in the National Archives. Later, Jameson told Mahan that the Institution would not make great demands on his time; that they only wanted him to pursue, in their sight, his own most important work.

1. If Mahan wrote such an article for *Youth's Companion*, it has not been found.

1. Mary Elizabeth Phillips, *James Fenimore Cooper*. New York: John Lane Company, 1913.

It is a very interesting and valuable addition to what I already knew about Cooper. There is something very fascinating in being admitted to the intimacies of the life of so well known an author, the association with whose books have added so many happy hours to my life.

To know the circumstances under which library works have been conceived, with the places and conditions under which they were written adds greatly to the charm with which in memory as mine of Cooper's books they are associated. I well recall my first reading of the *Last of the Mohicans* when I was fifteen. My favorite among his books I think is *Wing and Wing*, but it is only chief among many.

It is needless to add how much the profuse illustration adds to the value which I shall attach to your much appreciated present, for which I again make my thanks.

[P.S.] I have to regret that on leaving home this morning I could not lay my hand upon your letter, & so am obliged to send through your publishers.

To Bouverie F. Clark

University Club, New York, March 12, 1914 [LC]

My dear Clark: I see there is a steamer sailing to-morrow, but I fear she is a 7-day boat and that this, meant for March 19, will not make as good a hit [as] yours did on September 27. All the same, I can wish you Rip Van Winkle's toast—May you live long and prosper!

I follow the European news with my usual interest, or rather care; for, for the moment it is not as interesting to me as usual. *I* am, and always have been a convinced anti-Home ruler, and I greatly disadmire the methods by which your present Government has reduced Great Britain not only to a single-chamber State, but one without an executive somewhat independent of parliament. This business of the lower house of the legislature assuming all power to itself for five years seems to me despotism like that of the French National Convention of 1792, only not tempered, as that was, by Revolution.

I am more interested, however, personally, in the Balkan and near Eastern situation. I fear you all in Europe will find a trememdous rumpus on your hands, unless all the Great Powers can agree upon some arrangement, and then sit down hard upon all the small states thereabouts, and make them observe it and do as they are bid. We also have our problem of somewhat similar character in Mexico; for both here and there the question is really one of intervention—or non-intervention. Our party now in power has always been weak in external policy, doctrinaire in the worst sense of the word, in that they refuse to recognize that self government is not practicable for all peoples, merely because the English speaking peoples have made it work.

As regards the Balkans, our papers have stated recently that 55,000 Greeks are expected back to this country shortly, who have been home to fight.[1] Allowing for exaggeration as to number, it speaks well for them that a large number did throw up their jobs here and go back. We are spending this winter in the same hotel that we did two years ago, and the other day the head waiter showed us a photograph he had received of the man who was our waiter then, taken in uniform. He said he was a captain in the Greek army. He certainly showed very well.

I have nothing to report of ourselves, except that I feel that I am distinctly less vigorous than two years ago; cannot walk as fast or as far. This may be partly due to grip, but I had noticed it before my attack. The snow too made matters worse, for it compelled me to wear an overcoat which I could otherwise have dispensed with. We went till February 10—about—without snow; then in a fortnight three falls in rapid succession, aggregating two feet. I had been out some days before with the thermometer between zero and 5°, quite comfortable, but the chill of the snow penetrated with a much higher temperature. Snow is the one thing I cannot abide. They say it is good for the crops, but in the city it has not a single merit.

Barring diminution of strength, I am very well; and fairly busy, but with small matters for the most part. I am planning a book, but whether I shall begin it, much more complete it remains to be seen.[2] I trust this will find you well in health, fortune, and surroundings.

To Frederick Burgess[1]

Draft   45 West 35th Street, New York, April 6, 1914 [LC]

My dear Bishop Burgess: Referring to our brief conversation last Wednesday, I am preparing, and will send you in a day or two, certain views and suggestions on the matter of Prayer Book Revision.[2] I being resident in your Diocese, it is suitable that I should lay them before the Committee through you.

It has seemed to me that previous revisions have confined themselves to what might be called tinkering; that is introducing small changes here and

---

1. *The New York Times*, March 12, 1914, p. 5, carried a story on Greek-American soldiers returning to America.
2. He had barely begun his book on the "Expansion" of the United States when he died.
1. Episcopal Bishop of the Diocese of Long Island.
2. He published articles on this subject in *The Churchman* for October 10 and 17, 1914. *See* Mahan to Gilbert, September 10, 1914.

there, each doubtless for a reason that seemed sufficient; but without regard to what I conceive to be the chief general principle controlling Prayer Book Construction: namely, that the worship of the Church be *common*.

The papers I will send you comprise (1) a general argument for the supreme consideration to be given this principle in any contemplated changes. This carries with it the corollary that permissive omissions or changes, now authorized, should be diminished as far as possible. As a matter of fact almost all recent revision has borne the stamp of increased permission to the officiating minister to change at his sole discretion the features of what should be a service common to the Church at large. Instances are, the increased number of selections of psalms, the using a hymn in place of the Gloria in Excelsis, and (though this is part of the Revision of 1789) the option to use the Apostles' or Nicene Creed in the Communion Office. I hold that the common worship of the Church, through the length and breadth of the land, demands that in the major services of the week all should use the same order of service with one voice and one form of words.

(2) I hope to send you also several numbered suggestions for changes, with reasons in each case. I intend to send these detached, each from the others; to facilitate handling, if the Committee should entertain them.

Finally, these various papers were drawn up by me with a view to publishing in such way as to bring them before the Church in general, so far as I could. This will account for some of the phraseology. I wish to retain the right so to act, while at the same time recognizing the privilege granted me of thus placing the papers before the Committee through you.

To Francis V. Greene

University Club, New York, April 15, 1914 [LC]

My dear Greene: Thank you so much for your words of appreciation for my article,[1] which reached me this morning. English speaking people talk little to each other on such matters, and I had not known that you felt so strongly. It is a great satisfaction to know that my treatment of the subject commended itself to a man of your intelligence and training.

You are quite right in doubting what Unitarianism has effected. I made inquiry before I began to write; and besides statistics, and assurances from those in a position to know, I had sent me by one of my informants several pages from a Unitarian statistical publication. The contents showed nothing but lists of Unitarian societies in various parts of Europe and America, pos-

---

1. "Twentieth Century Christianity," *North American Review* (April 1914).

sibly claiming some of the individualistic movements in India as cognate; but of sustained missionary effort nothing but one small body in Japan. That the history of churches in Asia and Africa will, in their course, illustrate the deflections from the faith, here and there, that have characterized Christian history throughout, is of course probable; but there is substantially no Unitarian Missionary effort anywhere in the foreign field—neither religious nor benevolent. The motive is lacking.

You may be interested to know that the article was offered the *N.Y. Times,* and could have appeared there three weeks after Eliot's;[2] but they refused without reading it. I gave them a piece of my mind.[3]

To Elihu Root

University Club, New York, April 22, 1914 [LC]

Dear Mr. Root: I see in the reports of your yesterday's speech that you pronounce Huerta's government as *de facto* over the greater part of Mexico. The following verification may interest you, if you have not already made it.

A chance phrase in Rives's *United States and Mexico*[1] led me to investigate the distribution of population to-day. Drawing a line from Torreon to Tampico, assuming that to be the military dividing line at present, and taking the population of the several states south of that line to be under Huerta's control, I found from the *Statesman's Year Book* that 11,000,000 out of the 15,000,000 total were obedient to him; and that quietly, so far as appears.

Though my calculation was made deliberately, it should perhaps require going over; but I believe it substantially correct.

To J. Franklin Jameson

45 West 35th Street, New York, April 27, 1914 [NA]

My dear Dr. Jameson: I am indebted to you for the pamphlet containing the obituary of Prof. Whitman Bailey.[1] I do not think we had met since

2. Charles W. Eliot, "Twentieth Century Christianity," *The New York Times,* January 11, 1914. Eliot had earlier read this paper before the General Convention of the Unitarian Church in Buffalo on October 6, 1913.
3. Not published by *The Times.*
1. George Lockhart Rives, *The United States and Mexico.* 2 vols. New York: C. Scribner's Sons, 1913.
1. William Whitman Bailey, professor of botany at Brown University, was born at West Point in 1843.

we were boys, and my recollection had been that he was so much a smaller boy than I, that I was surprised to find he was within three years of my age. An inconsequential error in the notice is that he was in an accident to a boat going *up* the Hudson, in 1852. She was going down. I was curiously associated with that occurrence. The Bailey family & my grandmother, a woman then well along in her sixties, were both going to N.Y. I went with her to the dock to see her off. There were two boats racing; the *Armenia* and the *Henry Clay*. She being nervous and timid, asked *me* which she had better take; I being not quite twelve. I replied the *Armenia*, the *Clay* being in my childish mind in the proverbial position of a boy with a bad name. The stage driver concurring, she took the *Armenia*. The *Clay* caught fire and was burned, with a loss of eighty lives; Bailey's mother and sister being among these. His father and he escaped; he alone, his father, who was supporting the two ladies, being dragged from them by one of the drowning.

I have also to thank you for the paper by yourself on the subject of the expansion of the United States,[2] which I read with much instruction as well as interest. I do not know whether I made clear to you that my new present enterprise, long entertained, is a history of the United States in which Expansion should play the part which Sea Power did in certain other of my historical works. In some ways the ground is already very well taken up; so much that I feel as if research on my part will be rather gleaning after reapers. Henry Adams has covered the Louisiana purchase, and George Rives the acquisition of Texas and what we took from Mexico. My line therefore would be in these cases a presentation rather of motives, and tendencies which they have not neglected, but which perhaps I can the more elicit by paying less attention to the mere narrative of transactions.

Florida, Alaska, and the acquisitions of 1898, have not, so far as I know, received the exhaustive attention given by Adams and Rives to their themes. It has occurred to me also that the Northwestern Boundary and Oregon disputes, on which I am imperfectly informed, may be congruous to the present subject, although they seem less instances of expansion than of boundary adjustment.

I mention these matters because it has occurred to me that you and Dr. Putnam of the Congressional Library might, before my coming to Washington, decide upon archives most promising for my beginning. After beginning my experience hitherto has been that research propagates itself, like cancer.

Please thank Putnam for his suggestion as to apartments. This winter has wearied me much with that mode of living, but in the general lookout to

---

2. A paper which Jameson had delivered at the Historical Congress in London a year earlier. He enclosed it in Jameson to Mahan, February 23, 1914, in the Library of Congress.

be made next fall this will receive consideration. If practicable, I should prefer a house.

I shall at all times, and especially when I reach Washington, be very grateful for any suggestions from you or Putnam, such as I outline above.

To Josephus Daniels[1]

University Club, New York, May 4, 1914 [LC]

Dear Mr. Daniels: I beg to thank you sincerely for your kind words of appreciation for my article in the April *North American*.[2]

To Spencer Gordon

Draft Quogue, Long Island, May 20, 1914 [LC]

Dear Sir: I enclose herewith copy of my orders to the Naval War College, with endorsements, to report, in writing, October 31, 1908. My claim for fuel and light attendant upon my allowance for quarters extends from that date to the end of the then current fiscal year, June 30, 1909. After that time I received the customary allowances.

My claim for this allowance was made in October 1909, to the Fourth Auditor, and never withdrawn by me.[1]

For your personal guidance certain explanations are advisable.

My orders were issued with the clear understanding that I was not to reside at the College but to go there when my services were needed. I was accordingly ordered to report by letter, which I did, as shown by the endorsement. My established residence then was, and for some time had been, here: Quogue, N.Y.; but for reasons of convenience I received express permission from the Department to remove to Lawrence (Long Island), N.Y. from November 1, 1908, to May 1, 1909. For the remaining period of my claim, May and June, 1909, I was at Quogue.

Fuel: The fuel bills enclosed belong with one exception to the Lawrence period. The dealers, Both and Weston, being livery men, as well as in coal

---

1. Secretary of the Navy.
2. "Twentieth Century Christianity."

1. At this point in the manuscript the following sentences appear, but they are struck through: "I enclose also receipted bills for fuel and light, paid by me during the period named. These as they stand require some explanation."

and wood, the monthly bills contain various items. I have therefore, for convenience, marked with red pencil the fuel items in each.

The one bill at Quogue, of B. T. Carter for $153.01, December 3, 1908, is for coal laid in wholesale at that time by me against the following summer. Of course, no claim for that full amount is advanced. The bill serves only to show that I paid for my allowance for the two months May and June, 1909.

It will be remembered in all this action, and during this time, I was ignorant of the fact that there were allowances of fuel and of light; owing to my having been many years retired, I had had no occasion to know.

After first presenting my claim to the Fourth Auditor by letter, dated Quogue, Oct. 11, 1909, some correspondence with him ensued which ended in an opinion from him, November 2, 1909, and February 14, 1910, that my orders of October 23, 1908 (to report *by letter* on October 31) did not assign me "to such duty as to entitle him (me) to quarters." This decision was reversed by the Assistant Comptroller (Appeal No. 18472 ... CCM 8 D), on April 14, 1910. I then wrote—through the Navy Department—to the Comptroller, April 17, asking whether a decision signed by the Assistant Comptroller might be considered the final disposition of the case by the Treasury Department. The Secretary of the Navy replied that my letter had been placed on file, but not forwarded; "the Comptroller of the Treasury having heretofore decided that decisions of the Assistant Comptroller, in cases assigned to him in accordance with the terms of existing law, are final so far as the Treasury Department is concerned."

Light: Between the two opinions of the Fourth Auditor, November 2, 1909 and Feb. 14, 1910, he sent me, on November 22, 1909, a blank form upon which application for allowances for heat and light were to "be filled out by the party furnishing the heat and light." This was due to the fact that the *gas* bills at *Quogue* were made out by the Gas Company to E. L. Mahan (my wife), debtor, and she thus appeared as the party furnishing *me* the light. With the letter the Auditor returned me three gas bills thus made out. As I can find *none* of my light bills for the period, I presume that the three went back to the Auditor's office, along with the filled out blank, which I forwarded on November 30; and that the others, for *electric* light furnished me at *Lawrence*, not being returned to me, are still on file in the Auditor's office. If so, probably between October 11 and December 1, 1909.

I think of nothing to add to this, except that, if anything remain doubtful, or information imperfect, I conceive that in the Assistant Comptroller's very full review of the case, already quoted, and my own letter to him of March 9, 1910, presenting the case, every point of importance is fully stated.

In summary, the law establishing allowances shows the amount of fuel and light to which I was entitled during the period of the claim; the enclosed bills show the amount received of fuel, and that the price was paid by me.

As regards the number of rooms occupied by me, the house in Lawrence contained 14 and 2 bathrooms; that in Quogue 17, and 5 bathrooms. In the matter of deduction on account of number of rooms in a house, if we are up against an established ruling of the Treasury, there we are. It is, however, purely arbitrary. They might as well require a statement of my family habits as to going to bed. One family sits up till eleven in one room, another scatters to lie in bed in separate rooms reading to all hours, etc. Many rooms are unoccupied for months. All these things affect light and fuel consumption as really as the number of rooms. In both houses, in some rooms, there was practically no consumption.

As regards my claim for 1906 I find that the bills for that year, being outlawed, were destroyed last year. With this loss of necessary papers, the claim cannot be presented.

To Charles W. Stewart

Marshmere, Quogue, Long Island, May 23, 1914 [NA]

My dear Mr. Stewart: I fear I must open with an apology for neglecting to thank you for the last answer you made to one of my inquiries. I make it now; and on the principle of the man who settled his debt to tradesmen by giving a new order, I am going to intrude again on your kindness.[1]

1. Cooper, in his account of the Battle of L. Champlain, gives an elaborate account of the arrangement of kedges and hawsers, additional to the more usual springs, prepared by Macdonough for winding the *Saratoga*. My recollection is that M. in his report of Sept. 13 (Captains Letters) 1814 does not mention this; simply speaks of springs. Would you verify this recollection as to both the report and Cooper?

2. My second will be more troublesome. I think that Chevalier, *Histoire de la Guerre Maritime de 1778*, apropos of DeGrasse's sailing from Brest in March, 1781, states that the French Government had decided that naval operations *on the American coast* must be undertaken. They had been trivial in 1779, and in 1780 null. Washington had represented that the Americans could not hold out unaided much longer; hence, as I remember, the French decision. But my memory needs confirmation by reference. DeGrasse did come, we all know; but does Chevalier state the purpose as at the initiation of the campaign?

---

1. Mahan was preparing his "Commodore MacDonough at Plattsburg," *North American Review* (August 1914).

If too troublesome to you, you might send me the book itself to consult; but it seems hardly worth while to give it the two journeys, here and back.

If I have been too thankless in acknowledgment, I assure you I have not been in appreciation of your kindnesses.

To Charles W. Stewart

Marshmere, Quogue, Long Island, May 29, 1914 [NA]

My dear Mr. Stewart: Your letter of May 23 reached me here two days ago. As ten years have elapsed since I used the London Records Office, I fear my recollections now are too vague for precise reply to your questions. If your memory is accurate as to my saying that the probable expense of copying would be $500, my estimate was based on data now forgotten by me in *details*.

In *general*, my procedure was that I visited the office daily during some time in London, made extracts (for my specific treatment), and memoranda for subsequent copying. All this copying was done for me through Stevens and Brown, who engaged the copyists and sent me the bills. I found them always satisfactory. I was able to indicate precisely the documents I wished copied, from my previous examination. There is a vague impression in my mind that when I had finished with the copies, after my *1812* was complete, I sent them to you.

As regards the publication hitherto, I know nothing. I think the Navy History Society has drawn upon the In and Out Letters, but am not sure they have published.

It is probable that among the numerous letters of the period many are valueless; but it is hard to say how to select. It needs a specially competent man for selection, because often what seems trivial is important. I think therefore that your best course would be to ask Stevens & Brown, or any other competent party, to examine the mass of papers, and to submit an estimate of cost of copying the whole. That received, you can estimate the chance of carrying the work through, as the present Administration has nearly three years yet to run. In any case, half a loaf will be good. Perhaps it might be judicious to require, first, a memorandum of letters, from whom and to whom, with dates & general purpose. Some of Stevens' men were competent to this. My own preference, however, would be to have all, and selection then to be made of what should be *published*, if publication be contemplated.

Might not the Carnegie Institute, Historical Department, help in this, even to supplying what may be deficient in funds to the Navy Department? In your place I would consult Prof Jameson, who is Head of that Research Dept.

To Charles W. Stewart

Marshmere, Quogue, Long Island, May 30, 1914 [NA]

My dear Mr. Stewart: Thank you very much for the enclosures, and for the trouble taken in looking through Chevalier. The quotations confirm my memory, but I was afraid to trust it unconfirmed. I am to have an article on Macdonough at Plattsburg in the *North American* for August,[1] and am determined Macd. shall have the full credit, direct and indirect which he deserves.

You will, I hope, have received by this my reply about the In and Out Letters. I regret I could not be more positive and so more satisfactory, but trust my letter is not wholly useless.

[Memorandum]

Quogue, Long Island, May 1914[1]

Charge fifty dollars for 700; 700 being harder than 1000.[2]

To Spencer Gordon

Draft   Quogue, Long Island, June 19, 1914 [LC]

Dear Sir: I received on Tuesday, June 11, from Fourth Auditor's Office, a copy (unsigned) of a letter addressed to you, disallowing claim. There are in it errors of date inexplicable to me. The claim represented to you was for heat and light from October 31, 1908, to June 30, 1909, inclusive; and for that period only. This leaves me at a loss to understand "Claim for heat and light from October 1, 1909 to June 6, 1912." No such claims were ever entertained by me.

I have delayed writing till today, thinking I might hear from you, for I assume you received the original of the Auditor's letter. My own opinion

---

1. "Commodore MacDonough at Plattsburg."

1. From Charles C. Taylor, *Life of Admiral Mahan*, p. 280. Reprinted by permission.

2. This comment was written by Mahan on a letter he received from Wilmot Atherton Brownell, founder and president of the Century Syndicate, asking him to write twelve articles of 700 words each on "current and timely events" during the coming year. These pieces were to be "published on the editorial page of a large chain of papers (dailies)" over Mahan's signature. Because of Mahan's heart attack in August, the proposition came to nothing. *See* Mahan to Brownell, September 21, 1914.

is that it is scarcely worthwhile to carry the matter to the Comptroller; that, to use the common expression, it would cost more than it could come to.

I should add that, accompanying the letter was a slip, quoting section 8, Act of July 31, 1894 "Any person accepting payment under settlement by an Auditor etc."

To William H. Short[1]

Marshmere, Quogue, Long Island, June 24, 1914 [LC]

Dear Sir: Replying to your letter of June 22, just received, I am glad to enclose herewith a copy of the article you refer to, the rough draft of which I have fortunately preserved.

You will observe that the title given by me was not "The Folly of the Hague"; but, "Why Not Disarm?"[2] The change of title was made by the agent of the syndicate of papers for which the article was written, without consulting me, or giving me time to prevent the publication in that way. Not only so; but changes were made in the text—by omission—which in my opinion materially injured the argument. I remonstrated sharply but, as I said above, the wrong was done before I could stop it.

I am glad to put the matter right to you. The enclosed expresses my views, then and now.

To Spencer Gordon

Draft   Quogue, Long Island, June 25, 1914 [LC]

Dear Sir: Replying to your letter of June 22, the question as to further prosecution of claim, before the Court of Claims, involves first, for you and for me, the question of your compensation. Do I understand that, as in the case of the other claim, suggested by you, the remuneration is dependent upon recovery, in which case an agreed percentage of the amount becomes due you?

Your understanding of the case, in paragraph 3 of your letter of June 22, is not quite correct. The divergence is probably immaterial, but it is best to be quite clear.

---

1. Secretary of the New York Peace Society, delegate to the Peace Congresses of 1910 and 1912, and member of the committee that drafted the covenants for the League of Nations.
2. *See* Mahan to Griffith, September 15, 1913, Footnote 2.

About August, 1909, I first learned that there was a fuel and light allowance. Application about August 26 to the General Storekeeper at New York Yard, and through him to the Bureau of Supplies and Accounts resulted in my obtaining my fuel allowance for the fiscal year beginning July 1, 1909; my light allowance also, after November 1, 1909. The fuel allowance was thus recoverable, because cumulative. In November, 1909, I was entitled to all fuel allowance from July 1, if none had so far been received.

For the period October 31, 1908 to June 30, 1909, I was referred by the Bureau to the Fourth Auditor. My application to him was dated October 11, 1909. Some correspondence as to details results in his first suspending, (November 22, 1909), and then disallowing (February 15, 1910), payments already made to me for commutation of quarters during the period Oct. 31, 1908, to March 31, 1909, on the ground that my "orders of Oct. 23, 1908 directed me to report for duty by letter." Upon this followed an appeal to the Second Comptroller, who decided in my favor by decision dated April 14, 1910.

The above corrects your impression that when I was first put on active duty, Oct. 31, 1908, my allowances were held up. Further, whatever may have been the case as to light, I did receive fuel allowance for the whole fiscal year 1909–1910.

Referring to paragraph 4 of your letter the bill of Quogue Gas Company was made out to my wife, E. L. Mahan who thus, in the estimation of the Fourth Auditor was the supplier of the gas.

Paragraph 5. I have no receipts for fuel bought at Quogue between May 1 and June 30, 1909. The coal had been laid in the previous November or December, in wholesale quantity, as before said.

As the policy of filing the suit in the Court of Claims is to some extent pecuniary, may it not be well to bear in mind the Auditor's rule to scale down where more or fewer rooms than those allowed are occupied? What is the Court likely to hold? Bearing on this may be noted that where no meters exist the full allowance is conceded, both of heat and light. This I learned when occupying an apartment in an apartment hotel in New York, November, 1911, to May, 1912,[1] Every month, on my certificate that no means of measuring existed, cheque for full allowance was sent to the proprietor. The just rule of course is full allowance; conditioned only by certification that it is *used* by officer, *not sold* or exchanged, in whole or in part.

I enclose memorandum of light bills paid for months November, 1908, to September 30, 1909. These were paid by myself, not by government, and form part of the claim. That for one month, April, 1909, is missing, though doubtless paid about May 1. I would suggest that you total this

1. Hotel Collingwood, 45 West 35th Street.

amount with the fuel deducible from bills now in your hands, and judge whether, with your estimate of chances in the Court, it will probably pay to prosecute the claim. The question is rather for your decision than mine, as the time and trouble will be yours, except the asking for bills from the Light Companies, which I greatly dislike to do.

To Spencer Gordon

Quogue, Long Island, June 29, 1914 [LC]

Dear Sir: I have your letter of June 26,—postmarked 27,—and am of course entirely satisfied with the percentage you name. Mrs. Mahan has today gone over not only the stubs, memorandum of which was sent you, but the checks themselves. They bear of course the endorsement of the companies. I should let you know that Mrs. Mahan settles all our household bills, and that the checks consequently bear her signature, not mine. For the rest I retain what I think is a complete file of my correspondence with the Treasury on this subject, so that if any point of doubt arise I can probably inform you.

While I *dislike* to address the companies for certificates of bills, it is only due you that I should do so, if you think it advisable. I must take my share of the trouble, regretting that yours has been so much.

You have my acquiescence in your filing the suit. It may be convenient for you to know that I now expect to be in Washington from about November 1 next to the following May.

To John Bassett Moore

Marshmere, Quogue, Long Island, July 22, 1914 [LC]

My dear Mr. Moore: In an article I have just written upon the distribution of our naval force, as affected by the Panama Canal, I have used the expression "Concerted action against U.S. by an Atlantic naval power in cooperation with one in the Pacific is unlikely. This is indicated by known conditions qualifying the treaty relations of Great Britain and Japan, etc."[1]

I have here no reference, and therefore apply to you as the encyclopaedia of information on international relations. I dont want to trouble you with

---

1. "The Panama Canal and the Distribution of the Fleet," *North American Review* (September 1914).

any elaborate account of the modifications which my memory tells me Japan accepted as to the obligations of Great Britain under their treaty alliance, I wish only to be sure that I am right in assuming that there was such modification *lessening* the liability of Great Britain being drawn into any hostility with us through the alliance.

I was tempted, at the time of your resignation from the State Department to write you a letter expressive of my great chagrin. Independent of the fact that I knew you would know it, I felt that I should probably be drawn into assumptions and expressions concerning the matter in which I would not be justified, and which would reflect my sentiments rather than any accuracy of information as to the causes. You will believe, however, that I deeply regretted your retirement, and I continue to do so.

To Spencer Gordon

Draft   Quogue, Long Island, July 24, 1914 [LC]

Dear Sir: Replying to your letter of July 21, received yesterday, let me first call your attention to a wrong date "1898" in paragraph 2. It is meant to be 1908.

As to the calculations, there is one error; namely, as to fuel allowance not received. As I mentioned in my letter of June 25, the fuel allowance is cumulative. I therefore was able, upon discovering my claim in the autumn of 1909, to require for, and did receive, my fuel allowance from July 1 of that year, when the fiscal year began. My claim for fuel therefore runs only from October 31, 1908 to June 30, 1909.

The light allowance on the other hand is not cumulative, and I could not recover through the pay officer, as in the case of fuel. Therefore light claim, from Oct. 31, 1908, to September 30, 1909, had to be referred to the Auditor, together with the fuel claim up to June 30, 1909, because the latter was in a fiscal year then closed.

As regards the counter-claim, which you suggest the Government may set up, namely, that I received too large an allowance during the remaining period of my service in connection with the Naval War College, owing to excess of rooms occupied, the same thought had occurred to me. I find, however, in the *Navy Register* for 1914, page 303, section j under heading of "Allowances," that the Comptroller, by Decision September 6, 1913, decided that "when quarters occupied consist of a greater number of rooms than his rank entitles him to, payment for heat and light is authorized, provided the amounts consumed do not exceed the respective maximum amounts allowed for the number of rooms to which the rank of said officer entitles him." This seems fairly conclusive, as well as recent; but perhaps you had

[533]

best read this section yourself. In any event, I prefer the suit should go on, as I had rather lose by counter-claim than retain if not entitled.

As regards the detailed arithmetical calculation of your letter, I submit instead the following, based upon the table in *Navy Register*, 1914, p. 304:

Fuel

October 31, 1908–April 30, 1909, six months	$165.00
May 1–June 30, 1909, two months	12.00

Light

October 31, 1908–April 30, 1909, six months	57.60
May 1, 1909–August 31, 1909, four months	23.04
September 1–30, 1909, one month	9.60
	$267.24

Please verify these before filing. It may be that 1909 *Register* differs from 1914. A 1909 can be had at Navy Department Library.

To John Bassett Moore

Marshmere, Quogue, Long Island, July 25, 1914 [LC]

My dear Mr. Moore: Thank you very much for your prompt reply. I am glad that the coincidence reduced your trouble in the matter to a minimum. Although less decisive of my own needs than I had hoped, that belongs to the facts of the case and not to your very full answer to my questions.

I see you date from the city. I hope you are not shut up in it for the summer, although after Washington, as I have known it at this season, New York in temperature may pass as a reasonable summer resort.

To John Bassett Moore

Marshmere, Quogue, Long Island, N.D., circa July 27, 1914 [LC]

My dear Mr. Moore: Being in the city yesterday, I took up the *Round Table* for June.[1] This you doubtless know is a quarterly, begun some four years ago, dealing with questions of "Imperial Policy." In it I found the following passage:

"The second Treaty of Alliance with Japan made no provision for the possibility of War between U.S. and Japan: but British statesmen realized that in it there lay a challenge to public sentiment throughout the British

---

1. "Naval Policy and the Pacific Question," *Round Table* (June 1914).

democracies which would in a crisis have broken the alliance and ranged all British opinion on the side of Japan's white foe. It was accordingly provided" (here follows the provisions of Art. IV). "The possibility that the Empire might be drawn by its obligations into conflict with U.S. was thus ruled out. This new provision was highly unpopular in Japan. It led to some open demonstrations when the treaty was made public. The fact that Japanese statesmen nevertheless renewed the treaty is therefore strong prima facie evidence that they regard it as necessary from their own point of view."

This is of course not official, nor is the article, "Naval Policy and the Pacific Question," signed. Had I seen it I think I would in my own article have retained the expression that the clause (Art. IV) "indicated" known conditions qualifying the treaty relations between Great Britain and Japan, instead of changing to "may be inferred." I think the *Round Table* is written largely by persons having sources of inside information. I found it useful as well as suggestive, but stopped my subscription this year simply because there is a limit to my power of reading.

To the Editor of The Churchman

Draft   Quogue, Long Island, July 28, 1914[1] [LC]

In your issue of July 25, the Rev. Dr. Walker Gwynne,[2] in an article entitled "Sources of the Church's Strength and Weakness," enumerates first among the weaknesses that which he summarizes under the word "starch"; itself ill chosen, as lacking in the seriousness and reverence with which the subject should be treated. "Starch," it appears, consists in the "respectability and uniformity" characteristic of the set services; and the remedy proposed is expressed in the hope that the present Joint Commission on the Revision of the Prayer Book "will take out some of the starch," by giving "more freedom in the use *especially* of the Psalter, the Lectionary and the Canticles." "Especially" indicates that the hope extends beyond these.

If the *Venite* be reckoned a Canticle, and it is strictly of that character, the proposition of Dr. Gwynne is that in the Morning and Evening Prayer —Sundays not excepted—the entire service from the Lord's Prayer to the Creed is to be at the discretion of the officiating clergyman; not as regulated by the Church for a *common* devotion of her members throughout the land. Full half of the service is thus to be withdrawn from the class of what can

---

1. Published in *The Churchman*, (September 8, 1914), p. 189.
2. Walker Gwynne, "Sources of the Church's Strength and Weakness," *The Churchman* (July 25, 1914). Aside from "starch," Gwynne criticized ministerial classical education, a system of primary education based on the Bible alone, the secularization of higher education, lack of respect for the liturgy, and the modern sectarian spirit.

be called *common* worship, and be made merely that of the particular congregation; disconnected in fact, as in form, from all other congregations. It thus dismisses the catholicity of St. Paul, that "with one accord ye may with one mouth glorify God" (Rom. XV, 6); a oneness of utterance which he connects explicitly with oneness of mind or purpose—likemindedness. For completeness, Dr. Gwynne's suggestion needs only the addition—entirely congruous—that, when the officiating clergyman prefers, he shall substitute extemporary prayer for the prayers following the Creed. Under such a system no congregation can know what form the worship of another is taking, and there will be no common praise or prayer beyond the four walls of the building. We shall then have abandoned the catholic practice of the Church and adopted that of the purely Protestant separatist bodies that surround us.

In nothing is this more grievous than in the matter of the Canticles; for they represent the common praise, which is a nobler function than even that of Common Prayer. That anyone with a moderately intelligent understanding of the structure and association of the Canticles can find them— notably the *Venite* and *Te Deum*—monotonous or wearisome, is impossible, even in a daily service; much less in that of once a week, to which most of us are confined. The trouble is that the clergy do not put their own minds to the comprehension of these great hymns, much less instruct their people. Whatever "starch" there is, is in the uninstructed intelligence and apathetic imagination of the worshippers; and this fault will not be remedied by the Church abandoning her own function of governance of worship to a body of dissociated clergymen, acting independently from Sunday to Sunday.

As for the laity, under the system—if adopted—I trust they have imagination enough to fancy what they will get. We already have a certain amount of experience.

To the Committee on Admissions, Century Club

Draft   N.P., N.D. Possibly, Quogue, Long Island, August 1914 [LC]

Gentlemen: I observe on the list of candidates, for Non-Resident membership, the name of Mr. F. A. Richardson, Burlington, Vermont, formerly editor of the *International Monthly*; now styled, I believe, the *International Quarterly*.

The Committee will judge from the following statement whether Mr. Richardson, in gentlemanly integrity, meets the high standard which the Century attaches to membership.

Mr. Richardson having made more than one request to me to write for the *International*, I proposed to him, in January, 1902, that I should prepare articles to be published simultaneously by it and the English *National Review*. He accepted January 28, in these words: "Your suggestion is pleasing to me. I do not see why such arrangements cannot be of mutual advantage, and I am very glad of the opportunity to publish more of your work." In accordance with this Mr. R selected three out of several topics suggested by me. I then prepared before April 1 an article which appeared in the two magazines in May,[1] and proceeded with the second. On April 14, Mr. R. wrote me, "I shall be in New York the latter part of this week or the first of next and hope then to have the pleasure of talking over plans for the future essays." He did not however appear, and my next communication from him was May 15, to this effect: "I have been recently making changes in my plans for the Journal, and it will not be practical for me to continue further in the present arrangement with the *National Review*. I regret exceedingly to lose the next essay to the Journal, but this syndicate plan is no longer practicable."

The second article was then substantially ready, and was forwarded to England on May 23d, appearing there in July.[2] Mr. Richardson thus, without prior warning, threw back upon my hands work contracted for and done, according to agreement made over three months before. In reply, I simply denied his right thus to repudiate his agreement, but have never since heard from him.

I will add that a gentleman in this city who has done work for the *International* told me he had difficulty in getting his money.

From one or two interviews with Mr. Richardson, I can safely say there is no evidence of any such social[3] merit as to recommend exceptional allowance for demerit otherwise.

·

To Otis F. Wood Co., Inc.[1]

Quogue, Long Island, August 6, 1914 [LC]

Gentlemen: Replying to yours of August 4, it is not probable that I can undertake the weekly article you ask, in view of the several other propositions previously made me.

As I do not reach a final decision till Saturday evening you may wish to

---

1. The article, "The Military Rule of Obedience," appeared in the March 1902 issues of *International Monthly* and *National Review*.
2. "Conditions Governing the Disposition of Navies," *National Review* (July 1902).
3. The word "clubbable" was replaced by the word "social" here.

1. Otis F. Wood Newspaper Syndicate.

notify me more precisely as to terms. I should wish also some specific knowledge as to papers included in the syndicate; especially, in view of a most unpleasant experience at the hands of a syndicate within the twelvemonth,[2] I should require explicit assurance that my articles should be published as I send them as regards both heading and text.

To Spencer Gordon

Quogue, Long Island, August 7, 1914 [LC]

Dear Sir: Replying to your letter of August 4, I have signed the enclosed Power of Attorney, and also read the copy of the petition, which I assume I am to retain. I have gone over the amounts, and find them correct, by *Navy Register* Tables, 1914. In the petition I notice two errors; not material to the case, but better corrected. On pages 1 & 2 the Expiration of my duty at War College is given as June 7, 1910. It should be 1912.[1]

To Ralph Pulitzer[1]

Marshmere, Quogue, Long Island, August 10, 1914 [LC]

Dear Sir: Since writing you on Saturday I have received from the Navy Department a "Special Order" the gist of which is simply the transmission of the President's letter of August 6 to the Secretaries.[2] Although the President's letter simply *"suggests"* to the Secretaries that they *"advise* and *request"* officers to abstain from public comment etc., the Secretary of the Navy, beside the above heading, speaks of the letter as an "order." Neither "suggest," "request," nor "advise," can bear that con-

---

2. *See* Mahan to Short, June 24, 1914.

1. A few days later Gordon filed *Alfred T. Mahan vs. The United States* in the Court of Claims in Washington, the claim amounting to $240.96. The suit was pending at the time of Mahan's death.

1. President of the Press Publishing Company, which published the *New York World*, and vice-president of the Pulitzer Publishing Company, publishers of the *St. Louis Post-Dispatch*.

2. The President's letter read: "I write to suggest that you request and advise all officers of the service, whether active or retired, to refrain from public comment of any kind upon the military or political situation on the other side of the water. I would be obliged if you would let them know that the request and advice comes from me. It seems to me highly unwise and improper that officers of the Navy and Army of the United States should make any public utterances to which any color of political or military criticism can be given where other nations are involved."

struction of meaning; yet the word "order" binds me, till otherwise instructed.[3]

I mention these things because they seem to show some hesitancy on the part of the President to *order*; and because, as he is not to return to Washington till Thursday, you will have opportunity to consider whether the above considerations may be useful.

[*Memorandum*]

Quogue, Long Island, August 11, 1914[1]

Returned "advanced check" Aug. 11 A.T.M.[2]

To the Editor of The New York Times

Quogue, Long Island, August 14, 1914[1]

In your issue of Aug. 7 a correspondent, "A.H.W.," asks that some intelligent, sincere Christian answer the question, "What has Christianity done toward civilizing the world?"

I would reply that if "A.H.W." will compare the conditions of the countries in which Christianity has existed with those where it has only begun to touch, in such matters as the status of women, the administration of Justice, the conditions of settled government, he (or she) will find an answer. Such inquiry must be made by one capable of distinguishing substantial general results amid numerous perplexing details.

There is no such thing as "Christian Europe" or a Christian State. There is a Europe, and there are States, in which exists a large body of persons who hold the Christian faith and earnestly, if imperfectly, try to practice it in their lives. The presence of these through the centuries has been the

---

3. On February 11, 1915, Frederick A. Mahan wrote to Theodore Roosevelt: "My sister writes me that there is no doubt in her mind that his death was hastened by the worry caused through not being able to show our people, as this wretched war goes on, the necessity for preparedness, by illustrating the subject from the events of the day, his mouth being closed and his pen being stopped by the Executive Order forbidding our officers of the army and navy to express their opinions in public or through the medium of the press."

1. From Charles C. Taylor, *Life of Admiral Mahan*, p. 278. Reprinted by permission.

2. This comment was written on a letter, dated August 9, 1914, which Mahan received from William B. Howland, editor of *The Independent*, thanking Mahan for his willingness to write an article for *The Independent* on the "Naval Strategy of the War," and enclosing an advance of $100.

1. From *The New York Times*, August 16, 1914, under the heading "Christian Progress."

leaven which has effected what is called Christian civilization. The result, Christian civilization, is found only where the Christian leaven is found; from which may certainly be inferred that to this cause it is due.

If "A.H.W." wishes further development he can find it in an article in the April *North American*, "Twentieth Century Christianity."

To Josephus Daniels

Draft   Quogue, Long Island, August 15, 1914 [LC]

1. I have received the Department's Special Order of August 6, 1914, with reference to public comment by officers upon the existing European War.

2. I would represent that the status of a retired naval officer is by law so detached from employment by the Government, that his relation to the course of the Government, and the consequent responsibility of the Government for his published opinions, differs scarcely at all from the case of a private citizen.

This consideration is reinforced by the fact that all the weight attached to the judgment of any particular officer is purely personal to him, and therefore private. If I were to resign from the Navy tomorrow, my opinions on professional matters would be valued neither less nor more than they now are.

3. Assuming that the reason of the Government for the Order was to forestall any appearance of bias on its own part toward either belligerent—for not otherwise can a personal expression affect it—I submit that the published opinion of a retired officer can in no wise compromise the just sensitiveness of the Government as to the clear and evident impartiality of its own attitude.

4. Public opinion being in the last analysis the determining force in our national polity, the effect of the Order is to disable a class of men best qualified by their past occupation, and present position, to put before the public considerations which would tend to base public opinion in matters of current public interest, upon sound professional grounds.

5. Personally, at the age of seventy-four, I find myself silenced at a moment when the particular pursuits of nearly thirty-five years the results of which have had the approval of the naval authorities in almost all countries, might be utilized for the public. I admit a strong feeling of personal disappointment, but that necessarily must be of less consequence in any reconsideration that may be granted. I may state that I have applications more than I could attend to, if permitted, from Great Britain and from our own coun-

try, couched in terms of strong appreciation of my particular fitness for the work, and which may consequently be assumed to indicate a popular want.

6. I believe that the terms of the Order exceed in stringency the rules of any of the great naval states notably those of Great Britain. The Office of Naval Intelligence can probably inform the Department on this point.

7. On my own behalf, I request the withdrawal of the Order as far as applicable to retired officers.

To Josephus Daniels

Marshmere, Quogue, Long Island, August 15, 1914 [LC]

Dear Mr. Daniels: I venture to address you a personal letter, in connection with the official request forwarded for a reconsideration of the President's letter, to which you have given the force of an order.

The best ability of the active lists of our Army and Navy are doubtless on the Boards which under our system correspond to General Staffs elsewhere. They are bound to silence by the proprieties of their position. Why then cut off from the public the supply of other competent criticism of passing military events—and the political, as having military bearings? Why even deny the criticism of the moral side of political action, which weighs so heavily in public opinion, but which needs always to be emphasized?

Touching questions that call for comment, take, for example, Why did the German battle-cruiser *Goeben* take refuge in Turkish waters, instead of joining the Austrians in the Adriatic, which she could have done, and brought them a very valuable reinforcement?

Again, why not permit comment, of military character, upon the military decision of Italy? She remains neutral, which enables Austria to detach heavily to the support of Germany on the Rhine, where the French barely equal the Germans, if [they do] at all. Does Italy suppose that her neutrality now will save her from the punishment she will surely receive, if Germany and Austria win? They resent her neutrality as much as they would her hostility, though the injury is less. On the barest calculation of ultimate safety Italy owes to herself to occupy Austria, and divert part of France's enemies.

When I was in France eighteen months ago, a leading French statesman, a member of the present cabinet, told me that Germans had said to him that if they got France down again they would bleed her white. If a nation of that temper gets full control on the continent, which is what she is trying for, do you suppose it will long respect the Monroe Doctrine? At this moment Germany suffers from lack of coaling stations here. If she downs France, why not take Martinique? or if Great Britain, some Canadian port?[1]

To the Editor of The New York Times

Quogue, Long Island, August 31, 1914[1]

In an editorial of Aug. 29, "The American Example," you urge that "the unguarded frontier between the United States and Canada suggests the real reason why the United States has for a century maintained peace with Great Britain." As developed, the argument runs that preparation for war leads to war.

The statement is one that is running trippingly from hundreds of pens at the present moment. Let us examine it in the light of history.

In the last century the most protracted war, the one consequently most expensive in blood and treasure, was the war of secession between the North and South of our own country. In what way did "guarded frontiers" or other preparation for war contribute to the outbreak? What trained soldiery, what fortifications on either side, that in any way affected the determination to fight? The remote cause of the war was slavery; the immediate occasion popular emotion; fervid nationalism, patriotism, truly or falsely so-called, aroused on either side.

In 1812 the United States declared war on Great Britain. To what extent did preparations for war affect this decision? Our unpreparation was notorious, so that our own performance, except a few naval successes, was ludicrous, even grotesque, as an exhibition of military inadequacy. I know that war.

In 1846 we went to war with Mexico. Were the determining causes then in any sense preparation for war? During the past Winter I had the pleasure of reading twice George L. Rives's exhaustive and instructive work, *Relations of the United States with Mexico*. If anyone will read the same and find therein that sustained military armaments, beyond those originating

---

1. Daniels replied on August 18, justifying the President's "order": Mahan's work, he said, had been criticized as pro-English, Chadwick's as pro-German; but since both were naval officers, they "trench upon the line of American neutrality." Prior to the prohibition of August 6, Mahan had written and mailed his "Sea Power in the Present European War," which *Leslie's Weekly* published on August 20, 1914. This has been included in the Papers in this collection.

1. From *The New York Times*, September 10, 1914, p. 8. *See* Mahan to Miller, September 6, 1914.

[542]

with the immediate menace of war, had anything to do with bringing on that conflict, he will be more acute than I can flatter myself with being.

The war with Spain, which resulted in the liberation of Cuba, is of recent memory. In what sense, with any truth, can it be alleged that preparations for war—armaments—were an influential motive to that collision?

These instances are from our own history, and, naturally, unpreparedness for war is the American tradition, and, to some extent, the American boast. In every instance the causes were of the class we call "moral," which, of course, includes immoral. That is, the motives which led to war were popular and national interests, convictions, emotions, and sympathies, although they may have been bad or good, wise or unwise, in any particular instance.

Per contra, the State whose name is the synonym for systematic preparation for war, Germany, has had sustained peace for forty-three years—nearly a half century—despite her huge armament. Though armed to the teeth, the European Continent during the same period until 1912 did not see war, except between Russia and Turkey in 1877. Those who remember that war, and the antecedent occurrences which led to it, will have difficulty in assigning preparation for war as a principal cause. I myself have always believed that not the reluctant Czar, but the passionate Russian people, in that instance forced hostilities on behalf of their persecuted co-religionists; men, too, of their own blood.

I am not prepared to maintain that armaments never cause war; but, if space permitted, I should be prepared to argue that they do so only when some other exciting cause, of either interest or national feeling, comes into play. The hackneyed phrase, "Vital interests or national honor," really sums up the motives that lead nations to war. Armament is simply the instrument of which such motives avail themselves. If there be no armament, there is war all the same.

To B. F. Stevens and Brown

N.P., N.D. Probably, Quogue, Long Island, August 1–3, 1914[1]

I take this opportunity to express to you the vivid interest with which I am following Great Britain's course in this war. But the testimony to the uprightness and efficiency of her Imperial rule, given by the strong adhesion and support of India and the Dominions, is a glory exceeding that of pitched battle and overwhelming victory.

---

1. From Charles C. Taylor, *Life of Admiral Mahan*, p. 281. Reprinted by permission. The Stevens and Brown archives were destroyed only recently.

To George B. M. Harvey[1]

Quogue, Long Island, September 3, 1914 [LC]

Dear Sir: Contrary to the usual custom of the *Review*, I have not yet received the honorarium for the article "Commodore Macdonough at Lake Champlain" in the August issue.

As I see by the press that the article "The Panama Canal and the Distribution of the Fleet" has been published, in the September number, it has occurred to me that, unless contrary to office methods, it might be convenient to the *Review* to make both payments by the same check.

May I add that I had to write in order to get the copy of the August number, in accordance with the custom by which contributors receive such copies; and that similarly I have not received as yet any copy of the September issue.

To Charles R. Miller[1]

Draft   N.P., N.D. Probably, Quogue, Long Island, September 6, 1914 [LC]

Dear Sir: On August 31st I mailed from here to the *Times* a letter in reply to an editorial in your issue of August 29, "The American Example."

As several letters of later date than the above, notably a two column one from Dr. Eliot dated Sept 1, at Bar Harbor, have been published, I have to infer that it is inconvenient to the *Times* to publish my letter near the date of the editorial to which it referred.

I request therefore that, if my letter is not to appear the day after date of receipt of this, which I assume will be Tuesday, Sept 8, that *The Times* will return my letter in enclosed envelope, in order that I may seek some other channel of communication with the public; the matter being one of public importance on a subject the depths of misapprehension concerning which is shown by the *Times'* editorial.[2]

---

1. Editor of the *North American Review*.

1. Editor-in-Chief of *The New York Times*.
2. The letter was published by *The Times* on September 10, 1914, under the heading "Unguarded Frontiers: Not Factors in Preventing Wars, Admiral Mahan Says."

To the Editor of the New York Sun

Draft   Fragment   N.P., N.D. Probably, Quogue, Long Island, circa September 7, 1914 [LC]

... If the *Sun* can spare the space, I would like to add the following.[1]

The Times' editorial ended with the words, "Both countries prepared for nothing but peace and in the words of the late Prof. Sumner, what we prepare for we shall get."[2]

Doubtless, as a rule. Before 1812 we prepared nothing, and we got it. Hull's surrender at Detroit; the ignominious land campaigns of 1812 and 1813; the capture of Washington and the burning of the Capitol. Neither of the two causes for which we went to war was conceded in the peace negotiations.

In the War with Mexico, no armaments had been prepared, but we had prepared men. Our Commander in Chief, General Scott, attributed, not perhaps the entirety of success, but the dispatch and admirable execution of the operations, to the professional ability of the officers graduated from West Point, of which Academy he was not himself a pupil.

In the War of Secession it was these prepared men who steered the ship through. To name only the best known, Grant, Sherman, Sheridan on the Union side, Lee and the two Johnstones [*sic*] on the Confederate were all West Pointers. The Naval Academy was even then of too recent establishment to affect the larger operations, but they were entirely in the hands of men trained by long years to be military seamen, Farragut, Porter and their seconds.

In the War with Spain, it was Spain most markedly who got that for which she prepared. The brave but unfortunate Cervera wrote some months before Santiago, "Unless I am given the means for practice I shall go to a Trafalgar"; and he went.

Lack of proper preparation will not prevent war, but it is pretty sure to make war disastrous.

To Levi Gilbert[1]

Draft   Quogue, Long Island, September 10, 1914 [LC]

My dear Mr. Gilbert: I find it was on July 30 I wrote you with regard to proposed papers on the subject of Prayer Book Revision. I now en-

---

1. Mahan apparently drafted this to the *Sun* while waiting for *The New York Times* to publish his similar letter of August 31. He seems not to have completed or sent it. *See* Mahan to Miller, September 6, 1914; and Mahan to Reynolds, September 11, 1914.
2. *The New York Times*, Editorial, "The American Example," August 29, 1914.
1. Editor of *The Churchman* and delegate to various church conferences.

close them—two—for your examination and decision.[2] I have the feeling that I am perhaps intruding myself and opinions too much. On the other hand the subject is one that ought to interest churchmen generally.

Upon the whole, I hope you will exercise your judgment freely. I have enlarged on the *Venite*, because (1) I apprehend distinctive opposition to change, (2) because it offers itself to analysis as instructive as the *Te Deum*; (3) because, being the opening suggestion, I want as far as possible to gain readers at the outset.

The Committee meets again in October, I believe. Both papers were before it in the spring, substantially as they stand, though in II there are some additions. Could you eventually, yourself or some other, discuss the subject editorially? Only public discussion can effect anything. The Convention has neither time nor interest, as a body.

To Paul R. Reynolds[1]

Draft   N.P. Probably, Quogue, Long Island, September 11, 1914 [LC]

Dear Sir: Your letter of Sept. 5 was duly received, but the preoccupations of which I spoke have prevented a sooner reply.

The order of President Wilson—August 6—prevents me, in common with all naval officers, from comment upon the current war. I could probably write an article, which would possess considerable interest for readers of a certain class, upon the general lines of the enclosed letter of mine to the *New York Times*.[2] Both *Times* and *Evening Post* have retorted to it; the latter in an editorial a column long, trying to sustain the disproof to which you allude as its argument, while attributing to me extravagancies which I have asked it to substantiate by quotation.

If you see fit to bring the matter before Mr. Ellsworth,[3] you may say that the general argument of the enclosed, hasty and necessarily brief, will admit of enlargement to five thousand words or more. The matter I consider interesting, and demonstrative that, while absence of preparation does not avert war, preparation shortens it and is so less expensive of blood and money.

I had prepared some such elaboration for a daily paper,[4] because the *Times* delayed publication over a week, and I purposed publishing its action in printing my letter so far from its criticised editorial.

---

2. Published in *The Churchman*, October 10 and 17, 1914. *See* Mahan to Burgess, April 6, 1914.

1. Probably, Paul Revere Reynolds, senior partner in Paul R. Reynolds & Son, who founded in 1893, the first literary agency in America.
2. *See* Mahan to *The New York Times*, August 31, 1914.
3. William Webster Ellsworth, President of the Century Company.
4. *See* Mahan to the New York *Sun*, September 7, 1914.

To Charles R. Miller

Draft N.P., N.D. Probably, Quogue, Long Island,
circa September 12, 1914 [LC]

Dear Mr. Miller: Yours of the 9th was duly received. It is evident that a reply to an editorial, to be effective, needs to follow promptly. Mine was mailed August 31, doubtless received next day. It was not published till Sept. 10.

As regards the space for letters, you found room for a two-column one from Dr. Eliot, dated Bar Harbor, Sept 1, consequently received after mine, and no more pertinent to these times than my own short one. I followed the matter through the week, and think space could easily have been found. I noted especially another of nearly two columns. As regards the change in the Sunday issue, your letter gives no account why room was not found in the three following days, Sept. 7, 8, 9.

Your explanation is as little to the real point as that of Mr. Ochs[1] to the refusal to print a reply from me to Dr. Eliot last winter. *The Times* is master of its columns, it is not master of the reputation such acts earn it....

To Wilmot Atherton Brownell

Draft Quogue, Long Island, September 21, 1914 [LC]

Dear Sir: Referring to our correspondence in the early summer, concerning certain short articles to be contributed by me from time to time, I have since then suffered from a rather sharp heart attack, occasioned by a pressure of work connected with the outbreak of the current war in Europe.

The warning necessitates my withdrawing from the promise I gave you, for I have reason to fear recurrence of such attacks under similar pressure, which an obligation undertaken beforehand may entail, when maturing. If in the future you should wish an article, or articles, from me, I can consider each in connection with my work at the moment, but a definite engagement ahead has become impossible.

As I have momentarily mislaid your address, I have to send in care of Mr. Morse.[1]

---

1. Adolph S. Ochs, owner and publisher of *The New York Times*.

1. Edwin Wilson Morse, Secretary and Director of the book department of Charles Scribner's Sons.

To J. Franklin Jameson

Marshmere, Quogue, Long Island, September 26, 1914 [LC]

My dear Dr. Jameson: I have postponed acknowledging your kind note of the 14th till you should have arrived in Washington. Our plans, as decided by Mrs. Mahan for the family, are that she will arrive in Washington Oct. 25 or 26, and will stay at the Grafton while looking for a house,—unless you know anything about that hotel which would lead you to advise us against it. She hopes to settle speedily. I myself will go to Washington, Sunday, Nov. 1, from near Philadelphia where I expect to spent a few preceding days with relatives.

Needless to say that, if you know any good things in the way of furnished houses, Mrs. Mahan will be delighted by any assistance. She has one in prospect, recommended by friends, and she has been put in communication with a Mr. Tuckerman, an agent, whose wife has spent the summer here; but otherwise everything is in the inchoate state attendant upon prospective househunting.[1]

I shall hope to call on you at your office, Nov. 2.

To Bouverie F. Clark

Marshmere, Quogue, Long Island, October 1, 1914 [LC]

My dear Clark: Your good letter for my birthday was a little ahead of time but appreciated all the same. As I found at Palermo, eighteen months ago, one's memory cant keep all things. Being now three weeks since you wrote, the face of the campaign has changed a good deal. I am at the moment a little concerned lest the Germans nab the Belgians in Antwerp with their heavy siege guns, before the Allies turn their right on the Aisne. It looks like possibly close work; but all will have been solved, probably, before you get this. Our papers here are spending money wildly on cables, I fancy, for I find in them all the essentials day by day, which I get ten days later in *The Mail* (not Daily). Our interest remains strong, though naturally less excited than the first few days. All my entourage is strongly pro-Ally; it would be more correct to say anti-German; and I think that is the tone of our people generally, barring the "German-Americans" and some Irish. Our President, in his zeal for neutrality, has forbidden army and navy men to speak or write for publication. Luckily, I had fired off my mouth all I needed before the order came out. It has done me out of dollars only, of which a good many were in sight; but it is all for the best, for the pressure

---

1. Mrs. Mahan finally found a furnished house at 2025 Hillyer Place.

to write all that was asked of me brought on a heart attack. At least I think that the cause, and I have been obliged ever since to cut down my exercise. In fact, I feel as if I have definitely turned a corner downhill, but only in the way of more careful living. I believe I have told you that we are to pass the winter in Washington, I being employed to do some research work at good pay; an offer not to be disregarded in these hard times. The winter there is shorter and milder than in New York, and I am glad my daughters are to have a chance to know the capital familiarly. The sinking of your three cruisers[1] did not greatly impress me from the military standpoint. I have always held that torpedo protection is a matter of scouting—watchfulness, and lapses there will occur. The result will show if I am greatly wrong. Your fleet holds the balance & I trust will be wide awake.

To J. Franklin Jameson

Marshmere, Quogue, Long Island, October 6, 1914 [LC]

My dear Dr. Jameson: Mrs. Mahan has heard through friends of one house, more or less in the same general quarter of the city,[1] for $150 per month; but, while the account of accommodations is satisfactory, we cannot judge of conditions till we see it. Mrs. M. will not stick at $175. if the advantage of a house justify to her the additional sum. We want four rooms, for the four members of the family; and if possible four for servants—one a man—for we hope to take the four we now have, and bring them back here in the spring.[2] This is a large expectation of permanency in servants, but, despite many disappointments, we hope on. Other things being equal, we would like to be near a line of cars running near the Capitol, for I cant walk as I once did.

With regard to the expectations from me that you mention, I can only hope that I may fill the bill. I am much indebted for your care to secure for me a working room.

As regards the Marcy papers, I know Mrs. Sperry well enough to give a letter to her to any person whom you will recommend to me.[3] I can think of

---

1. The *Cressy, Hogue,* and *Aboukir,* sunk by a German submarine on September 22.

1. O Street, near New Hampshire Avenue. Jameson to Mahan, October 3, 1914, in the Library of Congress.

2. Jameson relayed this information to Charles Hague, a real estate agent in Washington, D.C.

3. Jameson had written that Professor Justin Smith, of Harvard, wished to consult the papers of William L. Marcy, Secretary of State in the Pierce Administration. Some of the papers were in the possession of Mrs. C. S. Sperry, Marcy's daughter, who, after Admiral Sperry's death in 1911, had gone to live in Boulder, Colorado. Jameson to Mahan, October 3, and November 19, 1914, in the Library of Congress.

no other mode of approach,—or, at least, no better. I have lost sight of her entirely since her husband's death, but doubtless she can be recovered without recourse to a detective.

[P.S.] Mrs. Mahan tells me that I should have laid stress on condition of plumbing, and also would like to know whether generally, or in a particular instance, kitchen utensils are part of the furnishing.

To George B. M. Harvey

Draft   Quogue, Long Island, October 9, 1914 [LC]

Dear Sir: Upon receipt of check for the Article, "The Panama Canal and the Distribution of the Fleet," I am surprised to find the amount tendered to be one hundred dollars; instead of the one hundred and fifty paid for all my articles heretofore, with a single exception.

That exception was for "Twentieth Century Christianity," in April last. Concerning that the *Review* notified me before hand that only one hundred could be paid, leaving me at liberty to reject or accept. In this case no similar intimation was given to me and I may add that my choice to offer the article to the *North American* traversed the advice given me by the person at whose suggestion the article was written.

To Roy B. Marston

Quogue, Long Island, October 14, 1914[1]

Dear Mr. Marston: Since you wrote, the misfortune to the three A.C.'s has occurred, and I saw yesterday that the Russians had also lost the *Pallada*. I have been surprised myself that such attempts have not been more frequent, and doubtless, if a full return of all submarine prowlings were obtainable, we should find many failures against each success. I have not shared Sir Percy Scott's dismal forebodings, believing that the question of the submarine would reduce itself to one of scouting and look-out; yet I have not ventured so positive an adverse opinion as sometimes I see attributed to me. As regards the inactivity of the German Main Fleet, it is to be remembered that it is numerically much inferior. In an article written for one of our weeklies early in the war[2] I gave the opinion that the Germans

---

1. From Charles C. Taylor, *Life of Admiral Mahan*, pp. 293–294. Reprinted by permission. Published also, in slightly different form, in *The New York Times*, December 8, 1914.
2. "Sea Power in the Present European War," *Leslie's Weekly* (August 20, 1914).

would first try to reduce the margin against them by torpedo attacks, and possibly by airships, and I have been accordingly surprised that no more has been attempted in the two months intervening. As regards the general course of the war, today's news is superficially discouraging, and I am disappointed that the Allies should have made so little impression on the lines of the Germans in France, while these were able to spare men enough to reduce Antwerp. Nevertheless, numbers and money will eventually tell, as in our Civil War, if the Allies persist to the end; and in any case the British Fleet holds the decision in its hands, as in the days of Napoleon. I do not permit myself anxiety, though it is hard to avoid when so interested; besides, I am sure that if Germany wins by a big margin she is likely to be nasty to us. Lord Roberts has a fine chance for "I told you so" as regards the need of your Army for greater numbers, if he wished to be disagreeable.

Myself and family are very well, though my seventy-four years, now complete, make themselves felt more and more. I have lost perceptibly in physical vigour during the summer. This winter we are to spend in Washington instead of New York, I having been asked to do some research work there.

With my most earnest interest in your nation's present and future, and my personal regards to yourself.

To Little, Brown and Company

Marshmere, Quogue, Long Island, October 23, 1914 [LC]

Gentlemen: Acknowledging your letter of October 19, doubtless there will be something, and there may be much to be said about the naval operations of the current war, but as yet so little has happened and the information concerning that little is so meagre that it is impossible to anticipate what can be made of it all. Plans cannot yet be formed.

I expect to be in Washington Nov 1 to May 1 and it is possible that there I may be able to acquire much data. I note your wish to bring out the book if I am able.

To Evarts B. Greene[1]

Washington, D.C., November 6, 1914 [LC]

Dear Sir: I regret that I will not be able to accept the kind invitation of Messrs. McLaughlin, James Schouler, and Charles Francis Adams, to the dinner to be given at the Metropolitan Club, in New York, on November 27.

---

1. Secretary of the American Historical Association.

To Rebecca Lewis Evans[1]

2025 Hillyer Place, Washington, D.C., November 10, 1914 [NWC]

My dear Rebecca: When I first arrived Ellie undertook to write you for both of us, for the moment, and I since then have been so overcome by general good for nothingness, due mainly to sleeping badly, though to other causes as well, that I have dragged on from day to day without energy to take up my pen. This remains the only drop of bitterness in our general conditions, for we really are very pleasantly and conveniently placed; could scarcely have been more so. The girls too seem to like Washington, so that all promises well for the venture, except in my own case, for which it was undertaken; and perhaps that too will come out right though I am not sanguine.

It is amazing the number of people who have turned up, and continue to turn up, with whom we have some affiliation in the past. As General Phipps said the place is one where you scarcely turn a corner, without meeting a chance acquaintance. The fact has for me its bad side as well as its good; or at least its awkward side. I have succeeded today in working off two duty calls; one on the Secretary,[2] and a card left at the door of the White House; which acts are I trust the end as well as the beginning of the transactions.

The rest of Haverford was very welcome and refreshing to me, coming between the two upsets, and I much enjoyed also seeing you all, and hearing the boys talk. We are all women in this establishment, & though it would not be possible to have better, or more acceptable to me, quite independent of my love for them, it is pleasant occasionally to drop into a household differently constituted.

Love to Allen & all others.

To J. Franklin Jameson

2025 Hillyer Place, Washington, D.C., November 21, 1914 [LC]

My dear Dr. Jameson: Being obliged to remain at home today, to receive a visit from the doctor, I have utilized the opportunity to write Mrs. Sperry. I have enclosed to her your letter, with that of Prof. Smith, as best explaining the situation, adding thereto my own recommendation & endorsement.[1]

---

1. Wife of Allen Evans, who was a first cousin of Mrs. A. T. Mahan.
2. Josephus Daniels, Secretary of the Navy.

1. *See* Mahan to Jameson, October 6, 1914, Footnote 3.

PAPERS
of
ALFRED THAYER MAHAN

All the world knows, gentlemen, that we are building a new navy—the process has begun, is going on, and its long continuance is an avowed purpose. We are to have a navy adequate to the sense of our needs; and that sense is bound to expand as our people appreciate more and more, as they are beginning to realize more and more, that a country's power and influence must depend upon her hold upon regions without her own borders, and to which the sea leads. The influence of the little British islands gives a lesson our people will surely learn.

Alfred Thayer Mahan
From Practical Words: An Address

Another curious obliquity of vision is that which sees in great armaments the cause of war; that, if nations were not armed, they would not fight. Needless to say that the getting the better of others is one of the large occupations of the human race, in business, in lawsuits, as well as in international affairs. . . . The cause of war is the human heart, and its passions, more often noble than simply perverse.

Alfred Thayer Mahan
From About What Is The War?

Memorandum of a Conversation With James E. Jouett on the Battle of Mobile Bay, August 5, 1864[1]

N.P., N.D. Probably, March 1883 [NA]

The *Brooklyn* appeared to be aground but soon saw that she was backing and fell off with her head pointing fair toward Fort Morgan. The Admiral ordered the *Metacomet* to back hard while the *Hartford* went ahead and so cleared the head of the two vessels and passed to port of the *Brooklyn*. While thus detained, the *Brooklyn* was suffering from the raking fire of Fort Morgan, wood flying out of her, her own battery of little use, the *Hartford's* (bow of *Hartford* 20 yds. from *Brooklyn*) also, and the *Richmond* piling up on top. Jouett says that the rebel gunboats were standing away from the fleet using their stern guns, so as to maintain a pretty steady distance from the head of our line, and that they kept throwing empty shell boxes over and that these were the buoys which Alden[2] speaks of as suspicious. Jouett accounts for the fleet passing over torpedoes safely because the caps of the torpedoes were close together on top—with a flood tide they pointed from the vessels. When he [Jouett] cast off from the *Hartford*, the *Gaines* soon turned and made for the fort, her damage having been mainly received from the *Hartford*. The two others kept on ahead, the *Metacomet* steering between them; the *Selma* on the port hand. *Metacomet* yawed two or three times to fire but finding that she lost way ceased and kept on. When quarter of a mile astern (about—perhaps more) a very heavy rain squall came on obscuring the two vessels. (Before this the *Selma* two or three times showed a disposition to close on the *Metacomet*; but the *Morgan* not doing so, she kept away again.) During the squall the *Morgan* ran aground and the *Metacomet* passed her in pursuit of the *Selma* and when the squall passed she was ahead of the latter, cutting off her retreat. One shot from the *Metacomet* killed the 1st Lieut &c, and the *Selma* surrendered. Surrender nearer West shore. *Metacomet* was drawing 9 feet.

---

1. The editors have reconstructed this account from Mahan's rough notes of his interview with Captain Jouett. Jouett commanded the *Metacomet*.
2. Captain James Alden, commanding officer of the *Brooklyn*.

Jouett says that he cautioned Craven[3] not to pass to the windward of the big buoy, and attributes his doing so to his intentness on the *Tennessee*. After firing, the *Tecumseh* loaded with steel shot and the heaviest service charge and turned her ports from the fort. As she was drawing near the buoy of the *Tennessee*, which had been lying behind Fort Morgan, stood out and crossed the channel. Jouett thinks that Craven in his anxiety to get at the *Tennessee* took a short cut across, and that that was Buchanan's[4] idea to decoy him. Thinks that the torpedoes were moored to a heavy line. Mentioned that the *Tennessee* stood for the *Hartford* and the latter moved her helm to avoid it.

3. Commander T.A.M. Craven, commanding officer of the *Tecumseh*.
4. Commodore Franklin Buchanan, CSN, commander of the Confederate Squadron.

Answers to Questions on Examination
for Promotion to Captain[1]

Washington, D.C., October 15, 1885 [LC]

Question 2: What are the general duties of a Naval Commdn. in Chief?

To acquaint himself with the qualities of each ship under his command; to ascertain by frequent (half yearly) inspection that her condition and discipline is such that she is good for all her qualities should fit her for. To keep himself in communication with diplomatic representatives of the United States on his station and to learn through them or otherwise the political conditions of the countries within his command. To afford protection to American interests, commerce and citizens, whenever he can properly interfere, acting as a diplomatic representative when none is present. To fulfill the official courtesies demanded by his position. In time of war to see that his subordinate commanders, besides being efficient themselves and in their vessels, have such knowledge of his orders, private signals and general intentions as may enable them with full intelligence to carry out their share of them. In case of actual expected battle, it is generally expedient that its plan and method should be explained to them, when possible. In all these matters he is to keep the Navy Department constantly informed, both by his own communications and those he may exact from his subordinates in their own spheres.

Question 5: How many formations are employed for a fleet in order of battle?

There are 3 principal formations.
(1) The line ahead (or column) in which the vessels are arranged in the line of the course.
(2) The line abreast (or simply line) in which the vessels are arranged on a bearing from each other of eight points from the course.

---

1. Questions for which Mahan's answers have not survived were: 1. Give the law of storms in both hemispheres; 3. What constitutes an efficient blockade?; and 4. Explain the right of search.

(3) The échelon (old time bow and quarter line) in which the ships bear from one another on a compass bearing of four points from the course.

There are several modifications of these as the double column, a double line, which may be indented; a double échelon as the old order of pursuit and retreat in which part of the ships are on the port and part on the starboard line of bearing from a designated ship. The vertex of the angle forward by the two lines of bearing is commonly supposed to be turned toward the enemy whether in pursuit or retreat.

Contingency Plan of Operations
in Case of War with Great Britain

New York, December 1890 [OANHD]

The subject for consideration is, the first steps to be taken in case of a threatened outbreak of war with Great Britain. The question posed refers to our present naval means, and must be principally so treated; but an outline of the general strategic position of the two countries will properly preface the answers.

Any attempts against the British Islands themselves, in the present relative strength of the two navies, is plainly impracticable. The belligerents will meet in the Western Hemisphere.

With the length of time that intervenes between the threat of war and the actual commencement of hostilities, it is probable that, when this occurs, the British fleet in America will exceed our own. The assumption of the defensive by us will therefore first be treated.

There are four methods by which an enemy may be supposed to act against us:

1. Invasion by a land force landed from ships.
2. The attack of harbors for the purpose of entering.
3. Bombardment.
4. Blockade of an important part of the coast line.

1. The first may be dismissed as unlikely to occur. Purely maritime operations will be less risky and more decisive.

2. The second case, an attempt to enter one of our harbors: Our present naval means of resistance are summed up in the report (No. 1178) made by the House Naval Committee, April 1, 1890. They are, for the Atlantic coast, four monitors awaiting completion; six of the larger new cruisers; the *Yorktown* and *Petrel*, the *Vesuvius*, *Stiletto* and *Cushing*. Of the larger cruisers the *Baltimore* is abroad.

Whatever else may be said as to the disposition of this force, it seems evident that to divide it among the Atlantic seaports would be to neutralize wholly whatever power it may possess.

(The Bureau of Ordnance may be able to state the means which it can dispose of within a year to assist the defense of our seaports by torpedoes.)

3. Bombardment is a modification of the second mode of attack. By

it the assailant tries to attain his end with less risk than by forcing a passage. The former remark, as to the division of our small mobile force, applies equally here.

One general remark also applies to both these attacks. The enemy in them takes an active offensive, for a fixed *limited* time. Any efforts of our own therefore will be made when he is on the alert, the most unfavorable conditions for the smaller force.

4. Blockade. There is an undeniable reluctance on the part of civilized nations now to resort to the bombardment of unarmed cities. While we would be foolish to rely upon an immunity not yet guaranteed by the so-called "laws" of war, the enemy may be influenced by it to resort to a means of annoyance equally efficient, and less likely to leave a general embittered feeling, viz: Blockade. It will be more expensive to him, but perhaps less risky. In case of adequate coast-defense he may be forced to this mode of action.

For the purposes of our consideration, the Atlantic coast of the United States may be divided into three sections:

1. From the Canadian boundary to, and including, the Chesapeake.
2. From Cape Henry to the Gulf.
3. The Gulf Coast.

The first of the three, containing the great commercial centres of Boston, New York, Philadelphia, and Baltimore, evidently offers the greatest advantages; and in the present state of our navy involves for the enemy no more risk than any other part of the coast. It will therefore naturally be chosen as the scene for his most extensive and thorough operations. But, with the existing disparity between the two navies, there will be no reason why the gulf ports and those on the southern Atlantic coast should not be at least watched, by a sufficient force to make a technically efficient blockade.

It is unlikely indeed that any foreign power could effect such a blockade as ours against the Confederacy. But the United States will be deeply humiliated by finding herself powerless to maintain her coasting trade, and with her foreign commerce practically annihilated. There will be no alleviation in the fact of a few isolated steamers running the blockades. Our immense system of export and import can certainly be brought to a standstill by the British navy, causing a derangement which, in the closely knit and far extending relations of commerce, will be felt, not merely in the seaboard centres, but through the length and breadth of the land.

The length of time and distribution of effort required by a blockade will give the operations the character of a campaign, and by the breathing spell thus afforded will allow our navy to contemplate some offensive operations. This last fact, however, and still more any invasion of Canada by us, will justify the enemy, in his own eyes and in those of the world, in proceeding to bombardment, if he feel the risk of forcing a passage to be too great.

The breathing spell required by the weaker navy should be secured by the adequate fortification of our chief ports. Much may be done by the weaker force, if not preoccupied by caring for the safety of the ports.

Assuming a breathing time, either by the delay of the enemy, or by the formidable character of our defenses, it is evident that with an inferior force, particularly when so very small as that now contemplated by Congress, it will be necessary to use the whole of it together. In other words, at the first serious threat of hostilities the fighting navy, as distinguished from mere cruisers, should be concentrated in one port.

We here pass to the consideration of those offensive operations, by the sagacity and vigor of which, and by them only, can the weaker country validly defend itself. Before quitting the subject of a passive defense, in itself the precursor of ruin, a remark may be permitted upon the utter hopelessness of our present plight, which must be felt by anyone cognizant of the facts and carefully reading the skeleton analysis of the situation given above. For the United States Navy to do anything, the chief home ports must have some reasonable security. Even the old fossils, *Lancaster*, *Pensacola*, &c. may be conceived as doing something in an offensive move, choosing their own time and method, and laying down their lives, if need be; but awaiting attack on the enemy's terms, their self devotion would not be heroism, but butchery and madness.

Offensive movements imply action on our part. To be efficient this must first be wisely directed, and then vehement. The weaker party must have recourse to action vigorous to desperation. So only can he reverse the odds.

Let us analyze the situation.

Canada lies at our mercy, unless the British navy by action on our coasts can stay our hand. If our coast defenses can hold the enemy in check a month, two months, we may obtain decisive advantages. If for six months, we can overrun Nova Scotia, and hold the enemy's only Cis-Atlantic coal field.

The part of the navy in such a case would be so to occupy and harass the enemy, by well conceived and rapid movements, as should force him either, (1) to an immense increase of his fleet here, injurious to his European position; or, (2), to leave positions unprotected; or, (3), to disperse his fleet so as to leave detachments open to our attack in superior force.

The three principal military ports of Great Britain on this side of the Atlantic are Halifax, Bermuda, and Kingston in Jamaica. The latter may be dismissed under the present conditions of the United States in naval preparation. It would be impossible for us seriously to affect it without controlling the sea. On the other hand, the exposed position of Canada and its value to the Empire, combine to tie the British fleets to that part of our territory which most menaces the Dominion.

The controlling element of modern naval strategy is fuel—coal. The great coal fields of British North America are in Nova Scotia and Cape Breton Island. Bermuda and Jamaica depend upon imported coal. If we can turn the British out of Nova Scotia, the fuel of the fleet must be brought three thousand miles, from England. Then, indeed, there would be a field for commerce destroyers. To protect the coal fields from seizure, or from maritime raids, will be one of the great cares of the British admiral.

Besides this, however, there are many imperfectly defended, yet important, ports to weigh on his mind. St. John's, N. B.; St. John's, New-foundland; the cable stations in Placentia Bay; Pictou Harbor and coal mines; Louisburg and the Cape Breton towns are points more important to them than—say Charleston—is to us. There are, besides, the British West Indies, and the scattered detachments of the British fleet, if such there be. The destruction of light-houses on the Nova Scotia coast would, from its fogs and dangerous character, be more injurious to them, than the destruction of ours to us.

The recently completed cable between Bermuda and Halifax will be a most important element in the combinations of the British fleet. Its position throughout its length should be at once ascertained by the Intelligence Office with precision, and the points at which it can be grappled to advantage determined. The cable steamers available for grappling should also be known in the Intelligence Office. If three can be had, three simultaneous attempts should be made; escorted in each case by an armed vessel sufficient to prevent interruption by a single hostile cruiser.

What is our strategic position—*assuming reasonable Coast Defense?*

Our chief seaport, New York, is nearly equidistant, 600 miles, from Halifax and Bermuda; the latter being the more remote, but by less than 100 miles.

Taking the distance from Bermuda to New York, and describing a circle with the island as a centre, the circumference will pass through the Cape Fear River, the Chesapeake [Bay], Delaware Bay, and Narragansett Bay. In other words these points are at the same distance from Bermuda. Charleston, S. C., is 100 miles farther. If the British lose their base at Halifax, or the free use of the coal fields of Nova Scotia and Cape Breton, they are thrown upon Bermuda for all operations. Bermuda must be kept constantly supplied by a stream of colliers from Europe. How numerous these must be, may be judged from the fact that 39,000 tons of coal were used in three weeks summer manoeuvres this year. A French writer in an extensive treatise on "Combined Operations of Fleets and Armies," estimates at 600 tons per diem the consumption of a fleet investing a fortified harbor. This is doubtless a minimum.

The vessels we have, whether of war or merchant, fit for commerce destroying, should be distributed among the ports before named and arrangements made for their rapid coaling and repairing—especially for cleaning bottoms. Bermuda, the point of arrival of the colliers, would be the centre of their operations, though of course the island itself would be belted by the enemy's cruisers; but, as it is only 600 miles from the ports named, a very large area around the island would be within the limit of their coal endurance, while ready always to reach their highest speed.

Even if the enemy be not forced from its Nova Scotian coal supply, all vessels available by their speed as commerce destroyers should be put into service, and disseminated among our ports, so as to compel the enemy to watch all, and so to scatter his ships. This division of his force will increase the opportunities for our fighting ships to strike successful, even if partial, blows. Worrying the opposing admiral, so as to perplex his judgment and lead him to make false dispositions, is our first effort.

The commerce destroyers being thus purposely scattered, the fighting ships should be concentrated in one port. The dictum is absolute and unqualified, so long as the battleships remain fewer in number than suggested by the present Secretary, viz: twelve for the Atlantic coast. When your force is concentrated you can divide it, if you wish; but when it is divided, you cannot certainly unite it. Imagine for instance six ships in Norfolk and six in New York. You wish to attempt a move with the whole force. It is not open to fleets, as it often is to armies, to move for concentration through a friendly country. The fleets must go to sea in order to concentrate, whether they move towards a common rendezvous, or whether one detachment tries to enter the port where the other is. By either effort they run the gauntlet of the enemy, supposed superior; they can unite only by a successful evasion. There is no need to enlarge upon the difficulties of *simultaneous* successful evasion, or the various dangers to a successful meeting. The foul bottoms, and numerous repairs of our new cruisers sufficiently testify to a class of impediments which steamers are going to encounter, and which will probably induce uncertainties in the movements of steam fleets quite equal to those proceeding from the wind. These remarks, however, are only the application to naval war of the perfectly established principle, that the point of concentration of armed forces should not be within the enemy's lines.

The point of concentration of the battle-ships is eminently and unqualifiedly New York. It is very central. It commands great resources. It gathers up into a cluster all the great lines of communication, North, East, West, and South. The Hudson River, in case of the enemy forcing a passage, offers retreat to a point where safety can be ensured by torpedo defenses and a continual menace be presented to an enemy below. The Hudson also will probably afford, within reasonable distance of the city, water fresh enough to keep clean bottoms; nearer than League Island for example. Though brackish, it is drinkable at West Point. Above all, New York has two entrances.

As our navy will probably always be inferior to that of England, such a port, properly fortified, will be an invaluable element in the offensive operations to which the inferior navy should resort. Let us assume our twelve battle-ships concentrated in New York. They can go to sea by either of two passages, the exits of which are over a hundred miles apart (from Montauk to Sandy Hook). To close both of these with any degree of security would require at least twentyfour ships of size equal to our own. For, it must be kept in mind that the task of the British admiral would be not only to whip our fleet if he met it, but to be sure and meet it, in order to protect British possessions from its attacks. To do this the methods of land warfare apply imperfectly. To occupy a central position with 18 of his ships, intending to fall upon us as we came out by either entrance, would be a fair disposition, but very liable to evasion; and with twenty-four hours' start there could be no telling where we were gone, nor what harm we would do.

If the above argument be reasonably correct, Great Britain would need twenty-four ships constantly before New York. As these require repairs frequently, there must be a reserve at Halifax. Probably some others will be wanted to supplement poorly provided Coast Defenses. Let us say 30 battleships at least. How long could England spare such a number and not lose her weight in Europe?

The use to be made of such torpedo vessels as we may have demands attention. There is such a reasonable probability of these small light-draught craft being able to move unseen along the Sound at night, that they could safely be accumulated at New London and in Narragansett Bay; without, however, wholly stripping New York. From the former positions they will operate on the enemy's most exposed flank; and, if he venture into the Sound, upon his rear. If by nightly attacks they accomplish nothing else, they will so harass and fatigue the enemy, as to reduce their morale. The wear and tear of constant watchfulness will be a potent factor in the deterioration of the enemy. The Thames and Narragansett Bay both afford retreat up narrow rivers; and if it should be desired to rally the boats at New York there will be no serious difficulty in so doing. The effect of this action will tend to keep the ground between Montauk and Fisher's Island clear of hostile cruisers and so facilitate a sortie of our fleet to the eastward, inside Nantucket.

So much for the Atlantic seaboard. Our Lake frontier will also demand immediate protection. Assuming that our great danger lies in the entrance of British men-of-war by the St. Lawrence canals, it follows that the control of Lake Ontario and the destruction of the canal system is the first of our cares. The latter, the canal system, should be the objective of the land forces; but, in the present state of military unreadiness both in Canada and the United States, the Marine Corps, rapidly concentrated, might be an invaluable assistance to such an attack, which is really aimed at the hostile navy. How quickly could the police of our great cities relieve the guards at navy yards?

The Office of Naval Intelligence should know the vessels on the Lakes available for extemporizing a naval force and the Bureau of Ordnance should have armaments prepared for them. Till better can be had, even smooth-bores will be equal to much of the work these ships would have to do.

Care should be taken that these vessels rendezvous soon on the lakes assigned to them; *but especially that those intended for service on Lake Ontario be kept there, from the time the danger becomes serious, lest by injury to the Welland Canal we lose them altogether.*

Lake Ontario is evidently the key of the whole Lake system. Our merchant shipping on the lakes being much more numerous than the Canadian, we can be everywhere superior on the upper lakes, and by controlling Ontario keep that superiority from being affected. If necessary in order to [maintain] superiority on Ontario, the shipping on the other lakes should be reduced.

Chaumont Bay from its position, its size, and the character of its entrance seems best suited for the base of our naval operations in Lake Ontario; but it may be that the lack of railroad communication may introduce a difficulty. If we can keep the enemy's ships of war from entering from the ocean, our superiority on the lakes should depend only upon the rapidity with which guns can be accumulated, to arm the vessels and protect their base.

While the navy is entitled to expect that the army should act against the St. Lawrence canal system, and also should protect the naval base of operations at Sackett's Harbor, or Chaumont Bay on Lake Ontario, the matter is too vital to the naval campaign to trust absolutely to any but ourselves. The locality about these two harbors should be studied, and also that part of the St. Lawrence, near Ogdensburg, when [where] the canals come under range of our frontier; the positions for batteries noted, and the number of guns determined. Plans for the batteries should be elaborated in the Intelligence Office. The Bureau of Ordnance should provide and keep on hand the guns, and the special shore mounts required for them, ready for immediate shipment. The whole safety of the Lake frontier rests on these points.

The first objective of our military operations should be to secure Montreal which, like New York, focuses the lines of communication in all directions; but if the city cannot be quickly reduced, seizing the railroad between it and Coteau Junction, where the Canadian Pacific comes in, will effectually sever Montreal from the West. The tongue of land between the St. Lawrence and the Ottawa rivers appears to be the decisive point for our army to hold, interposing thus not only between Kingston and Montreal, but also between the latter and the capital, Ottawa. But in such a position a subsidiary naval force would be of great value, to keep down that of the enemy on both rivers and to protect the bridges we would probably have across the St. Lawrence. There are resources of tugs or other light draught vessels that could be made available for this purpose, and their names, tonnage, and fitness for light guns should be ascertained.

The reasoning so far has been based upon the supposition that the enemy is not unprepared; but while lack of preparation can never be assumed, it is yet well to be ready in case such good luck should befall us.

If we have made, on the Atlantic, the preparations indicated, and it should appear that Halifax was inadequately garrisoned, the following facts may be noted:

Boston (or Portland) is distant from Halifax about 350 miles. We have many steamers, not properly sea-going, that could make this trip, well-loaded, if with a probability of tolerable weather for forty-eight hours (e.g. the Fall River and Sound lines, especially the freight steamers of the Sound lines, the Penobscot River line, &c. besides others more properly *sea* steamers). St. Margaret's Bay gives a good and unfortified landing, fifteen miles west of Halifax. Judging from the maps, the approach thence to the city is easy, but on this point the Intelligence Office should have information. The city of Halifax is dominated by the citadel, which being 270 feet above the water, commands also the navy yard and all the other works of the inner harbor. If carried by a *coup de main* the fall of the citadel would probably result in the fall of the place.

Another feature is that the water supply of Halifax is drawn from the Chain Lakes, well outside the defenses of the city and on the road from St. Margaret's Bay (See B. A. Chart 2410). It would be well to learn how far the loss of this could be remedied by wells or other internal sources of water supply.

Nova Scotia, being almost an island, and, by the only land approach from the United States, distant from three to four hundred miles (Halifax is over 400 miles from Bangor) is, granting reasonable precaution, wholly secured by that control of the sea which England will have. The approach by land, though certainly within our power, would be long and difficult.

An attempted surprise could be justified only by the extreme importance to us of success, and by some carelessness on the part of the enemy. Such an opportunity ought not to occur, if it does, it will disgrace him; but, on the other hand, we should be prepared for it, both by arrangements made, and by the firm conviction that the propriety of such an attempt is to be measured, not by the chances of failure, but by the vital importance to us of success. Failure, with the loss of two or three ships and ten thousand men, should not condemn such an undertaking, if there should appear to be one chance in five in our favor.

The outlines of such an attempt would be as follows: The two conditions essential to a chance of success, are the weakness of the British garrison, and of the British squadron at Halifax. We should naturally have a number of men under arms, particularly if the unguarded state of the place occurred some little time after the outbreak of the war. Having always in mind the chance of such an opportunity occurring, the details of the *number of troops to be embarked, days' food to be taken,* ammunition, scaling ladders &c. would have to be worked up and kept ready. If the opportunity offer there need be no delay for these. The transports would be assembled quietly at ports from Boston to Bangor, according to the disposition of the hostile fleet off the coast. *If possible,* a division should be drawn from the ships-of-war in New York, proportioned to the force that might be encountered at Halifax, for the convoy of the transports. The commerce destroyers in the northern ports would also be assigned to this duty. The question of simultaneous, or nearly simultaneous, starting can easily be managed, though it will be far more difficult to ensure the necessary junction. The effecting of the latter is, however, one of the difficulties inseparable from such an undertaking. If accomplished, a small division would be detached to make a serious demonstration at Pictou Harbor, with a view of drawing off the enemy's ships-of-war from Halifax, and thus facilitating the disembarkation in St Margaret's Bay. The attempt on the citadel must be made by a rush, to support which the ships of war would, having seen the landing assured, make an attack upon the forts. A weak garrison is presupposed.

In case of success the guns of the citadel would be turned upon the works beneath, and the navy yard destroyed; the fleet converting its attack at once into one much more serious. If the surrender of the city and forts can be compelled, measures to destroy them will at once be taken, and the transports will return home to bring out more troops; the idea being to establish ourselves, if possible, in control of the peninsula, living off the country. A body of fifteen thousand good troops, if such could be assembled and ammunitioned, should have no difficulty in living there. They would be but a small addition to the population.

Nevertheless, as history testifies that such occupations are most precarious without permanent control of the sea, the issue may well be that the force thus landed may have to surrender at last; but if they should have destroyed the works at Halifax, the navy yard, and a part of the railroad system (e.g. the bridge crossing the narrows), the sacrifice of their liberty till exchanged will be a small price. The future defense of the port for that war will devolve upon the fleet, which means its weakening elsewhere, and the difficulties of coaling will be vastly increased.

In proposing and sketching the outline of such an attempt, the great difficulties and the unfavorable chances attending it are admitted. The sufficient reply is that military and naval history abounds with instances of no less desperate attempts resulting successfully; and that the gain to us would be so great, and the loss from failure *comparatively* so small, as to justify this. It must be remembered that a desperate effort is not the same thing as a reckless or careless one. Desperation is consistent with the utmost painstaking to ensure success. Over confidence on the part of the enemy, pressure in some other quarter, the carelessness or stupidity of an admiral or general, a maritime disaster, hurricane or what not, may afford the opportunity. On the other hand we are, and probably will continue, so inferior in naval strength, that we can only redeem ourselves by a vigorous offensive that is not over cautious in weighing chances.

As regards our southern and Gulf coast, twelve battleships, concentrated in New York Bay, will so enforce the presence before that port of all the ships Great Britain can dare to send over here, that the other ports will be relatively safe, if provided with reasonable coast defenses. This same is true of Boston, Philadelphia, and Baltimore.

Let us suppose that Charleston, the nearest port south of the Chesapeake, can keep the enemy at bay for a week. He detaches six ships out of the twenty-four before New York to attack it. They must be drawn either from the Montauk or the Sandy Hook division, or else equally from both. In either case, one or the other becomes weaker than our force inside. If to avoid this, he draws the 18 together, he uncovers one entrance or both. We get away; if with only six or eight hours start, the division at Charleston may be overwhelmed before he can come up. In any event, if we are once lost sight of, the clearest headed admiral will be puzzled, and the ordinary man, the great majority that is, will make a blunder. His ships watching the Delaware, the Chesapeake, Boston, those in the Gulf are all exposed. He experiences all the perplexities of the defense, we have the privileges of the offense. We may be gone for Jamaica, or possibly for Sta. Lucia, which are one thousand miles apart; or we may be bound for the Pictou coal mines. Bermuda is pretty safe, yet to an anxious admiral even that will be doubtful.

To a person familiar with naval history the perplexities of the defense, and the advantages open to the escaped squadron, are clear, and numerous instances will at once occur. A conspicuous one, generally little appreciated, may be cited. In May 1799 Admiral Bruix escaped from Brest with 25 ships of the line. The Channel fleet, whose duty it was to watch him, was out of the way, and the admiral did not hear of his escape for one or two days. He immediately drew together all his available ships, a force much superior to Bruix, and covered Ireland. As Bruix had gone south, some thirty-odd British ships were for three or four weeks as useless as if they had been at the North Pole.

Bonaparte at this time was in Syria. The British Admiral Jervis, commanding the Mediterranean fleet, was at Gibraltar. A detachment of his, under Keith, of 15 ships, was watching Cadiz. Nelson, junior to Keith, had another subordinate command extending from Sicily to the Levant. His ships were scattered everywhere, two in the Levant, two or three blockading Malta, a couple with his flag at Palermo, one or two on the coast of Naples, contending with the French troops that had lately seized the city. Besides these, there was a small division of two or three ships of the line at Minorca, which had lately been seized by Duckworth, under Jervis' orders.

Bruix, though a brave and active fellow, did nothing with all these chances; but the greatness of his opportunities is evident. He fell in with Keith off Cadiz, 25 ships to 15; but it was blowing a gale, and he simply ran through the straits under the eyes of Jervis. All was now hurry and fluster among the British. Keith was recalled to Gibraltar, despatches sent off to Nelson and Duckworth. The correspondence of Jervis and Nelson is full of anxiety and speculation, sometimes guessing right, sometimes wrong —but it was all hit or miss. None *knew* where Bruix had gone. Those 25 ships might land 10,000 men in Egypt. They might have gobbled every one of the scattered detachments enumerated above. They might have relieved Malta, which could be subdued only by famine. Of course concentration was the first thing for the British; but that took time, and Bruix had the start. After a time the Admiralty learned where he was and a large division, of some 12 or 15 ships, was sent from the Channel to the Mediterranean, about July 1st; but, with all their chasing to and fro, the British never got sight of Bruix. He called off Cartagena, joined to himself, there and at Cadiz, some 15 or 20 Spanish ships, which he took back to Brest, where they remained as hostages of the somewhat uncertain Spanish alliance. The British combined Mediterranean and Channel divisions, of some forty ships, reached the neighborhood of Brest twenty-four hours after him.

For Brest read New York, for Ireland Nova Scotia, and, for the scattered divisions in the Mediterranean, Pictou, Louisburg, Jamaica, Bermuda, &c. &c. and you have your parallel. Twelve serviceable battle-ships, well manned and officered in New York, threaten every exposed British port, every small detachment. Uncover its exits and you uncover the whole British position. Therefore the twelve ships contribute to defend every port of the United States which has reasonable permanent works and do so far more efficiently by being collected in New York than they could possibly do by being divided among the other ports. The trouble with Bruix was that his ships were neither well equipped, well manned, nor well officered.

On the Pacific, so long as there is no canal, the eight battle-ships recommended by the Secretary of the Navy for that coast will be sufficient to control the situation. Great Britain cannot afford to maintain, even with the China fleet, an equal number there. As in all cases, reasonable coast defense must be supposed for San Francisco. Our ships should concentrate at Puget Sound; for in Vancouver alone, under existing conditions, can Great Britain get coal adequate to operations of war. A position threatening Vancouver, the navy yard at Esquimalt and the Nanaimo coal mines, protects San Francisco absolutely—granting of course that the latter can hold out for a fortnight. There is no use whatever in discussing military operations without some permanent and fortified bases, that can look out for themselves for a time.

Port Orchard and the San Juan Islands are the strongest natural positions on the Pacific coast, and among the strongest in the world. Great Britain has nothing like them in British Columbia. Based on them, we so menace her coal and communications as to paralyze her.

For the same reason that the ground surrounding Ogdensburgh and Chaumont Bay should be studied, the approaches to Port Orchard and Griffin's Bay should be at once examined, the positions for batteries, the number of guns, and the submarine mines required should be determined. This is the army's proper business, but the position of Port Orchard is so essential to the Navy's operations that we should be ready to assume the work, if the army, as likely, is not. The Bureau of Ordnance should keep in store on the Pacific coast the guns and carriages, as well as torpedo cases, charges, cables &c. necessary for Port Orchard.

The question of the strategic points of the northwest coast are fully discussed in a paper by Captain Mahan on file in the Intelligence Office.

Some detached suggestions as to our preparations for war are hereto appended.

1st. As fast as our battle-ships and coast defense ships are completed, they should be commissioned and kept permanently in commission. It should be a fixed rule that they never leave the coast of the United States, or the Caribbean Sea, except for an imperative necessity. They should habitually be stationed in one harbor (unless the number becomes greatly increased), and the harbor should be New York. Half or quarter crews only need be maintained, according to the allowance of men for general service.

These guard ships should serve as constant drill ships for the better (that is, most seaman-like) class of naval reserve. Whatever number of men the rolls of that reserve may show, should be sub-divided, so that each party should form, with the half crews of the guard ships, a full crew. Their drill, at least in the first years, should not be less than one month in the twelve, of constant living on board and instruction. For this time government must be prepared to pay, in our money making country, the full wages they would earn in their employment, *plus* an additional sum for the inconvenience; and the men must be secure of not losing the regular employment which they, for the time, drop.

The inconvenience to employers must also be met, for there will be many objections to parting for a time with valuable hands. To ensure the best solution of the many difficulties in the way of thus realizing a reserve, which will be at all worthy of the name, the general command of these ships should be invested in an officer of suitable rank, responsible *directly* to the Navy Department, and with a staff specially chosen for organizing faculty. There is always danger in our country that a naval reserve will become a mere paper force, useless in war, never ready, yet serving as an excuse for not increasing the regular naval force. The surest, if not the only, way to make it efficient and dependable, is to entrust its organization and management to a capable naval officer, having no other duty, and who shall hoist his flag on a ship kept ready for sea as the flagship of the naval reserve.

If the roll of the naval reserve shall contain as many men as will fill the complement of the guard ships six times, then these ships will have six months of naval reserve drill. If the roll will give twelve complements, drill will go on all the year round. Times and seasons will be made as far as possible to suit the convenience of all, but as the government *pays*, it will be less bound than otherwise. It may be well that for certain seasons a ship may be sent to Boston, or to Baltimore, because the section of the reserve to be drilled resides there.

As the reserve will embrace an engineer force, much of the time will be spent underway, even did not other considerations enjoin this. This means a coal bill.

It is very likely that, for the efficient enrollment and organization of the reserve, the coast will have to be divided into maritime districts, each under a captain or commander, whose business will be to know all about the men in his district suited by their pursuits to service in the fleet, whether they enter the reserve or not. He should also know all about the merchant steamers belonging to the ports in his district, and their fitness for naval use, whether as cruisers or transports. But whatever the extent of duty assigned to district commanders, their connection with and subordination to the flag officer commanding the coast-guard ships will be the great and vital circumstance of their functions.

While the drill of the reserve and their own proper crews is an essential part of the coast-guard work there is another no less important purpose the ships should subserve, in no way incompatible, but rather furthering, the former. The great distinguishing feature of the battle-ship is action *combined* with other ships. A battle-ship *alone* is out of its normal and proper place. But, for combined action, much drill is needed—a drill which concerns only the admiral, the captains, and some few of the senior officers who may have to succeed to command. There is no reason whatever why the gun and other exercises should not be going on uninterruptedly, while the fleet drills are occupying admiral and captains. On no point does naval history speak more clearly, or more loudly, than on the supreme importance, in battle, of precise, uniform, combined action. Without this no plans can be successfully carried out; and it is so rarely found, that the fleet possessing this faculty will easily double its power. This faculty can only be had by constant drilling together; therefore, these fleet drills should be continually going on, and the captains should be long continued in command. There is no reason to fear that they will become slaves to precise formations. On the contrary, in the hour of battle, the experiences of the drill ground will increase their aptitude for remedying confusion and restoring order. Vital as is the efficiency of each unit of the fleet, its efficiency as a whole is yet more important. The drill of the captains is more important than the drill of the guns and torpedoes.

By some such system, rigidly adhered to, the government will have in its hand at all times a force ready to act with intelligence, vigor, and skill at the first outbreak of hostilities. It should never leave the country, and as far as possible the units composing it should be kept together. The power of such a well drilled, flexible organization on the field of battle cannot be exaggerated.

2. Information concerning the positions of an enemy off the coast, and the usual distribution of his forces would be essential to a well concerted attack upon any part of them, or to an attempted evasion. Our coast being generally low, could not balloons, fitted with telescopes, be advantageously placed at certain points of the coast, e.g. eastern end of Long Island and toward Barnegat, for day observations? For night reconnaissances a submarine boat might venture well into an enemy's fleet. A reconnoitering boat in danger of being overtaken could release carrier pigeons.

3. Experience has shown that treasonable communication with an enemy's fleet can always be bought. The Department should be informed as to the ability of the detective force of the country to watch such efforts. The Life-Saving Service, as now organized, ought to contribute much to the surveillance of the coast.

4. On the other hand we should have a system of informers in Great Britain, in communication with agents on the continent, by whom information could be cabled to us of the enemy's purposes or movements.

5. In the matter of commerce destroying, we ought to know by practical test, and not by calculation only, how far our cruisers can go, and how long occupy a cruising station. Judging from the map of Commerce Routes furnished me by the Intelligence Office, there is no place where

we can effectively strike British commerce except that which leaves the West Indies and the Gulf of St. Lawrence. The latter will be greatly reduced from its present dimensions by a war with us, which will also, of course, annihilate at once all the British trade from our seaports. A glance at the map referred to will show the hopelessness of serious injury to British shipping, while we have no assured coal supplies abroad.

6. We have no coaling port east of Portland. The best plan for supplying cruisers to the eastward would be to accumulate a sufficient quantity at Bangor, and send it by rail thence to the head of Frenchman's Bay, as wanted. As the bay is not likely to be fortified, the amount on the shore should not be great. Soames Sound is a good maritime position, but it has no railroad.

An undefended coaling station can never be reliable; nor are we likely to need this eastward coaling station unless carrying on operations towards Nova Scotia and the Gulf of St. Lawrence. Such a contingency overthrows the whole basis on which the previous reasoning is founded, and can arise only from the naval superiority passing into our hands, of which there is no present likelihood. If it did arise, such a station would then be fairly secure and a great convenience. It is distant from Seal Island, at southwest extremity of Nova Scotia, about 120 miles; Boston being 250 miles from the same point.

7. Allusion has been made to mobilizing the Marine Corps in certain contingencies. If this corps be kept up to the standard of its former efficiency, it will constitute a most important re-enforcement, nay, backbone, to any force landing on the enemy's coast. Measures should be framed by which the whole body could be collected, and the care of the yards turned over to the local police, within a week.

8. Halifax is the type, as it is the chief, of all possible objectives of maritime expeditions on our part; (save of course the enemy's ships). Faint as the prospect is of a successful attempt against it, it should never be out of our minds. Every material preparation should be at all times ready for instant use. The transport of 20,000 men is a great undertaking. Chances often occur, but they are evanescent, and must be seized at once. Our maxim should be: "Always ready to take advantage of a chance at Halifax." In those depots of reserves which every well organized army has, and in the garrisons of maritime ports, the responsible officers should be prepared within twelve hours to embark the troops needed. On our part, besides other preparations, the old ships *Lancaster, Pensacola, Brooklyn,* and *Richmond,* must for a term be held on to. In tow, their own engines assisting, and spars down, they could be got over the ground with ten knots speed. If only as transports, they would be useful; but they still have no inconsiderable fighting power when speed is not in question. As being less valuable, they could be more properly risked in exposed posts, e.g. leading

a forlorn hope, when a torpedo line is to be passed, or shoved close against a work to beat down its fire with grape.

SUMMARY

The following statements summarize the steps to be taken by the Navy Department in case of a war with Great Britain, and are applicable both to our present circumstances, and to our condition when all the force shall have been realized which Congress now seems disposed to give. The reasoning on which these conclusions are based is appended.

1. No attempt can be made to carry the war to the other side of the Atlantic, or against a *fortified* island in the West Indies. In the latter quarter maritime raids may be attempted under favorable circumstances.

2. The battle-ships, including coast-defense ships, should be *concentrated* in one port, in order that they may be used to their full effect in such offensive operations as may be practicable. With them should be such cruisers as are essential to their organization as a fleet.

3. All other cruisers, whether naval or taken from the merchant service, should be *disseminated* through the fortified seaports, in order by their dispersion to provoke a scattering of the enemy's forces to watch them, and generally by their activity to increase the cares of the enemy. They will be constantly employed in commerce destroying or other cruising.

4. The point of concentration of the battle-ships should, on the Atlantic coast, be New York. On the Pacific coast, Puget Sound; and in Puget Sound, Port Orchard should be fortified by torpedoes and scattered guns; a defense which can be made very efficacious owing to the character of the channel and the shore line, and could probably be applied in short time. (The details of this should be studied out.)

5. Boston, Philadelphia, Baltimore, and the Atlantic and Gulf coast cities generally, should be thrown for defense purely upon permanent works, in which I include torpedoes. To these torpedo-boats should be added, if we have enough of them. In the appended paper reasons are given for believing that, if these cities can hold out a short time with permament defenses, they will be better protected by our fighting ships being concentrated in New York than by any dispersion of them for local defense.

6. The character of San Francisco harbor and entrance necessitates the permanent stationing there of local coast-defense ships.

7. The bulk of our torpedo-boats on the Atlantic should be concentrated about New York; preferably in the Thames River and Narragansett Bay.

8. The vital point in the British strategic position on this side of the Atlantic is the peninsula of Nova Scotia with its coal fields. Next to that comes the fortified harbor of Halifax, with its navy yard and docking facilities. The possibilities of action against these are outlined in the appended paper.

9. The vital point in the British strategic position on the Pacific is Van-

couver Island with its coal mines—especially at Nanaimo. The Esquimalt yard is a small affair.

We are infinitely more advantageously situated, as regards Great Britain, on the Pacific than on the Atlantic; nor are her preparations there much in advance of ours—except in naval force. It will be a great embarrassment to her to keep ships in the Pacific, if we have in New York a strong concentrated body.

10. The course of action to which the above dispositions look is a constant offensive action by the force in New York, directed against the enemy before that port; or, by evading his watch, against his scattered detachments before our other ports; or, lastly, against his numerous possessions. For this we divert his attention by commerce destroyers, and concentrate our whole fighting force for attack.

11. The harbor and navy yard at Norfolk should be kept in full efficiency so that in case of a successful sortie by our fleet, it need not be bound down to New York as its only port of return. It is impossible to lay too much stress on the importance of Chesapeake Bay and its approaches to the defense of the sea coast. It commands the approach to the capital and to one of our chief commercial cities, as well as lays open, if unprotected, access to a large interior country. To the navy it is, next to New York, the most important base of operations. The superior advantages of New York as a point for offensive operations, and the probably limited size of our navy, continue to forbid us to violate the established principle of concentration of force, by dividing our battleships between these points. *But*, when our fleet has gone to sea on an offensive errand, it is of the first importance that it should not have only one point on which to retreat. If it has only one, the enemy knows where, by waiting, it must sooner or later be found, and can concentrate there. While therefore it would be a mistake to divide our fighting ships with a view to defense of the Chesapeake, its defense by other means is essential to the navy acting offensively. The Navy Department should insist to the War Department that New York and the Chesapeake are the two principal strategic points of our seaboard.

12. At the close of the appended paper are given a number of details which are important to our efficiency, but not necessary to enumerate here.

The following steps conducive to our readiness for war should be at once undertaken.

1. Detailed information as to Lake steamers suitable for naval purposes should at once be collected, either by the Board now organized in New York for the inspection of merchant steamers, or by a special Board; the same details as are obtained for sea-going steamers should be filed in Intelligence Office.

2. Schemes for commanding the St. Lawrence canals from near Ogdens-

burg, and for protecting Chaumont Bay on Lake Ontario by naval guns and torpedoes should be perfected in the Intelligence Office.

3. A similar scheme for defending Port Orchard, Puget Sound, should also be prepared.

4. The Bureau of Ordnance should be instructed to keep on hand, ready for immediate shipment, the guns, carriages, ammunition and other equipments necessary to carry out 2 and 3.

5. The Bureau of Ordnance should also be directed to form a reserve of guns for the equipment of lake steamers, of merchant sea-going steamers taken up for the navy, and to supply losses due to action or to wear and tear. This reserve should contain . . . [remainder of manuscript missing].

Practical Words

An Address Delivered at the Naval War College

Newport, Rhode Island, September 1892 [NWC]

I must congratulate you upon the idea, which I consider a distinct advance upon what was done by me—an advance I always contemplated.

A problem like the one you propose involves, in its solution, the constructive work for which my own analyses in my published works form the logical preparation.[1]

It will be an immense advantage and educative influence to grapple with a problem, so closely connected with our vital interests. Might I suggest, if time allows, that the class should consider also the effect upon our coasting trade of such a hostile force, and how far railroads would be able to take up the interrupted transportation. I believe this is too much overlooked. I can therefore only express my strong general approval of the conception and terms of the problem, as admirably adapted to fix the attention, and draw out the strategic and tactical capacities of the officers.

I come now to the matter upon which I wish more particularly to speak; and here again I will illustrate by one of those casual conversations, which, like straws, often show more clearly than deliberate utterances how the wind of professional prejudice is blowing. I was in Washington a few months ago, and coming out of one of the clubs I met on the door steps a couple of naval officers. We stopped to talk, and one asked me: "Do you expect a session of the college this year?" I replied that I hoped so. "Well," he said, "are you going to do anything practical?" I recognized my enemy at once in the noble word "practical," which has been dropped like an angel of light out of its proper sphere and significance and made to do duty against its best friends, as a man's foes are often those of his own household. I endeavored to get out of the scrape, which would involve an extempore discussion of the true scope and meaning of the word practical by resorting to the Socratic method, liberally practiced by the modern Irish, which would throw the burden of explanation upon my questioner. "What do you mean by practical?" I said. The reply was a little hesitating,

---

1. The problem concerned a possible enemy attack on Narragansett, Gardiners, and Buzzards Bays.

as is apt to be the case to a categorical question, and after a moment's pause he said: "Well, torpedo boats and launches and that sort of thing."

Of course, I knew in a general way what was coming, when I asked my question; nor did I in the least contest the application of the word practical to torpedo boats or launches. Concerning the latter, in fact, it was a recommendation of my first report as president of the college, that such should be provided for practising the far more delicate and difficult management of the ram in action—a problem with which, I am bold to say, the naval mind has not begun to deal. But, while willing to concede this positive meaning, given to the word practical, I do most decidedly object to the implied negative limitation, which confines it to tangible utilitarian results, to that which can be touched, weighed, measured, handled, and refuses to concede the honor of "practical" to those antecedent processes of thought and reflection, upon which the results of rational human effort always depend, and without which they cannot be reached—unless, indeed, by the bungling, tedious and painful method which is called "butt end foremost." It is to this view of the matter, and to the full legitimate force of the word "practical," that I wish today to direct your attention; for the limitation so frequently imposed on it, and so generally accepted by thoughtless prejudice, is the greatest stumbling block in the way of the college, just as I have tried to show that the word "obsolete," so long held the United States navy in a state of suspended animation.

In discussing the word "practical," I do not of course propose to go into its etymology, for the sake of making a barren argument as to what it ought to mean. I intend to accept it in its common significance, as familiar to us in current speech; and I propose to maintain that, in that sense, it is just as applicable to the processes of thought which precede action, as it is to the action which follows thought and reflection, the only difference being that, taking the whole process of thought and action together, the thought which dictates the action is more practical, is of a higher order of practicalness than the result and action itself. Of this the old and common proverb "Look before you leap," is a vigorous presentment. The word "practical," however, has become so warped—not in its meaning, but in its application—that the practical man is he who disdains the theoretical process of looking—that is who will have no study, no forethought, no reflection—but simply leaps—that is, acts.

Of course, when one reaches a reductio ad absurdum—if you do—the victim cries out: He never meant any such thing. Neither does the man who leaps without looking mean to reach the possibly uncomfortable berth in which he lands. But let it be observed, it is not the man's nature to leap without looking; the irrational brute don't do that. Men leap without looking, because they have failed to prepare, because they have neglected the previous processes of thought and reflection, and so, when the sudden call

[578]

for action comes, it is "leap at all hazards"; and so, to quote the Holy Writ, while they are saying peace and safety, "sudden destruction comes upon them like travail upon a woman with child and they cannot escape." How often have we—I speak at least to men of my own time—been told that presence of mind consists largely—for the average man mainly—in preponderance of mind, "When you take the deck, think what you will do in any emergency likely to arise—a man falls overboard, a collision threatens from this or that quarter, land or reef may be unexpectedly sighted." Good. But is the thought which is simply study without books less practical than the resultant action? Is it less practical, even if no call for action arises?

Let us, for illustration, draw upon an art which has supplied many useful analogies to describe processes of gradual developments—that of the architect. Before erecting a building, be it one of simple design and unpretentious appearance, like that in which we are now seated, or be it one of the complicated and elaborate designs which decorate the Cliffs of Newport—what careful study, plotting and planning, goes on in the offices of the architect! What calculations to ensure convenience—to economize space—to please the eye. It is pure student's work, behind which lie, not merely the experience of the architect, but also years of patient study, devoted to mastering the principles of his art as embodied in the experience of his predecessors. Before a brick is laid, perhaps before the sod is turned, the complete design—the future house—exists upon paper.

Is all this prior labor of the architect in his office, and all the varied study that has enabled him to perform it not "practical," and does the "practical" work begin only when the carpenter and the bricklayer put their hands to it? If you think so, gather your mechanics and your hod carriers, provide your material of bricks and mortar, and then, setting to work without your designs and calculations, rejoice in the evidence of practical efficiency you have displayed to the world.

All the world knows, gentlemen, that we are building a new navy—the process has begun, is going on, and its long continuance is an avowed purpose. We are to have a navy adequate to the sense of our needs; and that sense is bound to expand as our people appreciate more and more, as they are beginning to realize more and more, that a country's power and influence must depend upon her hold upon regions without her own borders, and to which the sea leads. The influence of the little British islands gives a lesson our people will surely learn. Well, when we get our navy, what are we going to do with it? Shall we, like the careless officer of the deck, wait for the emergency to arise? If we do, we shall pretty surely leap without much looking. Or do you think that when a time of war comes you will find a vade mecum, a handy pocket manual, the result of other men's labors, which will tell you just what to do; much like one of those old seamanship problems: Riding to a single anchor and ebb tide with the wind on the starboard bow and a shoal on the port quarter, get underway and start out to sea. A remark to that effect was made by an officer, a commander now afloat, who I think is regarded by all as one of our most intelligent, as he certainly is one of our most advanced men. "I thought," he said, in discussing some naval problems of the kind with which the College proposes to grapple, "that, the case arising, I could turn to some work where the dispositions of a fleet, of a convoy, and other various questions connected with maritime expeditions would be treated and their solutions stated; but I find there is none and I myself do not know."

If, therefore, the line of thought, study and reflection, which the war college seeks to promote, is justly liable to the reproach that it leads to no useful end, can result in no effective action, it falls justly under the condemnation of not being "practical." But it must be frankly and fearlessly said that the man who is prepared to apply this stigma to the line of the college effort must also be prepared to class as not "practical" men like Napoleon, like his distinguished opponent, the Austrian Archduke Charles, and like Jomini, the profuse writer on military art and military history—whose works, if somewhat supplanted by newer digests, have lost little or none of their prestige, as a profound study and exposition of the principles of warfare.

Jomini was not merely a military theorist, who saw war from the outside. He was a distinguished and thoughtful soldier, in the prime of life during the Napoleonic wars, and of a contemporary reputation such that, when he deserted the cause of the emperor, he was taken at once into a high position as a confidential adviser of the allied sovereigns. Yet what does he say of strategy? Strategy is to him the queen of military sciences; it underlies the fortunes of every campaign. As in a building, which, however fair and beautiful the superstructure, is radically marred and imperfect if the foundation be insecure, so, if the strategy be wrong, the skill of the general on the battlefield, the valor of the soldier, the brilliancy of victory, however otherwise decisive, fail of their effect. Yet how does he define strategy, whose effects, if thus far reaching, must surely be esteemed "practical"? "Strategy," he says, "is the art of making war upon the map." It precedes the operations of the campaign, the clash of arms on the field. It is done in the cabinet, it is the work of the student, with his dividers in his hand and his information lying beside him. It originates, in other words, in a mental process, but it does not end there, therefore it is practical.

Most of us have heard an anecdote of the great Napoleon, which is nevertheless so apt to my purpose that I must risk the repetition. Having had no time to verify my reference I must quote from memory, but of substantial accuracy I am sure. A few weeks before one of his early and most decisive campaigns, his secretary, Bourrienne, entered the office and found the general, as he then was, stretched on the floor with a large map before him. Scattered over the map, in what to Bourrienne was confusion, were a number of red and black pins. After a short silence the secretary, who was an old friend of school days, asked him what it all meant. The general laughed good naturedly, called him a fool, and said, "This set of pins represents the Austrians and this the French. On such a day I shall leave Paris. My troops will then be in such positions. On a certain day, naming it, I shall be here, pointing, and my troops will have moved there. At such a time I shall cross the mountains, a few days later my army will be here, the Austrians will have done thus and so; and at a certain date I will beat them here," placing a pin. Bourrienne said nothing, perhaps he may have thought the matter not "practical"; but a few weeks later, after the battle, (Marengo I think) had been fought, he was seated by the general's side in his military travelling carriage. The programme had been carried out, and he recalled the incident to Bonaparte's mind. The latter himself smiled at the singular accuracy of his predictions in the particular instance.

The question I would like to pose will, in the light of such an incident, receive of course but one answer. Was the work the general was engaged on in his private office, this work of a student, was it "practical"? Or can it by any reasonable method be so divorced from what followed, that the word "practical" only applies further on. Did he only begin to be practical when he got into his carriage to drive from the Tuileries, or did the practical begin when he joined the army, or when the first gun of the campaign was fired? Or, on the other hand, if he had passed that time, given to studying the campaign, in arranging for a new development of the motived war, and so gone with his plans undeveloped, would he not have done a thing very far from "practical"?

But we must push our inquiry a little further back to get the full significance of Bourrienne's story. Whence came the facility and precision with which Bonaparte planned the great campaign of Marengo? Partly, unquestionably, from a native genius rarely paralleled; partly—but not by any means wholly. Hear his own prescription: "If any man will be a great general, let him study. Study what? Study history. Study the campaigns of the great generals—Alexander, Hannibal, Caesar," (who never smelt gunpowder, nor dreamed of iron clads) "as well as those of Turenne, Frederick, and myself, Napoleon." Had Bonaparte entered his cabinet to plan the campaign of Waterloo, with no other preparation than his genius, without the mental equipment and the ripened experience that came from knowledge of the past acquired by study, he would have come unprepared. Were, then, his previous study and reflection, for which the time of action had not come, were they not "practical," because they did not result in immediate action? Would they ever have been not "practical" had the time for action never come to him?

As the wise man said, "there is a time for everything under the sun," and the time for one thing cannot be used as the time for another. There is a time for action—all concede: few consider duly that there is also a time for preparation. To use the time of preparation for preparation, whatever the method, is practical; to postpone preparation to the time for action is not practical. Our new navy is preparing now; it can be scarcely said, as regards its material, to be yet ready. The day of grace is still with us—or with those who shall be the future captains and admirals. There is time yet for study; there is time to imbibe the experience of the past, to become imbued, steeped, in the eternal principles of war, by the study of its history and of the maxims of its masters. But the time of preparation will pass—some day the time of action will come. Can an admiral sit down, and reenforce his intellectual grasp of the problem before him, by a study of history—which is simply a study of past experience? Not so; the time for action is upon him, and he must trust to his horse sense (and be thankful if it does not turn out to be jackass sense).

The Battle of the Yalu

An Interview with The Times

London, September 25, 1894[1]

A representative of Dalziel's Agency had an interview on Sunday afternoon [September 23] at Southampton with Capt. Mahan shortly before
the American man-of-war *Chicago* left for Havre.

Captain Mahan said that, although the Japanese claimed the victory
at the Yalu River, there did not seem to be any certainty as yet as to the
capture of the Chinese transports. There was, however, no reason to doubt
the substantial accuracy of the reports, according to which the Japanese
claimed the victory.

Asked to give his opinion as a naval authority upon the lessons to be
learned from the encounter, Captain Mahan said that the great thing to be observed by a fleet in charge of transports was to prevent anything like a
surprise. A warship ought never, unless it were impossible to prevent it, to
be placed in a position of embarrassment, and the prominent feature that
presented itself to his mind in the attempt to convoy a number of transports
was that the convoying fleet should be distinctly superior to that of the
enemy. The Chinese appeared to have been considerably embarrassed by
the presence of the transports, and he was inclined to believe that the reason
the Chinese Admiral accepted battle with his fleet so close to the shore was
because, had he gone out to meet the Japanese fleet, which was his proper
course in ordinary circumstances, he would have been obliged to uncover
the entrance to the bay or river. He was, in consequence, obliged to draw
up his fleet close to the shore, and was thus embarrassed in the manoeuvering
of his vessels. He was afraid, in the position in which he found himself, to
advance to meet the enemy, and accordingly gave them an immense advantage. Had his force been much larger than that of the Japanese his
proper course would have been to advance and at the same time leave behind sufficient force to cope with any rush which might have been made
by the Japanese vessels to force the entrance of the river. The whole position illustrated the extreme difficulty of successfully resisting an attacking

---

1. From *The Times*, London, September 25, 1894. The engagement, a turning point
in the Sino-Japanese War, took place on September 17, 1894.

movement unless the defending fleet had absolute control of the water. Whether the Chinese altogether succeeded in their primary object of landing the troops did not appear to be clear, and the question as to whether it was worth while to take such a risk for the sake of landing the troops remained to be seen. It was undeniably bad management to fight the Japanese fleet so close to the shore, but the Chinese Admiral was obliged to do it, because he knew that if he moved out into the open he would uncover the approach to the transports. That appeared to be one reason why the Japanese did not attempt to break through the defending fleet. It was stated that some of the ships actually did make the attempt, but the information was at present incomplete upon that point. The Japanese would doubtless before long publish the fullest accounts of the encounter. It was not at present clear what was the formation of the Chinese fleet at the time of the attack. All that seemed clear was that the Japanese made the attack and that it was diverted by the Chinese, and therefore while the Japanese assumed the offensive the Chinese fleet acted strictly on the defensive. He supposed the Japanese were afraid that if they succeeded in breaking through the Chinese line of defence they would get into shallow water and would be unable to extricate themselves.

Turning to the effect which the battle was likely to have upon European naval armaments, Captain Mahan said that the engagement was undoubtedly an important one for modern warships, but there was no information at present to lead him to suppose that the encounter would bring about a reconstruction and remodelling of European fleets. The details to hand were exceedingly slight. They did not, for instance, know anything as to the manner of the attack, though, doubtless, the information would be forthcoming in due course. He only wished he had more time to reduce what he had to say in writing. What interested him more than anything was the manner in which the battle was fought, but that was a point on which they got no information. They had, however, an important lesson in regard to the attempt to carry a body of troops in transports across hostile waters. As a general rule it was an unsafe thing to make such an attempt. It was impossible, however, to lay down an absolute rule in regard to the matter. At the same time, he thought the battle went to show that the mere existence of a hostile fleet did not constitute such a deterrent force upon the movements of a resolute man as had recently been supposed in this country. That a hostile fleet was "in being" was doubtless a most important fact to be considered in accomplishing such an operation as that which the Chinese admiral undertook, but it was plain, as he had always contended, that the existence of such a fleet would not deter a bold and resolute commander who believed that the object of his attempt was of sufficient importance to justify such a risk as was taken by the Chinese admiral at the Yalu River. What remained to be seen was whether the result accomplished by the Chinese was sufficient to justify the risk. To a naval man, the most interesting piece of information would be to know in what way the Japanese attack was made, and whether they concentrated their fire upon a portion of the Chinese fleet or distributed it throughout the entire line of defence.

Memorandum on the Cost of Coal at Gibraltar

USS *Chicago*, Gibraltar, November 20, 1894 [LC]

Being directed by the admiral to coal ship as speedily as possible, I directed Messrs. Allen, Kenny[1] and Clover, to go ashore at 9 AM today and see to quality & prices, submitting result to me. On their return at 1 PM three bids were submitted viz: Messrs Turner at 18s. 3d, per ton, Messrs Onetti at 18.9, and Messrs Rougervai at 20s.; all delivered alongside. The Chief Engr. expressed the opinion that 5 tons of the Rougervai coal would give results equal to six tons of the other bids and I ordered it bought. Mr. Clover seemed unconvinced of the accuracy of Mr. Allen's judgment but after careful consideration I decided to be governed by it.

That afternoon a letter was recd. from Messrs. Turner saying that they expected a collier that evg. from which they could give us coal at 17s. per ton. The admiral wished the ship coaled at once—moreover 17s x 6=102s while 20s x 5=100s. I.E. the Rougervai coal by Allen's estimate would be cheaper. Not to speak of the fact that the collier was *not* yet in—only expected.

---

1. Chief Engineer Louis J. Allen and Pay Inspector Albert S. Kenny.

Memorandum on the Cost of Alcohol at Málaga

USS *Chicago*, November 23, 1894 [LC]

On Sunday aftn., about 5 P.M., Nov. 18, I having just roused from a sleep, Pay Insptr. Kenny came in and told me that he had learned from Mr. Bevan that the proper price for alcohol was 66 cts per gallon instead of 85 which he had bought it of Troughton for. That he had ordered the alcohol from Troughton without getting competitive bids, because he wished to hasten the delivery, the requisitions having been recd. late. That he had instructed Van Brunt who was ashore settling the bills to ask Troughton to make out the public bill for 66 cents, and that he, Kenny, would stand the loss. This Troughton refused to do, saying that 85 was the fair regular market price, as he could prove by the certificate of three firms of standing before the U.S. Consul. These certificates were subsequently sent to Gibraltar. On the strength of them, after taking 24 hours to consider, I approved the bill, the words "after public competition" being struck out of the customary form. As the ship was to sail early next morning, I could not have Kenny make the further personal investigation I would otherwise have insisted on.

Memorandum on the Cost of Coal at Algiers

USS *Chicago*, Algiers, February 19, 1895 [LC]

As regards the purchase of coal yesterday the Paymr., Ex Off. & Chief Engn.[1] spent the forenoon, 9–12, examining. Upon their return had a consultation in the cabin. The Chief Engn. objected decidedly to the lowest priced coal of Legembre & Co. at Fs. 20.60 as likely to injure our boilers. While having preferences among the other coals, they were not sufficiently important to reject them and the next lowest offer that of Prosper Durand Fs 21.50 was accepted and coal ordered from that firm.

[P.S.] Read above to Paym. Kenny before putting my initial to it.

---

1. A. S. Kenny, R. Clover and L. J. Allen, respectively.

Memorandum on the Cost of Coal at Gibraltar

USS *Chicago*, Gibraltar, March 6, 1895 [NA]

The Paym., Allen & Clover went as usual [ashore at Gibraltar on February 27]. One firm offered coal from a collier alongside at 17s—and there was one lower bid than that accepted. The *collier had not arrived* at the time of my consulting with the three officers—and as regards the one other lower bid the state of the sea prevented the officers from getting on board, but the Chief Engineer was satisfied from the looks of the dust that it was Newport, not Cardiff, coal. As time pressed, and I required for our long passage good coal, I took that of Bongeroni at 19s. 9d.

Memorandum recorded March 6, 1895, after refreshing my memory by interview with Paym. who has memoranda of bids.

A Statement on Behalf of the Church Missionary Society to Seamen in the Port of New York[1]

New York, April 10, 1897 [SCI]

There is no condition of life that should appeal more strongly to the sympathy of the fortunate than that of the homeless; not merely, nor even chiefly, of those who are without home in the sense of lacking physical shelter or comfort, but of the more numerous class, who have the things necessary to the body, but are separated from the family ties and affections which protect innocence and hallow life. No form of Christian activity is wiser, or more fruitful, than that which seeks to stop the beginnings of evil, by providing the surroundings of home for youths launched alone in the midst of our great cities.

To be homeless, in the last named sense, is the inevitable condition and the sore temptation of the seaman in every port; save, possibly, in some one, where a relative or a friend may visit. In this one fact is summed up the trials and the dangers, which most distinctly separate him from other members of society. Of the latter, even those who, arriving strangers, do not form family ties in the city of their adoption, nevertheless gradually gather round them, as time passes, affections or friendships; which, in part at least, take the place of the family fireside and influence existence happily. The shortness of the seaman's stay and the uncertainty of his return to the same spot, preclude the possibility of a like issue to him. He arrives a wanderer, flits for a few days through the streets, and then, again a wanderer, he departs.

It is upon this distinctly friendless condition, which needs but a moment's reflection to be realized by any one, that the appeal of this Society, and of the others of kindred aim in the City and Port of New York, must rest. Men who are not touched by this will be touched by nothing. These societies aim to afford a home as well for the body as for the soul; and as well for the soul as for the body. If they cannot provide the wanderer with father and mother, brothers and sisters, they strive at least to supply a

---

1. Mahan joined the Society (later called the Seamen's Church Institute) in 1867, and was active on various committees in addition to serving as manager, 1867–1896, corresponding secretary, 1897–1898, and lay vice president, 1898–1914. He became a "patron" of the organization in 1875, which obligated him to a contribution of not less than $100 annually.

friend or friends, who at some well known spot, and surrounded with some degree of modest comfort and convenience, stand ready to welcome, to assist, and—far beyond this material help, though that too is extended—to show unpretentious sympathy and to promote comradeship among those who go out and in. Clubs and associations are imperfect substitutes for home; but, though imperfect, they can in part supply its place, by bringing man in contact with man under genial surroundings. Under such conditions the power of external evil is minimized. The individual has not to seek debauching in mere weariness and aimlessness of monotony. He has, indeed, still to resist the evil within, as well; but reasonable employment of mind and decent companionship remove in great measure the crowd of temptations that spring from mere disoccupation.

Such centers of influence this Society—with others—has established in New York and has long sustained; and, alongside of the home, unobtrusive but open, refraining from solicitation but stretching out its arms to those who will come, stands the Church, ready to minister to spiritual wants as well. But, great commercial city though this is and freehanded as are its citizens, the very wandering of the wayfarer, which constitutes his privations, removes him also from men's thoughts. Money is not given in amount adequate to the continuance of the simple work, on the lines so far, though with difficulty, maintained. Let those, therefore, of our household of faith put it to themselves on these grounds, when in the happiness of their own homes; that there are those ever coming and going in this city, ministers to its wealth who are homeless; that members of their own communion are making organized effort for the benefit of such; and that the work languishes for want of means.

The Sinking of the USS *Maine*

Remarks to the New Jersey Chapter of the Society of the Cincinnati

Princeton Inn, February 22, 1898[1]

[No other speaker is quoted in the *Times* account, although the ex-minister to Italy, William Potter, was one of them. Mahan was cheered as he rose to speak. He began by praising Captain Charles Sigsbee and the behavior of the survivors of the *Maine* explosion.]

We should be very cautious in forming hasty conclusions in reference to such things as this disaster. People are liable to jump at conclusions at a great national crisis like this which might involve them seriously. The elements of danger to a modern warship, danger external or danger internal, are not such as can be wholly eliminated. In war this goes without saying.

Of course, it is part of the business of all those who have to do with the designing of navies and their management also in times of peace and of war to provide against every method of attack and against sources of internal troubles as far as human foresight and pains can provide, but there are risks that have to be taken.

For instance, accepting, for the sake of argument, one of the assumptions already made by the newspaper(s) that the accident to the *Maine*[2] was an explosion of a magazine caused by spontaneous combustion in the coal bunkers or by some other internal cause, we cannot deduce from that that either coal or powder or high explosives are not to be carried.

The only inference is that if any precautions whatever remain to be taken, that precaution must be applied. Consider, however, the number of warships, analogous in character if not in particular detail to the *Maine*, which are traversing the ocean and having on board coal and powder year in and year out without accident, and you will realize at once how preposterous it is to assume that because the effects are fearful the danger of the explosion is great. Recur, for instance, to the experience of passenger steamers.

---

1. From *The New York Times*, February 23, 1898.
2. A 324-foot, 6,648-ton armored cruiser mounting four 10-inch and six 6-inch guns. Commissioned in 1895, she carried 374 officers and men. She exploded in Havana Harbor on February 15, 1898.

How many yearly, for the past decade, have crossed the ocean bearing their thousands of human freight unharmed. Suddenly in a moment—literally in a moment—the *Elbe*[3] is struck by a small freight steamer, and, like the *Maine*, plunges to the bottom. Do any of you propose to abandon going to Europe on that account? I assure you, speaking as a seaman and as a naval officer, that I believe that no man crosses the ocean in a passenger steamer without undertaking in a week greater risk of collision than any seaman on board a ship of war does from explosion in the course of a year.

There is another hasty inference from the disaster to the *Maine* which I would warn you against, and that is the disposition shown in many quarters to condemn the modern battleship, even as a fighting ship, as a frightful mistake, because it appears under the circumstances not yet at all understood she may meet with a terrible accident involving many lives. It is the old story of generalizing from a single instance.

The present battleship is the product of a gradual evolution, directed by experience and controlled in her development by the best thought of many expert constructors and seamen, both in constant communication at all times with the best thought of the naval world throughout the civilized world.

In short, I think I may say without necessary offense that the disposition to condemn the battleship offhand as a fighting machine, whether the assumption be that the *Maine* perished from internal causes or from external, can proceed only from ignorance of the facts of the battleship construction in general and consequent mistaken inferences as to the result of future naval battles.

There has been in years still recent one great naval calamity which may illustrate my leading thought now, namely, the necessity of knowledge to correct the statement. I mean the upsetting and sinking of the *Victoria*.[4] I do not refer to the fault, wherever it lay, that caused the accident or the collision, but to what happened after the collision.

The unprofessional world was startled breathless to learn how speedily such a ship could go down, first turning bottom up. Professional men knew before that such ships had a narrow margin of stability, and they know also that that narrow margin, quite sufficient for safety under ordinary circumstances, might under unusual conditions cause what then happened.

But that narrow margin of stability constituted a necessary risk. Ships of that character sway with an easier movement than those which are stiffer; they are therefore better gun platforms and give better shooting, and to shoot straight to the mark is an end so primary in a ship of war as to justify some risk to attain it.

---

3. The *Elbe*, of the North German Lloyd Steamship Company, was sunk by the *Crathie* off Lowestoft, England, in January 1895.
4. HMS *Victoria* was accidentally rammed and sunk by HMS *Camperdown* in June 1893.

I might give other illustrations of risks necessary to undertake in ships of war, but I imagine these will be sufficient to suggest, which is all I desire, that first we must wait to learn what really did happen to the *Maine*, or at least, what probably happened, and then view those facts in the light of at least some acquaintance with all the multitudinous conditions which a modern ship of war has to satisfy. Above all, remember she exists to meet danger, and that some risk must necessarily be taken.

Expenses Incurred While Traveling Under Orders from Rome, Italy, to New York, April 27-May 7, 1898[1]

N.P., N.D. Probably, Washington, D.C., May, 1898 [LC]

In Italy

Telegram to B. F. Stevens for Navy Dept.	*Lire*	5.70
R.R. Ticket to London		273.80
Sleeper to Paris		47.95
Postage		.50
Baggage (R.R. charge)		21.25
Meals en route		10.00
Total *Lire*		361.00[2]

In France

Meals en route	*Francs*	15.00
Cabs in Paris		6.50
Total		21.50

In England

Cabs. London		8ˢ 6ᵈ
Porters "		2.0
Hotel "		11.2
R.R. to Liverpool	£ 1	9.0
Lunch en route		4.10
Steamer Fare to N. Y.	£30	0.0
Total	32	15.6

---

1. *See* Mahan to the Comptroller of the Treasury, October 18, 1898.
2. The sum is actually 359.20.

A Distinction Between Colonies and Dependencies

Remarks to the New York State Chapter of the Colonial Order

New York, November 30, 1898[1]

. . . There is a close connection between a country's colonies and its navy. In France, which has no very great colonial system or very great navy, the colonial and naval systems are combined under one head. There is an association of ideas between the navy, that binds the colonies to the mother country, and the colonies themselves.

But I would like to point out that the word colony, as applied to our new acquisitions, is a misnomer. We can't have colonies. The original Roman colony was an outpost of the mother country—an extended Rome in the fullest sense of the word. A colony must be a country qualified by its natural conditions, climatic or otherwise, to become incorporated with the mother country.

This country of ours cannot assimilate itself with these "new territories." They are not colonies. They should more properly be termed dependencies. And what an appealing word it is. What an appeal it makes to us. It reminds us that we must keep a sharp eye upon them. The difficulties of our own political system, under which so many charges of political corruption are made—how likely it is that they will spring up with increased virulence in these countries unless we watch them. . . .

We officers of the army and navy deal continually with men who are our dependents. I speak of men whose one thought in life is not merely that they do their duty, but that those men under them should be looked after in every way whatever.

It is the profession of these officers to look after the men under them. They are trained to it. The American officers of the navy and army are the best possible guardians you can give to these dependencies which have come to us under the treaty of peace. We have the opportunity of bestowing upon them a beneficence which they have never known. The officers of the army and navy are better qualified to deal with these subject races than men engaged in the hard fight of ordinary existence.

---

1. From *The New York Times*, December 1, 1898, p. 5. Full text of speech not found.

Presentation to the Annual Meeting of the Church Missionary Society to Seamen in the Port of New York

New York, December 13, 1898 [UNC]

The general missionary work of the Church has long and naturally been divided under two chief heads—Domestic and Foreign Missions; but as is the case in matters secular, so in this sacred duty, that space of the globe's surface which unites the two great sub-divisions, at the same time that it constitutes the boundary separating the one from the other,—the sea,—has been overlooked by the Church at large as a field for missions. Properly, one would say, considering the vast number of persons now daily embarked upon the deep, and their dependence upon the conscientious fidelity of seamen, the sea should form, in the consciousness of the Church, a third special department, additional to the two great land sub-divisions—the Foreign and the Domestic. That it is not so—that we forget—constitutes the imperative necessity for the existence and activity of the Church Missionary Society to Seamen in the Port of New York. When the Church as a body recognizes that the sea as well as the land demands her motherly care, that she should seek to build up the character of seamen by spreading among them the light of the gospel, the need for the separate and highly specialized effort of our Society may cease.

Till then, the Church Missionary Society to Seamen, feeble in resources because the members of the Church, as experience shows, pay little heed to seamen, strives to occupy the ground as best it may. Its chief stations are equipped not only for spiritual service, but for social benefit as well; for physical comfort and mental cheer, other than in the streets and saloons. They stand on the water-fronts, where, as in all great maritime cities, temptation abounds. They serve seamen, not only by direct ministration to them, but indirectly, by the elevating effect upon the neighborhoods which is exerted by whatever stands for good, or actively works for it, as the Church and her missionaries do. Help is asked to maintain and to extend this beneficent work. Whose duty is it to aid?

Address Delivered at Holy Trinity Episcopal Church, Brooklyn, New York

Brooklyn, New York, March 1899 [LC]

When a man is called upon to speak before an audience which has assembled for a specific purpose, as you all have today, it is to be expected naturally that he should have some special knowledge or experience of the subject, in which his hearers, by their very presence, testify their interest. I have questioned myself, therefore, what I could have to say to a number of persons, who by their coming together thus, on a secular day, show their interest in our Christian Religion; or, at the least, their willingness to hear what another man may have to say about it. I am not an expert in theology; nor am I, on the other hand, an expert in the natural sciences which at this day stand, in popular consciousness, as the special antagonists of traditional Christian beliefs. An expert means one who has had experience, to a high degree; while for a man to talk to others of that whereof he has no experience, is a waste of his time and of theirs; if, indeed, it be not an impertinence.

There is, however, an experience which all men gain,—some more, some less,—according as they go through life with the eyes of their understanding open or shut; and that is the *personal* experience of the battle of life, and of the effect upon that battle of the things which each has done or failed to do; and also the effect exerted upon his life by the views,—the beliefs—which have influenced his actions; for what we really believe certainly affects our action. Christianity is perfectly philosophical in putting faith at the foundation of successful life. To a reasonable reflective man, the record of successes and failures upon which he looks back means something; he sees in them not merely the results, but the antecedent causes which led to the results; and in those causes few indeed must they be, and most thoughtless, who do not find in them reflected, not mere external circumstance, but the error or truth of those general principles—those beliefs—upon which they have based their personal action throughout life. Experience of this sort may be very narrow or very broad, according to a man's position. The private soldier knows little of the battle-field beyond the range of his own movement; his experience, however vivid, is narrow. Those above him, according to their several spheres, see and know more; their broader experience has the value which science allows to generalization, which in turn depends upon wide observation. Similarly in life the breadth of a man's circle of experience tends to give greater value to his conclusions; but whether it be broad or narrow, the experience of each is his *own*, in a way which nothing else is.

"Remember," has said that eminent historian, Mandell Creighton, the present Bishop of London, "that there is only one thing we can give to another, and that is the principles that animate our own life. Is not that the case in private life? Is not that the case in your relationship with those with whom you come in contact? Do you not feel, increasingly, that the one thing that you can give to your brother is a knowledge of the principles upon which your own life rests? It is assuredly the most precious possession that you have. It is assuredly the one that is the most easily communicated."

It is, therefore, of my personal experience that I mean to speak to you today; for indeed what else do I know that I should speak of, except those things that have most deeply affected my life. Do not, however, think that I propose to speak of what are most commonly called religious experiences, emotional chiefly in character. With the utmost reverence for religious emotion, and conviction of its power, I conceive it to be a matter not usually to be talked of, or exhibited. My purpose is to speak of religious experience as a purely practical matter; what religion has been to me; what it has done for me; in what light, after thirty years of trial, it now appears to me; what in other words my present hope—or rather my present *expectation*—is, that it will continue to do for me. This is the testimony of one man to that which he believes he has found God do for him, and in him. My hope certainly is that the avowal of my experience may strengthen some fellow man in his own battle. That result, however, depends not upon the speaker chiefly. Whenever man speaks to man earnestly, on matters relating to the spirit, there is renewed the miracle of the first Pentecost. The hearer hears not in the tongue of the speaker; but every man hears in his own tongue wherein he was born; or better, in many cases, in that tongue into which he has been reborn by his baptism and by the Holy Ghost. In today's result it will not be what I say, so much as the manner of man each one is who listens. It is to this, I doubt not, that is due much of the bad preaching whereof we hear.

Here let me briefly say—to define my position at once clearly—that my experience of life is that of one who has based his practice upon a full intellectual acceptance of the Christian Faith, as explicitly set forth in the historic Creeds—the Apostles' and the Nicene Creeds. In those, and in the Word of God, I have found, and find, not merely comfort and strength but intense intellectual satisfaction.

This being so, now that I am verging on old age, for I am now not far from sixty, and for more than thirty years now have held this Faith, and to it committed my future, what have I to say of my experience? I should reply, in brief, in the words of the Psalmist: "Thou, Lord, hast never failed them that trust Thee." It is, I think, the hopefulness of Religion that has most impressed itself as the result of my experience—and I am not naturally of sanguine temper. As a matter of experience, starting in life with a fearful and apprehensive mind, I find constantly growing the feeling of hopeful confidence. God has stood by me so often, surely I can trust Him now. Like the Israelites I have seen God's works; unlike them, on the occasion of their great offence, it has been granted me thence to learn something of His ways. But I should do small justice to what I conceive to be God's working, if I limited my foundation of increasing confidence to mere rational deductions from experience, and to them only. If so, as occurs often in science, some sudden instance seemingly to the contrary, which cannot be accounted for by the intellect, might bring the whole previous conviction of God's faithfulness into doubt. What I find, God be thanked, and which I believe to be the direct gracious work of God the Holy Ghost in the spirit of man, is the growth of conviction, for which intellect can give no account. "The Spirit itself," says St. Paul, "beareth witness with our spirit." I dont account for this, I only know it. For this, beyond all other things, I value such reputation for intellectual power as I have attained—that I can say, with all boldness and assurance, that there is wrought in me increasingly, as years go by, a thing of which my intellect takes cognizance, but for which it cannot account. This too, is a matter of experience; but it is an experience which no man can have for another, and which no man can impart to another. I can tell you I have it, and you know me at least not to be a fool; but beyond my assertion I can give you no proof.

The old Jewish law, like our own, held that the witness of more than one is necessary. "It is written in your law," said our Lord, "that the witness of two men is true." I read the experience of my life, I see how God in circumstance after circumstance has dealt with me. Doubtless, I don't see all: perhaps at times I see amiss; but even if it be as through a glass, darkly, I do see, and I see enough. No man can fully read the experience of another; each must read his own; but when a man has lived many years, trusting God, he can trace sufficiently the evidence in his own case that something not himself has guided his course, overruling. Of this Shakespeare speaks: "the Divinity that shapes our ends." This is one witness, intellectual mainly, not safely to be trusted alone, and, I say with sorrow, not certainly to be recognized, except by those whose will is to serve God. This is one witness, that of the intellect spiritually enlightened. Of this witness, too, our great, sober-minded, observant, fellow countryman, Washington, the perspicuity as well as the moderation of whose judgments grow ever more apparent as one studies them more, has spoken words many of you may recall. "No people more than the people of the United States can be bound to acknowledge and adore the invisible hand which conducts the affairs of man.

[600]

Every step by which they have advanced to the character of an independent nation seems to have been distinguished by some token of providential agency. The reflections arising out of the present crisis have forced themselves strongly upon my mind"; and from them he humbly dares to "anticipate the future blessings which the same seems to presage." But besides this testimony of the natural intellect, quickened by God's Spirit, watching the course of external events there is the other witness, perfectly distinct from the first, clearly to be recognized, the testimony of the man's consciousness that he is growing in belief, in hope, quite independent of the visible, sensible, grounds of hope. Either of these witnesses alone might be doubted. I at least hesitate not to say that to me the two prove the case.

And may I point out to you that this double witness, of external demonstration and internal illumination, is clearly taught us by the Bible. In this teaching, and in the evident oneness of the Mind, which runs through the centuries separating Genesis from St. John, and underlies the individualities of the various writers, are two chief sources of the gratification I find in that Book. The Apostles appeal freely to their experience of external things. "That which we have seen and heard declare we unto you," said John. "We were eye-witnesses," said St. Peter. "We did eat and drink with Him after He rose from the dead." "The *works* which I do bear witness," said our Lord. All these are avouched by the one witness—the external. The other witness, not to quote St. Paul's frequent utterances, received the repeated sanction of Jesus Christ; as, for instance, in the memorable words to St. Peter. "Flesh and blood"—the senses—"hath not revealed it unto thee, but my Father which is in Heaven"—the internal light, the witness of God the Holy Ghost.

It is almost unnecessary to say that Hope, as a consequence of experience and of reflection, was one of the first fruits of the Christian Faith; and we may be thankful that after these ages it remains the reward of him who believes. Hope, said St. Paul, abideth; and it *has* abode. I say not that Hope is not to be found outside of Christian believers, though I think that even there it is the gift of the Christian centuries; but it is the dominant note of Christian Faith, and it is not the dominant note of unbelief. We all remember St. Paul's words of glowing hope just before his death; "I am now ready to be offered; the time of departure is at hand. . . . Henceforth there remaineth for me the crown of glory"; but I think we take less heed of his assertion, in mid-career, of the practical results of Christian experience to him: "Patience worketh experience, and experience worketh Hope." What greater blessing can be offered a man, in this life or in the next, than growing hope following growing experience.

Contrast with these words of the great Believer, where Patience is tied to Hope by the constant bond of blessed Experience, contrast with this the sorrowful utterance of that gifted man, whose relations to Christianity have been sympathetically traced, from one point of view, by a distinguished priest of our Church. After a moving description of the battle against the sorrows of life, of the sources in which men, who have not the faith, are forced to seek for strength to endure the bitterness of Experience, he continues:

> This for our wisest! and we others pine;
>   And wish the long unhappy dream would end;
> And waive all claim to bliss, and try to bear,
>   With close-lipped patience for our only friend,
> Sad patience, too near neighbor to despair.

So, to return to the Pentecost simile, every man hears in that tongue which has become his own, whether by the Spirit of God, or by his own refusal of the Spirit. In that tongue Life speaks to him; in that tongue Experience speaks to him. To St. Paul Experience speaks, and the sorely tried Apostle hears—Patience, Hope; to the modern poet who, concerning Christ, knows only that:

> He is dead; far off He lies
>   By the lone Syrian town;
> And on His grave, with shining eyes,
>   The Syrian stars look down:

to him Experience speaks also, and he hears "Patience, sad Patience, too near neighbor to Despair."

When I was asked to address you I . . . [illegible phrase].
time which could be allowed admitted of no arguments. The only thing of value that could be contributed, was a brief, positive, statement, to which would attach whatever weight might derive from the personality of the speaker, of the faith that was in him, and of the grounds of his confidence. I sum it all up in the reiteration of my sure and joyful confidence, that I have tried God these many years and found Him ever faithful; faithful not only in the ordering of my external life, but still more faithful in the gradual increase to me of that knowledge of God, in which standeth our eternal life; a knowledge of whose growth I can give no account, except that I do know.

I thank you greatly for listening to me, and your Rector for asking me to speak. I value beyond words the opportunity, once in my life, before God's people, to avow my faith, that to me He is, and has been,—not in my imperfect service, but in His own perfect faithfulness,—Alpha and Omega, the Beginning and the End, the First and the Last. I rejoice that once at least I am able publicly to lay at His feet in words—however poor my deeds—the confession that all that I have, all that I am, all that I have accomplished, has been of Him and through Him; and that, as the end draws near, there abides, what only my own demerit can forfeit, the Hope, which experience of His faithfulness renews day by day.

The Navy and the Philippines

Remarks to the Associate Alumni
of the College of the City of New York

Savoy Hotel, New York, February 24, 1900[1]

Captain Mahan said that he had had no idea of what he was to speak about when he came to the dinner, and that it had only been suggested to him by the sentiment placed opposite his name and which he had written fifteen years ago. "It is, however, in these wider operations, which embrace a whole theatre of war, and in a maritime contest may cover a large portion of the globe, that the teachings of history have a more evident and permanent value." Captain Mahan, making these words of his own his text, said that the United States, "pitchforked as it was into the Philippines," and in its position in the Nicaragua or Panama Canal, was committed to a development of sea power little dreamed of when the words quoted were written. Regarding the Philippine question, Captain Mahan said he did not believe that if Bryan were elected tomorrow he could recede from the islands. He said he ventured upon the prophecy that the world struggle was to be divided between the power of the sea and the land, and urged that the country should have a standing navy, which was needed quite as much if not more than a standing army, and that it was not alone ships that were needed, but men trained and habituated in the use of the instruments of navigation and naval warfare.

---

1. From *The New York Times*, February 25, 1900. Full text of speech not found.

The English-Speaking Race

Summary of an Address to a McGill University Convocation

Montreal, May 18, 1900[1] [MCGUA]

He remarked that he came to us as a foreigner, but in one thing we had a common possession: we spoke the same tongue, and the time had come when the unity of tongue was going to become one of the greatest factors in the development of the world. All of us speaking English looked forward to the day when the English-speaking race was to be the great predominating factor of the world. The dwellers on the North American continent, divided into two communities, probably held the key of the situation as regards the future of the English race. We fronted Europe on the one hand, and the Pacific and Asia on the other. We held that central position which, whether it be in diplomacy, or statesmanship, or military art, was the commanding situation. But, because of that it was not necessary for us to truckle or be false in the least to our own particular nation or yield for one moment anything that really concerned the honor or vital interest of the country. Nothing of that sort. Differences would arise between us, and they could not be helped. He was not speaking with reference to present troubles, but we must remember that we, beyond all other members of the English-speaking race, were in the highest degree responsible to see that the strength of that great race did not suffer in our hands. It was, therefore, a matter of pleasure to him that he had been able to side, heart and soul, with Great Britain in the present contest. He believed that she was substantially in the right, and if he had not believed this firmly, he would never have taken up his pen and raised his voice as he had done. He had rejoiced to see the growing greatness of the British Empire, and he had rejoiced to see colonial help coming forward. He was pleased to have had the opportunity of saying what he had. They would not misunderstand him. He was not one bit less a citizen of the United States. "Let us all," he said, in conclusion, "as we go away from here, and particularly you young men, remember how all-important it is that these two nations—how essential it is to the welfare of each, how essential it is to the future of the world, that differences do not ripen into quarrels."

---

1. From the *Montreal Gazette*, May 19, 1900. Text of speech not found.

The Well Being of the Seaman in Port

A Speech Delivered to the Church Missionary Society to Seamen in the Port of New York[1]

New York, March 21, 1902 [NWC]

Bishop Potter, Ladies and Gentlemen: I came here this afternoon with the purpose of attempting what I rarely do, speak to you extempore, but I thought I would bring the manuscript of what I had written this morning, with the idea of having two strings to my bow. However, as I come between two speakers, both of whom have addressed and will address you in that manner, and you perhaps need a little variety, if I stick to the plan of reading what I have to say, I hope you will bear with me.

The subject assigned me and accepted by me, the Seaman in Port, suggests many ideas, ideas of temptation, dissipation, etc., among which I conceive one to be not only obvious but conspicuous. The one distinctive characteristic is the transiency of his stay in any one place. He comes, he remains at the most a short time, and he goes—perhaps never to return—perhaps to go and come at stated intervals, like the crews of the great liners, but in any case, never a permanent resident. He is never one of the population. Many of you will remember the story associated with the dawn of Christianity for our English speaking race. An English thane, listening to the message of the Gospel, before unheard by him, remarked that the life of man to him resembled what they had all often noticed in their feasts of a winter night. A bird, attracted by the warmth and light, flew in through one of the many openings left by the rude architecture of those days, flitted about a few moments picking up the crumbs, and then flew out again to the outer darkness and cold.[2] It is precisely so with the seaman in relation to civilization and all it means to us. I don't mean to exaggerate the material hardships of his life—these are much less than

---

1. Printed in *Report of Address Delivered at a Meeting Held at Sherry's, New York, March 21, 1902. . . .* Pamphlet. New York: The Protestant Episcopal Church Missionary Society to Seamen in the City and Port of New York, N.D. [1902], pp. 8–11.
2. From Bede's *Ecclesiastical History of the English Nation.* The passage occurs in Book II, Chapter 13, in which Edwin holds council with his chief men about embracing the faith of Christ.

they were, thanks in great part to benevolent societies such as this now appealing to you; though severe, the material conditions are perhaps not worse than in some other callings, but the great difficulty is to supply and maintain for him the moral and spiritual influences which, to say the least, are not very far from most who live on shore, however little they may use them.

Then, again, the places where seamen congregate on shore, the shore line, the water front of seaboard cities, are out of sight of those most able to give. None of your parishes extend effectively to the water line of New York. You don't see them, and even if you did, there is little so distinctive as to attract your attention. You scarcely realize that there are some 50,000 men moving about, practically homeless as regards even material surroundings, only their berth on board the ship, and quite homeless in that which makes home home—family ties, surroundings and occupations. The day's work over, or his discharge given, he is practically on the street, for everything that life craves, except the bare eating, drinking and sleeping.

I don't propose to enter into the details of our endeavors to meet and combat this state of things. I hope that the gentleman who speaks after me, Mr. Johnson,[3] will tell you enough about this. No one, let me say, has labored more unceasingly or more sagaciously than he has for years past, to my personal knowledge. The beneficial changes that owe their origin to him are very many. Stated shortly, we seek to occupy the water line with a line of posts and agencies—benevolent and spiritual in character— which afford at least a refuge from the homelessness and lack of occupation which force many to resorts injurious at once to their health and their character. The same sort of thing you are familiar with in the city at large— the coffee and reading room system, resting further in this case upon churches, where unoccupied hours may be spent innocently and even profitably.

We have, however, not only to protect the seamen by these offered refuges, we have a certain aggressive warfare to carry on against those whose livelihood depends largely on anticipating our benevolent work, getting hold of the seamen before they know where they are and manipulating their stay in port to their own pecuniary gain. It is to facilitate the access of our missionaries and agents to ships entering port, or at anchor in the stream, or in any way inaccessible, that we want a launch. It is to extend our sphere of operations, aggressive and protective.

But I feel, in addressing an audience like yourselves, living far from the scene of action, and busy with your many occupations, that the chief thing, for *me*, at least, is to ask you not to go away and forget; but to give this effort of ours a recollection and a *systematic* support, which it greatly needs.

---

3. Jeremiah Augustus Johnson, a New York lawyer who was President of the Confederated Council of Good Government in New York City.

Seamen have a particular claim in a great commercial city like ours, and yet they are particularly forgotten because they go and come in constant flitting. The needed launch will be a good thing; but if you, then, dismiss the matter from your mind that will be a very bad thing. We accomplish a good deal, but we don't begin to cover the ground. If you help us never so much and regularly we shall not be able to keep up. For you this, so far from being a reason for neglecting us, should be a stimulus to action. Every good work grows, expands, with what it feeds on. Benevolence—Christian benevolence—can and should place no limit to its ambition save the extent of evil to be relieved. This applies, of course, to all the benevolent objects which you now pursue, and not only to our Mission for Seamen, but this stands peculiar in two things:

1.—It is for most of you out of sight and therefore out of mind.

2.—From its nature it partakes the double character of Domestic and Foreign Missions—Domestic because at our doors; Foreign because, of its own spontaneous action, the good done is carried to the several quarters of the world by the migratory career of the seaman.

We cannot always know and trace the work done; the men come and go; impressions received in one port bear fruit elsewhere. This is one of the discouragements, but enough is known to give assurance of spiritual success as well as of temporal benevolent result.

Personality and Influence

A Commencement Address at Dartmouth College

Hanover, New Hampshire, June 24, 1903 [LC]

Man cannot escape the spirit of his age. It surrounds him as an atmosphere. It bears him onward like a current, sweeping him continually into new conditions. These, which constitute his changeful environment, even if they do not essentially, though gradually, modify his native character. This a power not to be withstood successfully; yet it by no means follows, necessarily, that it is a force which should in no wise be resisted, for, like all human impulses it will be found in every generation to be a strange mixture of good and evil. It has therefore both that which is to be embraced and fostered, and also that which is to be shunned and eliminated. Without, however, affirming that direct conflict with it, resistance, even unto death, may not at times be required, the modification of that which is bad, victory over it, even, if need so be, is better sought by the promotion of an opposing good than by direct antagonism. To overcome evil with good is a counsel of human experience, as well as of inspired wisdom.

It may be urged that the phrase, spirit of the age, assumes a proposition which cannot be conceded; namely, that there is such a thing as a simple, easily recognized, tendency, to which this name can be applied. Let this be granted. I am not here to deny the complex texture of human history, past or present; to ignore the interaction of forces, be they two or many, the resultant of which determines the direction of movement. Neither do I propose an analysis of present impulses, with a view to a quantitative determination of their relative strengths. I seek only to recognize, and to fix attention upon, a single prominent, and to my mind predominant, tendency, fraught with both good and evil, to the modification of which for good the matter of my words shall be addressed. We are here, young and old together, not impotent playthings of fortune, but actors in a series of events, great and small. We may not dam the stream, to arrest its progress; but we may, each in his measure, contribute to modify its direction, to convert to beneficent ends that which might prove a rushing desolating torrent, by imparting to its course a deflection such as we continually find nature or art effecting, by the interposition of controlling factors.

To effect this end in a sphere of moral action, there must be introduced a moral agent; and forasmuch as we are here dealing, not with the unconscious forces of external nature, but with the wills of intelligent beings, this moral agent must be the moral purpose of men like ourselves, realized in the mass because first embraced, professed, and consciously nourished by individuals here and there. Such, I conceive, is the history of all moral movement; here and there, one or two, the leaven leavening the lump, the coral barrier building up from the bottom, little by little, strong ultimately to withstand even the fury of the ocean. In this light I see Personality, the supreme moral influence, itself of mixed good and evil, but after all the great redemptive factor, directive, controlling, upon which the hopes of the race are staked. If this be so, to each man his personal character, the fibre of his own individuality, is not only his own greatest interest, but is the one thing he has supremely in trust for the welfare of the community and of the world; of his brother man, in the widest sense of that phrase.

It will scarcely be questioned that a leading characteristic of contemporary movement, confirmed by a duration extending now over more than the life-time of a generation, and still predominant in the political, industrial, and social activities of to-day, is the tendency to concentration; to the combination of many into one. This unification implies, as its necessary complement, increasing strength of organization; and this again carries with it a certain submersion of the individual, of individual initiative, and individual power of self-disposal, which are personal liberty of action. These tend to wither and decay beneath the predominant power of the mass, to which the man is a captive, and often an unwilling captive.

In the political sphere we see this tendency in the absorption of small states, with their separate independence of action, into huge aggregations of communities, more or less closely bound together, so as to constitute a single political unit for internal or external action. In our own country, the Civil War of forty years ago fixed certain limitations, previously denied by a large part of the nation, upon the independent rights of the several states. Within the following decade was accomplished the unification of Germany and Italy, the history of which for centuries back had been that of independent, rival, and often warring communities. The groups of British colonies in Canada and in Australia have combined into great federations; and a movement in the same direction is plainly discernible in the one remaining large aggregation of colonies in South Africa. The as yet unfulfilled movement towards a federation of the British Empire, between the Mother Country and the great colonial groups; the aspirations in Germany and in Russia, which have received the somewhat uncouth names of Pan-Germanism and Pan-Slavism, and which look to a political union founded on and embracing the units of the same race, may or may not result successfully; but their very existence as ideals proves that the conception of combination and concentration in the political sphere still possesses the surest quality of vitality,—growth, expansion. The widening area of conquest by the greater nations, of appropriation of territory and of peoples foreign to their own native sphere, even though it may appear an illegitimate form of activity, bears nevertheless the same impress of concentration of political control. The invidious word "Imperialism" has so far proved powerless even to *check* the outward manifestation of an inward impulse, which, whether good or bad in essence, is congruous with the spirit of the age.

In the industrial sphere, the question of concentration is attracting at present so much attention, that it is superfluous for a speaker to cite instances. It is perhaps the most imminent and politically critical internal question of the day. I would be untrue to my present object, however, should I not seek to fasten your attention, as my own is fastened, upon a feature strictly and closely cognate to my present line of thought, and purpose in this address. I suppose it will be generally conceded that the tendency, nay, even the conscious aim, of the so called Trusts movement, and of the antagonistic concentrations in the ranks of labor, is the elimination of the independent individual; of the small producer and the middle man in the sphere of production and distribution; of the free workman in the ranks of labor. Between producer and consumer, between the walking delegate and the men who buy wages by work,—the consumers of wages, if I may so say,—there is to be no intervention of a class of men who stand on their own bottom. Competition and the middle man, it is explained, cause increased expense to the consumer, because concentration of control promotes efficiency of administration, with consequent reduction of cost in the product and to the consumer. I do not dispute the statement, though I recognize another side to the question; namely, that the same process strengthens indefinitely the political power of concentrated authority, and weakens proportionately the political strength of the unorganized consumers.

But besides, although myself interested as a consumer, I cannot look otherwise than apprehensively and sympathetically upon the disappearance,—if such it prove,—of any middle class; for what disappears is not the physical existence, the mere natural life, of so many men, but their free industrial selves, and, in consequent proportion, their political individualities. They pass under masters, upon whose direct and immediate action their livelihood depends. The political power they have represented as a class, and as individuals, and which was healthfully distributed, because diffused, becomes by this relation of immediate dependence unhealthfully concentrated, because too easily and surely exerted by the few who now more or less control it. The danger of excessive standing armies is precisely in that organization, of dependence and control, by which power is concentrated without adequate balance. That the instrument of power is arms is but a detail; it matters not what the instrument, provided the overbearing power exists. Personality, the true counterpoise of concentration, decays as dependence grows, and its healthful influence is proportionately lost.

No man doubtless is wholly independent. Such a condition of entire relief from social coercion is a dream, as vain as its realization would be unwholesome; but in the relative degrees of interdependence, upon which the social organism rests, there are grades of more or less, easily susceptible of recognition. To draw lines is proverbially difficult; but to see a gap as wide as that occasioned by the disappearance of a middle class, be it yeomen or shopmen, is not hard; nor yet to realize that the gap may be so great as to constitute a breach of continuity, between the extremes of the body social and politic,—a condition dangerous indeed.

In the social order, apprehended as logically distinct from the political and industrial, I presume the supreme conception of concentration by organization is that commonly known as Socialism. This, in final analysis, if I rightly understand, proposes such subordination of the individual to the community, as amounts to entire deprivation of initiative and of free action. The man's place, and sphere and scope of action, no more no less, are to be determined for him. There is no logical stopping place short of this ultimate conclusion. To the individual choice there is to be left only that which the community, by its appointed organs, decides it does not require. What effect upon personality such an environment, if it ever come to pass, will have, we need not stop to inquire. Nature is strong; but as in the past she has been modified by conditions, so doubtless it will be in the future. The personality which will remain, after a few generations of such surroundings, may retain qualities enough to give it definition; but influence (political, industrial, or social) that it assuredly will not possess. It will have ceased to be a force. Yet it may well be questioned whether the same tendency does not already exist in the industrial combinations of the day; whether their present continued tolerance of personality, and the scope still afforded to it, are not mere temporary alleviations, deriving from the greatness of the field of action remaining to be occupied; whether the pooling of enterprises, whatever its advantage as a productive or administrative measure, has not a drawback which more than counterbalances, in the inevitable dwarfing of personality in the mass of men, and the concentration of its powers among a favored or gifted few, in whom it is enormously and dangerously exaggerated. There is, in my judgment, ground for the fears of those, who see in unchecked industrial combination, the necessary and inevitable forerunner of that social concentration, which, as yet an unrealized idea, we know as Socialism.

You will by this [time] have recognized, I think, that I discern in the various movements of the day, which I have passed under review, a common impulse towards concentration and organization of power, so marked and so general as to constitute a prominent, if not the predominant, tendency of the times,—the spirit of the age. It is no new thing in spirit, even if it be in form. Collectivism and individualism, to use the terminology of to-day, are at another date despotism and freedom; at a third they are authority and license; they are order and anarchy at a fourth.

I have chosen these terms designedly, to show that I recognize clearly that at one era the evil preponderates in one scale of the balance, and at another in the opposite. Collectivism and despotism may be interchangeable terms; for it makes scant difference where the power is collected, in the hands of one or of a board, if it be excessive and unbalanced. So also individualism and anarchy may become equivalent terms, if the interests of the individual man are able unduly to assert themselves against those of the community. As the younger Pitt said, with his happy knack for impressive statement, "It is the union of liberty with law, raising a barrier equally firm against the encroachments of power and the violence of popular commotion"—against over-concentration of power as well as against excess of individualism,—"which is our first and most essential object. Let us preserve this, and all else is in our power." To the men to whom he spoke, the two abstract ideas,—liberty and law,—presented in union by Pitt, were concrete in opposition, as seen then in the ordered government of Great Britain and the wild license of the opening French Revolution; but, under one form or another, this opposition is ever with us. The tendency of power to exaggerate itself into tyranny, of liberty to degenerate into license, is perennial. Where the one or the other predominates, the contemporary generation must see its call to watchfulness.

It has seemed necessary first to emphasize and substantiate the prevalence, not in one direction only but in many, of the contemporary tendency to exaggerated concentrations of power, by combination and organization, in order to lay the foundation for insistence upon that modifying factor, which I style Personality, the very existence of which, as an influence held in honor, is to-day imperilled. For, chaotic and confused as popular movements often appear, they are the outward and visible sign, not of blind *unconscious* forces, but of a living inward spirit, conscious of sentiment and purpose, even though only dimly aware of the issue towards which impulse is urging it. The assertion of the rights that inhere in personality, and which constitute its value and dignity, are met by a demand at once imperious and contemptuous, that they be surrendered for the alleged good of the community; that good being often but the expression of the will, not of the instructed community itself, but of those who have contrived, by this means or by that, by manipulation or by violence, to organize into their own hands the power of obedient masses, of capital or of men. Even in the name

[612]

of religion, man's obligation to his own personality is stigmatized as selfishness.

I have been led despite myself, certainly despite my first intention, to speak of personality from the point of view of its rights rather than its duties; for not the assertion of personality, but its consecration, was and is the theme which I proposed to myself. Yet, so far as that which I have said has a foundation of truth, it conduces to my argument; for if it be so that the tendency of the day is to depress personality as an influence in the community, it follows directly that to restore this needed modifying factor is a duty, of the highest order. And it is a duty involved in no such obscurity as at times hangs over the public contests of the day, through the mingled stream of good and ill found on both sides, intensified by the strife of tongues concerning them. The vindication of personality as a public influence begins, and finds its one enduring justification, in the purification and exaltation of personal character. "This above all,—to thine own self,"—not, mark we, to thine own interests, commonly so understood, but

> —To thine own self, Be true,
> And it must follow, as the night the day,
> Thou canst not then be false to any man.

It is in this sublime, deep-searching, truth that man's duties to himself and to his fellow find perpetual reconcilement. This is the expansion of that terser, briefer, and much abused proverb, "Charity begins at home." If it so begins *in truth*, it will not stop there.

I have been young and now am old, and I feel therefore that I have some claim, as a matter of personal experience, to affirm for all stages of life the conviction, that what a man is, that he does. Personality influences, because it cannot but transpire, as fragrance issues from a flower; because it cannot avoid continual expression in actions, small and great alike. To *be* is man's highest duty, because to *do* follows on it, "as the night the day." What weary labors cannot most of us who are old look back on, in trying to force ourselves to action,—good action, I mean,—to which the inner man did not correspond. I will not be understood to disparage such self-coercion; it is part of the inevitable discipline of life to the personality yet undeveloped. Still, so far as effort has been expended upon the compulsion of outward act, rather than upon conversion of the inward temper, it is in the long run but labor lost, because misdirected.

We owe it to ourselves, each of us, to realize to ourselves, to make it part of our deepest conviction, the worth and dignity—they are but the English and Latin words for the same quality—of personal character. It is, under the service of God, with which it readily associates itself, the one undying motive, the one unfailing consolation, the one assured reward.

[613]

Other men may disappoint, the noblest causes apparently fail, and certainly linger; but whatever of distress and sorrow these may legitimately cause, neither faith, nor hope, nor love, can long languish in the heart of him who has realized, by spiritual conviction, what is the force of personality, the widespreading power of character in the individual to uplift his fellow man. Concerning the august Personality whose influence upon our civilization transcends that of all others, whatever our individual reply to the question, "Who say ye that I am," History has affirmed the truth of the impassioned cry of a contemporary, "If I may but touch the hem of His garment, I shall be whole." A more intense, graphic, and truthful tribute to the power of personality to uplift others, to be the salt of public life, has perhaps never been framed; yet in its essence it was no new thought. Pagan and Christian, the natural man and the spiritual man, have alike divined it. Christianity has but fulfilled the aspiration of heathen philosophy, as for the Jew it fulfilled the law and the prophets, in presenting to the one and to the other idealized humanity, concrete in a perfect personality; one in which private virtue and universal influence met, not as independent qualities linked in closest union, but in the indissoluble sequence of deepest cause and highest effect.

To each of us in measure it is open to realize in our own selves the same ideal; to be, and, because we are, to do and to influence. It is misdirection of effort, lost motion, as the mechanicians style it, to aim first at doing and influencing, and afterwards at being. To see in external action and results the test and proof of personal success, is to sow a harvest of disappointment.

> Force not thine upward growth, but first of all
> Deepen thy roots.

Look within, and find there that which, duly tended, shall of itself bring forth in due season the words and acts you owe your fellow man, as surely as a seed brings forth its plant, or leaven leavens a lump. Nor is this merely the surest way: it is the only certain way. Few things, perhaps, are more difficult, as the experience of millionaires has testified, than to be sure that apparent good done is real good achieved; but it is indisputable and irreversibly certain that, if you sow figs, you will not reap thistles; neither, if you plant thorns, will you gather grapes.

I see before me, as I speak, the figure of a man in the prime of life, as years ago, who from his youth has been by unforeseen illness and pain cut off from all the activities of life; from all those doings in which our age sees not only personal success, but beneficent action. An existence, some would say, fruitless, blighted. So it might be, but so it is not. It is not what he does, for he can do little, but what he is. Because he is patient, considerate, cheerful, uncomplaining, amid the protracted heart sickness of hope deferred, the roots of truest life within bear abundant fruit without; in the graciousness towards others, and thought for them, that call for the constant return of the like graces towards him. In no affectation, no mere assumption of a smiling exterior, but heart answering to heart, like brings forth like, provoking to love and to good works; renewing the temper and disposition of the mind, in him who endures, and in those who minister. Blessing and blessed, are these no results? The man has *not* lived in vain, who has so influenced because he so is.

It is therefore, I conceive, the root of greatest service we can render to our age, to look carefully to the inward springs of our personal being, to that inward spirit which, as it strengthens or decays, for good or for evil, makes us through life what we are, determining and coloring our action towards others. At the bottom of all such good dispositions lies unquestionably Faith; belief in human nature, one's own and that of others. Faith, the remedy for the disquiet of life, never greater, never I believe so great, as now. If we have it not, we are without excuse, for the world's record bears testimony to the good in man, and to progress. Yet it is not to be had, nor to be preserved, without diligent care. Immediate environment, now as always, is not promotive of faith. In that with which we are in close contact, it is more easy to see the evil, and by it to be impressed, than the good. It is more easy to despond; or, what is far worse, cheerfully to acquiesce in, and to accept, the predominance and power of evil. But in proportion as faith prevails, every other virtue strengthens; for it brings with it an assurance, a confidence, a power, which are as the rain and sunshine to a growing plant. The man that believes can wait; that is patience. He can be cheerful, that is joy,—a virtue too rarely recognized as such. Anxiety, feverish haste, fretting over trouble, with all their miserable brood of petulance, irritability, peevishness, moroseness, that mar the happiness of so many homes to which no condition of true happiness is really wanting, and retard the progress of so many otherwise willing feet, will be recognized not as merely weaknesses, which they doubtless are, but as weaknesses that should shame a man as cowardice does; faults grave, discreditable, ruinous. Whatever place Christianity may occupy in our individual thoughts, as a Divine Revelation, as a philosophical system it is profoundly, searchingly, right, in the matter of course, seemingly unconscious, assumption, with which it places Faith at the foundation of all virtue. Not merely the Christ, but no man, can do mighty works, in his own heart or among his fellows, where faith is absent. What Christianity has contributed to this truth, which exists independent of it, is the example of a Personality, whose absolute faith revolutionized the history of mankind, and also has given to the lesser personalities, of those who have accepted it indeed, a motive force, the faith of which knows no such thing as failure.

No such thing as failure. A bold assertion in this world of trials and disappointments; of careers cut short, of expectations blighted. Yet how

[615]

absolutely true for the man whose faith in human nature, and in himself as partaker in it, looks not to this or that external result, but to the consecration of personality, to the development and growth of character. That the race can progress, can grow better, is proved by the fact that it has grown better; I mean not in material surroundings merely, but in the accepted ideals and realized practice of justice, mercy, and truth. Through the ups and downs of two millenniums, human character has advanced; there have been failures innumerable, but there is not failure. Hence is Hope. Hope abides with us for the race, and this is the justification of hope in the individual. Hope, which finds the necessity, as well as the justification, of its being, in the fact that the end is not reached, but is sure to be reached. "Hope that is seen," says a Christian philosopher, "is not hope; for what a man seeth, why does he yet hope for? But if we hope for that we see not, then do we with patience wait for it." Hope the cause, patience the consequence, success the outcome. What influence cannot but exhale from the man whose personality breathes the hope and patience, which prolonged exercise of those qualities has made part of his being. Success in life—true success—has to me never been so forcibly expressed as in two brief sequent phrases, of the same Christian philosopher I have just quoted, to whom Hope was not merely a privilege or a happiness, but among the first of duties. I claim not for him here divine inspiration, but sublime human insight and wisdom. "Patience," said he, "works experience, and experience works hope." I say with profoundest personal conviction, that the man whose experience of life leaves him more hopeful at its end than at its beginning, is a man successful, in the happiest as well as the highest sense. But let it be noted that the experience which works hope, is not experience begrudged, a lot fiercely resisted or invidiously repined at. Every scientific man will echo St. Paul, that patience is the condition of fruitful experiment; and for what experiment is to science, that experience is to life. The science of life can be learned on no more easy terms than the science of matter.

Finally, who has not felt that it is far easier to be kind, benevolent, loving to others, when we ourselves are happy. The sunshine within communicates sunshine to those without; the very presence of joy is contagious, but not only in a passive sense. It seeks to convey itself to others, it expresses itself readily in loving words and acts. It was no mere collocation of independent virtues, but a direct logical and practical sequence, that Paul the Apostle stated in the well known conjunction, Faith, Hope, Love. There is the root, trunk, and branches of personal character; of a personality which, realized in the individual, is, and cannot but be, for the healing of mankind. Faith in the good in men and in ourselves; good potential in all, and realized to our view in so many, gives the patience that waits on experience; and experience in this spirit will eternally yield hope, for he who thus looks for good will find it. Find it abundantly, in such measure as shall bury the evil in men out of sight.

> I've heard of hearts unkind, kind deed
> With coldness still returning.
> Alas! the gratitude of men
> Hath oftener left me mourning.

And thus it comes to pass that to him who preserves his faith and hope, the end of life is better and brighter than the beginning. The window called Peace, that looketh toward the sunrising, is in the west where the sun sets. That good shall prevail over evil is as assured, as that that setting sun shall again appear where the man's gaze is fixed. The classical proverb, "They whom the gods love are young still when they die," finds its echo in the Christian assurance, "At evening time there shall be light." Light, not for the man himself alone, but for those who are privileged to come within the radiance of his hope and peace.

Personality, it is claimed, lags far behind the needs of the case. This cry, common to every period, is particularly marked now, it is part of the disquiet that noticeably distinguishes this age; the demand for quick and evident results, the impatience, the absence of that patience which works experience, and upon which, therefore, hopefulness depends. Who shall determine what sphere is narrow, and what broad? Who shall affix bounds to influence once set in motion? The greatest, as the least, had once a beginning. My reply would be: Kindle first your light, consecrate your personality, establish within that abundance of the heart out of which the mouth speaketh, and the hand worketh, and trouble not yourself whence the candlestick for the light is to come, where the words which the mouth shall speak, where the acts for the hands to do. Take time. "He that believeth shall not make haste." You may question the inspiration of the proverb, but you cannot deny its profound wisdom. Fear not, if you are faithful where you begin, within, but that a place will open to the outer work to which you are fitted. For that matter, the work is not far from any of us, in the tending of which we shall educate our personality for its effect upon the world. Untrained personality cannot operate for good, except possibly as a beacon for warning.

For, after all, you who would see the world influenced, you to whom opening youth or early prime holds out still fair visions of work for others to be done, of wide influence to be transmitted, we, whose work approaches its end, may well ask you, with tenderest sympathy for your highest aspirations—"Who is the world to you? Who is your neighbor?" Shall your projected career of beneficence be exempt from the rule of every other calling, that it shall begin with little and go on to more? You who have ideals for the world, what are your ideals for the home? What neighbor so close, what world so near, what influence so inevitable, or so great, as that of personality within the four walls of the house? You may for a time disguise to the outer world the inner personality under the outer demeanor; in no bad sense, I mean, in no conscious hypocrisy; but by mistaken effort, you may pass off good bearing for good will; making clean the outside of cup and platter, and thinking it then matters little about the inside. But you cannot do this at home; you cannot there avoid the penalties, or fail to reap the fruit, of personality. Father, mother, wife, child, will know you as you are; possibly not to the very depths of your being, but that which proceeds from those depths will be inevitably visible; not only affecting them, but influencing them. Only by grappling with your own personality, in its mingled good and evil, only by insisting with yourself that you shall be within what you would fain seem without, only by loving that which is good, and believing it can be wrought in yourself, shall you be to your home the influence you should. And, believe me, the home will recognize the struggle, the uplifting personality, quite as clearly as the original defects; will imitate, and will carry out into the world a radiating influence, the outward circles of which only the eye of Omniscience can trace. For self propagates itself, like begets like; and Christian philosophy is again perfectly accurate in its insight, "We shall be like Him, when we shall see Him as He *is*."

I hope I speak strongly, for it has been my privilege to witness that whereof I speak; the deepening of the roots, the silent upward, and beneficent, growth of gracious persons, and the influence they exercise; as it has been too my portion, as of us all who live long, to see the slow declension, and the blight spread around, by those who have not kept watch over their own hearts. For, as that which a man is, that he does; so that which a man loves, thither he continually tends. Errors, stumbles, falls, there may be—there almost surely will be; but that which he loves, to that will he return; if good, to good; if evil, to evil. Herein then, in the redemption and renewal of personality, more than, though not exclusive of, organized and concentrated movement in mass against the material evil of the world, let us see the hope of humanity. Let us cherish the ideal of consecrated Personality, of personality dedicated to the purification of its inner self, just because, and all the more that, the movement of the day is towards that concentration of organization, which tends to belittle the value and influence of personality. The two are not in themselves essentially opposed. They are rather complementary to one another, and certainly no military man will speak lightly of concentration; but just as, in the political world, man seems unable to hold a just balance except by opposition of parties, whereof one predominates to-day and the other to-morrow, so is it in that moral movement which has for its aim the uplifting of our race. At one time, respect for personal excellence tends to degenerate into a selfish regard for mere individual culture; at another, and I hold it is the case to-day, the impressive power of combination tends to shut men's eyes to the surpassing influence of personality, as the expression of inward character.

We shall never regenerate mankind unless we see success in the regeneration of its units, any more than you can insure a good building by ingenious plan completed with bad bricks. The simile is imperfect, in that the bricks of the human building are, to recur again to Christian imagery, "living stones," "growing into a holy temple." Growth, the expression and summary of all life, commends itself both to St. Peter and St. Paul as the fitting word for the advance of humanity towards perfection, although by each the simile is applied to the progress of a building. For this house is not made with hands, and its parts are fitted to their place, not by mechanical fashioning from without, but by the development of personality from within.

Statement Before the Senate Commission on the Merchant Marine

Washington, D.C., November 25, 1904[1]

Mr. Chairman and gentlemen of the Commission, everything connected with the economical and industrial features of a merchant marine concerns the work of the Commission, but it is a matter as to which I am not at all in a position to speak.

In listening to Mr. Parker's[2] address I do not know whether I understood him correctly, but I did not understand him to lay stress upon the necessity of developing the carrying trade of the country as well as the personnel. It may be that he took that for granted and that the personnel was his issue.

Of course it is obvious, a priori, to everybody that the greater the number of people existing in a particular country who are accustomed to the water in one shape or another and the more intimately they are connected with it, as the old-fashioned seaman or sailor was, the larger the reserve that that country will have and the greater the development possible to its navy. That is what I call the obvious view of the matter. It is scarcely necessary to enlarge upon that. It is like any other occupation in life. The larger the number of people interested in it and the greater their practical knowledge of it the easier expansion comes to that particular industry if there is any call for such an expansion to take place.

But in addition to that which is obvious and might be assumed beforehand, we have very strong historical testimony. It has fallen in my way in the last few months to go to some extent into the question of the old English navigation laws;[3] and in the first place it is to be remarked that after a very short time, if not in their very beginning, the navigation laws of Great Britain were regarded as a military matter, and only incidentally a commercial matter.

It may not be generally known—I suppose it scarcely should be—that when the navigation system of England went into operation some two

---

1. From the Merchant Marine Commission *Hearings*, 1904, Vol. 3, p. 1745ff.
2. Richard Wayne Parker, Representative from New Jersey. He and Luce preceded Mahan in presenting their views.
3. Mahan was writing his *The Influence of Sea Power in its Relation to the War of 1812* which Little, Brown and Company published in October 1905.

hundred and fifty years ago, England was in the same plight we ourselves are in now; that is, although she was an island and had every inducement to become a great maritime nation, yet more than half of the carrying trade of Great Britain was done by foreigners; and that is the reason why she resorted to the navigation system—or the navigation laws.

The navigation act was passed for that very reason. They found that their carrying trade had gone away from them; and of course if they had not ships they necessarily did not have seamen, or if they did have seamen those seamen were in foreign employ and consequently were not at the disposal of the Government at the time the Government needed them.

From that condition the navigation act took its issue; and, in my judgment, from following the question historically, it was really an immense success. It was a great protective measure. I do not speak as a protectionist, because I am not one, but it was a great protective measure for the development of the transportation trade and facilities of Great Britain; but coupled with that there is one provision upon which Mr. Parker was enlarging before you, that not only should the ships be English, but the seamen should be English as well.

I think there can be very little doubt, from following the development of that system through one hundred and fifty or more years—it lasted really for two hundred—that the effect was to develop the carrying trade of the nation, to largely develop their resources of seamen, and that to that, largely—chiefly—is due the fact that Great Britain attained to that supremacy of the seas, which, for a long time historically she is known to have held.

I mention that, although it is a very old story now, as it seems to me it is strictly applicable to us at the present time, not as regards the particular legislation, the particular methods, that England adopted at that time, but as to the fact that it was a system of nursing and developing a particular British industry—the carrying trade. They followed it out, although they knew it at some times and in some ways injured another kindred industry, which was that of commerce. That actually their commerce suffered by reason of the assistance they rendered the carrying trade, that it actually lost to a certain extent, they all conceded. As a matter of commercial exchange the country lost, but they were willing to undergo loss in order to build up this one particular industry, the carrying trade, which was fortified by the requirement that not only the ships, but that a certain percentage of the seamen, a very large proportion—three-fourths was the number—should be native British subjects, and this they did avowedly that they might have at easy command a strong reserve available for the navy in case of war. I do not know really that there is anything for me to add to that, but I may give an apt quotation from the correspondence of John Adams when envoy to Great Britain in 1785 and seeking to obtain concessions to American ships: "Every consideration has been repeatedly urged to no effect. Seamen, the navy, and power to strike an awful blow to their enemies at sea at the first outbreak of war are the ideas which prevail above all others."

As I say, on the face of things it seems reasonable to suppose that the larger the number of Americans who are engaged in seafaring pursuits the greater will be the reserve for the Navy, and that in order to have a large number of Americans so engaged you must also have a very large American shipping, which, in some way or other, and that is for the Commission to decide, is to be encouraged to come into existence and to compete with the other industries of the country, which at present it seems unable to do.

One of the great reasons why our shipping industry has declined is because of the large competition which inland industries have offered for the employment of capital. But that is a question for the Commission.

There is only one thing I should like to say in addition, and that is a bit of a warning which we should regard. In such a development, if it should be decided upon, as the development of reserves, as the development of a plan upon which we may count, from which we may expect something, we must be on our guard not to expect too much. One of the great troubles with all reserves is that people look to them as such and such a number, and they think they are going to realize the whole of that number, whereas as business men you gentlemen know that you rarely realize all you expect in any undertaking.

The value of them undoubtedly would be immense. How large I do not know. In Great Britain at the most flourishing period of the navigation acts they had practically 50,000 skilled seamen reserves, on whom they could call for the enlargement of the navy. But the warning I wanted to offer is that I would not like to see anything adopted which would seem to militate against the necessity of maintaining a large regular naval force, as the nucleus to which the reserves can go. It is not quite as true in these days as in the old days that a seaman in the merchant service is immediately available for service on naval shipboard; but a seaman coming from the merchant service, with the habit of the sea and accustomed to its ways, can be broken in with very great rapidity, not as rapidly as once, but still with considerable rapidity, provided you have a large trained regular naval service, such as you have in the Regular Army.

I think that should be kept in view. Otherwise any question of reserves will disappoint you, and you will expect more from them than you ought to. This is an important qualification; but for large available reserves the one way to command them is to develop your foreign shipping trade, and after that to reserve it in some manner or other to American seamen.[4]

---

4. In the questioning that followed the formal testimony, Senator Lodge elicited from Mahan the admission that Britain's forfeited commerce was eventually retrieved.

Comments on the Seizure of Private Property at Sea

Pau, France, February–March 1906[1]

It is only in the broad light of effect upon the resources of war,—the sinews of war, to use a common expression,—that the propriety of interference with an enemy's commerce can be adequately weighed. As commonly posed, the statement is that such action is the seizure of private property at sea. The expression is entirely misleading, in so far as it seeks to fix opprobrium on this method of warfare; an opprobrium probably due largely to the practice of prize money, awarded to stimulate the activity of cruisers. That such reproach is unreal, and inconsistent, will appear immediately by transferring it to the permitted practices of confiscation of contraband of war, or of property attempting to run a blockade. A vessel is seized on the high seas, bound to a belligerent port, laden with guns and powder. Is this public property? It may be, but by no means necessarily. It often is a private venture, in hopes of high profits, such as was provoked by the strenuous wants of the Confederate States during the American Civil War. No one disputes the propriety of confiscating such a cargo, yet the property is "private." It is confiscated because, conducing to the belligerent cause, it has acquired a belligerent stamp. It is engaged in an operation inconsistent with the neutral character, unlawful therefore to a neutral, and being thus engaged in unlawful practice is subject to the confiscation which the law in many instances inflicts upon the property of individuals engaged in unlawful civil pursuits. So again, property of a character not at all usually contraband, dry goods, food stuffs, articles even conducing only to luxury, is forfeited, if caught trying to enter or leave a port, the blockade of which has been declared and maintained by an adequate force. The articles of a character ordinarily innocent which were run into the Confederate harbors during the blockade by the Union navy, the cotton which was run out, were not necessarily public property. They were "private property," embarked by individuals with a single view to personal gain in a commercial transaction. Yet, if caught, they were confiscated, because engaged in a transaction admittedly

---

1. Enclosed in Mahan to Root, April 20, 1906. *See also* Mahan's "The Hague Conference: The Question of Immunity of Belligerent Merchant Shipping," *National Review* (June 1907).

unlawful, in virtue of a command issued by the belligerent; a command to which he was perfectly competent, because in pursuance of the rights permitted to him by international law.

In the cases of contraband and blockade running, International Law permits this practice and punishment, because both attempts are in contravention of neutrality, in that they assist the one belligerent at the expense of the measures taken by the other in order to win his fight. In the matter of contraband this may seem clear enough; but why should the exchange of cotton against dry goods and various other articles, of notoriously innocent character so far as the direct maintenance of war is concerned, have been prevented by the United States, with the consent of the rest of the civilized world, neither the sympathies nor the interests of which then went with the Union? Let the finances and general condition of the Southern Confederacy answer the question. To the downfall of the Confederacy, no single cause conduced more than did the entire destruction of its commerce. True, this was effected by blockade, rather than by the efforts of cruisers on the deep sea,—though these somewhat contributed; but in what essential respect is there difference? The destruction of the Confederacy's commerce was but one cause in the result, and it was indirect in action; but, like some deep-seated local disease, it poisoned the springs of life, spreading with remorseless certainty through innumerable hidden channels into every part of the political frame, till the whole was faint unto death.

Between the fact that property embarked in commercial venture is private in ownership, and the assumption that therefore it is not sustaining the enemy's cause, is not really belligerent, there is a gap in the reasoning. Its influence is indirect superficially; that is, it is not immediately seen and therefore to many remains untraceable. Nevertheless the effect is clear and substantial, as should be immediately recognized by anyone who has even casual opportunity to note the effect of fluctuations of trade upon the welfare of a community, which in turn affects the public income in an infinitude of ways. But the essence of trade is transportation. Stop transportation, and where is your trade? Were it in the power of one belligerent to paralyze the principal railroad system of his opponent, does any one believe that he would refrain from doing so? that he would ignore the effect upon the power to continue the war of the consequent embarrassment and suffering of the people at large, of the falling of the public revenue because of wide-spread diminution of private means? But what is ordinarily impossible within the territories of a nation, becomes to a greater or less extent possible exteriorily, and especially on the broad common we call the sea. The propriety of exercising the power depends not upon the fact that the property, to which transportation is denied, is private in ownership,—

all that is necessarily done to it is to bid it stay at home, under penalty of seizure,—but upon the consideration whether the act of forbidal really conduces to the purposes of war. If it does, it should be permissible; but the only way to enforce the prohibition is the penalty of confiscation for transgression. That it has, when exercised, an important, though often secondary, effect upon the issues is historically certain. The practice has been given a bad name of late, partly by the emphasis laid on the phrase "private property," partly doubtless because it is in direct descent from the old freebooting system prevalent when there were no standing navies, when war at sea was carried on by private venture wholly, or at best by private vessels impressed for the occasion; but in the course of centuries of adjudication it has been systematized and codified, brought under the full control of law.

If this argument is sound, the question is not one of essential righteousness, but of expediency, of policy; policy international, as well as of the individual state. For the latter, the question is not merely, what shall our people escape by the abandonment of this time-sanctioned practice? It is rather what power to overcome the enemy shall we surrender? It is a question of balance. As Jefferson said, when threatened with a failure of negotiations, "We shall have to begin the irrational process of trying which can do the other most harm." As a summary of war, the sentence is a caricature; but it incidentally embodies Farragut's aphorism, "The best defence is a rapid fire from our own guns." For the objects of war, offence is better than defence. It is to be remembered, also, that the effort of commerce destruction requires smaller numbers and cheaper vessels than are imposed upon the defendant, who has to protect his commerce everywhere. This was abundantly shown in the War of 1812 between the United States and Great Britain; the reason being that above advanced in the case of Russia and Japan. It constitutes therefore a powerful diversion, a double danger, like that of two ports, and in this respect has military value. From the international point of view, it is worth enquiring whether it is well to contract the area upon which the pressure of war may be brought to bear; to confine its effects more and more to the armies, or navies, and exempt the people at large from their portion of the burden, which would incline them to demand peace; whether war should be made to mean only killing men, and no longer take the more merciful method of crippling resources? Which will most promote, and maintain, a steady aversion to war? No people should be more qualified to answer this query than that of Great Britain, with her constant experience of small distant hostilities, almost incessant in one or other quarter of the empire. Which impression comparatively is the deepest and most lasting, that of the men killed here and there, from time to time, or the big bill that remains as a charge for the Boer War? Depend upon it, the interest of humanity demands that war is not to be a mere question of champions, land or sea, but that the whole people should be made to feel, individually, that the war will find its way to them, in purse as well as sorrow.

The Work of the
Naval War Board of 1898

A Report to the General Board of the Navy

Woodmere, Long Island, October 29, 1906 [NWC]

In obedience to the Department's orders of June 20, and July 1, 1906, I submit herewith the following narrative account of the work of the Naval War Board of 1898, giving, as nearly as can now be ascertained, the reason for its formation, the scope and nature of its duties, and their relation to the administration of the Navy Department; together with the general conclusions on strategical situations developed by the studies of the Board.

2.   In its first form, as stated by the Secretary of that time, Hon. J. D. Long, (*The New American Navy*, vol. 1, p. 162),[1] the Board consisted of Assistant Secretary Theodore Roosevelt, Captains A. S. Crowninshield and A. S. Barker, and Commander Richardson Clover, who *"were asked to act in that capacity just before the war began."* It appears from the recent letters to me of Admirals Barker and Crowninshield that other officers also were at times present, officially yet informally, and afterwards dropped out, with equal informality. The words underlined [italicized] imply an informal commencement; which corresponds to the recollection of Captain (now Rear Admiral) Barker, that, until the late Rear Admiral Sicard replaced Assistant Secretary Roosevelt, no definitive orders were given to those who thus met as a Board. Rear Admiral Sicard's own orders, April 16, 1898, were simply to report for such duty as might be assigned him in the Secretary's office; the nature of his duties was not specified, nor has any order specifying them been found. Captain Barker being then attached to the office of the Secretary, Captain Crowninshield being Chief of the Bureau of Navigation, and Commander Clover of the Office of Naval Intelligence, points also to the conclusion that, as originally constituted, the Board was simply a meeting of the officers whose other particular duties indicated them to be the proper persons for fruitful consultation, and for coordination of the many and speedy steps which had to be taken, outside and above Bureau action, in the pressing preparation for war. As such steps would need the Secretary's sanction, in whatever was

---

1. Published in two volumes by The Outlook Company of New York in 1903.

given, the Board fell naturally into the position of an advisory body; to which function, as far as my observation went, it was limited throughout its existence.

3. This function of advice constituted the *relation* of the Board to the administration of the Navy Department throughout my acquaintance with it; and from my communications with President Roosevelt, ex-Secretary Long, and Rear Admirals Barker and Crowninshield, I gather that, although perhaps never formally stated in orders, such was its office from the beginning. It possessed neither original nor executive powers. To this correspond the following words of Mr. Long, taken from the passage before cited: "The Secretary lacking professional experience, *and the Navy being without a General Staff*, it was necessary that he should have the assistance of such a Board." The underlining [italicization] is mine; and the well understood limits upon the authority of a General Staff designate exactly that exercised by the body to which it is here likened, in its *relations* to the head of the Navy Department.

4. The Secretary's lack of professional experience, together with the non-existence of a General Staff to supply that lack, mentioned in the words just quoted, contain the *reasons* for the organization of the Board, as apprehended by the person who had the most direct knowledge of such reasons. Further on, he states explicitly the *scope* and *nature* of the duties intrusted to the Board; thereby defining, implicitly, the particular kind of professional experience in which the Secretary considered himself lacking, to supply which the Board was created. "The Board was eminently fitted to coordinate the work of the Department and the Fleet, and to keep a general surveillance over the larger strategical and technical questions, which could not be dealt with by the Commander-in-chief of the several squadrons."

5. Mr. Long's book having been written for popular information, he has probably not submitted all his expressions to close scrutiny; and I should be inclined myself to eliminate the word "technical" from the above quotation. Undoubtedly, any Board created by the Department will consider any subject submitted to it by the Secretary, and I do not challenge "technical" as not being among his intentions; but actually I cannot recall the Board dealing with any such question, and it is obvious that almost every technical matter, strictly so called, which demands naval consideration, falls under the charge of one of the Bureaus. These for the most part are technical administrative bodies, whereas the War Board was neither technical nor administrative, even in its limited advisory capacity. I should add, however, that Admiral Sicard in his final report, August 24, 1898, states that "numerous matters, some verbal, some written, were placed before the Board for its information and action. Those submitted in writing, which have been chiefly from the Office of Naval Intelligence, have been

returned to that Office for file." Of these matters I have no specific recollection.

6. Before leaving this part of the subject committed to me by the Department, it should be remarked that not only is ex-Secretary Long, by official position at the time, the person best fitted to know the purposes of the Department, but that his statement, being made in 1903, is by three years nearer the date to which it refers than any other personal unwritten information now to be attained.

7. As regards the *work* of the Board, a history of which the Department's letter of June 20 names as a principal object of the orders to me: I was in Europe at the time the war began, and returning, in obedience to the Department's telegram, did not reach New York until Saturday, May 7th, six days after the Spanish fleet in Manila Bay had been destroyed by the fleet of Commodore (now Admiral) Dewey. May 9th I reported for duty. Prior to that date I had no knowledge of the proceedings of the Board; but, having reason to infer I was to be a member, in passing through Paris I telegraphed to the Navy Department certain opinions of my own,[2] elicited by the popular clamors in America, as reported in the foreign press. Through the courtesy of General Porter, then Ambassador to France, this message was transmitted through the State Department, and in its cipher. I have ascertained that a copy of this cablegram is on file in the State Department. I could not find it in that of the Navy.

8. With regard to the Department's specification that I should include in my statement, as part of "the history of the work," "the general conclusions on strategical situations developed by the studies of the Board," I must premise that the only such conclusions of which I know are those embodied in the daily action of the Board, as an advisory body in the operations of the existing war. I have therefore thought I should best meet the wish of the Department by stating currently the sequence of events in which the Board took advisory action, the advice given, and the particular conditions and reason governing it in the several instances.

9. When I reported, the late Rear Admiral Sicard was President of the Board. The Spanish Manila fleet having been destroyed, attention was centered upon Cervera's squadron, which had not yet turned up on this side of the Atlantic. The dispositions then existing are commonly known. Commodore Schley's "Flying" Squadron was waiting in Hampton Roads; Rear Admiral Sampson was en route for San Juan, Porto Rico, with his fleet; the *Oregon* was still on her way from the Pacific; and two fast ships, taken from the American Steamship Line, were scouting eighty miles to windward of Martinique and Guadaloupe, on the lookout for Cervera. That these ships did not sight the enemy was due, not to error in this dis-

---

2. *See* Mahan to Day, April 29, 1898.

position, but to the fact that the delay in the passage of the Spanish division exceeded the extreme calculation as to time made by the Board. The two ships, which cruised on a north and south line, and communicated daily, were ordered to remain to May 10. That day Cervera's squadron hove to 130 miles east of Martinique; that is 50 miles east of our lookouts' cruising ground. At 4 p.m. May 11, it was off Martinique.

10. The conditions on May 9, just stated, and the subsequent transactions as far as the Board was concerned, are with me now a matter of recollection, refreshed or corrected by reference to a series of papers written by me for *McClure's Magazine*, within six months of the end of the war, and afterwards published in book form under the title *Lessons of the War with Spain*.

11. It is obvious, and notorious, that such a body as the War Board, irresponsible, because without authority, yet possibly influential, behind the Secretary, occupies a somewhat invidious position; and that its relations to Commanders-in-Chief, though indirect, are real and extremely delicate. For this reason, and because of my fixed opinion that official responsibility should be individual, (not only responsibility in action, but responsibility for advice), I addressed a letter to the Secretary immediately after reporting, recommending that there should be but one responsible adviser to him. This adviser might consult with any numbers, and by any methods, that the Department desired; but I submitted that the ultimate conclusion, tendered to the Secretary as advice in a professional matter, in which the Secretary "lacked experience," should be the responsibility of one man. My letter was forwarded through the President of the Board. No action was taken upon it. The only reply given was a verbal interview between the Secretary and myself, in the course of which he asked me the question "Has the Board, as now constituted, made any mistake that you can point out?" At so early a date I could not have familiarized myself with all the conditions, and I replied "No"; but, with my already formed military views, and with due reflection, I can scarcely imagine that I could personally have approved the movement of Sampson's fleet against San Juan, then in process. In the papers referred to I criticized that action, after the event, for reasons that should have been obvious before it; but, having made the reply I did to the Secretary, I felt bound afterwards to assume my acquiescence in a step taken and beyond recall before I joined. As far as I can remember, the non-action of the Department in this matter of responsibility was due, not to any decision as to the principle advanced in my letter, but to its satisfaction with the working of the existing plan.

12. The question of individual responsibility for advice is, I think, worthy of the Department's consideration. As regards the particular movement towards San Juan, this illustrates precisely the difficulty and delicacy of the adviser's position, and his, or their, responsibility. My memory, con-

firmed by reference, is, that to proceed farther east than the Windward Passage, which was a central position in reference to San Juan, Cienfuegos, and Havana, was Admiral Sampson's own decision; and that the Department's telegram of May 9 betrayed doubt as to its expediency, but yielded in deference to the Commander-in-Chief on the spot. Reference to the telegrams may verify the extent of the Department's action, whether mandatory or consentant only; but my recollection is quite clear as to the subsequent uneasiness of the Board.

13.   When Cervera was reported off Martinique, May 12, the Board advised the immediate concentration of Sampson's and Schley's divisions at Key West; the latter to call off Charleston en route, to receive any modifying instructions necessitated by later intelligence. A steamer was detailed at Charleston to communicate with the squadron without causing delay. The Commandant at Key West was notified to be ready for recoaling the arrivals there; the purpose being to send one division of the armored fleet before Cienfuegos the instant that the Havana position—incidental to which was the protection of Key West—was properly reinforced by Sampson's return. Two cruisers, the *Minneapolis* and *St. Paul*, were sent, one to lookout between Haiti and the Caicos Bank, the other between Haiti and Jamaica. This action was reported to Sampson, the telegram adding that "it was important his fast cruisers should keep touch with the enemy." No interference was made with his cruisers; but he himself sent the *Harvard* and *Yale*, of his command, one to the Mona Passage, the other between Haiti and Jamaica. This placed two vessels, *St. Paul* and *Yale*, at the latter station, not too many for its importance at the moment; but, from later intelligence received at the Department, the *St. Paul's* destination was changed to Key West.

14.   Coincidently with this, Sampson and the Department both telegraphed Remey at Key West with reference to the Cienfuegos blockade; Sampson to have it warned, while the Department directed the withdrawal of all vessels except one to maintain the continuity of the blockade, if possible. Captain McCalla, in charge of that blockade, withdrew all the vessels. The instance is interesting, as showing three different decisions; and also as illustrating that the existence and advice of the Board did not necessarily cramp the initiative of local commanders,—the most dangerous tendency of such a body.

15.   These two principal actions—concentration and the disposition of lookouts—were advised by the Board. As military measures they were too obvious to invite either criticism or commendation. The points to be noted, as part of the experience of the Board, are:

(a)   During Sampson's return to Key West with his division, there were periods long enough to be of importance at such an instant, in which he was out of touch with the situation; whereas the Department, stationary at Washington, could and did receive continual information, and could take necessary steps. Such a condition not only may, but almost certainly will, recur hereafter; for telegrams can always outrun vessels, and in a passage of a week most serious action may need to be taken, for reasons which the Admiral cannot know soon enough. The need of a central authority is evident; that authority is the Government; if it "lack professional experience," it must have a professional adviser. Time and opportunity cannot be lost in deference to the prerogatives of a Commander-in-chief. Respect for the latter will be observed, if there be common sense and tact in the conduct of the central authority; and it may be remarked that the professional sympathy of a competent professional adviser will intuitively avoid needless occasions of friction, which a civilian may not foresee.

(b)   That the fact of the Department's control need not seriously affect the initiative of the Admiral is clear, from the fact that Sampson with his Flagship *New York* left his division, and hastened forward to Key West, just six hours before receiving a telegram from the Department to send thus ahead his most suitable armored ship. The same action was repeated by Captain Evans, whom Sampson had left in command. Soon after the Admiral's departure, there came by dispatch vessel a telegram showing the urgency of the situation. This Evans received. He left the others, and hurried with his own ship, the *Iowa*, to Key West; whence she was dispatched by Sampson to reinforce the Flying Squadron, which she joined twelve hours after it reached Cienfuegos. The entire action of the Department, largely the dissemination of intelligence, was advised by the Board, without in these instances fettering the judgment or injuring the initiative of the officer in command; while its previous action, in acquiescing in the ex-centric movement to San Juan, shows at least consideration for his views and position.

(c)   The present extension of telegraphic systems has modified very seriously the relations of central governments with their functionaries all over the world; as well diplomatic as naval. As regards the latter, however, the change rests chiefly upon the superior facility for receiving and utilizing information, possessed by a stationary authority over one that is moving. Vital adjuncts of the telegraph are the vessels employed in gaining and disseminating intelligence, or in carrying orders; for in war there will always be many points which no telegraph reaches. The experience and history of the Board proved that, in case of war, commanders of such vessels, whether occupying a station for lookout, or on mission, need to be very positively instructed that they individually are parts of an interdependent system; to the efficient working of which it is essential that both the center at Washington, and their particular commander-in-chief, know just where to look for each member. There is a class of mind easily fascinated by the idea of action taken independent of orders, or even contrary to them. That such action is sometimes most commendable is true; but the responsibility taken must be clearly enforced in the general orders issued to each cruiser, that the commander may understand clearly that he will be held to strict account to justify difficulty in finding him, in consequence of such action. The getting and distributing of information is of such prime importance that eccentric movement in a cruiser is much more likely to do harm than good.

(d)   The experience of the Board would go to show that facility for rapid coaling is an essential element in the celerity required of cruisers, and suggests that minute subdivision in compartments sacrifices such rapidity, as well as diminishes space. Also, it might be suggested that not every mission demands headlong speed, and that the efficiency and ultimate coal endurance of a cruiser might be extended, by notifying the commander by what time he was to reach a particular point, e.g.: to be at such a point by such a time, prepared either to observe for so long as possible the enemy's fleet, should it there appear, or to reach a certain point with the news.

16.   Before the first concentration at Key West was effected, it was known that Cervera had appeared off Curaçao and there received some coal. In this there was nothing to change the advice already given, viz: to place one division of armored ships before Havana, and the other before Cienfuegos. The entry of the Spaniards to Santiago was deemed scarcely probable, considering the inaccessibility of the place by land; and this forecast of the Board received justification by the subsequent statement of the Spanish Minister of Marine in the Cortes, that the squadron went there simply because there was no other port to which it could go,—an inability, real or presumed, which the Board could not know. But, even should it go there, the steps to be taken would be precisely as for San Juan de Porto Rico, which had been in the contemplation of the Board. That is, did Cervera enter San Juan, Cienfuegos and Havana being guarded by fighting squadrons, provision had been advised for immediate assembling before San Juan the four or more cruisers, which in the event were placed before Santiago. This number would provide not only for speediest news of the enemy's leaving port, but also for following and reporting the direction taken by him. It was further recommended that two fast cruisers should be held ready at Key West to proceed simultaneously at top speed off Cienfuegos, (two to provide against one breaking down), to dispatch the Flying Squadron off San Juan, should that be thought desirable. I do not recall whether or not this last precaution was taken; I imagine not; there were not cruisers enough available, both for the blockades and for such urgent occasions. It may be permissible here to say, incidentally, that while the strength of a Navy is its battleships, numerous scouts are the eyes and

messengers of the battle force, and form an equally necessary part of war preparation. We had not enough scouts in the war, and had to use torpedo vessels as dispatch vessels.

17. It will be recognized that this action, contemplated for San Juan, was that subsequently taken for Santiago. The question of sending the Havana division to the same point was reserved; Havana being considered the most important of all of the enemy's possible destinations. My own opinion is that, had the Flying Squadron succeeded in anticipating a departure from Porto Rico, the whole of the armored ships would next have been assembled there, as was done at Santiago.

18. From the day, May 22, that the two divisions were assembled before Cienfuegos and Havana, at which latter point the *Oregon* also joined on May 28, up to the concentration of the whole armored fleet (except the *Indiana*) before Santiago, June 1, the action of the Board is reflected in the telegrams; the particulars of which will be found on examination, I think, to show that naval minds were studying the conditions. But, as illustrating the relations of the Department to the Board, it should be said that the language of the telegram of May 27, quoted by ex-Secretary Long in his *New American Navy*, (vol. 1, p. 270), is largely that of the Secretary himself. As regards movements, most, if not all, were in accordance with the advice of the Board; but the peremptory wording, although the Board was in full sympathy with it, was that of the Secretary, who on that occasion sat down in the Board room and himself phrased the telegram. It should be added that, as far as I remember, there was no divergence of opinion between the Department and the Board, as a board, during that trying period of uncertainty as to the movements of Commodore Schley.

19. The telegram just quoted shows that the movement of the Army to Santiago had been decided by May 27, on the strength of information, increasing in probability, that Cervera was there. Commodore Schley, however, did not sight the two Spanish armored vessels until May 29, and the fact was not known in Washington until the evening of that day. Prior to that, our most positive information came through an agent of the Army Signal Corps, in Havana. The feeling of the Board, as I recall it, was that the probabilities all tended to confirm this intelligence; but, while the indications were sufficient to order Schley's division to Santiago, and to impose immediate *preparations* to transport an Army, the possibility of deception made it necessary not to move the latter until more certain. It is almost needless to say that not only the advice of the Board, but the concurrence of the War Department, is shown by the telegram.

20. In consequence of Schley's uncertain course, Sampson was ordered May 29, the same day that Schley's telegram announced seeing the enemy, to go in person to Santiago. His arrival there with the *New York* and *Oregon*, June 1, completed the investment of the port by sea. It is proper

to add that Admiral Sampson's orders so to proceed were at his own personal request. This anticipated the issuance of his orders, but not, I think, the intention of the Department. As I remember, Commodore Schley's vacillating action, as shown by his telegrams, had destroyed the confidence of the Department and of the Board in him, as a Commander-in-Chief.

21.   From the time of Sampson's arrival, the entire management of the blockade, with the accessories of landing the troops and cooperating with the Army, were left to him. That the Department did not abandon its right to supervise is shown by the fact that on the morning of the battle, his absence at the beginning was due to specific orders from Washington to consult personally with General Shafter. A further instance of interference was the order given him to send two fast armored vessels to Key West, to help convoy the Army. This order proceeded from a mistaken report, from two of our cruisers on the north side, that they had seen there at night a large ship of war, with smaller consorts, cruising. Improbable though this seemed, there were two witnesses, who confirmed the report when referred back for confirmation; and so far only two armored Spaniards had been seen in Santiago. The Board was responsible for the advice to reinforce the convoy by two armored ships. Admiral Sampson did not obey the order, having experience of a similar error lately made by an officer of coolness and judgment. The country is indebted to the Admiral for correcting the mistake of the Board; for such it was, though I have not myself been able since to condemn the decision.

22.   While citing these two instances of interference, it seems proper to associate with them the question of moving Admiral Sampson with the *New York* and *Oregon* to Santiago; for this, although first requested by the Admiral, was the act of the Department. I presume that the Department today wishes the history of the proceedings of the Board of 1898 mainly with a view to settle the value and functions of such board hereafter. Ought, then, Admiral Sampson to have asked, and awaited, authority for such a move? or should he have moved at once? Is there any principle at stake which would determine this, limiting or extending the advisory function of a board? or must this and similar cases rest each on its own merits?

23.   On this general question, no formal conclusion was taken nor advice given, by the Board. Had Admiral Sampson been out of telegraphic touch, even for twelve hours, he doubtless would, as Commander-in-chief, have acted in the manner taken. But it seems to me that, in view of the general plan of campaign having to be decided by the Government, a departure from the plan, so serious as the removal of the division from before the principal Cuban port, was a responsibility which the Department, because of its close communication, could not shirk, nor the Commander-in-chief assume. Yet the matter was so immediate in its demand for action, and so entirely interior to the command of the Commander-in-chief, as to

constitute a difficult question. It does not, for instance, stand upon the same ground as the Department's orders to him that the armored ships must not be risked, except upon a reasonable probability of destroying or injuring those of the enemy; for that simply laid down a broad line of general policy, dictated by international conditions, of which the Government must be the sole judge; and, besides, the "reasonable probability" left the Admiral his proper discretion. Nor, again, is it parallel to the decision of the Department to form a squadron out of Sampson's fleet to go to the East after Camara; or that to send the whole fleet to Europe, when Spain seemed inclined to hold out after Cervera's defeat. Both these decisions went outside of Sampson's station, (though they affected his fleet); and, as they appertained to the war as a whole, belonged rightly and solely to the Government.

24. The order to Sampson to send two fast armored vessels to Key West reflects exactly the spirit of the advice given to the Department by the Board concerning the transport of the Army. The defective organization of the transport service, the rawness and probable lack of military interest on the part of the transport captains, and the fact that almost all the immediately available trained troops were to be intrusted to this exposed transit, decided the Board to advise that all the cruisers which could by any possibility be spared from the blockade should be assembled for the convoy. As regards the behavior of the transport captains, in the event,—at the time of landing,—and their need of whipping in, Captain F. E. Chadwick, the Naval Chief of Staff, afterwards wrote, "Great difficulty was experienced through the wretched conduct of the transport captains, who were under no proper control and wandered the sea at will. Hours were spent in finding some of them, and when found they would insist upon laying miles from a shore which they could have approached with safety within a few ship's lengths." (*Encyclopaedia Americana*, 1904, vol. XVI.) It may be imagined what might have occurred, had an alarm of attack started among such men, and the consequent necessity of forestalling the occurrence of such alarm, and of controlling them if it arose. Hence the need of many convoyers, which had to be drawn from the blockaders; for it was not yet possible to use the cruisers on our northern coast, under Commodore Howell, which were afterwards released by Camara's sailing, and by the knowledge that all Cervera's division was in Santiago. The mistaken report, before mentioned, determined merely that the convoy should be still further strengthened by the two armored vessels, despite the inevitable delay thus occasioned. Although little apprehension was actually felt of injury by Spanish gunboats, known to be lurking among the reefs on the north coast of the island, the possibility existed; and they were sure to know of the movement, which would pass close before their stations.

25.   The management of the passage, the order in which the transports and convoying vessels should be formed, and all other details, were left entirely to Captain H. C. Taylor, of the *Indiana*, the senior Naval Officer in the expedition. Is it not most incongruous that the transports did not come under naval direction until they sailed, and then only for convoy? Everything connected with transportation is a particular feature of maritime activity; when of military transportation, of naval activity. Internal discipline of a ship, and proper control of her movements in a convoy, can only be insured by naval organization, and naval command. The committing of transport service to the Army is radically vicious in theory, and directly contrary to the practice of the most experienced nation, Great Britain. It may result disastrously.

26.   The transports sailed from Tampa June 14, and arrived off Santiago June 20. From this time forward, until the destruction of Cervera's squadron and surrender of Santiago, operations about the place were in the hands of the Army and Navy commanders on the spot. During the passage of the convoy, June 16, Camara's division sailed from Cadiz for the East. These two coincident events mark, therefore, the transfer of active intervention on the part of the Department, and of the Board as advisory, back from the West Indies to the Philippines, which after Dewey's victory had required little or no direct action, beyond occasional suggestion. The absence there of an enemy's naval force, the antecedent improbability of a movement, such as Camara's, being pushed to a conclusion, when leaving the seaboard cities of Spain open to the action of the American armored fleet, and the felt expediency of not dividing the latter, but insuring the complete destruction of Cervera,—these three considerations,—had centered attention upon the Spanish West India squadron. Its destruction or paralysis was the surest protection for our interests in the Far East. The *Monterey*, however, had been preparing to reinforce Dewey's squadron, and had sailed from San Francisco June 11, five days before Camara. The *Monadnock* sailed June 25. These two monitors arrived in the Philippines August 4 and 16 respectively; the former having been obliged to put back to Honolulu after leaving that port. But for this mishap it seems fairly probable that the *Monterey* would have reached Dewey before Camara, had he gone on; but the *Monadnock* not, unless favored by his delays.

27.   Whether resulting from necessary preparations, or lack of early forethought on the part of the Department, or its advisers, or from concession to popular alarms, prevalent on the Pacific as on the Atlantic, the tardy despatch of these two vessels has remained on my mind as the only serious oversight chargeable to the Board. Had harm resulted, the question of responsibility would have arisen; and I think it pardonable here again to suggest the consideration of individual responsibility for advice, as contrasted with the corporate responsibility of a Board. It is probable, how-

ever, that a Board previously constituted in time of peace, and permanent in organization, would have entered upon a war with preparations more fully made, with minds familiarized by study of the particular conditions, and a consequent all-round grasp of the situation, and of the recourses open to it under particular circumstances. The Board of 1898 was composed of officers hastily assembled, without previous study of the whole subject; dependent only upon their personal general knowledge of military questions, and confronted with popular demands which they recognized as unreasonable, yet could not wholly disregard.

28. Under the conditions the Board advised that a division of two armored vessels and four cruisers should be at once constituted from Sampson's fleet, to pursue Camara, who in the East would be without a protected harbor, and in force inferior to this proposed. The utmost publicity was allowed to the orders issued to Sampson to this effect; Commodore Watson was hurried with equal publicity to Santiago, to command this detachment; the purpose being avowed to take advantage of Camara's absence, and the unprotected Spanish coast, to bombard some of their principal cities. Everything was done to impart apparent imminency to a movement which it was intended to postpone to the last moment, or until Cervera was destroyed. I trust it may not appear pedantic, if, in considering the effect of all this upon Camara's procedure, I here quote Nelson. "There are those who think, if you leave the Sound open, that the Danish fleet may sail from Copenhagen to join the Dutch or French. I own I have no fears on that subject, for it is not likely that whilst their capital (sea-coast) is menaced with an attack, nine thousand of their best men should be sent out of the Kingdom." The Philippines could not weigh against Cadiz, Málaga, or Barcelona. In fact, had Camara got as far as Ceylon, Watson, appearing before any of those ports, and demanding his recall under penalty of bombardment, would have carried his point. There would have been no bombardment.

29. There here arises, incidentally but inevitably, the question, particularly appropriate to the approaching Hague Conference: should bombardment, or such a kindred measure as the capture of so-called private property at sea, be forbidden? Both, if carried into execution, fall on property which is private in ownership. Which is more humane or more effective, that Camara proceed to deadly battle with Dewey, or that he be recalled under threat of bombardment? Should bombardment take place, under customary notice for withdrawal of non-combatants, which nation is the offender? the one who insists on the fleet's proceeding, or the one who has sought to prevent it? I will not answer my own questions, beyond the general suggestion that the more widely distributed the incidence of the sufferings of war upon a belligerent people, the greater the guarantee for peace; the more speedy also the restoration of peace.

30. As I remember, a number of telegrams passed between the Department and Commodore Dewey, the former suggesting that, should Camara persist, and the *Monterey* not arrive in time, the fleet, having no armored vessel, should leave Manila and be drawn back to meet the *Monterey*; cruisers being sent to seek her on her probable courses, and direct her to a point of junction. Such an expedient is obvious and common; and the *Monadnock*, sailing later, was given a prescribed course which would insure finding her. Coupled with the exposure of the Spanish coast, it could not fail to weigh with the enemy that he would have two monitors to meet; and if successful, after engagement with the fleet they reinforced, must still await Watson.

31. The threat involved in the formation of Watson's division was the proper and only remaining strategic step to take under the circumstances. In the Pacific there was nothing further available to change conditions. What effect the threat had cannot certainly be known, unless the Spaniards should reveal their counsels. A plausible reading of Camara's move would be, that at no time did they intend that there should be between him and Spain a distance as great as that of the United States fleet in the West Indies; that they meant to recall him if, and when, such a threat should pass into execution. For instance, had Watson sailed, diminishing Sampson's force by two armored vessels, probably of the fastest, he would in two days have gone over 500 miles, quite beyond timely return. Camara could then be recalled to Spain, while Cervera took advantage of Sampson's diminished numbers to make his dash. The non-departure of Watson's division could for some days be attributed to its lack of preparation, or to hesitation; and this may have induced the prolonged pow-wows about coaling at Suez. There could be no difficulty in coaling there, outside neutral limits. Shoal water extends far to seaward, and the Mediterranean summer weather is notoriously propitious. Time was there spun out in apparent negotiations for coal, while testing the American intentions about Watson. The subsequent passage of the canal by the division, July 2, being succeeded by its almost immediate return, was at the time to me incomprehensible; but now, in analogy with the above reasoning, it seems possibly to have been a last effort to draw Watson away, and so facilitate Cervera's escape. If so, it should have been made two days sooner, and the passage of the Red Sea begun; but this increased distance might have enabled Watson to reach Spain before Camara could.

32. The question of coaling Camara,—or Watson, had his division gone, —was one that engaged my personal attention closely, and I presume that of other members of the Board; but I cannot recall that any conclusions were reached by it as a body, or tendered as advice. My own opinion at the time was, that anchorage ground could be found off Cadiz, and again off the mouth of the Nile, in the latter case outside neutral limits; and dur-

ing the Civil War I had so often been engaged in coaling in the open, off the Texas coast, at anchor, as to feel assured that in summer at least there would be no difficulty, or even serious delay, due to sea conditions at either of these points. The same is abundantly true of the Straits of Malacca. Of course, I did not then reckon upon such complaisance on the part of any neutral state as was shown to the Russian fleet in its passage to Japan, in 1905.

33.   The general military situation, constituted by Camara's movement eastward, is to my apprehension the most important and instructive of the whole war. Admiral Dewey's fleet, with the probable exception of the *Monterey*, was unarmored; Camara had two armored vessels; while, as compared with Cervera's numbers, the armored vessels under Sampson, counting in Watson's division, did not exceed the proportion which had been recently estimated to be necessary for such a blockade by a board of British admirals. That is, Sampson had not more than enough to distribute properly, allow for necessary absences, or temporary disabilities, and yet be able to meet the enemy in such wise as to assure "annihilation." For such an end, Sampson's monitors, because of their slowness, were useless against armored cruisers; although vessels of the same class, acting defensively, might have shown good fight against Camara's armored ships. The Department was confronted throughout with the dilemma of diminishing Sampson's squadron, with consequent risk of Cervera's escape, or of exposing Dewey to attack by superior force. It is obvious that this danger, and this exposure, existed from the beginning, or at least from the date, whatever it may have been, when Camara was ready; for his fleet occupied an interior position between the two American admirals. It is, however, equally obvious that, the Spanish sea coast cities being inadequately fortified, Spain was continually open to the check which we used, by the menacing organization of a division directed against them. To quote precedents for such a situation, and authorities for the proper course of either party, would be pedantic; but it is open to comment that the same unfortified condition of our own coast imposed the improper station of the Flying Squadron in Hampton Roads, with its consequent too late arrival at Cienfuegos; and also the retention of Howell's vessels in the north, to the narrowing and the comparative ineffectiveness of the commercial blockade of Cuba.

34.   Camara's return through the Canal, July 7, removed all possible apprehension concerning Dewey, while the destruction of Cervera's squadron decided the control of the sea in the Caribbean, and thus the ultimate issue of the war, even should Santiago hold out. The intention still remained to send Watson, and preparations continued; but as it was possible that, in a movement of desperation like Cervera's, Camara might attack him, if he had but two armored vessels, it was thought best now to send the whole armored fleet—except the *Texas* and monitors—to see him through

the Straits of Gibraltar. At no time during the war, or in the advice of the Board, was sight lost of the unfriendly sympathies of several naval powers, and the consequent inexpediency of incurring the weakening of our armored fleet by needless risks. To this action concurred the advisability of getting the armored fleet out of the sweep of the already begun hurricane season; and there was also contemplated the possibility of threatening a sea coast bombardment, should a mistaken feeling of national honor lead Spain to refuse submission to the now evident facts. Admiral Sampson was to continue commander-in-chief until the separation of the two bodies, which presumably would not take place till after the question of bombardment was decided. In order to insure touch with the fleet during passage, should occasion arise to modify its orders, one or more rendezvous were decided, at which dispatch vessels would await it at fixed dates. There was then no wireless.

35.   This expedition became unnecessary; but pending the decision of Spain to open negotiations, and coincident with the preparation of the armored vessels for departure, the Board advised the occupation by the Marine battalion of the Isle of Pines, in order to base thereon a careful patrol of the shoal water between it and Cuba by very small vessels, in furtherance of the blockade. This expedition had already started under command of Captain Goodrich, but on the way turned aside to attack Manzanilla. The island was, therefore, not occupied, but a study of the chart between it and Cuba will show that it would have become necessary to do so had the war continued.

36.   The preceding contains all that I am now able to supply of the advice of the Board, which constitutes the history of its work; and of the reasons for that advice, which represented its conclusions upon the successive situations of the war.

37.   I recall only one subject of particular importance upon which the Board was directed to advise, outside the immediate operations of the war, and that was upon coaling stations abroad. Senator Chandler of New Hampshire came in informally one day, to ask whether any definite views on this general subject had been reached. It was not within the understood scope of the Board's duties; but a special order of the Department subsequently required a report, which was submitted. I believe a copy now exists in the records of the Board. The Bureau of Equipment had a plan of its own, which I afterwards saw mentioned in the press; and I gained the impression that the Bureau had been governed chiefly by views of convenient distribution and economical efficiency, whereas the plan of the Board had looked to the question of military security and military action. Each conclusion might naturally be expected from the particular function of a Bureau and a War Board.

38.   It was in connection with this report, I think, that the Board made

and submitted a study of the defensible character of the anchorage at St. Thomas. A high estimate was expressed of the facility for defenses, as a coaling station, or even as a base of operations; near to Porto Rico, but much superior to its harbors. Such a study trenched on the province of the sea-coast military engineer, and would require his consideration; but it satisfied me that, if practicable, St. Thomas ought to be acquired by the United States in support of our general Caribbean position, and of Porto Rico in particular.

39. It will be readily understood that, in preparing this report, I have not been able after such a lapse of time to distinguish absolutely between my personal opinions and reasons of the Board, as such. I believe, however, that no substantial mistake has been made, and that I have not intruded as official the specifically personal points of view which I elaborated in my *Lessons of the War with Spain*, immediately after the events.

40. It may be permissible, and advantageous to the object of my present orders, to mention some matters that impressed themselves on my personal observation:

(a) On at least one occasion, feeling was manifested by a Chief of Bureau, because instructions to him concerning the dispatch of stores conveyed no knowledge on which he personally could base estimates and requirements, other than those indicated by the Department upon advice of the Board. It is obvious that such a view raises the question whether, not one, but all the Bureau Chiefs, administrative officers, should know the military movements contemplated by the Department, and how far such disseminated knowledge would consist with secrecy. Personally I found some difficulty in maintaining secrecy; not against press agents, to whom a flat refusal could be given, but against persons whose position commanded a certain deference, yet who questioned closely, and apparently thought themselves entitled to a reply.

(b) As regards press indiscretions: There should be a specified organ for giving such information as may be thought proper. Except this, all officers should be forbidden, not merely to give information, but to converse with any one on matters pertaining to the war. It protects a man,— and more important still, the country,—to be able to allege orders. A similar censorship should be established in each fleet. Possibly all leaks cannot be stopped, but the information distributed to the enemy by press indiscretions, through lack of supervision, can be much controlled. We may thank the Japanese for proving this.

(c) In matters touching the advice given by the Board to the Secretary concerning the conduct of the war, the Board cannot but be in certain relations, though wholly indirect, to Bureau Chiefs, to Commanders-in-chief, and to cruisers, regarded as part of the general intelligence system. The consequent attitude of the Department, the division of responsibilities and powers, need to be thought out, and formulated with some precision, antecedent to war.

(d)   As a matter of general strategical conclusion, nothing was more powerfully shown than the necessity of proper coast defense, as complementary to naval offensive action. In a popular government, it is of no avail to try and calm people's fears by rational military considerations. They clamor to be visibly defended. This is now the debated naval question in Australia. But, irrespective of popular outcry, the Navy should support generously the requirements of sea-coast defense, in the interest of its own freedom of action.

(e)   It should be remembered always that the Board of 1898 was an entirely new creation, extemporized on the moment for an urgent felt necessity. As a body, it had had no previous connection with the preparations of the Government, nor influence upon them; and the association with them of the individual members had been slight. The Board therefore approached the questions submitted to it without a formulated policy,—other than such knowledge as its members possessed of the leading principles of war,—and without previous mature consideration of the effect of this or that disposition on the whole theater of war,—of the relations of the parts to the whole. Among conflicting opinions of capable men,—and there were conflicts,—and divers considerations of policy, the Board had only the general leading principles just spoken of to guide it; it began with no digested appreciation of those special conditions, in the two countries, which might modify the application of principles. An example much in point is the retention of the Flying Squadron in Hampton Roads. On the one hand, this squadron quieted people as to defense; on the other, it arrived off Cienfuegos so late that Cervera could have entered there; within rail communication of Havana, and in support of an Army, to overcome which would have needed much more force than the division sent to Santiago. In other words, to quiet the people as to sea-coast safety, hostilities might have been prolonged by a year. Fortunately, the war was short and simple. Had it lasted longer, with a more efficient enemy, there could not but be mistakes, which careful previous study would have prevented.

Some Practical Considerations Concerning the Spiritual Life

An Address Before the Episcopal Church Club of Philadelphia

Philadelphia, February 25, 1907 [LC]

Perhaps the very first most practical consideration concerning the spiritual life is to ascertain whether we really believe that there is such a thing; that life spiritual is a substantial reality, as real, as vital, as susceptible as life physical is of beginning, of growth, and of death. Whatever spiritual death may mean, do we really believe there is such a thing? However spiritual growth may manifest itself, do we, do you, each one of you, or any particular one of my hearers to-night, believe that there is such a vital process; to be wrought in us day by day as really as are the physical changes of increasing years, or those induced in our bodies and our corporal functions by the observance or non-observance of the laws of bodily health? Unless you so believe, the matter evidently does not concern you; but if you do, are you, each one, as a practical man observing a course of life which fosters spiritual growth, and will therefore result in the attainment of a spiritual efficiency so strong as to carry, by the grace of God and the power of the Resurrection of Jesus Christ, the promise of eternal life?

For, in the practical issue, I presume the life everlasting, in which we affirm our belief as often as we repeat the Creed, may be considered as a condition of spiritual efficiency, dependent upon union with God through Jesus Christ. This is maintained by the habitual coöperation of our will with His; and, so assured, progresses endlessly towards the perfection of God, to which, being Infinite, our individual life can indeed never attain, but towards which it may continually approach. The mathematical and philosophical conception of the Infinite, of Infinity, which is absolute in God only, is metaphysical in character; but it is extremely practical for this purpose. It supplies to Eternity an adequate motive and an adequate employment, viz: increase in the knowledge of God and in likeness to Him; a process endless in duration, because the finite created being, though he may continually approach, yet can never attain. And if some caviller would say that such subjective development of the individual self is no worthy aim,— and there is a superabundance of such idle talk in this day,—let it be remembered that God is unceasing benevolent activity. He is Love, not quiescent, but active; and the more we are like Him, through spiritual growth, the more active for good shall we continually be. The Only Begotten Son, the Son of His Love, affirmed, "My Father worketh hitherto, and I work." The sons of adoption shall be like Him,—like the Only Begotten; He without limit or measure, we according to our measure, a measure increasing continually, world without end. Amen.

If such be the practical issue of eternal life, an ever progressive increase in the knowledge of God,—and our Blessed Lord Himself has affirmed that to know the only true God and Jesus Christ Whom He has sent *is* eternal life,—it is surely worth while for us as practical men, with a big proposition before us, to clear our heads as to what we believe, and then to ask ourselves how far our individual life, as now ordered, is calculated practically to favor the growth of spiritual life. The first thing is to be sure that we do believe in the spiritual life with a certain distinctness of grasp; practice follows on belief. Had we it not on the best authority that Faith is the foundation of Christian life; that he who begins by coming to God must believe that He is; had we not learned this by revelation, our own experience of life would affirm it to us. The man of profound convictions is the most potent worker; when doubt enters, the knees become feeble and the hands hang down.

Of course, no one will affirm that conviction necessarily rests upon refined intellectual processes,—upon them only. Daily experience would refute such a statement; and to such processes many persons are unequal, who nevertheless may and do hold the essentials of the faith with a tenacity and clearness which colors their whole life. Nevertheless, to those who can think efficiently, it remains a practical, and an imperative, task to do some thinking, in order that to the extent of their ability, they may clearly apprehend, and so the more intelligently guide their course of life. Understanding facilitates and betters any action we undertake; the failure to exercise understanding by servants is one of our greatest troubles; and, moreover, to seek to understand is part of that love we servants owe to God, to love Him with all our mind, which I apprehend to mean not merely our purpose, but our intellect.

How then are we to conceive of the spiritual life? There is a tendency on the part of many to represent the manifestations which we recognize as spiritual as being merely indications of bodily action. Some good people, it has been said,—I believe by Sydney Smith,—think they are pious when they are only bilious. There are again those of whom we have had painful illustration lately, who practically revive the old heresy of the essential evil of the body; going so far as to affirm a horror of a bodily resurrection, and of the idea that our Lord Jesus Christ now exists in bodily form, in glorious body. Human opinion seems to shuttlecock back and forth between

[645]

a qualified materialism, which traces all spiritual feeling to physical processes, and a false spiritualism which, recognizing the drag of the present body of our humiliation upon spiritual action, its perpetual rebellion, rejects with contumely the hope of the glorified body. This school of thought not only does not expect, it does not wish, the fulfilment of the promise that if the Spirit of Him that raised up Jesus from the dead dwell in you, He that raised up Christ from the dead shall also quicken your mortal bodies —give life to these bodies of humiliation.

At this point of writing I was tempted for a few moments to a digression, which might have led me farther than I purposed, in order to consider the relations of the spiritual life to the physical, and wherein consists that unity which embraces both. But such discussion, even were I fitted for it, is evidently inconsistent with my theme, which is the practical bearings of the spiritual life, and of our own actions as affecting it. It is sufficient for such practical object to note the duality internal to us, to which our own consciousness bears witness; the perpetual conflict which St. Paul characterizes as the lusting of the flesh against the spirit and of the spirit against the flesh. This antithesis appears in another form in our Lord's summary statement, "Except a man be born again, he cannot enter into the kingdom of God." The unity, which embraces in itself both the natural and the spiritual life, is, I apprehend, conserved and affirmed by the phrase "a man"; while the dual creature, thus embraced in the unity, is expressed by the words "that which is born of the flesh is flesh, and that which is born of the Spirit is spirit." But birth is not maturity. Birth necessarily involves progress, growth; or else it may involve decay and death. As in natural life, so in the spiritual; too many die in infancy, whatever their earthly years.

Spiritual growth on the one hand, resulting in an ever increasing knowledge of God, in an ever increasing Godlikeness, in activities ever increasing in scope and excellence to the ages of ages; or on the other hand spiritual decay and death, which means at the least the cessation and loss of all these possibilities, even if it do not further mean continual recession in the opposite direction, away from God, under the impulse of that lower nature which lusteth against the Spirit; against the Divine Spirit, and equally against that spiritual existence born in us at Baptism. From and in consequence of this perpetual departure is a continual development of the evil propensities— establishing and widening the "great gulf fixed."

I have drawn as strongly as I can, consistently with sobriety of language, the comprehensive results of spiritual growth and spiritual decay; for, in considering a matter of practical conduct, it is unquestionably practical to consider the issue—the outcome. The two great alternatives had to be stated, because my theme is the bearing of daily life upon them. Let me next as a practical matter draw your attention to the potency of spirit over matter, a consideration which I do not think enters at all sufficiently into those intellectual processes, those meditations or reflections, formal or spontaneous, which should in some manner characterize and shape the conduct of an earnest Christian. I say the potency of spirit over matter, the moulding of the flesh by the spirit, when duly nourished by devotional life. In order of time I presume the spiritual birth in man follows the natural birth. Our Lord's expression "born again," implies subsequency; and I apprehend that when St. Paul says, "first that which is natural, afterwards that which is spiritual," the affirmation holds not merely of the spiritual body, of which he is immediately speaking, but also of the order in which the completeness of man's being is constituted,—first natural, then spiritual. Nevertheless, it is written, "the elder shall serve the younger"; not otherwise can there be perfection.

The potency of spirit over matter. Think! God is a Spirit; God's word brought matter into existence, the first great and utterly incomprehensible miracle. Truly, as we contemplate that, we may echo St. Paul's words, "Why should it be thought incredible that God should raise the dead?" That first great sign of God's power, the mere existence of the universe, dwarfs in its grandeur every other sign recorded. We were not privileged to witness this, though we have before us always those processes of nature to which St. Paul appealed, as evidence of the "invisible things of God." Concerning these, however, it is possible to waste our understandings by halting upon the laws of nature, which it is perfectly conceivable may have been impressed unchangeable upon matter from the beginning. I do not myself so read Scripture; but granting to the fullest that the universe runs on lines of secondary causes, let us go back of them to the one great fact of the mere existence of matter. Spirit made it, and having made afterwards fashioned it, and the power which so wrought inheres in our own spiritual life, which according to our measure derives from God. Why emasculate our Lord's words, "If ye have faith, ye shall say to this mountain remove, and it shall remove." Of course, it needs but a moment's thought to see that such power is inconsistent with a capricious exercise, a mere wanton putting forth, a getting a mountain out of the way as a kind of circus show, or resort of indolence. God, the Spirit, is not capricious; the spirit born from Him cannot but be like Him. The perfect Man, the elder Brother of us all, expressed this necessity; this to Him limit of possibility: "Man does not live by bread alone." He in whom the Spirit dwelt without measure was incapable of capricious action, or of impatience of God's time. Yet, when occasion demanded, He, the Man, sharing at the moment the body of our humiliation, put in exercise the power of Spirit over matter; I need not in this company recall instances.

So, in the Virgin Birth, it is a strong argument that this action of Spirit upon matter was congruous to the occasion; corresponded in method to the character and singularity of the fact to be accomplished: the Incarnation of God. This congruity is indeed an important element in the belief in the Virgin Birth. As a matter of human testimony, however satisfactory may be the demonstration that the record in the Gospels is contemporary with the life of those who knew the Virgin, the establishment of the conditions of the Conception rests, humanly speaking, upon her sole evidence, and can rest nowhere else. It receives important circumstantial confirmation, however, in the fact that the definitions as to the nature and Being of Jesus Christ, made in the Creeds and Councils, were not framed specially to safeguard the Virgin Birth. It was not in dispute, yet the definitions given by the Creeds are consistent only with the condition of such birth. They are incompatible with mere human generation. In this view, the Virgin Birth was no capricious manifestation of power, but a necessary action of Spirit upon matter, of which the Incarnation is a direct, unmediated, instance.

The spirit of man is born of the Spirit of God, and to the measure of God's purpose, and of the man's correspondence to that purpose, shares also the power of spirit over matter. Let us, therefore, pass from the striking and singular instances of Creation, of the fashioning of the Earth, of the Incarnation, the works of the Spirit we call God, to one which touches the generality of our common human nature, which is indeed in line with the action of the grace of God that comes to every man. Take Inspiration. I am not going into any such thorny question as defining Inspiration, its particular method, quality, quantity, or degree. These are matters of argument, concerning which I see little prospect of finality; but, whatever the method or degree, this we may very surely hold: that Inspiration is a message from God the Spirit to man; that its first recognizable condition is thought; and that thought is a movement of matter, of the brain tissues. Whether the process is by communion of the Spirit of God to the spirit of man in the invisible hidden recesses of personality, or whether it is the direct action of the Divine Spirit upon the material organ, the brain, matters little. Personally, I believe that the vision of angels, or significant dreams such as recorded in the Bible, are the result of a brain process directly caused by the action of the Divine Spirit on the matter of the brain; and I believe also there are occasions now when a timely message in words is conveyed to man, by such direct action, traversing the line of his own thought in such wise as to forbid attributing its origin to himself,—to his precedent mental action. As a case in point, many will recall St. Augustine's recorded experience, in his agony of hesitation about forsaking his sin and giving himself to God, hearing the words, "Take up and read," with the consequences thereof. The case is more complicated where prolonged thought issues in sudden light upon the particular problem; the action of the human personality is more apparent. He who has been seeking has found. His own spirit is implicated, has coöperated in a spiritual process acting on the matter of the brain, the issue being to him a revelation. But there are indisputably cases where the suggestion is in subject and characteristics out of line with the course and direction of the man's perplexities or aspirations at the moment; where for a solution we are driven back upon mere chance, or upon the direct unmediated action of God the Spirit. This is as true now as ever it was; as true of the humblest child of God to whom it may happen, as of a prophet like Isaiah; to both it is Inspiration.

Is such action of the Divine Spirit therefore irrespective of the man's conduct, because in the particular instance there is no direct connection between its manifestation and his momentary occupation; perhaps even with his usual tone of mind? Is it, so to say, arbitrary on the part of God? I think not; for if it be thus, there would seem no motive for us to entertain those practical considerations concerning the spiritual life towards which I am working. It is true there have been instances of sudden and permanent conversion, by mental impressions produced by the Spirit upon men hitherto apparently godless. We do not need to explain exceptions; yet to me it seems clear that in them the man's future has been to God present, and that that future justified and demanded His inspirative message. "Whom He did foreknow, them He did predestinate"; whether to be conformed to the image of His Son, or, like Pharaoh, to be lifted up as a conspicuous example of what may betide him who to ten messages hardens his heart. The case of Pharaoh is a usual one of repeated opportunities, whether embraced or neglected; and the issue is in accordance with the man's own action. There is in the vast majority of cases such preparative action on the part of man, conducive or inimical to the growth of the spiritual life; of that life which holds in it the promise of the future here as well as hereafter; promise not only of the world to come, but also of effect upon the material conditions of this present world. "Manifold more in this present world," are our Lord's own words; and His servant repeats, "Godliness is profitable in all things, having the promise of the world that now is and also of that which is to come." I hope it is not necessary here to say that the promise, of the world that now is, is not of those things which are valued by this present world which is not God's; the world the standards of which we have renounced in our baptism.

May we not, however, believe that Christ's promise for this present world is that of a growing *conformity* of the sin-stricken flesh, of the body of our humiliation, to the redeemed and progressive spiritual life? Such correspondence of the body to the spirit the Gospel speaks of as liberty. "The creature itself shall be delivered from the bondage of corruption into the glorious *liberty* of the children of God." Like our common word contentment, liberty is a correspondence between the environment and the man, the result of spiritual discipline, the power of the spirit reacting on the flesh, and, it may be permitted to believe, changing even our present mortal bodies. Is not this an inspiring practical thought? Conscious of the frequent depressing influence of the flesh upon the spiritual life, do we give broad enough interpretation to the words, "The Spirit shall quicken your mortal bodies?" Raise them at the last day, doubtless; but no more? Is the Spirit incapable of so affecting the flesh here in this life, as to make it more obedient to the man's spirit? its own processes more conducive to spiritual excellence? Consider what we call moods, in which we accurately recognize reflex action of bodily conditions. Dare we not hope, and that reasonably, that the Spirit may alter these conditions, conforming moods more and more to the Spirit of Christ? Must we limit, to the great deliverance of the general Resurrection, the promise that "the creature shall be delivered from the bondage of corruption into the glorious *liberty* of the children of God?" This liberty will be the entire conformity of the spiritual body to the demands of the Spirit; the ending of the bondage, of the struggle between the Spirit and the flesh. May not the enfranchisement begin here? If this be incredible, how account for the miracles of Christ, healing the bodily ills of the sick?

Preparation therefore becomes us, and it is a very practical matter, for the issues are great and certain. The practical consideration for each one of us is that in our daily life we are working up to a day of judgment; a day of opportunity greater or smaller, but as decisive in results to us personally as was the call to St. Paul, or to the Pharaoh of the Exodus. St. Paul was, so to speak, taken by the shoulders and whirled suddenly right round; in a moment, in the twinkling of an eye, as at the last trump. Such was the outer fact that arrests our attention, but what the inner history? Honest purpose, though ignorantly in unbelief; faithful to the truth he saw; no slack hand in the work, but breathing out threatenings and slaughter; persecuting evil as he saw it even to strange cities; relentless in stamping out. In faithfulness to duty, in zeal towards God, as he himself says, there was as little of half service in St. Paul before his conversion, as there was when he became the chosen vessel, instrumental beyond all men in extending the faith which once he destroyed. Unconscious of the issue, as any one of you now listening may be of the opportunity towards which you are moving, St. Paul's life had been one long preparation of faithfulness to the right he knew, and in such condition to him came the day of opportunity which is a day of judgment. He was faithful on the way to Damascus; he was faithful when he stood before Festus; and how practical his fidelity tested by the issue! the servant of the five talents administering the same. So the overthrow of Pharaoh was the sudden coming of the day, up to which daily obstinacy and rejection had been leading.

"After a long time the Lord of those servants cometh and reckoneth with them." We are quite right in thinking of a day of final reckoning, whatever of imagery we attribute to our Lord's words concerning it; but we are wrong in failing to see in the spiritual life that recurrent opportunity we so continually note in earthly life, taken at the flood or missed. Opportunity is reckoning, is judgment. It shows where the man stands in temporal affairs or in spiritual. It is a question of character rather than of means; yet of both, just as heredity and environment, the past and the present, both have their share in shaping destiny. Have you ever thought, in the parable of the talents, of the force of the word "trading"? how much every man had gained by trading? The little gains of the shopkeeper, we have had thousands of cases in our country,—dollar by dollar laid up, yard by yard sold, article by article fashioned, and so building up little by little, not only nor chiefly capital, which is the means, but character also, which is efficiency. At last, suddenly, comes a great opportunity, or a great crisis; the present tests the past; to-day judges yesterday; the Lord cometh and reckoneth. Then how much has been gained by trading tells; the opportunity can be improved, or the crisis tided over, because of what day by day has been gained by trading. Nay, more important, the man himself has been built up, or undermined, as the case may be, for the opportunity which meets and tests him,—a day of judgment because one of opportunity.

That it is so in the spiritual life we have assurance from our Lord's using the parallel. Spiritual efficiency is the demand. The call for chosen vessels! How in the business world the cry goes up for chosen vessels, fit men, and how few they are compared to the demand; the men of one talent, and often also of more, drifting idly, neglecting to use, neglecting to trade with the same. And we shall miss the full lesson of the parable if we fail to see that the man of five talents, and the man of one, are not always separate individuals. The same man often has five talents in one direction, and but one in another; a test doubly searching. It is easy to say let the one go, and pay attention only to the five. St. Paul apparently concedes of himself, at least in some degree, that his bodily presence was weak and his speech contemptible,—one talent; his letters weighty and powerful, five talents, which have been rolling up at compound interest for now twenty centuries. Yet he abandoned not preaching, and for one listener who in his own life heard one of his letters, a hundred must have heard speeches such as those on Mars Hill, the farewell address to the elders of Ephesus, or his apologia before Festus and Agrippa.

The secret of success in spiritual trading is of course the clear and single eye to God's service. When a man is content that God should reap—so to seem, for it is not true—reap where He has not sown, content that to God there should be abundant return for a seemingly small gift; when the steady cry of his heart is, "Not unto me, Oh Lord! not unto me, but unto Thy Name be the praise," he cannot be slack in trading. That there shall be abundant harvest unto God will be motive enough; that God is pleased, reward enough. Yet how attain this most practical of working spirits, a loving heart? how penetrate the open secret, and make it one's own sure guide, that there is no motive so powerful as love, nor reward so satisfying as loving. What condition of mind and heart so efficient spiritually—or in the natural world —as loving? How then as a practical matter shall we attain unto it?

We say that Love is independent of man's will; it comes and it goes, like the wind, blowing where it listeth. Is this quite true? Have we not a very trite proverb about propinquity? I do not mean indeed to assert that that apt expression of common experience summarizes all truth on a weighty matter; but I do maintain that it is a lump of raw ore with an unusually large percentage of pure gold. For the gist of the proverb is that where the raw material for loving exists, communion with a fitting object will bring it to life and quicken life into flame. In every man exists the raw material, the capacity for loving God; in God Himself is the fitting object. "Thou hast made us for Thyself, and our hearts find no rest save in Thee."

I fear I have made weary the road we have traveled to bring you to the goal of practical action in order to gain spiritual efficiency. Communion with God will quicken love to God, kindling love into flame; into a passion and a force which, to manifest its devotion, demands expression in act, and finds content, perfect satisfaction, in the simple thought of Him who is loved. This may sound more mystical than practical, but it is not; it is just as practical, and much more so, than a mother's love for her child. Who by universal admission, of unbeliever as of believer, is the greatest of human characters, and has brought about the greatest result—in practical effect? Jesus Christ. What His human secret? "My meat, the support of my life, is to do the will of Him who sent Me." "I do always the things that please Him." This the motive, this the happiness of work; this the daily deed; and the reward,—constant communion: "The Father has not left Me alone." It is the echo of the early promise to the father of all the faithful. God said unto Abraham, not only "I am thy Shield,"—that is, I will not leave thee alone,—but more: "I—Myself—am thine exceeding great reward." So St. Paul, the most effective of all Christ's servants, reveals the spring of his efficiency, "I count all things but loss for the excellency of the knowledge of Christ Jesus my Lord." With such examples we need not hesitate to paraphrase the words of St. John: Jesus Christ is the First and the Last; the Alpha of motive, the Omega of reward.

Jesus Christ, yes; for in order that we might the more certainly enter into communion with God, God has in Christ revealed Himself unto us in terms of human flesh, terms which we can understand to the full measure of our mental and spiritual faculties. It is as though God had been translated from some strange foreign tongue into one understood of the people. In the Man Jesus Christ, in His Life, His Acts, His Words, stands revealed to us the brightness of God's glory and the express image of His Person, to the utmost extent that a sinless human nature can manifest them. Thus we can enter into communion with Him; can apprehend, if we cannot comprehend; can advance in knowledge, drawing near continually; increasing in love as in communion; increasing thereby in efficiency; beginning and maintaining here the approach which all the long ages of eternity can never complete.

Here is the way; how shall we enter in? Has our will nothing to do with love? Ah! we may not be able to make ourselves love; but we cannot help loving if we will draw near, if we will commune, if we will learn. There is our fault; the fault very especial to our own times, though by no means confined to them only. Because we cannot do God's part of that great communion, cannot bring love into being, we will not do ours. How unpractical! Indeed what unpractical folly, to forego the power and the delight of loving the All Worthy by mere neglect of simple things we can do. Not long ago I had occasion to ask a Christian, ill and in distress of mind: Do you ever read the Bible? No. How much time do you give to prayer? Ten minutes. No time to hear what God has to say to you, and ten minutes of communion from you to Him. What preparation is that for a day of reckoning?

Consider what an armory of instruments for communion with God His prophetic love has fashioned for us in the New Testament; in the Psalter; in the less difficult of the prophets, notably Isaiah. These chiefly; yet throughout the Old Testament, how often and unexpectedly light flashes out of darkness. Take that word from the Proverbs, "The path of the just is as the shining light which shineth more and more unto the perfect day." Beautiful! but who dare claim for himself the deserts or the reward of the just. Change it a little, a most lawful change; The path of the Just One, the way in which Jesus Christ walked, is as the shining light; and we can follow, though far off, and following we shall find the light grow more and more; a precise analogue with the slow gains of the trader, though a metaphor far more lovely. In His Word God communes with us, speaks to us messages apt to the varying fortunes of life; for courage, for endurance, for joy, for thankfulness. Then again the liturgy of the Church, especially the collects, supply a wealth of formulated prayer, ready to practised lips— but not to the neglectful—in those dark hours when the surge of temptation, or sorrow, or weariness, reduces almost to nothing the mental power to frame prayers. With what face can we expect God to be even able to help us to make a good fight, if we have neglected to master such resources. People speak of reading as formal, of prayer as formal. It is a commonplace to remark on the power of forms; but the true point of view is that such daily use is a slow process of accumulation of spiritual stores available in a day of visitation—whether of grief or joy.

Let us be practical and recur to the thought of trading. As unmarked days succeed one another, there may be the constant turning over of our spiritual capital by repeated acts of communion, even apparently formal. The daily reading, the daily prayer, the daily thought, the daily watchfulness over acts, to conform them to Christ's words; all this organized as a careful man organizes his business. They seem little, these little gains, but they roll up spiritual capital of knowledge, of habits, of prayer, of trained powers ready to be put forth on demand. In such quiet patience of effort, in such long trading, you are, to use our Lord's words, "winning your souls," your personality, for Jesus Christ; foot by foot, step by step, like the Israelites of old, you are entering in and possessing that good land, your personality, with all its undeveloped possibilities, which the Lord your God has given you. You are doing it not for yourself, but for Him; holding the ground won as a feudal retainer held his land for military service, to your Lord. And, though unmarked by striking event, the progress is hard enough, God knows; but then are you not pleasing Him? And is not that thought both motive and reward? Believe you will find it so, for experience demonstrates it. No matter how weary the flesh drags, He knoweth it all. When all seems deadest, the greater His delight in you; for He has shared the burden, knows its weight; and though footsore and weary the ground is being won. For yourself perhaps it seems almost useless, scarcely worth while; but then, for Christ? Surely, surely.

And then at last comes the day of reckoning, of some stern contest, a storm in which the winds blow, and the rains descend, and the floods come and beat upon the house. The days of small things are brought to the test of a great day. Recall again our Lord's words concerning him who digged deep, with pick and spade, penetrating deeply into the words of Christ, and founding the house of his spiritual fortunes upon this constant communion with Him. It fell not, for it was founded upon the Rock, the rock of Christ's words and Christ's Being, not neglected, but pondered, prayed over, acted upon, and made one's own. Then, though the waters of trial rage and swell, and the mountains quake at the tempest of the same, "the rivers of the flood thereof shall make glad the City of God; the holy place where the Most High tabernacles." "Then the righteous shall shine forth as the sun in the kingdom of the Father." The great cloud of witnesses shall rejoice, not only over the fighter himself, but still more in Him to Whom after all the victory redounds; and the victor shall celebrate the triumph in the self-forgetting words: Blessed be the Lord, my Strength! which teacheth my hands to war and my fingers to fight; my Hope and my Fortress; my Castle and Deliverer; my Defender; in Whom I trust; Who subdueth my people—all my faculties and my powers—that are under me.

Such are the rare great days for which the little days prepare, which indeed their littleness has rehearsed. Concerning them let me note one thing: that at such times words of Jesus Christ, often ill understood before, perhaps, as has been my own case, accepted by sheer authority asd scarcely thought practicable, clear up extraordinarily. Light shines where before no light was, and just at the moment of need; the Spirit touches the brain, the mortal body is quickened. But I must hasten to end. How far is our modern practice, nay our accepted modern standards, conformed to the very practical requirements of daily preparation? Our Sundays, our church going, our communions, our private prayer and reading of God's words, the ordered habits of our Christian life? Is it not a sign ominous of failure in the day of reckoning that not only is there neglect, or a miserable apportionment of such ordered effort at communion; but that this neglect is being formulated into recognized standards which minimize the importance of these things? worst of all, under the specious misleading plea of organized institutional benevolence being the first great duty of Christianity? Let us at least consider these matters carefully. If a man will work for God he must love Him: if he would love Him, he must know Him; if he would know Him, he must commune with Him. For spiritual advancement there must be spiritual communion; for spiritual growth there must be spiritual sowing and watering. There can be no reason to hope that the law concerning time and prayer will differ from that concerning money. "He that soweth sparingly shall reap also sparingly, and he that soweth plenteously shall reap also plenteously." Conditions indeed differ with individuals, but here also we have our rule: "If there be first a willing heart, it is accepted; according to that a man hath, and not according to that he hath not." There is a widow's mite of time, as well as of money. Unhappily, men and women with abundant time think a mite of it enough; look at our Sundays and our churches, and let each man search his own private devotion. What is our personal rule in this matter? and how by our words are we affecting the course of thought? a most serious practical question. Are we keeping on the whole armor of God that we may be able to stand in the evil day, the day of reckoning? or in present sunshine have we laid it aside, and encouraged others to do the same, trusting we can hurry it on when the enemy appears? If we are, we shall find, like David, that we have not proved it. David's stone was the widow's mite; its efficacy does not excuse the fully equipped warrior from his armor. It is too late to dig down to the rock when the flood is already roaring down the valley; to try to uplift our hearts with the war songs of Zion, the trumpet tones of Scripture, in the strange land of unfamiliarity to which we have exiled ourselves. He that is godly makes his prayer in a time when God may be found; otherwise, in the great water floods they shall not come nigh him. If the Lord by our willing choice has been continually on our right hand, we shall find Him still there, covering our heads, in the day of battle; but if we have forgotten or ignored communion with Him, His love indeed will not be less, nor His ear heavy, nor His arm shortened, but we shall find ourselves in the pitiable condition which the prophet characterizes as stumbling at noonday as in the night; starving in the midst of plenty; defenceless amid the abundance of weapons which we have not proved; our house left unto us desolate, for Jesus has gone out and departed from the temple of him who would have none of Him.

Excerpt from a Statement
to the American Movement[1]

Bad Nauheim, Germany, circa May 28, 1907[2]

The Power of the Gospel of our Lord is, I believe, signally manifested in this particular step. . . . As I believe that Englishmen and Americans when distant from home find themselves less distinctively party men, and more purely and simply national in feeling, so I believe that in the activities of the mission field, face to face with conditions alien to Christ, Christians will ultimately find the solution of the worst of our home problems—namely, our corporate separateness from one another. . . . I beg to join my own appeal to that which my friends and the organization behind them are about to make to our brethren in Great Britain.

---

1. This organization, dedicated to lay and foreign missions, invited Mahan to attend its meeting in Queens Hall, London, on May 28. He explained that his physician would not allow him to attend the meeting, but he sent a statement, the full text of which has not been found.
2. From *The Times*, London, May, 30, 1907. Among these who contributed statements of support were Silas McBee and Elihu Root.

[657]

The Advantages of Subig Bay Over Manila
as a Base in the Philippine Islands

Lawrence, Long Island, October 25, 1907 [NWC]

1. The question of the defense of the Philippine Islands assumes differing phases according as the United States has as an enemy (1) a European or (2) an Asiatic power.

2. If the enemy be a European power, operations in the Philippines will play a minor part in the war and will not have a material effect upon its ultimate result; moreover, there will be no such disparity in the strength of the contending fleets in Asiatic waters as will give to the enemy that control of the sea which alone could justify him in risking his ships in an attack upon land defenses.

3. If the enemy be an Asiatic power, the main theater of war will be in Asiatic waters, and the fate of the Philippines may decide the terms of peace. Such an enemy might be expected to have the advantage of overwhelming superiority in the strength of his fleet at the outbreak of hostilities and would hold such superiority for a period of at last three months—the time required to transfer our main fleet to Asiatic waters. If, during this period, he can capture our naval base in the Philippines, destroy the drydock, coal-pile, machine-shops, and other means of maintenance of our fleet, so that our ships upon arrival would find no sources of supply or repair (the facilities of neutral ports being closed to them), the effectiveness of our naval force would be crippled in a manner that would undoubtedly have an important bearing upon the outcome of the war.

4. It is therefore evident that, so far as relates to the Philippines, defense against an Asiatic enemy is the most important requirement, and that the United States must have in the islands at least one port capable of withstanding, for a considerable period, powerful combined attacks by land and sea, wherein may be sheltered the inferior force of American naval vessels together with the drydock and other resources of the fleet, and at which may be rallied, for their own protection and for contributing to the defense, all the land forces in the islands. In other words, all available means of defense must be concentrated in holding this one point against the enemy until the arrival of the Atlantic Fleet relieves the situation and places the United States in control of the sea. Until the United States possesses such

a stronghold, it is considered that all available funds should be devoted to creating one,—that division of appropriations for the installation of defenses of minor value at several different places would be a fatal mistake, clearly equivalent to the action of the commander of a military force who, scattering his units before going into action in such manner that only one part could be engaged at a time, laid open each part to defeat in detail.

5. Accepting the view that every effort must be devoted to creating one impregnable port, it follows that the port chosen must be that one which, regardless of nonmilitary considerations, lends itself most readily to defense; and this, it is contended, is Subig Bay. This bay has its entrance divided into two parts by Isla Grande; the channel to the eastward of the island is but 0.5 mile wide, and, having a maximum depth of 6 fathoms, could be completely and effectively blocked by mines, in which case there would be needed for its protection only a mine-defense battery of small caliber guns; or it might even be obstructed by sunken hulks, and further thought as to its defense dismissed. The channel to the westward is but 1.1 miles wide, its depth being such that mine defenses could not be depended upon. Comparing this with Manila Bay, we find the narrower of the two entrance channels at that place 1-¾ miles wide, and the larger, 4-½ miles wide,—both with depths incapable of effective mining. In addition to the more favorable conditions thus existing at Subig Bay for protection from attack by sea, the topographical conditions likewise lend themselves more naturally to land defense; the hills rise from the bay in an amphitheater in such manner that a minimum number of troops could hold it against attack, being much more favorably situated in this respect than Manila. The location of Port Olongapo, the naval station, in a pocket surrounded by high hills and thus protected from long-range bombardment, is a still further advantage which finds no equivalent in any site that could be selected in Manila Bay. This brief reference to the natural features for defense of the respective bays might be greatly elaborated, but it is assumed that the superiority of Subig Bay from a military view-point will not be questioned.

6. If Subig Bay be selected as the point at which our fortifications are concentrated, with the object of defense against an Asiatic enemy of markedly superior seapower, it is claimed that it would be none the less advantageous as a stronghold in the event of war with a European power. It is true that such an enemy might send its fleet into Manila Bay; but, besides being open to constant harrowing attacks from our surface and submarine torpedo boats based upon Subig Bay, it is to be assumed that its landing parties could no more reduce the city of Manila than could those of the American squadron in 1898; and unlike the conditions of the Spanish war, the enemy would not possess that control of the sea which would permit him to transport hither an army of occupation. Indeed, it is doubtful

if he could even maintain his fleet for any considerable time with the American ships at Subig Bay upon the flank of his communications. It may therefore be asked what, from a military point of view, could an enemy gain by entering Manila Bay, leaving unreduced an American base only 35 miles distant? We have passed the day of firing and looting unresisting cities; even the day of demanding ransom for withholding bombardment is waning. That commercial interests at Manila would suffer with the enemy in the Bay is conceded; but would they suffer less if the Philippines fell as a whole, or even if, with Manila Bay amply fortified, the enemy should occupy Subig Bay? And is it not possible that the effect of assigning to Manila a pre-eminent military importance would be to invite attack which, as a mere commercial port, it might escape?

7. As evidence of the weight of opinion favoring the adoption of Subig Bay for a naval base as against Manila, the following resumé of previous action upon the matter is submitted:

October, 1900: Secretary of Navy appointed a board of five officers under Admiral Remey, then commander-in-chief; the board reported unanimously in favor of Subig Bay.

September, 1901: The General Board, after seven months' study and consideration of this report and of the subject in general, earnestly recommended the establishment of a strong naval base at Subig Bay.

November, 1901: Secretary Long approved the report and recommendation referred to.

June and July, 1903: The General Board urged the importance of permanent fortifications to guard entrance at Subig Bay, in letters from which the following extracts are taken:

First, the Manila region is the all-important strategic area in the Philippines and should have the first attention. Second, Subig Bay is the key (from a naval standpoint) of that region and should be made an impregnable naval base of the first order immediately.

Subig Bay, whose entrance is only 30 miles from that of Manila Bay, must be considered as part of the Manila region in any discussion of the defenses of the Philippines, or of their advantages as a base for naval operations, because it is so valuable a position that it would surely be seized as a base by the enemy if it were not strongly occupied by ourselves in the event of war. Moreover, if it be made a strong base for an adequate fleet, Manila will be better defended than it could be were our naval station situated in its immediate vicinity. With the two, Manila and the station, close together, an attack on one would be an attack on both; with the station at Subig, Manila could not be attacked until Subig was reduced.

November, 1903: Secretary Moody in his annual report stated: "Commanders-in-Chief, two Boards, and the Admiral of the Navy all agree that our naval base should be within Subig Bay. It would seem as if this body of opinion ought to be deemed conclusive. I know of no other military question upon which such unanimity exists."

December, 1903: A committee of the Joint Board, of which Brigadier-General G. L. Gillespie, U. S. Army, was senior member, agreed upon certain fundamental points that may be summarized as follows: "That a protected base in the Philippines is essential for keeping open lines of communication, including those of the Army; that Manila is not suitable for such a base, but Subig Bay is suitable; that the fortification of the bay is essential to the security of a naval station at that place, and would likewise contribute to the defense of Manila."

December, 1903: The Joint Board reiterated the foregoing principles as its unanimous expression of opinion, and stated that both Army and Navy are united in demanding the fortification of Subig Bay as essential to any plan of defense.

May, 1904: Joint Board recommended that the whole of an appropriation of Congress of $700,000 (made April 21, 1904) be devoted to the fortification of Subig Bay, without devoting any portion to Manila.

July, 1904: Acting Secretary of War, in a letter to the Joint Board, explained that it was impracticable to comply with this recommendation, but approved project for the emergency defense of that place involving expenditure of $450,000.

February, 1906: The National Coast Defense Board of which Secretary Taft was president, placed Subig Bay ahead of Manila in order of importance for defense.

March, 1906: The President of the United States, in a message transmitting the report of the National Coast Defense Board to Congress, stated: "In the insular possessions the great naval bases at Guantanamo, Subig Bay, and Pearl Harbor, and the coaling stations at Guam and San Juan require protection, and, in addition, defenses are recommended for Manila Bay and Honolulu because of the strategic importance of these localities."

January, 1907: The General Board of the Navy, in submitting a plan of operations in view of possible hostilities with Japan, stated that the primary object of the United States, pending the arrival in Asiatic waters of the Atlantic fleet, should be to concentrate all troops, supplies, and naval coast defense forces at Subig Bay and "to fortify and hold Olongapo to the last."

March, 1907: A plan prepared with a similar object by a committee of the Army War College made like recommendations as to the essential necessity of holding Subig Bay with all available forces.

March, 1907: The Secretary of the Navy addressed a letter to the Secretary of War inviting the attention of the War Department to the urgent necessity for devoting an appropriation of $500,000 made by Congress on March 2, 1907, to the construction of such land defenses at Subig Bay as would successfully defend it against any enemy.

May, 1907: In accordance with the foregoing recommendation, the Secretary of War, after a conference with the Chiefs of Engineers, Artillery and Ordnance, by direction of the President approved a project for the "complete seacoast gun defense of Subig Bay," which involved the expenditure at that place of the whole of the $500,000 appropriation of 1907, together with certain other available funds, the correspondence in the matter indicating the entire concurrence of all Army authorities in the Subig Bay project.

June, 1907: The Joint Board submitted a plan for operations in the contingency of war with Japan, in which was embodied the following: "As the land and naval forces now in the Philippines are not sufficiently strong to afford adequate protection to more than one place, and as it would be impracticable, with our present resources in that section, to prevent a hostile fleet from entering Manila Bay and commanding the city, all available sources for defense should be placed at or around the naval base, Subig Bay, to protect the dry dock, the coal supply, and other utilities necessary for the most efficient use of the battle fleet upon its arrival."

Reminiscences of Service at the Naval War College

Lawrence, Long Island, March 24, 1908 [NWC]

My orders to the War College were issued in October, 1885, Rear Admiral Luce being then its President; but as there were no quarters ready, and my immediate duty of preparing lectures did not necessitate being in Newport, I did not go into residence until the following August.

Before that time, in the Spring of 1886, Admiral Luce had been detached, to command the North Atlantic fleet. I do not think I received any orders to succeed him, but simply fell into the presidency as a first lieutenant does into command after the captain's removal.

When I joined, in August, the building—formerly the Newport Almshouse—was unoccupied and unready. Lieutenant L. C. Logan was in charge, in the general capacity of an Executive Aide, but he lived in the city, there being no other place for him.

Upon my arrival I found that, although my quarters were not ready, there was a place to sleep. I therefore went into residence, being the sole occupant of the building. I may add that when my family joined me, in October, the repairs were still incomplete; we had to use some of the rooms on the second floor, afterwards turned into offices. This awkward condition lasted through part, at least, of the course of 1886. We had to get out of the way before the hour for lectures. The equipment was still so modest that I had but one lamp, a single student, which I had to carry with me from room to room at night.

The only other officer then attached to the College,—except Logan, who was not concerned with instruction—was Captain Tasker H. Bliss of the army, now Brigadier General. All other lecturers came from the outside service. I cannot be sure of recalling every name, but will mention those my memory retains. Professor Jas. R. Soley, then Librarian of the Navy Department, later Assistant Secretary of the Navy, on International Law; Lieut. Comdr. W. B. Hoff, who delivered a somewhat patch-work compilation of the utterances on Naval Tactics of various officers, foreign and American; Lieut. John F. Meigs, on Naval Gunnery,—not Naval Ordnance; Medical Director R. C. Dean, on Naval Hygiene. Captain Bliss dealt with Land Warfare. My own lectures of that year have since been printed in the book: *The Influence of Sea Power upon History, 1660–1783.*

Besides this list, which may not be complete, there were occasional single lectures by individuals. Admiral Luce opened the session with an address; and the well known military historian, John C. Ropes, gave a critical narration of (I think) the Gettysburg Campaign.

This Autumn session of 1886 lasted about two months, and I have reason to believe made an excellent impression on the officers in attendance, which so far was transmitted to the service. But the College was still a new thing, eyed with some suspicion; and there was besides a strong formulated opposition under two principal heads. The Bureau of Equipment, having under its charge the Training Station for apprentices, had at first possessed the whole island and all its buildings. It objected strongly to the intrusion of the College, and wished it removed; anywhere, so long as it went. Allied to this was a line of thought which argued that the College was a postgraduate school, and should therefore be near the under-graduate Academy, at Annapolis. The old marine hospital there was spoken of as a suitable location. Others again suggested the Naval Station at New London.

The then Secretary of the Navy, Mr. Whitney, had found the College already started by the action of his predecessor, Mr. Chandler, and it was believed that he was at the least indifferent, if not opposed, to the new institution. The Chairman of the House Naval Committee, Mr. Herbert, was resolutely inimical, and it soon became known that he would use his powerful influence against any appropriation. For these reasons it became necessary for me, as soon as relieved of the immediate pressure of the course of 1886, to consider the reasons that could be used most forcibly for the existence of the College; and upon that consideration to develop a line of policy, which, when advanced in argument with opponents, might tend to their conversion.

In the views of the objectors I recognized only one dangerously plausible contention, viz: that the College was in the nature of a post-graduate course, and therefore best placed at Annapolis, where there was a large equipment available for such purpose. I knew that there was a disposition, even among the friendly, to enhance the importance of the College by dwelling upon electricity, steam, ordnance, and other studies dependent upon the mechanical and physical sciences, as being part of the service it might do the Navy. It appeared to me that once impress upon the College that characteristic, it would inevitably predominate over the study of Warfare, because the disposition, alike of the Navy and of the age, is to insist upon material perfection as the chief end of military effort. Consequently, the only way to preserve the College at all, for its particular end, was resolutely to put away all thought of the material of the service; and this discardment destroyed also at once the argument for removal to Annapolis, the result of which would have been the inevitable strangulation of the younger and weaker institution by the older and stronger, much as a mother suffocates a baby by overlying.

Consequently, from that winter onward I was at pains, whenever occasion offered, to put forward this view; that the College would entertain no questions except such as concerned the carrying on of War. Perfected material, I urged, is but the foundation of our investigation; with the antecedent methods of its production we have no concern. If a gun will do a certain amount of work, it may be made of pasteboard, so far as the College is concerned; if an engine will give a certain speed, the fuel may be a tallow candle. Our only interest is to know what the implements will effect in the conduct of War. That such study was essential was demonstrable from the known opinions of great general officers; that no other agency than the College existed for its pursuit was on the face of things. This position dictated all my actions while remaining president of the College. In negotiating for the next course I kept it steadily in view. The largeness of the field thus assigned assured that year by year, as professional vision expanded, the course would increase like a rolling snowball, by gathering to itself questions of warlike activity, concerning which men would never think but for the stimulus of the College, existing for such ends only.

There was an appropriation for the fiscal year ending June 30, 1887, but the disfavor at Washington threatened the College with a discontinuance, unless the opposition of Mr. Herbert could be overcome. This I failed to accomplish, although no better argument for the need of the institution could be found than that furnished by the fact that a man so influential upon the interests of the Navy had no apparent conception of the necessity for studying the Art of War. An appeal to General Wheeler,[1] a representative from the same state as Herbert, met with instant comprehension and sympathy, for Wheeler was an educated as well as a practical soldier; but he could make no headway with Herbert. No appropriation was granted for the ensuing year, a result which left no doubt as to the indifference of the Secretary.

The College accordingly was run on a vacuum during the fiscal year 1887–88. The course, however, was extended to three months and a half. There were lectures on the Tactics of the Ram, by Commander P. F. Harrington; on those of the Torpedo, by Lieut-Comdr. Duncan Kennedy; and on the Strategical Conditions of the Pacific, by Lieut-Comdr. Stockton, who at a later day was himself president of the College. Besides those of the year before, there must have been others read, which now have escaped my memory, except Captain Bixby of the Engineer Corps of the Army. His subject, I think, was Coast Fortification.

During the succeeding winter, 1887–1888, our struggle for an appropriation was conducted with greater energy and system. My own failure of the year before dictated the employment of wider and more persistent

---

1. Joseph Wheeler.

effort. Several officers engaged in helping me, notably Commander Stockton, whose position in one of the Bureaus of the Department kept him continuously on the ground, and also Commander Harrington. Beyond occasional suggestion from me, every man worked as he could; I myself spent the better part of a fortnight at Washington. Mr. Herbert remained immovable; but despite these odds against us, a decisive majority,—ten to three, I think,—was won over in the Committee, and the appropriation passed both Houses. I may add that when I saw Mr. Whitney to ask his permission to work for the appropriation, he received what I said with evident annoyance, and replied, "I will not oppose you, but I do not authorize you to express any approval from me." The controlling head of the Navy had absolutely no appreciation of the necessity for systematic study of Warfare.

A course was held in the late summer and fall of 1888, and I myself was very sanguine that the future of the College was now assured; but, as is known, Mr. Whitney overthrew the whole undertaking by an order depriving the College of its building, and transferring such existence as was left it to the care of the Commander of the Torpedo Station, Commander Casper F. Goodrich. I myself was detached, and ordered as senior officer of a Commission to select a site for a Navy Yard on Puget Sound; a duty which, in actual performance, writing the report, and settling accounts, occupied me until the end of the summer of 1889. I may add that, finding the College thus deprived of its normal conditions, I had utilized what time was left me in drawing up instructions for a number of large maps which I knew would be useful in the future.

Thus, a map of our North Atlantic Coast, to and including Chesapeake Bay, and one of the approaches to the Mississippi, in which depths of water were distinguished by colors, were meant to illustrate a study of offensive and defensive operations possible to contending parties; and a great map of Northern Italy, to illustrate Bonaparte's campaigns.

A large part of the $10,000 appropriation was in this manner realized. I also had book cases contracted for, to take the place of those in the old building. The irregular size of the new ones, which may have attracted curiosity in the new building, was due to their being meant for the spaces in the old, to which at that time I thought the College might return. In any case, I aimed to save the appropriation by thus employing it for legitimate objects other than current expenses, for which under the circumstances there could be little need.

Meanwhile, President Harrison's Administration had been inaugurated, and the new Secretary, Mr. Tracy, was believed to be friendly to the College idea, as proved to be the case. Consequently, when I had finished the Puget Sound business, I was ordered on special duty, to continue the preparation of further lectures on Naval History, which afterwards were published under the title of *The Influence of Sea Power on the French Revolution and Empire*. Nothing, however, was for the time done towards restoring the College to an abiding place of its own. A course was held at Goat Island, in the summer of 1889, of which I know nothing except that I myself took part, giving, if I rightly recall, only the six lectures embraced in the subject of Naval Strategy, which I understand are still in use at the College.

I am not perfectly clear as to when the appropriation of $100,000 for a college building was made; but I think in the winter of 1889–1890. At all events it was expected that there would be a course the following summer; and to be at hand I took for the summer a house in the city of Newport. Actually, no course was held, and I simply continued working at the naval history of the French Revolution, together with some other special temporary matters assigned to me by the Department. I am quite sure, however, that during these months, acting under instructions from the Department, I, in cooperation with Civil Engineer MacKay, drew up plans for the present building, and selected the site; our recommendations being, of course, subject to the approval of the Chief of the Bureau of Navigation, Rear Admiral Ramsay.

I thus continued on special duty, connected with the College, but without any responsibility for the building beyond that above stated, until the summer of 1892. During these years I lived in New York City. The Department, though favorable, was engrossed with other matters, and it was not till the spring of 1892 was well advanced that it rather hurriedly decided that, as the building was ready, it must be utilized. I was ordered to prepare for a course, in which fortunately I had little difficulty, many of the old lecturers being still available. As my memory serves me, I went to Newport in July, occupying at once the quarters of the President in the building.

I retain little or no recollection of that year's course, except that one was held. More interesting, as pertaining to the history and progress of the College, is the fact that the four sets of quarters provided for resident instructors were all occupied by officers selected by the President of the College. Commander Charles H. Stockton, and Lieutenants James H. Sears and Washington I. Chambers were the three, besides myself, and all of them took part in the lectures of that year.

I continued President of the College during the ensuing winter, and remained in residence; but in April, 1893, I was detached, and ordered to the *Chicago*. Since that time my only connection with the institution has been that of an occasional outside lecturer.

I may add that in a book recently published by me, *From Sail to Steam*, I have embodied some other recollections which have not seemed to me of sufficient pertinence to be embraced in this account.

Jottings from Pocket Notebook, May-August 1908

N.P., N.D. Probably, Quogue, Long Island, May 29–August 18, 1908 [LC]

May

29	Telegram	.25
30	Stage to Station	.25
	R.R. to N.Y.	1.56
	Parlor Car	.50
	Ferry (both ways)	5
	Cab to 29th St & Club	1.30
	Return to Washn.	10.00
	Parlor Car	1.25
	Bag expressed to Washn.	1.00
	Lunch	.80
	Dinner	1.20
31st	Bkft	.40
*	Church	1.00
	Lunch	.75
	Cab to 23 St	1.10
	Porter	.10
	Dinner	1.35
	Carried over	22.86
	Pullman Porter	.10
	Porter (station)	.10
	Cab to Hotel	.75
	Porter	.10
June 1	Car Tickets	.25
2	Pullman seat	1.25
	Elevator man	.25
	Dining Room waiter	.50
	Porter (hotel)	.10
	Cab to station	.75
	R.R. porter	.15
	Hotel bill	7.95
May 30	Room at Club	3.00

June 2	Pullman porter	.10
	Dinner	1.35
	Porter to boat	.10
	Porter to hack	.10
		39.76
	Carried over	39.76
June		
2d	Hack to Club	1.00
	Room at Club	3.00
3d	Breakfast	.50
	Lunch	.65
	Hack to 34 St	1.10
	Railroad to Quogue	1.56
	Stage to house	.25
		47.82

$47.82 Total
Cost of trip to + fr. Washington
Bag from Station 25¢
   Total 48.07

Construction
Regulation
Management
Neutralization that of Suez
   Canal 3 mile limit
10 A.M. Friday
————xx————
Lunch Library
Dinner, 7 P.M. Teacup Inn,
   1623 H Street

Friday. Aug. 14. Feeling heavy yet not very, that by precaution because Sunday 3d, took ¾ gr. calomel. Seidlitz 7:10 A.M.

Sat. Aug. 15. Optd. thrice—by 3 p.m. last. Head clear and active for writing. Bathed 12–1. Stomach a little heavy. Ate rather less than usual. Tea, 5:30

Sunday. 16. Dozed a little on porch. In Bed, 10:30. Slept to 3:50, rousing once at 12:30. Could not sleep after 4, evident gastritis, also expectation of having to wake (3d Sunday) Very restless, forenoon, indigestion, head dull, could not give attention.

Tea 5:45 Excessively sleepy evg. In Bed 10:10

Monday. 17 Slept heavily. Waked 12:40 and 4:10. Hot water at 4:15. Slept till 7. Very heavy and headachy. Wineglass Rubriat Atlan [illegible] hard to [illegible]. Bathed 12–1 much better and head clearer after lunch—also indig. gone. Bicycle to R.R. Cross Tea 5:45 Bed 10:45.

Tuesday 18 Waked 12;30, 2, 5. did not sleep after 5:30. Less nervous etc forenoon. Digestion better p.m. Bathed 12–1.

Analogy

The modern Ram to be efficient, as such, needs, above all, *tactical* qualities and must be of dimension in which the opposing elements of speed and handiness are best reconciled.

But the battle-ship must be big—relying primarily upon her military power.

Loss of tactical skill leads to development of fighting force, and consequent increase of size. Hence quadriremes(?), quinqueremes, etc.

"The evolution of naval construction is always slow." Therefore it is probable that the first quadriremes or quinqueremes did not depart from the trireme model. They were triremes (probably) having 4 or 5 men on each fighting oar.

Serres[1] Theory

The Greek system of rowing galley is characterized

1 By the employment in the same ship of *oars* of different lengths,

2 Established at different heights,

3 Manned by a number of rowers proportionate to their dimensions,

4 Employed separately or together, according to the size of the galley, and according as the object is to increase the radius of action by economy of force, to increase speed by increasing the propelling power.

Opposite Theories

We have contested as impracticable all attempts at reconstruction, 1, which rest upon a division of rowers into groups separated by decks

2 upon the employment of more than two tiers of oars

3 upon rowers placed one over the other

4 upon the employment of single oarsmen for oars of all dimensions.[2]

---

1. Paul Serre, *Marines de Guerre de l'Antiquité et du Moyen Age*. Paris, 1885.
2. These notes seem related to Mahan's continuing revision of his War College naval strategy lectures which Little, Brown and Company published in 1911 as *Naval Strategy*.

Statement on Naval History
Archives and Repositories[1]

November 24, 1908 [NA]

Printed documents respecting our naval history are chiefly to be found in Force's *American Archives, The American State Papers. Naval Affairs*, the British *Naval Chronicle* (1798–1818), Brannan's Official Letters (1823), Goldsborough's *Naval Chronicle* (1824), *Niles' Register*, the Canadian Archive Reports, Cruikshank's *Documentary History of the Campaigns Upon the Niagara Frontier*, the annual and occasional reports of the Secretary of the Navy, Reports and Dispatches (1849), and the Official Records of the Union and Confederate Navies now in course of publication by the Government. But other very important documents must often be sought in places widely scattered. The court of inquiry asked by Commander Elliott, in 1815, upon his conduct on Lake Erie, is printed in one unofficial work; Perry's voluminous specifications against him, in 1818, in another—neither by the Government; both are necessary to the historian. The British minister, Mr. Foster, wrote to Monroe reams upon the questions then pending between the United States and Great Britain; but a document printed in the life of the Marquis of Wellesley, his Instructions to Foster, sets forth the British position on the Continental System with a succinctness, logic, and force nowhere else to be found.

Further publication should for the present be confined to the military activities of the Navy, to the postponement of civil and administrative papers. In view of the extensive publication of naval records concerning the Civil War, now proceeding, we see no reason for recommendation, unless it be that the "Letters from Foreign Consuls" (United States consuls abroad) mentioned in Van Tyne and Leland (p. 190, item 26), should be printed. They touch on the blockade and kindred matters, and the blockade was one of the most important military measures of that war. The letters referred to represent in a degree its external aspect.

From the brief duration and limited action of the war of 1898 with

---

1. Section F of the *Report by the Committee on Department Methods on the Documentary Historical Publications of the United States Government*, transmitted to Congress by a message from the President, February 11, 1909. Senate Document No. 714, 60th Cong., 2nd Sess.

Spain, and from the voluminous publications already made, we infer that the greater part of the documents are already in print, though at some time a fuller publication of telegrams may be desired, since the part which the cable played in this war was exceptionally great.

Turning to the earlier naval conflicts, it is profitable to remark that there are in every war conspicuous features which should in part determine the course and nature of research. Thus, in the war of 1812, we have, first, the prevalence of battles between single ships, owing to the vast inferiority of American naval strength; second, owing to the same cause, the completeness of the blockade of the American coasts, producing an exhaustion of means in the midst of plenty, a financial catastrophe which compelled peace without obtaining the formal concession of any one of the points for which the nation went to war; third, the fact that naval preponderance on the Great Lakes, whether established by victories, as on Erie and Champlain, or held in uncertain balance by a cautious policy of shipbuilding, as on Ontario, protected the northern border of the United States and rendered fruitless the British land operations in that region. Now, whenever it is possible to recognize beforehand such determining features, a clue is placed in the hands of the searcher of archives as to what is comparatively important to print.

Revolutionary War.—The United States Navy, despite the brilliant action of Paul Jones and one or two others, exercised no effect upon the outcome of the war, except upon Lake Champlain, in 1776. The American control of that lake in that year postponed the British invasion to 1777, entailing thus the decisive consequences of Saratoga and its sequel in the French alliance. The documentary history of the operations on Lake Champlain, therefore, deserves fuller treatment, in which, besides the papers already printed in the *American Archives* and elsewhere, attention should be directed to additional papers possessed by the United States Government, state governments, the British Public Records Office, and the Archives of War and Marine, in Paris. In several other parts of the conflict land and naval operations were so closely interwoven that the papers relating to them should be fused into one whole. The actions of privateers were often brilliant, and in the mass they influenced the result; but our government has few of the necessary materials for their history, and it is doubtful if the matter can be illustrated by any general documentary publication.

Tripolitan war.—As the Barbary pirates were the immediate originating cause of the United States Navy, the hostilities against them derive thence an interest to our naval history quite beyond their petty scale or military value. To illustrate the subject properly, it should be considered as a whole, from the depredations on American shipping, immediately after our protection by the British navy ceased, down to the conclusion of the peace in 1816.

Documents should be selected to illustrate the depredations, the tribute paid by us to the several Barbary powers, our dependence on Portugal for protection, the dismay felt when Portugal made peace with the pirates, the legislation authorizing a naval force, the actual hostilities, including Decatur's action with the Algerine naval vessels in 1815. References, at least, might well be inserted to the already printed debates of Congress touching the institution of a navy; they are a part of naval history, broadly considered.

Closely allied with these topics is the general question of Mediterranean commerce, and that of the gunboat system of Jefferson. It is probable that the "Captains' Letters," "Commanders' Letters," etc., still mostly unprinted, would give much incidental light upon Mediterranean trade and piratical depredations, from which the Mediterranean littoral suffered much more than the United States shipping. It does not appear that the gunboat system has ever been illustrated by adequate and systematic publication. Yet, though utterly inconsequent in itself, the system has historical importance, because, under Jefferson's influence, it stunted the rising navy, and so at least aided to bring on the war of 1812.

War of 1812.—The documents printed in the *American State Papers, Naval Affairs*, are incomplete and unsatisfactory from the historical point of view. The series "Letters Received" and "Letters Sent" in the Navy Department should be carefully gone over for the years 1810–1816, inclusive, attention being specifically directed upon (1) the single-ship actions, which have obtained in popular recognition an esteem which we can not properly disregard; (2) upon reports of officers commanding naval stations, as to the blockade, and operations of the enemy's vessels on the coast, including especially all transactions in the Chesapeake; (3) upon the general history of preparations and of action upon the Great Lakes. When army and navy are both engaged, as in the Chesapeake and on the Lakes, military correspondence will sometimes contain an essential part of a common programme, or one side of a dispute. Pertinent documents in *Niles' Register* and similar publications, the originals of which are not in the files of the Department, should be either included in the publication, or adequately referred to.

The log books of United States vessels, where preserved, may furnish data of importance, although log books of that day, British and American, are commonly scanty in information. Court-martial records are far more valuable. The proceedings of the court held on the survivors of the *Chesapeake* have not been printed. The same is true of the courts on the officers of the *Guerrière, Macedonian,* and *Java,* and those of the British squadrons defeated on lakes Erie and Champlain. All these are very full and necessary to any historian discussing the actions. The instructions issued by the British Government to its officers, both military and naval, seaboard and lake, are as essential to an understanding of operations as are those of our own Government.

War with Mexico.—In the way of fighting, the Navy in its proper sphere had little to do in this war, for there was no Mexican navy. But the transactions on the west coast, having to do with the acquisition of the territory ceded by Mexico, are of national importance.

In naval material the principle that it is not enough to consult the materials possessed by one side is emphasized by the almost invariable naval practice of holding a court-martial in any case of serious disaster. The result of this procedure is the accumulation of a mass of sworn testimony by expert eyewitnesses. Few questions are asked of victors; they tell their story much as they will; the vanquished must furnish explanations, and at large. The beaten side thus furnishes the better field for the historian.[2]

---

2. The text of the *Report* was signed by all three members of the Committee (J. Franklin Jameson, Mahan, and J. B. McMaster). Section F is plainly Mahan's contribution.

Statement of Expenses on a February 4-6, 1909, Visit to Washington, D.C.

N.P., N.D. Probably, Lawrence, Long Island, March 1, 1909 [LC]

Feb. 4–5

Bag to Station—Lawrence	.25
Return ticket Lawce. to N.Y.	.80
Baggage transfer N.Y.	.50
Dinner	1.20
Carfare N.Y.	.05
Porter Pa. N.Y. Statn.	.10
Return ticket N.Y. to Wash.	10.00
Pullman Sleeper	2.00
Tip to Porter "	.25
Baggage to Hotel Washn.	.25
Carfare	.05
Hotel Bill Washn. & a Bkft.	5.15
Tips Hotel Waiters	.30
Hd. "	.50
Porter	.30
Elevator	.25
	21.75[1]

Feb. 6

	21.75
Carriage to Station	.80
Tip to driver	.10
Telephone for Carriage	.10
Porter at Station	.20
Lunch	.20
Transfer Valise in N.Y.	.50
Pullman seat	1.25
Tip to Porter	.10
Valise to house Lawrence	.25
	25.00[2]

Should Treasury disallow mileage—Church will owe me $1.75.

---

1. The correct sum is $21.95.
2. The correct sum is $25.45.

Testimony Before the House Committee
on the Library

Washington, D.C., January 5, 1910[1] [NA]

I have very little to say, Mr. Chairman, after the gentlemen who have spoken,[2] with all their experience, because I have no experience in the matter. I presume that the Government proposes to go on with publications of this character, and the question is how they are to get the best results with the money they are to spend.

I should not have spoken of it at all, but I find myself differing so much from Mr. Adams's point of view with regard to salaries that I think I ought to speak upon the matter. So far as I now remember of the movements of the Committee on Documentary Publications, which was our name, it was I who suggested the idea of compensation. These eminent gentlemen are to do a certain amount of work for the Government, and they should be remunerated. But the case is not the same, in my apprehension, as that of a historical society in a State, which is a purely voluntary society, not employed by the State in any way, but purely a voluntary association of men who come together voluntarily, and their own interest carries on this work.

I entirely agree with Mr. Adams that the active or working man must be the secretary. More will depend upon him than upon any one member, but you will call upon these other gentlemen to do a large amount of work for the Government, which will be in a measure a large economy for the Government if they do the work conscientiously, and I always experience the conscientious pressure that is put upon me when I feel that I am being paid for the work I am doing; I feel that I must do it better than I would do voluntary work. Of course the interest in the work comes in to encourage a man already disposed to do it. That is another matter. But these gentlemen will be called away from the work in which they are im-

---

1. From *The Archives of the United States Government. A Documentary History 1774–1934.* Vol. XII. Washington, D.C.: Government Printing Office, 1910–1911.
2. J. F. Jameson, Dr. H. T. Colenbrander (Secretary of the Dutch Commission on National Historical Publications), Charles Francis Adams (President of the Massachusetts Historical Society), A. T. Mahan, Charles M. Andrews, Herbert Putnam, and Ruth Putnam (specialist in Dutch history) spoke in that order on behalf of H.R.15428.

mediately interested to engage in one in which they cannot fail to have some interest; they will be called to meet sometimes, because as historical students they can not fail to wish to see the thing carried on to the very best advantage. But the Government, in intending to employ a number of men, ought to give them some moderate compensation as representing the time they give and their experience in the matter, and also to exert that influence that comes to a man when he is receiving money and who expects that he must give work in return.

As regards the methods and personnel of the commission, I presume that the commission will be chosen, as the expression here is, of men of the highest standing and judgment. Of course, that is a matter of opinion, but it can be assumed that men of high standing would seek and get the appointment. We must assume that a certain amount of discretion would be used by the persons who appoint them. I think that the secretary should be adequately salaried, but beyond that I think there is nothing for me to say.

Statement of Expenses on a January 4-6, 1910, Visit to Washington, D. C.[1]

N.P., N.D. Probably, Lawrence, Long Island, circa January 7, 1910 [LC]

R.R. Ticket. (return)	10.00
Pullman's "	2.50
Hotel Bill	3.35
Room at Club Jan 5–6	3.00
Meals en route (four)	1.90
Tips (Hotel)	.40
Carfares (N.Y. 3 Washn. 4)	.35
R.R. Lawrence to N.Y. (return)	1.60
Cab to Statn. & back (Lawrence)	.50
	23.60

---

1. On January 4, Mahan was ordered to report to the Navy Department on January 5, to appear before the House Committee on the Library. He reported as ordered, and returned to Lawrence on January 6.

Comments on the Armament of Battleships[1]

New York, November 17 and 18, 1910[2]

My comment upon the paper, which I have read carefully, must be confined to a brief expression of my general agreement with the conclusions of Sir William White (page 16)[3] and the following summary of the leading principles I conceive to be involved in the controversy between the all-big-gun ship, which, barring torpedo defense, is to carry no armament except a few of the very heaviest caliber used by its nation, and the mixed battery vessel, which, to fewer of the heaviest guns, adds a proportioned number of comparatively light pieces variously called secondary or intermediate. This is the type which commands the adhesion of Sir William White.

The argument for the all-big-gun ship, briefly, is that it and the squadron to which it belongs will always be able to keep at its own desired range; and that, being so able, it can and will always choose such a distance that the smaller guns of its opponents will be practically "out of action," an aim which Sir William White accurately quotes as that of all ship fighting. Under this condition, the circumstances of the two fleets are reduced to the most heavy guns of the all-big-gun fleet opposed to the fewer of the mixed-battery fleet.

The reply to this is, that the fleet speed of any body of vessels is the speed of the slowest among them; and the maintenance of the all-big-gun distance presupposes a perpetual avoidance of close action by the fleet depending upon it, that is, constant withdrawal; that any mishap lessening the speed of a single member of the fleet entails the abandonment of that member or the acceptance of close action, within the range of the mixed battery.

1. Mahan's reply to "Notes on the Armament of Battleships," written by Sir William Henry White, former Chief Constructor of the Royal Navy.
2. White's paper and Mahan's comment upon it were read at the eighteenth meeting of the Society of Naval Architects and Marine Engineers in New York on November 17 and 18, 1910. Mahan's contribution was published in the Society's *Transactions*, XVIII (1910), pp. 20–22.
3. Sir William's conclusions on p. 16 read: "In no case is it desirable to carry more than eight heavy guns in a single ship, that these guns are best arranged in four positions as in the *Michigan* class, and that they should be supplemented by a powerful and well protected secondary armament."

The pursuing fleet follows with its best speed, because its slower members are in no danger, and will come up as a reserve.

Much stronger assertion is made as to the inferior accuracy of the smaller caliber, under conditions of modern action. Sir William White tells us (page 5) that naval officers having full and accurate information on this subject have assured him that the percentage of hits obtained with 6-inch guns under service conditions is not inferior to percentages obtained with guns of larger caliber. Accepting this, and also that, as was the case with battleships but a few years ago, three 6-inch are carried for one 12-inch gun, the number of 6-inch hits "under service conditions" would be to 12-inch as three to one. This is "volume of fire." Considering the large amount of surface penetrable, and of crew accessible to 6-inch projectiles, it is a very material consideration. It is to be remembered that the 6-inch projectile weighs 100 pounds, and that the repeated near burstings of such in rapid succession, even where they do not penetrate, is a tremendous nervous strain upon men subjected to them. This the Russians experienced at Tsushima.

The very striking success of the system of fire control developed within the past few years has led those to whom the credit of this belongs to insist much upon the difficulty of observation of the fall of projectiles, where two calibers are used. The splash of the 12-inch and of the 6-inch are often indistinguishable. I think this argument presupposes a deliberateness of fire control which will not obtain after the action becomes "hot." Till then, like two fencers measuring each other's strength, there may be "passes" with the 12-inch on each side to ascertain distance, and this will and should continue as long as possible. How long, is the question.

The all-big-gun conception leads necessarily to the wish for as many such guns as possible; or, what in aggregate impact is much the same, to each gun being made of as large caliber as possible. We have now risen from four big guns to twelve or thirteen, and from 12-inch to 14-inch. The notorious difficulty of placing several pairs, shown by Sir William White, necessarily of itself impels to fewer pairs of heavier guns. This means of course proportionately fewer discharges and fewer hits. All is staked on the disastrous effect of the large projectile, hitting less often; just as against a mixed battery all is staked on the secondary (or intermediate) battery— the 6-inch guns—being kept out of action by superior speed.

The assumptions of the advocates of all-big-gun ships are precarious though plausible. Chief among them is the assured ability to choose distance, at least for a time, long enough to cripple the assailant decisively. This is the cornerstone of the whole edifice. Upon this is built up the entire program—more and more big-gun fire, therefore bigger guns with fewer emplacements; bigger and bigger ships and fewer of them. Sight is lost of the fact, which Sir William brings forward, that the guns in three ships can be brought to bear effectively on the same number in two ships. This is concentration of fire; while the three ships, as compared with the two, give dispersion of target, a defensive provision entailing little offensive loss. This is exactly as in harbor defense; guns bearing from numerous positions on a critical point concentrate fire, yet gain comparative immunity through their separateness—dispersion of target.

The efficacy of bigger ships and fewer of them depends in part upon the considerations of concentration of fire—upon a few ships, and upon dispersion of target—among several ships, or gun emplacements. A bigger ship has an evident advantage over a smaller in a ship duel. In a fleet action the bigger ship reinforces proportionately the position in the fleet in which she is placed. But it does not follow that, in a combat of two ships against three, or eight against twelve, the same inequality continues. The dispersion of the target among twelve ships, the localization of a severe injury in one smaller ship instead of one bigger, the larger power of combination in twelve units over that in eight, all tend not only to compensate but to overcome the concentrated power (not concentrated fire) of the larger vessel, which is conspicuous in a ship duel.

The question ultimately is the difficult one of drawing a line. No one, for instance, wants one-gun ships, but a respectable school revolts at the twelve all-big guns; and the revolt is greater when more are proposed with increasing size of vessel and reduced numbers in the fleet. Collateral questions arise, e.g., dockage for such vessels and their use of navigable waters. Already Chesapeake Bay is too shoal for the increased draughts of battle-ships.

In conclusion Sir William White mentions that the Japanese have not abandoned the secondary or intermediate battery. I believe that this is also true of the German Navy, if not indeed of all save the British.

Thoughts on the Words of St. Peter

Quogue, Long Island, July 7, 1913 [LC]

Two thoughts occurred to me today while walking. One the words of St. Peter, "Lord, to whom shall we go? Thou hast the words of eternal life." A reply to unbelief, St. Peter's experience of Christ—and our experience—was that He had the words of eternal life, that if there be a God, not only the testimony of Jesus concerning Him, but also His words concerning our relations to Him, are such as fully satisfy our needs and our powers of conception concerning Him. Other disciples had not been so satisfied, and they went away in professed unbelief—"hard (?) sayings, who can hear them." Is it not the division of today anticipated?

I suppose the line of my thought derived from the opening chapters of *The Inside of the Cup*,[1] for the other thought bore also on unbelief, or rather upon a temporary inability to realize truth, hitherto held. The cry of Chirst on the Cross, "My God, why hast Thou forsaken Me" voiced a real, if brief, experience of the Man, Jesus Christ.* It may therefore very well voice occasional lesser, if longer, experiences of other believing men; and at such moments the words of St. Peter may supply the foundation upon which to base successful resistance: He has the words of eternal life; "will we then, can we, go away from Him?" It is not merely "whither else?" as though He, though unsatisfying, was the best to be had. It is the positive He *has* the actual best, He *has* the words of eternal life, and because of those words we hold fast to Him, even if for the moment, as to Him on the Cross, the reality of His Being, and the Father be veiled from our apprehension.

> * Here of also it is true
> Christ leads us through no darker rooms
>   Than He went through before;
> And he who to Christ's Kingdom comes
>   Must enter by this Door.

---

1. Winston Churchill, *The Inside of the Cup*. New York: Macmillan, 1913.

Thoughts on the Righteousness of War

N.P., N.D. Probably, Quogue, Long Island, circa July 23, 1913 [LC]

"All they that take the sword shall perish by the sword" has always seemed to me a difficult saying, partly because of the immediately preceding command "He that hath no sword &c" and because of the, to me, necessity of maintaining public right by public force. It has occurred to me, however, in relation to the progressive downfall of the Turk, and of Islam as a political power, which will entail also its downfall, as a religious power, as also it has stopped its progress wholly as an ameliorative power in Islamic peoples,—it has occurred to me that our Lord's meaning is that those who rely upon the sword, upon force, as a main principle of action and of achievement, as compared with moral and spiritual forces, will perish thereby by moral, mental, and spiritual paralysis—creeping over them, as men, or as nations, e.g. Napoleon. Moral and spiritual forces are the great elements of progress; of this the Lord Jesus is himself the great illustration.

Shameful and distressing as is the present internecine strife among those who lately fought side by side, the questions at stake are not wholly those of mere greed, but involve national interests, and racial sympathies, very difficult for an outsider to appreciate. Nor should we forget the ages of bondage they underwent as affective of character.

The immense disappointment now felt by many who sympathized deeply with the former victims of Turkish misrule may tend to a violent reaction of opinion. It seems therefore useful to quote here a very recent statement by an eminent English lawyer resident in Constantinople as to the effect of the displacement of Turkish authority over these communities which after a fine display of military efficiency have lapsed momentarily into unreason and savagery attendant and resultant upon continuous bondage.

"Twelve years ago I concluded a *historical* study with a sentence with which I venture to close this article. 'Wherever the deadweight of Turkish misrule has been removed, the young Xn. states have been fairly started on the path of civilzn., and justify the reasonable expectations of the statesmen, (of the) historians and (of the) scholars of the West, who sympathized with, and aided them in, their aspirations for freedom.' I still hold the same

[683]

opinion (after 12 years more of historical experience)." Sir Edwin Pears in *Contemporary*, June/13 (p.773).[1]

Sir E. P. has lived in Constantinople since 1873. Practised there in Consistory Courts & is President of the European Bar there.[2]

---

1. "Turkey, Present and Future."
2. This manuscript may have been a draft for Mahan's letter to *The New York Times* of the same date. *See also* Mahan to Clark, October 6, 1913.

Why Not Disarm?[1]

N.P., N.D. Probably, Quogue, Long Island, September 1913 [LC]

When considering the question of Disarmament with its handmaid Arbitration, in the various forms suggested for that method of adjusting international disputes, men are apt to look upon War as a fortuitous evil, regardless that it is a manifestation of deep seated causes, which must be removed if the effect is to be obviated. Because clearly recognizing that in many cases arbitration cannot remove the causes underlying war, the statesmen responsible for the welfare of nations persist in continuing or enlarging armament, as the only certain means of maintaining peace. It is an irony of the present situation, that one of the most noisy and self-advertising advocates of disarmament and arbitration has admitted that the chief effective champion of peace is the "War-Lord" of the greatest army and of the second largest navy now existing.

Armament is the organization and consecration of force as a factor in the maintenance of justice, order, and peace. It is the highest expression of that element in civilization—force—which has created and now upholds society, giving efficacy to the pronouncements of law, whether by the legislature or in the courts. Organized force, alone, enables the quiet and the weak to go about their business, and to sleep securely in their beds, safe from the violent without or within. That parts of New York City are esteemed unsafe at times to the ordinary citizen is due to inadequacy of organized force for his protection, to whatever that inadequacy be attributed. This social assurance has become so essential to men that they will submit to much restriction of liberty, if not otherwise can daily security for life and property be had. The despot follows hard on the heels of anarchy.

Nations have the same need for quiet that each man feels; and the necessity is the more urgent by so much as the welfare of millions exceeds that of an individual. Although under imperfect police conditions many are exposed to violence, comparatively the sufferers are few; while, if the incidents be frequent the community becomes aroused and support follows. But War not only affects many directly, by death, but through the

---

1. Published, possibly in different form, in the *National Sunday Magazine* for September 28, 1913, under the title, "The Folly of the Hague." *See* Mahan to Griffith, September 15, 1913; and Mahan to Short, June 24, 1914.

complicated network of social and economical relations involves indirectly all members of the state.

Why then not arbitrate, instead of fight? Because arbitration in a large minority of instances if not in an actual majority, is incompetent to pronounce upon the conflicting claims of nations. It is incompetent, sometimes because there is no existing law applicable; sometimes, because such law as does exist is so far behind the necessities of the case, that it is inapplicable, or worse. But if the question be posed otherwise, Why not devise some other means to avoid the fight, the reply is instant: Arm!

> Beware
> Of entrance to a quarrel; but being in,
> Bear't that the opposed may beware of thee,
> For, if thus ware, he will not attack.

This is the whole theory of Armament, which has kept the peace in a half dozen quarrels in Europe during the past decade.

Comprehensive abstract discussion within a thousand words is impossible. Take a current case,—the late conflicts in the Balkans. What were the causes? The political incapacity of Turkey, permitting or inflicting hideous social satrapy in her territory; the wrath of neighboring kindred peoples over these sufferings; and the incompetency of European diplomacy during thirty years to induce or compel Turkey to adequate reforms, contemplated by the Treaty of Berlin. Let any interested look up in the London *Times* the history of Young Turk government in the provinces during the years 1909–1912.

In six months war swept away an iniquity which had shamed Europe for thirty years; and in the regions desolated by Turkish misgovernment would have followed the control of states concerning which a competent observer, on the spot through forty years, has said that "When the dead weight of Turkish misrule is removed the young Christian states justify the expectations formed for them." Unhappily, the European Powers, which had acquiesced in the miseries of the Turkish provinces, intervened with a peaceful arbitrament on their own account, in their own interests. By removing Albania from the results of the war they secured their own peace, but so disconcerted the expectations of the allies as to contribute greatly to the break that occurred among them. It is of course impossible to say what would otherwise have happened, but if Europe had used its armaments throughout and imposed an adjustment as nearly as possible equitable all round, there need not have been the second Balkan War nor the scandal of the partial return of "Turkish misrule" over European soil. Dread of each other's armaments forced the European states to maintain peace among themselves. The arbitrament which they imposed, unsought, led to a most cruel war; for the prevention of which there was armament in abundance, if firmly used.

The Council of the Ambassadors in London was an extemporized Court of Arbitration. It preserved European peace because, in view of the universal armaments, each nation feared above all war. Armaments secured peace. The arbitrary interference which adjusted Albania, could with equal right—or unright—have gone farther, and settled all the territorial results; but it stopped short because, no law warranting action, intervention might have provided dissensions which only fear of existing armament could compose. So the Powers followed their old policy to let anything happen in the Balkans if thereby they themselves risked nothing. Arbitration broke down when most needed.

A condition analogous to the Balkan obtained in Cuba in 1898: oppression of a people by an alien rule. Armament put an end to this; the United States rejecting arbitration in any form. From time to time, frequently, wretchedly disturbed social conditions recur in and about the Caribbean. Our Monroe Doctrine imposes a veto upon interposition by non-American states. Arbitration cannot uphold the Doctrine because it has no legal status. Armament alone can sustain, and to be bloodless it must be sufficient, "that the opposed may be ware of thee."

Introduction to K. Asami's Biography
of Tasuka Serata[1]

N.P., N.D. Probably, Quogue, Long Island, Summer 1913, [LC]

I have been asked to write an introduction to the life of the late Vice Admiral Tasuka Serata, of the Imperial Japanese Navy. I have acceded to this request the more willingly because I had the pleasure of knowing the Admiral in his early life, during his career at the United States Naval Academy. It so happened that in the year of his admission there, in company with the present Admiral, Baron Uriu, in 1877—I was ordered to the Academy as head of the Department of Ordnance and Gunnery. Soon after beginning my duties I learned that three Japanese young men had entered with the new class; one, Enouye,[2] to take the Engineer course, the two others that usual then to deck officers.

It was then less than ten years since I had spent some time in Japan, in all quite a twelvemonth, between 1867 and 1869. I had seen a good deal of both the people and the country from Nagasaki in the south to Hakodate in the north, and had received of both a pleasant and interested impression which had remained with me, and remains to the present day, although I have never had opportunity to return. With these recollections it was natural that I should ask them to visit in my family, then limited to my wife and myself, and during the three following years I often had the pleasure of entertaining them in my home.

I bring therefore to my present writing pleasant personal memories. I can see now Serata's face scarcely less plainly than when we sat talking together, although the subjects of our conversations have mostly passed out of my mind. I remember only some discussion on the relations between ventilation and health, which were less clearly recognized thirty-five years ago than they now are. When I left the Academy, in 1880, Serata had still a year to remain, in order to complete his course. I never saw him afterward again, although I had the pleasure of again meeting Admiral Uriu, who, when in America a few years ago, did me the honor of calling upon me.

But, now that I am old, I feel, even more than I did in those distant days,

---

1. *See* Mahan to *The Times*, London, June 13, 1913, Footnote 3.
2. Yonoske Enouye.

that there was, and is, between Serata and myself a bond stronger than ordinary friendship. He was then, and until death continued to be, an avowed Christian; as I, too, then was and still am. In Christ there is for His followers a unity exceeding other ties. There is in the Japanese character, and certainly not least among their naval officers, a trait to which Christianity, rightly presented and realized, should appeal strongly. Christianity, summed up, is loyalty in thought and act to a Person, recognized as being worthy of all the sacrifice and devotion that a man can show Him. When every admission has been made of many shameful acts done by men undeservedly called Christians, the history of Christianity since its beginnings assures us, beyond all contradiction, that simple devotion to Jesus Christ has led innumerable men and women in every age to live and die nobly for His sake; content to be themselves unknown, if He can be honored through their acts or in their deaths.

In this respect, in personal self-devotion, the Christian gives to Christ all that the Japanese gives to the Emperor. Between these two devotions, to the eternal Christ and to the temporal Sovereign, there is no antagonism; nothing that could place a man like Serata in the position of trying to serve two opposing masters. In the early days of Christianity, the Roman Emperors at times imagined that there was such opposition, and tried therefore to make Christians renounce Christ; rather than do which thousands of Christians died by the sword, or by the lion. The story of what these men, and many women too, bore rather than deny Christ, would strongly move the admiration of Japanese, who would recognize in it a spirit kindred to their own. So far from antagonism, between Christ and the Sovereign, the law of Christ enjoins that for Christ's sake, for Christ's honor, the man shall give to the Ruler under whom he lives, shall give to the country, of which in Japanese eyes the Emperor is the embodiment, the fullness of hearty service. Throughout all persecution of Christians by the Roman Emperors, Christians continued to give them obedience, and to pray for them; for so it is commanded by Christ.

Because Christ, once crucified for men, now lives forever, He binds in one not only the men of today but those of all past time who have given themselves to Him. Serata, and all who serve Christ, are fellow-citizens in Christ's Kingdom with Stephen,—the first who died for Christ; with the great leaders Peter and Paul; with the ten thousands of others who in eighteen centuries have gladly laid down their lives for Him; or, what is a severer proof of loyalty, have lived long lives in constant conscious obedience to His commands.

To Christians, Christ is not only the Sovereign of all mankind, demanding obedience and devotion. He is the one who before all gave the example Himself of obedience and devotion. He is the Hero, who for the sake of others, for the sake of all men, was Himself loyal and devoted, and laid down His life. When He knew death awaited Him, He refused to turn back or aside; He went straight forward, met it, and accepted it. When His enemies seized Him, He asked only that His friends and followers should be spared. When crucified, He prayed to God that those who killed Him should be pardoned; for He willed that even those who harmed Him should benefit by His death. Such was the Christian leader, our great and noble example, when He lived upon earth, a man's life among men. Such He is now, when, as Christians believe, He is the Ruler of the Universe. As He loved us then, so He loves us now.

It is Christ's own loyalty to God, whom He called His Father, His loyalty to the cause of men, whom He called his brethren, His willingness to die for the honor of God and for the welfare of men, that made Him the worthy object of the personal devotion which true Christians now give Him. We love Him, said one of his greatest followers, because He first loved us. As His death was the expression of His love, so now that He lives for ever His care is ever for us men. He stands beside all who seek Him; He fights with them the fight against wrong; and walks with them throughout their lives on earth.

In view of the much wickedness and the great shortcomings which still mark European history, it may seem rash to appeal to it as proof of what Christ's love and present life has meant to those who seek Him. Nevertheless, the appeal can be made. It must be remembered that from the first, and throughout the eighteen centuries since He died on the Cross, those who in countries called Christian have given Him personal devotion have been the exception; not the rule. Yet in those countries and through His followers—Christians—He has wrought the civilization, the progress, which have gathered round His Cross, and have gathered nowhere else. A competent English observer,[3] resident for forty years in Constantinople, has recently affirmed, and repeated, that "whenever the deadweight of Turkish misrule has been removed, the young Christian states have moved forward on the path of civilization, and justified all expectations formed for them." But Turkish misrule is not because they are Turks, but because Mahomet has blinded their eyes to the Person of Christ, and to the Cross which showed His courage and fidelity. Japan has recognized the progress of Christendom, has adopted its fruits, and since so doing has herself contributed to the development much which the European world fully and explicitly admits.

It is the glory of that faith which Admiral Serata professed, in which he lived, and in which he died, that it impresses upon the group of nations in which it is held a solidarity, a unity, which survives and transcends all differences between them. It has the quality of immortality, of universality,

---

3. Sir Edwin Pears.

and of unity of character, which is to be found in no other feature of their various national lives. Through that faith, in the devotion of Christians to Christ, there is ever present within the Christian states a Kingdom not of this world, the King of which died that He might establish it; and having died now lives for ever, the Sovereign of a nation which shall have no end. Wherever on earth now the Christian Faith is accepted among men, Christ's Kingdom dwells among them; and from it, according to the promise of the King, flow the benefits which everywhere accompany its spread, as the records of the past and of today abundantly prove to those who are willing carefully to study. Wherever that Kingdom is found, throughout the whole earth, whatever the nation in which it is, the Kingdom is one, and all the members of it are one in the King.

The Kingdom is in this world, but not of this world. Everywhere, in all peoples, it stands separate, yet among them; warring for right, though not with the sword; of every nation, and yet of none; held together everywhere by the devotion and loyalty of its subjects to the King who died for them. Yet, while thus separate, it gives to each nation the patriotic fervor, and to all mankind the universal love, which the King commanded His followers to give. A Jew Himself, He as a good patriot loved and served above all the Jews in the time of His mortal life. When He departed from among us, He commanded the leaders whom He left behind to go into all the world and bring into His Kingdom from all earthly nations all men that were willing to come. Those who so enter become subjects of the Kingdom which has no end; but, also like Him, they recognize that for His sake, beyond every other reason, they must be good patriots, servants to the earthly Ruler of their own country.

The time will come when this earth shall pass away and with it all its own Kingdoms. But the Kingdom of the Christ shall remain for ever. No longer in this world, in the world to come it will not find itself as now, dispersed among many peoples, from whom it differs in most important respects, but shall itself be the One only Kingdom under the One King; with a citizenship which shall have a truly universal type of character, for there all shall be like Him. That will be the national type of that Kingdom; man differing from man as we now do, yet with a national characteristic such as is observable in those who have common ancestral antecedents. That characteristic will be likeness to Christ.

To that Kingdom they pass who die Christians, when they die to this earthly life. There we, who still remain in the Kingdom on earth, know that now Serata is; the loyal Japanese, the loyal Christian, who, having in his day served Christ and his Emperor, now, to use the Christian phrase, sleeps in Jesus. His condition is not that of unconsciousness. It is called sleep, because it is a perfect rest from sorrows and cares, such as healthful sleep gives; but in itself it is the most vivid life, face to face with Christ Himself, in the perpetual presence of the Person to whom loyalty has been given, and in whom all Christians are for ever one. "To depart and to be with Christ is far better," said His great servant Paul, who for the love of Christ suffered all things, fought a good fight, and died by the sword, because he would not deny his Lord.

The Purpose of a Life Work

*An Essay Written for the Board of Missions
of the Episcopal Church*

N.P., N.D. Probably, 1913 [NWC]

The word "purpose," etymologically one with "propose," and in thought cognate with "pursuit," indicates consciousness of an object which a man sets before himself, and which he proposes to accomplish. What then is the comprehensive object which men in general may be said to set before themselves, to follow during life? For, taking mankind at large, we find not one aim, but many, differing from one another in scope, quality, and dignity, which constitute the purposes of their several life-works. These purposes they realize to themselves with varying degrees of clearness, of initiative, and of sustained energy. Still, though thus differing in species, these various aims have one common factor which ranges them in one order of classification. This common factor is that satisfaction with one's self and one's surroundings which we call happiness.

The Declaration of Independence, the output of a man who was a bit of a philosopher, ranges the pursuit of happiness—the purpose of a life-work—with life and liberty; these three he selected for mention among the great inalienable rights of the individual. I remember to have read some quaintly mocking, yet sympathetically sad, remarks by the late Charles Dudley Warner upon the doubtful desirableness of the right to *pursue* happiness. For as a matter of experience and observation happiness is not over-taken by pursuit; it comes oftener unbidden to him who seeks it not. As was said of God Himself, under certain conditions of seeking, "I was found of them who sought not after me." Our Lord, Who, putting His Divinity apart, was the most profound of human philosophers, affirms the same: Seek first the Kingdom of God and His righteousness; these other things will come to you by the way.

While, therefore, happiness is a lawful object, proposed by Christ Himself, to pursue happiness, by any of those paths commonly followed in that aim by men,—pleasure, wealth, power, knowledge, reputation, amusement, ease, and whatever others there be,—is not the way to gain it. Happiness is to be found, it is not to be overtaken. The nautical proverb has it that a stern chase is a long chase; the experience of men through generations affirms that the chase of happiness is rarely successful. The issue often resembles those other chases, of which naval history records many, where night closes down, and the chaser's straining eyes see the lights, or the waving shadow which he takes to be the prize, still before him. He struggles on in pursuit and in his intentness passes it, turned to one side, and loses it forever.

That "man never is, but always to be, blessed," is not true; but it is in the main true of those who seek the end by other than the one Way. "Thou hast made us for Thyself, and our souls find no rest till they find it in Thee." Thus Saint Augustine; and Jesus Christ, "Peace I leave unto you, My peace I give unto you; not as the world (in its pursuit of happiness) giveth, give I unto you. Let not your heart be troubled." Again, there is the direct antithesis, "In the world ye shall have tribulation, in Me ye shall have peace; for I have overcome the world."

"In Me peace" is the reiteration of the peace which was the human life-experience of the Man of Sorrows. "The Father hath not left Me alone, for I do always those things which please Him." This was the purpose of His life-work: I came not to do Mine own will, but the will of Him Who sent Me. Not Self, but Another. The unrest of the world is proverbial, as is its unsuccess. The irony of its gains, when grasped, provokes now tears, now laughter. "Carlyle has surpassed my utmost hopes," wrote his wife, "and I am miserable." At the summit of achievement, possessed of world wide fame, the first man of his profession, and assured of that which is called an "immortal" name, Nelson wrote, "I have known little happiness, only rare gleams of pleasure." In the hour of death he solaced himself, not with his glory attained, but with "Thank God, I have done my duty," the testimony of his conscience. That a man should say he is willing to live his life over again, with all its experiences, is thought singular. Yet each successive generation, unprofited by its predecessors, goes forth to pursue happiness by the old misleading tracks. Christ with unerring finger points the way, which is Himself. "Not to be ministered unto, but to minister." This is the Christian philosophy of life; this the pronouncement of its purpose.

The term "minister" thus is consecrated, stamped with the Divine image of the Divine Man—our pattern. Its application to a particular calling, though fully justified when the spirit of that calling is realized in practice, tends to throw into the background of men's thoughts the primary meaning of the word, "a servant"—of God—doing God's work; and because a servant of God therefore a servant of others, as Christ was. One would not indeed limit the significance of the term to those classified as ministers by common speech. Every lawful calling, every natural or social relation, can be consecrated by this spirit; first God, then man for God's sake. This does not put Self, the happiness, the peace, the rest, for which we long and which the world pursues, wholly out of court. It recognizes simply that he who seeks Self will never find self; that the true self is not caught, even by self-culture, but comes to him who seeks God's kingdom and righteousness, within himself, and for others. Thus all are ministers, if they have the spirit of Christ. Yet the use of the term minister, in our ordinary phraseology, to indicate the men who embrace that calling is justified; because for the purpose of their life-work they take that of ministry solely, concentrating their effort upon the work of service.

One hesitates to recommend such a choice by indicating advantages; for consideration of these, and influence by them, may seem to detract from the pure unselfishness of that self surrender, which after all, from the worldly point of view, is great. Nevertheless, self and its influence is a part of God's plan for the ordering of the world, which is His world because it is His creation. It is not the use of those tendencies which Self comprises, but the abuse of them, which is to be avoided. Jesus Christ, both in deed and as teacher, represents the perfectness of self-surrender, ending in self-sacrifice; but Jesus Christ for the joy set before Him endured the Cross, despising the shame. That His joy was of the noblest type possible to a perfect being does not invalidate the fact that it was His very own joy. That it was rejoicing in the fruits of His Ministry, in the glory of God and the redemption of men, does not make it any the less His joy. Thus His great forerunner also says; "This my joy is fulfilled; I stand and hear His voice." The joy is in Another, yet still it is "mine."

It is not necessary to philosophize overmuch to see that He Who constituted Self, constituted it in such wise that Self can know no joy equal to that which it finds in another. Jesus Christ and John the Baptist, in the utterances quoted, show their brotherhood with us all. There can scarcely be any one so young, of experience so limited, as not to have known in himself the exquisite flavor of an unselfish act. It is not indeed to be obtained by doing the unselfish thing in order to experience the joy; that is a mere pursuit of happiness, and in quality selfish. He who seeks the Kingdom of God because desiring the other things to be added unto him, does not truly seek it. Yet, in determining the purpose of the life work, it is reasonable and proper to remember that he who abandons self will find self as in no other way he can; that he who loses his life shall find it. As a motive, the reward can be entertained; but as an object to be followed for its own sake, it will prove as delusive as the more transient happiness which it is the inalienable right of the natural man to pursue.

In undertaking a work of ministry, therefore, as a life-work, it is fully permissible to be moved thereto in part by the assurance that, faithfully followed as a service to God and man, it will bring a joy more certain, superior in quality, more enduring, and possibly greater in quantity even

[695]

here on earth, than that which any success in the pursuit of happiness, commonly so estimated, can bestow. Also, to this no unsuccess is possible. My rejoicing, says St. Paul, is this, the testimony of my conscience. Nothing can deprive a man of this; and who can say the same of the utmost the world can give of that which it has to give?

I do not wish for a moment to seem to undervalue as the purpose of a life-work, its aim and object, that degree of absolute self-surrender, self-devotion, in which self so far disappears as to find its sole expression and happiness in love, and in loving service for others. Only I doubt whether such a condition is not rather the crown of a life's work than the possible sole sustaining motive of a beginner, in those days of youth when the natural life in the full vigor of its desires clamors for recognition of earthly aims. I fear mistake; the error of taking warm impulse for attained purpose, the self-deception of the inexperienced. I cannot but feel that the appeal to the beginner should be somewhat on the lines which our nature, imperfect though it be, suggests; the motive to which our Lord Himself did not disdain to appeal—"What shall it profit?"

Until touched by grace, the simple human aim to which we are born is summed up in the words "success" and "happiness." Grace does not reject this, as suited to beginnings, but it points out the error in the natural estimate of what success is, and what happiness; how impossible it is for earthly measures of either to satisfy the demands of the spiritual nature, which is the essence of man's being. But it does not stop with showing error; it reveals also truth. It shows that whereas to labor for the things in which the world sees success, and imagines happiness, is to spend money for that which is not bread, and labor for that which satisfieth not, there nevertheless does exist that which yields full sustenance and inexhaustible gratification. There really is a condition which, attained, gives a joy that man, or the world, can no more take away than it can bestow. "Ye shall see Me, and your joy shall be full, and no man shall take it from you"; the joy of the Baptist as he saw himself superseded by Christ, his work complete in Another.

"In the world ye shall have tribulation" is no bald repetition of the universal knowledge that the world is full of sorrow, frustration, disappointments, failures. It is the stamp on the coin that affixes its value, declares the little worth of the aspirations confined to the world's rewards, their inadequacy to the purpose of a reasonable being's life. To announce this alone is to proclaim despair, even though disguised under the hollow philosophy of enjoying while you can; let us eat and drink, for to-morrow we die. But the declaration does not stand alone. Side by side is the other assurance, "In Me ye shall have Peace." "In My Presence is the fulness of joy." "I am with you always." As their context shows, these several affirmations are not to be understood simply of a distant hereafter called Heaven. They doubtless imply that increase in the blessings of peace and the consciousness of the Presence which we associate with the hereafter; but they are for the now of this world, and to those who understand what Peace in its comprehensive sense implies, and what the Presence is, they offer the purpose of a life's work which can know neither failure nor lack of satisfaction.

It is with such an appreciation of the truths of existence that men with life before them should approach the question which all pose to themselves, consciously or unconsciously,—the purpose of a life's work. The specific claim of the ministry is that it is the highest, completest, realization of an exclusive self-devotion, of a concentrated purpose. It has been so since the first Christian ministers, Andrew and Peter, called by One who, though their God, was also like themselves Man, left all and followed Him.

The Origins of the European War

Interview with the New York Evening Post

Quogue, Long Island, August 3, 1914[1]

The aggressive violence of Austria's ultimatum to Servia, taken with the concession by the latter of all the demands except those too humiliating for national self-respect, indicate that the real cause of the war is other than set forth by the ultimatum.

Knowing from past experience how the matter must be viewed by Russia, it is incredible that Austria would have ventured on the ultimatum unless assured beforehand of the consent of Germany to it. The inference is irresistible that the substance of the ultimatum was the pretext for a war already determined on as soon as plausible occasion offered.

The cause of this predetermination is to be found in the growing strength of Russia on recovering from her war with Japan. With the known deficiencies of French armaments which were recently admitted, the moment was auspicious for striking down France and Russia before they regained strength. The motives are to be found in Austria's apprehension of the growing Slav power in the south and that of Germany concerning Russia on the east.

Great Britain as the third member of the entente finds herself in the position of Prussia in 1805, when she permitted Napoleon to strike down Austria unaided, and was herself struck down the following year at Jena. Or of that of France in 1866 when she stood by while Prussia crushed Austria and was herself overwhelmed in 1870.

Germany's procedure is to overwhelm at once by concentrated preparation and impetuous momentum. If she fail in this she is less able to sustain prolonged aggression, as was indicated in the Franco-Prussian war during and after the siege of Paris.

The British fleet, which is superior to that of Germany, has the power to prevent all commerce under the German flag, and, by blockade, to close against neutrals all the rivers properly German except those emptying into the Baltic. The British fleet is not strong enough to divide for blockade

---

1. From the *New York Evening Post*, August 3, 1914, p. 1.

in both Baltic and North Seas. The Rhine, emptying through central Holland, cannot be blockaded.

If the German rush proves indecisive or prolonged, the financial pressure thus in the power of Great Britain may determine the issue, or may force the German fleet to fight, in which case the issues will be determined by battle.

If Germany succeeds in downing both France and Russia, she gains a respite by land, which may enable her to build up her sea force equal, or superior to that of Great Britain.

In that case the world will be confronted by the naval power of a state, not, like Great Britain, sated with territory, but one eager and ambitious for expansion, eager also for influence. This consideration may well affect American sympathies.

In my judgment, a right appreciation of the situation should determine Great Britain to declare war at once. Otherwise, her entente engagements, whatever the letter, will be in spirit violated, and she will earn the entire distrust of all possible future allies.

Italy likewise owes it to herself to declare war against her recent allies. In cooperation with France, and with Greece, reinforced by the two American battleships just purchased, she can doubtless maintain the balance of maritime power in the Mediterranean, prevent the Turks giving their expected support to Germany, keep quiet the Bulgarians, if these are so ill-advised as to purpose a diversion in favor of Austria, and, in brief, consolidate the opposition of the Balkan States to Austria-Hungary, whose ambitions are notoriously inconsistent with those of Italy.

Undoubtedly, the North Sea will be the theatre of the naval battles. The German fleet, so far as we know, steamed immediately from Kiel to the North Sea, ready to strike. For a long time it has been the German policy to keep her navy ready, and virtually cleared for action, and we may expect any minute, apparently, to get word of a great engagement, and should expect the British fleet to win.

The Kiel Canal will undoubtedly be used in Germany's naval strategy, as affording access to the North and the Baltic Seas, but not as the deciding movement. England cannot, as I have said, throw a preponderating fleet into both seas, and Germany's hope is to strike immediately. It is a question of existence for her. The stagnation of her carrying trade on the seas must threaten her very life, and the neutral shipping, already taxed to its limits, cannot bear the additional burdens of supplying Germany.

The suggestion made that Germany might demonstrate with her fleet in the Baltic is not tenable. The Russian fleet, with only eight pre-Dreadnoughts, and no Dreadnoughts and battle-cruisers—however much of an absurdity that type may be—is negligible. Germany could achieve nothing with her fleet in the Baltic, for it is a principle of warfare that under modern conditions no nation can afford to waste its navy in operations against fortifications.

[Admiral Mahan said that the most important questions to be answered would be those of the increased efficiency of submarines and torpedoes, and of aircraft.]

And believe me, the English fleet, which sailed with sealed orders, is at present in the North Sea, with the purpose of being just out of the effective range of submarines. I do not know, definitely, what the effective cruising range of such submersible craft is, but I should estimate it to be 200 miles. To accomplish that distance they must travel for a long way upon the surface, and so be in sight of the scouts which the British fleet, of course, has posted.

This question of the use of the increased efficiency of the submarine is assuredly one of the most important to be tested in actual warfare. They had, of course, no opportunity in the Russo-Japanese War, but in the present confined theatre of operations should be seen at their best. I do not share Sir Percy Scott's views of the surpassing power of the submarine to the complete effacement of the battleship.

The torpedoes, as used in the Russo-Japanese War, were utilized chiefly to put a finish to a ship almost silenced already by gun fire, and for such purposes they are effective. But torpedo boats are night craft. They cannot be effective in daylight against modern guns. Germany apparently does not place much faith in them.

But most of these problems of the technical science of warfare are too abstruse for the general observer. They are really even too technical for the experts to agree on. As Gen. Sherman said: "One may demonstrate something in manoeuvres, but you really need the element of human fear to be conclusive."

The mooted question of the big guns will also be tested. For my own part, I have always believed that the volume of fire was the determining fact. The number of hits, and not single shots, is the most important element, I believe. However, all those things we shall soon know, perhaps any minute.

The British Navy

Fragment of a Newspaper Interview

N.P., N.D. [Early August 1914][1]

You people in England do not realise the immense admiration felt all over the world, yes, and in Germany also, for the British Navy. Speaking from my standpoint, as an American, I tell you that there is only one navy in the world, and that the others are mere striplings by comparison. I do not mean to underrate the American and other fleets, but, by comparison with the British, every other navy still has much to learn. Whether the morale of the officers and men is as good to-day as in the time of Nelson remains to be proved, but, personally, I hold that the British Navy to-day, in all essentials, remains as incomparably superb as ever.

---

1. From Charles C. Taylor, *Life of Admiral Mahan*, p. 281. Reprinted by permission.

About What Is The War?

Draft of an Unpublished Article

N.P., N.D. Probably, Quogue, Long Island, Mid-August 1914 [NWC]

In the solemn pause which of necessity intervenes between declarations of war and the actual clash of great armies with occurrences of really important events, as distinguished from the relatively petty excursions and alarms which first fill the newspapers, the moment seems apt to recall and to consider the underlying causes which find their issue in war. Southey's familiar poem runs:

> What they fought each other for
> I could not well make out. . . .[1]

and such in good measure is the attitude of the world at large towards war in general. By a peculiar confusion of thought some seem to imagine that war is the result of a mere love of fighting, and in this there is a residuum—a very small residuum—of plausibility, because, once a nation has risen to the fighting pitch, the enthusiasm and the uproar reproduce in the populace the symptoms peculiar to individual men when heated in personal quarrel.

Another curious obliquity of vision is that which sees in great armaments the cause of war; that, if nations were not armed, they would not fight. Needless to say that the getting the better of others is one of the large occupations of the human race, in business, in lawsuits, as well as in international affairs; and that, if the superiority of one nation to another is two hundred to one hundred, they will under sufficient provocation fight, as certainly as if that superiority were two millions to one with all the organization characteristic of modern states. If a concrete instance be wanted, our War of Secession—erroneously styled Civil War—is immediately in point. What armament, what preparation, was there, in the least commensurate to the passions—the motives—on either side? Of the first encounter on any large scale—the first Bull Run—a southern officer engaged said after the war to a fellow-graduate of West Point, "I never in my life saw men as frightened as ours,—except yours." This proves, if proof were needed, the absence of that preparation of which armament is the accom-

---

1. Robert Southey's "The Battle of Blenheim."

paniment. The regular armies now about to engage in Europe are composed in large part of men who never saw a shot fired in anger, yet, in virtue of their training, it is not likely that any such comment will be passed on them, subject though even the best troops at times are to panic. But the unarmed and untrained men of our North and South flew to arms as readily as the Germans and French to-day, though in less orderly fashion.

It is the mistake of most pronounced advocates of peace and arbitration that, in their commendable effort to minimize war, they rely mainly upon methods which are essentially secondary, and overlook the underlying causes which when aroused defy their methods, and will continue so to do so long as they exist and come on occasion into operation. The primitive elemental passions of human nature are to be controlled only by principle or by force, and arbitration is essentially force, in that it aims to control by external pressure. There are motives which can be thus controlled, because not of the deepest or strongest; but others, as, for instance, national or race sympathy, once stirred, will shake off arbitration with a violence that cannot be withstood. Unless the inward feeling is changed, the only force that can control these is physical; that of numbers and of organization. In a word arbitration is adequate so far, and no farther.

The Secretary of the "American Association for International Conciliation" in a recent letter intimates that "bloated armament is not likely to provide insurance against anything except prosperity and peace." "Bloated" is of course an adjective characteristic of the point of view. Three or four times already in this century, armament—preparation for war—has insured peace, if averting war can be so called. No thoughtful man, I suppose, ever claimed that because it did so thrice it infallibly would always. That war shows that something is wrong somewhere is as certain as the same remark applied to an epidemic, but while the cure of actual sufferers has a place in such conditions a homely proverb tells us that immunity is to be had not in treatment but in removing causes.

The cause of war is the human heart, and its passions, more often noble than simply perverse. Serbia is in arms to-day because men of the same race in Serbia and in Austria have longed to be under a common government, an end which the States of Germany attained by war a generation ago. Austria is in arms because the realization of the Slav wish would mean a dismemberment—amputation—of her empire; the motive of the North in the war for the Union. Russia is in arms because of the threatened oppression of men of her race—Slavs—by Austria; the cause of British action in the Boer War. Germany is in arms for the avowed motive of fidelity to a contract of alliance with Austria for mutual defence; probably also because she feels herself restricted in possibilities of national growth, and barred from free access to the sea and from room to expand beyond the seas. Belgium is in arms because Germany has invaded her territory, after

[703]

a demand that she should dishonor her national character by permitting her soil to be used as a means of attacking a friendly nation that dwelt securely by her. Great Britain is in arms because of the violation of Belgian neutrality, which she in the general interest of Europe had guaranteed; as had Germany, the offender. That a fore-most nation of to-day should thus deliberately violate not only international law, but its own pledges, by an act evidently premeditated, in plans long formed, demonstrates that there still exists evil of a character which can be met only by physical repression. The opinion may persist that arbitration could control; so might the opinion that black is white, or that we have in a nation which has just flagrantly disregarded law, the probability of willing submission to a law-court.

"Bloated" armaments alone are adequate to meet their kind, and the doubt that still prevails as to issues is due to the fact that those of the opposition may not be bloated enough, that German thoroughness of preparation may sweep away resistance as a sudden jerk breaks a chain, and may thus bring Europe to the feet of a simple conqueror, dictating terms.

In the interlinked series of causes here sketched, it is alluring to seek the first cause. In a sense, of course, no such first cause can be assigned; it would itself be the result of history—of a past antecedent to itself. Yet there are such things as epochs, of which it may be said that responsible action decided the wrong way; when, to quote the late Lord Salisbury, "the wrong horse was backed."

Of the immediate present, among the causes above assigned, it is probably true that the discontent of the southern Slavs of Austria and of their brethren in Serbia is the fountain of ill. Hated racially by both the Germans and Hungarians of the dual Kingdom,—Austria-Hungary,—oppressed in the combination, and divided one from the other by artificial political arrangements, their longing for fair terms, for kindred association, and for the power that comes from aggression, inspires unappeasable restlessness, against which Austria exercises repression. Resistance may have taken criminal shape in instances; it is the note of the political resistances of the hopelessly weak. The assassination of the Archduke may be in point; but it is to be recalled that the trial at Agram of the fifty-three Southern Slavs, by Austria, in 1907, for high treason, was a judicial scandal, and that the distinguished Austrian Historian, Priedjung, two years later, was proved to have used forged documents, to substantiate a charge of treason against Slavs, which documents were furnished—it is to be assumed innocently— by the Austro-Hungarian Foreign Office.

When we regard the present European status—France, Great Britain, Russia—it seems probable that the resistance of the two former to the latter thus thwarting the natural expulsion of the Turks from Europe—the Crimean War,—was the most potent factor in leading up to the present situation. United Germany has since come into being, and Bismarck who presided at its conception and birth, was also prominent in the councils which again checked Russia in 1877, giving to Austria the administration of Bosnia and Herzegovina, though sovereignty remained with Turkey. The jealousies of southeastern Europe ministered to the security of Germany and to the weakness of Austria. The general result has been the prolongation of unrest and dissatisfaction, with continued oppression of Slavs by Turkey. There followed the Balkan War of 1912; after which persistence in disregard of Slav wishes, but, as it is understood, in obedience to those of Austria-Hungary, framed the treaty which disappointed both Bulgarians and Serbians. Upon this upset to their plans came the unhappy "Second Balkan War," freely ascribed by many to the meddling of the Powers, concerned only for their own peace, the partial return of the Turks, and the present situation. With all our sympathies for Great Britain and wishes for her success in the present conjuncture, it is to be hoped that her lingering sympathy with the Turkish Empire will be succeeded by a determination that Austria-Hungary no longer meddle with the Balkans; that at the worst those little states be left to work out their own salvation among themselves. No other state can do it for them. Europe now is reaping the harvest of past blunders which even at the time of their occurrence it was difficult to reconcile with sound statesmanship.

Sea Power in the Present European War

An Article Published in Leslie's Illustrated Weekly Newspaper,
CXIX *(August 20, 1914).*

N.P., N.D. Probably, Quogue, Long Island, August 1–3, 1914[1]

The fundamental principles of warfare are the same on land and on sea. Military war, commonly so called, and naval war, are the two great principal subdivisions,—specializations,—of the military art. Each contains within itself certain minor specializations which it is needless here to name.

One of the chief factors entering the conduct of war is the question of communications. The now somewhat familiar saying that "an army like a snake moves on its stomach" means in last analysis that the communications of an army with its sources of food supply are vital to its action. The problem applies to all other necessaries of daily military exertion—reinforcements, ammunition, and so forth; in the case of a navy, its coal supply also.

On a broader scale, that which is true of armies is true also of the countries to which they belong, as soon as those countries emerge from the most primitive stage of existence. It becomes increasingly so as civilization advances. The paralysis that has spread through the business world within the last fortnight testifies to the insecurity of communications—intercourse of every kind—between nations, due to imminent war.

Water being the greatest, simplest, and easiest mode of communication between countries, imparts to naval warfare its most determinative feature. This applies not only to the severance of communications but to the characteristic method of action. The battles of naval warfare are few compared with those of land; it is the unremitting daily silent pressure of naval force, when it has attained control of the sea against an opponent,—the sustained blocking of communication,—which has made sea power so decisive an element in the history of the world. To realize this, we have only to consider a few of the items upon which highly organized nations depend for the well-being of their population: food, raw materials for manufacture, exports to pay for imports, the carriage of specie in moments of emergency. By far the greater part of these is effected by sea, by lake, or by river.

---

1. Because this article cannot be readily found, it is reprinted here as a service to Mahan scholars.

Attention having been fixed upon this factor in history, it has brought into existence what is now in point of power the second greatest navy of the world. Before 1870 Germany was in the main an agricultural country, capable in great measure of living off itself, and in so far independent of the sea. Its commerce, outside of the then free cities, was mostly carried by other than German ships; its navy was negligible in any great European combination. But since 1879, with the installation of the protective system, manufactures have increased vastly, the national wealth has grown, the population has flowed increasingly from the fields to the city, a great mercantile marine has grown up under the imperial flag.

With the merchant shipping, though lagging somewhat behind in point of time, has come the navy. The general necessity for such protection was emphasized to imperial Germany by the geographical position of Great Britain, which lies across all the sea communications of Germany, except the relatively trivial intercourse with the Baltic. In case of war between the two countries, the whole carrying trade under the German flag would be stopped immediately; of which fact we at this moment are receiving striking instances. War would remove both British and German merchant ships, as sea-carriers for the maintenance of Germany's commercial system, thus disorganizing the entire social structure as resting upon industries.

Not only so, but neutral merchantmen could be debarred from entrance to German ports by blockade, a recognized method of war. In war, Germany would have to depend, for all that she drew from the sea in peace, upon adjacent neutral ports, such as those of the Rhine, the mouth of which is in Holland, whence by the stream access is to be had to the interior of Germany. It is evident, however, that communication thus limited resembles the sudden substitution of a single track railroad for one of four. All ships of Germany and Britain, the two chief carriers, are eliminated, and neutrals restricted, not to mention that the said neutrals are already largely occupied in other commercial relations.

Such in broad outline were the reasons which determined Germany to undertake a navy which, to use the official definition, should be so strong that the greatest naval Power would hesitate to provoke hostilities. Yet such a moment has arrived, and under circumstances of conduct on the part of Germany which seem to show that she deliberately provokes the hostility; that, instead of hesitation, Great Britain is compelled not to dare to hesitate.

Having given the general features of the situation, let us turn now to the specific conditions in the North Sea, beyond any possible doubt the chief theatre of this great naval war. Within the last year Germany has adopted the policy of keeping in full commission, prepared for instant action, a much larger part than before of her available fleet. The coincidence of this system with the recent transactions seems to emphasize the deliberate preparation with which she has flung her glove into the face of the world. I have not at hand as precise information as I could wish, nor the means of obtaining it at once; but I believe I am right in saying that Great Britain has, also in commission, a force with sufficient margin of strength, in all arms, over that of Germany, having regard only to a collision between the two fleets. Germany, therefore, might wish to postpone action till a happy blow, or happy chance, diminish the inequality. Great Britain for the same reason should desire to force action, though it is possible she may wish to delay, in order that her fleet may be reinforced by units already approaching readiness. In the balance of such considerations so much depends upon individual judgment, and upon particular circumstances, that it is impossible to speak positively as to probable action. Great Britain's reserves of force much exceed those of Germany.

Blockade, for reasons given above, is the readiest means of forcing action. It will bring the pressure of sea power directly and continuously upon the daily life of Germany. More than any other one means, blockade crushed the South in our War of Secession. By international law, a blockade requires only the presence, before the port blockaded, of vessels sufficient to constitute a real danger for a neutral attempting to enter. Light cruisers are sufficient for this. That they may not be driven off, the main fleet must be near enough to meet that of the enemy if it come out; for, if driven off, the blockade is legally removed. But it is not necessary that the main fleet keep so close as to be seriously exposed to submarine by day, or to torpedo by night, for the above definition of blockade is very elastic.

Let us suppose that Great Britain has thus established a formal blockade of the German North Sea coast, from the boundary of Holland to that of Denmark, and that the German battle fleet for reasons of its own chooses not to leave its port for immediate battle. There are two chief positions in which it can rest securely: either the entrance to the Kiel Canal on the east, or at the new great naval base at Wilhelmshaven, twenty miles west of the mouth of the Elbe. Whichever it choose, the fleet will be to-gether—concentrated. It will not risk division, with the chance that in seeking to unite one part may be overwhelmed by the whole British force. It being probable that even when united the total is less than the British aggregate, it is natural to suppose that the time of waiting will be signalized by attempts to reduce this margin by attacks of torpedo boats, of submarines, and very probably of air-craft. In this war we may look for fairly decisive tests of the actual value of these new means of warfare, for the opponents are skilled, enterprising, and trained, which was not the case with the Russians in the naval war of ten years ago.

I should anticipate that the blockade proper would be maintained by a very numerous body of light cruisers and torpedo vessels, so near the entrance as effectually to watch all attempts of hostile torpedo vessels to come out. The main fleet, the necessary object of the enemy's torpedoes, would remain out of sight by day; and after dusk would change position, to be less readily found by any submarine that should elude its own scouts. Air-craft will be met by air-craft. Most current reasoning on the new weapons of war proceeds on the vicious assumption that these new weapons will encounter only the battleship, overlooking that they must meet also their own kind.

A very serious danger to the British blockade will be the island of Heligo-land, twenty-eight miles off the German coast, between the mouths of the Elbe and the Weser. Great Britain held this from the days of Napoleon to the year 1890, when it was ceded to Germany by the government of the late Lord Salisbury in exchange for the relinquishment of the German claim to the island of Zanzibar. It is told of Lord Salisbury, a very wise man, that he said of military precaution that soldiers would wish to fortify the moon against an invasion from Mars. I apprehend that during some weeks British naval officers will wish that this particular moon had not been surrendered as an outpost to the German Mars. The island, though little over a mile in length and a third of a mile across, is now a heavily fortified torpedo base; and as it projects the German torpedo defences so far seaward, it will modify the position possible to the British fleet, while the need to watch it will diminish the force available for closing torpedo ports on the main-land. Such is the effect of Heligoland. For the rest, granted clear weather, the task of watching torpedo exits is arduous; but yet practicable to the degree to which military security can ever extend. War cannot be made without running risks. Of these fog probably is the greatest, but in it po-sition can be changed unseen.

After the preliminaries follows the possible encounter of the main fleets. About this it is impossible to predict. I believe the probabilities all are that when the collision comes the British numbers will be superior; that, whether soon or late, the Germans, if they fight at all, must accept this very serious disadvantage. Of course the question of relative efficiency enters. I know no reason to believe that of the Germans to be greater. Their thoroughness is known, and I have had described to me, by a British officer of German family relations, the mode of imparting knowledge practiced on their con-scripts. It suggested to me somewhat the process of fattening turkeys for Christmas. The advantage the British have, in my judgment, is that their enlistment system for the crews is voluntary and continuous; that of the Germans conscript and short service. So far as this is true, the contrast is that between a lifelong profession, with its acquired second nature, and that of an episodical period in the main course of life. A French officer once said to me of their conscription, "We keep our men too short a time." In general, the officers of the two services may be assumed to be equal. Men of particular ability can be revealed only by war.

The North Sea naval situation is of such absorbing interest that we too easily lose sight of the Mediterranean, where the trouble arose. The Turks are said to favor Germany and therefore Austria; and would naturally desire to seize this opportunity to regain some of their recent loss. Greece is said to intend aiding the Servians, to which Austria replies that in that event she will blockade the coast of Greece, which she has the ships to do. Unhindered, the Greek navy can so molest the transportation of Turks from Asia Minor as to render their action in large measure nugatory. Prevented, the Bulgarians, with Turks at hand, may rise against their recent allies. The French navy can control the Mediterranean, and stop the Austrian blockade with its indicated consequences; and by so doing increase the solid force of Servians, Greeks, and Montenegrins, who in the Balkans not only fight their own battle and that of Russia, but by the same action divert and greatly lessen the power of Germany's ally and France's enemy. Whether the Italian government can in such case control the traditional hatred of their people for the Austrian, inherited from the years of oppression which ended only in 1859, and exasperated by the modern cry of "unredeemed" Italy—Trieste and Trentino—will remain to be seen. I should doubt it; and, considering the wantonness with which Austria has provoked this general war, and the apparent complicity of Germany, I see no moral obligation to deter.

In short, while the most important naval transactions may be looked for in the North Sea, the questions of the Mediterranean are by so far the more interesting as they involve more doubtful points and are more intricate. The determinative bearing of sea power, military and commercial, is clear; and if anything more were needed the curious appeal issued from the German Embassy in London, for British neutrality, would confirm. The English might well reply, Fas est ab hoste doceri (it is right to be taught by an enemy).

Summary of a *New York Times* Editorial[1]

N.P., N.D. Probably, Quogue, Long Island, circa August 30, 1914 [LC]

A dispatch fr. Toronto contrastg. 3000 miles unguarded frontr. wh. divide U.S. fr. Can wth bristling frontrs. of Eur. suggests real reason why U.S. hs for centy. maintd. peace wth G.B. x x x Disarmg. frontrs removd suspicions. Fortifying Eur. boundaries has invited suspicn & attk. They are being attkd & elab. Eur. prepns as insurance agst war hv made war inevit. The hundred mills. of peop ths side C. frontr. do not molest 8.000.000 on tht side, not because occasns internatl jealousy hv. not arisen, but because in absence of brute force reason has invariably prevailed. (Instances cited) In 1864 when Fedl. Gvt. was suspectd of entertaining designs of invadg. Can., and later during revival of distrust over *Alabama* incident, one of deciding factors for continuance of peace was this mutually unguarded frontr. Both ctries had prepared for nothing but peace, and, in words of late Prof. Sumner, what we prepare for that we shall get.

---

1. The editorial appeared in *The New York Times* on August 29 under the title "The American Example." *See* Mahan to Miller, September 6, 1914.

Woman's Suffrage

A Speech

N.P., N.D [LC]

It has been said that, owing to Great Britain having no written Constitution as a check upon the powers of her Legislature, there is nothing which Parliament cannot do, except *to make a woman a man*. To define this object as the end of the suffrage movement would probably be called a caricature; yet a moment's reflection will show that it is true, in the sense of breaking down and removing for ever the line of demarcation, which the general sense of the world and the course of history have drawn, as the barrier separating the respective spheres of men and women. It is obvious that the movement cannot stop with the mere grant of the vote; that logically, and inevitably, it goes on to the full entrance of women upon the whole field of political activity; upon the legislative field, from the National Congress down, and upon the Executive, from the President of the United States to the smallest political office in the gift of the Government.

This is not merely to establish equality of consideration upon which so much argument is based, with the implication that the withholding of suffrage is an imputation of the inferiority of women to men. The result, stated above as inevitable, if the vote be once obtained, is not *equality* in any sense, but *identity* of social function between women and men. It means that women shall no longer concentrate their ambitions and affections upon the home, the children, and all the sacred relationships attaching to these words, but shall disperse their energies and modify their characters, and entire personality as a sex, by entering upon the outside hurly burly of masculine life.

The question before us then—in the light of which the remarks of the speaker of the evening should also be regarded—is whether it is, or can be, good for the community to sacrifice, wholly or even in great measure, the special social function of woman which throughout the Christian era has been hers in the Christian household. The equality of the sexes has been the teaching of Christianity from the beginning; and nowhere else than where Christianity enters has that equality been found, because women have neither the physical nor the moral energy to compel it by brute force. But Christianity—which is the cornerstone of European civilization—while inculcating equality, emphasizes differentiation and denies identity of function. Such identity is the end of the present women's movement. It promises and is already accompanied by, a lessening esteem for home and child-bearing. Is it probably for the good of the community? For the true test to be applied to every social and political demand is the good of the community; not the gratification of a very small section of it—which the suffragists now are.

Before the speaker of the evening begins, I would like to suggest to you a very few broad general considerations which seem to me to underlie determinations of the merits of the suffrage question.

1.   Is the effect upon the community at large. Voting is a communal action, for the welfare of the community. The argument that it is a personal right is the one usually—almost exclusively—advanced; on the familiar ground of taxation. But the Taxation without Representation is Tyranny applies to the community. The principle was recognized long ago, and the phrase formulated by men who were not thinking even of universal male suffrage. Minorities even now are not represented, or very imperfectly. The same line of thought applies to the alleged grievance of obeying laws in voting in which you have no part. The question who makes the laws—that is, who votes—is for the community to determine.

2.   The question of right disappearing, that of expediency follows. In this case—Is it expedient for the welfare of the community that women should have the ballot? Here we must recognize and remember that we face a far reaching proposition. You cant stop with the vote. There follows necessarily the full range of all the political activities. These at present are confined to men. Will it be to the advantage of the community—of the State—that women enter this arena also from President of the United States to [words missing]. Are political activities so consonant to women's sphere as to make this advisable? Or is it more probable that as actually men do and superintend all the commercial and business activities, all that constitutes the prosperity and order of the state, to them also should be confined the political action which regulates business, commerce, transport, manufactures.

3.   With these consequences in view the proposition to give women the vote breaks down the constant practice of the past ages by which to men is assigned the outdoor rough action of life and to women that indoor sphere which we call the family. There is no drawing a line here other than that of sex. Remove that barrier as is proposed and you reverse what has heretofore been fundamental in our society.

The Christian Doctrine of the Trinity

An Essay

N.P., N.D. [LC]

The coordinate, and in large degree mutually independent branches of our Government may be thought of abstractly; that is, separate from the particular incumbents who from time to time occupy, or are charged with, the several functions. Thus the Executive, the Legislative, the Judiciary, are "Powers that be, ordained of God," as really as those of which St. Paul affirmed. In this perpetual existence, as distinguished from the transiency of occupancy by particular men, there attaches to the several branches a kind of personality, a tripartite personality; yet, despite the difference of function attaching to the three, they form an organic whole, and that not by combination but by the essential unity which underlies and manifests itself in these coordinate existences. Each is an expression of the national life,—which is not divided among them, nor its unity in any way impaired by trinality.

We seem therefore to find here a certain analogy to the Blessed Trinity, which, like all analogies, must not be pressed too far, to the extent of affirming a precise parallel. It may nevertheless serve to illustrate, make more comprehensible, the Trinity in Unity; the undivided substance being the national life, the Persons being the three powers or forms in which, with corresponding separate functions, that life is manifested.

It is needless to say that in the Christian scheme of belief, along with unity of substance and of will, particular functions are attributed to each Person of the Trinity. There is also a certain representative capacity of the (entire) Godhead in the Person of the Father, to Whom therefore, *generally*, prayer is addressed. So in the unity of the national life, of the national sovereignty which is the chief attribute of the life, a representative capacity attaches to the Executive, in relation to all matters or persons external to the nation. God—The Trinity—is indeed immanent in creation, but He is also transcendent; in Nature, yet also beyond Nature. In this latter sense He is external to Nature, though perhaps it cannot be said that Nature is external to Him. Yet to each single man, and consequently to all humanity, He is not only immanent, but transcendent—external. In this relation, God the Father is to man the representative Person *commonly*; but not so as to exclude prayer to either the Son or the Holy Spirit.

The words of Jesus Christ concerning Himself and the Father: "If the Father be glorified in Me, He also will glorify Me in Myself and will straightway glorify Me," were fulfilled in that "hour" upon which He was even then entering. "The hour," He said, "is come." In that hour, of the Agony, the Father was glorified in Him by the perfectness of His submission to, acquiescence in, and, finally, acceptance of the Father's Will. The whole process, the full "hour," was one of constant glorifying of God; and the consequence followed God glorified Him in Himself, not merely the glory and honor thereafter attributed to Him by men unto this day, nor yet only the glory given by the keener eyed spiritual witnesses, but, and above all, the Lord Jesus was glorified in Himself, made more and exceedingly glorious in His personality, a more glorious being in His humanity, than ever before; to a degree also, we may believe, beyond which even His humanity could not attain, the fullness of His glory; for He therein was "made *perfect*."

I apprehend that this which was true of the Master may and will be true, in measure, of each follower. Whereinsoever occasion arises, as likewise in the less eventful even tenor of daily life, if God be glorified in a man, God also will glorify that man in himself; will crown him with glory and honor, not primarily with that glory which consists in the homage of others, but in that glory which consists in *being* glorious—the glory of character of intrinsic worth.

And so is constituted a perpetual reciprocal process. God glorified in the man, in his being and conduct, in his bearing fruit; and God glorifying the man in himself in the development of being, in the bearing more fruit even—as was the case also of Christ—by purging, pruning, suffering.

The Wife, the priestess in the home, filling it with the beauty of holiness; the intercessor, between God and the other members—the husband, the children, and most especially toward the servants. Recognizing and consecrating the relationship to all in the spirit of constant intercession, in prayer, in conduct, in inward cultivation of holiness of spirit. The little homely cares of children by the mother, priestly.

Intercessor—one who stands between—*inter*.

The man's *house* his *career*; to carry into it the like spirit of intercession—betweenness. Thus a priest has his official priesthood, his career, but he has also a natural priesthood common to all baptized to carry into & characterize his intercourse with others, his attitude toward them. Each believer a priest, not only in intercessory prayer, but in attitude and conduct toward others.

Thus the home, and the career, become the temple in which the woman and the man serve; as the body of the Christian is the temple—and his whole personality of the Holy Ghost. St. Paul is speaking of the body specifically as the temple, because dealing with the question of desecrating the body.

The development of a man's own spiritual character is somewhat like the corner stone of a building. Contracted in immediate dimension and scope, as compared with the completed structure, it nevertheless is the essential basis on which all rests and from which all develops. It is somewhat like—much like—the relation of the small seed to the full grown plant. Yet, also like them, how vast and more imposing the full field of Christian interest and activity outside the personal spiritual life of the individual. Outside this lies the whole Realm of Intercession, and of the activities which are the outward and visible sign—the Embodiment—of the spirit which Intercession voices.

Appendices

Recollections
of
Ellen Kuhn Mahan

circa 1937–1938 [NWC]

Note: *The form of these recollections, with their numerous unconnected paragraphs, indicates that they are answers to questions put by Captain W. D. Puleston, USN, when he was preparing his biography of Mahan (1939). The questions, now lost, are in most cases self-evident. The use of* we *in some of the answers suggests that Helen Evans Mahan assisted her younger sister in formulating replies. These recollections initially included a letter dated October 18, 1884, written to Ellen Kuhn Mahan by her father. This has been printed among the letters in these volumes.*

75 East 54th St. was an old-fashioned walk-up apartment of which we occupied the flat over-looking Park Avenue. We were there when my father went on the *Chicago*, but we cannot remember if we were there in 1889 or '90.[1] Lyle went to Groton from there. We did not own the flat.

489 West End Avenue was a house lent us by the architect until 160 West 86th Street should be ready for occupancy. We were there for a few months only from the fall of 1895 to early in 1896.

We moved in January or February, we think.[2]

We do not remember ever renting 160. My brother and his wife and her parents spent the summer of 1905 there, and my nephew was born there in July.[3] My mother sold the house soon after that but we don't remember just when. We sailed in Oct. or Nov.

1st house in 1894; 2nd finished in spring of 1909.[4]

Family returned in fall. We remained in Europe throughout the period of the war.[5] None of us went to Washington while my father was on the Board. Mr. Theodore Roosevelt lent him his house while he had to be in Washington.

---

1. Mahan joined the *Chicago* in May 1893. The family had moved to 75 East 54th Street in October 1890.
2. The family moved from West End Avenue to 160 West 86th Street during the last week of January 1896.
3. Madeleine Johnson Mahan, wife of Lyle Evans Mahan, gave birth to Alfred Thayer Mahan II in July 1905 at Quogue. The West 86th Street house was leased from 1906 to 1913 and was sold in 1915.
4. "Slumberside" in Quogue; and "Marshmere" in Quogue.
5. The Spanish-American War, during which Mahan served on the Naval War Board.

This trip was taken in 1905. We spent a night or two at Algeciras and went on to Granada, Cordova & Madrid where E.K.M. came down with scarlet fever. We were delayed about a month then went to Toledo, Burgos and San Sebastian where E.K.M. developed rheumatic fever and was carried on to trains and taken to Pau to Mamma's sister and brother-in-law.[6] In April or May we left for San Remo, thence to Nauheim via Milan and Strassburg. Home in May or June.

No. Europe, Autumn of 1912.

We went to Woodmere, to Mamma's brother's house—Mr. H. K. Evans—in 1906, for the winter. Spent the next four winters in Lawrence[7] and, we think, the winter of 1911–1912 at the Hotel Collingwood.[8] (We were there when the *Titanic* sank, we are sure of this, as a niece of my mother's[9] went down with her.)

4 weeks in hospital, 11 weeks with nurses at home, convalescence much longer.

1912–1913 London, Paris, Bourges, Clermont-Ferrand, Brives, Toulouse, Pau, Carcassonne, Marseille, San Remo, Florence, Sicily, home Southern trip. Latter part of winter Papa uneasy lest war break out. He considered the difficulty of getting gold at the banks a significant sign.

Born February 12th 1881. Divorced end of August or early September 1924.[10]

Grandma Mahan died in March 1893. Grandmother Evans April 11th 1894.[11]

My mother's aunt, Margaret Evans, left her something but chiefly personal things. Her Uncle, Charles Kuhn, who lived at Nice, died October 28th, 1899, left her money.

Lyle entered Groton 1892 or 3.[12] He was very ill there during his second term —1st year—and seems to have had some trouble left over from that, at any rate his masters were very anxious to have him lay off for a while and it was arranged for him to take an upper sixth at Groton and go abroad in 1898. He graduated from Columbia in 1902.

We just came out, four years apart.

As to my father's routine it was very much the same throughout his writing period after leaving the Navy. Up at half past six, breakfast at eight, walk—or

---

6. Rosalie Evans Brown and her husband, Francis Leonard Brown, M.D. The illnesses occurred in November–December 1905 during Ellen's second trip to Europe that year. She had accompanied her mother to Nauheim, Germany, in March–July 1905. The second trip, October 1905–June 1906, was made by the parents and both daughters.
7. In a rented house in Lawrence, Long Island.
8. At 45 West 35th Street in New York City.
9. Angelina ("Lina") Evans, daughter of Cadwalader and Angelina Corse Evans.
10. Lyle Evans Mahan (1881–1966) was divorced by Madeleine Johnson Mahan in 1924. He subsequently married Millicent Moore and Marion McCallum.
11. Mary Helena Okill Mahan; Ellen Kuhn Evans.
12. It was in September 1894.

bicycle—work, mail, paper, lunch, rest and more reading, walk, tea, rest, dinner, reading, bed. In town the work period would be varied by weeks of reading at the Astor or Public libraries, particularly before the summer or a trip to Europe for, even in Europe, if we were some time in one place—at my aunt's,[13] for instance—he would continue this routine of work rest and exercise.

In Europe he would take great interest in showing us cathedrals, fortifications and in walking with us about the streets of towns. He was tireless when it came to walking. Driving was the only thing that seemed to tire him.

I never heard him speak of Admiral Evans,[14] nor of any of his friends except Mr. Ashe and Sir Bouverie Clark. He seemed to feel a strong affection for both of these men. I wonder if you have seen any likeness in the characters of these two? They seem to me two chips from the same block. He thought very highly of John Bassett Moore, I know, and very poorly of Wilson.[15] My father was essentially "The Cat That Walked By Himself." My mother was the only person who loomed very large in his life and he was always happiest when we were all gathered together with some of our friends, especially the girls. But friends of his own were practically nonexistent. The crowds in N.Y. stimulated him, but individuals, outside the family and its small circle of friends, did not seem to be necessary to his happiness.

My father felt under obligations to do his part, dining out, entertaining & going to the club, but it was almost always because he thought he ought and his pleasure was not keen.

My father always went to the nearest church so it happens there are ten that we can remember easily.

New York, from grandmother's apartment, 2 E. 15th St., St. George's, Rector: Rainsford[16]

New York, from 75 E. 54, Holy Trinity, Rector: E. Walpole Warren

New York, from 160 W. 86th St., All Angels, Rector: S. DeLancey Townsend

Newport War College, St. John's (now Zabriskie Memorial), Rector: Moran[17]

Hewlett, from Woodmere, Trinity, Rector: Martin[18]

Far Rockaway, from Lawrence, St. John's, Rector: Henry Mesier

New York, from [Hotel] Collingwood, Incarnation, Rector: Howard Chandler Robbins

Washington, from Hillyer Pl., St. Thomas, Rector: Ernest Smith

Quogue, Atonement: Various clergymen.

---

13. Rosalie Evans Brown, Mrs. Mahan's sister, who lived in Pau, France.
14. Admiral Robley D. ("Fighting Bob") Evans.
15. Woodrow Wilson.
16. William S. Rainsford.
17. Samuel W. Moran.
18. Thomas W. Martin.

We called our parents "Pa-pa" and "Mam-ma." This was their official name, the one taught us and adhered to through life; but in the family variations, even absurd and incongruous names, were allowed as long as they did not violate the law of love. "Respect," with a capital "R" was not highly thought of in our family and I think that Grannie—my mother's mother—expressed my parents' feelings on the subject when she said "I don't care if the children call me 'Pig' if they love me."

My father had a bad temper, if anything so checked and bridled, and driven with such care and judgment, could be called bad. Perhaps it was with this fault in mind that all whippings (of which he heartily approved as being "quickly over") were administered by my mother, and with the hand only, on that part of the anatomy which could be reasonably supposed uninjurable.

My mother's tendency was toward the autocratic, we must do as she said, and we did. But by the time I became aware of her in relation to myself the rule of the house had become "Few orders, absolute obedience." My father was fond of adorning this moral with the following tale: A certain father had trained his children to obey him instantly. One day, when the family were assembled at dinner, the father exclaimed suddenly "Under the table" and with one accord they obeyed, just in time to be saved from the falling ceiling. With this insistence upon obedience, however, went a genuine respect for our personalities and for our rights as individuals. His sense of justice made it impossible for him to be tyrannical.

It will be seen that both our parents had strong wills and strong characters. As I look back and realize the effect each had on the other, how the character of each developed and expanded under the influence of the other, I am reminded of the principle underlying Gothic architecture. The perfect harmony of their lives was never marred, because, where there was a strain on one side the other inevitably rose to meet the situation.

I have seen my father angry with my mother. I have never seen her angry with him, nor did she ever look the martyr. On these rare occasions she knew exactly what to do and without any fuss all was soon fair weather again. We knew, as she did, that some unusual strain, either physical or in the outer realm of his work, was the cause of the small burst of temper. It never went beyond a very small flash.

Our parents shared in our bringing up; and here, again, there was perfect outward accord although I am quite sure that, behind the scenes, the case would be discussed calmly resulting, at times, in a change of method on the part of one or the other, but I was nearly grown up before I realized this.

When about two years old I contracted malaria at Annapolis. The family made a hurried exodus north which my father described to me a few years later in this letter. . . .[19]

---

19. See Mahan to Ellen Kuhn Mahan, October 18, 1884.

The rest of the letter seems not to have been kept, at any rate I have not found it.

My father used to sing us to sleep with hymns. It had amused Mrs. Hoskins[20] very much to hear him singing "Art thou weary, art thou languid, art thou sore distressed?" to my infant sister in Montevideo. Another favorite was "On the other side of Jordan, in the sweet fields of Eden," dubbed by my sister "les chères petites filles," alluded to in the preceding letter.

After this illness of mine my father contributed regularly to the fresh air fund of the Protestant Episcopal City Mission Society, of New York, as a thank offering for my recovery and was still doing so when I was nearly grown. Probably he continued to the end of his life.

My earliest recollections come in the form of pictures. In one of these my father and I are in Church and I still feel the prickle of the lingerie ruffle on my cap as I knelt with my forehead pressed against the pew in front. Perhaps this was the occasion on which my father saw tears rolling down my cheeks and hastily retreated to the street with me. It seems to have been his habit to go to Church at 8 and 10.30 or 11 in the morning and then to take us little ones in the afternoon, staying until we were tired.

My father attended entirely to my religious education when he was at home, and it was at his knee my prayers were said. Once I forgot the Lord's Prayer. He gave me my lead but nothing could bring the words back to me and I can hear his voice—shocked it seemed to me but, more likely, strange because he was struggling to keep his face straight—"Why, Nellikin, what *is* the matter?"

Papa often seemed more stern than he really was; it was his desire, I think, to treat serious subjects seriously; that we should know that our conduct was a matter of supreme importance. I remember that I had committed a great sin one day, I can't remember what it was but I was desperately miserable and when Papa came to kiss me good night I decided to confess. I will never forget his tenderness, his whole body seemed to melt as he bent over me and I knew that everything was all right.

He was much given to getting "a rise" out of us and our friends, when we were little, and my mother used to tell how he said to my sister one day, in a loud and angry voice, "Your mother is an *admirable* woman!" and my sister's tearful reply, "O! non, Papa, elle n'est pas." At the end of the day, his work behind him, he was ready for any frivolity with us although I do not remember that he played games with us.

He early taught us to tithe what money we received. He would tell us about the poor little Indians or Chinese until we longed to help; the rest was easy.

---

20. Mary S. Hoskins, wife of the Reverend Thomas R. Hoskins, Anglican clergyman in Montevideo when Mahan commanded the *Wasp* there. Helen Evans Mahan was born in Montevideo on August 6, 1873. Her sister, Ellen, was born on July 10, 1877, in Pau, France.

When pay, or money for articles or books came in, 10% was always deducted for the Church and for charitable objects, all the rest was turned over to my mother and she used it as she saw fit. My father never questioned her about it.

We were expected, as we grew older, to go to the two morning services with our parents and my father never read the newspaper until after the second one. The afternoon and evening were ours, to do as we pleased, and he encouraged our playing games and reading secular books if we chose. He maintained that Sunday was a day of recreation and rest, as well as of worship, and that it was instituted for these two purposes. He had suffered much in his youth from the abnormal amount of piety required on that day and always protected our rights in this respect.

We were never sent to Sunday School, as my father greatly distrusted the ability of the average teacher, but he took great pains to see that we knew and understood the catechism and wrote my confirmation instructions himself. It was as well, for my confirmation class, conducted by the rector himself, was composed of all ages from twelve—my own—to grown up candidates and I doubt if I learned anything there at all.

My father recommended, but never tried to enforce, our not going out on Saturday evenings but, rather, going to bed early and thus ensuring a reasonably alert mind on Sunday morning. On the other hand, we were expected to read our Bibles regularly and to pray night and morning and what he expected of us he did himself. It was his custom to read the Bible to my mother every morning and, immediately after breakfast, he had family prayers which lasted exactly five minutes.

My father's was an intensely nervous disposition. He bore pain badly and seemed to be completely unnerved by it. Very methodical, and making careful preparations for any move, an upset in his plans was all the more difficult for him to bear. Shortly before his death, when my mother and sister had gone to Washington to take a house for the winter, he was to go to my Philadelphia cousins[21] while I closed this house.[22] A friend was to take him to the train, he was to lunch at the club and take an afternoon train to Philadelphia. He was ready, we waited, the minutes rolled by until it was too late to catch the bus, then we heard the train come and go. He made no complaint but turning to me he said "Oh! Miss Nellikin, a double minded man is unstable in all his ways." I think he was blaming himself for not having insisted on the bus from the beginning, but I felt that while there was time I should have telephoned for the bus. One of my cousins, speaking to me about it later said "You know that should never have happened."

---

21. Probably Allen and Rebecca Evans, who were among many of Ellen's Philadelphia cousins.
22. "Marshmere" in Quogue.

If any sudden call for action came, such as putting out a spark from the fire, he would fairly leap from his chair and stamp until he had put it out; St. George could not have put forth more energy in slaying the dragon. He could not modulate his voice and if he wanted to call us, or stop us at something he thought dangerous, what my mother called his "quarter deck voice" would come bellowing out as if he were very angry. He wasn't, and we knew it and were not disturbed by it.

I cannot remember ever wanting to disobey my father; he was so reasonable, so just and I had the highest respect for his opinion. Until I was twenty, or more, I would ask him if I might read certain books, and I remember asking him about one called *A Blameless Woman*. "Why certainly, my dear, only remember, she isn't a blameless woman." Somehow, I think I must have suspected that.

At this time a friend came to stay with me and my father spoke of a magazine story which he said he hoped I wouldn't read. My friend started in at once and read it, and I still have a feeling of contempt for one who could have so disregarded his opinion.

We were very young when my father was first ordered to the Naval War College at Newport. After the very first, I knew it as the one place in all the world that was most like Heaven and felt, in some strange way, that no period in my life would ever quite equal it. At first, however, this was not the case. The ex-poorhouse was very cold and scantily furnished. Either there was no hot water or the heating apparatus was inadequate but my father had some rubber tubing attached to the valve in the radiator and cut the right length to lie in the bath tub. I can hear the comforting gurgle of the steam as it kindly heated the water to a comfortable temperature for my shivering body. Until this had been done, screens were put in front of the fire in the dining room and we had our baths between these and the fire.

This was my first experience of life on a government station, and though agreeable I was soon to learn that there were responsibilities connected with it. It appeared that Uncle Sam's property was to be treated as the apple of one's eye and that what might be overlooked, in the case of one's parents' property, was a great offense if "Government Property" was involved. On this subject my father was adamant and it never occurred to any of us to question his rulings. His attitude was the same with regard to the Custom House and I can hear the weary customs official who said to him "Well, Admiral, you've declared $150.00 worth and we can find only $100.00 worth and, anyway you are entitled to $200.00 worth," (for him and my mother).

My parents bought a second-hand typewriter while we were at Newport, and my mother began the task—never laid down until my father's death—of copying his manuscripts for him. I hope we appreciated her utter self-abnegation, if one can call such selflessness by a name that seems to savor a trifle of self-consciousness.

[725]

It was at Newport that Jomini was born. His mother had been given us by a friend of my mother's and great was the excitement when her five puppies were born. My brother and I went out to inspect them and, when older, each had to be picked up solemnly by the tail; for had we not been told on good authority that if one could pick up a puppy by the tail it *must* be a thoroughbred?

Jomini became a member of the family at once and so much was this the case that friends of mine said he *looked* like my father. I can see what they meant, the dog intent on his own thoughts, as the man was on his. I, too, soon learned, when walking with my father and Jomini, to be intent on *my* thoughts also.

My father was exerciser-in-chief to all our dogs. He had the habit, so dear to the doggie heart, of absolute regularity. Breakfast, walk, newspaper, work, lunch, rest, reading and another walk. This routine was varied by long periods of reading at a library where he took copious notes, enough to last for six or eight months when he would take up his writing again, in Quogue and even in Europe.

Papa never willingly got into a carriage. He walked, if the distance was at all possible; if not he would take a street car. One exception, when he would rather have died than be seen in the street in his dress uniform, was when Prince Henry of Prussia had invited him to lunch on the *Hohenzollern*.[23] Not only did a cab have to be called but my mother had to drive with him to the dock to give him moral support. When bicycling came into fashion he would take part of his exercise on his wheel. In summer he and my mother rode together, their favorite ride being to the railroad crossing at Good Ground—now Hampton Bays—where they would sit on a woody bank and watch the afternoon train go by.

My mother learned to ride while my father was at sea, on the *Chicago*, and she insisted on his learning when he came home. Always awkward, he gave himself many a bump which annoyed him extremely and he told my mother one day that, if anything could make him hate her, this would.

When my father took command of the *Chicago* we were living in a small walk-up flat, at the top of the house at 75 East 54th Street, on the corner of Park Avenue. It was a very different looking district from what it is today. The letters that began to come were very interesting, the flamboyant headlines most exciting, but we were not so devoid of humor that we couldn't get a good chuckle out of the contrast between his life and ours.

That summer was our first in Quogue, and the only house my mother could afford was a long way from beach or club, so she bought a horse—a centenarian I should judge—and a vehicle the like of which I had never seen before. There were two seats, out of which the stuffing protruded, a top supported by iron cords at the four corners and trimmed with a fringe all round. A "stable" was

---

23. Prince Henry visited New York in February 1902.

[726]

provided and, nothing doubting, the family started out to take complete charge of a horse. Fortunately his age was in our favor and even when he eluded us he didn't go far, our chief difficulty being to keep him out of the stable as the hay was much to his liking and he soon found out how to get the peg out of the hasp.

The first few months of being feted my father found very agreeable. He was much interested in the people he met and made a few good friends. Naturally the honors given him gratified him very much but I only remember one anecdote regarding these, the time Oxford—I think—gave him the D.C.L. He had been warned that the undergraduates were in the habit of making personal and often uncomplimentary remarks to those receiving honorary degrees. As my father drew near some one called out "Why don't you get your hair cut?" My father, being preceded by a bushy haired foreigner thought the remark made to him and only learned the following day that it was meant for himself.

Always fond of young girls he wrote of his pleasure at finding that his rank placed him, as a rule, next to young, and often pretty, girls. He became very fond of two of these, whose families were very kind to him, and whom some of us met later on.

Toward the end of his cruise, in the Mediterranean, he became very much irked by the life of the ship and the impossibility of getting off to see his friends at Nice. About this time, too, my brother became very ill at Groton. Measles followed by pneumonia and a relapse. My mother went to him at once and was there for weeks. She made the mistake of not telling my father about the illness while my brother's life hung in the balance, as she did not want to worry him while he was so far away, and knowing that she would not be able to avoid revealing her state of mind in her letters she did not write at all during this period. I think it was harder on both of them than if she had told all, for it stopped the natural outflow of her feelings while he, poor thing, depressed already, wrote pathetically "Your mother never neglected me like this before."

But the *Chicago* was on her way home now and soon the whole family was reunited and at peace—except for the reporters!

In looking back, it seems strange how little our family life was affected by the furor over my father's books. My mother suffered most for now the Four Hundred took them up and there were a succession of dinners to which my father and, therefore, my mother were invited. The women seem to have been less interesting, and certainly more frigid, than the men; besides, she had only one dress, made at home and of a material that no woman would have bought for a dress, so I suspect it was designed for other purposes. Time after time she went, never a word of complaint, just a quiet patient look, for she knew it pleased Papa.

We children, at least, enjoyed to the full every detail of every dinner and my mother brought us home interesting descriptions whenever she could.

[727]

They had arrived at one house after an old lady who went up the stairs just ahead of my mother to the dressing room. As they climbed the stairs my mother said to herself, "I suppose that's the kind of person they think good enough for us." At dinner she asked her partner who the old lady was with all the jewels. She said he looked at her in astonishment and said "Why, don't you know who *that* is? It's Mrs. Z."

On another occasion she asked her dinner partner to tell her who every one was, as the children would be sure to ask when she got home. "Do you mean to say that your children will be *interested?*" was his reply. One thing always disgusted my mother and that was affectation of any sort. After dinner one evening a woman said "I really never see my husband until the afternoon." "Oh!" said my mother, "I always get up at half past six and light the fire for mine." Eventually the Four Hundred got bored and went after other Lions while we resumed the even tenor of our ways.

My father was invited to join a group of men calling themselves the "Round Table Club." Here were always found men of distinction in their own line—indeed only such were invited to join—and they were a great stimulus to my father, he enjoying the meetings very much. He also joined the Century Club and the University Club. He used the former chiefly at their monthly meetings, but he went much oftener to the University where I think he found their library a good place for work. It was here, I think, that he saw Mr. Wilson—later President—sitting thoughtfully with his finger in the leaves of a book. As he was not reading, my father ventured to speak to him and said "Mr. Wilson, if your friend, Bryan, wants to save his soul alive he had better get out of politics." Mr. Wilson, my father said, did not answer immediately but in a moment replied "Yes, and his face shows it." I might explain that when my father said "Your friend" he usually meant someone whose ideas, principles and/or personality were either alien or antipathetic to the one to whom he was speaking, so that his remark in this case could not have been interpreted as insulting.

By this time Grannie[24] had died and left Mamma money enough with which to buy the house at 160 West 86th Street and we lived here very happily for twelve years. Then my parents received a blow which altered everything for us. From my mother and father something had gone which they were never to get back. Papa took command of the situation at once, his faith never faltered, he pointed out the way which we, as a family, should take. He showed us the true balance between head and heart which a Christian should keep and, above all, he kept it himself. Like the wholesome blood that was in his veins the wholesome stream of confidence in God—the conduits of which he had kept clean through years of devotion—rushed to his aid. Never have I admired my father more than in this long, last struggle when his natural impatience became a beautiful patience, and his character sweetened and ripened toward the harvest.

---

24. Ellen Kuhn Evans, who died on April 11, 1894.

He had one illness during this period, a very serious operation,[25] and was months getting back his strength, but it was the amusing thing that happened which comes oftenest to my mind. He was taken up to the operation, presumably in the state of mind engendered by lack of food and the awe of a new and, perhaps, terrible experience. On arrival, seeing no one about, he asked where the doctors were and was told that they had not yet arrived. Upon that he ordered himself taken back to his room and said he would go back to the operating room when the doctors had arrived; and he put it over. So much for forty years in the United States Navy.

An uncle of my mother's, Mr. Charles Kuhn, who lived at Nice, had taken a great fancy to my father while the *Chicago* was in the vicinity and when he died left my mother rather more than he did her sister and cousins.[26] These relatives were very fond of my father and none bore any grudge for what all felt was really an expression of regard for him, not that it would have been possible for them to behave other than generously.

My mother's cousins were, many of them, devoted to my father and he was a welcome visitor in their houses from the first. Also very religious, they understood each other perfectly and were friends to the end of their lives.

My parents decided to build another house in Quogue, which would have a furnace and so make it possible for us to make long seasons there, with a few months either in New York or abroad during the winters. We had previously, in 1894 I think, while my father was at sea, built a house here with money left him from his mother.[27] It was his particular desire that there should be no furnace as he did not wish to be "tempted"—did he mean over persuaded?—to spend the winters here. It would have been madness for he greatly needed the stimulus of town. There seems to have been something about the moving crowds, the seeing people all about him, even if he did not speak to them, which his mind required. He usually read in the evenings, but even then he liked to have us about and did not at all object to talking; it was only while he was writing that he required perfect quiet. In this house[28] there are two doors between his study and the front hall, and the walls between it and the living room were sound-proofed. It took my father some time to get used to this house, Marshmere; he rather hankered after the older house,[29] but gradually the beauty of the views and peacefulness of the surroundings appealed and I think he became quite reconciled.

Our life was very quiet, but happy, as we were all great lovers of home. My father had early instituted the custom of afternoon tea—I never remember a

---

25. A prostatectomy in late September 1907, followed by further surgery for related adhesions in early December 1907.
26. Charles Kuhn died on October 28, 1899.
27. Mary Helena Okill Mahan died in March 1893.
28. "Marshmere" in Quogue.
29. "Slumberside" in Quogue.

time when we didn't have it—which he always made himself. In summer he would ride his bicycle in the afternoon and on his return would dress for the evening, except that he wore a morning coat, only changing to the Tuxedo at dinner time; then he would make the tea and listen to us and our friends, one or two of whom were usually on hand. He was particularly fond of the younger women and they always got on very well together. The important business of brewing the tea over he would then take his part in the conversation. Both he and my mother were popular with young people and though she never became reconciled to tea she was always present with knitting or sewing and seemed to enjoy herself.

The outbreak of the war, his sympathy with the allies and anxiety on their behalf, added to pressure from outside in the way of extra articles and interviews, the attitude of the President and the move to Washington put a strain on my father's heart, already affected seriously, which it could not withstand. He must have felt very ill indeed for, when Lord Roberts died, about two weeks before my father, he stood looking out of the window and drumming on the pane, saying, "Lucky Bobs, lucky Bobs." [30]

My father stopped work only a week before his death. His decline was very rapid but he cheered up for a while when two nice young orderlies came to take him to the Naval Hospital. His whole expression was that of one who felt that everything was going to be all right and, as he was taken down stairs in a stretcher, he looked at me and winked. His mind was clear to the very end and he had just spoken to his nurse when he died. [31]

---

30. Field Marshal Frederick Sleigh ("Bobs") Roberts (1832–1914), 1st Earl Roberts of Kandahar, Pretoria, and Waterford.
31. Mahan died on December 1, 1914. His wife, Ellen, lived until November 15, 1927. Ellen Kuhn Mahan died on December 27, 1947. Her sister, Helen, lived until March 19, 1963. Lyle Evans Mahan, born in New York in 1881, died there in 1966.

Note on
Mahan's Bibliography

Almost all of Mahan's published works have been listed in George K. Kirkham, *The Books and Articles of Rear-Admiral A. T. Mahan, U.S.N.* (New York: Ballou Press, 1929); William D. Puleston, *Mahan: The Life and Work of Captain Alfred Thayer Mahan, U.S.N.* (New Haven: Yale University Press, 1939), pp. 359–364; and William E. Livezey, *Mahan on Sea Power* (Norman: University of Oklahoma Press, 1947), pp. 301–326.

However, the following published Mahan materials have not previously been listed:

Comment on Erasmus Weaver, "The Armament of the Outside Line of Defense," *Journal of the Military Service Institution of the United States*, IX (June 1888), pp. 169, 288–289.

"Report of the Commission to Select a Site For a Navy Yard on the Pacific Coast North of the Forty-Second Parallel of North Latitude," September 15, 1889, in *Report of the Secretary of the Navy. 1889.* With C. M. Chester and C. H. Stockton. (Washington, D.C.: Government Printing Office, 1890), Part 2, pp. 124–167.

"An Old Time Frigate," *Youth's Companion*, LXXII (September 22, 1898), pp. 436–437.

"The Youth of Admiral Farragut," *Youth's Companion*, LXXIV (June 28, 1900), pp. 328–329.

Review of *The War in South Africa*, by the Editors of *The Times* (London: The Times, 1902). Published in *The New York Times*, May 30, 1902.

Hare, James H., ed., *A Photographic Record of the Russo-Japanese War . . . With an Account of the Battle of the Sea of Japan by Captain A. T. Mahan. . . .* New York: P. F. Collier & Son, 1905.

"Tactics of Trafalgar," *Army and Navy Gazette* (July 29, 1905), p. 708.

"The Consistency of Nelson as a Tactician," *The Graphic*, LXXII (October 21, 1905), p. 514.

"The Personal Factor in Naval History," *Youth's Companion*, LXXXI (October 29, 1907), pp. 559–560.

"Christian Convictions," *The Churchman* (August 21, 1909), p. 282.

Memorandum Communicated to the Society of Naval Architects and Marine Engineers on Sir William White's Paper, "Notes on the Armaments of Battleships," Society of Naval Architects and Marine Engineers, *Transactions*, XVIII (1910), pp. 20–22.

"Why Not Disarm?" Edited and published under the title "The Folly of the Hague," *National Sunday Magazine* (September 28, 1913).

"The Seaman," *Youth's Companion*, LXXXVII (November 6, 1913), pp. 603–604.

"The Mediatorial Office of the Church Toward the State," *The Churchman* (August 29, 1914), p. 279.

Index of Omitted Letters

The editors have elected not to publish in this collection Mahan letters of a routine sort which add little to an understanding of the man, his historical works, or the navy in which he served.

Some of these are Department of the Navy form letters, reports, and quarterly returns signed by Mahan. Others are official letters written by clerks, signed by Mahan, dealing with the minor details of daily administration at sea and ashore. Still others, written to his publishers, concern mechanical problems associated with getting his numerous books and articles through press. Samples of all these letters have been included;[1] the rest have been omitted. Copies of all omitted letters have been deposited in the U.S. Naval War College Naval Historical Collection in Newport, Rhode Island. The originals may be found in the repositories indicated below.

In the interest of completeness the editors list these omitted letters, noting in each instance the name of the recipient, the date, the repository, and the general subject matter(s) dealt with. The subject-matter information has been coded as follows:

Code Number	Subject Matter
1	Acknowledgments and information related to the receipt or non-receipt of communications, orders, instructions, equipment, or stores.
2	Requisitions or requests for equipment or stores.
3	Letters transmitting information on periodic ships' drills, returns, reports, and cruising schedules.
4	Financial matters relating to competitive bids, bills and wages paid, ship and station debts incurred, freight and forwarding charges, and the cost of equipment and stores.
5	Invoices and receipts for equipment and stores forwarded or received.
6	Letters relating to the order, delivery, lading, forwarding, condition, available quantity, storage, and disposition of stores and equipment.

---

1. In this regard *see* Mahan to Whiting, July 15, 1880, Footnote 2; and Mahan to Little, Brown & Company, June 14, 1911, Footnote 2.

7	Correspondence concerning the repair, testing, quality, and maintenance of equipment.
8	Letters pertaining to the appointments, ratings, enlistments, promotions, discharges, desertions, deaths, transfers, replacements, and deportment of officers, enlisted men, and civilian employees of the Navy.
9	Acceptance or rejection of social invitations, and routine notes of thanks.
10	Letters to editors and publishers relating to textual changes, pagination, galley and page-proof corrections, illustrations, maps, and battle plans.

Recipient	Date	Repository	Subject
T. A. Jenkins	September 30, 1865	NA	1
T. A. Jenkins	December 5, 1866	NA	1
J. Alden	September 15, 1869	NA	6
W. R. Rogers	February 20, 1873	NA	2
W. R. Taylor	February 28, 1873	NA	6,2
W. R. Taylor	March 3, 1873	NA	8
W. R. Taylor	March 6, 1873	NA	2
W. R. Taylor	March 16, 1873	NA	8
J. J. Almy	March 17, 1873	NA	1
W. Reynolds	March 17, 1873	NA	2
W. R. Taylor	March 21, 1873	NA	1
W. R. Taylor	March 21, 1873	NA	2
W. R. Taylor	March 25, 1873	NA	2
W. R. Taylor	March 28, 1873	NA	7,2
D. Ammen	March 31, 1873	NA	3
G. M. Robeson	March 31, 1873	NA	3
W. R. Taylor	March 31, 1873	NA	3
A. L. Case	March 31, 1873	NA	3
W. Reynolds	March 31, 1873	NA	3
O. C. Badger	April 2, 1873	NA	1
O. C. Badger	April 7, 1873	NA	3
W. R. Taylor	April 30, 1873	NA	3
G. M. Robeson	May 1, 1873	NA	8
G. W. Smith	May 1, 1873	NA	8
W. R. Taylor	May 3, 1873	NA	2
W. R. Taylor	May 3, 1873	NA	2
W. R. Taylor	May 3, 1873	NA	2
W. R. Taylor	May 3, 1873	NA	4,2
W. R. Taylor	May 4, 1873	NA	1

Recipient	Date	Repository	Subject
O. C. Badger	May 5, 1873	NA	2
W. R. Taylor	May 15, 1873	NA	2
W. R. Taylor	May 31, 1873	NA	3
W. R. Taylor	May 31, 1873	NA	3,6
W. R. Taylor	June 26, 1873	NA	1
W. R. Taylor	June 28, 1873	NA	3
W. R. Taylor	June 30, 1873	NA	3
G. M. Robeson	June 30, 1873	NA	3
A. L. Case	June 30, 1873	NA	3
D. Ammen	June 30, 1873	NA	3
G. M. Robeson	July 2, 1873	NA	8
W. R. Taylor	July 7, 1873	NA	3
W. R. Taylor	July 7, 1873	NA	1
W. R. Taylor	July 14, 1873	NA	2
W. R. Taylor	July 14, 1873	NA	2
W. R. Taylor	July 24, 1873	NA	2
W. R. Taylor	July 27, 1873	NA	1
O. C. Badger	July 27, 1873	NA	2
W. R. Taylor	July 30, 1873	NA	1
W. R. Taylor	July 31, 1873	NA	3
W. R. Taylor	August 1, 1873	NA	1
O. C. Badger	August 1, 1873	NA	2
O. C. Badger	August 7, 1873	NA	1,2
F. Barrett	August 8, 1873	NA	5
D. Ammen	August 8, 1873	NA	5
O. C. Badger	August 9, 1873	NA	2,6
W. R. Taylor	August 13, 1873	NA	2
W. R. Taylor	August 25, 1873	NA	2
W. R. Taylor	August 28, 1873	NA	1
W. R. Taylor	August 31, 1873	NA	3
W. N. Jeffers	September 5, 1873	NA	2
O. C. Badger	September 8, 1873	NA	4
W. R. Taylor	September 13, 1873	NA	2
W. R. Taylor	September 18, 1873	NA	2
W. R. Taylor	September 30, 1873	NA	3
G. M. Robeson	September 30, 1873	NA	3
G. M. Robeson	September 30, 1873	NA	3
W. Reynolds	September 30, 1873	NA	3
D. Ammen	September 30, 1873	NA	3
W. R. Taylor	October 15, 1873	NA	2
W. R. Taylor	October 20, 1873	NA	2
W. R. Taylor	October 21, 1873	NA	2

Recipient	Date	Repository	Subject
W. R. Taylor	October 31, 1873	NA	3
W. R. Taylor	November 3, 1873	NA	2
W. R. Taylor	November 3, 1873	NA	1
W. R. Taylor	November 11, 1873	NA	2
W. R. Taylor	November 19, 1873	NA	2
J. H. Strong	November 25, 1873	NA	1
J. H. Strong	November 26, 1873	NA	3,4,2
J. H. Strong	November 26, 1873	NA	2
W. Reynolds	November 29, 1873	NA	8
J. H. Strong	November 30, 1873	NA	3
J. H. Strong	November 30, 1873	NA	3
J. H. Strong	December 14, 1873	NA	2
J. H. Strong	December 31, 1873	NA	2
J. H. Strong	December 31, 1873	NA	2,4
J. H. Strong	December 31, 1873	NA	3
W. W. Wood	December 31, 1873	NA	2
W. Reynolds	December 31, 1873	NA	3
G. M. Robeson	December 31, 1873	NA	3
D. Ammen	December 31, 1873	NA	3
A. W. Bacon	January 15, 1874	NA	1
D. P. Wight	January 26, 1874	NA	1,4
G. M. Robeson	February 7, 1874	NA	8
D. P. Wight	March 5, 1874	NA	1,4
G. M. Robeson	March 31, 1874	NA	3
A. W. Bacon	April 4, 1874	NA	1
D. P. Wight	May 4, 1874	NA	1,4
A. W. Bacon	June 15, 1874	NA	1
G. M. Robeson	June 18, 1874	NA	8
G. M. Robeson	June 30, 1874	NA	3
S. W. Very	July 2, 1874	NA	2
D. P. Wight	July 11, 1874	NA	1,4
A. W. Bacon	July 16, 1874	NA	1
W. Reynolds	August 6, 1874	NA	1
A. W. Bacon	August 14, 1874	NA	1
F. A. Roe	August 14, 1874	NA	1
A. W. Bacon	September 15, 1874	NA	1
G. M. Robeson	September 30, 1874	NA	3
W. M. Preston	October 5, 1874	NA	1
G. M. Robeson	December 31, 1874	NA	3
G. H. Cooper	July 16, 1880	NA	4
G. H. Cooper	July 17, 1880	NA	1
G. H. Cooper	July 19, 1880	NA	1,6,7

Recipient	Date	Repository	Subject
G. H. Cooper	July 19, 1880	NA	1,6
G. H. Cooper	July 20, 1880	NA	1,5
G. H. Cooper	July 20, 1880	NA	5,6
G. H. Cooper	July 24, 1880	NA	2
G. H. Cooper	July 24, 1880	NA	5
E. T. Nichols	July 26, 1880	NA	6
G. H. Cooper	July 29, 1880	NA	2,6
G. H. Cooper	July 31, 1880	NA	6
G. H. Cooper	August 2, 1880	NA	6
G. H. Cooper	August 5, 1880	NA	6
G. H. Cooper	August 7, 1880	NA	1,5
G. H. Cooper	August 9, 1880	NA	1,6
G. H. Cooper	August 13, 1880	NA	6
G. H. Cooper	August 27, 1880	NA	1
G. H. Cooper	October 14, 1880	NA	1,5,7
G. H. Cooper	October 15, 1880	NA	7
G. H. Cooper	October 30, 1880	NA	2,6
G. H. Cooper	November 8, 1880	NA	1,2
G. H. Cooper	November 13, 1880	NA	1
G. H. Cooper	November 15, 1880	NA	1
G. H. Cooper	November 16, 1880	NA	7
G. H. Cooper	November 22, 1880	NA	2
G. H. Cooper	December 1, 1880	NA	7
G. H. Cooper	December 1, 1880	NA	6
G. H. Cooper	December 6, 1880	NA	1
G. H. Cooper	December 7, 1880	NA	2
G. H. Cooper	December 7, 1880	NA	2
G. H. Cooper	December 14, 1880	NA	7,1
G. H. Cooper	December 20, 1880	NA	2
G. H. Cooper	December 21, 1880	NA	6
G. H. Cooper	December 21, 1880	NA	6,4
G. H. Cooper	December 21, 1880	NA	6
G. H. Cooper	December 22, 1880	NA	5,6
G. H. Cooper	December 30, 1880	NA	5,6
G. H. Cooper	January 6, 1881	NA	6
G. H. Cooper	January 8, 1881	NA	2
G. H. Cooper	January 18, 1881	NA	1
G. H. Cooper	January 20, 1881	NA	4
G. H. Cooper	January 24, 1881	NA	4
G. H. Cooper	January 28, 1881	NA	6
G. H. Cooper	February 4, 1881	NA	6,4
G. H. Cooper	February 9, 1881	NA	6

Recipient	Date	Repository	Subject
G. H. Cooper	February 11, 1881	NA	6
G. H. Cooper	February 28, 1881	NA	4
G. H. Cooper	March 1, 1881	NA	6
G. H. Cooper	March 1, 1881	NA	7
G. H. Cooper	March 11, 1881	NA	1
G. H. Cooper	March 21, 1881	NA	2
G. H. Cooper	March 24, 1881	NA	6
G. H. Cooper	April 1, 1881	NA	5
G. H. Cooper	April 1, 1881	NA	6
G. H. Cooper	May 7, 1881	NA	7
G. H. Cooper	May 13, 1881	NA	4,6
G. H. Cooper	May 14, 1881	NA	6
G. H. Cooper	May 20, 1881	NA	4
G. H. Cooper	May 27, 1881	NA	6
G. H. Cooper	June 3, 1881	NA	6
G. H. Cooper	June 3, 1881 (Enclosure)	NA	7
G. H. Cooper	June 4, 1881	NA	6
G. H. Cooper	June 7, 1881	NA	7
G. H. Cooper	June 11, 1881	NA	2,4
G. H. Cooper	June 13, 1881	NA	1
G. H. Cooper	June 16, 1881	NA	2
G. H. Cooper	June 20, 1881	NA	4
G. H. Cooper	June 20, 1881	NA	7
G. H. Cooper	June 22, 1881	NA	7
G. H. Cooper	June 22, 1881	NA	6
G. H. Cooper	June 22, 1881	NA	6,4
G. H. Cooper	June 23, 1881	NA	7
G. H. Cooper	June 24, 1881	NA	7
G. H. Cooper	June 24, 1881	NA	2,7
G. H. Cooper	July 1, 1881	NA	4,7
G. H. Cooper	July 9, 1881	NA	1,6
G. H. Cooper	July 11, 1881	NA	7,6
G. H. Cooper	July 12, 1881	NA	6
G. H. Cooper	July 20, 1881	NA	7,6
G. Brown	July 20, 1881	NA	7
G. H. Cooper	July 23, 1881	NA	6
G. H. Cooper	July 23, 1881	NA	2,6
G. H. Cooper	July 26, 1881	NA	7,6
G. H. Cooper	July 27, 1881	NA	6
G. H. Cooper	July 28, 1881	NA	6
G. H. Cooper	July 29, 1881	NA	4
G. H. Cooper	July 29, 1881	NA	7

Recipient	Date	Repository	Subject
G. H. Cooper	August 2, 1881	NA	4,6
G. H. Cooper	August 6, 1881	NA	6
G. H. Cooper	August 6, 1881	NA	7,6
G. H. Cooper	August 9, 1881	NA	6
G. H. Cooper	August 12, 1881	NA	7
G. H. Cooper	August 17, 1881	NA	1
G. H. Cooper	August 23, 1881	NA	4,6
G. H. Cooper	October 8, 1881	NA	7
G. H. Cooper	October 8, 1881	NA	6
G. H. Cooper	November 1, 1881	NA	6
G. H. Cooper	November 4, 1881	NA	2,6
G. H. Cooper	November 12, 1881	NA	6,7
G. H. Cooper	November 12, 1881	NA	6
G. H. Cooper	November 14, 1881	NA	6
G. H. Cooper	November 14, 1881	NA	7
G. H. Cooper	November 16, 1881	NA	7
G. H. Cooper	November 16, 1881	NA	7
G. H. Cooper	November 17, 1881	NA	2,6
G. H. Cooper	November 21, 1881	NA	7
G. H. Cooper	November 21, 1881	NA	7
G. H. Cooper	November 22, 1881	NA	6
G. H. Cooper	November 23, 1881	NA	7
G. H. Cooper	December 5, 1881	NA	6
G. H. Cooper	December 6, 1881	NA	4,7
G. H. Cooper	December 6, 1881	NA	6
G. H. Cooper	December 7, 1881	NA	7
G. H. Cooper	December 7, 1881	NA	4
G. H. Cooper	December 22, 1881	NA	6
G. H. Cooper	December 22, 1881	NA	7
G. H. Cooper	December 23, 1881	NA	7
G. H. Cooper	December 28, 1881	NA	6
G. H. Cooper	January 4, 1882	NA	6
G. H. Cooper	January 5, 1882	NA	4,6
G. H. Cooper	January 7, 1882	NA	7
G. H. Cooper	January 7, 1882	NA	6
G. H. Cooper	January 7, 1882	NA	6,7
G. H. Cooper	January 9, 1882	NA	6
G. H. Cooper	January 10, 1882	NA	1
G. H. Cooper	January 10, 1882	NA	6
G. H. Cooper	January 19, 1882	NA	6
G. H. Cooper	February 3, 1882	NA	7
G. H. Cooper	February 8, 1882	NA	1,4,6

Recipient	Date	Repository	Subject
G. H. Cooper	February 8, 1882	NA	7
G. H. Cooper	February 9, 1882	NA	4
G. H. Cooper	February 9, 1882	NA	6,7
G. H. Cooper	February 9, 1882	NA	4,6
G. H. Cooper	February 10, 1882	NA	7
G. H. Cooper	February 11, 1882	NA	4,7
G. H. Cooper	February 18, 1882	NA	6
G. H. Cooper	February 20, 1882	NA	7
G. H. Cooper	March 2, 1882	NA	7
G. H. Cooper	March 2, 1882	NA	6,7
G. H. Cooper	March 4, 1882	NA	6
G. H. Cooper	March 6, 1882	NA	1
G. H. Cooper	March 7, 1882	NA	2
G. H. Cooper	March 9, 1882	NA	1
G. H. Cooper	March 11, 1882	NA	7
G. H. Cooper	March 22, 1882	NA	2
G. H. Cooper	March 27, 1882	NA	6
G. H. Cooper	March 29, 1882	NA	6
G. H. Cooper	March 30, 1882	NA	6
J. H. Upshur	April 1, 1882	NA	6
G. Brown	April 6, 1882	NA	7
J. H. Upshur	April 10, 1882	NA	6
J. H. Upshur	April 12, 1882	NA	4
J. H. Upshur	April 12, 1882	NA	7
J. H. Upshur	April 14, 1882	NA	7
J. H. Upshur	April 18, 1882	NA	6
J. H. Upshur	April 19, 1882	NA	4
J. H. Upshur	April 20, 1882	NA	6
J. H. Upshur	April 25, 1882	NA	7
J. H. Upshur	April 25, 1882	NA	6
J. H. Upshur	April 25, 1882	NA	6
J. H. Upshur	April 27, 1882	NA	6
J. H. Upshur	May 9, 1882	NA	4
J. H. Upshur	May 9, 1882	NA	6
J. H. Upshur	May 11, 1882	NA	6,7
J. H. Upshur	May 12, 1882	NA	4,7
J. H. Upshur	May 13, 1882	NA	6
J. H. Upshur	May 19, 1882	NA	2
J. H. Upshur	May 20, 1882	NA	6,7
J. H. Upshur	May 22, 1882	NA	4,7
J. H. Upshur	May 22, 1882	NA	2
J. H. Upshur	May 26, 1882	NA	6

Recipient	Date	Repository	Subject
J. H. Upshur	June 3, 1882	NA	6
J. H. Upshur	June 5, 1882	NA	6,7
J. H. Upshur	June 6, 1882	NA	6
J. H. Upshur	June 6, 1882	NA	5
J. H. Upshur	June 6, 1882	NA	6
J. H. Upshur	June 10, 1882	NA	7
J. H. Upshur	June 14, 1882	NA	7
J. H. Upshur	June 15, 1882	NA	6,4
J. H. Upshur	June 15, 1882	NA	1
J. H. Upshur	June 26, 1882	NA	7
J. H. Upshur	June 27, 1882	NA	1
J. H. Upshur	July 1, 1882	NA	1
J. H. Upshur	July 8, 1882	NA	1,6
J. H. Upshur	July 11, 1882	NA	6
J. H. Upshur	July 13, 1882	NA	4,7
J. H. Upshur	July 14, 1882	NA	1
J. H. Upshur	July 18, 1882	NA	7
J. H. Upshur	July 19, 1882	NA	5
J. H. Upshur	July 19, 1882	NA	7
J. H. Upshur	July 20, 1882	NA	7
J. H. Upshur	July 21, 1882	NA	7
J. H. Upshur	July 21, 1882	NA	6,7
J. H. Upshur	July 21, 1882	NA	6
J. H. Upshur	July 21, 1882	NA	7
J. H. Upshur	July 26, 1882	NA	6,7
J. H. Upshur	August 4, 1882	NA	6
J. H. Upshur	August 4, 1882	NA	2
J. H. Upshur	August 5, 1882	NA	6
J. H. Upshur	August 8, 1882	NA	6
J. H. Upshur	August 9, 1882	NA	2
J. H. Upshur	August 11, 1882	NA	6
J. H. Upshur	August 15, 1882	NA	7,6
J. H. Upshur	August 16, 1882	NA	6
J. H. Upshur	August 16, 1882	NA	6
J. H. Upshur	August 16, 1882	NA	4,6
J. H. Upshur	August 17, 1882	NA	7
J. H. Upshur	August 22, 1882	NA	6
J. H. Upshur	August 22, 1882	NA	6,7
J. H. Upshur	August 22, 1882	NA	2,4
J. H. Upshur	August 23, 1882	NA	4
J. H. Upshur	August 24, 1882	NA	6
J. H. Upshur	August 26, 1882	NA	6

Recipient	Date	Repository	Subject
J. H. Upshur	August 29, 1882	NA	1,6
J. H. Upshur	August 31, 1882	NA	7,4
J. H. Upshur	August 31, 1882	NA	5
J. H. Upshur	October 4, 1882	NA	7
J. H. Upshur	October 6, 1882	NA	6
J. H. Upshur	October 6, 1882	NA	4
J. H. Upshur	October 16, 1882	NA	4
J. H. Upshur	October 16, 1882	NA	6,7
J. H. Upshur	October 17, 1882	NA	6
J. H. Upshur	October 19, 1882	NA	7
J. G. Walker	October 20, 1882 (Telegram)	NA	6
J. H. Upshur	October 20, 1882	NA	4,6
J. H. Upshur	October 20, 1882	NA	6
J. H. Upshur	October 26, 1882	NA	6
J. H. Upshur	November 1, 1882	NA	7
G. Brown	November 3, 1882	NA	6
J. H. Upshur	November 22, 1882	NA	6,7
J. H. Upshur	December 1, 1882	NA	6
J. H. Upshur	December 21, 1882	NA	6
J. H. Upshur	December 21, 1882	NA	7
J. H. Upshur	January 9, 1883	NA	4,6
J. H. Upshur	January 17, 1883	NA	6,7
J. H. Upshur	January 17, 1883	NA	7
J. H. Upshur	January 20, 1883	NA	7
J. H. Upshur	January 22, 1883	NA	7
J. H. Upshur	January 22, 1883	NA	6
J. H. Upshur	January 29, 1883	NA	6,4,7
J. H. Upshur	February 3, 1883	NA	6
J. H. Upshur	February 7, 1883	NA	6
J. H. Upshur	February 12, 1883	NA	1
J. H. Upshur	March 3, 1883	NA	4,6
J. H. Upshur	March 3, 1883	NA	7
J. H. Upshur	March 7, 1883	NA	6
J. H. Upshur	March 16, 1883	NA	4
J. H. Upshur	March 20, 1883	NA	7
G. Brown	April 3, 1883	NA	6
J. H. Upshur	April 23, 1883	NA	7
J. H. Upshur	April 26, 1883	NA	7
J. H. Upshur	April 30, 1883	NA	6
J. H. Upshur	May 2, 1883	NA	2
J. H. Upshur	May 3, 1883	NA	6

Recipient	Date	Repository	Subject
J. H. Upshur	May 7, 1883	NA	6
J. H. Upshur	May 8, 1883	NA	6
J. H. Upshur	May 9, 1883	NA	7
J. H. Upshur	May 9, 1883	NA	6,7
J. H. Upshur	May 14, 1883	NA	2
J. H. Upshur	May 17, 1883	NA	5
J. H. Upshur	June 1, 1883	NA	6
J. H. Upshur	June 11, 1883	NA	8
J. H. Upshur	June 13, 1883	NA	6
J. H. Upshur	June 13, 1883	NA	7
J. H. Upshur	June 14, 1883	NA	2,4
J. H. Upshur	June 18, 1883	NA	6
J. H. Upshur	June 21, 1883	NA	6
J. H. Upshur	June 21, 1883	NA	7
J. H. Upshur	June 22, 1883	NA	5,6
J. H. Upshur	June 23, 1883	NA	7
J. H. Upshur	July 19, 1883	NA	6,4
J. H. Upshur	July 20, 1883	NA	2,6
J. H. Upshur	July 21, 1883	NA	6
J. H. Upshur	July 24, 1883	NA	2,8
J. H. Upshur	July 25, 1883	NA	7
J. H. Upshur	August 1, 1883	NA	7,6
J. G. Walker	September 9, 1883	NA	1
J. G. Walker	September 13, 1883	NA	2,6
J. G. Walker	September 13, 1883	NA	3
J. G. Walker	September 21, 1883	NA	3
E. English	September 22, 1883	NA	8
W. E. Chandler	[October 1883]	NA	3
J. G. Walker	October 10, 1883	NA	3
W. E. Chandler	October 11, 1883	NA	3
J. G. Walker	December 3, 1883	NA	2
J. G. Walker	December 5, 1883	NA	1
J. G. Walker	December 12, 1883	NA	2
E. English	December 12, 1883	NA	4,8
E. English	December 14, 1883	NA	2
E. English	December 14, 1883	NA	8
E. English	December 21, 1883	NA	2
M. Sicard	December 21, 1883	NA	2
J. G. Walker	December 24, 1883	NA	8
J. G. Walker	January 8, 1884	NA	2
W. E. Chandler	January 8, 1884	NA	3
E. English	January 22, 1884	NA	2

Recipient	Date	Repository	Subject
J. G. Walker	January 23, 1884	NA	7
M. Sicard	January 30, 1884	NA	5
M. Sicard	February 13, 1884	NA	2
M. Sicard	February 20, 1884	NA	6,2
E. English	February 20, 1884	NA	1
J. G. Walker	March 3, 1884	NA	1,5
M. Sicard	March 15, 1884	NA	1
J. G. Walker	March 18, 1884	NA	1,3
E. English	March 21, 1884	NA	8
W. E. Chandler	April 1, 1884	NA	3
J. R. Bartlett	April 18, 1884	NA	1
J. G. Walker	April 18, 1884	NA	1
J. R. Bartlett	May 5, 1884	NA	1
M. Sicard	May 9, 1884	NA	1
J. R. Bartlett	May 9, 1884	NA	1
E. English	June 11, 1884	NA	1
E. English	June 17, 1884	NA	1,2
J. G. Walker	July 9, 1884	NA	1
J. R. Bartlett	July 14, 1884	NA	1
J. G. Walker	July 15, 1884	NA	2
E. English	July 15, 1884	NA	2
E. English	August 27, 1884	NA	1
E. English	September 3, 1884	NA	1
J. G. Walker	September 4, 1884	NA	2
M. Sicard	October 12, 1884	NA	3
W. E. Chandler	October 12, 1884	NA	3
W. S. Schley	October 23, 1884	NA	8
J. R. Bartlett	October 28, 1884	NA	1
W. S. Schley	October 28, 1884	NA	1
W. E. Chandler	October 29, 1884	NA	3
W. S. Schley	November 4, 1884	NA	6
W. S. Schley	November 5, 1884	NA	8
J. R. Bartlett	November 27, 1884	NA	1
W. S. Schley	December 3, 1884	NA	8
W. E. Chandler	January 8, 1885	NA	3
W. C. Whitney	July 3, 1885	NA	3
W. C. Whitney	July 14, 1885	NA	8
W. C. Whitney	September 9, 1885	NA	8
F. M. Ramsay	August 5, 1892	NA	2
F. M. Ramsay	August 19, 1892	NA	4
F. M. Ramsay	August 24, 1892	NA	1
F. M. Ramsay	September 9, 1892	NA	2

Recipient	Date	Repository	Subject
B. F. Tracy	February 13, 1893	NA	1
H. A. Herbert	March 20, 1893	NA	1
J. R. Soley	April 20, 1893	NA	1
H. A. Herbert	May 19, 1893	NA	1
H. A. Herbert	May 23, 1893	NA	8
H. A. Herbert	May 24, 1893	NA	8
H. A. Herbert	May 25, 1893	NA	8
H. A. Herbert	June 13, 1893	NA	8
H. A. Herbert	June 16, 1893	NA	8
H. A. Herbert	July 1, 1893	NA	8
H. A. Herbert	July 3, 1893	NA	8
H. A. Herbert	July 17, 1893	NA	8
H. A. Herbert	August 19, 1893	NA	8
W. T. Sampson	August 23, 1893	NA	1,2
H. A. Herbert	August 28, 1893	NA	8
H. A. Herbert	August 28, 1893	NA	8
H. A. Herbert	September 2, 1893	NA	8
W. G. McAdoo	September 4, 1893	NA	1
H. A. Herbert	September 19, 1893	NA	8
H. A. Herbert	September 22, 1893	NA	8
F. M. Ramsay	September 27, 1893	NA	8
F. E. Chadwick	September 30, 1893	NA	1
H. A. Herbert	September 30, 1893	NA	8
H. A. Herbert	October 3, 1893	NA	3
F. M. Ramsay	October 19, 1893	NA	4
H. A. Herbert	October 25, 1893	NA	8
H. A. Herbert	October 31, 1893	NA	8
F. M. Ramsay	November 18, 1893	NA	8
H. A. Herbert	November 30, 1893	NA	8
F. M. Ramsay	December 7, 1893	NA	8
F. M. Ramsay	December 8, 1893	NA	8
W. T. Sampson	December 21, 1893	NA	7
F. M. Ramsay	December 28, 1893	NA	8
F. M. Ramsay	December 31, 1893	NA	8
F. M. Ramsay	December 31, 1893	NA	8
F. M. Ramsay	January 1, 1894	NA	6
F. M. Ramsay	January 12, 1894	NA	8
F. M. Ramsay	January 20, 1894	NA	8
F. M. Ramsay	January 26, 1894	NA	8
H. A. Herbert	January 26, 1894	NA	8
H. A. Herbert	January 31, 1894	NA	8
F. M. Ramsay	February 6, 1894	NA	2

Recipient	Date	Repository	Subject
H. A. Herbert	February 28, 1894	NA	8
H. A. Herbert	March 2, 1894	NA	3,8
H. A. Herbert	March 8, 1894	NA	8
H. A. Herbert	March 22, 1894	NA	8
H. A. Herbert	March 31, 1894	NA	3,8
F. M. Ramsay	March 31, 1894	NA	6
F. M. Ramsay	March 31, 1894	NA	8
H. A. Herbert	April 11, 1894	NA	1,2
H. A. Herbert	April 11, 1894	NA	1,6
H. A. Herbert	April 19, 1894	NA	8
H. A. Herbert	April 26, 1894	NA	8
H. A. Herbert	April 30, 1894	NA	8
H. A. Herbert	May 1, 1894	NA	3,8
H. A. Herbert	June 24, 1894	NA	8
H. A. Herbert	June 24, 1894	NA	8
H. A. Herbert	June 26, 1894	NA	8
F. M. Ramsay	June 30, 1894	NA	6
F. M. Ramsay	June 30, 1894	NA	8
H. A. Herbert	July 1, 1894	NA	8
H. A. Herbert	July 3, 1894	NA	8
H. Erben	August 3, 1894	NA	8
H. A. Herbert	August 29, 1894	NA	8
H. Erben	September 6, 1894	NYHS	1
W. A. Kirkland	September 15, 1894	NA	8
F. M. Ramsay	September 30, 1894	NA	6
F. M. Ramsay	September 30, 1894	NA	8
H. A. Herbert	October 10, 1894	NA	3,8
H. A. Herbert	November 12, 1894	NA	8
F. M. Ramsay	November 15, 1894	NA	8
H. A. Herbert	December 9, 1894	NA	1,8
H. A. Herbert	December 13, 1894	NA	6,1
H. A. Herbert	December 17, 1894	NA	3,8
H. A. Herbert	December 31, 1894	NA	3
H. A. Herbert	December 31, 1894	NA	6
H. A. Herbert	December 31, 1894	NA	8
H. A. Herbert	January 4, 1895	NA	8
H. A. Herbert	January 24, 1895	NA	3
[Memorandum]	February 27, 1895	LC	4
H. A. Herbert	March 23, 1895	NA	8
H. A. Herbert	March 23, 1895	NA	8
H. A. Herbert	March 25, 1895	NA	8
H. A. Herbert	March 25, 1895	NA	8

Recipient	Date	Repository	Subject
H. A. Herbert	March 26, 1895	NA	8
H. A. Herbert	April 4, 1895	NA	6
M. Sicard	April 4, 1895	NA	6
H. A. Herbert	April 6, 1895	NA	8
H. A. Herbert	April 6, 1895	NA	8
H. A. Herbert	April 12, 1895	NA	8
H. A. Herbert	April 13, 1895	NA	8
H. A. Herbert	April 15, 1895	NA	8
H. A. Herbert	April 16, 1895	NA	5
H. A. Herbert	April 16, 1895	NA	6
H. A. Herbert	April 18, 1895	NA	8
H. A. Herbert	April 25, 1895	NA	6
H. A. Herbert	April 30, 1895	NA	5
H. A. Herbert	April 30, 1895	NA	6
H. A. Herbert	April 30, 1895	NA	8
H. A. Herbert	April 30, 1895	NA	3
M. Sicard	May 1, 1895	NA	8
Bureau of Navigation	May 1, 1895	NA	8
H. A. Herbert	May 6, 1895	NA	6
H. A. Herbert	May 16, 1895	NA	6
H. A. Herbert	August 10, 1895	NA	6
K. Bowlker	January 6, 1904	HUL	9
Little, Brown & Co.	September 5, 1907	LC	10
J. P. Merrell	March 19, 1908	NWC	10
Little, Brown & Co.	September 17, 1908	LC	10
Little, Brown & Co.	April 5, 1909	LC	10
Little, Brown & Co.	April 19, 1909	LC	10
Little, Brown & Co.	May 4, 1909	LC	10
Little, Brown & Co.	September 21, 1910	LC	10
Little, Brown & Co.	October 1, 1910	LC	10
Little, Brown & Co.	June 26, 1911	LC	10
Little, Brown & Co.	June 28, 1911	LC	10
Little, Brown & Co.	June 29, 1911	LC	10
Little, Brown & Co.	July 18, 1911	LC	10
Little, Brown & Co.	July 20, 1911	LC	10
Little, Brown & Co.	July 24, 1911	LC	10
Little, Brown & Co.	July 31, 1911	LC	10
Little, Brown & Co.	August 3, 1911	LC	10
Little, Brown & Co.	August 5, 1911	LC	10
Little, Brown & Co.	August 9, 1911	LC	10
Little, Brown & Co.	August 12, 1911	LC	10
Little, Brown & Co.	August 22, 1911	LC	10

Recipient	Date	Repository	Subject
Little, Brown & Co.	August 26, 1911	LC	10
Little, Brown & Co.	August 26, 1911	LC	10
Little, Brown & Co.	September 1, 1911	LC	10
Little, Brown & Co.	September 2, 1911	LC	10
Little, Brown & Co.	September 6, 1911	LC	10
Little, Brown & Co.	September 11, 1911	LC	10
Little, Brown & Co.	September 14, 1911	LC	10
Little, Brown & Co.	September 19, 1911	LC	10
Little, Brown & Co.	September 19, 1911	LC	10
Little, Brown & Co.	September 23, 1911	LC	10
Little, Brown & Co.	September 26, 1911	LC	10
Little, Brown & Co.	September 26, 1911	LC	10
Little, Brown & Co.	September 26, 1911	LC	10
Little, Brown & Co.	September 27, 1911	LC	10
Little, Brown & Co.	September 29, 1911	LC	10
Little, Brown & Co.	September 30, 1911	LC	10
Little, Brown & Co.	October 2, 1911	LC	10
Little, Brown & Co.	October 3, 1911	LC	10
Little, Brown & Co.	October 4, 1911	LC	10
Little, Brown & Co.	October 4, 1911	LC	10
Little, Brown & Co.	October 6, 1911	LC	10
Little, Brown & Co.	October 7, 1911	LC	10
Little, Brown & Co.	October 9, 1911	LC	10
Little, Brown & Co.	October 10, 1911	LC	10
Little, Brown & Co.	October 11, 1911	LC	10
Little, Brown & Co.	October 11, 1911	LC	10
Little, Brown & Co.	October 12, 1911	LC	10
Little, Brown & Co.	October 12, 1911	LC	10
Little, Brown & Co.	October 12, 1911	LC	10
Little, Brown & Co.	October 13, 1911	LC	10
Little, Brown & Co.	October 13, 1911	LC	10
Little, Brown & Co.	October 17, 1911	LC	10
Little, Brown & Co.	October 24, 1911	LC	10
Little, Brown & Co.	November 4, 1911	LC	10
Little, Brown & Co.	October 12, 1912	LC	10
Little, Brown & Co.	October 19, 1912	LC	10
Little, Brown & Co.	October 21, 1912	LC	10
Little, Brown & Co.	January 10, 1913	LC	10
Little, Brown & Co.	April 25, 1913	LC	10
Little, Brown & Co.	May 7, 1913	LC	10
Little, Brown & Co.	May 13, 1913	LC	10
Little, Brown & Co.	May 19, 1913	LC	10

Recipient	Date	Repository	Subject
Little, Brown & Co.	May 20, 1913	LC	10
Little, Brown & Co.	May 29, 1913	LC	10
Little, Brown & Co.	June 28, 1913	LC	10
Little, Brown & Co.	July 1, 1913	LC	10
Little, Brown & Co.	July 7, 1913	LC	10
Little, Brown & Co.	July 8, 1913	LC	10
Little, Brown & Co.	July 25, 1913	LC	10
Little, Brown & Co.	July 28, 1913	LC	10
A. T. Gillender	May 2, [?]	HUL	9

Collections and Libraries Searched for Mahan Materials Without Success

Every major research center of American history in the United States was queried about possible Mahan holdings. Manuscript collections of persons known to be connected with Mahan and his career were specifically searched. Libraries and other institutions that might reasonably have been expected to harbor Mahan items were also searched, or officials there asked to aid in the search for relevant materials. The following is a list of places in which Mahan manuscript materials were *not* found. It is submitted by the editors in the interest of preventing duplication of effort by other historians interested in Alfred Thayer Mahan.

Collection or Institution	*Location*
American Bible Society	New York, N. Y.
T. F. Bayard Collection	Library of Congress
C. E. and R. Belknap Collection	Library of Congress
T. H. Bliss Collection	Library of Congress
C. J. Bonaparte Collection	Library of Congress
British Museum	London
Brown University Library	Providence, R. I.
A. Carnegie Collection	Library of Congress
S. Casey Collection	Library of Congress (Naval Historical Foundation—NHF)
F. E. Chadwick Collection	University of West Virginia Library
W. E. Chandler Collection	Library of Congress (NHF)
C. M. Chester Collection	Library of Congress (NHF)
City College of New York Library	New York, N. Y.
Columbia Historical Society	Washington, D. C.
G. A. Converse Collection	Library of Congress (NHF)
A. C. Dayton Collection	University of West Virginia Library
C. W. Eliot Collection	Harvard University Library
W. H. Emory Collection	Library of Congress (NHF)
R. D. Evans Collection	Library of Congress (NHF)
W. F. Fullman Collection	Library of Congress (NHF)
General Theological Seminary Library	New York, N. Y.

Collection or Institution	*Location*
A. Gleaves Collection	Library of Congress (NHF)
C. F. Goodrich Collection	Library of Congress (NHF)
N. Goff Collection	University of West Virginia Library
A. B. Hart Collection	Duke University Library
H. A. Herbert Collection	University of North Carolina Library
W. H. Hunt Collection	Library of Congress
Henry E. Huntington Library	San Marino, Calif.
L. A. Kimberly Collection	Library of Congress
D. Knox Collection	Library of Congress
E. S. Land Collection	Library of Congress
H. C. Lodge Collection	Library of Congress
S. B. Luce Collection	Naval War College Library, Newport, R. I.
D. H. Mahan Collection	U.S.M.A. Library West Point, N Y.
Marine Historical Society	Portland, Maine
Marine Historical Association	Mystic, Conn.
Maryland Historical Society Library	Baltimore, Md.
Mayo Collection	Minnesota Historical Society Library, Minneapolis, Minn.
McCook Family Collection	Library of Congress
C. B. McVay Collection	Library of Congress (NHF)
G. von L. Meyer Collection	Massachusetts Historical Society, Boston, Mass.
G. von L. Meyer Collection	Library of Congress
Military Historical Society of Massachusetts	Boston, Mass.
J. T. Morgan Collection	Library of Congress
Navy Records Society	London
Newberry Library	Chicago, Ill.
C. O. Paullin Collection	Library of Congress
D. D. Porter Collection	Library of Congress
W. Pratt Collection	Division of Naval History, Navy Yard, Washington, D.C.
Public Record Office	London
Quogue Public Library	Quogue, Long Island, N. Y.
P. Reinsch Collection	State Historical Society of Wisconsin, Madison, Wis.
G. C. Remey Collection	Library of Congress (NHF)
G. C. Remey Collection	University of Iowa Library (Remey Collection closed until 1995)
Rhode Island Historical Society	Providence, R. I.

Collection or Institution	Location
R. P. Rodgers Family Collection	Library of Congress (NHF)
W. L. Rodgers Collection	Library of Congress (NHF)
Royal Commission on Historical Manuscripts	London
Royal United Services Institute	London
M. Schoonmaker Collection	Library of Congress (NHF)
H. E. Scudder Collection	Massachusetts Historical Society, Boston, Mass.
T. O. Selfridge, Sr. and Jr. Collection	Library of Congress (NHF)
R. W. Shufeldt Collection	Library of Congress (NHF)
M. Sicard Collection	Library of Congress (NHF)
W. H. Taft Collection	Library of Congress
H. C. Taylor Collection	Library of Congress (NHF)
Virginia Theological Seminary Library	Alexandria, Va.
J. G. Walker Collection	Library of Congress (NHF)
J. C. Watson Collection	Library of Congress (NHF)
W. C. Whitney Collection	Library of Congress
Woodrow Wilson Collection	Library of Congress

Lost or Destroyed

The back correspondence files of the following persons, publishers, journals, and institutions with whom and which Mahan is known to have corresponded in the 1875–1914 period have been destroyed or lost or are for other reasons unobtainable.

The Army and Navy Journal
The Churchman Magazine
W. Clowes & Sons, Ltd. (including the files of *Brassey's Annual*)
Colliers Magazine
English Historical Review
The Forum Magazine
Groton School
Harper & Row
W. O'Connor Morris
Revue Maritime
Scientific American Magazine
B. F. Stevens and Brown, Ltd.
Charles H. Stockton

Index

To facilitate its precise use, this index is divided, at the cost of some redundancy, into four sections:

I General

II Ships

III Bibliography—books, articles, and other items written by, read by, or used by Mahan, or cited by Mahan and the editors.

IV Judgments and opinions—persons, subjects, concepts, and events on which Mahan expressed various opinions, judgments, and attitudes. Mahan's personal beliefs, problems, and family relationships are also included in this section.

SECTION I—GENERAL

A&M's store: 97
Abbot, Henry L.: 656, 665
Abbott, Francis Lemuel: **II**, 484
Aberdeen, W. T.: 674
Aberdeen Herald (Aberdeen, Wash. Ter.):
    letter to editor, 673–675
Aboukir, Egypt: **II**, 600
Aboukir Bay, Egypt: **II**, 480
Acapulco, Mex.: 598, 599, 611, 612
Ackerman, J. E.: **II**, 53
A'Court, Col. Charles: **II**, 658; **III**, 109
Adair, Mrs. Cornelia Wadsworth: **II**, 137
Adam, Charles Fox: **II**, 296
Adam, Graeme Mercer: letter to, **II**, 580
Adam, Juliet Palmer (Mrs. Charles Fox
    Adam): **II**, 296
Adams, Miss: 15, 16, 17, 18, 20, 26, 49, 56, 57,
    70
Adams, Charles Francis: **II**, 474; **III**, 196, 551,
    676
Adams, Charles Kendall: **III**, 43
Adams Express: **III**, 241
Adams, Henry: **III**, 43, 47, 112, 159, 286, 524
Adams, John: **III**, 621
Adams, John Quincy: **III**, 114, 115
Adamson, Thomas: 567, 591, 594, 609
Aden, Arabia: 98, 110, 111, 141, 146; M.
    describes, 112–113
Admiralty Inlet, N.W.T., Canada: 673, 686
Admiralty Islands, Bismarck Archipelago:
    III, 383
Admiralty Library: **II**, 722
Adrianople, European Turkey: **III**, 511
Adriatic Sea: **III**, 541
Aetna, Mt., Sicily: **II**, 237
Afghanistan: **II**, 129
Africa: 101, 113; **II**, 18, 357, 529, 568, 582,
    589, 674, 698; **III**, 420, 502, 508, 523
Agram, Croatia: trial at, **III**, 704
Ahaja, Alonzo D.: 598
Aisne River, France: **III**, 548
Alaska: **III**, 390, 524; boundary question, **III**,
    471
Albania: **III**, 686, 687
Albany, N.Y.: **III**, 63, 76, 364
Albi, France: 463
Alcazar Palace, Seville, Spain: **II**, 358
Alden, Henry: **II**, 496
Alden, James: letters to, 355, 356, 358, 359,
    367–368, 369; mention, 357; **III**, 555
Aldens, Mrs. Jane: **II**, 123
Alderman, Edwin A.: letter to, **III**, 478
Aldershot, England: **II**, 328
Aldrich, Nelson W.: letter to, 639; mention,
    664, 665; **II**, 58, 59, 60, 62, 63, 64
Alexander the Great: 607; **III**, 581
Alexander I, Czar: **II**, 197
Alexander III, Czar: **II**, 359, 360; **III**, 543
Alexandretta, Turkey: **II**, 245, 246, 247, 248,
    249

Alexandria, Egypt: 53; **II**, 226, 245, 248, 249,
    250, 251, 254, 255, 262, 368, 413, 414
Alford, Dean: **II**, 115
Algeciras, Spain: **III**, 148, 720
Algeciras Conference of 1907: **III**, 342
Algeciras Bay, Spain: 619
Alger, Philip R.: letter to, **III**, 201
Alger, Russell A.: **II**, 690, 691, 692, 718, 719,
    728
Algiers, French Morocco: **II**, 92, 257, 258,
    259, 262, 365, 371, 374, 375, 376, 377, 379,
    381, 382, 383, 384, 385, 387, 388, 394, 396,
    399, 401, 404, 405, 408, 418, 419; **III**, 118,
    473, 588; governor general, **II**, 383; M. de-
    scribes, **II**, 402
Algeria: **III**, 473
Algonquin Club: **III**, 286
Alhambra, The: **II**, 164, 169, 358
Alicante, Spain: **II**, 167
Alien Land Bill: **III**, 496
All Angels Episcopal Church (New York):
    II, 618; **III**, 721
"All-Big-Gun" Ship Controversy: mention,
    III, 178, 281, 284, 285, 291, 342, 679, 680,
    700. *See* Index Section IV, U.S. Navy:
    Ships
Allderdice, Mrs.: **II**, 389
Allen, Ethan: **III**, 470
Allen, Louis J.: **III**, 586, 587, 588, 589
Allied Powers (1914): **III**, 548, 551, 730
Allmond, Douglas A.: 684
All Souls College, Oxford: **II**, 290
Almeida, Portugal: **III**, 191
Almirante Bay, Colombia: **II**, 589, 590
Alporter family: 91
Alps: 606
Alsina, Adolfo: 414
Alvine, Vice Adml.: 398, 399
Amami O Sima, Ryukyu [Lu-Chu] Islands,
    China Sea: **III**, 384
Amazon River: **III**, 54
Amazon, Valley of, Brazil: **III**, 446
America: 44, 65, 74, 75, 101, 107; **II**, 443,
    567, 569, 583, 589; **III**, 354, 394, 411, 442,
    443, 445, 446, 453, 460, 487, 497, 499, 521,
    522, 559, 629, 688
American Academy of Arts and Letters:
    III, 85, 300
American Academy of Arts and Sciences:
    II, 410
American Association for International Con-
    ciliation: **III**, 703
American Baptist Foreign Mission Society:
    III, 507
American-Canadian Reciprocity Treaty of
    1911: **III**, 427
American Chilean Crisis of 1891–1892: **II**,
    59, 62, 63, 64, 65, 68
American Church [Protestant Episcopal]
    Institute for Negroes: **III**, 190

American Historical Association: **II**, 701, 741; **III**, 4, 24, 42, 45–46, 51, 131, 240, 552

American Japanese Treaty of Commerce and Navigation: **III**, 226, 412

American-Japanese war scare of 1907: **III**, 221, 222

American and Mexican Pacific R.R.: 596. *See* Kansas City, Mexico & Orient R.R.

American Movement: **III**, 657

American Peace and Arbitration League: **III**, 433

American Philosophical Society: **II**, 527

American Revolution: mention, 629, 636, 659; **II**, 92, 510, 518, 556, 608, 724, 725; **III**, 119, 394, 467, 519, 671

American Revolution Centennial: 452, 454, 455, 457

American Society for Judicial Settlement of International Disputes: **III**, 436

American Steamship Line: **III**, 629

American Surety Co.: **II**, 727

Ames, Sullivan Dorr ("Dunker" or "Dunk"): 18, 30, 31, 34, 52, 54, 55, 88

Amherst County, Va.: 31

Ammen, Daniel: letters to, 370, 371, 372, 373, 430, 435–436, 436, 457, 460, 461–462, 463, 466; mention, 370, 462, 474; **II**, 97

Ancud, Chile: 565

Anderson, Mr.: 297

Anderson, Charles G.: **II**, 317

Anderson, Thomas: 383, 384

Andes Mts.: 572; **III**, 54

Andrews, Charles M.: **III**, 676

Andrews, Philip: letter to, **III**, 352–358; mention, **III**, 352

Angell, Norman: **III**, 448, 449

Anglesey, Lady (née Minnie King Wodehouse): **II**, 202

Anglo-American General Arbitration Treaty: **II**, 450, 498, 504

Anglo-French Expedition into China in 1860: **II**, 92

Anglo-French rivalry in the Sudan: **II**, 620

Anglo-Japanese Treaty: **III**, 12, 226, 308, 358, 533, 534, 535

Anglo-Nicaraguan tension: **II**, 444

Anglo-Saxon race: **II**, 442, 545, 557

Annapolis, Md.: 19, 39, 40, 46, 47, 55, 62, 63, 65, 70, 71, 80, 82, 84, 357, 433, 460, 464, 466, 469, 476, 483, 486, 487, 578, 645; **II**, 53, 55, 108, 148, 179, 349; **III**, 270, 664, 721

Antilles: **III**, 472

Anti-Taurus Mts., Turkey: **II**, 247

Antofagasta, Chile: 560, 564

Antwerp, Belgium: **II**, 256, 260, 286, 287, 288, 290, 291, 292, 296, 299, 309, 310, 317, 327, 345, 414; **III**, 548, 551; mosquitoes in, **II**, 306; M. describes, **II**, 293, 304

Apennines: **II**, 229

Appleton, Francis Henry: **II**, 533

Appleton and Company: letter to, **II**, 69–70; mention, 507; **II**, 46, 55; **III**, 303

Appleton, Nathan: letter to, **II**, 171

Apra, Guam: **III**, 398, 399

Arabia: 113

Arabs: 108, 109, 113; language, **II**, 357

Arbitration, Permanent Tribunal of, **II**, 445, 450

Arbitration, treaties with Great Britain and France: **III**, 422, 433, 434, 435, 437, 438, 440, 441, 442, 443, 444, 445, 450, 458; Carnegie Hall meeting on, **III**, 438, 443

Arbuthnot, Marriot: **III**, 472

Arctic: 86; **II**, 621

Ardois Night Signals: **II**, 338

Arequipa, Peru: 560, 572

Argentina: 385, 386, 389, 399, 401, 408–409, 409, 414, 415, 416, 419, 420, 422–423, 424, 425; **II**, 341, 680

Arica, Chile, earthquake at: 240

Arkansas State Legislature: **II**, 159

Arles, France: **II**, 174, 175, 176, 560

Arlington, English estate: **II**, 325, 327

Armor belt: **III**, 281

Army and Navy Club (Washington): **II**, 396, 400

Arnim, von, Count: **II**, 130

Arnold, Benedict: **II**, 92; **III**, 470

Arnold, C. H.: 383, 388, 389, 400, 404

Arnold, Matthew: **II**, 115

Arthur, Mr.: 195

Artillery Institute: **II**, 138

Arun, John: 184

Asami, Lt. Cmdr. K., IJN: **III**, 499

Ashe, Elizabeth Emerson (Mrs. George B. Flint): 451

Ashe, George Bamford: 451; **III**, 271, 273

Ashe, Hannah Emerson Willard (Mrs. Samuel A'C. Ashe): 367, 434, 451, 464, 649, 451

Ashe, Hannah Willard (Mrs. William H. Bason): 451

Ashe, John Grange: 451

Ashe, Josephine Grange (Mrs. Joseph E. Graef): 451, 544; **III**, 271, 464

Ashe, Mary Porter: 451; **III**, 190

Ashe, Samuel A'Court: letters to, 5–9, 9–14, 15–17, 17–20, 20–24, 25–27, 27–32, 32–36, 36–39, 39–50, 50–51, 52–53, 54–56, 56–59, 59–61, 61–63, 63–64, 64–65, 65–68, 68–70, 70–72, 73–75, 75–77, 77–79, 80–81, 81–82, 82–83, 84–85, 85–86, 87–88, 336–338, 338–341, 347–349, 350–351, 351, 352, 352–354, 354–355, 356–358, 359–360, 364–365, 367, 432–433, 433–434, 435, 436–439, 440–442, 442–443, 450–452, 453–454, 454–456, 456–457, 458–459, 463–464, 464–466, 466–469, 469–471, 472–474, 474–475, 476–477, 481–483, 486–489, 491–492, 543–544, 554–556, 557–558, 571–574, 591–594, 620–621, 624–625, 635–636, 641–642, 646, 647–648, 648–

649, 652, 653–655; **II**, 181–183, 470, 482–483, 658; **III**, 53–58, 190, 227–228, 230–231, 270–271, 272–273, 464–466; mention, 3, 5, 13, 14, 26, 59, 81, 163, 169, 205, 235, 295, 329, 434; **III**, 190, 721. *See* Index Section IV, Ashe
Ashe, Samuel A'Court, Jr.: 434, 451
Ashe, Thomas Martin: 451
Ashe, Thomas Samuel: 470
Ashe, William Shepperd: 59
Ashe, William Willard: 451
Asheville, N.C.: 470, 475
Ashley, Roscoe Lewis: **II**, 680
Asia: **II**, 506, 582, 583, 658; **III**, 12, 35, 206, 411, 458, 465, 508, 522, 604, 658, 661
Asia Minor: **II**, 245, 246, 247; **III**, 710
Aspinwall, Panama: 572, 590, 595
Asquith, Herbert Henry. *See* Oxford and Asquith
Assistant Comptroller: **III**, 526
Associate Alumni of the College of the City of N.Y.: **III**, 603
Astor Foundation: **II**, 517
Astoria Gas bill: **II**, 668
Astoria, Ore: 674
Astoria, Oregon: letter to mayor of, 673–675
Asunción, Paraguay: 386, 395, 396, 397, 398, 399, 400, 402, 403, 405, 415–416, 423, 424
Athanasius: **II**, 172
Athenaeum Club (London): **II**, 267, 271, 345
Athenian attack on Syracuse: **II**, 138, 434
Athens, Greece: **II**, 238
Atlantic: **II**, 67, 261, 381, 384, 394, 395, 405, 506, 566, 584, 621, 680; **III**, 53, 77, 78, 80, 146, 206, 380, 381, 383, 384, 385, 400, 401, 402, 403, 410, 439, 445, 458, 489, 495, 532, 561, 566, 574, 575, 629, 637
Atlantic Coast: 568; **II**, 551, 553, 567, 584, 683; **III**, 206, 353, 354, 355, 372, 559, 560, 563, 564, 574
Atlantic Transport Co.: **III**, 484
Atonement Episcopal Church (Quogue, N.Y.): **III**, 721
Attalus I: 354
Attica, Greece: **II**, 238
Auckland, New Zealand: 385
Augagneur, Victor: **III**, 502, 508
Australia: 142, 662; **II**, 18, 270, 583; **III**, 13, 16, 214, 216, 217, 221, 225, 308, 376, 377, 384, 397, 402, 411, 427, 448, 449, 452, 468, 609, 643
Austria-Hungary: **III**, 342, 499, 500, 541, 698, 699, 703, 704, 705, 710; Emperor, **III**, 10; Empress, **III**, 389; empire, **III**, 498; military activities, **III**, 344, 388, 581; Balkan annexation, **III**, 342; Foreign Office, **III**, 704; ultimatum to Serbia, **III**, 698
Authors' Club of New York: letter to, **II**, 697
Author's Syndicate: **III**, 237
Avellaneda, Nicolas: 414, 424

Averett College (Danville, Va.): **III**, 55
Averett, Samuel W.: 6, 8, 11, 12, 56, 66–67, 73–74, 78, **III**, 53, 55
Aviation: **II**, 75; **III**, 410, 551, 572, 700, 708, 709
Avignon, France: **II**, 174, 175, 176, 233, 560
Aylesbury, English estate: **II**, 141
Azores: 3; **II**, 67

Babcock, O. E.: 459
Bache, Huston: 287; **II**, 188, 195
Backus, John H.: 172, 186, 208, 209, 210, 211, 213, 271
Bacon, Albert W.: letter to, 413–414; mention, 413
Badger, Oscar Charles: letters to, 390, 390–391, 391–392, 392, 392–393, 393, 394, 395, 395–396, 396; mention, 376, 396, 397, 406
Badham, F. P.: **II**, 619, 624, 630; **III**, 48, 118
Bad Nauheim, Germany: **III**, 100, 127, 209, 212, 214, 215, 225, 657, 720
Bagley, J. R.: letter to, 673–675
Bahia, Brazil: 428
Bahia, Ecuador: 588, 589, 605
Bailey, Mr. (at Little, Brown Co.): **II**, 502, 621
Bailey, Mr. (in Yokohama): 148, 161, 324
Bailey, William Whitman: **III**, 523–524
Bainbridge Id., W. T.: 680, 683, 695
Bainbridge, William: **III**, 61, 69, 103
Baird, Mrs.: **II**, 194
Baiz, Jacob: 526, 528
Baker, Benjamin: **III**, 205–206
Balch, George B.: letters to, 478–481; **III**, 237–238; mention, 478, 486–487; **III**, 237
Balch Price Co.: **III**, 504
Baldwin, E. F.: **III**, 240
Balfour, Arthur James: **II**, 105, 110, 131, 273, 445, 674; **III**, 244
Balkan states: **II**, 710, 744; **III**, 687, 699, 705; people, **III**, 510; situation, **III**, 520, 521; wars, **III**, 495, 505, 521, 683, 686, 705
Ballard, Kings: **II**, 345
Ballenita, Costa Rica: 589
Baltic Sea: 619; **II**, 55, 621; **III**, 91, 372, 698, 699, 707
Baltimore, Md.: 38, 40, 47, 49, 62, 355, 356, 357, 477, 714; **III**, 560, 568, 571, 574
Banana Point, Water Island, Lesser Antilles: **II**, 586
Bangor, Me.: **III**, 566, 573
Bangkok, Siam: 307
Banning, Henry Blackstone: 454
Bantry Bay, Ireland: **II**, 119
Barbados, Windward Islands: **II**, 629
Barbary pirates: **III**, 672
Barbary States, N. Africa: **III**, 673
Barber, F. M.: **II**, 95
Barbour, Thomas S.: **III**, 507, 508, 509

Barcelona, Spain: **II**, 160, 165, 166, 168, 169, 173, 174, 175, 176, 177, 178, 188, 213, 360, 363, 367, 369, 370, 371, 372, 373, 564; **III**, 638
Barclay, John Judson: **II**, 357, 358
Barclay, Robert Heriot: **III**, 118, 122, 135, 141, 150, 162, 313, 673
Barclay Street Seminary for Young Ladies: 41, 46
Bar Harbor, Me.: 613, 614, 631, 632, 633, 634, 688, 689, 690, 693; **II**, 14, 148, 159, 304, 355, 455; **III**, 544, 547
Barker, Albert S.: **II**, 27, 28, 57, 507; **III**, 162, 627, 628
Baring Co. of New York: **III**, 220
Barnegat, N.J.: **III**, 572
Barnes, James: **II**, 544
Barnes, John S.: letters to, **II**, 558, 562, 566–567, 578, 623, 627, **III**, 222; mention, 700, 707, 712, **II**, 578, **III**, 222
Barney, Miss: **III**, 247
Barrett, Seaman, 495
Barrington, Samuel: 629; **III**, 472
Barrios, Justo Rufino: 599, 600
Barron, James: **III**, 61
Barrow, Sir Edmund: **III**, 153
Barry, Mrs. Smith: **II**, 137
Bartlett, John Russell: **II**, 577
Barus, F. S.: letter to, 484; mention, 485
Bastia, Siege of, 1794: **II**, 419
Batcheller, Oliver A.: 325
Bathurst, Henry, 3rd Earl: **III**, 136, 137
Battles
  Aboukir: **II**, 600
  Algiers: **III**, 118
  Beachy Head (Beréziers): **III**, 368
  Bull Run: 98; **II**, 699; **III**, 702
  Cape Finisterre: **II**, 66
  Cape St. Vincent: **II**, 576
  Cavite: **II**, 600
  Chancellorsville: **II**, 699
  Copenhagen: **II**, 437, 444, 514, 600, 638. *See* Index Section III, Bibliography
  Four Days (1666), 633
  Fredericksburg: **II**, 699
  Gettysburg: 637
  Glorious First of June (1794): **II**, 279
  Hampton Roads: **III**, 56
  Lake Champlain: **III**, 167, 170, 527, 672
  Lake Erie: **III**, 67, 70, 672
  Manila Bay: **II**, 564, 566, 567; **III**, 629, 637
  Marengo: **III**, 581
  Minorca: 629
  Mobile Bay: 118, 551; **II**, 56; **III**, 56, 555–556
  Newbury: **II**, 327
  New Orleans: 118; **II**, 56; **III**, 81, 143, 167, 170
  Nile: **II**, 419, 463, 577
  Plattsburg: **III**, 136

Port Royal: 89, 90
Salamanca: **III**, 326
Santiago Bay: **II**, 569, 571, 573–577, 591, 600, 623, 632, 670, 690, 691, 692, 703–704, 720, 727–728
Saratoga: **III**, 672
Toulon: **II**, 722, 723
Trafalgar: 714; **II**, 9, 66–67, 150, 160, 415, 422, 430, 447, 454, 458, 465, 574; **III**, 155–156
Tsushima: **III**, 153, 154, 182, 201, 202, 680
Vicksburg: 546, 550; **III**, 388
Yalu: **II**, 416; **III**, 583–585
Yorktown: **III**, 519
"Battleship Conference." *See* Newport Conference
Batum, Russia: **II**, 300
Bayard, Thomas Francis, Sr.: letter to, 443; mention, 443, 482, 604; **II**, 131, 275, 277, 278, 284, 285, 335, 339
Beach, Consul General: 589
Beachy Head, England: **II**, 337
Beatrice, Princess of Battenberg: **II**, 140
Beauchamp, Lady: **II**, 152
Beaulieu, France: **II**, 203, 313, 321, 346, 355, 399
Beaumont, Mrs.: **II**, 277, 280, 284
Beckwith, Mr.: **II**, 354, 358
Beech, Mr.: 286, 287, 288
Beechey, Sir William: **II**, 484
Beira, Portugal: **II**, 688
Beirut, Lebanon: **II**, 245, 248, 262
Belden, Charles L.: 591, 595, 597
Belgium: flags, 510; people, **II**, 304, **III**, 221, 548, 703, 704
Belknap, Mr. & Mrs. Robert Lenox: **II**, 374
Belknap, William W.: 459
Bell, Charles H.: 94, 95
Bell, Henry Haywood: 118, 139, 192, 334; M. describes accidental death of, 122–123; funeral of, 124–125, 136
Bell, James Franklin: **III**, 6, 282
Belmont, Mass.: **II**, 500
Benham, E. A. K.: **II**, 740
Benjamin, Park: **II**, 739, 739–740; **III**, 2, 4
Benoit, Mr.: 517
Benson, William Shepherd: 520
Beresford, Lord Charles: **II**, 136, 270, 272, 274, 275, 523; **III**, 16, 263, 283, 315
Berg, Mr.: **II**, 522
Berlin and Milan Decrees: **III**, 115, 116, 122, 123, 124, 126
Bermuda: 96; **II**, 402, 405, 407, 408, 622; **III**, 561, 562, 563, 568, 569
Bernadou, John: **II**, 219
Berry, Albert Gleaves: 388–389, 400
Berry, Sir Edward: **II**, 419
Berutich, Mr.: 588
Bevans, Mr.: **II**, 363; **III**, 587

Bevington, Louisa S.: **II**, 115
Bicknell, George Augustus: 163, 170, 179, 185, 199, 200, 201, 203, 208, 227, 243, 254, 261, 293, 310, 311
Bigelow, George A.: 51
Bigelow, Poultney: **II**, 267, 270, 273
Billings, John S.: letters to, **II**, 517–518, 695, 721; **III**, 32, 37, 48–49, 50, 51, 52, 111, 112, 118–119, 119–120, 121–122, 131–132, 138–139, 200–201, 202, 242, 279, 282; mention, **II**, 517; **III**, 139, 140
Billings, Mr.: **II**, 400
Bingham, Lady Anne: **II**, 383
Bingham, Mrs.: **II**, 346, 392
Birmingham, England: **III**, 71
Biscay, Bay of: **II**, 1, 67, 264, 342, 352
Bishop, Joseph Bucklin: **III**, 28
Bishop, Mrs.: **II**, 221
Bismarck, von, Prince Otto Eduard Leopold: **III**, 32, 705
Bixby, W. H.: 637; **III**, 665
Bizen, Prince of: 127, 128
Black Bay, N.Y.: **III**, 85, 86
Black, Mrs.: 143
Blackburne, R. F.: **III**, 9
Blackie and Son, Ltd.: **II**, 610; **III**, 360–361
"Black Swamp," Ohio: **III**, 78
Blackwood, Mr.: **II**, 484
Blackwood, Sir Henry: **II**, 318
Bladens of Maryland: **II**, 724
Blaine, James G.: 455, 459, 477, 482, 544, 571, 572, 573, 591–592, 624, 655; **II**, 25, 126
Blake, Francis B.: 365, 433; **II**, 117, 135, 230, 275
Blake, George S.: letters to, 4–5, 5; mention, 4, 15, 18, 19, 24, 29, 30, 34, 38, 39, 60, 69, 76, 78, 81, 82, 433
Blake, Mrs. George S.: 69, 433
Blake, Mrs. Henry Jones: **II**, 230, 267, 269, 270, 272, 273, 275, 280
Blake Id., W. T.: 680, 681, 690, 696, 699
Blake, Sallie Spencer (Mrs. Francis B. Blake): 365, 433; **II**, 275
Blanco y Erenas, Ramon: **II**, 554
Bland-Allison Silver Act: 467–468, 469
Blarney Castle, Ireland: **II**, 118
Blenheim, Germany: **III**, 388
Bliss Taffrail Log: 495
Bliss, Tasker: 619, 637, 640, 651, 708, 712; **II**, 74; **III**, 663
Blodgett, George M.: 79
Bloemfontein Conference: **II**, 678; **III**, 51
Blomfield, Sir Richard Massie: **II**, 255
BLR guns: **II**, 303
Bluefields, Nicaragua: **II**, 435
Blunt, Wilfred: **II**, 115, 137
Board House (Annapolis): **II**, 6, 23, 30
Boers: **II**, 656, 666, 674, 677, 678, 679, 680, 689, 698, 722; **III**, 40, 51, 498, 499

Boer War: **II**, 656–657, 664, 670–671, 674, 677, 678, 688, 690, 698; **III**, 9, 10, 51, 604, 625–626, 703
Bogan, Charles H.: 583; **II**, 320
Boisse, M.: **II**, 218, 306, 525
Boissondy, Vice Adm.: **II**, 217
Bolivia: 526
Bombay, India: 112, 113, 114, 119, 141, 332, 351, 352, 556
Bonaparte, Charles J.: letter to, **III**, 161–162; mention, **III**, 142, 158, 164
Bonaparte, Napoleon: Italian Campaign, **II**, 445, **III**, 345, 412, 413, 426, 666; Egyptian Campaign, **II**, 138; wars, **II**, 29, **III**, 580; mention, 57, 71, 207, 252, 336, 607; **II**, 66, 126, 150, 197, 201, 252, 277, 337, 438, 595; **III**, 114, 116, 126, 191, 323, 325–326, 326, 356, 388, 392, 410, 551, 569, 580–581, 683, 709
Bonhomme Richard–Serapis action: **II**, 540, 544, 545, 546, 547; **III**, 487
Boone University, Wuchang, China: **III**, 418
Borchert, George A.: 6, 12, 13, 31, 37, 56, 78, 79; **III**, 55
Bordeaux, France: 427, 429, 430, 464
Borden, Sir Robert Laird: **III**, 427
Bormann fuzes: 562
Borneo: **III**, 377
Borokenhagen, Capt.: **II**, 218
Boscawen, Edward: 629
Bosnia and Herzegovina, Austria-Hungary: **III**, 342, 705
Boston, Mass.: 359, 364, 366, 367, 469, 527, 530, 562, 613, 622, 707; **II**, 124, 132, 133, 300, 396, 420, 421, 468, 497, 499, 500, 505, 530, 534, 537, 539, 592, 596, 604, 629, 666, 671, 676, 680; **III**, 63, 64, 81, 82, 83, 84, 85, 97, 145, 240, 356, 357, 425, 560, 566, 567, 568, 571, 573, 574
Boston Athenaeum: **III**, 119
Boston Public Library: **II**, 461; **III**, 470
Both and Weston: **III**, 525–526
Boudinot, W. E.: 22
Boulder, Colo.: **III**, 549
Bourgeois, M.: **II**, 651, 652
Bourges, France: **III**, 720
Bourrienne, M.: **III**, 580–581
Bowers, Charles S.: letter to, 405; mention, 405
Bowlby, J. J. A.: letter to, 674–675
Bowles, Thos. Gibson: **II**, 396
Bowyer, John Marshall: 569
Boxer Rebellion: **II**, 693
Boyle, Patrick: **II**, 208, 209, 210, 232
Bradford, Robert Forbes: 79
Bradford, Royal B.: 151, 164, 166, 175, 177, 194, 213, 226, 268, 279, 281, 290, 294, 296, 298, 314, 315, 317, 323, 329; **II**, 33, 95; **III**, 39

Bradley, Miss Rider: 62, 83

Brainard, Fred Roland: 478, 480–481

Brassey, Thomas, 1st Earl: **III**, 16, 184, 187

Brava Point Light, River Plate, So. America: 419

Brazil: 98, 385, 386, 399, 409, 413, 414, 415, 415–416, 509, 512, 530; **II**, 537

Breese, Marcy (née Curtin): **II**, 194

Bremen, Germany: **III**, 160, 214, 215

Bremerton, W. T.: **III**, 356, 383, 384, 385, 401, 402, 403

Brent, Bishop Charles Henry: **III**, 10

Brest, France: 671; **III**, 527, 568

Brewer, Ellen Kate: 7, 15, 17, 18, 22, 24, 27, 31, 38, 40, 50, 53, 57, 62

Brewer, John: 40–41, 49

Brewer, Lucy: 7, 15, 17, 18, 19, 22, 27, 31, 38, 40, 50–51

Bridge, Sir Cyprian A. G.: letters to, **II**, 332, 359; mention, **II**, 332; **III**, 154, 180, 455

Bridge, Edward W.: 531, 536, 538, 603

Bridgeman, William R.: **II**, 98

Bridport, Alexander N. Hood, Viscount: **II**, 594

Bridport Collection (British Museum): **II**, 623, 624

Bristow, Benjamin H.: 455

British Columbia, Canada: **II**, 538; **III**, 225, 226, 252, 376, 377, 449, 570

British Guiana: **II**, 442

British Museum: **II**, 467, 594, 632

British Public Record Office: **III**, 135, 528, 672

Brito, Nicaragua: **II**, 583, 584

Brive, France: **III**, 720

Brodie family: **II**, 363

Broke, Philip B. V.: **III**, 70

Brookline, Mass.: **III**, 146

Brooklyn, N.Y.: **III**, 598

Brooks, Henry: 86–87

Brown, Allan D.: 282, 474

Brown, the Rev. A. J.: **III**, 509

Brown, Bishop Edward Harold: 442

Brown, F. Leonard: **III**, 146, 429, 481, 484, 720

Brown, George: 148, 155, 172, 173, 548

Brown, Henry Billings: **II**, 566, 567

Brown, Isaac N.: 554–555

Brown, Jimmie: **II**, 120

Brown, John M.: letters to, **II**, 107, 109–110, 110–111, 207–208, 419–420, 421, 424–425, 440–441, 450–451, 458–459, 459, 460, 460–461, 461–462, 462–463, 463, 465–466, 466, 467, 468, 468–469, 469–470, 472, 473, 474–475, 476–477, 477–478, 478, 479–480, 481, 481–482, 484–485, 485, 486, 487, 487–488, 490, 491, 491–492, 492–493, 495, 495–496, 497–498, 499–500, 500, 500–501, 501, 502, 503–504, 511–512, 513, 516–517, 519–520, 523, 532, 532–533, 533, 536, 543–544, 547–548, 561, 568, 571–572, 593, 593–594, 596, 596–597, 598, 606, 610, 614, 615, 615–616, 618–619, 621–622, 623–624, 626, 630–631, 632, 633, 634, 641, 655, 676, 686–687, 688, 702–703, 716–717, 720–721, 723–724, 724–725, 729, 736, 738–739; **III**, 23–24, 80–81, 84, 85, 127, 128, 133–134, 135, 139–140, 147–148, 156, 161, 173, 176–177, 199–200, 208, 224, 226–227, 228–229, 229–230, 239, 241–242; mention, 712, 713, **II**, 207, 245, 246, 525, 534, 535, **III**, 88, 230, 241, 274, 293, 302, 303

Brown, Mrs. John M.: **II**, 421, 501, 533

Brown, Rosalie Evans (Mrs. F. Leonard Brown) ("Rosie," "Dodie," "Marraine"): 363; **II**, 14, 158, 169, 174, 186, 193, 211, 220, 254, 257, 258, 260, 262, 264, 265, 271, 277–278, 293, 302, 304, 305, 308, 311, 340, 355, 356, 371, 374, 380, 381, 382, 384, 385, 386, 387, 388, 389, 392, 393, 395, 396, 397, 399, 400, 401, 404, 560; **III**, 146, 484, 491, 720, 721, 729

Brown, Samuel Francis: 88

Brown University: **II**, 422

Brownell, William Crary: **III**, 73

Brownell, Wilmot Atherton: letter to, **III**, 547; mention, **III**, 529

Brownson, Willard H.: letters to, 678, 681–682; **II**, 557, 561; mention, 678, 680, 689, 691, 698, 700–701; **II**, 563, 569, 571, 574; **III**, 236

Brueys, François Paul: **III**, 323, 394

Bruinsburg, Miss.: 546

Bruix, Eustache: **III**, 568–569, 569

Brussels, Belgium: **II**, 658

Bryan, William Jennings: **II**, 465, 466, 470, 602, 694–695, 697; **III**, 514, 603, 728

Bryce, James: **II**, 142, 144, 275, 532, 533

Bryce, Lloyd Stephens: **II**, 305, 314

Buchanan, Franklin: **III**, 556

Buchanan, James: 555

Buckingham Palace: **II**, 284

Budd, George: **III**, 70

Buel, Clarence C.: letters to, **II**, 444; **III**, 416; mention, **II**, 444, 447

Buenaventura, Colombia: 591, 595

Buenos Aires, Argentina: 375, 377, 378, 382, 396, 397, 400, 401, 403, 404, 405, 409, 410, 415, 419, 422, 423, 424, 425, 426, **II**, 47, 680; letter to Captain of the Port, 425

Buffalo, N.Y.: **III**, 76

Bulgaria: **III**, 699, 705, 710

Buller, Sir Redvers Henry: **II**, 325, 698, 699; **III**, 10

Bunce, Francis M.: **II**, 38, 52, 71, 74, 89, 108, 136, 144, 145, 193, 212, 222, 244, 251, 265, 371

Bunting, Sir Percy: **III**, 63

Burdon, Captain of the *Drake*: **II**, 547

Burger, Rosalie Evans (Mrs. Van V. Burger): 487
Burgess, Frederick: letter to, III, 521–522; mention, III, 521
Burgos, Spain: III, 720
Burgoyne, John: II, 92
Burke, Edmund: II, 616
Burlingame, Edward L.: letters to, II, 511, 518, 519, 520, 521, 522, 523, 524, 524–525, 526, 527, 539–540, 541, 545–546, 547, 548, 549, 560, III, 246; mention, II, 511, III, 77, 82
Burnside, Ambrose Everett: II, 699
Burrish, George: II, 722, 723
Burroughs, A. C.: 612
Burton, Clarence M.: III, 129
Butler, Arthur J. Wellington Foley: II, 326, 329, 334
Butler, Benjamin: 537, 635
Butler, Lady (née Ellen Stager): II, 326
Butler, Henry: 86–87
Butler, Nicholas Murray: III, 3, 18, 438
Butler, Sigourney: letter to, 672; mention, 672
Butt, Walter R.: 11, 31, 38, 51, 57, 70; III, 54–55
Buzzard's Bay, Mass.: 469; III, 577
Byng, John: 629; II, 704
Byron, George Gordon, 6th Baron: II, 352–353
Byron, John: 629

Caamaño, José Maria Placido: 588
Caballero, Bernardino: 398, 399, 409
Cabell, Mary Virginia Ellet: 548
Cadiz, Spain: 59; II, 125, 160, 331, 359, 369, 553, 564, 565; III, 404, 569, 637, 638, 639; Cadiz division, II, 553, 554
Cadore, Jean Baptiste Nompère de Champagny, Duc de: III, 121, 124
Cadore Letter, III, 121, 124
Caesar, Julius: 607; III, 434, 581
Caicos Bank, Bahama Islands: III, 631
Cairo, Egypt: II, 251, 368
Calalan Bank, Guam: III, 398
Calcutta, India: 351
Caldera, Chile: 560, 564
Caldwell, Albert: 564
Caldwell, Charles Henry Bromedge: 384
Caldwell, John C.: letters to, 423–424, 426; mention, 423
Calhoun, John C.: III, 123
California: 488, 568, 587, 590; III, 55, 225; III, 377
California, Gulf of: 590
Calkins, Carlos Gilman: 640, 644
Callahan, E. W.: III, 174
Callao, Peru: 240, 341, 342, 557, 560, 561, 563, 570, 572, 573, 581, 590, 592, 594, 596; II, 424
Calvert, Mr.: II, 69

Calvinist theocracy of Geneva and early New England: III, 434
Cámara, Manuel de la: II, 563, 567; III, 188, 191, 192, 636, 637, 638, 639, 640
Cambon, Jules: II, 577–578
Cambridge, Duke of: II, 284, 325, 326, 327, 329, 691
Cambridge, Mass.: II, 421
Cambridge University: II, 285, 290, 291, 294, 297, 298, 319, 397
Campbell Bannerman, Sir Henry: III, 203, 205, 207, 216, 225–226
Canada: 142; II, 18, 426, 684, 732; III, 82, 83, 84, 136, 174, 176, 221, 222, 226, 252, 291, 345, 388, 397, 427, 448, 449, 452, 459, 468, 496, 499, 542, 560, 561, 565, 609
Canadian Pacific Railroad: II, 25; III, 566
Canadian Records (Archives) Office: III, 65, 82, 83–84, 111, 136, 340–341
Canary Islands: II, 67, 568, 570
Cannes, France: II, 230
Canning, George: III, 124, 125, 128, 129, 130
Cannon, Joseph G.: III, 370
Canterbury, Archbishop of: II, 297; III, 305
Canterbury Cathedral: 365
Canton, China: 278; II, 582
Cape Breton Island, Canada: III, 562
Cape Cod, Mass.: 344, 348, 470, 487; II, 427, 428; III, 357
Capes of the Chesapeake: II, 585
Cape Fear River, N.C.: III, 562
Cape Gallo, Greece: II, 237
Cape Guardafui, Africa: 110, 111
Cape of Good Hope, South Africa: 98, 100, 101, 103, 104, 105, 141; II, 18, 589, 674
Cape Sable Island, N.S., Canada: II, 425
Cape St. Roque [C. de São Roque, now Cabo do Calcanhar], Brazil: 98
Capetown, South Africa: 88, 100, 103, 105, 107, 141, 346; M. describes, 106
Capture of Private Property at Sea: III, 112–113, 157–158, 158, 164, 165, 192, 210, 216, 221, 284, 623–626, 638
Cape Verde Islands: II, 67; Cape Verde Fleet, II, 553, 554
Cap Martin, France: II, 389
Carcassonne, France: 463; II, 174, 175, 560; III, 720
Carden, John S.: III, 118, 121, 131, 135, 140, 673
Carden, Sir Lionel: III, 512
Cardiff coal: III, 589
Careenage Cay, Colombia: II, 589
Caretas Bank, River Plate: 407, 411
Caribbean: II, 37, 82, 127, 582, 583, 584, 585, 588, 589, 590, 683; III, 80, 312, 354, 357, 369, 375, 377, 378, 426, 459, 570, 640, 642, 687
Carkett, Robert: II, 730, 733

Carl: **II**, 113, 122, 135, 146, 159, 176, 181, 206, 240
Carleton, Guy: **III**, 470
Carlyle, Thomas: **III**, 694
Carnavon, George Edward Stanhope Molyneux Herbert, 5th Earl of: **II**, 275
Carnavon, Lady: **II**, 275
Carnegie, Andrew: **II**, 283, 305; **III**, 72, 223, 308, 438, 474
Carnegie Hall: **III**, 438, 443
Carnegie Foundation for Advancement of Teaching, The: **III**, 224
Carnegie Institution of Washington, D.C., The: **II**, 422, 517, 605; **III**, 116, 123, 129, 134, 505, 516, 517, 518, 519, 528, 549, 551
Caroline Islands: **II**, 569; **III**, 165, 377
Carpenter, George R.: letter to, 687; mention, 687
Carr, Dr.: **II**, 167; **III**, 138
Carroll, Miss Carrie: 62
Carroll, Charles: 146, 148, 149, 155, 164, 165, 168, 171, 172, 173, 180, 203, 211, 216, 217, 221, 223, 318, 319, 331
Carroll, Mrs. Charles: 140, 142
Cartagena, Spain: **III**, 569
Carter, B. T.: **III**, 526
Carter, James C.: **III**, 364
Carter, Samuel P.: 7, 13, 18, 19, 20, 34, 39, 50, 155, 158, 173, 179, 284, 288, 304, 319, 320, 325, 326
Carthaginians: **II**, 161
Casco Bay, Me.: **II**, 425
Case, Augustus L.: letters to, 376–377, 387; mention, 376
Casey, Silas: 38
Casey, Thomas L.: letter to, 673; mention, 673
Cashart, James: 134
Cass, Louis: 387–388, 390
Castellammare, Italy: **II**, 234
Castlereagh, Robert Stewart, Viscount. *See* Londonderry, 2nd Marquis of
Castro, Cipriano: **III**, 50
Caswell, Thomas T.: 505
Cathay: **II**, 33
Cathedral Church (Capetown): 107
Cauca River, Colombia: 609
Cavite, Philippine Islands: **II**, 600, 612, **III**, 236
Cecil, Lady Gwendolen: **II**, 130–131, 203, 206
Celebes, Indonesia: **III**, 377
Cenas, Hilary: 6, 7, 8, 12, 13, 14, 15, 17, 18, 27, 28, 29, 31, 32, 36, 39, 40, 41, 48, 49, 59, 61, 64, 65, 68, 69, 71, 75, 78, 80, 81, 85, 86, 89–90; **III**, 53, 54
Central America: 595, 597, 599, 601, 606, 608, 641, 643; **II**, 26, 354, 435, 537; **III**, 377
Central Europe: **II**, 77
Central Powers (1914): **III**, 703

Century Club (New York): letter to, **III**, 536–537; mention, **II**, 461, 539, 696, **III**, 252, 728
Century Co.: **II**, 397–398, 491, 497, 499, 600, 632; **III**, 546
Century Syndicate: **III**, 529
Cervera y Topete, Pascual: **II**, 556, 562, 563, 567, 569, 571, 574, 575, 576, 590, 605, 727; **III**, 31, 188, 545, 629, 630, 631, 633, 634, 636, 637, 638, 639, 640, 643
Ceylon: **III**, 489, 638
Chaco region, S.A.: 400
Chadwick, French Ensor: 640; **II**, 34, 37, 38, 56–57, 58, 59, 60, 62, 141, 143, 144, 148, 371, 402, 601, 602, 603, 604, 607, 672, 673; **III**, 69, 178, 271, 454, 455, 456, 542, 636
Chaffee, Adna R.: **II**, 708
Chain Lakes, N.S., Canada: **III**, 566
Chamberlain, Joseph: **III**, 9, 71, 72, 149, 154, 203
Chambers, James Julius: letter to, **II**, 508; mention, **II**, 508
Chambers, Washington I: letters to, **II**, 75–77, 108–109; mention, **II**, 75, 82, 94, 201, 223, **III**, 667
Champlain, Lake: **II**, 92, 524, 525, 725, **III**, 101, 118, 167, 170, 470, 471, 488, 514, 672, 673
Chandler, L. E.: letter to, 436; mention, 436
Chandler, Lloyd H.: **III**, 262, 265
Chandler, William Eaton: letters to, 556, 557, 559, 561, 563, 566, 567, 567–568, 569, 570, 579, 583, 583–584, 587–589, 589–590, 590, 590–591, 591, 594; mention, 544, 556, 562, 568, 596, 655, **II**, 673, 680, **III**, 178, 219, 641, 664
Chang Tau harbor, Chusan Archipelago, China: **II**, 583
Channel (English) tunnel: **II**, 93; **III**, 98–99
Chapin, Joseph H.: letters to, **III**, 76–77, 77–78, 78, 81–82, 82, 487; mention, **III**, 76
Charles I: **II**, 327, 502
Charles Louis, Archduke of Austria: **II**, 526; **III**, 306, 308, 344, 421, 580
Charleston, S.C.: 444; **III**, 77, 357, 562, 568, 631
Charlotte Amalie, St. Thomas: **II**, 586
Chart, Edwin: **II**, 143
"Chase of the *Constitution*," by Stephen Salisbury Tuckerman, painting used as frontispiece to Mahan's *War of 1812*: **III**, 89
Chase, Richard M.: 76
Chatto and Windus, Messrs.: **III**, 243
Chaumont Bay, N.Y.: **II**, 36; **III**, 86, 565, 570, 576
Chauncey, Isaac: **III**, 78–79, 79, 86, 313, 467
Chauvenet, William ("Chauvy"): 13, 25, 34, 52, 58, 59, 60, 68, 71, 73; **III**, 182

Chemical Bank (New York): **II**, 132

Cherbourg, France: 59, **II**, 124, 125; **III**, 96, 97

Chesapeake Bay: 59, 76; **II**, 554; **III**, 77, 88, 120, 354, 355, 356, 357, 400, 560, 562, 568, 575, 666, 673

Chesapeake-Shannon action: **III**, 68, 69, 70, 103–104

Chesney Gold Medal: **II**, 691

Chester, Colby Mitchell: letters to, 680, 682, 682–683, 683–685, 686, 686–687, 687–688, 688, 691, 692–693, 694, 695, 696–697, 698, 698–699, 703, 704–705, 705–706, 706, 707, 708–709, 709, 710, 711, 713–714, 714–715; mention, 676, 688, 690, 692, 694, 700, 701, 702, 714

Chester, Pa.: 639

Chestnut Hill, Pa.: 455; **III**, 517

Chevalier de Caylus, correspondence of: **III**, 132

Chicago, Ill.: 613; **II**, 173

Chicago Republican Convention (1888): 652

Chicarene Point, La Union, Salvador: 598, 612

Chief of Engineers, USN: **II**, 72; at Mare Island, 698

Chile: 526, 572, 607, **II**, 47, 63, 65; flags, 510; navy, 544, **II**, 507; port authorities, 560; civil war in, **II**, 82; crisis with U.S., **II**, 59–65, 734

Chilean imbroglio 1891–1892: **II**, 734

Chile-Peru War: **II**, 422

China: people, 116–117, **II**, 92–93; emigration-immigration issue, 355, **II**, 92–93, 337, **III**, 449; relations with the West, **II**, 537, 584, 658, 708; missionary work in, **III**, 508; Boxer Rebellion in, **II**, 693, 700; mention, 107, 115, 118, 385, **II**, 315, 346, 358, 463, 464, 508, 509, 521, 567, 582, 583, 619, 693, 707, **III**, 12, 13, 35, 49, 113, 251, 312, 353, 377, 459, 509

Chios, Greece: **II**, 246

Chiosin: 126, 127, 128, 130

Chiriqui Lagoon, Colombia: **II**, 588

Chirol, Sir Valentine: **III**, 485, 496, 497, 498, 499, 500, 503

Choate, Joseph H.: letters to, **II**, 580, **III**, 448–449, 451; mention, **II**, 580, 606, **III**, 207, 209, 210, 216, 438

Christ Church College, Oxford: **II**, 290, 297, 298

Christobal Island, Colombia: **II**, 589

Chrystler's [Field], Ont., Canada: **III**, 83

Church, George Hurlbut: 300, 301

Church, William C.: letters to, 460, 460–461; mention, 460

Church of the Advent (Boston): **III**, 294

Church of England: **III**, 274

Church of the Holy Communion (New York): **III**, 294

Churchill, John, 1st Duke of Marlborough: **III**, 388

Churchill, Winston: **III**, 491, 514

Chusan [Chushan] Archipelago, China: **II**, 583, 590

Ciara, Brazil: 98, 100

Cienfuegos, Cuba: 558, 630, 673; **II**, 553, 554; **III**, 31, 631, 632, 633, 634, 640, 643; Cienfuegos division, **II**, 554

Cilicia, Turkey: **II**, 247

Cilley, Greenleaf: 294

Cintra, Portugal: **II**, 159

Citizens' National Committee [for Arbitration]: **III**, 438

Citizens' Union: **II**, 667, 671

City Hotel (Annapolis): **II**, 180

Ciudad Rodrigo, Spain, **III**, 326

Civil War: 90, 118, 172, 574; **II**, 470, 699; **III**, 10, 53, 71, 163, 165, 196, 203, 228, 278, 285, 315, 342, 352, 385, 487, 498, 542, 545, 551, 609, 623, 640, 671, 702, 708

Claiborne, Henry B. ("Billy"): 6, 7, 8, 12, 13, 14, 17, 19, 22, 30, 31, 32, 34, 36, 37, 40, 41, 45, 48, 49, 51, 52, 59, 61, 66, 67, 69, 75, 78, 80, 81, 84, 85, 89–90; **III**, 53, 54

Clark, Alonzo H.: letter to, **III**, 42; mention, **III**, 42

Clark, Bouverie F.: letters to, **II**, 47–48, 418–419, 443–444, 699–700, 721–722; **III**, 8–10, 31, 47–48, 97–98, 197–198, 202–203, 211–212, 225–226, 232–233, 262–263, 277–278, 307–308, 314–315, 333–334, 426–428, 438–439, 447–448, 484–485, 491–492, 510–511, 511–512, 515–516, 520–521, 548–549; mention, **II**, 47, 133, 140, 285–286, 286, 343, 344, 345, 346, 349, 700–701, **III**, 28, 36, 721

Clark, Mrs. Bouverie F.: **II**, 418, 419, 444, 720; **III**, 10, 31, 48

Clark, Charles Edgar: 598, 599, 602

Clark, Frank H.: **II**, 242

Clark, George R.: 567–568; **III**, 365

Clark, James Beauchamp ("Champ"): **III**, 388–389, 427, 465

Clarke, George Sydenham: letters to, **II**, 83–85, 305, 336–338, 394–395, 543, 556, 579–580; mention, **II**, 83, 133, 146, 256, 283, 495, 530, 546, 665, **III**, 201

Clarke, Mrs. George Sydenham: **II**, 133, 146, 267, 270, 282, 305, 337, 345, 395, 543, 556

Clarke, Herbert E.: **II**, 115

Clasen, Mr.: 568

Clausewitz, von, Karl: **III**, 394

Clayton-Bulwer Treaty: **II**, 126, 153, 683; **III**, 45, 431

Clear Cape, Clear Island, Ireland: **II**, 113

Clemenceau, Georges: **III**, 485

Clermont-Ferrand, France: **III**, 720

Cleveland, Grover: letter to, **II**, 208; mention, 574, 591–592, 624–625, 655, **II**, 138, 207, 210, 235, 328, 361, 406, 407, 443, 482, 506, **III**, 54, 299, 434, 476

Cleveland, Ohio: **II**, 329

Cliff-at-Hoo, England: **II**, 289, 290

Clover, Richardson: letters to, **II**, 42–43, 44, 48, 54, 55, 66–67, 67; mention, **II**, 42, 226, 249, 250, 251, 306, 310, 323, 342, 351, 353, 360, 365, 384, 398–399, **III**, 23, 586, 588, 589, 627

Clover, Mrs. Richardson: **II**, 306, 360

Clowes David: **II**, 267, 268, 282, 320, 394

Clowes, Sir William Laird: **II**, 510, 513, 518, 531, 543–544; **III**, 177, 514

Clowes, William, and Sons: **III**, 389

Clymer, Mrs.: **II**, 181

Coaster's Harbor Island, R.I.: 620, 664, 671, 672, 676, 716; **II**, 4, 5, 20, 22, 23, 31, 66, 244; **III**, 664

Coates, Mr.: 106, 107, 132

Cobb, A. H.: **III**, 174

Cochrane, Sir Alexander Inglis: **III**, 136, 143

Cochrane, Thomas, 10th Earl of Dundonald: **II**, 279, 297; **III**, 143

Cockran, William Bourke: **II**, 664

Coelho, Mr.: 91

Coffin, John H. C.: 26

Colahan, Charles Ellwood: 382

Colbert, Jean-Baptiste: 650

Coldstream Guards: **II**, 345

Colenbrander, H. I.: **III**, 676

Colenso, John William: 103–104, 107

Coleridge, Hartley: **II**, 115

Coley, F. E.: 561

Colgate family: **II**, 262, 263

Colhoun, John: 78

Coliseum (Rome): 354

College of the City of New York: **III**, 603

Colley, Sir George Pomeroy: **II**, 280

Collingwood, Lord: **II**, 574; **III**, 155, 156

Colomb, Philip H.: 630, 669, 670; **II**, 9, 135, 191, 665

Colombia: 530–531, **II**, 589; **III**, 463, 486; Cauca battalion of, 609

Colon, Panama: **III**, 377, 401

Colonia, Uruguay: 375, 378, 379, 380, 383, 386, 387, 401, 414, 417, 425, 426

Colonial Club (New York): **II**, 620

Colonna, B. A.: letters to, 688–689, 692, 693, 694, 696, 697, 700–701, 701, 702; mention, 687–688, 688, 695, 706

Colonna, Cape, Greece: **II**, 238

Colorado: **II**, 470

Columbia River, W.T.: 673

Columbia University: 2, 33; **II**, 102, 234, 321, 449, 687, 689, 690; **III**, 3, 28, 112, 720

Columbus, Christopher: 576; **II**, 102

Columbus Exposition in Madrid: **II**, 222

Columbus Island, Colombia: **II**, 589

Combattants naufragés: **II**, 639–641

Comité d'Examen (Hague Conference): letter to, **II**, 637–639; mention, **II**, 639–641, 643, 644, 645, 710, 711, 712, 713, 715, 731, 737, 738, 741, 744, **III**, 13, 14, 18, 19, 20

Comité de Rédaction (Hague Conference): **II**, 645, 646, 647, 648

Commemorative naval medals: **II**, 79

Commerell, Sir John Edmund: **II**, 129, 311, 312

Committee on Documentary Historical Publications of the United States Government: **III**, 240, 266, 279, 329, 339, 671, 674, 676

Comoro Islands: 108

Comptroller of the Treasury: letter to, **II**, 601–604; mention, **II**, 604, 607, **III**, 530, 533, 595; Second Comptroller, 691, 698, **III**, 531

"Concert of Europe": **II**, 505; **III**, 346

Confederate States of America: 483, 554; **III**, 545, 560, 623, 624

Confederate States Army: 652

Confederate States Navy: 43, 196, 299, 331, 333, 471, 473, 554, 555; **III**, 53, 54, 55, 57

Confederate Council of Good Government in New York City: **III**, 606

Conkling, Roscoe: 455, 477

Connally, John Kerr: 60

Connaught, Arthur William Patrick Albert, Duke of: **II**, 130, 140, 284, 319, 328

Constant. See Estournelles de Constant

Constantinople, Turkey: **II**, 217, 222, **III**, 12, 226, 505, 511, 683, 684, 690; capture of, by Turks, **II**, 169

Constitution (U.S.): **II**, 556, 663; **III**, 280, 427, 434, 437, 444

Continental System: **II**, 150

Converse, George A.: **II**, 95, 136

Cook, Francis Augustus: 480; **II**, 574

Cook Company: **II**, 385

Cooke, Augustus P.: letters to, 564–565, **II**, 47; mention, 79, 81, 564

Cooper, G. H.: letters to, 485, 485–486, 489, 489–491, 491, 493, 493–494, 497–498, 498, 498–501, 501–502, 502–503, 503, 503–504, 504–505, 505–506, 506–507, 508, 508–509, 509–510, 511–512, 512–513, 513–515, 515, 516, 517, 518–520, 520, 521, 521–522, 522, 523; mention, 460, 484, 507, 524

Cooper, James Fenimore: **III**, 520

Cooper, Philip H.: 556; **II**, 350

Copenhagen, Denmark: **II**, 437, 573, 576, 600; **III**, 638

Copernicus: **II**, 342

Coppa, Angelo: 22, 39, 57

Copples and Upham: **III**, 295

Coquimbo, Chile: 560, 564, 590; **II**, 157, 159

Corbett, Sir Julian S.: letter to, **III**, 223; mention, **II**, 723, **III**, 223, 224, 225, 227, 230, 231, 232, 273, 304, 394
Corbin, Henry C.: **II**, 692
Cordova, Spain: **III**, 151, 720
Corfu, Ionian Islands, Greece: **II**, 426
Corinto, Nicaragua: 597, 599, 602
Cork, Ireland: **II**, 116, 118, 119
Cornell, Alonzo Barton: 477
Cornwallis, Charles, 1st Marquis: **III**, 341, 472
Corregidor, Luzon, Philippines: **III**, 381, 393, 400, 401, 402, 403, 404
Corrientes, Argentina: 398, 403
Cortelyou, George: **II**, 693; **III**, 7
Coslidge, T. J.: **III**, 240
Costa Rica: 599; **II**, 584, 590
Coteau Junction, Canada: **III**, 566
Cotting, Dr.: **II**, 472
Coston Signals: 505, 527, 538
Couden, A. R.: **II**, 82
Coudert, Frederic R.: **III**, 438
Council of Ambassadors in London: **III**, 687
Council of National Defense (U.S.): **III**, 374, 408
Council of Nicaea (325 A.D.): **II**, 172
County Cork, Ireland: **II**, 119
County Kerry, Ireland: **II**, 119
Courts-martial: of Anderson, Thomas, 383, 384; Barclay, Robert H., **III**, 118, 122, 135, 141, 673; Barrett, 495; Barron, James, **III**, 61; Boyle, Patrick, **II**, 208-210, 232; Burdon, Capt., **II**, 547; Burrish, George, **II**, 722; Byng, John, 629; Carden, John S., **III**, 118, 121, 131, 135, 140, 673; Dacres, James D., **III**, 118, 121, 131, 135, 140, 673; Davis, Daniel W., 556; Dotty, 452-453; Downie, George, **III**, 118, 122, 135, 141, 673; Hawkins, William, 245, 246; Hope, Harry, 312-313, 313, 314; Hull, William, **III**, 130; Johnson, Henry L., **II**, 89, 90; Laffan, John, **II**, 208-210, 232; Lambert, Henry, **III**, 673; Marston, John, 493; Matthews, Thomas, **III**, 119; Moore, John, 312-313, 313, 314; Pearson, Sir Richard, **III**, 118, 121, 131, 139, 140; Quackenbush, John N., 404; Simpson, J. A. G., **II**, 208-210, 232; Sumner, George W., **II**, 431; Torrington, Arthur Herbert, Earl of, **II**, 337; general court-martial at Richmond, Va., **II**, 67, 68
Cowell Point, St. Thomas, Lesser Antilles: **II**, 586
Cowen, John: 242
Cowes, Isle of Wight: **II**, 126, 128, 130, 132, 133, 140, 309, 310, 327
Cowes Regatta: **II**, 306, 309, 313
Cowles, William Henry Harrison: 620-621, 624

Cowles, William S.: **II**, 124, 130, 134; **III**, 282
Cox, W. W.: **III**, 339
Crafts, James H.: **III**, 240
Craig, Joseph E.: letters to, **II**, 540-541, 596, 629, 666; mention, **II**, 540
Craik, Dinah Maria: **III**, 356
Craven, Anne ("Nannie"): 7, 15, 18, 19, 20-21, 24, 25, 26, 27, 28-29, 31, 32, 34-35, 36, 40-41, 42, 45, 47-48, 49, 52, 54, 55, 56, 57, 58, 60, 61, 62, 64, 65, 66, 68, 70, 76
Craven, Henry Smith ("Harry"): 35, 36, 49, 60
Craven, Thomas A. Tingey: 7, 13, 15, 16, 17, 18, 19, 22, 24, 29, 33, 34, 40, 41, 54, 55, 57, 59, 60, 65, 66, 68, 69, 80, 82; **III**, 556
Creighton, Johnston B.: 136
Creighton, Bishop Mandell: **III**, 599
Cresap, James C.: **II**, 215, 220, 240
Crete: **II**, 505
Crichton, Col.: **II**, 146, 148
Crimean War: **III**, 511, 704
Croke, Sir Alexander: **III**, 88
Crossman, Alexander Foster: **III**, 222
Crowninshield, Arent S.: **II**, 591, 595; **III**, 135, 162, 627, 628
Crozier, William: letter to, **II**, 744-745; mention, **II**, 642, 708, 713, **III**, 18, 38, 102, 106, 429, 450
Cruikshank, Ernest Alexander: **III**, 389
Cruikshank, Mr.: **II**, 149
Cuba: **II**, 532, 554, 567, 579, 588, 590, 596, 619, 625, 635, 664, 691; **III**, 221, 377, 543, 640, 641, 687
Culebra, West Indies: **II**, 587, 590; **III**, 396
Cummings, Amos J.: **II**, 207, 210, 246
Curaçao, West Indies: **II**, 27; **III**, 377, 633
Curruth, Mr.: **II**, 159
Curry, Mr.: 283
Curtis, Lionel: **III**, 396-397, 414-415, 452
Cushing, William B.: 296, 307, 308, 310, 312, 313, 314; **II**, 517, 568, 571, 593
Cushing, Mrs. William B.: **II**, 517, 568, 593
Cushman, Charles H.: 24
Cutler family: **II**, 199
Cutting, Mr.: **II**, 159
Czolgosz, Leon: **III**, 9-10

Dacres, James D.: **III**, 118, 121, 131, 135, 140, 673
Dadi Beach, Guam: **III**, 398
Daimyos: 125, 127, 127-128, 128, 136, 137
Daiozaki, Japan: 165
Dale, Alfred Taylor: **II**, 408, 409, 419
Dallari, Gino: **III**, 517
Daly, Kiernan: 679
Daly, William R.: letter to, **II**, 551; mention, **II**, 551, 567, 568, 572, 579, 635
Dalziel's Agency: **III**, 583
Damascus, Syria: **III**, 650

Daniels, Josephus: letters to, III, 525, 540–541, 541–542; mention, III, 525, 538, 542, 552

Danish Islands (Virgin Islands): II, 586, 587, 588; III, 445

Danton, Georges Jacques: III, 393

Darien Isthmus Expedition: 541

Darrieus, Gabriel: III, 273

Dartmouth College: III, 63, 608

Darwin, Charles R.: II, 146

Darwin, Sir Francis: II, 146

Darwin, Sir George Howard: II, 146

Daveluy, René: III, 273

Davenport, England: II, 286

Davidson, A. C.: 714

Davidson, R. H. M.: 714

Davidson, Archbishop Randall Thomas: III, 305

Davis, Charles H.: letters to, II, 17–18, 35–37; mention, II, 17, 38, 68, 69, 234

Davis, Daniel W.: 556

Davis, Jefferson: 70–71

Davis, William H.: II, 289–290

Dawes, Henry Laurens: 651

Dayton, Alston G.: III, 278, 282

Dazol Bay, Philippines: II, 582

Dean, R. C.: 637, 647, 659; II, 83; III, 663

de Camp, C. B.: letter to, III, 513; mention, III, 513

Decatur, Stephen: III, 61, 64, 70, 79, 673

Deception Pass, W.T.: 680, 695

Declaration of Independence: II, 724, III, 693

Declaration of London: III, 366

Declaration of Paris: III, 366

Dedham, Mass.: III, 85

Defender Committee: II, 440

De Florez, Sr.: II, 420

de Gainza, Sr.: 385, 398, 408–409

de Glanville, James: 561

DeGolver-McClelland Co.: 488

DeGroot family: II, 197, 199, 200

De Guichen, Luc Urbain du Bouëxic, Comte: III, 472

De Koven, Dr.: 429

de la Gravière, Jurien: 649

Delaware: III, 221

Delaware Bay: II, 36; III, 76, 77, 562, 568

Delcassé, Théophile: III, 342

Delehanty, Daniel: 192, 196, 478–479, 480–481

Delhi, India: 352

Demarest, Garrett: letter to, III, 504; mention, III, 504

Demerara, British Guiana: II, 485

de Martens, Feodor: II, 645, 649

Democratic Party (U.S.): 157, 338, 455, 457, 459, 470, 473, 477, 482, 488–489, 543–544, 556, 571–572, 625, 655; II, 205, 235, 361, 665, 696; III, 75, 271, 364, 365, 370, 414, 445, 448, 452, 453, 457, 458, 463, 464, 465, 466, 467, 468, 469, 474, 475, 476, 477, 478, 484, 484–485, 512, 514, 520–521

Denmark: III, 638, 708

Dennis, Mr.: 688

Depew, Chauncey M.: III, 438

Derby, Dr.: III, 206–207, 210

Derby, Eloise: II, 302

de Ruiz, Alberto: 565

De Ruyter, Michel Adriaanszoon, 633; III, 73–74

Descamps, M.: II, 710

de Sillac, Jarousse: letters to, II, 712–713, 731–732; mention, II, 712, III, 14

Desina, Japan: 299, 303

D'Estaing, Charles: 629, 636; III, 467, 472, 488

de Staal, Baron: II, 645

de Suffren, Pierre André: 629; II, 92; III, 467, 472

Detroit, Mich.: III, 129

Detroit River, Mich.: III, 78

DeVeaux, Jackson S.: II, 227, 239

de Vere, Aubrey Thomas: II, 115

de Villeneuve, Pierre Charles: II, 66–67

Devonport, England: 662; II, 343, 345

Devonshire, England: II, 419, 443; III, 36, 100

DeWet, Christian Rudolf: II, 722

Dewey, George: letters to: II, 717–718, III, 106–107, 164, 166, 169, 174–175; mention, 365, 452, 556, 557, II, 564, 565, 566, 567, 589, 612, 613, 619, 634, 656, 659, 673, 681, 684, 703, 704, 740, 744, III, 4, 55, 74, 158, 161, 163, 191, 191–192, 195, 206, 209, 216, 281, 423, 529, 637, 638, 639, 640

Dewey, Theodore Gibbs: II, 169, 179, 180, 206, 215, 220, 240

Dicey, Albert Van: III, 279

Dicey, Edward: III, 279

Dickins, Francis William: 480

Diehl, S. W. B.: II, 82

Diesbach, Dr.: II, 218, 525, 593, 594, 619

Disraeli, Benjamin: III, 263

Dives, France: III, 97

Dix, John Alden: III, 364, 365

Dix, Morgan: II, 123, 308, 321

Dixey, John: 157

Doane, Bishop William Croswell: II, 617; III, 302

Dobie, Armistead Mason: III, 478

Dodge, Mr.: letter to, II, 675–676

Dodsworth, Mr.: II, 251

Dog Fish Bay, W.T.: 683

Dohrman, Horatio G.: letters to, III, 463–464, 468–469, 476–478

Dolph, Joseph Norton: 698, 710, 714–715

Done, Dr.: 282, 283

Dorn, Edward J.: II, 360

Dornin, Thomas Lardner: 15, 17, 18, 19, 70
Dorothea, Czarina of Russia: **II**, 197
Dotty, Charles: 452–453
Douglas, Sir Charles: **III**, 470
Dover Straits: **II**, 126
Downe, Hugh Richard Dawnay, 8th Viscount: **II**, 325, 326
Downer Oil Co.: 533, 534, 535
Downie, George: **III**, 118, 122, 135, 141, 313, 673
Doynel Rock, River Plate, South America: 414
Drake, Sir Francis: 594
Drake, Franklin J.: 516, 517, 525–526, 526, 530, 531, 532, 536; **II**, 82
Draper, William Franklin: **II**, 234
Drayton, Percival: letters to, 91, 91–92, 92; mention, 90, 91, 92, **III**, 201, 237, 393
Drennan, M. C.: 390
Driggs, William Hale: 406
Drummond Co.: **II**, 736
Dry Tortugas, Fla.: **II**, 585
Dublin [Kingstown], Ireland: **II**, 117, 118, 121, 124, 125, 126
Du Cane, Lady: **III**, 131
Duckworth, Sir John Thomas: **III**, 569
Duke, J. Maurice: 598, 610
Dumail, Nicholas: 389, 408, 410
Dunraven, Earl of: **II**, 474
Dupuy Company: **III**, 488
Durand, George R.: 296
Durand, Sir Henry Mortimer: **III**, 130
Durham, John George Lambton, 1st Earl: **III**, 176
Dutch Commission on National Historical Publications: **III**, 676
Dutch Harbor, Aleutian Islands: **III**, 383
Dye's Inlet, W.T.: 680

East Indies: **II**, 618
Eastlake, Mr.: 172
Eastman, Robert L.: 42, 48
Eastman, Thomas H.: 42, 79, 438
Eaton, Joseph Giles: **III**, 69
Ebbs, Mr. and Mrs.: **II**, 389
Eccles, Mrs.: **II**, 485, 492, 500
Ecuador: 588, 594, 603–604, 605; **III**, 376
Edinburgh, Duke of: **II**, 327
Edinburgh, Scotland: **III**, 508
Edward VII, **III**, 160; coronation of, **III**, 26
Edwin, King of England: **III**, 605
Eggemoggin Reach, Penobscot Bay, Me.: **II**, 425, 427, 428
Egypt: 259, 260; **II**, 226, 529, 607, 674; **III**, 49, 383, 569; M. describes, **II**, 251–253
Ekins, Sir Charles: **III**, 118
Elbe River: **III**, 708, 709
Eldridge, Frank Harold: **II**, 164
Eliot, Charles W.: 474; **III**, 474, 544, 547

Elizabeth Islands, Mass.: **II**, 427
Elizabeth, N.J.: 370, 432, 455, 457, 458, 462, 471, 576, 578, 583, 613, 626, 647, 686, 687, 711; **II**, 10, 97, 139, 159, 168, 293, 330, 376, 380; **III**, 504
Elizabeth, Princess: **II**, 299
Ellet, Charles, Jr.: 548
Ellicott, John: **II**, 219
Elliot Islands, Japan: **II**, 387, 402
Elliott, Jesse Duncan: **III**, 65; court of inquiry on, **III**, 671
Elliott, John: **III**, 107
Elliott, Mrs. (née Wheeler): **II**, 143, 146
Elliott, William: 652
Ellis Island, N.Y.: 538
Ellsworth, William Webster: **III**, 546
Elsinore, Denmark: **II**, 514
Emery, Paymaster: 280, 287
Emory, William Hemsley: 149
Endicott Board of Fortifications: 651
Endicott, William Crowninshield: 651–652, 660
England: 74, 115, 142, 252, 262, 353, 434, 457, 608, 640, 671, 707; **II**, 35, 36, 37, 38, 84, 93, 105, 109, 110, 111, 137, 148, 149, 152, 156, 168, 180, 182, 186, 204, 224, 226, 259, 260, 265, 287, 297, 300, 306, 313, 317, 323, 325, 334, 337, 343, 344, 351, 367, 394, 395, 396, 401, 405, 406, 407, 429, 430, 437, 444, 445, 452, 465, 466, 467, 472, 509, 519, 529, 532, 536, 543, 544, 545, 546, 550, 573, 608, 610, 615, 656–657, 658, 661, 662, 664, 665, 670–671, 674, 677, 678, 679, 680, 683, 684, 685, 686, 688, 691, 698, 707, 736; **III**, 6, 9, 81, 96, 100, 125, 135, 153, 156, 159, 165, 184, 192, 198, 205, 207, 210, 213, 214, 216, 221, 222, 226, 251, 273, 277, 291, 307, 341, 342, 345, 346, 366, 368, 371, 374–375, 375, 378, 380, 385, 394, 410, 420, 427, 431, 432, 438, 442, 449, 452, 454, 457, 459, 462, 465, 475, 476, 483, 487, 491, 493, 496, 500, 514, 520, 532, 533, 535, 537, 540, 541, 542, 543, 559, 561, 562, 564, 566, 568, 570, 572, 574, 575, 579, 604, 612, 620, 621, 622, 625, 637, 657, 671, 674, 698, 699, 701, 704, 707, 708, 709, 711, 712. *See* Great Britain; and Index Section IV, Great Britain
Englehardt, Dr.: 258
English Channel: 363; **II**, 36, 125, 187, 256, 264, 343, 412; **III**, 77, 392, 394, 410, 529
English, Earl: letters to, 559, 568, 569, 571; mention, 101, 109, 110, 111, 114, 116, 124, 126, 131, 149, 150, 153, 154, 155, 156, 157, 158, 162, 164, 166, 167, 168, 171, 175, 177, 178, 179, 180, 182, 184, 185, 186, 187, 189, 191, 192, 193, 194, 195, 196, 198, 200, 201, 202, 203, 205, 206, 207, 208, 209, 211, 212, 214, 217, 220, 221, 222, 223, 224, 225, 226, 228, 229, 230, 232, 233, 234, 235, 236, 237,

English, Earl (*cont.*)
238, 239, 241, 242, 247, 248, 249, 250, 254, 261, 263, 266, 268, 272, 275, 279, 280, 281, 295, 309, 310, 311, 316, 318, 326, 344, 346, 347. *See* Index Section II, Ships: *Iroquois*; and Section IV, English

English "Narrow Seas" doctrine: **III**, 445, 454

English Navigation Laws: **III**, 620, 621, 622

English-speaking race: **III**, 604, 605

Enouye, Yonoske: **III**, 688

Ensor, Mr.: 300, 301, 309, 310

Entre Rios, Argentina: 381, 384–385, 386, 389, 404–405, 408–409, 409–410

Episcopal Church: **III**, 336, 434, 522, 535, 536, 591, 597, 602, 721, 723, 724; annual convention of, **II**, 159, **III**, 231; Board of Missions of, **III**, 693; Missionary Diocese of Philippines, **III**, 10–11

Episcopal Church Club of Massachusetts: **II**, 671

Episcopal Church Club of Philadelphia: **III**, 644

Episcopal Church of the Holy Trinity (Middletown, Conn.): **III**, 286

Episcopal Foreign and Domestic Missionary Society: **II**, 726

Erben, Henry: letters to, **II**, 153–154, 164–165, 227–228, 241–243; mention, **II**, 113, 114, 116, 117, 121, 128, 134, 135, 140, 141, 144, 148, 149, 150, 151, 159, 160, 162, 163, 165, 178, 180, 186, 188, 190, 191, 192, 195, 199, 204, 206, 209, 210, 211, 212, 213, 214, 215, 216, 217, 218, 219, 221, 222, 223, 225, 227, 228, 229, 231–232, 234, 235, 236, 239, 240, 243–244, 246, 248, 249, 250, 251, 253, 254, 255, 256, 257, 263, 266, 267, 268, 269, 272, 278, 279, 281, 282, 283, 284, 285, 287, 292, 297, 300, 301, 302, 303, 306, 309, 310, 311, 313, 322, 322–323, 323, 324, 325, 340, 341, 343, 344, 399, 403, 435 703–704, **III**, 203, 586. *See* Index Section II, Ships: *Chicago*; and Section IV, Erben

Erben, Mrs. Henry: **II**, 165, 191, 313

Erie, Lake: **III**, 67, 70, 78, 82, 83, 101, 118, 671, 672, 673

Erie, Pa.: **III**, 77

Erskine, David Montagu, 2nd Baron: **III**, 124, 125, 127, 128, 129, 130

Esdaile, Col.: **II**, 485, 492, 500

Esquimalt, B. C.: 698; **III**, 570, 575

Esterbrook, John James: **II**, 403–404

Estournelles de Constant, Paul Henri Benjamin, Baron d': **III**, 13, 72–73

Eton School, headmaster of: **II**, 297

Euphrates River: **III**, 12

Europe: 16, 44, 101, 319, 328, 332, 350, 352, 372, 430, 432, 463, 623; **II**, 33, 42, 92–93, 110, 115, 182, 195, 196, 230, 302, 309, 315, 501, 506, 508, 535, 541, 546, 551, 560, 568, 578, 589, 601, 604, 633, 683, 684, 722; **III**, 12, 32, 89, 96, 127, 140, 141, 145, 147, 167, 195, 209, 217, 307, 312, 342, 346, 410, 428, 465, 477, 479, 480, 484, 493, 495, 515, 522, 539, 543, 562, 564, 593, 595, 604, 636, 686, 703, 704, 705, 719, 720, 726

Europe: navies of, **II**, 428, **III**, 6, 372, 584; power and powers in, **II**, 566–567, 568, **III**, 202, 212, 444, 658, 659, 686, 687; nations, **II**, 582, 611, 652, 737, **III**, 454, 502; system of polity, **II**, 582, 589; control of Chinese territory, **II**, 582, questions purely European, **II**, 651, 737; politics, **III**, 13, 43, 49, 80, 366; wars, **III**, 445; immigration, **III**, 458; civilization, **III**, 489, 496, 497

European Bar [of Law] in Constantinople: **III**, 505, 511, 684

Evalard family: 91

Evans, Allen: **II**, 302; **III**, 340, 552, 724

Evans, Angelina ("Lina"): **III**, 454, 720

Evans, Angelina Corse (Mrs. Cadwalader Evans): **II**, 188; **III**, 720

Evans, Cadwalader: 487; **II**, 258; **III**, 720

Evans, Charlotte Taylor (Mrs. Robley D. Evans): **II**, 143

Evans, Edith: 455

Evans, Edmund C.: **II**, 302; **III**, 340

Evans, Ellen Kuhn (Mrs. Manlius Glendower Evans): 359, 363, 366, 368, 369, 430, 431, 432, 433, 458, 473, 487, 615, 620; **II**, 14, 30, 156, 157, 160, 164, 169, 195, 221, 254, 257, 258, 259, 260, 261, 262, 271, 315, 349, 355; **III**, 720, 721, 722, 728

Evans, Emma Totteral (Mrs. William E. Evans): **II**, 311

Evans, Grace: 455; **II**, 235

Evans, Hartman Kuhn ("Hart"): 443, 487, 576; **II**, 132, 137, 141, 150, 156, 160, 169, 206–207, 210, 211, 235, 257, 265, 293, 371, 374, 380, 381, 382, 384, 387, 388, 392, 395, 396, 401, 404, 405; **III**, 177, 197, 204, 720

Evans, Hartman Kuhn, Jr.: 487

Evans, Lillian: **II**, 261

Evans, Mabel E. Curtis (Mrs. Hartman K. Evans): 487

Evans, Manlius Glendower: 359, 369, 430, 433, 443, 455, 458, 463, 467, 473; **II**, 114, 258

Evans, Margaret: 455; **II**, 351, 354, 355, 357; **III**, 720

Evans, Rebecca Lewis (Mrs. Allen Evans): letter to, **III**, 551; mention, **II**, 302, 383, **III**, 724

Evans, Robley Dunglison: **II**, 109, 143, 212, 474, 672; **III**, 262, 263, 267, 282, 652, 721

Evans, William E.: **II**, 261, 311

Evans, W. I.: 412, 413

Evarts, William Maxwell: **III**, 120, 143

Everett, Edward: **III**, 44

Exeter Cathedral, England: 364, 365

Exmouth, Edward Pellew, Viscount: **II**, 92, 724, 725, 730; **III**, 470
Eze, France: **II**, 190, 355, 365, 371, 375, 376

Fairchild, Charles Stebbins: letter to, **II**, 696; mention, **II**, 109, 111, 207, 208, 246, 696
Facpi Point, Guam: **III**, 398
Fajardo, Porto Rico: **II**, 565
Falconer, William: **II**, 238, 476
Falkland Islands: 142
Fall River Line: **III**, 313, 328, 566
Far East: 310–311; **II**, 566, 581, 619; **III**, 6, 13, 27, 80, 91, 96, 99, 113, 202, 206, 259, 372, 500, 637, 638
Fareham, England: **II**, 317, 318
Farmer, Edward: 390, 393
Farnam, Henry Walcott: **II**, 515
Farquhar, Francis U.: 42
Farquhar, Norman H. ("Quack"): 6, 7, 10, 31, 34, 42, 48, 55, 59, 67–68, 79, 83; **III**, 55, 228
Farragut, David Glasgow: 118; **II**, 61, 69, 528, 595, 628, 704; **III**, 183, 393, 545, 555, 625
Farragut, Loyall: **II**, 225; **III**, 55; personal life of, **III**, 464
Farrington, Thomas Putnam: 38, 50, 51
Far Rockaway, N.Y.: **III**, 721
Fawkes, Sir William Hawksworth: **III**, 28
Fayal, Azores: 3; squadron, **III**, 143
Federal Reserve System: **III**, 512
Ferdinand & Isabella: **II**, 169, 576
Ferrol, Spain: **II**, 67
Fez, Spanish Morocco: **II**, 357
Fiennes, Geoffrey Cecil T-W.: **III**, 397
Fiji Islands: **III**, 377
Fillmore, Millard: **III**, 45
Finisterre, Cape, Spain: **II**, 67, 352, 353
Finland: **III**, 99, 230
Finley, Henry Marzette: 478–479, 480
Fish, Hamilton: 395, 396, 420
Fisher, Miss: **II**, 193
Fisher, Mr.: **III**, 178
Fisher-Beresford imbroglio: **III**, 263
Fisher of Kilverstone, John A., 1st Baron: letters to, **II**, 639–641, 643–644, 645; mention, **II**, 639, 649, 658, **III**, 263, 285, 315, 334, 492
Fisher's Island, N.Y.: **III**, 564
Fisher's Island Sound: **III**, 194
Fiske, Bradley: **III**, 178
Fister, Thomas D.: 23, 75, 77, 83
Fitch, Henry W.: **II**, 153, 211, 268, 296
FitzGeorge, Col.: **II**, 325, 326
Fitz, George, Mrs.: **I**, 325–326
FitzHugh, Carter: letters to, **III**, 410, 446, 483, 489–490; mention, **III**, 446
Fitzroy, Robert O'Brien: **II**, 419
Fiume, Austria: 408, 410
Flamborough Head, England: **II**, 540

Flamingo Point, Water Island, Lesser Antilles: **II**, 586
Fletcher, Arthur Henry: 167, 168, 170, 171, 172, 174, 179, 184, 185, 186, 188, 191, 192, 195, 196, 199, 200, 203, 204, 205, 206, 209, 210, 211, 212, 213, 214, 215, 219, 220, 222, 226, 227, 228, 229, 232, 234, 235, 236, 237, 238, 239, 241, 245, 247, 249, 250, 252, 254, 265, 272, 276, 277, 278, 279, 283, 290, 296, 328
Fletcher, Montgomery: 596
Flint, Frank P.: **III**, 371
Florence, Italy: **II**, 234; **III**, 491, 720
Flores Island, River Plate, South America: 401, 407, 408, 411, 412, 413, 419, 424
Florida: **III**, 76, 524
Flushing, N.Y.: **III**, 377
Folger, William Mayhew: **II**, 8, 35, 36–37, 38, 63, 94, 95, 734; **III**, 282
Fonseca, Gulf of, Salvador: **II**, 584, 590
Foochow, China: M. describes, 116
Foote, Henry D.: 75, 77–78, 78, 81
Force, Alfred: 261
Ford, Worthington Chauncey: **III**, 240, 317
Forde, Thomas G.: 19, 50, 76, 77
Formosa: 247, 250, 593; **III**, 56, 377, 386
Forrest, Rutherford W.: 471–472
Fort Erie, Ontario, Canada: **III**, 84
Fort George, Quebec, Canada: **III**, 84
Fort Jackson, New Orleans, La.: 547, 548
Fort Lafayette, Boston, Mass.: 89
Fort Morgan, Mobile, Ala.: 551, 555; **III**, 555, 556
Fort Moultrie, Charleston, S.C.: 619; **II**, 725; **III**, 489
Fort, W. S.: letter to, 374; mention, 374, 376, 382
Fortier, Alcée: **III**, 42
Foss, George Edmund: **III**, 204, 374
Foster, Sir Augustus John: **III**, 122, 124, 128, 671
Foulweather Point, W.T.: 682
"Four Hundred," **III**, 727, 728
Fournier, Gaston: letter to, **II**, 525; mention, **II**, 525, 593, 614, 618, 619, 622, 702, 703
Fourth Auditor of the Treasury: letter to, **III**, 316, 318, 320, 321–322; mention, 716, **II**, 239, 404, **III**, 316, 319, 320, 322, 327, 331, 525, 526, 529, 530, 531
Fox, Charles James: **II**, 298; **III**, 87
Fox, Gustavus Vasa: letter to, 88–89; mention, 88
France: flags, 510; hatred of Britain, 617; admirals, 629; navy, 573, 593, 616, 629, 649, 670, 671–672, **II**, 217, 337, 426, **III**, 368, 493, 519, 710; language, **II**, 158; Rapide, **II**, 175–176; working class, **II**, 178; at Hague Conference, **II**, 745; in Panama, **III**, 9; in North Africa, **III**, 473; in Canada, **III**, 498; Revolution (1789), **II**, 56, 89, 197,

France (*cont.*)

384, **III**, 520, 612, 667, (1871) 364; relations with Britain, **II**, 620, **III**, 12; relations with Germany, **III**, 342; relations with Russia, **II**, 380, 620; relations with U.S., 636, **II**, 556; mention, 74, 359, 364, 372, 458, 640, 649–650, **II**, 2, 3, 37, 42, 125, 150, 152, 175, 176, 179, 323, 339 384, 389, 395, 481, 529, 543, 545, 548, 556, 560, 593, 620, 744, **III**, 32, 34, 37, 45, 72, 80, 97, 115, 123, 124, 128, 221, 381, 383, 442, 452, 453, 459, 465, 490, 493, 527, 541, 551, 569, 581, 595, 596, 638, 698, 699, 703, 704. *See* Index Section IV, France

Francis Ferdinand, Archduke of Austria-Hungary: **III**, 704

Franco-Prussian War: **III**, 698

Francovitch, L.: letter to, 410; mention, 410

Frank, Gen.: 191, 193

Franklin, Miss Anna: 60, 62

Franklin, Benjamin: **II**, 724

Franklin, Charles Love: 53

Fraser, Sir Charles: **II**, 326

Fraser, W. L.: **II**, 432, 437, 514

Frazer, Reah: 589

Frederick the Great: **II**, 580, 581

Fredericksen, Nils: **II**, 405–406

Frelinghuysen, Frederick T.: 604

Fremantle, Sir Charles: **II**, 503

French, Major: **II**, 199

Frenchman's Bay, Me.: **III**, 573

French running lights: 533, 534

Frendo, Emmanuel: **II**, 334

Frontside, Me.: 613

Fullam, William F.: **III**, 178, 284

Fuller, James Fullerton: 75, 77

Fuller, Loie: **II**, 296

Fuller, Mr.: 111

Fullerton, Rear Adm.: **II**, 140, 312

Fullerton, W. Morton: **III**, 415

Fulton Centennial Celebration: **III**, 313, 315

Funchal, Madeira: **II**, 407

Funck burner: 550

Funck, Mr.: 541

Funk and Wagnalls Company: **III**, 428, 430

Furey, John: 493

Galapagos Islands: **III**, 376, 377

Gallatin, Albert: **III**, 114, 475

Galveston, Texas: **II**, 527; **III**, 354

Gardiner, Samuel Rawson: **II**, 637; **III**, 48, 159

Gardiners Bay, N.Y.: **III**, 577

Garfield, James A.: 487–488, 488, 491–492

Gatewood, R.: 637, 639, 647, 660

Gauss, Mr.: letter to, **III**, 67; mention, **III**, 67, 79

General Storekeeper (USN): **III**, 316, 331, 531

General Board (USN): **III**, 158, 174, 175, 191, 206, 281, 395, 627, 660, 661

General & International Flag Signals: **II**, 338

Geneva Convention: **II**, 638, 646, 647

Geneva Cross Convention: **II**, 643, 659

Geneva, Switzerland: **III**, 434

Genoa, Italy: **II**, 85, 178, 181, 183, 184, 185, 186, 187, 188, 219, 221, 222, 223, 225, 232, 234, 313, 346, 358, 382, 388, 470

George, Charles H.: letter to, **III**, 2; mention, **III**, 1, 2, 5

George, Lake: **III**, 470

George, Lloyd: **III**, 516

George III: **III**, 123

German North Sea Coast: **III**, 708

German Southwest Africa: **III**, 442

Germany: commerce and commercial routes, **II**, 18, **III**, 35, 159, 192, 205, 213, 221, 284, 445; interest in annexation of Holland, **II**, 27, **III**, 377; emigration, **II**, 537; navy, **II**, 681, **III**, 345, 377, 410, 412, 444, 451, 457, 459, 468, 490, 548, 550, 551, 681, 689, 699, 707, 708; naval building, **III**, 12, 291, 334, 412, 707; naval strategy, **III**, 699–700; intervention in China, **II**, 536; threat to Monroe Doctrine, **III**, 291–292, 307–308, 345, 445, 541–542; imperial expansion, **II**, 529, 536–537, **III**, 34, 446; Anglo-German tension, **III**, 12, 63, 307, 334; German-American tension, **II**, 566, 567, **III**, 165, 291–292; Franco-German tension, **III**, 342; German-Russian tension, **III**, 342; role in origin of European War, **III**, 698, 707, 710; use of submarines and airplanes, **III**, 549, 550–551, 708–709; General Staff, **III**, 218; Pan-Germanism, **III**, 609; mention, 592, 640, **II**, 37, 38, 529, 683, **III**, 13, 17, 23, 32, 50, 97, 184, 210, 211, 216, 251, 277, 333, 343, 344, 350, 360, 371, 380, 420, 442, 443, 452, 453, 465, 499, 514, 543, 701, 703, 704, 705. *See* Index Section IV, Germany

Germany, Empress of: **II**, 129

Gettysburg Campaign: **III**, 664

Ghent, Belgium: **III**, 115

Ghent, Treaty of: **III**, 115, 137; American commissioners, **III**, 132; British commissioners, **III**, 132

Gherardi, Bancroft: **II**, 154, 231

Gibbon, Edward: **III**, 159

Gibbon, John: 143, 709, 710

Gibbs, Richard: 560

Gibraltar: 53, 142, **II**, 36, 84, 85, 125, 148, 156, 157, 159, 160, 163, 254, 257, 258, 259, 312, 338, 356, 358, 359, 360, 363, 365, 367, 369, 370, 371, 372, 385, 386, 388, 393, 401, 402, 404, 405, 407, 408, 412, 419, **III**, 146, 153, 356, 392, 394, 569, 586, 589; Artillery Mess, **II**, 162; Colonial Hospital, **II**, 406; North Front Cemetery, **II**, 406; Rock of,

II, 161, 368, 369; Straits of, II, 162, 168, 564, 565, 566, 570, 572, 589, III, 641; governor of, II, 365, 366, 367, 409; M. describes, II, 161; M. entertained by RN at, II, 162

Gibson, Mr.: 299, 307

Gifford, Benjamin: 163, 224

Gift, George: 555

Gilbert, Levi: letter to, III, 545–546; mention, III, 545

Gilder, Richard Watson: II, 542; III, 25

Gill, Anne: 25, 75, 76, 78

Gill family: II, 179, 180

Gill, Mary Esther: 25, 64, 76, 78

Gillender, Augustus T.: letters to, II, 112, 112–113, 416, 417, 436, 439, 440, 444, 447, 448, 453, 461, 463, 464, 464–465, 465, 467, 499, 510–511, 515–516, 522, 549–550, 620, 656, 720, 726–727, 728, III, 11, 75–76; mention, 429, II, 141, 210, 241, 351, 361, 370, 438, 440, III, 504

Gillender, Mrs. Augustus T.: II, 447; III, 76

Gillespie, G. L.: III, 661

Gillett, Simon Palmer: 88

Gillmore, James C.: 644

Gillpatrick, William W.: II, 138, 218, 223, 224, 226, 227, 240, 249, 250, 251, 282, 323

Gilman, Daniel C.: letters to, II, 605, 607–608; mention, II, 605

Ginn Company: III, 258, 259

Gironde, France: 429, 430

Gladstone, William Ewart: 434; II, 26, 105, 110, 131, 298, 319, 388–389, 674

Gladstone, Mrs. William Ewart: II, 135

Glass, Henry: II, 213–214

Gleaves, Albert: letter to, III, 105; mention, III, 103–104

Glengariff, Ireland: II, 119

Glidden, George Dana Boardman: 215

Goat Island, R.I.: 676, 716; II, 8, 11, 21, 23, 25, 31; III, 667

Goble, Edgar: II, 317–318, 328

Goddard, E. T.: 588, 589

Godkin, Edwin Lawrence: II, 146, 501; III, 580

Goff, Nathan, Jr.: letters to, 492–493, 493; mention, 492

Gold Island [Coaster's Island], R.I.: 671, 672

Goldsborough, John: 84, 88, 90

Goldsborough, Louis M. ("Old Goldy"): letter to, 86–87; mention, 84, 85, 87, 371, III, 61

Good Ground [Hampton Bays], N.Y.: III, 726

Goodrich, Caspar F.: letter to, III, 263–264; mention, 474, 577, 637, 654, 677, 678, 689, 700, 708, 712, 713, 714, II, 84, 146, 244, 251, 349, 371, III, 178, 219, 263, 264, 265, 266, 316, 641, 666

Gordon, Charles G. ("Chinese"): II, 674

Gordon, Jacob: 224

Gordon, Spencer: letters to, III, 287–289, 525–527, 529–530, 530–532, 532, 533–534, 538; mention, III, 287

Gore, Mrs.: II, 294

Goshen, N.Y.: 2

Gough, Charles G.: 476

Goulburn, Henry: III, 132

Gould, George J.: II, 310–311

Gould Island, R.I.: 671

Gower, Leveson: II, 652

Grace Episcopal Church (New York): II, 617; III, 302

Grafton Hotel (Washington): III, 548

Granada, Spain: II, 162, 165, 167, 169, 170, 174, 233, 357, 358, III, 151, 720; M. describes Alhambra, II, 164

Granada Cathedral: II, 169

Grand Hotel Axenfels, Lake Lucerne, Switzerland: III, 100

Grand Hotel (Nice): II, 202

Grand River, Ontario, Canada: III, 82

Grant, J. W.: 383

Grant, Ulysses Simpson: 439, 443, 450, 477, 482, 487, 546, 592; II, 605; III, 388, 393, 545

Grantly, Lord: II, 392

Granville, George Leveson-Gower, 2nd Baron: II, 652

Grasse, Francois Joseph Paul, Comte de: 629; III, 467, 472, 488, 519, 527

Graves, Charles Iverson: 69

Gravesend, England: II, 259, 261, 264, 287, 288, 289, 414

Gray, James: 479

Gray, Bishop Robert: 103–104, 107

Great Britain: Admiralty, 497, III, 276, 315, 375, 438, 491; army, III, 551; Boer War, II, 657, 664, 678, 688–689; Church of England, II, 280; commerce, II, 18, III, 16, 621, 622; Commonwealth, III, 397, 415; consuls, 311, II, 255; election (1906), III, 133; Empire, 112, II, 529, 607, 617, III, 72, 543, 604, 625; Foreign Office, III, 128, 132; France, historical conflict with, 74, 87, 91, II, 26, 545; Home Rule, III, 520; House of Commons, II, 275, 277, 298, III, 370, 520; House of Lords, III, 370, 427, 486; Imperial defence, III, 397, 439; Imperial Federation, III, 13, 23, 27, 28, 72, 100, 221, 609; Navigation Acts, III, 154; Navy League, II, 550; Orders-in-Council (1807), III, 114, 115, 116, 122, 123, 124, 125, 126, 127–128, 130, 340, (1904), III, 281; Parliament, II, 122, 406, III, 63, 98, 116, 370, 409, 514, 520, 712; people, II, 161, 330; press, 91, II, 606, III, 16, 276; Royal Navy, 36, 47, 444–445, 446, 448, 482, 497, 573, 593, 629, 658, 659, 670, II, 84, 92, 93, 99, 141, 273–274, 337, 359, 360, 405, 408,

Great Britain (*cont.*)
435, 481, 514, 577, **III**, 167, 170, 458, 459, 460, 493, 519, 551, 559, 560, 562, 563, 565, 567, 568, 569, 570, 674, 698, 699, 700, 701, 707, 708, 709; sea power, **II**, 93, 126, **III**, 449; Staff College, **II**, 199; U.S.A., attitudes toward, **II**, 171, 546, 556; War of 1812, **III**, 71, 87, 116, 130. *See* Index Section IV, Great Britain
Great Harbor, Culebra, West Indies: **II**, 587
Great Lakes: **III**, 458, 564, 565, 672, 673
Great Round Shoal Light, Nantucket Sound, Mass.: **II**, 426
Greece: **II**, 237, 241, 495, 505, **III**, 699, 710; flags, 510; language, **II**, 513; people, **III**, 521, 710; army, **III**, 521; navy, **III**, 710
Greek Archipelago: **II**, 238, 241, 247
Greeley, Horace: 457, 591–592; **II**, 697
Greely relief expedition: 582
Green, I. F.: 4, 5, 7
Greene, Evarts B.: letter to, **III**, 551; mention, **III**, 551
Greene, Francis V.: letters to, **II**, 630, 692–693, 694–695, **III**, 522–523; mention, **II**, 630, 636, 692
Greene, George: 231, 261, 315, 322
Greene, Samuel Dana: 8, 41, 58, 60, 66, 68, 464, 593; **III**, 56
Greenland: **II**, 618
Greenman, Charles T.: 183
Green Mountain: **II**, 119
Greenwich, England: **II**, 273
Greenwich Savings Bank (N.Y.C.): **II**, 132
Greer, Bishop David H.: **III**, 302
Grenville, William Wyndham, Baron: **III**, 126
Grey, Sir Edward: **III**, 412, 420, 439, 512
Greytown, Nicaragua: **III**, 222
Gridley, Charles V.: 471
Griffin's Bay, W.T.: 682; **III**, 570
Griffith, William: letter to, **III**, 506–507; mention, **III**, 506
Grimball, John: 555; **III**, 58
Grimes, James Wilson: 475
Groix, Ile de, France: **II**, 544
Grote, George: **III**, 371
Groton School: **II**, 49, 101, 315, 331, 341, 374, 405, 501, 542, 560; **III**, 719, 720, 727
Guadeloupe, Leeward Islands: 97, 100; **II**, 37; **III**, 442, 629
Guajan [Guam]: **II**, 582, 583, 590; **III**, 356, 357, 358, 377, 380, 381, 382, 383, 384, 385, 386, 387, 391, 392, 393, 396, 398–399, 402, 661
Guánica, Porto Rico: **II**, 612
Guantanamo, Cuba: **II**, 575, 576, 588, 590; **III**, 354, 355, 356, 357, 376, 377, 396, 400, 402, 403, 404, 661

Guatemala: 523, 526, 528, 598, 599, 600, 601, 602, 605, 606, 607; **II**, 47
Guayaquil, Ecuador: 577, 589, 602, 603, 605, 606, 607, 608, 611
Guiana, South America: **II**, 18
Guildford, England: **II**, 318
Gulf Stream: **III**, 454
Gurdon, Lt.: 161, 165, 183, 286, 287
Gurney, Mrs.: **II**, 181
Gwynne, Walker: **III**, 535, 536

Hackett, Samuel Holland ("Ding"): 6, 13, 17, 19, 34, 37, 38, 48, 59, 60, 61, 65, 66, 67, 78; **III**, 53, 55
Haeseler, Francis Joy: 479
Hague, The, Netherlands: **II**, 633, 634, 658, 667, 691, 702; **III**, 8, 106
Hague Peace Conference (First), 1899: Second Committee of, **II**, 646, 647, 648, 649; Third Committee of, **II**, 705, 710, 713, 719, 738, 744, 745, **III**, 21; Ten Articles recommended by, **II**, 659; Article 27, **II**, 709, 710–711, 712, 713, 714, 715, 719, 737–738, 741, 744, 745, **III**, 14, 16, 18, 19, 20, 21, 22, 73, 139, 450; mention, **II**, 631, 632, 633, 634, 643, 645, 646, 647, 648, 649, 650, 651, 652, 653, 658, 659, 660, 663, 664, 670, 693, 705, 710, 712, 713, 714, 719, 728, 731, 737, 738, 741, **III**, 18, 19, 20, 21, 25, 72, 73, 139, 442, 450, 451
Hague Peace Conference (Second), 1907: **III**, 72, 112, 139, 157, 158, 164, 172, 184, 192, 204, 205, 207, 213, 214, 221, 223, 442, 658
Hainan, Gulf of, China: 264
Haines, Hubert: **II**, 30
Hains, Peter C.: **III**, 9
Haiti: 510, 530; **II**, 435, 588; **III**, 631
Hakodate, Japan: 225, 226, 229, 232, 233, 236, 322, 336, 341, 343, 344, 346, 347, 348, **III**, 383, 384, 688; M. describes, 342, 344, 348; lake country, 231, 345, 349
Hakodate volcano: M. visits, 231, 342–343, 344–346, 348–349
Hakodate Head: 231, 344, 348
Hale, Eugene: 650; **II**, 302; **III**, 98, 204, 334
Halifax, N.S.: **II**, 425; **III**, 88, 561, 562, 564, 566, 567, 573, 574
Hall, Bishop: **II**, 245
Hall, Charles: 600, 601
Hall, Harriot Ingraham (Mrs. Wilburn B. Hall): **II**, 179, 180
Hall, Wilburn B.: 13, 19, 30, 31, 39, 42, 59, 196, 364, 476–477; **II**, 178–179, 180, 181, 182, 183, 185, 200, 470; **III**, 55, 228
Hamburg (S.C.) "Massacre": 459
Hamilton, Lady Emma: **II**, 227, 328, 333, 441, 462, 478, 481, 485, 514
Hamilton, Lord Claud: **II**, 273

Hamilton, Lord George Francis: **II**, 135, 278, 462

Hamilton, Sir Vesey: **II**, 279

Hamilton, William: **II**, 115

Hammett, Charles E., Jr.: letter to, 671–672; mention, 671

Hammond, Capt.: **II**, 419

Hampton Roads, Va.: **III**, 267, 412, 629, 640, 643

Hancock, Winfield Scott: 487, 488

Hanford, Franklin: **II**, 32, 365, 384

Hanna, Marcus Alonzo: **II**, 621

Hannay, David: **II**, 594

Hannibal: 606, 607; **II**, 167, 493; **III**, 581

Hanover, N.H.: **III**, 608

Hanscom, Isaiah: 437, 442, 442–443, 481

Hanson, James Christian Meinich: **II**, 514

Happin, Charlie: 130

Hard Times, La.: 547

Hardee, William Joseph: 43

Hardy, Thomas W.: **II**, 318; **III**, 472

Hare, Mrs.: **II**, 381, 383, 385

Harison, William Beverley: **II**, 295, 723, 724

Harmony, David B.: letter to, 673; mention, 672, 698

Harper Brothers: letter to, **III**, 173; mention, **III**, 173, 227, 466, 486, 552; reasons for declining to publish *Influence*, **II**, 295

Harriman, E. H.: **III**, 440

Harrington, P. F.: 644, 660, 663; **II**, 82; **III**, 665, 666

Harris, Benjamin Winslow: 475

Harris, Frank: **II**, 325

Harris, Mrs. Frank: **II**, 325

Harris, Joseph Whipple: 48, 79

Harrison, Benjamin: **II**, 707; **III**, 299, 666

Harrison, Thomas Locke: 17, 19, 31, 52, 55, 61, 70

Hastings-on-the-Hudson, N.Y.: **III**, 464

Hart, Albert Bushnell: letters to, **II**, 701, 716; mention, **II**, 701, 716

Hartpence, Minnie. *See* Sands

Harvard University: 474; **II**, 49, 420, 421, 534, 716; **III**, 85, 244, 474, 549

Harvey, Bertie: **II**, 117

Harvey, George B. M.: letters to, **III**, 544, 550; mention, **III**, 544

Haskins, Charles H.: letter to, **III**, 45–46; mention, **III**, 45

Hatfield House, English estate: **II**, 274, 275, 298, 313

Hatteras, Cape: 90

Haupt, Louis M.: **II**, 9

Havana, Cuba: **II**, 551, 553, 554, 571, 630; **III**, 31

Havana Harbor, Cuba: **II**, 544; **III**, 592, 631, 633, 634, 643

Haverford, Pa.: **II**, 9–10, 415; **III**, 340, 552

Hawaii: **II**, 361 506, 532, 538–539, 583, 619, **III**, 54, 80, 202, 251, 355, 356, 357, 377, 380, 381, 382, 383, 384, 385, 386, 387, 388, 458, 465, 477; revolution in, **II**, 92; annexation question, **II**, 94

Hawke, Edward: 618, 619, 629, 671; **II**, 724, 730

Hawke, J. A.: letter to, 404; mention, 390

Hawkins, William: 243, 244, 245, 246, 287, 288

Haxtun, Milton: 491–492

Hay, John Milton: **II**, 635, 680, 706; **III**, 157, 213, 411, 431, 462, 463

Hay Open Door Policy: **II**, 708; **III**, 346, 353, 355, 356

Hay-Pauncefote Treaty (First), 1900: **II**, 683; **III**, 421, 431, 437, 450, 486

Hay-Pauncefote Treaty (Second), 1901: **III**, 432, 433, 477, 486, 487, 490

Hayden, Edward Daniel: 648

Hayden, Edward Everett: **II**, 44, 48, 49

Haydn, Joseph: **II**, 197, 200

Hayes, Rutherford B.: 455, 457, 459, 470; vetoes appropriation bill, 473, 475

Hayes, Samuel: 304, 314, 315, 316, 339, 352

Hays, J. M.: letter to, **II**, 527; mention, **II**, 527

Hayter, Lady: **II**, 135, 137, 141, 269

Hayter, Sir George: **II**, 135

Hazeltine, Mayo Williamson: **III**, 156

Heard, Mrs.: 327

Hearne, Mr.: **II**, 523

Hearst, William Randolph: **II**, 508, 598

Heligoland, Germany: **III**, 709

Henderson, Sir William Hamilton: letters to, 662–663, 669–671, 677–678, **II**, 9, 344–345, 509–510, 546, **III**, 27–28, 36, 203–204, 284–285, 341–343, 369–371; 451–452, 513–515; mention, 662, **II**, 226, 255, 509, 546, **III**, 28, 100, 284

Henderson, Mrs. William H.: **III**, 341, 371, 452, 515

Henderson's Harbor, N.Y.: **III**, 86

Hendricks, Thomas A.: 457, 459

Hendrickson, W. W.: 471

Henry, Cape, Va.: **III**, 560

Henry, Prince of Battenberg: **II**, 140

Henry, Prince of Prussia: **III**, 726

Hepburn, Mrs.: 315, 323, 330

Herbert, Hilary A.: letters to, **II**, 103–104, 106, 106–107, 112, 171, 179, 187, 192, 205, 239, 254, 289–290, 291, 303, 314, 317, 320, 322–323, 324, 338, 339, 362, 372, 389–392, 403–404, 405–406, 406–407, 407, 409, 410–411, 412, 413, 414, 415, 431, 434, 435, 436–437; mention, 648, 650–651, 652, **II**, 32, 62, 98, 99, 100, 102, 105, 108, 109, 138, 142, 144, 147, 160, 168, 182, 201, 207, 208, 210, 217,

Herbert, Hilary A. (*cont.*)
   222–223, 225, 232, 236, 239–240, 244, 248,
   250, 263, 275, 282, 291, 294, 302, 306, 313,
   314, 341, 349, 359, 409, 437, 474, 595, **III**,
   299, 664, 665, 666. *See* Index Section IV,
   Herbert; U.S. Navy: Naval War College
Herschell, Lord: **III**, 411
Hessel, Max: **II**, 192
Hewlett, N.Y.: **III**, 721
Hibbert, Mr.: 287
Hibbler & Rausch Co.: 490
Higginson, Francis J.: **II**, 302, 575, 613, 672
Hildebrand, Pope Gregory: 571
Hill, C. F.: **II**, 314
Hill, Henry J.: 295
Hill, Mr.: **II**, 546
Hill, Mr. and Mrs. W. B.: 91
Hindoos: **II**, 129
Hingham, Mass.: **II**, 719
Hiogo [Kobe], Japan: 119, 121, 122, 123,
   125, 126, 127, 128, 131, 134, 136, 140, 150,
   183, 187, 188, 191, 194, 195, 199, 200, 202,
   203, 206, 208, 211, 217, 220, 221, 223, 224,
   297, 307, 336, 337, 338, 341
Historical Congress in London (1913): **III**,
   524
Hitchcock Lamp Co.: 502, 503, 504, 527,
   529, 532, 534, 541, 550
Hitchcock, Robert B.: 356
Hoar, George F.: **II**, 680
Hobson, Richmond P.: **III**, 465
Hoche, Lazare: **II**, 337
Hodges, Harry M.: **II**, 241, 242–243
Hoff, William Bainbridge: 632, 637; **III**, 663
Hogg, John: 602; **II**, 25
Hokkaido, Japan. *See* Yezo
Holden, R. M.: letter to, **III**, 44; mention,
   III, 44
Holguín, Cuba: **II**, 612
Holland: flags, 510; character of people, **II**,
   260, 304; school of painting, **II**, 304; in
   South America, **II**, 698; empire, **III**, 377;
   language, **III**, 490; navy, **III**, 493; German
   threat to, **II**, 27, **III**, 292; foreign policy,
   III, 368; mention, **II**, 27, 304, 419, **III**, 59,
   638, 699, 707, 708
Holland, Henry Richard Fox, 3rd Baron:
   III, 125–126
Hollinger and Rockey Co.: **II**, 499
Hollis, I. N.: **II**, 77, 83
Holls, George Frederick William: letters to,
   II, 697, 704–706, 709–712, 714–715, 737–
   738, 741, **III**, 13–14, 15; mention, **II**, 633,
   675, 706, 708, 709, 710, 712, 713, 714, 731–
   732, 744–745, 745, **III**, 1, 15, 16, 17–22, 73,
   74, 449, 450. *See* Hague Peace Conference
   (First); and Index Section IV, Hague
   Conference (First): Mahan-Holls Con-
   troversy
Holt family: **II**, 220

Holt, Hamilton: letters to, **II**, 739–741, 744,
   III, 1–2, 3; mention, **II**, 739, **III**, 2, 4, 5
Holy Trinity Episcopal Church (Brooklyn,
   N.Y.): **III**, 598
Holy Trinity Episcopal Church (New
   York): 107; **II**, 364; **III**, 721
Honduras: 526, 599
Hong Kong, China: 115, 117, 120, 122, 130,
   133, 136, 137, 139, 140, 141, 262, 264, 274,
   275, 276, 279, 280, 281, 282, 283, 284, 285,
   287, 288, 292, 293, 294, 296, 298, 332, 333,
   334, 350, 351, 352; **II**, 555, 582, **III**, 192
Honolulu, Hawaii: **II**, 583; **III**, 380, 383,
   384, 401, 637, 661
Hood, John, **III**, 178
Hood, Sir Samuel: 629; **III**, 472
Hood's Canal, W.T.: 696
Hooker, Edward: 303, 311
Hooker, Mrs. Edward: 312
Hooker, Joseph: **II**, 699
Hoole, James Lingard: 59
Hope, Harry: 312–313, 313, 314
Hopkins, Sir John: **II**, 408
Hopkins, William F. ("Poppy"): 13, 54, 56,
   59, 62, 63, 70–71, 85
Hopkins, William R. ("Bull Pup"): 63, 71
Hoppner, John: **II**, 484, 490
Hornby, Sir Geoffrey Thomas Phipps: **II**, 9
Horse Island, N.Y.: **III**, 86
Horwitz, Phineas J.: 172
Hoskins, the Rev. Thomas R.: 432; **III**, 723
Hoskins, Mrs. Thomas R.: 432; **II**, 268, 275,
   286, 289; **III**, 723
Hotchkiss Co.: **II**, 287, 339
Hotel Collingwood (45 W. 35th St.,
   N.Y.C): **III**, 427, 428, 429, 436, 439, 445,
   447, 448, 452, 512, 514, 521, 531, 720, 721
Hotel Reina Cristina, Algeciras, Spain: **III**,
   148
Hotel St. George, Algiers: **II**, 389
Hotel Vieux Doelen, The Hague: **II**, 633, 636
Houghton, Baron. *See* Milnes, Robert
Houghton, Mifflin and Co.: **II**, 111–112, 119,
   169, 296, 729; **III**, 487
Houston, Edwin S.: **II**, 404
Howard, Thomas W.: letters to, 415, 419,
   420; mention, 415, 416
Howe, Frederic C.: **II**, 708
Howe, Richard, Earl: 629, 670; **II**, 1, 2, 92,
   724, 725, 730; **III**, 467, 472
Howell, Commodore: **III**, 636, 640
Howell, John Adams: 53, 464, 548
Howell torpedo: **II**, 82, 95
Howells, William Dean: letter to, **III**, 300;
   mention, **III**, 300
Howison, Henry L.: 464, 471; **II**, 534
Howland, William B.: **III**, 539
Howland, Mrs.: 281
Hudson River, N.Y.: 106; **III**, 194, 524, 563
Hudson River Valley, N.Y.: **III**, 464

Huerta, Victoriano: **III**, 512, 523
Hughes, Aaron K.: letter to, 561–562; mention, 559, 562, 587, 608
Hughes, Sir Edward: 629; **III**, 467, 472
Hughes, the Rev. Stanley C.: letter to, **III**, 423; mention, **III**, 423
Hull, William: **III**, 64, 65, 78, 129, 130, 545
Hunker, John Jacob: **II**, 625, 628
Hunt, Gaillard: **III**, 166, 167, 168, 169, 170, 171–172, 318
Hunt, William H.: letters to, 495, 496–497; mention, 487, 495
Hunter, Sir William Wilson: **III**, 159
Huntington, Dr. William Reed: **II**, 617; **III**, 302
Huron, Lake: **III**, 79
Huxley, Thomas Henry: **II**, 297

Iglesias, Miguel: 573
Impressment: **II**, 109–110
Incarnation Episcopal Church (New York): **III**, 721
India: 113, 351, 352, 629; **II**, 529, 607, 608; **III**, 7, 12, 13, 27, 34, 489, 502, 523
Indiana: 488; **III**, 78
Indian Ocean: **II**, 384
Indians (American): **II**, 159, 616, 636; **III**, 723
Ingraham, Duncan N.: **II**, 179
Innisfallen, Lake, Ireland: **II**, 120
International Marine Conference (1889): **II**, 406
International Naval Review (1893): **II**, 102, 267
Inter-Parliamentary Union (1910): **III**, 366
Ireland: **II**, 36, 115, 118, 119, 120, 123, 131, 137, 173, 268, 337, 544, 572; **III**, 520, 569
Ireland, F. G.: **II**, 49, 250, 267, 365
Irondale, Port Townsend, W.T.: 698
Irving, Washington: 576
Irwin, John: letters to, **II**, 89, 90; mention; **II**, 89, 90, 555
Iselin, C. Oliver: **II**, 474
Isla Grande, Subic Bay, Philippines: **III**, 659
Islam: **III**, 683
Ismay, J. Bruce: **III**, 454, 455
Israelites: **II**, 543; **III**, 600
Isthmian Canal, 482; **II**, 82, 584, 683, 684; **III**, 80, 431, 432; railroad across, **II**, 25; policy of U.S., 593, 643, **II**, 171. See Index Section IV, Isthmian Canal
Isthmian Canal Commission: 507, 609; **III**, 9
Italy: 126–127, 353, 573; **II**, 157, 180, 186, 413–414, 543; **III**, 383, 388, 442, 500, 595, 609, 666. See Index Section IV, Italy
Ito, Sukenori: **II**, 422; **III**, 583–585
Ives, Mr.: 189, 231
Iznaga, Constance: **II**, 311
Izoulet, M.: **III**, 151

Jaccaci, August F.: **II**, 615, 616
Jackson, Francis James: **III**, 121, 125, 128, 134, 168, 169, 171, 172
Jackson, Helen: 265–266
Jacobs, Enoch: letters to, 387–388, 390, 396, 405; mention, 381, 385, 387, 390, 405, 415
Jacobs, William Cloyd: 26
Jalpataqua, Guatemala: 600
Jamaica: 71, 662; **II**, 546; **III**, 143, 204, 568, 569, 631
James River, Va.: 687
James, William: 445
Jameson, J. Franklin: letters to, **II**, 422–423, 428–429, 429, 432, 469, 476, 477, 485, 497, 502, 513, 533, 546, 550, 608–609, 622, 631, 663, 668, 674–675, 696, 702, **III**, 4, 24, 85, 134, 136, 136–137, 147, 148, 162–163, 166, 169–170, 171–172, 175–176, 208–209, 246, 316, 328–329, 339, 504–505, 506, 515, 516, 518–519, 523–525, 548, 552; mention, **II**, 422, **III**, 134, 208, 519, 524, 528, 549–550, 674, 676
Jameson Raid: **III**, 32
Jamestown, Va.: **III**, 166, 170
Janvier, Thomas A.: letter to, **II**, 378
Japan: 122, 125, 126, 133, 154, 212, 213, 332, 343, 344, 345, 348; **II**, 358, 538, 593; **III**, 27, 32, 56, 182, 183, 322, 356, 363, 372, 377, 412, 427, 498, 502, 503, 508, 514, 523, 532, 533, 534, 535, 583, 584, 585, 625, 640, 642, 661, 662, 681, 689, 690, 691. See Index Section IV, Japan; War: Sino-Japanese, Russo-Japanese
Japan, Emperor of: 126, 128, 134, 138; **III**, 689, 691
Japan, Sea o: 117–118, 335, 338; **III**, 387
Jardin da Estrella, Lisbon, Portugal: **II**, 157
Jasper, Robert T.: 472; **II**, 179, 180
Java: **II**, 582; **III**, 377
Jayne, Joseph L.: letter to, **III**, 358–359; mention, **III**, 358
Jefferson, Thomas: **II**, 205, 361; **III**, 94, 114, 116, 132, 414, 454, 475, 484, 625, 673
Jekyll, Col.: **II**, 117
Jena, Germany: **III**, 698
Jenkins, Thornton A.: letters to, 92–93, 93, 94, 94–95, 96; mention, 92
Jertsen Basin, W.T.: 693, 706
Jerusalem, Ottoman Empire: **II**, 249, 380
Jervis, John, Earl of St. Vincent. See St. Vincent
Jeune, Lady: **II**, 136, 267, 269, 273, 324, 325, 328–329, 330–331, 334, 335, 343
Jeune, Sir Francis Henry: **II**, 136, 269, 270, 275, 325, 331, 334, 512, 513
Jewell, Theodore Frelinghuysen: **II**, 8, 20, 38, 44, 82
Jews: 113, 258; **II**, 190, 356, 371, 456; **III**, 600, 614, 691
"Jingo": **II**, 580, 605, 607

Joan of Arc: **II**, 151
Johanna Island, Comoro Islands: 107, 107–108, 108, 109, 146; M. describes, 108–110
Johns Hopkins University: **II**, 605
Johnson, President Andrew: 198, 307
Johnson, Andrew: 404
Johnson, Capt.: 297
Johnson, Emory: **III**, 9
Johnson, Henry L.: **II**, 89, 90
Johnson, Jeremiah Augustus: **III**, 606
Johnson, the Rev. J. W.: **II**, 617
Johnson, Mortimer: 452
Johnson, Reverdy: 262, 267
Johnson, Robert U.: letters to, **II**, 410, 411, 415, 416, 417, 417–418, 418, 421–422, 423–424, 429, 430, 431, 432, 433–434, 437, 438, 447, 449, 450, 453, 453–454, 454–455, 462, 469, 480, 501, 514–515, 525–526, 535–536, 537, 538, 542, 548–549, 552, 555, 559, 631–632, 671–672, 672, 688, **III**, 24–25, 322, 369, 376, 376–377, 388–389, 395–396, 396–397, 405; mention, **II**, 410, 418, 556
Johnston, Albert Sidney: **III**, 545
Johnston, Joseph Eggleston: **III**, 545
Jomini, Baron Henri: **II**, 526, 595; **III**, 276, 580
"Jomini": **II**, 148, 252, 253, 311, 354, 699; **III**, 726
Jones, David P.: **II**, 25
Jones, Fanny: **II**, 187
Jones, George ("Old Slicky"): 8, 9, 11, 19, 22–23, 25, 26, 30, 33–34, 38, 43, 51, 57, 58, 60, 69, 76
Jones, John Paul: **II**, 539, 540, 541, 544, 545, 547; **III**, 118, 672
Jones, Richard: **II**, 300
Jones, William: **III**, 103, 104
Jordan, David Starr: **II**, 661, 663
Jordán, Ricardo Lopez: 381, 382, 385, 398, 404–405, 408–409, 409, 409–410
Jouett, James E.: **III**, 555–556
Jourdan, Comte Jean Baptiste: **III**, 344
Jovellanos, President: 401
Jurien de La Gravière, Jean Baptiste Edmond: **II**, 394

Kane, Elisha Kent: 86
Kane, Theodore F.: 19, 30, 62, **III**, 55–56; post-USNA career, **III**, 53–54; one of last survivors of class of 1859, **III**, 228
Kaneko, Baron Kentaro: **III**, 117–118
Kansas City, Mexico, and Orient Railway: 590. See American and Mexican Pacific R.R.
Keats, John: **II**, 115, 196
Keet, Alfred Ernest: letter to, **II**, 479; mention, **II**, 479
Keith, George Keith Elphinstone, Viscount: **III**, 569
Kellogg, Augustus G.: 320

Kellogg, Wainwright: 383, 400
Kelly, E.: **II**, 487, 492
Kelly, John: 477
Kelly, J. J.: **II**, 210
Kelly, John W.: 14, 52, 69
Kelvin, William Thompson, 1st Baron: **II**, 297
Kemble family: 110
Kempff, Louis: **II**, 213–214
Kennedy, Crammond: **III**, 430, 431
Kennedy, Duncan: **II**, 296, 424, 501; **III**, 665
Kenny, Albert S.: **II**, 180, 398, 406; **III**. 586, 587, 588, 589
Kent, Julia: 22, 27, 29, 37, 40, 48, 52, 56, 57, 60, 61, 63, 65, 66, 68, 70, 71, 73, 76, 77, 78, 83
Kent, Mrs.: 37, 40, 60, 76–77
Keppel, Augustus: 618, 619
Keppel, Sir Henry: **II**, 129, 312
Kern, Richard: 682, 683, 688, 691, 692, 693, 694, 697, 698, 699, 705, 709
Key, Francis Scott: 64
Key, Philip Barton: 64
Key West, Fla.: 115, 362; **II**, 559, 585, 625, 673; **III**, 191, 354, 355, 357, 402, 404, 413, 631, 632, 633, 635, 636
Khartoum, Anglo-Egyptian Sudan: **II**, 674
Kiaochow, China: **II**, 536; **III**, 97
Kiel Canal, Germany: **III**, 699, 708
Killarney, Lakes of, Ireland: **II**, 115, 117, 118, 120, 121, 123
Kimberley, Earl of: **II**, 406
Kimberley, South Africa: **II**, 699
King, Ben: 61
King, Charles: 2
King, John P.: **II**, 202, 219
King, Rufus: **III**, 142
Kingston, Jamaica: 362; **III**, 120, 143, 204, 561
Kingston, Ontario: **III**, 76–77, 566
Kioto, Japan: 138
Kirkland, William Ashe: letters to, 427, 430; mention, 426, **II**, 294, 322, 324, 325, 331, 334, 339, 340, 341, 342, 344, 345, 346, 351, 352, 353, 354, 355, 357, 358, 360, 361, 363, 365, 368, 369, 370, 371, 373, 374, 375, 376, 377, 379, 380, 381, 383, 385, 386, 388, 399, 402, 403, 404, 406, 417, 435
Kiska, Aleutian Islands: **III**, 380, 381, 382, 383, 384, 385, 386
Kitchener, Horatio: **II**, 658; **III**, 153
Kitsap County, W.T.: 680, 684, 695, 698, 706
Kitsap, Lake, W.T.: 698, 702, 704, 705, 706, 711
Kittele, Sumner E.: letter to, **III**, 191–192; mention, **II**, 219, 227, **III**, 191
Kittredge, Mr.: 710
Kiushu, Japan: **III**, 386
Knapp, John J.: 567
Knollys, Sir Francis: **II**, 298

Knowles, Sir James Thomas: **III**, 231–232
Knox, Philander Chase: **III**, 436, 437, 467
Koelble, Alphonse G.: **III**, 438
Korea: **II**, 306, 506; **III**, 99, 230, 355, 377, 411, 502
Koweit, Arabia: **III**, 35
Kroll, George F.: 693, 694
Kruger, Stephanus Johannes Paulus: **II**, 678, 679; **III**, 9, 32
Kruger Telegram: **II**, 444
Kuhn, Charles: **II**, 181, 187, 188, 190, 191, 194, 194–195, 197, 199, 211, 216, 217, 220, 221, 222, 223, 322, 346, 352, 366, 371, 373, 374, 375, 376, 377, 380, 382, 384, 387, 393; **III**, 729
Kuhn, Pia: **II**, 187, 221
Kure, Japan: **III**, 387
Kuroki, Tamemoto: **III**, 109
Kuropatkin, Aleksei N.: **III**, 103, 108, 109
Kyle, James H.: letter to, **II**, 538–539; mention, **II**, 538

Ladrone Islands: **II**, 569, 582, 583, 590; **III**, 377
Ladysmith, South Africa: **II**, 699; **III**, 10, 201
Laffan, John: **II**, 208, 209, 210, 232
La Gravière, Jurien de. *See* Jurien
La Hougue, France: **III**, 368
Laird, John: 262
Lake, Atwell Peregrine Macleod: **II**, 161, 337, 364, 366, 367
La Libertad, Salvador: 598, 599, 600, 602, 610
Lambert, Bruce: 75–77
Lambert, Henry: **III**, 673
Lambton, Sir Hedworth: **III**, 201
Lammasch, Heinrich: **III**, 13
Lamorvonnais, M.: 381
Landquist, Capt.: **III**, 469
Lane Co.: **III**, 520
Langhorne, Mr.: 316
Lanman, L.: 404
Lansdowne, Henry Charles Keith Petty-Fitzmaurice, 5th Marquis: **III**, 432, 486
La Paz, Bolivia: 560
La Paz, Entre Rios, Argentina: 397, 398, 404–405
Latouche-Tréville, Louis René Madeleine Le Vassor, Comte de: **II**, 489
Laughton, John Knox: 629; **II**, 29, 32, 33, 34, 37, 101, 135–136, 230, 477–478, 500, 503, 504, 547, 733–734, 739; **III**, 132, 154, 176, 429, 438, 467
La Union, Salvador: 594, 597, 598, 599, 602, 612
Laurie, Dr.: **II**, 341
Laurie, Mrs.: **II**, 341
Law, Richard L.: 80, 318, 322, 491–492
Lawrence, James: **III**, 65, 69, 70, 103–104

Lawrence, L.I., N.Y.: **III**, 232, 241, 268, 269, 272, 275, 287, 288, 297, 299, 316, 318, 320, 322, 362, 369, 405, 525, 526, 527, 658, 663, 675, 678, 720, 721
Lawrence Literary Society (USNA): 7, 19, 59, 68, 71, 73
Lawton, Mr.: **II**, 136, 138, 150
Leach, Thomas Walter: 164, 178, 199, 203, 219, 221, 233, 254, 261, 271, 278, 293, 299, 320
League Island, Pa.: 501; **III**, 357, 564
League of Nations: **III**, 530
Leary, Mr.: 319
Lecky, William Edward Hartpole: **II**, 277, 298
Lee, Albert: **III**, 90
Lee, John T.: letter to, **III**, 126
Lee, Robert E.: **II**, 194; **III**, 545
Lee, Col.: **II**, 635
Lee, Dr.: 146, 148, 151, 156, 161, 164
Lee, Miss: **II**, 194, 216, 221
Lee, Mrs.: 140
Leeward Islands Station: **III**, 488
Legembre and Company: **III**, 588
Le Havre, France: **II**, 84, 125, 134, 144, 146, 148, 149, 152, 156, 159, 167, 330, 331, 334, 335, 336, 339, 344, 354, **III**, 583; M. describes, **II**, 151
Leland Stanford University: **II**, 661
Leland, W. G.: **III**, 671
Lenox Foundation: **II**, 517
Lenox Library: **II**, 478; **III**, 79, 81, 83, 84
LeRoy, William E.: letters to, 422–423, 424–425; mention, 422, 423, 424, 425, 430, **II**, 190
Lesseps, de, Viscount Ferdinand Marie: 572; attempts to build canal in Panama, 572
Lestock, Richard: **II**, 722, 723, 731; **III**, 119
Levant, The: **II**, 219, 220, 246, 249, 256, 331, 354, 368, 674; **III**, 35, 49, 569
Levrault, Berger: **II**, 619
Lewis, Charles: 42
Lewis, Elizabeth ("Libbie"): letter to, 2–4; mention, 2, 21, 26, 36, 41, 42, 45, 46, 48, 49, 51, 52, 54, 57, 58, 62, 132
Lewis, Enoch E.: 374
Lewis, James H.: 134
Lewis, Mary ("Maime") (Mrs. Stevens Parker): 45, 50, 111–112, 132; **II**, 124
Lewis, Mr.: 238
Lewis, William Fisher: 111, 132
Lexow, Clarence: **II**, 343
Liaotung Peninsula, Manchuria: **III**, 342
Liao-Yang, Manchuria: **III**, 109
Library of Congress: **III**, 105, 108, 117, 132, 240, 506, 524
Life-Saving Service: **III**, 572
Light House Board: 698, 706, 708; **II**, 235
Light House inspectors: **III**, 253
Lima, Peru: 573
Lincoln, Abraham: 303, 304, 506; **III**, 498

Lippincott Co.: 463–464

Lisbon, Portugal: 53, 428, 429, **II**, 114, 125, 148, 149, 151, 152, 154, 155, 159, 160, 161, 162, 167, 175, 259, 264, 331, 334, 339, 349, 350, 351, 353, 356, 357, 358, 367, 412; M. describes, **II**, 157–158; cholera epidemic at, **II**, 261–262, 263

Littell, Eliakim: **III**, 214

Little, Brown and Company: letters to, 717–718, **II**, 303, 397–398, **III**, 145–146, 151–152, 180–181, 195, 200, 206, 215, 224, 225, 228, 229, 230, 231, 231–232, 238, 244–245, 246, 249–250, 253–254, 255, 256, 256–257, 257, 257–258, 258, 258–259, 259, 259–260, 260, 260–261, 261, 262, 264, 266, 267, 268, 290, 292–293, 293, 294, 294–295, 295–296, 297, 298, 299, 302, 302–303, 303, 304–305, 305, 305–306, 306, 309, 310, 337, 348–349, 349, 350, 351, 351–352, 358, 360, 361, 361–362, 362, 365, 373, 375, 377–378, 378–379, 407, 408, 415, 416, 417, 418, 418–419, 422, 424–425, 425–426, 428, 428–429, 429–430, 430, 436, 440, 443, 444, 446, 451, 456, 460–461, 466–467, 469, 469–471, 471, 471–472, 479–480, 480–481, 481, 482, 482–483, 483, 485–486, 488, 488–489, 490, 493, 494, 495, 499–500, 507, 509, 513, 517, 551; mention, 712, 714, **II**, 115, 117, 122, 124, 168, 186, 193, 217, 277, 286, 295, 300, 311, 356, 389, 396, 454, 455, 462, 490, 531, 535, **III**, 40, 89, 127, 223, 231, 320, 360, 362, 367, 376, 407, 410, 421, 426, 441

"Little Englanders": **III**, 222

Little, William McCarty: letter to, **III**, 368; mention, 689, 708, **II**, 259, 526, **III**, 237, 314, 324, 326, 335, 338, 340, 343, 347, 348, 351, 359, 367, 412, 413, 417, 419, 429, 441

Liverpool, England: 454, 462, **II**, 116, 122, 300, **III**, 595; M. on filth of, 366

Liverpool, Robert Banks Jenkinson, 2nd Earl of: **III**, 136, 137

Livingston, Charles S.: 32

Livingston, Emily Evans: **II**, 261, 262

Livingston, John H.: **II**, 261, 293–294, 294

Livingston, Katherine: **II**, 261, 293–294, 294

Lloyd, Arthur S.: letter to, **II**, 726; mention, **II**, 726

Lloyds of London: **II**, 531

Lobos Island, Uruguay: 376

Locker, William: **II**, 484

Lockett, S. H.: 546

Lockhart, Mrs. Graeme Alexander Sinclair: **II**, 366

Lockwood, Henry H.: 17, 31, 39, 52, 62, 63

Lodge, Henry Cabot: letters to, **II**, 11, 236, 282–283, 562–563, 569, 571, 572, 600, 627, 698–699, 703–704, **III**, 441–443, 443–444; mention, **II**, 11, 17, 208, 234, 237, 239–240, 240, 250, 281, 563, **III**, 435, 441, 622

Lodge, Mrs. Henry Cabot: **II**, 563, 627

Loeb, William: letter to, **III**, 265–266; mention, **III**, 265

Logan, John A.: 459

Logan, Leavit Curtis: 480, 628; **III**, 663

Loire River, France: **II**, 544

London Convention (1884): **III**, 51

Londonderry, Lord: **III**, 115, 137

Londonderry, Robert Stewart, 2nd Marquis of (Viscount Castlereagh): **III**, 115, 132, 137

London, England: 103, 360, 364, 429, 431, 433, 491, 588, 640, 646; **II**, 124, 130, 131, 133, 134, 135, 137, 138, 139, 140, 141, 142, 146, 147, 168, 186, 200, 203, 204, 206, 259, 261, 268, 269, 270, 273, 280, 285, 286, 291, 292, 293, 319, 325, 327, 334, 335, 339, 343, 345, 360, 392, 395, 443, 452, 460, 466, 478, 548; **III**, 9, 97, 100, 102, 115, 118, 128, 133, 136, 145, 156, 160, 203, 299, 334, 342, 397, 427, 484, 485, 492, 510, 528, 595, 720

Long Branch, N.J.: 368, 369

Long, John Davis: letters to, **II**, 551–552, 555, 558, 559, 567–568, 569–570, 572–573, 577–578, 581–591, 594–595, 597–598, 599, 605–606, 607, 609, 609–610, 612–613, 620–621, 624–626, 626–627, 628–629, 634, 635–636, 636, 653–654, 659–660, 673, 680–682, 682, 718–720, 727–728, **III**, 4–5, 10–11; mention, **II**, 506, 548, 556, 562, 563, 570, 591, 592, 600, 669–670, 690, 691, 634, **III**, 162, 164, 627, 628, 629, 630, 634, 642, 660

Long Island, Me.: **II**, 427

Long Island, N.Y.: **II**, 120; **III**, 195, 215, 478, 572

Long Island Railroad: **III**, 478–479, 480

Long Island Sound, N.Y.: 538; **III**, 194, 325, 354, 399, 564

Long Island Sound Line: **III**, 566

Longmans, Green and Company: **II**, 453; **III**, 274, 305, 306

Long Point, St. Thomas: **II**, 586

Long's Hotel (London): **II**, 133, 134

Lotos Club (New York): **II**, 620

Lott, J. W.: **III**, 418

Louis, Prince of Battenberg: **II**, 396, 398–399

Louis XIV: **II**, 398

Louisburg, Cape Breton Island, Canada: **III**, 562, 569

Louisiana Historical Society: **III**, 42

Love, Alfred Henry: **II**, 671

Lovell, Mansfield, Court of Inquiry: 546

Low, A. Maurice: **III**, 486

Low, Seth: letters to, **II**, 449–450, 498, 670–671, 682–684, 685, 689, 690–691, 692, 713–714, **III**, 28, 43, 85; mention, **II**, 449, 635, 659, 660, 675, 706, 708, **III**, 3, 18, 43, 438, 450, 507, 509

Low, William Franklin: 594, 595

Lowell, Augustus: letters to, **II**, 410, 415, 445, 446, 447–448, 472–473, 530; mention, **II**, 410, 534

Lowell Institute: **II**, 410, 445, 446

Lowell Institute Lectures: **II**, 410, 446, 472, 498, 499, 503, 505, 507, 530, 615; **III**, 81, 82, 83, 84, 97, 198, 200

Lowell, James Russell: **II**, 270

Lowell, Miss: **II**, 530

Luce, Stephen B.: letters to, 577–578, 581–582, 597, 603, 606–607, 607–608, 610–611, 613, 614, 615, 615–616, 616, 616–617, 617–618, 618–619, 619, 621–622, 622, 622–624, 626, 626–627, 628–630, 630–631, 632, 632–634, 664–665, 676–677, 677, 700, 707–708, 711–713, 714, 716, 718, **II**, 1–2, 2–3, 9–10, 19, 19–20, 20–21, 24–25, 29–30, 32–33, 33–35, 37–38, 39, 40, 43, 56–57, 57, 58–59, 59, 60, 60–61, 62, 63, 64–65, 105, 144, 145, 473–474, 526, 591–592, 734–735, **III**, 31, 52, 61, 64–65, 68, 68–69, 70, 88, 89, 163, 194–195, 198–199, 199, 216–217, 217–218, 219–220, 233–234, 235 [from Ellen E. Mahan], 236–237, 239, 250, 282–283, 283–284, 299, 319, 321, 325, 423–424, 424, 445–446, 468; mention, 577, 614, 615, 635, 637, 638, 644, 655, **II**, 22, 23, 76, 125, 155, 208, 222, 274, 302, 493, **III**, 52, 103, 178, 245, 248, 282, 298, 303, 429, 620, 663, 664

Luce, Mrs. Stephen B.: 578, 615, 700, 708, 714; **II**, 2, 21, 40, 57, 65, 735; **III**, 199, 235, 239

Luce Board: **II**, 76

Lucerne, Lake, Switzerland: **III**, 100, 103

Lu-Chu [Ryukyu] Islands, China Sea: **III**, 387

Ludlow, Augustus C.: **III**, 69, 103, 104

Ludlow, Nicoll: 146, 151, 157, 161, 194, 211, 215, 216, 222, 228, 249, 251, 271, 276, 281, 282, 283, 284, 297, 298, 308, 316, 322; **II**, 235

Luther, Martin: **II**, 169

Luzon, Philippines: **II**, 569, 579, 583, 590, 635, 636

Lyceum (USNA): 26, 61

Lycia District, Turkey: **II**, 247

Lydenberg, H. M.: letter to, **III**, 242; mention, **III**, 242

Lynnfield, Mass.: **II**, 344, 468, 663, 668

Lyon, Mr.: **II**, 49, 102

Lyons, Algernon M'Lennan: 561; **II**, 343, 346

Lyons, Gulf of, France: **II**, 372, 481

Lyons, Richard Bickerton Pemell, 1st Earl: 65, 70

Lytton, Edward George Earle Bulwer, 1st Baron: 11

McAdoo, William G.: **II**, 107, 108; **III**, 438

McBee, Silas: letters to, **II**, 508, 616–617, 617–618, 618, 654, 654–655, 656, 656–657, 664, 671; mention, **II**, 508, 671, **III**, 657

McCalla, Bowman Hendry: **II**, 2, 3, 145, 525, 672; **III**, 631

McCarty, Stephen A.: 75, 77, 166

McClellan, George Brinton: 656; **II**, 699; **III**, 10

McClelland, James: 172

McClure, S. S.: **II**, 552, 559; **III**, 25, 237, 346–347, 348

McClure Co.: **II**, 615, 616, 619

McCook Chandlers binnacle: 501

McCook, Roderick S.: 6, 13, 30, 37, 57, 66, 67, 68; **III**, 57

McCrea, Charles: **II**, 199, 342, 365

McCrea, Mrs. Charles: **II**, 190–191, 194

McCrea, the Misses: **II**, 219, 220, 221, 224

McCrea, Edward P.: 318, 319, 320, 325, 326, 327, 328, 329, 331

McCubbin, Miss: 27

McCullom, Lt. Cmdr.: 715

McDonald, M. M.: letters to, 546, 549, 549–550; mention, 546, 548

McFarland, John: 47, 149, 155, 160, 167, 173, 174, 216, 222, 239

McGiffin, Philo N.: **II**, 416

McGill University, Montreal: **II**, 684; **III**, 604

McGlensey, John F.: 251; **II**, 104

McGruder, Mary C. ("Mrs. M."): 111, 132

McGunnegle, Wilson M.: 8, 64

McIntyre, James W.: letters to, **III**, 274, 285–286, 296, 297–298, 346, 346–347, 348; mention, 712, **II**, 502

McJunkin, Ira: 471–472

McKee, Llewelyn T.: 471, 472

McKenna, Reginald: **III**, 333

MacKenzie, Alexander Slidell: 7, 31, 68, 593; **III**, 56

McKinley, William: letter to, **II**, 656; mention, **II**, 569, 570, 579, 592, 610, 612, 613, 634, 636, 653, 659, 665, 669, 670, 671, 673, 683, 685, 690, 691, 692, 708, 719, 727, 728, **III**, 5, 9, 10, 113, 431, 432

McLaughlin, Andrew C.: letters to, **III**, 46, 51, 114–115, 116–117, 121, 122–123, 123–125, 126–127, 127–128, 129–130, 130–131, 132; mention, **III**, 46, 47, 51, 116, 123, 129, 131, 147, 551

McLean, Mrs.: **II**, 375

McLean, T. C.: **II**, 82; **III**, 178

McMaster, John Bach: **II**, 4, 674

McNair, Frederick Vallette: 471; **II**, 213, 349

McVay, Charles Butler: **II**, 162, 220

McVickar, Kitty: **II**, 392

Macao, China: 341, 392

Macauley, Frank: **II**, 234

Macauley, T. B.: **III**, 430

Maccoun, Robert T.: 282, 311, 319, 326, 327

Macdonell, Sir John: **III**, 218–219

Macdonough, Thomas: **III**, 101, 110, 111, 167, 527
Mackay, George: **II**, 19, 20, 21, 22–23, 24, 25, 27, 28, 30, 31, 32, 45; **III**, 667
Macklin, Charles Searns: **II**, 162
Madagascar: 107; **II**, 384; **III**, 502, 508
Madeira Islands: 49; **II**, 67, 331, 405, 408, 629
Madison, James: **III**, 116, 121, 122, 123, 124, 125, 126, 128, 129, 130, 132, 168, 169, 171, 475
Magaw, Samuel: 46, 47
Magdalena Bay, Mexico: **III**, 254, 263, 265, 267
Magellan, Ferdinand: **III**, 392
Magi Bay, Nagasaki, Japan: 299
Mahan, Alfred Thayer II ("Tim"): **III**, 719
Mahan, Dennis Hart, Sr.: letters to, 107–110, 115–117, 343–347; mention, 2, 6, 19, 24, 30–31, 36, 41, 43–44, 45, 54, 59, 67, 82, 88, 90, 117, 133, 235, 367, 369, 450, 620, **II**, 190–191, 198, 276, 299, 313, 348, 598
Mahan, Dennis Hart, Jr.: 35, 122, 301, 492; **II**, 135, 172, 174, 241, 402, 436, 438–439, 440, 444, 447, 448, 463, 464, 499, 515–516, 522, 597–598, 599, 620
Mahan, Ellen Kuhn ("Nellie," "Nellikin," "Nell"): letters to, 566–567, 580–581, 584; **II**, 118–121, 128–130, 139–141, 151–152, 161–162, 173–174, 187–189, 201, 202–204, 237–238, 251–254, 261–262, 272–274, 307–309, 325–327, 347–348, 357–359, 367–368, 372–373, 380–382, 388–389, 401–402, **III**, 137–138; Recollections of, **III**, 719–730; mention, 464, 473, 475, 487, 556, 566, 567, 580, 642, 676, 700, **II**, 114, 115, 121, 122, 125, 133, 139, 141, 148, 150, 154, 155, 159, 164, 168, 185, 187, 189, 194, 201, 206, 223, 230, 235, 241, 243, 259, 262, 264, 268, 274, 276, 277, 285, 286, 288–289, 289, 293, 294, 296, 304, 305, 310, 320–321, 324, 333, 334, 335, 339–341, 342, 344, 345, 348, 350, 354, 356, 362, 364, 369, 373, 377, 386, 392, 397, 402, 405, 408, 409, **III**, 127, 151, 152, 153, 156, 307, 549, 552
Mahan, Ellen Lyle Evans (Mrs. Alfred Thayer Mahan) ("Deldie," "Elly"): letters to, 359, 360–361, 362–363, 363, 363–364, 365–366, **II**, 113–115, 117–118, 121–122, 122, 123–124, 127–128, 130–132, 132–133, 134–136, 136, 136–139, 139, 141, 141–143, 146–147, 149–151, 154–155, 155–156, 158–160, 160–161, 162–163, 163–164, 164, 165–166, 166–168, 171–173, 174–176, 177, 177–179, 179–181, 185–186, 187, 189–192, 193–195, 198–200, 204–205, 210, 210–212, 215–216, 216–217, 218, 221–222, 222–224, 224, 225–227, 231–233, 233–235, 235, 239–241, 243–246, 246, 248–249, 249–251, 254–255, 255–256, 256–257, 257–258, 258–259, 262–263, 264–265, 266, 269–271, 274–

276, 276, 277–278, 284–286, 286, 288–289, 290, 290–291, 292, 292–293, 295–296, 300–301, 302, 306–307, 310–313, 314–315, 315–316, 320–322, 324, 330–331, 334–335, 335, 335–336, 341–342, 343, 345–346, 348–350, 351–352, 354–356, 357, 360–362, 364–367, 369–370, 370–372, 373–374, 374, 375, 379–380, 382–384, 386–387, 387, 387–388, 392–393, 398–400, 400, 402–403, 404, 405, 407–408, 408–409; mention, 368–369, 374, 380, 381, 428, 429, 430, 431, 432, 433, 435, 454, 455, 456, 457, 458, 464, 465, 473, 475, 487, 556, 557, 566, 569, 575, 576, 580, 584, 585, 586, 593, 614, 615, 620, 631, 635, 636, 676, 679, 700, 713, 714, **II**, 2, 15, 17, 57, 63, 110, 111, 112, 113, 115, 116, 118, 119, 121, 125, 130, 134, 141, 147, 148, 151, 152, 153, 157, 158, 161, 162, 168, 169, 170, 173, 174, 183, 184, 185, 187, 189, 198, 204, 219, 220, 229, 230, 231, 237, 246, 251, 253, 259, 260, 261, 268, 269, 272, 274, 656, 699, 728, **III**, 36, 74, 76, 96, 97, 100, 127, 137, 138, 156, 160, 197, 204, 212, 236, 278, 293, 307, 311, 321, 367, 452, 484, 492, 518, 526, 531, 532, 548, 549, 550, 552, 688, 719, 720, 721, 722, 723, 724, 725, 726, 727, 728, 729, 730
Mahan, Frederick Augustus: letter to, **II**, 438–439; mention, 1, 35, 103, 104, 121–122, 352, 620, 621, **II**, 83, 148, 172, 207, 235, 244, 439, 440, 447, 448, 464, 465, 720, **III**, 103, 151, 484, 491, 539
Mahan, Helen: 21
Mahan, Helen Evans ("Hennie," "Henny"): letters to, 574–577, 585–587, 700, **II**, 13–15, 15–17, 115–117, 125–126, 133–134, 147–148, 157–158, 168–170, 183–185, 195–198, 200–201, 219–220, 229–231, 246–248, 259–260, 266–269, 278–281, 304–305, 309–310, 317–320, 332–334, 343–344, 352–354, 362–364, 375–377, 378–379, 384–386, 395–397, 455–458; mention, 428, 429, 430–431, 431–432, 433, 434, 435, 454, 473, 475, 487, 556, 566, 567, 580, 584, 642, 676, **II**, 2, 114, 118, 124, 131, 132, 133, 137, 138, 139, 142, 146, 149, 150, 152, 159, 162, 164, 172, 173, 174, 179, 185, 187, 189, 193, 205, 217, 226, 231, 243, 245, 246, 248, 249, 254, 256, 264, 274, 277, 284, 288, 293–295, 302, 310, 320, 321, 341, 342, 343, 345, 346, 348, 350, 351, 355, 356, 357, 359, 365, 367, 368, 371, 373, 379, 381, 382, 386, 387, 389, 393, 402, 403, 404, 405, 408, 409, **III**, 128, 137, 138, 307, 549, 552, 719, 723, 724, 730
Mahan, Jane Leigh ("Jenny"): letters to, 104–107, 121–125, 134–137, 139–143, 334–336, 341–343, **II**, 296–300, 515; mention, 35, 111, 113, 120, 132, 137, 138, 205, 272, 281, 333, 340, 346, 347, **II**, 157, 172, 183, 217, 241, 288, 293, 302, 330, 336, 351, 355, 376, 380, 440, 656, 720, **III**, 539

Mahan, Jeannette Katherine Murat (Mrs. Dennis H. Mahan, Jr): **II**, 363, 463, 464, 465, 515–516, 516

Mahan, Lyle Evans ("Buster," "Laddie," "Major"): letters to, 569, 584; mention, 566, 567, 586, 642, 676, 700, **II**, 14, 49, 101, 125, 134, 137, 142, 146, 147, 152, 155, 156, 159, 162, 164, 166, 168, 172, 173, 174, 184, 185, 189, 198, 199, 220, 222, 224, 225, 230, 231, 251, 255, 257, 258, 259, 261, 264, 267, 274, 276, 277, 290, 291, 292, 293, 298, 302, 304, 305, 310, 311, 313, 315, 331, 333, 335, 341, 342, 344, 345, 346, 348, 354, 356, 363, 365, 368, 373, 374, 377, 379, 384, 386, 395, 400, 402, 403, 404, 405, 407, 408, 409, 419, 541, 560, 687, **III**, 28, 149, 195, 295, 451, 719, 720, 726, 727, 730

Mahan, Madeleine Johnson (Mrs. Lyle Evans Mahan): **III**, 719, 720

Mahan, Marion McCallum (Mrs. Lyle Evans Mahan): **III**, 720

Mahan, Mary: 1, 21

Mahan, Mary Griffitts Fisher Lewis (Mrs. Milo Mahan): 2, 50, 111, 132

Mahan, Mary Helena Okill (Mrs. Dennis H. Mahan, Sr.): letters to, 1, 96–97, 98, 99–104, 111–114, 117–121, 125–130, 131–133, 134, 137–139, 333–334, 368–369, 427–429, 430–431, 431–432; mention, 1, 8, 10, 14, 15, 17, 18, 19, 24, 36, 42, 44, 45, 49, 54, 57, 59, 66, 68, 69, 88, 104, 105, 107, 110, 117, 121, 135, 143, 147, 161, 162, 281, 306, 338, 340, 341, 367, 451, 455, 458, 465, 471, 475, 575, 620, 626, 639, 686, **II**, 97, 100, 160, 190, 262, 276, 351, 355, 448, 720, **III**, 295, 504, 720, 729

Mahan, Mary Morris (Mrs. Frederick A. Mahan): **II**, 464

Mahan, May: **II**, 439

Mahan, Millicent Moore (Mrs. Lyle Evans Mahan): **III**, 720

Mahan, the Rev. Milo: 2, 24, 45, 50, 104, 130, 133, 141, 167, 356, 358; **II**, 172

Mahan's Valley, Hiogo, Japan: 203, 217

Mahomet: 36; **III**, 690

Mahoney, John: **II**, 268

Maine: **II**, 426; **III**, 98

"Major": **II**, 311

Majuba Hill, South Africa: **II**, 674

Makaroff, Stephen O.: **III**, 92

Malacca, Straits of: **III**, 640

Málaga, Spain: **II**, 160, 162, 163, 165, 166, 167, 169, 171, 358, 359, 360, 363, 364, 366, 564, **III**, 587, 638; cathedral, **II**, 169, 363

Malampaya Sound, Palawan, Philippines: **III**, 387

Malea, Cape, Greece: **II**, 237

Mallory, Stephen Russell: 474–475

Malplaquet, France: **III**, 388

Malta: 142; **II**, 36, 84, 133, 146, 168, 200, 217, 219, 221, 235, 248, 254, 255; **III**, 358, 381, 383, 569

Mañá Dock, Montevideo, Uruguay: 417–418, 420, 424

Manchester, Duchess of: **II**, 311

Manchuria: **III**, 12, 27, 99, 109, 214, 221, 226, 264, 347, 355, 377, 411

Manhattan Brass Co.: 550

Manila, Luzon, Philippines: 247, 250, 253, 255, 262; **II**, 555, 564, 567, 582, 583, 590; **III**, 206, 267, 386, 402, 629, 639, 658, 659, 660, 661, 662

Mann, Edward C.: letter to, **II**, 347

Manorville, N.Y.: **III**, 478

Manta, Ecuador: 588, 589

Manton, Benjamin: 417

Maranhão, Brazil: 98

Marcy, Samuel: 13, 60, 79

Marcy, William L.: **III**, 549

Marengo, Italy: **III**, 388

Marie Antoinette: **II**, 197

Marie Galante, Leeward Islands: 629

Marlborough Club (London): **II**, 134

Marlborough, John Churchill, 1st Duke of: **III**, 388

Marmont, de, Auguste Frederic: **III**, 325, 326; at Salamanca, **III**, 191

Marrowstone Point, W.T.: 715

Marryat, Frederick: 445; **II**, 264, 279, 297

Marseilles, France: 139, 352; **II**, 171, 173, 174, 175, 176, 178, 360, 363, 368, 371, 372, 373, 374, 376, 377, 381, 397, 402, 481, 482, 489, **III**, 720

Marsh, Othniel Charles: **II**, 515

Marshall, Charles H.: **II**, 234

Marshall Islands: **III**, 377

Marshall, John: **III**, 158

Marshall, W. L.: **III**, 282

Marshfield, Ore.: 673

Marston, John: 493

Marston, Roy B.: letters to, **II**, 93, 493–494, 531, **III**, 530–531; mention, **II**, 93, 135, 178, 179, 186, 191, 270, 271, 272–273, 274, 275, 277, 295–296, 319, 321, 349, 460, 466, 467, 473, 475, 478, 479, 485, 487, 489, 490, 495, 497, 498, 500, 502, 513, 517, 518, 519, 521, 522, 523, 532, 548, 549, 596, 598, 610, 616, 618, 621, 622, 623, 626, 632, 633, 703, 716, 729, **III**, 35, 81, 99, 150, 151, 176, 177, 199, 296, 377

Martens, M.: **II**, 675; **III**, 13

Martha's Vineyard, Mass.: **II**, 427

Martin, the Rev. Thomas W.: **III**, 721

Martinez, Antonio: 588

Martin Garcia Island, Argentina: 402, 403

Martinique, Windward Islands: **II**, 37, 556, 723; **III**, 441, 445, 452, 453, 489, 542, 629, 630, 631

Mary, Queen of Scots: **II**, 299

Maryland: 90; **II**, 562, 563

Maryland Hotel (Annapolis): 475

Mason, George C., Jr.: **II**, 45, 46

Mason, George C., and Son: **II**, 45, 46, 49, 50, 51, 52

Mason family: **II**, 366

Mason, Theodorus Bailey Meyer: **II**, 424

Mason, William Pinckney: 555

Massachusetts Institute of Technology: **III**, 224

Matamoros, Mexico: **II**, 527, 528

Matapan, Cape, Greece: **II**, 237

Mathews Thomas: **II**, 722, 723, 725, 731; **III**, 119

Mathias Point, Va.: 90

Matinicus Rock, Me.: **II**, 427

Matthews, Edmund Orville: 493

Matthews, James Brander: letters to, **III**, 3, 43, 44; mention, **III**, 3

Matthews, Mr.: **II**, 245

Maturin, Basil William: **II**, 221

Maudslay, Mrs.: **II**, 541

Maurice, Sir John Frederick: **II**, 105; **III**, 90

Maurice, Prince of Orange: **II**, 384

Mauritius, Indian Ocean: **II**, 384

Maxse, Leopold J.: letters to, **II**, 732, 735, 735–736, 742–743, **III**, 5–6, 7, 8, 11–12, 12–13, 15–16, 17, 22–23, 25–26, 26–27, 29, 30, 32–33, 33–34, 34–36, 37, 37–38, 40, 49–50, 52–53, 58–59, 60–61, 62, 63–64, 71–73, 96–97, 98–99, 100, 101, 102, 102–103, 109, 131, 141, 144–145, 146–147, 148–149, 152–153, 172, 181–182, 192, 204–205, 207, 209, 210, 211, 213–214, 215–216, 220–222, 242, 243–244, 251–252, 485, 486–487; mention, **II**, 732, **III**, 23, 33, 60, 315

Mayne, Richard Charles: **II**, 117

Mazet, Robert: **II**, 667, 668, 671

Meade, Richard Worsam: 325; **II**, 302

Medanich, Rocco A.: 389, 408, 410

Mediterranean: 607; **II**, 1, 35, 44, 48, 49, 84, 114, 148, 167, 178, 186, 188, 237, 247, 254, 330, 334, 345, 350, 354, 368, 369, 380, 382, 384, 388, 391, 408, 412, 418, 570, 572, 581, 589, 618, 621, 683; **III**, 49, 492, 529, 639, 699, 710, 727

Medley, Vice Adm.: **III**, 132

Meigs, J. F.: 637, 657, 716; **II**, 3, 12, 33, 40, 43, 82; **III**, 663

Meiji, Era of the: **III**, 499

Melby, Mr.: 170

Melville, George Wallace: **II**, 528

Memphis, Tenn.: 548, **III**, 388

Mendell, George H.: 715

Mentone, France: **II**, 206

Mercantile Library Association: **II**, 340

Merrell, John P.: letters to, **III**, 233, 238, 247, 248, 269, 269–270, 271–272, 272, 273, 298, 300, 300–301, 303, 303–304, 308, 309–310, 310–311, 311, 312, 314; mention, **III**, 233,

248, 299, 309, 316, 317, 318, 319, 320, 322, 324, 327, 330, 331, 332

Merrell, Mrs. John P.: **III**, 311

Merrell, Miss: **III**, 312

Merrimon, Augustus Summerfield: 434, 436–437, 438, 439, 440, 442, 451, 470, 474

Mersin, Turkey: **II**, 246, 247, 248

Mesier, the Rev. Henry: **III**, 721

Messina, Italy: **II**, 331

Messina, Straits of: **II**, 237

Metcalf, Victor H.: **III**, 236, 269, 662

Metropolitan Club (New York): **II**, 623; **III**, 551

Mexico: 599; **III**, 377, 512, 514, 520, 523

Mexico, Gulf of: 111, 547, 548, 607; **II**, 37, 38, 127, 584, 618; **III**, 312, 353, 354, 355, 357, 369, 426, 458, 560, 568, 574; international tension in (1858), 35–36

Mexican Revolution (1913): **III**, 512

Mexican War: **III**, 542, 545, 674

Meyer Code: **II**, 338

Meyer, George von Lengerke: letters to, **III**, 319, 332, 374–375, 399–404; mention, **II**, 634, **III**, 289, 317, 319, 334, 349, 360, 367, 369, 373, 526

Michie, Peter S.: **II**, 535

Michigan, naval reserve units in Spanish-American War: **II**, 577

Milan, Italy: **III**, 720

Miles, Charles R.: letter to 666–669; mention, 666

Miles, Nelson A.: **II**, 573, 612, 613, 620, 653, 684, 692, 727; **III**, 74

Military Historical Society of Massachusetts: **II**, 417, 534, 604, 666; **III**, 676

Millard, Thomas F.: **II**, 708

Miller, Charles R.: letters to, **III**, 544, 547; mention, **III**, 544

Miller, Jack: **II**, 146

Miller, Joseph N.: **II**, 38

Miller, Merrill: **II**, 507

Mills, Thomas B.: 299

Milner, Sir Alfred: **II**, 678; **III**, 9, 51

Milnes, Robert Offley Ashburton Crewe, 2nd Baron Houghton: **II**, 116, 117, 118, 135, 140, 267, 297

Milton, John: 576; **II**, 308; **III**, 273

Mincio, Italy: **III**, 412

Mineola, N.Y.: **III**, 478, 480

Minerva, Temple of, Cape Colonna, Greece: **II**, 238

Minnesota: 451

Minor, Benjamin Blake: 710

Minorca: **II**, 377, 381; **III**, 569

Mintoyne, William L.: 442

Missions, Christian, relationships with governments: **III**, 501, 502, 507, 508, 509

Mississippi River: 548, 675; **III**, 357, 388, 666

Mitchell, Edward P.: letters to, **II**, 530, **III**, 89–90; mention, **II**, 530

Mitchell, John Hipple: 698, 710, 714–715
Mitchell, Richard: 404
Mitchell, Silas Weir: **II**, 474, 491
Mito clan: 128
Mitré, Bartolomé: 389, 399, 400, 422, 425
Mittler and Son: **III**, 444, 451, 456
Mobile, Ala.: 548, 555; **III**, 354
Mocha, Yemen: 112
Mollendo, Peru: 560
Moltke, von, Helmuth: **II**, 450; **III**, 410
Moluccas Indonesia: **III**, 377
Molyneux Harbor, Chile: 564, 565
Mommsen, Theodor: **II**, 17, 493
Monomoy, Mass.: **II**, 427
Monro, Hugh R.: letters to, **III**, 210–211, 335–336; mention, **III**, 210
Monroe Doctrine: 482, 573; **II**, 442, 452, 529, 536, 566–567, 589, 710, 711, 714, 715, 719, 737, 744, 745; **III**, 1, 5, 6, 14, 19, 20, 49, 50, 58–59, 60, 80, 139, 291, 292, 307, 342, 345, 346, 353, 357, 408, 412, 420, 428, 435, 436, 442, 443, 444, 445, 446, 452, 453, 454, 457–459, 464, 474, 477, 542, 687
Monroe, James: **III**, 122, 123, 124, 125, 126, 127, 128, 132, 454, 671
Montauk, N.Y.: **II**, 426; **III**, 564, 568
Monte Carlo, Monaco: **III**, 356
Monte Cristo, Ecuador: 588
Montevideo, Uruguay: 89, 90, 91, 333, 375, 376, 377, 378, 379, 380, 381, 382, 383, 385, 386, 387, 388, 391, 392, 394, 395, 397, 401, 403, 405, 406, 407, 410, 411, 412, 413, 414, 415, 416, 417, 422, 423, 424, 425, 426, 427, 429, 432, 433, 573; **II**, 157, 159; **III**, 723
Montgomery, William S.: **II**, 227, 228
Montoya, Gen.: 609
Montpelier, Vt.: 557
Montreal, Quebec: **II**, 524, 685; **III**, 76, 565, 566, 604
Montserrat, Leeward Islands: **II**, 173
Moody Commission: **III**, 278–279, 279, 280–281, 282, 283, 284, 285, 286, 288, 309, 320
Moody, William H.: letters to, **III**, 41–42, 278–279, 280–281, 283, 286, 290; mention, **III**, 41, 110, 282, 288, 289, 661
Moon Temple, Hiogo, Japan: 222, 335
Moon, William S.: 84
Moore, John: 312–313, 313, 314
Moore, John Bassett: letters to, **II**, 688–689, 689, 690, 695, **III**, 16, 17–22, 44, 44–45, 45, 87, 87–88, 109–110, 114, 115–116, 117–118, 120, 122, 123, 125–126, 129, 149–150, 444, 444–445, 456, 461–463, 532–533, 534, 534–535; mention, **II**, 579, **III**, 434, 438, 444, 514, 533, 721
Moore, Thomas: 388
Moore, Thomas (poet): 23
Moors: **II**, 161, 164
Moran, the Rev. Samuel W.: **III**, 721
Mordecai, Mrs.: 140

Moreau, Jean Victor: **III**, 344
Morey, H. L.: 488
Morgan, E. D.: **II**, 474
Morgan, Harjes and Co.: **II**, 548, 550
Morgan, J. Pierpont: 707, 712; **II**, 159, 474; **III**, 438
Morgan, J. S., and Co.: **II**, 548, 549
Morgan, Mrs.: **II**, 170, 377
Morialdi, Vincente: 415
Morley, Albert W.: letters to, 416, 421; mention, 393, 402
Morley, John, Viscount Morley of Blackburn: **II**, 131, 141, 142, 144, 277, 278
Mornit Light, River Plate: 419
Morocco: **II**, 162, 358; **III**, 342, 459, 473
Morris, Capt.: **III**, 88
Morris, Carrie (Mrs. James Cheston): 576
Morris family: **III**, 138
Morris, Charles: **III**, 253
Morris, Eugenia (Mrs. Radcliff Cheston): 576
Morris, Gouverneur, papers of: **II**, 541
Morris, William O'Connor: **II**, 116, 123, 149, 479, 490, 512, 610
Morrison, Alfred: **II**, 476, 500, 512, 513; **III**, 119
Morristown, N.J.: 626; **II**, 388
Morse, Edwin Wilson: **III**, 547
Morton, James St. C.: 43–44
Morton, Levi P.: 455; **II**, 290, 474
Morton, Paul: **III**, 282, 283, 287, 288
Moseley, James C.: 78, 79
Moses, W. B., and Son: **II**, 71, 73
Motley, John Lothrop: 267; **II**, 260, 304
Mott, John R.: **III**, 335
Mount Desert Island, Me.: 435, 454, 455, 487, 620, 621, 633; **II**, 119
Mt. Edgecumbe, Plymouth, England: **III**, 28, 35
Mt. Hope Bay, R.I.: 671
Mountsier, Robert: letters to, **III**, 253, 255–256
Mozambique Channel: 107
Muldaur, Alonzo W.: 299, 321, 354
Mullan, Dennis W.: 316
Mullan, Horace E.: 316
Muller, Lt.: **II**, 672
Mumford, W. W.: letter to, **III**, 295; mention, **III**, 11
Muñoz, J. M.: letters to, 417–418, 420; mention, 417
Murdock, J. B.: **II**, 82
Murphy, Charles F.: **III**, 364
Murray, Ambrose S.: letters to, 2; mention, 2
Murray, John, Co.: **III**, 296, 377
Murviedro, Spain: **II**, 167
Muscat, Arabia: 110, 112, 113; **III**, 35; M. describes appearance and politics of, 114
Muskegat Channel, Nantucket Sound: **II**, 426
Mussulmans: 108; **II**, 129, 248, 357

Nagasaki, Japan: 115, 117, 119, 120, 123, 124, 224, 225, 226, 236, 298, 299, 300, 301, 304, 309, 310, 311, 312, 313, 314, 317, 339, 341, 348, **III**, 688; consuls at, 311, 312
Nahant, Mass.: 366
Nanaimo, B. C.: **III**, 570, 575
Nantes, France: **II**, 144
Nantucket, Mass.: **II**, 425, 427, 428; **III**, 564
Nantucket Shoals: 538
Nantucket Sound: **II**, 425, 426, 427, 428
Napier, Robert Cornelis, 1st Baron Napier of Magdala: 65, 70; **III**, 1
Naples, Italy: **II**, 84, 178, 200, 217, 219, 220, 222, 223, 224, 232, 236, 237, 239, 250, 252, 259, 331, 379, 383, 543, 545, 548, **III**, 569; M. describes, **II**, 225, 227, 234
Narragansett Bay, R. I.: **II**, 4; **III**, 77, 194, 195, 325, 354, 400, 488, 489, 562, 564, 574, 577
Natal, South Africa: 103; **III**, 51
National Arbitration and Peace Congress: **III**, 208
National Archives (U.S.): 641, 698
National Coast Defense Board (U.S.): **III**, 661
Navy History Society: **III**, 528
Navy League: **II**, 205
Navy Records Society: 700; **II**, 485, 674; **III**, 119
Nazro, Arthur Phillips: **II**, 140, 169, 174, 180, 194, 206, 211, 218, 233, 238, 282, 311, 323, 342, 366, 398, 399
Neeser, Robert W.: letter to, **III**, 22; mention, **III**, 22, 157
Negril Bay, Jamaica: **III**, 120, 143
Negroes: 33, 76, 113, 120, 235, 338, 355; **II**, 206, 616, 617; **III**, 190, 214, 498
Negus Company: 494–495, 529
Nelson, Horatio, Viscount: 17, 629; **II**, 67, 89, 110, 116, 136, 138, 143, 147, 227, 230, 268, 273, 297, 318, 328, 332, 347, 359, 377, 419, 426, 430, 432, 434, 441, 453, 454, 462, 463, 470, 476, 477, 478, 481, 486, 488, 492, 507, 514, 571, 574, 576, 577, 580, 594, 616, 618, 621, 660, 681; **III**, 48, 118, 138, 149, 155, 276, 337, 394, 404, 569, 638, 694
Nelson, Horatio, 3rd Earl: **II**, 318, 320, 328, 500; **III**, 119
Nelson, Lady: **II**, 332, 333, 349, 478, 485, 486, 487, 491, 492, 495, 623, 624, 626
Nelson, Maurice Horatio: **II**, 318
Nelson, the Rev.: 38
Nelson, the Rev. Dr.: 238, 241, 242, 243
Neptunite: 492–493
Netherlands: **II**, 304
Nevada: **III**, 221
Nevin, the Rev. Robert Jenkins: **II**, 234, 316, 319, 328
Nevis, Leeward Islands: **II**, 660

Newberry, Truman H.: **III**, 236, 275
Newbury, England: **II**, 325, 327
Newcome, C. S.: letter to, 89–91; mention, 89
Newel, Stanford: **II**, 706, 708, 713; **III**, 18; letter to John Hay, **II**, 706
Newell, John Stark: **II**, 32, 95, 405
New England: **II**, 239, 341, **III**, 434; temperance in, 256
New England Bunting Co.: 521
New Forest, England: **II**, 333
Newfoundland: **II**, 1
New Guinea: **II**, 18; **III**, 377
New Haven, Conn.: **II**, 516
New Jersey: **II**, 251, 306; **III**, 488
New Jersey Central Railroad: **II**, 293
New Jersey Chapter of the Society of the Cincinnati: **III**, 592
New London, Conn.: 556; **III**, 564, 664
Newman, John Henry: 434
Newman, William B.: letters to, 388–389, 400; mention, 388, 404, 416, 505
New Nationalism: **III**, 364
New Orleans Expedition (British): **III**, 120, 142, 143
New Orleans, La.: 94, 546, 547, 548, 656, 700; **III**, 54, 56, 120, 143, 167, 170, 354, 371, 393
Newport, R.I.: 525, 613, 614, 620, 621, 625, 627, 635, 636, 642, 677, 687, 691, 692, 700, 714, 715, 716, **II**, 2, 5, 7, 12, 13, 28, 30, 33, 34, 43, 44, 45, 58, 64, 66, 70, 71, 72, 74, 89, 90, 94, 97, 120, 147, 150, 230, 240, 277, 288, 417, 420, 421, 432, 445, 459, 460, 466, 467, 478, 523, 592, **III**, 306, 312, 313, 314, 318, 327, 328, 329, 349, 411, 412, 415, 423, 440, 500, 663, 667, 721, 725, 726; Almshouse, **III**, 663; cliffs, **III**, 579; Library, **III**, 312; Town Council, 664
Newport Conference: **III**, 284, 301
Newport Town Council: 664
New York City: 1, 2, 33, 36, 41, 42, 43, 44, 45, 46, 55, 78, 82, 91, 96, 107, 121, 129, 335, 337, 342, 348, 355, 356, 357, 429, 455, 514, 534, 536, 556, 557, 568, 583, 588, 602, 614, 615, 621, 629, 630, 633, 647, 686, 687, 713, 714, **II**, 20, 22, 25, 27, 34, 35, 39, 49, 52, 54, 55, 57, 62, 64, 70, 90, 94, 101, 105, 114, 119, 123, 124, 128, 138, 140, 155, 157, 158, 159, 163, 170, 176, 177, 186, 190, 197, 219, 224, 229, 231, 233, 240, 245, 257, 271, 280, 292, 296, 313, 321, 322, 325, 331, 333, 339, 343, 346, 354, 355, 365, 371, 373, 378, 386, 395, 397, 400, 401, 402, 403, 404, 405, 407, 408, 414, 415, 416, 418, 419, 420, 421, 426, 428, 434, 435, 443, 460, 464, 468, 471, 482, 509, 511, 523, 527, 534, 543, 559, 585, 596, 601, 605, 606, 680, 690, 725, 732, **III**, 55, 56, 57, 58, 62, 63, 76, 88, 96, 97, 127, 137, 138, 144, 145, 147, 148, 160, 161, 177, 194, 197, 216, 232, 233, 241, 242, 272, 277, 284, 287, 288,

289, 299, 301, 307, 311, 312, 313, 314, 325, 328, 340, 353, 354, 355, 356, 357, 362, 364, 371, 397, 399, 400, 405, 426, 427, 428, 429, 436, 445, 447, 452, 464, 478, 486, 493, 504, 505, 506, 510, 512, 513, 514, 515, 516, 517, 518, 524, 531, 534, 537, 549, 551, 560, 562, 563, 564, 565, 567, 568, 569, 570, 574, 575, 591, 595, 596, 597, 598, 605, 606, 629, 667, 668, 675, 678, 679, 685, 719, 720, 721, 726, 729, 730; Chamber of Commerce, **II**, 611; harbor, 538, **II**, 153, **III**, 194, 472, 568; Police Board, **II**, 449

New-York Historical Society: **II**, 314

New York Lyceum: 617, 627; **II**, 33

New York Peace Society: **II**, 739; **III**, 530

New York Public Library (Astor Library): M. donates collected Nelson materials to, **III**, 48–49, 50, 138–139; offers collected Boer War materials to, **III**, 51; advises on building collection, **III**, 118–120, 121–122, 131–132; assists in building collection, **III**, 140, 389; mention, 630, 634, 650, **II**, 2, 33, 386, 430, 478, 511, 517, 695, 721, **III**, 32, 37, 49, 51, 52, 138, 139, 140, 200, 242, 279, 326, 389, 721

New York State: 457, 459, 488, **III**, 221, 271, 364, 365, 409, 488, 489; Volunteers, **II**, 533

New York State Chapter of the Colonial Order: **III**, 596

New York State Public Service Commission: letters to, **III**, 478–479, 480; mention, **III**, 479, 480

New York State Senate: **III**, 365

New York Stock Exchange: **II**, 504

New York Telephone Co.: letter to, **III**, 495

New York University, alumni dinner of: **III**, 18

New York Yacht Club: **II**, 474

New Zealand: **III**, 216, 217, 377, 427, 468

Niagara Falls, N.Y.: **III**, 78, 81, 82, 83, 84

Niblack, A. P.: **II**, 82

Nicaragua: 357, 599; **II**, 101, 444

Nicaraguan Canal: **II**, 75, 82, 506, 584, 588–589, 589, 590; **III**, 9, 603

Nicaraguan Canal Commission: 507

Nice, France: 352; **II**, 125, 155, 160, 162, 172, 178, 181, 182, 185, 186, 188, 190, 191, 192, 195, 196, 199, 217, 219, 220, 221, 223, 230, 233, 244, 260, 313, 318, 321, 331, 342, 344, 346, 351, 352, 356, 365, 368, 373, 374, 375, 376, 377, 378, 382, 383, 384, 385, 388, 389, 392, 393, 396, 397, 399, 400, 401; **III**, 727, 729

Nichols, Edward T.: 436, 437

Nichols, Mr.: 164

Nicholson, Stuart James: **II**, 260

Nickels, J. A.: **II**, 341

Niebuhr, Barthold George: **II**, 514

Niigata, Japan: 225, 229, 341

Nile River: **II**, 1, 251, 253, 571, 577; **III**, 639

Nimes, France: **II**, 174, 175, 560

Nineveh, Assyria: **II**, 356

Nipe, Bay of, Cuba: **II**, 588, 590

Noble, Alfred: **III**, 9

Noel, Capt.: **II**, 285

Noel, Florence Kirkland (Mrs. York Noel): **II**, 341, 360, 380, 381, 383, 399

Noel, York: **II**, 341, 360, 364, 381, 383, 399

Nones, Henry Beauchamp: 147, 149, 152, 180, 192, 193, 199, 203, 223, 225, 226, 247, 268, 284, 296

Norfolk, Va.: 528, 687; **II**, 726; **III**, 357, 562, 575

Norman, Mr.: **II**, 501

Norris, Sir John: **II**, 722

North, the (U.S., Civil War): 26, 29, 88, 434, 625, 636; **II**, 380; **III**, 196, 542, 703

North Atlantic coast: **II**, 590; **III**, 666

North Atlantic Ocean: 101; **II**, 12, 38, 621; **III**, 98

Northbrook, Thomas George Baring, 2nd Baron: **II**, 135

North Carolina: 3, 26, 367, 465, 470

Northcliffe, Alfred Charles William Harmsworth, 1st Viscount: **III**, 213

Northcliffe, Lady: **III**, 213

North German Lloyd Steamship Co.: **III**, 593

North Pacific Ocean: **II**, 92

North Pole: **III**, 569

North Sea: **III**, 699, 700, 707, 710

Northwestern boundary dispute: **III**, 524

North Western Hotel (Liverpool): 366

Norton, Albert L.: **II**, 242

Norton, Miss: **II**, 326

Nourse, Joseph E. ("Holy Joe," "Old Joe"): 10, 11, 13, 18, 19, 26, 54, 56, 60, 83

Nova Scotia: **II**, 426; **III**, 77, 561, 562, 563, 566, 569, 573, 574

Noyes, Mrs. Boutelle: 714; **II**, 2, 57

Nuku Hiva, Marquesas Islands: **III**, 383

Oahu, Hawaiian Islands: **III**, 382, 391, 392, 393

Oak Bay, W.T.: 715

O'Brien, John: 162, 225, 261

Ochs, Adolph S.: **III**, 547

O'Connor, William: 568

Ogden, Cadwalader: **II**, 114

Ogden, Mrs. Cadwalader: **II**, 114

Ogden, David B.: **II**, 210, 211, 212, 217, 224, 225, 231, 237, 239, 240, 266; **III**, 102, 364

Ogden, Edith: **II**, 131, 145, 333

Ogden family: **II**, 203

Ogden, Frank: **II**, 197

Ogden, Mrs. Frank: **II**, 197

Ogden, Gouverneur Morris ("Gouv"): letter to, **II**, 144–145; mention, **II**, 114, 131, 133, 135, 147, 207, 210, 211, 234, 266, 324, 333, 404

Ogden, Harriet Verena Evans (Mrs. Gouverneur M. Ogden) ("Aunt O."): 435; **II**, 114, 134, 145, 329, 331, 333, 364, 404
Ogden, Morgan Lewis: 75, 77
Ogden, Tom: **II**, 349
Ogdensburg, N.Y.: **III**, 565, 570, 575–576
Oglesby, Miss: 315, 322, 326
Ohio: 455; **III**, 221, 478
O'Kane, James ("Jim"): 13, 19, 20, 22, 23, 26, 31, 33, 34, 37; **II**, 38
Okill, James: **II**, 448, 720, 727
Okill, Mary Jay: letter to, 1; mention, 1, 41, 46, 48, 51, 576, **II**, 351, 447, 448, 720, **III**, 524
Old Corner Bookstore in Boston: 707
Old Point Comfort, Va.: 43
Oliphant's (Shanghai): 242, 283, 284, 286, 288
Oliver, James H.: 591
Oliver, Mrs.: **II**, 309
Olney, Richard: **III**, 286, 434, 437, 440
Olson, Edward M.: letters to, 383, 384; mention, 380, 389
Olson, Mrs. Edward M.: 380, 381
Olympia, W.T.: 673, 688, 699; letter to mayor of, 673–675
160 W. 86th St.: **II**, 416, 419, 468, 527, 690, 732; **III**, 55, 138, 140, 141, 150, 160, 161, 177, 197, 204, 216, 232, 233, 284, 299, 371, 439
Oneida, Lake, N.Y.: **III**, 76
O'Neil, Charles: letters to, 416, 418–419, 421, 423; **III**, 66–67, 67; mention, 416
O'Neil, Charles, Jr.: 416
O'Neil, Richard Frothingham: 416
Onetti Company: **III**, 586
Ontario, Canada: **III**, 82, 83
Ontario, Lake: **II**, 36; **III**, 78, 82, 565, 576, 672
Oregon: 51, 710; **III**, 377
Oregon Dispute: **III**, 524
O'Reily, Timothy: **II**, 291
Oriental Association of Tokyo: **II**, 511, 513
Orote Peninsula, Guam: **III**, 398, 399
Osaka, Japan: 117, 119, 122, 125, 126, 127, 128, 136, 150, 183, 195; M. describes, 334–335, 337
Osborn, Thomas O.: letters to, 419–420, 425, 426; mention, 419, 422
Osborne, Mr.: 330
Osborne, royal estate, England: **II**, 128, 144, 310, 327
Ostrom, H. R.: **II**, 677, 679
Ottawa, Ontario: **III**, 65, 81, 83, 136, 145, 566
Ottawa River, Canada: **III**, 566
Oudenaarde, Belgium: **III**, 388
Ovtchinnikow, de Vaissian: **II**, 636
Owens-Glass Act (1913): **III**, 512
Owens, Miss: 77
Oxford and Asquith, Herbert Henry Asquith, 1st Earl of: **II**, 131; **III**, 370

Oxford Movement: 188
Oxford University: **II**, 285, 286, 290, 291, 294, 297, 298, 327, 397; **III**, 34, 727
Oyster Bay, L.I.: **III**, 74, 164, 169
Oysterville, W.T.: 674

Pacific: 572; **II**, 26, 82, 93, 286, 343, 345, 346, 365, 506, 529, 538, 570, 582, 583, 584, 590; **III**, 77, 80, 109, 113, 165, 205, 206, 226, 353, 355, 356, 357, 369, 371, 373, 382, 383, 385, 388, 390, 393, 400, 401, 402, 403, 404, 410, 439, 458, 532, 570, 574, 575, 604, 629, 637, 639
Pacific Cable Co.: **II**, 555
Pacific Coast: 672; **II**, 93, 538, 539, 567, 583, 684; **III**, 217, 221, 226, 263, 334, 353, 355, 356, 367, 372, 383, 384, 385, 388, 390, 392, 400, 420, 436, 452, 453, 500
Pacific Journal (Oysterville, W.T.): letter to editor of, 673–675
Pacific Mail (P.M.S.S.): 121, 132, 134, 137, 139, 162
Pacific Steam Navigation Co.: 567
Paddock, J. D.: 33
Padgett, Lemuel: **III**, 414
Page and Williams Co.: 533
Page, Charles H.: 118
Page, Thomas Nelson: letter to, **III**, 321; mention, **III**, 321
Page, Walter Hines: letters to, **II**, 520, 521, 524, **III**, 41; mention, **II**, 155, 479, 505, 507
Pago-Pago, Samoa: **II**, 583, 590
Paine, Frederick Henry: 212, 293, 298
Pakenham, Sir Edward Michael: **III**, 143
Palermo, Sicily: **II**, 331, 379, **III**, 491, 493, 510, 569
Palfrey, J. C.: 637
Palisades property. *See* Tenafly, N.J.
Palmer, Aulick: **II**, 296
Palmer House (Chicago): 613, 614
Palmer, James C.: **II**, 296
Palmley, Miss: 46
Palos Lagoon, Almirante Bay, Colombia: **II**, 589
Panama: 46, 482, 589, 594, 595, 597, 598, 599, 602, 606, 607, 608, 609, 610, 612, 615, 626, 646; **II**, 583, 584, 684; **III**, 9, 355, 377, 390, 400, 401, 462, 463, 477
Panama Canal: **II**, 584, 588; **III**, 159, 202, 307, 355, 373, 377, 383, 385, 388, 396, 400, 401, 402, 403, 404, 409, 414, 430, 432, 437, 445, 452, 453, 458, 459, 464, 474, 477, 486, 487, 532, 603
Panama Canal Act: **III**, 476–477, 483, 489, 490
Panama, Isthmus of: 572, 595; **II**, 583, 588, 590; **III**, 353, 371, 401, 463
Panama Railroad Co.: 595
Panic of 1873: 430
Pan-Slavism: **III**, 609
Papacy: **II**, 591; **III**, 59

Para, Brazil: **III**, 54
Paraguay: 381, 386, 389, 395, 398, 399, 401, 415–416
Paraguay River: 402, 403, 404
Paraná, Argentina: 382, 385, 397, 398, 402
Paraná River, Argentina: 357, 377, 378, 397, 402, 403, 416
Paris, France: 351, 352, 353, 329; **II**, 125, 171, 175, 185, 360, 440, 560, 570, 579, 626; **III**, 484, 485, 491, 581, 595, 629, 720
Paris, siege of: **III**, 698
Parker, Alexis duPont: **II**, 393
Parker, Foxhall Alexander: letter to, 471–472; mention, 458, 466, 471, 472, 473
Parker House (Boston): 613
Parker, Sir Hyde: **II**, 484, 577
Parker, Mary Lewis (Mrs. Stevens Parker): 50; **II**, 256, 257, 264, 277–278, 393. See Lewis, Mary
Parker, Sir Peter: **II**, 484
Parker Publishing Co.: **III**, 274
Parker, Richard Wayne: **III**, 620
Parker, the Rev. Stevens: 50; **II**, 256
Parker, Sir William, Sr.: **II**, 317; **III**, 472
Parker, Sir William: **II**, 317–318, 480, 481, 485, 487, 491, 500
Parker, William Harwar: 471; **III**, 57
Parkes, Sir Harry Smith: 138
Parkes, Lady: 157
Parkin, Sir George Robert: **II**, 654, 671; **III**, 28
Parnell, Charles Stewart: **II**, 313
Parrish, Samuel L.: letter to, **III**, 466
Pass, F. W.: 679
Passaic Bay, N.J.: **II**, 293
Patagonia, Argentina: 587
Patmos, Dodecanese Islands: **II**, 246, 247
Patuxent River: **III**, 132–133
Pau, France: 428, 429, 430, 462, 463, 464, 473; **II**, 560; **III**, 141, 145, 146, 148, 149, 151, 152, 156, 481, 484, 485, 487, 488, 489, 490, 491, 509, 623, 720, 723
Paul I, Czar of Russia: **II**, 197
Paulding family: 110
Pauncefote, Sir Julian: **II**, 406, 690
Pavilion Hotel (Sharon Springs, N.Y.): 368
Payn, Louis F.: **II**, 676
Payne, O. H.: **III**, 240
Paysandú, Uruguay: 381
Payta, Peru: 581, 589, 609, 610
Peabody, Endicott: letters to, **II**, 49, 101–102, 103, 542, 560; mention, **II**, 49
Peabody, Mrs. Endicott: **II**, 542, 560
Peabody, George Foster: **III**, 190, 302
Peace Congresses of 1910 and 1912: **III**, 530
Peace movement: **III**, 207, 223, 277, 308, 444, 474, 489, 516
Pearl Harbor, Hawaii: **III**, 356, 357, 380, 381, 382, 396, 400, 401, 402, 403, 404, 661

Pears, Sir Edwin: **III**, 505, 506, 511, 683–684, 686, 690
Pearson, Frederick: 559, 562, 584
Pearson, Sir Richard: **II**, 545, 547; **III**, 118, 121, 131, 139
Pease, Mr.: **II**, 410–411
Peekskill, N.Y.: 693, 695, 697
Peel, Sir Robert: **III**, 132
Peking, China: **II**, 582, 693, 708
"Pelicans" (USNA): 18, 33
Pell, Edith Harris: 111, 333
Pellew, Edward, Viscount Exmouth. See Exmouth
Pendergast, Austin: **III**, 61
Pendleton, George Hunt: **III**, 143
P. & O. [Peninsula and Orient] Steamship Co.: 112, 121, 132, 139, 334
Peninsula Campaign of 1862: 637
Pennington, Harper: **III**, 104–105
Penn's Cove, W.T.: 680
Pennsylvania: 455; **III**, 78, 221
Penobscot Bay, Me.: **II**, 425
Penobscot River Line: **III**, 566
Pensacola, Fla.: 700; **III**, 357
Pepper, George Wharton: **III**, 302
Perigueux, France: 464
Perkins, George C.: letter to, **III**, 371–372; mention, **III**, 371
Perkins, George Hamilton: 452
Perkins, Lyman B.: 471, 472
Permanent Court of Arbitration at the Hague: **III**, 514
Pernambuco, Brazil: 428
Perry, Bliss: letters to, **III**, 47, 51–52; mention, **III**, 47
Perry, Oliver Hazard: **III**, 67, 70, 101, 110, 111, 167, 313, 671
Perry, Thomas: **II**, 405
Persian Gulf: 110; **III**, 5, 6, 8, 12, 13, 26, 27, 32, 35, 96, 99, 109, 226
Persians: **III**, 492
Peru: 342, 421, 572; flags, 510
Pescadores Islands, Formosa: **III**, 387, 402
Peters, Horatio: 163, 176, 177, 248, 252–253
Peters, Ralph: **III**, 480
Peterson, William: letters to, **II**, 684, 685; mention, **II**, 684
Petropolis, Brazil: 99
Phelan, John Rogers: 321, 354
Phelps, Capt.: 281
Phelps, Edward John: **II**, 452, 474
Phelps, Mrs.: 140, 142, 151, 165, 181, 304, 316, 322, 323, 326, 327, 328
Philadelphia, Pa.: 46, 84, 91, 92, 454, 455, 457; **II**, 46, 258, 445, 486; **III**, 4, 45, 46, 77, 160, 484, 490, 548, 560, 568, 574, 644, 724
Philip, John W.: **II**, 623, 717, 717–718
Philippine Islands: **II**, 553, 555, 566, 567, 569, 579, 606, 619, 634, 635, 680, 722; **III**, 5, 7, 10–11, 80, 202, 205, 206, 355, 356, 357, 377,

Philippine Islands (*cont.*) 382, 384, 385, 387, 392, 401, 442, 477, 603, 637, 638, 658, 659, 660, 661, 662
Philippine Commission: **III**, 6
Philips, Col.: **II**, 311
Philips, George Morris: **II**, 368
Philips, John S.: **II**, 615
Philips, Mary E.: letter to, **III**, 519–520
Phillips, Paul: 81, 83
Phinney, William: 225
Phipps, Gen.: **III**, 552
Phythian, Robert L.: 715, 716; **II**, 53
Piacenza, Italy: **III**, 388
Pichilinque, Mexico: 611
Pictou Harbor, N.S., Canada: **III**, 562, 567, 568, 569
Pierce, Franklin: **III**, 549
Pigeons, carrier: **III**, 572
Pillsbury, John E.: **III**, 236, 304, 330
Pines, Isle of, Cuba: **III**, 641
Pingree, Hazen S.: **II**, 577
Pinkney, Ninian: 17, 59
Pinkney, William: **III**, 114, 125, 129, 130
Pitt, William (The Elder): **II**, 26, 507; **III**, 276
Pitt, William (The Younger): **II**, 26, 507; **III**, 612
Pittsburgh, Pa.: 355, 356
Placentia Bay, Newfoundland: **III**, 562
Plata, Rio de la [River Plate], So. America: 375, 377, 378, 383, 386, 387, 396, 397, 403, 411, 413, 414, 419, 423, 425, 426
Platt, Mr.: **II**, 416
Platt, Thomas C.: 715; **II**, 676, 692
Plattsburg, N.Y.: **III**, 83
Playa de Santa Rosa, Argentina: 413
Playfair, Lyon, 1st Baron of St. Andrews: **II**, 135
Playfair, Lady Edith Russell: **II**, 135
Pleven, Bulgaria: 469
Plimpton House (Watch Hill, R. I.): 557
Plum Gut, L. I. Sound: **II**, 426
Plum Island, L. I. Sound: **III**, 194
Plymouth, England: 363, 364; **II**, 133, 325, 335, 339, 343, 349, 352; **III**, 8, 10, 36, 203
Plutarch: **II**, 549
Poerras Lagoon, Almirante Bay, Colombia: **II**, 589
Point Balandra, St. Thomas: **II**, 587
Point Bucco, River Plate: 412
Pt. Glover, W.T.: 683
Pt. Jefferson, W.T.: 680
Pt. Judith, R.I.: 671; **III**, 325
Pt. Peninsula, N.Y.: **III**, 86
Point San José, River Plate: 393
Point Turner, W.T.: 681, 683, 715
Pt. Wilson, W.T.: 715
Pointe-à-Pitre, Guadeloupe: 97, 117, 130
Poland: **III**, 499

Pollock, Alsager: **III**, 389, 394
Pollock Rip, Nantucket Sound: **II**, 426
Pollonnais, Mayor: **II**, 190, 203, 221
Pollonnais, Mme.: **II**, 245
Pomfret, Conn.: **II**, 172, 176, 177, 314–315, 324
Pompeii, Italy: M. describes, **II**, 233
Ponsonby, Sir William Francis: **II**, 129
Popa Island, Colombia: **II**, 589
Pope, John: **II**, 699
Poppenac, Count: **II**, 143
Porcheit, Jules: 100
Port Arthur, Manchuria: **III**, 27, 92, 93, 94, 99, 101, 102, 103, 107, 109, 153, 155, 206, 245, 314
Port Culebra, Costa Rica: **II**, 584, 590
Port Elena, Costa Rica: **II**, 584, 590
Porteños Party: 381
Porter, Adm.: **II**, 474
Porter, David: **III**, 61, 64, 65, 545
Porter, David Dixon: 546, 656; **II**, 528, 704; **III**, 393
Porter, Hobart: **III**, 240
Porter, Horace: **II**, 551; **III**, 629
Porter, Thomas K.: 80
Porter's Sons, Chandlers: 489, 529, 533, 534, 535, 541
Port Gamble, W.T.: 679
Port Hudson, La.: **II**, 56
Portland, Me.: **III**, 103, 566, 573
Portland, Ore.: 673, 675, 699; letter to mayor of, 673, 675
Portland, William Henry Cavendish Bentinck, 3rd Duke of: **III**, 126
Port La Union, Salvador: **II**, 584
Port Mahon, Minorca: **II**, 160, 163, 572
Port Masinglock, Luzon, Philippines: **II**, 582
Port Matalvi, Luzon, Philippines: **II**, 584
Port Olongapo, Luzon, Philippines: **III**, 659, 661
Port Orchard, W.T.: 680, 681, 688, 695, 698, 699, 715; **III**, 570, 574, 576
Porto Rico: **II**, 551, 553, 554, 564, 565, 572, 584, 585, 586, 588, 612, 635; **III**, 357, 442, 634, 642
Port Royal, S.C.: **III**, 357
Portsmouth Conference: **III**, 117
Portsmouth, England: 662; **II**, 318
Portsmouth, N.H.: 53, 94, 114, 538; **III**, 357
Port Townsend, W.T.: 673, 698, 715; letter to mayor of, 673, 675
Portugal: **III**, 673, 688; flags, 510; coast, **II**, 67; language, **II**, 158; Boer War relationship, **II**, 689
Potomac River: 90
Potter, Bishop Henry Codman: **II**, 617; **III**, 605
Potter, William: **II**, 233, 234; **III**, 592
Potter, William P.: **II**, 149, 150, 180, 255

Powel, Mary Edith (Mrs. Samuel Powel, Jr.): letter to, II, 699; mention, II, 150, 302, 304, 468, 525
Powel, Samuel, Jr.: II, 150, 355, 468, 699
Pratt, John Francis: letters to, 680–681, 681, 685–686, 689, 690, 693–694, 704, 710–711; mention, 678, 691, 692, 693, 695, 696, 697, 698, 699, 701, 702, 703, 704, 705, 706, 709, 710
Pratt, Mrs. John Francis: 681, 686, 690, 704, 711
Prentiss, Roderick: 17, 30; III, 56
Presbyterian Church: 44, 57; Board of Foreign Missions of, III, 509
President Roads, Boston, Mass.: III, 104
Press Publishing Co.: III, 538
Preston, W. M.: 382, 394
Pretoria Convention (1881): III, 51
Pretti, Joseph C.: II, 414
Prevost, Sir George: III, 136
Prince, Albert H.: 200
Princeton University: 659; II, 605; III, 449
Priory School: 143
Pritchard, William Tarn: II, 733
Pritchett, Henry S.: III, 224, 225, 230
Progressive (Bull Moose) Party: III, 466, 467, 468
Prosper Durand Co.: III, 588
[Protestant Episcopal] Church Board of Missions: III, 190
[Protestant Episcopal] Church Missionary Society to Seamen in the Port of New York: III, 590, 591, 597, 605
Protestant Episcopal City Mission Society, of New York: III, 723
Prothero, Rowland Edmund Ernle, 1st Baron: III, 487
Providence, R.I.: II, 427, 502; III, 63
Provincetown, Mass.: II, 425
Provision Island, Colombia: II, 589
Prudence Island, R.I.: 671
Prussia: III, 32, 698, 726
Puerto Rico. See Porto Rico
Puget Sound, W.T.: 680, 682, 686, 687, 689, 695, 702; II, 683; III, 356, 357, 381, 570, 574, 576, 666
Puleston, W. D.: III, 719
Pulitzer, Joseph: II, 194
Pulitzer Publishing Co.: III, 538
Pulitzer, Ralph: letters to, II, 631, III, 538–539; mention, III, 538
Punic War (Second): II, 167
Punta Brasa, River Plate: 401
Punta Caretas, River Plate: 408
Punta Rosa, Paraná River: 397, 398, 402
Punta Sacate Island, Gulf of Fonseca, Salvador: II, 584, 590
Putnam, Herbert: letters to, III, 60, 105, 107, 108, 117, 132–133, 133, 317, 318, 517–518; mention, III, 60, 255, 524, 525, 676

Putnam, Ruth (Mrs. Herbert Putnam): III, 676
Pyrenees: 431

Quackenbush, John N.: 373, 374, 375, 389, 398, 404, 438, 439, 443
Quebec, Que.: II, 524; III, 77
Queen of Sheba: II, 167
Queen's [Victoria] Birthday, May 26, 1894: II, 276, 279, 297
Queens Hall (London): III, 657
Queenstown, Ireland: II, 113, 114, 115, 118, 122, 123, 124, 126, 127, 131, 140, 153, 213, 215
Quincy, Josiah: II, 138; III, 299
Quito, Ecuador: 589
Quogue, L.I.: II, 111, 112, 113, 114, 120, 124, 138, 140, 144, 146, 147, 151, 153, 155, 165, 167, 168, 173, 184, 197, 204, 206, 230, 243, 248, 260, 263, 264, 268, 271, 280, 281, 285, 290, 292, 293, 296, 299, 311, 321, 387, 415, 416, 417, 419, 420, 421, 453, 459, 460, 509, 511, 513, 591, 594, 606, 641, 689, 725; III, 29, 62, 71, 121, 160, 161, 162, 191, 198, 214, 215, 216, 242, 247, 268, 269, 297, 298, 299, 305, 307, 313, 315, 316, 318, 320, 322, 337, 338, 340, 362, 389, 404, 405, 406, 410, 427, 429, 440, 445, 456, 461, 464, 478, 480, 491, 493, 510, 512, 513, 514, 525, 526, 527, 531, 544, 668, 669, 682, 683, 685, 698, 706, 719, 721, 724, 726, 729
Quogue Gas Co.: III, 526

Radford, William: 95
Radstock, Lord: II, 142, 148, 152, 226, 233, 347, 349, 500
Raffalovich, A.: II, 641
Rainsford, the Rev. William S.: III, 721
Raleigh, N.C.: 451; III, 190, 464
Raleigh, Sir Walter: 50
Rams, detachable: II, 95
Ramillies, Belgium: III, 388
Ramsay, Francis M.: letters to, II, 3–7, 8, 11–12, 12, 13, 20, 22, 22–24, 27, 27–28, 30–31, 31, 31–32, 44, 45–46, 46, 49, 50–51, 51, 52, 53, 54, 55, 57, 62–63, 65, 65–66, 66, 67, 68, 69, 70, 71, 72, 72–73, 73, 74, 78, 78–79, 79, 80, 86, 87, 87–88, 88–89, 89, 90, 91, 98, 100, 102, 103, 177, 411, 414, 420, 421, 431, 432; mention, II, 3, 19, 27, 30, 32, 33, 34, 40, 41, 43, 44, 46, 48, 54, 55, 57, 58, 59, 60, 61, 62, 68, 74, 78, 105, 107, 108, 109, 142, 143, 144, 160, 163, 193, 212, 222, 223, 230, 236, 239, 240, 244, 248, 249, 261, 265, 292, 294, 302, 303, 306, 313, 314, 322, 349, 354, 363, 369, 371, 734, 740, III, 299, 667
Randolph, E. & C., Co.: III, 150
Randolph, Wallace: II, 626–627
Rapid-fire ammunition: II, 287

Rawson, Edward K.: letters to, **II**, 660, 679, 690, 702, 722–723, 725, 725–726, 730, 730–731, 735, **III**, 30, 33; mention, **II**, 660, 673

Raymond, George: **III**, 69

Raymond, Henry Warren: **II**, 39

Read, Charles William: 555

Read, Edmund Gaines: 11, 20, 24, 31, 55, 70, 331, 332, 350, 555

Reade, Charles: **III**, 309

Redmond, Mr.: 130, 133

Red River, U.S.A.: 547; **II**, 528

Red Sea: **III**, 35, 639

Redwood Library (Newport, R.I.): **II**, 1, 33, 40; **III**, 312

Reed, John Henry: 122, 124–125

Reed, Mr.: 282, 295

Reid, Stuart J.: **II**, 500

Reid, Whitelaw: letter to, **III**, 71; mention, **III**, 71

Reinberg, Mr.: 589

Reinsch, Paul Samuel: **III**, 258, 259, 260, 428

Reiss, Mr.: 318, 319, 328

Reiss, Mrs.: 170, 181, 324

Remey, George C. ("Jack"): 7, 13, 37, 471, 593; **II**, 57, 625; **III**, 55, 191, 228, 341, 631, 660

Renault, Louis: **II**, 645, 647

Rennes, France: **II**, 66

Republican Club (New York): **III**, 444

Republican insurgent reform movement: **III**, 370

Republican National Committee: **III**, 440

Republican Party: 157, 340, 442, 455, 456, 457, 459, 470, 473, 477, 482, 543, 625, 655; **II**, 205, 234, 235, 361, 669, 694; **III**, 75, 116, 271, 363, 365, 370, 371, 448, 457, 465, 467, 468, 484, 512

Reynolds, Paul R.: letter to, **III**, 546; mention, **III**, 546

Reynolds, Paul R., Co.: **III**, 546

Reynolds, William: letters to, 379, 389, 408; mention, 379, 380, 410

Rhine River: **III**, 344, 541, 699, 707

Rhoades, Archibald C.: 119, 120

Rhode Island: **II**, 4; **III**, 221

Rhode Island naval reserve unit in Spanish-American War: **II**, 577

Rhodes, Dodecanese Islands: **II**, 246, 247

Rhodes, James Ford: letters to, **II**, 503, 527–528, 531, 534, 629, 633, 636–637, 666, 667, 679–680, 696–697, 701, 742, **III**, 43, 112, 159–160, 240, 241, 252, 266, 277, 286, 367; mention, **II**, 503, 534, 680, **III**, 46, 47

Rhodes, Mrs. James Ford: **II**, 666; **III**, 43, 160

Rhodesia: **II**, 688

Rice, Mr.: 226, 322, 324

Richard Coeur de Lion: **II**, 151

Richards, Benjamin S.: 583

Richards, G. E.: **II**, 135

Richardson, Frederick A.: **II**, 743; **III**, 7, 8, 11, 26, 29, 536–537

Richelieu, Cardinal: **II**, 253

Richfield Springs, N.Y.: **II**, 52, 53, 55, 250

Richmond, Va.: **II**, 67, 54; **III**, 230

Rick's Passage, W.T.: 681

Rideing, William H.: letters to, **II**, 628, 652–653, **III**, 101, 236, 519; mention, **II**, 628

Rigaud, John Francis: **II**, 484

Riley, James: 200, 201

Rio de Janeiro, Brazil: 98, 99, 100, 101, 103, 104, 346, 373, 376, 390, 393, 399, 410, 416, 427, 455, **II**, 260, **III**, 54; M. describes, 87

Ripon, George Frederick Samuel Robinson, Marquis of: **II**, 135, 277, 281

Rivasola, Sr.: 409

Riverside Press: **II**, 166

Rives, George L.: **II**, 474, 714, 715; **III**, 524

Rives, William Cabell: **III**, 44

Riviera: **II**, 343, 352, 355, 375, 376, 377, 384, 389, 396; **III**, 481, 484

Rivington's Press: **III**, 274

Rixey, Presley M.: **III**, 236

Robbins, the Rev. Howard Chandler: **III**, 721

Roberts, Frederick Sleigh, 1st Earl Roberts of Kandahar, Pretoria and Waterford: **II**, 129, 276; **III**, 551, 730

Robertson, the Rev. F. W.: 258

Robertson, James Patterson: 75, 77

Robeson, George M.: letters to, 372, 374, 380–381, 387, 402, 411–412, 426, 452–453, 655; mention, 362, 374, 411, 437–438, 439, 440, 442–443, 443, 445, 446, 447, 452–453, 456, 457, 458, 459, 462, 463, 470, 475, 481, 557, 558, 592

Robeson, Henry Bellows: 23, 324, 326, 329, 331, 332, 634

Robiglio, de, Comtesse: **II**, 198, 244

Robiglio family: **II**, 194, 197, 198, 199, 221

Robiglio, Robina: **II**, 194

Robinett, Mr.: 324

Robins, Capt.: **II**, 535

Rochefort, France: 671

Rockefeller, John Davison, Sr.: **III**, 193

Rockwell, Alaska: 570

Rocky Mountains: **III**, 221, 226, 453

Rodgers, C. R. P.: 460, 461, 463, 465, 466, 470

Rodgers, John: **III**, 61, 64

Rodgers, Raymond P.: letters to, 627–628, 630, 640, 649–650, 656, 658, 659, 664, 679, 689, **III**, 317–318, 322–323, 323–324, 325, 325–326, 326, 327–328, 328, 329, 332–333, 335, 336–337, 337–338, 338, 339, 339–340, 340, 343–344, 347–348, 349, 350, 351, 359–360, 362, 367, 380–388, 389–394, 395, 396, 398–399, 404, 405, 406, 406–407, 407, 408, 412, 413–414, 417, 418, 421, 426; mention, 627, **II**, 220, 221, 222, **III**, 273, 301, 309, 324, 332, 358, 360, 373, 407, 412, 429, 445

Rodgers, Thomas Slidell: **II**, 164, 165, 169, 179, 180, 190, 196, 206, 211, 215, 218, 220, 233, 240, 346, 392

Rodgers, William L.: letter to, **III**, 460; mention, **III**, 445, 446

Rodjestvensky, Zinovi Petrovitch: **III**, 206, 335, 347, 372

Rodman, Hugh: 561

Rodney, George: 618, 619, 629; **II**, 724, 726, 730, 733; **III**, 142–143, 467, 472, 488

Roe, Francis Asbury: 268, 548

Rogers, C. C.: 645, 656, 689; **II**, 12

Rogers, John: 372

Roget, Edward ("Jennie," "Old Don"): 48, 59, 66, 79

Roman Catholic Church: 99, 258, 434; **III**, 503

Roman Emperors: **III**, 689

Romans: **II**, 161, 398

Rome, Italy: 75, 352, **II**, 365, 383, 560, 601, 604, **III**, 595, 596; M. describes, 353–354

Romeike Co.: **III**, 435

Ronda, Spain: **III**, 151

Ronins (Japan): 128, 138

Rood, Henry E.: letters to, **III**, 196, 209; mention, **III**, 196

Rooke, Sir George: **II**, 723

Rooney, Wm. R. A.: 565, 566; **II**, 22

Roosevelt, Edith Kermit Carow (Mrs. Theodore Roosevelt): letter to, **II**, 563; mention, **III**, 74

Roosevelt, Theodore: letters to, **II**, 96–97, 98–99, 100–101, 281, 505–506, 507, 676, 706–708, 708, **III**, 6–7, 38–40, 73–74, 112–114, 139, 164–165, 178–180, 182–189, 189–190, 202, 273–275, 279–280, 290, 411–412, 412–413, 414, 420–421, 422, 435–436, 438, 439–440; mention, **II**, 94, 102, 122, 207, 208, 212, 215, 217, 218, 224, 225, 231, 234, 236, 237, 239, 240, 490, 506, 563, 600, 668, 692, **III**, 5, 10, 64, 68–69, 106, 117, 157, 158, 169, 170, 178, 192, 199, 204, 206, 207, 209, 210, 211, 216, 221, 232, 236, 239, 247, 251, 265, 281, 282, 283, 284, 285, 290, 291, 300, 309, 320, 363, 365, 370, 378, 408, 409, 415, 434, 440, 462, 463, 465, 465–466, 466, 467, 468, 477, 484, 500, 627, 628, 661, 662, 720

Root, Elihu: letters to, **III**, 157–159, 503–504, 523; mention, **II**, 474, **III**, 7, 74, 181, 207, 209, 210, 216, 434, 437, 440, 623, 657

Roper, Jesse M.: 617

Ropes, John C.: letters to, 648, 650–651, **II**, 533–534, 535, 539, 604; mention, 637, 711–712, **II**, 56, 534, 537, 666, **III**, 664

Rosario, Sante Fé, Argentina: 375, 378, 397, 398, 401, 403

Rosebery, Archibald Philip Primrose, Earl of: **II**, 276, 277, 278, 280, 291, 297–298, 298, 299

Rose Island, R.I.: 671

Rossetti, Christina: **II**, 115

Rossetti, Dante Gabriel: **II**, 115

Rothschild, Baron Ferdinand: **II**, 141

Rothschild, Nathan Meyer, 1st Baron: **II**, 290

Rouen, France: **II**, 151, 159; cathedral, **II**, 151

Rougervai Co.: **III**, 586

Round Table Club: **II**, 539; **III**, 282, 448, 728

Rover affair: **III**, 56

"Rovie": **III**, 137–138

Rowan, Stephen Clegg: 139, 171, 178, 210, 225, 242, 244, 246, 247, 255, 280, 283, 288, 289, 297, 307, 309, 319, 326, 327, 329, 331, 332, 336, 339; **II**, 704

Rowell, Newton W.: letters to, **III**, 501–503, 507–509

Roy, Kate: 40

Royal Military Academy, Sandhurst, England: **II**, 105

Royal Military Tournament: **II**, 284

Royal Naval Barracks, Devonport, England: **II**, 345

Royal Naval College, Greenwich, England: 678; **II**, 9, 273

Royal Navy Club: **II**, 279; **III**, 203, 212

Royal United Service Institution: 630, 663; **II**, 734; **III**, 44

Rubens, Peter Paul: **II**, 304

Rupert, Prince: **II**, 327

Russell, Sir Baker Creed: **II**, 325, 326

Russell, Clark: **II**, 533

Russell, Henry: **II**, 235

Russell, Hope Ives (Mrs. Henry Russell): **II**, 235

Russell, John Scott: **III**, 40

Russell, Jonathan: **III**, 115, 116

Russell, Lord John, 1st Earl Russell of Kingston Russell: **II**, 26

Russell, Robert Lee: **II**, 431

Russia: people, 99; navy, 638, **II**, 636, 643, **III**, 91, 92, 94, 155, 640, 680, 699, 708; the czardom, **II**, 591, **III**, 13; mention, 464, 469, 608, **II**, 389, 506, 537, 593, 620, 658, 693, 707, **III**, 12, 27, 32, 34, 72, 96, 97, 99, 102, 103, 108, 109, 206, 214, 221, 226, 322, 342, 355, 357, 384, 496, 609, 625, 698, 703, 710. *See* Index Section IV, Russia; and War: Russo-Japanese

Russian Circular Letter (1898): **II**, 646, 647, 650, 652

Russo-Japanese Convention of July 4, 1910: **III**, 347

Russo-Japanese War (1904–1905): **III**, 96, 97, 98, 99, 100, 101, 102, 103, 107–108, 108, 109, 141, 149, 153, 245, 247, 248, 254, 273, 301, 306, 308, 309, 342, 367, 372, 375, 378, 385, 402, 406, 698, 700, 708

Russo-Turkish War (1877–1878): 469; **III**, 543

Rutteybeggar, Justinianus: 90

Ryan, Charles O.: **II**, 372
Ryan, George P.: 465–466
Ryan, William Thomas: **II**, 317
Ryde, England: **II**, 324
Ryukyu [Lu-Chu] Islands: **III**, 387

Sabine Pass, Texas: **II**, 527, 557
Sacket's Harbor, N.Y.: **II**, 36; **III**, 83, 85, 86, 565
Saddle Hill, Almirante Bay, Colombia: **II**, 589
Sado Island, Japan: 227, 228, 229, 341, 343–344, 346, 348
Sagasta, Práxedes Mateo: **II**, 570
St. Albans Cathedral (England): 365
St. Anne's Episcopal Church (Annapolis): **II**, 180
St. Augustine School (Raleigh, N.C.): **III**, 190
St. Botolph Club (Boston): **III**, 85
St. Catharines Island, Brazil: 87
St. Clements Episcopal Church (Philadelphia): **II**, 221
St. George's Episcopal Church (New York): **III**, 721
St. George's School (Newport, R.I): **II**, 231
St. Helena, S. Atlantic Ocean: **III**, 83
St. John's Episcopal Church (Far Rockaway, N.Y.): **III**, 721
St. John's Episcopal Church (Newport): **II**, 143; **III**, 312, 721
St. John's Episcopal Church (Wilmington, Del.): 30, 50; **II**, 256
St. John, Henry Craven: **II**, 117
St. John, N.B.: **III**, 562
St. John's, Newfoundland: **III**, 562
St. Kitts, Leeward Islands: 629
St. Lawrence canals: **III**, 564, 565, 575
St. Lawrence, Gulf of: **III**, 573
St. Lawrence River: **II**, 524; **III**, 470, 565, 566
St. Lorenzo Point, Bay of Samana, Santo Domingo: **II**, 587
St. Louis, Mo.: 652
St. Lucia, Windward Islands: 629; **III**, 488, 568
St. Luke's Episcopal Church (Norfolk Va.): **II**, 726
St. Malo, France: **II**, 309
St. Margaret Bay, N.S.: **III**, 566, 567
St. Martin's summer: **II**, 355
St. Paul's American Church (Rome): **II**, 234
St. Paul's College (Hong Kong): 286, 287
St. Peters (Rome): 353
St. Polycarp, Tomb of, Smyrna, Turkey: **II**, 241
St. Stephens Episcopal Church (Boston): **III**, 11
St. Thomas, Danish Islands: 96; **II**, 572, 585, 586, 587, 590; **III**, 642

St. Thomas Episcopal Church (Washington): **III**, 721
St. Vincent, Cape, Portugal: **II**, 161, 576
St. Vincent, John Jervis, Earl of: 22, 618, 670; **II**, 161, 486, 724, 730; **III**, 98, 569
Salamanca, Spain: **III**, 191, 326
Salem, Mass.: 114
Salinas Bay, Costa Rica: **II**, 584, 590
Salisbury Cathedral: 364
Salisbury, Lady: **II**, 202–203, 276, 299
Salisbury, Robert Arthur Talbot Gascoyne-Cecil, 3rd Marquis of: **II**, 130–131, 202–203, 206, 274, 275, 278, 298, 299, 313, 482; **III**, 511, 704, 709
Salmon, Sir Nowell: **III**, 203
Saltonstall, Henry: letter to, 651–652; mention, **II**, 185, 241, 342, 344, 369, 371, 375
Saltonstall Mrs. Henry: 652, **II**, 468, 500, 596, 663, 666
Saltonstall, Miss W.: **II**, 370
Salvador: 510, 523, 526, 599, 600, 610; **II**, 584, 590
Samana, Santo Domingo: **II**, 585, 587, 590
Samoa Islands: 572; **II**, 583, 590; **III**, 57, 377, 380, 381, 382, 385, 392
Samos, Greece: **II**, 246
Sampson Low, Marston & Company: **II**, 93, 135, 295, 300, 305, 473, 517, 519, 520; **III**, 35, 81, 149, 180, 200, 208, 238, 239, 270, 274, 296, 309, 337, 377, 378, 379, 416, 444, 446, 460
Sampson-Schley controversy: **II**, 562, 573–577, 578, 656–657, 669–670, 673, 703–704, 740, 744; **III**, 2, 4, 74, 423, 424. *See* Index Section IV, War: Spanish-American
Sampson, William Thomas: letters to, **II**, 94–95, 95–96, 287; mention, 464, 471, 644, 645, **II**, 94, 145, 147, 212, 225, 558, 559, 562, 563, 569, 571, 572, 573, 574, 575, 576, 577, 578, 605, 612, 620, 659, 669, 670, 671, 673, 681, 690, 692, 703–704, **III**, 31, 188, 191, 219, 248, 249, 252, 254, 270, 271, 423, 424, 629, 630, 631, 632, 634, 635, 636, 638, 639, 640, 641
Sanderson, Gardner F.: **II**, 185
Sanderson, Sir Percy: **III**, 212
Sands, Joshua: 85
Sands, Minnie Hartpence (Mrs. Mahlon Sands): **II**, 315–316, 319, 328, 334, 340, 352, 371
Sandusky River, Ohio: **III**, 78
Sandwich Islands [Hawaiian Islands]: **II**, 92
Sandy Creek, N.Y.: **III**, 86
Sandy Hook, N.J.: **II**, 113, 426; **III**, 195, 564, 568
San Francisco, Calif.: 133, 137, 350, 516, 557, 572, 578, 590, 594, 595, 608, 611, 673, 675, 680, 681, 683, 699; **II**, 90, 195, 376, 583, 683; **III**, 214, 221, 226, 263, 267, 356, 357, 380,

381, 383, 384, 385, 401, 402, 403, 404, 570, 574, 637
San José, Guatemala: 599, 601, 602
San Juan Islands, W.T.: III, 570
San Juan, Porto Rico: II, 554, 558, 564, 565, 584, 585, 586, 587, 630; III, 31, 629, 630, 631, 632, 633, 634, 661
San Luis harbor, Guam: III, 393
San Remo, Italy: III, 491, 720
San Sebastian, Spain: III, 151, 720
Santa Ana, Salvador: 600
Santa Barbara, Calif.: III, 390
Santa Ceraz, Rio de Janeiro, Brazil: 87
Santa Cruz, Lesser Antilles: II, 572
Santa Elena, Cape, Costa Rica: 589
Santiago, Cuba: II, 558, 559, 562, 563, 569, 571, 573, 574, 588, 590, 600, 612, 620, 653, 672, 673, III, 31, 188, 191, 236, 545, 633, 634, 635, 636, 637, 638, 640, 643; agreement of surrender (1898), II, 590; White House conference to consider surrender terms, II, 653, 654
Santiago Bay, Funchal, Madeira: II, 67
Santo Domingo: 362, 523, 530, 531; II, 587; III, 45
Santo Domingo Commission: III, 106
Santos, Elias: 588
Santos, Flavio: 588
Santos, Julio Romano: 587–589, 590, 594, 603, 604–605, 605, 611
Saratoga, N.Y.: II, 92, 672
Sargent, Aaron A.: 459
Sargent, Charles S.: II, 534
Sargent, Nathan: III, 191
Sargent, W.: 354
Sasebo, Japan: III, 387
Saskatchewan, Canada: III, 377
Satow, Sir Ernest Mason: III, 221
Satsuma clan: 126, 128, 129, 130, 138
Saumarez, James: 618, 619; II, 91–92, 500, 724, 725, 730
Saunders, George: III, 485
Savannah, Ga.: III, 77
Savoy Hotel (New York): III, 603
Scales, Dadney Minor: 555
Scheldt River, Belgium: II, 293
Scheveningen, Belgium: II, 636, 637
Schiff, Mr. and Mrs. George: II, 190, 194, 195, 196, 197, 198, 199, 203, 204, 206, 217, 219, 220, 221, 222, 223, 224, 230, 250, 267, 270, 273, 274, 276, 278, 280, 284, 285, 290, 292, 306, 310, 313, 335, 342, 343, 346, 352, 355, 365, 366, 373, 374, 375, 376, 377, 383, 392, 395, 396, 404, 405
Schiff, Marie: II, 194, 196, 232, 392
Schiff, Rosie: II, 194, 196, 203–204, 220, 222, 230, 254, 265, 294, 344, 348, 356, 371, 382
Schleswig-Holstein, Germany: II, 141
Schley Court of Inquiry: II, 740

Schley, Winfield Scott: letters to, 582, 583; mention, 8, 33, 48, 54, 582, 655, 664, 676, 716, II, 265, 558, 559, 562, 563, 573, 574, 575, 576, 578, 612, 620, 669, 670, 671, 672, 673, 703–704, 739, 740, III, 135, 423, 424, 629, 631, 634, 635
Schofield, John M.: 619, 651, 708; II, 74, 474
Schoomaker, Cornelius Marius: 11, 246, 332; III, 57
Schott, Miss: III, 104
Schouler, James: III, 551
Schroeder, Seaton: III, 262
Schurz, Carl: II, 605, 662, 697
Schuyler, Philip John: III, 470
Scilly Isles: 363
Scott, James Brown: III, 449
Scott, Mrs.: 295
Scott, Sir Percy: III, 263, 550, 700
Scott, Robert N.: 550
Scott, Sir Walter: II, 366
Scott, William Lawrence: 652
Scott, Winfield: III, 545
Scribner, Charles: letter to, III, 494; mention, III, 494
Scribner's Sons: letters to, 547–548, 548, 553, 657–658, 658–659, II, 697; mention, 551, 658, II, 522, III, 294, 303, 547
Scribner and Welford Co.: 552
Scribner's Magazine: letters to, III, 82–84, 84, 85–86
Scrymser, James A.: II, 555
Scudder, Horace: letters to, II, 22, 26, 27, 28, 29, 42, 44, 85, 85–86, 91–92, 94, 97, 99–100, 102, 104–105, 111–112, 126–127, 153, 166, 313–314, 350, 409, 505; mention, II, 22, 118, 122, 123, 131, 132, 133, 139, 141, 147, 148, 150, 151, 155, 156, 310, 311
Scylla and Charybdis, Messina Straits: II, 237
Seager, Edward: 353
Seal Island, N.S.: III, 573
Seamen's Church Institute of New York: II, 172
Seamen's Church (Shanghai): 240
Sea Power: II, 494, 717; III, 369, 373, 505, 524, 708
Searchlights: II, 338
Sears, James H.: II, 82, 193, 201, 223; III, 667
Seattle, W.T.: 673, 683, 687, 698, 699; letter to mayor of, 673–675; U.S. Land Office records at, 684, 698
Seawell, Molly Elliott: letter to, II, 606; mention, II, 410, 411, 434, 449, 606
Sebree, Uriel: 683, 698, 706, 709, 710
Secession movement: 483, 574
Sedgwick, William Parker, Jr.: II, 210, 220, 231
Seeley, Sir John Robert: III, 34, 246, 249, 254
Segovia, Spain: III, 151

Selborne, Lord: **III**, 28
Selfridge, Thomas O.: 436, 548, 715
Selkirk, Lord: **II**, 541
Semmes, Raphael: 110
Sepoy Mutiny (1857–1858): **II**, 92
Serata, Tasuka: **III**, 499, 688, 689, 690, 691
Serbia [Servia]: **III**, 698, 703, 704, 705, 710
Serbian War: 457
Seville, Spain: **II**, 358, **III**, 151 Alcazar palace, **II**, 358
Seward, Mr.: 242
Seward, William Henry: **III**, 463
Sewell, Mr.: 461
Seymour, Sir Edward Hobart: **III**, 315
Seymour, Dr.: 428
Shafter, William R.: **II**, 588, 626, 653, 690, 727; **III**, 635
Shakespeare, William: 576; **II**, 308; **III**, 458, 600
Shanghai, China: 171, 174, 195, 225, 233, 238, 239, 241, 243, 249, 289, 292, 304, 341, 347; **II**, 508, 582, 708
Sharon Springs, N.Y.: 114, 355, 357, 366, 367, 369; **II**, 235
Shaw, Albert: **II**, 715
Shaw-Lefevre, George John, Baron Eversley: **II**, 270, 275, 277
Sheldon, George Rumsey: **III**, 440
Sheldon, Mr.: **III**, 105
Shelley, Percy Bysshe: **II**, 196
Shepard, Edward M.: **III**, 364
Shepard, Edwin Malcolm: 480; **II**, 403
Shepard's Harbor, Almirante Bay, Colombia: **II**, 589
Sheppard, Augustine: 76
Sheppard, Francis Edgar: 76, 77, 80–81, 82, 83
Sheridan, Philip Henry: **III**, 545
Sherman, F. F.: **II**, 164–165
Sherman, William Tecumseh: **III**, 220, 388, 393, 545, 700; March to the Sea, **III**, 388
Shetland Islands: **II**, 544
Shilshop Bay, W.T.: 688, 689
Shock, W. H.: 474
Short, William: letter to, **III**, 530; mention, **III**, 530
Shorthouse, Joseph Henry: **II**, 377
Shrewsbury, Lady: **II**, 275
Shuttleworth, William L.: 149
Sicard, Montgomery: letters to, 562–563, 565, 567, **II**, 413, 553–555; mention, 562, 611, 708, 713, 714, **II**, 474, 591, 592, **III**, 175, 627, 628, 629, 630
Sicily: **II**, 178, 237, 503; **III**, 484, 491, 510, 569, 720
Sickles, Daniel E.: 64
Sidney, W. T: 684, 693
Sidon, Phoenicia: 264
Siegfried, C. A.: **II**, 83

Siglin, J. M.: letter to, 673–675; mention, 673
Sigsbee, Charles: **III**, 592
Silesia, Germany: **III**, 32
Silveira, Antonio: letter to, 413; mention, 413
Silver question: **II**, 483
Similk Bay, W.T.: 695
Simons, Mr.: 194
Simon's Bay, South Africa: 104, 105
Simonstown, South Africa: 163
Simpson, Edward: 18, 19, 22, 23, 24, 26, 38, 40, 41, 47, 48, 51, 60, 70
Simpson, J. A. G.: **II**, 208, 209, 210, 232
Sims, William S.: letters to, **III**, 170, 177–178, 193; mention, **III**, 170, 178, 182, 183, 184, 185, 187, 204, 205, 234, 236, 264
Sinclair, Arthur: **III**, 79
Sinclair Harbor, W.T.: 681–682, 685, 696
Singapore: 141
Singer, Frederick: letter to, **II**, 99; mention, **II**, 99
Sino-Japanese War: **II**, 342, 345, 422; **III**, 342, 583–585
Sippican, Cape Cod, Mass.: 469
Sitka, Alaska: 570
Skagit River, W.T.: 695
Slamm, Jefferson A.: 84, 88; **III**, 53, 54, 227–228
Slamm, Levi D.: 84; **III**, 53
Slattery, the Rev. Charles L.: letter to, **III**, 461; mention, **III**, 461
Slavs: **III**, 13, 705; provinces of Austria, **III**, 499; power, **III**, 698, 703
Sloane, William Mulligan: **III**, 112, 241, 252
Small lamps: 490
Smalley, George Washington: **II**, 299, 452, 679
Smith, Adam: **II**, 507; **III**, 462
Smith, Beatty Peshine: 6, 78; **III**, 56–57
Smith, Charles William: **II**, 291
Smith, Dr.: **III**, 63
Smith, Edward J.: **III**, 454
Smith, Elsie: **II**, 293, 294, 296, 311, 371, 388, 395
Smith, the Rev. Ernest: **III**, 721
Smith, Frederick R.: 314
Smith, Goldwin: **II**, 26; **III**, 498
Smith, Henry C.: 508
Smith, Justin: **III**, 549, 552
Smith, Melancthon: 359, 370
Smith, M. L.: 546
Smith, Sally: **II**, 366
Smith, Sir William Sidney: 618; **III**, 645
Smyrna, Turkey: **II**, 222, 230, 235, 236, 238, 239, 246, 247, 248, 249, 262, 358; M. describes, **II**, 241, 245
Snowden, Archibald Loudon: **II**, 105, 110, 138
Soames's Sound, Me.: **II**, 119; **III**, 573
Socialism: **II**, 483; **III**, 611

Society of Naval Architects and Marine Engineers: **III**, 679
Society of the Sons of the Revolution: **III**, 519
Soley, James Russell: letters to, **II**, 77, 78, 79, 80–83, 83; mention, 622, 634, 635, 637, 707, 712, **II**, 8, 32, 34, 58, 60, 62, 77, 107, 231, 295, **III**, 274, 663
Soley, John C.: 471; **II**, 82
Solomon Islands, Pacific Ocean: **III**, 383
Somali, East Africa: 113, 114
Somerset Club (Boston): **III**, 147
Sorel, Quebec: **III**, 470
Soudan [Anglo-Egyptian Sudan]: **II**, 658
Soult, Nicolas Jean de Dieu: **III**, 326
South, the (C.S.A, Civil War): 26, 88, 89, 90, 434, 473, 488, 625; **II**, 336, 662; **III**, 53, 54, 55, 57, 71, 75, 196, 271, 444, 465, 467, 542, 703, 708
South Africa: 106; **III**, 396, 499, 609
South America: 240, 432, 621; **II**, 149, 157, 508, 581; **III**, 291
Southampton, England: 364; **II**, 114, 117, 118, 120, 124, 125, 127, 130, 131, 134, 142, 146, 148, 149, 152, 215, 226, 233, 309, 327, 330, 331, 334, 335, 336, 344, 345, 347, 349, 350, 367; **III**, 583
South Atlantic Ocean: 101; **II**, 12
South Carolina: 90, 337
Southerland, William Henry Hudson: **II**, 625, 628
Southern Pacific Railroad: **II**, 527
Southey, Robert: **II**, 470
Spain: Cuban flurry, 496; flags, 509; trade, 570; court and chivalry, 576; cities and towns, 577, **II**, 233; language, **II**, 158, **III**, 462; mails and post offices, **II**, 162, 166; women, **II**, 169, 363; people, **II**, 570; possessions, **II**, 570, 583; soldiery, **III**, 7; war in Morocco, **II**, 170; Moors, **II**, 357; navy, 482, 544, **II**, 553, 554, 556, 558, 564, 571, 575, 576, 625, **III**, 143, 493, 569, 629, 630, 633, 637, 639, 640; mention, 410, 439, **II**, 37, 38, 148, 161, 165, 167, 331, 405, 410, 544, 565, 567, 568, 569, 577, 588, 653, 654, 691, **III**, 146, 150, 151, 153, 191, 545, 636, 638, 641. *See* Index Section IV, War: Spanish-American
Spanish Academy: **III**, 462
Spanish-American War: **II**, 551, 553–555, 556, 563, 567, 569, 571, 600, 606, 609, 612, 617, 626–627, 631–632, 658, 670, 680, 708, 727; **III**, 25, 31, 56, 98, 139, 165, 174, 245, 369, 412, 464, 543, 545, 629, 630, 636, 640, 641, 642, 643, 659, 671, 719
Spanish Morocco: sultan of, **II**, 357, 358
Spartel, Cape, Tangier: **II**, 67
Spartivento, Cape, Italy: **II**, 237
Star torpedoes: **II**, 95

Speer, Robert E.: **III**, 302
Spencer, John Poyntz Spencer, 5th Earl: **II**, 120, 121, 122, 123, 133, 135, 140, 144, 267, 277
Spencer, Lady: **II**, 140
Spencer, Mr.: **III**, 138
Spencer, Sallie. *See* Sallie Spencer Blake
Spencer, Thomas Starr ("Blondy," "Fan," "Kate"): 3, 7, 11, 13, 17, 19, 20, 31, 34, 54, 57, 67, 78–79, 89, 90, 451; **III**, 53, 54
Speonk, N.Y.: **III**, 478, 480
Sperry, Charles Stillman: letter to, **III**, 104–105; mention, **II**, 103, 104, 323, **III**, 102, 178, 233, 248, 265, 267, 268, 282, 439, 549, 550
Sperry, Mrs. Charles S. (née Marcy): **III**, 549–550, 552
Spezia, Italy: **II**, 181
Spicer, William F.: **II**, 360
Spion Kop, Natal, S. Africa: **III**, 10
Spooner, Mr.: 171, 180, 319
Sprague, H. J.: **II**, 161, 341, 364, 365, 406
Sprague, J. W.: letter to, 673–675
Spurgeon, Charles Haddon: **III**, 335–336
Squadron of Evolution: **II**, 57
Squire, Watson C.: letter to, 673–675; mention, 673, 710
Staal, Dr.: **II**, 745
Stacker, Mr.: 166
Stadly, G. W., & Company: letter to, **II**, 433; mention, **II**, 433
Stager, Anson: **II**, 326
Stanhope, Countess: **II**, 655
Stanley, Col.: **II**, 273, 329
Stanley, Dorothy: **II**, 326, 329, 330, 331, 334, 344
Stanley, Henry Morton: **II**, 275
Stanley, Lady, of Alderley: **II**, 273, 275
Stanley, Madeline: **II**, 326, 329, 330, 331, 334, 344, 348, 371, 382
Stanton, Oscar F.: **II**, 25
Starkey Company: **II**, 136–137, 141, 152, 155
Staten Island, N.Y.: 516, 519, 553; **II**, 293
Staunton, Sidney Augustus: 649, 650; **III**, 9
Stead, William Thomas: **III**, 207, 223, 457
Stearns, Mr.: 331
Stedman, Edmund Clarence: **II**, 697
Steece, Tecumseh: 26
Steedman, Charles: 367, 368
Stein, Robert: letter to, **III**, 193; mention, **III**, 193
Sterling, J. B.: letters to, **II**, 301, 445–446, 451–452, 504–505, 512, 545, 619–620; mention, **II**, 301, 345, 546, 665
Stevens, Benjamin Franklin: 360, 361, 517, 707; **II**, 84, 87, 111, 112, 121, 124, 127, 128, 132, 133, 136, 137, 139, 141, 183, 189, 220, 264–265, 269, 283, 345, 347, 350, 368, 387, 500, 618, 621, 626, 632; **III**, 96, 102, 103, 128, 129, 133, 135, 145, 209, 528, 543, 595

Stevens, Durham W.: **III**, 251
Stevens, John Leavitt: 381, 396
Stevens, T. H.: letter to, 551; mention, 548, 551
Stevenson, Paymaster: 505
Stevenson, Robert Louis: **II**, 200
Stewart, Charles W.: letters to, **III**, 65–66, 69–70, 76, 78–79, 103–104, 110–111, 135–136, 140, 141–142, 142–143, 143, 144, 145, 157, 177, 196, 217, 218, 240, 245, 247, 252, 253, 265, 290–292, 313, 340–341, 345–346, 368–369, 394, 394–395, 397, 416, 421, 441, 443, 472, 473, 527–528, 528, 529; mention, **III**, 65, 304
Stewart, Edwin: 493
Stewart, Sir Houston: **II**, 279, 279–280, 281
Stewart, Mr.: **II**, 667
Stewart, Paul: **II**, 393
Stewart, Scott: 307, 316
Stewart, William F.: 131, 185, 284, 285, 299, 323, 325, 354
Stimson, Henry Lewis: **III**, 364, 365, 409
Stirling, Yates: 609, 611
Stitt, F. R.: **II**, 164–165
Stockton, Charles Herbert: letter to, 676; mention, 646, 657, 676, 686–687, 694, 709, 718, **II**, 26, 32, 52, 56, 57, 59, 60, 62, 66, 70, 71, 72, 82, 88, 108, 136, 143, 144, 145, 147, 150, 163, 201, 202, 222, 244, 255, 256, 330, 509, 521, 695, 696, **III**, 71, 316, 334, 665, 666, 667
Stockton, Cornelia Carter (Mrs. Charles H. Stockton): **II**, 201, 202
Stockton, Nelie: **II**, 201
Stockton, Pauline Lentilhon King (Mrs. Charles H. Stockton): **II**, 202
Stoddard, Mr.: **II**, 398
Stoessel, Anatoli M.: **III**, 103, 107–108
Stoney Creek, N.Y.: **III**, 86
Stoney Island, N.Y.: **III**, 86
Stonington, Conn.: 633
Storer, Horatio R.: letter to, **II**, 79–80; mention, **II**, 79
Stovel and Company: **II**, 136–137, 139, 141, 152, 155
Strachey, John St. Loe: **III**, 43, 44, 216
Strassburg, Germany [France]: **III**, 720
Straus, Oscar: **III**, 438
Strode, Capt.: 390
Stromboli, Italy: **II**, 237
Strong, James H.: letters to, 405–406, 406–407, 407–408, 408, 408–409, 409, 409–410, 410, 411, 411–412, 414, 415–416, 416–417; mention, 405, 417, 420, 422
Strong, Mayor: **II**, 474
Strong, William C.: 319
Sturdivant, Theodore: 37
Sturdy, Edward William: letters to, 416, 421; mention, 406

Subic Bay, Philippines: **II**, 582, 590; **III**, 236, 658, 659, 660, 661, 662
Submarines: **III**, 549, 572, 659, 700, 708
Suez Canal: **II**, 581–582, 589, 684; **III**, 16, 35, 431, 639, 640
Suez, Egypt: 331, 332; **III**, 387, 392, 639
Sugarloaf, Rio de Janeiro, Brazil: 87
Sumatra: **II**, 582; **III**, 376, 377
Sumner, George W.: **II**, 431
Sumner, William Graham: **III**, 545, 711
Super-dreadnoughts: **III**, 514
Superior spy glasses: 507
Sutherland, Mr.: 537
Sutphen, Edson Webster: 563
Suydam, John Howard: **II**, 266
Swan, Mr.: **II**, 593
Swann, William: 41
Swasey, Charles Henry: 6, 6–7, 19, 31, 68, 593; **III**, 56
Swatow, China: 292, 293, 295
Swedenborg, Emanuel: 358
Swift, James: 1; **II**, 448
Swift, Mrs. James: 1
Swift, Jane Leigh Okill (Mrs. John L. Swift) ("Aunty"): letter to, **II**, 327–329; mention, 1, 14, 21, 24, 46, 51, 107, 129, 243, **II**, 138, 139, 172, 241, 300, 336, 349, 351, 355, 438, 440, 448, **III**, 295
Swift, John L.: 1, 21
Switzerland: **II**, 181; **III**, 221
Syle, Mr.: 243, 244, 292
Symonds, John Addington: **II**, 115
Syria: **II**, 245; **III**, 569

Table Mountain, Capetown: 106
Tacoma, W.T.: 673, 679, 683, 687; letter to mayor of, 673–675
Taft, Mr.: 217
Taft, William Howard: **III**, 6, 7, 290, 364, 370, 408, 409, 422, 423, 424, 427, 433. 434, 437, 439, 443, 454, 457, 465, 467, 468, 477, 483, 490, 661, 662
Tahiti, Society Islands: 587
Tai Shei Shan, Chushan Archipelago, China: **II**, 583
Tammany Hall: 488; **II**, 667, 668, 671, 680, 692–693; **III**, 75, 364, 365
Tampa, Fla.: **II**, 625; **III**, 637
Tampico, Mexico: **III**, 523
Tanaka, M. S.: **II**, 718
Tangier, Spanish Morocco: **II**, 148, 162, 163, 356, 357, 358, 360, 361; governor of, **II**, 358
Tan-shui, Formosa: 250
Tansill, Robert: 89–90
Tarascon, France: **II**, 175
Tarbell, J. F.: 404
Tarsus, Turkey: **II**, 246, 247, 248
Tate's (Annapolis): 27, 40, 76
Tayloe, James Langhorne: 31, 55
Taylor, D. W.: **II**, 83

Taylor, Henry Clay: letters to, **II**, 425–428, **III**, 79–80; mention, **II**, 143, 144, 145, 147, 163, 201, 206, 210, 222, 241, 246, 256, 265, 386, 417, 593, 594, 595, 596, 681, **III**, 41, 68, 79, 637

Taylor, Mrs.: **III**, 137

Taylor, William Rogers: letters to, 373, 375, 376, 377–378, 378–379, 379, 380, 381–382, 382–383, 383–384, 384–385, 385, 386, 386–387, 391, 394–395, 395, 396, 397, 398, 399–400, 400–401, 401, 402–403, 403, 403–404, 404–405; mention, 373, 374, 378, 379, 393, 404, 405, 406

Taylor, Zachary: **III**, 45

Tejedor, Carlos: 415

Temple, Bishop Frederick: 365

Temple, William G.: 362

Tenafly, N.J., property ("Palisades property"): **II**, 351, 436, 438–439, 440, 448, 461, 464, 511, 515–516, 516, 720, 726–727, 728

Tenerife, Canary Islands: 428

Tennyson, Alfred, Lord: **II**, 271

Terrell, H. L.: **III**, 240

Terry, Silas Wright: 464, 465, 470–471

Teutonism vs. Slavism: **III**, 13

Texas: **II**, 527; **III**, 640

Texel, W. Frisian Islands, Netherlands: **II**, 544

Thames River, Conn.: 556; **III**, 564, 574

Thames River, England: **II**, 259, 264, 289

Thomas, Chauncey: **II**, 219, 229, 231, 233, 256

Thomas, Charles M.: **II**, 165, 180, 250

Thomas Hunt & Company: 130, 133

Thomas, Mr.: 91

Thompson, Horatia Nelson: **II**, 476, 477

Thompson, Miss: 41, 64

Thompson, Richard W.: letter to, 475–476; mention, 470, 471, 475, 481–482, 486, 491–492, 592, 715

Thorn, Miss: 170

Thornton, Gilbert E.: 705

Thucydides: **II**, 549

Thursfield, James R.: letters to, **II**, 271, 272, 281–282, 283, 287, 435–436, 437, 441–442, 494–495, 509, 529–530, 536–537, 622–623, 637, 664–665, 673–674, **III**, 153–154, 154–156; mention, **II**, 271, 345, 436, 437, 504, **III**, 34, 317, 318

Thursfield, Mrs. James R.: **II**, 282, 283, 287, 436, 441, 495, 509, 530, 623, 637

Thwaites, Reuben G.: letter to, **II**, 608; mention, **II**, 608

Tientsin, China: **II**, 693

Tiffany and Co.: **II**, 264, 295, 315

Tilden Foundation: **II**, 517

Tilden, Samuel J.: 457, 459

Tillman, Benjamin R.: **III**, 280

Tillman, Prof.: 666

Tilton, Clara: 62

Timmons, Joseph: 134

Tobago, West Indies: 200

Todd, Henry Davis: 471

Togo, Marquis Heihachiro: **III**, 153, 154, 155, 182, 183, 245

Tokiti, Japan: 124

Toral, José: **II**, 588, 653, 654

Tokyo. See Yeddo

Toledo, Spain: **III**, 720

Tompkinsville, Staten Island, N.Y.: **II**, 403, 404, 408

Topolobampo, Mexico: 590, 595

Toronto, Ont., Canada: **III**, 76, 711

Torreon, Mexico: **III**, 523

Torres, Sr.: **II**, 357

Torrington, Arthur Herbert, Earl of: **II**, 337, 509

Toucey, Isaac: 29, 35, 69, 75, 77

Toulouse, France: 463; **III**, 720

Tourville, Anne Hilarion de Cotentin, Comte de: **II**, 92, 337, 509; **III**, 368

Towing torpedoes: **II**, 95

Townsend, the Rev. S. DeLancey: **II**, 618; **III**, 721

Townshend, Mr.: **II**, 508

Towson, Nathan: **III**, 65

Tracewell, R. J.: letters to, **III**, 327, 330–332; mention, **III**, 327, 329, 330, 331, 332, 339, 526

Tracy, Benjamin F.: letters to, 718, **II**, 10, 18–19, 38–39, 40–41, 46, 54–55, 59, 66, 74, 80, 89, 90, 91; mention, 676, 688, 691, 692, 698, 707, 708, 709, 710, 714, 718, **II**, 8, 18, 19, 21, 34, 36, 37, 39, 40, 43, 57, 58, 59, 60, 61, 62, 64, 65, 79, 98, 109, 182, 237, 239, 474, 680, 734, **III**, 75, 299, 563, 570, 666

Tracy, Charlie: **II**, 267

Tracy family: 366

Tracy, Julia: **II**, 393

Trafalgar, Cape: 714; **II**, 9, 160, 161, 465, 574; **III**, 155, 545

Trafalgar, English estate: **II**, 318, 320, 328

Transit of Venus expedition (1874): 466

Transvaal, South Africa: **II**, 656, 657, 677, 678, 679, 722; **III**, 9

Treaty, Monroe-Pinkney (1806): **III**, 125

Treaty of Berlin (1878): **III**, 686

Treaty of General Arbitration with Great Britain (1912): **III**, 420, 421; proposed Joint High Commission of Inquiry under, **III**, 420, 436, 442

Treaty of Naturalization (1873): 588

Treaty of Paris (1898): **II**, 611, 627; U.S. Peace Commission to, **II**, 579

Treaty of Portsmouth (1905): **III**, 263

Treaty of Shimonoseki (1895): **III**, 342

Treaty of Transit (Bidlack Treaty, U.S.-New Granada, 1846): **III**, 462

Trench, Major: **II**, 481

Trench, Richard Chenevix: 274

Trentino, Austria [Italy]: **III**, 710

Trevelyan, Sir George Otto: **II**, 142, 144
Trieste, Austria: **III**, 710
Trinidad, West Indies: **III**, 263, 265
Trinity College, Oxford: **II**, 290
Trinity Episcopal Church (Hewlett, N.Y.): **III**, 721
Trinity Episcopal Church (Newport): **III**, 423
Triple Entente: **III**, 698, 699
Tripolitan War: **III**, 672–673
Tristan da Cunha, South Atlantic Ocean: **III**, 83
Tromp, Cornelius van: 633
Troubridge, Sir Thomas: **II**, 486, 487, 502
Troughton Co.: **III**, 587
Troupe, A. H.: 684, 710
Tryon, Sir George: **II**, 114, 161, 168, 275
Tryon, J. R.: 676
Tsugaru Strait, Japan: 230, 348
Tuck, Rosamund: **II**, 184
Tucker, William J.: letter to, **III**, 62–63; mention, **III**, 62
Tucker, Mrs. William J.: **III**, 62
Tuckerman, Mr.: **III**, 548
Tuckerman, Stephen Salisbury: **III**, 89
Tullamore, Ireland: **II**, 123
Tunisia: **III**, 473
Turenne, Henri de La Tour d'Auvergne, Vicomte de: **III**, 581
Turkey: foreign policy, **II**, 495, 505, **III**, 710; captures Constantinople, **II**, 169; government, **III**, 492, 510; imperial administration, **III**, 489, 505–506, 511, 683, 686, 690; military capability, **III**, 510; mention, 457, 469, 482, **II**, 246, 247, 248, 744, **III**, 350, 494, 508, 541, 699, 704, 705
Turner Co.: **III**, 586
Turner, Frederick Jackson: letter to, **III**, 244; mention, **III**, 240, 244
Tuskegee Institute: **II**, 617
Twain, Mark: **II**, 167, 267, 273
Tycoon: 125–126, 126, 127, 128, 130, 136, 137, 138, 334
Tycoon's Palace, Osaka, Japan: 334
Tyndall, John: **II**, 273
Tyndall, Louisa Hamilton [Mrs. John Tyndall]: **II**, 273, 275
Tyng, the Rev. Mr.: 429
Tyre, Phoenicia: 264
Tyrell, Mr.: **III**, 200, 208

Ubico, Don Arturo: 526
Uitlanders: **II**, 677, 678, 679
Ulm, Germany: **III**, 388
Unalaska, Aleutian Islands: **III**, 382, 383, 384, 385
Underwood, Oscar Wilder: **III**, 463, 465
Underwood Tariff Act (1913): **III**, 512
Unitarian Church: **III**, 211, 522, 523

United Service Club (London): **II**, 134, 345
U.S. Army: 43, 44, 84, 85, 444, 454, 637, 651, 665; **II**, 562, 565, 566, 569, 578, 579, 598, 612, 613, 625, 628, 635, 636, 683, 692, 727; **III**, 276, 375, 401, 403, 410, 538, 541, 565, 570, 596, 603, 622, 634, 635, 636, 637, 661, 662
U.S. Army Corps of Engineers: **II**, 235
U.S. Army, Military Academy (West Point): 9, 30, 42, 43, 44, 50, 52, 59, 61, 88, 123, 355, 558, 660, 666; **II**, 74, 535, 545, 702
U.S. Army, Signal Corps: **III**, 634
U.S. Army, War College: **III**, 662
U.S. Civil Service Commission: **II**, 96
U.S. Coast and Geodetic Survey: 678, 680, 681, 682, 686, 687, 688, 690, 691, 692, 693, 694, 698, 701, 702, 704, 705, 706, 708, 710, 717; **III**, 86, 470
U.S. Commission to the First Hague Conference: letters to, **II**, 646–649, 650–652; mention, **II**, 643, 645, 648, 649, 650, 651, 652, 654, 659, 704–706, 708, 709, 709–712, 712, 714, 715, 719, 741, 745, **III**, 13, 14, 15, 17, 18, 19, 20, 21, 22, 73, 106, 450
U.S. Congress: 41, 51, 52, 434, 438, 439, 458, 458–459, 464, 469, 473, 544, 591, 620, 635–636, 642, 648, 661, 672, 673, 676, 684, 686, 691, 694, 709, 714, 715; **II**, 8, 24, 101, 532, 587, 602, 603, 612, 681; **III**, 50, 98, 123, 129, 203, 291, 370, 374, 375, 453, 474, 512, 574, 661, 662, 666, 673, 712
U.S. Consuls: Antwerp, **II**, 294; Beirut, **II**, 396; Castellammare, **II**, 234; Gibraltar, **II**, 161, 341, 364, 365, 406; Hakodate, 232; Hiogo, 187; Le Havre, **II**, 148, 149, 150, 152, 163, 339; Lisbon, **II**, 154, 155, 161; Málaga, **III**, 587; Nagasaki, 298, 300, 301, 304, 310; Naples, **II**, 234; Nice, **II**, 178–179, 191–192, 221; Colombia, 558; Queenstown, **II**, 124; Swatow, 292, 295; Tangier, **II**, 357, 358
U.S. Court of Claims: **III**, 530, 531, 522, 538
U.S. Department of State: 589, 602, 603, 604, 611; **II**, 413, 414, 626; **III**, 16, 106, 124, 629
U.S. Department of the Treasury: letter to, 716–717; mention, 680, 681, 688, 690, 691, 693, 694, 717, **III**, 287, 320, 327, 328, 339, 526, 532
U.S. Department of War, 651, 656; **II**, 587, 591; **III**, 129, 130, 369
U.S. Fish Commission: 546
U.S. House of Representatives: 437, 438, 439, 442, 456, 458, 475, 557–558, 642, 648, 650, 652, 654, 655, 663; **II**, 8, 11, 32, 205, 427, 439, 448, 452, 454, 462, 465, 469, 475, 512
U.S. House Committee on Appropriations: 540, 652; **III**, 290–291, 375, 459, 476
U.S. House Committee on Foreign Affairs: **III**, 374, 466

U.S. House Committee on the Library: **III**, 676, 678

U.S. House Committee on Naval Affairs: 438, 443–444, 451–452, 453, 455–456, 457, 470, 648–649, 650, 652, 654, 676; **II**, 11, 92, 206, 207, 208, 246; **III**, 204, 291, 375, 408, 414, 466, 559, 664, 665

U.S. Marine Corps: 4, 60, 149, 568; **II**, 360, 372, 435, 493; **III**, 565, 573, 641

U.S. Merchant Marine, 558; **III**, 620–622

U.S. Naval Institute: 436, 474, 666, 668, 669, **II**, 533; **III**, 266

U.S. Navy, Auxiliary Defense Fleet (1898): **II**, 558

U.S. Navy, Boards: Academic (USNA), 58, 70, 71, 79, 80; Bureau Chiefs, **II**, 682; Construction, **II**, 680, 681, 682; Examiners (USNA), 460, 466, 472; Examining and Retiring, 74, 372, **II**, 56 (Stagnation); Inspection, 656, **II**, 212, 240, 391; Line Officers (Promotion), **II**, 53, 55, 68, 214; Luce (NWC), **III**, 219–220; Pythian, 716, 718; Visitors (USNA), 471, **III**, 465; Wainwright (Spanish-American War), **II**, 688; Joint Army and Navy, **III**, 236, 661, 662

U.S. Navy, Bureaus: **II**, 62, 581, 680, **III**, 275, 281, 282, 284; Construction and Repair, 437, 562, **II**, 346, **III**, 281; Equipment and Recruiting, 101, 379, 389, 408, 517, 541, 559, 571, 581, 582, 583, 613, 616, 640, **II**, 540, 559, **III**, 39, 641, 664; Medicine and Surgery, 172, **II**, 559; Navigation, 91, 92, 93, 94, 95, 355, 356, 359, 367, 369, 370, 371, 372, 373, 430, 435, 436, 460, 461, 461–462, 462, 463, 466, 472, 483, 484, 485, 489, 491, 494, 498, 501, 502, 503, 504, 505, 506, 507, 508, 509, 511, 513, 514, 515, 516, 517, 518, 519, 520, 521, 522, 523, 524, 525, 526, 527, 528, 530, 531, 532, 533, 534, 535, 536, 537, 538, 539, 540, 541, 542, 543, 544, 545, 549, 553, 556, 559, 560, 563, 564, 565, 568, 618, 634, 638, 652, 653, 656, 657, 701, 708, 711, 714, **II**, 4, 5, 8, 13, 18, 27, 42, 45, 46, 50–51, 51, 69, 73, 78, 79, 80, 86, 87, 89, 90, 102, 103, 109, 143, 291, 324, 362, 389, 411, 413, 414, 420, 421, 431, 591, 594, 595, **III**, 79, 174, 236, 275, 289, 330, 405, 406, 407, 417, 441, 627, 667; Ordnance, 376, 502, 517, 520, 562, 563, 567, 677, **II**, 8, 11, 94, 95, 339, **III**, 66, 281, 559, 565, 570, 576; Steam Engineering, 501, 596, **II**, 296; Supplies and Accounts, **II**, 324, **III**, 316, 531; Yards and Docks, 487, 672, 691, 697, 698, 703, 705, **II**, 19

U.S. Navy, Department of the Navy: letters to, 371–372, 372, **II**, 208–210, 228–229; mention, *passim*

U.S. Navy, Engineer Corps: 558, 656, 698; **II**, 528

U.S. Navy, Gulf of Mexico and South Atlantic Coast Navy Yard Site Commission: 688, 690, 700, 710

U.S Navy, Hydrographic Office: 369, 516, 680, 715; **II**, 42, 43, 55, 56, 407; **III**, 396, 470

U.S. Navy, Naval Academy: 3, 4, 5, 7, 8, 17, 31, 38, 40, 41, 45, 46, 47, 50, 53, 55, 61, 68, 70, 73, 74, 76. 81, 83, 84, 160, 192, 196, 208, 353, 371, 450, 460, 461–462, 462, 463, 464, 465, 471, 473, 475, 476, 478, 483, 486, 496, 518, 558, 618, 625, 644, 645, 710; **II**, 3, 21, 23, 25, 39, 84, 106, 108, 178, 341, 349, 350, 595, 660; **III**, 42, 222, 248, 249, 254, 266, 270–271, 271, 341, 423, 499, 664, 688

U.S. Navy, Naval Asylum: **II**, 26

U.S. Navy, Naval Observatory: 715

U.S. Navy, Naval Reserve: 649; **II**, 82; **III**, 42, 570–571

U.S. Navy, Naval War College: 577, 603, 606, 607, 608, 611, 613, 616, 620, 621, 622, 624, 625, 626, 627, 628, 634–635, 635, 636–639, 639, 640, 641, 642, 642–644, 644, 645, 646, 647, 648, 649, 651, 652–653, 653, 654, 656, 657, 659, 660, 661–662, 662, 663, 664, 665, 666, 667, 668, 669, 676, 677, 677–678, 689, 692, 700, 708, 710, 712, 716; **II**, 3, 3–5, 5, 5–6, 6–7, 8, 9, 10, 11, 12, 19, 20–21, 22–24, 24–25, 27, 27–28, 30, 30–31, 31, 32, 34, 37–38, 39, 40, 40–41, 42, 43, 45–46, 48, 50–51, 51, 52, 54, 55, 56–57, 58, 59, 60, 60–61, 62, 63, 64, 65–66, 66, 68, 69, 70, 71, 72, 73, 74, 75–77, 77, 78, 79, 80, 80–83, 86, 88, 89, 91, 94, 95, 96, 99, 100, 101, 106, 107, 108, 109, 123, 127, 136, 142, 143, 144, 145, 147, 148, 150, 155, 163, 193, 206, 207, 208, 210, 212, 219, 222–223, 225, 230, 234, 240–241, 244, 256, 265, 279, 285, 349, 386, 414, 417, 419, 420, 421, 425, 432, 445, 459, 468, 472, 474, 526, 594, 595, 597, 598, 599, 600, 636; **III**, 68, 104, 137, 191, 198, 199, 216, 218, 219–220, 233, 234, 245, 248, 269, 299, 300, 301, 303, 304, 308, 309, 310–311, 311, 312, 314, 317, 318, 319, 320, 321, 322, 323, 324, 325, 327, 330, 331, 332, 334, 338, 340, 343, 349, 351, 358, 360, 369, 370, 372, 373, 375, 389, 390, 391, 393, 395, 406, 410, 411, 412, 416, 417, 425, 426, 440, 441, 445, 460, 464, 465, 525, 533, 538, 577, 578, 580, 663–667, 670, 721, 725

U.S. Navy, Naval War College Library: **II**, 62, 69, 70, 100; **III**, 31, 270, 271, 304, 312, 421

U.S. Navy, Naval War Board (1898): letter to, **II**, 563–566; report of, **III**, 627–643; mention, **II**, 551–552, 553, 555, 556, 558, 559, 561, 562, 572, 581, 581–591, 591, 592, 595, 596, 609, 628, 653, 692, 727, **III**, 161, 162, 163, 164, 169, 174, 175, 191, 192, 234, 276, 418, 627, 628, 629, 630, 631, 632, 633, 634, 635, 636, 637, 638, 639, 641, 642, 643, 719

U.S. Navy, North West Coast Navy Yard Site Commission: 646, 672, 672–673, 673, 674, 675, 676, 677, 678, 679, 682, 683, 684, 689, 690, 691, 692, 694, 696, 697, 698, 700, 701, 702, 705, 710, 711, 713, 714–715, 717; **II**, 54; **III**, 666

U.S. Navy, Office of Naval Intelligence: 630, 640, 641, 656, 659, 679, 696, 707, 713, 715, **II**, 5, 12, 95, 437, **III**, 273, 301, 308, 309, 541, 562, 565, 566, 570, 575, 576, 627, 628–629; Officer of Naval Intelligence, 564, 627, 640, 644, **II**, 17, 99

U.S. Navy, Office of Naval Records and Library: 710; **II**, 591, 660, 722; **III**, 65, 118, 135, 139, 140, 141, 142, 144, 196, 217, 313, 368. 389, 534

U.S. Navy, Pay Office and Paymasters: letter to, **III**, 247; mention, 641, 680–681, 691, 705, **II**, 26, 52, 114, 292, **III**, 234, 316, 319, 327, 331, 405

U.S. Navy, Squadrons: Asiatic, 88 (China), 101, 118, 215, 225, 268, 282, 372, **II**, 567, **III**, 381; European, 101, 408, 410, 456, **II**, 150, 268, 272; Farragut's, 546, 551, **II**, 56; Flying (1898), **II**, 625, **III**, 412–413, 629, 632, 633, 634, 640, 643; North Atlantic, 251, 590, 644, **II**, 354, 437, 561, 587, 625, **III**, 205, 206, 658, 661, 663; Pacific, 559, 573, **II**, 506, 538, 567, **III**, 381; South Atlantic, 85, 294 (Brazil), 372, 379; South Atlantic Blockading, 371; South Pacific, 172; Training (Newport), 524, 525, **II**, 3, 4, 5, 24, 25, 73, 74, 87–88, 106, 108, 136, 420, **III**, 664; West Gulf Blockading, 172, 372

U.S. Navy, Stations: Asiatic, 101, 268, 644, **II**, 98; China, **III**, 55; Coaling, **II**, 581–591; European, 101, **II**, 368; New London, Conn., **III**, 664; North Atlantic, 528, 530, **II**, 154, 302; Pacific, 530, 557, 564, 579, 608, 617, **II**, 47; South Atlantic, 101, 373, 376, 384, 405, 422, 423, **II**, 38; Torpedo (Newport), 603, 628, 641, 654, 661–662, 663, 677–678, **II**, 8, 11, 20, 21, 23, 30–31, 73, 74, 95, 265, **III**, 666

U.S. Navy, Surgeon General: **II**, 559

U.S. Navy Yard, Boston: 220, 367, 436, 441, 442, 446, 452, 456, 457, 458, 527

U.S. Navy Yard, Mare Island (San Francisco): 492, 505, 561, 568, 582, 587, 589, 590, 591, 594, 596, 608, 611, 613, 622, 627, 690, 698; **II**, 89, 213, 302; **III**, 356

U.S. Navy Yard, New York (Brooklyn): 90, 93, 94, 358, 359, 483, 484, 486, 487, 489, 493, 505, 506, 507, 509, 512, 513, 515, 517, 524, 525, 536, 537, 538, 543, 549, 553, 555–556, 570; **II**, 113, 153, 213, 404, 408, 413, 431; **III**, 325, 531

U.S. Navy Yard, Washington, D.C.: 95, 502, 506, 507; **II**, 3, 32, 360

U.S. Revenue Service: 81, 83; **III**, 228

U.S. Secretary of War: 712; **II**, 589, 592, 596, 621, 734; **III**, 575, 634, 662

U.S. Senate: 438, 439, 470, 474–475, 492, 651, 654, 663, 687, 690; **II**, 8, 704; **III**, 18, 291, 420, 421, 422, 424, 427, 428, 430–431, 432, 433, 434, 435, 437, 439, 450, 452, 462, 464

U.S. Senate Commission on the Merchant Marine: **III**, 110, 112, 620–622

U.S. Senate Committee on Appropriations: 650

U.S. Senate Committee on Foreign Affairs: **III**, 374, 433–434, 466

U.S. Senate Committee on Naval Affairs: 38, 650; **II**, 581; **III**, 98, 466

U.S. Supreme Court: 604; **III**, 411, 427, 428

U.S. Volunteer Navy (1861): 299, 311

United States and *Macedonian* action: **III**, 82

Universal Peace Union: **II**, 670–671

University Club (Boston): **II**, 503

University Club (New York): **II**, 623, 703; **III**, 12, 17, 43, 44, 52, 96, 112, 117, 228, 233, 240, 252, 269, 277, 284, 298, 299, 307, 334, 349, 376, 395, 405, 424, 491, 493, 669, 678, 721, 728

University of Michigan: **III**, 253

University of Pennsylvania: **III**, 4

University of Tennessee: 546

University of Virginia: 33; **III**, 478

University of Wisconsin: **III**, 45, 244

Unwin, Fisher: **III**, 377

Uphens, Frank: **II**, 199

Upper Canada College, Toronto: **II**, 654

Upshur, John H.: letters to, 524, 524–525, 525, 525–526, 527, 527–528, 528, 528–529, 529, 529–530, 530, 530–531, 531, 532, 533–535, 535, 536, 537, 538, 539, 540, 540–541, 541–542, 542, 543, 544–545, 545–546, 547, 549, 550, 552, 552–553, 553, 581, 587; mention, 524, 537, 539, 579, 581, 584, 587, 589, 590, 591, 595, **II**, 214

Uriu, Baron Sotokichi: **III**, 688

Uruguay: 409, 410, 414, 415, 416, 420, 428, 433; flags, 510, 530

Urquiza, Justo José: 381

Ushant Island, France: 619; **II**, 352

Usher, George R.: 395, 396, 399

Utsaladdy, W. T.: 683

Vail, Abraham H.: 578, 582, 601, 618

Valcour Island, Lake Champlain, N.Y.: **III**, 470

Valencia, Spain: **II**, 167

Vallejo, Calif.: **II**, 90

Valparaiso, Chile: 557, 560, 564, 566, 567, 571, 572, 587, 589; **II**, 424; **III**, 77

Van Allen, James: **II**, 234

Van Brunt, Mr.: **III**, 587

Vance, Zebulon B.: 647

Vancouver Island, B.C.: 680, **III**, 570, 574–575

Vanderbilt, Mr.: **III**, 197

Van der Hyde, Mr.: 191

Van Noppen, Charles Leonard: **II**, 272

Van Noppen, Leonard Charles: **II**, 272–273

Van Schaick, Mr. and Mrs.: **II**, 522

Van Tyne, C. H.: **III**, 671

Van Valkenburgh, Robert Bruce: 125, 126, 148, 149, 150, 165, 166, 167, 168, 169, 172, 177, 178, 315, 322, 327

Van Valkenburgh, Mrs. Robert Bruce: 140

Vashon Island, W.T.: 680

Vatican: 353

Venezuela: flags, 512, 515, 530; Anglo-American tension over, **II**, 441, 442, 443, 452, 472, 482, 506, **III**, 476; Anglo-German punitive action against, **III**, 50, 53, 445; U.S. boundary study commission in, **II**, 442; U.S policy in, **II**, 452

Venice, Italy: 334

Very, Samuel W.: 645

Very signals: 553

Vesuvius: **II**, 225, 227

Viceroy of Ireland. *See* Milnes

Vickers family: **II**, 226

Vicksburg, Miss.: 546, 547, 549, 555; **II**, 56, 69; **III**, 388, 393

Victoria Club (Boston): **III**, 140, 141, 145, 146, 147, 148–149

Victoria, Princess of Schleswig-Holstein: **II**, 140

Victoria, Queen: **II**, 124, 128–129, 140, 142, 144, 284, 299, 312, 327; Diamond Jubilee of, **II**, 537

Vienna, Austria: **III**, 137

Villa Albion, Bad Nauheim, Germany: **III**, 209, 212, 214, 215, 225

Villard, Henry: letter to, **II**, 516; mention, **II**, 516

Villefranche, France: **II**, 182, 187, 188, 194, 202, 203, 205, 223, 230, 243, 245, 250, 260, 313, 321, 322, 342, 346, 365, 370, 376, 377, 379, 383

Villegas, Clara: 90, 91, 333

Vinal Haven Island, Me.: **II**, 427

Vineyard Sound, Mass.: **II**, 426

Virginia: 26, 31, 88, 90; **III**, 55

Virginia Capes: 3

Virginia Company: **III**, 24

Virginia Military Institute: 88

Virgin Islands. *See* Danish Islands

Virginius affair: 410, 439

Vladivostok, Russia: **III**, 108, 392

Voorhees, Daniel Wolsey: **III**, 120, 143

Waddell, James Iredell ("Jas. I." or "Jass-eye"): 13, 19, 39, 40, 47, 59, 76, 80–81, 81

Waddell, Mrs. James Iredell: 13, 22, 76

Wadsworth, James Samuel: **II**, 137

Wainwright, Richard: 191; **II**, 688; **III**, 236, 262, 282

Waldegrave, Miss: **II**, 148

Waldegrave, Mr.: **II**, 143

Wales, Albert Edward, Prince of: **II**, 279, 284, 297, 300, 314, 317, 327; **III**, 16

Walke, Henry: 554

Walker, Edward A. ("Tom"): 452; **III**, 54

Walker, John G.: letters to, 507, 536, 556, 557, 559, 559–560, 560, 563–564, 564, 565–566, 570, 615, 634, 634–635, 635, 636–639, 639, 642–644, 644, 645, 646, 647, 648, 652–653, 653, 657, 659, 660, 660–662, 679, 689, 692, 701, 711, 715; mention, 507, 540, 541, 608, 611, 648, 656, 665, 677, 691, 708, 712, **II**, 38, 39, 109, 154, 222, 231, 232, 595, 680, **III**, 9

Walker Taffrail Log: 494–495

Wallace, Sir Donald: **II**, 536, 637

Wallace, Rush Richard: **II**, 420, 432

Walter, Mr.: **II**, 57

Walter, Mrs. Caroline Luce: **II**, 57

Walton, J. J., lamps: 489, 490, 528, 529, 533, 534, 540

Wanamaker, John: **II**, 234

War of the Pacific (Chile vs. Peru): 572, 573

Ward, Annie: 364, 366; **II**, 180

Ward, Mr.: 211, 283, 287

Ward, Mrs.: 366

Ward, Nelson: **II**, 500

Warner, Charles Dudley: **III**, 693

Warren, Sir Charles: **III**, 10

Warren, the Rev. E. Walpole: **II**, 364; **III**, 721

Warren, Sir John Borlase: **III**, 135, 136

Washington, Booker Taliaferro: **II**, 617

Washington, D.C.: 2, 8, 41, 48, 62, 64, 74, 81, 83, 89, 160, 368, 371, 451, 456, 464, 487, 505, 538, 550, 553, 555, 577, 578, 599, 620, 630, 648, 673, 676, 680, 686, 687, 691, 693, 695, 697, 699, 702, 703, 707, 714; **II**, 19, 35, 40, 43, 52, 59, 61, 62, 63, 64, 68, 127, 218, 224, 409, 552, 560, 567, 575, 591, 594, 601, 604, 654, 680, 691, 703, 707, 709, 719, 734; **III**, 10, 38, 55, 57, 69, 74, 79, 81, 88, 110, 112, 116, 122, 124, 125, 126, 175, 209, 247, 275, 287, 288, 289, 322, 328, 329, 342, 371, 478, 505, 512, 518, 524, 525, 532, 534, 539, 548, 549, 551, 552, 577, 595, 632, 634, 635, 665, 666, 668, 669, 675, 678, 719, 721, 724, 730

Washington, George: **II**, 234, 358; **III**, 527, 600

Washington, Lake, W.T.: 680, 683, 687

Washington Naval Hospital: **III**, 730

Washington Sound, W.T.: 694

Washington, State of: **III**, 377

Washington Territory: 710

Watch Hill, R.I.: 580; M. describes, 556

Waterbury, David: **III**, 470

Water Island, Lesser Antilles: **II**, 586

Waterloo, Belgium: **III**, 581

Watson, John Crittenden: 17, 19; **II**, 561, 565, 567, 570; 572; **III**, 188, 191, 638, 639, 640

Watterson, Henry: **III**, 438

Weather: levanters, **II**, 163, 370; mistrals, **II**, 174, 373

Weaver, Aaron Ward: **II**, 241

Webb, Mrs. (née Remsen): 44

Webber, John: 84

Wednesday Evening Century Club (Boston): **II**, 534, 535

Weir, Allan: letter to, 673–675

Weld, Stephen Minot: **III**, 85

Welland Canal, Ont., Canada: **III**, 565

Weller, Mr.: 364

Welles, Gideon: 89

Wellesley, Richard Colley, 1st Marquis: **III**, 124, 125, 128, 130, 671

Wellington, Arthur Wellesley, 1st Duke of: **III**, 137, 191, 326

Wells, David Ames: **II**, 452

Wells, Edwin: 404

Wells, Fargo and Co.: 133, 567

Welsh, Charles W.: 48

Wemyss, Francis Wemyss Charteris Douglas, Earl of: **II**, 131

Wemyss, Lady Elcho: **II**, 131

Weser River, Germany: **III**, 709

West, Benjamin: **II**, 3

West, Mr.: 392, 417

West, William: 224, 228

Western Electric Co.: 529

Westhampton, N.Y.: **III**, 478

West Indies: 91, 97, 121, 142; **II**, 38, 67, 264, 354, 426, 546, 560, 565, 587, 621, 670, 733; **III**, 143, 392, 394, 562, 573, 574, 637, 639

Westphalia, Peace of (1648): 623

West Point, N.Y.: 1, 2, 24, 34, 35, 36, 39, 41, 42, 44, 46, 48, 49, 50, 51, 84, 90, 91, 92, 94, 104, 105, 133, 280, 317, 320, 354, 355, 356, 357, 367, 369, 660; **III**, 76

Whalen, James: **II**, 412

Whatcom, W.T.: 680

Wheeler, Everett P.: **II**, 667, 668; **III**, 476

Wheeler, Joseph: 652; **III**, 665

Wheeler, Mrs.: **II**, 143

Whichelo, C. John M.: **II**, 484, 484–485, 486, 487, 490

Whidbey Island, W.T.: 695

White, Andrew D.: letters to, **III**, 709, 712, 716, **III**, 1, 15; mention, **II**, 705, 706, 708, 709, **III**, 1, 15, 21, 450, 451

White, Mrs. Andrew D.: **III**, 15

White, Charles H.: 314

White, Dr.: 317

White, Edwin: 480

White, George B.: 691, 703, 705, 709

White, Henry: letters to, **II**, 117, **III**, 467–468; mention, **II**, 110, 117, 120, 121, 122, 123, 130, 131, 134, 135, 141, 144, 315, 315–316, 318–319, 328, 474, **III**, 160

White, Mrs. Henry (née Rutherford): **II**, 130–131, 316, 319, 328; **III**, 468

White, Julius: 389, 396, 397, 398, 401, 403, 415, 424

White, Richard Dace: **III**, 182

White, W. H.: letter to, 679; mention, 679, 684

White, Sir William Henry: **III**, 679, 680, 681

Whitehead torpedoes: 633; **II**, 82, 95

Whitehead, William: 88

Whitehorne, H. B.: 147, 166, 167, 168, 169

Whitehouse, Henry Remsen: 599, 600; **II**, 685

White Star Line: **III**, 454, 455

Whiting, William D.: letters to, 472, 483, 484, 486, 505, 506; mention, 472

Whitney, William C.: letters to, 595, 596, 597, 597–598, 599, 599–601, 601, 602, 603–605, 605, 605–606, 608–609, 609, 609–610, 610, 611, 612, 613–614, 614, 617, 625, 641, 651, 653, 656, 660, 665, 666, 672, 672–673; sponsors M. retirement dinner, **II**, 474; mention, 595, 608, 615, 651, 654–655, 655, 656, 663, 664, 665, 672, 673, 676, 677, 678, 716, **II**, 20–21, 61, 244, 278, 279, 474, **III**, 664, 665, 666

Whittaker, E. J.: 165, 596

Whitthorne, Washington C.: letter to, 443–450; mention, 443, 453, 455, 456, 470, 475, 652

Whitworth, W. H.: 684

Wickes, Joseph L.: 475–476

Wickes, Judge: 475

Wight, Isle of: **II**, 124

Wilhelm, Crown Prince of Germany: **III**, 487

Wilhelm II, Kaiser: **II**, 124, 128–129, 310, 312, 319–320, 327–328, 444, 529, 536–537, 665; **III**, 32, 487, 514

Wilhelmina, Queen of Holland: **III**, 292

Wilhelmshaven, Germany: **III**, 358, 708

Wilkinson, Spenser: **III**, 34

Will, James F.: 471, 472

Willett, William F.: **III**, 280

William the Conqueror: **II**, 333

William the Silent: **II**, 384; **III**, 368

Williams Basin, W.T.: 693, 706

Williams, Edward P. ("Barney"): 301, 306, 307, 310, 322, 326

Williams, Mr.: **II**, 367

Willing, Mrs. Tom (née Lee): **II**, 194, 216, 221

Williston and Lucas Co.: 489–491

Wilmington, Del.: 50, 172; **II**, 393

Wilmington, N.C.: 115, 355, 451; **II**, 36, 482; **III**, 76
Wilson, Sir Arthur: **III**, 333
Wilson, H. W.: **II**, 523
Wilson, James: **II**, 708
Wilson, James G.: letters to, **II**, 55–56, 63–64; mention, **II**, 55
Wilson, Josiah Mann: 284, 298
Wilson, Mr.: **II**, 490, 495
Wilson, T. S.: 89–90
Wilson, Woodrow: **III**, 465, 469, 475, 477, 478, 512, 514, 528, 538, 539, 541, 542, 546, 548, 721, 728, 730
Wiltse, Gilbert C. ("Gil" or "Old Gil"): 13, 23–24, 56–57, 68, 78, 79, 89, 90; **III**, 53, 54
Winchester, England: **II**, 133, 146, 325; cathedral, 364, 365; **II**, 146
Windom, William: 691, 716
Windward Islands: **II**, 67
Windward Passage, West Indies: **II**, 588; **III**, 376, 631
Wingate, Charles E. L.: letters to, **II**, 499, 510; mention, **II**, 499
Winslow, C. McR.: **III**, 282
Winslow, John A.: 406
Winsor, Justin: **II**, 528
Winterburn, Mr.: **II**, 447
Winterthur (Del.): **II**, 393
Wisconsin State Historical Society: **II**, 608
Wisser, J. P.: 660, 666
Witherspoon, W. W.: **III**, 282
Wolcott, Roger: **II**, 534
Wolseley, Sir Garnet: **II**, 92, 471, 481
Wood, Leonard: **III**, 382, 429
Wood, Otis F., Newspaper Syndicate, Inc.: letter to, **III**, 537–538
Woodmere, L.I.: **III**, 177, 181, 189, 194, 197–198, 204, 627, 720, 721
Wood's Hole, Cape Cod, Mass.: **II**, 427
Woodward, J. J.: **II**, 83
Woodward, Robert Simpson: letter to, **III**, 517; mention, **III**, 516, 517
Woolverton, Theron: mention, 149, 155, 155–156, 156, 157, 158, 158–159, 160, 161, 162, 163, 165, 166, 167, 168, 169, 170, 171, 172, 173, 174, 174–175, 177, 178, 179, 182, 195, 209, 215, 216, 217, 218, 219, 220, 221, 222, 223, 224, 229, 245, 284, 285, 286, 287, 288, 290, 292, 293–294, 294, 295, 296, 297, 298, 301, 302, 304, 305, 306, 307, 308, 309, 310, 311, 312, 313, 314, 315, 316, 317, 317–318, 318, 319, 320, 321, 322, 323, 327, 329, 330, 332, 339–340, 340; **II**, 260

Woolwich, England: **II**, 305
Woosung, China: 245, 247
Wordsworth, William: **II**, 115, 249
World's Fair (1892): **II**, 84
World War I: **III**, 539, 540, 543, 547, 548, 550, 551, 698–700, 701–705, 730
Wright, Evelyn Evans (Mrs. John B. Wright): 487
Wurbs-Dundas, Major: **II**, 191, 199, 202
Wurbs-Dundas, Mrs. (née Lippincott): **II**, 191, 199
Wyckoff, A. B.: 715
Wyman, Robert H.: letter to, 421–422; mention, 369
Wyndham, William: **III**, 146

XYZ affair: **III**, 116

Yakunins (Japan): 126, 128, 136, 138, 335
Yale University: **II**, 515, 516; **III**, 157
Yalu River: **II**, 337, 416; **III**, 109, 583, 584
Yangtze River, China: 237, 247; **II**, 583, 590, 666, 707, 708; **III**, 6
Yaquina City, W.T.: 673
Yates, Arthur R.: 296, 317
Yazoo River, Miss.: 555
Yeddo, Japan: 125, 130, 137, 138, 330
"Yellow" journalism: **II**, 580
"Yellow peril": **III**, 214, 216, 217, 221, 222, 225, 252, 277, 308, 334, 355, 408, 411, 427, 436, 448, 449, 452, 496–499
Yeo, Sir James Lucas: **III**, 135, 136, 313, 467
Yezo, Japan: 344
Yokohama, Japan: 119, 120, 125, 130, 131, 132, 133, 134, 138, 141, 142, 146, 155, 164, 168, 170, 171, 172, 173, 178, 180, 181, 185, 188, 284, 304, 308, 314, 315, 316, 318, 319, 320, 323, 324, 326, 327, 328, 329, 330, 331, 336, 339, 343, 346, 350, 351, 491; **III**, 380, 383, 384, 392
Yorke, John Manners: **II**, 146, 148, 268, 320
Yorktown, Va.: 553, 636; **III**, 394
Youmans, Mr.: **II**, 511, 515, 516, 520
Yukon, Canada: 690
Young, James C.: **III**, 241, 243
Zabriskie, Mrs. George: **III**, 302
Zaldivar y Lazo, Don Rafael: 599, 600
Zanzibar, E. Africa: **III**, 709
Zasulich, Gen.: **III**, 109
Zoebisch, Mr.: 485
Zola, Émile: **II**, 168–169

Vessels listed are warships unless otherwise designated: H (hospital); M (merchant or passenger); Pvt (privateer); T (tender); Y (yacht).

Nationality is U.S. unless noted as: Ar (Argentine); Br. (British); Bra (Brazilian); Ch (Chilean); CSA (Confederate); Fr. (French); Ger (German); Itl (Italian); J (Japanese); P (Peruvian); Rus (Russian); or Sp (Spanish).

Aboukir (Br): **III**, 549, 550
Abtas (Ch): 564
A. C. Bear (M): 415
Adams: 608
Adventure (Br): 332
Agamemnon (Br): **II**, 491
Alabama (CSA): 110, 262, 267, 406; **II**, 644, 647, 659; **III**, 711
Albatross (Ger): 564
Albemarle (CSA): **II**, 517
Alexander III (Rus): **III**, 184
Alliance: **II**, 544
Anganicos (Ch): 564
Annapolis: **II**, 625
Annapolis Packet (M): 76
Arethusa (Br): 662
Arkansas (CSA): 554, 555; **III**, 58
Armenia (M): **III**, 524
Aroostook: 110, 145, 323, 326, 372; M. ordered to command of, 314; entertains aboard, 316, 320, 321; eagerness to be quit of, 316, 317, 319, 320, 330, 332, 350; little to do aboard, 318; personal isolation aboard, 330; threatened by storm, 329; sale of, 316, 317, 319, 320, 330, 332, 350; M. removes guns from, 332; ordered home from, 332; plans trip home from via Europe, 328, 331, 332; departs for home from, 332, 350
Ashuelot: 215; M. ordered to command of, 314; illness prevents taking command, 314; attends survey upon, 332
Atlanta: **II**, 38, 156
Aurora (M/Br): **II**, 238
Azov (M/Br): **II**, 300–301

Badger: **II**, 597; Dennis M. involved in incident aboard, **II**, 597–598, 599
Bayan (Rus): **III**, 94
Baltimore: **II**, 98, 103; **III**, 559
Barbarossa (M/Ger): **III**, 160
Bennington: **II**, 156, 165, 179, 180, 195, 219, 220, 221
Blake (Br): **II**, 408
Blanco Encalado (Ch): 564
Bonhomme Richard: **II**, 518, 540, 544, 545, 547; **III**, 487
Boston: **II**, 33, 39
Braconnot (Bra): 390
Brandywine: **III**, 252
Brooklyn: 36, 497–498, 498, 501, 507, 551; **II**, 564, 566, 574; **III**, 555, 573
Bustard (Br): 297

Cambrian (Br): **II**, 396
Campania (M/Br): **III**, 160
Camperdown (Br): **II**, 114; **III**, 593
Canada (M/Br): 491
Captain Prat (Ch): **II**, 63, 507
Carlos V (Sp): **II**, 565
Carondelet: 554, 555
Castine: **II**, 405
Cayalti (M): U.S. registry with Peruvian officers and crew, 341; *Iroquois* investigates mystery of, 225, 341–342, 346–347; mutiny aboard, 342, 347
Cebarozo (Bra): 386
Ceres (Sp): 410
Charleston: **II**, 57
Charlotte (Br): M. visits, 287
Chesapeake: **III**, 61, 65, 68, 69, 70, 103–104, 673; inquiry on loss of, **III**, 69–70, 673
Chicago: particulars, **II**, 103, 351, **III**, 218; M. ordered to command, **II**, 103, 104; takes command, **II**, 103; detached, **II**, 414; anticipates short cruise, **II**, 112, 182, 198; hope for short cruise dashed, **II**, 147, 256, 261, 263, 275, 292, 295, 296, 302, 305; dislike of duty aboard, **II**, 114, 178, 182, 226–227, 230, 249, 255, 260, 300, 356, 370, 375, 377, 378, 381; disinterest in cruise, **II**, 163, 250, 292; urge to return home, **II**, 200, 230, 255, 256, 265, 272, 275, 276, 291, 295, 313, 331, 348, 352, 366, 370; wastes two years of his life in, **II**, 300, 324, 370; difficulty of adjusting to modern ship, **II**, 139–140, 331, 394, 407; harassed by petty details of shipboard administration, **II**, 139–140, 141, 142, 153, 160, 226–227, 257, 288, 300, 309, 313, 315, 332, 334, 335–336, 347, 350, 352, 370, 382, 394; fears breakdown under command pressure, **II**, 224, 311, 342, 345, 364, 365, 372, 374; fear of collision, **II**, 160; constantly on bridge while underway, **II**, 162, 167–168, 241; collision with *Azov*, **II**, 300–301; USN rules on collision, **II**, 406; leg injury, **II**, 113, 115, 117, 118, 121, 122, 123, 124, 125, 126, 127, 131, 140, 213; ship movements, **II**, 111, 113, 114, 117, 118, 121, 125, 127, 134, 144, 146, 148, 149, 151, 152, 156, 160, 162, 173, 174, 178, 219, 221, 222, 235, 238, 245, 246, 259, 260, 261, 287, 309, 331, 334, 339, 352, 356, 363, 371; general condition of ship, **II**, 214–215, 323; poor condition of boilers, **II**, 153–154, 186, 260, 263, 268, 287, 295, 301, 304, 306, 411, 413; poor condition of engines, **II**, 346, 360, 369, 381,

384, 394, 399, 408, 411; coal consumption and cost, **II**, 153, 402, 405, 407, 408, **III**, 586, 588, 589; ammunition shortages, **II**, 287, 324, 339; seamanship accidents, **II**, 241–243, 249; routine drills, **II**, 154, 173, 177, 227, 338, 389–392, 412; crew vacancies, **II**, 106; crew recruitment abroad, **II**, 154; crew discharges abroad, **II**, 154, 192, 320; crew fitness reports, **II**, 320; foreign crewmen aboard, **II**, 145, 362; crew discipline, **II**, 154, 208–210, 232, 367, 373, 374, 413; crew health, **II**, 154, 412, 418–419; outbreak of measles, **II**, 162–164; crew desertions, **II**, 289, 317, 372, 410–411; crew deaths, **II**, 239, 289–290, 314, 405–406; officers rotated, **II**, 219, 220; M. comments on officers, **II**, 138, 150, 194, 206, 219, 221, 223, 398; M. entertains officers, **II**, 159, 169, 179, 180, 181, 398–399; disrespect for chaplain aboard, **II**, 164–165; officers entertained ashore, **II**, 190, 191; officers entertain aboard, **II**, 121, 195, 203, 401; M. entertains aboard, **II**, 152, 219, 220, 277, 281–282, 294, 320, 334, 364; M. violates USN regulations, **II**, 192; church attendance ashore, **II**, 138, 180, 197, 280, 299, 327; sight-seeing experiences ashore described, **II**, 115, 117, 118, 119, 120, 151, 157–158, 159, 161, 164, 169–170, 174–176, 188, 233, 237–238, 241, 246–248, 251–253, 293, 357–358; rumored deployment to China, **II**, 315, 346; rumored deployment to Korea, **II**, 306; homeward bound, **II**, 354, 357, 359, 360–361, 363, 365, 367, 369, 373, 381, 386, 393, 394, 399, 401, 402, 404, 405, 407, 408; anxiety over decommissioning inspection, **II**, 236, 239, 240, 396, 397, 399, 400, 403, 405, 407, 408; ship decommissioned, **II**, 418.
Research and Writing Aboard: social distractions interfere with, 204–205; ship duties interfere with, **II**, 107, 110, 112, 113, 139–140, 145, 147, 148, 151, 153, 155, 159, 160, 178, 189, 223, 233, 258, 301, 303, 313, 332, 350, 397; declines offers to write articles, **II**, 138, 189, 311, 332, 342, 355; minimizes literary output while aboard, **II**, 214; Nelson biography, **II**, 114, 135–136, 138, 143, 148, 153, 155, 156, 159, 168, 172, 178, 183, 189, 193, 200, 204, 205, 223, 258, 259, 265, 303, 317–318, 328, 332, 347, 349, 359, 397, **III**, 119–120; stops work on Nelson after Erben criticism, **II**, 227; uncompleted Nelson manuscript sent home, **II**, 229, 231, 233; anger at having to discontinue work on Nelson, **II**, 258–259; Howe article, **II**, 114, 118, 121, 124, 126, 127, 132, 135, 155, 166; Two Maritime Expeditions article, **II**, 138, 142, 143, 147; Blockade and Naval Strategy article, **II**, 276, **301**; Possibilities of Anglo-American

Reunion article, **II**, 295, 300, 301, 303, 305, 307, 310, 311, 314, 332, 334, 338, 342, 350, 355; mention, **II**, 38, 167, 171, 179, 211, 212, 216, 217, 225, 267, 269, 270, 273, 274, 325, 341, 376, 380, 383, 409, 420, 431, **III**, 203, 218, 238, 299, 583, 587, 667, 719, 726, 729
See Index Section III, Bibliography; and Index Section IV, Mahan, A. T.: Naval Career; Sea Duty; Sea
Chickasaw: 551
China (M/Br): 171, 173, 318
City of Paris (M/Br): **II**, 131, 348
Cizaba (Bra): 409
Colon (Sp): **II**, 574
Colorado: 540
Columbia: **II**, 368, 431, 435, 553
Comus (Br): 563
Concord: **II**, 349
Confeanza (Itl): 398
Congress: 89, 90, 91, 294, 371, 426, **III**, 53, 227; M. first active duty, **II**, 54; likes ship and crew, 84; assigned charge of Powder Division, 85; reports crewmen for disobedience, 86–87
Connecticut: **III**, 358–359
Conquest (Br): 662
Constellation: 79; **II**, 84, 85
Constitution: 445, 538; **III**, 61, 77, 83, 84, 89, 145, 319
Cormorant (M/Br): M. visits, 219
Costa Rica (M/Br): 121, 195, 196, 212
Crathie (M/Br): **III**, 593
Cressy (Br): **III**, 549, 550
Curaçoa (Br): 70, 75
Cushing: **III**, 559

Dacotah: 87–88
Dart (Br): 385
Dayot (Fr): 600
Deerhound (Y/Br): **II**, 644, 647, 659
Defender (Y): **II**, 474
Despatch (Y): 508, 517
Detroit: **II**, 367, 369, 406
Devastation (Br): 662, **II**, 509
Dolphin: **II**, 145
Dorothea (Y): **II**, 558
Dorsetshire (Br): **II**, 722
Drake (Br): **II**, 547
Dreadnought (Br): **III**, 171, 178, 185, 204
Duke of Wellington (Br): 662

Eagle (Y): **II**, 625, 673
Edgar (Br): 662; **II**, 226, 255
Elbe (M/Ger): **III**, 593
Elephant (Br): **II**, 514
Enchantress (Y/Br): **II**, 117, 140
Enterprise: 515; **II**, 2; **III**, 196
Epervier: **III**, 83
Essex: **III**, 61, 77, 196

Etruria (M/Br): **II**, 114
Euryalis (Br): **II**, 318

Formidable (Fr): **II**, 217, 221
Fredonia: 240
Furst Bismarck (M/Ger): **II**, 365, 386, 387, 402

Gaines (CSA): **III**, 555
Galena: 645
General Armstrong (Pvt): **III**, 120, 143
Germanic (M/Br): 534
Glencartney (M/Br): 351; M. takes passage in, 351–352
Goeben (Ger): **III**, 541
Great Republic (M): 137, 139, 139–140, 279, 316
Guerrière (Fr): 445; **III**, 77, 83, 84, 118, 673
Guiscardo (Itl): 382

Hartford: 118, 122, 124, 140, 182, 217, 225, 338, 530, 551, 561, 567, 597, 607, 608; **III**, 555
Harvard: **III**, 631
Henry Clay (M): **III**, 524
Heroine (Br): 595; **III**, 9
Hogue (Br): **III**, 549, 550
Hohenzollern (Ger): **III**, 726
Huascar (Ch): **II**, 422, 423, 424
Huron: **III**, 196; loss of in gale, 465; loss of reflects adversely upon USNA, 465, 466

Idaho: 311, 312, 313
Independence: Dennis M. serves in, 492
Independencia (P): **II**, 423
Indiana: **II**, 566, 630; **III**, 634, 637
Iowa: **II**, 143, 564, 566; **III**, 632
Iroquois: particulars, 78, 96, 101–102, 103, 105 107, 115, 346, 348; M. seeks assignment to, 78; ordered to as XO, 95; loses orders, 96; seeks command of, 280; takes command as acting CO, 283; detached, 314; neglect of duty, 167, 182, 239; objections to boredom of routine duty, 182, 191, 194, 195, 201, 211, 225, 230, 261, 278, 301; self-analysis as XO, 291; social life aboard, 149, 150, 154, 180; disliked by officers aboard, 99, 192; problems with officers' mess aboard, 97, 106, 110, 164, 166, 168, 208, 253, 257; desire to return home, 336, 341, 350; dislike of subordinates, 192, 198; conflicts with officers aboard, 271, 298, 328; ship movements, 150, 183, 195, 203, 224, 225, 229, 233, 245, 247, 250, 253, 262, 264, 292, 296, 298, 336, 338, 339, 341, 343, 347; problems with engines, 98, 114, 152, 226, 272, 284, 338, 339, 348; coaling problems, 98, 116, 266; food aboard, 163, 199, 205, 236, 272, 276, 287; routine drills, 147, 150, 153, 159, 168, 180, 182, 188, 192, 196, 201, 211,

219, 226, 229, 251, 254, 268, 298, 311; courts-martial duty, 182, 187, 245–246, 248, 262, 312, 313, 314, 323, 326; punishment of crew members, 176–177, 210, 231; crew crimes ashore, 129; desertions, 100, 138, 165, 184; deaths, 103, 110, 111, 134, 135; M. tension with crew, 147, 157, 162, 163, 174, 176, 177, 183, 186, 213, 224, 235, 241, 248, 252, 261, 277, 296, 299; crew discipline, 147; laziness of crew, 255; drunkenness of crew, 129, 200, 208, 231, 239, 255, 257; liberty parties ashore, 171, 238, 239, 240, 255, 256, 257; enlistment of foreign seamen abroad, 162; shorthanded crew, 176, 177; discharges of crew, 224, 225; outbreak of smallpox aboard, 134, 135, 137–138, 140; profanity, 100, 101; competitions with other ships in squadron, 118, 182, 198, 200, 202, 207, 208, 209, 211, 212, 213, 221, 306, 311, 336; gambling, 211; pets, 280; rats, 283, 312; small church attendance, 300; M. lectures crew on church attendance aboard, 193; religious interests of crew, 244, 282; church services aboard, 146, 151, 156, 161, 188, 193, 199, 203, 207, 210, 214, 218, 221, 267, 310; M. non-religious reading aboard 152, 155, 158, 167, 173, 174, 179, 183, 189, 192, 195, 199, 204, 208, 209, 210, 211, 213, 214, 221, 224, 226, 232, 233, 234, 235, 245–246, 255, 258, 266, 270, 276, 285, 293, 294, 309, 312, 321, 322, 323, 325, 328, 330, 331; time spent reading, 197; *Cayalti* investigation, 225, 341–342, 346–347; search for *Letrouge*, 264, 289; participation in Japanese treaty port openings, 117, 119; Tycoon takes refuge aboard, 125–126; evacuation of Japanese soldiers from Osaka, 126–127; landing party to avenge Japanese firing on Europeans, 127; landing parties to maintain order ashore, 153, 197, 212, 213; Japanese visit aboard, 153, 154; life of CO aboard, 285; M. performance as CO, 295; greater leisure time as CO, 296; loneliness of command, 297, 307; anxieties of command, 297, 307; duties as CO, 302, 311; Law relieves English as CO of, 318; M. visits aboard, 326; replaces *Wachusett* in Santos case representation, 611; mention, 78, 79, 131, 145, 146, 170, 171, 178, 185, 217, 222, 223, 227, 228, 237, 249, 274, 281, 304, 308, 316, 320, 342, 372, 599, 603, 646. *See* Index Section IV, English; Fletcher; Japan; Woolverton; Mahan, A. T.: Alcohol, Health, Religion, Sea, Seamanship, Sex, Sin, Temper, Vanity
Ivahy (Bra): 390

James Adger: 88, 372; M. ordered detached from, 91
Jamestown: 530, 531

Jennie Cushman (M): 114
Jibaro (Sp): 425
John Adams: 79
Juniata: 352, 539, 557
Jupiter (Fr): 425

Kaiser Wilhelm (Ger): **II**, 361
Kansas: **III**, 222
Kearsarge: 406
Kendrick Fish (M): 240
Kerguelen (Fr): 564

Lackawana: 551, 564, 608, 609; **II**, 47
Lancaster: 6, 79, 384, 407; **III**, 561, 573
Lawrence: **III**, 85
Leander (Br): **II**, 486
Leibnitz (M/Br): 413
Leopard (Br): **III**, 61
Letrouge (Fr): *Iroquois* searches for, 264, 289
Levant: 79, 81; M. rejects possible assignment to, 78; seeks assignment to, 80
Limicos (Bra): 563
Lord Nelson (Br): **III**, 185
Loyall (T): 551

Macedonian: 53, 371, 633, **III**, 61, 64, 82, 118, 217, 673; M. serves as Lt. in on USNA summer (1863) training cruise, **II**, 125, 408
Machias: **II**, 358, 360, 404, 405, 463
Maine: **II**, 543, 544, 546, 567, 675; M. reaction to sinking, **II**, 545; M. speech on sinking, **III**, 592–594
Manhattan: 551
Manzanita (T): 705
Marblehead: **II**, 435, 525, 672
Maria Teresa (Sp): **II**, 571
Marion: 644
Marlborough (Br): **II**, 722
Massachusetts: **II**, 566, 575, 576, 592, 630
Maumee: 206, 296, 312; M. critical of officers aboard, 280; M. visits, 307
Mearim (Bra): 386
Merrimac (CSA): **III**, 56
Metacomet: **III**, 555
Michigan: **III**, 679
Minneapolis: **II**, 553; **III**, 631
Minnesota: 38–39, 495, 524, 633; **II**, 290
Missouri: **III**, 177
Mohican: 608; **II**, 89
Monadnock: **II**, 566; **III**, 191, 637, 639
Monarch (Br): **II**, 514
Monitor: **III**, 56
Monocacy: 166, 171, 172, 179, 215, 219, 220, 222, 305, 308, 316, 318, 320, 332, 339; M. visits, 149, 152, 155, 158, 164, 173, 284, 288, 304, 325, 328, 331; criticizes dissipation of officers, 178, 180; criticizes seamanship aboard, 165; attends survey on, 331; movements of, 174, 304; smallpox outbreak, 314

Monongahela: 251, 551; **II**, 156; **III**, 56
Montcalm (Fr): 564
Monterey: **II**, 566; **III**, 637, 639, 640
Morgan (CSA): **III**, 555
Muscoota: 119, 149, 372; M. detached from, 94; orders to distasteful, 97; attempts to bring crew to God, 99–100; notes two religious conversions among crew members, 100; malaria sweeps ship, 139; canine mascot aboard, 142
Mutina (Br): 563

Narvaez (Sp): 381, 391, 410
Nedda (M/Br): **II**, 405
Nelson (Br): 662
Neptune (Fr): **II**, 221
Newark: **II**, 553; **III**, 191
New Hampshire: 524, 641
New Orleans: **II**, 553
New York: 304, 640; **II**, 143, 566, 574, 575, 672; **III**, 632, 634, 635
Nile (Br): 662; **II**, 509
Nipsic: 549
Normannia (M/Danish): **II**, 219, 385, 386, 387

Oneida: 124, 136, 298, 301, 306, 311, 321, 336; smallpox aboard, 140; M. visits, 198, 214, 217, 285, 299, 300, 303, 325, 326; beats *Iroquois* in sail-furling exercise, 213; M. criticizes officers of, 214; dispatched to Bangkok, 307; lost at sea, 185, 354
Onward: 561, 562
Oregon: 630; **II**, 553, 566, 567, 581, 630; **III**, 629, 634, 635
Orel (Rus): **III**, 184
Osborne (Y/Br): **II**, 140

Pallada (Rus): **III**, 550
Pavon (Ar): 425
Peacock (Br): **III**, 83
Pelayo (Sp): **II**, 565
Pelican (Br): **III**, 83
Pensacola: 79, **II**, 32, **III**, 561, 573; M. seeks assignment to, 78
Petrel: **III**, 559
Petropavlovsk (Rus): **III**, 90, 93, 95
Pinta: 564, 565, 568, 587
Pique (Fr): 385
Piscataqua: 192, 296, 311, 314, 316, 317, 318–319, 321, 324, 338; M. duty visits aboard, 225, 246, 280, 283, 309, 322, 328, 331; relieves *Hartford* as flagship of squadron, 225; M. social visits to, 277, 280, 325, 326; English transferred to command of, 280; M. lives aboard while awaiting transfer to *Aroostook*, 315; M. entertains aboard, 315
Plymouth: 83; M. takes USNA summer (1857) training cruise in, 2–4

Pocahontas: 371, **III**, 237; M. describes, 89; serves as XO in, 89; participates in abortive Matthias Point (Va.) operation, 90; prepares to join Port Royal operation, 89, 90

Portsmouth: 79, **II**, 290; M. seeks assignment to, 78

Potosi (M/Br): 427, 430, **II**, 250; M. family takes passage in, 427–430

Powhatan: 240, 538, 595

Preble: M. takes USNA summer (1858) training cruise in, 19, 23, 43, 59

President: **III**, 61, 64, 319

Prinzess Alice (M/Ger): **III**, 90, 214–215

Pylades: (Br): 385, 390

Rainbow: 76

Ranger (1776): **II**, 544, 547

Ranger (1873): 598, 599, 602

Ready (Br): 398

Release: 86

Resaca: 94

Restless: **II**, 558

Revenge: **III**, 470

Richmond: 503, 664, 665; **II**, 136; **III**, 555, 573

Rocket (Br): 385

Rodney (Br):118

Rover (M): **III**, 56

Royal Savage: **II**, 525

Royal Sovereign (Br): **III**, 155–156

Russia (M): **II**, 235

Sabine: M. urged to seek assignment to, 81–82; Dennis M. serves in as midshipman, 352

St. Louis: **II**, 624

St. Mary: 46

St. Paul: **II**, 553; **III**, 631

San Francisco: **II**, 354, 357, 360, 361, 363, 365, 368, 369, 371, 372, 374, 375, 376, 377, 379, 381, 383, 384, 386, 393, 394, 397, 402, 403, 404, 431

Saratoga: 525; **III**, 527

Satellite (Br): 564

Saxonia (M/Br): **III**, 491, 510

Scioto: 161; **III**, 56

S. Curling (M): 240

Selma (CSA): **III**, 555

Seminole: 371–372; M. recalls technique of coaling at sea, **III**, 557

Serapis (Br): **II**, 540, 544, 545, 547; **III**, 118, 121, 131, 139, 140, 487

Servia (M/Br): 534

Shannon (Br): **III**, 68, 69, 104

Shenandoah: 119, 124, 217, 528, 591; M. duty visit to, 219; critical of procedures aboard, 220; *Iroquois* beats in sail-furling exercise, 221

Snap (Br): 178; M. gets drunk aboard, 175

Solace (H): **II**, 559

Sterling Castle (Br): **II**, 730

Stiletto: **III**, 559

Stonewall (J): 148, 173; *Iroquois* supplies with crewmen, 168; arrives in Yokohama, 333

Suavaroff (Rus): **III**, 184

Sumter (CSA): 88–89

Supply: 365

Suwonada (M): 240

Swatara: 556; **II**, 22

Swiftsure (Br): 561, 563

Tallapoosa: 512, 523, 524, 527, 538

Tecumseh: 551; **III**, 556

Tennessee (CSA): **III**, 556

Tennessee: 362, 502, 551, 553, 637, 639; M. participates in survey on, 507

Texas: **II**, 565, 566; **III**, 640

Thetis: 646, 709, 718; **II**, 26

Ticonderoga: 376, 382, 390, 391, 393, 395, 413

Titanic (M/Br): M. criticizes Ismay role in disaster as near cowardice, **III**, 454–457; cousin of Mrs. M. lost in sinking, **III**, 720

Trenton: 507; first in USN to be fitted with electric lights, 549

Union (P): 382

United States: 633; **III**, 61, 64, 82, 217

Valkyrie III (Y/Br): **II**, 474

Vandalia: **III**, 57

Vermont: 540, **II**, 290; M. ordered to duty in, 370; requests detachment to get married, 371

Vesuvius: **III**, 559

Victoria (Br): **II**, 114, 161, 168; **III**, 593

Victory (Br): **II**, 317, 465, 491

Vigilant (Br): **II**, 310

Virginia (CSA): 84

Virginius (M): 410, 439

Vittore Pisani (Itl): 385, 563

Wabash: 452

Wachusett: particulars, 556–557, 559, 560; M. ordered to command of, 556; reports on board, 559; detached, 613, 614; dislike of duty aboard, 578, 605, 611, **II**, 256; worst Commander's command in USN, 605; pending promotion suggests short tour aboard, 557; ship movements, 559–560, 572, 591, 594, 597–598, 601, 602, 612; poor condition of, 561–562, 570, 578, 584, 587, 590, 596, 597, 607, 608, 609; unseaworthiness, 587, 590, 595, 601; obsolete as warship, 592, 594; poor condition of equipment, 562–563, 596, 602; condition of guns, 565; coal consumption, 594, 597, 598, 599, 601, 602; cost of coal, 594; short steaming radius, 598, 599, 611; animals aboard, 566; deaths aboard, 561; fear for health of crew, 605–606, 609, 610; runs aground, 598, 612; collision, **II**, 160; courts-martial, 581; court of inquiry, 581; routine exercises, 565; earlier Alaskan deployment, 570; crew discharges, 568, 571, 583; crew vacancies, 559, 569, 571, 581, 583, 584, 603; crew reenlistment, 581; crew recruitment, 559, 569, 571, 582, 616; crew pay, 582, 583, 589–590; crew fitness reports, 612; officer vacancies, 565, 559, 589, 590–591, 594, 595; officer fitness reports, 561, 563, 566, 567, 568, 569, 591, 617; officer personnel changes, 565, 584; M. fails to submit intelligence reports, 564; reports on Central American war, 598–600, 601; involvement in U.S. diplomacy, 587–589, 590, 591, 594, 595, 597, 598, 599, 600, 601, 602, 603–604, 609, 610; preliminary work on *Influence* book aboard, 606–607, 616, **II**, 493–494; ordered home to Mare Island, 589, 590, 591, 611; M. protests delay in returning home, 590–591, 596, 601; seeks detachment to take up NWC duty, 578, 581–582, 583–584, 597, 603, 605, 607, 608; sees conspiracy to keep him aboard, 607, 608; decommissioning inspection, 613, **II**, 213; M. enjoyed peace and obscurity of South American ports, **II**, 149; mention, 556–567, 569–571, 574, 578–579, 581–584, 587, 589–592, 594–603, 605–606, 608–609, 611–614, 616–617; **II**, 47, 213, 214, 256, 362, 363, 375; **III**, 365. *See* Index Section IV, Chile; Colombia; Ecuador; Guatemala; Luce, Stephen B.; Peru.

Wasp: particulars, 373; seakeeping qualities, 427; M. ordered to command of, 373; assumes command, 373; detached, 426, 427, 430; unable to move wife aboard, 374; ship movements, 375, 377–378, 379, 380, 383, 386–387, 396, 397, 400–401, 402, 403, 407, 411, 419, 424–425, 426; general condition of, 375, 376–377, 379, 380, 385, 387, 391, 394–395, 397, 402–403, 406–407, 411; survey on hull, 416, 417, 418, 419, 421, 427; poor condition of ship's boats, 382, 385, 406, 407, 408, 414; boiler and engine problems, 375, 379, 380, 382, 390, 391, 392, 395,
402, 404, 405, 406, 414, 424; coaling, 384, 394, 395, 397, 403, 407, 410, 414; replenishment of stores, 393, 413, 414; illness aboard, 374, 376, 382; courts-martial aboard, 383, 384; routine exercises, 379, 380, 385, 388–389, 397, 403, 411, 418, 419; difficulty recruiting seamen abroad, 379, 383, 385, 387–388, 390; ignorance of crew, 388; instruction of crew, 388; conduct of crew, 389, 408, 410; discharge of crew, 389; crew personnel changes, 408, 410; officer personnel changes, 390, 406; collision, 394; trapped in drydock, 417–418, 420, 424; runs aground, 397, 398, 402, 403, 407, 411, 412; shows flag in Paraguay, 396, 397, 399; hydrographic surveys, 400, 401, 406, 407, 408, 411, 412, 413, 414, 419, 421–422, 424; yellow fever drives from Montevideo, 401; assistance to U.S. merchant vessels, 404, 415, 416; assistance to U.S. diplomacy, 405, 423, 425; salutes Argentine flag, 419–420; non-participation in Peruvian independence ceremony, 421; off-limits to Argentine citizens, 423; M. protests dangerous anchorage; mention, 373–407, 410–412, 414–427, 430, 438, **III**, 723. *See* Index Section IV, Argentina; Brazil; Paraguay

Wateree: 240

Wieland (M/Ger): **II**, 231, 233

Winnebago: 551

Worcester: 365, 367, 369, 372, **II**, 146; M. assigned duty in, 359; ordered to France with grain, 360; seakeeping qualities, 360, 362, 363; deadly explosion of boiler, 361, 362; cargo sold in London, 364; M. goes to church ashore, 364; visits London, 364; dislike of duty aboard, 366; crew desertions, 366; M. detached from, 369, 370

Wyoming: 215

Yale: **III**, 631

Yankee: **II**, 557

Yorktown: **II**, 34, 143; **III**, 559

Yosemite: **II**, 577

Ypiranga (Bra): 390

Zebra (Br): 198, 209

SECTION III—BIBLIOGRAPHY

Note: *This section consists of books, articles, and other items written by, read by, or used by Mahan, or cited by Mahan and the editors.*

BOOKS

Books (General): gain M. no entrée into American social circles, **II**, 122; win Chesney Medal, **II**, 691; copyright considera-
tions, **II**, 415, 424, 460–461, 466, 472, 492, 522, 526, 610, **III**, 200, 232, 237, 269, 305, 361, 428, 430, 461; translations of, **II**, 108, 179, 186, 218, 306, 511, 513, 525, 593–594, 596, 614, 619, 622, 702, 703, 716, **III**, 151,

Books, General (*cont.*)

331, 444, 451, 456, 490, 491; no point writing what few will read, **II**, 510; M. pleased his books contribute to welfare of Britain and English-speaking race, **II**, 691; better received in Britain than U.S., **II**, 47, 105, 182, 305, 395, **III**, 190; reception and reputation of in Britain, **II**, 47, 85, 97, 105, 110, 116, 117, 129, 131, 135, 142, 144, 146, 149–150, 166, 182, 199, 203, 207, 265, 270, 271, 273, 277, 279, 281, 319, 327, 342, 366, 395, 402, **III**, 203, 375; M. popularity in England stimulates sales of, **II**, 277, 295–296, 300, 305, 306, 392; considers lowering price of in England, **III**, 293; economics of serialization, **II**, 398, **III**, 200; prices sold at, **III**, 418; M. recognizes vogue as author is over, **III**, 492; Fisher dubs M. extinct volcano as author, **III**, 492; sales of books, **II**, 168, 186, 240, 274, 277, 285, 286, 295–296, 300, 303, 305, 306, 319, 321, 349, 392, 397, 451, 462, 467, 472, 490, 511, 519, 536, 594, 596, 633, 655, 729, 739, **III**, 135, 156, 190, 200, 238, 362, 373, 407, 417; royalty payments to M., 553, **II**, 110, 111, 115, 117, 124, 133, 186, 193, 205, 291, 293, 306, 389, 459, 460, 466, 467, 519, 536, 549, 568, 626, 633, 641, 655, 676, **III**, 135, 150, 156, 173, 199, 206, 360, 361, 362, 375, 378, 490, 517; books projected or considered but unwritten: Naval History of the Civil War, **II**, 96, 110, 178, 459; History of the U.S. Navy, **II**, 510; Collection (Essays) of Famous Naval Battles, **II**, 434, 449, **III**, 25; Life of William B. Cushing, **II**, 517, 568, 571, 593, 596; Textbook on Sea Power, **II**, 517, 561, 568, 641, 655, 676, 686–687, 688, 703, 716, 717, 724, 743; Children's History of the U.S., **II**, 723–724, 743; History of U.S. Expansion, **III**, 161, 461, 477, 505, 521, 524; Collected Works of A. T. Mahan, **III**, 173, 181, 199, 200, 301, 302, 303; Naval Operations in European War (1914), **III**, 551. *See* Historiography, History, Publication Procedures; Index Section IV, Mahan, A. T.: Financial Problems

Historiography (*General*): popularization of materials, 712, 713, **II**, 9, 433, 497, **III**, 25, 246, 249, 254; influence of public opinion through, **II**, 234, 685, 701, **III**, 204–205, 346; subordinationist methodology, **II**, 42, 61, 394, 441, 465, 494, 549, **III**, 161, 246, 249, 254, 286; research techniques, **II**, 32–33, **III**, 528; handling of factual material, **II**, 26, 42, 43, 465, 520; writing style and techniques, 575–576; **II**, 42, 308, 320–321; bias in, **II**, 26, 340, 478, 491, **III**, 64; anecdote in, **II**, 486; requires access to personal letters, **II**, 517; comparisons of private letters most productive of truth, **III**, 116–

117; court transcripts productive of truth, **III**, 130; importance of contemporary documents, **III**, 191; importance of the index, **III**, 133; speed of execution, 554, 621, **II**, 27, 46, 57, 94, 101, 105, 460, **III**, 73, 131; importance of continuity of application to task, **II**, 68, 91, 96, 98; M. required absolute quiet when writing, **III**, 729; M. considers his primary profession, **II**, 377, 394; a naval historian rather than statesman, **II**, 531; more useful to USN as historian than ship's officer, **II**, 91, 97, 98, 107, 160, 165, 182, 217, 230, 281; writing biography more difficult than philosophizing about history, **II**, 436, 441, 451; M. flattered to be recognized as an historian, **II**, 701; sees early exhaustion of naval subjects on which to write, **III**, 111; over-abundance of useless data threatens future historians, **III**, 247; pleasure of reading books must yield to the business of writing them, **III**, 41; sadness on having completed a book, **III**, 159. *See* History; Books; Articles; Index Section IV, American Historical Association, American Historical Review

History (*General*): M. belief in "lessons" of past, 623, 625, 659, **II**, 9; influence of sea power upon, **II**, 9, and *passim*; origin of sea power concept, **II**, 320, 493–494; experience of past should shape opinions and policy of future, 623, 628, **II**, 11; reading of aboard *Iroquois*, 266, 270, 276, 285, 293, 294, 312, 331; New Testament as, 190; historicity of the Bible, **III**, 648; role of Christian standards in progress of Christian nations, **III**, 489; Christ the motive power behind civilization and progress, **III**, 690; regeneration of mankind is the regeneration of individual men **III**, 619; concept of inevitable progress in, **II**, 483, 543, **III**, 616; men control and are controlled by events, **II**, 629, **III**, 608; study of war is study of, **III**, 273; reading of by officers important to well-being of USN, **III**, 304; future world struggle will be between land power and sea power, **III**, 603; M. charged with having no philosophy of, **II**, 671; M. work on U.S archival publications project, **III**, 240, 244; 1815–1850 period in U.S. a terra incognita, **III**, 159. Naval History: analogy between land warfare and naval warfare, 619, 624, 631, 633, 637, 638, 651, **II**, 9, **III**, 71, 91, 220, 387–388, 706; courts-martial records more valuable in than ships' logs, **III**, 673–674; archival sources for U.S., **III**, 671–674; battles rendered intelligible by historical context, **II**, 449. *See* Historiography; Publication Procedures; Books; Articles

Literary References: "Algernon," in Moore, *The Leycesters*, **II**, 125; "Sir Sedley Beaudesert" in Lytton, *The Caxtons*, 23; "Caspar," in Southey, "Battle of Blenheim," **II**, 549; "Lucy Dashwood," in Lever, *Charles O'Malley*, 9, 11, 12; "Sir George Dashwood," *ibid.*, 9, 12; "Hamlet," in Shakespeare, *Hamlet*, **III**, 450; "Josiah Hartopp," in Lytton, *op. cit.*, 71; "D. Leycester," in Moore, *op. cit.*, **II**, 125; "Charles O'Malley," in Lever, *op. cit.*, 12, 628; "Sancho Panza," in Cervantes, *Don Quixote*, **II**, 364; "Bishop Proudie," in Trollope, *Barchester Towers*, **II**, 236; "Don Quixote," in Cervantes, *op. cit.*, 348, **II**, 364; "Mr. Seladine," in Moore, *op. cit.*, **II**, 125; "Sam Weller," in Dickens, *Pickwick Papers*, **II**, 273. Poets and Poems: Dean Alford, "Easter Eve," **II**, 115; Louise S. Bevington, "Love's Depth," **II**, 115; Lord Byron, *Childe Harold's Pilgrimage*, 354; Herbert E. Clark, "Assignation," **II**, 115; Samuel Taylor Coleridge, *The Rime of the Ancient Mariner*, 105; William Falconer, "Shipwreck," **II**, 238; Lytton, "Lucifer in Starlight," **II**, 115; Robert Southey, "The Battle of Blenheim," **II**, 549; **III**, 702

Publication Procedures: multiple publication (republication, prepublication, serialization) of same written materials, **II**, 26, 42, 44, 85, 86, 91, 92, 94, 97, 100, 102, 111–112, 122, 350, 397–398, 422, 424, 429, 430, 431, 432, 433–434, 437, 453, 454, 486, 491, 492–493, 496, 497, 498, 518, 519, 520, 521, 523, 524, 526, 529, 531, 552, 615, 634, 655, 666, 687, 720, **III**, 23, 29, 30, 31, 36, 46, 59, 76, 89–90, 136–137, 141, 147, 152, 173, 205, 234, 241–242, 245, 246, 248, 294, 389, 428, 466; simultaneous publication of same written materials, **II**, 522, 526, 549, 615, 699, 743, **III**, 5, 7, 8, 17, 131, 141, 152, 172, 180, 181, 205, 214, 256, 537; use of book and magazine materials in lectures, **II**, 35, 410, 446, 534, **III**, 97, 141, 146. *See* Articles, Books

Books Written by Mahan

Mahan, A. T., *Armament and Arbitration, or The Place of Force in International Relations of States*. New York: Harper Brothers, 1912: **III**, 466, 483, 486

Mahan, A. T., *From Sail to Steam*. New York: Harper Brothers, 1907: **III**, 203, 231, 233, 234, 241, 243, 264, 302, 314, 667; purpose of **III**, 232; M. flattered by offer to write autobiography, **III**, 161, 198; financial motivation to write, **III**, 161, 216, 225; serialization and royalty arrangement, **III**, 173, 198; sees articles comprising through press, **III**, 209, 222; research on, **III**, 177,

216, 217–218, 219–220, 222; sees book through press, **III**, 224, 227; serialization delayed, **III**, 225; complimentary copies sent, **III**, 232; reviews, III, 237

Mahan, A. T., *The Gulf and Inland Waters*. New York: Charles Scribner's Sons, 1883: 658, **II**, 55, **III**, 303; research on, 546, 548, 549, 550, 551, 554, 555, **III**, 57–58; map work for, 547–548; submits to publisher, 547, 554; copies ordered by USN, 552; advance on royalties, 553; financial motive for writing, 554; speed of writing, 554; sectional viewpoints in, 554–555; writing style employed, 575–576

Mahan, A. T., *The Harvest Within: Thoughts on the Life of a Christian*. Boston: Little, Brown and Company, 1909: **II**, 735, **III**, 296, 298, 418; M. contemplates writing, **III**, 234; gives high priority on writing schedule, **III**, 248; interests Little, Brown in publishing, **III**, 274; search for title, **III**, 274, 293, 295, 297, 303; service on Moody Commission delays, **III**, 285; organized around a central idea, **III**, 286; book the expansion of an 1899 lecture, **III**, 286, 294; sees through press, **III**, 286, 290, 292–295, 297, 299; complimentary copies sent, **III**, 302, 305; cover design embarrasses M., **III**, 304; difficulty finding English publisher, **III**, 305, 306; reviews, **III**, 305, 306, 310

Mahan, A. T., *The Influence of Sea Power upon History, 1660–1783*. Boston: Little, Brown and Company, 1890 [*Influence #1*]: 614, 711, 718, **II**, 12, 26, 54, 84, 85, 108, 129, 186, 217, 303, 349, 460, 467, 476, 489, 511, 513, 525, 549, 691, **III**, 81, 113, 373, 418, 479, 481, 489, 663; origin of underlying idea, **II**, 493; **III**, 220; theme of, **II**, 9; initial thoughts on content and structure, 606–607, 622–624; chooses NYC as research base, 615; research for NWC lectures comprising, 615–619, 621, 624, 627, 628, 630, 632–634, **II**, 526; lectures at NWC lead to, 641, **II**, 9; daily work schedule on, 618; mental strain occasioned by, 621; work slowed by illness, 626; fear of failure, 621, 628; anticipates originality of, 624; affirms originality of, 658; purpose of, **II**, 10, 11; hopes will raise status of his profession, 625; attempts to find publisher for, 657–659, 707, 708, 712, **II**, 295, **III**, 274; reasons for refusing to publish lectures comprising in USNI *Proceedings*, 666–669; attempts to publish privately, 700, 707, 708, 712; attempt to publish initially in England, 707; secures pre-publication commitments to purchase, 708, 712, 714; popular nature of, 712, 713; **II**, 9; usefulness to NWC curriculum, 712–713, **II**, 69; Seeley

Books Written by Mahan (*cont.*)
article similar to thrust of, 713; profit motive in publication of, 714, **II**, 9; sees through press, 717, 718, **II**, 2; complimentary copies to friends and USN political allies, **II**, 9, 10, 11; reviews of, **II**, 34, 94, 138, 189, 191; links fame of with importance of NWC, **II**, 41, 60–61; better received in England than U.S., **II**, 47; orders copies for NWC library, **II**, 69; title phrase "sea power" chosen for impact, **II**, 494; surprised at success of, **II**, 494; sales of, **II**, 240, 462, 596, 655

Mahan, A. T., *The Influence of Sea Power upon the French Revolution and Empire, 1793–1812*. Boston: Little, Brown and Company, 1892 [*Influence #2*]: **II**, 38, 86, 110, 129, 147, 186, 349, 389, 392, 433–434, 453, 460, 462, 489, 490, 493, 525, 596, 619, **II**, 227, 418, 667; research on, **II**, 1, 2, 3, 9, 26, 29, 32, 33, 37, 39, 42, 44, 48, 49, 54, 55, 66–67, 531; use of material in magazine articles, **II**, 26, 42; use of materials in NWC lectures, **II**, 35; lectures at NWC lead to, **II**, 54; asserts originality of viewpoint, **II**, 26, 42; scope and material covered in part by Henry Adams, **II**, 42; seeks avoidance of USN duty unrelated to writing of, **II**, 53, 67; wants sea duty postponement to complete, **II**, 54–55; urged by Tracy to complete, **II**, 64; attributes completion to Tracy's protection, **II**, 89; publication of, **II**, 42, 47–48, 84, 85; anxiety over British reception, **II**, 85; complimentary copies to friends and USN political allies, **II**, 89; Herbert reads and converts to pro-NWC stance, **II**, 142, 144, 145; Morris comment on, **II**, 149–150; advertised for sale in Britain, **II**, 115; sales of, **II**, 240, 462, 596, 655; length of, **II**, 466; reviews of, **II**, 94, 105, 116, 138, 189, 191; M. considers final three chapters his best work, **II**, 494

Mahan, A. T., *The Influence of Sea Power in its Relation to the War of 1812*. Boston: Little, Brown and Company, 1905: **II**, 178, 517, 548, 568, 571, 694, 717, **III**, 59, 71, 101, 134, 136, 139, 147, 149, 150, 151, 154, 159, 176, 208, 239, 313, 340–341, 385, 416, 467, 475–476, 542, 545, 620, 625, 672, 673; first considered, **II**, 96; initial conception of, **II**, 492; inquires about possible commercial success of, **II**, 110; will be his last book, **II**, 110; will write next after *Nelson*, **II**, 395, 510; Century Company proposes prepublication serialization, **II**, 491, 492–493, 497; M. sees possibility of two complementary books on subject, **II**, 492–493, 497; derives articles from, **II**, 521–522, **III**, 76, 81, 97; suspends work on, **II**, 561, 694;

pecuniary interest in, **III**, 141; sees small commercial prospects for, **II**, 561; aimed at U.S. rather than British market, **II**, 724, **III**, 152; research on, **II**, 679, 724, **III**, 30, 33, 61, 64–70, 73, 76, 78–79, 81, 85, 87–88, 103–104, 105, 107–111, 114–117, 120–130, 132–133, 137, 144; main thesis of, **III**, 52; M. bias on subject, **III**, 58, 64; sees serialized articles comprising through press, **III**, 76–78, 81–84, 85–86, 97, 103; length, **III**, 80–81; reviews, **III**, 88, 152, 155, 156, 161, 162, 166, 167–172, 195; sends Roosevelt proof pages to argue maritime neutral rights historical point, **III**, 113, 157; argues immunity of capture of private property at sea issue in, **III**, 158; writing of, **III**, 127, 133; found writing of a dry task, **III**, 155; sees book through press, **III**, 128, 133, 135, 137, 139–140; material is similar to that in Henry Adams book, **III**, 128, 133, 137; complimentary copies sent, **III**, 140, 145, 148, 428; M. pleased with format, **III**, 145; thinks it the best of his three *Influence* books, **III**, 195; sales of, **III**, 152, 156, 190, 200; Roosevelt quotes from in Annual Message, **III**, 195; serialization produced main payment for work on, **III**, 200; flatness of theme caused commercial failure, **III**, 200; M. questions sale price of, **III**, 418

Mahan, A. T., *Sea Power Series*: **II**, 9, 461, 479, 491, 510, 655, 676, 679, 724, **III**, 48, 140, 159, 161, 181, 195, 257, 274, 286, 373, 425

Mahan, A. T., *The Interest of America in International Conditions*. Boston: Little, Brown and Company, 1910: **III**, 347, 418, 446; purpose in writing, **III**, 346, 348; McClure rejects serialization proposal, **III**, 348; M. sees through press, **III**, 348–352, 358, 360; last minute updating of text of, **III**, 350, 358, 360; complimentary copies sent, **III**, 361; royalty rate on reduced, **III**, 361, 362

Mahan, A. T., *The Interest of America in Sea Power, Present and Future*. Boston: Little, Brown and Company, 1897: **II**, 496, 523, 524, 684, **III**, 52, 71, 151, 261, 418; motive in compiling, **II**, 529; complimentary copies sent, **II**, 529–531, 533; M. urges advertisements for, **II**, 532–533; reviews of, **II**, 532

Mahan, A. T., *Lessons of the War with Spain and Other Articles*. Boston: Little, Brown and Company, 1899: **II**, 530, 594, 657, 716, 739, **III**, 4, 31, 38, 191, 261, 418, 630, 642; conceived during war, **II**, 552; motive for writing articles comprising, **II**, 582; research on, **II**, 596, 605, 609, 610, 625; conflict over republication rights, **II**, 615; Long assists M. in research on, **II**,

625; Hague assignment halts work on book version, **II**, 632, 641; advertisements for, **II**, 634; Hague article included in, **II**, 652–653, 655; passages republished by A. B. Hart, **II**, 716

Mahan, A. T., *Life of Admiral Farragut.* New York: D. Appleton Co., 1892: **II**, 55, 57, 115, 186, 204, 205, 489, **III**, 227, 303; speed of preparation, **II**, 46, 57; purpose of, **II**, 46; relation of M. sea duty to writing, **II**, 46, 47; uses materials from *Gulf and Inland Waters* in, **II**, 56; links with usefulness of NWC, **II**, 57, 80; sees through press, **II**, 63–64, 69–70; works on during Chilean crisis, **II**, 64; complimentary copies sent to friends and USN political allies, **II**, 80, 245; commercial failure, **II**, 497, 517, 568, 593, **III**, 156; blames failure of on anti-navalism in U.S., **II**, 497; Morris praises, **II**, 116, 123, 225, 497; reviews, **II**, 116, 170, 225; inadequacy of research materials for, **II**, 517; derives article from, **II**, 628; cites in reference to possible U.S.-Japan war, **III**, 393

Mahan, A. T., *The Life of Nelson, the Embodiment of the Sea Power of Great Britain.* 2 vols. Boston: Little, Brown and Company, 1897: **II**, 153, 155, 159, 168, 178, 199, 231, 233, 265, 272, 395, 398, 496, 523, 525, 532, 637, 691, 739, **III**, 85, 118; M. inquires about possible commercial success of, **II**, 110; initial conception of, **II**, 110, 230; urged to write, **II**, 116; research, **II**, 114, 135–136, 138, 143, 147, 317–318, 328, 332–333, 347, 349, 359, 397, 419, 437, 440–441, 444, 461–462, 463, 468, 469, 475, 478, 514, 690, **III**, 119–120; writing of, **II**, 148, 156, 172, 183, 189, 193, 200, 205, 245, 259, 441, 465, delays in finishing, **II**, 303, 311, 314, 359, 396; London *Chronicle* interview on, **II**, 138, 473; financial success predicted for, **II**, 182, 204, 205, 258, 460, 471; anxiety over reviews, **II**, 191, 489, 495, 509; Little, Brown reports great interest in, **II**, 193; M. thinks it the great work of his life, **II**, 229, 470, 509; theme of, **II**, 488, 494; resumes work on after *Chicago* duty, **II**, 386, 419, 421, 446; derives articles from for *Century Magazine*, **II**, 422, 424, 429, 430, 431, 432, 434, 437, 447, 449, 450, 453–454, 458, 465, 480; solicits illustrations for in England, **II**, 430, 463, 467, 473, 481; articles derived from will help sales of, **II**, 434, 447, 458, 462, 465, 488; concern for Christmas sales of, **II**, 451, 454, 458; completes first volume, **II**, 450–451; precautions against destruction of manuscript by fire, **II**, 453, 463; England the best sales market for, **II**, 459, 461, 465, 466, 471; seeks to raise royalty rate on, **II**, 459, 460;

publication date advanced, **II**, 458, 460, 462; length of, **II**, 466, 482; sees through press, **II**, 469, 472–475, 477–478, 481–482, 484–492, 495; M. designs cover and title page, **II**, 479–480, 488–489; reviews of, **II**, 471, 473, 479, 481, 490, 500, 502, 504, 509, 594, 619, 622, 624, 630; Laughton book on Nelson draws on similar materials, **II**, 476–477; fears possible war in Europe will hurt sales, **II**, 495; typographical errors in, **II**, 503–504; complimentary copies sent, **II**, 500, 512, 513, 610. M. pleased with reception of, **II**, 509, 512; blames poor reviews on professional jealousy, **II**, 594; Nelson death scene, **III**, 337; sales of, **II**, 490, 511, 519, 536, 594. *See* Index Section **II**, Ships: *Chicago*

Mahan, A. T., *The Life of Nelson, the Embodiment of the Sea Power of Great Britain*, 2nd ed., revised. Boston: Little, Brown and Company, 1899: **II**, 511, 641, 702, **III**, 162, 425, 469; revised cheaper edition, **II**, 616, 618, 621, 624, 630, 633, **III**, 118; research on revised edition, **II**, 623–624, 626, 632, **III**, 49; thinks the subject of Nelson has been overworked, **III**, 148; M. confesses errors in first edition, **II**, 622; revision responds to criticism of M. handling of Nelson in Naples, **II**, 619, 622, 624, 626, 630–631, 632, 637, **III**, 48–49, 85, 118; sales of, **II**, 633, 729; M. donates Nelson materials to NYC Public Library, **III**, 48–49, 50; questions lowering sale price of, **III**, 418

Mahan, A. T., *The Major Operations of the Navies in the War of American Independence.* Boston: Little, Brown and Company, 1913: Century Company proposes serialization, **II**, 491; initially written for and published in Clowes, *Royal Navy*, **II**, 497, 510, 513, 520, 524, 543, 596; M. derives articles from, **II**, 518–524, 526–527, 531, 540–541, 544; anticipates poor reviews, **II**, 596; research for, **II**, 531, 540, 541; payment for Clowes version of, **II**, 199, 200, 208, 296, 378, 379; separate publication of in U.S., **II**, 616, **III**, 176–177, 180, 199–200, 208, 239, 296, 377–378, 379, 416, 460; financial dimensions of separate publication, **III**, 176, 296; little money to be made by separate publication in U.S., **III**, 416; no additional research for separate publication, **III**, 460, 467; rearranges organization for U.S. publication, **III**, 470, 512; additional research on, **III**, 472, 473, 512; sees through press (Little, Brown), **III**, 466–467, 469–472, 479–483, 485–486, 488–490, 493–494, 495, 499–500, 509, 513; sale of, **III**, 494; final book on naval history, **III**, 511–512, 514; Balkan War reference in-

Books Written by Mahan (*cont.*)
serted in preface to, **III**, 495; complimentary copies sent, **III**, 507, 511, 513

Mahan, A. T., *Naval Administration and Warfare, Some General Principles.* Boston: Little, Brown and Company, 1908: **III**, 46, 141, 258 259, 260, 261, 262, 269, 270, 406, 418, 428, 430; M. suggests collection of his articles, **III**, 241–242; governing idea of, **III**, 246, 249, 254; arrangements relating to collecting articles for, **III**, 243, 245, 246, 247, 249–250, 251, 254, 255, 256; difficulty choosing title, **III**, 246, 249, 256, 257; sees through press, **III**, 253–262, 264, 267, 268; M. argument with Goodrich delays publication, **III**, 264–266; reviews, **III**, 305

Mahan, A. T., *Naval Strategy, Compared and Contrasted with the Principles of Military Operations on Land.* Boston: Little, Brown and Company, 1911: **III**, 220, 299, 311, 312, 327, 331, 337, 340, 343, 347–350, 375, 378, 418–419, 439; contemplated, **II**, 96, 526, 615; Luce urges M. to update and publish NWC strategy lectures, **III**, 163, 198, 216, 234, 245, 250; financial considerations in writing, **III**, 163, 198, 234, 248, 414; recalled to temporary active duty to write, **III**, 198, 234, 248, 269, 317, 330, 367; problems connected with, **III**, 199, 234, 250, 359–360, 404; M. takes up project reluctantly, **III**, 234, 248, 250; research on, **III**, 245, 247, 248, 270, 271–272, 273, 301, 304, 306, 308, 309, 314, 323, 325–326, 335, 338, 368, 369, 394–395, 397, 404, 406, 416, 421; revision of NWC strategy lectures comprising, **III**, 269, 300–301, 303, 306, 309, 317–318, 330, 334, 351, 367, 368, 370, 670; writes new NWC lectures to be included in, **III**, 298, 300, 301, 304, 306, 308, 309, 310, 318, 323, 334, 337; NWC assists in preparation of manuscript of, **III**, 309–311, 322–324, 326, 328–329, 332, 336–340, 349, 351, 404; M. opposes use of simplified spelling in manuscript of, **III**, 325; finds writing difficult and nerve-wracking, **III**, 334, 417, 426; approaches Little, Brown on publication of, **III**, 373; sees through press, **III**, 359–360, 377, 379, 389, 404, 405, 407–408, 410–415, 417, 421–422, 425–426, 429–430; USN pre-publication purchase commitments, **III**, 362, 373, 407, 417, 421; M. includes previously published articles in, **III**, 389; asserts it will be his last magnum opus, **III**, 422, 447; index of, **III**, 422, 424–425, 430; complimentary copies sent, **III**, 428–429, 436; thinks strategic parts weak, **III**, 436; charged for excessive changes in galley and page proof, **III**, 436; an uninteresting book which M. came to loathe, **III**, 439, 440; hopes reputation will survive

it, **III**, 447; typographical errors in, **III**, 440, 441, 443; German translation, **III**, 444, 451; poor French translation, **III**, 491; Corbett writes on same subject, **III**, 451; too technical to be remunerative, **III**, 491; read by Winston Churchill, **III**, 491

Mahan, A. T., *Nelson at Naples.* Pamphlet, 1900: **III**, 49

Mahan, A. T., *The Problem of Asia and its Effect upon International Policies.* Boston: Little, Brown and Company, 1900: **II**, 666, 687, 703, 718, 742, **III**, 12, 35, 71, 348, 360, 418, 517; research on, 666; problems in Asia could lead to war, **II**, 688; M. considers book his swan song on contemporary politics, **II**, 707, 708; thinks it as good as anything he has written, **III**, 135; translated into Japanese, **II**, 716; outline of arguments in, **III**, 27; sale of, **III**, 135

Mahan, et al., "Report of the Commission to Select a Site for a Navy Yard on the Pacific Coast North of the Forty-second Parallel of North Latitude," September 15, 1889; in *Report of the Secretary of the Navy. 1889. In Two Parts.* Washington, D.C.: Government Printing Office, 1890. Part 2: 672, 673, 679–683, 686–689, 692, 694, 696, 697–700, 702–710, 714, 718, **III**, 570

Mahan, A. T., *Retrospect and Prospect, Studies in International Relations, Naval and Political.* Boston: Little, Brown and Company, 1902: **II**, 732, **III**, 23, 26, 71, 162, 245, 261, 418, 517; Little, Brown suggests publishing, **III**, 24; M. sends complimentary copies, **III**, 40

Mahan, A. T. and Sims, William S., *Size of Battleships . . . Naval Papers*: **III**, 178

Mahan, A. T., *Some Neglected Aspects of War.* Little, Brown and Company, 1907: **II**, 735, **III**, 172, 261, 418; Corbett contributes to, **III**, 223, 224; purpose of, **III**, 223, 225; arrangements relating to publication, **III**, 224, 225, 227, 231–232; sees through press, **III**, 225–228, 230–232; sales, **III**, 238; reviews, **III**, 238

Mahan, A. T., *The Story of the War in South Africa, 1899–1900.* London: Sampson Low, Marston and Company, Ltd., 1900. [The illustrated American edition was titled: *The War in South Africa; a Narrative of the Anglo-Boer War from the Beginning of Hostilities to the Fall of Pretoria.* New York: P. F. Collier and Son, 1900]: **II**, 687, 702, **III**, 10, 270; offer of high flat commission payment attracts M. to writing, **II**, 686; rushes to completion, **II**, 688; describes book as brief outline, **II**, 690; length of, **II**, 699; research on, **II**, 688, 699–700, **III**, 51; Clark provides data for, **II**,

699–700; asks J. B. Moore for assistance on, **II**, 688; sends complimentary copies, **II**, 699–700; reviews, **II**, 700; offers materials collected for to NYC Public Library, **III**, 51; donates materials to University Club library, **III**, 52

Mahan, A. T., *Types of Naval Officers: Drawn from the British Navy*. Boston: Little, Brown and Company, 1901: **II**, 717, **III**, 162, 215, 418, 472; initial conception of, **II**, 111–112, 123, 153, 496; attempt to interest Little, Brown in publishing, **II**, 496; length, **II**, 498, 729; concern over pre-emption of scope and concept of book, **II**, 720–721, 723; research on new material in, **II**, 722–723, 725, 726, 730–731, 735; American connections of British officers treated mentioned, **II**, 724–725; M. assistance to other historians working in same materials, **II**, 732–734; regards it as supplement to Nelson biography, **II**, 739; sees through press, **II**, 736; complimentary copies sent, **II**, 738–739; review of related to Sampson-Schley controversy, **II**, 739–740; sales of, **II**, 739

Other Books

Abbot, Gen. Henry L., *Memoir of Dennis Hart Mahan (1802–1871)*: 656

Adams, Henry, *History of the United States of America*: **II**, 37, 42
———, *History of the United States during the Administrations of Jefferson and Madison*: **III**, 121, 128, 133, 134, 137, 524

Admiral Mathew's Charge against Vice-Admiral Lestock Dissected and Confuted. By a Kings Letterman: **II**, 725, 731

Ady, Julia Mary (Cartright), *Madame, a Life of Henrietta, Daughter of Charles I and the Duchess of Orleans*: **II**, 217, 219
———, *Sacharissa; Some Account of Dorothy Sidney, Countess of Sunderland, Her Family and Friends, 1617–1648*: **II**, 189, 196, 219

Agathos and Other Sunday Stories: 1

Alcock, Sir Rutherford, *The Capital of the Tycoon. Narrative of a Three Years' Residence in Japan*: 179

Alderman, Edwin A., ed., *Library of Southern Literature*: **III**, 478

Alford, Henry, *Meditations in Advent: Creation and Providence*: 210

American State Papers: **II**, 110, 115, **III**, 115, 121, 122, 123, 124, 125, 126, 127, 132, 671; Naval Affairs, **III**, 673

Ammen, Daniel, *The Atlantic Coast*: 552

Angell, Norman, *The Great Illusion*: **III**, 448–449, 450, 487

Annual Report of the Secretary of the Navy: (1882) 544; (1889) 718; (1895)

II, 411, **III**, 397, 671. "Appendix to the Report of the Bureau of Navigation (1897–1898)": **II**, 605, 609, 671–672; (1898) **II**, 624

Appleton's Cyclopedia of American Biography, J. G. Wilson, ed.: **II**, 55

Arabian Nights: 108; **II**, 357

[Archduke Charles] Karl Ludwig, Archduke of Austria, *Grundsätze der Kriegskunst für die Generäle*: **II**, 526
———, *Grundsätze der Strategie erläutert durch die Darstellung des Feldzugs 1796*: **II**, 526
———, *Gesch. des Feldzugs von 1799*: **II**, 526

Archives of the United States Government. A Documentary History 1774–1934: **III**, 676

Army and Navy Register: **II**, 275

Asakawa, Kanichi, *The Russo-Japanese Conflict. Its Causes and Issues*: **III**, 406–407

Asami, Lt. Cmdr. K., IJN, *Biography of Vice Admiral Tasuka Serata*. Introduction by A. T. Mahan: **III**, 499, 688. *See* **III**, 688–692

Ashe, Samuel A'Court, *History of North Carolina*: **III**, 272

Autobiography of Commodore Charles Morris: **II**, 541, **III**, 252. *See* Soley, J. R., ed., "The Autobiography of Commodore Charles Morris," U.S. Naval Institute *Proceedings*, VI, No. 12

Babcock, Malthie Davenport, *Fragments That Remain from the Ministry of Malthie Davenport Babcock*: **III**, 295

Badham, F. D., *Nelson at Naples*: **III**, 49

Barnes, James, *David G. Farragut*: **II**, 631
———, *Drake and His Yeomen*: **II**, 631
———, *Naval Actions of the War of 1812*: **II**, 469, 476, 544

Barnsby, K. C., *The Royal Institution of Naval Architects, 1860–1960*: **III**, 40

Barrow, Sir John, *Autobiography*: **III**, 30, 33

Beatson, Robert, *Naval and Military Memoirs of Great Britain from 1727 to 1783*: **II**, 517–518

Beatty, Sir William, *Authentic Narrative of the Death of Lord Nelson*: **II**, 469

Beckford, William, *The History of the Caliph Vathek*: **II**, 462

Bede's *Ecclesiastical History of the English Nation*: **III**, 605

Beer, George, *British Colonial Policy 1754–1765*: **III**, 395
———, *The Commercial Policy of England Toward the American Colonies*: **III**, 395
———, *The Old Colonial System*: **III**, 395

Other Books (*cont.*)
———, *The Origins of the British Colonial System, 1578–1600*: **III**, 395
Benet, Stephen V., *A Treatise on Military Law and Practice of Courts-Martial*: 453
Biddle, James E., ed., *Autobiography of Charles Biddle, Vice President of the Supreme Executive Council of Pennsylvania, 1745–1821*: **II**, 609
Bigelow, Poultney, *The Borderland of Czar and Kaiser*: **II**, 267
Blake, E. Vale, ed., *Arctic Experiences: Capt. G. E. Tyson's Wonderful Drift on the Icefloe.* . . . : 552
Blameless Woman, A: **III**, 725
Bonfils, Léonard Léonce La Peyrouse, *Histoire de la Marine Française*: 617
Book of Common Prayer, revision of, by Joint Commission: **III**, 521, 522, 535, 545–546
Boswell, James, *Life of Johnson*: **II**, 200; **III**, 426, 492
Bowditch, Nathaniel, *The New American Practical Navigator*: **III**, 196
Bowles, Thomas Gibson, *Maritime Warfare*: **II**, 396
Brackenridge, Henry Marie, *Voyage to South America, Performed by Order of the American Government, in the Years 1817 and 1818, in the Frigate Congress*: **II**, 478
Brandt, Gerard, *Life of De Ruyter*: **III**, 73
Brassey, Thomas, *Brassey's Naval Annual*: **II**, 79, 437, 735; **III**, 16, 153, 358
Brenton, Edward Pelham, *Life and Correspondence of John, Earl of St. Vincent*: **II**, 735
British *Naval Chronicle (1798–1818)*: **III**, 671
British Parliamentary Blue Books: **III**, 51, 52
Brown, Allan D., *Jack Haultaut, Midshipman, United States Navy; or Life at the Naval Academy*: 474
Brown, G. Latham, *Nelson, His Public and Private Life*: **III**, 119
Bryce, James, *American Commonwealth*: **II**, 144
———, *Impressions of South Africa*: **II**, 673–674
Buel, C. C. and Johnson, Robert U., eds., *Battles and Leaders of the Civil War*: **II**, 410
Buell, Augustus C., *Paul Jones, Founder of the American Navy: a History*: **II**, 697; **III**, 317
Burgess, Tristram, *The Battle of Lake Erie, with Notice of Commodore Elliott's Conduct in that Engagement*: **III**, 66
Burgoyne, Sir John Montagu, *A Short History of the Naval and Military Operations in Egypt from 1798–1802*: 616
Burrows, M., *Life of Edward, Lord Hawke*: 618
Burton, Clarence M., *Early Detroit: A Sketch of Some of the Interesting Affairs of the Olden Time*: **III**, 130
Butler, Joseph, *The Analogy of Religion, Natural and Revealed, to the Constitution and Course of Nature* . . . : 147, 148, 150, 154, 159, 159–160, 162, 163, 164, 168, 169, 173, 174, 176
Byng's Court Martial: **II**, 726

Callwell, Charles Edward, *The Effect of Maritime Command on Land Campaigns Since Waterloo*: **III**, 270
Campbell, John, *Naval History of Great Britain, including the History and Lives of the British Admirals*: **II**, 178; **III**, 368
Canadian Government Archive Reports: **III**, 671
Captains' Letters: (1812), **III**, 416; (1813), **III**, 67, 389; (1814), **III**, 69, 78, 527, 673
Castex, R. V. P., *Théories stratégiques*: **III**, 491
Century Atlas: **III**, 77, 86
Cervantes, Miguel, *Don Quixote*: 348; **II**, 364
Chadwick, French Ensor, *The New American Navy*: **II**, 672
———, *The Relations of the United States and Spain: Diplomacy*: **II**, 672
———, *The Relations of the United States and Spain: The Spanish-American War*: **II**, 672
Charnock, John, *Biographia Navalis; or, Impartial Memoirs of the Lives and Characters of Officers of the Navy of Great Britain from the Year 1660 to the Present Time* . . . : 618; **II**, 730
Chevalier, Louis Edouard, *Histoire de la guerre maritime de 1778*: **III**, 527, 529
———, *Histoire de la marine française pendant la guerre de l'indépendance americaine*: **III**, 472
———, *Sous la première republique*: **III**, 473
Chiles, Rosa P., ed., *Letters of Alfred Thayer Mahan to Samuel A'Court Ashe*: 5, 9, 84
Churchill, Awnsham, comp., *A Collection of Voyages and Travels*: **II**, 679
Churchill, Winston, *The Inside of the Cup*: **III**, 682
Clark, *Combination Lock*: 542
Clark, George Ramsey, Stevens, William O., Alden, Carroll S., and Kraft, Herman F., *A Short History of the United States Navy*: **III**, 365

Clarke, Sir George Sydenham, *Russia's Sea-Power, Past and Present, or, The Rise of the Russian Navy*: **II**, 609

Clarke, Sir George Sydenham, and Thursfield, James R., *The Navy and the Nation*: **II**, 494–495

Cleveland City Council, *Inauguration of the Perry Statue, at Cleveland, on the Tenth of September, 1860, Including the Addresses and Other Proceedings, with a Sketch of William Walcutt, the Sculptor*: **III**, 144

Clowes, Sir William Laird, *The Royal Navy: a History from the Earliest Times to the Present ... assisted by Sir Clements Markham ... Capt. A. T. Mahan, U.S.N., H. W. Wilson, Theodore Roosevelt, E. Fraser*: **II**, 510, 513, 518, 519, 520, 521, 522, 523, 524, 531, 543, 594, 596, 597, 614, 616, 619; **III**, 176, 208, 239, 296, 378, 471, 473, 511, 514

Collins, Wilkie, *The Moonstone*: 245, 246

Colomb, Sir John, *Naval Intelligence and the Protection of Commerce*: 630

Colomb, P. H., *Naval Warfare: its Ruling Principles and Practice Historically Treated*: **II**, 189

Colton, George Woolworth, *Colton's General Atlas*: 124, 506

Commentaires de Napoleon: **III**, 323

Cooper, James Fenimore, *The Battle of Lake Erie; or, Answer to Messrs. Burgess, Duer and MacKenzie*: **III**, 66, 76

——, *History of the Navy of the United States of America*: 445; **III**, 65, 527

——, *The Last of the Mohicans*: **III**, 520

——, *Wing and Wing*: **III**, 520

Corbett, Sir Julian Stafford, *The Campaigns of Trafalgar*: **III**, 223

——, *Drake and the Tudor Navy*: **II**, 497; **III**, 223

——, *England in the Mediterranean; a Study of the Rise and Influence of British Power Within the Straits, 1603–1713*: **III**, 271, 273, 338, 416, 421

——, *England in the Seven Years' War; a Study of Combined Strategy*: **III**, 273, 276, 338, 374

——, ed., *Fighting Instructions, 1530–1816*: **II**, 722

——, *Some Principles of Maritime Strategy*: **III**, 223, 451

——, *Successors of Drake*: **III**, 223

Cortissoz, Royal, *The Life of Whitelaw Reid*: **III**, 71

Craik, George Lillie, and MacFarlane, C.: *Pictorial History of England*: **II**, 2

Creasey, Sir Edward Shepherd, *Fifteen Decisive Battles of the World, from Marathon to Waterloo*: **II**, 449

Cruikshank, Ernest Alexander, *Documentary History of the Campaigns upon the Niagara Frontier*: **III**, 671

——, *Documents Relating to the Invasion of Canada and the Surrender of Detroit, 1812*: **III**, 389

Curtis, Lionel, et al., *The Government of South Africa*: **III**, 396

Custance, Sir Reginald Neville, *The Ship of the Line in Battle*: **III**, 239

Dallas, George M., *Defense*: **III**, 65

Dante Alighieri, *The Divine Comedy*, translated by Henry W. Longfellow: 189

Darrieus, Gabriel, *La guerre sur mer, stratégie et tactique. La doctrine*: **III**, 235, 239, 272

Daveluy, René, *Étude sur la stratégie navale*: **III**, 272

Davies, C.: *Elements of Surveying and Levelling*: 400

Davis, Calvin DeArmond, *The United States and the First Hague Conference*: **II**, 633

Davis, Richard Harding, *Exiles and Other Stories*: **II**, 368

——, *Gallagher and Other Stories*: **II**, 368

Dearborn, Henry Alexander Scammell, *Defense of Gen. Henry Dearborn, Against the Attack of Gen. William Hull*: **III**, 130

De Hart, William C., *Observances on Military Law*: 453

de la Roncière, Charles, *Histoire de la marine française*: **II**, 631, 663, 668

de Rémusat, Claire Elizabeth Jeanne Gravier de Vergennes, *Memoirs of Madame de Rémusat*: **II**, 201

Deschanel, A. P., *Electricity and Magnetism*: 518, 519

de St. Amand, Arthur Léon Imbert, *Famous Women of the French Court*: **II**, 196

Dickens, Charles, *David Copperfield*: **II**, 358

d'Oberkirch, Henriette Louise, *Memoires of the Baroness d'Oberkirch, Countess de Montbrison*: **II**, 197

Dominions Office and Colonial Office List ... Comprising Historical and Statistical Information Respecting the Overseas Dominions and Colonial Dependencies of Great Britain: **II**, 79

Drayton, Percival, *Naval Letters from Captain Percival Drayton, 1861–1865*: **III**, 200, 202

Drinkwater, John, *A History of the Late Siege of Gibraltar, with a Description and Account of that Garrison, from the Earliest Periods*: **II**, 730

——, *A Narrative of the Battle of St. Vincent with Anecdotes of Nelson, Before and After the Battle*: **II**, 430

Other Books (*cont.*)

Dumas, A., *I Borboni di Napoli*: **III**, 49

Du Moncel, Theodose Achille Louis, *The Telephone, the Microphone and the Phonograph*: 519

Duncan, Robert Adam Philips Haldane, *Admiral Duncan*: **II**, 550

Dwight, Timothy, *Theology: Explained and Defended, in a Series of Sermons . . . with a Memoir of the Life of the Author*: 201

Edwards, Jonathan, *An Account of the Life of the Late Rev. David Brainerd*: 10

Ekins, Sir Charles, *The Naval Battles of Great Britain, from the Accession of the Illustrious House of Hanover to the Throne to the Battle of Navarin*: 616; **III**, 118

Eliot, Sir George Augustus, *A Treatise on Future Naval Battles and How to Fight Them*: 616

Eliot, Frances Minto, *Old Court Life in France*: **II**, 219

——, *Old Court Life in Spain*: **II**, 219

Emmons, George Foster, *The Navy of the United States, from the Commencement, 1775 to 1853, with a Brief History of Each Vessel's History and Fate*: **III**, 66, 177

Encyclopaedia Americana: **III**, 637

Encyclopaedia Britannica: **II**, 384, 641

Estournelles de Constant, Paul Henri Benjamin, *A French Plea for Limitation of Naval Expenses*: **III**, 72

——, *International Conciliation: The Organization of Peace*: **III**, 72

——, *Program of the Association for International Conciliation*: **III**, 72

——, *The Results of the Second Hague Conference*: **III**, 72

Evans, Robley D., *An Admiral's Log*: **II**, 143

——, *A Sailor's Log*: **II**, 143

Farragut, Loyall, *The Life of David Glasgow Farragut, First Admiral of the United States Navy, Embodying His Journals and Letters*: **II**, 55, 56, 225

Field, Edward, *Esek Hopkins, Commander-in-Chief of the Continental Navy, 1775–1778*: **II**, 608, 622

Fiennes, Geoffrey Cecil T.-W.: *Reminiscences*: **III**, 397

Fiennes, Gerard Yorke Twisleton-Wykham, *The Ocean Empire, its Dangers and Defences*: **III**, 397

Findlay, Alexander George, *Sailing Directory for the Ethiopic or South Atlantic Ocean*: 412

Fiske, John, *Old Virginia and Her Neighbors*: **III**, 166

Foote's Vindication: **III**, 49

Force, Peter, ed., *American Archives*: **III**, 671

Foreign Relations of the United States: **II**, 406

Fraser, Sir William Augustus, *Hic et Ubique*: **II**, 476

Freeman, Edward Augustus, *The Historical Geography of Europe*: **III**, 312

Froissart, Jean, *Cronycles*: 72

Froude, James Anthony, *English Seamen in the Sixteenth Century. Lectures Delivered at Oxford, Easter Terms, 1893–1894*: **II**, 422, 428–429

——, *Oceana, or England and her Colonies*: 626

Fullerton, William Morton, *Problems of Power, a Study of International Politics from Sadowa to Kirk-Kilissé*: **III**, 494

Fyffe, Charles Alan, *A History of Modern Europe*: **II**, 42

Gardiner, Samuel Rawson, *The History of England from the Accession of James I to the Outbreak of the Great Civil War, 1603–1642*: **III**, 159, 166

Gibbon, Edward, *The Decline and Fall of the Roman Empire*: **III**, 159

Gilder, William Henry, *Schwatka's Search: Sledging in the Arctic in Quest of the Franklin Records*: 552

Gleaves, Albert, *James Lawrence, Captain, United States Navy, Commanding the Chesapeake*: **III**, 103–104, 105

Gleig, George Robert, *A Narrative of the Campaigns of the British Army at Washington, Baltimore and New Orleans, under Generals Ross, Pakenham, and Lambert, in the years 1814 and 1815*: **III**, 120, 143

Goldsborough, Charles Washington, *The United States Naval Chronicle*: **III**, 30, 671

Goodrich, Samuel G., *Peter Parley's Tales of Animals*, 1

Gordon, James Edward Henry, *A Physical Treatise on Electricity and Magnetism*: 518, 519, 520

Goulburn, Edward Meyrick, *An Introduction to the Devotional Study of the Holy Scriptures*: 197, 204, 210, 256, 302, 308, 311

——, *Thoughts on Personal Religion, being a Treatise on the Christian Life in its Two Elements, Devotion and Grace*: **II**, 458

Grant, Ulysses S., *Personal Memoirs of U.S. Grant*: **III**, 388

Griffis, William Elliott, *Corea. The Hermit Nation*: 553

——, *Unbeaten Tracks in Japan*: 553

Guérin, Léon, *Histoire maritime de la France ... depuis le règne de Louis XIV jusqu'à l'année 1850*: **III**, 472

Guettée, René François Wladimir, *The Papacy ...* : 130

Guizot, François Pierre Guillaume, *The History of Civilization, from the Fall of the Roman Empire to the French Revolution*: 331

Hall, Charles Mercer, *The Life of a Christian; Some Suggestions for Short Studies on the Spiritual Life*: **III**, 293

Halleck, Henry W., *Treatise on International Law and the Laws of War*: 618, 619

Hamersly, Lewis R., *The Records of Living Officers of the United States Navy and Marine Corps*: 591; **II**, 250; **III**, 249

Hamilton, Sir Richard Vesey, *Naval Administration: The Constitution, Character, and Functions of the Board of Admiralty, and of the Civil Departments it Directs*: **III**, 30, 33

Hamley, Sir Edward Bruce, *The Operations of War Explained and Illustrated*: 621, 624; **II**, 526; **III**, 343, 421

Hannay, David, *Rodney*: **II**, 723, 726

Harraden, Beatrice, *Ships that Pass in the Night*: **II**, 294

Harrison, Benjamin, *Views of an Ex-President*: **II**, 707

Harrison, James, *Life of Nelson*: **II**, 478

Hart, Albert Bushnell, *American History Told by Contemporaries*: **II**, 716

———, *Foundations of American Foreign Policy*: **II**, 701

Harwood, Andrew A., *The Law and Practice of United States Naval Courts-Martial*: 453

Hayes, Isaac Israel, *Arctic Boat Journey, in the Autumn of 1854*: 552

———, *Land of Desolation, being a Personal Narrative of Observation and Adventure in Greenland*: 552

Higginson, Thomas Wentworth, *Cheerful Yesterdays*: **II**, 505

Higgs, Robert, *The Electric Light in its Practical Application*: 519

Hildreth, Richard, *The History of the United States of America*: **III**, 159

Hoff, William Bainbridge, *Examples, Conclusions, and Maxim's of Modern Naval Tactics*: 627–628

Holls, George Frederick William, *The Peace Conference at the Hague and its Bearing on International Law and Policy*: **II**, 697, 704–706, 706, 710–712, 713, 714, 715, 719, 738; **III**, 16, 18, 19, 20, 21, 22, 449

Holmes, Oliver Wendell, *The Guardian Angel*: 158, 159

Hull, William, *Memoirs of the Campaign of the North Western Army of the United States A.D. 1812. In a Series of Letters Addressed to the Citizens of the U.S.*: **III**, 130

Hull, William, *The Two Hague Conferences and Their Contributions to International Law*: **III**, 449

Hunt, Gaillard, ed., *The First Forty Years of Washington Society*: **III**, 166

———, ed., *The Writings of James Madison*: **III**, 166

Hymnal of Protestant Episcopal Church: 266, 300

Imperial Dictionary and Cyclopedia, ed., Robert Hunter: **II**, 486, 499

Ingersoll, Charles Jared, *Historic Sketch of the Second War between the United States of America and Great Britain*: **III**, 66

In Memoriam, Samuel Wooten Averett, President of Judson Institute: **III**, 55

Irving, Washington, *The Alhambra*: 576

———, *The Conquest of Granada*: 576; **II**, 159

———, *A History of the Life and Voyages of Christopher Columbus*: 577

———, *History of New York ... by Diedrich Knickerbocker*: 23

Jackson, T. S., ed., *Logs of the Great Sea Fights, 1794–1805*: **II**, 663, 673

James, William, *A Full and Correct Account of the Chief Naval Occurrences of the Late War between Great Britain and the United States of America*: **II**, 694; **III**, 83, 86, 103

———, *The Naval History of Great Britain, from the Declaration of War by France in 1793, to the Accession of George IV*: **II**, 484, 694; **III**, 66, 68, 69, 69–70, 70

James II, King of Great Britain, *Memoirs of the English Affairs, Chiefly Naval, from the Year 1660 to 1673*: **II**, 723

Janvier, Thomas A., *In Old New York*: **II**, 378

Jeaffreson, J. C., *Lady Hamilton and Lord Nelson*: **II**, 476

———, *Queen of Naples and Lord Nelson*: **II**, 476

Jefferson, Thomas, *Writings*, Paul L. Ford, ed.: **III**, 114

Johnson, Robert U. and Buel, C. C., eds., *Battles and Leaders of the Civil War*: **II**, 410

Other Books (*cont.*)
Jomini, Henri, *The Art of War*: 616, 618, 619, 624, 633
————, *Histoire critique et militaire des guerres de la révolution*: **III**, 343, 421
Journal of Rear-Admiral Bartholomew James, 1752–1828. Laughton and Sullivan, eds.: **II**, 485

Keble, John, *The Christian Year; Thoughts in Verse for the Sundays and Holydays throughout the Year*: 586
Kent, James, *Commentaries on American Law*: Part I, *International Law*; Part II, *Constitution of the United States*: 60
Klado, Nikolai Lavrentievich, *The Battle of the Sea of Japan*: **III**, 182, 406
————, *The Russian Navy in the Russo-Japanese War*: **III**, 406
Knight, Austin M. and Puleston, William D., *History of the United States Naval War College*: 654

Laughton, John Knox, *Nelson*: **II**, 475, 477
————, *The Nelson Memorial, Nelson and his Companions in Arms*: **II**, 475, 476, 477, 478
Lecky, Thornton Stratford, *"Wrinkles" in Practical Navigation*: 529–530
Leech, Margaret, *In the Days of McKinley*: **II**, 690
Leighton, Robert, *The Whole Works of Robert Leighton*: 146, 147
Lemoni, *Nelson e Caracciolo e La Rep. Nap. 1799*: **III**, 49
Le Nain de Tillemont, *Ecclesiastical Memories of the First Six Centuries*: **II**, 172
————, *The History of the Arians and of the Council of Nicea*: **II**, 172
Lestock's Vindication, as Spoke by Him at the Bar of the Hon. House of Commons: **II**, 725
Lever, Charles James, *Charles O'Malley*: 9, 11, 12, 628
Long, John D., *The New American Navy*: **III**, 164, 627, 628, 634
Loss of Minorca, The: **II**, 723
Love, Alfred Henry, ed., *The Bond of Peace*: **II**, 671
————, ed., *The Voice of Peace*: **II**, 671
Lucas, Sir Charles Prestwood, *The Canadian War of 1812*: **III**, 174, 175–176
Lytton, Edward George Earle Bulwer-Lytton, *The Caxtons*: 23, 71

McLaughlin, Andrew C., ed., Publication #22, *Report of the Diplomatic Archives of the Department of State, 1789–1840*: **III**, 114–115

Macaulay, Thomas Babington, *Essays*: **II**, 308, 321, 488
————, *The History of England from the Accession of James II*: **II**, 340
Mackenzie, Alexander Slidell, *The Life of Commodore Oliver Hazard Perry*: **III**, 66, 110, 144, 389
Maclay, Edgar Stanton: *A History of American Privateers*: **III**, 65
————, *Life and Adventures of "Jack" Philip, Rear Admiral, U.S.N.*: **II**, 717
Macpherson, David, *Annals of Commerce, Fisheries, and Navigation . . . from the Earliest Accounts to the Meeting of the Union Parliament in 1801 . . .*: **II**, 2, 29
Manning, Cardinal Henry Edward, *Caesarism and Ultramontanism*. Pamphlet: 435
————, *The Vatican Decrees in their Bearing on Civil Allegiance*. Pamphlet: 435
Marder, Albert J., ed., *Fear God and Dread Nought: The Correspondence of Admiral of the Fleet, Lord Fisher of Kilverstone*: **III**, 492
Maresca, B., *Gli Avvenimenti di Napoli, June 13–July 12, 1799*: **III**, 49
————, *Il Cavaliere Antonio Micheroux*: **III**, 49
Marindin, George Eden, *Our Naval Heroes*: **II**, 720, 723
Markham, Sir Albert H., *Great Frozen Sea; a Personal Narrative of the Voyage of the "Alert" during the Arctic Expedition of 1875–76*: 552
Marryat, Frederick, *Mr. Midshipman Easy*: **II**, 721
————, *Peter Simple*: 109; **II**, 721
Martin, Henri, *A Popular History of France from the First Revolution to the Present Time*: 617
Master Commanders' Letters: **III**, 110, 416, 673
Maurice, Sir John Frederick, *Military History of the Campaign of 1882 in Egypt*: **II**, 105
Memoirs of Lady Hamilton: **II**, 469, 478
Miles, Jeaffreson, *Vindication of Lord Nelson's Proceedings in the Bay of Naples*: **III**, 119
Millis, Walter, *The Martial Spirit*: **II**, 690
Milton, John, *Paradise Lost*: **III**, 273
Mitchell, Silas Weir, *Hugh Wynne, Free Quaker*: **II**, 491, 492
Mommsen, Theodor, *The History of Rome*: 606–607; **II**, 493
Monson, Sir William, *Naval Tracts*: **II**, 679, 702
Moore, Frances, *The Leycesters*: **II**, 125
Moore, John Bassett, *American Diplomacy, Its Spirit and Achievements*: **III**, 149

————, *Contraband of War*. Pamphlet: **III**, 456

————, *A Digest of International Law*: **III**, 150, 462, 486

————, *Four Phases of American Development—Federalism—Democracy—Imperialism—Expansion*: **III**, 456, 461

————, *History of Arbitrations*: **III**, 116, 120

————, *International Arbitrations to which the United States Has Been a Party*: **III**, 16

Morison, E. E., *Letters of Theodore Roosevelt*: **III**, 74

Morris, William O'Connor, *Napoleon and Revolutionary France*: **II**, 149

Morrison, Alfred, *Catalogue of the Collection of Autograph Letters and Historical Documents formed between 1865 and 1882 by A. Morrison*: **II**, 476; **III**, 119.

Motley, John Lothrop, *History of the Dutch Republic*: 285, 293, 294

Mundy, Godfrey Basil, *Life and Correspondence of the Late Admiral Lord Rodney*: **III**, 142

Murray, Sir George, *The Letters and Despatches of John Churchill, First Duke of Marlborough*: **III**, 368

Naval Annual: **II**, 417

Nares, Sir George Strong, *Narrative of a Voyage to the Polar Sea during 1875–76 in H.M. Ships 'Alert' and 'Discovery'*: 552

Naval Chronicle [British]: **II**, 1, 37

Naval Miscellany [British]: **III**, 143, 144

Navy Register: 149, 355, 370, 404, 491, 496, 557, 582, **III**, 196; (1842): **III**, 177, 217; (1843; 1844): **III**, 217; (1857): **III**, 177, 217; (1859): **III**, 57; (1909): **III**, 534; (1911): **III**, 403; (1914): **III**, 533, 534, 538

Neeser, Robert W., *Our Navy and the Next War*: **III**, 22

————, *Ship Names of the U.S. Navy*: **III**, 22

————, *Statistical and Chronological History of the United States Navy*: **III**, 22, 240

Nelson, Horatio, *The Letters of Lord Nelson to Lady Hamilton; with a Supplement of Interesting Letters, by Distinguished Characters*: **II**, 481

Newcomb, Simon, *Astronomy*: 552

Newman, J. H., *Letter to the Duke of Norfolk*. Pamphlet: 434, 435

New York (State) Lake Champlain Tercentenary Commission. *The Champlain Tercentenary*: **III**, 470

Nicolas, Sir Nicholas Harris, ed., *The Dispatches and Letters of Vice-Admiral Lord Viscount Nelson*: **II**, 468, 474, 690; **III**, 337

Niles' Weekly Register: **III**, 37, 65, 68, 76, 110, 120, 144, 389, 671, 673

Norman, Charles Boswell, *The Corsairs of France*: **II**, 33, 37

Norton, Charles Eliot, ed., *Letters of James Russell Lowell*: **II**, 200

Official History of the Russo-Japanese War: Part III, *The Siege of Port Arthur*: **III**, 314

O'Neil, Charles, Manuscript Diary (January 1874 to January 1875): 416

Oppenheim, M., *History of the Administration of the Royal Navy and of Merchant Shipping in Relation to the Navy, 1509–1660*: **II**, 477, 485, 497, 502

Overman, *History of Europe 1598–1715*: **II**, 340, 356

Oxford Book of Eighteenth Century Verse: **II**, 238

Page, Thomas Nelson, *The Burial of the Guns*: **II**, 368

————, *Meh Lady*: **II**, 189

Page, Walter Hines, *The Rebuilding of Old Commonwealths, being Essays towards the Training of the Forgotten Man in the Southern States*: **III**, 41

Paget, John, *Paradoxes and Puzzles, Historical, Judicial, and Literary*: **II**, 475, 476

Pahl, G. G., *Storia della Republica Partenopea*: **III**, 49

Palgrave, Francis Turner, *The Golden Treasury of the Best Songs and Lyric Poems of the English Language*: **II**, 125, 196

Palmer, Frederick, *Bliss, Peacemaker: The Life and Letters of Tasker H. Bliss*: 640

Palumbo, R., *Maria Carolina, Carteggio con Lady Hamilton*: **III**, 49

Papers for Continuation Committee, November 1913; Report of Committee Appointed to Draw Up a Statement of Recognized Principles Underlying the Relations of Missions and Governments. Pamphlet: **III**, 501–503, 507–509

Pardoe, Julia, *Louis XIV and the Court of France in the 17th Century*: **II**, 201, 340

Parker, Foxhall A., *Fleet Tactics Under Steam*: 577

Parker, William Harwar, *Recollections of a Naval Officer, 1841–1865*: **III**, 57

Parliamentary Debates From the Year 1803 to the Present Time (Hansard): **II**, 32

Parry, Sir Charles Hubert Hastings, *Art of Music*: **II**, 230, 294

Parsons, G. S.: *Nelsonian Reminiscences*: **II**, 440, 441

Paullin, Charles Oscar, *The Battle of Lake Erie . . . Documents*: **III**, 66

Other Books (*cont.*)

——, *Commodore John Rodgers, Captain, Commodore, and Senior Officer of the American Navy*: **III**, 328

Pears, Sir Edwin, *The Destruction of the Greek Empire and the Story of the Capture of Constantinople by the Turks*: **III**, 505, 684

Penhoat, Vice-Admiral, *Eléments de tactique navale*: 626, 627

Penn, Granville, *Memorials of the Professional Life and Times of Sir William Penn ... from 1644 to 1670*: **II**, 726, 730

Pettigrew, Thomas Joseph, *Memoirs of the Life of Vice-Admiral Lord Viscount Nelson*: **II**, 462, 476; **III**, 120

Philip, George, *Philips' Mercantile Marine Atlas*: **III**, 395

Phillips, Mary Elizabeth, *James Fenimore Cooper*: **III**, 519

Pollonnais, Amélie, *A travers les mansardes et les écoles*: **II**, 245

Pometti, F., *Vigliena*: **III**, 49

Poole, William Frederick, and Fletcher, William I., *Poole's Index to Periodical Literature*: **III**, 449

Porter, David Dixon, *Memoir of Commodore David Porter, of the United States Navy*: 542; **II**, 33

Prescott, George Bartlett, *The Speaking Telephone, Electric Light, and Other Recent Electrical Inventions*: 519

Price, E. D., ed., *Hazell's Annual Cyclopedia, 1891–1895*: **II**, 79

Pritchard, William Tarn, *Digest of Admiralty and Maritime Law*: **II**, 733

Puleston, W. D.: *Mahan: The Life and Work of Captain Alfred Thayer Mahan, U.S.N.*: 278, 314; **II**, 512; **III**, 719

Putnam, Edward, *An Exposition of the Apocalypse of Saint John the Apostle*: 171

Rawson, Edward K., *Twenty Famous Naval Battles*: **II**, 660, 674–675

Reade, Charles, *Dora*: 270

——, *Peg Woffington*: 173

Record of Proceedings of a Court of Inquiry in the Case of R. Adm. Winfield S. Schley, U.S.N.: **II**, 688

Redding, Cyrus, *Memoirs of William Beckford of Fonthill*: **II**, 462, 463

Reinsch, Paul Samuel, *Readings on American Federal Government*: **III**, 258

——, *The Young Citizen's Reader*: **III**, 258

Remains of Late Reverend Richard Hurrell Froude: 187, 198

Remains of the Late Mrs. Trench, being selections from Her Journals, Letters and Other Papers: **II**, 481

Renan, Ernest, *The Apostles*: 207

Reply to Hints on the Reorganization of the Navy. An answer to Hints on the Reorganization of the Navy, Including an Examination of the Claims of its Civil Officers to an Equality of Rights: **III**, 30

Report of Address Delivered at a Meeting Held at Sherry's, New York, March 21, 1902. Pamphlet. The Protestant Episcopal Church Missionary Society to Seamen in ... New York. See **III**, 605–607

Report of a Committee of the Privy Council concerning the condition and Trade of the British West Indies, 1787: **III**, 105, 107, 108, 117

Report on the Manuscripts of Lady Du Cane: **III**, 131–132

Repplier, Agnes, *A Book of Famous Verse*: **II**, 196

——, *Essays in Idleness*: **II**, 196

——, *Essays in Miniature*: **II**, 196

——, *Points of View*: **II**, 196

Revised Statutes of the United States (1875): 507

Rhodes, James Ford, *History of the United States from the Compromise of 1850*: **II**, 503, 667; **III**, 159

Rink, Hinrich Johannes, *Danish Greenland, Its People and Products*: 552

Ripley, G. and Dana, C., eds., *New American Cyclopedia: Popular Dictionary of General Knowledge*: 506–507

Rives, George Lockhart, *The United States and Mexico*: **III**, 523, 524, 542

Robertson, Frederick William, *Sermons on St. Paul's Epistle to the Corinthians*: 166, 173

Roosevelt, Theodore, *The Naval Operations of the War Between Great Britain and the United States, 1812–1815*: **III**, 379

——, *The Naval War of 1812*: **III**, 64, 68–69

Rowell, Newton W., *The British Empire and Independence*: **III**, 501

Ruffo, Fabrizio, *Rivoluzione e Contro. Riv. 1798–1799*: **II**, 632; **III**, 49

Russell, Clark, *Horatio Nelson and the Naval Supremacy of England*: **II**, 533

——, *William Dampier*: **II**, 533

Sacchinelli, D., *Memorie Storiche sulla vita del Cardinale Ruffo*: **III**, 49

Sadler, Ferrebee, *Emmanuel*: 188, 189, 190, 301, 303, 304, 308, 312

Sailing and Fighting Instructions, London, 1741: **II**, 723, 725, 731

——, London, 1742: **II**, 722

——, London 1782: **II**, 723, 725–726

Saint Denys, *Histoire de la Revolution Dans les deux Siciles*: **III**, 49

Saunders, Albert, *Maritime Law*: **III**, 485
———, *The Neutral Ship in War Time: Rights, Duties and Liabilities*: **III**, 485
Schouler, James, *History of the United States of America, under the Constitution*: **III**, 159
Scientific American Reference Book: 507
Scott, James Brown, *The Hague Peace Conferences of 1899 and 1907*: **III**, 449
———, *Instructions to the American Delegates to the Hague Peace Conference and Their Official Reports*: **II**, 638, 646–649, 650–652
Scott, Sir Walter, *Familiar Letters of Sir Walter Scott*: **II**, 200
———, *Ivanhoe*: 33
———, *John Graham of Claverhouse*: 72
———, *Old Morality*: 72
Seawell, Molly Elliot, *The Loves of Lady Arabella*: **II**, 606
———, *Twelve Naval Captains*: **II**, 606
Seeley, Sir John Robert, *Ecce Homo: a Survey of the Life and Works of Jesus Christ*: 294, 295
———, *The Expansion of England*: **III**, 34, 249
Segre, C., *Il Cattivo Genio di Nelson*: **III**, 49
Selections from the Works of Jeremy Taylor: 182, 229, 262, 288
Semenov, Vladimir Ivanovitch, *The Battle of Tsu-shima between the Japanese and Russian Fleets, Fought on 27th May, 1905*: **III**, 201, 335
———, ed., *Rasplata (The Reckoning); by Commander Vladimir Semenoff . . . His Diary During the Blockade of Port Arthur and the Voyage of Admiral Rojestvensky's Fleet*: **III**, 335
Serre, Paul, *Marines de Guerre de l'Antiquité et du Moyen Age*: **III**, 670
Sewell, Elizabeth Missing, *Margaret Percival*: 99
Sharp, William, *Sonnets of This Century*: **II**, 115–116
Sketches of the War, between the United States and the British Isles, Intended as a Faithful History of All the Material Events from the Time of the Declaration in 1812, to and including the Treaty of Peace in 1815 . . .: **III**, 66
Sloane, William Milligan, *The Life of Napoleon Bonaparte*: **II**, 398, 493
Smiles, Samuel, *The Huguenots, their Settlements, Churches, and Industries in England and Ireland, with an Appendix Relating to the Huguenots in America*: 312
Soley, James Russell, *Admiral Porter*: **III**, 393

———, *The Blockade and the Cruisers*: 553; **II**, 528
———, *The Boys of 1812 and Other Naval Heroes*: **III**, 66
———, *Report on Foreign Systems of Naval Education*: 640
Spears, John Randolph, *History of Our Navy from Its Origins to the Present Day*: **II**, 497, 533, 546
Speech of Commodore Jesse Duncan Elliott, U.S.N., delivered in Hagerstown, Md., on 14th November, 1843. Pamphlet: **III**, 66
Spencer, George John, *Private Papers of George, Second Earl Spencer, First Lord of the Admiralty, 1794-1801*: **III**, 515
Spurgeon, Charles Haddon, *John Ploughman's Talk; or Plain Advice for Plain People*: **III**, 336
Staunton, G. F., *Memoir* [of John Barrow]: **III**, 30
Stedman, Edmund Clarence, *American Anthology*: **II**, 697
Stewart, Charles W., ed., *The Official Records of the Union and Confederate Navies in the War of Rebellion*: 88; **III**, 65, 313, 671
Strategic Geography, The Theaters of War of the Rhine and the Danube: **II**, 62
Suydam, John Howard [Knickerbocker, Jr.] *Cruel Jim*: **II**, 266
———, *The Wreckmaster*: **II**, 266

Taylor, Charles C., *Life of Admiral Mahan*: **II**, 511, 529, 578; **III**, 173, 415, 529, 539, 543, 550, 701
Temple, Dorothy Osborne, *The Letters of Dorothy Osborne to Sir William Temple, 1852-5*: **II**, 196
Tennyson, Alfred, Lord, *Idylls of the King*: 222
———, *Locksley Hall*: **II**, 33
Terhune, Mary Virginia (Hawes), *The Story of Mary Washington*: **II**, 119
Thackeray, William Makepeace, *The Newcomes; Memoirs of a Most Respectable Family*: 321, 322, 323, 325
———, *Pendennis*: 209, 210, 211
Thomas à Kempis, *The Imitation of Christ*: 243, 317; **II**, 244
Thursfield, James R. and Clarke, George Sydenham, *The Navy and the Nation*: **II**, 494–495
Thursfield, James R., *Nelson and Other Naval Studies*: **III**, 317
Thwaites, Reuben G., ed., *Jesuit Relations and Allied Documents*: **II**, 608
———, ed., *Original Journals of the Lewis and Clark Expeditions*: **II**, 608
Torrington, Lord (George Byng), *Life of*: **II**, 30

Other Books (*cont.*)

Treanor, Thomas Stanley, *Heroes of the Goodwin Sands*: **II**, 189

Trench, Richard Chenevix, *Notes on the Parables of Our Lord*: 176, 177, 178, 179, 204, 207, 268, 273, 293

Trials of Burrish and Others, 1799: **II**, 722, 725, 730

Trollope, Anthony, *Barchester Towers*: **II**, 236

Troude, O., *Batailles navales de la France*: **III**, 368, 394, 472

Turner, Frederick Jackson, *Preliminary Report of Professor Turner, Committee on the Documentary Historical Publications of the United States Government, May 9, 1908*: **III**, 244

U.S., Congress, House, *Hearings Before the House Naval Affairs Committee*, 61st Cong., 3d Sess.: **III**, 374–375
——, *Reports 788 and 789*: 438
——, Misc. Document 170, 44th Cong., 1st Sess.: 438
——, Misc. Document No. 1705, Pt. 8 [1876]: 443–450
U.S., Congress, Senate, Merchant Marine Commission *Hearings, 1904*: **III**, 110. See **III**, 620–622
——, *Report by the Committee on Department Methods on the Documentary Historical Publications of the United States Government*. Senate Document No. 714, 6oth Cong., 2d Sess.: **III**, 671
U.S. Navy, *Fleet Drill Book, 1891*: **II**, 431
U.S. Navy, *General Board Document No. 404*: **III**, 352–358
U.S. Navy, *General Orders and Circulars of the Navy Department*: 445; **II**, 78
U.S. Navy, *Naval Regulations*: 373, 374, 375, 376, 377, 394, 402, 411, 427, 539, 579, 582, 612; **II**, 103–104, 192, 282, 682
U.S. Navy, Office of Naval Intelligence, *Information from Abroad, General Information Series, No. 3*: 627

Vaillant, J. B. P., et al., eds., *Correspondance de Napoleon I*: **II**, 526; **III**, 191, 325
Van Tyne, C. H., and Leland, W. G., *Guide to the Archives of the Government of the United States in Washington*: **III**, 240
Villari, P., *Nelson, Caracciolo e la Rep. Nap.*: **III**, 49
von Bernhardi, Friedrich Adam Julius, *Germany and the Next War*: **III**, 485
von Chamiso, Adelbert, *Peter Schlemihl's Wunderbare Geschichte*: 98
Vondel, Joost van den, *Lucifer*: **III**, 272, 273

von Ranke, Leopold, *The History of the Popes, their Church and State, and Especially of their Conflicts with Protestantism in the Sixteenth and Seventeenth Centuries*: 266, 270, 276

Waldo, Samuel Putnam, *The Life and Character of Stephen Decatur*: 250
Walsh, Robert, *A Letter on the Genius of the French Government*: **II**, 33, 37, 39, 40
War in the Far East, 1904–1905, by the Military Correspondent of the London *Times*: **III**, 154
Webster's International Dictionary: **III**, 462
Wharton, Francis, ed., *The Revolutionary Diplomatic Correspondence of the United States*: **III**, 44
Wheaton, Henry, *Elements of International Law*: 604
White, Andrew Dickson, *Autobiography*: **III**, 451
White, Thomas, *Naval Researches, or a Candid Inquiry into the Conduct of Admirals Byron, Graves, Hood and Rodney, in the Actions off Grenada, Chesapeake, St. Christophers, and of the Ninth and Twelfth of April, 1782. Being a Refutation of the Plans and Statements of Mr. Clerk, Rear Adm. Ekins, and Others*: **III**, 119
Wiggins, Kate Douglas, *A Cathedral Courtship*: **II**, 296
Wilkinson, Spencer, *Britain at Bay*: **III**, 34
Wilson, Herbert Wrigley, *Ironclads in Action, 1855–1895 . . .* with an Introduction by Capt. A. T. Mahan: **II**, 441
Wilson, James G., ed., *Appleton's Cyclopedia of American Biography*: **II**, 55
——, ed., *The Memorial History of the City of New York*: **II**, 55, 86
——, ed., *The Great Commanders Series*: **II**, 55, 123
Wood, William, ed., *The Logs of the Conquest of Canada*: **III**, 316
Worcester Dictionary: **II**, 486, 499

Young, *Voyage of the Pandora*: 552

Papers Written by Mahan

Mahan, A. T., Paper, Comments on the Seizure of Private Property at Sea (February–March, 1906): **III**, 158; 182. See **III**, 623–626
Mahan, A. T., Paper, Contingency Plan of Operations in Case of War with Great Britain (December 1890): **II**, 18, 35, 38, 734. See **III**, 559–576
Mahan, A. T., Paper, Introduction to K. Asami's Biography of Tasuka Serata. (Summer 1913): **III**, 499. See **III**, 688–692

Mahan, A. T., Paper, Personality and Influence: A Commencement Address at Dartmouth College (June 24, 1903): **III**, 63. *See* **III**, 608–619

Mahan, A. T., Paper, The Practical in Christianity: An address delivered in the Episcopal Church of the Holy Trinity, Middletown Conn. (March 22, 1899): **III**, 286, 294, 297

Mahan, A. T., Paper, Practical Words: An Address Delivered at the Naval War College (September 1892): **III**, 533. *See* **III**, 577–582

Mahan, A. T., Paper Read by Captain Mahan Before the Second Committee of the Peace Conference on June 20, 1899, in James Brown Scott, *Instructions to the American Delegates to the Hague Peace Conference and Their Official Reports*: **II**, 638, 646–649, 650–652

Mahan, A. T., Paper, The Relations of the Church to the State: An Address to the Episcopal Club of Massachusetts (October 1899): **II**, 671

Mahan, A. T., Paper, Reminiscences of Service at the Naval War College (March 24, 1908): **III**, 233, 238. *See* **III**, 663–667

Mahan, A. T., Paper, Statement Before the Senate Commission on the Merchant Marine (November 25, 1904): **III**, 110. *See* **III**, 620–622

Mahan, A. T., Paper, Thoughts on the Righteousness of War (July 23, 1913): **III**, 505. *See* **III**, 683–684

Mahan, A. T., Paper, The Work of the Naval War Board of 1898 (October 29, 1906): **III**, 161, 163, 164, 174. *See* **III**, 627–643

ARTICLES

Articles (General): M. hopes to influence public opinion with, **II**, 234, 685, 701, **III**, 204–205, 207, 214, 246, 346; specializes in and emphasizes current events, **II**, 86, 94, 471, 496, **III**, 60, 73; Venezuela crisis stimulates M. interest in contemporary international affairs, **II**, 452; international affairs are M. chief interest, **III**, 494; lacks knowledge of diplomatic subjects for, **III**, 17; plans those relating USN to general national policy, **II**, 347; subjects geared to newspaper headlines, **III**, 73, 131; too many illustrations inhibit flow of text, **II**, 424, 467, 493, 699; executed rapidly, **III**, 73; M. racks brain to produce, **III**, 8; large circulation of U.S. magazines, **III**, 172; tailored to fit editorial demands, **II**, 438, 450, 524, **III**, 396; produced at request of editors,

II, 524, 529, **III**, 5, 8, 11–12, 36, 37, 59; declines offers to write, **II**, 138, 189, 311, 332, 342, 355, 479, 505, 520, 598, 641, **III**, 397, 537, 538–539, 547; two a year will pay for family dinner fund, **II**, 383; price of related to amount of labor in, **II**, 430, 482; more lucrative than books, **II**, 86, 110–111, 471, 568, 655, **III**, 48; sees as necessary pot-boiling, **II**, 459, 461, **III**, 216; negotiations related to payment for, **II**, 26, 277, 292, 423, 429, 430, 496, 521, 522, 535–536, 549, 743, **III**, 5, 17, 29, 35, 36, 38, 47, 89, 146, 149, 172, 259, 369, 430, 513, 529, 538; payments for, **II**, 111, 132, 133, 137, 138, 147, 151, 153, 156, 160, 181, 204, 206, 276, 277, 295, 300, 307, 311, 355, 383, 418, 447, 496, 515, 522, 530, 568, 652, 676, 732, 736, **III**, 17, 23, 30, 33, 37, 58, 63, 89, 96, 98, 146, 147, 152, 214, 215, 220, 544, 550; prohibited by USN from writing on European War, **III**, 538–539, 546; requests withdrawal of writing prohibition, **III**, 540–541, income lost by USN writing prohibition, **III**, 548; feels preparedness article falls outside writing prohibition order, **III**, 546; heart attack slows writing of, **III**, 547, 549; articles projected but unwritten or unpublished, 460, 461, 463, **II**, 86, 92, 99, 126, 153, 310, 311, 488, 535, 548–549, 600, 617–618, 631–632, **III**, 25, 63, 181, 192, 322, 513, 519, 523. *See* Historiography; History; Publication Procedures; Index Section IV, Mahan, A. T., Financial Problems

Articles Written by Mahan

Mahan, A. T., "About What Is the War?" unpublished article, mid-August 1914: **III**, 533. *See* **III**, 702–705

Mahan, A. T., "Admiral the Earl of St. Vincent (Jervis)," *Atlantic Monthly* (March 1893): **II**, 85, 94, 496, 724, 729

Mahan, A. T., "Admiral Lord Exmouth (Pellew)," *Atlantic Monthly* (July 1893): **II**, 92, 100, 101, 102, 111, 122, 123, 125, 127, 169, 172, 496, 724, 729

Mahan, A. T., "Admiral Lord Howe," *Atlantic Monthly* (January 1894): **II**, 92, 101, 111, 114, 118, 121, 124, 127, 132, 133, 135, 147, 150, 160, 166, 172, 180, 210, 314, 350, 496, 724, 729; M. thinks it a heavy article, **II**, 155; brings larger payment than expected, **II**, 206

Mahan, A. T., "Admiral Saumarez," *Atlantic Monthly* (May 1893): **II**, 91, 94, 97, 101, 496, 724, 729

Mahan, A. T., "Appreciation of Conditions in the Russo-Japanese Conflict," Part I, *Collier's Weekly* (February 20, 1904); Part II, *ibid.* (April 30, 1904): **III**, 89;

Articles Written by Mahan (*cont.*)
Part II also in *The Times*, London: **III**, 96, 98

Mahan, A. T., "Armaments and Arbitration," *North American Review* (May 1911): **III**, 395, 411

Mahan, A. T., "The Battle of Copenhagen," *Century Magazine* (February 1897): **II**, 411, 415, 422, 424, 429, 430, 447, 449, 453, 465, 469, 486, 514, 535

Mahan, A. T., "The Battle of Trafalgar," Military Historical Society of Massachusetts, *Proceedings*, I (1898): **II**, 534, 537

Mahan, A. T., "The Battleship of All Big Guns," *World's Work* (January 1911): **III**, 359

Mahan, A. T., "Blockade in Relation to Naval Strategy," Royal United Service Institution *Journal* (November 1895); also in U.S. Naval Institute *Proceedings* (December 1895): **II**, 276, 441; pressure of *Chicago* duty slows writing of, **II**, 301

Mahan, A. T., "The Boer Republic and the Monroe Doctrine," *The Independent* (May 10, 1900): **II**, 740

Mahan, A. T., "Britain and World Peace," *The Daily Mail*, London, October 31, 1910: **III**, 345, 347, 348

Mahan, A. T., "Christian Progress," *The New York Times*, August 16, 1914: **III**, 539–540

Mahan, A. T., "Commodore Macdonough at Plattsburg," *North American Review* (August 1914): **III**, 527, 529, 544

Mahan, A. T., "Conditions Governing the Dispositions of Navies," *National Review* (July 1902): **III**, 6, 11, 23, 25, 26, 29, 33, 35, 36, 40, 537

Mahan, A. T., "The Consistency of Nelson as a Tactician," *The Graphic* (October 21, 1905): **III**, 144, 155, 156

Mahan, A. T., "Current Fallacies upon Naval Subjects," *Harper's Monthly* (November 1899): **II**, 657

Mahan, A. T., "Declares British Navy Weak," *The Daily Mail*, London, January 4, 1914: **III**, 516

Mahan, A. T., "The Deficiencies of Law as an Instrument of International Adjustments," *North American Review* (November 1911): **III**, 395

Mahan, A. T., "Diplomacy and Arbitration," *North American Review* (July 1911): **III**, 395

Mahan, A. T., "Distinguishing Qualities of Ships of War," Scripps-McRae Newspaper League (November 1898): **II**, 530, 681

Mahan, A. T., "The Effect of Deficient Coast Defense on the Movement of the Navy," *McClure's Magazine* (January 1899): **II**, 625

Mahan, A. T., "Effects of Asiatic Conditions upon World Policies," *North American Review* (November 1900): **II**, 687

Mahan, A. T., Walker, John G., Evans, R. D., and Staunton, S. A., "The Engineer in Naval Warfare," *North American Review* (December 1896): **II**, 528

Mahan, A. T., "The Folly of the Hague," *National Sunday Magazine*, September 28, 1913: **III**, 506, 530, 685. *See* Paper, Why Not Disarm, **III**, 685–687

Mahan, A. T., "For More Battleships," *The New York Times*, April 4, 1912: **III**, 453–454, 483

Mahan, A. T., "The Future in Relation to American Sea Power," *Harper's New Monthly Magazine* (October 1895): **II**, 496

Mahan, A. T., "Germany's Naval Ambition," *Collier's Weekly* (April 24, 1909): **III**, 307

Mahan, A. T., "The Great Illusion," *North American Review* (March 1912): **III**, 449, 486

Mahan, A. T., "The Guard Set Over Cervera and the Watch Kept on Camara," *McClure's Magazine* (April 1899): **II**, 629

Mahan, A. T., "The Hague Conference and the Practical Aspects of War," *National Review* (July 1907); also in *Living Age* (July 27, 1907): **III**, 172, 205, 207, 209, 210, 213, 214, 216, 217, 220, 223, 229

Mahan, A. T., "The Hague Conference; the Question of Immunity of Belligerent Merchant Shipping," *National Review* (June 1907); also as "Maritime Capture in War," *Living Age* (July 6, 1907): **III**, 158, 172, 205, 207, 209, 210, 211, 213, 214, 215, 217, 218, 219, 220, 223, 230, 231, 623

Mahan, A. T., "Hawaii and Our Future Sea Power," *The Forum* (March 1893): **II**, 496, 506, 522; motive for writing, **II**, 94, 507, 520, 524; done speedily, **II**, 101; M. thinks led to banishment to sea in *Chicago*, **II**, 138, **III**, 299

Mahan, A. T., "The Immunity from Capture of Private Property at Sea," *The New York Times*, November 4, 1910: **III**, 366

Mahan, A. T., "Influence de la puissance maritime sur l'histoire," *Revue Maritime et Coloniale* (February–December 1894): **II**, 306–307

Mahan, A. T., "The Influence of the South African War upon the Prestige of the British Empire," *National Review* (December 1901): **II**, 732, 735, 736; **III**, 40, 245

Mahan, A. T., "The International Signifi-
cance of German Naval Development,"
The Daily Mail, London, July 4; 6, 1910:
III, 345, 347

Mahan, A. T., Introduction to Edgar Stanton Maclay, et al., *Life and Adventures of
"Jack" Philip, Rear Admiral, U.S.N.*: **II**,
717

Mahan, A. T., Introduction to William F.
Tilton, "The Spanish Armada," *Century
Magazine* (June 1898): **II**, 514

Mahan, A. T., "The Isthmus and Sea Power," *Atlantic Monthly* (October 1893):
II, 101, 105, 111, 124, 125, 127, 132, 137,
138, 147, 148, 151, 153, 156, 160, 169, 180,
496

Mahan, A. T., "John Paul Jones in the
Revolution," *Scribner's Magazine* (July;
August 1898): **II**, 518, 522, 524, 540, 542,
544, 545, 546, 547

Mahan, A. T., "Japan Among the Nations.
Admiral Mahan's Views," *The Times*,
London, June 23, 1913: **III**, 495–499, 500,
503

Mahan, A. T., "Lessons from the Yalu
Fight," *Century Magazine* (August 1895):
II, 342, 415; research on, **II**, 416; exceeds
agreed upon length, **II**, 417; payment for,
II, 418

Mahan, A. T., "Letter to the Editor,"
American Historical Review (October
1906): **III**, 167–169

Mahan, A. T., "Letter to the Editor," *The
Churchman* (September 9, 1899): **II**, 661;
(September 8, 1914): **III**, 535; (October
10; 17, 1914): **III**, 521, 546

Mahan, A. T., "Letter to the Editor," *Contemporary Review* (September 1907):
III, 218–219

Mahan, A. T., "Letter to the Editor," *The
Daily Mail*, London, July 4; 6, 1910: **III**,
345

Mahan, A. T., "Letter to the Editor," *The
New York Evening Post*, November 11,
1911: **III**, 430; April 27, 1912: **III**, 454–456

Mahan, A. T., "Letter to the Editor," The
New York *Sun*, August 7, 1898: **II**, 573–
577, 578; January 31, 1907: **III**, 205–206;
circa September 7, 1914: **III**, 545, 546

Mahan, A. T., "Letter to the Editor," *The
New York Times*, March 17, 1897: **II**, 499;
October 29, 1897: **II**, 527; November 17,
1898: **II**, 610–612, 613; November 23, 1898:
II, 613–614; November 2, 1899: **II**, 667–
668; November 18, 1899: **II**, 669–670;
January 22, 1900: **II**, 677, 679, 680; January 26, 1900: **II**, 677–679, 680; February
12, 1904: **III**, 86; November 16, 1904: **III**,
107–108; June 15, 1907: **III**, 214–215; October 26, 1910: **III**, 363–365, 409; June 5,

1911: **III**, 408–409, 411; November 24,
1911: **III**, 433–435; December 8, 1911: **III**,
436–437; May 24, 1912: **III**, 457–459, 483;
August 17, 1912: **III**, 473; July 25, 1913:
III, 505–506, 684; October 15, 1913: **III**,
511; August 31, 1914: **III**, 711; September
10, 1914: **III**, 542–543, 544, 546, 547

Mahan, A. T., "Letter to the Editor," *The
New York Times*, November 24, 1911;
also in *The New York Evening Post*, November 23, 1911: **III**, 433–435

Mahan, A. T., "Letter to the Editor, *Philadelphia Ledger*," in *Army and Navy Journal* (June 16, 1906): **III**, 160

Mahan, A. T., "Letter to Lt. Charles R.
Miles," U.S. Naval Institute *Proceedings*
No. 48 (1889): 666–669

Mahan, A. T., "Letter to the Secretary,"
Royal United Service Institution *Journal*
(1902): **III**, 44

Mahan, A. T., "Letters to William Peterson," *Montreal Gazette*, March 22, 1900:
II, 684, 685; in *The Times*, London, March
14, 1900: **II**, 686

Mahan, A. T., "Letter to the Editor," *The
Times*, London, June 13, 1913: **III**, 500,
504, 688

Mahan, A. T., "The Military Rule of Obedience," *National Review* (March 1902);
also in *International Monthly* (March
1902): **II**, 743; **III**, 7, 8, 537

Mahan, A. T., "Misrepresenting Mr. Roosevelt," *The Outlook* (June 17, 1911); also
in *The New York Times*, June 5, 1911:
III, 408–409, 411, 415

Mahan, A. T., "The Monroe Doctrine,"
National Review (February 1903): **III**, 5,
11, 37, 44, 49, 52, 58, 59, 242, 243, 250, 254,
255, 256, 267, 428, 446

Mahan, A. T., "Motives to Imperial Federation," *National Review* (May 1902): **II**,
743; **III**, 5, 11, 12, 15, 17, 22, 25, 27, 33

Mahan, A. T., "The Naval Campaign of
1776 on Lake Champlain," *Scribner's
Magazine* (February 1898): **II**, 520, 521,
523, 524, 525, 527, 540, 549

Mahan, A. T., "Naval Education," U.S.
Naval Institute *Proceedings* (December
1879): 474; **III**, 263

Mahan, A. T., "Naval Ships," New York
Sun, March 3, 1901: **II**, 707

Mahan, A. T., "The Naval War College,"
North American Review (July 1912):
III, 446

Mahan, A. T., "Navies as International Factors," *North American Review* (September 1911): **III**, 395, 422

Mahan, A. T., "Our Navy Before the War
of Secession," *Harper's Monthly* (May
1907): **III**, 196

Articles Written by Mahan (*cont.*)

Mahan, A. T., "The Neapolitan Republicans and Nelson's Accusers," *English Historical Review* (July 1899): **II**, 632, 637

Mahan, A. T., "The Necessity and Objects of a Naval War College," U.S. Naval Institute *Proceedings* (December 1888): 662, 667, 670; **III**, 247, 250

Mahan, A. T., "Negotiations at Ghent in 1814," *American Historical Review* (October 1905): **III**, 117, 121, 130, 131, 137, 147

Mahan, A. T., "Nelson at the Battle of the Nile," *Century Magazine* (January 1897): **II**, 411, 415, 422, 424, 429, 430, 434, 437, 438, 449, 450, 454, 465, 486, 535

Mahan, A. T., "Nelson at Cape St. Vincent," *Century Magazine* (February 1896): **II**, 415, 422, 424, 429, 430, 432, 433, 434, 453, 454, 535

Mahan, A. T., "Nelson at Naples," *English Historical Review* (October 1900): **III**, 148

Mahan, A. T., "Nelson at Trafalgar," *Century Magazine* (March 1897): **II**, 411, 415, 422, 424, 429, 430, 431, 447, 454, 458, 465, 469, 480, 535

Mahan, A. T., "An Old Time Frigate," *Youth's Companion* (September 22, 1898): **II**, 628

Mahan, A. T., "The Panama Canal and the Distribution of the Fleet," *North American Review* (September 1914): **III**, 532, 544, 550

Mahan, A. T., "The Panama Canal and Sea Power in the Pacific," *Century Magazine* (June 1911): **III**, 395, 446; payment for, **III**, 369; partial treatment of the subject, **III**, 372–373; sees through press, **III**, 376–377, 389, 396–397, 405; reconsiders passages on Canada in light of Clark annexation statement, **III**, 388–389; British interest in in conjunction with Imperial defence, **III**, 396–397, 414–415; reactions to, **III**, 415

Mahan, A. T., "The Peace Conference and the Moral Aspect of War," *North American Review* (October 1899): **II**, 652, 655, 657, 658, 665, 675; **III**, 72, 229, 450

Mahan, A. T., "The Persian Gulf and International Relations," *National Review* (September 1902): **III**, 6, 12, 17, 23, 29, 30, 32, 33, 35, 37, 245

Mahan, A. T., "The Personal Factor in Naval History," *Youth's Companion* (October 29, 1907): **II**, 628

Mahan, A. T., "The Personality of Nelson," *United Service Magazine* (October 1905): **III**, 141

Mahan, A. T., "The Philippines and the Future," *The Independent* (March 22, 1900): **II**, 740

Mahan, A. T., "Pitt's War Policy," *The Quarterly Review* (July 1892): **II**, 26, 44

Mahan, A. T., "The Place of Force in International Relations," *North American Review* (January 1912): **III**, 446

Mahan, A. T., "Possibilities of an Anglo-American Reunion," *North American Review* (November 1894): **II**, 305, 337, 396; undertaken for the payment promised, **II**, 295, 300, 303, 314, 334, 355; difficulty coordinating ideas in, **II**, 301, 350; withdraws from publication for personal and political reasons, **II**, 307, 310, 311, 314, 332, 338; tones down and resubmits, **II**, 334, 338, 342; predicts criticism of, **II**, 350

Mahan, A. T., "The Practical Character of the United States Naval War College," U.S. Naval Institute *Proceedings* (June 1893): **III**, 245, 247, 248, 250. See **III**, 577–582

Mahan, A. T., "Preparedness for a Naval War," *Harper's New Monthly Magazine* (March 1897): **II**, 496

Mahan, A. T., "Principles of Naval Administration," *National Review* (June 1903): **III**, 60, 60–61, 62, 109, 242, 250

Mahan, A. T., "Principles of Naval Administration—American and British," *Scribner's Magazine* (May 1903): **III**, 250

Mahan, A. T., "The Probability of the Survival of the Battleship: Captain Mahan's Conclusions," the New York *Sun*, May 11, 1904: **III**, 89, 90–95, 98

Mahan, A. T., "The Problem of Asia," *Harper's Monthly* (March; April; May 1900): **II**, 666, 676, 684, 687

Mahan, A. T., "The Problems That Rozhdesvensky and Togo Must Solve," *The Times*, London, May 13, 1905; also in *Collier's Weekly* (May 13, 1905): **III**, 131

Mahan, A. T., "Reflections, Historic and Other, Suggested by the Battle of the Japan Sea," U.S. Naval Institute *Proceedings* (June 1906); also in Royal United Service Institution *Journal* (November 1906): **III**, 178, 180, 182, 188, 204, 239

Mahan, A. T., "Relations of the United States to Their New Dependencies," *Review of Reviews* (March 1899): **II**, 715

Mahan, A. T., Response to F. P. Badham, *The Athenaeum* (July 8; 22, 1899); also in *English Historical Review* (July 1899; October 1900): **II**, 619

Mahan, A. T., Review of L. S. Amery, ed., *Times History of the War in South Africa*, *The New York Times*, May 30, 1902: **III**, 35

Mahan, A. T., Review of J. Barnes *Naval Actions of the War of 1812, American Historical Review* (April 1897): **II**, 497

Mahan, A. T., Review of M. Oppenheim *History of the Administration of the Royal Navy, American Historical Review* (July 1897): **II**, 497

Mahan, A. T., Review of J. R. Spears *History of Our Navy from Its Origins to the Present Day, American Historical Review* (October 1897–January 1898): **II**, 497, 546

Mahan, A. T., "Sampson's Naval Career," *McClure's Magazine* (July 1902); also as "Rear Admiral Wm. T. Sampson," *Fortnightly Review* (August 1902): **III**, 248

Mahan, A. T., "Sandwich Islands Annexation by U.S. as Barrier against Chinese Invasion," *The New York Times*, February 1, 1893: **II**, 92–93, 520, 524

Mahan, A. T., "The Seaman," *Youth's Companion* (November 6, 1913): **II**, 628

Mahan, A. T., "Sea Power in the Present European War," *Leslie's Illustrated Weekly Newspaper*, August 20, 1914: **III**, 542, 550. See **III**, 706–710

Mahan, A. T., "Some Considerations of the Principles Involved in the Present War," *National Review* (September 1904): **III**, 100, 102, 242, 243, 249, 250, 251, 254

Mahan, A. T., "Some Reflections Upon the Far Eastern War," *National Review* (May 1906); also in *Living Age* (July 14, 1906): **III**, 141, 152, 153, 158, 182, 184, 242, 250

Mahan, A. T., "Strategic Features of the Caribbean Sea and the Gulf of Mexico," *Harper's Monthly* (October 1897): **II**, 127, 153, 496, 498, 523

Mahan, A. T., "The Strength of Nelson," *National Review* (November 1905): **III**, 141, 144, 145, 146, 148, 152, 242

Mahan, A. T., "Subordination in Historical Treatment," American Historical Association *Annual Report* (1902); also as "Writing of History," *Atlantic Monthly* (March 1903): **III**, 46, 47, 51, 52, 60, 245, 246

Mahan, A. T., "Tactics of Trafalgar," *The Army and Navy Gazette*, July 29, 1905: **III**, 144

Mahan, A. T., "Time Ill Chosen for a Weak Navy," *The New York Times*, August 21, 1912: **III**, 473–476, 476, 483

Mahan, A. T., "Torpedo Craft vs. Battleships," *Collier's Weekly* (May 21, 1904): **III**, 89, 90, 93

Mahan, A. T., "The Transvaal and the Philippine Islands," *The Independent* (February 1, 1900): **II**, 680, 740

Mahan, A. T., "Twentieth Century Christianity," *North American Review* (April 1914): **III**, 522, 525, 540, 550

Mahan, A. T., "A Twentieth Century Outlook," *Harper's New Monthly Magazine* (September 1897): **II**, 523

Mahan, A. T., "Two Maritime Expeditions," *United Service Magazine* (October 1893): **II**, 143, 155, 337, 434, **III**, 389; cribbed from NWC lecture notes, **II**, 138, 142, 147; receives larger payment for than expected, **II**, 181

Mahan, A. T., "The United States Looking Outward," *Atlantic Monthly* (December 1890): **II**, 28, 29; M. dissents from isolationist viewpoint, **II**, 19–20; Luce assists with, **II**, 19, 22, 25; M. recommends to G. S. Clarke, **II**, 84

Mahan, A. T., "The United States Navy Department," *Scribner's Magazine* (May 1903): **II**, 60, 60–61, 62, 242, 246, 250

Mahan, A. T., "The Value of the Pacific Cruise of the U.S. Fleet, 1907. Prospect," *Scientific American* (December 12, 1907): **III**, 234, 245, 250, 254

Mahan, A. T., "The Value of the Pacific Cruise of the U.S. Fleet, 1908. Retrospect," *Collier's Weekly* (August 28, 1908): **III**, 245, 250, 254, 255, 256, 257, 262, 263, 264, 265, 266, 267, 268

Mahan, A. T., "War from the Christian Standpoint," November 1900, in *Some Neglected Aspects of War* and *The Harvest Within*: **II**, 735; **III**, 223, 228, 229

Mahan, A. T., "The War on the Sea and Its Lessons. Part I. How the Motive of the War Gave Direction to Its Earliest Movements," *McClure's Magazine* (December 1898): **II**, 625

Mahan, A. T., "Was Panama a Chapter of National Dishonor?" *North American Review* (October 1912): **III**, 486, 489

Mahan, A. T., "Why Fortify the Panama Canal?" *North American Review* (March 1911): **III**, 373

Mahan, A. T., "The Youth of Admiral Farragut," *Youth's Companion* (June 28, 1900): **II**, 628

Other Articles

A.B.C. Etc., "British Foreign Policy," *National Review* (November 1901): **III**, 13

Alison, A., "Armed Europe: Sea Power," *Blackwood's Edinburgh Magazine* (February 1894): **II**, 222

"The American Example," *The New York Times*, August 29, 1914: **III**, 542, 544, 545, 711

Appleton, Nathan, "Clayton-Bulwer Treaty and the Ship Canal," *Harper's Weekly* (September 30, 1898): **II**, 171

Other Articles (*cont.*)

Badham, F. P., "Nelson and the Neapolitan Republicans," *English Historical Review* (April 1898): **II**, 619, 630

Baker, Benjamin, "The Philippines, the Key to the Open Door," *The Navy* (January 1907): **II**, 205–206

"The Balkan Danger and Universal Peace," *The Round Table* (March 1912): **III**, 449

"The Banquet to the American Naval Officers at St. James Hall," *The Graphic* (London), June 2, 1894: **II**, 285

Barrow, Sir Edmund, "The New Balance of Power in the Far East," *National Review* (October 1905): **III**, 153

Benjamin, Park, "A Casuistry in Naval Ethics," *The Independent* (December 19, 1901): **II**, 739; **III**, 4

———, "The Schley Court of Inquiry," *ibid.* (September 5, 1901): **III**, 2, 3

Blind, Karl, "Transvaal Independence and England's Future," *Fortnightly Review* (November 1899): **II**, 673–674

Bridge, Sir Cyprian A. G., "The Centenary of Trafalgar," *Cornhill's Magazine*, XCII: **III**, 155

———, "Recent Caluminiators of Nelson," *United Service Magazine*, XXXII: **III**, 155

"British Policy in Persia and Asiatic Turkey," *Edinburgh Review* (April 1902): **III**, 34

"Captain Mahan," *Saturday Review* (May 12, 1894): **II**, 270

"Captain Mahan on Anglo-American Relations," *The Times*, London, April 12, 1898: **II**, 550; March 24, 1900: **II**, 686

Carnegie, Andrew, "A Look Ahead," *North American Review* (June 1893): **II**, 283

Chadwick, French Ensor, "Address to the Naval War College, June 4, 1902," U.S. Naval Institute *Proceedings*, XXVIII: **III**, 69

———, "Letter to the Editor," U.S. Naval Institute *Proceedings*, XXVIII: **III**, 69

———, "United States—War with Spain," *Encyclopedia Americana*, 1927 ed.: **III**, 236, 636

"Chicago: Antwerp Visited; Boilers Will be Repaired; Salute Acknowledged," *The New York Times*, June 14, 1894: **II**, 295

Chirol, Sir Valentine, "Japan Among the Nations: The Bar of Race," *The Times*, London, May 19, 1913: **III**, 496, 503

Clarke, George Sydenham, "Captain Mahan's Counsels to the United States," *Nineteenth Century* (February 1898): **II**, 543

———, "A Naval Union with Great Britain: Reply to Mr. Andrew Carnegie,"

North American Review (March 1894): **II**, 283, 305

———, "A Plea for a Policy," *United Service Magazine* (September 1894): **II**, 338

———, Review of *Influence of Sea Power upon the French Revolution and Empire, 1793–1812*, *The Guardian*, London (June 7, 1893): **II**, 116

Clowes, W. L. [Nauticus], "Sea Power, Its Past and Its Future," *Fortnightly Review* (December 1893): **II**, 189, 191

Colomb, P. H., "The Manoeuvring Powers of Ships," Royal United Service Institution *Journal* (March 31, 1882): 669–670

———, "Naval Defense of the United Kingdom," Royal United Service Institution *Journal* (May 18, 1888): 662

———, Review of A. T. Mahan, *Life of Nelson*, *Saturday Review*, LXXXIII: **II**, 502

Corbett, Julian S., "The Capture of Private Property at Sea," *Nineteenth Century* (June 1907): **III**, 223, 224, 228, 229, 231, 232

[Custance, Sir R.], "The Growth of the Capital Ship," *Blackwood's Magazine* (May 1906): **III**, 180

———, "Lessons from the Battle of Tsu Sima," *ibid.* (February 1906): **III**, 180

———, "The Speed of the Capital Ship," *ibid.* (October 1906): **III**, 180

Davis, Richard Harding, "The Exiles," *Harper's Magazine* (May 1894): **II**, 361

De Koven, Anna Farwell, "A New Page in the History of John Paul Jones," *Harper's Weekly* (April 7, 1906): **III**, 317

Eaton, Joseph Giles, "The *Chesapeake* and the *Shannon*," Military Historical Society of Massachusetts *Papers*: **III**, 69

Editorial, *Manchester Guardian*, July 20, 1899: **II**, 705

Editorial, *The New York Times*, October 30, 1897: **II**, 528; August 8, 1911: **III** 420; December 3, 1911: **III** 436

Editorial, "A Roosevelt Incident," *The New York Times*, June 1, 1911: **III**, 408–409

Editorial, *The Washington Post*, July 31, 1898: **II**, 576

E. G. D., "Uncle Sam's Naval Schools," *The New York Times*, May 29, 1893: **II**, 108

Eliot, Charles W., "Twentieth Century Christianity," *The New York Times*, January 11, 1914: **III**, 523

Ellicot, J. M., "With Erben and Mahan on the *Chicago*," U.S. Naval Institute *Proceedings* (September 1941): **II**, 296

"The Emigration Question in Japan," *The Round Table*, I, No. 3: **III**, 411

"Erben and Capt. Mahan," *Army and Navy Register*, April 21, 1894: **II**, 282

"Faith in Action," *The Guardian*, London (August 18, 1909): **III**, 310

Fiennes, Geoffrey C. T.-W. [Excubitor], "Command of the German Ocean," *Fortnightly Review* (September 1906): **III**, 184, 397

"Genesis of the War," *Weekly Times*, London, June 3, 1904: **III**, 99

"Ghent and Portsmouth; Some Observations on the Russian Czar's Part in Our Peace of 1814," The New York *Sun*, August 10, 1905: **III**, 136–137

Gibbon, John, "Puget Sound—a Sketch of its Defenses," *Journal of the Military Service Institution of the United States* (September 1889): 713

Gildersleeve, B. L., "My Sixty Days in Greece," *Atlantic Monthly* (February; March; May 1897): **II**, 505

Gilman, Daniel C., "Books and Politics," *The New York Times*, October 23, 1898: **II**, 605

Gracie, Archibald, "Account of *Titanic* Sinking," *The New York Times*, April 25, 1912: **III**, 455

Gwynne, the Rev. Dr. Walker, "Sources of the Church's Strength and Weakness," *The Churchman* (July 25, 1914): **III**, 535

Harrison, Benjamin, "Musings upon Current Topics," *North American Review* (February–March 1901): **II**, 707
———, "Status of Annexed Territory and its Inhabitants," *ibid.* (January 1901): **II**, 707

Hobson, Richmond Pearson, "Fortification Bill." U.S. Government Printing Office, 1909: **III**, 421

Hoff, William Bainbridge, "A View of Our Naval Policy and a Discussion of its Factors," U.S. Naval Institute *Proceedings* (1886): 632

Hunt, Gaillard, Review of A. T. Mahan, *War of 1812*, *American Historical Review* (July 1906): **III**, 166, 167

Kennedy, Crammond, "Admiral Mahan and the Canal," *The New York Evening Post*, November 7, 1911: **III**, 430

Laughton, John Knox, "Captain Mahan on Naval Power," *Edinburgh Review* (October 1890): **II**, 34
———, "The Earl of St. Vincent," *Army and Navy Gazette*, London, November 22, 1890: **II**, 721
———, "Notes on the Last Great Naval War," *Royal United Service Institution Journal* (1885): 619
———, Review of A. T. Mahan, *The Life of Nelson*, *Edinburgh Review* (July 1897): **II**, 504

Loft, Peter, "The Battle of Copenhagen," *United Service Magazine* (January 1893): **II**, 514

"Lombard Street and War," *The Round Table* (March 1912): **III**, 449

Low, A. Maurice, "American Affairs," *National Review* (December 1912): **III**, 486

Low, Seth, "The International Conference of Peace," *North American Review* (November 1899): **III**, 450

Loyson, Charles Jean Marie, "Eight Months of the Vatican Council," *The Guardian*, London (July 5, 1876): 457

Luce, Stephen B., "Naval Administration," U.S. Naval Institute *Proceedings*, XIV (1888); XXVIII (1902); XXIX (1903): **III**, 68
———, "On the Study of Naval Warfare as a Science," U.S. Naval Institute *Proceedings*, XII (1886): 627
———, "Naval History (Grand Tactics)," *ibid.*, XIII (1887): 627
———, "The Spanish-American War," *North American Review* (October 1911): **III**, 424
———, "The United States Naval War College," *The United Service Magazine* (January 1885): **III**, 219
———, "War Schools," U.S. Naval Institute *Proceedings*, IX (1883): **III**, 219

McAdoo, W. G., in *The New York Times*, May 26, 1894: **II**, 285

McBee, Silas, "Captain Mahan's Interpretations of the Faith," *The Churchman* (August 21, 1909): **III**, 310

McGiffin, Philo N., "The Battle of the Yalu," *Century Magazine* (August 1895): **II**, 416, 417

Macdonnell, Sir John, "Note on the Hague Conference," *Contemporary Review* (July 1907): **III**, 218

Mackinder, Halford J., "The Geographical Pivot of History," *The Geographical Journal* (April 1904): **III**, 99

Marston, R. B., "Captain Mahan and Our Navy," *The Sphere* (June 11, 1904): **II**, 93, 493; **III**, 99

Martens, F., "International Arbitration and the Peace Conference at the Hague," *North American Review* (November 1899): **III**, 450

INDEX

Other Articles (*cont.*)

Maurice, Sir John Frederick, "Army and Civil War," *Blackwood's Magazine* (May 1893): **II**, 116

———, Review of A. T. Mahan, *The Influence of Sea Power upon the French Revolution and Empire, 1793–1812, United Service Magazine* (May 1893): **II**, 105

Maxse, Leopold J., "Germany's Next War," *National Review* (December 1912): **III**, 487

———, Review of A. T. Mahan, "Monroe Doctrine," *ibid.* (February 1903): **III**, 58

Millard, William Salter, "Battle of Copenhagen," *Macmillan* (June 1895): **II**, 514

Morris, W. O'C., Review of A. T. Mahan, *Life of Farragut, Academy* (February 1894): **II**, 225

———, Review of A. T. Mahan, *Life of Nelson, Fortnightly Review* (June 1, 1897): **II**, 479

"The Mystery of the Status Quo," *Nineteenth Century* (September 1910): **III**, 358

"Naval Policy and the Pacific Question," *The Round Table* (June 1914): **III**, 534–535

"Naval Program of Japan," *The Times*, London, April 12–17, 1897: **II**, 506

"Our American Visitors," *The Graphic*, June 9, 1894: **II**, 285

"Our Naval Supremacy; Captain Mahan's Opinion," *Pall Mall Gazette*, May 10, 1894: **II**, 268

"The Panama Canal," *Quarterly Review* July; October 1912): **III**, 486–487

Parkin, Sir George Robert, Review of David Starr Jordan, *Imperial Democracy, The Churchman* (September 9, 1899): **II**, 654, 661

Pears, Sir Edwin, "Turkey, Present and Future," *Contemporary Review* (June 1913): **III**, 505, 511, 684

"Persia and the Persian Gulf," *Quarterly Review* (January 1902): **III**, 12, 13

"Powers and the War—The Boer Peace Mission—Portugal and the Beira Route," *The Standard*, London, April 27, 1900: **II**, 689

Pritchett, Henry S., "The Power that Makes For Peace," *Atlantic Monthly* (July 1907): **III**, 224, 227, 228, 229, 231

"The Question of Manchuria," *The Times*, London, August 6, 1910: **III**, 358

Review of A. T. Mahan, *Life of Farragut, Spectator* (February 1894): **II**, 225

Review of A. T. Mahan, *Life of Nelson* in *Athenaeum* (April 17, 1897): **II**, 504

"A Review of the Naval Situation," *The Navy* (January 1908): **III**, 236

Roosevelt, Theodore, "Expansion and Peace," *The Independent* (December 21, 1899): **II**, 676

———, "A Great Public Servant," *The Outlook* (January 13, 1915): **II**, 671

———, Review of A. T. Mahan, *The Influence of Sea Power upon the French Revolution and Empire, 1793–1812, Atlantic Monthly* (April 1893): **II**, 94

———, Review of A. T. Mahan, *The Influence of Sea Power upon History, Atlantic Monthly* (October 1890): **II**, 94

Root, Elihu, "Letter to the Editor," *The New York Times*, October 30, 1899: **II**, 668

Sampson, W. T., "The Atlantic Fleet in the Spanish War," *Century Magazine* (April 1899): **II**, 630

Seawell, Molly Elliot, "Paul Jones," *Century Magazine* (March 1894): **II**, 410

Seeley, John R., "War and the British Empire," *Journal of the Military Service Institution of the United States* (September 1889): 713

Shearman, Mr., "Letter to the Editor," *The New York Times*, January 17, 1900: **II**, 677

Sims, William S., "The Inherent Tactical Qualities of All-Big-Gun, One-Calibre Battleships," *U.S. Naval Institute Proceedings* (December 1906): **III**, 171, 178, 182–185, 188, 193

"So-Called Naval Questions," Royal United Service Institution *Journal* (1885): 634

Soley, James Russell, ed., "The Autobiography of Commodore Charles Morris, U.S.N.," *U.S. Naval Institute Proceedings*, VI, (1880): **II**, 541; **III**, 30, 32, 252

Stockton, Charles Herbert, "Capture of Enemy Merchant Vessels at Sea," *North American Review* (February 1899): **III**, 71

" 'Superior Speed' in Battleships," The New York *Sun*, October 19, 1906: **III**, 187, 189

Temple, Bishop Frederick, "The Education of the World," *Essays and Reviews* (1860): 365

Thursfield, James R., "Nelson," *Quarterly Review* (January 1898): **II**, 537

———, "The Nelson Touch," *Spectator*, XCV: **III**, 155

———, Review of A. T. Mahan, *Life of Nelson, Quarterly Review* (January 1898): **II**, 504

Tryon, Sir George, "National Insurance," *United Service Magazine* (July 1890): **II**, 29

"The United States, the President, and the Congress," *The Times*, London, January 21, 1910: **III**, 279–280

Wells, David Ames, "Great Britain and the United States, Their True Relations," *North American Review* (April 1896): **II**, 452

Wetmore, C. H., "Famous Sea-fight; The Engagement in 1879 off the Bolivian Coast between Peruvian and Chilean Ironclads,"

Century Magazine (April 1898): **II**, 422

White, Richard Dace, "With the Baltic Fleet at Tsushima," *Scientific American* (August 11, 1906): **III**, 182, 182–183, 183, 184

White, Sir William Henry, "The Naval Situation," *Nineteenth Century* (April 1909): **III**, 333–334

———, "Notes on the Armament of Battleships." Unpublished article read at meeting of Society of Naval Architects and Marine Engineers, New York, November 1910: **III**, 679

SECTION IV—JUDGMENTS AND OPINIONS

Abbot, Henry L.: M. tribute to, 665

Adams, Henry: M. impressed with as an historian, 37; treats same subjects as M., **II**, 42, **III**, 128, 133, 137

Adams, Miss: appearance, 15; M. characterizes, 15, 16, 18; M. attracted to, 18, 20; separates from, 26; M. disliked by, 49; M. dislike of, 57

Administration. *See* U.S. Navy: Administration

Alabama claims: M. supports U.S. position in, 262; reads Motley speech on, 267

Alcohol. *See* Mahan, A. T.: Alcohol

Aldrich, Nelson W.: interest in NWC, 639; M. enlists in fight to save NWC, 664, **II**, 58, 59, 62, 64

All-Big-Gun Ship controversy. *See* U.S. Navy: Ships

American Historical Association: M. becomes vice president of, **II**, 701; wants no administrative duties as president, **II**, 701; opposes moving annual meeting to Nashville, **II**, 742; accepts presidency of, **III**, 4; supports publication projects of, **III**, 24; M. ignorant of membership procedures of, **III**, 42; M. subordinates events of annual meeting in Philadelphia to social calls in the area, **III**, 46; M. knows little about personnel of, **III**, 45, 131; M. arrangements to publish presidential address to, **III**, 46, 47, 51, 52, 60; serves on Committee on Documentary Historical Publications of U.S. Government, **III**, 240, 244, 266, 279, 339, 676; insists on payment for members of Committee, **III**, 339, 676

American Historical Review: M. learns of existence of, **II**, 422; asks pay for reviewing books for, **II**, 423; declines to review books, **II**, 428–429, 477, 485, 513, 533, 550, 608, 622, 631, 663, 668, **III**, 174, 175–176,

316, 328–329, 515; reviews books for, **II**, 469, 476, 477, 485, 497, 502, 533, 546; declines invitation to submit article, **II**, 429, 433, 476, 696, 702, **III**, 166, 170; asks to review Clarke book in, **II**, 609; refuses to review poor book written by friend, **II**, 674–675; accepts invitation to publish article in, **III**, 117, 121, 130, 131, 134, 136–137, 147; negotiates payment for article, **III**, 147, 148; responds to critical review of his War of 1812 book in, **III**, 167–170, 171–172

American Revolution Centennial Celebration: 452; M. hopes to visit, 454–455; high quality of, 457

Ames, Sullivan Dorr: supports M. in Hackett Affair at USNA, 31; M. opinion of, 31

Animals. *See* Mahan, A. T.: Animals

Annapolis, Md.: M. social life in, 7, 15, 17, 18, 19, 22, 24, 27, 37, 40–41, 48, 50–51, 64, 65–66, 75–76, 76–77; M. like of, 63–64; M. dislike of, 65, 70, 80, 84; Army officers at social disadvantage in, 62; outbreak of scarlet fever in, 474; M. opposed to daughters living in, **II**, 350

Arbitration: M. opposes Anglo-American arbitral tribunal or treaty, **II**, 445, 450, 498, 504, 512, **III**, 420–421, 422, 433–437, 438, 440, 441–444; questions of national honor, conviction and conscience cannot be arbitrated, **II**, 445, 449, 658, 676; incapable of settling certain questions, **III**, 207, 225, 408, 420, 685, 686; interest in stems from maudlin anti-war sentimentality, **II**, 504; concept mocked by morally necessary Spanish and Boer wars, **II**, 675; useful only on questions of fact, **II**, 685; would not have prevented Spanish-American War, **III**, 139; movement for ignores international realities, **III**, 308; impossible

Arbitration (*cont.*)
to arrange in face of aroused national opinion, **III**, 376, 703; M. explains Taft stance on, **III**, 408–409; Grey sees Monroe Doctrine exempt from treaties of, **III**, 412; M. objects to clerical support of, **III**, 433–435; cannot sustain Monroe Doctrine, **III**, 687; M. despairs endorsement of by eminent citizens, **III**, 438; cannot insure peace, **III**, 469; helpless to stay outbreak of Balkan War, **III**, 495; a handmaiden of disarmament sentiment, **III**, 685. *See* Armaments, Peace (Peace Movement), War

Argentina: M. reports on revolution in, 381, 382, 384–385, 386, 389, 398, 404–405, 408, 409, 410, 422–426; tension with Brazil, 399, 409, 413, 414, 416; tension with Paraguay, 401; tension with Uruguay, 414, 415; internal political difficulties in, 414; political character of people, 422–423. *See* Index Section II, Ships: *Wasp*

Armaments: armed preparedness the surest way to preserve international peace and justice, 593, **II**, 65, 507, **III**, 195, 217, 469, 474, 489, 685, 686, 687, 703; larger USN would have deterred Spain and insured peace, **II**, 544; existence of put end to oppressive alien rule in Cuba, **III**, 687; limitations on naval arms constrict future action, **III**, 72; limitation on tonnage of single ships would help relieve financial burden of, **III**, 113–114; lack of would expose white world to attack by non-whites, **III**, 193, 285; lack of on both sides did not prevent Civil War, **III**, 278, 285, 315, 342, 487, 542, 702; did not bring on War of 1812, Mexican War, or Spanish-American War, **III**, 542–543, 545; existence of contained expansion of Balkan War, **III**, 495; existence of preserved peace in Europe from 1871 to 1912, **III**, 343, 703; existence of shortens wars and minimizes bloodshed and expense, **III**, 546; an effect rather than a cause of conditions, **III**, 315, 474, 543, 702; navies are only means to ends, **III**, 459; disarmament no guarantor of peace, **III**, 342, 546, 553; balance of lead to peaceful accommodations, **III**, 343; working-class demands for social welfare render financial burden of insupportable, **III**, 371; U.S. unilateral reduction of impractical, **III**, 474; support national policies in time of crisis, **III**, 474; unfortified boundary with Canada no argument against, **III**, 542, 711. *See* Arbitration, Peace (Peace Movement), War

Ashe, Samuel A'Court: M. affection for, 3, 5, 8, 9, 10, 12, 13, 14, 32, 69, 339, 571, **III**, 721; supports M. in Hackett Affair, 6; did not think M. conceited, 66; resignation from USNA, 3, 13, 14, 17, 26, 29, 59; family life of, 10, **II**, 183; marriage, 367; children of, 434, 451, 544; M. visits son of at USNA, **III**, 271, 273; daughter of marries, **III**, 464; study and practice of law, 9, 85, 86; enters newspaper business, 488; M. correspondence with, 16, 17, 18, 163, 169, 205, 235, 295, 352, 367, 574; M. attempts to arrange visits with, 367, 455, 457, 459, 464, 465, 466, 469, 476, 483; M. visits in Wilmington, N.C. (1871), **II**, 482; M. visits in Raleigh, N.C. (1906), **III**, 190; M. wants him to meet Woolverton, 340; M. lends money to, 351, 432–433, 472–473, 474; M. seeks loan repayment from, 432–433, 472–473, 474; repays M., 433–434, 474; assists M. in USN reform movement, 434, 437, 438, 439, 440, 442, 443, 452; renders assistance to NWC, 646, 647, 648, 649, 652, 653, 654; illness, 451; M. advises against medicinal use of whiskey, 451; M. informs on officer pay inequities, 454; view on origin of Civil War, 625; M. splits with on national political issues, 457, 487, 591, **II**, 470; M. congratulates on 1882 Democratic victory, 543; M. seeks aid on mother's pension legislation, 620–621, 624; becomes Postmaster of Raleigh, N.C., 624; politically powerful in N.C., **II**, 183; death of USNA roommate, **III**, 227; M. advises on health problems, **III**, 271; sends M. copy of his *History of North Carolina*, **III**, 272; M. life-long friendship with, **III**, 721

Asquith, Herbert H.: M. dines with, **II**, 131

Asuncion, Paraguay: *Wasp* arrives at, 398, 399; M. salutes Paraguay flag at, 399; mosquito season in, 424

Australia: must increase population, the basis of state power, **III**, 16; workingmen in discourage immigration to, **III**, 16; threat of Japanese immigration to, **III**, 221; dislike of Anglo-Japanese alliance, **III**, 308; M. declines to write article on necessity of immigration to, **III**, 397; Japanese emigrants have economic advantage over whites in, **III**, 411; need of British connection binds to Empire, **III**, 427; shares U.S. anti-Japanese immigration stance, **III**, 448; would oppose Chinese immigration with force, **III**, 449; slow white population growth endangers, **III**, 451–452; U.S. power related to security of, **III**, 468

Averett, Samuel W.: breaks with M. on Hackett Affair at USNA, 11, 12, **III**, 53; appearance, 66; character, 66, 67; M. predicts poor career ahead of, 73–74; post-Civil War career, **III**, 55

Balfour, Arthur James: impressed with M. *Influence* books, **II**, 105, 110; M. dines with, **II**, 131

Bases. *See* U.S. Navy: Yards (Bases)

Bayard, Thomas F., Sr.: M. prefers as GOP candidate in 1880, 482

Benson, William S.: M. blames inventory error on, 520

Bible. *See* Mahan, A. T.: Religion

Bicknell, George A.: M. curt to, 200; M. criticism of, 254; conversation about religion with, 259; M. has to dinner, 293

Blaine, James J.: M. condemns imperialistic policies of, 544, 573; nomination for presidency would drive M. out of GOP, 571, 655; M. fears his unscrupulous character, 572; hopes for his defeat in 1884 election, 572, 573, 624; M. thinks "insane," 591–592; no statesman, **II**, 25

Blake, Francis B.: appearance, 365, 433; resignation from USN, 365; in banking business in London, 433; marriage of, 433; social connections in England, **II**, 117; M. dines with in London, **II**, 275

Blake, George S.: supports M. in Hackett Affair, 24, 82; predicts rapid promotions for M., 69; critical of Colhoun of *Portsmouth*, 78; assists M. in securing desirable duty assignment, 82; death of, 433

Bliss, Tasker H.: suggests to M. analogy between land and naval warfare, 619; lectures at NWC, 637, **II**, 74; interest in NWC, 640; M. tribute to, 651, **II**, 74; assists with sale of *Influence*, 712

Boer War. *See* War: Boer War

Borchert, George A.: supports M. in Hackett Affair at USNA, 12; M. predicts famous career for, 73; post-Civil War career, **III**, 55

Boston Navy Yard. *See* U.S. Navy: Yards (Bases)

Bradford, Royal B.: M. anger toward, 151, 166, 175, 213; M. invites to dinner, 294; M. conflict with, 177, 279, 298; slowness in firing gun, 268; conflict with Ludlow, 298; M. respect for, **III**, 39

Brazil: M. reports on intervention in Argentine revolution, 385, 386, 398; tension with Paraguay, 399; M. reports on intervention in Paraguay revolution, 386, 398, 399, 415–416; tension with Argentina, 399, 409, 413, 414, 416; tension with Uruguay, 414; elaborate design of national ensign, 509, 512. *See* Index Section II, Ships: *Wasp*

Brewer, Ellen K. ("Kate"): appearance, 7; M. opinion of, 7; tricks M., 53; personality, 62

Brewer, Lucy: appearance, 7; M. opinion of, 7

Brooklyn (N.Y.) Navy Yard. *See* U.S. Navy: Yards (Bases)

Brown, Mrs. Francis Leonard. *See* Evans, Rosalie

Brown, John M.: M. approaches personally on publication of *Influence*, 712; M. enlists in fight for NWC appropriations, **II**, 207, 208, 246; M. sends complimentary tickets to Lowell Lectures, **II**, 498, 499; suffers serious accident, **II**, 501; M. birthday greetings to, **III**, 23–24; M. sends special copy of War of 1812 book to, **III**, 140; death, **III**, 274

Bryan, William Jennings: election of will lead to currency depreciation, **II**, 466; campaign speeches criticized, **II**, 470; M. thinks him a revolutionary, **II**, 694–695; M. distrust of approaches terror, **III**, 271; diplomatic faddist, **III**, 514; could not abandon Philippines even if elected in 1900, **III**, 603

Buenos Aires, Argentina: cholera in, 409, 410, 413; M. comment on political disturbances in, 422–423, 424, 425; M. critical of dangerous anchorage at, 425

Bunce, Francis M.: M. suggests as NWC president, **II**, 38; relieved by M. at NWC, **II**, 74; M. dislike of, **II**, 108, 144, 265; hostility to NWC, **II**, 144, 193, 208, 244; M. hopes will leave NWC, **II**, 145; M. assumes animus of in fight with Erben, **II**, 212; vexed over M. reception in Britain, **II**, 222; criticizes M. *Influence* books, **II**, 251; M. bears no lasting grudge against, **II**, 371. *See* U.S. Navy: Naval War College

Butt, Walter R.: breaks with M. on Hackett Affair, 11; M. characterizes, 11; hatred of M., 38; wants to resign from USNA, 51; post-Civil War career, **III**, 54–55

Canada: ONI studies war resources of, 656; M. lauds role of troops in Boer War, **II**, 684, **III**, 604; Japanese immigration to, **III**, 221, 449; shares U.S. anti-Japanese immigration stance, **III**, 448; opposition to Japanese immigration, **III**, 225–226, 252, 277, 496; will someday embrace USN as ally, **III**, 252; hostage to U.S. in event of Anglo-American war, **III**, 291, 345, 468; U.S. invasion of projected in contingency war plan for Britain, **III**, 560–561, 565–566, 567–568, 573, 574; Clark statement on U.S. annexation of, **III**, 388–389, 427; should remain British to keep Britain right on Japanese immigration question, **III**, 427; M. does not understand U.S. Reciprocity Treaty with, **III**, 427; inclines toward independence from Britain, **III**, 427

Carnegie, Andrew: M. finds his views on Anglo-American union vaporous, **II**, 283, 305; advocates Anglo-American political union, **II**, 283; M. dismisses views of on British imperial preferential tariffs, **III**, 72; M. opposes his peace movement activities, **III**, 223; gets on M. nerves, **III**, 308

Carnegie Institution (Washington, D.C.): M. disinclined to accept research appointment at, **III**, 504–505, 506; considers research appointment at, **III**, 516; accepts appointment at, **III**, 517, 518; pecuniary considerations determine acceptance of appointment to, **III**, 518, 549; duties at, **III**, 518–519, 524

Carter, Samuel P.: M. criticizes, 155, 179; M. dislike of, 158, 173, 284, 320, 325; M. calls officially upon, 304

Cenas, Hilary: supports M. in Hackett Affair, 12; class standing at USNA, 13; imprisoned in Fort Lafayette, 89; post-Civil War dissipation, III, 54

Century Club: M. membership in, **II**, 461; membership rules, **II**, 461; inferior to University Club, **III**, 252; opposes Richardson admission into, **III**, 536–537

Century Company: proposes pre-publication serialization of future M. books, **II**, 491, 497

Century Magazine: M. screens manuscripts for, **II**, 422, 423, 424, 514; negotiates publication of articles in, **II**, 415, 422, 424, 429; raises question of pay for articles, **II**, 429, 515

Chadwick, French Ensor: possible successor to M. as president of NWC, **II**, 34, 56–57, 58; interest in NWC perfunctory, **II**, 58; ambivalent on NWC presidency, **II**, 59; supports M. for NWC presidency, **II**, 60; informs M. of Herbert's conversion to pro-NWC stance, **II**, 142, 143, 144, 148; informs M. that Ramsay has not read *Influence* books, **II**, 371; M. cites in travel expenses argument with Treasury Dept., **II**, 601–604, 607; books written by, **II**, 672; supports Ismay role in *Titanic* disaster, **III**, 454, 455; condemns behavior of merchant marine transport captains during Spanish-American War, **III**, 236, 636

Chambers, Washington I.: opposition to NWC consolidation, **II**, 108, 193, 201; criticized by Herbert, **II**, 223

Chandler, William E.: M. lauds personnel policies of, 556; M. criticism of, 592; patronage abuses of, 655; thinks USN ships too large to be easily deployable, **II**, 680; approves establishment of NWC, **III**, 664

Chauvenet, William: M. opinion of, 71, **III**, 182

Chester, Colby M.: M. respect for, 713

Chile: superiority of navy to USN, 544, 592; M. describes, 572–573; women not beautiful, 573; incapacity for self-government, **II**, 47; civil war in studied at NWC, **II**, 82

Crisis with U.S.: M. called to Washington to assist in, **II**, 59, 60, 68, 734; utilizes presence in Washington during to fight for NWC, **II**, 59–64; Government of wants no war, **II**, 63; naval capability, **II**, 63, 507; difficulty of fighting Chile at such distances, **II**, 63; M. works on Farragut biography during, **II**, 64; war possibility fades, **II**, 64, 65; USN preparedness insures peace, **II**, 65; Tracy ran USN during, **II**, 734; M. worked on problems connected with in virtual isolation, **II**, 734

China: M. describes people, 116–117; a barbaric people, **II**, 92–93; immigration into U.S., 355; natives sought for enlistment in USN, 582; U.S. exclusion laws compromise USN enlistment, 582; emigration to Hawaii dangerous to U.S., **II**, 92; expansion into Pacific Ocean predicted, **II**, 92–93, 619; Russian and German imperialism in contributes to Anglo-American identity of interest, **II**, 537; European penetration of raises important commercial questions for U.S., **II**, 582; U.S. Open Door policy in, **II**, 658, 708; U.S. participation in lifting Boxer siege at Peking, **II**, 693; M. equates Boxer behavior with that of children, **II**, 700; M. fearful of Russian ambitions in, **II**, 693; can be saved by penetration of European ideas and trade, **II**, 208; naval power in Yangtze can check Russian expansion in, **II**, 707–708; recognizes U.S. good will, **III**, 251; has reason for complaint against treatment of nationals in California, **III**, 251

Christianity. *See* Mahan, A. T.: Religion (Christianity)

Churchman Magazine, The: M. reads, 429; urges right thinking on Boer War issues, **II**, 656

Civil War (U.S.). *See* War: Civil War

Claiborne, Henry B. ("Billy"): M. opinion of, 6; supports M. in Hackett Affair, 12; low academic standing at USNA, 13; imprisoned in Fort Lafayette, 89; Civil War service, **III**, 54; death, **III**, 54

Clark, Bouverie F.: congratulates M. on *Influence*, **II**, 47; M. met while in *Wachusett*, **II**, 133, 285–286, **III**, 9; M. dines with in London, **II**, 285; provides M. with data for Boer War book, **II**, 699–700; named for K.C.B., **II**, 721; retirement of, **III**, 8; appearance, **III**, 10; death of wife, **III**, 31; Boer War service, **III**, 48; assists

M. with autobiography, **III**, 202–203; M. affection for, **III**, 721

Clark, James Beauchamp ("Champ"): advocates U.S. annexation of Canada, **III**, 388, 427; M. thinks him an alcoholic, **III**, 389, 427; M. hatred of, **III**, 465; M. served with on USNA Board of Visitors, **III**, 465

Clarke, Sir George Sydenham: M. dines with wife of, **II**, 133, 146; M. dines with in Malta, **II**, 256; M. entertains aboard *Chicago*, **II**, 282; M. congratulates on assignment to Woolwich, **II**, 305; highly critical of M. book, **II**, 543; asks M. to review his book on Russian navy, **II**, 609; sustains M. all-big-gun ship arguments, **III**. 201, 202; role in British imperial defense planning, **III**, 201

Cleveland, Grover: M. supports in 1884 elections, 574, 624; cheers election of, 592; defeat of in 1888 benefits NWC, 665; banishes M. to sea because of Hawaii article, **II**, 138; **III**, 299; M. will not be silenced by Administration, **II**, 138; M. organizes political pressure on in NWC appropriations fight, **II**, 207; M. writes asking support in NWC appropriations fight, **II**, 208; awkwardness of as a diplomat, **II**, 443–444; should have annexed Hawaii when opportunity presented, **II**, 506

Clover, Richardson: assists M. with research on *Influence #2*, **II**, 42, 44, 48, 49, 54, 55, 66–67; serves as USN Hydrographer, **II**, 49; ordered to *Chicago* as XO, **II**, 226; M. criticism of, **II**, 226, 306; joins *Chicago* as XO, **II**, 249; M. hopes to leave *Chicago* details in hands of, **II**, 250, 251; M. evaluates as an officer, **II**, 306; connection with Ramsay noted, **II**, 306; Erben praises in anti-Mahan context, **II**, 323; advises publication of M. Anglo-American Reunion article, **II**, 342; socially dull, **II**, 398; sends M. clipping from British newspaper, **III**, 23

Coaling Stations. *See* U.S. Navy: Coaling Stations

Colhoun, John: M. on Blake's critical opinion of, 78

Colombia: conflict with U.S. over arrest of consul in Buenaventura, 591, 592, 597; U.S. intervention in Panama (1885), 594, 595, 597, 609, **III**, 9; purchase of Almirante Bay from as USN coaling station, **II**, 589, 590

Columbia University: M. attends, **II**, 234

Commerce: immunity of private property at sea in wartime issue, **II**, 610–612, 613–614, **III**, 112–114, 157–159, 164–165, 172, 192, 210, 213, 218–219, 366, 623–626; relationship of to USN, 643, **II**, 81; importance of international, 112; M. studies routes, **II**, 12, 18; control of key to Anglo-American power in Far East, **III**, 113; destruction of in wartime strategically secondary, **II**, 531; control of important to policies of naval states, **III**, 155; British control over German, **III**, 159, 165, 192; U.S. control of routes at Panama, **III**, 159; as sinews of war, **III**, 219, 623. *See* Hague Conference (Second); U.S. Merchant Marine

Corbett, Julian S.: M. criticism of, **III**, 273, 394; M. praises book of, **III**, 276, 338, 374–375; complements Jomini, **III**, 276; relies on Clausewitz, **III**, 394; writes book on principles of naval strategy, **III**, 451

Craven, Anne ("Nannie"): appearance, 15, 28, 53, 76; M. attraction to, 18, 20–21, 24, 28–29, 32, 34, 36, 52, 57, 68, 70; an enigma to M., 55, 64; encourages M. academically at USNA, 56; snubs M., 60; thinks M. conceited, 66

Craven, Thomas T.: M. opinion of, 19, 35, 55; Ashe opinion of, 19; supports M. in Hackett Affair, 19, 24, 82; personal interest in M., 54; high opinion of M. academic potential at USNA, 60; defends M. personality, 66

Cuba: need for USN coaling station in, **II**, 588, vision of a free Cuba under U.S. control, **II**, 619; strategic importance of Guantanamo to USN, **III**, 354; coaling capability at Guantanamo needed, **III**, 400, 402

Cushing, William B.: M. entertains aboard *Iroquois*, 307, 310; plays billiards with, 308, 310, 312, 313

Cushman, Charles H.: M. opinion of, 24

Daniels, Josephus: compliments M. on religious article, **III**, 525; M. asks withdrawal of order prohibiting officers from writing on European War, **III**, 540–541; denies M. request to write on European War, **III**, 542

Davis, Charles H.: responds to M. contingency plan for war with Britain, **II**, 35–37; works on NWC maps, **II**, 68, 69; sees conspiracy against M. in Erben fight, **II**, 234

Delehanty, Daniel: M. loses temper with, 192; conflict with Midn. Finley at USNA, 478–481

Democratic Party: M. knows little about, 157; M. has no faith in, 338; considers voting for in 1876, 455; in election of 1876, 459; in election of 1880, 488; M. predicts defeat of, 473; predicts end of Solid South, 473; existence of Solid South, 477; M. alienated by, 477; M. opposes economic policies of, 477, 489; M. predicts defeat of in 1880, 477; fears pro-

Democratic Party (*cont.*)
motions of Southern officers if returned to power, 482–483; majority of USN officers belong to, 482; should abandon states' rights issue, 488, 571–572; should embrace Civil Service reform, 489; should support free trade, 489; M. hopes will take interest in USN, 544, 556; anticipates victory of in 1884, 571; should stand for strict construction of Constitution, 571; M. leans toward in 1888, 655; victory in 1890 not good for NWC, **II**, 32; anticipates victory in 1892, **II**, 47; buried in the tomb of Jefferson, **II**, 205, 361, **III**, 414; anti-Navy stance of, **II**, 205, **III**, 448, 457, 467, 474, 475, 476, 484, 512; has no appreciation of sea power, **II**, 235; 1896 platform wrong and revolutionary, **II**, 470; leads attack on Britain in Boer War issue, **II**, 665; platform undermined by Bryan personality, **III**, 271; international events will force support of military expenditures, **III**, 371; M. fears will retreat from Panama Canal fortification, **III**, 414; represents least rich and least educated, **III**, 448; has no broad view of external policy, **III**, 448, 467, 469, 477; naval attitudes imperil Monroe Doctrine and security of Panama Canal, **III**, 463–464; unfortunate Panama Tolls Act, **III**, 476–477; will mismanage foreign policy, **III**, 477, 478; naval unpreparedness of in 1812 disastrous, **III**, 475–476; nation threatened by accession to power of in 1912, **III**, 484; once led by incompetent named Jefferson, **III**, 484; has placed U.S. in hands of the Philistines, **III**, 500; M. feels insecure while party is in office, **III**, 512; will be captivated by Churchill's naval-holiday notion, **III**, 514

Department of the Navy. *See* U.S. Navy: Department of the Navy

Department of the Navy Library. *See* U.S. Navy: Office of Naval Records and Library

Dewey, George: attends E. A. Walker funeral, 452; M. jealousy of, 557; service on Santo Domingo Commission, **III**, 106; would lean to Schley if controversy with Sampson reopened, **III**, 423

Diplomacy. *See* Canada; Chile; France; Germany; Great Britain: Diplomacy; Isthmian Canal; Japan; Monroe Doctrine; U.S.A.: Diplomacy; War

Dixey, John: M. loses temper with and criticizes, 157

Dotty, Charles: M. conflict with Robeson on court-martial of, 452–453

Drake, Franklin J.: experience with photometric tests, 516; draws devices for foreign national ensigns, 517, 525–526, 531, 532; invents appliance for taking bearings, 536; lectures at NWC, **II**, 82

Eastman, Thomas H.: dishonesty of, 438

Ecuador: conflict with U.S. on Santos case, 587–589. 590, 594, 602, 603–605; demonstrations in against U.S. lease of Galapagos Islands, **III**, 376

Elections. *See* Democratic Party; Republican Party; U.S.A.: Congressional Elections; Presidential Elections

Emory, William H.: criticizes Earl English, 149; M. disciplines, 149

English, Earl: comments on beauty of Maime Lewis Parker, 111; criticized by Ens. Emory, 149; brings drunken boat crew back to ship, 239; M. criticisms of, 150, 153, 154, 155, 156, 157, 175, 177, 179, 184, 185, 186, 189, 191, 195, 196, 201, 202, 206, 207, 212, 220, 221, 222, 230, 235, 236, 237, 238, 239, 241, 248, 251, 254, 266, 275, 278, 279, 346; M. conflict with, 162, 164, 165, 166, 167, 168, 187, 191, 205, 207, 263, 279, 281; M. approval of, 189, 221, 232, 295; transferred to command of *Piscataqua*, 280; visits M. aboard *Iroquois*, 310; M. discusses Line vs. Staff with, 311; visits M. aboard *Aroostook*, 316; relieved as CO of *Iroquois*, 318

Episcopal Church. *See* Mahan, A. T.: Religion

Erben, Henry: social gaucherie of, **II**, 134; M. feeling of social superiority toward, **II**, 231–232, 244; poor health of, **II**, 232, 278, 279, 297; M. overshadows during *Chicago* visit to England, **II**, 135, 267, 278, 297, **III**, 203; frets about trifles, **II**, 151; M. doubts Civil War record of, **II**, 250; joined by family abroad, **II**, 181; hatred of Walker, **II**, 232; hosts reception aboard *Chicago*, **II**, 287; departs *Chicago*, **II**, 324; popular with *Chicago* officers, **II**, 324; supports Sampson in controversy with Schley, **II**, 703–704

Erben vs. Mahan Fitness Report Controversy: **II**, 210–216, 217, 224, 228, 231–232, 234, 236, 239, 240, 243–244, 250, 282–283, 302, 322–323, 435; offers to transfer M. home, **II**, 228; harassment of M., **II**, 216, 272; M. criticism of personality and habits of, **II**, 134, 211, 212, 217, 229, 231–232, 239, 243–244, 254, 263, 292, 340, 361; M. criticism of as an officer-administrator, **II**, 218, 223, 227, 229, 232, 236, 254, 263, 303; M. feels himself vindicated in Erben fight, **II**, 240, 246; M. blames problems with on envy in USN, **II**, 225; M. pays closer attention to shipboard duties during controversy with, **II**, 226, 228, 233, 248; fears split in USN on Erben issue along pro- and anti-NWC lines, **II**, 234, 250; M. doubts actual conspiracy involved in Erben fight, **II**, 234, 245; M. anticipates retirement of, **II**, 249, 309; M. fears will poison Kirkland against him, **II**, 322; M. uses British reception to counter, **II**, 266; service confidence in M. unshaken by controversy with, **II**, 403. *See* Index Section II, Ships: *Chicago*

Evans, Ellen Kuhn (Mrs. Manlius Glendower) (mother-in-law): opposes M. engagement to Ellen Lyle Evans, 368, 369; resides in Pau for reasons of economy, 433, 473; declining health of, 473, **II**, 257, 260; returns to U.S. from Pau, 487; death of, **II**, 257, 258, 259, 261, 262; conflict with daughter Rosalie, **II**, 257; Lyle Mahan's love for, **II**, 257, 258; M. considers her death a blessed release, **II**, 262; M. inherits her estate, **II**, 271; estate settlement, **II**, 315, **III**, 728

Evans, Hartman Kuhn (brother-in-law): assists M. in naval reform movement, 443; assists Mrs. M. with financial problems, **II**, 132, 137, 139, 150; assists M. in NWC appropriations fight, **II**, 206; suffers business failure, **II**, 371; visits Europe, **II**, 371; proposes settling abroad, **II**, 380, 381, 388; plans to live with Charles Kuhn in Nice, **II**, 371, 374, 380, 382, 392, 401; M. lives in house leased by, **III**, 177, 197, 204

Evans, Manlius Glendower (father-in-law): poor health of, 369, 473, 615; introduces M. to Sen. Bayard, 443; advises M. on national currency issues, 467; business failure of, 473; returns to U.S. from Pau, 487

Evans, Margaret (wife's aunt): death, **II**, 351, 354; death a merciful release, **II**, 351; Mrs. M. anticipates inheritance, **II**, 355, **III**, 720; will of, **II**, 357

Evans, Robley D. ("Fighting Bob"): M. enlists in fight with Erben, **II**, 212

Evans, Rosalie (Mrs. Francis L. Brown) wife's sister) ("Dodie," "Rose," "Rosie," "Marraine"): lives with and takes care of her mother, **II**, 193, 257, 271; resorts to stimulants, **II**, 193; conflict with her mother, **II**, 257; mother's death a necessary relief, **II**, 262; visits Quogue after mother's death, **II**, 271; M. thinks she should be specially provided for in her mother's will, **II**, 355; breakdown after mother's death, **II**, 371, 380, 384, 385; takes trip to Europe, **II**, 374, 381, 382, 384; M. thinks she may settle permanently abroad, **II**, 381, 388; M. terms her an invalid, **II**, 384, 385; M. sees her briefly in Algiers, **II**, 385, 386, 387, 388; appearance, **II**, 388; settles initially in Nice, **II**, 395, 401; health im-

proves in Nice, **II**, 404; marries, **II**, 560, **III**, 484; M. visits at home in Pau, **III**, 484, 491

Farquhar, Norman H.: breaks with M. on Hackett Affair at USNA, 67–68; post-USNA career, **III**, 55; death, **III**, 228

Financial Problems. *See* Mahan, A. T.: Financial Problems and Considerations

Fister, Thomas D.: participates in Foote Incident at USNA, 75, 77–78, 81, 83; M. on political influence of, 81; commissioned in Revenue Service, 83

Fletcher, Arthur Henry: M. criticism and dislike of, 167, 168, 170, 179, 185, 186, 191, 192, 196, 200, 203, 204, 206, 210, 211, 212, 214, 215, 219, 220, 222, 226, 227, 229, 232, 234, 235, 236, 237, 241, 245, 250, 265, 272, 276, 277, 278, 328; M. attempts to bring to God, 170, 247, 252, 253–254, 267; reported to be an agnostic, 247; M. conflict with, 171, 184, 188; M. tries to change hostile attitude toward, 171, 290; M. invites ashore, 239, 279, 283; reports Nones to M., 296

Folger, William M.: participates in contingency war planning, **II**, 35–38; supports aims of NWC, **II**, 63; interest in materials of war, **II**, 63,

Foote Incident. *See* U.S. Navy: Naval Academy

Foreign Languages. *See* Mahan, A. T.: Foreign Languages (study and use)

France: tests Monroe Doctrine in Mexico, 94; revolution in (1871), 364; U.S. isthmian policy dictates a USN equal to France's, 593; naval war with Britain, 629; Franco-American alliance (1778), 636, **II**, 556; cannot be great on land and sea unless Britain permits, 671; U.S. contingency plan for war with not needed, **II**, 37; reception of *Chicago* in, **II**, 148, 152; few pretty women, **II**, 178; M. hopes Italians will defeat in coming war, **II**, 179; M. reputation in navy, **II**, 218; musical implications of alliance with Russia, **II**, 380; M. criticizes in Sudan rivalry with Britain, **II**, 620; Russia does not support in Sudan, **II**, 620; thinks French a peculiar people, **II**, 620; Panama canal rights negotiations with U.S., **III**, 9; inevitable enemy of Britain, **III**, 12; Delcassé incident, **III**, 342; Algeciras crisis, **III**, 342; tension with Germany, **III**, 342; presence in Algeria and Tunisia economically beneficial to native populations, **III**, 473

Garfield, James A.: weakness of character, 488

General Staff concept. *See* U.S. Navy: Administration

Germany: navy superior to USN, 592; M. advocates drawing up contingency plans for war with, II, 37, 38; German opinions of *Influence* books, II, 129–130; translation of *Influence* books into German, II, 179, 186; M. reputation in German Navy, II, 218; Kaiser's interest in M. books, II, 312; personality of Kaiser, II, 537; imperial expansion of portends future tension with U.S., II, 529, 536; expansion a temporary phenomenon, III, 34; population growth dictates imperial expansion, II, 536–537; expansion of natural and laudable, III, 446; emigrants make poor colonists abroad, II, 537; U.S. tension with during Spanish-American War, II, 566, 567; M. urges expansion of into Middle East to counterbalance Russia, III, 12; growth of sea power of, III, 12, 334; ultimate alliance with Britain, III, 17; association with Britain in punitive action in Venezuela, III, 50, 445; American dislike of Germans, III, 29; shameless opportunism of diplomacy of, III, 32–33; difficult diplomatic position of, III, 32, 34; hatred of U.S., III, 32–34, 35; naval building program alarms Britain, III, 63, 307, 334; ambitions threaten U.S., III, 165, 291–292; M. did not oppose acquisition of Carolines by, III, 165; M. condemns treatment by North German Lloyd Co., III, 214–215; new building program will produce larger navy than USN by 1912, III, 291, 334, 412; ambitions in Latin America threaten Monroe Doctrine, III, 291–292, 307–308, 445; naval strength permits challenge of Monroe Doctrine, III, 345; ambitions not turned toward W. Hemisphere, III, 334; tension with France, III, 342; tension with Russia in Balkans, III, 342; social framework well supports future armaments growth, III, 371; German-Americans, III, 548; territorial designs on Holland and Dutch Empire, II, 27, III, 377; Moltke on invasion of Britain, III, 410; USN parity with needed, III, 410; M. wants no U.S. general arbitration treaty with, III, 420; German-Americans disrupt pro-arbitration treaty rally, III, 438; large merchant shipping influences Caribbean (Panama) territorial ambitions, III, 445; article in magazine attacks Monroe Doctrine, III, 459; Bernhardi advocates brute force of, III, 487; harsh war (1914) aims of, III, 541; victory in Europe will threaten Monroe Doctrine, III, 541–542; victory in Europe will increase hostility toward U.S., III, 551; M. concerned over early German successes in European War, III, 548, 551; German use of submarines and airplanes, III, 549, 550–551, 708–709; principal instigator of European War, III, 698, 707, 710; German naval strategy in European War, III, 699–700; reasons for building German navy, III, 707. *See* Great Britain: Diplomacy; U.S.A.: Diplomacy; War

Gill, Mary Esther: M. attraction to, 25

Gillender, Augustus T.: legal and financial work for M., 429, II, 112–113, 139, 361, 416, 417; M. enlists in NWC appropriations fight, II, 210; handles Tenafly-Palisades property inheritance problem, II, 351, 436, 438, 444, 447, 448, 461, 463, 464, 465, 467, 720, 726, 728; handles squatters on Tenafly-Palisades property, II, 499, 511, 515–516, 522, 620; M. social exchanges with, II, 447; M. proposes for membership in Century Club, II, 461; M. refuses to support for public office, III, 75; suffers paresis, III, 504

Gillpatrick, William W.: desk-bound aboard *Chicago*, II, 138; M. blames *Chicago* command pressures on inadequacy of, II, 223, 224, 226; M. blames inadequacies as XO on presence of wife, II, 224; M. criticism of, II, 249; M. blames condition of *Chicago* on, II, 250–251; supports M. in Erben fight, II, 282; M. praises in anti-Erben context, II, 323

Gladstone, William Ewart: impressed with M. *Influence* books, II, 105, 110; M. describes Mrs. G., II, 135; snubs M., II, 298; M. books encourage resignation of, II, 298

Goldsborough, John: quoted on decision to remain loyal to U.S. in Civil War, 90; M. lauds his decision to fight for U.S. in Civil War, 90

Goldsborough, Louis M.: M. criticizes cautious seamanship of, 87

Goodrich, Caspar F.: heads combined NWC and Torpedo Station, 677, 678; M. has confidence in, 678; assists with sale of *Influence*, 712; M. criticism of, 713; seeks superintendency of USNA, II, 349; M. wants no rivalry with, II, 371; sides with Sims in all-big-gun ship controversy, III, 178; criticizes M. Great White Fleet article, III, 263–264; breaks with M., III, 264; mind more eccentric than original, III, 316

Grant, Ulysses S.: surrounded by corrupt friends, 439; not a serious candidate in 1880, 482; M. criticism of, 487; compromised by military background, 592

Great Britain: class reasons for glory of, 74; M. critical of press handling of U.S. Civil War, 91; press watch-dog function in,

III, 16; bearing and behavior of military abroad, 107, 141–142; superior mail service to Far East, 139; a selfish nation, 593; M. impressed by servants in, II, 299; frequency of titles, II, 329; wealthy Americans pursue English titles, II, 451; M. anglophilia, II, 395, 441, 444, 445, 451, 504, III, 27–28, and *passim*; M. defends mercantilist system of, III, 461–462; view of Navigation Acts, III, 620–621; M. enjoys being lionized in, II, 142, 144, 166, 267–268, 270, 281, 286, 291, 299, 342, 344, 346, 366, 493; laments ending of lionization in, II, 293, 327, 342, 343, 344; misses society of, II, 370; social harassment and fatigue in, II, 136, 148, 270, 272, 274, 284, 286, 299; lingering reputation of M. in, III, 500

Diplomacy: M. supports imperialism at Aden, 112; critical of Near Eastern policy of, 457; U.S.-Irish vote in relations with U.S., 593, II, 84, 664, 665, 679, 685, 686; cooperation with U.S. in Panama intervention, 595; policy of in Venezuela Crisis with U.S., III, 476; racial and political identity with U.S., 593, II, 84, 171, 504, 529, 685; leadership of English-speaking race, II, 445; organic union with U.S., II, 283; brings civilization out of barbarism, II, 503, 504; beneficence of imperial expansion of, II, 529; M. critical of stance in Greco-Turkish tension over Crete, II, 505; M. criticizes support of Turkey, III, 511; M. impressed with commonwealth system, II, 537, III, 427; supports imperial federation idea, II, 743, III, 13, 15, 23, 27, 71–72, 100, 153–154, 609; supports imperial preferential tariff proposal, III, 71–72, 149, 154; organization of Imperial defence, III, 397; Anglo-Japanese Treaty, III, 12, 532–533, 534–535; danger to U.S. of alliance with Japan, III, 214, 216, 221–222, 226, 308, 533, 534–535; M. supports in Sudan tension with France, II, 620; growing tension with Germany, III, 12, 32; Germany less a threat to than Russia, III, 29; M. sees ultimate Anglo-German alliance, III, 17; association with Germany in punitive action in Venezuela, III, 50; importance of geographic and strategic control over German commerce, III, 159, 165, 192, 205, 211, 213, 284, 707; Free Ships-Free Goods doctrine weakens control of over German commerce, III, 192, 205, 210, 221, 366; acceptance of Free Ships-Free Goods would force U.S. tilt toward Germany, III, 216; competition with Germany inclines G. B. toward U.S., III, 468; should encourage Russian involvement in Far East (Manchuria) to reduce pressure in Persian Gulf and elsewhere, III, 99,

109, 214, 221, 226; Persian Gulf more vital to than Far Eastern concerns, III, 12, 27, 96, 99, 109; Persian Gulf key to strategic posture of, III, 13, 34, 35, 109; Russia as natural enemy of, III, 12, 29, 34; Russian-German tension in Middle East useful to, III, 12, 13; mishandling of Alaska boundary question with U.S., III, 411; inevitability of Anglo-American Imperial Democracy, III, 263; Empire of the Sea produced British Empire, III, 154; foreign policy of determined by sea power capability, III, 439. *See* U.S.A.: Diplomacy; Germany; Japan; Russia; War (Boer)

Domestic Affairs: M. avoids involvement in Irish issue, II, 268; adopts anti-Home Rule stance, III, 333, 520; favors Chamberlain in 1906 elections, III, 153–154; has no confidence in Liberal Government, III, 203, 205, 207, 216, 307; pleased with Conservative gains in 1908 elections, III, 244; views on free trade identical with Balfour's, III, 244; sees socialist bent in Liberal Cabinet, III, 315; doubts wisdom of reduction of power of House of Lords, III, 370, 427, 520; miners strike, III, 447

Entertainment (Formal) of M. in: Lord Lieutenant of Ireland (Milnes), II, 116, 117, 118, 140–141; First Lord of the Admiralty (Spencer), II, 120, 121, 122, 123, 133, 135, 140–141, 144, 277; Queen Victoria, II, 128–129, 140, 142, 144, 166, 310, 311–312, 327; Secretary of U.S. Legation (White), II, 130, 131; honorary memberships in private clubs, II, 134, 267; St. James Hall banquet, II, 266, 267, 270, 276, 278, 297, 342; Sampson Low, Marston dinner, II, 272–273, 274, 275; Royal Naval College tour, II, 273; Cabinet dinner (Queen's Birthday), II, 274, 275, 276, 297–298; Treasury Lords dinner, II, 275; Bayard dinner, II, 277, 278; Royal Navy Club dinner, II, 277, 279–280, 297, 396, III, 203; Royal Military Tournamant invitation, II, 284; Queen's State Ball, II, 279, 284–285, 286; Foreign Office reception, II, 298; Trinity House dinner, II, 300, 327; dinner on royal yacht, II, 310, 327

Entertainment (Private) of M. in: Clark weekend, II, 133, 140, 343, 344, 345, 419, III, 36; Clarke lunch, II, 133, 146; Cowles dinner, II, 134; White dinner, II, 134; Laughton dinner, II, 135; Jeune dinner, II, 136, 269; Hayter weekend, II, 137–138, 140, 269; Spencer dinner, II, 141; Crichton dance, II, 146, 148; Yorke dinner, II, 146, 148; Radstock dinner, II, 148; Jeune weekend, II, 267, 269, 324, 325–326, 327, 328–329, 330, 331; Blake lunch, II, 267, 270, 272, 273, 280; Clarke dinner, II, 267, 270; Bige-

Great Britain (*cont.*)

low dinner, **II**, 267, 270, 273; Beresford weekend, **II**, 270, 274; Lefevre dinner, **II**, 270, 272, 277; Jeune dinner, **II**, 273; Salisbury weekend, **II**, 274, 275, 276, 298; Bryce lunch, **II**, 275; Rosebery dinner, **II**, 277, 278, 297, 298, 396; Beaumont dinner, **II**, 277, 280, 284; Rothschild lunch, **II**, 298; White weekend, **II**, 315–316, 319, 328; Nelson weekend, **II**, 320, 328

Royal Navy: M. lauds discipline in, 74; favors command structure of, 444–445; favors midshipmen recruitment policy, 497; assists with burial of USN midn. in Callao, 561; admirals lack scientific approach, 629; maneuvers studied by ONI, 658, 659, 664, 670, **II**, 99; M. appeals to for support of NWC, 662, 663, 669; sympathy for NWC goals within, 669, 670; M. contingency plan for USN war with, **II**, 18, 35–37, **III**, 559–576; availability of coaling stations, **II**, 36; reception of *Influence* books within, **II**, 47, 161, 168, 194, 255, 285, 312; channel tunnel would weaken defensive capability of, **II**, 93, **III**, 98–99; *Victoria* disaster, **II**, 114, 161, 168, 188, 593; M. books influence building program, **II**, 186, 255, 266, 276, 298, 471; M. reluctance to fire upon in war, **II**, 444; rejects honorary rank in, **II**, 512; strength of benefits U.S., **III**, 27–28; M. supports changes in policies in, **III**, 204; Fisher-Beresford controversy within, **III**, 263, 284–285, 307, 315, 334; German naval growth rivals, **III**, 291, 333; two-power standard a national rather than party question, **III**, 457; cruisers sunk by German submarines, **III**, 549, 550; key to victory in European War, **III**, 551; must bring German fleet to battle, **III**, 699, 708; strategy of in European War, **III**, 698–699, 707–708; M. eulogy to, **III**, 701. *See* U.S. Navy

Great White Fleet cruise. *See* U.S. Navy: Great White Fleet

Greece: tension with Turkey over Crete, **II**, 495, 505; Greek-Americans, **III**, 521

Greeley, Horace: M. calls "honest lunatic," 591

Greene, Dana: suffers brain tumor, 593; death by suicide, **III**, 56; heroism in *Monitor* vs. *Merrimac* fight, **III**, 56

Guatemala: defeat in war, 598, 599, 600; disorders in, 598, 599; *Wachusett* shows flag in, 599, 600; *Wachusett* affects diplomacy of, 601; *Wachusett* officers given leave in, 602

Hackett, Samuel H.: M. break with, 6; hatred of, 6; opinion of, 6, 37, 66; appearance, 17; drinking habits, 48; M. competes for Julia Kent with, 78; roomed with Ashe at USNA, **III**, 53; resignation from USN, **III**, 53

Hackett Affair. *See* U.S. Navy: Naval Academy

Hague Conference (First): M. appointed to U.S. delegation to, **II**, 631; interrupts M. literary work, **II**, 632; financial arrangements for M. participation, **II**, 633; purpose of Conference obscure, **II**, 633; neutral vessels rescuing men from water at scene of naval engagement should do so at own risk, **II**, 638, 639–641, 643, 644, 645, 646–649, 654, 659–660; M. opposes size limitations on USN, **II**, 643, 652; opposes limitations on use of poison gas projectiles, **II**, 650–651; derives article from experiences at, **II**, 652–653; Russian motives at suspect, **II**, 658; McKinley cannot support M. stance at, **II**, 659; U.S. opposition to Article 27 triggered by chance news article, **III**, 139

Mahan-Holls Controversy: **II**, 697, 704–706, 708–716, 719–720, 731–732, 737–738, 741, 744–745; **III**, 1, 13–14, 15, 16, 17–22, 73, 74, 450

Hague Conference (Second): M. wants U.S. to abandon traditional Free Ships-Free Goods position at, **III**, 112–114, 157–159, 210, 213, 221, 638; seeks freedom as officer to speak out publicly on issues at, **III**, 158, 164–165, 172, 192; M. hopes will limit size of warships, **III**, 184; seeks to influence outcome of with articles on capture of private property at sea, **III**, 204–205, 207, 209, 210, 211, 214, 216, 221; M. pleased with British position on capture of private property at sea, **III**, 213; small nations favor immunity from capture concept, **III**, 221

Hall, Wilburn B.: class standing at USNA, 13; **II**, 178; visits M. aboard *Iroquois*, 196; appearance, 476, **II**, 180, 181; conducts school in Baltimore, 477; serves as U.S. Consul in Nice, **II**, 178, **III**, 55, 228; visits M. aboard *Chicago*, **II**, 178–179, 180, 181; appearance of Mrs. Hall, **II**, 179, 180, 181, 200; Southern sympathies of, **II**, 179; M. meets in Genoa, **II**, 470

Hanscom, Isaiah: corruption of, 437, 442, 443, 481

Hawaii: Chinese immigration to dangerous to U.S., **II**, 92; strategic key to containment of Chinese expansion, **II**, 93; M. advocates U.S. annexation of, **II**, 93, 506, 532; annexation of implies large USN, **II**, 93; article on, **II**, 94, 101, 138, **III**, 299; key to future American-Japanese relations, **II**, 506; Mongolian inundation of, **II**, 507;

N.Y. Times opposition to Hawaiian annexation, **II**, 532; M. arguments for annexation of, **II**, 538–539; Dewey victory at Manila brings annexation of, **II**, 619; Japanese reaction to U.S. annexation of, **III**, 251; Pearl Harbor as secondary naval base, **III**, 356, 357; Japanese population in threatens security of base at Pearl Harbor, **III**, 357, 385; vulnerability of to Japanese seizure, **III**, 385, 465; Pearl Harbor as USN base, **III**, 380–381, 383, 391, 393, 400, 402; military importance of, **II**, 583

Hayes, Samuel: M. correspondence with, 304, 314; reports to M. on Woolverton's behavior, 304; announces conversions and confirmations of Chinese in Shanghai, 304; M. asks to pray for Woolverton, 314; M. dines with, 315; M. affection for, 339; serves in *Juniata*, 352

Haxtun, Milton: promotion controversy, 491–492

Health. *See* Mahan, A. T.: Health

Hearst, William Randolph: M. turns down dollar-a-word offer from, **II**, 598

Henderson, William H.: visits M. aboard *Chicago*, **II**, 226, 255; tribute to M. *Influence* books, **II**, 255; congratulates M. on *Nelson*, **II**, 509; congratulates M. on article, **III**, 36; disagrees with M. on immunity of private property in war, **III**, 284

Herbert, Hilary A.: opposes NWC, 648, 650–651, 652, **III**, 664, 666; M. criticism of, 650, **II**, 105, 109; M. maintains personal connection with, **II**, 62; disposed not to assign M. to further sea duty, **II**, 100; forces M. to sea, **II**, 102, **III**, 299; M. attempts to convert to pro-NWC view, **II**, 108; thinks M. had political and social hold over Tracy, **II**, 109; conversion to pro-NWC stance, **II**, 142, 143, 144, 145, 147, 208, 239–240, 595; M. designates as saviour of NWC, **II**, 144; wants M. to resume writing after *Chicago* duty, **II**, 145; wants M. to return to NWC after *Chicago* duty, **II**, 147, 223; congratulates M. on *Influence* books, **II**, 168, 239–240; M. writes to on NWC consolidation issue, **II**, 201; ambivalence of in Mahan-Erben fight, **II**, 208, 222; supports NWC in appropriations issue, **II**, 222; supports M. in Erben fight, **II**, 239–240; M. doubts constancy of support in Erben fight, **II**, 250; fails to write promised private letter of support to M., **II**, 263; M. thinks will move NWC to Annapolis, **II**, 349; M. conversation with about a leave for resumption of writing, **II**, 409; assigns M. to temporary duty at NWC to resume writing, **II**, 414; assigns M. to duty at Quogue to write, **II**, 421

Hill, Henry J.: M. urges temperance upon, 295

Hiogo, Japan: M. on decision of Europeans to hold treaty concession in at all costs against Japanese attacks, 127–128; M. dislike of, 150, 206; visits ashore, 191, 194, 203, 207, 208, 211, 219, 220, 221, 222

Hobbies. *See* Mahan, A. T.: Hobbies

Holls, George F. W.: sends M. copy of Hague Conference book, **II**, 697; M. personal dislike of, **II**, 745, **III**, 73; relationship with Roosevelt, **III**, 74; M. controversy with, **II**, 697, 704–706, 708–716, 719–720, 731–732, 737–738, 741, 744–745, **III**, 1, 13–14, 15, 16, 17–22, 73, 74, 450. *See* Hague Conference (First)

Hong Kong, China: political tension, 275; M. plays billiards in, 276, 279, 283, 284; attends church in, 277, 279, 282, 283, 285, 286, 288; visits St. Paul's College, 286, 287; takes up residence ashore, 297; U.S. Consul in, 297

Honorary degrees: Cambridge, **II**, 290, 291, 294, 297, 298, 397; Columbia, **II**, 689, 690; Dartmouth, **III**, 62–63; Harvard, **II**, 420, 421; McGill, **II**, 684, 685; Oxford, **II**, 285, 286, 290, 291, 294, 297, 298, 397, **III**, 727; Yale, **II**, 515, 516

Hopkins, William F. ("Old Poppy"): suffers epileptic seizure at USNA, 62; diplomatic appointment, 70–71; M. opinion of, 71

Hopkins, William R. ("Bull Pup"): M. opinion of, 71

Ireland (Irish): M. describes, **II**, 115–120; M. Irish background, **II**, 116; vote in U.S., 593, **II**, 84, 120; pro-Boer movement among, **II**, 679; Irish-Americans, **II**, 685, 686; mention, **II**, 268, 665, **III**, 370, 548, 577

Isthmian Canal: prospect of construction of will end U.S. isolation, 482, 643; existence will require USN equal to Britain's, 482, 593; expedition to isthmus, 541; M. observes French construction of, 572; strategic implications of studied at NWC, 643, **II**, 82; articles on, **II**, 101, 105, 111, 124, 126, 127, 148, **III**, 372–373; sea power key to control of, **II**, 126, 171; need for USN coaling facilities near, **II**, 584, 588–589, 590, **III**, 400, 401, 403; existence of would obviate need for USN coaling facilities in Africa and Mediterranean, **II**, 589–590; building of would advance U.S. Atlantic frontier to Pacific, **II**, 506; non-fortification provision in first Hay-Pauncefote Treaty with Britain, **II**, 683, **III**, 430–433, 486–487; non-fortified canal will require USN equal to Germany's,

Isthmian Canal (*cont.*)

II, 684; Taft supports fortification of, **III**, 409; Senate preserves U.S. fortification interests, **III**, 430–433, 437; Naval War Board (1898) urges Nicaraguan route, **II**, 589; M. prefers Nicaragua to Panama route, **III**, 9; existence of will increase strategic importance of Caribbean, **III**, 80; U.S. commercial control of, **III**, 159; strategic relationship to Hawaii, **III**, 385, 388; security of key to USN prosecution of war in Pacific, **III**, 401; German naval growth threatens U.S. position in, **III**, 307, 453–454, 459; legality of U.S. recognition of Republic of Panama, **III**, 462–463, 486; security of dependent on adequate armaments, **III**, 474; Panama Tolls Act will require powerful USN to sustain, **III**, 476; M. thinks Tolls Act obnoxious legislation, **III**, 489–490; importance of to U.S. dictates further development of sea power, **III**, 603. *See* Colombia; Germany; Nicaragua; Index Section II, Ships: *Wachusett*; Index Section III, Articles

Italy: navy superior to USN, 592, 594; abundance of attractive women in, **II**, 178; M. hopes will defeat France in coming war, **II**, 179; neutrality of in 1914 helps Austria and Germany, **III**, 541; should invade Austria, **III**, 541; national interests dictate war declaration on Central Powers, **III**, 699, 710

Jameson, J. Franklin: assists M. on War of 1812 book, **III**, 85; editor of *American Historical Review*, **III**, 134; M. social relations with, **III**, 506

Japan: M. descriptions of countryside and cities, 119, 120, 165, 334–338; climate, 129; people and customs, 118, 119–120, 123–124, 135–136, 137, 335, 337, 350; military personnel and bearing, 120, 126, 128, 335; hari-kari, 136; smallpox vaccination unavailable in, 134, 135; M. dislike of people, 310–311; quaintness and charm of people, **III**, 499; character of people conducive to conversion to Christianity, **III**, 689

Civil War (Meiji Restoration) in: aspects of, 125–128, 130, 134, 136, 137, 138, 140, 150; clash with French seamen at Hiogo, 126, 134, 136; murder of French seamen at Osaka, 136, 138; attack on British minister, 138; inflation caused by war, 337

Modern Japan: navel building program, **II**, 506, 507; ambitions in Hawaii, **II**, 506; American-Japanese rivalry benefits Russia, **II**, 506; IJN superior to USN, **II**, 507; IJN officers translate *Influence* into Japanese, **II**, 511, 513, **III**, 331; counterweight to Russia in Manchuria, **III**, 12; treaty

with Britain, **III**, 12, 214, 221; reaction to Treaty of Portsmouth, **III**, 263; USN and RN can contain Japanese ambitions, **III**, 277; capability of invading U.S. Pacific coast, **III**, 355, 384, 385, 454; will attack U.S. without warning, **III**, 381; will not attack Pearl Harbor if USN is there, **III**, 396; M. comment on NWC contingency plan for war with, **III**, 380–388, 389–394; vulnerability of Guam to seizure by, **III**, 386; capability of temporarily controlling Pacific, **III**, 390; division of USN battle fleet would lead to capture of Philippines and Hawaii by, **III**, 202, 206; criticism of 1911 trade treaty with U.S. in, **III**, 412; U.S. tension with over immigration issue, **III**, 214, 216, 217, 221–222, 226, 263, 277, 334, 355, 400, 411, 436, 448, 465; M. opposes immigration on cultural rather than racial grounds, **III**, 221, 436; overextension of power of, **III**, 251; radical political changes within, **III**, 263; U.S. wealth would eventually overwhelm in war, **III**, 391; emigrants cannot compete economically with Koreans or Manchurians, **III**, 411; emigrants will flood U.S. continent west of Rockies, **III**, 448, 453, 500; relationship between immigration and U.S. naturalization, **III**, 496; racial differences render immigrants from unassimilable, **III**, 497, 499; immigration leads to colonization and annexation, **III**, 436; great-power status does not confer immigration rights, **III**, 496; M. evaluation of best USN attack route in war with, **III**, 382–384, 392; dependence of on the sea, **III**, 407; need of room to expand, **III**, 407, 465; historical future lies with Asiatics, **III**, 452; U.S. tension with stretches into an uncertain future, **III**, 500, 504; M. personal relations with Admiral Serata, **III**, 688–689. *See* Philippines; Strategy; U.S.A.: Diplomacy; U.S. Navy: Great White Fleet; War: Russo-Japanese War; Index Section II, Ships: *Iroquois*

Jews. *See* Mahan, A. T.: Religion

Johnson, Andrew: M. critical of, 198, 303, 304, 307

Kent, Julia: M. attraction to, 27, 63, 65; appearance, 40, 61, 63; M. escorts to USNA dance, 60, 61; kindness to M., 63; M. calls upon often, 73; M. competes with Hackett for attentions of, 78

Kirkland, William A.: ordered as Erben's replacement on European Station, **II**, 294; M. on personality and habits of, **II**, 322, 341, 376, 399; appearance, **II**, 331; interferes less with M. than had Erben, **II**, 331, 334, 376; suffers gout, **II**, 334, 360, 365;

hauls *Chicago* out of dry dock for ceremonial purposes, **II**, 339; M. impressed favorably with, **II**, 340, 341, 361, 365, 380, 399; dislike of mess dinners, **II**, 360; hosts dance aboard *Chicago*, **II**, 363, 385; anticipates promotion to admiral, **II**, 365; enjoys disappointing others, **II**, 373; M. criticizes for not taking *Chicago* to Nice, **II**, 383, 385, 388, 389, 399; illness of daughter, **II**, 381, 383, 399; writes good fitness report on M., **II**, 403, 435; thinks Erben was unjust to M., **II**, 403

Kuhn, Charles (wife's uncle): visits aboard *Chicago*, **II**, 187, 188; M. visits and stays with in Villefranche (Nice), **II**, 187, 190, 211, 217, 220, 221, 371, 374, 376; appearance, **II**, 187, 221, 375; residence in Nice, **II**, 191; carriage accident, **II**, 194–195; death, **III**, 720, 729; leaves money in will to Mrs. M., **III**, 720, 729

Laughton, John Knox: Luce enlists assistance for M. on *Influence #2*, **II**, 29, 32, 33; reviews *Influence*, **II**, 34; M. criticizes, **II**, 34; M. asks for research assistance, **II**, 37; corresponds with M., **II**, 101; M. dines with in London, **II**, 135–136; gives M. pointers on Nelson biography, **II**, 135–136; informs M. he too is writing a biography of Nelson, **II**, 230; beats M. to press with certain Nelson materials, **II**, 476–477, 478; M. considers his Nelson book sketchy, **II**, 477; assists M. on John Paul Jones articles, **II**, 547; assists M. on Russo-Japanese war articles, **III**, 154; urges separate publication of M. *Major Operations*, **III**, 176; assists M. on *Major Operations*, **III**, 467

Law, Richard L.: relieves English as CO of *Iroquois*, 318; promotion controversy, 491–492; M. dislike of, 492; assists Dennis H. Mahan, Jr., 492

Lawrence Literary Society (USNA): M. opinion of, 19, 54, 73; Hackett president of, 59; declining fortunes of, 59

Lawrence, L.I., N.Y.: M. leases house in, **III**, 231, 299; advantages of living in, **III**, 284, 362, 371; size of house in, **III**, 527

Leach, Thomas Walter: M. conflict with, 254; M. criticizes, 271; accuses M. of partiality toward Ludlow, 271; visits Canton, 278; M. visits aboard *Iroquois*, 320

Lee, Dr.: joins M. in praying for Woolverton, 161

Lewis, Elizabeth ("Libbie") (uncle's stepdaughter): M. love for, 21, 36, 41, 45; M. kisses, 45, 48; taught Sunday School, 42; appearance, 45, 48, 49, 62; M. considers marriage to, 49, 54; aware of M. social life in Annapolis, 49; M. invites to USNA

dance, 58, 62; pursued by other men, 62; M. lauds her support of W. F. Lewis-Mary C. McGruder marriage, 132

Lewis, Mary ("Maime") (Mrs. Stevens Parker) (uncle's step-daughter): M. on kissing terms with, 45; appearance, 50; opposed marriage of her mother to Milo Mahan, 50, 132; opposed marriage of her brother to Mary C. McGruder, 111, 132; M. criticizes lack of sweetness and softness, 111–112; M. criticizes her lack of manners toward Mrs. McGruder, 132; death of her husband, **II**, 256, 257; M. sympathy note to, **II**, 277–278

Lewis, Mary Griffitts Fisher (Mrs. Milo Mahan) (uncle's wife): marriage to Milo Mahan, 2; marriage opposed by Mary Lewis, 50; opposes marriage of son William Fisher Lewis to Mary C. McGruder, 111; conflict with Mrs. McGruder, 111

Lewis, William Fisher ("Will") (uncle's stepson): controversial marriage of to Mary C. McGruder, 111, 132

Lewis, Mrs. William. *See* McGruder, Mrs. Mary C.

Liberal Republican Party: in 1872 election, 457, 591–592; in 1876 election, 457; M. hails defeat in 1872, 591–592

Line vs. Staff controversy. *See* U.S. Navy: Line vs. Staff

Little, Brown and Company: agree to publish *Influence*, 714; report on sale of *Influence* books, **II**, 168; urges M. to complete *Nelson* manuscript speedily, **II**, 193, 396, 397; M. criticizes for lack of enterprise, **II**, 295; M. averse to serializing *Nelson*, **II**, 398; raise M. royalty payments on *Nelson*, **II**, 460; M. evaluates manuscript submissions to, **II**, 476; provides M. with drawings for Lowell Lectures, **II**, 498; M. signals end of joint Sea Power project with, **III**, 140; notifies M. that public interest in naval topics has declined, **III**, 362; M. instructs in proper grammar, **III**, 425–426

Little, William McCarty: early association with NWC, 689; perfects *Kriegspiel* studies at NWC, 689; assists M. in searching for publisher of *Influence*, 708; reads M. lectures to NWC classes, **III**, 314, 338, 340, 347; assists M. with *Naval Strategy*, **III**, 326, 335, 368, 412, 413, 417, 419; assists M. with NWC lectures, **III**, 343–344, 347–348, 351

Lodge, Henry Cabot: intervenes for M. with Herbert in Erben fight, **II**, 234, 236, 239–240, 250, 283; sees conspiracy against M. in Erben fight, **II**, 234; M. asks for advice in Erben fight, **II**, 282–283; M. social connection with during Spanish-American

Lodge, Henry Cabot (*cont.*)
  War, **II**, 563; M. enlists in Sampson-Schley controversy, **II**, 569, 571, 703; M. notes similarity of diplomatic views with, **II**, 698; M. urges arguments on to be used against General Arbitration Treaty with Britain, **III**, 441–444
Long, John D.: M. criticism of, **II**, 581, 582; M. makes final plea for NWC to, **II**, 594–595, 600; intercedes for Dennis H. Mahan, Jr., in *Badger* incident, **II**, 599; assists M. with book on Spanish-American War, **II**, 609, 610, 625; M. assists with book on the New Navy, **II**, 625, 626–627; supports American expansion, **II**, 634; involvement in Sampson-Schley controversy, **II**, 669–670; M. cites book on Navy, **III**, 627, 628, 634
Lowell Institute: M. declines invitation to lecture at, **II**, 410, 415; M. solicits invitation to lecture at, **II**, 445; agrees to lecture at, **II**, 446, 447–448; uses NWC lectures at, **II**, 472; delivers Lowell Lectures at, **II**, 497, 498, 503, 507, 530, **III**, 81, 85, 97; uses magazine articles for lectures at, **III**, 97, 200; considers publication of lectures at, **III**, 198; financial advantages of lecturing at, **III**, 200
Luce, Stephen B.: offers M. position at NWC, 577; M. seeks aid in getting detached from *Wachusett*, 581, 597, 603, 607; M. gives credit to for founding NWC, **III**, 68, 216, 220; lectures at NWC, 626–627, 631, 637, 644, **III**, 299, 664; assists M. with *Influence*, 627, 631, 632; helps M. find publisher for *Influence*, 711; asked to help with sales of *Influence*, **II**, 10; M. attributes his success to, 714, **II**, 10, **III**, 198, 216, 220; assists M. with articles, **II**, 19, 22, 25; assists M. with *Influence #2*, **II**, 2–3, 29–30, 32, 33, 39; M. solicits advice on NWC, **II**, 57; M. asks aid on NWC presidency appointment, **II**, 58, 59; rejoices over Herbert's support of NWC, **II**, 155; M. sees in Nice, **II**, 222; vacations in London, **II**, 274; M. fears overreaction of in Erben fight, **II**, 302; asks M. to approach Long on General Staff concept, **II**, 591–592; assists M. on War of 1812 book, **III**, 61, 64–65, 68–69, 70, 88, 89, 319–320; urges M. to update and publish NWC strategy lectures, **III**, 163, 198, 216, 220, 234, 245, 250; sides with Sims in all-big-gun ship controversy, **III**, 178; assists M. with autobiography, **III**, 216, 217–218, 219–220; assists M. with *Naval Strategy*, **III**, 299; works to reform naval administration, **III**, 68; would reopen Sampson-Schley controversy after Schley's death, **III**, 423–424

Ludlow, Nicoll: dislikes M., 211; M. dislike of, 249, 251, 276, 281, 282; M. accused of partiality toward, 271; replaces M. as XO of *Iroquois*, 283; M. invites to dinner, 284; conflict with R. B. Bradford, 298; vulgar and profane, 308; gets drunk, 308; serves on Light House Board, **II**, 235; attacks F. A. Mahan, **II**, 235

McCalla, Bowman H.: writes M. that NWC is saved, **II**, 145; M. introduces as prospective author, **II**, 525
McCook, Roderick S.: breaks with M. in Hackett Affair, 6; USNA class standing, 13; M. opinion of, 37, 67, **III**, 57; character and behavior, 68, **III**, 57; death, **III**, 57
McFarland, John: M. criticizes, 155, 167
McGruder, Mrs. Mary C.: M. thinks unprepossessing, 132
McIntyre, James W.: role in publication of M. *Influence #1*, **III**, 274; M. attempts to interest in publishing *Harvest Within*, **III**, 274
MacKenzie, Alexander S.: killed in Formosan punitive expedition (1867), 593, **III**, 56; broke with M. over Hackett Affair, **III**, 56
McKinley, William: M. impressed with handling of Spanish-American War, **II**, 579, 691; invites M. to Dewey dinner at White House, **II**, 656, 703; differs with M. on Hague Conference maritime issues, **II**, 659; M. thinks assassination of secures his place in U.S. history, **III**, 10
McLaughlin, Andrew C.: assists M. with research on War of 1812 book, **III**, 114–115, 116–117, 121, 122, 123, 124–125, 126–130, 132; offers M. research grant for work on War of 1812, **III**, 116
Mahan, Alfred Thayer: boyhood interests, 1, **III**, 520; early religious training, **III**, 724; boyhood recollections, **III**, 523–524; poor at dancing, 7, 125, **II**, 197; wishes he had sister, 21, 25, 28–29; pride in family talents, 21, 24; personal isolation and aloneness, 99, 160, 161, 163, 165, 192, 309, 322, 330; unpopularity of, **II**, 376; introvertedness, **II**, 150, 299, 311, 376, **III**, 721; dislike of public speaking, **II**, 275, 294, 539, 666; **III**, 43, 461; poor public speaker, **III**, 148–149, 461; declines speaking invitations, **III**, 253, 300, 301, 461; Irish background, **II**, 116, 313, 346; social aspirations, **II**, 122, 348, 361, 362; interest in folktales, **II**, 192, 363–364; love within family, **II**, 179–180; homesickness, **II**, 195, 333; no understanding of American football, **II**, 199; man of thought rather than action, **II**, 507, **III**, 284; rescues brother from USN scrape, **II**, 597–598, 599; tension of American life, **III**, 9; dis-

like of yellow journalism, **II**, 508, 578, 597–598; non-joiner, **III**, 266; shore residences, **III**, 719, 720 and *passim*; travel to Europe, **III**, 719–720, 721 and *passim*; criticism of American tourists abroad, **II**, 252; discipline in home, **III**, 722, 728; methodical personality, **III**, 724; concern for Government property, **III**, 725; fond of pretty young girls, **III**, 727, 730; family unaffected by furor over books, **III**, 727; death, **III**, 730

Alcohol: excessive use of, 88, 146, 148, 149, 150, 158, 161, 168, 172, 175–176, 178, 182, 193, 199, 204, 216, 217, 218, 222–223, 227, 230, 231, 236, 237, 240, 252, 255, 256, 260, 272, 277, 281, 283, 289, 299, 301, 305, 306, 308, 330, 332; craving for, 155, 166, 170–171, 183, 187, 200, 203, 208–209, 219, 305; rationalizations for use of, 164, 260, 281, 282, 285; hangovers, 146, 215, 218, 223, 240, 255, 281, 305, 306; rejects as medical aid, 451; daily with coffee, 483; thinks wine an aid to good health, **II**, 243

Animals: buys horse in Japan, 133, 326, 333; proper treatment of dogs, **II**, 311; "Jomini," **II**, 148, 253, 311, 354, 699, **III**, 138, 726; "Major," **II**, 311; death of "Rovie," **III**, 137–138; aboard *Muscoota*, 142; aboard *Iroquois*, 280; aboard *Wachusett*, 566

Appearance: physical, 43, 46, 55, 56, 340; baldness, **II**, 220, **III**, 492, 727; photographs, **II**, 292; portraits, **III**, 104–105; "quarterdeck voice," **III**, 725; taste in clothes, **II**, 186

Financial Problems and Considerations: family financial arrangements, 429; petty economies, 630, **II**, 166; avoids duty in expensive Washington, D.C., 714; family has small means, **II**, 47, worry about money, **II**, 132, 348; cost of maintaining horse, 333; carelessness in handling money, 333, 474; seeks loan repayment from Ashe, 472–473, 474; pay and allowances at Boston Navy Yard, 454; put on waiting-orders pay, 456; put on furlough pay, 458, 463; high cost of living on East Coast, 463, 469, 544; problems increase while at New York Navy Yard, 487; chooses inexpensive vacation resort, 556; subsidy to live in NYC while writing *Influence #1*, 615; importance of being paid well for writing, **II**, 26, 110, 115, 117, 124, 132–133, 147, 151, 153, 160, 181, 186, 193, 204, 206, 217, 274, 277, 285, 286, 292, 293, 300, 302, 315, 349, 355, 356, 383, 392, 423, 429, 430, 459, 461, 467, 482, 488, 517, 535, 548, 561, 633, 676, 687, 743, **III**, 84, 147, 161, 163, 172, 248, 361, 548; son's tuition at Groton, **II**, 102, 311, 560; cannot afford two residences, **II**, 64, 65, 66; monthly allotment to wife,

II, 112, 114, 292; cash problems while aboard *Chicago*, **II**, 118, 146, 204, 243, 259, 261, 269, 271, 286, 291, 292, 302, 315, 330; bequests ease financial situation, **II**, 189, 349, 355, 361, 395, *viz*: Mary Helena Okill Mahan bequest, **II**, 160, 355, **III**, 295; Ellen Kuhn Evans bequest, **II**, 271, 315, **III**, 728; Jane Leigh Okill Swift bequest, **II**, 349, 355, 436, 438–439, 440, 464, 726–727, 728, **III**, 295; Margaret Evans bequest, **II**, 355, 357, **III**, 720; anticipates increased problems during retirement years, **II**, 184, 205, 258, 333, 370, 482; fears pay of retired officers will be cut, **II**, 333; money prevents family from mixing into society, **II**, 348; hopes not to write chiefly for money in retirement, **II**, 395; problems will be intensified by Bryan's election, **II**, 466, 467; will supplement retirement pay with literary income, **II**, 482, **III**, 163; expense of living in NYC, **II**, 482; raises price of his magazine articles, **II**, 535; promotion to Rear Admiral raises pay, **III**, 203; fight for retirement pay, **III**, 234; fights and sues Government for quarters allowances, **III**, 316, 318, 319, 320, 321, 322, 327–328, 329, 330–332, 333, 339, 405, 525–527, 529–532, 533–534, 538; members of historical commission should be paid, **III**, 339, 676; passing of vogue as author reduces financial security, **III**, 492; decisions must yield to pecuniary considerations, **III**, 518; accepts Carnegie Institution position for financial reasons, **III**, 518, 549

Foreign Languages (study and use): French, 174, 226, 233, 251, 252, **II**, 158, 190, 217, 383, 641–642; German, **III**, 211; Greek, 179, 180, 185, 189, 191, 192, 194, 195, 196, 197, 204, 213, 215, 216, 217, 221, 262, 263; Latin, 50, **II**, 657, **III**, 74, 710; Spanish, 206, 211, **II**, 158

Health: re-vaccinated for smallpox, 135, 137; medications taken, 209, 211, 233, 238, 239, 327, 355, 476, 483, **II**, 408, **III**, 669; recommended cholera treatment, **II**, 155; hospitalized, 14, 49, 61, 314, **III**, 230, 231, 233, 234, 235, 236, 241, 244, 262, 271, 278, 284, 289, 341; would remain sick to insure and hasten return home from Japan, 320–321; seeks medical survey and detachment from *Aroostook*, 327, 328, 330; visits springs for cures, 367, **III**, 212, 225; bore pain badly, **III**, 724; aging (problems of), 133, **II**, 182, 370, 380, 407, **III**, 190, 212, 216, 228, 233, 238, 241, 262, 284, 301, 333, 341, 367, 426, 492, 515, 521; biliousness, **II**, 190, 195; bunions, 174, 201; catarrhal attack, **III**, 152; colic, 319; dental problems, 476, **II**, 195, 216, 217, 243, 271,

Mahan, Alfred Thayer (*cont.*)

275, 334, 335; diarrhea, 239, 240; dyspepsia, 129, 198, 199, 225, 227, 268, 272; earache, **II**, 251; gout, **II**, 193; grippe, **III**, 515, 516, 521; heart disease, **III**, 212, 228, 529, 547, 549, 730; leg injury, **II**, 113, 115, 117, 118, 121, 122, 123, 124, 125, 126, 127, 131, 140, 213; malaria, 91–93, 311, 357, 476, 626, **II**, 196, 408; melancholia (despondency, mental depression), 150, 155, 156, 159, 160, 161, 162, 183, 207, 209, 220, 229, 236, 242, 244, 249, 255, 260, 263, 266, 278, 304, 306, 313, 323, 330, 450, **II**, 255; mumps, 676; nervousness, 155, 156, 157, 159, 165, 168, 172, 185, 189, 198, 204, 225, 232, 237, 238, 247, 258, 260, 276, 282, 287, 288, 303, 309, **III**, 515, 724; nervous headaches, 107, 157, 186, 201; neuralgia, 476, **II**, 468; prostate disorder (prostatectomy), **III**, 230–231, 232, 233, 234, 235, 236, 241, 244, 262, 271, 278, 284, 289, 341, 728, 729; rheumatism, 114, 150, 247, 260; seasickness, 27, 263; skin eruptions, 157, 227; stomach disorders, 131, 157, 186, 196, 208, 210, 212, 214, 217, 226, 227, 238, 239, 243, 244, 253, 263, 286, 309, 311, 312, 314, 320, 321, 322, 323, 324, 325, **III**, 669

Hobbies: billiards, 238, 243, 276, 279, 283, 284, 293, 308, 309, 310, 312, 313, 324, 329, 634; bicycling, **III**, 720–721, 726; horseback riding, 107, 125, 129, 133, 135, 140, 146, 147, 148, 157, 171, 178, 219, 223, 301, 326, 331, 355; mishaps while riding, 181, 207, 327, 336, 349; walking, 162, 192, 286, **II**, 212, 262, 278, 370–371, 427, 448, 510, **III**, 720–721, 726

Letters (Letter-Writing): prides himself on skill, 18, 340; asks recipients to save, 44–45, **II**, 298; chore of, 117, 135, 334, 336, 338, 341, 476; admits poor penmanship, 121; undertakes personal diary, 146, 187; becomes more burdensome with age, 476; complains of lack of mail from home, *passim*; difficulties and uncertainties in receipt of mail abroad, 120–121, 132, 137, 138, 139, 140, 334, and *passim*; urges wife to repeat important information in hers to him abroad, **II**, 127 ff.

Marriage: affirms will never marry, 22; distrust of young love leading to, 121; cost of maintaining a wife, 333; attitudes toward, 34, 76, **II**, 15–17; passion needed in, 357; expects difficulty adjusting to daily routine of, 358; proposes to Ellen Lyle Evans, 368; Miss Evans not beautiful, 368; has little passion for Miss Evans, 369; settles for her character, 368; M. married, 359; married love, **II**, 125–126; his own, **II**, 286, 330, 364, 515; wants more children from,

544; advice to daughter on, **II**, 13–17, 125–126. *See* Women

Naval Career: wants out of USN, 248; wants no son of his to join, 434, 584, **II**, 249; growth of USN would improve personal prospects, 558; plans career out of, 298; uselessness of naval service, 584; loneliness of naval service, 584, **II**, 183; youthful folly caused choice of profession, **II**, 183, 366; washes hands of, **II**, 123; dislike of, 355, **II**, 131, 163, 230, 249; dislike of engineers in, 299, 328; disinterested in reorganization of, 310; disinterest in Line vs. Staff controversy in, 311; NWC work sneered at in, **II**, 107; historical work rejected by, **II**, 105; more useful to USN as historian than as ship's officer, **II**, 91, 97, 98, 107, 160, 165, 182, 217, 230, 281; career marked by no incidents of special interest, **II**, 493; drawbacks balanced by certainties of, **III**, 273; career summary, 371–372

Promotion: M. anticipates early, 29; prospects for, 69; Civil War assists rapid, 89; M. requests, 92; examination for, 371, 372, 614, **III**, 557–558; examinations for too easy, 445; M. promoted, 372, 387, 624, 625, **II**, 213–214, **III**, 163, 195, 198, 203; briskness of because of deaths, 433; fears promotion of Southern officers if Democrats come to power, 482–483; hopes promotion to Captain will shorten *Wachusett* tour, 557, 584; thirteen years as Commander, 578; slower in lower ranks than before Civil War, 624; fortunate in having received regular, 624; would rather retire than wait for to Rear Admiral, **II**, 178, 313; title of Rear Admiral confuses *nom de plume*, **III**, 203, 425; financial implications of to Rear Admiral, **III**, 233–234, 248. *See* U.S. Navy: Officers

Retirement: considers in 1896, **II**, 47, 91, 96, 98, 101, 182; laws governing, **II**, 47, 91, 92, 96, 98, **III**, 464; promises in return for no further sea duty, **II**, 96, 98, 101; *Chicago* cruise stimulates interest in, **II**, 165, 250, 300, 324, 369, 408; Erben controversy strengthens desire for, **II**, 223; hopes for year's paid leave ashore prior to, **II**, 258, 265, 303, 349, 370, 395, 397, 414; no further separations from wife, **II**, 348, 471; plans literary career during, **II**, 265, 303, 333, 370; will devote all energies to Nelson book in, **II**, 386, 395; hopes for full family social life in, **II**, 387; decides to retire in 1896, **II**, 419, 471; applies for after Venezuela crisis with Britain settled, **II**, 472, 482; naval duties during year's leave prior to, **II**, 431; future promotion and pay increases lost by, **II**, 482, **III**, 163; Whitney dinner marking, **II**, 474; retirement from all further possible duty (1912), **III**, 460, 464; daily routine following, **III**, 720–721, 726, 729, 730. *See* Financial Problems and Considerations

Sea Duty: requests delay of, 95; seeks to avoid, 355, **II**, 39, 91, 95, 98; writing *Gulf* delays, 556; seeks near NYC, 557, **II**, 38; near Boston, **II**, 39; hopes for near San Francisco, 572; NWC duty offers early end to, 578, 581–582, 603, 607, 608; denies using NWC position to escape, 611; asks to be recalled from, 583, 605; sees conspiracy to keep him at, 607, 608; fears Whitney may punish him with, 664–665; Tracy postpones, **II**, 40, 47; Farragut book related to postponement of, **II**, 46, 47; too old to go on, **II**, 47; requests early decision on, **II**, 54; requests postponement of to finish *Influence #2*, **II**, 55, 57; position on roster renders likely, **II**, 57; will not ask not to be assigned to, **II**, 57; assignment to *Charleston* rumored, **II**, 57; relationship of to reassignment to NWC presidency, **II**, 58, 60; compares his with Farragut's, **II**, 61; hopes *Influence #2* will lead to extended shore duty, **II**, 89; continuation of writing depends on no further, **II**, 96, 98; assignment to *Baltimore* rumored, **II**, 98; Herbert disposed not to assign M. further, **II**, 100; M. forced to sea by Herbert, **II**, 102; M. thinks ships are beastly things, **II**, 114; Herbert insists M. serve full tour in *Chicago*, **II**, 145, 147. *See* Mahan: Sea; Seamanship; Index Section II, Ships: *Chicago, Iroquois, Wachusett, Wasp*

Profanity: embarrassed by midshipmen use of at USNA, 41; cannot control aboard ship, 100–101; use of, 29, 32, 156, 187, 277, 289, 296, 301, 310

Religion:
Bible: admiration for, 61, **III**, 601; chronology in Old Testament unhistorical and not mathematical, 259–260; nature and purpose of Gospels, 190; nature and purpose of Epistles, 190; opinions and interpretations of parables, 177, 268–269, 273–274; New Testament as history, 190, **III**, 648; M. rejects Genesis version of creation, 218, 258; supports necessity of war, **III**, 229

Christianity: need for regular moral and spiritual self-analysis, 72, 147, 164, 288, 289, 290, 291, 292, 296, 297, 329; urge to convert others, 99–100, 292, 296,

304, **II**, 231; avoids science vs. religion arguments, 191–192; avoids public discussions of, 193, 293; distrusts intellectual approach to, 216; deems Renan rationalism unfair, 207; defends inadequately, 313; conflict between religious study and naval duty, 195; reads and rejects Swedenborg, 358; religious reading, 99, 130, 133, 146, 148, 150, 151, 153, 154, 159, 160, 162, 163, 164, 165, 168, 169, 171, 173, 176, 177, 179, 183, 187, 188, 189, 197, 198, 201, 204, 207, 210, 243, 254, 256, 262, 268, 272, 279, 282, 285, 292–293, 294, 295, 301, 303, 306, 308, 312, 325; finds religious reading sleep-inducing, 198, 204, 214, 300, 323; spiritual life most influenced by reading Goulburn, **II**, 458; shuns non-believers, **II**, 220; Christianity satisfies his intellect, **II**, 220, **III**, 599; piety breaks down during prostatectomy and hastens writing of spiritual autobiography (*The Harvest Within*), **III**, 234; condemns secularization of Sunday in U.S., **III**, 423; clergy should not intervene in U.S. diplomacy, **III**, 433–435; Christian standards influence progress of Christian nations, **III**, 489; comments on Church vs. State relationships, **III**, 507–509; role of Christianity in civilizing world, **III**, 539–540; practical impact of Christianity on leading his life, **III**, 599, 602; cannot be viewed from standpoint of rationality, **III**, 600; superiority of Christianity, **III**, 614; explains in simple terms to Japanese readers, **III**, 689–691; Christian philosophy of life, **III**, 694

Episcopal Church: superiority of, 44, 107; dislike of Low Church, 366; preference for High (Anglo-Catholic) Church, 429; dislike of evangelical homiletics, 188, 243, 310; attendance, *passim*; inattention at divine services, 146, 151, 161, 170, 182, 240, 244, 257, 277, 285, 315, 324, 327, 330; private services, devotions and prayers aboard *Iroquois*, Diary, *passim*; contributions and tithes, 182, 256, 334, **II**, 132, 148, 172, 174, 204, 205, 381, **III**, 723, 724; subscriptions to publications, 133, 429, **III**, 310; weak publishing capability of, **III**, 274; critical of Anglican service in Capetown, 107; English upper classes casual about church attendance, **II**, 280; poor church attendance on board HMS *Rodney*, 118; protective of clergy, **II**, 364; discrimination against Negro Episcopalians, **II**, 617; participation in Annual Convention, **III**, 231;

Mahan, Alfred Thayer (*cont.*)
small attention by to *Harvest Within*, **III**, 310; criticizes N.Y. Diocesan Convention for endorsing Anglo-American arbitration treaty, **III**, 434–435; seeks to revise *Book of Common Prayer*, **III**, 521–522, 535–536, 545–546; various churches regularly attended, **III**, 721

Jews: murderers of Christ, 113; Covenant with God, 258, 259–260; attitude toward, **II**, 202; errors of, **II**, 456

Missions: Episcopal, **II**, 508; among U.S. Negroes at home, **III**, 190; in Philippines, **III**, 10–11; strength of home churches affects overseas effort, **III**, 335; sends copies of his books to Boone University in China, **III**, 418; need for closer relationships with relevant governments, **III**, 501–503, 508; functions complicated by Church vs. State issues, **III**, 508; Christians of all nations brought closer together in mission fields, **III**, 657; true Christians are inherently missionaries, **III**, 694–695

Mohammedanism: lauds temperance of, 108; backward and oppressive political regimes under, **III**, 511, 683; Mohammed blinded eyes of Turks to Christ, **III**, 690

Presbyterian Church: inferior to Episcopal, 44

Roman Catholic Church: false temptations of, 99; corruption of priests in Philippines, 258; attends services in Manila, 275; false doctrine of absolution, 303; idolatry, 303, false doctrine of Papal Infallibility, 434, 435; false view of the Virgin, 435; civil allegiance compromised by, 435; Vatican Council, 457; intrudes into civil sphere, **III**, 503

Seaman's Church Institute: chapel dedication, 359; contributes to, **II**, 172; importance of work, **III**, 590–591, 597, 605–607; membership in, **III**, 590

Sins (Personal): weighed down by sense of, 306; distraction at prayers, 147, 152, 153, 155, 165, 166, 170, 180, 203, 205, 211, 227, 236, 263, 283; purveyor of gossip and scandal, 149, 158, 170, 172, 180, 185, 193, 215, 232, 234, 257, 280, 283, 287, 296–297, 300, 303, 307, 314, 315, 319, 325, 332; boastfulness, 206, 216, 221, 309, 316; overbearingness, 192; lack of humility, 75, 154, 181, 183, 289; pridefulness, 181, 182, 202; spiritual pride, 159, 165, 178, 186, 291; uncharitableness, 168, 183; self-righteousness, 177; self-centeredness, 180, 181, 195, 222; procrastination, 292, 294; reading novels, 159, 186, 196, 224, 232; lack of concentration on sacred

matters, 197, 203; attempts to overcome sins (Plan for the Day), 202–203, 207, 237, (1869 New Year's Resolution), 256, 259, 260, 261, 262, 263, 264, 265, 266, 267, 270, 271, 272, 273, 275, 276, 277, 278, 279, 284, 286

Theology: youthful agnosticism, 25, 34, 38, 58; Communion, 132, 324, 325; role of priest in absolution, 302–303; immortality, 306, 338, **III**, 644, 645, 647, 682; personal resurrection, 97, 104–105, **III**, 644, 645; Confirmation, 585–586; Trinity, **II**, 172, **III**, 211, 714–715; confession, 180; Baptism, 189–190, 191, 257–258, 302, **II**, 456; salvation, 267–268, 269–270, 273–274; predestination vs. free will, 264–265; circumcision, 257–258; pre-Adam race of sinless men (original sin problem), 218; eucharistical adoration, 429; possession by the Devil, 149, 172, 199, 201, 251, 287, 585; theology and history, 190; faith vs. works, **II**, 457–458; Christ died for animals, **III**, 138; Christ died for the salvation of sinful mankind, **III**, 335–336; Incarnation, **III**, 211, 647–648; affirms he is no expert in, **III**, 598; Holy Ghost, **III**, 600–601; God's hand in the affairs of man, **III**, 600–601; individual will moves toward perfection in God, **III**, 644; importance of faith, **III**, 645; Virgin Birth, **III**, 647–648; revelation, **III**, 652–653; prayer, **III**, 653; final judgment, **III**, 653–654; abandonment of self, **III**, 695

Unitarian Church: false teachings, **III**, 211; lack of missionary effort, **III**, 522–523

Sea: youthful love of, 4, 78, 83; danger of death at, 59; storms at described, 101–103, 131, 233, 343–344, 346, 348, **II**, 237–238, 377; fear of, 96, 184, 185, 203, 206, 227, 228, 229, 230, 233, 234, 236, 248, 249, 251, 264, 265, 270, 271, 292, 297, 351, 428; anxiety over going to, 226, 229, 250, 262, 297, **II**, 113; relief at returning from, 205, 206, 228, 230, 237, 238, 248; less anxiety on large ship, **II**, 113; collision of passenger liners at, **III**, 160

Seamanship: failures in, 80, 154, 156, 164, 166, 174, 181, 187, 188, 195, 201, 204, 213, 230, 238, 268, 307–308; critical of failures by others, 465–466; successes in, 168, 169, 170, 171, 194, 201, 206, 214, 221, 298

Servants: opinion of civilian, 14; British impress M., **II**, 299; family, **II**, 147, 189–190, **III**, 599; opinion of USN stewards, 100, 172, 186, 208, 209, 210, 211, 213, 271, **II**, 113; overtime pay for USN stewards, 582; critical of personal steward Backus in *Iroquois*, 172, 186, 208, 209, 210, 211,

213, 271; satisfaction with personal steward Carl in *Chicago*, **II**, 113, 120, 135, 146, 159, 176, 181, 206, 240; personal mess attendant in *Chicago* a syphilitic, **II**, 334

Sex: punishment for adultery, 64; Scottish hand-fasting, 76; genitals, 86, 91, 337; prostitution, 169, 173; morals of American working girls, 188, 220; affairs, 217, 307; impure thoughts, 270, 271, 272, 275, 277, 289, 299, 308, 332; temptations, 276, 277, 279, 312; excited by women, 280, 573; impurities of USN officers, 310, 316; bare breasts not alluring, 337; on sanitary precautions against syphilis, 312; celibacy an unnatural state, 357; prostatectomy, **III**, 728–729

Temper: exhibitions of, 130, 146, 149, 152, 154, 157, 162, 176, 183, 186, 188, 192, 200, 206, 213–214, 217, 221, 224, 225, 233, 237–238, 241, 242, 245, 247, 253, 254, 257, 264, 277, 279, 289, 290, 297, 313, 330, 332, **II**, 156, **III**, 243, 722

Tobacco: excessive use of, 150, 156, 172, 199, 204, 216, 217, 218, 237, 238, 301, 305, 308, 311, 330, 332

Vanity: physical appearance, 46, 55, 56, 340, **II**, 349; expects life-long persecution, 51; family favorite, 51; smartest man in USNA class, 55; admits conceit, 55, 56, 151, 154, 158, 159, 178, 179, 185, 253, 268, 284, 287, 294, 298, 301; lack of humility, 56, 75, 151, 154, 181, 183, 289; superior character, 56; attractiveness to women, 62; thought to be conceited, 66; rapid promotion, 69; self-centeredness, 132, 180, 181, 195, 222; universal genius, 574; lauds self as NWC president, 654; denies vaingloriousness, **II**, 61; leading authority on naval warfare, **II**, 108, 207, **III**, 331, 333; literary excellence, **II**, 108; publications chief assets of NWC, **II**, 108–109; modesty about *Influence* books, **II**, 129; attack on M. is attack on entire USN, **II**, 214; fearful flattery may be habit-forming, **II**, 275, 277; apologizes for singing own praises, **II**, 275, 277, 312; craves and dislikes adulation, **II**, 291; M. compared with Copernicus, **II**, 342; not vain about success of books, **II**, 366; excellence of work on Naval War Board, **II**, 582; lasting contribution to NWC, **III**, 220; minimizes ego in autobiography, **III**, 225; definitive article claimed, **III**, 428; comments on European War awaited, **III**, 540–541

Mahan, Dennis H., Sr. (father): supports and advises M. in Hackett Affair at USNA, 6, 30–31, 67, 82; critical of M. academic effort at USNA, 19, 36; conflict with Lt. Morton, 43–44; as fortifications engineer, 44; visits M. at USNA, 54, 59;

M. love for, 55; examines VMI cadets, 88; prefers Southern women to Northern, 88; attachment to South, 88; mental depression and suicide, 450; attitude toward servants, **II**, 189–190; eye for pretty women, **II**, 197–198; tendency to social withdrawal, **II**, 299; loved the young, **II**, 348; M. evokes memory of to Long in defense of Dennis, Jr., **II**, 598

Mahan, Dennis H., Jr. (brother): serves in *Sabine*, 352; serves in *Independence*, 492; M. visits in Nice, 352; helped out of difficulties by Law, 492; wants to sell Tenafly-Palisades property, **II**, 436, 438, 439, 444, 447; M. has little confidence in business sense of, **II**, 438; poor promotion prospects, **II**, 438–439; drinking problem, **II**, 439; agrees to division of Tenafly-Palisades inheritance, **II**, 448, 464; wants Tenafly-Palisades share prior to leaving for China, **II**, 463; leaves for China in *Machias*, **II**, 464, 465; squatters on his Tenafly-Palisades property, **II**, 511, 515–516, 522, 620; M. intercedes with Long on behalf of in *Badger* incident, **II**, 597–598, 599; threatened with court-martial, **II**, 597, 599; promotion to Lt. Cmdr. questioned, **II**, 597

Mahan, Ellen Kuhn (daughter) ("Nellie," "Nellikin," "Nell"): birth, 464; religious training, **III**, 723–724; childhood, **III**, 723; life at NWC, **III**, 137, 725; contracts scarlet fever, 473–474, 475; near-fatal malarial attack, 487, 580–581, **II**, 148, **III**, 722; attends children's play, 566; M. corrects grammar, **II**, 122; socially shy and backward, **II**, 150, 155, 276, 288, 294, 311, 381; M. urges her to seek and make friends, **II**, 150, 161, 188, 263, 264, 288, 320, 381; M. sends and recommends books, **II**, 189, 294–295, 296, 340, 356, 368; M. shields from improper reading, **III**, 725; M. on social advantages of Quogue for, **II**, 230, 263, 264; M. urges assertion of individuality, **II**, 245; suffers attacks of mental depression, **II**, 288, 289, 373; studies drawing, **II**, 288, 307–308, 354, 358; M. advises on needed skills of artists and writers, **II**, 308–309; M. advises on study of literature, **II**, 320–321; M. unwilling for her to live in Annapolis, **II**, 350; takes dancing lessons, **II**, 381; accompanies mother to Europe, **III**, 127; falls ill in Europe, **III**, 151, 152, 153, 156, 720; death, **III**, 730

Mahan, Ellen Lyle Evans (wife) ("Ellie," "Elly," "Deldie"): invites M. to church, 359; marries M., 359; summers in Sharon, N.Y., 366; M. proposes to, 368; M. thinks her not beautiful, 368; M. has little passion for, 369; character, 368; reliance on M., 369; evacuated from Montevideo in

Mahan, Ellen Lyle Evans (*cont.*)
Wasp, 380; lives briefly aboard *Wasp*,
380–381; financial resources, 429; M. wants
another child by, 454; suffers miscarriage,
454; pregnancy, 464; plans visit to parents
in Pau, France, 473, 475; M. on separations
from, **II**, 114; M. instructions to on financial matters, **II**, 132, 136–137, 139, 141,
170, 190, 204; M. misses her advice, **II**,
134, 158; unsafe apartment, **II**, 149; searches
unsuccessfully for another NYC apartment, **II**, 157, 158, 159, 162, 163, 164; M.
writes on advantages of 75 E. 54th St., **II**,
163, 170, 173, 177, 345, 348; plans and builds
summer home at Quogue (*see* Quogue);
M. criticizes grammar, **II**, 176; suffers
gout, **II**, 176, 250; suffers sciatica, **II**, 387;
nervous disorders, **II**, 393, 395; M. criticizes newsless letters, **II**, 177; casual spending habits, **II**, 193; M. enlists in NWC appropriations fight, **II**, 210; M. enlists aid
of in fight with Erben, **II**, 210–212, 217;
stands behind M. in Erben fight, **II**, 232;
considers joining M. in Europe, **II**, 224,
313; M. advice to on proposed trip to
Europe, **II**, 224, 313, 321–322, 345–346, 348–
349, 351, 355, 361, 399; transfers her mother's estate to M., **II**, 271; M. warns against
walking NYC streets after dark, **II**, 343;
questions M. affection for her, **II**, 352;
M. thinks family needs more social life,
II, 361, 362, 387; decides to buy NYC
townhouse, **II**, 355, 361, 364, 370, 383, 393;
M. advises on proper location of NYC
townhouse, **II**, 361, 381, 385–386, 387; M.
advises on appointments of NYC townhouse, **II**, 380; M. instructs on social advantages of NYC townhouse, **II**, 381, 383,
385–386; attends Lyle during illness at
Groton, **II**, 419, **III**, 727; goes to Europe
for health, **III**, 96, 97, 100, 127, 141, 156,
212; abandons NYC townhouse for health
reasons, **III**, 284, 307; types M. manuscripts, **III**, 311, 725, and *passim*; handles
all household bills, **III**, 532; searches for
housing in Washington, D.C., **III**, 548,
549; autocratic tendencies, **III**, 722; death,
730. *See* Quogue, N.Y.
Mahan, Frederick Augustus (brother):
graduates from USMA, 103; matrimonial
prospects, 103; M. thinks should delay
marriage, 121–122; lectures at NWC, **II**,
83; conversation with Chadwick about
NWC, **II**, 148; M. enlists in fight for
NWC, **II**, 207; ardent Cleveland support-
er, **II**, 235; controversy on Light House
Board, **II**, 235; authors paper on light-
houses, **II**, 235; M. fears his falling away
from God, **II**, 244; agrees to division of
Tenafly-Palisades inheritance, **II**, 447, 448,

464; assists M. in book-translation negotiations, **III**, 151
Mahan, Helen (sister): early death of, 21
Mahan, Helen Evans (daughter) ("Hennie," "Henny"): birth in Montevideo,
428; infancy, 428, 429, 430, 431, 432,
433, 434, 437, **II**, 157, 309–310, **III**, 723;
early religious training, **III**, 723–724; M.
religious advice to, 585–587, **II**, 170, 197,
378–379, 456–458; accompanies parents to
Europe, 428; M. wants additional children
after, 454; raised easily to adulthood, **II**,
133–134; M. teaches history to, 542; M.
instructs in writing style, 575; studies
music (piano), **II**, 2; teaches music, **II**, 170,
184, 193, 197, 281, 321, 350, 377; M. advice
to on love and marriage, **II**, 13–17, 125–
126; little interest in young men, **II**, 150;
social shyness, **II**, 124, 142; M. instructs
on proper reading, 574–575, **II**, 115–116,
125–126, 168–169, 196–197, 200–201, 217,
219; books sent to by M., **II**, 119, 189, 196,
230, 294, 368; cautioned on surfbathing,
II, 120; M. cautions against overwork as
teacher, **II**, 134, 150, 197, 198, 269, 281,
321, 333, 378; M. thinks not physically
mature enough to work steadily, **II**, 150,
184, 197, 205, 269, 281, 321, 378; M. thinks
teaching income of will be useful to family
in retirement years, **II**, 184, 205, 333; urged
to take more students, **II**, 377, 379; social
advantages of Quogue for, **II**, 230; M.
urges assertion of individuality, **II**, 245;
M. hopes she will develop sense of humor,
II, 259; takes over running of home, **II**,
346, **III**, 307; M. unwilling for her to live
in Annapolis, **II**, 350; cautioned against
speaking negatively about Episcopal clergyman, **II**, 364; receives gift of baby
grand piano, **II**, 371; takes up fencing, **II**,
381; M. instructs on need for selflessness
in the home, **II**, 455–456; nervous disorders, **III**, 128; goes to Europe (Pau) for
health, **III**, 141; death, **III**, 730
Mahan, Jane Leigh (sister) ("Jennie," "Jenny"): M. lauds her confirmation, 104–
105; M. sends her book, 132; M. correspondence with, 205, 272, 281, 333, 334;
took care of her mother and aunt for
years, **II**, 355; additional bequest provided
for in Swift will, **II**, 355; lonely life of,
II, 376, 380; travel in Europe, **II**, 440; Swift
inheritance, **II**, 440
Mahan, Lyle Evans (son) ("Major," "Buster," "Laddie"): birth, 566; M. love for,
569, **II**, 335; discouraged from military
career, 584, **II**, 249; early education, **II**,
49, 267, 293; physical awkwardness of as
child, **II**, 251; home religious training, **II**,
152, 172; attends Groton School, **II**, 101–

102, 103, 302, 315, 331, 335, 341, 363, 374, 386, 542; M. visits at Groton, **II**, 501; attends Columbia, **II**, 102, 687, **III**, 28; M. insists on rigid disciplining of, **II**, 142; cautioned on owning and using a rifle, **II**, 184; books recommended and sent to by M., **II**, 189; studies French, **II**, 198; M. urges to concentrate on studies rather than football, **II**, 199; M. wishes he was right age for a match with Rosie Schiff, **II**, 220; love for his grandmother Evans, **II**, 257, 258, 259; aggressive independence of, **II**, 365; nearly dies at Groton from measles and subsequent complications, **II**, 400, 402, 403, 404, 405, 419, **III**, 727; withdrawn from Groton to accompany parents abroad, **II**, 542, 560; M. sponsors for club membership, **III**, 28; prolonged illness of, **III**, 195; M. turns family estate and inheritance problems over to, **III**, 295; writes article on arbitration, **III**, 451; M. visits at residence in Paris, **III**, 484, 491; death, **III**, 730

Mahan, Mary (sister): mental retardation of, 21

Mahan, Mary Helena Okill (mother): wanted M. to enter ministry, 10; visits M. at USNA, 14, 15, 17, 18, 19, 54; urges M. to mingle in female society, 19; acts as liaison for M. in Eliz. Lewis romance, 49; doubtful of M. taste in women, 68; M. writes to, 161, 281, 306, 326, 338; poor eyesight, 121; M. love for, 340; seeks arrears of pension through legislation, 620–621, 624; aids M. pursuit of Ellen Evans, 368–369; calm attitude toward death, 451; death, **II**, 97, 100; bequest, **II**, 160, 448, **III**, 295, 504; her death a relief to her loved ones, **II**, 262; legal affairs handled by Gillender, **III**, 504

Mahan, Milo (uncle): marriage to Mary G. F. Lewis, 2; marriage opposed by Mary Lewis, 50; M. correspondence with, 104, 167; M. seeks advice of in ordering books, 130; founder and editor of *Church Journal*, 133; instructs M. in religion, 358, **II**, 172; M. fondness for, 358; death, 356; M. attends funeral of in Baltimore, 356, 357

Mahan, Mrs. Milo. *See* Mary G. F. Lewis

Manila, Philippines: M. attends church in, 253, 257; dislikes, 255

Marriage. *See* Mahan, A. T.: Marriage

Marseilles, France: M. regards as the commonest cheapest city in the world, **II**, 372

"Marshmere." *See* Quogue, N.Y.

Marston, Roy B.: visits aboard *Chicago*, **II**, 277; assists M. with Nelson biography, **II**, 467, 473, 475, 489, 492; cautions M. against suggested British reviewer of *Nelson*, **II**, 481; M. approaches on separate publica-

tion of *Major Operations*, **III**, 176. *See* Sampson Low, Marston & Co.

Maxse, Leopold J.: suggests magazine article subjects to M., **III**, 5, 8, 11, 12, 37, 71; sends M. British comments on articles, **III**, 33, 34, 37, 38; M. solicits advice of on suitable articles for *National Review*, **III**, 36; sends M. Bernhardi book, **III**, 485; arranges M. contact with Clemenceau, **III**, 485; M. sends copy of *Armaments and Arbitration* to, **III**, 486

Merrimon, Augustus S.: M. seeks assistance of in naval reform movement, 434, 436–437, 438, 439, 440, 442, 470; supports M. on naval reform, 474

Mexico: M. participates in naval buildup against France in, 94; war with U.S. not brought on by existence of armaments, **III**, 542–543, 545. *See* U.S.A.: Diplomacy

Mills, Thomas B.: M. criticism of, 299

Missions. *See* Mahan, A. T.: Religion

Mohammedanism. *See* Mahan, A. T.: Religion

Monroe Doctrine: France violates in Mexico, 94; size of USN related to, 482; defense of at Isthmus related to larger USN, 482, 643; *Wachusett* upholds, 573; harbinger of U.S. imperialism, 574; implications of in possible German annexation of Curaçao, **II**, 27; U.S. shows fidelity to in Venezuelan crisis with Britain, **II**, 442; not related to Philippine annexation question, **II**, 566–567; prohibits U.S. involvement in Europe, **II**, 589; German challenge of anticipated, **III**, 291–292, 307–308, 345, 377, 443–444, 446, 453–454, 459; no-transfer corollary of threatened by German interest in French Martinique, **III**, 445, 453–454; German magazine attack on, **III**, 459; German victory in Europe (1914) will undermine, **III**, 541–542; Western Hemisphere a natural and necessary U.S. sphere, **II**, 443; Americans will fight to sustain, **II**, 529, **III**, 457; safeguarded at first Hague Conference by M., **II**, 710, 719, **III**, 73, 139, 450; application of varies with changing circumstances, **III**, 37; M. articles on, **III**, 37, 49, 52–53, 58, 428; Britain should support in her own interest, **III**, 50; Anglo-German punitive action against Venezuela does not contravene, **III**, 50; contributes to international peace, **III**, 60, 342, 445, 458; can only insure peace if USN force is behind it, **III**, 452; no European nation strong enough to challenge, **III**, 80; a national symbol supportable only with a superior USN, **III**, 291, 292, 457, 458, 474; a policy of national interest rather than international legality, **III**, 342, 458; lack of legal

Monroe Doctrine (*cont.*)
status exempts from arbitration, **III**, 687; should be exempt from general arbitration treaties, **III**, 412, 443–444, 445, 450, 458, 687; Asiatic immigration threatens, **III**, 436; no need to extend application of south of Amazon Valley, **III**, 446; British support of may weaken in face of German importunities, **III**, 459; Panama Canal Tolls Act embarrasses, **III**, 476. *See* Germany; Hague Conference (First): Mahan vs. Holls Controversy; U.S.A.: Diplomacy; Index Section II, Ships: *Wachusett*

Montevideo: yellow fever in, 380, 386, 401; M. apartment ashore in, 381; M. protests change of mooring off, 391, 392–393; Spanish Minister at, 392; fixed moorings at, 412; recommends lease of mooring at, 412; Mañá Dock in, 417

Moody Commission: *See* U.S. Navy: Administration

Moody, William H.: heads Commission to reorganize Navy Department, **III**, 278, 282, 283

Moore, John Bassett: Spanish-American War Peace Commission, **II**, 579; assists M. on Boer War book, **II**, 688–689; sends own books to M., **II**, 695, **III**, 16, 149, 456, 461; assists M. with research on articles, **III**, 44–45; assists M. with War of 1812 book, **III**, 87–88, 110, 114, 115–116, 120, 122, 125–126, 129, 150; M. advises on where to live in NYC, **III**, 129, 150; M. social relations with, **III**, 444; supports General Arbitration Treaty with Britain, **III**, 434, 444; assists M. on proposed U.S. expansion book, **III**, 461–463; capable legist, **III**, 514; M. thought highly of, **III**, 721

Morris, William O'Connor: praises M. *Farragut*, **II**, 116, 123; appearance, **II**, 123; wants to publish in U.S., **II**, 123; asks M. to read and criticize his Napoleon book, **II**, 149; praises M. *Influence* #2, **II**, 149–150; reviews M. *Nelson*, **II**, 479, 490; praises *Nelson*, **II**, 512

Morton, James St. C.: conflict with Dennis H. Mahan, Sr., 43–44

Mount Desert Island (Bar Harbor), Maine: M. family vacations at, 435, 454, 487, 614, 620, 621, 631, 632, 633, 634, 688; climate of beneficial to health of M. daughters, 487; M. works on *Influence* #1 at, 620, 621, 632, 633, 634, 635, 700; works on N.W. Coast Navy Yard Site Commission report at, 689

Nagasaki, Japan: M. goes ashore in, 225, 226, 300, 301, 303, 304, 309, 313; calls on U.S. Consul at, 298, 310; calls on British Consul at, 311; sight-seeing excursion, 299; at-

tends church in, 300; plays billiards ashore in, 308, 309, 310, 312, 313

Naval Academy. *See* U.S. Navy: Naval Academy

Naval War Board (1898). *See* War: Spanish-American War: Naval War Board

Naval War College. *See* U.S. Navy: Naval War College

Nazro, Arthur P.: friend of Dennis Hart Mahan, Jr., **II**, 174; death of wife, **II**, 174, 180; a lieutenant at age 45, **II**, 174; M. likes, **II**, 194; amateur journalist, **II**, 194; supports M. in fight with Erben, **II**, 211, 218, 233, 282; advises publication of M. Anglo-American Reunion article, **II**, 342

Negroes: M. critical of U.S. abolitionists, 33; "niggers," 33, 355, **II**, 349; "darkies," 76; mixed bloods, 108; Negro soldiers, 108; improvement of Southern during Reconstruction, 338; M. critical of Negro cadet at USMA, 355; minstrel show aboard *Chicago*, **II**, 206; childhood of races concept, **II**, 605, 700; discrimination against Negro Episcopalians, **II**, 617; status of introduced into Philippine annexation debate, **II**, 616; progress of in U.S. noted, **II**, 617; M. interest in Episcopal missions among in U.S., **III**, 190; racial questions involving linked with Japanese immigration issue, **III**, 214, 453, 498; Civil War not fought over Negro slavery issue, **III**, 498; Negro not a white man with the accident of black skin, **III**, 498; affirms Japanese racial superiority over, **III**, 497, 498; affirms white racial superiority over, **III**, 498

New York City, N.Y.: political corruption in, 475; Tammany Hall political role in, 488; M. opposition to Tammany, **II**, 667–668, 680, 693, **III**, 364–365; M. search for townhouse in, **II**, 355, 361, 362, 364, 370, 374, 380, 381, 383, 385, 386, 387, 389, 393, 400, 416, 443; purchase and remodeling of 160 W. 86th St., **II**, 416, 417, 435, 443; best residential section in, **III**, 129, 150; education of children ties M. to, **II**, 34, 39, 54; living arrangements in, **II**, 54; appointment of Police Board members, **II**, 449–450; streets unsafe after dark, **II**, 343; M. involvement in local politics, **II**, 667–668, 671; effective municipal administration endangered by partisan approach to local politics, **III**, 75; importance of subway to living in, **III**, 129, 150; M. leases his townhouse in, **III**, 138, 140, 141, 150, 160, 161, 177, 197, 204, 216, 233, 284, 299, 371, 439; townhouse sold, **III**, 299; bus transportation in, **III**, 197; transportation improvements in, **III**, 371; M. doubts he will live in again, **III**, 233; M. family lives at residential Hotel Collingwood (1911–1912, 1913–1914), **III**, 427, 428, 439, 512, 514, 521; advantages of Collingwood (W. 35th St.) apartment in, **III**, 439, 447–448, 452; M. attends opera and theater in, **III**, 447; protests high taxi fares in, **III**, 511; din of city wearisome, **III**, 514; M. dislike of apartment living, **III**, 524; social life in, **III**, 727–728

New York (Brooklyn) Navy Yard. *See* U.S. Navy: Yards (Bases)

New York State: gubernatorial election in (1878), 477; M. supports Roosevelt reform actions in, **II**, 676; supports Republican Party ticket in (1900), **II**, 692–693; supports Stimson for governor of (1910), **III**, 364, 409; M. complains to about service on Long Island R.R., **III**, 478–479, 480

New Zealand: need of British connection binds to Empire, **III**, 427; U.S. power related to security of, **III**, 468

Nicaragua: M. turns down duty assignment in, 357; proposed ship canal in, 357; internal disturbances in, **II**, 435; Marines land in Bluefields to protect U.S. lives and property, **II**, 435; M. favors canal in, **III**, 9. *See* Isthmian Canal

Niigata, Japan: M. goes ashore in, 228; dislike of, 228

Nones, Henry Beauchamp: vexes M., 152; horseback rides with M., 223; goes ashore with M. in Nagasaki, 225; reports Fletcher's agnosticism to M., 247; tension with Fletcher, 296

"Nonpareille": M. love for, 278, 340, 353; M. faithfulness to, 278; M. sees and courts in Nice, 352; rejects M., 352, 352, 354

Northwest Coast Navy Yard Site Selection Commission. *See* U.S. Navy: Yards (Bases)

Officers. *See* U.S. Navy: Officers

Ogden, David B. (wife's cousin): M. enlists in NWC appropriations fight, **II**, 210; M. enlists in fight with Erben, **II**, 211, 212, 217, 224, 225, 231, 240, 266; briefs Tracy on M. fight with Erben, **II**, 239

Ogden, Frank (wife's cousin): M. visits with in Nice, **II**, 197

Ogden, Gouverneur Morris ("Gouv") (wife's aunt's husband): M. visits with in London, **II**, 134–135; assists M. in NWC fight, **II**, 206–207; M. asks assistance in Erben fight, **II**, 266; dines with in London, **II**, 329, 331, 333; death of, **II**, 404

O'Kane, James: M. opinion of, 22, 37; supports M. in Hackett Affair at USNA, 22, 31

Okill, Mary Jay (maternal grandmother): friendship with Washington Irving, 576;

children inherit Tenafly-Palisades property from, **II**, 351, 447; provisions of will, **II**, 448, 720

O'Neil, Charles: reports aboard *Wasp*, 416; diary of, 416; correspondence with M., 416; granted leave, 423; assists M. with War of 1812 book, **III**, 66–67

Open Door Policy: M. defines, **III**, 353; relationship to location of naval installations, **III**, 353; Russo-Japanese tension contributes to maintenance of, **III**, 355. *See* U.S.: Diplomacy

Paine, Frederick H.: M. criticizes, 212, 298; has to dinner, 293

Pacific Ocean: seat of future American war, **III**, 80; removal of U.S. battle fleet from a confession of weakness and isolationism, **III**, 80

Paraguay: M. reports on revolution in, 381, 386, 399, 415–416; refuses recognition of U.S. Consul at Asuncion, 395, 396; *Wasp* shows flag in, 396, 397, 399; Brazilian intervention in revolution in, 399; internal conditions in, 399; tension with Brazil, 399; tension with Argentina, 401. *See* Index Section II, Ships: *Wasp*

Parker, Foxhall: M. criticism of, 471; drunken habits of, 471; breakdown of health of, 473

Parker, Mrs. Stevens. *See* Mary Lewis

Pau, France: M. visits, 428, 429, 431, 433, 462, and *passim*; describes Evans home in, 431; describes town, 431; M. plans visit to to survive pay cut, 458, 462, 463; Evans family returns to U.S. from, 487

Peace (Peace Movement): surest way to maintain is preparedness for war, 593, **II**, 65, 507; M. disinterest in movement, **II**, 670–671; M. opposition to movement, **III**, 223, 277; Monroe Doctrine contributes to international, **III**, 60, 342, 445, 458; lack of armaments does not insure, **III**, 553; no plan for can insure, **III**, 193; only change in hearts of men can insure, **III**, 217, 449; movement people ignore facts, **III**, 277, 308, 342, 449; Congress petitioned against USN increase, **III**, 277; can only be preserved by use of force, **III**, 278; Civil War proves wrong-headedness of, **III**, 278, 487; public opinion and public virtue alone can maintain, **III**, 342; capture of private property at sea would hasten, **III**, 366; M. attacks Angell's arguments for, **III**, 448–449, 486, 487; Stead sees British two-power naval standard as peace measure, **III**, 457. *See* Arbitration; Armaments; War

Peru: M. describes coast of, 572–573; beauty of women in Lima, 573; incapacity for

Peru (*cont.*)
self-government, 573; occupation by Chilean forces, 573; revolution in, 573; M. suggests USN base in Payta, 609, 610
Peters, M.: M. criticizes, 252–253
Philadelphia, Pa.: M. dislike of, 84, 455, 457
Philippines: reinforcement of Dewey squadron a diplomatic decision, **II**, 565, 567; Monroe Doctrine not related to annexation of, **II**, 566–567; M. would annex only Luzon and Ladrones from Spain, **II**, 569; not earlier considered as a U.S. outpost, **II**, 619; U.S. military presence in encourages Filipino revolt against Spain, **II**, 569; annexation forced on U.S. by Filipino insurgents, **II**, 579; M. supports annexation of, **II**, 617; U.S. popular support for annexation, **II**, 634; Naval War Board indecisiveness on how much to be annexed, **II**, 590; U.S. pitchforked into, **III**, 603; M. opposition to anti-imperialist movement, **II**, 580, 605, 679–680; American aptitude for colonial administration, **II**, 607–608, 661–662; Christian arguments for annexation, **II**, 661–663; annexation a Constitutional issue comparable to secession, **II**, 663; M. interest in Episcopal missionary activities in, **III**, 10–11; vulnerability to Japanese invasion, **III**, 384–385; Corregidor as USN base and coaling station in, **III**, 400, 401, 402, 403; impregnable USN base in is key to defense of against Japan, **III**, 658–659, 661; enemy naval landing party could not take Manila, **III**, 659. *See* Japan; U.S. Navy: Coaling Stations, Yards (Bases); War: American-Philippine War, Spanish-American War
Philippine Insurrection. *See* War: American-Philippine War
Pittsburgh, Pa.: M. ordered to ordnance duty at, 355, 356; detached from duty at, 356; dislike of duty at, 357
Prentiss, Roderick: appearance, 17; killed in Civil War, **III**, 56
Presbyterian Church. *See* Mahan, A. T.: Religion
Profanity. *See* Mahan, A. T.: Profanity
Progressive (Bull Moose) Party: existence of can only assure Democratic victory in 1912, **III**, 467
Promotion. *See* Mahan, A. T.: Naval Career

Quackenbush, John N.: USN investigation of drunkenness of, 404, 438; court-martial, 404; restored to service, 439, 443; M. criticism of, 438, 443
Quogue, Long Island, N.Y.: M. wife and children summer at, **II**, 111, 112, 115; lease and remodeling of summer home at, **II**,

112; considers renewing lease at, **II**, 138–139, 146, 147; considers permanent summer place at, **II**, 140; struck by hurricane, **II**, 145, 148, 150; social advantages of, **II**, 146–147, 167, 173, 188, 230, 263; Mrs. M. plans to build permanent summer home at, **II**, 165, 168, 173, 204, 243; economics of building "Slumberside," **II**, 167, 185, 206, 292, **III**, 729; details of "Slumberside," **II**, 184; first real home M. ever owned, **II**, 243; M. suggestions for writing desk in house at, **II**, 243; search for a name for house, **II**, 245, 260; "Slumberside" name an unnecessary frill, **III**, 29; "Slumberside" sold, **III**, 299, 307; "Marshmere" built, **III**, 299, 307, 313, 315, 729; "Slumberside" too small for family needs, **III**, 307; M. grants telephone line easement across property in, **III**, 495; beauty of "Marshmere," **III**, 510; new house an expensive undertaking, **II**, 292, 307, 311; site of house at, **II**, 419, **III**, 726; family horse and carriage at, **III**, 726; size of "Marshmere," **III**, 527; four servants required to staff "Marshmere," **III**, 549

Ramsay, Francis M.: refuses to assist M. with *Influence #1*, 634; M. dislike of, **II**, 33, 34, 40, 58, 60, 62, 105, 109, 160, 223, 230, 248, 250, 265, **III**, 299; M. conflict with on new NWC building, **II**, 40, 41; postpones M. sea duty for one year, **II**, 40; M. circumvents on new NWC building, **II**, 40–41; M. circumvents on orders, **II**, 54–55; ambivalent on M. orders to sea, **II**, 54; hostility toward NWC, **II**, 58, 61, 108, 109, 144, 163, 208, 244; dislike of M., **II**, 163, 222, 313; indecisive on NWC presidency assignment, **II**, 60; refuses to excuse M. from court-martial duty, **II**, 68; thwarts M. on NWC equipment requisition, **II**, 78; sends M. to San Francisco on court-martial duty at Christmas time, **II**, 89; M. asks to be excused from sea duty, **II**, 98, 99, 182; orders M. to sea, **II**, 102; would keep M. at sea, **II**, 163; told that Herbert has shifted to support of NWC, **II**, 142, 144; vexed over M. reception in Britain, **II**, 222; M. assumes animus of in fight with Erben, **II**, 212; secret access to and influence on Herbert, **II**, 236, 248, 302, 314; rumored replacement for Erben in *Chicago*, **II**, 292, 294; M. considers a gentleman socially, **II**, 292; M. blames for keeping *Chicago* abroad, **II**, 302, 313, 314, 354; fails to read M. books, **II**, 314, 371
Read, Edmund G.: breaks with M. on Hackett Affair at USNA, 11, 24; M. opinion of, 55; M. visits with in Yokohama, 350

Religion. *See* Mahan, A. T.: Religion

Remey, George C.: class standing at USNA, 13; broke with M. over Hackett Affair, **III**, 55; quits Lawrence Literary, 7; post-Civil War career, **III**, 55; one of last survivors of USNA '59, **III**, 228

Renan, Ernest: M. critical of, 207

Republican Party: M. knows little about, 157; opposes Reconstruction policy of, 338; dislikes Black Republicans, 340; relationship to corruption in Navy yards, 442; M. favors on free silver issue, 455; compromised by Robeson in 1876 elections, 456; M. supports in 1876, 457; corruption in and 1876 elections, 459; M. supports economic policies of, 477; deserves losing 1882 elections, 543; corruption in, 543; M. welcomes return to power of in 1888, 669, **II**, 9; M. thinks more progressive than Democrats, **II**, 205; U.S. imperial aspirations best fulfilled by, **II**, 234–235, 361; M. contributes to campaign chest in 1900, **II**, 694; M. cautious in endorsing candidates of, **II**, 700; appeals more to Independents, 477; weak candidates offered by, 477; future of NWC turns on, **II**, 62; M. became a Republican when Cleveland refused Hawaiian annexation, **II**, 361; M. anticipates folly of in 1908 election, **III**, 271; demoralized and sinking in 1910, **III**, 363; M. supports Insurgent movement within, **III**, 370; real brains found in, **III**, 448; predicts victory of in 1912, **III**, 448; M. votes for Senate and House candidates of in 1912 but not for Taft, **III**, 484

Retirement. *See* Mahan, A. T.: Naval Career

Rhodes, James Ford: M. assists with research problem, **II**, 527–528; M. social relations with, **II**, 629, 636, 696, **III**, 277, 286, 367; sends M. copy of his *History of the U.S.*, **II**, 667; M. nominates for membership in University Club, **III**, 112, 240, 241, 252; compliments M. on War of 1812 book, **III**, 159

Richfield Springs, N.Y.: M. spends 1891 summer vacation at, **II**, 52, 53; M. recommends to wife for gout cure, **II**, 250

Robeson, George M.: M. criticism of policies of, 437, 450, 456, 592, 655; corruption of, 437, 438–439, 442, 443, 457, 458, 459, 475, 481, 544, 592; demoralizes USN officers, 438; M. fears retaliation by, 439, 456; M. demands investigation of, 440; undermines role of Executive Officer, 445; M. conflict with, 452–453; overrules M. assignment to USNA, 462; Whitthorne attacks, 475

Robeson, Henry B.: M. plays billiards with, 324; assists M. with *Influence #1*, 634

Rodgers, C. R. P.: M. criticizes as USNA Superintendent, 465

Rodgers, Thomas S.: supports M. in fight with Erben, **II**, 211, 218, 233

Roe, Francis A.: M. dislike of, 268

Roman Catholic Church. *See* Mahan, A. T.: Religion

Roosevelt, Theodore: favorably reviews *Influence* books, **II**, 94; M. enlists aid in attempt to avoid further sea duty, **II**, 96–97, 98–99; asks Herbert to excuse M. from sea duty, **II**, 100; fails to stay M. assignment to sea duty, **II**, 102; M. enlists in fight for NWC appropriations, **II**, 207; coordinates M. allies in Erben fight, **II**, 212, 215, 217, 218, 224, 234, 236, 281; sees conspiracy against M. in Erben fight, **II**, 234; M. hopes will review his *Nelson*, **II**, 490; M. advises on international relations, **II**, 506, 507; M. advises on naval affairs, **II**, 506, 507, **III**, 178–180, 182–189, 202, 439; M. lives in home of during Spanish-American War, **II**, 552, **III**, 720; M. social relations with, **II**, 676; M. views election to vice presidency as period of professional rest, **II**, 706–707; M. lauds Naval General Staff bill, **III**, 74; will be a better President than McKinley, **III**, 10; disagrees with M. on capture of private property at sea issue, **III**, 157; M. argues Free Ships-Free Goods issue with, **III**, 165, 211, 216; opposes M. in all-big-gun ship controversy, **III**, 171, 204; permits M. to speak out publicly on Second Hague Conference issues, **III**, 172, 192; quotes M. in Annual Message, **III**, 190, 195; loses spelling-reform fight, **III**, 197; M. confidence in, **III**, 197, 210, 232; thought M. underpaid for book, **III**, 199; personal characteristics, **III**, 251; M. critical of in Brownson controversy, **III**, 236; awake to German ambitions, **III**, 251; interest in maintaining USN at full force, **III**, 251, 500; M. appeals to on Great White Fleet controversy with Goodrich, **III**, 265–266; baited by Congressmen, **III**, 280; heads off Congressional scheme to divide USN battle fleet, **III**, 291, 439; advises Taft not to divide battle fleet, **III**, 290, 439; calls and attends Newport conference on battleship design, **III**, 301; M. defends political activity of in 1910, **III**, 363, 409; accused of trying to provoke war with Japan, **III**, 363; M. sees bright political future for, **III**, 370; author, **III**, 378; M. defends from *N.Y. Times* attack, **III**, 408–409; solicits M. arbitration articles for *Outlook* magazine, **III**, 422; M. rejects Roosevelt-Harriman political charge, **III**, 440; unquestionably the Republican choice in 1912,

Roosevelt, Theodore (*cont.*)
III, 465, 467; M. supports in 1912, III, 465–466, 467, 484; only candidate in 1912 with grasp of foreign policy issues, III, 466, 468; M. prefers as a man to Taft, III, 477; recommends fortification of seven key overseas naval bases and coaling stations, III, 661; political rally for, II, 696; 1906 Annual Message, III, 195; spelling reform, III, 197; Secret Service message, III, 280

Ropes, John C.: lectures at NWC, 637, III, 664; assistance to NWC, 648, 650; offers to support private publication of *Influence #1*, 711–712; M. visits in Boston, II, 534; death, II, 666

Rosebery, Archibald Philip Primrose, Earl of: congratulates M. on simultaneous Oxford and Cambridge honorary degrees, II, 291, 298; M. has private dinner with, II, 277, 278, 297, 298

Rowan, Stephen C.: M. critical of secretiveness of, 210, 225, 242, 244, 247, 255, 289; orders changes in court-martial records, 246; M. thinks behavior foolish, 307; M. impatience with, 283; M. lies to, 319; kindnesses to M., 326

Royal Navy. *See* Great Britain: Royal Navy

Russia: USN has poor reproductions of national ensign of, 509; M. likes national anthem of, II, 380; benefited by American-Japanese rivalry, II, 506; no support for ally France in Sudan, II, 620; study of NWC curriculum, II, 636; called First Hague Conference to counteract Anglo-American rapprochement, II, 658; ambitions in Asia, II, 658, 693, 707, III, 12; must have access to warm-water ports, III, 27, 99; fears U.S. Open Door Policy in China, II, 658; naval power in Yangtze can check expansion of in China, II, 707–708; strategic threat to Britain in Middle East, III, 12, 99; counterbalanced by Japan in Manchuria, III, 12, 27; more dangerous to Britain than Germany, III, 13; M. distrust of the Slav, III, 13; less dangerous to Britain in Far East than in Middle East, III, 27

Russo-Japanese War. *See* War: Russo-Japanese War

Russo-Turkish War. *See* War: Russo-Turkish War

Ryan, George P.: M. critical of seamanship of, 465–466; death of in *Huron*, 465

Salisbury, Robert Gascoyne-Cecil, Marquis of: M. entertains aboard *Chicago*, II, 206; describes Lady Cecil, his daughter, II, 206; appearance, II, 206; M. sympathizes with politics of, II, 275; foolishly ceded Heligoland to Germany, III, 709

Saltonstall, Henry: assists M. in NWC appropriations fight, II, 241; M. sends photograph to, II, 344; fatal illness of, II, 369–370, 371, 375

Saltonstall, Mrs. Henry: M. visits, II, 468, 500, 596, 666

Salvador: U.S. diplomats biased against, 600; participation in Central American war, 598–600; disturbances in, 610; M. urges warship sent to La Libertad, 610. *See* Index Section II, Ships: *Wachusett*

Sampson Low, Marston & Co.: report on sale of *Influence* books in England, II, 178; M. rejects proposal of, II, 178; advertise *Influence* books, II, 191, 319; entertain M. in London, II, 272–273, 274, 275; suggest new and cheaper editions of *Influence* books, II, 274; suggest promotional linking of *Nelson* to *Influence* books, II, 479; M. satisfaction with, III, 81; M. negotiations with for separate publication of *Major Operations*, III, 180, 199, 200, 208, 239, 296, 377–378, 379, 416, 446, 460; company changes management, III, 239; M. dislike of new management, III, 274, 296, 297–298, 337; M. dispute with on *Major Operations*, III, 208, 239, 297. *See* Index Section III, Bibliography

Sampson-Schley Controversy. *See* War: Spanish-American War: Sampson-Schley Controversy

Sampson, William T.: M. enlists in fight with Erben, II, 212, 225; death, III, 248; M. speech to memory of, III, 248, 249, 270, 271; M. praises for good judgment in disobeying an order during Spanish-American War, III, 635. *See* War: Spanish-American War

Santo Domingo: proposed U.S. annexation of, 362; prospects of a USN coaling station in, II, 587; U.S. involvement in (1852) an aberration, III, 45; commission to study debt structure of, III, 106

Schiff, Mr. and Mrs. George: entertain M. in Villefranche, II, 190, 194, 195, 206, 217, 221, 374, 375, 376; entertain *Chicago* officers, II, 190; appearance, accomplishments and social sophistication of daughters of, II, 194, 196, 198, 200, 203–204, 220, 222, 230, 265, 294, 344, 371, 382; Mrs. S. suffers heart attack, II, 206, 223, 285, 392, 396; M. exchanges photographs with, II, 219, 220; entertained aboard *Chicago*, II, 219, 220; M. family critical of M. interest in daughter Rosie Schiff, II, 265; entertain M. in London, II, 267, 273, 284, 285, 290, 313, 335

Schley, Winfield Scott: pranks at USNA, 8, 33, 54; home life, 48; influences Whitney against NWC, 655, 664, 716; M. dislike of, 655; seizure of NWC building suspected, 676; supports NWC consolidation, 716; M. notes attractiveness to women and amusing nature, **II**, 265; death, **III**, 423; USNA battalion attends funeral of, **III**, 423; Taft sympathy on death of, **III**, 423. *See* War: Spanish-American War: Sampson-Schley Controversy

Schoonmaker, C. M.: breaks with M. on Hackett Affair at USNA, 11; visits M. aboard *Iroquois*, 246; death aboard *Vandalia* in Samoan hurricane, **III**, 57; personality of, **III**, 57

Scribner's, Charles, Sons: reject M. *Influence #1* manuscript, 658–659

Sea. *See* Mahan, A. T.: Sea

Sea Duty. *See* Mahan, A. T.: Naval Career

Seamanship. *See* Mahan, A. T.: Seamanship

Seamen's Church Institute. *See* Mahan, A. T.: Religion

Sears, James H.: opposition to NWC consolidation, **II**, 193, 201

Secretary of the Navy. *See* U.S. Navy: Secretary of the Navy

Servants. *See* Mahan, A. T.: Servants

Sex. *See* Mahan, A. T.: Sex

Shanghai, China: M. sight-seeing in, 238; visits ashore, 238, 241, 243; considers attending dance in, 238; plays billiards in, 238, 243; attends Seamen's church ashore, 240; prayer meeting ashore, 242; attends church ashore, 244; M. orders clothes in, 241; observes missionary activities in, **II**, 508

Ships. *See* Index Section II, Ships

Sickles-Key murder case: M. comment on, 64

Sims, William S.: defeats M. in all-big-gun ship controversy, **III**, 170–171; M. coolness toward, **III**, 177–178, 193; publications on all-big-gun ships, **III**, 178, 204–205; M. conflict with on all-big-gun ship issue, **III**, 178–180, 182–189, 193; M. enraged by, **III**, 234; M. withdraws from debate with, **III**, 204. *See* U.S. Navy: Ships

Sin. *See* Mahan, A. T.: Religion

Sino-Japanese War. *See* War: Sino-Japanese War

Slamm, Jefferson: M. opinion of, **III**, 227–228

"Slumberside." *See* Quogue, N.Y.

Smith, Beatty Peshine: M. criticism of, **III**, 56; post-USNA career, **III**, 56–57; passed over and dropped from USN, **III**, 56

Soley, James Russell: lectures at NWC, 622, 635, **II**, 8, 82; assists M. with *Influence #1*, 634; helps arrange publication of *Influence #1*, 707, 712, **II**, 295, **III**, 274; interest in NWC wanes, **II**, 58, 60, 62; M. criticism of, **II**, 62; not approached to help

M. in Erben fight, **II**, 231; M. cites book of, **III**, 393

Spanish-American War. *See* War: Spanish-American War

Spencer, Thomas Starr: M. rooms with at USNA, 3; M. dislike of, 31, 34, 54, 57, 67, 78, 79, 452; M. like of, **III**, 54; Civil War duty, 90; marriage of sisters of, 452, **III**, 54; drinking habits of, 452, **III**, 54; resignation from USN, **III**, 54; death, **III**, 54

Stations. *See* U.S. Navy: Stations

Spain: USN has poor reproductions of national ensign of, 509; superiority of navy to USN, 544; M. draws up contingency plan for war with, **II**, 37, 38, 734; lacks pretty women, **II**, 167, 169, 363; smelly towns in, **II**, 167, 169; war with Morocco, **II**, 170; anticipated movement of navy in war with U.S., **II**, 553–554, 558; naval movements in war with U.S., **II**, 558, 563, **III**, 629–630, 633. *See* Philippines; War: Spanish-American War

Stockton, Charles H.: serves with M. on N.W. Coast Navy Yard Site Commission, 676 ff.; lectures at NWC, 657, **II**, 82; M. recommends as author, **II**, 26, 521, 696; M. confides in on NWC matters, **II**, 57, 59; directs construction of NWC building, **II**, 66; duty as XO at NWC, **II**, 32, 70, 71, 72, 88; succeeds M. as president of NWC, **II**, 136; informs M. of Herbert's conversion to pro-NWC stance, **II**, 143, 145, 147; opposes NWC consolidation, **II**, 201; petulance of, **II**, 201; bitterness over NWC fights, **II**, 244; babysitter for M. children, **II**, 330; breadth and acuteness of intellect, **II**, 510; studies international law, **II**, 695; publications of, **III**, 71; M. recommends as book reviewer, **III**, 316; appearance, **III**, 334

Strategy: possession of sea power crucial in, 623; commerce destruction as factor in, **II**, 531, **III**, 113; blockade as a form of commerce destruction in determining, **III**, 71; lessons of past useful to proper understanding of, 623, 625, 627, **II**, 10; principles of, 671; relationship of new weapons to, 638; fleet-in-being concept, **II**, 336–338, 504, 509, **III**, 584; Jomini definition of, **II**, 580, 595, Napoleon definition of, **II**, 595, **III**, 580–581; control of sea main issue in, **III**, 95, 567; in defense of U.S. Northeast Coast, **III**, 194–195, 325; role of Guam in USN in Western Pacific, **III**, 356, 357, 358, 382, 386, 387; base in Lu-Chus (Ryukyus) important to USN in war with Japan, **III**, 387; M. favors northern Pacific route for USN counter-attack on Japan, **III**, 382–384, 392; M. objections to southern Pacific route in counter-attack on

Strategy (*cont.*)

Japan, **III**, 392; importance of coaling stations to USN in counter-march across Pacific against Japan, **III**, 392–393; relation of coaling stations to, **III**, 399; controlling element of modern is fuel (coal), **III**, 562, 563, 633; impact of telegraph on, **III**, 632; impact of wireless on, **III**, 403–404. *See* Tactics; U.S. Navy: Coaling Stations; War

Swasey, Charles H.: M. opinion of, 6–7; killed in Civil War, 593, **III**, 56; M. served as pallbearer at funeral of, **III**, 56

Swatow, China: M. goes ashore in, 292, 293, 295; plays billiards in, 293; missionaries in visit M. aboard *Iroquois*, 296

Swift, Jane Leigh Okill (aunt): M. writes to from Shanghai, 243; silver service divided, **II**, 172, 241; death, **II**, 336; lived in a world of illusions, **II**, 336; M. saddened by death of, **II**, 336; estate of, **II**, 349, 351, 355, 436, 438–439, 440, 448, **III**, 295; special bequest to Jane Leigh M., **II**, 355

Tactics: role of commerce raiding in, 593, **III**, 563, 567, 574, 575; role of ram in, 638; M. confesses ignorance of, 607; M. not up to date in, **III**, 180; lessons of past useful to understanding of, 623, 625, 627, **II**, 10; lack of systematic in Anglo-Dutch wars, 632; concept of the defensive-offensive, 631, 633, **II**, 625; continuing importance of blockade in, 670, **II**, 551, **III**, 560; relationship between weapons and, 625, 628, 629, 637–638, **II**, 9; relationship of naval to land, 619, 624, 631, 633, 637, 638, 651, **II**, 9, **III**, 71, 91, 220, 387–388, 393, 419, 706; historical tactical analogies, **III**, 568–569; M. concept of and insistence on tactical concentration, **II**, 428, 551, 553, 554, **III**, 93, 94, 95, 188, 202, 205–206, 290, 291, 372, 386–387, 563, 568, 570, 574, 575; USN battle fleet must not be divided, **III**, 202, 205–206, 290, 291, 371–372; offensive capability of coast defense fortresses, **III**, 314; torpedo craft vs. battleships in, **III**, 89, 90–95; problems in supporting troop landings with naval gunfire, **III**, 391–392; enemy should be attacked where strongest, **III**, 394; possible impact of aviation on, **III**, 410, 708, 709; role of torpedoes in, 628, 631, 633, **II**, 94–95, **III**, 86, 564. *See* Strategy; U.S. Navy: Ships

Taft, William Howard: M. questions military sense of, **III**, 290; M. attempts to bridge political split with Roosevelt, **III**, 408–409; M. lauds naval building policy of, **III**, 409, 477; inadvertently errs on Canadian annexation statement, **III**, 427; can be nominated but not elected in 1912,

III, 465; diplomatic record of administration of not impressive, **III**, 467, 477; M. closer to on domestic issues in 1912 than to Roosevelt, **III**, 467, 468, 477; M. will vote for if Bull Moose party seems to help Democrats gain power, **III**, 468

Tangier, Spanish Morocco: M. describes, **II**, 357–358; criticism of U.S. Consul in, **II**, 358

Tayloe, James L.: supports M. in Hackett Affair at USNA, 31

Taylor, Henry C.: opposition to NWC consolidation, **II**, 201; informs M. of attack on NWC, **II**, 206; informed on Mahan-Erben fight, **II**, 246; M. promises guest lecture at NWC when able, **II**, 265; steps down from NWC presidency in despair, **II**, 594

Temper. *See* Mahan, A. T.: Temper

Terry, Silas W.: M. critical of as USNA Commandant, 465

Theology. *See* Mahan, A. T.: Religion

Thompson, Richard W.: too old for job as SecNav, 470, 481; lowers academic standards at USNA, 470; weak administration of, 471; M. criticism of as SecNav, 475, 492, 592; M. fears retaliation by, 475; attempts to reform Dept. of Navy, 481–482; intervenes in Law promotion controversy, 491–492

Thursfield, James R.: M. entertains aboard *Chicago*, **II**, 282; solicits information on USN maneuvers for Brassey article, **II**, 436–437; M. thanks for favorable reviews, **II**, 495; sends M. copy of his book on RN, **II**, 494; compliments M. on *Nelson*, **II**, 509; visits M. in NYC, **II**, 622–623; assists M. with Russo-Japanese War articles, **III**, 153, 154; taken in by spurious Buell book on John Paul Jones, **III**, 317, 318

Tobacco. *See* Mahan, A. T.: Tobacco

Tracy, Benjamin F.: supports M. on N.W. Site Commission funding, 688; reopens NWC consolidation decision, 692; upholds administrative separateness of NWC, 718; supports transfer of NWC from Goat Island to Coaster's Harbor Island, **II**, 8; receives M. *Influence #1* book, **II**, 10; employs M. in contingency war planning capacity, **II**, 18, 35–37, 734; thinks highly of Chadwick, **II**, 34; postpones M. sea duty, **II**, 40, 47; M. enlists support of on new NWC building, **II**, 40–41; urged to appoint a president for NWC, **II**, 58, 60, 62; overly impressed with Materials of War arguments, **II**, 59; calls M. to Washington in Chilean Crisis, **II**, 59, 734; handling of Chilean Crisis, **II**, 62, 65, 734; M. asks to help arrange continued shore duty, **II**, 91; reasons for assisting M. writing projects, **II**, 109; M. has high regard for, **II**, 109; M. seeks private conversation with, **II**, 41; M. asks about sea-duty status, **II**, 54-55; orders M. to presidency of NWC, **II**, 64; urges M. to finish *Influence #2*, **II**, 64; M. acknowledges indebtedness to, **II**, 80, 89

Turkey: dirty towns, **II**, 248; tension with Greece over Crete, **II**, 495, 505; M. condemns atrocities of, **III**, 489; people hopelessly unfit for self-government, **III**, 492, 510; perpetual source of trouble in Europe, **III**, 492; individual Turks superior to Persians, **III**, 492; M. scores misrule of in Balkans, **III**, 505-506; 511, 686; government administratively incompetent, **III**, 510; army of a disorganized mob, **III**, 510; Balkan Wars speedily swept away iniquities of, **III**, 686; probable role in European War (1914), **III**, 710

Twain, Mark: M. meets in London, **II**, 273; appearance, **II**, 273; M. dislikes books of, **II**, 273

Uruguay: tension with Brazil, 413; tension with Argentina, 414, 415

Unitarian Church. *See* Mahan, A. T.: Religion

United States of America:
Congressional Elections: M. comments on, *1882*, 543; *1890*, **II**, 32; *1894*, **II**, 360, 361; *1898*, **II**, 610; *1906*, **III**, 191; *1910*, **III**, 363, 370, 371

Diplomacy: M. opposes U.S. imperial policy, 574; colonies lead to strong central government at home, 574; M. participation in Santos case (Ecuador), 587-589, 590, 602, 603-605; protection of U.S. citizens abroad, 591, 595, 610; intervention in Panama (1885), 595, 597, 609; U.S. diplomats sympathize with nations to which accredited, 600; influence of warships on, 601, **II**, 565; naval officers need briefings on, 605, **II**, 507; Anglo-American relations compromised by Irish vote, 593, **II**, 84, 664, 665, 679, 685, 686; Anglo-American friendship and cooperation, **II**, 550, **III**, 113; Anglo-American identity of interests, **II**, 171, **III**, 27-28, 165; Anglo-American (English-speaking) race, 593, **II**, 84, 442, 445, 685, 691, 736, **III**, 604, 605; Anglo-American naval union, **II**, 283, 305; Anglo-American political union, **II**, 283; concept of Anglo-American Imperial Democracy, **III**, 153-154, 263; prophets needed to awaken U.S. to imperial possibilities, **II**, 28; Americans must be converted to imperialism gradually, **II**, 305; definition of imperialism, **III**, 462; M. advocates U.S. territorial expansion, **II**, 507,

627; U.S. emergence onto world stage necessary, **II**, 443; U.S. imperialism benefits world, **II**, 627; condemns American isolationism, **II**, 442, 503, 558; M. opposes formal entangling alliances, **II**, 569, 700, **III**, 28; U.S. should abandon traditional Free Ships-Free Goods doctrine, **II**, 610-612, 613-614, **III**, 112-114, 157-159, 164-165, 172, 192, 210, 213, 218-219, 366, 623-626; military opinion needed in decision-making, **II**, 683-684, **III**, 375; inequality of Clayton-Bulwer Treaty, **II**, 126; non-interference in British-German tension in South Africa, **II**, 444; non-interference in British-Nicaraguan tension, **II**, 445; unfortunate Venezuelan Crisis with Britain, **II**, 441-442, 443, 452, **III**, 476; Venezuelan Crisis delays M. retirement from USN, **II**, 472, 482; peaceful settlement of Venezuelan Crisis should reorient USN toward Pacific, **II**, 506; M. opposes General Arbitration Treaty with Britain, **II**, 445, 450, 498, 504, **III**, 420-421, 422, 433-437, 438, 441-444; U.S. and Britain natural allies in Pacific, **II**, 529; American-Japanese tension and war scare over immigration issue, **III**, 214, 216, 217, 221-222, 226, 263, 277, 334, 355, 400, 411, 436, 448, 465; M. scorns distinction between military and diplomatic considerations, **III**, 276, 466; four new USN battleships needed annually to sustain, **III**, 291; Alaska boundary question with Britain, **III**, 411; large USN is nation's only security in face of German and Japanese expansion, **III**, 465; size of USN a diplomatic rather than naval question, **III**, 466, 483; split with Britain on Mexican issues, **III**, 512; Wilson mismanagement of Mexican policy, **III**, 520-521, 523. *See* Canada; Chile; France; Germany; Great Britain: Diplomacy; Isthmian Canal; Japan; Monroe Doctrine; Open Door Policy; Russia; War

Economic Issues: M. critical of 8-hour workday law, 438, 537; impact of depression on USN, 454; M. opinion on silver (currency) issue, 455, 467-468, **II**, 483; Bland-Allison Act, 467, 468, 469; M. G. Evans advises M. on, 467; admits superficial knowledge of, **II**, 483; Morey letter scandal, 488; advocates hard money position, 489; thinks hand-sewing superior to sewing machine, 521; civilian employees of USN supply own tools, 524, 525; pay reduction accompanies 8-hour day, 537; female pay at N.Y. Navy Yard, 539; opposes movement toward trusts, 655, **III**, 610; regulation of domestic industrial relations necessary, **III**, 477; M. criticism of U.S. millionaires, **II**, 443; distrust of

United States of America (*cont.*)

Rockefeller business methods, **III**, 193; supports free trade, 489, 572, **III**, 154, 244, 263; free trade no longer possible, **III**, 263, 307; fears impact of Bryan election on economy, **II**, 466; M. fixed income will be hard hit by inflation, **II**, 466; effect of inflation on sale of M. books, **II**, 467; M. opposes high protective tariffs, 655, **II**, 483, 503, **III**, 16; tariff protection a form of isolationism, **II**, 503; government should not support private banking, **II**, 483; U.S. population growth increases domestic consumption, **III**, 16; M. inadequate grasp of international economics, **III**, 71, 427; commercial wickedness causes wars, **III**, 315; workers' pensions weaken economic resources of nations, **III**, 371; coal-mining unions control nations, **III**, 447; individual initiative submerged in tendency toward industrial concentration, **III**, 609; both socialism and corporate concentration endanger individual initiative, **III**, 611–612

Political Opinions: despotism, 72; weakness of republics, 74; tyranny of majority, 625, **II**, 470; Civil Service reform, 489; advantages of bicameralism, **III**, 462; doubtful about initiative, referendum, and recall, **III**, 468; concept of the Union, 554, 555, 574, **II**, 40, 662, 663, **III**, 157, 498, 624, 703; nationalism vs. states' rights, **III**, 475; self-government not practicable for all peoples, **III**, 520; power tends toward tyranny and liberty toward license, **III**, 612; M. arguments against women's suffrage, **III**, 712–713; compares U.S. Constitution and Doctrine of the Trinity, **III**, 714; government everywhere fallen into the hands of lawyers, **III**, 411

Presidential Elections: M. comments on, *1872*, 591–592, **II**, 697; *1876*, 455, 456, 457, 459; *1880*, 477, 482, 487–488; *1884*, 571–572, 574, 591–592, 624–625; *1888*, 655, 665, 669; *1892*, **II**, 47; *1896*, **II**, 463, 465, 466, 470, 694; *1900*, **II**, 692, 694–695, 696, 697, 706, **III**, 603; *1904*, **III**, 440; *1908*, **III**, 271; *1912*, **III**, 388, 448, 457, 459, 463–464, 465–466, 467–468, 474–475, 476–478, 484. *See* Democratic Party; Progressive (Bull Moose) Party; Republican Party

Reconstruction Policy in the South: M. opposes, 338, 434; critical of congressional role in, 434; interpretation of Hamburg Massacre, 459; misjudged racial inferiority of the Negro, **III**, 498; enfranchisement of Negro an humanitarian impulse, **III**, 498. *See* Negroes

Social Issues: class superiority, 72; capital punishment, 279; public schools, 281; socialism seen as the new slavery, **II**, 483; worthless U.S. leisure class undermines national capacity to endure challenges, **III**, 452; fears disappearance of U.S. middle class, **III**, 610

U.S. Army: Military Academy (West Point): M. compares and contrasts with USNA, 9, 30, 42–43, 50; disapproves of Negro cadet at, 355; skills of graduates insured victory in Mexico and in Civil War, **III**, 545

U.S. Congress: M. critical of, 434; M. critical of 8-hour law in Navy Yards passed by, 438; private business more efficient than, 438; investigation of U.S. Navy Dept., 438, 456; slashes USN appropriation, 456, 458, 459; passes USN deficiency bill, 464; uncertainty of on USN pay issue, 469; conflict with President Hayes, 473; passes USN appropriations bill (1882), 540; indifference to NWC, 635, 647–648; provides funds for new NWC building, **II**, 23; incompetent to judge on division of USN battle fleet, **III**, 291; Naval Appropriation Bill of 1909, **III**, 291–292; M. does not know name of his congressman, **III**, 339; Naval Appropriation Bill of 1912, **III**, 476

U.S. House Committee on Naval Affairs: M. asks Merrimon to work for naval reform through, 438; M. participates in investigation of USN by, 443–450, 455–456; M. responds to questions by, 443–450, 451–452, 455–456; studies size and character of USN, 453–454; M. critical of precipitateness of, 455; recommends USN budget cuts, 457; M. favors Whitthorne as chairman of, 470; M. lobbies for NWC, 648–649; opposition to NWC, 650–651, **II**, 206; majority favors NWC, 652, **III**, 666; NWC consolidation issue, 676; recommends new building for NWC, **II**, 3; passes 30-year retirement law, **II**, 92; deletes appropriation for NWC, **II**, 206, 207; headed by incompetent small-navy Democrat, **III**, 414; M. tells that size of USN is not a naval question but a diplomatic one, **III**, 414; M. organizes political pressure on to restore NWC appropriation, **II**, 206–207, 208; hearings on Council of National Defense proposal, **III**, 375; Roosevelt prevents vote in to divide USN battle fleet, **III**, 291, 439

U.S. House of Representatives: slashes USN appropriation, 458; distrust of Robeson, 458; kills NWC appropriation, 642; passes NWC appropriation, 654; transfers NWC from Goat Island to Coasters' Harbor

Island, **II**, 8; hostile attitude of toward USN, **III**, 448; Democratic-controlled refuses appropriation for battleships, **III**, 452, 453, 454, 458, 465, 466

U.S. Merchant Marine: need for as source of trained USN reserve seamen in wartime, 558, **III**, 620, 622; conversion of ships to USN cruisers, **II**, 36, **III**, 575, 629; conversion of ships to troop transports, **II**, 99, **III**, 575; confusion and cowardice of transport captains off Santiago, **III**, 236, 636; coastal trade does not require additional protection of Panama Tolls Act, **III**, 490; decline of related to wage competition from shore industries, **III**, 622; jobs in must be reserved for American seamen, **III**, 622

U.S. Naval Institute: M. election to membership in, 436; feebleness of, 474; essay contest sponsored by, 474; M. wins honorable mention in contest sponsored by, 474; M. will not publish sea power lectures in *Proceedings* of, 666–669; M. disinterest in, **III**, 266

U.S. Navy: politics in, 74; need for rigid discipline in, 74, 75, 192; building program proposals (1858), 38, (1876), 449; corruption in, 74; policies unsettled, 434; deplorable condition of, 437, 481, 482, 486, 544, 558, 592, **III**, 391; inadequate funding of, 437, 544; diplomatic and commercial purposes for existence of, 441; relationship to commercial expansion, 643; main purpose of is to fight, 441, 448; lacks accurate designs of foreign flags, 523, 526, 528, 530, 531; equity with European navies unlikely, **II**, 428; too small and dispersed for fleet maneuvers, **II**, 435, 437; U.S. must have two-ocean, **III**, 206; can prevent invasion of continental U.S., **III**, 410; must be second only to Britain's, **III**, 483; must increase by at least two battleships per year, **III**, 483; role and importance of Naval Reserve, **III**, 570–572; enlisted men in equated with U.S. colonial subjects, **III**, 596; M. unable to keep up with modern naval matters, **III**, 203, 391–392, 494; has no experience with the New Navy, **III**, 237–238; General Signal Book, **II**, 338
Administration (General Staff Concept): M. attacks Bureau system, 445, 448; German example cited, 444, **III**, 218; RN example cited, 444–445, **III**, 279, 285; Board of Admiralty needed in USN, 449; M. recommends centralization of decision-making power in a single officer, **II**, 551–552, 592, **III**, 195, 281, 285; supports Roosevelt's Naval General Staff bill, **III**, 74; General Board should advise on immunity

of private property at sea issue, **III**, 158; Newberry support of General Staff, **III**, 275; M. discusses concept of, **III**, 275–277; would unify diplomatic and military considerations, **III**, 276; should advise on ship types and armaments, **III**, 276, 281; should advise on all-big-gun ship issue, **III**, 281; military, naval, diplomatic functions must be exercised by one person during war, **III**, 374–375; M. supports Council of National Defense proposal, **III**, 374–375; need for General Staff during Spanish-American War, **III**, 628, 630, 632, 637–638
Moody Commission to Reorganize USN: **III**, 278, 282, 284; M. suggests study procedures, **III**, 278–279, 282–283; examines British organization, **III**, 279; M. suggests reorganization plan, **III**, 280–282, 286; suggests membership of, **III**, 283; finds service on distasteful, **III**, 284; expenses of serving on challenged, **III**, 287–289; accepts report modifications, **III**, 286; service on delays writing of *Naval Strategy*, **III**, 309. See U.S. Navy: Secretary of the Navy
Coaling Stations: need for on western Central American coast, 598–599, 611, **II**, 584; lack of on western European coast, **II**, 36; Naval War Board on future location of, **II**, 581–591, **III**, 641; M. comment on optimum strategic location of, **III**, 399–404; security and economy of, **III**, 404; coaling from colliers in wartime, **III**, 402; oil depot policy, **III**, 403. See Strategy; U.S. Navy: Yards (Bases)
Department of the Navy: investigates Quackenbush, 404, 438; orders honors paid Winslow, 406; corruption in, 437, 438, 440; M. works to reform, 434, 439, 440, 442, 452; reforms recommended, 443–450; congressional investigation of, 438; officers losing power to civilians in, 440; takes credit for making M. *Influence* books possible, **II**, 285; M. urges support of in quarters allowance issue with Treasury Dept., **III**, 333; orders USNA battalion to attend Schley funeral, **III**, 423; Special Order of prohibits officers from publicly commenting on European War issues, **III**, 538–539, 540
Great White Fleet Cruise: purpose logistical rather than diplomatic-military, **III**, 226; Mahan-Sims conflict on, **III**, 234; M. updates article on, **III**, 268; M. sources of information on, **III**, 262, 265, 267, 268; anticipates hostile Japanese reaction to, **III**, 263; inaccuracies in M. articles on charged, **III**, 263–264; research on, **III**, 265, 267, 268; M. enlists Roosevelt aid in

U.S. Navy (*cont.*)
argument with Goodrich about, **III**, 265–266; Roosevelt accused of ordering to provoke war with Japan, **III**, 363
Hydrographic Office: M. reports for duty at, 369
Line vs. Staff Controversy: M. disinterest in, 311; criticizes assimilated staff ranks, 440–441, 450; conflict aboard ship, 441; criticizes pretensions of staff officers, 440–441, 445, 461, **II**, 528; M. dislike of engineers, 448; need for reform of relationships between, 440, 444; advocates establishment of Corps of Machinists, 460; comparison of sizes of line and staff groups, 558; implicit in Brownson controversy, **III**, 236
Naval Academy: M. appointment to as midshipman, 2; expansion of size expected, 53; physical plant, 65, 464; M. boasts of career at, 316; *Huron* shipwreck reflects adversely upon, 465, 466; overproduction of officers, 470, 496–497; administrative changes, 470–471; M. rumored for superintendency of, **II**, 341–342, 349, 350; has no interest in becoming Superintendent of, **II**, 349, 350; M. never particularly interested in, **III**, 266; serves on Board of Visitors, **III**, 465; befriends Japanese midshipmen at, **III**, 688
Academic: M. grades, 10, 13, 35, 56, 60; M. class standing, 13, 25, 36, 49, 56, 61; jealousy of M. academic success, 56; study habits, 14, 60–61; curriculum, 60; departmental politics, 62–63, 71; examinations, 54, 56, 58, 79, 80, 81, 82–83; lack of academic challenge at, 14, 35; non-academic reading, 9–10, 11, 12, 14, 23, 71, 72, 628; M. anticipation of graduation, 64, 77; M. examines midshipmen for promotion, 466, 467, 472; decline of standards, 470; academic dishonesty at, 471–472; Delehanty-Finley confrontation, 478–481; study of electricity, 518; changes in admission policy, 558; naval history library holdings, 618, 619; seamanship course, 633; M. would have teach all advanced ordnance and mechanics courses, **II**, 3, 21, 23; suggestion that all USN postgraduate education be centered at, **II**, 108, **III**, 664; need for introductory course in naval history at, **II**, 595. See Honorary degrees
Class of 1859: Mahan vs. Hackett Affair within, 6, 11–12, 13, 22, 24, 26, 30–31, 37–38, 67, 82, 470, **III**, 53, 55, 56; M. high opinion of, 3; friendships within, 3, 9; low opinion of, 73; few friends within, 51, 470; M. comments on individual members of, 196, 476–477, 593, **II**, 178,

179, 180, 181, **III**, 53–57, 227–228, 341; comment on class of 1856, 70, 80; comment on 1841 date, **III**, 177, 217; mentioned, 4, 7, 23, 29, **III**, 341
Cruises: M. summer cruise in *Plymouth* (1857), 2–4, **II**, 717–718; summer cruise in *Preble* (1858), 19, 23, 43, 59, **II**, 125; training cruise in *Macedonian* (1863), **II**, 125, 408
Discipline: lack of midshipmen discipline, 7, 13; midshipmen pranks, 7, 8, 18, 33, 54; M. violation of regulations, 4–5, 71; threatened with dismissal, 5; reported for hazing, 26; critical of regulations, 51; M. on need for more discipline, 74; chills and exercises, 17, 23–24, 30, 31, 33, 39, 51, 52, 83; Foote Incident, 75, 77–78, 81, 83; double standard of, 470; hazing scandal, 475–476
Duty Assignment: M. turns down assignment to Dept. of Astronomy, 357; ordered to headship of Dept. of Gunnery, 461, 462, 463; Gunnery Dept. orders cancelled, 461; M. challenges orders cancellation, 462; living quarters, 464; M. disappointment with duty at, 465; detached from duty at, 483, 486–487
Religion: M. dislike of chapel services, 8–9, 22–23; dislike of religion at, 10, 11, 18–19, 22–23, 26, 29–30, 58–59; church attendance policy, 57; pressure to conform in chapel, 69; dislike of Chaplain Jones, 8–9, 11, 22–23, 33–34, 51, 60, 69; dedicates chapel window to Sampson, **III**, 248, 249, 270, 271. See Ashe; Mahan, A.T.: Naval Career, Religion
Naval War College: origins of, **III**, 218, 219–220; purpose of, 642, 643, 646, 661, 662, 667, 668, **II**, 24; M. offered position at, 577; M. accepts position at, 577–578; seeks detachment from *Wachusett* to take position at, 578, 581–582, 583–584, 597, 603, 605, 607, 608; insists on preparation time prior to commencing duty, 577–578, 603, 607, 610, 611; not prepared for 1885 session, 613; ordered to, 613; reports for duty at, 615, **II**, 74, 75, **III**, 663; continued in duty at, 657; detached, **III**, 667; future development of, **II**, 75–77, 82; curriculum at, 577–578, **II**, 8, 20, 32, 41, 107, **III**, 577–582; docility of students at, 663, 668; war games study at, 639, 689, **III**, 372; Art of War vs. Materials of War issue at, 643, 644, 651, 653, 661, 667, 678, 716, **II**, 3, 9, 19, 23, 25, 56, 59, 75–77, 91, 96, 595, **III**, 664–665; working relationship with ONI, 630, 641, 656, 657, 658, 664, **II**, 99; M. would merge with ONI, **II**, 95; M. lobbies congressmen for support of, 647, 648, 649, 650, 652, **III**, 665, 666; revival of under Repub-

licans, **II**, 9, 61, 64; physical plant, 635, 638, 676, **II**, 3-4, **III**, 663; site of, 676, 716, **II**, 3, 4, 8, 22-23, 24, 25; quarters at, 619, 620, 636, 676, **II**, 5-7, 70, 106, 108, **III**, 663, 667; planning and construction of new building, **II**, 3-7, 19, 20, 21, 22, 23, 24, 25, 27, 28, 30, 31, 32, 33, 40, 41, 43, 45, 46, 49, 50-51, 52, 66, 71, 72, 73, 79, 81, **III**, 667; M. orders maps for, **II**, 11-12, 18, 42, 44, 55, 68, 69, 77, **III**, 666; books for library, 615, 616, 617, 618, 620, 622 626, **II**, 62, 69, 70, 79, 87, 100, **III**, 304; uniforms at, 627, 628, **II**, 73; Bureau of Navigation attacks on, **II**, 594-595; congressional opposition to, 635, 642, 647, 648, 650, 651, **II**, 206, **III**, 665-666; M. work for sneered at in USN, **II**, 107; threatened consolidation with Torpedo Station, 654, 661, 663, 664, 665, 676, 677, 678, 716, **II**, 3, 8, 11, 20, 30, 244, **III**, 666; threatened consolidation with Training Station, **II**, 106, 109, 136, 193, 201, 223, 255, **III**, 664; relations with Training Station, **II**, 73, 74, **III**, 664; threatened deletion of appropriation, **II**, 206-208, 210, 222-223, 230, 240-241, 246; suggestion that USN postgraduate education be moved to USNA, **II**, 108, **III**, 664; M. fights for preservation of, 661, 663, 664, 665, 669, 670, 676, 677, 716, **II**, 56, 57, 58, 59, 60, 61, 64, 206-207, 208, **III**, 665; Pythian Board study of, 716; importance of faculty to, **II**, 41; support personnel and pay at, **II**, 71, 78, 83, 86, 88; routine administration of, **II**, 71, 78, 83, 86, 87, 88; M. seeks clarification of president's role, **II**, 74; possible successors to M. as president of, **II**, 34, 37-38, 41, 56, 58, 60, 62; M. reappointment as president of, **II**, 38, 54, 58, 59, 60, 62, 64, 65; suggests sea pay for president of, **II**, 39, 40; would not again accept presidency of, **II**, 223, 265; M. pleased with survival and growth of, **II**, 244; M. washes hands of, **II**, 123, 163, 255-256; rumor of abolition of saddens M., **II**, 142; Herbert shifts to support of, **II**, 142, 143, 144, 147, 208, 239-240, 595; *Influence* books save, **II**, 145, 147; M. links usefulness of to fame of self and publications, **II**, 41, 59, 60-61, 77, 80, 107, 108-109, 207, 279; pioneers movement to reform naval administration, **III**, 68; role of in Spanish-American War, **II**, 600; proposal for M. portrait at, **III**, 104-105; M. writes reminiscences of service at, **III**, 233, 238, 663-667; M. ends all association with, **III**, 460

Annual Sessions (Conferences): *1885*, 613; *1886*, 636-639, **III**, 664; *1887*, 642-644, 645, 646, 647, 655, **III**, 665; *1888*, 649, 650, 652, 653, 656, 657, 659, 660-662, 665, 666, **III**, 247, 248, 666; *1889*, 649, **III**, 667; *1890* (no session), **II**, 8, 19, **III**, 667; *1891* (no session), **II**, 19, 32; *1892*, **II**, 43, 44, 56, 58, 61, 62, 64, 65, 66, 72, 75, 77, 79, 80, 81-83, **III**, 247, 667; *1893*, **II**, 106, 108; *1894*, **II**, 296; *1895*, **II**, 386, 416, 417, 419, 420, 421, 425, 432, 445; *1896*, **II**, 445, 459, 468; *1899*, **III**, 299; *1909*, **III**, 300-301, 347, 350, 351; *1910*, **III**, 317, 340, 343, 349, 358; *1911*, **III**, 375, 410, 411, 415

Lectures and Lecturers: M. lectures at lead to books, 641, **III**, 663, 666-667; Little reads M. lectures at, **III**, 303, 314, 330, 338, 340; M. lectures at, 622, 637, 641, 646, 700, **II**, 82, 127, 386, 419, 420, 421, 432, 445, 459, 460, 468, 470, 472, 523, 526, **III**, 300, 301, 304, 308, 309, 311, 312, 314, 317, 324, 330, 338, 340, 343-344, 347, 349, 350, 358, 410, 411, 415, 663; lecturers and lectures at (1886-1892), 622, 637, 640, 644, 645, 646, 647, 649, 650, 656, 657, 659, 660, 668, **II**, 8, 12, 43, 44, 56, 75, 77, 81-83, **III**, 663, 665

War Game Problems: *1892*, M. reference to USN defense of Buzzards, Narragansett, Gardiners bays, **III**, 577; *1895*, M. comment on war with Britain off New England coast, **II**, 425-428; *1907*, M. comment on Philippine defense in war with Japan (Orange vs. Blue) in Pacific, **III**, 658-662; *1911*, M. comment on war with Japan (Orange vs. Blue) in Pacific, **III**, 378, 380-388, 389-394, 395. *See* Herbert; Luce; Ramsay; Tracy

Office of Naval Intelligence: M. seeks information from, 627-628; assistance of to NWC, 630, 641, 656, 657, 658, 664, **II**, 99; studies war resources of Canada, 656; studies foreign naval capabilities, 657; studies RN maneuvers, 658, 659, 664, 670, **II**, 99; interest in strategic character of N.W. coast, 679, 696, 713, 715; M. writes strategic study of N.W. coast for, 715; sends copies of NWC lectures to, 679; interest in Kriegspiel studies at NWC, 689; close working relationship with NWC, **II**, 12, 17, 99; M. would merge with NWC, **II**, 95; role in Spanish-American War, **III**, 628-629; assists M. with research on *Naval Strategy*, **III**, 273, 301, 306, 309; sends M. Russo-Japanese War materials, **III**, 301, 306, 308; USN intelligence concepts in 1890, **III**, 562, 572. *See* U.S. Navy: Stations

Office of Naval Records and Library: M. advises purchases for, **III**, 135-136, 142, 145, 528; historical advice to, **III**, 143, 144; M. gifts to, **III**, 118, 135, 139, 140, 141-143, 313, 340-341, 389, 416, 528; authorized to collect naval records, **III**, 110, 142; M. sends copy of article to, **III**, 345-346

Officers: expansion of corps proposed, 69;

U.S. Navy (*cont.*)
M. on needed qualities of, 73; superior-inferior relationships in USN, 75, 192, 290, **II**, 256; incompetent tolerated, 79; inadequate time notification of first lieutenants assigned to sea, 94–95; number of compared to number in Army, 454; pay scales, 454; should be paid allowance for quarters ashore, 444; status of ships' executive officers, 444–445; rigid weeding-out of young needed, 445–446, 497; reasons poor retained in USN, 445–446; more rapid promotion of able needed, 446, **III**, 49; retirement plan for needed, 446; courts-martial harsher on young, 449; power of commanding should not be checked by boards, 449; most belong to Democratic Party, 482; return of Southern feared, 482–483; enjoy superior education, 558; too few ships for number of, 486; slowness of promotion, 496–497, 624; reduction in non-combatant aboard ships, 558; ensigns should stand watch, 579; hopes *Influence #1* will raise status of, 625; scarcity of in 1888, 660; right of as citizens to comment publicly on national issues, **II**, 20, **III**, 158, 164–165, 333–334; have greater interest in foreign affairs than other citizens, **II**, 28; few interested in the Art of War, **II**, 56, 75; drilled in subordination of military to civil authority, **II**, 75, 507; expression of political opinions not encouraged by politicians, **II**, 305; should not publicly discuss pending Administration matters, **II**, 682–683; should not publish opinions on current naval subjects, **III**, 1, 2, 333–334; adequate supply of senior, **III**, 41; inadequate supply of division and watch, **III**, 41; M. espouses Naval Reserve officer plan, **III**, 42; interpretation of treaties beyond scope of most, **III**, 483; best possible guardians of subject races in new U.S. colonies, **III**, 596; rear admirals should not command one-ship squadrons, **II**, 370–371. *See* U.S. Navy: Line vs. Staff Controversy
Secretary of the Navy: inferior to most Cabinet members, 592; usually incompetent to make strategic decisions, **III**, 195; Roosevelt fills position with figureheads, **III**, 236; USN too big to be run by other than first-class, **III**, 236; inadequacies of corrected by Bureau system, **III**, 275; must have ultimate power over Chief of General Staff, **III**, 277; Chief of General Staff should be sole responsible advisor to, **III**, 281
Ships: inferiority of USN to RN, 448; compared unfavorably with foreign, 544, 592; trend toward long, low gunboats, 88;

design needs of USN, 448–449; M. opposes larger guns on, 448–449; great guns, **633**; supports balanced battery on, 449; cannot compete with foreign ironclads, 482; most USN worthless, 492, 544, 558, 592; rams, 630, 638, 639; torpedo vessels, 631; twin-screw armored, 627–628; armored cruisers, **III**, 239; technological problems solved by other navies, 558, **II**, 621; types of new needed, 593; modern too complicated for M., **II**, 98, 394; M. has difficulty adjusting to *Chicago*, **II**, 139–140, 331, 394, 407; efficiency of declines as administrative details aboard multiply, **II**, 394; Pacific interests dictate building on West Coast, **II**, 506; building program must continue, **II**, 621; battleship size must be studied, **II**, 680–681, 682, **III**, 38–40; M. would limit size of battleships, **III**, 91, 95, 179, 184, 185, 204, 285, 342; balanced fleet concept, **II**, 681, **III**, 179; Bureau system inadequate in determining sizes and capabilities, **II**, 682, **III**, 74; M. laments passing of age of sail, **II**, 718; relationship of design to naval policy and strategy, **III**, 74, 95; the All-Big-Gun Ship controversy, **II**, 95, 682, **III**, 171, 177–180, 182–189, 193, 201, 202, 204–205, 239, 281, 284, 285, 342, 358–359, 679–681, 700; Hale would have Congress determine types, **III**, 98; Navy General Staff should determine types, **III**, 276; M. accepts limitation on tonnage of single ships, **III**, 113–114; M. confesses lack of knowledge of contemporary technology, **III**, 188, 201, 390, 403; M. unable to keep up with modern naval matters, **III**, 203, 391–392, 494; has had no experience with the New Navy, **III**, 237–238; Newport Conference on battleship design, **III**, 301; shift from coal to oil, **III**, 403; submarines and submarine operations, **III**, 403, 572, 700; *Maine* disaster should not shake confidence in battleship type, **III**, 593
Stations:
European: ceremonial functions on a nuisance and bore, **II**, 150–151; admiral on commands but a single ship, **II**, 272
Pacific: foreign ships on, 573; intelligence reports on foreign warship movements on, 563–564; intelligence reports on harbors on, 564, 567; inadequate coaling facilities on, 598, 599
South Atlantic: intelligence reports on foreign warship movements on, 382, 385, 386, 390, 398, 410, 414
Yards (Bases): M. urges administrative reforms in, 440, 443, 447; political influence in, 446; inadequate inspection in, 447; contractor system in permits fraud, 448; exist only for war, 448, **III**, 353; related

to how USN is used, **III**, 352; strategic considerations should determine choice of, **III**, 353; consideration of locations of, **III**, 353–358, 369; locations dictated by sectional political considerations, **III**, 369; defensibility of, **III**, 356–357; potential and importance of Guam as, **III**, 356, 357, 358, 380–381, 382, 384, 386, 391, 393, 396, 398–399, 402; potential and importance of Pearl Harbor as, **III**, 380–381, 385, 391, 393, 400, 402; potential and importance of Kiska as, **III**, 382, 384, 386; advantages of Subic Bay over Manila as, **III**, 658–662

Boston Navy Yard: M. seeks duty assignment to, 436; assigned to duty at, 436; detached from duty as economy measure, 456, 457; corrupt contractors at, 437; workmen employed at election time, 437, 446; corruption in, 441; courts-martial duty at, 452; pay while on duty at, 454

New York (Brooklyn) Navy Yard: M. seeks assignment to, 357, 358, 487; ordered to duty at, 359, 483, 486; reports for duty at, 484, 487; denied quarters at, 487; commutes to work, 543; tests new inventions at, 484, 485, 492, 493, 494, 495; attempts to achieve economy and efficiency in operations at, 485, 486, 499, 501, 502, 505, 506, 508, 509, 510, 513, 514, 517, 523, 524, 525, 539; supplies USN ships from, 491, 503, 505, 538; courts-martial duty, 493, 556; court of inquiry duty, 527; M. tests lamps and lanterns at, 489, 490, 491, 502, 503, 504, 516, 527, 528, 529, 540, 541, 550; tests compasses, 497–498, 539, 545, 546; tests flag bunting, 498, 499, 500, 501, 511, 512, 521, 523, 528; tests lamp oil, 516, 531, 532, 533, 534, 535, 542; tests voice trumpets, 543, 544, 545; storage of fireworks at, 553; inventory problems at, 504, 505, 514, 520, 527; books ordered at, 506, 507, 517, 518, 519, 529, 530, 552–553; M. urges study of applied electricity at, 507, 517, 518, 519, 520; problems with manufacturing and supplying foreign flags, 509, 510, 512, 513 515, 516, 523, 526, 528, 530, 531, 532, 547; inadequacy of work force in Navigation Office at, 514, 536, 541, 549; civilian employees at, 524, 525, 536, 537, 539; M. critical of civilian employees, 527; M. admits error, 542; charts needed, 538; inadequate dry dock at, 549

Northwest Coast: M. heads Navy Yard Site Selection Commission, 672, 676, 677, 711, 713; factors involved in site selection, 674–675, 678, 679, 684, 685, 686, 687, 688, 690, 693, 695, 698, 699, 701, 703, 704;

M. would change name of Puget Sound, 686; costs and expenditures of Site Selection Commission, 673, 678, 680, 681, 688, 689, 690, 691, 692, 693, 694, 697, 701, 705, 706, 717; strategic implications of site selected, 673, 679, 687, 713, 715; Port Orchard site, 682, 688, 695, 698, 702, 715; opposition to selection of Port Orchard site, 683, 687, 709, 714–715; commercial and military necessity of N.W. Yard, 687, 694, 696, 697, 698; writing the Report of the N.W. Coast Navy Yard Site Selection Commission, 672, 673, 679, 680, 681, 682, 683, 686, 687, 688, 689, 692, 694, 696, 697, 698, 699, 700, 702, 703, 704, 705, 706, 707, 708, 709, 710, 714, 718

Washington (D.C.) Navy Yard: M. ordered to duty at, 95; duty at, 333; M. suffers mental depression at, 160; M. would locate all advanced USN ordnance and mechanics instruction at, **II**, 3

U.S. Senate: transfers NWC from Goat Island to Coaster's Harbor Island, **II**, 8; votes to divide USN battle fleet between coasts, **III**, 439

U.S. Senate Committee on Foreign Relations: M. thinks USN should be put under control of, **III**, 466

U.S. Senate Committee on Naval Affairs: requests study on USN coaling stations by Naval War Board, **II**, 582

University Club (NYC): superior to Century Club, **III**, 252

Vanity. *See* Mahan, A. T.: Vanity

Van Valkenburgh, Robert Bruce: M. dislike and criticism of, 148, 150, 182; calls on socially, 149

Victoria, Queen: M. describes dinner with at Osborne, **II**, 128–129, 311–312; appearance, **II**, 312; knowledge of M. books, **II**, 129, 144; commands M. presence at State Ball, **II**, 284; M. confidence in presence of, **II**, 299

Villefranche (Nice), France: M. describes, **II**, 188; M. social life ashore in, **II**, 188–189, 190, 191, 193, 197, 198–199, 202–203, 221; fatigued by social responsibilities in **II**, 200, 201, 202. *See* Schiff, Mr. and Mrs. George; Index Section II, Ships: *Chicago*

Villegas, Clara: M. infatuation with, 90, 91, 333; beauty of, 333; engaged to be married to another, 333; recollection of stimulates M., 573

Virginius Affair: Spanish-American tension over, 410; M. supplies naval intelligence on Spanish Navy, 410, M. thinks used to

Virginius Affair (*cont.*)
divert Congressional investigation of Navy
Dept., 439

Walker, Edward A.: naval career of, 452;
married to Spencer sisters, 452; death of,
452; funeral of, 452; M. attends funeral
of, 452
Walker, John G.: supports M. on NWC
consolidation issue, 665; assigns M. to
special duty to encourage his writing,
708, 711; agrees to purchase copies of *Influence #1* if published, 708; M. considers
approaching for help in Erben fight, **II**,
231
War: concept of the Art of War, 643, 644,
651, 653, 663, 667, 668, 669, 670, 678, 716,
II, 23, 25, 41, 56, 76, 81, 106, 332, 549, 582;
shortened by prior existence of armaments, **III**, 546; preparedness for insures
peace, 593; unpreparedness stimulates, **II**,
37; unpreparedness for an American tra-
dition, **III**, 543; principles of, **II**, 9, 41, **III**,
582; M. contingency plan for with Britain,
II, 18, 35–37, 38, 41, 734, **III**, 559–576; M.
contingency plans for with Germany and
Spain, **II**, 37, 38, 734; M. contingency plan
for with Japan, **III**, 380–388, 389–394; disaster of possible Anglo-American, **II**, 441,
444; concept of the just, **II**, 556, 675; Bible
supports necessity of, **III**, 229; Christian
dimensions of, **III**, 223, 228–229; sometimes
a moral imperative, **II**, 658, 665, 675, **III**,
683, 686; evils of should not obscure moral
character of, **II**, 675, **III**, 9, 489; achievement of justice by, **II**, 664; observations
on righteousness of, **III**, 683; some questions can only be settled by, **III**, 225;
civilized nations must be prepared for
against barbarian nations, **II**, 446; stems
from human impulse to fight, **III**, 113,
553, 703; inherent in nationalism, **II**, 611,
III, 193; inevitable, **III**, 217, 223; costliness of justified by proper results from,
III, 9; legalization of private property capture at sea in wartime would deter, **II**,
611, 614, **III**, 113, 366; offence in is the
best defence in, **III**, 392; study of is a
study of history, **III**, 273; difference between war and peace a semantic one, **III**,
276; acquisition of territory by a legitimate international transaction, **III**, 291;
the result rather than cause of conditions,
III, 315; commercial wickedness causes,
III, 315; nations do not engage in for material gain, **III**, 487; spirit of modern involves making war on entire populations,
III, 366, 626; the greater the suffering
visited on belligerent civilians the shorter
the war, **III**, 638; modern must be quickly

and decisively mounted, **III**, 387; mainly
caused by vital interests or national hon-
or, **III**, 543; unguarded frontiers do not
prevent, **III**, 542, 544; more likely in Pacific than Atlantic for USN, **III**, 400; era
of burning and looting unresisting cities
is over, **III**, 660. *See* Arbitration; Armaments; Peace (Peace Movement); Strategy; Tactics; U.S. Navy: Naval War College
American-Philippine War (*1899–1902*):
Filipinos in childhood stage of race development, **II**, 627; U.S. offensive operations must be maintained, **II**, 635; rawness
of U.S. troops in, **II**, 635; U.S. tactics
should draw on experience with American
Indians, **II**, 636; sees end of fighting near,
II, 722; links Filipinos and Boers, **II**, 722;
must maintain U.S. military force in islands after, **III**, 6–7. *See* Philippines
Boer War (*1899–1902*): U.S. newspaper
condemnation of Britain needs study, **II**,
656, 665; M. emphasizes suffrage issue in
Transvaal, **II**, 657, 674, 677, 678–679, 698;
M. sympathy for British cause, **II**, 664, 674,
736, **III**, 604; Anglo American rapprochement related to, **II**, 657, 664, 665; compares
Britain in South Africa with U.S. in Cuba,
II, 664; M. urges U.S. non-involvement in,
II, 670–671, 677; distressed by British military setbacks in, **II**, 674, 698–699; British
tactical failures in, **III**, 10; backward Boer
political system deserves to die, **II**, 674;
a just war, **II**, 675, 677, 736; British re-
spond to Boer aggression, **II**, 698; M. iden-
tifies Uitlanders with American Revolu-
tionists, **II**, 679; links pro-Boer sentiment
in U.S. with Philippine anti-annexation
movement, **II**, 679–680; McKinley flound-
ering on mediation issue, **II**, 685; high payment offered M. for book on **II**, 686; M.
sees early end of, **II**, 722, **III**, 9; M. would
exclude Boer leaders and language from
future society of South Africa, **III**, 40.
See Great Britain: Diplomacy; U.S.A.:
Diplomacy; Index Section III, Bibliography: Books, Articles
Civil War (*1861–1865*): M. preference for
Southerners as friends, 26; critical of ultra-
abolitionists, 33; hopes for exciting duty
in event of, 78; plan to capture CSS *Sumter*, 88–89; stimulates rapid promotion, 89;
criticizes Maryland's stance in, 90; reports morale of Union people high, 90;
critical of British press handling of, 91;
trial by battle saves U.S., 483; M. blockading duty, 90, **II**, 369, 527, 557; numbers and
money produced U.S. victory, **III**, 551;
USN blockade main factor in victory,
III, 157, 165, 624; coaling at sea on block-

ade, **III**, 639–640; success of Hatteras Inlet operation, 90; abortive Mathias Point (Va.) operation, 90; Port Royal operation, 89, 90; M. veneration of concept of The Union, 574, **II**, 743; a clash of militarily unprepared nations, **III**, 278, 285, 342, 487, 542; Constitutional clause denying right of secession might have avoided, **III**, 443; not fought over Negro slavery issue, **III**, 498, 542; Battle of Mobile Bay, **III**, 555–556; meets Lee's daughter and cousin in France (1893), **II**, 194, 216, 221

Russo-Japanese War (1904–1905): M. interest in stimulated by payment for articles on, **III**, 98; hopes it will remain live topic for articles, **III**, 141; torpedo craft vs. battleships in, **III**, 91–95, 98; Russian consul in NYC blames origins of on Germany, **III**, 97; M. supports Russian decision to defend Port Arthur, **III**, 102–103, 107–108, 109, 155; condemns Russian expansion in Far East, **III**, 99; justifies Japan's war declaration, **III**, 108; research on, **III**, 99, 109, 149, 152, 153, 154; asks editor to send him material for article on, **III**, 152; publications on, **III**, 89, 90–95, 96, 98, 100, 102, 141, 146, 149; Battle of Tsushima, **III**, 178, 182–183, 184, 204, 680; division of battle fleet insured Russian defeat, **III**, 206, 372; Treaty of Portsmouth, **III**, 263; ONI collects materials on, **III**, 301, 306, 308; Japan regains earlier losses in Shimonoseki treaty, **III**, 342; concentration of Russian fleet might have avoided war, **III**, 372; Japanese peace moves dictated by economic exigencies, **III**, 384; Japanese experience in with coaling from colliers, **III**, 402. *See* Japan; Russia; Index Section III, Bibliography: Books, Articles

Russo-Turkish War (1877–1878): M. wants Turks driven from Eastern Europe, 457; Russian successes in, 464, 469; passion of Russian people forced war for religious reasons, **III**, 543

Sino-Japanese War (1894–1895): M. opinion solicited on, **II**, 335, 336, **III**, 583–585; Battle of the Yalu, **II**, 337, 415, 416, **III**, 583–585; declines offer to write on, **II**, 342; not newsworthy in Tangier, **II**, 358; writes article on, **II**, 415, 416, 417; Japan denied fruits of victory in, **III**, 342. *See* Index Section III, Bibliography: Articles

Spanish-American War (1898): M. trip to Europe on eve of, **II**, 535, 541, 542, 543, 545, 548, 549–550, 601; recalled to duty, **III**, 464; returns to U.S., **III**, 629; Treasury Dept. questions M. travel expenses from Rome to NYC, **II**, 601–604, 607, **III**, 595; U.S. has no fear of Spain, **II**, 544, **III**, 643; calm M. reaction to *Maine* disaster, **II**, 545, **III**, 592–594; *Maine* sinking promotes Anglo-American understanding, **II**, 545, 546; British support of U.S. cause in, **II**, 556, 579, 657; movement toward Anglo-American entente during, **II**, 556, 657, 664; tension with Germany during, **II**, 566, 567; M. deems it a just war, **II**, 556; considers and negotiates post-war articles on, **II**, 552, 559, 560, 582, 594, 600, 606, **III**, 630; public fear of Spanish naval attacks on coastal cities, **II**, 551, 554, 625, **III**, 98, 412–413, 414, 637, 643; Spanish naval movements, **II**, 558, 563, **III**, 629–630, 633; Army landings at Santiago delayed by report of Spanish naval movements, **II**, 625, 626–627, 628, 629, **III**, 636, 637; inefficiency of Spanish Navy in, **II**, 590; M. recommends USN strategy in, **II**, 551, 553–554; 563–566, 569–570, 626, **III**, 188, 191, 629, 639; critical of USN eccentric movements, **III**, 31, 632; critical of Army strategy in Puerto Rico, **II**, 573, 612; criticizes Army control of troop transports, **III**, 637; Army strategy at Santiago, **II**, 562, 621; surrender of Spanish garrison at Santiago issue, **II**, 612, 653–654, 691, 692, 719, 727–728; M. seeks credit for providing formula for Spanish garrison surrender at Santiago, **II**, 653–654, 691, 692, 718–720, 728; shift of U.S. public opinion to imperial expansion during, **II**, 556, 579, 605, 610; role of NWC in, **II**, 595, 600, **III**, 191; USN coaling problems in, **II**, 557, 581; construction of useless ships during, **III**, 98; role of ONI in, **III**, 628–629; intelligence reports during, **III**, 191; difficulty of maintaining secrecy during, **II**, 642; press indiscretions during require future censorship system, **III**, 642; plan to bombard Spanish coast, **III**, 638, 639, 640; plan to occupy Isle of Pines with Marine battalion, **III**, 641; USN ship and fleet movements during, **III**, 630–631, 634, 637, 638, 639; M. recommends local armistice with Spain in Europe, **II**, 570; advocates speedy peace to insure USN efficiency, **II**, 572–573, 577–578; Protocol ending war, **II**, 583; treaty of surrender in Cuba, **II**, 588; Treaty of Paris, **II**, 627; arbitration would not have prevented, **III**, 139; non-preparedness insured Spain's defeat in, **III**, 545; colonies acquired by called dependencies, **III**, 596; M. did not oppose German acquisition of Carolines after, **III**, 165. *See* U.S.A.: Diplomacy; Index Section III, Bibliography: Books, Articles

Naval War Board: M. recommends abolition of, **II**, 551–552, 556, 581, **III**, 276, 630; duties and functions of vague, **III**, 627–628, 643; personnel of hastily assembled,

War (*cont.*)

III, 638; guesses wrong on Spanish naval movements, II, 558, 630, III, 633; surprised by Cervera's run into Santiago, III, 633; erred in speedy reinforcement of Dewey at Manila, III, 637; Camara fleet movement toward Manila major strategic problem faced by, III, 639–640; decisions and recommendations of, II, 555, 558, 559, 561, 581–591, 620–621, 628, 692, III, 191, 631, 632, 638; criticism of, II, 556, 579, 592; work complimented, II, 609; M. work on guided by his studies at NWC, II, 595, 600, III, 191; M. writes history of, III, 161–162, 163, 164, 169, 174–175, 191–192, 234, 627–643; M. history of based on *McClure's Magazine* articles, III, 630, 642; recommends purchase of St. Thomas, II, 572, 585–586, III, 642; recommends location of postwar coaling stations, II, 581–591, III, 641; recommends Nicaraguan canal route, II, 589; M. confuses personal opinions with those of Board, III, 642. *See* U.S. Navy: Administration

Sampson-Schley Controversy: M. comments on, II, 562, 563, 569, 571, 573–577, 578, 612, 620, 657, 669–670, 671–672, 673, 688, 703–704, 739–741, 744, III, 2, 3, 4–5, 74, 423–424, 634–635

War of 1812: U.S. unpreparedness insured defeat II, 37, III, 475–476; U.S. lucky to survive, III, 115, 137, 476, 545; not brought on by existence of armaments, III, 542, 545; U.S. war aims not achieved, III, 545. *See* Armaments; Peace (Peace Movement); Index Section III, Bibliography: Books, Articles

War of the Pacific (1879–1884): mentioned, 572; issues involved in, 573; outcome, 573; clash of ironclads in, II, 422, 423–424. *See* Chile

World War I (1914–1918): M. ethics on criticized, II, 671; M. fears outbreak of in 1913 while traveling in Europe, III, 720; Balkan contribution to outbreak of, III, 520; U.S. officers enjoined from public comment on, III, 538, 546; M. cheers Commonwealth participation in, III, 543; pressure of work and worry relating to causes M. heart attack, III, 547, 549; concerned over initial German successes in Belgium, III, 548, 551; M. strongly pro-Ally and anti-German in, III, 548; notes very little naval action in, III, 551; contemplates writing book about, III, 551; German support of Austrian ultimatum to Serbia principal cause of, III, 698, 710; causes of, III, 703–705; Britain must declare war on Germany, III, 698–699; German naval strategy

in, III, 699–700, 708–709; British naval strategy in, III, 698–699, 707–708; Italian policy in, III, 699, 710; M. scorns pro-German stance of Irish-Americans and German-Americans, III, 548; numbers and money will eventually produce Allied victory, III, 551; wishes British Army were larger, III, 551; RN key to British victory, III, 551; will test All-Big-Gun Ship question, III, 700; M. not alarmed over submarine sinkings of three RN cruisers, III, 549, 550; Germany will employ air and submarine attacks to reduce RN surface margin, III, 550–551, 708–709; effectiveness of submarines and aircraft are still unanswered questions, III, 700, 708–709; visualizes war in the air, III, 709

War of 1812. *See* War: War of 1812

War of the Pacific. *See* War: War of the Pacific

Washington, D.C.: always distasteful to M., III, 518; search for living accommodations in, III, 524–525, 548, 549, 550; M. family plans to take four servants to, III, 549; M. final illness in, III, 551, 552

Washington Navy Yard. *See* U.S. Navy: Yards (Bases)

West Point, N.Y.: M. flirtation with young lady of, 84

Whitehorne, H. B.: M. conflict with, 147; criticism of, 167

Whitney, William C.: shortens 1888 NWC session, 653, 656; urges consolidation of NWC with Torpedo Station, 654, 663, 676, 716, II, 21; indifferent to NWC, III, 664, 666; M. dislike of, 654, 655, II, 61, 244; political corruption of, 655; M. fears retaliation by, 664; dismisses M. from NWC without comment, 678; secures funds for NWC building, II, 244; M. attends banquet with in London, II, 278; compliments M. on his books, II, 278; hosts retirement dinner for M., II, 474; M. serves with in America Cup races investigation, II, 474

Whitthorne, Washington C.: M. criticism of on reduction of USN officers corps, 453; M. criticizes procedures of, 455; M. confidence in, 470; holds favorable opinion of M., 470; attacks Robeson, 475; supports NWC, 652

Wilhelm II, Kaiser: M. meets personally, II, 312; interest in M. books, II, 312

Williams, Edward P.: M. bored by, 306; M. criticizes, 307

Wilson, Josiah M.: M. invites to dinner, 284; M. critical of as an officer, 298

Wilson, Woodrow: economic policies of, III, 512; amateurish diplomacy in Mexico, III, 512, 514; M. dislike of, III, 721; forbids officers to comment publicly on European War issues, **III**, 538, 546, 548; M. death hastened by his gag order, **III**, 539; M. reports his humorous statement about Bryan, **III**, 728; M. thinks personal interests of will predominate over duty to presidential office, **III**, 465, 477; M. a convert away from, **III**, 469; M. feels his conversion to progressivism to be opportunistic, **III**, 469; unconcerned about naval dimensions of foreign policy, **III**, 475; vagueness of acceptance speech, **III**, 478

Wiltse, Gilbert C.: appearance, 23, 24; M. opinion of, **III**, 54; low academic standing at USNA, 56; teased by classmates, 57; Civil War duty, 90; post-Civil War career, **III**, 54; death, **III**, 54

Wisser, J. P.: M. tribute to, 666

Women: M. youthful disinterest in, 3; kissing hands of, 16; short duration of attachments to, 31–32; inconstancy toward, 32–33; neither angels nor instruments of evil, 85; uncomfortable in presence of, 15, 18, 20, 27, 37, 355; M. dislike of female society, 333; liking for female society, 76, 78, 333; need for female society, 84, 106; prefers men to, 340; judge of beauty of, 353–354; dislike of Secesh, 90, 140–149; inferior to men, 34, 366; men should be kind toward, 584; do not fully mature until mid-twenties, **II**, 150, 184, 197, 205, 269, 281, 321; M. eye for pretty women, **II**, 184, 197, 280, 348, 382; need the support of a man in the house, **II**, 288; approves bicycling, fencing, horseback-riding for, **II**, 381; opposes suffrage for, **II**, 662, **III**, 712–713; place is in the home, **III**, 712, 713. *See* Mahan, A.T.: Marriage; Sex

Woodmere, Long Island, N.Y.: social advantages of living in, **III**, 197; disadvantages of living in, **III**, 204

Woolverton, Theron: M. affection for, 156, 158, 165, 168, 169, 174, 175, 179, 209, 223, 284, 285, 290, 291, 293, 294, 295, 302, 305, 306, 307, 308, 309, 310, 313, 314, 316–317, 318, 327, 339–340; does not reciprocate M. affection, 223, 224, 302, 323, 330; M. en-tertains aboard *Iroquois*, 149, 215, 216, 305; aboard *Piscataqua*, 315; aboard *Aroostook*, 316; M. visits aboard *Monocacy*, 216, 219, 222, 284, 288, 304; M. correspondence with, 156–157, 167, 169, 209, 218, 222, 229, 245, 296, 307, 317, 329, **II**, 260; M. writes his mother about, 162, 306; M. wants Ashe to meet, 340; lends M. books, 219, 222; lends M. book of sermons, 339; M. social life ashore with, 155, 217, 220, 221, 284; physical nervousness of, 168; M. attends church with, 170, 285; M. considers him a backsliding Christian, 156, 297, 314; M. indifference toward, 287, 314, 322, 330; M. criticizes sins of, 156, 216, 217, 293, 297, 308, 314, 317, 327, 330, 340; M. prays for, 161, 165, 169, 174, 175, 310, 327; agrees to pray for M., 306, 308, 311, 312; criticizes M., 315; deceives M., 322, 323; attachment to M.; 322; M. efforts at religious conversion of, 156, 158, 159, 160, 161, 163, 169, 170, 173, 174, 175, 182, 216, 220, 285, 286, 287, 288, 290, 292, 294, 295, 301, 305, 307, 308, 309, 315, 317, 318, 321, 339–340; M. disappointed with spiritual progress of, 163, 165, 166, 195, 216, 223, 245, 290, 304, 305, 320, 329, 332; M. sorrow at parting with, 305–306, 317, 318, 327; relief for arrives in Yokohama, 316; M. plans to accompany back to U.S. via California, 316, 319, 331; M. on future prospects of, 323; handling of smallpox outbreak aboard *Monocacy*, 314; retirement from USN, **II**, 260

World War I. *See* War: World War I

Yards. *See* U.S. Navy: Yards (Bases)

Yates, Arthur R.: M. invites to lunch, 296

Yokohama, Japan: M. social life ashore in, 140, 141, 142, 143, 146, 148, 149, 151, 157, 164, 165, 181, 315, 318, 319, 322, 323, 324, 326, 327, 328, 331, 333; attends church in, 151, 156, 161, 164, 180, 182, 319, 324, 327, 330; plays billiards in, 324, 329; new U.S. Consul arrives in, 328; M. criticism of U.S. Consul in, 328

This far from cle
convey the idea. You
seem officers

may without
you, confidentially, the
qualities have influe